THE BLAIR READER

EXPLORING CONTEMPORARY ISSUES

SIXTH EDITION

EDITED BY

LAURIE G. KIRSZNER

University of the Sciences in Philadelphia

STEPHEN R. MANDELL

Drexel University

Upper Saddle River, New Jersey 07458

Library of Congress Cataloging-in-Publication Data

The Blair reader / edited by Laurie G. Kirszner, Stephen R. Mandell. — 6th ed.
   p. cm.
   Includes index.
   ISBN-13: 978-0-13-230869-4
   ISBN-10: 0-13-230869-X
  1. College readers. 2. English language—Rhetoric—Problems, exercises, etc.
  3. Report writing—Problems, exercises, etc. I. Kirszner, Laurie G.
  II. Mandell, Stephen R.
   PE1417.B54 2007
   808'.0427—dc22   2006038590

Editorial Director: Leah Jewell
Senior Acquisitions Editor: Brad Potthoff
Editorial Assistant: Megan Dubrowski
Production Liaison: Joanne Hakim
Senior Marketing Manager: Windley Morley
Marketing Assistant: Kimberly Caldwell
Assistant Manufacturing Manager: Mary Ann Gloriande
Permissions Specialist: Kathleen Karcher
Cover Art Director: Jayne Conte
Cover Design: Bruce Kenselaar
Cover Images: (a) University students—Steve Raymer/Corbis; (b) French fries—
  Matthias Schrader/dpa/Corbis
Director, Image Resource Center: Melinda Patelli
Manager, Rights and Permissions: Zina Arabia
Manager, Visual Research: Beth Brenzel
Manager, Cover Visual Research & Permissions: Karen Sanatar
Photo Coordinator: Nancy Seise
Photo Researcher: Rachel Lucas
Full-Service Project Management: John Shannon/Pine Tree Composition, Inc.
Composition: Laserwords Private Limited
Printer/Binder: RR Donnelley & Sons Company
Cover Printer: Phoenix Color

Credits and acknowledgments borrowed from other sources and reproduced, with permission, in this textbook appear on pages 799–810.

Pearson Education LTD., London
Pearson Education Singapore, Pte. Ltd
Pearson Education, Canada, Ltd
Pearson Education–Japan
Pearson Education Australia PTY, Limited

Pearson Education North Asia Ltd
Pearson Educación de Mexico, S.A. de C.V.
Pearson Education Malaysia, Pte. Ltd
Pearson Education, Upper Saddle River,
  New Jersey

10 9 8 7 6 5 4 3 2
ISBN 978-0-13-230869-4
ISBN 0-13-230869-X

CONTENTS

■ ■ ■ ■ □ ■ ■ ■ ■

TOPICAL CLUSTERS   VIII

RHETORICAL TABLE OF CONTENTS   XVI

PREFACE   XXIV

INTRODUCTION: BECOMING A CRITICAL READER   1

CHAPTER 1   FAMILY TIES   12

Robert Hayden, "Those Winter Sundays"   15
Gary Soto, "One Last Time"   16
E. B. White, "Once More to the Lake"   23
Maxine Hong Kingston, "No Name Woman"   29
Alice Walker, "Beauty: When the Other Dancer
    Is the Self"   40
Sherman J Alexie, Jr. "The Unauthorized
    Autobiography of Me"   47

Fiction: Harlan Coben, "The Key to My Father"   56

Focus: Does Gay Marriage Threaten the Family?   61
Ralph Wedgwood, "What Are We Fighting For?"   62
Maggie Gallagher, "What Marriage Is For"   65
Kerry Howley, "Marriage Just Lets the State Back In"   72

CHAPTER 2   ISSUES IN EDUCATION   80

Lynda Barry, "The Sanctuary of School"   83
John Holt, "School Is Bad for Children"   86
Daniel H. Pink, "School's Out"   91
Maya Angelou, "Graduation"   103
Bich Minh Nguyen, "The Good Immigrant
    Student"   113
Christina Hoff Sommers, "For More
    Balance on Campuses"   121

Fiction: Edward P. Jones, "The First Day"   124

**Focus: How Much Do a College's Facilities Really Matter?
    (Photo essay)   129**

CHAPTER 3   THE POLITICS OF LANGUAGE   134

Jim Sagel, "Baca Grande"   137
Richard Rodriguez, "Aria"   139
Louise Erdrich, "Two Languages in Mind, But Just
    One in the Heart"   146
Frederick Douglass, "Learning to Read and Write"   150
Diane Ravitch, "You Can't Say That"   155
Alleen Pace Nilsen, "Sexism in English: Embodiment
    and Language"   158
Amy Tan, "Mother Tongue"   170
Jonathan Kozol, "The Human Cost of an Illiterate Society"   175
Aldous Huxley, "Propaganda Under a Dictatorship"   183
George Orwell, "Politics and the English Language"   189

Focus: How Free Should Free Speech Be?   201

Stanley Fish, "The Free-Speech Follies"   202
Tim Robbins, "A Chill Wind Is Blowing in This Nation"   206
Stuart Taylor, Jr., "It's Time to Junk the Double Standard
    on Free Speech"   211

CHAPTER 4   MEDIA AND SOCIETY   218

Edward R. Murrow, Speech to Radio-Television News
    Directors Association   221
Marie Winn, "Television: The Plug-In Drug"   231
Salman Rushdie, "Reality TV: A Dearth of Talent
    and the Death of Morality"   239
Charles W. Moore, "Is Music Piracy Stealing?"   242
Mary Eberstadt, "Eminem Is Right"   250
James Fallows, "Who Shot Mohammed al-Dura?"   257

Fiction: Amanda Holzer, "Love and Other Catastrophes:
A Mix Tape"   272

Focus: Has the Internet Doomed the Newspaper?   274

Richard A. Posner, "Bad News"   275
Reuven Frank, "A Loser's Game"   285
Jack Shafer, "Not Just Another Column
    about Blogging"   290

CHAPTER 5   LIFE AND LIFESTYLE   298

William Wordsworth, "The World Is Too Much with Us"   301
Richard Florida, "The Transformation of Everyday Life"   302
Ellen Ruppel Shell, "The Boredom Effect"   310
Edward J. Blakely and Mary Gail Snyder, "Putting Up the
    Gates"   314

Greg Critser, "Supersize Me"   318
Michelle Lee, "The Fashion Victim's Ten Commandments"   326

Focus: Can We Build Real Communities Online?

Barry Wellman, "Connecting Communities:
On and Offline"   341
Brent Staples, "What Adolescents Miss when We Let Them
Grow Up in Cyberspace"   349
Tom Standage, "The Internet in a Cup"   351

CHAPTER 6   GENDER AND IDENTITY   362

Marge Piercy, "Barbie Doll"   365
Sharon Olds, "Rite of Passage"   366
Michael Nava, "Gardenland, Sacramento, California"   367
E. J. Graff, "The M/F Boxes"   374
Judy Brady, "Why I Want a Wife"   380
Glenn Sacks, "Stay-at-Home Dads"   382
Leah Hager Cohen, "Without Apology: Girls,
Women, and the Desire to Fight"   385
Deborah Tannen, "Marked Women"   393

Focus: Is There a Gender Crisis in Education?   399

Christina Hoff Sommers, "The War Against Boys"   400
Ann Hulbert, "Boy Problems"   405
Rosalind C. Barnett and Caryl Rivers, "Men Are
from Earth, and So Are Women"   408

CHAPTER 7   THE AMERICAN DREAM   418

Chief Seattle, "We May Be Brothers"   421
Alexis de Tocqueville, "Why the Americans Are So
Restless in the Midst of Their Prosperity"   423
Richard Wright, "The Library Card"   427
Dinesh D'Souza, "Becoming American"   435
Judith Ortiz Cofer, "The Myth of the Latin Woman:
I Just Met a Girl Named Maria"   442
Gish Jen, "Coming Into The Country"   447
Brent Staples, "Just Walk On By"   450
Lars Eighner, "On Dumpster Diving"   454

Fiction: Amy Tan, "Two Kinds"   465

Focus: What Is the American Dream?   476

Thomas Jefferson, The Declaration of Independence   477
Emma Lazarus, "The New Colossus"   480
John F. Kennedy, Inaugural Address   481
Martin Luther King, Jr., "I Have a Dream"   485

CHAPTER 8 WHY WE WORK 492
Andrew Curry, "Why We Work" 495
Virginia Woolf, "Professions for Women" 500
Arlie Hochschild, "The Second Shift" 505
Eric Schlosser, "Behind the Counter" 511
Barbara Ehrenreich, "Selling in Minnesota" 519
Henry Louis Gates, Jr., "Delusions of Grandeur" 523
Suzanne Gordon, "What Nurses Stand For" 526

Fiction: Jamaica Kincaid, "Girl" 536

Focus: Is Outsourcing Bad for America? 538
Cullen Murphy, "Let Someone Else Do It: The Impulse
Behind Everything" 539
Clay Risen, "Missed Target: Is Outsourcing Really
So Bad?" 542
Albino Barrera, "Fair Exchange: Who Benefits from
Outsourcing?" 548

CHAPTER 9 SCIENCE AND HUMAN VALUES 558
Elizabeth Alexander, "Apollo" 561

Focus 1: Is Global Warming Fact or Fiction? 563
Mark Lynas, "Global Warming: Is
It Already Too Late?" 564
Fred Pearce, "Climate Change: Menace or Myth?" 569
Tom Bethell, "The False Alert of Global Warming" 575

Focus 2: Can the Energy Crisis Be Solved? 581
Paul Roberts, "Over a Barrel" 582
Dennis Behreandt, "Energy's Future" 592
James Howard Kunstler, "The End of Oil" 602

Focus 3: Are Men Better in Math and Science than Women? 611
Lawrence Summers, Remarks at NBER Conference on
Diversifying the Science & Engineering Workforce 613
Women in Science and Engineering Leadership Institute,
Response to Lawrence Summers 622
Katha Pollitt, "Summers of Our Discontent" 627
Andrew Sullivan, "The Truth about
Men and Women" 630

CHAPTER 10 RELIGION IN AMERICA 636
Langston Hughes, "Salvation" 639
Tenzin Gyatso (Dalai Lama XIV), "Our Faith
in Science" 641

Tayari Jones, "Among the Believers"   644
David Brooks, "Kicking the Secularist Habit"   647
William J. Stuntz, "Turning Faith into Elevator
    Music"   652
Jeffery Sheler and Michael Betzold, "Muslim in
    America"   655
William C. Symonds, Brian Grow, and John Cady, "Earthly
    Empires"   659

Fiction: Raymond Carver, "Cathedral"   666

Focus: Is There Intelligent Design in Nature?   679
Christoph Schönborn, "Finding Design in Nature"   680
H. Allen Orr, "Why Intelligent Design Isn't"   682
Kenneth R. Miller, "Finding Darwin's God"   692

CHAPTER 11   MAKING CHOICES   706
Robert Frost, "The Road Not Taken"   709
Linda Pastan, "Ethics"   710
Annie Dillard, "The Deer at Providencia"   711
George Orwell, "Shooting an Elephant"   715
Henry David Thoreau, "Civil Disobedience"   722
Martin Luther King, Jr., "Letter from Birmingham Jail"   741
Claire McCarthy, "Dog Lab"   756
Stanley Milgram, "The Perils of Obedience"   764

Fiction: Ursula K. Le Guin, "The Ones Who Walk Away
    from Omelas"   777

Focus: Can We Be Both Free and Safe?   783
Eric Foner, "The Most Patriotic Act"   784
Declan McCullagh, "Why Liberty Suffers in
    Wartime"   786
Jay Tolson, "Imbalance of Power"   790

CREDITS   799

INDEX OF AUTHORS AND TITLES   811

TOPICAL CLUSTERS

■ ■ ■ ■ □ ■ ■ ■ ■

Classic Essays

Note: Essays are listed in alphabetical order by author's last
   name.

Maya Angelou, "Graduation"   103
Judy Brady, "Why I Want a Wife"   380
Annie Dillard, "The Deer at Providencia"   711
Frederick Douglass, "Learning to Read and Write"   150
John Holt, "School Is Bad for Children"   86
Aldous Huxley, "Propaganda under a Dictatorship"   183
Thomas Jefferson, The Declaration of Independence   477
Maxine Hong Kingston, "No Name Woman"   29
Martin Luther King, Jr., "Letter from Birmingham Jail"   741
George Orwell, "Politics and the English Language"   189
George Orwell, "Shooting an Elephant"   715
Brent Staples, "Just Walk On By"   450
Henry David Thoreau, "Civil Disobedience"   722
Alexis de Tocqueville, "Why the Americans Are So Restless
   in the Midst of Their Prosperity"   423
E. B. White, "Once More to the Lake"   23
Virginia Woolf, "Professions for Women"   500
Richard Wright, "The Library Card"   427

Belief and Doubt
   Langston Hughes, "Salvation"   639
   Tenzin Gyatso, "Our Faith in Science"   641
   Tayari Jones, "Among the Believers"   644
   David Brooks, "Kicking the Secularist Habit"   647
   William J. Stuntz, "Turning Faith into Elevator Music"   652
   Raymond Carver, "Cathedral" (fiction)   666
   Kenneth R. Miller, "Finding Darwin's God"   692
   Robert Frost, "The Road Not Taken" (poetry)   709
   Linda Pastan, "Ethics" (poetry)   710

Civil Rights and Liberties
   Ralph Wedgwood, "What Are We Fighting For?"   62
   Maya Angelou, "Graduation"   103
   Diane Ravitch, "You Can't Say That"   155

Stanley Fish, "The Free-Speech Follies" 202
Tim Robbins, "A Chill Wind Is Blowing in This Nation" 206
Stuart Taylor, Jr., "It's Time to Junk the Double Standard
  on Free Speech" 211
Martin Luther King, Jr., "Letter from Birmingham Jail" 741
Declan McCullagh, "Why Liberty Suffers in Wartime" 786

The College Years
"How Much Do a College's Facilities Really
  Matter?" (photo essay) 129
Stanley Fish, "The Free-Speech Follies" 202
Stuart Taylor, Jr., "It's Time to Junk the Double Standard on
  Free Speech" 211
Christina Hoff Sommers, "For More Balance on Campuses" 121
Rosalind C. Barnett and Caryl Rivers, "Men Are from Earth,
  and So Are Women" 408

Conformity and Rebellion
John Holt, "School Is Bad for Children" 86
Maya Angelou, "Graduation" 103
Bich Minh Nguyen, "The Good Immigrant Student" 113
Aldous Huxley, "Propaganda under a Dictatorship" 183
Michelle Lee, "The Fashion Victim's Ten Commandments" 326
Michael Nava, "Gardenland, Sacramento, California" 367
Leah Hager Cohen, "Without Apology" 385
Thomas Jefferson, The Declaration of Independence 477
Langston Hughes, "Salvation" 639
George Orwell, "Shooting an Elephant" 715

Costumes and Masks
Bich Minh Nguyen, "The Good Immigrant Student" 113
Michelle Lee, "The Fashion Victim's Ten Commandments" 326
Marge Piercy, "Barbie Doll" (poetry) 365
Michael Nava, "Gardenland, Sacramento, California" 367
E. J. Graff, "The M/F Boxes" 374
Deborah Tannen, "Marked Women" 393

Exiles
Maxine Hong Kingston, "No Name Woman" 29
Sherman J. Alexie Jr., "The Unauthorized Autobiography
  of Me" 47
Amy Tan, "Mother Tongue" 170
Michael Nava, "Gardenland, Sacramento, California" 367
Chief Seattle, "We May Be Brothers" 421
Gish Jen, "Coming Into the Country" 447
Lars Eighner, "On Dumpster Diving" 454

Jeffery Sheler and Michael Betzold, "Muslim in America"   655
Ursula K. Le Guin, "The Ones Who Walk Away from
    Omelas" (fiction)   777

Fear and Courage
Maxine Hong Kingston, "No Name Woman"   29
Edward P. Jones, "The First Day" (fiction)   124
Richard Rodriguez, "Aria"   139
Leah Hager Cohen, "Without Apology"   385
Virginia Woolf, "Professions for Women"   500
Brent Staples, "Just Walk On By"   450
Langston Hughes, "Salvation"   639
Claire McCarthy, "Dog Lab"   756
Ursula K. Le Guin, "The Ones Who Walk Away from
    Omelas" (fiction)   777
Eric Foner, "The Most Patriotic Act"   784

Generation Gap
Robert Hayden, "Those Winter Sundays" (poetry)   15
E. B. White, "Once More to the Lake"   23
Harlan Coben, "The Key to My Father" (fiction)   56
Gary Soto, "One Last Time"   16
Sharon Olds, "Rite of Passage" (poetry)   366
Gish Jen, "Coming Into the Country"   447
Amy Tan, "Two Kinds" (fiction)   465
Langston Hughes, "Salvation"   639
Tayari Jones, "Among the Believers"   644

Government and Misgovernment
Kerry Howley, "Marriage Just Lets the State Back In"   72
Aldous Huxley, "Propaganda under a Dictatorship"   183
Tim Robbins, "A Chill Wind Is Blowing in This Nation"   206
Thomas Jefferson, The Declaration of Independence   477
John F. Kennedy, Inaugural Address   481
Martin Luther King, Jr., "I Have a Dream"   485
William J. Stuntz, "Turning Faith into Elevator Music"   652
George Orwell, "Shooting an Elephant"   715
Henry David Thoreau, "Civil Disobedience"   722
Ursula K. Le Guin, "The Ones Who Walk Away from
    Omelas" (fiction)   777
Jay Tolson, "Imbalance of Power"   790

Innocence and Experience
E. B. White, "Once More to the Lake"   23
Sherman J. Alexie, Jr., "The Unauthorized
    Autobiography of Me"   47
Lynda Barry, "The Sanctuary of School"   83

John Holt, "School Is Bad for Children"   86
Edward P. Jones, "The First Day" (fiction)   124
Richard Rodriguez, "Aria"   139
Ellen Ruppel Shell, "The Boredom Effect"   310
Brent Staples, "What Adolescents Miss When We Let Them
    Grow Up in Cyberspace"   349
Sharon Olds, "Rite of Passage" (poetry)   366
Michael Nava, "Gardenland, Sacramento, California"   367
Gish Jen, "Coming Into the Country"   447
Langston Hughes, "Salvation"   639
Claire McCarthy, "Dog Lab"   756
Ursula K. Le Guin, "The Ones Who Walk Away from
    Omelas" (fiction)   777

Law and Justice
Ralph Wedgwood, "What Are We Fighting For?"   62
Kerry Howley, "Marriage Just Lets the State Back In"   72
Aldous Huxley, "Propaganda under a Dictatorship"   183
Stanley Fish, "The Free-Speech Follies"   202
Stuart Taylor, Jr., "It's Time to Junk the Double Standard
    on Free Speech"   211
Charles W. Moore, "Is Music Piracy Stealing?"   242
Thomas Jefferson, The Declaration of Independence   477
Martin Luther King, Jr., "I Have a Dream"   485
Albino Barrera, "Fair Exchange: Who Benefits from
    Outsourcing?"   548
William J. Stuntz, "Turning Faith into Elevator Music"   652
Henry David Thoreau, "Civil Disobedience"   722
Martin Luther King, Jr., "Letter from Birmingham Jail"   741

Mother Tongues
Bich Minh Nguyen, "The Good Immigrant Student"   113
Richard Rodriguez, "Aria"   139
Louise Erdrich, "Two Languages in Mind, but
    Just One in the Heart"   146
Amy Tan, "Mother Tongue"   170
Gish Jen, "Coming Into the Country"   447

Music
Sherman J Alexie, Jr., "The Unauthorized
    Autobiography of Me"   47
Charles W. Moore, "Is Music Piracy Stealing?"   242
Mary Eberstadt, "Eminem Is Right"   250
Amanda Holzer, "Love and Other Catastrophes:
    A Mix Tape" (fiction)   272
Amy Tan, "Two Kinds" (fiction)   465

Names and Naming

Maxine Hong Kingston, "No Name Woman"   29
Sherman J. Alexie Jr., "The Unauthorized
   Autobiography of Me"   47
Judy Brady, "Why I Want a Wife"   380
Alleen Pace Nilsen, "Sexism in English: Embodiment and
   Language"   158
Michael Nava, "Gardenland, Sacramento,
   California"   367
E. J. Graff, "The M/F Boxes"   374
Judith Ortiz Cofer, "The Myth of the Latin Woman:
   I Just Met a Girl Named Maria"   442

Nationalism and Patriotism

Aldous Huxley, "Propaganda under a Dictatorship"   183
Tim Robbins, "A Chill Wind Is Blowing in This Nation"   206
Stuart Taylor, Jr., "It's Time to Junk the Double
   Standard on Free Speech"   211
Alexis de Tocqueville, "Why the Americans Are
   So Restless in the Midst of Their Prosperity"   423
Dinesh D'Souza, "Becoming American"   435
Gish Jen, "Coming into the Country"   447
Thomas Jefferson, The Declaration of Independence   477
Emma Lazarus, "The New Colossus"   480
John F. Kennedy, Inaugural Address   481
Martin Luther King, Jr., "I Have a Dream"   485

Prejudice

Ralph Wedgwood, "What Are We Fighting For?"   62
Maya Angelou, "Graduation"   103
Bich Minh Nguyen, "The Good Immigrant Student"   113
Brent Staples, "Just Walk On By"   450
Amy Tan, "Mother Tongue"   170
Marge Piercy, "Barbie Doll" (poetry)   365
Alleen Pace Nilsen, "Sexism in English:
   Embodiment and Language"   158
Michael Nava, "Gardenland, Sacramento,
   California"   367
Christina Hoff Sommers, "The War Against Boys"   400
Gish Jen, "Coming Into the Country"   447
Elizabeth Alexander, "Apollo" (poetry)   561
Jeffery Sheler and Michael Betzold,
   "Muslim in America"   655
George Orwell, "Shooting an Elephant"   715
Raymond Carver, "Cathedral" (fiction)   666

Reading and Writing

Sherman J. Alexie, Jr., "The Unauthorized
Autobiography of Me"   47

Bich Minh Nguyen, "The Good Immigrant Student"   113

Frederick Douglass, "Learning to Read and Write"   150

Diane Ravitch, "You Can't Say That"   155

Jonathan Kozol, "The Human Cost of an
Illiterate Society"   175

George Orwell, "Politics and the English Language"   189

Aldous Huxley, "Propaganda under a Dictatorship"   183

Martin Luther King, Jr., "Letter from Birmingham Jail"   741

Rural Life

E. B. White, "Once More to the Lake"   23

Maxine Hong Kingston, "No Name Woman"   29

Alice Walker, "Beauty: When the Other
Dancer Is the Self"   40

Maya Angelou, "Graduation"   103

Louise Erdrich, "Two Languages in Mind, but
Just One in the Heart"   146

Gary Soto, "One Last Time"   16

Self Image

Maxine Hong Kingston, "No Name Woman"   29

Alice Walker, "Beauty: When the Other Dancer
Is the Self"   40

Bich Minh Nguyen, "The Good Immigrant Student"   113

Frederick Douglass, "Learning to Read and Write"   150

Michelle Lee, "The Fashion Victim's Ten
Commandments"   326

Marge Piercy, "Barbie Doll" (poetry)   365

Sharon Olds, "Rite of Passage" (poetry)   366

Michael Nava, "Gardenland, Sacramento, California"   367

E. J. Graff, "The M/F Boxes"   374

Leah Hager Cohen, "Without Apology"   385

Rosalind C. Barnett and Caryl Rivers, "Men Are
from Earth, and So Are Women"   408

Gish Jen, "Coming Into the Country"   447

Langston Hughes, "Salvation"   639

Tayari Jones, "Among the Believers"   644

Raymond Carrer, "Cathedral" (fiction)   666

Social and Economic Class

"How Much Do a College's Facilities Really Matter?" (photo
essay)   129

Jim Sagel, "Baca Grande" (poetry)   137
Gary Soto, "One Last Time"   16
Richard Rodriguez, "Aria"   139
Jonathan Kozol, "The Human Cost of an
    Illiterate Society"   175
Alexis de Tocqueville, "Why the Americans Are So
    Restless in the Midst of Their Prosperity"   423
Lars Eighner, "On Dumpster Diving"   454
Albino Barrera, "Fair Exchange: Who Benefits from
    Outsourcing?"   548

Stereotyping
Maya Angelou, "Graduation"   103
Bich Minh Nguyen, "The Good Immigrant
    Student"   113
Michael Nava, "Gardenland, Sacramento,
    California"   367
E. J. Graff, "The M/F Boxes"   374
Leah Hager Cohen, "Without Apology"   385
Ann Hulbert, "Boy Problems"   405
Rosalind C. Barnett and Caryl Rivers, "Men Are
    from Earth, and So Are Women"   408
Judy Brady, "Why I Want a Wife"   380
Glenn Sacks, "Stay-at-Home Dads"   382
Judith Ortiz Cofer, "The Myth of the Latin Woman"   442
Gish Jen, "Coming Into the Country"   447
George Orwell, "Shooting an Elephant"   715
Jeffery Sheler and Michael Betzold,
    "Muslim in America"   655

Suburban Life
Ellen Ruppel Shell, "The Boredom Effect"   310
Edward J. Blakely and Mary Gail Snyder,
    "Putting Up the Gates"   314
Barry Wellman, "Connecting Communities:
    On and Offline"   341
Michael Nava, "Gardenland, Sacramento, California"   367
Glenn Sacks, "Stay-at-Home Dads"   382

Teenage Wasteland
Richard Rodriguez, "Aria"   139
Mary Eberstadt, "Eminem Is Right"   250
Brent Staples, "What Adolescents Miss When
    We Let Them Grow Up in Cyberspace"   349
Christina Hoff Sommers, "The War Against Boys"   400
Ellen Ruppel Shell, "The Boredom Effect"   310

Urban Life

Harlan Coben, "The Key to My Father" (fiction)   56
Edward P. Jones, "The First Day" (fiction)   124
Brent Staples, "Just Walk On By"   450
Lars Eighner, "On Dumpster Diving"   454

Violence

Maxine Hong Kingston, "No Name Woman"   29
Salman Rushdie, "Reality TV: A Dearth of Talent and the
   Death of Morality"   239
Lean Hager Cohen, "Without Apology"   385
Mary Eberstadt, "Eminem Is Right"   250
James Fallows, "Who Shot Mohammed al-Dura?"   257
Stanley Milgram, "The Perils of Obedience"   764

Speeches

Note: Speeches are listed in alphabetical order.

John F. Kennedy, Inaugural Address   481
Martin Luther King, Jr., "I Have a Dream"   485
Edward R. Murrow, Speech to RTNDA Convention   221
Tim Robbins, "A Chill Wind Is Blowing in
   This Nation"   206
Chief Seattle, "We May Be Brothers"   421
Lawrence Summers, Remarks at NBER Conference on
   Diversifying the Science and Engineering
   Workforce   613
Amy Tan, "Mother Tongue"   170
Virginia Woolf, "Professions for Women"   500

Rhetorical Table of Contents

■ ■ ■ ■ □ ■ ■ ■ ■

Note: Essays are listed alphabetically within categories.

Narration

Sherman Alexie, "The Unauthorized
Autobiography of Me"   47
Maya Angelou, "Graduation"   103
Lynda Barry, "The Sanctuary of School"   83
Judith Ortiz Cofer, "The Myth of the Latin Woman"   442
Leah Hager Cohen, "Without Apology"   385
Dinesh D'Souza, "Becoming American"   435
Annie Dillard, "The Deer at Providencia"   711
Frederick Douglass, "Learning to Read and Write"   150
Lars Eighner, "On Dumpster Diving"   454
Barbara Ehrenreich,"Selling in Minnesota"   519
Louise Erdrich,"Two Languages in Mind, but Just
One in the Heart"   146
James Fallows, "Who Shot Mohammed al-Dura?"   257
Tayari Jones, "Among the Believers"   644
Maxine Hong Kingston, "No Name Woman"   29
Claire McCarthy, "Dog Lab"   756
Kenneth R. Miller, "Finding Darwin's God"   692
Michael Nava, "Gardenland, Sacramento, California"   367
George Orwell, "Shooting an Elephant"   715
Daniel H. Pink, "School's Out"   91
Tim Robbins, "A Chill Wind Is Blowing in
This Nation"   206
Richard Rodriguez, "Aria"   139
Glenn Sacks, "Stay-at-Home Dads"   382
Eric Schlosser, "Behind the Counter"   511
Ellen Ruppel Shell, "The Boredom Effect"   310
Christina Hoff Sommers, "For More Balance on
Campuses"   121
Gary Soto, "One Last Time"   16
Brent Staples, "Just Walk On By"   450
Amy Tan, "Mother Tongue"   170

E. B. White, "Once More to the Lake"   23
Richard Wright, "The Library Card"   427

Description

Edward J. Blakely and Mary Gail Snyder, "Putting
    Up the Gates"   314
Leah Hager Cohen, "Without Apology"   385
Greg Critser, "Supersize Me"   318
Louise Erdrich, "Two Languages in Mind, but Just
    One in the Heart"   146
James Fallows, "Who Shot Mohammed al-Dura?"   257
Richard Florida, "The Transformation of Everyday Life"   302
Langston Hughes, "Salvation"   639
Gish Jen, "Coming Into the Country"   447
Tayari Jones, "Among the Believers"   644
Michelle Lee, "The Fashion Victim's
    Ten Commandments"   326
Kenneth R. Miller, "Finding Darwin's God"   692
Michael Nava, "Gardenland, Sacramento, California"   367
George Orwell, "Shooting an Elephant"   715
Richard Rodriguez, "Aria"   139
Eric Schlosser, "Behind the Counter"   511
Ellen Ruppel Shell, "The Boredom Effect"   310
Tom Standage, "The Internet in a Cup"   351
E. B. White, "Once More to the Lake"   23

Process

David Brooks, "Kicking the Secularist Habit"   647
Greg Critser, "Supersize Me"   318
Barbara Ehrenreich, "Selling in Minnesota"   519
Lars Eighner, "On Dumpster Diving"   454
Gish Jen, "Coming into the Country"   447
Claire McCarthy, "Dog Lab"   756

Exemplification

Rosalind C. Barnett and Caryl Rivers, "Men Are from
    Earth, and So Are Women"   408
Albino Barrera, "Fair Exchange: Who Benefits from
    Outsourcing?"   548
Tom Bethell, "The False Alert of Global Warming"   575
Judith Ortiz Cofer, "The Myth of the Latin Woman"   442
Leah Hager Cohen,"Without Apology"   385
Andrew Curry, "Why We Work"   495
Mary Eberstadt, "Eminem Is Right"   250
Suzanne Gordon, "What Nurses Stand For"   526
E. J. Graff, "The M/F Boxes"   374

Thomas Jefferson, The Declaration of Independence   477
Gish Jen, "Coming into the Country"   447
Martin Luther King, Jr., "I Have a Dream"   485
Jonathan Kozol, "The Human Cost of an
    Illiterate Society"   175
James Howard Kunstler, "The End of Oil"   602
Michelle Lee,"The Fashion Victim's Ten
    Commandments"   326
Mark Lynas, "Global Warming: Is It Already too Late?"   564
Declan McCullagh, "Why Liberty Suffers in Wartime"   786
Cullen Murphy, "Let Someone Else Do It"   539
Bich Minh Nguyen, "The Good Immigrant Student"   113
Alleen Pace Nilsen, "Sexism in English: Embodiment and
    Language"   158
George Orwell, "Politics and the English Language"   189
Daniel H. Pink, "School's Out"   91
Richard A. Posner, "Bad News"   275
Clay Risen, "Missed Target: Is Outsourcing
    Really So Bad?"   542
Tim Robbins, "A Chill Wind Is Blowing in
    This Nation"   206
Paul Roberts, "Over a Barrel"   582
Jack Shafer, "Not Just Another Column about
    Blogging"   290
Ellen Ruppel Shell, "The Boredom Effect"   310
Tom Standage, "The Internet in a Cup"   351
Brent Staples, "Just Walk On By"   450
Lawrence Summers, Remarks at NBER Conference on
    Diversifying the Science and Engineering
    Workforce   613
William C. Symonds, "Earthly Empires"   659
Stuart Taylor, Jr., "It's Time to Junk the Double
    Standard on Free Speech"   211
Alice Walker, "Beauty: When the Other Dancer
    Is the Self"   40
Barry Wellman, "Connecting Communities:
    On and Offline"   341
Marie Winn, "Television: The Plug-In Drug"   231

Cause & Effect
Dennis Behreandt, "Energy's Future"   592
Tom Bethell, "The False Alert of Global Warming"   575
Edward J. Blakely and Mary Gail Snyder, "Putting
    Up the Gates"   314

Greg Critser, "Supersize Me"   318

Alexis de Tocqueville, "Why the Americans
    Are So Restless in the Midst of Their Prosperity"   423

Mary Eberstadt, "Eminem Is Right"   250

James Fallows, "Who Shot Mohammed al-Dura?"   257

Eric Foner, "The Most Patriotic Act"   784

Aldous Huxley, "Propaganda under a Dictatorship"   183

Jonathan Kozol, "The Human Cost of an
    Illiterate Society"   175

James Howard Kunstler, "The End of Oil"   602

Ann Hulbert, "Boy Problems"   405

Mark Lynas, "Global Warming: Is It
    Already too Late?"   564

Edward R. Murrow, Speech to RTNDA
    Convention   221

Fred Pearce, "Climate Change: Menace or Myth?"   569

Richard A. Posner, "Bad News"   275

Tim Robbins, "A Chill Wind Is Blowing in
    This Nation"   206

Paul Roberts, "Over a Barrel"   582

Salman Rushdie, "Reality TV: A Dearth of Talent and the
    Death of Morality"   239

Brent Staples, "Just Walk On By"   450

Brent Staples, "What Adolescents Miss when
    We Let Them Grow Up in Cyberspace"   349

Alice Walker, "Beauty: When the Other Dancer
    Is the Self"   40

Barry Wellman, "Connecting Communities: On and
    Offline"   341

E. B. White, "Once More to the Lake"   23

Marie Winn, "Television: The Plug-In Drug"   231

Richard Wright, "The Library Card"   427

Comparison & Contrast

Rosalind C. Barnett and Caryl Rivers, "Men Are from
    Earth, and So Are Women"   408

Dennis Behreandt, "Energy's Future"   592

Edward J. Blakely and Mary Gail Snyder, "Putting
    Up the Gates"   314

Leah Hager Cohen, "Without Apology"   385

Dinesh D'Souza, "Becoming American"   435

Stanley Fish, "The Free-Speech Follies"   202

Richard Florida, "The Transformation of
    Everyday Life"   302

Reuven Frank, "A Loser's Game"   285
Maggie Gallagher, "What Marriage Is For"   65
Henry Louis Gates, Jr., "Delusions of Grandeur"   523
E. J. Graff, "The M/F Boxes"   374
Tenzin Gyatso, "Our Faith in Science"   641
Arlie Hochschild, "The Second Shift"   505
Ann Hulbert, "Boy Problems"   405
Gish Jen, "Coming into the Country"   447
Michelle Lee, "The Fashion Victim's
    Ten Commandments"   326
Declan McCullagh, "Why Liberty Suffers in Wartime"   786
Alleen Pace Nilsen, "Sexism in English:
    Embodiment and Language"   158
Daniel H. Pink, "School's Out"   91
Katha Pollitt, "Summers of Our Discontent"   627
Richard A. Posner, "Bad News"   275
Glenn Sacks, "Stay-at-Home Dads"   382
Chief Seattle, "We May Be Brothers"   421
Jack Shafer, "Not Just Another
    Column about Blogging"   290
Ellen Ruppel Shell, "The Boredom Effect"   310
Christina Hoff Sommers, "For More
    Balance on Campuses"   121
Christina Hoff Sommers, "The War Against Boys"   400
Tom Standage, "The Internet in a Cup"   351
Andrew Sullivan, "The Truth about Men and Women"   630
Lawrence Summers, Remarks at NBER Conference on
    Diversifying the Science and Engineering Workforce   613
Deborah Tannen, "Marked Women"   393
Ralph Wedgwood, "What Are We Fighting For?"   62
Barry Wellman, "Connecting Communities:
    On and Offline"   341
Women in Science and Engineering Leadership Institute,
    Response to Lawrence Summers   622
Virginia Woolf, "Professions for Women"   500

Classification & Division

Rosalind C. Barnett and Caryl Rivers,
    "Men Are from Earth, and So Are Women"   408
Judy Brady, "Why I Want a Wife"   380
Andrew Curry, "Why We Work"   495
Richard Florida, "The Transformation of
    Everyday Life"   302
E. J. Graff, "The M/F Boxes"   374
Diane Ravitch, "You Can't Say That"   155

Glenn Sacks, "Stay-at-Home Dads"   382
Amy Tan,"Mother Tongue"   170

Definition

Tom Bethell, "The False Alert of Global Warming"   575
Judy Brady, "Why I Want a Wife"   380
Andrew Curry, "Why We Work"   495
Dinesh D'Souza, "Becoming American"   435
Louise Erdrich, "Two Languages in Mind, but Just
    One in the Heart"   146
Stanley Fish, "The Free-Speech Follies"   202
Revren Frank, "A Loser's Game"   285
Maggie Gallagher, "What Marriage Is For"   65
Suzanne Gordon, "What Nurses Stand For"   526
E. J. Graff, "The M/F Boxes"   374
Aldous Huxley, "Propaganda under a
    Dictatorship"   183
Charles W. Moore, "Is Music Piracy Stealing?"   242
Cullen Murphy, "Let Someone Else Do It"   539
Daniel H. Pink, "School's Out"   91
Diane Ravitch, "You Can't Say That"   155
Glenn Sacks, "Stay-at-Home Dads"   382
Deborah Tannen, "Marked Women"   393
Stuart Taylor, Jr., "It's Time to Junk the
    Double Standard on Free Speech"   211
Jay Tolson, "Imbalance of Power"   790
Alice Walker, "Beauty: When the Other Dancer
    Is the Self"   40
Barry Wellman, "Connecting Communities:
    On and Offline"   341
Virginia Woolf, "Professions for Women"   500

Argument & Persuasion

Rosalind C. Barnett and Caryl Rivers, "Men Are from
    Earth, and So Are Women"   408
Albino Barrera, "Fair Exchange: Who Benefits from
    Outsourcing?"   548
Dennis Behreandt, "Energy's Future"   592
Tom Bethelt, "The False Alert of Global Warming"   575
Judy Brady, "Why I Want a Wife"   380
Greg Critser, "Supersize Me"   318
Annie Dillard, "The Deer at Providencia"   711
Dinesh D'Souza, "Becoming American"   435
Mary Eberstadt, "Eminem Is Right"   250
Stanley Fish, "The Free-Speech Follies"   202

Eric Foner, "The Most Patriotic Act"   772
Reuven Frank, "A Loser's Game"   285
Maggie Gallagher, "What Marriage Is For"   65
Henry Louis Gates, Jr., "Delusions of Grandeur"   523
E. J. Graff, "The M/F Boxes"   374
Tenzin Gyatso, "Our Faith in Science"   641
Kerry Howley, "Marriage Just Lets the
   State Back In"   72
Ann Hulbert, "Boy Problems"   405
Thomas Jefferson, The Declaration of Independence   477
Martin Luther King, Jr., "Letter from Birmingham Jail"   741
Jonathan Kozol, "The Human Cost of an
   Illiterate Society"   175
James Howard Kunstler, "The End of Oil"   602
Mark Lynas, "Global Warming: Is It Already
   Too Late?"   564
Declan McCullagh, "Why Liberty Suffers in
   Wartime"   786
Stanley Milgram, "The Perils of Obedience"   764
Kenneth R. Miller, "Finding Darwin's God"   692
Charles W. Moore, "Is Music Piracy Stealing?"   242
Cullen Murphy, "Let Someone Else Do It: The Impulse
   Behind Everything"   539
Edward R. Murrow, Speech to RTNDA Convention   231
Alleen Pace Nilsen, "Sexism in English:
   Embodiment and Language"   158
Allen Orr, "Why Intelligent Design Isn't"   682
George Orwell, "Shooting an Elephant"   715
Fred Pearce, "Climate Change: Menace or Myth?"   569
Daniel H. Pink, "School's Out"   91
Katha Pollitt, "Summers of Our Discontent"   627
Richard A. Posner, "Bad News"   275
Clay Risen, "Missed Target: Is Outsourcing Really
   So Bad?"   542
Tim Robbins, "A Chill Wind is Blowing in
   This Nation"   206
Paul Roberts, "Over a Barrel"   582
Salman Rushdie, "Reality TV: A Dearth of
   Talent and the Death of Morality"   239
Glenn Sacks, "Stay-at-Home Dads"   382
Christoph Schönborn, "Finding Design in Nature"   680
Christina Hoff Sommers, "For More
   Balance on Campuses"   121
Brent Staples, "Just Walk On By"   450
Brent Staples, "What Adolescents Miss when We

Let Them Grow Up in Cyberspace"   349
Jack Shafer, "Not Just Another Column about
    Blogging"   290
William J. Stuntz, "Turning Faith into
    Elevator Music"   652
Andrew Sullivan, "The Truth about Men and
    Women"   630
Lawrence Summers, Remarks at NBER Conference on
    Diversifying the Science and Engineering
    Workforce   613
Stuart Taylor, Jr., "It's Time to Junk the Double
    Standard on Free Speech"   211
Henry David Thoreau, "Civil Disobedience"   722
Jay Tolson, "Imbalance of Power"   790
Ralph Wedgwood, "What Are We Fighting For?"   62
Barry Wellman, "Connecting Communities:
    On and Offline"   341
Marie Winn, "Television: The Plug-In Drug"   231
Women in Science and Engineering Leadership Institute,
    Response to Lawrence Summers   622

PREFACE

■ ■ ■ □ ■ ■ ■ ■

After more than twenty-five years of teaching composition, we have come to see reading and writing as interrelated activities: If students are going to write effectively, they must also read actively and critically. In addition, we see writting as is both a private and a public act. As a private act, it enables students to explore their feelings and reactions and to discover their ideas about subjects that are important to them. As a public act, writing enables students to see how their own ideas fit into larger discourse communities, where ideas gain meaning and value. We believe that students are enriched and engaged when they view the reading and writing they do as a way of participating in ongoing public discussions about ideas that matter to them. From the beginning, our goal in *The Blair Reader* has always been to encourage students to contribute to these discussions in the wider world by responding to the ideas of others.

The core of *The Blair Reader* is, of course, its reading selections. As we selected the readings for this book, our goal was to introduce students to the enduring issues they confront as citizens in the twenty-first century. Many of these readings are very contemporary; many are also quite provocative. Whenever possible, however, we include classic readings that give students the historical context they need. For example, Chapter 2, "Issues in Education," includes "School Is Bad for Children" by John Holt; Chapter 3, "The Politics of Language," includes "Learning to Read and Write" by Frederick Douglass; and Chapter 7, "The American Dream," includes "Why the Americans Are So Restless in the Midst of Their Prosperity" by Alexis de Tocqueville. It was also important to us that the selections in *The Blair Reader* represent a wide variety of rhetorical patterns and types of discourse as well as a variety of themes, issues, and positions. In addition to essays, *The Blair Reader* contains speeches; newspaper, magazine, and Internet articles; and short stories and poems. It is our hope that exposure to this wide variety of formats, topics, and viewpoints can help students to discover their own voices and express their own ideas.

As teachers, we—like you—expect a thematic reader to include compelling reading selections that involve instructors and students in spirited exchanges. We also expect readings that reflect the diversity of ideas that characterizes our society and questions that challenge students to think for themselves and to respond critically to what they have read. In short, we expect a book that stimulates discussion and that encourages students to discover new ideas and to see familiar ideas in new ways. These expectations guided us as we initially created *The Blair Reader,* and they continued to guide us as we worked on this new sixth edition.

What's New in the Sixth Edition?

In response to the thoughtful comments of the many instructors who generously shared with us their reactions (and their students' reactions) to the *The Blair Reader,* we have made many changes in this new edition, adding new thematic units, new readings, new study questions and writing prompts, and new visuals.

- **Two new thematic chapters**—"Science and Human Values" (Chapter 9) and "Religion in America" (Chapter 10)—provide background on important contemporary subjects. The "Science and Human Values" chapter consists of three Focus sections that serve as mini-casebooks on global warming, the energy crisis, and women's place in the world of science and mathematics. The "Religion in America" chapter includes essays by Langston Hughes and Tenzin Gyatso (the Dalai Lama), among others, and a Focus section on the question, "Is There Intelligent Design in Nature?"

- **New Focus sections** in chapters throughout the text showcase related essays that examine contemporary concerns. These Focus sections zero in on questions such as "Does Gay Marriage Threaten the Family?" "Has the Internet Doomed the Newspaper?" "Can We Build Real Communities Online?" "Is There a Gender Crisis in Education?" and "Is Outsourcing Bad for America?"

- **Expanded treatment of visual literacy** places additional emphasis on this important skill. In the Introduction to the text, a new section, "Reacting to Visual Texts," includes both a series of questions to help students approach and understand visuals and a sample visual with student annotations. In addition, we have added new visuals in the chapter openers and Focus sections.

- **A new photo essay** encourages students to react to the ideas communicated in images. In Chapter 2, "Issues in Education," a new full-color photo essay juxtaposes two Iowa college campuses—one richly endowed and the other less financially secure. Responding to the Images questions encourage students to consider the similarities and differences between the two schools and the impact these differences have on students' education.

- **New readings** have been added to stimulate student interest and to introduce them to some of the challenging issues that they confront as students and as citizens. Among the many essays that are new to this edition are Maggie Gallagher's "What Marriage Is For," Bich Minh Nguyen's "The Good Immigrant Student," Diane Ravitch's "You Can't Say That," Mary Eberstadt's "Eminem Is Right," Brent Staples's "What Adolescents Miss When We Let Them Grow Up in Cyberspace," Michael Nava's "Gardenland, Sacramento, California" Leah Hager Cohen's "Without Apology: Girls, Women, and the Desire to Fight," and Gish Jen's "Coming Into the Country." New fiction, such as Raymond Carver's "Cathedral"; new poetry, such as Elizabeth Alexander's "Apollo"; and new speeches, such as Edward R. Murrow's famous 1958 address to radio and television professionals, have also been added.

Resources for Students

We designed the apparatus in *The Blair Reader* to involve students and to encourage them to respond critically to what they read. These responses can lay the groundwork for the more focused thinking that they will do when they write. In order to help students to improve their critical reading and writing skills, we have included the following features:

- **Introduction: Becoming a Critical Reader** explains and illustrates the process of reading and reacting critically to texts (including visual texts) and formulating varied and original responses.

- **Paired visuals** introduce each thematic chapter. These visuals engage students by encouraging them to identify parallels and contrasts. In addition, they introduce students to the themes that they will be considering as they read the essays in the chapter.

- A brief **chapter introduction** places each chapter's broad theme in its social, historical, or political context, helping students to understand the complexities of the issues being discussed. This chapter introduction is followed by **Preparing to Read and Write,** a list of questions designed to help students to focus their responses to individual readings and to relate these responses to the chapter's larger issues.

- **Headnotes** that introduce each selection provide biographical information as well as insight into the writer's purpose.

- **Responding to Reading** questions following each selection address thematic and rhetorical considerations. By encouraging students to think critically, these questions help them to see reading as an interactive and intellectually stimulating process.

- A **Responding in Writing** prompt after each reading selection gives students the opportunity to write an informal response.

- A **Focus** section in each chapter is introduced by a provocative question related to the chapter's theme, followed by a visual that is accompanied by **Responding to the Image** questions and a writing prompt. The heart of the Focus section is a group of readings that take a variety of positions on the issue, encouraging students to add their voices to the debate and demonstrating that complex issues elicit different points of view. Each reading is followed by "Responding to Reading" questions and a "Responding in Writing" prompt.

- At the end of each chapter's Focus section, a **Widening the Focus** feature includes "For Critical Thinking and Writing," a writing prompt that asks students to tie the readings together; "For Further Reading," a list of essays in other chapters of the book that also address the issues raised by the Focus question; and "For Internet Research," an assignment that encourages students to explore the Focus topic more closely.

- **Writing** suggestions at the end of each chapter ask students to respond to one or more of the chapter's readings.

- A **Rhetorical Table of Contents,** located at the front of the book on pages xvi–xxiii, groups the text's readings according to the way they arrange material: narration, description, process, comparison and contrast, and so on.

- **Topical Clusters,** narrowly focused thematic units (pp. viii–xv), offer students and teachers additional options for grouping readings.

Additional Resources for Instructors and Students

Instructor's Manual (0-13-230870-3)

Because we wanted *The Blair Reader* to be a rich and comprehensive resource for instructors, a thoroughly revised and updated *Instructor's Resource Manual* has been developed to accompany the text. Designed to be a useful and all-inclusive tool, the manual contains teaching strategies, collaborative activities, and suggested answers for "Responding to Reading" questions. The manual includes Web and/or multimedia teaching resources for almost every reading. It also contains new questions for stimulating classroom discussions of the new chapter-opening images. Contact your local Prentice Hall representative for details.

Companion Website^{TM}: www.prenhall.com/kirszner

The Companion Website^{TM} provides additional chapter exercises, links, and activities that reinforce and build upon the material presented in the text.

The Web site includes the following features:

- Additional essay and short-answer questions for every reading
- Web links that provide additional contextual information
- Visual analysis questions for each chapter
- Web destinations for each essay topic

MyCompLab^{TM}

Created by composition instructors for composition instructors and their students, MyCompLab^{TM} offers the best multimedia resources for composition in one, easy-to-use place. Students will find guidelines, tutorials, exercises, and other help for writing, grammar, and research. Also included are Grade Tracker and access to the following resources

- Exchange, Prentice Hall's online peer and instructor review program
- Tutor Center, for book-specific tutoring by composition instructors via phone, e-mail, or fax
- MyDropBox.com, a leading Web-based plagiarism detection service

To package *The Blair Reader* with access to MyCompLab or MyCompLab CourseCompass, contact your local Prentice Hall representative.

Prentice Hall Pocket Readers

These compact readers include essays that have withstood the test of time and teaching, making them the perfect companions for any writing course. To package a *Prentice Hall Pocket Reader* with *The Blair Reader* for only a nominal additional cost, please contact your local Prentice Hall representative. Choices include:

THEMES: A Prentice Hall Pocket Reader
ARGUMENT: A Prentice Hall Pocket Reader
LITERATURE: A Prentice Hall Pocket Reader
WRITING ACROSS THE CURRICULUM: A Prentice Hall Pocket Reader
PATTERNS: A Prentice Hall Pocket Reader
PURPOSES: A Prentice Hall Pocket Reader

Dictionary and Thesaurus

To include a dictionary or thesaurus with *The Blair Reader* for only a nominal additional cost, please contact your local Prentice Hall representative.

Acknowledgments

The Blair Reader is the result of a fruitful collaboration between the two of us, between us and our students, between us and Prentice Hall, and between us and you—our colleagues who told us what you wanted in a reader.

At Prentice Hall we want to thank Brad Potthoff, Senior Acquisitions Editor, and Leah Jewell, Editorial Director. We also appreciate the efforts of Tara Culliney, Editorial Assistant, as well as our copyeditor, Patricia Daly.

Karen R. Smith, our wonderful developmental editor, spent a great deal of time and effort making this book as good as it is. As always, her patience, professionalism, and hard work are greatly appreciated. At Pine Tree Composition, Inc., we want to thank John Shannon, Production Editor, for seeing this book through to completion.

In preparing *The Blair Reader*, Sixth Edition, we benefited at every stage from the assistance and suggestions from colleagues from across the country: Charlene Bunnell, University of Delaware; Jason Chaffin, Cape Fear Community College; Anne Fernald, Fordham University; Ruth Gerik, University of Texas at Arlington; Janet Gerstner, San Juan College; Lu Ellen Huntley, University of North Carolina at Wilmington; Alan Kaufman, Bergen Community College; Robert Leston, University of Texas at Arlington; Andrea Penner, San Juan College; Darlene Smith-Worthington, Pitt Community College; Sharon Strand, Black Hills State University; and Diane Sweet, Wentworth Institute of Technology.

We would also like to thank the following reviewers of previous editions for their valuable insight: Derek Soles, Drexel University; Stephen R. Armstrong, Eastern Carolina University; Mary Williams, Midland College; Janet Eldred, University of Kentucky, Marguerite Parker, Eastern Carolina University; Pamela Howell, Midland College; Patricia Baldwin, Pitt Community College; Tara Hubschmitt, Lakeland

College; and David Holper, College of the Redwoods, Angie Pratt, Montgomery College; Chere Berman, College of the Canyons; Paul Northam, Johnson County Community College; Jennifer Vanags, Johnson County Community College; CC Ryder, West L.A. College; John Lucarelli, Community College of Allegheny County; Linda A. Archer, Green River Community College; Stephen H. Wells, Community College of Allegheny County; Terry Jolliffe, Midland College; Anthony Armstrong, Richland College; Dimitri Keriotis, Modesto Junior College; Robert G. Ford, Houston Community College; Carla L. Dando, Idaho State University; Lori Ann Stephens, Richland College; Debra Shein, Idaho State University; Cara Unger, Portland Community College; Dr. Emily Dial-Driver, Rogers State University; Jesse T. Airaudi, Baylor University; Camilla Mortensen, University of Oregon; Kathryn Neal, York Technical College; K. Siobhan Wright, Carroll Community College; Rosemary Day, Ph.D., Albuquerque Community College; Jacob Agatucci, Central Oregon Community College; Peggy Cole, Ph.D., Arapahoe Community College; and James Jenkins, Mt. San Antonio College.

On the home front, we once again "round up the usual suspects" to thank—Mark, Adam, and Rebecca Kirszner and Demi, David, and Sarah Mandell. And, of course, we thank each other: it really has been a "beautiful friendship."

INTRODUCTION: BECOMING A CRITICAL READER

In his autobiographical essay "The Library Card" (p. 427), Richard Wright describes his early exposure to the world of books. He says, "The plots and stories in the novels did not interest me so much as the point of view revealed. I gave myself over to each novel without reserve, without trying to criticize it; it was enough for me to see and feel something different. Reading was like a drug."

It is a rare person today for whom reading can hold this magic or inspire this awe. Most of us take the access to books for granted. As a student, you've probably learned to be pragmatic about your reading. In fact, "reading a book" may have come to mean just reading assigned pages in a textbook. Whether the book's subject is modern American history, principles of corporate management, or quantum mechanics, you probably tend to read largely for information, expecting a book's ideas to be accessible and free of ambiguity and the book to be clearly written and logically organized.

In addition to reading textbooks, however, you also read essays and journal articles, fiction and poetry (in print or online). These texts present special challenges because you read them not just for information but also to discover your own ideas about what the writer is saying—what the work means to you, how you react to it, why you react as you do, and how your reactions differ from the responses of other readers. And, because the writers express opinions and communicate impressions as well as facts, your role as a reader must be more active than it is when you read a textbook. Here, reading becomes not only a search for information, but also a search for meaning.

Reading and Meaning

Like many readers, you may assume that the meaning of a text is hidden somewhere between the lines and that you only have to ask the right questions or unearth the appropriate clues to discover exactly what the writer is getting at. But reading is not a game of hide-and-seek in which you search for ideas that have been hidden by the writer. As current reading theory demonstrates, meaning is created by the interaction of a reader with a text.

One way to explain this interactive process is to draw an analogy between a text—a work being read—and a word. A word is not the natural equivalent of the thing it signifies. The word *dog*, for example, does not evoke the image of a furry, four-legged animal in all parts of the world. To speakers of Spanish, the word *perro* elicits the same mental picture *dog* does in English-speaking countries. Not only does the word *dog* have meaning only in a specific cultural context, but even within that context it evokes different images in different people. Some people may picture a collie, others a poodle, and still others a particular pet.

Like a word, a text can have different meanings in different cultures—or even in different historical time periods. Each reader brings to the text associations that come from the cultural community in which he or she lives. These associations are determined by readers' experience and education as well as by their ethnic group, class, religion, gender, and many other factors that contribute to how they view the world. Each reader also brings to the text expectations, desires, and prejudices that influence how he or she reacts to and interprets it. Thus, it is entirely possible for two readers to have very different, but equally valid, interpretations of the same text. (This does not mean, of course, that a text can mean whatever any individual reader wishes it to mean. To be valid, an interpretation must be supported by the text itself.)

To get an idea of the range of possible interpretations that can be suggested by a single text, consider some of the responses different readers might have to E. B. White's classic essay "Once More to the Lake" (p. 23).

In "Once More to the Lake," White tells a story about his visit with his son to a lake in Maine in the 1940s, comparing this visit with those he made as a boy with his own father in 1904. Throughout the essay, White describes the changes that have occurred since his first visit. Memories from the past flood his consciousness, causing him to remember things that he did when he was a boy. At one point, after he and his son have been feeding worms to fish, he remembers doing the same thing with his father and has trouble separating the past from the present. Eventually, White realizes that he will soon be just a memory in his son's mind—just as his father is only a memory in his.

White had specific goals in mind when he wrote this essay. His title, "Once More to the Lake," indicates that he intended to compare his childhood and adult visits to the lake. The organization of ideas in the essay, the use of flashbacks, and the choice of particular transitional phrases reinforce this purpose. In addition, descriptive details—such as the image of the tarred road that replaced the dirt road—remind readers, as well as White himself, that the years have made the lake site different from what it once was. The essay ends with White suddenly feeling the "chill of death."

Despite White's specific intentions, each person reading "Once More to the Lake" will respond to it somewhat differently. Young male readers might identify with the boy. If they have ever spent a vacation at a lake, they might have experienced the "peace and goodness and jollity" of the whole summer scene. Female readers might also want to share these experiences, but they might feel excluded because only males are described in the essay. Readers who have never been on a fishing trip might not feel the same nostalgia for the woods that White feels. To them, living in the woods away from the comforts of home might seem an unthinkably uncomfortable ordeal. Older readers might identify with White, sympathizing with his efforts as an adult to recapture the past and seeing his son as naively innocent of the challenges of life.

Thus, although each person who reads White's essay will read the same words, each will be likely to interpret it differently and to see different things as important. This is because much is left open to interpretation. All essays leave blanks or gaps—missing ideas or images—that readers have to fill in. In "Once More to the Lake," for example, readers must imagine what happened in the years that separated White's last visit to the lake with his father and the trip he took with his son.

These gaps in the text create ambiguities—words, phrases, descriptions, or ideas that need to be interpreted by the reader. For instance, when you read the words "One summer, along about 1904, my father rented a camp on a lake," how do you picture the camp? White's description of the setting contains a great deal of detail, but no matter how much information he supplies, he cannot paint a complete verbal picture of the lakeside camp. He must rely on the reader's ability to visualize the setting and to supply details from his or her own experience.

Readers also bring their emotional associations to a text. For example, how readers react to White's statement above depends, in part, on their feelings about their own fathers. If White's words bring to mind a parent who is loving, strong, and protective, they will most likely respond favorably; if the essay calls up memories of a parent who is distant, bad-tempered, or even abusive, they may respond negatively.

Because each reader views the text from a slightly different angle, each may also see a different focus as central to "Once More to the Lake." Some might see nature as the primary element in the essay and believe that White's purpose is to condemn the encroachment of human beings on the environment. Others might see the passage of time as the central focus. Still others might see the initiation theme as being the most important element of the essay: each boy is brought to the wilderness by his father, and each eventually passes from childhood innocence to adulthood and to the awareness of his own mortality.

Finally, each reader may evaluate the essay differently. Some readers might think "Once More to the Lake" is boring because it has little action and deals with a subject in which they have no interest. Others might believe the essay is a brilliant meditation that makes an impact through its vivid description and imaginative figurative language. Still others might see the essay as a mixed bag—admitting, for example, that although White is an excellent stylist, he is also self-centered and self-indulgent. After all, they might argue, the experiences he describes are available only to relatively privileged members of society and are irrelevant to others.

Reading Critically

Reading critically means interacting with a text, questioning the text's assumptions and formulating and reformulating judgments about its ideas. Think of reading as a dialogue between you and the text: sometimes the author will assert himself or herself; at other times, you will dominate the conversation. Remember, though, that a critical voice is a thoughtful and responsible one, not one that shouts down the opposition. Linguist Deborah Tannen makes this distinction clear in an essay called "The Triumph of the Yell":

> In many university classrooms, "critical thinking" means reading someone's life work, then ripping it to shreds. Though critique is surely one form of critical thinking, so are integrating ideas from disparate fields and examining the context out of which they grew. Opposition does not lead to truth when we ask only "What's wrong with this argument?" and never "What can we use from this in building a new theory, a new understanding?"

In other words, being a critical reader does not necessarily mean quarreling and contradicting; more often, it means asking questions and exploring your reactions—while remaining open to new ideas.

Asking the following questions as you read will help you to become aware of the relationships between the writer's perspective and your own:

- **What audience does the writer address?** Does the work offer clues to the writer's intended audience? For example, the title of John Holt's essay on early childhood education, "School Is Bad for Children" (p. 106), not only states his position but also suggests that he is questioning his readers' preconceived notions about the value of a traditional education.

- **What is the writer's purpose?** Exactly what is the writer trying to accomplish in the essay? For example, is the writer attempting to explain, persuade, justify, evaluate, describe, debunk, entertain, preach, browbeat, threaten, or frighten? Or, does the writer have some other purpose (or combination of purposes)? For example, is the writer trying to explain causes and effects, as Marie Winn is in "Television: The Plug-In Drug" (p. 231)? To reflect on his or her life, as Sherman Alexie is in "The Unauthorized Autobiography of Me" (p. 47)? Or to move readers to action, as Arlie Hochschild is in "The Second Shift" (p. 505)? What strategies does the writer use to achieve his or her purpose? For example, does the writer rely primarily on logic or on emotion? Does the writer appeal to the prejudices or fears of his or her readers or in any other way attempt to influence readers unfairly?

- **What voice does the writer use?** Does the writer seem to talk directly to readers? If so, does the writer's subjectivity get in the way, or does it help to involve readers? Does the writer's voice seem distant or formal? Different voices have different effects on readers. For example, an emotional tone, like the one Martin Luther King, Jr., uses in "I Have a Dream" (p. 485), can inspire; an intimate tone, like the one Lynda Barry uses in "The Sanctuary of School" (p. 83), can create reader identification and empathy; a straightforward, forthright voice, like that of Edward R. Murrow in his 1958 speech to the Radio and Television News Directors Association (p. 221), can make the writer's ideas seem reasonable and credible. An ironic tone can either amuse readers or alienate them; a distant, reserved tone can inspire either respect or discomfort.

- **What emotional response is the writer trying to evoke?** In "We May Be Brothers" (p. 421), Chief Seattle maintains a calm, unemotional tone even though he is describing the defeat of his people and the destruction of their land. By maintaining a dignified tone and avoiding bitterness and resentment, he succeeds in evoking sympathy and respect in his readers. Other writers may attempt to evoke other emotional responses: amusement, nostalgia, curiosity, wonder over the grandeur or mystery of the world that surrounds us, and even anger or fear.

- **What position does the writer take on the issue?** The choice of the word *war* in Christina Hoff Sommers's title "The War against Boys" (p. 400) clearly reveals her position on society's attitude toward boys; Martin Luther King, Jr., conveys his position in equally unambiguous terms when, in "Letter from Birmingham Jail" (p. 741), he asserts that people have a responsibility to disobey laws they consider unjust. Keep in mind, though, that a writer's position may not always be as obvious as it is in these two examples. As you read, look carefully for statements that suggest the writer's position on a particular subject or issue—and be sure you understand how you feel about that position, particularly if it is an unusual or controversial one. Do you agree or disagree? Can you explain your reasoning? Of course, a writer's advocacy of a position that is at odds with your own does not automatically render the work suspect or its ideas invalid. Remember, ideas that you might consider shocking or absurd may be readily accepted by many other readers. Unexpected, puzzling, or even repellent positions should encourage you to read carefully and thoughtfully, trying to understand the larger historical and cultural context of a writer's ideas.

- **How does the writer support his or her position?** What kind of support is provided? Is it convincing? Does the writer use a series of individual examples, as Alleen Pace Nilsen does in "Sexism in English: Embodiment and Language" (p. 158), or an extended example, as Claire McCarthy does in "Dog Lab" (p. 756)? Does the writer use statistics, as Barry Wellman does in "Connecting Communities: On and Offline" (p. 341), or does he or she rely primarily on personal experiences, as Brent Staples does in "Just Walk On By" (p. 450)? Does the writer quote experts, as Deborah Tannen does in "Marked Women" (p. 393), or present anecdotal information, as Jonathan Kozol does in "The Human Cost of an Illiterate Society" (p. 175)? Why does the writer choose a particular kind of support? Does he or she supply enough information to support the essay's points? Are the examples given relevant to the issues being discussed? Is the writer's reasoning valid, or do the arguments seem forced or unrealistic? Are any references in the work unfamiliar to you? If so, do they arouse your curiosity, or do they discourage you from reading further?

- **What beliefs, assumptions, or preconceived ideas do you have that color your responses to a work?** Does the writer challenge any ideas that you accept as "natural" or "obvious"? For example, do the experiments described in Stanley Milgram's "The Perils of Obedience" (p. 764) shock you or violate your sense of fairness? Does the fact that you are opposed to the concept of home schooling prevent you from appreciating arguments presented in Daniel H. Pink's "School's Out" (p. 91)?

- **Does your background or experience give you any special insights that enable you to understand or interpret the writer's ideas?** Are the writer's experiences similar to your own? Is the writer like you in terms of age, ethnic background, gender, and social class? How do the similarities between you and the writer affect your reaction to the work? For example, you may be able to understand Amy Tan's "Mother Tongue" (p. 170) better than other students because you, too, speak one language at home and another in public. You may have a unique perspective on the problems Lynda Barry describes in "The Sanctuary of School" (p. 83) because you, too, had a difficult childhood. Or your volunteer work at a shelter may have helped you understand the plight of the homeless as described by Lars Eighner in "On Dumpster Diving" (p. 454). Any experiences you have can help you to understand a writer's ideas and shape your response to them.

Recording Your Reactions

It is a good idea to read a work at least twice: first to get a general sense of the writer's ideas and then to react critically to these ideas. As you read critically, you interact with the text and respond in ways that will help you to interpret it. This process of coming to understand the text will prepare you to discuss the work with others and, perhaps, to write about it.

As you read and reread, record your responses; if you don't, you will forget some of your best ideas. Two activities can help you keep a record of the ideas that come to you as you read: **highlighting** (using a system of symbols and underlining to identify key ideas) and **annotating** (writing down your responses and interpretations).

When you react to what you read, don't be afraid to question the writer's ideas. As you read and make annotations, you may disagree with or even challenge some of these ideas. Jot your responses down in the margin; when you have time, you can think more about what you have written. These informal responses may be the beginning of a thought process that will lead you to an original insight.

Highlighting and annotating helped a student to understand the passage on page 8, which is excerpted from Brent Staples's essay "Just Walk On By" (p. 450). As she prepared to write about the essay, the student identified and summarized the writer's key points and made a connection with another essay, Judith Ortiz Cofer's "The Myth of the Latin Woman" (p. 442). As she read, she underlined some of the passage's important words and ideas, using arrows to indicate relationships between them. She also circled a few words to remind her to look up their meaning later on, and she wrote down questions and comments as they occurred to her.

The fearsomeness mistakenly attributed to me in public places often has a perilous flavor. The most frightening of these confusions occurred in the late 1970s and early 1980s when I worked as a journalist in Chicago. One day, rushing into the office of a magazine I was writing for with a deadline story in hand, I was mistaken for a burglar. The office manager called security and, with an ad hoc posse, pursued me through the labyrinthine halls, nearly to my editor's door. I had no way of proving who I was. I could only move briskly toward the company of someone who knew me.

Still applies — today?

(Fear creates danger)

First experience

Another time I was on assignment for a local paper and killing time before an interview. I entered a jewelry store on the city's affluent Near North Side. The proprietor excused herself and returned with an enormous red Doberman pinscher straining at the end of a leash. She stood, the dog extended toward me, silent to my questions, her eyes bulging nearly out of her head. I took a cursory look around, nodded, and bade her good night. Relatively speaking, however, I never fared as badly as another black male journalist. He went to nearby Waukegan, Illinois, a couple of summers ago to work on a story about a murderer who was born there. Mistaking the reporter for the killer, police hauled him from his car at gunpoint and but for his press credentials would probably have tried to book him. Such episodes are not uncommon. Black men trade tales like this all the time.

Second experience

Compare with Ortiz Cofer's experience w/ stereo-types

Reacting to Visual Texts

Many of the written texts you read—from newspapers and magazines to textbooks like this one—include visuals. Some of these visuals (charts, tables, maps, graphs, scientific diagrams, and the like) are designed primarily to present information; others (fine art, photographs, cartoons, and advertisements, for example) may be designed to have an emotional effect on readers or even to persuade them.

Visuals may be analyzed, interpreted, and evaluated just as written texts are. You begin this process by looking critically at the visual, identifying its most important elements, and considering the relationships of various elements to one another and to the image as a whole. Then, you try to identify the purpose for which the image was created, and you consider your own personal response to the image.

As you examine a visual text, finding answers to the following questions will help you to understand it better:

- **What audience is the visual aimed at?** Does the visual seem to address a wide general audience or some kind of specialized audience, such as new parents, runners, or medical profession-als? Is it aimed at adults or at children? Does it seem likely to ap-peal mainly to people from a particular region or ethnic group, or is it likely to resonate with a broad range of people? Often, know-ing where a visual appeared—in a popular magazine, a profes-sional journal, or a trade publication, for example—will help you identify the audience the visual is trying to reach.

- **What is the purpose of the visual?** Is the visual designed to evoke an emotional response—fear or guilt, for example? Is it designed to be humorous? Or is its purpose simply to present information? To understand a visual's purpose, you need to consider not only its source but also what images it contains and how it arranges them. (Sometimes, you will have to consider written text as well.)

- **What elements does the visual use to achieve its purpose?** What is the most important image? Where is it placed? What other im-ages are present? Does the visual depict people? How much space is left blank? How does the visual use color and shadow? Does it include written text? How are words and images juxtaposed? For example, a visual designed to be primarily informative may use written text and straightforward graphics (such as graphs or sci-entific diagrams), while one that aims to persuade may use a sin-gle eye-catching image surrounded by blank space.

- **Does the visual make a point?** If so, how does it use images to get its message across? What other elements convey that message? Is the visual designed to convince its audience of something—for ex-ample, to change unhealthy behavior, donate to a charity, vote for a candidate, or buy a product? Exactly how does it communicate this message? For example, a photograph of starving people might con-vey the idea that a contribution will bring them food, but statistics about infant mortality might make the image even more persuasive. Moreover, a close-up of one hungry child might be more convincing than a distant photo of a crowd. Similarly, an ad might appeal to people either by showing satisfied customers using a product or by presenting a memorable slogan against a contrasting background.

- **Do you have any beliefs or assumptions that affect your re-sponse to the visual?** Is there anything in your background or ex-perience that influences your reaction? Just as with written texts, different people react differently to different visual texts. For ex-ample, if you have expertise in economics, you may approach a chart depicting economic trends with greater interest—or greater skepticism—than a general audience. If you know very little about fine art, your reaction to a painting is more likely to be emotional than analytical. And, as a loyal Democrat or Republican, you may react negatively to a political cartoon that is critical of your party.

Finally, if you or a family member has struggled with illness or addiction, you might not respond favorably to a visual that took a superficial, lighthearted, or satirical approach to such a problem.

The following visual is a parody of an ad for Marlboro cigarettes. The visual, which appeared on the Web site *www.adbusters.org*, was annotated by a student who was assigned to analyze it. As he examined the ad, he identified its key elements and recorded his reactions in handwritten notes.

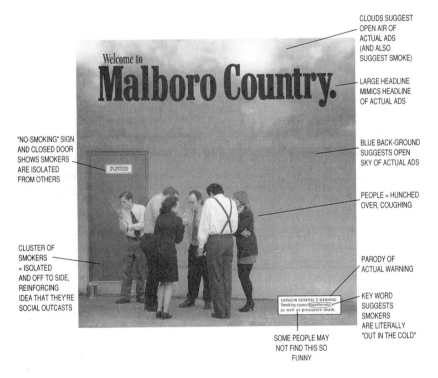

Reading to Write

Much of the reading you will do as a student will be done to prepare you for writing. Writing helps you focus your ideas about various issues; in addition, the process of writing can lead you in unexpected directions, thereby enabling you to discover new ideas. With this in mind, we have included in *The Blair Reader* a number of features that will help you as you read and prepare to write about its selections.

The readings in *The Blair Reader* are arranged in eleven thematic chapters, each offering a variety of different vantage points from which to view the chapter's central theme. Each chapter opens with a brief introduction, which provides a context for the chapter's theme and lists **Preparing to Read and Write** questions to guide your thinking as you read. These questions will help you to sharpen your critical skills and begin to apply those skills effectively. Each chapter introduction also includes a pair of contrasting visual images—newspaper photographs, advertisements, Web pages, and so on—designed to introduce you to the chapter's theme and to help you begin thinking about the issues it suggests.

Following each reading are three questions that encourage you to think about and respond to what you have read. These **Responding to Reading** questions ask you to think critically about the writer's ideas, perhaps focusing on a particular strategy the writer has used to achieve his or her purpose. In some cases, these questions may ask you to examine your own ideas or beliefs. Following the **Responding to Reading** questions is a **Responding in Writing** prompt that asks you to write a brief, informal response. These prompts may ask you to link the writer's experiences or ideas to your own; to do some kind of writing exercise, such as making a list, writing a summary, or drafting a letter; or to respond more critically to the writer's ideas.

Following the essays that develop aspects of each chapter's general theme is a **Focus** section that zeroes in on a specific issue related to that theme. The **Focus** section's central question—for example, "How Free Should Free Speech Be?" (Chapter 3) or "Has the Internet Doomed the Newspaper?" (Chapter 4)—introduces a cluster of thought-provoking essays that take different positions on a single complex issue; a related visual image is also included in this Focus section (Chapter 9, "Science and Human Values," is composed of three Focus Sections.) Each **Focus** essay is accompanied by three **Responding to Reading** questions and one **Responding in Writing** prompt; **Responding to the Image** questions follow each visual. The **Focus** section ends with **Widening the Focus**, which provides a writing prompt, identifies related readings in other chapters of the book, and gives an assignment for doing guided Internet research.

At the end of each chapter are suggestions for writing assignments that are longer and more formally structured than those suggested by the **Responding in Writing** prompts. These writing assignments ask you to examine some aspect of the chapter's theme by analyzing, interpreting, or evaluating ideas explored in various essays, sometimes considering parallels and contrasts with other essays in the book—or with your own life experiences.

As you read and write about the selections in this book, remember that you are learning ways of thinking about yourself and about the world. By considering and reconsidering the ideas of others, by rejecting easy answers, by considering a problem from many different angles, and by appreciating the many factors that can influence your responses, you develop critical thinking skills that you will use throughout your life. In addition, by writing about the themes discussed in this book, you participate in an ongoing conversation within the community of scholars and writers who care deeply about the issues that shape our world.

1

FAMILY TIES

The ties that bind us to family, and to our family history, are like no other human connections. In this chapter, writers search their memories, trying to understand, recapture, or re-create the past, to see across the barriers imposed by time. In some cases, memories appear in sharp focus; in others, they are blurred, confused, or even partially invented. Many writers focus on themselves; others focus on their parents or other family members, struggling to close generational gaps, to replay events, to see through the eyes of others—and thus to understand their families and themselves more fully.

In a sense, every child (even siblings) grows up in a different family. Depending on birth order and changing family circumstances—financial gains and losses, illness and death of family members, geographic

Family at beach at Margate, New Jersey, July 1955

relocation, divorce and remarriage—children will have different experiences, different challenges, and different memories.

Finally, the notion of what constitutes a family is very different from what it was a generation or two ago. In fact, for the past thirty years, the marriage rate has been declining in the United States; at the same time, the number of couples living together has been steadily rising. Now, the "nuclear family" exists alongside single-parent families, gay couples with children, "blended" families that combine unrelated children in a single household, couples or single people with adopted as well as biological children, and couples (gay or straight) without children. For many people, this diversity is a sign of healthy change; for other, it suggests the decline of the family.

In the Focus section of this chapter, "Does Gay Marriage Threaten the Family?" (p. 61), three writers consider the pros and cons of legalizing marriage between gay or lesbian partners. In "What Are We Fighting For?" Ralph Wedgwood argues that marriage is an important legal right for same-sex couples; without access to marriage, he believes, such couples will have second-class status in the eyes of their fellow citizens. Maggie Gallagher's "What Marriage Is For" takes a very different view, arguing that the purpose of marriage is to provide mothers and fathers for children; thus, by definition, marriage is an unsuitable arrangement for gays and lesbians. Gallagher believes that allowing same-sex couples to marry will threaten the institution of marriage as we know it. Finally, Kerry Howley, in "Marriage Just Lets the State Back In," rejects the notion of marriage as an ideal for same-sex couples, arguing that it

Family at beach, late 1990s

permits the state to impose its "dated social conventions" on such couples, who should seek control over their own commitment arrangements. Underlying all three essays is the sense that the gay marriage movement is gaining ground and may, perhaps, be inevitable.

——————— PREPARING TO READ AND WRITE ———————

As you read and prepare to write about the selections in this chapter, you may consider the following questions:

- How does the writer define *family?*

- Is the writer's focus on a particular family or on families in general?

- Does the writer focus on a single person, on a relationship between two people, or on larger family dynamics?

- Do you think the writer's perspective is *subjective* (shaped by his or her emotional responses or personal opinions) or *objective* (based mainly on observation and fact rather than on personal impressions)?

- Does the writer recount events from the perspective of an adult looking back at his or her childhood? If so, does the writer seem to have more insight now than when the events occurred? What has the writer learned—and how?

- Are the memories generally happy or unhappy ones?

- Are family members presented in a favorable, unfavorable, neutral, or ambivalent way?

- Does the writer feel close to or distant from family members? Does the writer identify with a particular family member?

- Does one family member seem to have a great influence over others in the family? If so, is this influence positive or negative?

- What social, political, economic, or cultural forces influence the way the family functions?

- What is the writer's primary purpose? For example, is the writer's purpose to observe, explore, discover, explain, or persuade?

- Do you identify with the writer or with another person described in the selection? What makes you identify with that person?

- Which selections seem most similar in their views of family? How are they similar?

- Which selections seem most different in their views of family? How are they different?

THOSE WINTER SUNDAYS
Robert Hayden
1913–1980

Robert Hayden's work includes poems about slave rebellions and the histori-
cal roots of racism as well as about more personal subjects. Hayden's first
book of poetry, Heart-Shaped in the Dust, *was published in 1940. Other*
works include Angle of Ascent; New and Selected Poems *(1975), in*
which "Those Winter Sundays" appeared, and Complete Poems *(1985).*
In the following poem, the speaker expresses his ambivalence about his fa-
ther's sacrifices.

Sundays too my father got up early
and put his clothes on in the blueblack cold,
then with cracked hands that ached
from labor in the weekday weather made
banked fires blaze. No one ever thanked him.   5

I'd wake and hear the cold splintering, breaking,
When the rooms were warm, he'd call,
and slowly I would rise and dress,
fearing the chronic angers of that house,

Speaking indifferently to him,   10
who had driven out the cold
and polished my good shoes as well.
What did I know, what did I know
of love's austere and lonely offices?

Responding to Reading

1. Other than having "driven out the cold," what has the father done for his
   son? To what might the "chronic angers" (line 9) refer?
2. What important lessons has the speaker learned? Do you see these lessons
   as primarily theoretical or practical?
3. In what respects does this poem sound like conversational prose? In what
   respects is it "poetic"?

Responding in Writing

What do you now know about your parents' responsibilities and sacrifices that
you did not know when you were a child? How has this knowledge changed
your feelings about your parents?

ONE LAST TIME

Gary Soto

1952–

Gary Soto grew up working along with his family as a migrant laborer in California's San Joaquin Valley. Soto often write s of the struggles of Mexican Americans, as he does in the following autobiographical essay, in which he describes his experiences picking grapes and cotton. This essay is taken from Living Up the Street: Narrative Recollections, *for which he won the American Book Award in 1985. The author of ten poetry collections, Soto has also published short story collections, novels, and picture books for children. He is also involved with two organizations that work for justice for migrant workers: California Rural Legal Assistance (CRLA) and the United Farm Workers of America (UFWA).*

Yesterday I saw the movie *Gandhi*[1] and recognized a few of the people—not in the theater but in the film. I saw my relatives, dusty and thin as sparrows, returning from the fields with hoes balanced on their shoulders. The workers were squinting, eyes small and veined, and were using their hands to say what there was to say to those in the audience with popcorn and Cokes. I didn't have anything, though. I sat thinking of my family and their years in the fields, beginning with Grandmother who came to the United States after the Mexican revolution to settle in Fresno where she met her husband and bore children, many of them. She worked in the fields around Fresno, picking grapes, oranges, plums, peaches, and cotton, dragging a large white sack like a sled. She worked in the packing houses, Bonner and Sun-Maid Raisin, where she stood at a conveyor belt passing her hand over streams of raisins to pluck out leaves and pebbles. For over twenty years she worked at a machine that boxed raisins until she retired at sixty-five.

Grandfather worked in the fields, as did his children. Mother also found herself out there when she separated from Father for three weeks. I remember her coming home, dusty and so tired that she had to rest on the porch before she trudged inside to wash and start dinner. I didn't understand the complaints about her ankles or the small of her back, even though I had been in the grape fields watching her work. With my brother and sister I ran in and out of the rows; we enjoyed ourselves and pretended not to hear Mother scolding us to sit down and behave ourselves. A few years later, however, I caught on when I went to pick grapes rather than play in the rows.

---

[1]The 1982 film biography of the nonviolent revolutionary Mohandas Gandhi (known as Mahatma), which was set in part among the peasants of India. [Eds.]

❧ Mother and I got up before dawn and ate quick bowls of cereal. She drove in silence while I rambled on how everything was now solved, how I was going to make enough money to end our misery and even buy her a beautiful copper tea pot, the one I had shown her in Long's Drugs. When we arrived I was frisky and ready to go, self-consciously aware of my grape knife dangling at my wrist. I almost ran to the row the foreman had pointed out, but I returned to help Mother with the grape pans and jug of water. She told me to settle down and reminded me not to lose my knife. I walked at her side and listened to her explain how to cut grapes; bent down, hands on knees, I watched her demonstrate by cutting a few bunches into my pan. She stood over me as I tried it myself, tugging at a bunch of grapes that pulled loose like beads from a necklace. "Cut the stem all the way," she told me as last advice before she walked away, her shoes sinking in the loose dirt, to begin work on her own row.

I cut another bunch, then another, fighting the snap and whip of vines. After ten minutes of groping for grapes, my first pan brimmed with bunches. I poured them on the paper tray, which was bordered by a wooden frame that kept the grapes from rolling off, and they spilled like jewels from a pirate's chest. The tray was only half filled, so I hurried to jump under the vines and begin groping, cutting, and tugging at the grapes again. I emptied the pan, raked the grapes with my hands to make them look like they filled the tray, and jumped back under the vine on my knees. I tried to cut faster because Mother, in the next row, was slowly moving ahead. I peeked into her row and saw five trays gleaming in the early morning. I cut, pulled hard, and stopped to gather the grapes that missed the pan; already bored, I spat on a few to wash them before tossing them like popcorn into my mouth.

So it went. Two pans equaled one tray—or six cents. By lunchtime ₅ I had a trail of thirty-seven trays behind me while mother had sixty or more. We met about halfway from our last trays, and I sat down with a grunt, knees wet from kneeling on dropped grapes. I washed my hands with the water from the jug, drying them on the inside of my shirt sleeve before I opened the paper bag for the first sandwich, which I gave to Mother. I dipped my hand in again to unwrap a sandwich without looking at it. I took a first bite and chewed it slowly for the tang of mustard. Eating in silence I looked straight ahead at the vines, and only when we were finished with cookies did we talk.

"Are you tired?" she asked.

"No, but I got a sliver from the frame," I told her. I showed her the web of skin between my thumb and index finger. She wrinkled her forehead but said it was nothing.

"How many trays did you do?"

I looked straight ahead, not answering at first. I recounted in my mind the whole morning of bend, cut, pour again and again, before answering a feeble "thirty-seven." No elaboration, no detail. Without looking at me she told me how she had done field work in Texas and Michigan as a child. But I had a difficult time listening to her stories. I played with my grape knife, stabbing it into the ground, but stopped when Mother reminded me that I had better not lose it. I left the knife sticking up like a small, leafless plant. She then talked about school, the junior high I would be going to that fall, and then about Rick and Debra, how sorry they would be that they hadn't come out to pick grapes because they'd have no new clothes for the school year. She stopped talking when she peeked at her watch, a bandless one she kept in her pocket. She got up with an "*Ay, Dios,*" and told me that we'd work until three, leaving me cutting figures in the sand with my knife and dreading the return to work.

10   Finally I rose and walked slowly back to where I had left off, again kneeling under the vine and fixing the pan under bunches of grapes. By that time, 11:30, the sun was over my shoulder and made me squint and think of the pool at the Y.M.C.A. where I was a summer member. I saw myself diving face first into the water and loving it. I saw myself gleaming like something new, at the edge of the pool. I had to daydream and keep my mind busy because boredom was a terror almost as awful as the work itself. My mind went dumb with stupid things, and I had to keep it moving with dreams of baseball and would-be girlfriends. I even sang, however softly, to keep my mind moving, my hands moving.

   I worked less hurriedly and with less vision. I no longer saw that copper pot sitting squat on our stove or Mother waiting for it to whistle. The wardrobe that I imagined, crisp and bright in the closet, numbered only one pair of jeans and two shirts because, in half a day, six cents times thirty-seven trays was two dollars and twenty-two cents. It became clear to me. If I worked eight hours, I might make four dollars. I'd take this, even gladly, and walk downtown to look into store windows on the mall and long for the bright madras shirts from Walter Smith or Coffee's, but settling for two imitation ones from Penney's.

    That first day I laid down seventy-three trays while Mother had a hundred and twenty behind her. On the back of an old envelope, she wrote out our numbers and hours. We washed at the pump behind the farm house and walked slowly to our car for the drive back to town in the afternoon heat. That evening after dinner I sat in a lawn chair listening to music from a transistor radio while Rick and David King played catch. I joined them in a game of pickle, but there was little joy in trying to avoid their tags because I couldn't get the fields out of my mind: I saw myself dropping on my knees under a vine to tug at a branch that wouldn't come off. In bed, when I closed my eyes, I saw the fields, yellow with kicked up dust, and a crooked trail of trays rotting behind me.

The next day I woke tired and started picking tired. The grapes rained into the pan, slowly filling like a belly, until I had my first tray and started my second. So it went all day, and the next, and all through the following week, so that by the end of thirteen days the foreman counted out, in tens mostly, my pay of fifty-three dollars. Mother earned one hundred and forty-eight dollars. She wrote this on her envelope, with a message I didn't bother to ask her about.

The next day I walked with my friend Scott to the downtown mall where we drooled over the clothes behind fancy windows, bought popcorn, and sat at a tier of outdoor fountains to talk about girls. Finally we went into Penney's for more popcorn, which we ate walking around, before we returned home without buying anything. It wasn't until a few days before school that I let my fifty-three dollars slip quietly from my hands, buying a pair of pants, two shirts, and a maroon T-shirt, the kind that was in style. At home I tried them on while Rick looked on enviously; later, the day before school started, I tried them on again wondering not so much if they were worth it as who would see me first in those clothes.

Along with my brother and sister I picked grapes until I was fif- 15 teen, before giving up and saying that I'd rather wear old clothes than stoop like a Mexican. Mother thought I was being stuck-up, even stupid, because there would be no clothes for me in the fall. I told her I didn't care, but when Rick and Debra rose at five in the morning, I lay awake in bed feeling that perhaps I had made a mistake but unwilling to change my mind. That fall Mother bought me two pairs of socks, a packet of colored T-shirts, and underwear. The T-shirts would help, I thought, but who would see that I had new underwear and socks? I wore a new T-shirt on the first day of school, then an old shirt on Tuesday, then another T-shirt on Wednesday, and on Thursday an old Nehru shirt that was embarrassingly out of style. On Friday I changed into the corduroy pants my brother had handed down to me and slipped into my last new T-shirt. I worked like a magician, blinding my classmates, who were all clothes conscious and small-time social climbers, by arranging my wardrobe to make it seem larger than it really was. But by spring I had to do something—my blue jeans were almost silver and my shoes had lost their form, puddling like black ice around my feet. That spring of my sixteenth year, Rick and I decided to take a labor bus to chop cotton. In his old Volkswagen, which was more noise than power, we drove on a Saturday morning to West Fresno—or Chinatown as some call it—parked, walked slowly toward a bus, and stood gawking at the winos, toothy blacks, Okies, *Tejanos*[2] with gold teeth, whores, Mexican families, and labor contractors shouting "Cotton" or "Beets," the work of spring.

---

[2]Descendants of early Mexican settlers in Texas. [Eds.]

We boarded the "Cotton" bus without looking at the contractor who stood almost blocking the entrance because he didn't want winos. We boarded scared and then were more scared because two blacks in the rear were drunk and arguing loudly about what was better, a two-barrel or four-barrel Ford carburetor. We sat far from them, looking straight ahead, and only glanced briefly at the others who boarded, almost all of them broken and poorly dressed in loudly mismatched clothes. Finally when the contractor banged his palm against the side of the bus, the young man at the wheel, smiling and talking in Spanish, started the engine, idled it for a moment while he adjusted the mirrors, and started off in slow chugs. Except for the windshield there was no glass in the windows, so as soon as we were on the rural roads outside Fresno, the dust and sand began to be sucked into the bus, whipping about like irate wasps as the gravel ticked about us. We closed our eyes, clotted up our mouths that wanted to open with embarrassed laughter because we couldn't believe we were on that bus with those people and the dust attacking us for no reason.

When we arrived at a field we followed the others to a pickup where we each took a hoe and marched to stand before a row. Rick and I, self-conscious and unsure, looked around at the others who leaned on their hoes or squatted in front of the rows, almost all talking in Spanish, joking, lighting cigarettes—all waiting for the foreman's whistle to begin work. Mother had explained how to chop cotton by showing us with a broom in the backyard.

"Like this," she said, her broom swishing down weeds. "Leave one plant and cut four—and cut them! Don't leave them standing or the foreman will get mad."

The foreman whistled and we started up the row stealing glances at other workers to see if we were doing it right. But after awhile we worked like we knew what we were doing, neither of us hurrying or falling behind. But slowly the clot of men, women, and kids began to spread and loosen. Even Rick pulled away. I didn't hurry, though. I cut smoothly and cleanly as I walked at a slow pace, in a sort of funeral march. My eyes measured each space of cotton plants before I cut. If I missed the plants, I swished again. I worked intently, seldom looking up, so when I did I was amazed to see the sun, like a broken orange coin, in the east. It looked blurry, unbelievable, like something not of this world. I looked around in amazement, scanning the eastern horizon that was a taut line jutted with an occasional mountain. The horizon was beautiful, like a snapshot of the moon, in the early light of morning, in the quiet of no cars and few people.

20   The foreman trudged in boots in my direction, stepping awkwardly over the plants, to inspect the work. No one around me looked up. We all worked steadily while we waited for him to leave.

When he did leave, with a feeble complaint addressed to no one in particular, we looked up smiling under straw hats and bandanas.

By 11:00, our lunch time, my ankles were hurting from walking on clods the size of hardballs. My arms ached and my face was dusted by a wind that was perpetual, always busy whipping about. But the work was not bad, I thought. It was better, so much better, than picking grapes, especially with the hourly wage of a dollar twenty-five instead of piece work. Rick and I walked sorely toward the bus where we washed and drank water. Instead of eating in the bus or in the shade of the bus, we kept to ourselves by walking down to the irrigation canal that ran the length of the field, to open our lunch of sandwiches and crackers. We laughed at the crackers, which seemed like a cruel joke from our Mother, because we were working under the sun and the last thing we wanted was a salty dessert. We ate them anyway and drank more water before we returned to the field, both of us limping in exageration. Working side by side, we talked and laughed at our predicament because our Mother had warned us year after year that if we didn't get on track in school we'd have to work in the fields and then we would see. We mimicked Mother's whining voice and smirked at her smoky view of the future in which we'd be trapped by marriage and screaming kids. We'd eat beans and then we'd see.

Rick pulled slowly away to the rhythm of his hoe falling faster and smoother. It was better that way, to work alone. I could hum made-up songs or songs from the radio and think to myself about school and friends. At the time I was doing badly in my classes, mainly because of a difficult stepfather, but also because I didn't care anymore. All through junior high and into my first year of high school there were those who said I would never do anything, be anyone. They said I'd work like a donkey and marry the first Mexican girl that came along. I was reminded so often, verbally and in the way I was treated at home, that I began to believe that chopping cotton might be a lifetime job for me. If not chopping cotton, then I might get lucky and find myself in a car wash or restaurant or junkyard. But it was clear; I'd work, and work hard.

I cleared my mind by humming and looking about. The sun was directly above with a few soft blades of clouds against a sky that seemed bluer and more beautiful than our sky in the city. Occasionally the breeze flurried and picked up dust so that I had to cover my eyes and screw up my face. The workers were hunched, brown as the clods under our feet, and spread across the field that ran without end—fields that were owned by corporations, not families.

I hoed, trying to keep my mind busy with scenes from school and pretend girlfriends until finally my brain turned off and my thinking went fuzzy with boredom. I looked about, no longer mesmerized by the beauty of the landscape, no longer wondering if the winos in the fields could hold out for eight hours, no longer dreaming of the clothes I'd buy with my pay. My eyes followed my chopping as the plants, thin as their shadows, fell with each strike. I worked slowly with ankles and arms hurting, neck stiff, and eyes stinging from the dust and the sun that glanced off the field like a mirror.

25   By quitting time, 3:00, there was such an excruciating pain in my ankles that I walked as if I were wearing snowshoes. Rick laughed at me and I laughed too, embarrassed that most of the men were walking normally and I was among the first timers who had to get used to this work. "And what about you, wino," I came back at Rick. His eyes were meshed red and his long hippie hair was flecked with dust and gnats and bits of leaves. We placed our hoes in the back of a pickup and stood in line for our pay, which was twelve fifty. I was amazed at the pay, which was the most I had ever earned in one day, and thought that I'd come back the next day, Sunday. This was too good.

Instead of joining the others in the labor bus, we jumped in the back of a pickup when the driver said we'd get to town sooner and were welcome to join him. We scrambled into the truck bed to be joined by a heavy-set and laughing *Tejano* whose head was shaped like an egg, particularly so because the bandana he wore ended in a point on the top of his head. He laughed almost demonically as the pickup roared up the dirt path, a gray cape of dust rising behind us. On the highway, with the wind in our faces, we squinted at the fields as if we were looking for someone. The *Tejano* had quit laughing but was smiling broadly, occasionally chortling tunes he never finished. I was scared of him, though Rick, two years older and five inches taller, wasn't. If the *Tejano* looked at him, Rick stared back for a second or two before he looked away to the fields.

I felt like a soldier coming home from war when we rattled into Chinatown. People leaning against car hoods stared, their necks following us, owl-like; prostitutes chewed gum more ferociously and showed us their teeth; Chinese grocers stopped brooming their storefronts to raise their cadaverous faces at us. We stopped in front of the Chi Chi Club where Mexican music blared from the juke box and cue balls cracked like dull ice. The *Tejano*, who was dirty as we were, stepped awkwardly over the side rail, dusted himself off with his bandana, and sauntered into the club.

Rick and I jumped from the back, thanked the driver who said *de nada* and popped his clutch, so that the pickup jerked and coughed blue smoke. We returned smiling to our car, happy with the money we had made and pleased that we had, in a small way, proved ourselves to be tough; that we worked as well as other men and earned the same pay.

We returned the next day and the next week until the season was over and there was nothing to do. I told myself that I wouldn't pick grapes that summer, saying all through June and July that it was for Mexicans, not me. When August came around and I still had not found a summer job, I ate my words, sharpened my knife, and joined Mother, Rick, and Debra for one last time.

Responding to Reading

1. In paragraph 1, Soto says he recognizes his relatives in the characters he sees in the film *Gandhi*. What does he mean?
2. Why would Soto at age fifteen "rather wear old clothes than stoop like a Mexican" (15)? Does the adult Soto understand the reasons for this sentiment? What does this comment reveal about the society in which Soto grew up?
3. What did Soto learn from the events he describes? What more do you think he had to learn?

Responding in Writing

Is there a film or TV show in whose characters you recognize your own family members as Soto recognizes his relatives in *Gandhi*? In what sense are your relatives like those you see on the screen?

Once More to the Lake

E. B. White
1899–1985

Well known for his children's stories, Elwyn Brooks White was also a talented essayist and a witty observer of contemporary society. His expansion of Will Strunk's The Elements of Style *remains one of the most popular and concise grammar and style texts in use today. White wrote for the* New Yorker *and* Harper's Magazine, *and his essays are collected in* Essays of E. B. White *(1977). In 1939, he moved to a farm in North Brooklin, Maine, where he wrote the children's classics* Stuart Little *(1945) and* Charlotte's Web *(1952). As a youth, White vacationed with his family on a lake in Maine. It is to this lake that he returned with his son, and he describes his experience in the following essay.*

One summer, along about 1904, my father rented a camp on a lake in Maine and took us all there for the month of August. We all got ringworm from some kittens and had to rub Pond's Extract on our arms and legs night and morning, and my father rolled over in a canoe with all his clothes on; but outside of that the vacation was a success and from then on none of us ever thought there was any place in the world like that lake in Maine. We returned summer after summer—always on August 1st for one month. I have since become a salt-water man, but sometimes in summer there are days when the restlessness of the tides and the fearful cold of the sea water and the incessant wind which blows across the afternoon and into the evening make me wish for the placidity of a lake in the woods. A few weeks ago this feeling got so strong I bought myself a couple of bass hooks and a spinner and returned to the lake where we used to go, for a week's fishing and to revisit old haunts.

I took along my son, who had never had any fresh water up his nose and who had seen lily pads only from train windows. On the journey over to the lake I began to wonder what it would be like. I wondered how time would have marred this unique, this holy spot—the coves and streams, the hills that the sun set behind, the camps and the paths behind the camps. I was sure the tarred road would have found it out and I wondered in what other ways it would be desolated. It is strange how much you can remember about places like that once you allow your mind to return into the grooves which lead back. You remember one thing, and that suddenly reminds you of another thing. I guess I remembered clearest of all the early mornings, when the lake was cool and motionless, remembered how the bedroom smelled of the lumber it was made of and of the wet woods whose scent entered through the screen. The partitions in the camp were thin and did not extend clear to the top of the rooms, and as I was always the first up I would dress softly so as not to wake the others, and sneak out into the sweet outdoors and start out in the canoe, keeping close along the shore in the long shadows of the pines. I remembered being very careful never to rub my paddle against the gunwale for fear of disturbing the stillness of the cathedral.

The lake had never been what you would call a wild lake. There were cottages sprinkled around the shores, and it was in farming country although the shores of the lake were quite heavily wooded. Some of the cottages were owned by nearby farmers, and you would live at the shore and eat your meals at the farmhouse. That's what our family did. But although it wasn't wild, it was a fairly large and undisturbed lake and there were places in it which, to a child at least, seemed infinitely remote and primeval.

I was right about the tar: it led to within half a mile of the shore. But when I got back there, with my boy, and we settled into a camp near a farmhouse and into the kind of summertime I had known, I could tell that it was going to be pretty much the same as it had been before—I knew it, lying in bed the first morning, smelling the bedroom, and hearing the boy sneak quietly out and go off along the shore in a boat. I began to sustain the illusion that he was I, and therefore, by simple transposition, that I was my father. This sensation persisted, kept cropping up all the time we were there. It was not an entirely new feeling, but in this setting it grew much stronger. I seemed to be living a dual existence. I would be in the middle of some simple act, I would be picking up a bait box or laying down a table fork, or I would be saying something, and suddenly it would be not I but my father who was saying the words or making the gesture. It gave me a creepy sensation.

We went fishing the first morning. I felt the same damp moss cov-   5 ering the worms in the bait can, and saw the dragonfly alight on the tip of my rod as it hovered a few inches from the surface of the water. It was the arrival of this fly that convinced me beyond any doubt that everything was as it always had been, that the years were a mirage and there had been no years. The small waves were the same, chucking the rowboat under the chin as we fished at anchor, and the boat was the same boat, the same color green and the ribs broken in the same places, and under the floor-boards the same freshwater leavings and débris—the dead helgramite,[1] the wisps of moss, the rusty discarded fishhook, the dried blood from yesterday's catch. We stared silently at the tips of our rods, at the dragonflies that came and went. I lowered the tip of mine into the water, tentatively, pensively dislodging the fly, which darted two feet away, poised, darted two feet back, and came to rest again a little farther up the rod. There had been no years between the ducking of this dragonfly and the other one—the one that was part of memory. I looked at the boy, who was silently watching his fly, and it was my hands that held his rod, my eyes watching. I felt dizzy and didn't know which rod I was at the end of.

We caught two bass, hauling them in briskly as though they were mackerel, pulling them over the side of the boat in a businesslike manner without any landing net, and stunning them with a blow on the back of the head. When we got back for a swim before lunch, the lake was exactly where we had left it, the same number of inches from the dock, and there was only the merest suggestion of a breeze. This seemed an utterly enchanted sea, this lake you could leave to its own devices for a few hours and come back to, and find that it had not stirred, this constant and trustworthy body of water. In the shallows, the dark, watersoaked sticks and twigs, smooth and old, were undulating in clusters on the bottom against the clean ribbed sand, and the track of the mussel was plain. A school of minnows swam by, each minnow with its small individual shadow, doubling the attendance, so clear and sharp in the sunlight. Some of the other campers were in swimming, along the shore, one of them with a cake of soap, and the water felt thin and clear and unsubstantial. Over the years there had been this person with the cake of soap, this cultist, and here he was. There had been no years.

---

[1]The nymph of the May-fly, used as bait. [Eds.]

Up to the farmhouse to dinner through the teeming, dusty field, the road under our sneakers was only a two-track road. The middle track was missing, the one with the marks of the hooves and the splotches of dried, flaky manure. There had always been three tracks to choose from in choosing which track to walk in; now the choice was narrowed down to two. For a moment I missed terribly the middle alternative. But the way led past the tennis court, and something about the way it lay there in the sun reassured me; the tape had loosened along the backline, the alleys were green with plantains and other weeds, and the net (installed in June and removed in September) sagged in the dry noon, and the whole place steamed with midday heat and hunger and emptiness. There was a choice of pie for dessert, and one was blueberry and one was apple, and the waitresses were the same country girls, there having been no passage of time, only the illusion of it as in a dropped curtain—the waitresses were still fifteen; their hair had been washed, that was the only difference—they had been to the movies and seen the pretty girls with the clean hair.

Summertime, oh summertime, pattern of life indelible, the fade-proof lake, the woods unshatterable, the pasture with the sweetfern and the juniper forever and ever, summer without end; this was the background, and the life along the shore was the design, the cottagers with their innocent and tranquil design, their tiny docks with the flag-pole and the American flag floating against the white clouds in the blue sky, the little paths over the roots of the trees leading from camp to camp and the paths leading back to the outhouses and the can of lime for sprinkling, and at the souvenir counters at the store the miniature birch-bark canoes and the post cards that showed things looking a little better than they looked. This was the American family at play, escaping the city heat, wondering whether the newcomers in the camp at the head of the cove were "common" or "nice," wondering whether it was true that the people who drove up for Sunday dinner at the farmhouse were turned away because there wasn't enough chicken.

It seemed to me, as I kept remembering all this, that those times and those summers had been infinitely precious and worth saving. There had been jollity and peace and goodness. The arriving (at the beginning of August) had been so big a business in itself, at the railway station the farm wagon drawn up, the first smell of the pine-laden air, the first glimpse of the smiling farmer, and the great importance of the trunks and your father's enormous authority in such matters, and the feel of the wagon under you for the long ten-mile haul, and at the top of the last long hill catching the first view of the lake after eleven months of not seeing this cherished body of water. The shouts and cries of the other campers when they saw you, and the trunks to be unpacked, to give up their rich burden. (Arriving was less exciting nowadays, when you sneaked up in your car and parked it under a tree near the camp and took out the bags and in five minutes it was all over, no fuss, no loud wonderful fuss about trunks.)

Peace and goodness and jollity. The only thing that was wrong 10 now, really, was the sound of the place, an unfamiliar nervous sound of the outboard motors. This was the note that jarred, the one thing that would sometimes break the illusion and set the years moving. In those other summertimes all motors were inboard; and when they were at a little distance, the noise they made was a sedative, an ingredient of summer sleep. They were one-cylinder and two-cylinder engines, and some were make-and-break and some were jump-spark,[2] but they all made a sleepy sound across the lake. The one-lungers throbbed and fluttered, and the twin-cylinder ones purred and purred, and that was a quiet sound too. But now the campers all had outboards. In the daytime, in the hot mornings, these motors made a petulant, irritable sound; at night, in the still evening when the afterglow lit the water, they whined about one's ears like mosquitoes. My boy loved our rented outboard, and his great desire was to achieve singlehanded mastery over it, and authority, and he soon learned the trick of choking it a little (but not too much), and the adjustment of the needle valve. Watching him I would remember the things you could do with the old one-cylinder engine with the heavy flywheel, how you could have it eating out of your hand if you got really close to it spiritually. Motor boats in those days didn't have clutches, and you would make a landing by shutting off the motor at the proper time and coasting in with a dead rudder. But there was a way of reversing them, if you learned the trick, by cutting the switch and putting it on again exactly on the final dying revolution of the flywheel, so that it would kick back against compression and begin reversing. Approaching a dock in a strong following breeze, it was difficult to slow up sufficiently by the ordinary coasting method, and if a boy felt he had complete mastery over his motor, he was tempted to keep it running beyond its time and then reverse it a few feet from the dock. It took a cool nerve, because if you threw the switch a twentieth of a second too soon you would catch the flywheel when it still had speed enough to go up past center, and the boat would leap ahead, charging bull-fashion at the dock.

We had a good week at the camp. The bass were biting well and the sun shone endlessly, day after day. We would be tired at night and lie down in the accumulated heat of the little bedrooms after the long hot day and the breeze would stir almost imperceptibly outside and the smell of the swamp drift in through the rusty screens. Sleep

---

[2]Methods of ignition timing. [Eds.]

would come easily and in the morning the red squirrel would be on the roof, tapping out his gay routine. I kept remembering everything, lying in bed in the mornings—the small steamboat that had a long rounded stern like the lip of a Ubangi, and how quietly she ran on the moonlight sails, when the older boys played their mandolins and the girls sang and we ate doughnuts dipped in sugar, and how sweet the music was on the water in the shining night, and what it had felt like to think about girls then. After breakfast we would go up to the store and the things were in the same place—the minnows in a bottle, the plugs and spinners disarranged and pawed over by the youngsters from the boys' camp, the fig newtons and the Beeman's gum. Outside, the road was tarred and cars stood in front of the store. Inside, all was just as it had always been, except there was more Coca-Cola and not so much Moxie and root beer and birch beer and sarsaparilla. We would walk out with a bottle of pop apiece and sometimes the pop would backfire up our noses and hurt. We explored the streams, quietly, where the turtles slid off the sunny logs and dug their way into the soft bottom; and we lay on the town wharf and fed worms to the tame bass. Everywhere we went I had trouble making out which was I, the one walking at my side, the one walking in my pants.

One afternoon while we were there at that lake a thunderstorm came up. It was like the revival of an old melodrama that I had seen long ago with childish awe. The second-act climax of the drama of the electrical disturbance over a lake in America had not changed in any important respect. This was the big scene, still the big scene. The whole thing was so familiar, the first feeling of oppression and heat and a general air around camp of not wanting to go very far away. In midafternoon (it was all the same) a curious darkening of the sky, and a lull in everything that had made life tick; and then the way the boats suddenly swung the other way at their moorings with the coming of a breeze out of the new quarter, and the premonitory rumble. Then the kettle drum, then the snare, then the bass drum and cymbals, then crackling light against the dark, and the gods grinning and licking their chops in the hills. Afterward the calm, the rain steadily rustling in the calm lake, the return of light and hope and spirits, and the campers running out in joy and relief to go swimming in the rain, their bright cries perpetuating the deathless joke about how they were getting simply drenched, and the children screaming with delight at the new sensation of bathing in the rain, and the joke about getting drenched linking the generations in a strong indestructible chain. And the comedian who waded in carrying an umbrella.

When the others went swimming my son said he was going in too. He pulled his dripping trunks from the line where they had hung all through the shower, and wrung them out. Languidly, and with no thought of going in, I watched him, his hard little body, skinny and bare, saw him wince slightly as he pulled up around his vitals the small, soggy, icy garment. As he buckled the swollen belt suddenly my groin felt the chill of death.

Responding to Reading

1. How is White's "holy spot" different when he visits it with his son from how it was when he visited it with his father?
2. Is this essay primarily about a time, a place, or a relationship? Explain.
3. Why does White feel "the chill of death" (13) as he watches his son? Do you identify more with White the father or White the child?

Responding in Writing

Write two short paragraphs about a place that was important to you as a child: one from the point of view of your adult self, and one from the point of view of your childhood self. How are the two paragraphs different?

No Name Woman

Maxine Hong Kingston
1940–

Maxine Hong Kingston was born in Stockton, California, the daughter of Chinese immigrants who ran a gambling house and, later, a laundry where she and her five siblings worked. Since her first book, The Woman Warrior: Memoirs of a Girlhood Among Ghosts *(1976), was published, Kingston has been acclaimed as a writer of fiction and nonfiction. Her most recent novel is* The Fifth Book of Peace *(2003). In the following autobiographical essay from* The Woman Warrior, *Kingston speculates about the life and death of a family member she has never met.*

"You must not tell anyone," my mother said, "what I am about to tell you. In China your father had a sister who killed herself. She jumped into the family well. We say that your father has all brothers because it is as if she had never been born.

"In 1924 just a few days after our village celebrated seventeen hurry-up weddings—to make sure that every young man who went 'out on the road' would responsibly come home—your father and his brothers and your grandfather and his brothers and your aunt's new husband sailed for America, the Gold Mountain. It was your grandfather's last trip. Those lucky enough to get contracts waved good-bye from the decks. They fed and guarded the stowaways and helped them off in Cuba, New York, Bali, Hawaii. 'We'll meet in California next year,' they said. All of them sent money home.

"I remember looking at your aunt one day when she and I were dressing; I had not noticed before that she had such a protruding melon of a stomach. But I did not think, 'She's pregnant,' until she began to look like other pregnant women, her shirt pulling and the white tops of her black pants showing. She could not have been pregnant, you see, because her husband had been gone for years. No one said anything. We did not discuss it. In early summer she was ready to have the child, long after the time when it could have been possible.

"The village had also been counting. On the night the baby was to be born the villagers raided our house. Some were crying. Like a great saw, teeth strung with lights, files of people walked zigzag across our land, tearing the rice. Their lanterns doubled in the disturbed black water, which drained away through the broken bunds. As the villagers closed in, we could see that some of them, probably men and women we knew well, wore white masks. The people with long hair hung it over their faces. Women with short hair made it stand up on end. Some had tied white bands around their foreheads, arms, and legs.

5   "At first they threw mud and rocks at the house. Then they threw eggs and began slaughtering our stock. We could hear the animals scream their deaths—the roosters, the pigs, a last great roar from the ox. Familiar wild heads flared in our night windows; the villagers encircled us. Some of the faces stopped to peer at us, their eyes rushing like searchlights. The hands flattened against the panes, framed heads, and left red prints.

"The villagers broke in the front and the back doors at the same time, even though we had not locked the doors against them. Their knives dripped with the blood of our animals. They smeared blood on the doors and walls. One woman swung a chicken, whose throat she had slit, splattering blood in red arcs about her. We stood together in the middle of our house, in the family hall with the pictures and tables of the ancestors around us, and looked straight ahead.

"At the time the house had only two wings. When the men came back, we would build two more to enclose our courtyard and a third one to begin a second courtyard. The villagers pushed through both wings, even your grandparents' rooms, to find your aunt's, which was also mine until the men returned. From this room a new wing for one of the younger families would grow. They ripped up her clothes and shoes and broke her combs, grinding them underfoot. They tore her work from the loom. They scattered the cooking fire and rolled the new weaving in it. We could hear them in the kitchen breaking our bowls and banging the pots. They overturned the great waist-high earthenware jugs; duck eggs, pickled fruits, vegetables burst out and mixed in acrid torrents. The old woman from the next field swept a broom through the air and loosed the spirits-of-the-broom over our heads. 'Pig.' 'Ghost.' 'Pig,' they sobbed and scolded while they ruined our house.

"When they left, they took sugar and oranges to bless themselves. They cut pieces from the dead animals. Some of them took bowls that were not broken and clothes that were not torn. Afterward we swept up the rice and sewed it back up into sacks. But the smells from the spilled preserves lasted. Your aunt gave birth in the pigsty that night. The next morning when I went for the water, I found her and the baby plugging up the family well.

"Don't let your father know that I told you. He denies her. Now that you have started to menstruate, what happened to her could happen to you. Don't humiliate us. You wouldn't like to be forgotten as if you had never been born. The villagers are watchful."

Whenever she had to warn us about life, my mother told stories 10 that ran like this one, a story to grow up on. She tested our strength to establish realities. Those in the emigrant generations who could not reassert brute survival died young and far from home. Those of us in the first American generations have had to figure out how the invisible world the emigrants built around our childhoods fit in solid America.

The emigrants confused the gods by diverting their curses, misleading them with crooked streets and false names. They must try to confuse their offspring as well, who, I suppose, threaten them in similar ways—always trying to get things straight, always trying to name the unspeakable. The Chinese I know hide their names; sojourners take new names when their lives change and guard their real names with silence.

Chinese-Americans, when you try to understand what things in you are Chinese, how do you separate what is peculiar to childhood, to poverty, insanities, one family, your mother who marked your growing with stories, from what is Chinese? What is Chinese tradition and what is the movies?

If I want to learn what clothes my aunt wore, whether flashy or ordinary, I would have to begin, "Remember Father's drowned-in-the-well sister?" I cannot ask that. My mother has told me once and for all the useful parts. She will add nothing unless powered by Necessity, a riverbank that guides her life. She plants vegetable gardens rather than lawns; she carries the odd-shaped tomatoes home from the fields and eats food left for the gods.

Whenever we did frivolous things, we used up energy; we flew high kites. We children came up off the ground over the melting cones our parents brought home from work and the American movie on New Year's Day—*Oh, You Beautiful Doll* with Betty Grable one year, and *She Wore a Yellow Ribbon* with John Wayne another year. After the one carnival ride each, we paid in guilt; our tired father counted his change on the dark walk home.

Adultery is extravagance. Could people who hatch their own 15 chicks and eat the embryos and the heads for delicacies and boil the feet in vinegar for party food, leaving only the gravel, eating even the gizzard lining—could such people engender a prodigal aunt? To be a woman, to have a daughter in starvation time was a waste enough. My aunt could not have been the lone romantic who gave up everything for sex. Women in the old China did not choose. Some man had commanded her to lie with him and be his secret evil. I wonder whether he masked himself when he joined the raid on her family.

Perhaps she encountered him in the fields or on the mountain where the daughters-in-law collected fuel. Or perhaps he first noticed her in the marketplace. He was not a stranger because the village housed no strangers. She had to have dealings with him other than sex. Perhaps he worked an adjoining field, or he sold her the cloth for the dress she sewed and wore. His demand must have surprised, then terrified her. She obeyed him; she always did as she was told.

When the family found a young man in the next village to be her husband, she stood tractably beside the best rooster, his proxy, and promised before they met that she would be his forever. She was lucky that he was her age and she would be the first wife, an advantage secure now. The night she first saw him, he had sex with her. Then he left for America. She had almost forgotten what he looked like. When she tried to envision him, she only saw the black and white face in the group photograph the men had had taken before leaving.

The other man was not, after all, much different from her husband. They both gave orders: she followed. "If you tell your family, I'll beat you. I'll kill you. Be here again next week." No one talked sex, ever. And she might have separated the rapes from the rest of living if only she did not have to buy her oil from him or gather wood in the same forest. I want her fear to have lasted just as long as rape lasted so that the fear could have been contained. No drawn-out fear. But women at sex hazarded birth and hence lifetimes. The fear did not stop but permeated everywhere. She told the man, "I think I'm pregnant." He organized the raid against her.

On nights when my mother and father talked about their life back home, sometimes they mentioned an "outcast table" whose business they still seemed to be settling, their voices tight. In a commensal[1] tradition, where food is precious, the powerful older people made wrongdoers eat alone. Instead of letting them start separate new lives like the Japanese, who could become samurais and geishas, the Chinese family, faces averted but eyes glowering sideways, hung on to the offenders and fed them leftovers. My aunt must have lived in the same house as my parents and eaten at an outcast table. My mother spoke about the raid as if she had seen it, when she and my aunt, a

---

[1]Eating at the same table; sharing meals as table companions. [Eds.]

daughter-in-law to a different household, should not have been living together at all. Daughters-in-law lived with their husbands' parents, not their own; a synonym for marriage in Chinese is "taking a daughter-in-law." Her husband's parents could have sold her, mortgaged her, stoned her. But they had sent her back to her own mother and father, a mysterious act hinting at disgraces not told me. Perhaps they had thrown her out to deflect the avengers.

She was the only daughter; her four brothers went with her father, husband, and uncles "out on the road" and for some years became western men. When the goods were divided among the family, three of the brothers took land, and the youngest, my father, chose an education. After my grandparents gave their daughter away to her husband's family, they had dispensed all the adventure and all the property. They expected her alone to keep the traditional ways, which her brothers, now among the barbarians, could fumble without detection. The heavy, deep-rooted women were to maintain the past against the flood, safe for returning. But the rare urge west had fixed upon our family, and so my aunt crossed boundaries not delineated in space. 20

The work of preservation demands that the feelings playing about in one's guts not be turned into action. Just watch their passing like cherry blossoms. But perhaps my aunt, my forerunner, caught in a slow life, let dreams grow and fade and after some months or years went toward what persisted. Fear at the enormities of the forbidden kept her desires delicate, wire and bone. She looked at a man because she liked the way the hair was tucked behind his ears, or she liked the question-mark line of a long torso curving at the shoulder and straight at the hip. For warm eyes or a soft voice or a slow walk— that's all—a few hairs, a line, a brightness, a sound, a pace, she gave up family. She offered us up for a charm that vanished with tiredness, a pigtail that didn't toss when the wind died. Why, the wrong lighting could erase the dearest thing about him.

It could very well have been, however, that my aunt did not take subtle enjoyment of her friend, but, a wild woman, kept rollicking company. Imagining her free with sex doesn't fit, though. I don't know any women like that, or men either. Unless I see her life branching into mine, she gives me no ancestral help.

To sustain her being in love, she often worked at herself in the mirror, guessing at the colors and shapes that would interest him, changing them frequently in order to hit on the right combination. She wanted him to look back.

On a farm near the sea, a woman who tended her appearance reaped a reputation for eccentricity. All the married women blunt-cut their hair in flaps about their ears or pulled it back in tight buns. No nonsense. Neither style blew easily into heart-catching tangles. And at their weddings they displayed themselves in their long hair for the last time. "It brushed the backs of my knees," my mother tells me. "It was braided, and even so, it brushed the backs of my knees."

25   At the mirror my aunt combed individuality into her bob. A bun could have been contrived to escape into black streamers blowing in the wind or in quiet wisps about her face, but only the older women in our picture album wear buns. She brushed her hair back from her forehead, tucking the flaps behind her ears. She looped a piece of thread, knotted into a circle between her index fingers and thumbs, and ran the double strand across her forehead. When she closed her fingers as if she were making a pair of shadow geese bite, the string twisted together catching the little hairs. Then she pulled the thread away from her skin, ripping the hairs out neatly, her eyes watering from the needles of pain. Opening her fingers, she cleaned the thread, then rolled it along her hairline and the tops of her eyebrows. My mother did the same to me and my sisters and herself. I used to believe that the expression "caught by the short hairs" meant a captive held with a depilatory string. It especially hurt at the temples, but my mother said we were lucky we didn't have to have our feet bound when we were seven. Sisters used to sit on their beds and cry together, she said, as their mothers or their slave removed the bandages for a few minutes each night and let the blood gush back into their veins. I hope that the man my aunt loved appreciated a smooth brow, that he wasn't just a tits-and-ass man.

Once my aunt found a freckle on her chin, at a spot that the almanac said predestined her for unhappiness. She dug it out with a hot needle and washed the wound with peroxide.

More attention to her looks than these pullings of hairs and pickings at spots would have caused gossip among the villagers. They owned work clothes and good clothes, and they wore good clothes for feasting the new seasons. But since a woman combing her hair hexes beginnings, my aunt rarely found an occasion to look her best. Women looked like great sea snails—the corded wood, babies, and laundry they carried were the whorls on their backs. The Chinese did not admire a bent back; goddesses and warriors stood straight. Still there must have been a marvelous freeing of beauty when a worker laid down her burden and stretched and arched.

Such commonplace loveliness, however, was not enough for my aunt. She dreamed of a lover for the fifteen days of New Year's, the time for families to exchange visits, money, and food. She plied her secret comb. And sure enough she cursed the year, the family, the village, and herself.

Even as her hair lured her imminent lover, many other men looked at her. Uncles, cousins, nephews, brothers would have looked, too, had they been home between journeys. Perhaps they had already been restraining their curiosity, and they left, fearful that their glances, like a field of nesting birds, might be startled and caught. Poverty hurt, and that was their first reason for leaving. But another, final reason for leaving the crowded house was the never-said.

She may have been unusually beloved, the precious only daughter, spoiled and mirror gazing because of the affection the family lavished on her. When her husband left, they welcomed the chance to take her back from the in-laws; she could live like the little daughter for just a while longer. There are stories that my grandfather was different from other people, "crazy ever since the little Jap bayoneted him in the head." He used to put his naked penis on the dinner table, laughing. And one day he brought home a baby girl, wrapped up inside his brown western-style greatcoat. He had traded one of his sons, probably my father, the youngest, for her. My grandmother made him trade back. When he finally got a daughter of his own, he doted on her. They must have all loved her, except perhaps my father, the only brother who never went back to China, having once been traded for a girl.

Brothers and sisters, newly men and women, had to efface their sexual color and present plain miens.[2] Disturbing hair and eyes, a smile like no other, threatened the ideal of five generations living under one roof. To focus blurs, people shouted face to face and yelled from room to room. The immigrants I know have loud voices, unmodulated to American tones even after years away from the village where they called their friendships out across the fields. I have not been able to stop my mother's screams in public libraries or over telephones. Walking erect (knees straight, toes pointed forward, not pigeon-toed, which is Chinese-feminine) and speaking in an inaudible voice, I have tried to turn myself American-feminine. Chinese communication was loud, public. Only sick people had to whisper. But at the dinner table, where the family members came nearest one another, no one could talk, not the outcasts nor any eaters. Every word that falls from the mouth is a coin lost. Silently they gave and accepted food with both hands. A preoccupied child who took his bowl with one hand got a sideways glare. A complete moment of total attention is due everyone alike. Children and lovers have no singularity here, but my aunt used a secret voice, a separate attentiveness.

She kept the man's name to herself throughout her labor and dying; she did not accuse him that he be punished with her. To save her inseminator's name she gave silent birth.

He may have been somebody in her own household, but intercourse with a man outside the family would have been no less abhorrent. All the village were kinsmen, and the titles shouted in loud

---

[2]Appearances. [Eds.]

country voices never let kinship be forgotten. Any man within visiting distance would have been neutralized as a lover—"brother," "younger brother," "older brother"—one hundred and fifteen relationship titles. Parents researched birth charts probably not so much to assure good fortune as to circumvent incest in a population that has but one hundred surnames. Everybody has eight million relatives. How useless then sexual mannerisms, how dangerous.

As if it came from an atavism[3] deeper than fear, I used to add "brother" silently to boys' names. It hexed the boys, who would or would not ask me to dance, and made them less scary and as familiar and deserving of benevolence as girls.

35   But, of course, I hexed myself also—no dates. I should have stood up, both arms waving, and shouted out across libraries, "Hey, you! Love me back." I had no idea, though, how to make attraction selective, how to control its direction and magnitude. If I made myself American-pretty so that the five or six Chinese boys in the class fell in love with me, everyone else—the Caucasian, Negro, and Japanese boys—would too. Sisterliness, dignified and honorable, made much more sense.

Attraction eludes control so stubbornly that whole societies designed to organize relationships among people cannot keep order, not even when they bind people to one another from childhood and raise them together. Among the very poor and the wealthy, brothers married their adopted sisters, like doves. Our family allowed some romance, paying adult brides' prices and providing dowries so that their sons and daughters could marry strangers. Marriage promises to turn strangers into friendly relatives—a nation of siblings.

In the village structure, spirits shimmered among the live creatures, balanced and held in equilibrium by time and land. But one human being flaring up into violence could open up a black hole, a maelstrom that pulled in the sky. The frightened villagers, who depended on one another to maintain the real, went to my aunt to show her a personal, physical representation of the break she had made in the "roundness." Misallying couples snapped off the future, which was to be embodied in true offspring. The villagers punished her for acting as if she could have a private life, secret and apart from them.

If my aunt had betrayed the family at a time of large grain yields and peace, when many boys were born, and wings were being built on many houses, perhaps she might have escaped such severe punishment. But the men—hungry, greedy, tired of planting in dry soil, cuckolded—had had to leave the village in order to send food-money home. There were ghost plagues, bandit plagues, wars with the Japanese, floods. My Chinese brother and sister had died of an

---

[3]The reappearance of a characteristic after a long absence. [Eds.]

unknown sickness. Adultery, perhaps only a mistake during good times, became a crime when the village needed food.

The round moon cakes and round doorways, the round tables of graduated size that fit one roundness inside another, round windows and rice bowls—these talismans had lost their power to warn this family of the law: a family must be whole, faithfully keeping the descent line by having sons to feed the old and the dead, who in turn look after the family. The villagers came to show my aunt and her lover-in-hiding a broken house. The villagers were speeding up the circling of events because she was too shortsighted to see that her infidelity had already harmed the village, that waves of consequences would return unpredictably, sometimes in disguise, as now, to hurt her. This roundness had to be made coin-sized so that she would see its circumference: punish her at the birth of her baby. Awaken her to the inexorable. People who refused fatalism because they could invent small resources insisted on culpability. Deny accidents and wrest fault from the stars.

After the villagers left, their lanterns now scattering in various di- 40 rections toward home, the family broke their silence and cursed her. "Aiaa, we're going to die. Death is coming. Death is coming. Look what you've done. You've killed us. Ghost! Dead ghost! Ghost! You've never been born." She ran out into the fields, far enough from the house so that she could no longer hear their voices, and pressed herself against the earth, her own land no more. When she felt the birth coming, she thought that she had been hurt. Her body seized together. "They've hurt me too much," she thought. "This is gall, and it will kill me." With forehead and knees against the earth, her body convulsed and then relaxed. She turned on her back, lay on the ground. The black well of sky and stars went out and out and out forever; her body and her complexity seemed to disappear. She was one of the stars, a bright dot in blackness, without home, without a companion, in eternal cold and silence. And agoraphobia[4] rose in her, speeding higher and higher, bigger and bigger; she would not be able to contain it; there would be no end to fear.

Flayed, unprotected against space, she felt pain return, focusing her body. This pain chilled her—a cold, steady kind of surface pain. Inside, spasmodically, the other pain, the pain of the child, heated her. For hours she lay on the ground, alternately body and space. Sometimes a vision of normal comfort obliterated reality: she saw the family in the evening gambling at the dinner table, the young people massaging their elders' backs. She saw them congratulating one another, high joy on the mornings the rice shoots came up. When these pictures burst, the stars drew yet further apart. Black space opened.

---

[4]Pathological fear of being helpless or embarrassed in a pubic situation, characterized by avoidance of public places. [Eds.]

She got to her feet to fight better and remembered that old-fashioned women gave birth in their pigsties to fool the jealous, pain-dealing gods, who do not snatch piglets. Before the next spasms could stop her, she ran to the pigsty, each step a rushing out into emptiness. She climbed over the fence and knelt in the dirt. It was good to have a fence enclosing her, a tribal person alone.

Laboring, this woman who had carried her child as a foreign growth that sickened her every day, expelled it at last. She reached down to touch the hot, wet, moving mass, surely smaller than anything human, and could feel that it was human after all—fingers, toes, nails, nose. She pulled it up on to her belly, and it lay curled there, butt in the air, feet precisely tucked one under the other. She opened her loose shirt and buttoned the child inside. After resting, it squirmed and thrashed and she pushed it up to her breast. It turned its head this way and that until it found her nipple. There, it made little snuffling noises. She clenched her teeth at its preciousness, lovely as a young calf, a piglet, a little dog.

She may have gone to the pigsty as a last act of responsibility: she would protect this child as she had protected its father. It would look after her soul, leaving supplies on her grave. But how would this tiny child without family find her grave when there would be no marker for her anywhere, neither in the earth nor the family hall? No one would give her a family hall name. She had taken the child with her into the wastes. At its birth the two of them had felt the same raw pain of separation, a wound that only the family pressing tight could close. A child with no descent line would not soften her life but only trail after her, ghost-like, begging her to give it purpose. At dawn the villagers on their way to the fields would stand around the fence and look.

45   Full of milk, the little ghost slept. When it awoke, she hardened her breasts against the milk that crying loosens. Toward morning she picked up the baby and walked to the well.

Carrying the baby to the well shows loving. Otherwise abandon it. Turn its face into the mud. Mothers who love their children take them along. It was probably a girl; there is some hope of forgiveness for boys.

"Don't tell anyone you had an aunt. Your father does not want to hear her name. She has never been born." I have believed that sex was unspeakable and words so strong and fathers so frail that "aunt" would do my father mysterious harm. I have thought that my family, having settled among immigrants who had also been their neighbors in the ancestral land, needed to clean their name, and a wrong word would incite the kinspeople even here. But there is more to this silence: they want me to participate in her punishment. And I have.

In the twenty years since I heard this story I have not asked for details nor said my aunt's name; I do not know it. People who can comfort the dead can also chase after them to hurt them further—a reverse ancestor worship. The real punishment was not the raid swiftly inflicted by the villagers, but the family's deliberately forgetting her. Her betrayal so maddened them, they saw to it that she would suffer forever, even after death. Always hungry, always needing, she would have to beg food from other ghosts, snatch and steal it from those whose living descendants give them gifts. She would have to fight the ghosts massed at crossroads for the buns a few thoughtful citizens leave to decoy her away from village and home so that the ancestral spirits could feast unharassed. At peace, they could act like gods, not ghosts, their descent lines providing them with paper suits and dresses, spirit money, paper houses, paper automobiles, chicken, meat, and rice into eternity—essences delivered up in smoke and flames, steam and incense rising from each rice bowl. In an attempt to make the Chinese care for people outside the family, Chairman Mao[5] encourages us now to give our paper replicas to the spirits of outstanding soldiers and workers, no matter whose ancestors they may be. My aunt remains forever hungry. Goods are not distributed evenly among the dead.

My aunt haunts me—her ghost drawn to me because now, after fifty years of neglect, I alone devote pages of paper to her, though not origamied into houses and clothes. I do not think she always means me well. I am telling on her, and she was a spite suicide, drowning herself in the drinking water. The Chinese are always very frightened of the drowned one, whose weeping ghost, wet hair hanging and skin bloated, waits silently by the water to pull down a substitute.

Responding to Reading

1. How accurate do you imagine Kingston's "facts" are? Do you think strict accuracy is important in this essay? Why or why not?
2. Kingston never met her aunt; in fact, she doesn't even know her name. Even so, in what sense is this essay about her relationship with her aunt (and with other family members, both known and unknown)?
3. In paragraph 49, Kingston says, "My aunt haunts me—" Why do you think Kingston is "haunted" by her aunt's story?

Responding in Writing

Write a one-paragraph biographical sketch of a family member whose memory "haunts" you. Or, write a short obituary of a deceased relative.

---

[5]Mao Zedong (1893–1976), founder and leader of the communist People's Republic of China from 1949 until his death. [Eds.]

BEAUTY: WHEN THE OTHER DANCER IS THE SELF

Alice Walker

1944–

Alice Walker, best known for her award-winning novel The Color Purple *(1982), is recognized as an important voice among African-American women writers. Born in Georgia, the daughter of sharecroppers, Walker received scholarships to Spelman College in Atlanta and Sarah Lawrence College in Bronxville, New York. Her work, which often focuses on racism and sexism, includes poetry, novels, short stories, essays, criticism, a biography of Langston Hughes, and an edition of Zora Neale Hurston's collection* I Love Myself When I Am Laughing *(1979). Walker's most recent work is the novel* Now Is the Time to Open Your Heart *(2004). Like much of her writing, the following essay moves from pain and despair to self-celebration.*

It is a bright summer day in 1947. My father, a fat, funny man with beautiful eyes and a subversive wit, is trying to decide which of his eight children he will take with him to the county fair. My mother, of course, will not go. She is knocked out from getting most of us ready: I hold my neck stiff against the pressure of her knuckles as she hastily completes the braiding and then beribboning of my hair.

My father is the driver for the rich old white lady up the road. Her name is Miss Mey. She owns all the land for miles around, as well as the house in which we live. All I remember about her is that she once offered to pay my mother thirty-five cents for cleaning her house, raking up piles of her magnolia leaves, and washing her family's clothes, and that my mother—she of no money, eight children, and a chronic earache—refused it. But I do not think of this in 1947. I am two and a half years old. I want to go everywhere my daddy goes. I am excited at the prospect of riding in a car. Someone has told me fairs are fun. That there is room in the car for only three of us doesn't faze me at all. Whirling happily in my starchy frock, showing off my biscuit-polished patent-leather shoes and lavender socks, tossing my head in a way that makes my ribbons bounce, I stand, hands on hips, before my father. "Take me, Daddy," I say with assurance; "I'm the prettiest!"

Later, it does not surprise me to find myself in Miss Mey's shiny black car, sharing the back seat with the other lucky ones. Does not surprise me that I thoroughly enjoy the fair. At home that night I tell the unlucky ones all I can remember about the merry-go-round, the man who eats live chickens, and the teddy bears, until they say: "That's enough, baby Alice. Shut up now, and go to sleep."

It is Easter Sunday, 1950. I am dressed in a green, flocked, scalloped-hem dress (handmade by my adoring sister, Ruth) that has its own smooth satin petticoat and tiny hot-pink roses tucked into each scallop. My shoes, new T-strap patent leather, again highly biscuit-polished. I am six years old and have learned one of the longest Easter speeches to be heard that day, totally unlike the speech I said when I was two: "Easter lilies/pure and white/blossom in/the morning light." When I rise to give my speech I do so on a great wave of love and pride and expectation. People in the church stop rustling their new crinolines. They seem to hold their breath. I can tell they admire my dress, but it is my spirit, bordering on sassiness (womanishness), they secretly applaud.

"That girl's a little *mess*," they whisper to each other, pleased.   5

Naturally I say my speech without stammer or pause, unlike those who stutter, stammer, or, worst of all, forget. This is before the word "beautiful" exists in people's vocabulary, but "Oh, isn't she the *cutest* thing!" frequently floats my way. "And got so much sense!" they gratefully add . . . for which thoughtful addition I thank them to this day.

It was great fun being cute. But then, one day, it ended.

I am eight years old and a tomboy. I have a cowboy hat, cowboy boots, checkered shirt and pants, all red. My playmates are my brothers, two and four years older than I. Their colors are black and green, the only difference in the way we are dressed. On Saturday nights we all go to the picture show, even my mother; Westerns are her favorite kind of movie. Back home, "on the ranch," we pretend we are Tom Mix, Hopalong Cassidy, Lash LaRue (we've even named one of our dogs Lash LaRue); we chase each other for hours rustling cattle, being outlaws, delivering damsels from distress. Then my parents decide to buy my brothers guns. These are not "real" guns. They shoot "BBs," copper pellets my brothers say will kill birds. Because I am a girl, I do not get a gun. Instantly I am relegated to the position of Indian. Now there appears a great distance between us. They shoot and shoot at everything with their new guns. I try to keep up with my bow and arrows.

One day while I am standing on top of our makeshift "garage"—pieces of tin nailed across some poles—holding my bow and arrow and looking out toward the fields, I feel an incredible blow in my right eye. I look down just in time to see my brother lower his gun.

Both brothers rush to my side. My eye stings, and I cover it with   10 my hand. "If you tell," they say, "we will get a whipping. You don't want that to happen, do you?" I do not. "Here is a piece of wire," says the older brother, picking it up from the roof; "say you stepped on one end of it and the other flew up and hit you." The pain is beginning to start. "Yes," I say, "Yes, I will say that is what happened." If I do not say this is what happened, I know my brothers will find ways to make me wish I had. But now I will say anything that gets me to my mother.

Confronted by our parents we stick to the lie agreed upon. They place me on a bench on the porch and I close my left eye while they examine the right. There is a tree growing from underneath the porch that climbs past the railing to the roof. It is the last thing my right eye sees. I watch as its trunk, its branches, and then its leaves are blotted out by the rising blood.

I am in shock. First there is intense fever, which my father tries to break using lily leaves bound around my head. Then there are chills: my mother tries to get me to eat soup. Eventually, I do not know how, my parents learn what has happened. A week after the "accident" they take me to see a doctor. "Why did you wait so long to come?" he asks, looking into my eye and shaking his head. "Eyes are sympathetic," he says. "If one is blind, the other will likely become blind too."

This comment of the doctor's terrifies me. But it is really how I look that bothers me most. Where the BB pellet struck there is a glob of whitish scar tissue, a hideous cataract, on my eye. Now when I stare at people—a favorite pastime, up to now—they will stare back. Not at the "cute" little girl, but at her scar. For six years I do not stare at anyone, because I do not raise my head.

Years later, in the throes of a mid-life crisis, I ask my mother and sister whether I changed after the "accident." "No," they say, puzzled. "What do you mean?"

15   *What do I mean?*

I am eight, and, for the first time, doing poorly in school, where I have been something of a whiz since I was four. We have just moved to the place where the "accident" occurred. We do not know any of the people around us because this is a different county. The only time I see the friends I knew is when we go back to our old church. The new school is the former state penitentiary. It is a large stone building, cold and drafty, crammed to overflowing with boisterous, ill-disciplined children. On the third floor there is a huge circular imprint of some partition that has been torn out.

"What used to be here?" I ask a sullen girl next to me on our way past it to lunch.

"The electric chair," says she.

At night I have nightmares about the electric chair, and about all the people reputedly "fried" in it. I am afraid of the school, where all the students seem to be budding criminals.

20   "What's the matter with your eye?" they ask, critically.

When I don't answer (I cannot decide whether it was an "accident" or not), they shove me, insist on a fight.

My brother, the one who created the story about the wire, comes to my rescue. But then brags so much about "protecting" me, I become sick.

After months of torture at the school, my parents decide to send me back to our old community, to my old school. I live with my grandparents and the teacher they board. But there is no room for Phoebe, my cat. By the time my grandparents decide there *is* room, and I ask for my cat, she cannot be found. Miss Yarborough, the boarding teacher, takes me under her wing, and begins to teach me to play the piano. But soon she marries an African—a "prince," she says—and is whisked away to his continent.

At my old school there is at least one teacher who loves me. She is the teacher who "knew me before I was born" and bought my first baby clothes. It is she who makes life bearable. It is her presence that finally helps me turn on the one child at the school who continually calls me "one-eyed bitch." One day I simply grab him by his coat and beat him until I am satisfied. It is my teacher who tells me my mother is ill.

My mother is lying in bed in the middle of the day, something I 25 have never seen. She is in too much pain to speak. She has an abscess in her ear. I stand looking down on her, knowing that if she dies, I cannot live. She is being treated with warm oils and hot bricks held against her cheek. Finally a doctor comes. But I must go back to my grandparents' house. The weeks pass but I am hardly aware of it. All I know is that my mother might die, my father is not so jolly, my brothers still have their guns, and I am the one sent away from home.

"You did not change," they say.

Did I imagine the anguish of never looking up?

I am twelve. When relatives come to visit I hide in my room. My cousin Brenda, just my age, whose father works in the post office and whose mother is a nurse, comes to find me. "Hello," she says. And then she asks, looking at my recent school picture, which I did not want taken, and on which the "glob," as I think of it, is clearly visible, "You still can't see out of that eye?"

"No," I say, and flop back on the bed over my book.

That night, as I do almost every night, I abuse my eye. I rant and 30 rave at it, in front of the mirror. I plead with it to clear up before morning. I tell it I hate and despise it. I do not pray for sight. I pray for beauty.

"You did not change," they say.

I am fourteen and baby-sitting for my brother Bill, who lives in Boston. He is my favorite brother and there is a strong bond between us. Understanding my feelings of shame and ugliness he and his wife take me to a local hospital, where the "glob" is removed by a doctor named O. Henry. There is still a small bluish crater where the scar tissue was, but the ugly white stuff is gone. Almost immediately I become a different person from the girl who does not raise her head. Or so I think. Now that I've raised my head I win the boyfriend of my dreams. Now that I've raised my head I have plenty of friends. Now that I've raised my head classwork comes from my lips as faultlessly as Easter speeches did, and I leave high school as valedictorian, most popular student, and *queen*, hardly believing my luck. Ironically, the girl who was voted most beautiful in our class (and was) was later shot twice through the chest by a male companion, using a "real" gun, while she was pregnant. But that's another story in itself. Or is it?

"You did not change," they say.

It is now thirty years since the "accident." A beautiful journalist comes to visit and to interview me. She is going to write a cover story for her magazine that focuses on my latest book. "Decide how you want to look on the cover," she says. "Glamorous, or whatever."

35 Never mind "glamorous," it is the "whatever" that I hear. Suddenly all I can think of is whether I will get enough sleep the night before the photography session: if I don't, my eye will be tired and wander, as blind eyes will.

At night in bed with my lover I think up reasons why I should not appear on the cover of a magazine. "My meanest critics will say I've sold out," I say. "My family will now realize I write scandalous books."

"But what's the real reason you don't want to do this?" he asks.

"Because in all probability," I say in a rush, "my eye won't be straight."

"It will be straight enough," he says. Then, "Besides, I thought you'd made your peace with that."

40 And I suddenly remember that I have.

I remember:

I am talking to my brother Jimmy, asking if he remembers anything unusual about the day I was shot. He does not know I consider that day the last time my father, with his sweet home remedy of cool lily leaves, chose me, and that I suffered and raged inside because of this. "Well," he says, "all I remember is standing by the side of the highway with Daddy, trying to flag down a car. A white man stopped, but when Daddy said he needed somebody to take his little girl to the doctor, he drove off.

I remember:

— I am in the desert for the first time. I fall totally in love with it. I am so overwhelmed by its beauty, I confront for the first time, consciously, the meaning of the doctor's words years ago: "Eyes are sympathetic. If one is blind, the other will likely become blind too." I realize I have dashed about the world madly, looking at this, looking at that, storing up images against the fading of the light. *But I might have missed seeing the desert!* The shock of that possibility—and gratitude for over twenty-five years of sight—sends me literally to my knees. Poem after poem comes—which is perhaps how poets pray.

On Sight

I am so thankful I have seen
The Desert
And the creatures in the desert
And the desert Itself.

The desert has its own moon
Which I have seen
With my own eye.
There is no flag on it.

Trees of the desert have arms
All of which are always up
That is because the moon is up
The sun is up
Also the sky
The stars
Clouds
None with flags.

If there were flags, I doubt
the trees would point.
Would you?

But mostly, I remember this:

I am twenty-seven, and my baby daughter is almost three. Since her birth I have worried about her discovery that her mother's eyes are different from other people's. Will she be embarrassed? I think. What will she say? Every day she watches a television program called "Big Blue Marble." It begins with a picture of the earth as it appears from the moon. It is bluish, a little battered-looking, but full of light, with whitish clouds swirling around it. Every time I see it I weep with love, as if it is a picture of Grandma's house. One day when I am putting Rebecca down for her nap, she suddenly focuses on my eye. Something inside me cringes, gets ready to try to protect myself. All children are cruel about physical differences, I know from experience, and that they don't always mean to be is another matter. I assume Rebecca will be the same.

But no-o-o-o. She studies my face intently as we stand, her inside and me outside her crib. She even holds my face maternally between her dimpled little hands. Then, looking every bit as serious and lawyerlike as her father, she says, as if it may just possibly have slipped my attention: "Mommy, there's a *world* in your eye." (As in, "Don't be alarmed, or do anything crazy.") And then, gently, but with great interest: "Mommy, where did you get that world in your eye?"

For the most part, the pain left then. (So what, if my brothers grew up to buy even more powerful pellet guns for their sons and to carry real guns themselves. So what, if a young "Morehouse man"[1] once nearly fell off the steps of Trevor Arnett Library because he thought my eyes were blue.) Crying and laughing I ran to the bathroom, while Rebecca mumbled and sang herself off to sleep. Yes indeed, I realized, looking into the mirror. There was a world in my eye. And I saw that it was possible to love it: that in fact, for all it had taught me of shame and anger and inner vision, I *did* love it. Even to see it drifting out of orbit in boredom, or rolling up out of fatigue, not to mention floating back at attention in excitement (bearing witness, a friend has called it), deeply suitable to my personality, and even characteristic of me.

That night I dream I am dancing to Stevie Wonder's song "Always" (the name of the song is really "As," but I hear it as "Always"). As I dance, whirling and joyous, happier than I've ever been in my life, another bright-faced dancer joins me. We dance and kiss each other and hold each other through the night. The other dancer has obviously come through all right, as I have done. She is beautiful, whole and free. And she is also me.

Responding to Reading

1. Although she is remembering past events, Walker uses present tense ("It is a bright summer day in 1947") to tell her story. Why do you think she does this? Is the present tense more effective than the past tense ("It *was* a bright summer day in 1947") would be? Explain.
2. At several points in the essay, Walker repeats the words her relatives used to reassure her: "You did not change." Why does she repeat this phrase? Were her relatives correct?
3. What circumstances or individuals does Walker blame for the childhood problems she describes? Who do you think is responsible for her misery? Would you be as forgiving as Walker seems to be?

Responding in Writing

Using present tense, write a paragraph or two about a painful incident from your childhood. Begin with a sentence that tells how old you are ("I am _____.").

---

[1]A student at Morehouse College, a historically black college in Atlanta, Georgia. [Eds.]

THE UNAUTHORIZED AUTOBIOGRAPHY OF ME
Sherman J. Alexie, Jr.
1966–

Sherman Alexie grew up on an Indian reservation in Wellpinit, Washington, about 50 miles northwest of Spokane. Alexie is a Spokane/Coeur d'Alene Indian whose works focus on tribal connections and draw upon the oral and religious traditions of his heritage. Although he began his writing career as a poet, Alexie has also written stories and novels. A story from his first collection, The Lone Ranger and Tonto Fistfight in Heaven *(1993), became the basis for the screenplay and film* Smoke Signals *(1998). Alexie has published fourteen books, most recently* Ten Little Indians *(2003). In his writings, Alexie often seems to be constructing a Native American web of life, weaving together elements of the personal, mythical, historical, and modern. In the following "unauthorized autobiography," he spins just such a web.*

Late summer night on the Spokane Indian Reservation. Ten Indians are playing basketball on a court barely illuminated by the streetlight above them. They will play until the brown, leather ball is invisible in the dark. They will play until an errant pass jams a finger, knocks a pair of glasses off a face, smashes a nose and draws blood. They will play until the ball bounces off the court and disappears into the shadows.

Sometimes, I think this is all you need to know about Native American literature.

Thesis: I have never met a Native American. Thesis reiterated: I have met thousands of Indians.

PEN American panel in Manhattan, November 1994, on Indian Literature. N. Scott Momaday, James Welch, Gloria Miguel, Joy Harjo, and myself. Two or three hundred people in the audience. Mostly non-Indians; an Indian or three. Questions and answers.

"Why do you insist on calling yourselves Indian?" asked a white 5
woman in a nice hat. "It's so demeaning."

"Listen," I said. "The word belongs to us now. We are Indians. That has nothing to do with Indians from India. We are not American Indians. We are Indians, pronounced In-din. It belongs to us. We own it and we're not going to give it back."

So much has been taken from us that we hold on to the smallest things with all the strength we have left.

Winter on the Spokane Indian Reservation, 1976. My two cousins, S and G, have enough money for gloves. They buy them at Irene's Grocery

Store. Irene is a white woman who has lived on our reservation since the beginning of time. I have no money for gloves. My hands are bare.

We build snow fortresses on the football field. Since we are Indian boys playing, there must be a war. We stockpile snowballs. S and G build their fortress on the fifty-yard line. I build mine on the thirty-yard line. We begin our little war. My hands are bare.

10 My cousins are good warriors. They throw snowballs with precision. I am bombarded, under siege, defeated quickly. My cousins bury me in the snow. My grave is shallow. If my cousins knew how to dance, they might have danced on my grave. But they know how to laugh, so they laugh. They are my cousins, meaning we are related in the Indian way. My father drank beers with their father for most of two decades, and that is enough to make us relatives. Indians gather relatives like firewood, protection against the cold. I am buried in the snow, cold, without protection. My hands are bare.

After a short celebration, my cousins exhume me. I am too cold to fight. Shivering, I walk for home, anxious for warmth. I know my mother is home. She is probably sewing a quilt. She is always sewing quilts. If she sells a quilt, we have dinner. If she fails to sell a quilt, we go hungry. My mother has never failed to sell a quilt. But the threat of hunger is always there.

When I step into the house, my mother is sewing yet another quilt. She is singing a song under her breath. You might assume she is singing a highly traditional Spokane Indian song. She is singing Donna Fargo's "The Happiest Girl in the Whole USA." Improbably, this is a highly traditional Spokane Indian song. The living room is dark in the late afternoon. The house is cold. My mother is wearing her coat and shoes.

"Why don't you turn up the heat?" I ask my mother.

"No electricity," she says.

15 "Power went out?" I ask.

"Didn't pay the bill," she says.

I am colder. I inhale, exhale, my breath visible inside the house. I can hear a car sliding on the icy road outside. My mother is making a quilt. This quilt will pay for the electricity. Her fingers are stiff and painful from the cold. She is sewing as fast as she can.

On the jukebox in the bar: Hank Williams, Patsy Cline, Johnny Cash, Charlie Rich, Freddy Fender, Donna Fargo.

On the radio in the car: Creedence Clearwater Revival, Three Dog Night, Blood, Sweat and Tears, Janis Joplin, early Stones, earlier Beatles.

20 On the stereo in the house: Glen Campbell, Roy Orbison, Johnny Horton, Loretta Lynn, "The Ballad of the Green Beret."

The fourth-grade music teacher, Mr. Manley, set a row of musical instruments in front of us. From left to right, a flute, clarinet, French horn, trombone, trumpet, tuba, drum. We had our first chance to play that kind of music.

"Now," he explained, "I want all of you to line up behind the instrument you want to learn how to play."

Dawn, Loretta, and Karen lined up behind the flute. Melissa and Michelle behind the clarinet. Lori and Willette behind the French horn. All ten Indian boys lined up behind the drum.

My sister, Mary, was beautiful. She was fourteen years older than me. She wore short skirts and nylons because she was supposed to wear short skirts and nylons. It was expected. Her black hair combed long and straight. 1970. Often, she sat in her favorite chair, the fake leather lounger we rescued from the dump. Holding a hand mirror, she combed her hair, applied her makeup. Much lipstick and eyeshadow, no foundation. She was always leaving the house. I do not remember where she went. I do remember sitting at her feet, rubbing my cheek against her nyloned calf, while she waited for her ride.

She died in an early morning fire in Montana in 1981. At the time, I 25 was sleeping at a friend's house in Washington. I was not dreaming of my sister.

"Sherman," asks the critic, "how does your work apply to the oral tradition?"

"Well," I say, as I hold my latest book close to me, "it doesn't apply at all because I type this. And I'm really, really quiet when I'm typing it."

Summer 1977. Steve and I want to attend the KISS concert in Spokane. KISS is very popular on my reservation. Gene Simmons, the bass player. Paul Stanley, lead singer and rhythm guitarist. Ace Frehley, lead guitar. Peter Criss, drummer. All four hide their faces behind elaborate makeup. Simmons the devil, Stanley the lover, Frehley the space man, Criss the cat.

The songs: "Do You Love Me," "Calling Dr. Love," "Love Gun," "Makin' Love," "C'mon and Love Me."

Steve and I are too young to go on our own. His uncle and aunt, 30 born-again Christians, decide to chaperon us. Inside the Spokane Coliseum, the four of us find seats far from the stage and the enormous speakers. Uncle and Aunt wanted to avoid the bulk of the crowd, but have landed us in the unofficial pot smoking section. We are overwhelmed by the sweet smoke. Steve and I cover our mouths and noses with Styrofoam cups and try to breathe normally.

KISS opens their show with staged explosions, flashing red lights, a prolonged guitar solo by Frehley. Simmons spits fire. The crowd rushes the stage. All the pot smokers in our section hold lighters, tiny flames flickering, high above their heads. The songs are so familiar. We know all the words. The audience sings along.

The songs: "Let Me Go, Rock 'n Roll," "Detroit Rock City," "Rock and Roll All Nite."

The decibel level is tremendous. Steve and I can feel the sound waves crashing against the Styrofoam cups we hold over our faces. Aunt and Uncle are panicked, finally assured that the devil plays a mean guitar. This is too much for them. It is too much for Steve and me, but we pretend to be disappointed when Aunt and Uncle drag us out of the coliseum.

During the drive home, Aunt and Uncle play Christian music on the radio. Loudly and badly, they sing along. Steve and I are in the back of the Pacer, looking up through the strangely curved rear window. There is a meteor shower, the largest in a decade. Steve and I smell like pot smoke. We smile at this. Our ears ring. We make wishes on the shooting stars, though both of us know that a shooting star is not a star. It's just a sliver of stone.

35 I made a very conscious decision to marry an Indian woman, who made a very conscious decision to marry me.

Our hope: to give birth to and raise Indian children who love themselves. That is the most revolutionary act possible.

1982. I am the only Indian student at Reardan High, an all-white school in a small farm town just outside my reservation. I am in the pizza parlor, sharing a deluxe with my white friends. We are talking and laughing. A drunk Indian walks into the parlor. He staggers to the counter and orders a beer. The waiter ignores him. Our table is silent.

At our table, S is shaking her head. She leans toward the table as if to share a secret. We all lean toward her.

"Man," she says, "I hate Indians."

40 I am curious about the Indian writers who identify themselves as mixed-blood. It must be difficult for them, trying to decide into which container they should place their nouns and verbs. Yet, it must be good to be invisible, as a blond, Aryan-featured Jew might have known in Germany during World War II. Then again, I think of the horror stories that a pale Jew might tell about his life during the Holocaust.

An Incomplete List of People Who I Wish Were Indian

1. Martin Luther King, Jr.
2. Robert Johnson
3. Meryl Streep
4. Helen Keller
5. Walt Whitman

6. Emily Dickinson
7. Superman
8. Adam
9. Eve
10. Muhammad Ali
11. Billie Jean King
12. John Lennon
13. Jimmy Carter
14. Rosa Parks
15. Shakespeare
16. John Steinbeck
17. Billy the Kid
18. Voltaire
19. Harriet Tubman
20. Flannery O'Connor
21. Pablo Neruda
22. Amelia Earhart
23. Sappho
24. Mary Magdalene
25. Robert DeNiro
26. Susan B. Anthony
27. Kareem Abdul-Jabbar
28. Wilma Rudolph
29. Isadora Duncan
30. Bruce Springsteen
31. Dian Fossey
32. Patsy Cline
33. Jesus Christ

Summer 1995. Seattle, Washington. I am idling at a red light when a car filled with white boys pulls up beside me. The white boy in the front passenger seat leans out his window.

"I hate you Indian motherfuckers," he screams.

I quietly wait for the green light.

1978. David, Randy, Steve, and I decide to form a reservation doo-wop group, like the Temptations. During recess, we practice behind the old tribal school. Steve, a falsetto, is the best singer. I am the worst singer, but have the deepest voice, and am therefore an asset.

"What songs do you want to sing?" asks David.

"'Tracks of My Tears,'" says Steve, who always decides these kind of things.

We sing, desperately trying to remember the lyrics to that song. We try to remember other songs. We remember the chorus to most, the first verse of a few, and only one in its entirety. For some unknown reason, we all know the lyrics of "Monster Mash," a novelty hit from the fifties. However, I'm the only one who can manage to sing with the pseudo-Transylvanian accent that "Monster Mash" requires. This dubious skill makes me the lead singer, despite Steve's protests.

"We need a name for our group," says Randy.

"How about The Warriors?" I ask.

50   Everybody agrees. We watch westerns.

We sing "Monster Mash" over and over. We want to be famous. We want all the little Indian girls to shout our names. Finally, after days of practice, we are ready for our debut. Walking in a row like soldiers, the four of us parade around the playground. We sing "Monster Mash." I am in front, followed by Steve, David, then Randy, who is the shortest, but the toughest fighter our reservation has ever known. We sing. We are The Warriors. All the other Indian boys and girls line up behind us as we march. We are heroes. We are loved. I sing with everything I have inside of me: pain, happiness, anger, depression, heart, soul, small intestine. I sing and am rewarded with people who listen.

This is why I am a poet.

I remember watching Richard Nixon, during the whole Watergate affair, as he held a press conference and told the entire world that he was not a liar.

For the first time, I understood that storytellers could be bad people.

Poetry = Anger • Imagination

55   Every time I venture into the bookstore, I find another book about Indians. There are hundreds of books about Indians published every year, yet so few are written by Indians. I gather all the books written about Indians. I discover:

1. A book written by a person who identifies herself as mixed-blood will sell more copies than a book written by a person who identifies herself as strictly Indian.
2. A book written by a non-Indian will sell more copies than a book written by a mixed-blood or Indian writer.
3. A book about Indian life in the pre-twentieth century, whether written by a non-Indian, mixed-blood, or Indian, will sell more copies than a book about twentieth-century Indian life.
4. If you are a non-Indian writing about Indians, it is almost guaranteed that Tony Hillerman will write something positive about you.

5. Reservation Indian writers are rarely published in any form.

6. Every Indian woman writer will be compared with Louise Erdrich. Every Indian man writer will be compared with Michael Dorris.

7. A very small percentage of the readers of Indian literature have heard of Simon J. Ortiz. This is a crime.

8. Books about the Sioux sell more copies than all of the books written about other tribes combined.

9. Mixed-blood writers often write about any tribe that interests them, whether or not the writer is descended from that tribe.

10. Most of the writers who use obviously Indian names, such as Eagle Woman and Pretty Shield, are usually non-Indian.

11. Non-Indian writers usually say "Great Spirit," "Mother Earth," "Two-Legged, Four-Legged, and Winged." Mixed-blood writers usually say "Creator," "Mother Earth," "Two-Legged, Four-Legged, and Winged." Indian writers usually say "God," "Earth," "Human Being, Dog, and Bird."

12. If an Indian book contains no dogs, then the book is written by a non-Indian or mixed-blood writer.

13. If there are winged animals who aren't supposed to have wings on the cover of the book, then it is written by a non-Indian.

14. Successful non-Indian writers are thought to be learned experts on Indian life. Successful mixed-blood writers are thought to be wonderful translators of Indian life. Successful Indian writers are thought to be traditional storytellers of Indian life.

15. Very few Indian and mixed-blood writers speak their tribal languages. Even fewer non-Indian writers speak their tribal languages.

16. Mixed-bloods often write exclusively about Indians, even if they grew up in non-Indian communities.

17. Indians often write exclusively about reservation life, even if they never lived on a reservation.

18. Non-Indian writers always write about reservation life.

19. Nobody has written the great urban Indian novel yet.

20. Most non-Indians who write about Indians are fiction writers. They write fiction about Indians because it sells.

Have you stood in a crowded room where nobody looks like you? If you are white, have you stood in a room full of black people? Are you an Irish man who has strolled through the streets of Compton? If you are black, have you stood in a room full of white people? Are you an African man who has been playing the back nine at the local country club? If you are a woman, have you stood in a room full of men? Are you Sandra Day O'Connor or Ruth Ginsburg?

Since I left the reservation, almost every room I enter is filled with people who do not look like me. There are only two million Indians in this country. We could all fit into one medium-sized city. We should look into it.

Often, I am most alone in bookstores where I am reading from my work. I look up from the page at a sea of white faces. This is frightening.

There was an apple tree outside my grandmother's house on the reservation. The apples were green; my grandmother's house was green. This was the game. My siblings and I would try to sneak apples from the tree. Sometimes, our friends would join our raiding expeditions. My grandmother believed green apples were poison and was simply trying to protect us from sickness. There is nothing biblical about this story.

60   The game had rules. We always had to raid the tree during daylight. My grandmother had bad eyes and it would have been unfair to challenge her during the dark. We all had to approach the tree at the same time. Arnold, my older brother, Kim and Arlene, my younger twin sisters. We had to climb the tree to steal apples, ignoring the fruit that hung low to the ground.

Arnold, of course, was the best apple thief on the reservation. He was chubby but quick. He was fearless in the tree, climbing to the top for the plumpest apples. He'd hang from a branch with one arm, reach for apples with the other, and fill his pockets with his booty. I loved him like crazy. My sisters were more conservative. They often grabbed one apple and ate it quickly while they sat on a sturdy branch. I always wanted the green apples that contained a hint of red. While we were busy raiding the tree, we'd also keep an eye on my grandmother's house. She was a big woman, nearly six feet tall. At the age of seventy, she could still outrun any ten-year-old.

Arnold, of course, was always the first kid out of the tree. He'd hang from a branch, drop to the ground, and scream loudly, announcing our presence to our grandmother. He'd run away, leaving my sisters and me stuck in the tree. We'd scramble to the ground and try to escape. If our grandmother said our name, we were automatically captured.

"Junior," she'd shout and I'd freeze. It was the rule. A dozen Indian kids were sometimes in that tree, scattering in random directions when our grandmother burst out of the house. If our grandmother remembered your name, you were a prisoner of war. And, believe me, no matter how many kids were running away, my grandmother always remembered my name.

"Junior," she'd shout and I would close my eyes in disgust. Captured again! I'd wait as she walked up to me. She'd hold out her hand

and I'd give her any stolen apples. Then she'd smack me gently on the top of my head. I was free to run then, pretending she'd never caught me in the first place. I'd try to catch up with my siblings and friends. I would shout their names as I ran through the trees surrounding my grandmother's house.

My grandmother died when I was fourteen years old. I miss her. I miss everybody. 65

So many people claim to be Indian, speaking of an Indian grandmother, a warrior grandfather. Let's say the United States government announced that every Indian had to return to their reservation. How many people would shove their Indian ancestor back into the closet?

My mother still makes quilts. My wife and I sleep beneath one. My brother works for our tribal casino. One sister works for our bingo hall, while the other works in the tribal finance department. Our adopted little brother, James, who is actually our second cousin, is a freshman at Reardan High School. He can run the mile in five minutes.

My father used to leave us for weeks at a time to drink with his friends and cousins. I missed him so much I'd cry myself sick. Every time he left, I ended up in the emergency room. But I always got well and he always came back. He'd walk in the door without warning. We'd forgive him.

I could always tell when he was going to leave. He would be tense, quiet, unable to concentrate. He'd flip through magazines and television channels. He'd open the refrigerator door, study its contents, shut the door, and walk away. Five minutes later, he'd be back at the fridge, rearranging items on the shelves. I would follow him from place to place, trying to prevent his escape.

Once, he went into the bathroom, which had no windows, while I 70 sat outside the only door and waited for him. I could not hear him inside. I knocked on the thin wood. I was five years old.

"Are you there?" I asked. "Are you still there?"

Years later, I am giving a reading at a bookstore in Spokane, Washington. There is a large crowd. I read a story about an Indian father who leaves his family for good. He moves to a city a thousand miles away. Then he dies. It is a sad story. When I finish, a woman in the front row breaks into tears.

"What's wrong?" I ask her.

"I'm so sorry about your father," she says.

"Thank you," I say. "But that's my father sitting right next to 75 you."

Responding to Reading

1. Why does Alexie call his memoir an "unauthorized autobiography"?
2. What is Alexie's attitude here toward his Indian heritage? Is this attitude consistent, or does he seem to have mixed feelings about his heritage?
3. What do you think Alexie is saying in this essay about the difference between fiction and nonfiction? Between storytelling and lying?

Responding in Writing

Alexie mentions many musicians and many songs in his "unauthorized autobiography." What do you think these references add to his memoir?

THE KEY TO MY FATHER

Harlan Coben

1962–

Harlan Coben is a well-known writer of mystery novels set in the glamorous worlds of the media and professional sports. Since 1990, Coben has published more than a dozen popular mystery novels, most recently The Innocent *(2005) and* Promise Me *(2006). In the following short story, which appeared in the* New York Times *on June 15, 2003—Father's Day—Coben considers how much and how little a son can know about his own father.*

Let's get something straight right away: my father was hopelessly unhip. He was the corporeal embodiment of an Air Supply eight-track. He'd come home from work, shed the powder-blue suit with reversible vest, the tie so polyester it would melt during heat waves, the V-neck Hanes undershirt of startling white, the gray socks bought by the dozen at Burlington Coat Factory. He'd don a logo T-shirt that was compulsorily a size too snug, if you know what I mean, and shorts that were, uh, short, like something John McEnroe wore at Wimbledon in 1979.

His sunglasses were big, too big. They might have worked on Sophia Loren but on Dad they looked like manhole covers.

He had thin legs. My mom teased him about this, this 6-foot-2 man with the barrel chest and olive skin, teetering on spindly legs. His hair, as described by my mother, was "tired," wispy and flyaway. He had big arms. To his children, they looked like oak branches. The biceps would grow spongy with the years. But they never had time to fully atrophy.

He would play ball with us, but he was a terrible athlete.

I remember going to that Little League coaches' softball game, the ₅ one they have at the end of every season, and watching my father— this man who had taught me to keep my elbow up and back foot planted—take to the plate and ground out weakly to third. Three times in a row. To his credit, he never made excuses. "You," he'd tell me. "You're an athlete. Me, I'm a spaz."

His after-shave was Old Spice. There had been a radical period when he tried an eau called Royal Copenhagen—someone had given him a gift set and damned if he was going to let it go to waste—but he veered back onto his Old Spice route. That is still my strongest bar mitzvah recollection—that smell.

No, I can't tell you what part of the haphtara I recited from the pulpit of B'nai Jeshurun. Something from Ezekiel, I think. But there's that part in the ceremony where the father blesses the son. My father bent down and whispered in my ear. He said something about loving me and being proud—much as I want to, I can't remember the exact words—and then he kissed me on the cheek. I remember the feel of his cheek on mine, the catcher's-glove hand cupping my head, and the smell of Old Spice.

On Saturday mornings, we went to Seymour's luncheonette on Livingston Avenue for a milkshake and maybe a pack of baseball cards. I'd sit on a stool at the counter and twirl. He'd stand next to me, always, as if that was what a man did.

He'd lean against the counter and eat—too quickly, I think. He was never fat but he was always on the wrong side of the weight curve. He was uneven about physical activity. He'd discover a work-out program, do it for three months, go idle for about six, find something new. Rinse, repeat. Like with shampoo.

He hated his job.

He never told me this. He dutifully went to work every day. But I ₁₀ knew. He didn't have a lot of friends either, but that was by choice. He could have been a popular man. People liked him. He could feign charm and warmth, but there was a coldness there. He cared only about his family and he cared with a ferocity that both frightened and exhilarated. You know those stories about someone lifting a car to save a trapped loved one? It took little to imagine him performing such a feat. The world was his family—the rest of the planet's inhabitants no more than the periphery, deep background, scenery.

The night was his domain. He slept lightly, too lightly. I wonder if that is to blame, the way he'd startle awake. I would try my hardest to tiptoe past his door, but no matter how great my stealth, he would jerk upright in his bed as if I'd dropped a Popsicle on his stomach. Every night the same thing:

"Marc?" he'd shout.

"Yes, Dad."

"Something wrong?"

15   "Just going to the bathroom," I'd say. "I've been going by myself since I was 14."

During my freshman year at college, after a particularly debauched frat party, I was struck by a strange realization: this was the first time I'd woken up sick without my father present. His hand was not on my forehead. He was not speaking softly or rubbing my back.

I was alone.

I blame myself for what happened.

Three days before my college graduation, I dropped my father off at the airport.

20   We were late. He ran to catch his flight. That is the image I can't shake all these years later. My father, hopelessly unhip and out of shape, running for that stupid flight so he could be at a meeting that meant nothing to anybody.

Six hours later, he called from the Comfort Suite in Tampa.

"Let me speak to your mother."

I handed her the phone.

I watched her listen. I saw her face turn white.

25   "What?" I asked.

"He's having chest pains, but he says he's fine."

And I knew.

And she knew. I called the front desk. I told them to send an ambulance. I called my father back. "I told the front desk to send someone up," and then my father said the most frightening thing of all: "O.K."

No argument, no brave front, no I'm fine.

30   "But I have to find the room key first," he added.

"What?"

"They'll be here soon. I have to go. I have to find the key."

"Forget the key."

"You might need it."

35   "For what?"

But he hung up. And again I knew. He had never been ill, but I knew. With my father's strength, you somehow still sensed the fragile.

My mother and I rushed to the airport. I called the hotel from a pay phone. They just wheeled him out the lobby, I was told.

Wheeled him out. I pictured the oxygen mask on his face. I imagined him as I had never seen him: afraid.

He liked building things, my father, but he was bad with his hands. He gardened on weekends, but our shrubs never looked right, not like the shrubs that belonged to the Bauers, who lived next door. Their lawn looked as if it'd been trimmed for a P.G.A. event.

40   Ours had dandelions tall enough to go on the adult rides at Six Flags.

My father fought in the Korean War but never talked about it.

I didn't even know he'd been in the military until I explored his junk drawer when I was 8 and found a bunch of medals in the bottom. They were loose in the drawer, mingling with spare change.

Our plane had a stopover at the Atlanta airport, the epicenter of the stopover. I called the hospital. The nurse assured me that my father was fine.

But I didn't believe her. She transferred me to the doctor. I told the doctor I was calling about my father, that I was his son. The doctor did that calm voice thing and asked me my name. He told me, Marc—using my name so often it became like an annoying tick—that my father was in serious condition, Marc, that they are going to operate in a few minutes. I felt my legs go. He's awake and comfortable, the doctor told me. He understands what is happening. I asked to speak to him. "The phone cord won't reach, Marc," the doctor said.

"Tell him we're on our way," I insisted.

"I will." But I didn't believe him.

My father always longed for a Cadillac. He got one when he turned 52.

He listened only to AM radio. Every once in a while a certain song would come on and he'd turn it up. His face would change. The lines would soften. He'd lean back and steer with his wrists and whistle.

By the time we arrived at the hospital, night had fallen. I sat in the waiting room. He was still in surgery. My mother did not speak, something that is usually accompanied by a parting sea or burning bush.

I began to make deals with whatever higher power would listen, you know the kind, about what I'd do, what I'd risk, what I'd trade, if only it could be morning again and we could leave for that damn plane a few minutes earlier and if he hadn't run to catch that flight, if he'd just walked instead, if he didn't devour his food, if he kept up with an exercise program, if I'd been an easier son.

At 4 a.m., that awful hospital beeping sound echoed down the still corridor, then a rush that stole our breath. The air was suddenly gone. And so, too, was my father.

We bury him on Father's Day.

The weather is, of course, spectacular, mocking my gloom. The men his age come up to me and tell me all about their own heart problems, about their close calls, about how lucky they've been. I look through them, wondering why they are the ones who get to stand before me, happily breathing. I wish them ill. I call his former boss, the one who sold the company and made my father stuff envelopes with his resume at the age of 56. I tell him that if he shows up at the funeral, I'll punch him in the face. He, too, is to blame.

I wonder if my father was scared near the end or if he went into surgery thinking it would be all be O.K. Don't know, of course.

There is a lot I don't know. I don't know what my father wanted out of life. I don't know what he wanted to be when he was a young

man, before I came around and changed everything. He never expressed any of that to me. And I never asked.

A week after the funeral, I call his doctor down in Tampa.

"He died alone," I say.

"He knew you were there."

60 "You didn't tell him."

"I did."

"What did he say?"

The doctor takes a second.

"He said for you to check his pocket."

65 "What?"

"You'd need a place to stay overnight. He said to check his
pocket."

Cradling the phone, I go to the closet where his belongings, still
in the plastic hospital bag the nurse handed me, are hanging. I break
the seal. The Old Spice scent is faint but there. I dig past the Hanes V-
Neck and find his pants.

"What else?" I ask.

"Pardon?"

"What else did he say?"

70 "That's it."

"Those were his final words? Check his pocket?"

His voice is suddenly soft.

"Yes."

75 My fingers slip into the pocket of his pants and hit something
metallic. I pull it out.

The hotel key. He'd found it after all. He put it in his pocket. His
last words, his last act, for us.

I still have the key.

I keep it in a drawer with his medals.

Responding to Reading

1. Why does the narrator blame himself for his father's death? Who (or what)
   else does he blame? What, specifically, do you think the narrator regrets?
2. What does the key in his father's pocket represent to the narrator? In what
   sense is it, as the story's title claims, "the key to [his] father"?
3. Paragraph 10 begins with the sentence, "He hated his job." Paragraph 11
   ends with the sentence, "The world was his family—the rest of the planet's
   inhabitants no more than the periphery, deep background, scenery." What
   is the significance of these two sentences in the story?

Responding in Writing

Coben uses many small physical details—for example, his gray socks and his
aftershave—to characterize the narrator's father. List as many of these details
as you can. Then, create a similar list of the physical details that characterize
one of your own parents.

Focus

Does Gay Marriage Threaten the Family?

Figures of two grooms on a wedding cake

Responding to the Image

1. The two male figures pictured on top of the wedding cake in this photo do not conform to most people's expectations. What is your reaction to this image? What elements of the image *do* conform to tradition?

2. The figures of the two men are identical. Do they have to be? What does their physical similarity suggest?

WHAT ARE WE FIGHTING FOR?

Ralph Wedgwood

Ralph Wedgwood, a lecturer in Philosophy at Merton College, Oxford University, has published numerous scholarly articles on ethics and metaethics (the study of ethical language), epistemology (the study of knowledge), and metaphysics. In "What Are We Fighting For?" Wedgwood explores the nature of marriage and argues that same-sex marriage, like heterosexual marriage, is an institution that upholds and protects the family.

The same-sex marriage debate raises some difficult questions. Is same-sex marriage really worth fighting for? What would same-sex marriage mean for us? What exactly is marriage anyway?

Many advocates of same-sex marriage seem to assume that marriage is a purely legal institution, consisting of a cluster of legal rights, obligations, and benefits. Married couples have mutual rights and obligations, such as the right to mutual financial support and (in the event of divorce or separation) to alimony and an equitable division of property; and they also receive certain state-provided benefits such as tax breaks, preferential immigration treatment, tenancy succession rights, health insurance benefits, and so on.

If marriage is no more than this, however, then it is not marriage itself that matters, but only its constituent rights and benefits. But the best way to secure these rights and benefits for same-sex couples may not be to try to get them through "marriage" as such. After all, the mutual rights and obligations of marriage can already be re-created by means of private contracts, wills, and power-of-attorney agreements. And some of the other legal benefits of marriage are already being split off from marriage and provided to same-sex couples. Even though same-sex marriage does not exist anywhere in the world, same-sex partners already receive health insurance benefits from many employers, preferential immigration treatment from some countries, tenancy succession rights in some cities, and so on. If these legal rights and benefits are all that matter, then it is probably a mistake to try to secure them all at once by fighting for full same-sex marriage.

As most people intuitively sense, however, marriage is more than just a cluster of legal rights and benefits. Of course the legal aspects of marriage are important. But marriage involves more than this. Marriage is a fusion of law and culture. It is a legal status that not only confers legal rights and obligations, but also has crucial effects on how the married couple is regarded by society.

5   The point is not that the law requires or encourages people to approve of and support the married couple's relationship—the law does

nothing to deter me from disapproving of a friend's marriage, or even from persuading my friend to get divorced, if I see fit to do so—but that society as a whole has certain generally shared expectations about the kind of relationship that married couples typically have (while it lacks any such clear expectations about relationships of other sorts). Once a couple is legally married, society will come to expect that their relationship is of this kind. These expectations include, at least in our society, that the couple engage in intimacy and probably sex; that they have shared finances and a shared household, or at least co-operate extensively in coping with the necessities of life; that they have a serious long-term commitment to their relationship; and that the relationship involves certain legal rights and obligations, notably the right to mutual financial support.

The legal aspects of marriage complement and undergird society's shared expectations of marriage. Marriage is a legal status: the question "Is Chris married to Jo?" is a legal question; it is the law that determines who is married and who is not. This means that there is general agreement about who is married and who is not, thus allowing the married couple to be regarded as married by society as a whole (not just by their particular circle or subculture). The legally binding mutual rights and obligations of marriage reflect society's expectations of marriage, and when necessary are enforced, thus providing an assurance that these expectations will be fulfilled. For example, rights such as the right to spousal support and (in the event of divorce or separation) to alimony and an equitable division of property reinforce the generally shared expectation that marriage involves a serious mutual commitment to long-term economic and domestic partnership. In this way, these legal aspects of marriage, together with the fact that marriage is so familiar, provide an assurance that society as a whole will share these generally shared expectations of marriage, and that the married couple's relationship will be regarded in the light of these expectations.

This helps to explain what attracts couples to the institution of marriage. Couples get married because they not only want to make a legally binding commitment to each other, but also want to get the rest of society to understand that they have a serious commitment to an intimate relationship, which involves long-term domestic and economic partnership. It is the public recognition of the status of "married" that constitutes the most important benefit of marriage, and what is most crucially abridged when the State discriminates against gay couples who want to marry.

Same-sex couples want to get married for the same reasons that heterosexual couples do. They not only want the legal rights and benefits of marriage; they also want to be regarded as married by society. It is all too easy for the rest of society to ignore same-sex relationships, and to assume that they are only sexual, or involve no serious long-term commitment or sharing of finances and household responsibilities. Many gay and lesbian couples want to make it clear to everyone that they have a relationship of the same general kind as society expects of married couples. Domestic partnerships are just less effective for this purpose. If you say, "Chris and I are domestic partners," your audience may wonder, "Do domestic partnerships expire every month unless they are renewed? Are the partners obliged to support each other financially? Do they have a sexual relationship— or are they just roommates who want to keep the rent-controlled apartment if the other dies?" For society at large, domestic partnerships and commitment ceremonies are less familiar than marriage; they lack the resonance of marriage.

Same-sex marriage would clearly not deprive anyone else of any important benefits of marriage, and would not fundamentally change its definition (intimacy, shared household, mutual commitment, and so on). Other elements that may be included in this definition, such as procreation, are far from being as categorical as the ones I've specified. Thus, for example, while there may be a general expectation that many couples will have children together, society has never expected all married couples to do so.

10   Some opponents of same-sex marriage are concerned that if marriage were extended to couples who obviously cannot procreate together, this would weaken the association between marriage and procreation, reducing married couples' motivation to have children. Others worry that same-sex marriages would be more liable to marital breakdown than heterosexual marriages, but this is mere speculation in the absence of any accumulated experience with same-sex marriage.

The ban on same-sex marriage certainly cannot be justified on the grounds that it serves to express and reinforce the view, which a number of people hold, that heterosexual unions are superior to homosexual unions, based on religious credos or moral statements. The State cannot justify its actions by appeal to such controversial moral or religious views, any more than it can justify them by appeal to the view that Christianity is superior to Judaism. The ban on same-sex marriage is opposed by some because it seems to install homosexual relations as equal in value to heterosexual ones. Technically, it does no such thing. The state allows convicted wife-murderers, child-abusers, and rapists to marry, even while in jail; it is not expressing any sort of approval of these relationships.

Once we understand what marriage is, we can see what marriage would mean for us, and why it is worth fighting for. Same-sex marriage would not force anyone to honor or approve of gay or lesbian relationships against their will. But it would enable those of us who are involved in gay or lesbian relationships to get the rest of society to understand that we take these relationships just as seriously as heterosexual married couples take theirs. And without marriage, we remain second-class citizens—excluded, for no good reason, from participating in one of the basic institutions of society.

Responding to Reading

1. In his essay's first paragraph, Wedgwood asks three questions. Briefly summarize his response to each of these questions. Do your own answers to these questions agree with his?
2. According to Wedgwood, marriage is "a legal status that not only confers legal rights and obligations, but also has crucial effects on how the married couple is regarded by society" (4). Do you think Maggie Gallagher (below) and Kerry Howley (p. 72) would agree with Wedgwood on this point? Would they agree that this public recognition is "the most important benefit of marriage" (7)?
3. In paragraphs 10–11, Wedgwood introduces objections raised by those who oppose same-sex marriage. Does he refute these objections effectively? If so, where? If not, how might he defend his position against these objections?

Responding in Writing

Wedgwood's key argument here, as stated in his conclusion, is that without the option of marriage, gays and lesbians are "second-class citizens." Do you agree that state-sanctioned marriage would elevate the status of gay and lesbian couples? Do you believe they have a right to this status?

WHAT MARRIAGE IS FOR

Maggie Gallagher

1960–

Maggie Gallagher is the editor of MarriageDebate.com *and president of the Institute for Marriage and Public Policy, whose motto is "strengthening marriage for a new generation." She is a frequent contributor to the same-sex marriage debate, and her articles have appeared in the* New York Times, *the* Weekly Standard, *the* National Review, *the* Wall Street Journal, *and numerous scholarly journals. She has published several books on marriage, most recently, with Linda J. Waite,* The Case for Marriage: Why Married People Are Happier, Healthier, and Better Off Financially *(2000). The following essay argues that marriage is by definition a social institution that includes mothers, fathers, and childern.*

Gay marriage is no longer a theoretical issue. Canada has it. Massachusetts is expected to get it any day. The Goodridge decision there could set off a legal, political, and cultural battle in the courts of 50 states and in the U.S. Congress. Every politician, every judge, every citizen has to decide: Does same-sex marriage matter? If so, how and why?

The timing could not be worse. Marriage is in crisis, as everyone knows: High rates of divorce and illegitimacy have eroded marriage norms and created millions of fatherless children, whole neighborhoods where lifelong marriage is no longer customary, driving up poverty, crime, teen pregnancy, welfare dependency, drug abuse, and mental and physical health problems. And yet, amid the broader negative trends, recent signs point to a modest but significant recovery.

Divorce rates appear to have declined a little from historic highs; illegitimacy rates, after doubling every decade from 1960 to 1990, appear to have leveled off, albeit at a high level (33 percent of American births are to unmarried women); teen pregnancy and sexual activity are down; the proportion of homemaking mothers is up; marital fertility appears to be on the rise. Research suggests that married adults are more committed to marital permanence than they were twenty years ago. A new generation of children of divorce appears on the brink of making a commitment to lifelong marriage. In 1977, 55 percent of American teenagers thought a divorce should be harder to get; in 2001, 75 percent did.

A new marriage movement—a distinctively American phenomenon—has been born. The scholarly consensus on the importance of marriage has broadened and deepened; it is now the conventional wisdom among child welfare organizations. As a Child Trends research brief summed up: "Research clearly demonstrates that family structure matters for children, and the family structure that helps children the most is a family headed by two biological parents in a low-conflict marriage. Children in single-parent families, children born to unmarried mothers, and children in stepfamilies or cohabiting relationships face higher risks of poor outcomes. . . . There is thus value for children in promoting strong, stable marriages between biological parents."

5   What will court-imposed gay marriage do to this incipient recovery of marriage? For, even as support for marriage in general has been rising, the gay marriage debate has proceeded on a separate track. Now the time has come to decide: Will unisex marriage help or hurt marriage as a social institution?

Why should it do either, some may ask? How can Bill and Bob's marriage hurt Mary and Joe? In an exchange with me in the just-released book *Marriage and Same Sex Unions: A Debate,* Evan Wolfson, chief legal strategist for same-sex marriage in the Hawaii case, *Baer v. Lewin,* argues there is "enough marriage to share." What counts, he says, "is not family structure, but the quality of dedication, commitment, self-sacrifice, and love in the household."

Family structure does not count. Then what is marriage for? Why have laws about it? Why care whether people get married or stay married? Do children need mothers and fathers, or will any sort of family do? When the sexual desires of adults clash with the interests of children, which carries more weight, socially and legally?

These are the questions that same-sex marriage raises. Our answers will affect not only gay and lesbian families, but marriage as a whole.

In ordering gay marriage on June 10, 2003, the highest court in Ontario, Canada, explicitly endorsed a brand new vision of marriage along the lines Wolfson suggests: "Marriage is, without dispute, one of the most significant forms of personal relationships. . . . Through the institution of marriage, individuals can publicly express their love and commitment to each other. Through this institution, society publicly recognizes expressions of love and commitment between individuals, granting them respect and legitimacy as a couple."

The Ontario court views marriage as a kind of Good Housekeeping   10 Seal of Approval that government stamps on certain registered intimacies because, well, for no particular reason the court can articulate except that society likes to recognize expressions of love and commitment. In this view, endorsement of gay marriage is a no-brainer, for nothing really important rides on whether anyone gets married or stays married. Marriage is merely individual expressive conduct, and there is no obvious reason why some individuals' expression of gay love should hurt other individuals' expressions of non-gay love.

There is, however, a different view—indeed, a view that is radically opposed to this: Marriage is the fundamental, cross-cultural institution for bridging the male-female divide so that children have loving, committed mothers and fathers. Marriage is inherently normative: It is about holding out a certain kind of relationship as a social ideal, especially when there are children involved. Marriage is not simply an artifact of law; neither is it a mere delivery mechanism for a set of legal benefits that might as well be shared more broadly. The laws of marriage do not create marriage, but in societies ruled by law they help trace the boundaries and sustain the public meanings of marriage.

In other words, while individuals freely choose to enter marriage, society upholds the marriage option, formalizes its definition, and surrounds it with norms and reinforcements, so we can raise boys and girls who aspire to become the kind of men and women who can make successful marriages. Without this shared, public aspect, perpetuated generation after generation, marriage becomes what its critics say it is: a mere contract, a vessel with no particular content, one of a menu of sexual lifestyles, of no fundamental importance to anyone outside a given relationship.

The marriage idea is that children need mothers and fathers, that societies need babies, and that adults have an obligation to shape their sexual behavior so as to give their children stable families in which to grow up.

CHAPTER 1 FOCUS

Which view of marriage is true? We have seen what has happened in our communities where marriage norms have failed. What has happened is not a flowering of libertarian freedom, but a breakdown of social and civic order that can reach frightening proportions. When law and culture retreat from sustaining the marriage idea, individuals cannot create marriage on their own.

15   In a complex society governed by positive law, social institutions require both social and legal support. To use an analogy, the government does not create private property. But to make a market system a reality requires the assistance of law as well as culture. People have to be raised to respect the property of others, and to value the traits of entrepreneurship, and to be law-abiding generally. The law cannot allow individuals to define for themselves what private property (or law-abiding conduct) means. The boundaries of certain institutions (such as the corporation) also need to be defined legally, and the definitions become socially shared knowledge. We need a shared system of meaning, publicly enforced, if market-based economies are to do their magic and individuals are to maximize their opportunities.

Successful social institutions generally function without people's having to think very much about how they work. But when a social institution is contested—as marriage is today—it becomes critically important to think and speak clearly about its public meanings.

Again, what is marriage for? Marriage is a virtually universal human institution. In all the wildly rich and various cultures flung throughout the ecosphere, in society after society, whether tribal or complex, and however bizarre, human beings have created systems of publicly approved sexual union between men and women that entail well-defined responsibilities of mothers and fathers. Not all these marriage systems look like our own, which is rooted in a fusion of Greek, Roman, Jewish, and Christian culture. Yet everywhere, in isolated mountain valleys, parched deserts, jungle thickets, and broad plains, people have come up with some version of this thing called marriage. Why?

Because sex between men and women makes babies, that's why. Even today, in our technologically advanced contraceptive culture, half of all pregnancies are unintended: Sex between men and women *still* makes babies. Most men and women are powerfully drawn to perform a sexual act that can and does generate life. Marriage is our attempt to reconcile and harmonize the erotic, social, sexual, and financial needs of men and women with the needs of their partner and their children.

How to reconcile the needs of children with the sexual desires of adults? Every society has to face that question, and some resolve it in ways that inflict horrendous cruelty on children born outside marriage. Some cultures decide these children don't matter: Men can have all the sex they want, and any children they create outside of marriage will be throwaway kids; marriage is for citizens—slaves and peasants need not apply. You can see a version of this elitist vision of marriage emerging in America under cover of acceptance of family diversity. Marriage will continue to exist as the social advantage of elite communities. The poor and the working class? Who cares whether their kids have dads? We can always import people from abroad to fill our need for disciplined, educated workers.

Our better tradition, and the only one consistent with democratic 20 principles, is to hold up a single ideal for all parents, which is ultimately based on our deep cultural commitment to the equal dignity and social worth of all children. All kids need and deserve a married mom and dad. All parents are supposed to at least try to behave in ways that will give their own children this important protection. Privately, religiously, emotionally, individually, marriage may have many meanings. But this is the core of its public, shared meaning: Marriage is the place where having children is not only tolerated but welcomed and encouraged, because it gives children mothers and fathers.

Of course, many couples fail to live up to this ideal. Many of the things men and women have to do to sustain their own marriages, and a culture of marriage, are *hard*. Few people will do them consistently if the larger culture does not affirm the critical importance of marriage as a social institution. Why stick out a frustrating relationship, turn down a tempting new love, abstain from sex outside marriage, or even take pains not to conceive children out of wedlock if family structure does not matter? If marriage is not a shared norm, and if successful marriage is not socially valued, do not expect it to survive as the generally accepted context for raising children. If marriage is just a way of publicly celebrating private love, then there is no need to encourage couples to stick it out for the sake of the children. If family structure does not matter, why have marriage laws at all? Do adults, or do they not, have a basic obligation to control their desires so that children can have mothers and fathers?

The problem with endorsing gay marriage is not that it would allow a handful of people to choose alternative family forms, but that it would require society at large to gut marriage of its central presumptions about family in order to accommodate a few adults' desires.

The debate over same-sex marriage, then, is not some sideline discussion. It *is* the marriage debate. Either we win—or we lose the central meaning of marriage. The great threat unisex marriage poses to marriage as a social institution is not some distant or nearby slippery slope, it is an abyss at our feet. If we cannot explain why unisex marriage is, in itself, a disaster, we have already lost the marriage ideal.

Same-sex marriage would enshrine in law a public judgment that the desire of adults for families of choice outweighs the need of children for mothers and fathers. It would give sanction and approval to

CHAPTER 1 FOCUS

the creation of a motherless or fatherless family as a deliberately chosen "good." It would mean the law was neutral as to whether children had mothers and fathers. Motherless and fatherless families would be deemed just fine.

25   Same-sex marriage advocates are startlingly clear on this point. Marriage law, they repeatedly claim, has nothing to do with babies or procreation or getting mothers and fathers for children. In forcing the state legislature to create civil unions for gay couples, the high court of Vermont explicitly ruled that marriage in the state of Vermont has nothing to do with procreation. Evan Wolfson made the same point in *Marriage and Same Sex Unions:* "[I]sn't having the law pretend that there is only one family model that works (let alone exists) a lie?" He goes on to say that in law, "marriage is not just about procreation—indeed is not necessarily about procreation at all."

Wolfson is right that in the course of the sexual revolution the Supreme Court struck down many legal features designed to reinforce the connection of marriage to babies. The animus of elites (including legal elites) against the marriage idea is not brand new. It stretches back at least thirty years. That is part of the problem we face, part of the reason 40 percent of our children are growing up without their fathers.

It is also true, as gay-marriage advocates note, that we impose no fertility tests for marriage: Infertile and older couples marry, and not every fertile couple chooses procreation. But every marriage between a man and a woman is capable of giving any child they create or adopt a mother and a father. Every marriage between a man and a woman discourages either from creating fatherless children outside the marriage vow. In this sense, neither older married couples nor childless husbands and wives publicly challenge or dilute the core meaning of marriage. Even when a man marries an older woman and they do not adopt, his marriage helps protect children. How? His marriage means, if he keeps his vows, that he will not produce out-of-wedlock children.

Does marriage discriminate against gays and lesbians? Formally speaking, no. There are no sexual-orientation tests for marriage; many gays and lesbians do choose to marry members of the opposite sex, and some of these unions succeed. Our laws do not require a person to marry the individual to whom he or she is most erotically attracted, so long as he or she is willing to promise sexual fidelity, mutual caretaking, and shared parenting of any children of the marriage.

But marriage is unsuited to the wants and desires of many gays and lesbians, precisely because it is designed to bridge the male-female divide and sustain the idea that children need mothers and fathers. To make a marriage, what you need is a husband and a wife. Redefining marriage so that it suits gays and lesbians would require fundamentally changing our legal, public, and social conception of what marriage is in ways that threaten its core public purposes.

Some who criticize the refusal to embrace gay marriage liken it to 30 the outlawing of interracial marriage, but the analogy is woefully false. The Supreme Court overturned anti-miscegenation laws because they frustrated the core purpose of marriage in order to sustain a racist legal order. Marriage laws, by contrast, were not invented to express animus toward homosexuals or anyone else. Their purpose is not negative, but positive: They uphold an institution that developed, over thousands of years, in thousands of cultures, to help direct the erotic desires of men and women into a relatively narrow but indispensably fruitful channel. We need men and women to marry and make babies for our society to survive. We have no similar public stake in any other family form—in the union of same-sex couples or the singleness of single moms.

Meanwhile, *cui bono?* To meet the desires of whom would we put our most basic social institution at risk? No good research on the marriage intentions of homosexual people exists. For what it's worth, the Census Bureau reports that 0.5 percent of households now consist of same-sex partners. To get a proxy for how many gay couples would avail themselves of the health insurance benefits marriage can provide, I asked the top 10 companies listed on the Human Rights Campaign's website as providing same-sex insurance benefits how many of their employees use this option. Only one company, General Motors, released its data. Out of 1.3 million employees, 166 claimed benefits for a same-sex partner, *one one-hundredth of one percent.*

People who argue for creating gay marriage do so in the name of high ideals: justice, compassion, fairness. Their sincerity is not in question. Nevertheless, to take the already troubled institution most responsible for the protection of children and throw out its most basic presumption in order to further adult interests in sexual freedom would not be high-minded. It would be morally callous and socially irresponsible.

If we cannot stand and defend this ground, then face it: The marriage debate is over. Dan Quayle[1] was wrong. We lost.

Responding to Reading

1. According to Gallagher, exactly what is marriage for? Do you think her notion of the purpose of marriage is accurate? Do you see it as too narrow? Do you think it is dated? Explain your views.
2. Gallagher's primary argument against gay marriage is that it would change the "legal, public, and social conception of marriage in ways that threaten its core public purposes" (29). What are these "core public purposes"? Do you think she is right to be alarmed?
3. In paragraphs 28 and 29, Gallagher argues that marriage does not discriminate against gays and lesbians but rather "is unsuited to [their] wants and

[1]Vice President of the United States under George H.W. Bush, Quayle was a staunch defender of the traditional family. [Eds.]

desires. . ." What does she mean? How might Ralph Wedgwood (p. 62) respond to this argument? How might he respond to Gallagher's explanation, in paragraph 30, of why gay marriage is not analogous to interracial marriage?

Responding in Writing

In paragraph 5, Gallagher asks, "Will unisex marriage help or hurt marriage as a social institution?" Clearly, Gallagher believes gay marriage will hurt the institution of marriage. Taking the opposing view, write a paragraph arguing that legalizing same-sex marriage could actually strengthen the institution of marriage.

MARRIAGE JUST LETS THE STATE BACK IN

Kerry Howley

1981–

Assistant editor at Reason *magazine, Kerry Howley writes articles and blog entries on topics ranging from U.S. healthcare, globalization, and corporate responsibility to same-sex marriage and divorce. In "Marriage Just Lets the State Back In," Howley argues that efforts to legalize same-sex marriage are misguided and that homosexual relationships can and should thrive without government approval.*

What do you do after you've won one of the most important Supreme Court cases in decades and shoved the state, kicking and screaming, out of your bedroom? Apparently, you beg the government to walk right back in. "The Marriage Revolution" has arrived, and homosexuals are the unlikely heroes of the quest to revive a fading institution.

Lawrence v. Texas, the most important Supreme Court decision in decades, was a victory for all Americans who consider their private, consensual sexual behavior to be beyond the legitimate realm of state control. But in the wake of *Lawrence,* the gay political establishment immediately began agitating for government regulation of its constituents' personal lives! The ironic message to legislators is as clear as it is misguided: we don't want government to censor our sexual relationships, but we are happy to have the government regulate our personal relationships.

Marriage, people tend to forget, is a three-way contract in which the power of one party, the state, greatly outweighs that of the other two. While marriage has some of the attributes of an ordinary contract— spouses enter into it voluntarily; they can agree to dissolve it; they both must obey its terms—many of the normal rules of a contractual agreement don't apply. The government can determine the circumstances under which marriage and divorce are undertaken, and it can change the terms whenever it likes. In 1996, when "no fault" divorce came under attack, several state legislatures considered making divorces much harder to obtain. Had these measures passed, couples who had entered into what they thought was a voluntary contract, subject to voluntarily dissolution, would have found themselves bound by a very different set of circumstances. To get married in America is to put oneself at the mercy of state legislators, many of whom believe that marriage is a social good, a sacred bond, and that divorce is a threat to social stability.

At present, Washington has concerned itself with formulating a relatively static definition of marriage. According to Senator Rick Santorum and House Majority Leader Bill Frist, marriage is, by definition, "a relationship between a man and a woman." If this sounds arbitrary, that's because it is. Marriage is whatever the state decides it is, at any given time, subject to change under any given administration.

That this Congress is threatening to write its definition into the   5 Constitution is not particularly revolutionary. The Defense of Marriage Act, signed by President Clinton, essentially defined marriage as between a man and woman for the purpose of federal benefits. The proposed Constitutional amendment, proposed by the Republican majority, would force states to adopt the same definition. Future legislators might further restrict marriage, or might expand the ranks of the eligible. As long as marriage remains a government program, its future will be subject to political whim.

Given the peculiar provisions of the marriage contract, the entangling, complex nature of divorce law, and the increasing acceptability of cohabitational arrangements, heterosexual couples are finding marriage less and less desirable. The marriage rate has been dropping since 1970, while the number of cohabiting couples has increased over 1000 percent since 1960. According to the 2000 census, eleven million Americans live with an unmarried partner and 41 percent of those households are raising children. In Europe, often a harbinger of social change in the U.S., the turn away from marriage has been even more dramatic. The youth of France have shown a particularly strong aversion toward state-sanctioned marriage, and the situation is even more marked in Eastern Europe, where a deep mistrust of government, fueled by years under coercive communist regimes, has led young people to keep their relationships private.

This is not to say that monogamy is out of vogue. Even the ultra-conservative Rutgers Marriage Project concedes that "high school seniors seem to believe in monogamy more than ever." In 1975, according to a report authored by the project, sixty percent of students "disagreed" or "mostly disagreed" with the proposition that "Having a close intimate relationship with only one partner is too restrictive for the average person." By 1995, seventy percent of students disagreed. Many of the doomsday statistics we hear about "single-parent families" include perfectly healthy couples that never sought the state's permission for their union. According to the Alternative to Marriage Project, an advocacy group for the unmarried, 41 percent of first births to supposedly single mothers are actually born to cohabiting couples. Though such unions are on average less permanent than traditional marriages, it is a mistake to equate a reluctance to embrace marriage with a refusal to commit. Marriage has simply ceased, quietly but definitively, to be an obvious step toward intimacy.

As entangling as marriage might be, it is still unarguably convenient for those deemed eligible. The best arguments for legal marriage, homosexual or otherwise, are not ideological but practical. They invoke the myriad of services and entitlements available to those who can claim that particular legal status—everything from health care to inheritance law to immunity from legal testimony. Such rights are of course key to a secure, stable, monogamous relationship. When California resident Keith Brandowski was denied compensation for the death of his domestic partner in the 9/11 terrorist attacks, it looked to many like a clear case of discrimination against gay men. But the problem is larger. If Brandowski's partner had been a woman who had chosen not to involve the state in her relationship, the problem would have been the same. What's needed is a way to secure basic rights between committed individuals without ceding too much authority to the state.

Putting partners in control of the contractual agreement is a way simultaneously to maintain their autonomy over the commitment process and to ensure their security. This is the "privatize marriage" proposal, popularized by the Cato Institute's David Boaz, in which adults can either draw up their own contract or choose from a number of ready-made generic contracts. The marriage agreement can therefore be tailored to the needs of specific relationships. In an arrangement where one partner stays home with children, it would probably be important to secure the economic stability of the homemaker in the event of divorce; for partners who will be gainfully employed, such a provision might not be necessary. Those with a religious commitment to marriage might make a separation difficult to obtain; others might terminate the arrangement with a simple signature. Rather than dictate the terms of the agreement, the state would merely ensure its enforcement. Religious institutions could continue to act as they always have, surrounding the marriages they accept with all the traditional trappings of ceremony and promises of permanence.

10   Privatization is an aggressively practical approach to the marriage problem, but for many homosexual couples, a legal marriage in the traditional sense would be a largely symbolic gesture. For those who see marriage as a magic ticket into mainstream society, state marriages for

everyone are the only solution. But it is not at all clear that the problems of being homosexual in a homophobic nation will soften under state-sanctioned marriage. According to a poll taken by the National Opinion Research Center, 53 percent of Americans think that homosexual relations are "always wrong"—regardless of whether they're undertaken by a conservative couple married in Canada or by a commune committed to free love. The majority of Americans seem to have problem with homosexuality as such, and many of them find the idea of homosexual marriage even more abhorrent.

In his 1995 book *Virtually Normal*, Andrew Sullivan writes, "until gay marriage is legalized, this fundamental element of person dignity will be denied a whole segment of humanity." Sullivan is a passionate and eloquent advocate for the gay community, but he has let his quixotic faith in state solutions eclipse his belief in individual dignity. It is not for government to bestow dignity on individuals, but to protect the basic dignity with which they are born. There's nothing remotely dignified about begging the state to regulate one's personal affairs, and it is a belittling view of personhood that assumes that citizens cannot navigate their own romantic relationships.

Seen in this light, the movement to legalize gay marriage is a profoundly conservative one. It is a movement that looks to dated social conventions as a means to acceptance and seeks a static solution to social evolution. The legal arguments against same-sex marriage are largely incoherent, and the current firewall against it probably will not last. But the real victory for couples lies in rejecting the need for government regulation and taking responsibility for their own commitments.

GLBT* people should not have to wait for public opinion to evolve to feel that their unions are legitimate. Heterosexual couples should not have to welcome a definition of marriage that clashes with their values, or invite the state into their personal lives to obtain basic benefits. In 2003, American men and women, whether hetero– or homosexual, have more choices in more facets of life than ever before. Individuals are empowered to shape ever more aspects of their lives, from the provider of long-distance phone service to the number of children they have. We should not leave our most fundamental choices to the whims of politicians and bureaucrats, nor rest our dignity on the government's sanctioning of our relationships.

Responding to Reading

1. In paragraph 1, Howley calls marriage a "fading institution." How does she support this claim? Do her arguments convince you?

---

*Gay, lesbian, bisexual, and transgendered.

2. Why does Howley see legalizing same-sex marriage as a "profoundly con-
    servative" movement (12)?
3. What is the "privatize marriage" proposal (9)? What does Howley see as
    its strengths and weaknesses? What reaction to this proposal would you
    expect from Ralph Wedgwod (p. 62)? From Maggie Gallagher (p. 65)?

Responding in Wrtiting

Kerry Howley, who dismisses the notion of gay marriage, writes from the perspective of a gay person. Do you think her sexual orientation gives Howley
greater or lesser credibility on this issue than a straight person? Does her sexual
orientation matter at all?

WIDENING THE FOCUS

For Critical Thinking and Writing

After reading the three essays in this Focus section, write an essay in which you answer the question, "Does gay marriage threaten the family?" In gathering support for your essay, you should consider information from Ralph Wedgwood's "What We're Fighting For," Maggie Gallagher's "What Marriage Is For," and Kerry Howley's "Marriage Just Lets the State Back In," but you may also wish to include information from your own personal experience or from the experience of friends and family members.

For Further Reading

The following readings can suggest additional perspectives for thinking and writing about the subject of divorce and the family:

- Judy Brady, "Why I Want a Wife" (p. 380)

- E. J. Graff, "The M/F Boxes" (p. 374)

- Arlie Hochschild, "The Second Shift" (p. 505)

For Internet Research

Does gay marriage threaten the family, or do all matrimonial unions serve to strengthen family ties and foster healthy, supportive environments for children and adults alike? As the readings in the Focus section suggest, Americans are divided on this question. Write an essay in which you take a position in the same-sex marriage debate, basing your argument on information from one of the following Web pages. Be sure to address the major arguments against your position.

- The *Intercollegiate Studies Institute* [*http://www.isi.org/lectures/lectures. aspx?SBy=search&SSub=speaker&SFor=Gallagher*] presents the online debate "Will Same-Sex Marriage Hurt America?" between Jonathan Rauch, Senior *National Journal* Writer and Columnist, and Maggie Gallagher, whose essay "What Marriage Is For" appears in the Focus section.

- The *Online NewsHour with Jim Lehrer* [*http://www.pbs.org/newshour/bb/ law/gay_marriage/debate.html*] outlines the responses of six experts to five key questions in the gay marriage debate.

CHAPTER 1 FOCUS

--- **WRITING** ---

Family Ties

1. What exactly is a family? Is it a group of people bound together by love? By marriage? By blood? By history? By shared memories? By economic dependency? By habit? What unites family members, and what divides them? Does *family* denote only a traditional nuclear family or also a family broken by divorce and blended by remarriage? Define *family* as it is presented in several of the readings in this chapter.

2. Leo Tolstoy's classic Russian novel *Anna Karenina* opens with the sentence, "Happy families are all alike; every unhappy family is unhappy in its own way." Write an essay in which you concur with or challenge this statement, supporting your position with references to several of the readings in this chapter.

3. In a sense, memories are like snapshots, a series of disconnected candid pictures, sometimes unflattering, often out of focus, eventually fading. Writers of autobiographical memoirs often explore this idea; for example, Alice Walker (p. 40) sees her painful childhood as a series of snapshots. Using information from your own family life as well as from your reading, discuss the relationship between memories and photographs. If you like, you may describe and discuss some of your own family photographs. (You may also want to examine the two photos that open this chapter.)

4. In "No Name Woman," Maxine Hong Kingston (p. 29) presents a detailed biographical sketch of a family member. Using her essay as a guide, write a detailed biographical essay about a member of your family. Prepare for this assignment by interviewing several family members.

5. In "The Unauthorized Autobiography of Me" (p. 47), Sherman Alexie uses song titles and names of musicians and groups to re-create a sense of the background music of his life. List the songs and musical artists that have been central to various stages of your own life. Then, write a musical autobiography that gives readers a sense of who you were at different times of your life. Using the music as the "sound track of your life," try to help readers understand the times you grew up in and the person you were (and became).

6. How do your parents' notions of success and failure affect you? Do you think your parents tend to expect too much of you? Too little? Explore these ideas in an essay, referring to essays in this chapter and in Chapter 7, "The American Dream."

7. Gary Soto comes to understand his parents better by seeing them in the role of workers (p. 16). Discuss his changing attitude toward his parents' work, comparing his views about work with ideas expressed in Chapter 5 and by one or more essays in Chapter 8. (You may also discuss how your experience as a worker has helped you to understand or appreciate your own parents.)

8. Many people have mixed feelings about their parents, and works of fiction and poetry, like essays, often express this ambivalence. Read Robert Hayden's poem "Those Winter Sundays" (p. 15) and Harlan Coben's short story "The Key to My Father" (p. 56), and write an essay explaining the mixed feelings these two works convey.

9. What traits, habits, and values (positive or negative) have you inherited from your parents? What qualities do you think you will pass on to your children? Write a letter to your parents in which you answer these two questions, incorporating the ideas of several of the writers in this chapter.

2

■ ■ ■ ■ □ ■ ■ ■ ■

ISSUES IN EDUCATION

■ ■ □ ■ ■

In the nineteenth century, most people had little difficulty defining the purpose of education: they assumed it was the school's job to prepare students for the roles they would play as adults. To accomplish this end, public school administrators made sure that the elementary school curriculum gave students a good dose of the basics: arithmetic, grammar, spelling, reading, composition, and penmanship. High school students studied literature, history, geography, and civics. At the elite private schools, students learned physics, rhetoric, and elocution—as well as Latin and Greek so that they could read the classics in the original.

Today, educators seem to have a great deal of difficulty agreeing on what purpose schools are supposed to serve. No longer can a group of school administrators simply proscribe a curriculum.

Elementary school children in traditional classroom

Parents, students, politicians, academics, special interest groups, and religious leaders all attempt to influence what is taught. The result, according to some educators, is an environment in which it is almost impossible for any real education to take place. In fact, in many of today's schools, more emphasis seems to be placed on increasing self-esteem, avoiding controversy, and passing standardized tests than on challenging students to discover new ways of thinking about themselves and about the world. In this milieu, classic books are censored or rewritten to eliminate passages that might offend, ideas are presented as if they all have equal value, and the curriculum is revised so that teachers can "teach to the test." The result is an educational environment that has all the intellectual appeal of elevator music. Many people—educators included—seem to have forgotten that ideas must be unsettling if they are to make us think. After all, what is education but a process that encourages us to think critically about our world and develop a healthy skepticism—to question, evaluate, and reach conclusions about ideas and events?

The Focus section of this chapter (p. 129) is a visual essay that addresses the question "How Much Do a College's Facilities Really Matter?" The pictures in this section contrast two colleges in Iowa—one with a very large endowment and the other with a relatively small one. In addition to pointing out some obvious differences between these two colleges, the pictures in this visual essay raise some important questions about higher education in the United States. For example, what educational advantages does a wealthy college provide? Do state-of-the-art

Children being home schooled

facilities, such as those at Grinnell, actually enhance learning, or do they exist primarily to attract students? Can students get a good education from a college with more modest facilities, such as Clarke? Finally, do affluent colleges actually perpetuate the educational divide that separates the rich from the poor in the United States?

PREPARING TO READ AND WRITE

As you read and prepare to write about the selections in this chapter, you may consider the following questions:

- How does the writer define *education?* Is this definition consistent with yours?

- What does the writer think the main goals of education should be? Do you agree?

- Which does the writer believe is more important, formal or informal education?

- On what aspect or aspects of education does the writer focus?

- Who does the writer believe bears primary responsibility for a student's education? The student? The family? The school? The community? The government?

- Does the writer use personal experience to support his or her points? Does he or she use facts and statistics or expert opinion as support? Do you find the writer's ideas convincing?

- What changes in the educational system does the writer recommend? Do you agree with these recommendations?

- Are the writer's educational experiences similar to or different from yours? How do these similarities or differences affect your response to the essay?

- In what way is the essay similar to or different from other essays in this chapter?

THE SANCTUARY OF SCHOOL
Lynda Barry
1956–

Lynda Barry grew up as part of an extended Filipino family (her mother was Filipino, her father an alcoholic Norwegian-Irishman). She majored in art— the first member of her family to pursue higher education—and began her career as a cartoonist shortly after graduation. Barry is known as a chronicler of adolescent angst both in her syndicated comic strip Ernie Pook's Comeek *and in collections like* My Perfect Life *(1992),* The Freddie Stories *(1997), and the semi-autobiographical* One Hundred Demons *(2002). Barry has also written a novel,* The Good Times Are Killing Me *(1988), which was turned into a successful musical. In the following essay, Barry remembers her Seattle grade school in a racially mixed neighborhood as a nurturing safe haven from her difficult family life.*

I was 7 years old the first time I snuck out of the house in the dark. It was winter and my parents had been fighting all night. They were short on money and long on relatives who kept "temporarily" moving into our house because they had nowhere else to go.

My brother and I were used to giving up our bedroom. We slept on the couch, something we actually liked because it put us that much closer to the light of our lives, our television.

At night when everyone was asleep, we lay on our pillows watching it with the sound off. We watched Steve Allen's mouth moving. We watched Johnny Carson's mouth moving. We watched movies filled with gangsters shooting machine guns into packed rooms, dying soldiers hurling a last grenade and beautiful women crying at windows. Then the sign-off finally came and we tried to sleep.

The morning I snuck out, I woke up filled with a panic about needing to get to school. The sun wasn't quite up yet but my anxiety was so fierce that I just got dressed, walked quietly across the kitchen and let myself out the back door.

It was quiet outside. Stars were still out. Nothing moved and no 5 one was in the street. It was as if someone had turned the sound off on the world.

I walked the alley, breaking thin ice over the puddles with my shoes. I didn't know why I was walking to school in the dark. I didn't think about it. All I knew was a feeling of panic, like the panic that strikes kids when they realize they are lost.

That feeling eased the moment I turned the corner and saw the dark outline of my school at the top of the hill. My school was made up of about 15 nondescript portable classrooms set down on a fenced concrete lot in a rundown Seattle neighborhood, but it had the most beautiful view of the Cascade Mountains. You could see them from anywhere on the playfield and you could see them from the windows of my classroom—Room 2.

I walked over to the monkey bars and hooked my arms around the cold metal. I stood for a long time just looking across Rainier Valley. The sky was beginning to whiten and I could hear a few birds.

In a perfect world my absence at home would not have gone unnoticed. I would have had two parents in a panic to locate me, instead of two parents in a panic to locate an answer to the hard question of survival during a deep financial and emotional crisis.

10　　But in an overcrowded and unhappy home, it's incredibly easy for any child to slip away. The high levels of frustration, depression and anger in my house made my brother and me invisible. We were children with the sound turned off. And for us, as for the steadily increasing number of neglected children in this country, the only place where we could count on being noticed was at school.

"Hey there, young lady. Did you forget to go home last night?" It was Mr. Gunderson, our janitor, whom we all loved. He was nice and he was funny and he was old with white hair, thick glasses and an unbelievable number of keys. I could hear them jingling as he walked across the playfield. I felt incredibly happy to see him.

He let me push his wheeled garbage can between the different portables as he unlocked each room. He let me turn on the lights and raise the window shades and I saw my school slowly come to life. I saw Mrs. Holman, our school secretary, walk into the office without her orange lipstick on yet. She waved.

I saw the fifth-grade teacher Mr. Cunningham, walking under the breezeway eating a hard roll. He waved.

And I saw my teacher, Mrs. Claire LeSane, walking toward us in a red coat and calling my name in a very happy and surprised way, and suddenly my throat got tight and my eyes stung and I ran toward her crying. It was something that surprised us both.

15　　It's only thinking about it now, 28 years later, that I realize I was crying from relief. I was with my teacher, and in a while I was going to sit at my desk, with my crayons and pencils and books and classmates all around me, and for the next six hours I was going to enjoy a thoroughly secure, warm and stable world. It was a world I absolutely relied on. Without it, I don't know where I would have gone that morning.

Mrs. LeSane asked me what was wrong and when I said "Nothing," she seemingly left it at that. But she asked me if I would carry her purse for her, an honor above all honors, and she asked if I wanted to come into Room 2 early and paint.

She believed in the natural healing power of painting and drawing for troubled children. In the back of her room there was always a drawing table and an easel with plenty of supplies, and sometimes during the day she would come up to you for what seemed like no good reason and quietly ask if you wanted to go to the back table and "make some pictures for Mrs. LeSane." We all had a chance at it—to sit apart from the class for a while to paint, draw and silently work out impossible problems on 11 × 17 sheets of newsprint.

Drawing came to mean everything to me. At the back table in Room 2, I learned to build myself a life preserver that I could carry into my home.

We all know that a good education system saves lives, but the people of this country are still told that cutting the budget for public schools is necessary, that poor salaries for teachers are all we can manage and that art, music and all creative activities must be the first to go when times are lean.

Before- and after-school programs are cut and we are told that 20 public schools are not made for baby-sitting children. If parents are neglectful temporarily or permanently, for whatever reason, it's certainly sad, but their unlucky children must fend for themselves. Or slip through the cracks. Or wander in a dark night alone.

We are told in a thousand ways that not only are public schools not important, but that the children who attend them, the children who need them most, are not important either. We leave them to learn from the blind eye of a television, or to the mercy of "a thousand points of light"[1] that can be as far away as stars.

I was lucky. I had Mrs. LeSane. I had Mr. Gunderson. I had an abundance of art supplies. And I had a particular brand of neglect in my home that allowed me to slip away and get to them. But what about the rest of the kids who weren't as lucky? What happened to them?

By the time the bell rang that morning I had finished my drawing and Mrs. LeSane pinned it up on the special bulletin board she reserved for drawings from the back table. It was the same picture I always drew—a sun in the corner of a blue sky over a nice house with flowers all around it.

Mrs. LeSane asked us to please stand, face the flag, place our right hands over our hearts and say the Pledge of Allegiance. Children across the country do it faithfully. I wonder now when the country will face its children and say a pledge right back.

Responding to Reading

1. What information about her school does Barry provide? What information does she not provide? How can you explain these omissions?

---

[1]Catchphrase for the first president George H. W. Bush's plan to substitute volunteerism for government programs. [Eds.]

2. In paragraph 22, Barry asks two questions. Why doesn't she answer them? What do you think the answers to these questions might be?
3. Barry's essay ends on a cynical note. How effective is this conclusion? What does Barry gain or lose with this concluding strategy?

Responding in Writing

Has school been a sanctuary for you as it was for Barry? Write a paragraph or two in which you answer this question.

SCHOOL IS BAD FOR CHILDREN

John Holt

1923–1985

John Holt, a teacher and education theorist, believed that traditional school-ing suppresses children's natural curiosity about life. In his writings about education, Holt suggested that students should be allowed to pursue what-ever interests them. Holt worked for an international peace group, traveled in Europe, and then worked at the private Colorado Rocky Mountain School in Carbondale, Colorado, where he taught high school English, French, and mathematics and coached soccer and baseball. His many books include How Children Fail *(1964),* How Children Learn *(1967),* Education *(1976), and* Learning All the Time *(1989). In the following essay, first published in 1969, Holt makes a plea to free children from the classroom, a "dull and ugly place, where nobody ever says anything very truthful," and to "give them a chance to learn about the world at first hand." He was also a major supporter of in the Home Schooling movement.*

Almost every child, on the first day he sets foot in a school building, is smarter, more curious, less afraid of what he doesn't know, better at finding and figuring things out, more confident, resourceful, persis-tent and independent than he will ever be again in his schooling—or, unless he is very unusual and very lucky, for the rest of his life. Al-ready, by paying close attention to and interacting with the world and people around him, and without any school-type formal instruction, he has done a task far more difficult, complicated and abstract than anything he will be asked to do in school, or than any of his teachers has done for years. He has solved the mystery of language. He has discovered it—babies don't even know that language exists—and he has found out how it works and learned to use it. He has done it by exploring, by experimenting, by developing his own model of the grammar of language, by trying it out and seeing whether it works, by gradually changing it and refining it until it does work. And while he has been doing this, he has been learning other things as well, in-cluding many of the "concepts" that the schools think only they can teach him, and many that are more complicated than the ones they do try to teach him.

In he comes, this curious, patient, determined, energetic, skillful learner. We sit him down at a desk, and what do we teach him? Many things. First, that learning is separate from living. "You come to school to learn," we tell him, as if the child hadn't been learning before, as if living were out there and learning were in here, and there were no connection between the two. Secondly, that he cannot be trusted to learn and is no good at it. Everything we teach about reading, a task far simpler than many that the child has already mastered, says to him, "If we don't make you read, you won't, and if you don't do it exactly the way we tell you, you can't." In short, he comes to feel that learning is a passive process, something that someone else does *to* you, instead of something you do for yourself.

In a great many other ways he learns that he is worthless, untrustworthy, fit only to take other people's orders, a blank sheet for other people to write on. Oh, we make a lot of nice noises in school about respect for the child and individual differences, and the like. But our acts, as opposed to our talk, say to the child, "Your experience, your concerns, your curiosities, your needs, what you know, what you want, what you wonder about, what you hope for, what you fear, what you like and dislike, what you are good at or not so good at—all this is of not the slightest importance, it counts for nothing. What counts here, and the only thing that counts, is what we know, what we think is important, what we want you to do, think and be." The child soon learns not to ask questions—the teacher isn't there to satisfy his curiosity. Having learned to hide his curiosity, he later learns to be ashamed of it. Given no chance to find out who he is—and to develop that person, whoever it is—he soon comes to accept the adults' evaluation of him.

He learns many other things. He learns that to be wrong, uncertain, confused, is a crime. Right Answers are what the school wants, and he learns countless strategies for prying these answers out of the teacher, for conning her into thinking he knows what he doesn't know. He learns to dodge, bluff, fake, cheat. He learns to be lazy. Before he came to school, he would work for hours on end, on his own, with no thought of reward, at the business of making sense of the world and gaining competence in it. In school he learns, like every buck private, how to goldbrick, how not to work when the sergeant isn't looking, how to know when he is looking, how to make him think you are working even when he is looking. He learns that in real life you don't do anything unless you are bribed, bullied or conned into doing it, that nothing is worth doing for its own sake, or that if it is, you can't do it in school. He learns to be bored, to work with a small part of his mind, to escape from the reality around him into daydreams and fantasies—but not like the fantasies of his preschool years, in which he played a very active part.

5   The child comes to school curious about other people, particularly other children, and the school teaches him to be indifferent. The most interesting thing in the classroom—often the only interesting thing in it—is the other children, but he has to act as if these other children, all about him, only a few feet away, are not really there. He cannot interact with them, talk with them, smile at them. In many schools he can't talk to other children in the halls between classes; in more than a few, and some of these in stylish suburbs, he can't even talk to them at lunch. Splendid training for a world in which, when you're not studying the other person to figure out how to do him in, you pay no attention to him.

In fact, he learns how to live without paying attention to anything going on around him. You might say that school is a long lesson in how to turn yourself off, which may be one reason why so many young people, seeking the awareness of the world and responsiveness to it they had when they were little, think they can only find it in drugs. Aside from being boring, the school is almost always ugly, cold, inhuman—even the most stylish, glass-windowed, $20-a-square-foot schools.

And so, in this dull and ugly place, where nobody ever says anything very truthful, where everybody is playing a kind of role, as in a charade, where the teachers are no more free to respond honestly to the students than the students are free to respond to the teachers or each other, where the air practically vibrates with suspicion and anxiety, the child learns to live in a daze, saving his energies for those small parts of his life that are too trivial for the adults to bother with, and thus remain his. It is a rare child who can come through his schooling with much left of his curiosity, his independence or his sense of his own dignity, competence and worth.

So much for criticism. What do we need to do? Many things. Some are easy—we can do them right away. Some are hard, and may take some time. Take a hard one first. We should abolish compulsory school attendance. At the very least we should modify it, perhaps by giving children every year a large number of authorized absences. Our compulsory school-attendance laws once served a humane and useful purpose. They protected children's right to some schooling, against those adults who would otherwise have denied it to them in order to exploit their labor, in farm, store, mine or factory. Today the laws help nobody, not the schools, not the teachers, not the children. To keep kids in school who would rather not be there costs the schools an enormous amount of time and trouble—to say nothing of what it costs to repair the damage that these angry and resentful prisoners do every time they get a chance. Every teacher knows that any kid in class who, for whatever reason, would rather not be there not only doesn't learn anything himself but makes it a great deal tougher for anyone else. As for protecting the children from exploitation, the chief and indeed only exploiters of children these days *are* the schools. Kids caught in the college rush more often than not work 70 hours or more a week, most of it on paper busywork. For kids who aren't going to college, school is just a useless time waster, preventing them from earning some money or doing some useful work, or even doing some true learning.

Objections. "If kids didn't have to go to school, they'd all be out in the streets." No, they wouldn't. In the first place, even if schools stayed just the way they are, children would spend at least some time there because that's where they'd be likely to find friends; it's a natural meeting place for children. In the second place, schools wouldn't stay the way they are, they'd get better, because we would have to start making them what they ought to be right now—places where children would *want* to be. In the third place, those children who did not want to go to school could find, particularly if we stirred up our brains and gave them a little help, other things to do—the things many children now do during their summers and holidays.

There's something easier we could do. We need to get kids out of the school buildings, give them a chance to learn about the world at first hand. It is a very recent idea, and a crazy one, that the way to teach our young people about the world they live in is to take them out of it and shut them up in brick boxes. Fortunately, educators are beginning to realize this. In Philadelphia and Portland, Oreg., to pick only two places I happen to have heard about, plans are being drawn up for public schools that won't have any school buildings at all, that will take the students out into the city and help them to use it and its people as a learning resource. In other words, students, perhaps in groups, perhaps independently, will go to libraries, museums, exhibits, court rooms, legislatures, radio and TV stations, meetings, businesses and laboratories to learn about their world and society at first hand. A small private school in Washington is already doing this. It makes sense. We need more of it.

As we help children get out into the world, to do their learning there, we get more of the world into the schools. Aside from their parents, most children never have any close contact with any adults except people whose sole business is children. No wonder they have no idea what adult life or work is like. We need to bring a lot more people who are *not* full-time teachers into the schools and into contact with the children. In New York City, under the Teachers and Writers Collaborative, real writers, working writers—novelists, poets, playwrights—come into the schools, read their work, and talk to the children about the problems of their craft. The children eat it up. In another school I know of, a practicing attorney from a nearby city comes in every month or so and talks to several classes about the law. Not the law as it is in books but as he sees it and encounters it in his cases, his problems, his work. And the children love it. It is real, grown-up, true, not *My Weekly Reader*, not "social studies," not lies and baloney.

Something easier yet. Let children work together, help each other, learn from each other and each other's mistakes. We now know, from the experience of many schools, both rich-suburban and poor-city, that children are often the best teachers of other children. What is more important, we know that when a fifth- or sixth-grader who has been having trouble with reading starts helping a first-grader, his own reading sharply improves. A number of schools are beginning to use what some call Paired Learning. This means that you let children form partnerships with other children, do their work, even including their tests, together, and share whatever marks or results this work gets—just like grownups in the real world. It seems to work.

Let the children learn to judge their own work. A child learning to talk does not learn by being corrected all the time—if corrected too much, he will stop talking. *He* compares, a thousand times a day, the difference between language as he uses it and as those around him use it. Bit by bit, he makes the necessary changes to make his language like other people's. In the same way, kids learning to do all the other things they learn without adult teachers—to walk, run, climb, whistle, ride a bike, skate, play games, jump rope—compare their own performance with what more skilled people do, and slowly make the needed changes. But in school we never give a child a chance to detect his mistakes, let alone correct them. We do it all for him. We act as if we thought he would never notice a mistake unless it was pointed out to him, or correct it unless he was made to. Soon he becomes dependent on the expert. We should let him do it himself. Let him figure out, with the help of other children if he wants it, what this word says, what is the answer to that problem, whether this is a good way of saying or doing this or that. If right answers are involved, as in some math or science, give him the answer book, let him correct his own papers. Why should we teachers waste time on such donkey work? Our job should be to help the kid when he tells us that he can't find a way to get the right answer. Let's get rid of all this nonsense of grades, exams, marks. We don't know now, and we never will know, how to measure what another person knows or understands. We certainly can't find out by asking him questions. All we find out is what he doesn't know—which is what most tests are for, anyway. Throw it all out, and let the child learn what every educated person must someday learn, how to measure his own understanding, how to know what he knows or does not know.

We could also abolish the fixed, required curriculum. People remember only what is interesting and useful to them, what helps them make sense of the world, or helps them get along in it. All else they quickly forget, if they ever learn it at all. The idea of a "body of knowledge," to be picked up in school and used for the rest of one's life, is nonsense in a world as complicated and rapidly changing as ours. Anyway, the most important questions and problems of our time are not *in* the curriculum, not even in the hotshot universities, let alone the schools.

Children want, more than they want anything else, and even after 15 years of miseducation, to make sense of the world, themselves, and other human beings. Let them get at this job, with our help if they ask for it, in the way that makes most sense to them.

Responding to Reading

1. In what ways does Holt believe schools fail children?
2. According to Holt, what should schools do to correct their shortcomings? Are his suggestions realistic or unrealistic?
3. In paragraph 13, Holt says, "Let's get rid of all this nonsense of grades, exams, marks." Do you agree? What would be the advantages and disadvantages of this course of action?

Responding in Writing

What would your ideal elementary school be like? How would it be like the schools you attended? How would it be different?

SCHOOL'S OUT

Daniel H. Pink

1964–

Daniel H. Pink worked from 1995 to 1997 as chief speechwriter to Vice President Al Gore. Pink writes mainly about business, work, and economic transformation. His articles and essays have appeared in Wired, *the* New York Times, *the* New Republic, Slate, *and other publications. Currently, he is a contributing editor to* Wired *magazine. His latest book is* A Whole New Mind: Moving from The Informational Age to the Conceptual Age *(2005). The following essay, taken from Pink's book* Free Agent Nation: How America's New Independent Workers Are Transforming the Way We Live *(2001), shows how traditional public schools are unable to prepare students for the challenges of the twenty-first century.*

Here's a riddle of the New Economy: Whenever students around the world take those tests that measure which country's children know the most, American kids invariably score near the bottom. No matter the subject, when the international rankings come out, European and Asian nations finish first while the U.S. pulls up the rear. This, we all know, isn't good. Yet by almost every measure, the American economy outperforms those very same nations of Asia and Europe. We create greater wealth, deliver more and better goods and services, and positively kick butt on innovation. This, we all know, *is* good.

Now the riddle: If we're so dumb, how come we're so rich? How can we fare so poorly on international measures of education yet perform so well in an economy that depends on brainpower? The answer is complex, but within it are clues about the future of education—and how "free agency" may rock the school house as profoundly as it has upended the business organization.

We are living in the founding of what I call "free agent nation." Over the past decade, in nearly every industry and region, work has been undergoing perhaps its most significant transformation since Americans left the farm for the factory a century ago. Legions of Americans, and increasingly citizens of other countries as well, are abandoning one of the Industrial Revolution's most enduring legacies—the "job"—and forging new ways to work. They're becoming self-employed knowledge workers, proprietors of home-based businesses, temps and permatemps, freelancers and e-lancers, independent contractors and independent professionals, micropreneurs and infopreneurs, part-time consultants, interim executives, on-call troubleshooters, and full-time soloists.

In the U.S. today, more than 30 million workers—nearly one-fourth of the American workforce—are free agents. And many others who hold what are still nominally "jobs" are doing so under terms closer in spirit to free agency than to traditional employment. They're telecommuting. They're hopping from company to company. They're forming ventures that are legally their employers', but whose prospects depend largely on their own individual efforts.

5   In boom times, many free agents—fed up with bad bosses and dysfunctional workplaces and yearning for freedom—leapt into this new world. In leaner times, other people—clobbered by layoffs, mergers, and downturns—have been pushed. But these new independent workers are transforming the nation's social and economic future. Soon they will transform the nation's education system as well.

The Homogenizing Hopper

Whenever I walk into a public school, I'm nearly toppled by a wave of nostalgia. Most schools I've visited in the 21st century look and feel exactly like the public schools I attended in the 1970s. The classrooms are the same size. The desks stand in those same rows. Bulletin boards preview the next national holiday. The hallways even *smell* the same. Sure, some classrooms might have a computer or two. But in most respects, the schools American children attend today seem indistinguishable from the ones their parents and grandparents attended.

At first, such déjà vu warmed my soul. But then I thought about it. How many other places look and feel exactly as they did 20, 30, or 40 years ago? Banks don't. Hospitals don't. Grocery stores don't. Maybe the sweet nostalgia I sniffed on those classroom visits was really the odor of stagnation. Since most other institutions in American society have changed dramatically in the past half-century, the stasis of schools is strange. And it's doubly peculiar because school itself is a modern invention, not something we inherited from antiquity.

Through most of history, people learned from tutors or their close relatives. In 19th-century America, says education historian David Tyack, "the school was a voluntary and incidental institution." Not until the early 20th century did public schools as we know them— places where students segregated by age learn from government-certified professionals—become widespread. And not until the 1920s did attending one become compulsory. Think about that last fact a moment. Compared with much of the world, America is a remarkably hands-off land. We don't force people to vote, or to work, or to serve in the military. But we do compel parents to relinquish their kids to this institution for a dozen years, and threaten to jail those who resist.

Compulsory mass schooling is an aberration in both history and modern society. Yet it was the ideal preparation for the Organization Man economy, a highly structured world dominated by large, bureaucratic corporations that routinized the workplace. Compulsory mass schooling equipped generations of future factory workers and middle managers with the basic skills and knowledge they needed on the job. The broader lessons it conveyed were equally crucial. Kids learned how to obey rules, follow orders, and respect authority—and the penalties that came with refusal.

This was just the sort of training the old economy demanded. 10 Schools had bells; factories had whistles. Schools had report card grades; offices had pay grades. Pleasing your teacher prepared you for pleasing your boss. And in either place, if you achieved a minimal level of performance, you were promoted. Taylorism—the management philosophy, named for efficiency expert Frederick Winslow Taylor, that there was One Best Way of doing things that could and should be applied in all circumstances—didn't spend all its time on the job. It also went to class. In the school, as in the workplace, the reigning theory was One Best Way. Kids learned the same things at the same time in the same manner in the same place. Marshall McLuhan once described schools as "the homogenizing hopper into which we toss our integral tots for processing." And schools made factory-style processing practically a religion—through standardized testing, standardized curricula, and standardized clusters of children. (Question: When was the last time *you* spent all day in a room filled exclusively with people almost exactly your own age?)

So when we step into the typical school today, we're stepping into the past—a place whose architect is Frederick Winslow Taylor and whose tenant is the Organization Man. The one American institution that has least accommodated itself to the free agent economy is the one Americans claim they value most. But it's hard to imagine that this arrangement can last much longer—a One Size Fits All education system cranking out workers for a My Size Fits Me economy. Maybe the answer to the riddle I posed at the beginning is that we're succeeding *in spite of* our education system. But how long can that continue? And imagine how we'd prosper if we began educating our children more like we earn our livings. Nearly 20 years ago, a landmark government report, *A Nation at Risk,* declared that American education was "being eroded by a rising tide of mediocrity." That may no longer be true. Instead, American schools are awash in a rising tide of irrelevance.

Don't get me wrong. In innumerable ways, mass public schooling has been a stirring success. Like Taylorism, it has accomplished some remarkable things—teaching immigrants both English and the American way, expanding literacy, equipping many Americans to succeed beyond their parents' imaginings. In a very large sense, America's schools have been a breathtaking democratic achievement.

But that doesn't mean they ought to be the same as they were when we were kids. Parents and politicians have sensed the need for reform, and have pushed education to the top of the national agenda. Unfortunately, few of the conventional remedies—standardized testing, character training, recertifying teachers—will do much to cure what ails American schools, and may even make things worse. Free agency, though, will force the necessary changes. Look for free agency to accelerate and deepen three incipient movements in education—home schooling, alternatives to traditional high school, and new approaches to adult learning. These changes will prove as pathbreaking as mass public schooling was a century ago.

The Home-Schooling Revolution

"School is like starting life with a 12-year jail sentence in which bad habits are the only curriculum truly learned." Those are the words of John Taylor Gatto, who was named New York state's Teacher of the Year in 1991. Today he is one of the most forceful voices for one of the most powerful movements in American education—home schooling.

In home schooling, kids opt out of traditional school to take control of their own education and to learn with the help of parents, tutors, and peers. Home schooling is free agency for the under-18 set. And it's about to break through the surface of our national life.

As recently as 1980, home schooling was illegal in most states. In the early 1980s, no more than 15,000 students learned this way. But Christian conservatives, unhappy with schools they considered God-free zones and eager to teach their kids themselves, pressed for changes. Laws fell, and home schooling surged. By 1990, there were as many as 300,000 American home-schoolers. By 1993, home schooling was legal in all 50 states. Since then, home schooling has swum into the mainstream—paddled there by secular parents dissatisfied with low-quality, and even dangerous, schools. In the first half of the 1990s, the home-schooling population more than doubled. Today some 1.7 million children are home-schoolers, their ranks growing as much as 15 percent each year. Factor in turnover, and one in 10 American kids under 18 has gotten part of his or her schooling at home.

Home schooling has become perhaps the largest and most successful education reform movement of the last two decades:

- While barely 3 percent of American schoolchildren are now home-schoolers, that represents a surprisingly large dent in the public school monopoly—especially compared with private schools. For every four kids in private school, there's one youngster learning at home. The home-schooling population is roughly equal to all the school-age children in Pennsylvania.

- According to *The Wall Street Journal*, "Evidence is mounting that home-schooling, once confined to the political and religious fringe, has achieved results not only on par with public education, but in some ways surpassing it." Home-schooled children consistently score higher than traditional students on standardized achievement tests, placing on average in the 80th percentile in all subjects.

- Home-schooled children also perform extremely well on nearly all measures of socialization. One of the great misconceptions about home schooling is that it turns kids into isolated loners. In fact, these children spend more time with adults, more time in their community, and more time with children of varying ages than their traditional-school counterparts. Says one researcher, "The conventionally schooled tended to be considerably more aggressive, loud, and competitive than the home educated."

"Home schooling," though, is a bit of a misnomer. Parents don't re-create the classroom in the living room any more than free agents re-create the cubicle in their basement offices. Instead, home schooling makes it easier for children to pursue their own interests in their own way—a My Size Fits Me approach to learning. In part for this reason, some adherents—particularly those who have opted out of traditional schools for reasons other than religion—prefer the term "unschooling."

The similarities to free agency—having an "unjob"—are many. Free agents are independent workers; home-schoolers are independent learners. Free agents maintain robust networks and tight connections through informal groups and professional associations; home-schoolers have assembled powerful groups—like the 3,000-family Family Un-schoolers Network—to share teaching strategies and materials and to offer advice and support. Free agents often challenge the idea of sepa-rating work and family; home-schoolers take the same approach to the boundary between school and family.

Perhaps most important, home schooling is almost perfectly con-sonant with the four animating values of free agency: having free-dom, being authentic, putting yourself on the line, and defining your own success. Take freedom. In the typical school, children often aren't permitted to move unless a bell rings or an adult grants them permis-sion. And except for a limited menu of offerings in high school, they generally can't choose what to study or when to study it. Home-schoolers have far greater freedom. They learn more like, well, chil-dren. We don't teach little kids how to talk or walk or understand the world. We simply put them in nurturing situations and let them learn on their own. Sure, we impose certain restrictions. ("Don't walk in the middle of the street.") But we don't go crazy. ("Please practice talking for 45 minutes until a bell rings.") It's the same for home-schoolers. Kids can become agents of their own education rather than merely re-cipients of someone else's noble intentions.

20   Imagine a 5-year-old child whose current passion is building with Legos. Every day she spends up to an hour, maybe more, absorbed in complex construction projects, creating farms, zoos, airplanes, space-ships. Often her friends come over and they work together. No one assigns her this project. No one tells her when and how to do it. And no one will give her creation a grade. Is she learning? Of course. This is how many home-schoolers explore their subjects.

Now suppose some well-intentioned adults step in to teach the child a thing or two about Lego building. Let's say they assign her a daily 45-minute Lego period, give her a grade at the end of each ses-sion, maybe even offer a reward for an A+ building. And why not bring in some more 5-year-olds to teach them the same things about Legos? Why not have them all build their own 45-minute Lego build-ings at the same time, then give them each a letter grade, with a prize for the best one? My guess: Pretty soon our 5-year-old Lego lover would lose her passion. Her buildings would likely become less cre-ative, her learning curve flatter. This is how many conventional schools work—or, I guess, *don't work*.

The well-meaning adults have squelched the child's freedom to play and learn and discover on her own. She's no longer in control. She's no longer having fun. Countless studies, particularly those by University of Rochester psychologist Edward L. Deci, have shown that kids and adults alike—in school, at work, at home—lose the intrinsic motivation and the pure joy derived from learning and working when somebody takes away their sense of autonomy and instead imposes some external system of reward and punishment. Freedom isn't a detour from learning. It's the best pathway toward it.

Stay with our Lego lass a moment and think about authenticity—the basic desire people have to be who they are rather than conform to someone else's standard. Our young builder has lost the sense that she is acting according to her own true self. Instead, she has gotten the message. You build Legos for the same reason your traditionally employed father does his work assignments: because an authority figure tells you to.

Or take accountability. The child is no longer fully accountable for her own Lego creating. Whatever she has produced is by assignment. Her creations are no longer truly hers. And what about those Lego grades? That A+ may motivate our girl to keep building, but not on her own terms. Maybe she liked the B− building better than the A+ creation. Oh well. Now she'll probably bury that feeling and work to measure up—to someone else's standards. Should she take a chance—try building that space shuttle she's been dreaming about? Probably not. Why take that risk when, chances are, it won't make the grade? Self-defined success has no place in this regime. But for many home-schoolers, success is something they can define themselves. (This is true even though, as I mentioned, home-schoolers score off the charts on conventional measures of success—standardized tests in academic subjects.)

To be sure, some things most kids should learn are not intrinsically 25 fun. There are times in life when we must eat our Brussels sprouts. For those subjects, the punishment-and-reward approach of traditional schooling may be in order. But too often, the sheer thrill of learning a new fact or mastering a tough equation is muted when schools take away a student's sense of control. In home schooling, kids have greater freedom to pursue their passions, less pressure to conform to the wishes of teachers and peers—and can put themselves on the line, take risks, and define success on their own terms. As more parents realize that the underlying ethic of home schooling closely resembles the animating values of free agency, home schooling will continue to soar in popularity.

Free Agent Teaching

Several other forces will combine to power home schooling into greater prominence. One is simply the movement's initial prominence.

As more families choose this option, they will make it more socially acceptable—thereby encouraging other families to take this once-unconventional route. The home-schooling population has already begun to look like the rest of America. While some 90 percent of home-schoolers are white, the population is becoming more diverse, and may be growing fastest among African Americans. And the median income for a home-school family is roughly equal to the median income for the rest of the country; about 87 percent have annual household incomes under $75,000.

Recent policy changes—in state legislatures and principals' offices—will further clear the way. Not only is home schooling now legal in every state, but many public schools have begun letting home-schoolers take certain classes or play on school teams. About two-thirds of American colleges now accept transcripts prepared by parents, or portfolios assembled by students, in lieu of an accredited diploma.

Another force is free agency itself. Thanks to flexible schedules and personal control, it's easier for free agents than for traditional employees to home-school their children. Free agents will also become the professionals in this new world of learning. A carpenter might hire herself out to teach carpentry skills to home-schoolers. A writer might become a tutor or editor to several home-schoolers interested in producing their own literary journal. What's more, the huge cadre of teachers hired to teach the baby boom will soon hit retirement age. However, perhaps instead of fully retiring, many will hire themselves out as itinerant tutors to home-schoolers—and begin part-time careers as free agent educators. For many parents, of course, the responsibility and time commitment of home schooling will be daunting. But the wide availability of teachers and tutors might help some parents overcome the concern that they won't be able to handle this awesome undertaking by themselves.

The Internet makes home schooling easier, too. Indeed, home-schoolers figured out the Internet well before most Americans. For example, my first Internet connection was a DOS-based Compuserve account I acquired in 1993. Before the wide acceptance of the Internet and the advent of the World Wide Web, the most active discussion groups on Compuserve were those devoted to home schooling. Using the Web, home-schoolers can do research and find tutors anywhere in the world. There are now even online ventures—for instance, the Christa McAuliffe Academy (www.cmacademy.org) in Washington state and ChildU.com in Florida—that sell online courses and provide e-teachers for home-schoolers. Physical infrastructure might also accelerate this trend. Almost three-fourths of America's public school buildings were built before 1969. School administrations might be more likely to encourage some amount of home schooling if that means less strain on their crowded classrooms and creaky buildings.

I don't want to overstate the case. Home schooling, like free 30
agency, won't be for everyone. Many parents won't have the time or
the desire for this approach. And home schooling won't be for all
time. Many students will spend a few years in a conventional school
and a few years learning at home—just as some workers will migrate
between being a free agent and holding a job. But home schooling is
perhaps the most robust expression of the free agent way outside the
workplace, making its continued rise inevitable.

The End of High School

One other consequence of the move toward home schooling will be
something many of us wished for as teenagers: the demise of high
school. It wasn't until the 1920s that high school replaced work as the
thing most Americans did in their teens. "American high school is obsolete," says Bard College president Leon Botstein, one of the first to
call for its end. He says today's adolescents would be better off pursuing a college degree, jumping directly into the job market, engaging in
public service, or taking on a vocational apprenticeship. Even the National Association of Secondary School Principals, which has blasted
home schooling, concedes that "high schools continue to go about
their business in ways that sometimes bear startling resemblance to
the flawed practices of the past."

In the future, expect teens and their families to force an end to
high school as we know it. Look for some of these changes to replace
and augment traditional high schools with free-agent-style learning—
and to unschool the American teenager:

- **A renaissance of apprenticeships.** For centuries, young people
  learned a craft or profession under the guidance of an experienced master. This method will revive and expand to include
  skills like computer programming and graphic design. Imagine a
  14-year-old taking two or three academic courses each week, and
  spending the rest of her time apprenticing as a commercial artist.
  Traditional high schools tend to separate learning and doing.
  Free agency makes them indistinguishable.

- **A flowering of teenage entrepreneurship.** Young people may become free agents even before they get their driver's licenses—and
  teen entrepreneurs will become more common. Indeed, most teens
  have the two crucial traits of a successful entrepreneur: a fresh way
  of looking at the world and a passionate intensity for what they do.
  In San Diego County, 8 percent of high school students already run
  their own online business. That will increasingly become the norm
  and perhaps even become a teenage rite of passage.

- **A greater diversity of academic courses.** Only 16 states offer basic economics in high school. That's hardly a sound foundation for the free agent workplace. Expect a surge of new kinds of "home economics" courses that teach numeracy, accounting, and basic business.

- **A boom in national service.** Some teenagers will seek greater direction than others and may want to spend a few years serving in the military or participating in a domestic service program. Today, many young people don't consider these choices because of the pressure to go directly to college. Getting people out of high school earlier might get them into service sooner.

- **A backlash against standards.** A high school diploma was once the gold standard of American education. No more. Yet politicians seem determined to make the diploma meaningful again by erecting all sorts of hurdles kids must leap to attain one—standardized subjects each student must study, standardized tests each student must pass. In some schools, students are already staging sit-ins to protest these tests. This could be American youth's new cause célèbre. ("Hey hey, ho ho. Standardized testing's got to go.")

Most politicians think the answer to the problems of high schools is to exert more control. But the real answer is *less* control. In the free agent future, our teens will learn by less schooling and more doing.

The Unschooling of Adults

For much of the 20th century, the U.S. depended on what I call the Thanksgiving turkey model of education. We placed kids in the oven of formal education for 12 years, and then served them up to employers. (A select minority got a final, four-year basting at a place called college.) But this model doesn't work in a world of accelerated cycle times, shrinking company half-lives, and the rapid obsolescence of knowledge and skills. In a free agent economy, our education system must allow people to learn throughout their lives.

35   Home schooling and alternatives to high school will create a nation of self-educators, free agent learners, if you will. Adults who were home-schooled youths will know how to learn and expect to continue the habit throughout their lives.

For example, how did anybody learn the Web? In 1993, it barely existed. By 1995, it was the foundation of dozens of new industries and an explosion of wealth. There weren't any college classes in Web programming, HTML coding, or Web page design in those early years. Yet somehow hundreds of thousands of people managed to learn. How? They taught themselves—working with colleagues, trying new things, and making mistakes. That was the secret to the Web's success. The Web flourished almost entirely through the ethic and practice of self-teaching. This is not a radical concept. Until the first part of this century, most Americans learned on their own—by reading. Literacy and access to books were an individual's ticket to knowledge. Even today, according to my own online survey of 1,143 independent workers, "reading" was the most prevalent way free agents said they stay up-to-date in their field.

In the 21st century, access to the Internet and to a network of smart colleagues will be the ticket to adult learning. Expect more of us to punch those tickets throughout our lives. Look for these early signs:

- **The devaluation of degrees.** As the shelf life of a degree shortens, more students will go to college to acquire particular skills than to bring home a sheepskin. People's need for knowledge doesn't respect semesters. They'll want higher education just in time—and if that means leaving the classroom before earning a degree, so be it. Remember: Larry Ellison, Steve Jobs, and Steven Spielberg never finished college.

- **Older students.** Forty percent of college students are now older than 25. According to *The Wall Street Journal*, "By some projections, the number of students age 35 and older will exceed those 18 and 19 within a few years." Young adults who do forgo a diploma in their early 20s may find a need and desire for college courses in their 40s.

- **Free agent teaching.** Distance learning (private ventures like the University of Phoenix, Unext, Ninth House Network, and Hungry Minds University) will help along this self-teaching trend. Today, some 5,000 companies are in the online education business. Their $2 billion of revenues is expected to hit $11 billion by 2003. And nontraditional teaching arrangements will abound. One lament of independent scholars—genre-straddling writers like Judith Rich Harris and Anne Hollander—is that they don't have students. Here's a ready supply. More free agent teachers and more free agent students will create tremendous liquidity in the learning market—with the Internet serving as the matchmaker for this new marketplace of learning.

- **Big trouble for elite colleges.** All this means big trouble in Ivy City. Attending a fancy college serves three purposes in contemporary life: to prolong adolescence, to award a credential that's modestly useful early in one's working life, and to give people a network of friends. Elite colleges have moved slowly to keep up with the emerging free agent economy. In 1998, 78 percent of public four-year colleges offered distance-learning programs, compared with only 19 percent of private schools. Private college costs have soared, faster even than health care costs, for the past 20 years. But have these colleges improved at the same rate? Have they improved at all? What's more, the students who make it to elite colleges are generally those who've proved most adroit at conventional (read: outdated) schooling. That could become a liability rather than an advantage. In his bestseller, *The Millionaire Mind*, Thomas J. Stanley found a disproportionately large number of millionaires were free agents—but that the higher somebody's SAT scores, the *less* likely he or she was to be a financial risk-taker and therefore to become a free agent.

- **Learning groupies.** The conference industry, already hot, will continue to catch fire as more people seek gatherings of like-minded souls to make new connections and learn new things. Conferences allow attendees to become part of a sort of Socratic institution. They can choose the mentor they will pay attention to for an hour, or two hours, or a day—whatever. In addition, many independent workers have formed small groups that meet regularly and allow members to exchange business advice and offer personal support. These Free Agent Nation Clubs, as I call them, also provide an important staging ground for self-education. At F.A.N. Club meetings, members discuss books and articles and share their particular expertise with the others. This type of learning— similarly alive in book clubs and Bible study groups—represents a rich American tradition. One of the earliest self-organized clusters of free agents was Benjamin Franklin's Junto, formed in 1727, which created a subscription library for its members, which in turn became the first public library in America.

The next few decades will be a fascinating, and perhaps revolutionary, time for learning in America. The specifics will surprise us and may defy even my soundest predictions. But the bottom line of the future of education in Free Agent Nation is glaringly clear: School's out.

Responding to Reading

1. What is a "free agent nation" (3)? In what sense is work in the United States undergoing a transformation? Why does Pink see this transformation as the "most significant transformation since Americans left the farm for the factory" (3)?
2. According to Pink, how are traditional public schools not meeting the challenges of the new economy? In what way does home schooling better prepare students for the new realities of "free agency?"
3. Do you think Pink is correct when he says that one of the consequences of home schooling will be "the demise of high school" (31)? What other changes does Pink see occurring in education?

Responding in Writing

List three advantages and three disadvantages of home schooling, and then write a paragraph in which you argue for or against it.

GRADUATION
Maya Angelou
1928–

Maya Angelou was raised in Arkansas by her grandmother, who ran a general store. She began a theatrical career when she toured with Porgy and Bess *in 1954–1955. Angelou is now a poet, writer, lecturer, and teacher. She read her poem "On the Pulse of Morning" at the 1993 presidential inauguration of Bill Clinton. Angelou's most recent book is,* A Song Flying Up to Heaven *(2002). In "Graduation," excerpted from her autobiography* I Know Why the Caged Bird Sings *(1969), Angelou remembers the anger and pride of graduation day at her segregated school in Stamps, Arkansas.*

The children in Stamps trembled visibly with anticipation. Some adults were excited too, but to be certain the whole young population had come down with graduation epidemic. Large classes were graduating from both the grammar school and the high school. Even those who were years removed from their own day of glorious release were anxious to help with preparations as a kind of dry run. The junior students who were moving into the vacating classes' chairs were tradition-bound to show their talents for leadership and management. They strutted through the school and around the campus exerting pressure on the lower grades. Their authority was so new that occasionally if they pressed a little too hard it had to be overlooked. After all, next term was coming, and it never hurt a sixth grader to have a play sister in the eighth grade, or a tenth-year student to be able to call a twelfth grader Bubba. So all was endured in a spirit of shared understanding. But the graduating classes themselves were the nobility. Like travelers with exotic destinations on their minds, the graduates were remarkably forgetful. They came to school without their books, or tablets or even pencils. Volunteers fell over themselves to secure replacements for the missing equipment. When accepted, the willing workers might or might not be thanked, and it was of no importance to the pregraduation rites. Even teachers were respectful of the now quiet and aging seniors, and tended to speak to them, if not as equals, as beings only slightly lower than themselves. After tests were returned and grades given, the student body, which acted like an extended family, knew who did well, who excelled, and what piteous ones had failed.

Unlike the white high school, Lafayette County Training School distinguished itself by having neither lawn, nor hedges, nor tennis court, nor climbing ivy. Its two buildings (main classrooms, the grade school and home economics) were set on a dirt hill with no fence to limit either its boundaries or those of bordering farms. There was a large expanse to the left of the school which was used alternately as a baseball diamond or basketball court. Rusty hoops on swaying poles represented the permanent recreational equipment, although bats and balls could be borrowed from the P.E. teacher if the borrower was qualified and if the diamond wasn't occupied.

Over this rocky area relieved by a few shady tall persimmon trees the graduating class walked. The girls often held hands and no longer bothered to speak to the lower students. There was a sadness about them, as if this old world was not their home and they were bound for higher ground. The boys, on the other hand, had become more friendly, more outgoing. A decided change from the closed attitude they projected while studying for finals. Now they seemed not ready to give up the old school, the familiar paths and classrooms. Only a small percentage would be continuing on to college—one of the South's A & M (agricultural and mechanical) schools, which trained Negro youths to be carpenters, farmers, handymen, masons, maids, cooks and baby nurses. Their future rode heavily on their shoulders, and blinded them to the collective joy that had pervaded the lives of the boys and girls in the grammar school graduating class.

Parents who could afford it had ordered new shoes and ready-made clothes for themselves from Sears and Roebuck or Montgomery Ward. They also engaged the best seamstresses to make the floating graduating dresses and to cut down secondhand pants which would be pressed to a military slickness for the important event.

5   Oh, it was important, all right. Whitefolks would attend the ceremony, and two or three would speak of God and home, and the Southern way of life, and Mrs. Parsons, the principal's wife, would play the graduation march while the lower-grade graduates paraded down the aisles and took their seats below the platform. The high school seniors would wait in empty classrooms to make their dramatic entrance.

In the Store I was the person of the moment. The birthday girl. The center. Bailey[1] had graduated the year before, although to do so he had had to forfeit all pleasures to make up for his time lost in Baton Rouge.

My class was wearing butter-yellow piqué dresses, and Momma launched out on mine. She smocked the yoke into tiny crisscrossing puckers, then shirred the rest of the bodice. Her dark fingers ducked in and out of the lemony cloth as she embroidered raised daisies around the hem. Before she considered herself finished she had added a crocheted cuff on the puff sleeves, and a pointy crocheted collar.

---

[1]Angelou's brother. The store was run by Angelou's grandmother, whom she called Momma, and Momma's son, Uncle Willie. [Eds.]

I was going to be lovely. A walking model of all the various styles of fine hand sewing and it didn't worry me that I was only twelve years old and merely graduating from the eighth grade. Besides, many teachers in Arkansas Negro schools had only that diploma and were licensed to impart wisdom.

The days had become longer and more noticeable. The faded beige of former times had been replaced with strong and sure colors. I began to see my classmates' clothes, their skin tones, and the dust that waved off pussy willows. Clouds that lazed across the sky were objects of great concern to me. Their shiftier shapes might have held a message that in my new happiness and with a little bit of time I'd soon decipher. During that period I looked at the arch of heaven so religiously my neck kept a steady ache. I had taken to smiling more often, and my jaws hurt from the unaccustomed activity. Between the two physical sore spots, I suppose I could have been uncomfortable, but that was not the case. As a member of the winning team (the graduating class of 1940) I had outdistanced unpleasant sensations by miles. I was headed for the freedom of open fields.

Youth and social approval allied themselves with me and we 10 trammeled memories of slights and insults. The wind of our swift passage remodeled my features. Lost tears were pounded to mud and then to dust. Years of withdrawal were brushed aside and left behind, as hanging ropes of parasitic moss.

My work alone had awarded me a top place and I was going to be one of the first called in the graduating ceremonies. On the classroom blackboard, as well as on the bulletin board in the auditorium, there were blue stars and white stars and red stars. No absences, no tardinesses, and my academic work was among the best of the year. I could say the preamble to the Constitution even faster than Bailey. We timed ourselves often: "WethepeopleoftheUnitedStatesinordertoformamoreperfectunion . . ." I had memorized the Presidents of the United States from Washington to Roosevelt in chronological as well as alphabetical order.

My hair pleased me too. Gradually the black mass had lengthened and thickened, so that it kept at last to its braided pattern, and I didn't have to yank my scalp off when I tried to comb it.

Louise and I had rehearsed the exercises until we tired out ourselves. Henry Reed was class valedictorian. He was a small, very black boy with hooded eyes, a long, broad nose and an oddly shaped head. I had admired him for years because each term he and I vied for the best grades in our class. Most often he bested me, but instead of being disappointed I was pleased that we shared top places between us. Like many Southern Black children, he lived with his grandmother, who was as strict as Momma and as kind as she knew how to be. He was courteous, respectful and soft-spoken to elders, but on the playground he chose to play the roughest games. I admired him. Anyone, I reckoned, sufficiently afraid or sufficiently dull could be polite. But to be able to operate at a top level with both adults and children was admirable.

His valedictory speech was entitled "To Be or Not to Be." The rigid tenth-grade teacher had helped him write it. He'd been working on the dramatic stresses for months.

15   The weeks until graduation were filled with heady activities. A group of small children were to be presented in a play about buttercups and daisies and bunny rabbits. They could be heard throughout the building practicing their hops and their little songs that sounded like silver bells. The older girls (nongraduates, of course) were assigned the task of making refreshments for the night's festivities. A tangy scent of ginger, cinnamon, nutmeg and chocolate wafted around the home economics building as the budding cooks made samples for themselves and their teachers.

In every corner of the workshop, axes and saws split fresh timber as the woodshop boys made sets and stage scenery. Only the graduates were left out of the general bustle. We were free to sit in the library at the back of the building or look in quite detachedly, naturally, on the measures being taken for our event.

Even the minister preached on graduation the Sunday before. His subject was, "Let your light so shine that men will see your good works and praise your Father, Who is in Heaven." Although the sermon was purported to be addressed to us, he used the occasion to speak to backsliders, gamblers and general ne'er-do-wells. But since he had called our names at the beginning of the service we were mollified.

Among Negroes the tradition was to give presents to children going only from one grade to another. How much more important this was when the person was graduating at the top of the class. Uncle Willie and Momma had sent away for a Mickey Mouse watch like Bailey's. Louise gave me four embroidered handkerchiefs. (I gave her crocheted doilies.) Mrs. Sneed, the minister's wife, made me an undershirt to wear for graduation, and nearly every customer gave me a nickel or maybe even a dime with the instruction "Keep on moving to higher ground," or some such encouragement.

Amazingly the great day finally dawned and I was out of bed before I knew it. I threw open the back door to see it more clearly, but Momma said, "Sister, come away from that door and put your robe on."

20   I hoped the memory of that morning would never leave me. Sunlight was itself young, and the day had none of the insistence maturity would bring it in a few hours. In my robe and barefoot in the backyard, under cover of going to see about my new beans, I gave myself up to the gentle warmth and thanked God that no matter what

evil I had done in my life He had allowed me to live to see this day. Somewhere in my fatalism I had expected to die, accidentally, and never have the chance to walk up the stairs in the auditorium and gracefully receive my hard-earned diploma. Out of God's merciful bosom I had won reprieve.

Bailey came out in his robe and gave me a box wrapped in Christmas paper. He said he had saved his money for months to pay for it. It felt like a box of chocolates, but I knew Bailey wouldn't save money to buy candy when we had all we could want under our noses.

He was as proud of the gift as I. It was a soft-leather-bound copy of a collection of poems by Edgar Allan Poe, or, as Bailey and I called him, "Eap." I turned to "Annabel Lee" and we walked up and down the garden rows, the cool dirt between our toes, reciting the beautifully sad lines.

Momma made a Sunday breakfast although it was only Friday. After we finished the blessing, I opened my eyes to find the watch on my plate. It was a dream of a day. Everything went smoothly and to my credit. I didn't have to be reminded or scolded for anything. Near evening I was too jittery to attend to chores, so Bailey volunteered to do all before his bath.

Days before, we had made a sign for the Store, and as we turned out the lights Momma hung the cardboard over the doorknob. It read clearly: CLOSED. GRADUATION.

My dress fitted perfectly and everyone said that I looked like a 25 sunbeam in it. On the hill, going toward the school, Bailey walked behind with Uncle Willie, who muttered, "Go on, Ju." He wanted him to walk ahead with us because it embarrassed him to have to walk so slowly. Bailey said he'd let the ladies walk together, and the men would bring up the rear. We all laughed, nicely.

Little children dashed by out of the dark like fireflies. Their crepe-paper dresses and butterfly wings were not made for running and we heard more than one rip, dryly, and the regretful "uh uh" that followed.

The school blazed without gaiety. The windows seemed cold and unfriendly from the lower hill. A sense of ill-fated timing crept over me, and if Momma hadn't reached for my hand I would have drifted back to Bailey and Uncle Willie, and possibly beyond. She made a few slow jokes about my feet getting cold, and tugged me along to the now-strange building.

Around the front steps, assurance came back. There were my fellow "greats," the graduating class. Hair brushed back, legs oiled, new dresses and pressed pleats, fresh pocket handkerchiefs and little handbags, all homesewn. Oh, we were up to snuff, all right. I joined my comrades and didn't even see my family go in to find seats in the crowded auditorium.

The school band struck up a march and all classes filed in as had been rehearsed. We stood in front of our seats, as assigned, and on a signal from the choir director, we sat. No sooner had this been accomplished than the band started to play the national anthem. We rose again and sang the song, after which we recited the pledge of allegiance. We remained standing for a brief minute before the choir director and the principal signaled to us, rather desperately I thought, to take our seats. The command was so unusual that our carefully rehearsed and smooth-running machine was thrown off. For a full minute we fumbled for our chairs and bumped into each other awkwardly. Habits change or solidify under pressure, so in our state of nervous tension we had been ready to follow our usual assembly pattern: the American national anthem, then the pledge of allegiance, then the song every Black person I knew called the Negro National Anthem. All done in the same key, with the same passion and most often standing on the same foot.

30   Finding my seat at last, I was overcome with a presentiment of worse things to come. Something unrehearsed, unplanned, was going to happen, and we were going to be made to look bad. I distinctly remember being explicit in the choice of pronoun. It was "we," the graduating class, the unit, that concerned me then.

The principal welcomed "parents and friends" and asked the Baptist minister to lead us in prayer. His invocation was brief and punchy, and for a second I thought we were getting on the high road to right action. When the principal came back to the dais, however, his voice had changed. Sounds always affected me profoundly and the principal's voice was one of my favorites. During assembly it melted and lowed weakly into the audience. It had not been in my plan to listen to him, but my curiosity was piqued and I straightened up to give him my attention.

He was talking about Booker T. Washington, our "late great leader," who said we can be as close as the fingers on the hand, etc. . . . Then he said a few vague things about friendship and the friendship of kindly people to those less fortunate than themselves. With that his voice nearly faded, thin, away. Like a river diminishing to a stream and then to a trickle. But he cleared his throat and said, "Our speaker tonight, who is also our friend, came from Texarkana to deliver the commencement address, but due to the irregularity of the train schedule, he's going to, as they say, 'speak and run.'" He said that we understood and wanted the man to know that we were most grateful for the time he was able to give us and then something about how we were willing always to adjust to another's program, and without more ado—"I give you Mr. Edward Donleavy."

Not one but two white men came through the door off-stage. The shorter one walked to the speaker's platform, and the tall one moved to the center seat and sat down. But that was our principal's seat, and already occupied. The dislodged gentleman bounced around for a long breath or two before the Baptist minister gave him his chair, then with more dignity than the situation deserved, the minister walked off the stage.

Donleavy looked at the audience once (on reflection, I'm sure that he wanted only to reassure himself that we were really there), adjusted his glasses and began to read from a sheaf of papers.

He was glad "to be here and to see the work going on just as it 35 was in the other schools."

At the first "Amen" from the audience I willed the offender to immediate death by choking on the word. But Amens and Yes, sir's began to fall around the room like rain through a ragged umbrella.

He told us of the wonderful changes we children in Stamps had in store. The Central School (naturally, the white school was Central) had already been granted improvements that would be in use in the fall. A well-known artist was coming from Little Rock to teach art to them. They were going to have the newest microscopes and chemistry equipment for their laboratory. Mr. Donleavy didn't leave us long in the dark over who made these improvements available to Central High. Nor were we to be ignored in the general betterment scheme he had in mind.

He said that he had pointed out to people at a very high level that one of the first-line football tacklers at Arkansas Agricultural and Mechanical College had graduated from good old Lafayette County Training School. Here fewer Amen's were heard. Those few that did break through lay dully in the air with the heaviness of habit.

He went on to praise us. He went on to say how he had bragged that "one of the best basketball players at Fisk[2] sank his first ball right here at Lafayette County Training School."

The white kids were going to have a chance to become Galileos 40 and Madame Curies and Edisons and Gauguins,[3] and our boys (the girls weren't even in on it) would try to be Jesse Owenses and Joe Louises.[4]

Owens and the Brown Bomber were great heroes in our world, but what school official in the white-goddom of Little Rock had the right to decide that those two men must be our only heroes? Who decided that for Henry Reed to become a scientist he had to work like George Washington Carver, as a bootblack, to buy a lousy microscope? Bailey was obviously always going to be too small to be an athlete, so which concrete angel glued to what country seat had

---

[2]Highly regarded, historicaly black university in Nashville. [Eds.]
[3]Inventors, scientists, and artists. [Eds.]
[4]The black track star and Olympic gold medalist, and the longtime world heavyweight boxing champion known as the "Brown Bomber." [Eds.]

decided that if my brother wanted to become a lawyer he had to first pay penance for his skin by picking cotton and hoeing corn and studying correspondence books at night for twenty years?

The man's dead words fell like bricks around the auditorium and too many settled in my belly. Constrained by hard-learned manners I couldn't look behind me, but to my left and right the proud graduating class of 1940 had dropped their heads. Every girl in my row had found something new to do with her handkerchief. Some folded the tiny squares into love knots, some into triangles, but most were wadding them, then pressing them flat on their yellow laps.

On the dais, the ancient tragedy was being replayed. Professor Parsons sat, a sculptor's reject, rigid. His large, heavy body seemed devoid of will or willingness, and his eyes said he was no longer with us. The other teachers examined the flag (which was draped stage right) or their notes, or the windows which opened on our nowfamous playing diamond.

Graduation, the hush-hush magic time of frills and gifts and congratulations and diplomas, was finished for me before my name was called. The accomplishment was nothing. The meticulous maps, drawn in three colors of ink, learning and spelling decasyllabic words, memorizing the whole of *The Rape of Lucrece*[5]—it was for nothing. Donleavy had exposed us.

45   We were maids and farmers, handymen and washerwomen, and anything higher that we aspired to was farcical and presumptuous.

Then I wished that Gabriel Prosser and Nat Turner[6] had killed all whitefolks in their beds and that Abraham Lincoln had been assassinated before the signing of the Emancipation Proclamation, and that Harriet Tubman[7] had been killed by that blow on her head and Christopher Columbus had drowned in the *Santa Maria*.

It was awful to be a Negro and have no control over my life. It was brutal to be young and already trained to sit quietly and listen to charges brought against my color with no chance of defense. We should all be dead. I thought I should like to see us all dead, one on top of the other. A pyramid of flesh with the whitefolks on the bottom, as the broad base, then the Indians with their silly tomahawks and teepees and wigwams and treaties, the Negroes with their mops and recipes and cotton sacks and spirituals sticking out of their mouths. The Dutch children should all stumble in their wooden shoes and break their necks. The French should choke to death on the Louisiana Purchase (1803) while silkworms ate all the Chinese with their stupid pigtails. As a species, we were an abomination. All of us.

---

[5]*The Rape of Lucrece* is a long narrative poem by Shakespeare. [Eds.]

[6]Prosser and Turner both led slave rebellions. [Eds.]

[7]Harriet Tubman (1820–1913) was an African-American abolitionist who became one of the most successful guides on the Underground Railroad. [Eds.]

Donleavy was running for election, and assured our parents that if he won we could count on having the only colored paved playing field in that part of Arkansas. Also—he never looked up to acknowledge the grunts of acceptance—also, we were bound to get some new equipment for the home economics building and the workshop.

He finished, and since there was no need to give any more than the most perfunctory thank-you's, he nodded to the men on the stage, and the tall white man who was never introduced joined him at the door. They left with the attitude that now they were off to something really important. (The graduation ceremonies at Lafayette County Training School had been a mere preliminary.)

The ugliness they left was palpable. An uninvited guest who   50 wouldn't leave. The choir was summoned and sang a modern arrangement of "Onward, Christian Soldiers," with new words pertaining to graduates seeking their place in the world. But it didn't work. Elouise, the daughter of the Baptist minister, recited "Invictus,"[8] and I could have cried at the impertinence of "I am the master of my fate, I am the captain of my soul."

My name had lost its ring of familiarity and I had to be nudged to go and receive my diploma. All my preparations had fled. I neither marched up to the stage like a conquering Amazon, nor did I look in the audience for Bailey's nod of approval. Marguerite Johnson,[9] I heard the name again, my honors were read, there were noises in the audience of appreciation, and I took my place on the stage as rehearsed.

I thought about colors I hated: ecru, puce, lavender, beige and black.

There was shuffling and rustling around me, then Henry Reed was giving his valedictory address, "To Be or Not to Be." Hadn't he heard the whitefolks? We couldn't *be,* so the question was a waste of time. Henry's voice came out clear and strong. I feared to look at him. Hadn't he got the message? There was no "nobler in the mind" for Negroes because the world didn't think we had minds, and they let us know it. "Outrageous fortune"? Now, that was a joke. When the ceremony was over I had to tell Henry Reed some things. That is, if I still cared. Not "rub," Henry, "erase." "Ah, there's the erase." Us.

Henry had been a good student in elocution. His voice rose on tides of promise and fell on waves of warnings. The English teacher had helped him to create a sermon winging through Hamlet's soliloquy. To be a man, a doer, a builder, a leader, or to be a tool, an unfunny joke, a crusher of funky toadstools. I marveled that Henry could go through with the speech as if we had a choice.

---

[8]An inspirational poem written in 1875 by William Ernest Henley (1849–1903). Its defiant and stoic sentiments made it extremely popular with nineteenth-century readers. [Eds.]
[9]Angelou's given name. [Eds.]

⁵⁵   I had been listening and silently rebutting each sentence with my eyes closed; then there was a hush, which in an audience warns that something unplanned is happening. I looked up and saw Henry Reed, the conservative, the proper, the A student, turn his back to the audience and turn to us (the proud graduating class of 1940) and sing, nearly speaking,

> "Lift ev'ry voice and sing
> Till earth and heaven ring
> Ring with the harmonies of Liberty . . ."

It was the poem written by James Weldon Johnson. It was the music composed by J. Rosamond Johnson. It was the Negro national anthem. Out of habit we were singing it.

Our mothers and fathers stood in the dark hall and joined the hymn of encouragement. A kindergarten teacher led the small children onto the stage and the buttercups and daisies and bunny rabbits marked time and tried to follow:

> "Stony the road we trod
> Bitter the chastening rod
> Felt in the days when hope, unborn, had died.
> Yet with a steady beat
> ⁵   Have not our weary feet
> Come to the place for which our fathers sighed?"

Each child I knew had learned that song with his ABC's and along with "Jesus Loves Me This I Know." But I personally had never heard it before. Never heard the words, despite the thousands of times I had sung them. Never thought they had anything to do with me.

On the other hand, the words of Patrick Henry had made such an impression on me that I had been able to stretch myself tall and trembling and say, "I know not what course others may take, but as for me, give me liberty or give me death."

⁶⁰   And now I heard, really for the first time:

> "We have come over a way that with tears
> has been watered,
> We have come, treading our path through
> the blood of the slaughtered."

While echoes of the song shivered in the air, Henry Reed bowed his head, said "Thank you," and returned to his place in the line. The tears that slipped down many faces were not wiped away in shame.

We were on top again. As always, again. We survived. The depths had been icy and dark, but now a bright sun spoke to our souls. I was no longer simply a member of the proud graduating class of 1940; I was a proud member of the wonderful, beautiful Negro race.

Oh, Black known and unknown poets, how often have your auctioned pains sustained us? Who will compute the lonely nights made less lonely by your songs, or the empty pots made less tragic by your tales?

If we were a people much given to revealing secrets, we might raise monuments and sacrifice to the memories of our poets, but slavery cured us of that weakness. It may be enough, however, to have it said that we survive in exact relationship to the dedication of our poets (include preachers, musicians and blues singers).

Responding to Reading

1. Angelou's graduation took place in 1940. What expectations did educators have for Angelou and her classmates? How were these expectations different from the expectations Angelou and her fellow students had?
2. In what way did Mr. Donleavy's speech "educate" the graduates? How did Angelou's thinking change as she listened to him?
3. In paragraph 62, Angelou says, "We were on top again." In what sense were she and the graduates "on top"? Do you think Angelou was being overly optimistic in light of what she had just experienced?

Responding in Writing

In the 1954 *Brown v. Board of Education* decision, the Supreme Court of the United States ruled that the "separate but equal" education that Angelou experienced was unconstitutional. How do you suppose her education would have been different had she attended high school in 1960 instead of in 1940?

THE GOOD IMMIGRANT STUDENT

Bich Minh Nguyen

1974–

Bich Minh Nguyen is a lecturer at Purdue University and winner of the PEN American Center's 2005 PEN/Jerard Award in nonfiction for her memoir, Stealing Buddha's Dinner *(2007). She has also written a novel, coedited three anthologies, and written for* Gourmet *magazine, the* Chicago Tribune, *and other publications. In the following essay, Nguyen explores the implications of bilingual education for immigrants in America.*

My stepmother, Rosa, who began dating my father when I was three years old, says that my sister and I used to watch *Police Woman* and rapturously repeat everything Angie Dickinson said. But when the show was over Anh and I would resume our Vietnamese, whispering together, giggling in accents. Rosa worried about this. She had the idea that she could teach us English and we could teach her Vietnamese. She would make us lunch or give us baths, speaking slowly and asking us how to say *water,* or *rice,* or *house.*

After she and my father married, Rosa swept us out of our falling-down house and into middle-class suburban Grand Rapids, Michigan. Our neighborhood surrounded Ken-O-Sha Elementary School and Plaster Creek, and was only a short drive away from the original Meijer's Thrifty Acres. In the early 1980s, this neighborhood of mismatching street names—Poinsettia, Van Auken, Senora, Ravanna—was home to families of Dutch heritage, and everyone was Christian Reformed, and conservative Republican. Except us. Even if my father hadn't left his rusted-through silver Mustang, the first car he ever owned, to languish in the driveway for months we would have stuck out simply because we weren't white. There was my Latina stepmother and her daughter, Cristina, my father, sister, grandmother, and I, refugees from Saigon; and my half-brother born a year after we moved to the house on Ravanna Street.

Although my family lived two blocks from Ken-O-Sha, my stepmother enrolled me and Anh at Sherwood Elementary, a bus ride away, because Sherwood had a bilingual education program. Rosa, who had a master's in education and taught ESL and community ed in the public school system, was a big supporter of bilingual education. School mornings, Anh and I would be at the bus stop at the corner of our street quite early, hustled out of the house by our grandmother who constantly feared we would miss our chance. I went off to first grade, Anh to second. At ten o'clock, we crept out of our classes, drawing glances and whispers from the other students, and convened with a group of Vietnamese kids from other grades to learn English. The teachers were Mr. Ho, who wore a lot of short-sleeved button-down shirts in neutral hues, and Miss Huong, who favored a maroon blouse with puffy shoulders and slight ruffles at the high neck and wrists, paired with a tweed skirt that hung heavily to her ankles. They passed out photocopied booklets of Vietnamese phrases and their English translations, with themes such as "In the Grocery Store." They asked us to repeat slowly after them and took turns coming around to each of us, bending close to hear our pronunciations.

Anh and I exchanged a lot of worried glances, for we had a secret that we were quite embarrassed about: we already knew English. It was the Vietnamese part that gave us trouble. When Mr. Ho and Miss Huong gave instructions, or passed out homework assignments, they did so in Vietnamese. Anh and I received praise for our English, but were reprimanded for failing to complete our assignments and failing to pay attention. After a couple of weeks of this Anh announced to Rosa that we didn't need bilingual education. Nonsense, she said. Our father just shrugged his shoulders. After that, Anh began skipping bilingual classes, urging me to do the same, and then we never went back. What was amazing was that no one, not Mrs. Eunice, my first grade teacher, or Mrs. Hankins, Anh's teacher, or even Mr. Ho or Miss Huong said anything directly to us about it. Or if they did, I have forgotten it entirely. Then one day my parents got a call from Miss Huong. When Rosa came to talk to me and Anh about it we were watching television the way kids do, sitting alarmingly close to the screen. Rosa confronted us with "Do you girls know English?" Then she suddenly said, "Do you know Vietnamese?" I can't remember what we replied to either question.

For many years, a towering old billboard over the expressway ₅ downtown proudly declared Grand Rapids "An All-American City." For me, that all-American designation meant all-white. I couldn't believe (and still don't) that they meant to include the growing Mexican-American population, or the sudden influx of Vietnamese refugees in 1975. I often thought it a rather mean-spirited prank of some administrator at the INS, deciding with a flourish of a signature to send a thousand refugees to Grand Rapids, a city that boasted having more churches per square mile than other city in the United States. Did that administrator know what Grand Rapids was like? That in school, everywhere I turned, and often when I closed my eyes, I saw blond blond blond? The point of bilingual education was assimilation. To my stepmother, the point was preservation: she didn't want English to take over wholly, pushing the Vietnamese out of our heads. She was too ambitious. Anh and I were Americanized as soon as we turned on the television. Today, bilingual education is supposed to have become both a method of assimilation and a method of preservation, an effort to prove that kids can have it both ways. They can supposedly keep English for school and their friends and keep another language for home and family.

In Grand Rapids, Michigan, in the 1980s, I found that an impossible task.

I transferred to Ken-O-Sha Elementary in time for third grade, after Rosa finally admitted that taking the bus all the way to Sherwood was pointless. I was glad to transfer, eager to be part of a class that wasn't, in my mind, tainted with the knowledge of my bilingual stigma. Third grade was led by Mrs. Alexander, an imperious, middle-aged woman of many plaid skirts held safe by giant gold safety pins. She had a habit of turning her wedding ring around and around her finger while she stood at the chalkboard. Mrs. Alexander had an intricate system of rewards for good grades and good behavior, denoted by colored star stickers on a piece of poster board that loomed over us all. One glance and you could see who was behind, who was striding ahead.

I was an insufferably good student, with perfect Palmer cursive and the highest possible scores in every subject. I had learned this trick at Sherwood. That the quieter you are, the shyer and sweeter and better-at-school you are, the more the teacher will let you alone. Mrs. Alexander should have let me alone. For, in addition to my excellent marks, I was nearly silent, deadly shy, and wholly obedient. My greatest fear was being called on, or in any way standing out more than I already did in the class that was, except for me and one black student, dough-white. I got good grades because I feared the authority of the teacher; I felt that getting in good with Mrs. Alexander would protect me, that she would protect me from the frightful rest of the world. But Mrs. Alexander was not agreeable to this notion. If it was my turn to read aloud during reading circle, she'd interrupt me to snap, "You're reading too fast" or demand, "What does that word mean?" Things she did not do to the other students. Anh, when I told her about this, suggested that perhaps Mrs. Alexander liked me and wanted to help me get smarter. But neither of us believed it. You know when a teacher likes you and when she doesn't.

Secretly, I admired and envied the rebellious kids, like Robbie Andrews who came to school looking bleary-eyed and pinched, like a hungover adult; Robbie and his ilk snapped back at teachers, were routinely sent to the principal's office, were even spanked a few times with the principal's infamous red paddle (apparently no one in Grand Rapids objected to corporal punishment). Those kids made noise, possessed something I thought was confidence, self-knowledge, allowing them to marvelously question everything ordered of them. They had the ability to challenge the given world.

10   Toward the middle of third grade Mrs. Alexander introduced a stuffed lion to the pool of rewards: the best student of the week would earn the privilege of having the lion sit on his or her desk for the entire week. My quantity of gold stars was neck and neck with that of my two competitors, Brenda and Jennifer, both sweet-eyed blond girls with pastel-colored monogrammed sweaters and neatly tied Dock-Sides. My family did not have a lot of money and my stepmother had terrible taste. Thus I attended school in such ensembles as dark red parachute pants and a nubby pink sweater stitched with a picture of a unicorn rearing up. This only propelled me to try harder to be good, to make up for everything I felt was against me: my odd family, my race, my very face. And I craved that stuffed lion. Week after week, the lion perched on Brenda's desk or Jennifer's desk. Meanwhile, the class spelling bee approached. I didn't know I was such a good speller until I won it, earning a scalloped-edged certificate and a candy bar. That afternoon I started toward home, then remembered I'd forgotten my rain boots in my locker. I doubled back to school and overheard Mrs. Alexander in the classroom talking to

another teacher. "Can you believe it?" Mrs. Alexander was saying. "A foreigner winning our spelling bee!"

I waited for the stuffed lion the rest of that year, with a kind of patience I have no patience for today. To no avail. In June, on the last day of school, Mrs. Alexander gave the stuffed lion to Brenda to keep forever.

The first time I had to read aloud something I had written—perhaps it was in fourth grade—I felt such terror, such a need not to have any attention upon me, that I convinced myself that I had become invisible, that the teacher could never call on me because she couldn't see me.

More than once, I was given the assignment of writing a report about my family history. I loathed this task, for I was dreadfully aware that my history could not be faked; it already showed on my face. When my turn came to read out loud the teacher had to ask me several times to speak louder. Some kids, a few of them older, in different classes, took to pressing back the corners of their eyes with the heels of their palms while they chanted, "Ching-chong, ching-chong!" during recess. (This continued until Anh, who was far tougher than me, threatened to beat them up.)

I have no way of telling what tortured me more: the actual snickers and remarks and watchfulness of my classmates, or my own imagination, conjuring disdain. My own sense of shame. At times I felt sickened by my obedience, my accumulation of gold stickers, my every effort to be invisible.

Yet Robbie Andrews must have felt the same kind of claustrophobia, 15 trapped in his own reputation, in his ability to be otherwise. I learned in school that changing oneself is not easy, that the world makes up its mind quickly.

I've heard that Robbie dropped out of high school, got a girl pregnant, found himself in and out of first juvenile detention, then jail.

What comes out of difference? What constitutes difference? Such questions, academic and unanswered, popped up in every other course description in college. But the idea of difference is easy to come by, especially in school; it is shame, the permutations and inversions of difference and self-loathing, that we should be worrying about.

Imagined torment, imagined scorn. When what is imagined and what is desired turn on each other.

Some kids want to rebel; other kids want to disappear. I wanted to disappear. I was not brave enough to shrug my shoulders and flaunt my difference; because I could not disappear into the crowd, I wished to disappear entirely. Anyone might have mistaken this for passivity.

20   Once, at the end of my career at Sherwood Elementary, I disappeared on the bus home. Mine was usually the third stop, but that day the bus driver thought I wasn't there, and she sailed right by the corner of Ravanna and Senora. I said nothing. The bus wove its way downtown, and for the first time I got to see where other children lived, some of them in clean orderly neighborhoods, some near houses with sagging porches and boarded-up windows. All the while, the kid sitting across the aisle from me played the same cheerful song over and over on his portable boom box. *Pass the doochee from the left hand side, pass the doochee from the left hand side.* He and his brother turned out to be the last kids off the bus. Then the bus driver saw me through the rearview mirror. She walked back to where I was sitting and said, "How come you didn't get off at your stop?" I shook my head, don't know. She sighed and drove me home.

I was often doing that, shaking my head silently or staring up wordlessly. I realize that while I remember so much of what other people said when I was a child, I remember little of what I said. Probably because I didn't say much at all.

I recently came across in the stacks of the University of Michigan library *A Manual for Indochinese Refugee Education 1976–1977*. Some of it is silly, but much of it is a painstaking, fairly thoughtful effort to let school administrators and teachers know how to go about sensitively handling the influx of Vietnamese children in the public schools. Here is one of the most wonderful items of advice: "The Vietnamese child, even the older child, is also reported to be afraid of the dark, and more often than not, believes in ghosts. A teacher may have to be a little more solicitous of the child on gloomy, wintery days." Perhaps if Mrs. Alexander had read this, she would not have upbraided me so often for tracking mud into the classroom on rainy days. In third grade I was horrified and ashamed of my muddy shoes. I hung back, trying to duck behind this or that dark-haired boy. In spite of this, in spite of bilingual education, and shyness, and all that wordless shaking of my head, I was sent off every Monday to the Spectrum School for the Gifted and Talented. I still have no idea who selected me, who singled me out. Spectrum was (and still is) a public school program that invited students from every public elementary school to meet once a week and take specialized classes on topics such as the Middle Ages, Ellis Island, and fairy tales. Each student chose two classes, a major and minor, and for the rest of the semester worked toward final projects in both. I loved going to Spectrum. Not only did the range of students from other schools prove to be diverse, I found myself feeling more comfortable, mainly because Spectrum encouraged individual work. And the teachers seemed happy to be there. The best teacher at Spectrum was Mrs. King, whom every student adored. I still remember the soft gray sweaters she wore, her big wavy hair, her art-class handwriting, the way she'd often tell us to close our eyes when she read us a particular story or passage.

I believe that I figured out how to stop disappearing, how to talk and answer, even speak up, after several years in Spectrum. I was still deeply self-conscious, but I became able, sometimes, to maneuver around it.

Spectrum may have spoiled me a little, because it made me think about college and freedom, and thus made all the years in between disappointing and annoying.

In seventh grade I joined Anh and Cristina at the City School, a seventh through twelfth grade public school in the Grand Rapids system that served as an early charter school; admission was by interview, and each grade had about fifty students. The City School had the advantage of being downtown, perched over old cobblestone roads, and close to the main public library. Art and music history were required. There were no sports teams. And volunteering was mandatory. But kids didn't tend to stay at City School; as they got older they transferred to one of the big high schools nearby, perhaps wishing to play sports, perhaps wishing to get away from City's rather brutal academic system. Each half semester, after grades were doled out, giant dot-matrix printouts of everyone's GPAs were posted in the hallways.

I didn't stay at City, either. When my family moved to a different suburb, my stepmother promptly transferred me to Forest Hills Northern High School. Most of the students there came from upper-middle-class or very well-to-do families; the ones who didn't stood out sharply. The rich kids were the same as they were anywhere in America: they wore a lot of Esprit and Guess, drove nice cars, and ran student council, prom, and sports. These kids strutted down the hallways; the boys sat in a row on the long windowsill near a group of lockers, whistling or calling out to girls who walked by. Girls gathered in bathrooms with their Clinique lipsticks.

High school was the least interesting part of my education, but I did accomplish something: I learned to forget myself a little. I learned the sweetness of apathy. And through apathy, how to forget my skin and body for a minute or two, almost not caring what would happen if I walked into a room late and all heads swiveled toward me. I learned the pleasure that reveals itself in the loss, no matter how slight, of self-consciousness. These things occurred because I remained the good immigrant student, without raising my hand often or showing off what I knew. Doing work was rote, and I went along to get along. I've never gotten over the terror of being called on in class, or the dread in knowing that I'm expected to contribute to class discussion. But there is a slippage between being good and being unnoticed, and in that sliver of freedom I learned what it could feel like to walk in the world in plain, unself-conscious view.

I would like to make a broad, accurate statement about immigrant children in schools. I would like to speak for them (us). I hesitate; I cannot. My own sister, for instance, was never as shy as I was. Anh disliked school from the start, choosing rebellion rather than silence. It was a good arrangement: I wrote papers for her and she paid me in money or candy; she gave me rides to school if I promised not to tell anyone about her cigarettes. Still, I think of an Indian friend of mine who told of an elementary school experience in which a blond schoolchild told the teacher, "I can't sit by her. My mom said I can't sit by anyone who's brown." And another friend, whose family immigrated around the same time mine did, whose second grade teacher used her as a vocabulary example: "Children, this is what a *foreigner* is." And sometimes I fall into thinking that kids today have the advantage of so much more wisdom, that they are so much more socially and politically aware than anyone was when I was in school. But I am wrong, of course. I know not every kid is fortunate enough to have a teacher like Mrs. King, or a program like Spectrum, or even the benefit of a manual written by a group of concerned educators; I know that some kids want to disappear and disappear until they actually do. Sometimes I think I see them, in the blurry background of a magazine photo, or in a gaggle of kids following a teacher's aide across the street. The kids with heads bent down, holding themselves in such a way that they seem to be self-conscious even of how they breathe. Small, shy, quiet kids, such good, good kids, *immigrant, foreigner,* their eyes watchful and waiting for whatever judgment will occur. I reassure myself that they will grow up fine, they will be okay. Maybe I cross the same street, then another, glancing back once in a while to see where they are going.

Responding to Reading

1. What does Nguyen mean when she says that today bilingual education is supposed to be "both a method of assimilation and a method of preservation" (5)? Does she believe this is true?
2. In paragraph 17, Nguyen asks, "What comes out of difference? What constitutes difference?" How does she answer these questions? In what way does her own sense of difference affect her education?
3. What is "the good immigrant student"? How did Nguyen's education reinforce this stereotype? How did it help her move beyond it?

Responding in Writing

In paragraph 28, Nguyen says, "I would like to make a broad, accurate statement about immigrant children in schools. I would like to speak for them (us). I hesitate; I cannot." What do you think she means? Why do you think she cannot make "a broad, accurate statement"?

FOR MORE BALANCE ON CAMPUSES
Christina Hoff Sommers
1956–

*Christina Hoff Sommers currently works as a fellow at the American Enter-
prise Institute. Sommers is the author of essays in a wide variety of periodicals and has published several books but is best known for* Who Stole
Feminism?: How Women Have Betrayed Women *(1994) and* The War
against Boys: How Misguided Feminism Is Harming Our Young Men
(2000). Her latest book, coauthored with Sally Satel, is One Nation Under
Therapy: How the Helping Culture is Eroding Self-Reliance *(2005). In
the following essay, the introduction to a longer essay that appeared in the*
Atlantic Monthly, *Sommers makes a plea for more political diversity on
America's college campuses.*

Washington—In a recent talk at Haverford College, I questioned the
standard women's studies teaching that the United States is a patriar-
chal society that oppresses women.

For many in the audience, this was their first encounter with a
dissident scholar. One student was horrified when I said that the free
market had advanced the cause of women by affording them unprecedented economic opportunities. "How can anyone say that capitalism has helped women?" she asked.

Nor did I win converts when I said that the male heroism of special forces soldiers and the firefighters at ground zero should persuade
gender scholars to acknowledge that "stereotypical masculinity" had
some merit. Later an embarrassed and apologetic student said to me,
"Haverford is just not ready for you."

After my talk, the young woman who invited me told me there
was little intellectual diversity at Haverford and that she had hoped I
would spark debate. In fact, many in the audience were quietly delighted by the exchanges. But two angry students accused her of providing "a forum for hate speech."

As the 2000 election made plain, the United States is pretty evenly   5
divided between conservatives and liberals. Yet conservative scholars
have effectively been marginalized, silenced, and rendered invisible
on most campuses. This problem began in the late '80s and has become much worse in recent years. Most students can now go through
four years of college without encountering a scholar of pronounced
conservative views.

Few conservatives make it past the gantlet of faculty hiring in
political-science, history, or English departments. In 1998, when a reporter from Denver's *Rocky Mountain News* surveyed the humanities
and social sciences at the University of Colorado, Boulder, he found
that of 190 professors with party affiliations, 184 were Democrats.

There wasn't a single Republican in the English, psychology, journalism, or philosophy departments. A 1999 survey of history departments found 22 Democrats and 2 Republicans at Stanford. At Cornell and Dartmouth there were 29 and 10 Democrats, respectively, and no Republicans.

The dearth of conservatives in psychology departments is so striking, that one (politically liberal) professor has proposed affirmative-action outreach. Richard Redding, a professor of psychology at Villanova University, writing in a recent issue of American Psychologist, notes that of the 31 social-policy articles that appeared in the journal between 1990 and 1999, 30 could be classified as liberal, one as conservative.

The key issue, Professor Redding says, is not the preponderance of Democrats, but the liberal practice of systematically excluding conservatives. Redding cites an experiment in which several graduate departments received mock applications from two candidates nearly identical, except that one "applicant" said he was a conservative Christian. The professors judged the nonconservative to be the significantly better candidate.

10   Redding asks, rhetorically: "Do we want a professional world where our liberal world view prevents us from considering valuable strengths of conservative approaches to social problems . . . where conservatives are reluctant to enter the profession and we tacitly discriminate against them if they do? That, in fact, is the academic world we now have. . . ."

Campus talks by "politically incorrect" speakers happen rarely; visits are resisted and almost never internally funded. When Dinesh D'Souza, Andrew Sullivan, David Horowitz, or Linda Chavez do appear at a college, they are routinely heckled and sometimes threatened. The academy is now so inhospitable to free expression that conservatives buy advertisements in student newspapers. But most school newspapers won't print them. And papers that do are sometimes vandalized and the editors threatened.

The classical liberalism articulated by John Stuart Mill in his book *On Liberty* is no longer alive on campuses, having died of the very disease Mr. Mill warned of when he pointed out that ideas not freely and openly debated become *dead dogmas*. Mill insisted that the intellectually free person must put himself in the *mental position of those who think differently* adding that dissident ideas are best understood *by hear[ing] them from persons who actually believe them*.

Several groups are working to bring some balance to campus. The Intercollegiate Studies Institute, Young America's Foundation, Clare Boothe Luce Policy Institute, and Accuracy in Academia sponsor lectures by leading conservatives and libertarians. Students can ask these groups for funds to sponsor speakers.

More good news is that David Horowitz's Center for the Study of Popular Culture has launched a "Campaign for Fairness and Inclusion in Higher Education." It calls for university officials to:

1. Establish a zero-tolerance policy for vandalizing newspapers or heckling speakers.
2. Conduct an inquiry into political bias in the allocation of student program funds, including speakers' fees, and seek ways to promote underrepresented perspectives.
3. Conduct an inquiry into political bias in the hiring process of faculty and administrators and seek ways to promote fairness toward—and inclusion of—underrepresented perspectives.

Were even one high-profile institution like the University of Col- 15 orado to adopt a firm policy of intellectual inclusiveness, that practice would quickly spread, and benighted students everywhere would soon see daylight.

Responding to Reading

1. Why does Sommers call herself a "dissident scholar" (2)? What generally accepted beliefs does she question? During her talk at Haverford College, why do her remarks cause such uneasiness?
2. According to Sommers, conservatives have been marginalized on most American college campuses. What does she mean? How has this occurred? What evidence does Sommers present to support her claim? Is her evidence persuasive?
3. In Sommers's view, what is the effect of excluding conservatives from the intellectual life of a college or university? What does Sommers say is being done "to bring some balance to campus" (13)?

Responding in Writing

Sommers says that students almost never hear campus talks by "'politically incorrect' speakers" (11). Do you agree with Sommers, or do you believe that at your college or university you are exposed to a cross section of ideas?

FICTION

THE FIRST DAY

Edward P. Jones

1950–

Edward P. Jones studied writing at the University of Virginia. His book Lost in the City *(1992) is a collection of stories set in the hometown of his childhood, Washington, D.C., a city of working-class black men and women who struggle heroically in their daily lives. The book was nominated for the National Book Award and lauded by critics both for addressing racial issues and for transcending them. His first novel,* The Known World, *published in 2003, was chosen as one of the year's nine best books (and four best novels) by the editors of the* New York Times Book Review. The Known World *also won the fiction prize of the National Book Critics Circle and the 2004 Pulitzer Prize for fiction. His latest book,* All Aunt Hagar's Children *(2006): is a collection of stories. The short story that follows, from* Lost in the City, *is the poignant story of a mother who takes her daughter to her first day of school.*

In an otherwise unremarkable September morning, long before I learned to be ashamed of my mother, she takes my hand and we set off down New Jersey Avenue to begin my very first day of school. I am wearing a checkeredlike blue-and-green cotton dress, and scattered about these colors are bits of yellow and white and brown. My mother has uncharacteristically spent nearly an hour on my hair that morning, plaiting and replaiting so that now my scalp tingles. Whenever I turn my head quickly, my nose fills with the faint smell of Dixie Peach hair grease. The smell is somehow a soothing one now and I will reach for it time and time again before the morning ends. All the plaits, each with a blue barrette near the tip and each twisted into an uncommon sturdiness, will last until I go to bed that night, something that has never happened before. My stomach is full of milk and oatmeal sweetened with brown sugar. Like everything else I have on, my pale green slip and underwear are new, the underwear having come three to a plastic package with a little girl on the front who appears to be dancing. Behind my ears, my mother, to stop my whining, has dabbed the stingiest bit of her gardenia perfume, the last present my father gave her before he disappeared into memory. Because I cannot smell it, I have only her word that the perfume is there. I am also wearing yellow socks trimmed with thin lines of black and white around the tops. My shoes are my greatest joy, black patent-leather miracles, and when one is nicked at the toe later that morning in class, my heart will break.

I am carrying a pencil, a pencil sharpener, and a small ten-cent tablet with a black-and-white speckled cover. My mother does not believe that a girl in kindergarten needs such things, so I am taking them only because of my insistent whining and because they are presents from our neighbors, Mary Keith and Blondelle Harris. Miss Mary and Miss Blondelle are watching my two younger sisters until my mother returns. The women are as precious to me as my mother and sisters. Out playing one day, I have overheard an older child, speaking to another child, call Miss Mary and Miss Blondelle a word that is brand new to me. This is my mother: When I say the word in fun to one of my sisters, my mother slaps me across the mouth and the word is lost for years and years.

All the way down New Jersey Avenue, the sidewalks are teeming with children. In my neighborhood, I have many friends, but I see none of them as my mother and I walk. We cross New York Avenue, we cross Pierce Street, and we cross L and K, and still I see no one who knows my name. At I Street, between New Jersey Avenue and Third Street, we enter Seaton Elementary School, a timeworn, sad-faced building across the street from my mother's church, Mt. Carmel Baptist.

Just inside the front door, women out of the advertisements in *Ebony* are greeting other parents and children. The woman who greets us has pearls thick as jumbo marbles that come down almost to her navel, and she acts as if she had known me all my life, touching my shoulder, cupping her hand under my chin. She is enveloped in a perfume that I only know is not gardenia. When, in answer to her question, my mother tells her that we live at 1227 New Jersey Avenue, the woman first seems to be picturing in her head where we live. Then she shakes her head and says that we are at the wrong school, that we should be at Walker-Jones.

My mother shakes her head vigorously. "I want her to go here," my mother says. "If I'da wanted her someplace else, I'da took her there." The woman continues to act as if she has known me all my life, but she tells my mother that we live beyond the area that Seaton serves. My mother is not convinced and for several more minutes she questions the woman about why I cannot attend Seaton. For as many Sundays as I can remember, perhaps even Sundays when I was in her womb, my mother has pointed across I Street to Seaton as we come and go to Mt. Carmel. "You gonna go there and learn about the whole world." But one of the guardians of that place is saying no, and no again. I am learning this about my mother: The higher up on the scale of respectability a person is—and teachers are rather high up in her eyes—the less she is liable to let them push her around. But finally, I see in her eyes the closing gate, and she takes my hand and we leave the building. On the steps, she stops as people move past us on either side.

"Mama, I can't go to school?"

She says nothing at first, then takes my hand again and we are down the steps quickly and nearing New Jersey Avenue before I can blink. This is my mother: She says, "One monkey don't stop no show."

Walker-Jones is a larger, newer school and I immediately like it because of that. But it is not across the street from my mother's church, her rock, one of her connections to God, and I sense her doubts as she absently rubs her thumb over the back of her hand. We find our way to the crowded auditorium where gray metal chairs are set up in the middle of the room. Along the wall to the left are tables and other chairs. Every chair seems occupied by a child or adult. Somewhere in the room a child is crying, a cry that rises above the buzz-talk of so many people. Strewn about the floor are dozens and dozens of pieces of white paper, and people are walking over them without any thought of picking them up. And seeing this lack of concern, I am all of a sudden afraid.

"Is this where they register for school?" my mother asks a woman at one of the tables.

10   The woman looks up slowly as if she has heard this question once too often. She nods. She is tiny, almost as small as the girl standing beside her. The woman's hair is set in a mass of curlers and all of those curlers are made of paper money, here a dollar bill, there a five-dollar bill. The girl's hair is arrayed in curls, but some of them are beginning to droop and this makes me happy. On the table beside the woman's pocketbook is a large notebook, worthy of someone in high school, and looking at me looking at the notebook, the girl places her hand possessively on it. In her other hand she holds several pencils with thick crowns of additional erasers.

"These the forms you gotta use?" my mother asks the woman, picking up a few pieces of the paper from the table. "Is this what you have to fill out?"

The woman tells her yes, but that she need fill out only one.

"I see," my mother says, looking about the room. Then: "Would you help me with this form? That is, if you don't mind."

The woman asks my mother what she means.

15   "This form. Would you mind helpin me fill it out?"

The woman still seems not to understand.

"I can't read it. I don't know how to read or write, and I'm askin you to help me." My mother looks at me, then looks away. I know almost all of her looks, but this one is brand new to me. "Would you help me, then?"

The woman says Why sure, and suddenly she appears happier, so much more satisfied with everything. She finishes the form for her daughter and my mother and I step aside to wait for her. We find two chairs nearby and sit. My mother is now diseased, according to the girl's eyes, and until the moment her mother takes her and the form to the front of the auditorium, the girl never stops looking at my mother. I stare back at her. "Don't stare," my mother says to me. "You know better than that."

Another woman out of the *Ebony* ads takes the woman's child away. Now, the woman says upon returning, let's see what we can do for you two.

My mother answers the questions the woman reads off the form. They start with my last name, and then on to the first and middle names. This is school, I think. This is going to school. My mother slowly enunciates each word of my name. This is my mother: As the questions go on, she takes from her pocketbook document after document, as if they will support my right to attend school, as if she has been saving them up for just this moment. Indeed, she takes out more papers than I have ever seen her do in other places: my birth certificate, my baptismal record, a doctor's letter concerning my bout with chicken pox, rent receipts, records of immunization, a letter about our public assistance payments, even her marriage license—every single paper that has anything even remotely to do with my five-year-old life. Few of the papers are needed here, but it does not matter and my mother continues to pull out the documents with the purposefulness of a magician pulling out a long string of scarves. She has learned that money is the beginning and end of everything in this world, and when the woman finishes, my mother offers her fifty cents, and the woman accepts it without hesitation. My mother and I are just about the last parent and child in the room.

My mother presents the form to a woman sitting in front of the stage, and the woman looks at it and writes something on a white card, which she gives to my mother. Before long, the woman who has taken the girl with the drooping curls appears from behind us, speaks to the sitting woman, and introduces herself to my mother and me. She's to be my teacher, she tells my mother. My mother stares.

We go into the hall, where my mother kneels down to me. Her lips are quivering. "I'll be back to pick you up at twelve o'clock. I don't want you to go nowhere. You just wait right here. And listen to every word she say." I touch her lips and press them together. It is an old, old game between us. She puts my hand down at my side, which is not part of the game. She stands and looks a second at the teacher, then she turns and walks away. I see where she has darned one of her socks the night before. Her shoes make loud sounds in the hall. She passes through the doors and I can still hear the loud sounds of her shoes. And even when the teacher turns me toward the classrooms and I hear what must be the singing and talking of all the children in the world, I can still hear my mother's footsteps above it all.

Responding to Reading

1. Why does the narrator's mother want to enroll her in Seaton Elementary School? Why is she unable to? What does the mother's reaction to this situation tell you about her?
2. What are the mother's limitations? What are her strengths?
3. Do you think that this story is primarily about the mother or her daughter? How do you explain the mother's reaction as she leaves her daughter? Why does the daughter still remember this reaction years later as she is telling this story? Why do you think the story ends with the sound of the mother's footsteps?

Responding in Writing

Write a paragraph describing your earliest memory of school.

——————— Focus ———————

How Much Do a College's Facilities Really Matter?

The eight photographs that follow show the campuses of two Iowa colleges: Grinnell College and Clarke College. In the April 7, 2006, issue of the *Chronicle of Higher Education,* a weekly publication for college faculty and administrators, these two schools were profiled in a special report entitled, "The Rich-Poor Gap Widens for Colleges and Students." As the report pointed out, Grinnell is an extremely wealthy college, with a 1.4 billion dollar endowment; Clarke, however, has a small endowment and therefore depends on tuition for most of its income. In one of the articles included in the report, the *Chronicle* noted, "By every statistical measure, the divide between the haves and the have-nots in higher education—among students as well as institutions—is growing." The pictures that accompanied the report (some of which are reproduced here) attempted to illustrate the have/have-not divide by contrasting various buildings and facilities on the two campuses.

Look closely at the photographs on the pages that follow, and read the captions that accompany them. Then, answer the questions below.

Responding to the Images

1. What do you consider to be a college's most important physical resources? Are any of these not pictured here?
2. On a tour of a college campus, what resources and facilities (other than the ones pictured here) would a tour guide show you? Are any of these items more important to you than the ones depicted on the pages that follow? Why?
3. On a sheet of paper, list the differences you see between the two labs, dining halls, fitness centers, and art galleries pictured here. Which differences are most striking in each case?
4. How important do you think a state-of-the-art fitness center is? Do you see it as important just for recruitment of new students, or do you think it adds in any way to the quality of a student's education?
5. Which of the items pictured here do you see as *most* important? Why? Which do you see as *least* important?
6. What kind of marketing efforts do you think a school like Clarke might use to recruit students? What kind of resources might be emphasized?

CHAPTER 2 FOCUS

7. Do you think it necessarily follows that the school with the more impressive physical plant offers a superior education? Why or why not?
8. Assuming that these pictures do indicate a significant disparity in the quality of the education the two schools offer, what do you see as the long-term consequences of such a gap?

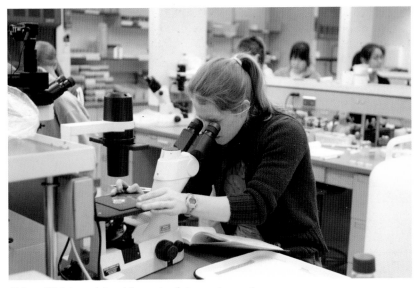

Grinnell biology lab with up-to-date equipment.

Clarke science lab, slated for updating when funds are available.

Traditional dining hall at Grinnell (to be replaced by dining venues in new student center).

Clarke dining hall.

Grinnell's state-of-the-art fitness center.

Clarke fitness center (in old gym).

Grinnell art museum, part of art center complex that includes three theaters.

Clarke art gallery.

WIDENING THE FOCUS

For Critical Thinking and Writing

Assume that you have been accepted at both Grinnell and Clarke. Your finances are limited, and neither school has offered you financial aid. You know that Grinnell has more resources and a bigger endowment, but Grinnell's tuition, fees, and room and board will cost you almost $10,000 a year more than Clarke's. Which school would you choose? Is it possible to get an equally strong education at either school? In making your decision, think carefully about whether it is worth the money to attend Grinnell instead of Clarke. What other factors—besides the physical appearance of the campus and the resources offered in the labs, dining halls, fitness centers, and art galleries depicted in this Focus section—would you consider in making your decision?

For Further Reading

The following readings can suggest additional perspectives for thinking and writing about the subject of inequality in education.

- Maya Angelou, "Graduation" (p. 103)

- Jim Sagal, "Baca Grande" (p. 137)

- Jonathan Kozol, "The Human Cost of an Illiterate Society" (p. 175)

- Robert Frost, "The Road Not Taken" (p. 000)

For Internet Research

To what extent does a college's Web site convey the college's quality of education? Visit Grinnell College's site at *<http://www.grinnell.edu/>* and Clarke College's site at *<http://www.clarke.edu/>* and read about some of the resources and facilities the two sites advertise. Then, write an essay in which you evaluate the schools' self-images as projected by the two sites. Which site makes its college more appealing? Be sure to support your position with examples and evidence from both sites.

WRITING

Issues in Education

1. Both Lynda Barry (p. 83) and Maya Angelou (p. 103) describe personal experiences related to their education. Write an essay in which you describe a positive or negative experience you have had with your own education. Be specific, and make sure you include plenty of vivid descriptive details.

2. Many of the essays in this chapter discuss the role of education in society. In the process, they try to define exactly what constitutes a "good" education. Write an essay in which you define a good education. Explain your view with specific references to essays in this chapter by john Holt (p. 86) and Daniel H. Pink (p. 91), as well as with examples from your own experience.

3. According to Christina Hoff Sommers (p. 121), instructors with conservative political views are being systematically excluded from many American colleges and universities. Write a letter to Sommers in which you agree or disagree with her contentions. Make sure that you address Sommers's specific points and that you use examples from both the essay and your own experience to support your position.

4. In his short story "The First Day (p.124)" Edward P. Jones tells the story of a child attending school for the first time. Write an essay in which you discuss your own first impressions of school. In what way have your impressions changed? How have they stayed the same? Do you agree with John Holt (p. 86) that traditional methods of education do more to hurt students than to help them?

5. In "School's Out" (p. 91), Daniel H. Pink quotes John Taylor Gatto, New York State's 1991 Teacher of the Year. According to Gatto, "School is like starting life with a 12-year jail sentence in which bad habits are the only curriculum truly learned" (14). Write an editorial for your school newspaper in which you agree or disagree with Gatto's observation—at least as it applies to the schools you have attended. Use your own experience as well as references to the essays in this chapter by Pink (p. 91) and by John Holt (p. 86).

6. In her essay "The Good Immigrant Student(p.113)," Bich Minh Nguyen discusses the difficulties immigrant students face in American schools. At one point in her essay she says that she has never "gotten over the terror of being called on in class, or the dread in knowing that I'm expected to contribute to class discussion" (27). Assume that you are a tutor in your school's writing center and that you have been asked to write an essay to be included in an orientation booklet. In this essay, your goal is to address the concerns

that Nguyen expresses. Be supportive, and give specific advice for overcoming these problems.

7. Define your educational philosophy. Then, choose one grade level, and design a curriculum that reflects your philosophy. Finally, write a proposal in which you present your ideal curriculum, referring to the ideas of at least one of the writers in this chapter.

8. All the writers in this chapter believe in the power of education to change a person. For many people, this process begins with a teacher who has a profound influence on them. Write an essay in which you discuss such a teacher. What, in your opinion, made this teacher so effective? In what ways did contact with this teacher change you?

9. Write an essay in which you develop a definition of good teaching, considering the relationship of the teacher to the class, the standards teachers should use to evaluate students, and what students should gain from their educational experience. Make sure you refer to the ideas of John Holt (p. 86) and Daniel H. Pink (p. 91) in your essay.

3

THE POLITICS
OF LANGUAGE

During the years he spent in prison, political activist Malcolm X became increasingly frustrated by his inability to express himself in writing, so he began the tedious and often frustrating task of copying words from the dictionary—page by page. The eventual result was that for the first time, he could pick up a book and read it with understanding: "Anyone who has read a great deal," he says, "can imagine the new world that opened." In addition, by becoming a serious reader, Malcolm X was able to develop the ideas about race, politics, and economics that he presented so forcefully after he was released from prison.

Abortion-rights demonstrators outside a Buffalo, New York, clinic

In our society, language is constantly manipulated for political ends. This fact should come as no surprise if we consider the potential power of words. Often, the power of a word comes not from its dictionary definition, or *denotation*, but from its *connotations*, the associations that surround it. Often these connotations are subtle, giving language the power to confuse and even to harm. For example, whether a doctor who performs an abortion is "terminating a pregnancy" or "murdering a preborn child" is not just a matter of semantics. It is also a political issue, one that has provoked not only debate but also violence. This potential for misunderstanding, disagreement, deception, and possibly danger makes careful word choice very important.

The Focus section of this chapter (p. 201) addresses the question, "How Free Should Free Speech Be?" As the essays in this section illustrate, the answer to this question is by no means simple. In "The Free-Speech Follies," Stanley Fish makes the point that the First Amendment is often misused and misinterpreted by those who seek to invoke it. In "A Chill Wind Is Blowing in This Nation," Tim Robbins implies that his constitutional rights were taken away after he spoke out against the war in Iraq. And finally, in "It's Time to Junk the Double Standard on Free Speech," Stuart Taylor, Jr. accuses the media of having a double standard when it comes to making the case for freedom of speech.

Antiabortion demonstrators outside a Buffalo, New York, clinic

PREPARING TO READ AND WRITE

As you read and prepare to write about the essays in this chapter, you may consider the following questions:

- Does the selection deal primarily with written or spoken language?

- Does the writer place more emphasis on the denotations or the connotations of words?

- Does the writer make any distinctions between language applied to males and language applied to females? Do you consider such distinctions valid?

- Does the writer discuss language in the context of a particular culture? Does he or she see language as a unifying or a divisive factor?

- In what ways would the writer like to change or reshape language? What do you see as the possible advantages or disadvantages of such change?

- Does the writer believe that people are shaped by language or that language is shaped by people?

- Does the writer see language as having a particular social or political function? In what sense?

- Does the writer see language as empowering?

- Does the writer make assumptions about people's status on the basis of their use of language? Do these assumptions seem justified?

- Does the writer make a convincing case for the importance of language?

- Is the writer's focus primarily on language's ability to help or its power to harm?

- In what ways are your ideas about the power of words similar to or different from the writer's?

- How is the essay like and unlike other essays in this chapter?

BACA GRANDE[1]

Jim Sagel

1947–1998

Poet, playwright, fiction and nonfiction writer, and bilingual educator, Jim Sagel often focused on the language and culture of northern New Mexico in his numerous works. The recipient of several awards, Sagel won the 1997 El Premio Literario Cuidad de San Sebastián, Spain, for the best Spanish play. The following poem, "Baca Grande," explores the ways in which language shapes experience.

> *Una vaca se topó con un ratón y le dice:*
> *"Tú—¿tan chiquito y con bigote?" Y le responde el ratón:*
> *"Y tú tan grandota—¿y sin brassiere?"[2]*

It was nearly a miracle
James Baca remembered anyone at all
from the old hometown gang
having been two years at Yale
    no less   5
and halfway through law school
at the University of California at Irvine
They hardly recognized him either
in his three-piece grey business suit
and surfer-swirl haircut   10
with just the menacing hint
of a tightly trimmed Zapata moustache
    for cultural balance
and relevance

He had come to deliver the keynote address   15
to the graduating class of 80
at his old alma mater
and show off his well-trained lips
which laboriously parted
    each Kennedyish "R"   20
and drilled the first person pronoun
through the microphone
like an oil bit
with the slick, elegantly honed phrases
that slid so smoothly   25

---

[1]*Baca Grande: Baca* is both a phonetic spelling of the Spanish word *vaca* (cow) and the last name of one of the poem's characters. *Grande* means "large."

[2]*Una . . . brassiere?:* A cow ran into a rat and said: "You—so small and with a moustache?" The rat responded: "And you—so big and without a bra?"

off his meticulously bleached
    tongue
He talked Big Bucks
with astronautish fervor and if he
30   the former bootstrapless James A. Baca
could dazzle the ass
off the universe
then even you
    yes you

35   Joey Martinez toying with your yellow
      tassle
and staring dumbly into space
could emulate Mr. Baca someday
      possibly
40   well
there was of course
such a thing
as being an outrageously successful
gas station attendant too
45   let us never forget
it doesn't really matter what you do
so long as you excel
never believing a word
50   of it
for he had already risen
        as high as they go

Wasn't nobody else
from this deprived environment
55   who'd ever jumped
      straight out of college
into the Governor's office
and maybe one day
he'd sit in that big chair
60   himself
and when he did
he'd forget this damned town
and all the petty little people
in it
65   once and for all

That much he promised himself

Responding to Reading

1. Who is the poem's speaker? What can you infer about the speaker from his
    language? How is his language different from James Baca's?

2. Why is Baca visiting the speaker's school? What ideas is he supposed to convey to his audience? What ideas do you think he actually conveys?
3. List the words and phrases that identify this poem's diction as informal. Do you think this informality is a strength or a weakness?

Responding in Writing

What comment does the poem make about James Baca? What comment does it make about the social divisions between the speaker and Baca? Do you think the speaker's observations are valid?

ARIA[1]

Richard Rodriguez

1944–

The son of Mexican-American immigrants, Richard Rodriguez earned a Ph.D. in Renaissance literature from the University of California at Berkeley (1975). His most recent books include Days of Obligation: An Argument with My Mexican Father *(1992) and* Brown: The Last Discovery of America *(2002). Currently a journalist and author, Rodriguez is a frequent contributor to National Public Radio and an editor for the Pacific News Service (PNS) as well as a contributing editor for* Harpers' *Magazine, U.S. News and World Report, and the* Los Angeles Times. *In 1997, he won a George Foster Peabody Award for his NewsHour Essays on American Life. The following selection is from Rodriguez's first book,* The Hunger of Memory: The Education of Richard Rodriguez *(1982). In this memoir, he writes about the experience of growing up in a Spanish-speaking home and adapting to the English-speaking community around him.*

Supporters of bilingual education today imply that students like me miss a great deal by not being taught in their family's language. What they seem not to recognize is that, as a socially disadvantaged child, I considered Spanish to be a private language. What I needed to learn in school was that I had the right—and the obligation—to speak the public language of *los gringos*.[2] The odd truth is that my first-grade classmates could have become bilingual, in the conventional sense of that word, more easily than I. Had they been taught (as upper-middle-class children are often taught early) a second language like Spanish or French, they could have regarded it simply as that: another public language. In my case such bilingualism could not have been so quickly achieved. What I did not believe was that I could speak a single public language.

---

[1]Solo vocal piece with instrumental accompaniment or melody. [Eds.]
[2]Foreigners, especially Americans. [Eds.]

Without question, it would have pleased me to hear my teachers address me in Spanish when I entered the classroom. I would have felt much less afraid. I would have trusted them and responded with ease. But I would have delayed—for how long postponed?—having to learn the language of public society, I would have evaded—and for how long could I have afforded to delay?—learning the great lesson of school, that I had a public identity.

Fortunately, my teachers were unsentimental about their responsibility. What they understood was that I needed to speak a public language. So their voices would search me out, asking me questions. Each time I'd hear them, I'd look up in surprise to see a nun's face frowning at me. I'd mumble, not really meaning to answer. The nun would persist, "Richard, stand up. Don't look at the floor. Speak up. Speak to the entire class, not just to me!" But I couldn't believe that the English language was mine to use. (In part, I did not want to believe it.) I continued to mumble. I resisted the teacher's demands. (Did I somehow suspect that once I learned public language my pleasing family life would be changed?) Silent, waiting for the bell to sound, I remained dazed, diffident, afraid.

Because I wrongly imagined that English was intrinsically a public language and Spanish an intrinsically private one, I easily noted the difference between classroom language and the language of home. At school, words were directed to a general audience of listeners. ("Boys and girls.") Words were meaningfully ordered. And the point was not self-expression alone but to make oneself understood by many others. The teacher quizzed: "Boys and girls, why do we use that word in this sentence? Could we think of a better word to use there? Would the sentence change its meaning if the words were differently arranged? And wasn't there a better way of saying much the same thing?" (I couldn't say. I wouldn't try to say.)

5   Three months. Five. Half a year passed. Unsmiling, ever watchful, my teachers noted my silence. They began to connect my behavior with the difficult progress my older sister and brother were making. Until one Saturday morning three nuns arrived at the house to talk to our parents. Stiffly, they sat on the blue living room sofa. From the doorway of another room, spying the visitors, I noted the incongruity—the clash of two worlds, the faces and voices of school intruding upon the familiar setting of home. I overheard one voice gently wondering, "Do your children speak only Spanish at home, Mrs. Rodriguez?" While another voice added, "That Richard especially seems so timid and shy."

That Rich-heard!

With great tact the visitors continued, "Is it possible for you and your husband to encourage your children to practice their English when they are home?" Of course, my parents complied. What would they not do for their children's well-being? And how could they have questioned the Church's authority which those women represented? In an instant, they agreed to give up the language (the sounds) that had revealed and accentuated our family's closeness. The moment after the visitors left, the change was observed, "*Ahora,* speak to us *en inglés,*"[3] my father and mother united to tell us.

At first, it seemed a kind of game. After dinner each night, the family gathered to practice "our" English. (It was still then *inglés,* a language foreign to us, so we felt drawn as strangers to it.) Laughing, we would try to define words we could not pronounce. We played with strange English sounds, often overanglicizing our pronunciations. And we filled the smiling gaps of our sentences with familiar Spanish sounds. But that was cheating, somebody shouted. Everyone laughed. In school, meanwhile, like my brother and sister, I was required to attend a daily tutoring session. I needed a full year of special attention. I also needed my teachers to keep my attention from straying in class by calling out, *Rich-heard*—their English voices slowly prying loose my ties to my other name, its three notes, *Ri-car-do.* Most of all I needed to hear my mother and father speak to me in a moment of seriousness in broken—suddenly heartbreaking—English. The scene was inevitable: One Saturday morning I entered the kitchen where my parents were talking in Spanish. I did not realize that they were talking in Spanish however until, at the moment they saw me, I heard their voices change to speak English. Those *gringo* sounds they uttered startled me. Pushed me away. In that moment of trivial misunderstanding and profound insight, I felt my throat twisted by unsounded grief. I turned away quickly and left the room. But I had no place to escape to with Spanish. (The spell was broken.) My brother and sisters were speaking English in another part of the house.

Again and again in the days following, increasingly angry, I was obliged to hear my mother and father: "Speak to us *en inglés*" (*Speak.*) Only then did I determine to learn classroom English. Weeks after, it happened: One day in school I raised my hand to volunteer an answer. I spoke out in a loud voice. And I did not think it remarkable when the entire class understood. That day, I moved very far from the disadvantaged child I had been only days earlier. The belief, that calming assurance that I belonged in public, had at last taken hold.

Shortly after, I stopped hearing the high and loud sounds of *los* 10 *gringos.* A more and more confident speaker of English, I didn't trouble to listen to *how* strangers sounded, speaking to me. And there simply were too many English-speaking people in my day for me to hear American accents anymore. Conversations quickened. Listening to persons who sounded eccentrically pitched voices, I usually noted

---

[3]"Now, speak to us in English." [Eds.]

their sounds for an initial few seconds before I concentrated on *what* they were saying. Conversations became content-full. Transparent. Hearing someone's *tone* of voice—angry or questioning or sarcastic or happy or sad—I didn't distinguish it from the words it expressed. Sound and word were thus tightly wedded. At the end of a day, I was often bemused, always relieved, to realized how "silent," though crowded with words, my day in public had been. (This public silence measured and quickened the change in my life.)

At last, seven years old, I came to believe what had been technically true since my birth; I was an American citizen.

But the special feeling of closeness at home was diminished by then. Gone was the desperate, urgent, intense feeling of being at home, rare was the experience of feeling myself individualized by family intimates. We remained a loving family, but one greatly changed. No longer so close; no longer bound tight by the pleasing and troubling knowledge of our public separateness. Neither my older brother nor sister rushed home after school anymore. Nor did I. When I arrived home there would often be neighborhood kids in the house. Or the house would be empty of sounds.

Following the dramatic Americanization of their children, even my parents grew more publicly confident. Especially my mother. She learned the names of all the people on our block. And she decided we needed to have a telephone installed in the house. My father continued to use the word *gringo.* But it was no longer charged with the old bitterness of distrust. (Stripped of any emotional content, the word simply became a name for those Americans not of Hispanic descent.) Hearing him, sometimes, I wasn't sure if he was pronouncing the Spanish word *gringo* or saying gringo in English.

Matching the silence I started hearing in public was a new quiet at home. The family's quiet was partly due to the fact that, as we children learned more and more English, we shared fewer and fewer words with our parents. Sentences needed to be spoken slowly when a child addressed his mother or father. (Often the parent wouldn't understand.) The child would need to repeat himself. (Still the parent misunderstood.) The young voice, frustrated, would end up saying, "Never mind"—the subject was closed. Dinners would be noisy with the clinking of knives and forks against dishes. My mother would smile softly between her remarks; my father at the other end of the table would chew and chew at his food, while he stared over the heads of his children.

15   My *mother!* My *father!* After English became my primary language, I no longer knew what words to use in addressing my parents. The old Spanish words (those tender accents of sound) I had used earlier—*mamá* and *papá*—I couldn't use anymore. They would have been too painful reminders of how much had changed in my life. On

the other hand, the words I heard neighborhood kids call their parents seemed equally unsatisfactory. *Mother* and *Father; Ma, Papa, Pa, Dad, Pop* (how I hated the all American sound of that last word especially)—all these terms I felt were unsuitable, not really terms of address for my parents. As a result, I never used them at home. Whenever I'd speak to my parents, I would try to get their attention with eye contact alone. In public conversations, I'd refer to "my parents" or "my mother and father."

My mother and father, for their part, responded differently, as their children spoke to them less. She grew restless, seemed troubled and anxious at the scarcity of words exchanged in the house. It was she who would question me about my day when I came home from school. She smiled at small talk. She pried at the edges of my sentences to get me to say something more. (What?) She'd join conversations she overheard, but her intrusions often stopped her children's talking. By contrast, my father seemed reconciled to the new quiet. Though his English improved somewhat, he retired into silence. At dinner he spoke very little. One night his children and even his wife helplessly giggled at his garbled English pronunciation of the Catholic Grace before Meals. Thereafter he made his wife recite the prayer at the start of each meal, even on formal occasions, when there were guests in the house. Hers became the public voice of the family. On official business, it was she, not my father, one would usually hear on the phone or in stores, talking to strangers. His children grew so accustomed to his silence that, years later, they would speak routinely of his shyness. (My mother would often try to explain: Both his parents died when he was eight. He was raised by an uncle who treated him like little more than a menial servant. He was never encouraged to speak. He grew up alone. A man of few words.) But my father was not shy, I realized, when I'd watch him speaking Spanish with relatives. Using Spanish, he was quickly effusive. Especially when talking with other men, his voice would spark, flicker, flare alive with sounds. In Spanish, he expressed ideas and feelings he rarely revealed in English. With firm Spanish sounds, he conveyed confidence and authority English would never allow him.

The silence at home, however, was finally more than a literal silence. Fewer words passed between parent and child, but more profound was the silence that resulted from my inattention to sounds. At about the time I no longer bothered to listen with care to the sounds of English in public, I grew careless about listening to the sounds family members made when they spoke. Most of the time I heard someone speaking at home and didn't distinguish his sounds from the words people uttered in public. I didn't even pay much attention to my parents' accented and ungrammatical speech. At least not at home. Only when I was with them in public would I grow alert to their accents. Though, even then, their sounds caused me less and less concern. For I was increasingly confident of my own public identity.

I would have been happier about my public success had I not sometimes recalled what it had been like earlier, when my family had conveyed its intimacy through a set of conveniently private sounds. Sometimes in public, hearing a stranger, I'd hark back to my past. A Mexican farmworker approached me downtown to ask directions to somewhere, "¿*Hijito* . . .?"[4] he said. And his voice summoned deep longing. Another time, standing beside my mother in the visiting room of a Carmelite convent, before the dense screen which rendered the nuns shadowy figures, I heard several Spanish-speaking nuns—their busy, singsong overlapping voices—assure us that yes, yes, we were remembered, all our family was remembered in their prayers. (Their voices echoed faraway family sounds.) Another day, a dark-faced old woman—her hand light on my shoulder—steadied herself against me as she boarded a bus. She murmured something I couldn't quite comprehend. Her Spanish voice came near, like the face of a never-before-seen relative in the instant before I was kissed. Her voice, like so many of the Spanish voices I'd hear in public, recalled the golden age of my youth. Hearing Spanish then, I continued to be a careful, if sad, listener to sounds. Hearing a Spanish-speaking family walking behind me, I turned to look. I smiled for an instant, before my glance found the Hispanic-looking faces of strangers in the crowd going by.

Today I hear bilingual educators say that children lose a degree of "individuality" by becoming assimilated into public society. (Bilingual schooling was popularized in the seventies, that decade when middle-class ethnics began to resist the process of assimilation—the American melting pot.) But the bilingualists simplistically scorn the value and necessity of assimilation. They do not seem to realize that there are *two* ways a person is individualized. So they do not realize that while one suffers a diminished sense of *private* individuality by becoming assimilated into public society, such assimilation makes possible the achievement of *public* individuality.

20   The bilingualists insist that a student should be reminded of his difference from others in mass society, his heritage. But they equate mere separateness with individuality. The fact is that only in private—with intimates—is separateness from the crowd a prerequisite for individuality. (An intimate draws me apart, tells me that I am unique, unlike all others.) In public, by contrast, full individuality is achieved, paradoxically, by those who are able to consider themselves members of the crowd. Thus it happened for me: Only when I was able to think

---

[4]"Little boy . . .?" [Eds.]

of myself as an American, no longer an alien in *gringo* society, could I seek the rights and opportunities necessary for full public individuality. The social and political advantages I enjoy as a man result from the day that I came to believe that my name, indeed, is *Rich-heard Road-ree-guess*. It is true that my public society today is often impersonal. (My public society is usually mass society.) Yet despite the anonymity of the crowd and despite the fact that the individuality I achieve in public is often tenuous—because it depends on my being one in a crowd—I celebrate the day I acquired my new name. Those middle-class ethnics who scorn assimilation seem to me filled with decadent self-pity, obsessed by the burden of public life. Dangerously, they romanticize public separateness and they trivialize the dilemma of the socially disadvantaged.

My awkward childhood does not prove the necessity of bilingual education. My story discloses instead an essential myth of childhood—inevitable pain. If I rehearse here the changes in my private life after my Americanization, it is finally to emphasize the public gain. The loss implies the gain: The house I returned to each afternoon was quiet. Intimate sounds no longer rushed to the door to greet me. There were other noises inside. The telephone rang. Neighborhood kids ran past the door of the bedroom where I was reading my school-books—covered with shopping-bag paper. Once I learned public language, it would never again be easy for me to hear intimate family voices. More and more of my day was spent hearing words. But that may only be a way of saying that the day I raised my hand in class and spoke loudly to an entire roomful of faces, my childhood started to end.

Responding to Reading

1. What distinction does Rodriguez make between public and private language? What point does this distinction help him make?
2. What does Rodriguez say he gains by speaking English? What does he say he loses? Do you agree with his assessment?
3. What is Rodriguez's main argument against those who support bilingual education? What evidence does he use to support his argument? How convincing is he?

Responding in Writing

Do you agree with Rodriguez's opposition to bilingual education, or do you think that children who do not speak English should be taught in their native language?

TWO LANGUAGES IN MIND, BUT JUST ONE IN THE HEART

Louise Erdrich

1954–

Of German and Chippewa descent, Louise Erdrich grew up in Wahpeton, North Dakota, on the Minnesota border, where her parents taught at the Bureau of Indian Affairs school. In 1972, Erdrich was among the first women admitted to Dartmouth College, where she majored in English and creative writing and took courses in Native American Studies. Erdrich's first collection of stories, published as the novel Love Medicine *(1979), won a National Book Critics Circle Award. Recent works include* The Master Butchers Singing Club *(2003);* The Game of Silence *(2005), a children's book; and* The Painted Drums: A Novel *(2005). Known for her moving and often humorous portrayals of Chippewa life, Erdrich draws on her heritage to portray the endurance of women and Native Americans. In the following essay, she writes about her enduring love for Ojibwe, the language of the Chippewa people.*

For years now I have been in love with a language other than the English in which I write, and it is a rough affair. Every day I try to learn a little more Ojibwe. I have taken to carrying verb conjugation charts in my purse, along with the tiny notebook I've always kept for jotting down book ideas, overheard conversations, language detritus, phrases that pop into my head. Now that little notebook includes an increasing volume of Ojibwe words. My English is jealous, my Ojibwe elusive. Like a besieged unfaithful lover, I'm trying to appease them both.

Ojibwemowin, or Anishinabemowin, the Chippewa language, was last spoken in our family by Patrick Gourneau, my maternal grandfather, a Turtle Mountain Ojibwe who used it mainly in his prayers. Growing up off reservation, I thought Ojibwemowin mainly was a language for prayers, like Latin in the Catholic liturgy. I was unaware for many years that Ojibwemowin was spoken in Canada, Minnesota and Wisconsin, though by a dwindling number of people. By the time I began to study the language, I was living in New Hampshire, so for the first few years I used language tapes.

I never learned more than a few polite phrases that way, but the sound of the language in the author Basil Johnson's calm and dignified Anishinabe voice sustained me through bouts of homesickness. I spoke basic Ojibwe in the isolation of my car traveling here and there on twisting New England roads. Back then, as now, I carried my tapes everywhere.

The language bit deep into my heart, but it was an unfulfilled longing. I had nobody to speak it with, nobody who remembered my grandfather's standing with his sacred pipe in the woods next to a box elder tree, talking to the spirits. Not until I moved back to the Midwest and settled in Minneapolis did I find a fellow Ojibweg to learn with, and a teacher.

Mille Lac's Ojibwe elder Jim Clark—Naawi-giizis, or Center of the Day—is a magnetically pleasant, sunny, crew-cut World War II veteran with a mysterious kindliness that shows in his slightest gesture. When he laughs, everything about him laughs; and when he is serious, his eyes round like a boy's.

Naawi-giizis introduced me to the deep intelligence of the language and forever set me on a quest to speak it for one reason: I want to get the jokes. I also want to understand the prayers and the adisookaanug, the sacred stories, but the irresistible part of language for me is the explosion of hilarity that attends every other minute of an Ojibwe visit. As most speakers are now bilingual, the language is spiked with puns on both English and Ojibwe, most playing on the oddness of gichi-mookomaan, that is, big knife or American, habits and behavior.

This desire to deepen my alternate language puts me in an odd relationship to my first love, English. It is, after all, the language stuffed into my mother's ancestors' mouths. English is the reason she didn't speak her native language and the reason I can barely limp along in mine. English is an all-devouring language that has moved across North America like the fabulous plagues of locusts that darkened the sky and devoured even the handles of rakes and hoes. Yet the omnivorous nature of a colonial language is a writer's gift. Raised in the English language, I partake of a mongrel feast.

A hundred years ago most Ojibwe people spoke Ojibwemowin, but the Bureau of Indian Affairs and religious boarding schools punished and humiliated children who spoke native languages. The program worked, and there are now almost no fluent speakers of Ojibwe in the United States under the age of 30. Speakers like Naawi-giizis value the language partly because it has been physically beaten out of so many people. Fluent speakers have had to fight for the language with their own flesh, have endured ridicule, have resisted shame and stubbornly pledged themselves to keep on talking the talk.

My relationship is of course very different. How do you go back to a language you never had? Why should a writer who loves her first language find it necessary and essential to complicate her life with another? Simple reasons, personal and impersonal. In the past few years I've found that I can talk to God only in this language, that somehow my grandfather's use of the language penetrated. The sound comforts me.

10   What the Ojibwe call the Gizhe Manidoo, the great and kind spirit residing in all that lives, what the Lakota call the Great Mystery, is associated for me with the flow of Ojibwemowin. My Catholic training touched me intellectually and symbolically but apparently never engaged my heart.

There is also this: Ojibwemowin is one of the few surviving languages that evolved to the present here in North America. The intelligence of this language is adapted as no other to the philosophy bound up in northern land, lakes, rivers, forests, arid plains; to the animals and their particular habits; to the shades of meaning in the very placement of stones. As a North American writer it is essential to me that I try to understand our human relationship to place in the deepest way possible, using my favorite tool, language.

There are place names in Ojibwe and Dakota for every physical feature of Minnesota, including recent additions like city parks and dredged lakes. Ojibwemowin is not static, not confined to describing the world of some out-of-reach and sacred past. There are words for e-mail, computers, Internet, fax. For exotic animals in zoos. Anaamibiig gookoosh, the underwater pig, is a hippopotamus. Nandookomeshiinh, the lice hunter, is the monkey.

There are words for the serenity prayer used in 12-step programs and translations of nursery rhymes. The varieties of people other than Ojibwe or Anishinabe are also named: Aiibiishaabookewininiwag, the tea people, are Asians. Agongosininiwag, the chipmunk people, are Scandinavians. I'm still trying to find out why.

For years I saw only the surface of Ojibwemowin. With any study at all one looks deep into a stunning complex of verbs. Ojibwemowin is a language of verbs. All action. Two-thirds of the words are verbs, and for each verb there are as many as 6,000 forms. The storm of verb forms makes it a wildly adaptive and powerfully precise language. Changite-ige describes the way a duck tips itself up in the water butt first. There is a word for what would happen if a man fell off a motorcycle with a pipe in his mouth and the stem of it went through the back of his head. There can be a verb for anything.

15   When it comes to nouns, there is some relief. There aren't many objects. With a modest if inadvertent political correctness, there are no designations of gender in Ojibwemowin. There are no feminine or masculine possessives or articles.

Nouns are mainly designated as alive or dead, animate or inanimate. The word for stone, asin, is animate. Stones are called grandfathers and grandmothers and are extremely important in Ojibwe philosophy. Once I began to think of stones as animate, I started to wonder whether I was picking up a stone or it was putting itself into my hand. Stones are not the same as they were to me in English. I can't write about a stone without considering it in Ojibwe and acknowledging that the Anishinabe universe began with a conversation between stones.

Ojibwemowin is also a language of emotions; shades of feeling can be mixed like paints. There is a word for what occurs when your heart is silently shedding tears. Ojibwe is especially good at describing intellectual states and the fine points of moral responsibility.

Ozozamenimaa pertains to a misuse of one's talents getting out of control. Ozozamichige implies you can still set things right. There are many more kinds of love than there are in English. There are myriad shades of emotional meaning to designate various family and clan members. It is a language that also recognizes the humanity of a creaturely God, and the absurd and wondrous sexuality of even the most deeply religious beings.

Slowly the language has crept into my writing, replacing a word here, a concept there, beginning to carry weight. I've thought of course of writing stories in Ojibwe, like a reverse Nabokov. With my Ojibwe at the level of a dreamy 4-year-old child's, I probably won't.

Though it was not originally a written language, people simply 20 adapted the English alphabet and wrote phonetically. During the Second World War, Naawi-giizis wrote Ojibwe letters to his uncle from Europe. He spoke freely about his movements, as no censor could understand his writing. Ojibwe orthography has recently been standardized. Even so, it is an all-day task for me to write even one paragraph using verbs in their correct arcane forms. And even then, there are so many dialects of Ojibwe that, for many speakers, I'll still have gotten it wrong.

As awful as my own Ojibwe must sound to a fluent speaker, I have never, ever, been greeted with a moment of impatience or laughter. Perhaps people wait until I've left the room. But more likely, I think, there is an urgency about attempting to speak the language. To Ojibwe speakers the language is a deeply loved entity. There is a spirit or an originating genius belonging to each word.

Before attempting to speak this language, a learner must acknowledge these spirits with gifts of tobacco and food. Anyone who attempts Ojibwemowin is engaged in something more than learning tongue twisters. However awkward my nouns, unstable my verbs, however stumbling my delivery, to engage in the language is to engage the spirit. Perhaps that is what my teachers know, and what my English will forgive.

Responding to Reading

1. Why did Erdrich want to learn Ojibwe? What difficulties did she have with this language? How did she overcome these difficulties?
2. Why did the Bureau of Indian Affairs and religious boarding schools punish and humiliate "children who spoke native languages" (8)?

3. What advantages does Ojibwe have over English? What effect has learning Ojibwe had on Erdrich? What does she mean when she says, "to engage in the language is to engage the spirit" (22)?

Responding in Writing

Does your family speak a language other than English? What emotional ties, if any, do you have to this language?

LEARNING TO READ AND WRITE

Frederick Douglass
1817?–1895

Frederick Douglass was born a slave in rural Talbot County, Maryland, and later served a family in Baltimore. After escaping to the North in 1838, he settled in Bedford, Massachusetts, where he became active in the abolitionist movement. He recounts these experiences in his most famous work, Narrative of the Life of Frederick Douglass *(1845). After spending almost two years in England and Europe on a lecture tour, Douglass returned to the United States and purchased his freedom. In 1847, he launched the antislavery newspaper* The North Star *and became a vocal supporter of both Abraham Lincoln and the Civil War. Throughout his life, Douglass believed that the United States Constitution, if interpreted correctly, would enable African Americans to become full participants in the economic, social, and intellectual life of America. In the following excerpt from his* Narrative, *Douglass writes of outwitting his owners to become literate, thereby finding "the pathway from slavery to freedom."*

I lived in Master Hugh's family about seven years. During this time, I succeeded in learning to read and write. In accomplishing this, I was compelled to resort to various stratagems. I had no regular teacher. My mistress, who had kindly commenced to instruct me, had, in compliance with the advice and direction of her husband, not only ceased to instruct, but had set her face against my being instructed by any one else. It is due, however, to my mistress to say of her, that she did not adopt this course of treatment immediately. She at first lacked the depravity indispensable to shutting me up in mental darkness. It was at least necessary for her to have some training in the exercise of irresponsible power, to make her equal to the task of treating me as though I were a brute.

My mistress was, as I have said, a kind and tender-hearted woman; and in the simplicity of her soul she commenced, when I first went to live with her, to treat me as she supposed one human being ought to treat another. In entering upon the duties of a slaveholder, she did not seem to perceive that I sustained to her the relation of a mere chattel,[1] and that for her to treat me as a human being was not only wrong, but dangerously so. Slavery proved as injurious to her as it did to me. When I went there, she was a pious, warm, and tender-hearted woman. There was no sorrow or suffering for which she had not a tear. She had bread for the hungry, clothes for the naked, and comfort for every mourner that came within her reach. Slavery soon proved its ability to divest her of these heavenly qualities. Under its influence, the tender heart became stone, and the lamblike disposition gave way to one of tigerlike fierceness. The first step in her downward course was in her ceasing to instruct me. She now commenced to practice her husband's precepts. She finally became even more violent in her opposition than her husband himself. She was not satisfied with simply doing as well as he had commanded; she seemed anxious to do better. Nothing seemed to make her more angry than to see me with a newspaper. She seemed to think that here lay the danger. I have had her rush at me with a face made all up of fury, and snatch from me a newspaper, in a manner that fully revealed her apprehension. She was an apt woman; and a little experience soon demonstrated, to her satisfaction, that education and slavery were incompatible with each other.

From this time I was most narrowly watched. If I was in a separate room any considerable length of time, I was sure to be suspected of having a book, and was at once called to give an account of myself. All this, however, was too late. The first step had been taken. Mistress, in teaching me the alphabet, had given me the *inch*, and no precaution could prevent me from taking the *ell*.

The plan which I adopted, and the one by which I was most successful, was that of making friends of all the little white boys whom I met in the street. As many of these as I could, I converted into teachers. With their kindly aid, obtained at different times and in different places, I finally succeeded in learning to read. When I was sent on errands, I always took my book with me, and by going one part of my errand quickly, I found time to get a lesson before my return. I used also to carry bread with me, enough of which was always in the house, and to which I was always welcome; for I was much better off in this regard than many of the poor white children in our neighborhood. This bread I used to bestow upon the hungry little urchins, who, in return, would give me that more valuable bread of knowledge. I am strongly tempted to give the names of two or three of those little boys, as a testimonial of the gratitude and affection I bear them; but prudence forbids;—not that it would injure me, but it might embarrass them; for it is almost an unpardonable offense to teach slaves to read in this Christian country. It is enough to say of the dear little fellows, that they lived on Philpot Street, very near Durgin and Bailey's

---

[1]Property. [Eds.]

ship-yard. I used to talk this matter of slavery over with them. I would sometimes say to them, I wished I could be as free as they would be when they got to be men. "You will be free as soon as you are twenty-one, *but I am a slave for life!* Have not I as good a right to be free as you have?" These words used to trouble them; they would express for me the liveliest sympathy, and console me with the hope that something would occur by which I might be free.

5   I was now about twelve years old, and the thought of being *a slave for life* began to bear heavily upon my heart. Just about this time, I got hold of a book entitled "The Columbian Orator."[2] Every opportunity I got, I used to read this book. Among much of other interesting matter, I found in it a dialogue between a master and his slave. The slave was represented as having run away from his master three times. The dialogue represented the conversation which took place between them, when the slave was retaken the third time. In this dialogue, the whole argument in behalf of slavery was brought forward by the master, all of which was disposed of by the slave. The slave was made to say some very smart as well as impressive things in reply to his master— things which had the desired though unexpected effect; for the conversation resulted in the voluntary emancipation of the slave on the part of the master.

In the same book, I met with one of Sheridan's might speeches on and in behalf of Catholic emancipation.[3] These were choice documents to me. I read them over and over again with unabated interest. They gave tongue to interesting thoughts of my own soul, which had frequently flashed through my mind, and died away for want of utterance. The moral which I gained from the dialogue was the power of truth over the conscience of even a slaveholder. What I got from Sheridan was a bold denunciation of slavery, and a powerful vindication of human rights. The reading of these documents enabled me to utter my thoughts, and to meet the arguments brought forward to sustain slavery; but while they relieved me of one difficulty, they brought on another even more painful than the one of which I was relieved. The more I read, the more I was led to abhor and detest my enslavers. I could regard them in no other light than a band of successful robbers, who had left their homes, and gone to Africa, and stolen us from our homes, and in a strange land reduced us to slavery. I loathed them as being the meanest as well as the most wicked of men. As I read and contemplated the subject, behold! that very discontentment which Master Hugh had predicted would follow my learning to read had already come, to torment and sting my soul to

---

[2]A popular textbook that taught the principles of effective public speaking. [Eds.]

[3]Richard Brinsley Sheridan (1751–1816), British playwright and statesman who made speeches supporting the right of English Catholics to vote. Full emancipation was not granted to Catholics until 1829. [Eds.]

unutterable anguish. As I writhed under it, I would at times feel that learning to read had been a curse rather than a blessing. It had given me a view of my wretched condition, without the remedy. It opened my eyes to the horrible pit, but to no ladder upon which to get out. In moments of agony, I envied my fellow-slaves for their stupidity. I have often wished myself a beast. I preferred the condition of the meanest reptile to my own. Any thing, no matter what, to get rid of thinking! It was the everlasting thinking of my condition that tormented me. There was no getting rid of it. It was pressed upon me by every object within sight or hearing, animate or inanimate. The silver trump of freedom had roused my soul to eternal wakefulness. Freedom now appeared, to disappear no more forever. It was heard in every sound, and seen in every thing. It was ever present to torment me with a sense of my wretched condition. I saw nothing without seeing it, I heard nothing without hearing it, and felt nothing without feeling it. It looked from every star, it smiled in every calm, breathed in every wind, and moved in every storm.

I often found myself regretting my own existence, and wishing myself dead; and but for the hope of being free, I have no doubt but that I should have killed myself, or done something for which I should have been killed. While in this state of mind, I was eager to hear any one speak of slavery. I was a ready listener. Every little while, I could hear something about the abolitionists. It was some time before I found what the word meant. It was always used in such connections as to make it an interesting word to me. If a slave ran away and succeeded in getting clear, or if a slave killed his master, set fire to a barn, or did any thing very wrong in the mind of a slave-holder, it was spoken of as the fruit of *abolition*. Hearing the word in this connection very often, I set about learning what it meant. The dictionary afforded me little or no help. I found it was "the act of abolishing"; but then I did not know what was to be abolished. Here I was perplexed. I did not dare to ask any one about its meaning, for I was satisfied that it was something they wanted me to know very little about. After a patient waiting, I got one of our city papers, containing an account of the number of petitions from the north, praying for the abolition of slavery in the District of Columbia, and of the slave trade between the States. From this time I understood the words *abolition* and *abolitionist*, and always drew near when that word was spoken, expecting to hear something of importance to myself and fellow-slaves. The light broke in upon me by degrees. I went one day down on the wharf of Mr. Waters; and seeing two Irishmen unloading a scow of stone, I went, unasked, and helped them. When we had finished, one of them came to me and asked me if I were a slave. I told him I was. He asked, "Are ye a slave for life?" I told him that I was. The good Irishman seemed to be deeply affected by the statement. He said to the other that it was a pity so fine a little fellow as myself should be a slave for life. He said it was a shame to hold me. They both advised me to run away to the north; that I should find friends there, and that I should be free. I pretended not to be interested in what they said, and treated them as if I did not understand them; for I feared they might be treacherous. White men have been known to encourage slaves to escape, and then, to get the reward, catch them and return them to their masters. I was afraid that these seemingly good men might use me so; but I nevertheless remembered their advice, and from that time I resolved to run away. I looked forward to a time at which it would be safe for me to escape. I was too young to think of doing so immediately; besides, I wished to learn how to write, as I might have occasion to write my own pass. I consoled myself with the hope that I should one day find a good chance. Meanwhile, I would learn to write.

The idea as to how I might learn to write was suggested to me by being in Durgin and Bailey's ship-yard, and frequently seeing the ship carpenters, after hewing, and getting a piece of timber ready for use, write on the timber the name of that part of the ship for which it was intended. When a piece of timber was intended for the larboard side, it would be marked thus—"L." When a piece was for the starboard side, it would be marked thus—"S." A piece for the larboard side forward, would be marked thus—"L. F." When a piece was for starboard side forward, it would be marked thus—"S. F." For larboard aft, it would be marked thus—"L. A." For starboard aft, it would be marked thus—"S. A." I soon learned the names of these letters, and for what they were intended when placed upon a piece of timber in the shipyard. I immediately commenced copying them, and in a short time was able to make the four letters named. After that, when I met with any boy who I knew could write, I would tell him I could write as well as he. The next word would be, "I don't believe you. Let me see you try it." I would then make the letters which I had been so fortunate as to learn, and ask him to beat that. In this way I got a good many lessons in writing, which it is quite possible I should never have gotten in any other way. During this time, my copy-book was the board fence, brick wall, and pavement; my pen and ink was a lump of chalk. With these, I learned mainly how to write. I then commenced and continued copying the Italics in Webster's Spelling Book, until I could make them all without looking on the book. By this time, my little Master Thomas had gone to school, and learned how to write, and had written over a number of copy-books. These had been brought home, and shown to some of our near neighbors, and then laid aside. My mistress used to go to class meeting at the Wilk Street meetinghouse every Monday afternoon, and leave me to take care of the house. When left thus, I used to spend the time in writing in the spaces left in Master Thomas's copy-book, copying what he had written. I continued to do this until I could write a hand very similar to that of Master Thomas. Thus, after a long, tedious effort for years, I finally succeeded in learning how to write.

Responding to Reading

1. What does Douglass mean in paragraph 2 when he says that slavery proved as harmful to his mistress as it did to him? In spite of his owners' actions, what strategies did Douglass use to learn to read?
2. Douglass escaped from slavery in 1838 and became a leading figure in the antislavery movement. How did reading and writing help him develop his ideas about slavery? In what way did language empower him?
3. What comment do you think Douglass's essay makes on the condition of African Americans in the mid-nineteenth century?

Responding in Writing

Does this essay, written over 150 years ago, have relevance today? Explain.

YOU CAN'T SAY THAT

Diane Ravitch

1938–

Formerly Assistant Secretary of Education and member of the National Assessment Governing Board, Diane Ravitch is currently Research Professor at the Steinhardt School of Education, New York University. Her numerous books and articles focus on issues in American education, particularly in urban settings. In her recent book The Language Police: How Pressure Groups Restrict What Students Learn *(2003), Ravitch examines the consequences of censoring textbook content, also the subject of the following essay.*

To judge by the magazines we read, the programs we watch or the music lyrics we hear, it would seem that almost anything goes, these days, when it comes to verbal expression. But that is not quite true.

In my book "The Language Police," I gathered a list of more than 500 words that are routinely deleted from textbooks and tests by "bias review committees" employed by publishing companies, state education departments and the federal government. Among the forbidden words are "landlord," "cowboy," "brother-hood," "yacht," "cult" and "primitive." Such words are deleted because they are offensive to various groups—feminists, religious conservatives, multiculturalists and ethnic activists, to name a few.

I invited readers of the book to send me examples of language policing, and they did, by the score. A bias review committee for the state test in New Jersey rejected a short story by Langston Hughes because he used the words "Negro" and "colored person." Michigan bans a long list of topics from its state tests, including terrorism, evolution, aliens and flying saucers (which might imply evolution).

A textbook writer sent me the guidelines used by the Harcourt/Steck/Vaughn company to remove photographs that might give offense. Editors must delete, the guidelines said, pictures of women with big hair or sleeveless blouses and men with dreadlocks or medallions. Photographs must not portray the soles of shoes or anyone eating with the left hand (both in deference to Muslim culture). To avoid giving offense to those who cannot afford a home computer, no one may be shown owning a home computer. To avoid offending those with strong but differing religious views, decorations for religious holidays must never appear in the background.

A college professor informed me that a new textbook in human 5 development includes the following statement: "As a folksinger once sang, how many roads must an individual walk down before you can call them an adult." The professor was stupefied that someone had made the line gender-neutral and ungrammatical by rewriting Bob Dylan's folk song "Blowin' in the Wind," which had simply asked: "How many roads must a man walk down before you call him a man?"

While writing "The Language Police," I could not figure out why New York State had gone so far beyond other states in punctiliously carving out almost all references to race, gender, age and ethnicity, including even weight and height. In June 2002, the state was mightily embarrassed when reports appeared about its routine bowdlerizing on its exams of writers such as Franz Kafka and Isaac Bashevis Singer.

The solution to the puzzle was recently provided by Candace deRussy, a trustee of the State University of New York. Ms. DeRussy read "The Language Police," and she too wondered how the New York State Education Department had come to censor its regents exams with such zeal. She asked the department to explain how it decided which words to delete and how it trained its bias and sensitivity reviewers.

At one point, state officials said that since June 2002 (the time of the debacle) they have adhered to only one standard: "Test developers should strive to identify and eliminate language, symbols, words, phrases, and content that are generally regarded as offensive by members of racial, ethnic, gender, or other groups, except when judged to be necessary for adequate representation of the domain." Ms. DeRussy guessed (correctly) that the state was holding back the specific instructions that had emboldened the bowdlerizers. She decided to use the state's freedom-of-information law to find out more. Months later, a state official sent her the training materials for the bias and sensitivity reviewers, which included a list of words and phrases and a rationale for language policing.

So here is how New York made itself an international joke. The state's guidelines to language sensitivity, citing Rosalie Maggio's "The Bias-Free Wordfinder," says: "We may not always understand why a certain word hurts. We don't have to. It is enough that someone says, 'That language doesn't respect me.'" That is, if any word or phrase is likely to give anyone offense, no matter how farfetched, it should be deleted.

Next the state asked: "Is it necessary to make reference to a person's age, ancestry, disability, ethnicity, nationality, physical appearance, race, religion, sex, sexuality?" Since the answer is frequently no, nearly all references to such characteristics are eliminated. Because these matters loom large in history and literature—and because they help us to understand character, life circumstances and motives—their silent removal is bound to weaken or obliterate the reader's understanding. 10

Like every other governmental agency concerned with testing, the New York State Education Department devised its own list of taboo words. There are the usual ones that have offended feminists for a generation, like "fireman," "authoress," "handyman" and "hostess." New York exercised its leadership by discovering bias in such words as "addict" (replace with "individual with a drug addiction"); "alumna, alumnae, alumni, alumnus" (replace with "graduate or graduates"); "American" (replace with "citizen of the United States or North America"); "cancer patient" (replace with "a patient with cancer"); "city fathers" (replace with "city leaders").

Meanwhile, the word "elderly" should be replaced by "older adult" or "older person," if it is absolutely necessary to mention age at all. "Gentleman's agreement" must be dropped in favor of an "informal agreement." "Ghetto" should be avoided; instead describe the social and economic circumstances of the neighborhood. "Grandfather clause" is helplessly sexist; "retoractive coverage" is preferred instead. The term "illegal alien" must be replaced by "undocumented worker."

Certain words are unacceptable under any circumstances. For example, it is wrong to describe anyone as "illegitimate." Another word to be avoided is "illiterate." Instead, specify whether an individual is unable to read or write, or both. Similarly, any word that contains the three offensive letters "m-a-n" as a prefix or a suffix must be rousted out of the language. Words like "manhours," "manpower," "mankind" and "manmade" are regularly deleted. Even "pen-manship," where the guilty three letters are in the middle of the word, is out.

New York identified as biased such male-based words as "masterpiece" and "mastery." Among the other words singled out for extinction were *white collar, blue collar, pink collar, teenager, senior citizen, third world, uncivilized, underprivileged, unmarried, widow or widower,* and *yes man.* The goal, naturally, is to remove words that identify people by their gender, age, race, social position or marital status.

15   Thus the great irony of bias and sensitivity reviewing. It began with the hope of encouraging diversity, ensuring that our educational materials would include people of different experiences and social backgrounds. It has evolved into a bureaucratic system that removes all evidence of diversity and reduces everyone to interchangeable beings whose differences we must *not* learn about—making nonsense of literature and history along the way.

Responding to Reading

1. What is "language policing"? Who engages in this activity? Does Ravitch supply enough examples to convince you that this activity is a problem?
2. Beginning in paragraph 11, Ravitch singles out New York State for criticism. How does New York go further than other states in eliminating "almost all references to race, gender, age, and ethnicity, including even weight and height" (6)? Why does New York follow such strict guidelines?
3. According to Ravitch, what is "the great irony of bias and sensibility reviewing" (15)? Do you agree with her conclusion that this activity is ultimately harmful to both literature and history?

Responding in Writing

Of the words Ravitch mentions in her essay, which do you agree should be deleted from textbooks and tests? Which should not be? Are there words that Ravitch does not mention that you consider unacceptable?

SEXISM IN ENGLISH: EMBODIMENT AND LANGUAGE

Alleen Pace Nilsen

1936–

Alleen Pace Nilsen is an educator and essayist. Her most recent books, coauthored with her husband, are the Encyclopedia of 20th-Century American Humor *(2000) and* Vocabulary Plus K–8: A Source-Based Approach *(2003). When Nilsen lived in Afghanistan in the 1960s, she observed the subordinate position of women in that society. When she returned to the United States, she studied American English for its cultural biases toward men and women. Nilsen says of that project, "As I worked my way through the dictionary, I concentrated on the way particular usages, metaphors, slang terms, and definitions reveal society's attitude toward males and females." The following essay is an updated version of Nilsen's findings from her dictionary study.*

During the late 1960s, I lived with my husband and three young children in Kabul, Afghanistan. This was before the Russian invasion, the Afghan civil war, and the eventual taking over of the country by the Taleban Islamic movement and its resolve to return the country to a strict Islamic dynasty, in which females are not allowed to attend school or work outside their homes.

But even when we were there and the country was considered moderate rather than extremist, I was shocked to observe how different were the roles assigned to males and females. The Afghan version of the *chaderi*[1] prescribed by Moslem women was particularly confining. Women in religious families were required to wear it whenever they were outside their family home, with the result being that most of them didn't venture outside.

The household help we hired were made up of men, because women could not be employed by foreigners. Afghan folk stories and jokes were blatantly sexist, as in this proverb: "If you see an old man, sit down and take a lesson; if you see an old woman, throw a stone."

But it wasn't only the native culture that made me question women's roles, it was also the American community within Afghanistan.

Most of the American women were like myself—wives and moth- 5 ers whose husbands were either career diplomats, employees of USAID, or college professors who had been recruited to work on various contract teams. We were suddenly bereft of our traditional roles: The local economy provided few jobs for women and certainly none for foreigners; we were isolated from former friends and the social goals we had grown up with. Some of us became alcoholics, others got very good at bridge, while still others searched desperately for ways to contribute either to our families or to the Afghans.

When we returned in the fall of 1969 to the University of Michigan in Ann Arbor, I was surprised to find that many other women were also questioning the expectations they had grown up with. Since I had been an English major when I was in college, I decided that for my part in the feminist movement I would study the English language and see what it could tell me about sexism. I started reading a desk dictionary and making note cards on every entry that seemed to tell something different about male and female. I soon had a dog-eared dictionary, along with a collection of note cards filling two shoe boxes.

The first thing I learned was that I couldn't study the language without getting involved in social issues. Language and society are as

---

[1]A *chaderi* is a heavily draped cloth covering the entire head and body. [Eds.]

intertwined as a chicken and an egg. The language a culture uses is telltale evidence of the values and beliefs of that culture. And because there is a lag in how fast a language changes—new words can easily be introduced, but it takes a long time for old words and usages to disappear—a careful look at English will reveal the attitudes that our ancestors held and that we as a culture are therefore predisposed to hold. My note cards revealed three main points. While friends have offered the opinion that I didn't need to read a dictionary to learn such obvious facts, the linguistic evidence lends credibility to the sociological observations.

Women Are Sexy; Men Are Successful

First, in American culture a woman is valued for the attractiveness and sexiness of her body, while a man is valued for his physical strength and accomplishments. A woman is sexy. A man is successful.

A persuasive piece of evidence supporting this view are the eponyms—words that have come from someone's name—found in English. I had a two-and-a-half-inch stack of cards taken from men's names but less than a half-inch stack from women's names, and most of those came from Greek mythology. In the words that came into American English since we separated from Britain, there are many eponyms based on the names of famous American men: Bartlett pear, boysenberry, Franklin stove, Ferris wheel, Gatling gun, mason jar, sideburns, sousaphone, Schick test, and Winchester rifle. The only common eponyms that I found taken from American women's names are Alice blue (after Alice Roosevelt Longworth), bloomers (after Amelia Jenks Bloomer), and Mae West jacket (after the buxom actress). Two out of the three feminine eponyms relate closely to a woman's physical anatomy, while the masculine eponyms (except for "sideburns" after General Burnsides) have nothing to do with the namesake's body, but, instead, honor the man for an accomplishment of some kind.

10   In Greek mythology women played a bigger role than they did in the biblical stories of the Judeo-Christian cultures, and so the names of goddesses are accepted parts of the language in such place names as Pomona, from the goddess of fruit, and Athens, from Athena, and in such common words as *cereal* from Ceres, *psychology* from Psyche, and *arachnoid* from Arachne. However, there is the same tendency to think of women in relation to sexuality as shown through the eponyms *aphrodisiac* from Aphrodite, the Greek name for the goddess of love and beauty, and *venereal disease* from Venus, the Roman name for Aphrodite.

Another interesting word from Greek mythology is *Amazon*. According to Greek folk etymology, the *a-* means "without," as in *atypical* or *amoral*, while -*mazon* comes from *mazos*, meaning "breast," as still seen in *mastectomy*. In the Greek legend, Amazon women cut off their right breasts so they could better shoot their bows. Apparently, the storytellers had a feeling that for women to play the active, "masculine" role the Amazons adopted for themselves, they had to trade in part of their femininity.

This preoccupation with women's breasts is not limited to the Greeks; it's what inspired the definition and the name for "mammals" (from Indo-European *mammae* for "breasts"). As a volunteer for the University of Wisconsin's *Dictionary of American Regional English (DARE),* I read a western trapper's diary from the 1830s. I was to make notes of any unusual usages or language patterns. My most interesting finding was that the trapper referred to a range of mountains as "The Teats," a metaphor based on the similarity between the shapes of the mountains and women's breasts. Because today we use the French wording "The Grand Tetons," the metaphor isn't as obvious, but I wrote to mapmakers and found the following listings: Nipple Top and Little Nipple Top near Mount Marcy in the Adirondacks; Nipple Mountain in Archuleta County, Colorado; Nipple Peak in Coke County, Texas; Nipple Butte in Pennington, South Dakota; Squaw Peak in Placer County, California (and many other locations); Maiden's Peak and Squaw Tit (they're the same mountain) in the Cascade Range in Oregon; Mary's Nipple near Salt Lake City, Utah; and Jane Russell Peaks near Stark, New Hampshire.

Except for the movie star Jane Russell, the women being referred to are anonymous—it's only a sexual part of their body that is mentioned. When topographical features are named after men, it's probably not going to be to draw attention to a sexual part of their bodies but instead to honor individuals for an accomplishment.

Going back to what I learned from my dictionary cards, I was surprised to realize how many pairs of words we have in which the feminine word has acquired sexual connotations while the masculine word retains a serious businesslike aura. For example, a callboy is the person who calls actors when it is time for them to go on stage, but a callgirl is a prostitute. Compare sir and madam. *Sir* is a term of respect, while *madam* has acquired the specialized meaning of a brothel manager. Something similar has happened to master and mistress. Would you rather have a painting "by an old master" or "by an old mistress"?

It's because the word *woman* had sexual connotations, as in "She's 15 his woman," that people began avoiding its use, hence such terminology as ladies' room, lady of the house, and girl's school or school for young ladies. Those of us who in the 1970s began asking that speakers use the term *woman* rather than *girl* or *lady* were rejecting the idea that *woman* is primarily a sexual term.

I found two-hundred pairs of words with masculine and feminine forms; for example, *heir/heiress, hero/heroine, steward/stewardess, usher/*

usherette. In nearly all such pairs, the masculine word is considered the base, with some kind of a feminine suffix being added. The masculine form is the one from which compounds are made; for example, from king/queen comes kingdom but not queendom, from sportsman/sportslady comes sportsmanship but not sportsladyship. There is one—and only one—semantic area in which the masculine word is not the base or more powerful word. This is in the area dealing with sex, marriage, and motherhood. When someone refers to a virgin, a listener will probably think of a female unless the speaker specifies male or uses a masculine pronoun. The same is true for prostitute.

In relation to marriage, linguistic evidence shows that weddings are more important to women than to men. A woman cherishes the wedding and is considered a bride for a whole year, but a man is referred to as a groom only on the day of the wedding. The word *bride* appears in *bridal attendant, bridal gown, bridesmaid, bridal shower,* and even *bridegroom. Groom* comes from the Middle English *grom,* meaning "man," and in that sense is seldom used outside of the wedding. With most pairs of male/female words, people habitually put the masculine word first: *Mr. and Mrs., his and hers, boys and girls, men and women, kings and queens, brothers and sisters, guys and dolls, and host and hostess.* But it is the bride and groom who are talked about, not the groom and bride.

The importance of marriage to a woman is also shown by the fact that when a marriage ends in death, the woman gets the title of widow. A man gets the derived title of widower. This term is not used in other phrases or contexts, but widow is seen in widowhood, widow's peak, and widow's walk. A widow in a card game is an extra hand of cards, while in typesetting it is a leftover line of type.

Changing cultural ideas bring changes to language, and since I did my dictionary study three decades ago the word *singles* has largely replaced such gender-specific and value-laden terms as *bachelor, old maid, spinster, divorcee, widow,* and *widower.* In 1970 I wrote that when people hear a man called "a professional," they usually think of him as a doctor or a lawyer, but when people hear a woman referred to as "a professional," they are likely to think of her as a prostitute. That's not as true today because so many women have become doctors and lawyers, it's no longer incongruous to think of women in those professional roles.

20   Another change that has taken place is in wedding announcements. They used to be sent out from the bride's parents and did not even give the name of the groom's parents. Today, most couples choose to list either all or none of the parents' names. Also it is now much more likely that both the bride and groom's picture will be in the newspaper, while twenty years ago only the bride's picture was published on the "Women's" or the "Society" page. In the weddings I have recently attended, the official has pronounced the couple "husband and wife" instead of the traditional "man and wife," and the

bride has been asked if she promises to "love, honor, and cherish," instead of to "love, honor, and obey."

Women are Passive; Men are Active

However, other wording in the wedding ceremony relates to a second point that my cards showed, which is that women are expected to play a passive or weak role while men play an active or strong role. In the traditional ceremony, the official asks, "Who gives the bride away?" and the father answers, "I do." Some fathers answer, "Her mother and I do," but that doesn't solve the problem inherent in the question. The idea that a bride is something to be handed over from one man to another bothers people because it goes back to the days when a man's servants, his children, and his wife were all considered to be his property. They were known by his name because they belonged to him, and he was responsible for their actions and their debts.

The grammar used in talking or writing about weddings as well as other sexual relationships shows the expectation of men playing the active role. Men *wed* women while women *become* brides of men. A man *possesses* a woman; he *deflowers* her; he *performs*; he *scores*; he *takes away* her virginity. Although a woman can *seduce* a man, she cannot offer him her virginity. When talking about virginity, the only way to make the woman the actor in the sentence is to say that "she lost her virginity," but people lose things by accident rather than by purposeful actions, and so she's only the grammatical, not the real-life, actor.

The reason that women brought the term Ms. into the language to replace Miss and Mrs. relates to this point. Many married women resent being identified in the "Mrs. Husband" form. The dictionary cards showed what appeared to be an attitude on the part of the editors that it was almost indecent to let a respectable woman's name march unaccompanied across the pages of a dictionary. Women were listed with male names whether or not the male contributed to the woman's reason for being in the dictionary or whether or not in his own right he was as famous as the woman. For example:

Charlotte Brontë = Mrs. Arthur B. Nicholls
Amelia Earhart = Mrs. George Palmer Putnam
Helen Hayes = Mrs. Charles MacArthur
Jenny Lind = Mme. Otto Goldschmit
Cornelia Otis Skinner = daughter of Otis
Harriet Beecher Stowe = sister of Henry Ward Beecher
Dame Edith Sitwell = sister of Osbert and Sacheverell[2]

---

[2]Charlotte Brontë (1816–1855), author of *Jane Eyre*; Amelia Earhart (1898–1937), first woman to fly over the Atlantic; Helen Hayes (1900–1993), actress; Jenny Lind (1820–1887), Swedish soprano; Cornelia Otis Skinner (1901–1979), actress and writer; Harriet Beecher Stowe (1811–1896), author of *Uncle Tom's Cabin*; Edith Sitwell (1877–1964), English poet and critic. [Eds.]

Only a small number of rebels and crusaders got into the dictionary without the benefit of a masculine escort: temperance leaders Frances Elizabeth Caroline Willard and Carry Nation, women's rights leaders Carrie Chapman Catt and Elizabeth Cady Stanton, birth control educator Margaret Sanger, religious leader Mary Baker Eddy, and slaves Harriet Tubman and Phillis Wheatley.

Etiquette books used to teach that if a woman had Mrs. in front of her name, then the husband's name should follow because Mrs. is an abbreviated form of Mistress and a woman couldn't be a mistress of herself. As with many arguments about "correct" language usage, this isn't very logical because Miss is also an abbreviation of Mistress. Feminists hoped to simplify matters by introducing Ms. as an alternative to both Mrs. and Miss, but what happened is that Ms. largely replaced Miss to become a catch-all business title for women. Many married women still prefer the title Mrs., and some even resent being addressed with the term Ms. As one frustrated newspaper reporter complained, "Before I can write about a woman I have to know not only her marital status but also her political philosophy." The result of such complications may contribute to the demise of titles, which are already being ignored by many writers who find it more efficient to simply use names; for example, in a business letter: "Dear Joan Garcia," instead of "Dear Mrs. Joan Garcia," "Dear Ms. Garcia," or "Dear Mrs. Louis Garcia."

25   Titles given to royalty show how males can be disadvantaged by the assumption that they always play the more powerful role. In British royalty, when a male holds a title, his wife is automatically given the feminine equivalent. But the reverse is not true. For example, a count is a high political officer with a countess being his wife. The same pattern holds true for a duke and a duchess and a king and a queen. But when a female holds the royal title, the man she marries does not automatically acquire the matching title. For example, Queen Elizabeth's husband has the title of prince rather than king, but when Prince Charles married Diana, she became Princess Diana. If they had stayed married and he had ascended to the throne, then she would have become Queen Diana. The reasoning appears to be that since masculine words are stronger, they are reserved for true heirs and withheld from males coming into the royal family by marriage. If Prince Phillip were called "King Phillip," British subjects might forget who had inherited the right to rule.

The names that people give their children show the hopes and dreams they have for them, and when we look at the differences between male and female names in a culture, we can see the cumulative expectations of that culture. In our culture girls often have names taken from small, aesthetically pleasing items; for example, Ruby, Jewel, and Pearl. Esther and Stella mean "star," and Ada means "ornament." One of the few women's names that refers to strength is Mildred, and it means "mild strength." Boys often have names with meanings of power and strength; for example, Neil means "champion"; Martin is from Mars, the God of war; Raymond means "wise protection"; Harold means "chief of the army"; Ira means "vigilant"; Rex means "king"; and Richard means "strong king."

We see similar differences in food metaphors. Food is a passive substance just sitting there waiting to be eaten. Many people have recognized this and so no longer feel comfortable describing women as "delectable morsels." However, when I was a teenager, it was considered a compliment to refer to a girl (we didn't call anyone a "woman" until she was middle-aged) as a cute tomato, a peach, a dish, a cookie, honey, sugar, or sweetie-pie. When being affectionate, women will occasionally call a man honey or sweetie, but in general, food metaphors are used much less often with men than with women. If a man is called "a fruit," his masculinity is being questioned. But it's perfectly acceptable to use a food metaphor if the food is heavier and more substantive than that used for women. For example, pin-up pictures of women have long been known as "cheesecake," but when Burt Reynolds posed for a nude centerfold the picture was immediately dubbed "beefcake," that is, a hunk of meat. That such sexual references to men have come into the language is another reflection of how society is beginning to lessen the differences between their attitudes toward men and women.

Something similar to the fruit metaphor happens with references to plants. We insult a man by calling him a "pansy," but it wasn't considered particularly insulting to talk about a girl being a wallflower, a clinging vine, or a shrinking violet, or to give girls such names as Ivy, Rose, Lily, Iris, Daisy, Camelia, Heather, and Flora. A positive plant metaphor can be used with a man only if the plant is big and strong; for example, Andrew Jackson's nickname of Old Hickory. Also, the phrases *blooming idiots* and *budding geniuses* can be used with either sex, but notice how they are based on the most active thing a plant can do, which is to bloom or bud.

Animal metaphors also illustrate the different expectations for males and females. Men are referred to as studs, bucks, and wolves, while women are referred to with such metaphors as kitten, bunny, beaver, bird, chick, and lamb. In the 1950s, we said that boys went "tom catting," but today it's just "catting around," and both boys and girls do it. When the term foxy, meaning that someone was sexy, first became popular it was used only for females, but now someone of either sex can be described as a fox. Some animal metaphors that are used predominantly with men have negative connotations based on the size and/or strength of the animals; for example, beast, bull-headed, jackass, rat, loanshark, and vulture. Negative metaphors used with women are based on smaller animals; for example, social butterfly, mousey, catty, and vixen. The feminine terms connote action, but not the same kind of large scale action as with the masculine terms.

Women are Connected with Negative Connotations; Men with Positive Connotations

30 The final point that my note cards illustrated was how many positive connotations are associated with the concept of masculinity, while there are either trivial or negative connotations connected with the corresponding feminine concept. An example from the animal metaphors makes a good illustration. The word *shrew* taken from the name of a small but especially vicious animal was defined in my dictionary as "an ill-tempered scolding woman," but the word *shrewd* taken from the same root was defined as "marked by clever, discerning awareness" and was illustrated with the phrase "a shrewd businessman."

Early in life, children are conditioned to the superiority of the masculine role. As child psychologists point out, little girls have much more freedom to experiment with sex roles than do little boys. If a little girl acts like a tomboy, most parents have mixed feelings, being at least partially proud. But if their little boy acts like a sissy (derived from *sister*), they call a psychologist. It's perfectly acceptable for a little girl to sleep in the crib that was purchased for her brother, to wear his hand-me-down jeans and shirts, and to ride the bicycle that he has outgrown. But few parents would put a boy baby in a white-and-gold crib decorated with frills and lace, and virtually no parents would have their little boy wear his sister's hand-me-down dresses, nor would they have their son ride a girl's pink bicycle with a flower-bedecked basket. The proper names given to girls and boys show this same attitude. Girls can have "boy" names—Cris, Craig, Jo, Kelly, Shawn, Teri, Toni, and Sam—but it doesn't work the other way around. A couple of generations ago, Beverly, Frances, Hazel, Marion, and Shirley were common boys' names. As parents gave these names to more and more girls, they fell into disuse for males, and some older men who have these names prefer to go by their initials or by such abbreviated forms as Haze or Shirl.

When a little girl is told to be a lady, she is being told to sit with her knees together and to be quiet and dainty. But when a little boy is told to be a man, he is being told to be noble, strong, and virtuous—to have all the qualities that the speaker looks on as desirable. The concept of manliness has such positive connotations that it used to be a compliment to call someone a he-man, to say that he was doubly a man. Today many people are more ambivalent about this term and respond to it much as they do to the word *macho*. But calling someone a manly man or a virile man is nearly always meant as a compliment. Virile comes from the Indo-European *vir,* meaning "man," which is also the basis of *virtuous*. Consider the positive connotations of both virile and virtuous with the negative connotations of *hysterical*. The Greeks took this latter word from their name for uterus (as still seen in *hysterectomy*). They thought that women were the only ones who experienced uncontrolled emotional outbursts, and so the condition must have something to do with a part of the body that only women have. But how word meanings change is regularly shown at athletic events where thousands of *virtuous* women sit quietly beside their *hysterical* husbands.

Differences in the connotations between positive male and negative female connotations can be seen in several pairs of words that differ denotatively only in the matter of sex. Bachelor as compared to spinster or old maid has such positive connotations that women try to adopt it by using the term *bachelor-girl* or *bachelorette*. Old maid is so negative that it's the basis for metaphors: pretentious and fussy old men are called "old maids," as are the leftover kernels of unpopped popcorn and the last card in a popular children's card game.

Patron and *matron* (Middle English for "father" and "mother") have such different levels of prestige that women try to borrow the more positive masculine connotations with the word *patroness,* literally "female father." Such a peculiar term came about because of the high prestige attached to patron in such phrases as a *patron of the arts* or a *patron saint*. Matron is more apt to be used in talking about a woman in charge of a jail or a public restroom.

When men are doing jobs that women often do, we apparently try 35 to pay the men extra by giving them fancy titles. For example, a male cook is more likely to be called a "chef" while a male seamstress will get the title of "tailor." The armed forces have a special problem in that they recruit under such slogans as "The Marine Corps builds men!" and "Join the Army! Become a Man." Once the recruits are enlisted, they find themselves doing much of the work that has been traditionally thought of as "women's work." The solution to getting the work done and not insulting anyone's masculinity was to change the titles as shown below:

> waitress = orderly
> nurse = medic or corpsman
> secretary = clerk-typist
> assistant = adjutant
> dishwasher = KP (kitchen police) or kitchen helper

Compare *brave* and *squaw*. Early settlers in America truly admired Indian men and hence named them with a word that carried connotations of youth, vigor, and courage. But for Indian women they used an Algonquin slang term with negative sexual connotations that are almost opposite to those of brave. Wizard and witch contrast almost as much. The masculine *wizard* implies skill and wisdom combined with magic, while the feminine *witch* implies evil intentions combined with magic. When witch is used for men, as in witch-doctor, many main-stream speakers feel some carry-over of the negative connotations.

Part of the unattractiveness of both witch and squaw is that they have been used so often to refer to old women, something with which our culture is particularly uncomfortable, just as the Afghans were. Imagine my surprise when I ran across the phrases *grandfatherly advice* and *old wives' tales* and realized that the underlying implication is the same as the Afghan proverb about old men being worth listening to while old women talk only foolishness.

Other terms that show how negatively we view old women as compared to young women are *old nag* as compared to *filly, old crow* or *old bat* as compared to *bird,* and being *catty* as compared to being *kittenish.* There is no matching set of metaphors for men. The chicken metaphor tells the whole story of a woman's life. In her youth she is a chick. Then she marries and begins feathering her nest. Soon she begins feeling cooped up, so she goes to hen parties where she cackles with her friends. Then she has her brood, begins to henpeck her husband, and finally turns into an old biddy.

I embarked on my study of the dictionary not with the intention of prescribing language change but simply to see what the language would tell me about sexism. Nevertheless, I have been both surprised and pleased as I've watched the changes that have occurred over the past three decades. I'm one of those linguists who believes that new language customs will cause a new generation of speakers to grow up with different expectations. This is why I'm happy about people's efforts to use inclusive languages, to say "he or she" or "they" when speaking about individuals whose names they do not know. I'm glad that leading publishers have developed guidelines to help writers use language that is fair to both sexes. I'm glad that most newspapers and magazines list women by their own names instead of only by their husbands' names. And I'm so glad that educated and thoughtful people no longer begin their business letters with "Dear Sir" or "Gentlemen," but instead use a memo form or begin with such salutations as "Dear Colleagues," "Dear Reader," or "Dear Committee Members." I'm also glad that such words as *poetess, authoress, conductress,* and *aviatrix* now sound quaint and old-fashioned and that *chairman* is giving way to *chair* or *head, mailman* to *mail carrier, clergyman* to *clergy,* and *stewardess* to *flight attendant.* I was also pleased when the National

Oceanic and Atmospheric Administration bowed to feminist complaints and in the late 1970s began to alternate men's and women's names for hurricanes. However, I wasn't so pleased to discover that the change did not immediately erase sexist thoughts from everyone's mind, as shown by a headline about Hurricane David in a 1979 New York tabloid, "David Rapes Virgin Islands." More recently a similar metaphor appeared in a headline in the *Arizona Republic* about Hurricane Charlie, "Charlie Quits Carolinas, Flirts with Virginia."

What these incidents show is that sexism is not something exist- 40 ing independently in American English or in the particular dictionary that I happened to read. Rather, it exists in people's minds. Language is like an X-ray in providing visible evidence of invisible thoughts. The best thing about people being interested in and discussing sexist language is that as they make conscious decisions about what pronouns they will use, what jokes they will tell or laugh at, how they will write their names, or how they will begin their letters, they are forced to think about the underlying issue of sexism. This is good because as a problem that begins in people's assumptions and expectations, it's a problem that will be solved only when a great many people have given it a great deal of thought.

Responding to Reading

1. What point is Nilsen making about American culture? Does your experience support her conclusions?
2. Does Nilsen use enough examples to support her claims? What others can you think of? In what way do her examples—and your own—illustrate the power of language to define the way people think?
3. Many of the connotations of the words Nilsen discusses are hundreds of years old and are also found in languages other than English. Given these widespread and long-standing linguistic patterns, do you think attempts by Nilsen and others to change this situation can succeed?

Responding in Writing

List some words and phrases that you routinely use that reinforce the stereotypes Nilsen discusses. What alternatives could you employ? What would be gained and lost if you used these alternatives?

MOTHER TONGUE

Amy Tan

1952–

Amy Tan was born to parents who had emigrated from China only a few years earlier. (Her given name is actually An-mei, which means "blessing from America.") A workaholic, Tan began writing stories as a means of personal therapy, and these stories eventually became the highly successful The Joy Luck Club *(1987), a novel about Chinese-born mothers and their American-born daughters that was later made into a widely praised film. Tan's other books include four more novels—*The Kitchen God's Wife *(1991),* The Hundred Secret Senses *(1995),* The Bonesetter's Daughter *(2001), and* Saving Fish from Drowning *(2005)—and a work of nonfiction,* The Opposite of Fate: A Book of Musings *(2003) as well as two illustrated children's books. In the following essay, which was originally delivered as a speech, Tan considers her relationship with her own mother, concentrating on the different "Englishes" they use to communicate with each other and with the world.*

I am not a scholar of English or literature. I cannot give you much more than personal opinions on the English language and its variations in this country or others.

I am a writer. And by that definition, I am someone who has always loved language. I am fascinated by language in daily life. I spend a great deal of my time thinking about the power of language—the way it can evoke an emotion, a visual image, a complex idea, or a simple truth. Language is the tool of my trade. And I use them all—all the Englishes I grew up with.

Recently, I was made keenly aware of the different Englishes I do use. I was giving a talk to a large group of people, the same talk I had already given to half a dozen other groups. The nature of the talk was about my writing, my life, and my book, *The Joy Luck Club.* The talk was going along well enough, until I remembered one major difference that made the whole talk sound wrong. My mother was in the room. And it was perhaps the first time she had heard me give a lengthy speech, using the kind of English I have never used with her. I was saying things like, "The intersection of memory upon imagination" and "There is an aspect of my fiction that relates to thus-and-thus"—a speech filled with carefully wrought grammatical phrases, burdened, it suddenly seemed to me, with nominalized forms, past perfect tenses, conditional phrases, all the forms of standard English that I had learned in school and through books, the forms of English I did not use at home with my mother.

Just last week, I was walking down the street with my mother, and I again found myself conscious of the English I was using, and the English I do use with her. We were talking about the price of new and used furniture and I heard myself saying this: "Not waste money that way." My husband was with us as well, and he didn't notice any switch in my English. And then I realized why. It's because over the twenty years we've been together I've often used that same kind of English with him, and sometimes he even uses it with me. It has become our language of intimacy, a different sort of English that relates to family talk, the language I grew up with.

So you'll have some idea of what this family talk I heard sounds 5 like, I'll quote what my mother said during a recent conversation which I videotaped and then transcribed. During this conversation, my mother was talking about a political gangster in Shanghai who had the same last name as her family's, Du, and how the gangster in his early years wanted to be adopted by her family, which was rich by comparison. Later, the gangster became more powerful, far richer than my mother's family, and one day showed up at my mother's wedding to pay his respects. Here's what she said in part:

"Du Yusong having business like fruit stand. Like off the street kind. He is Du like Du Zong—but not Tsung-ming Island people. The local people call putong, the river east side, he belong to that side local people. The man want to ask Du Zong father take him in like become own family. Du Zong father wasn't look down on him, but didn't take seriously, until that man big like become a mafia. Now important person, very hard to inviting him. Chinese way, came only to show respect, don't stay for dinner. Respect for making big celebration, he shows up. Mean gives lots of respect. Chinese custom. Chinese social life that way. If too important won't have to stay too long. He come to my wedding. I didn't see, I heard it. I gone to boy's side, they have YMCA dinner. Chinese age I was nineteen."

You should know that my mother's expressive command of English belies how much she actually understands. She reads the Forbes report, listens to *Wall Street Week,* converses daily with her stockbroker, reads all of Shirley MacLaine's[1] books with ease—all kinds of things I can't begin to understand. Yet some of my friends tell me they understand 50 percent of what my mother says. Some say they understand 80 to 90 percent. Some say they understand none of it, as if she were speaking pure Chinese. But to me, my mother's English is perfectly clear, perfectly natural. It's my mother tongue. Her language, as I hear it, is vivid, direct, full of observation and imagery. That was the language that helped shape the way I saw things, expressed things, made sense of the world.

Lately, I've been giving more thought to the kind of English my mother speaks. Like others, I have described it to people as "broken"

---

[1]Actress known for her autobiographical books, in which she traces her many past lives. [Eds.]

or "fractured" English. But I wince when I say that. It has always bothered me that I can think of no way to describe it other than "broken," as if it were damaged and needed to be fixed, as if it lacked a certain wholeness and soundness. I've heard other terms used, "limited English," for example. But they seem just as bad, as if everything is limited, including people's perceptions of the limited English speaker.

I know this for a fact, because when I was growing up, my mother's "limited" English limited *my* perception of her. I was ashamed of her English. I believed that her English reflected the quality of what she had to say. That is, because she expressed them imperfectly her thoughts were imperfect. And I had plenty of empirical evidence to support me: the fact that people in department stores, at banks, and at restaurants did not take her seriously, did not give her good service, pretended not to understand her, or even acted as if they did not hear her.

10   My mother has long realized the limitations of her English as well. When I was fifteen, she used to have me call people on the phone to pretend I was she. In this guise, I was forced to ask for information or even to complain and yell at people who had been rude to her. One time it was a call to her stockbroker in New York. She had cashed out her small portfolio and it just so happened we were going to go to New York the next week, our very first trip outside California. I had to get on the phone and say in an adolescent voice that was not very convincing, "This is Mrs. Tan."

And my mother was standing in the back whispering loudly, "Why he don't send me check, already two weeks late. So mad he lie to me, losing me money."

And then I said in perfect English, "Yes, I'm getting rather concerned. You had agreed to send the check two weeks ago, but it hasn't arrived."

Then she began to talk more loudly. "What he want, I come to New York tell him front of his boss, you cheating me?" And I was trying to calm her down, make her be quiet, while telling the stockbroker, "I can't tolerate any more excuses. If I don't receive the check immediately, I am going to have to speak to your manager when I'm in New York next week." And sure enough, the following week there we were in front of this astonished stockbroker, and I was sitting there red-faced and quiet, and my mother, the real Mrs. Tan, was shouting at his boss in her impeccable broken English.

We used a similar routine just five days ago, for a situation that was far less humorous. My mother had gone to the hospital for an appointment, to find out about a benign brain tumor a CAT scan had revealed a month ago. She said she had spoken very good English, her best English, no mistakes. Still, she said, the hospital did not apologize when they said they had lost the CAT scan and she had come for nothing. She said they did not seem to have any sympathy when she told them she was anxious to know the exact diagnosis, since her husband and son had both died of brain tumors. She said they would not give her any more information until the next time and she would have to make another appointment for that. So she said she would not leave until the doctor called her daughter. She wouldn't budge. And when the doctor finally called her daughter, me, who spoke in perfect English—lo and behold—we had assurances the CAT scan would be found, promises that a conference call on Monday would be held, and apologies for any suffering my mother had gone through for a most regrettable mistake.

I think my mother's English almost had an effect on limiting my 15 possibilities in life as well. Sociologists and linguists probably will tell you that a person's developing language skills are more influenced by peers. But I do think that the language spoken in the family, especially in immigrant families which are more insular, plays a large role in shaping the language of the child. And I believe that it affected my results on achievement tests, IQ tests, and the SAT. While my English skills were never judged as poor, compared to math, English could not be considered my strong suit. In grade school I did moderately well, getting perhaps B's, sometimes B-pluses, in English and scoring perhaps in the sixtieth or seventieth percentile on achievement tests. But those scores were not good enough to override the opinion that my true abilities lay in math and science, because in those areas I achieved A's and scored in the ninetieth percentile or higher.

This was understandable. Math is precise; there is only one correct answer. Whereas, for me at least, the answers on English tests were always a judgment call, a matter of opinion and personal experience. Those tests were constructed around items like fill-in-the-blank sentence completion, such as, "Even though Tom was , Mary thought he was ." And the correct answer always seemed to be the most bland combinations of thoughts, for example, "Even though Tom was shy, Mary thought he was charming," with the grammatical structure "even though" limiting the correct answer to some sort of semantic opposites, so you wouldn't get answers like, "Even though Tom was foolish, Mary thought he was ridiculous." Well, according to my mother, there were very few limitations as to what Tom could have been and what Mary might have thought of him. So I never did well on tests like that.

The same was true with word analogies, pairs of words in which you were supposed to find some sort of logical, semantic relationship— for example, "*Sunset* is to *nightfall* as is to ." And here you would be presented with a list of four possible pairs, one of which showed the same kind of relationship: *red* is to *stoplight, bus* is to *arrival, chills* is to *fever, yawn* is to *boring.* Well, I could never think that way. I knew what the tests were asking, but I could not block out of my mind the images already created by the first pair, "*sunset* is to *nightfall*"—and I would see a burst of colors against a darkening sky, the moon rising, the lowering of a curtain of stars. And all the other pairs of words—red, bus, stoplight, boring—just threw up a mass of confusing images, making it impossible for me to sort out something as logical as saying: "A sunset precedes nightfall" is the same as "a chill precedes a fever." The only way I would have gotten that answer right would have been to imagine an associative situation, for example, my being disobedient and staying out past sunset, catching a chill at night, which turns into feverish pneumonia as punishment, which indeed did happen to me.

I have been thinking about all this lately, about my mother's English, about achievement tests. Because lately I've been asked, as a writer, why there are not more Asian Americans represented in American literature. Why are there few Asian Americans enrolled in creative writing programs? Why do so many Chinese students go into engineering? Well, these are broad sociological questions I can't begin to answer. But I have noticed in surveys—in fact, just last week—that Asian students, as a whole, always do significantly better on math achievement tests than in English. And this makes me think that there are other Asian-American students whose English spoken in the home might also be described as "broken" or "limited." And perhaps they also have teachers who are steering them away from writing and into math and science, which is what happened to me.

Fortunately, I happen to be rebellious in nature and enjoy the challenge of disproving assumptions made about me. I became an English major my first year in college, after being enrolled as premed. I started writing nonfiction as a freelancer the week after I was told by my former boss that writing was my worst skill and I should hone my talents toward account management.

20   But it wasn't until 1985 that I finally began to write fiction. And at first I wrote using what I thought to be wittily crafted sentences, sentences that would finally prove I had mastery over the English language. Here's an example from the first draft of a story that later made its way into *The Joy Luck Club*, but without this line: "That was my mental quandary in its nascent state." A terrible line, which I can barely pronounce.

Fortunately, for reasons I won't get into today, I later decided I should envision a reader for the stories I would write. And the reader I decided upon was my mother, because these were stories about mothers. So with this reader in mind—and in fact she did read my early drafts—I began to write stories using all the Englishes I grew up with: the English I spoke to my mother, which for lack of a better term might be described as "simple"; the English she used with me, which for lack of a better term might be described as "broken"; my translation of her Chinese, which could certainly be described as "watered down"; and what I imagined to be her translation of her Chinese if she could speak in perfect English, her internal language, and for that I sought to preserve the essence, but neither an English nor a Chinese structure. I wanted to capture what language ability tests can never reveal: her intent, her passion, her imagery, the rhythms of her speech and the nature of her thoughts.

Apart from what any critic had to say about my writing, I knew I had succeeded where it counted when my mother finished reading my book and gave me her verdict: "So easy to read."

Responding to Reading

1. Why does Tan begin her essay with the disclaimer, "I am not a scholar of English or literature. I cannot give you much more than personal opinions" (1)? Do these opening statements add to her credibility or detract from it? Explain.
2. Tan implies that some languages are more expressive than others. Do you agree? Are there some ideas you can express in one language that are difficult or impossible to express in another? Give examples if you can.
3. Do you agree with Tan's statement in paragraph 15 that the kind of English spoken at home can have an effect on a student's performance on IQ tests and the SAT?

Responding in Writing

Do you think the English you speak at home has had a positive or a negative effect on your performance in school?

THE HUMAN COST OF AN ILLITERATE SOCIETY

Jonathan Kozol

1936–

In 1964, Jonathan Kozol took a teaching job in the Boston Public Schools System. In 1967, he published his first book, Death at an Early Age: The Destruction of the Hearts and Minds of Negro Children in the Boston Public Schools. *Based on his experiences as a fourth-grade teacher in an inner-city school, a position from which he was fired for "curriculum deviation," this book won the National Book Award in 1968 and led to a number of specific reforms. Since then, Kozol has divided his time between teaching and social activism. His books include* Illiterate America *(1985),* Savage Inequalities *(1991),* Ordinary Resurrections *(2000), and* The Shame of a Nation: The Restoration of Apartheid Schooling in America *(2005). In the following essay, a chapter of* Illiterate America, *Kozol exposes the problems facing the sixty million Americans who are unable to read and argues that their plight has important implications for the nation as a whole.*

PRECAUTIONS. READ BEFORE USING.
Poison: Contains sodium hydroxide (caustic soda-lye).
Corrosive: Causes severe eye and skin damage, may cause blindness.
Harmful or fatal if swallowed.
If swallowed, give large quantities of milk or water.
Do not induce vomiting.
Important: Keep water out of can at all times to prevent contents from violently erupting . . .

—warning on a can of Drano

Questions of literacy, in Socrates' belief, must at length be judged as matters of morality. Socrates could not have had in mind the moral compromise peculiar to a nation like our own. Some of our Founding Fathers did, however, have this question in their minds. One of the wisest of those Founding Fathers (one who may not have been most compassionate but surely was more prescient than some of his peers) recognized the special dangers that illiteracy would pose to basic equity in the political construction that he helped to shape.

"A people who mean to be their own governors," James Madison wrote, "must arm themselves with the power knowledge gives. A popular government without popular information or the means of acquiring it, is but a prologue to a farce or a tragedy, or perhaps both."

Tragedy looms larger than farce in the United States today. Illiterate citizens seldom vote. Those who do are forced to cast a vote of questionable worth. They cannot make informed decisions based on serious print information. Sometimes they can be alerted to their interests by aggressive voter education. More frequently, they vote for a face, a smile, or a style, not for a mind or character or body of beliefs.

The number of illiterate adults exceeds by 16 million the entire vote cast for the winner in the 1980 presidential contest. If even one third of all illiterates could vote, and read enough and do sufficient math to vote in their self-interest, Ronald Reagan would not likely have been chosen president. There is, of course, no way to know for sure. We do know this: Democracy is a mendacious[1] term when used by those who are prepared to countenance the forced exclusion of one third of our electorate. So long as 60 million people are denied significant participation, the government is neither of, nor for, nor by, the people. It is a government, at best, of those two thirds whose wealth, skin color, or parental privilege allows them opportunity to profit from the provocation and instruction of the written word.

---
[1]Basely dishonest. [Eds.]

The undermining of democracy in the United States is one "ex- 5 pense" that sensitive Americans can easily deplore because it repre- sents a contradiction that endangers citizens of all political positions. The human price is not so obvious at first.

Since I first immersed myself within this work I have often had the following dream: I find that I am in a railroad station or a large department store within a city that is utterly unknown to me and where I cannot understand the printed words. None of the signs or symbols is familiar. Everything looks strange: like mirror writing of some kind. Gradually I understand that I am in the Soviet Union. All the letters on the walls around me are Cyrillic. I look for my pocket dictionary but I find that it has been mislaid. Where have I left it? Then I recall that I forgot to bring it with me when I packed my bags in Boston. I struggle to remember the name of my hotel. I try to ask somebody for directions. One person stops and looks at me in a pecu- liar way. I lose the nerve to ask. At last I reach into my wallet for an ID card. The card is missing. Have I lost it? Then I remember that my card was confiscated for some reason, many years before. Around this point, I wake up in a panic.

This panic is not so different from the misery that millions of adult illiterates experience each day within the course of their routine existence in the U.S.A.

Illiterates cannot read the menu in a restaurant.

They cannot read the cost of items on the menu in the *window* of the restaurant before they enter.

Illiterates cannot read the letters that their children bring home 10 from their teachers. They cannot study school department circulars that tell them of the courses that their children must be taking if they hope to pass the SAT exams. They cannot help with homework. They cannot write a letter to the teacher. They are afraid to visit in the class- room. They do not want to humiliate their child or themselves.

Illiterates cannot read instructions on a bottle of prescription medicine. They cannot find out when a medicine is past the year of safe consumption; nor can they read of allergenic risks, warnings to diabetics, or the potential sedative effect of certain kinds of nonpre- scription pills. They cannot observe preventive health care admoni- tions. They cannot read about "the seven warning signs of cancer" or the indications of blood-sugar fluctuations or the risks of eating cer- tain foods that aggravate the likelihood of cardiac arrest.

Illiterates live, in more than literal ways, an uninsured existence. They cannot understand the written details on a health insurance form. They cannot read the waivers that they sign preceding surgi- cal procedures. Several women I have known in Boston have en- tered a slum hospital with the intention of obtaining a tubal ligation and have emerged a few days later after having been subjected to a hysterectomy.[2] Unaware of their rights, incognizant of jargon, intimidated by the unfamiliar air of fear and atmosphere of ether that so many of us find oppressive in the confines even of the most attractive and expensive medical facilities, they have signed their names to documents they could not read and which nobody, in the hectic situation that prevails so often in those overcrowded hospitals that serve the urban poor, had even bothered to explain.

Childbirth might seem to be the last inalienable right of any female citizen within a civilized society. Illiterate mothers, as we shall see, already have been cheated of the power to protect their progeny against the likelihood of demolition in deficient public schools and, as a result, against the verbal servitude within which they themselves exist. Surgical denial of the right to bear that child in the first place represents an ultimate denial, an unspeakable metaphor, a final darkness that denies even the twilight gleamings of our own humanity. What greater violation of our biological, our biblical, our spiritual humanity could possibly exist than that which takes place nightly, perhaps hourly these days, within such over-burdened and benighted institutions as the Boston City Hospital? Illiteracy has many costs; few are so irreversible as this.

Even the roof above one's head, the gas or other fuel for heating that protects the residents of northern city slums against the threat of illness in the winter months become uncertain guarantees. Illiterates cannot read the lease that they must sign to live in an apartment which, too often, they cannot afford. They cannot manage check accounts and therefore seldom pay for anything by mail. Hours and entire days of difficult travel (and the cost of bus or other public transit) must be added to the real cost of whatever they consume. Loss of interest on the check accounts they do not have, and could not manage if they did, must be regarded as another of the excess costs paid by the citizen who is excluded from the common instruments of commerce in a numerate society.

15   "I couldn't understand the bills," a woman in Washington, D.C., reports, "and then I couldn't write the checks to pay them. We signed things we didn't know what they were."

Illiterates cannot read the notices that they receive from welfare offices or from the IRS. They must depend on word-of-mouth instruction from the welfare worker—or from other persons whom they have good reason to mistrust. They do not know what rights they have, what deadlines and requirements they face, what options they might choose to exercise. They are half-citizens. Their rights exist in print but not in fact.

---

[2]A hysterectomy, the removal of the uterus, is a much more radical procedure than a tubal ligation, a method of sterilization that is a common form of birth control. [Eds.]

Illiterates cannot look up numbers in a telephone directory. Even if they can find the names of friends, few possess the sorting skills to make use of the yellow pages; categories are bewildering and trade names are beyond decoding capabilities for millions of nonreaders. Even the emergency numbers listed on the first page of the phone book—"Ambulance," "Police," and "Fire"—are too frequently beyond the recognition of nonreaders.

Many illiterates cannot read the admonition on a pack of cigarettes. Neither the Surgeon General's warning nor its reproduction on the package can alert them to the risks. Although most people learn by word of mouth that smoking is related to a number of grave physical disorders, they do not get the chance to read the detailed stories which can document this danger with the vividness that turns concern into determination to resist. They can see the handsome cowboy or the slim Virginia lady lighting up a filter cigarette; they cannot heed the words that tell them that this product is (not "may be") dangerous to their health. Sixty million men and women are condemned to be the unalerted, high-risk candidates for cancer.

Illiterates do not buy "no-name" products in the supermarkets. They must depend on photographs or the familiar logos that are printed on the packages of brand-name groceries. The poorest people, therefore, are denied the benefits of the least costly products.

Illiterates depend almost entirely upon label recognition. Many 20 labels, however, are not easy to distinguish. Dozens of different kinds of Campbell's soup appear identical to the nonreader. The purchaser who cannot read and does not dare to ask for help, out of the fear of being stigmatized (a fear which is unfortunately realistic), frequently comes home with something which she never wanted and her family never tasted.

Illiterates cannot read instructions on a pack of frozen food. Packages sometimes provide an illustration to explain the cooking preparations; but illustrations are of little help to someone who must "boil water, drop the food—*within* its plastic wrapper—in the boiling water, wait for it to simmer, instantly remove."

Even when labels are seemingly clear, they may be easily mistaken. A woman in Detroit brought home a gallon of Crisco for her children's dinner. She thought that she had bought the chicken that was pictured on the label. She had enough Crisco now to last a year—but no more money to go back and buy the food for dinner.

Recipes provided on the packages of certain staples sometimes tempt a semiliterate person to prepare a meal her children have not tasted. The longing to vary the uniform and often starchy content of low-budget meals provided to the family that relies on food stamps commonly leads to ruinous results. Scarce funds have been wasted and the food must be thrown out. The same applies to distribution of

food-surplus produce in emergency conditions. Government induce-
ments to poor people to "explore the ways" in which to make a tasty
meal from tasteless noodles, surplus cheese, and powdered milk are
useless to nonreaders. Intended as benevolent advice, such recommendations mock reality and foster deeper feelings of resentment and
of inability to cope. (Those, on the other hand, who cautiously refrain
from "innovative" recipes in preparation of their children's meals
must suffer the opprobrium of "laziness," "lack of imagination. . . .")

Illiterates cannot travel freely. When they attempt to do so, they
encounter risks that few of us can dream of. They cannot read traffic
signs and, while they often learn to recognize and to decipher symbols, they cannot manage street names which they haven't seen before. The same is true for bus and subway stops. While ingenuity can
sometimes help a man or woman to discern directions from familiar
landmarks, buildings, cemeteries, churches, and the like, most illiterates are virtually immobilized. They seldom wander past the streets
and neighborhoods they know. Geographical paralysis becomes a bitter metaphor for their entire existence. They are immobilized in almost every sense we can imagine. They can't move up. They can't
move out. They cannot see beyond. Illiterates may take an oral test for
drivers' permits in most sections of America. It is a questionable con-
cession. Where will they go? How will they get there? How will they
get home? Could it be that some of us might like it better if they
stayed where they belong?

25   Travel is only one of many instances of circumscribed existence.
Choice, in almost all its facets, is diminished in the life of an illiterate adult. Even the printed TV schedule, which provides most people with the luxury of preselection, does not belong within the
arsenal of options in illiterate existence. One consequence is that the
viewer watches only what appears at moments when he happens to
have time to turn the switch. Another consequence, a lot more common, is that the TV set remains in operation night and day. Whatever the program offered at the hour when he walks into the room
will be the nutriment that he accepts and swallows. Thus, to passivity, is added frequency—indeed, almost uninterrupted continuity.
Freedom to select is no more possible here than in the choice of
home or surgery or food.

"You don't choose," said one illiterate woman. "You take your
wishes from somebody else." Whether in perusal of a menu, selection
of highways, purchase of groceries, or determination of affordable enjoyment, illiterate Americans must trust somebody else: a friend, a
relative, a stranger on the street, a grocery clerk, a TV copywriter.

"All of our mail we get, it's hard for her to read. Settin' down and
writing a letter, she can't do it. Like if we get a bill . . . we take it over
to my sister-in-law . . . My sister-in-law reads it."

Billing agencies harass poor people for the payment of the bills for purchases that might have taken place six months before. Utility companies offer an agreement for a staggered payment schedule on a bill past due. "You have to trust them," one man said. Precisely for this reason, you end up by trusting no one and suspecting everyone of possible deceit. A submerged sense of distrust becomes the corollary to a constant need to trust. "They are cheating me . . . I have been tricked . . . I do not know . . ."

Not knowing: This is a familiar theme. Not knowing the right word for the right thing at the right time is one form of subjugation. Not knowing the world that lies concealed behind those words is a more terrifying feeling. The longitude and latitude of one's existence are beyond all easy apprehension. Even the hard, cold stars within the firmament above one's head begin to mock the possibilities for self-location. Where am I? Where did I come from? Where will I go?

"I've lost a lot of jobs," one man explains. "Today, even if you're a 30 janitor, there's still reading and writing . . . They leave a note saying, 'Go to room so-and-so . . .' You can't do it. You can't read it. You don't know."

"The hardest thing about it is that I've been places where I didn't know where I was. You don't know where you are . . . You're lost."

"Like I said: I have two kids. What do I do if one of my kids starts choking? I go running to the phone . . . I can't look up the hospital phone number. That's if we're at home. Out on the street, I can't read the sign. I get to a pay phone. 'Okay, tell us where you are. We'll send an ambulance.' I look at the street sign. Right there, I can't tell you what it says. I'd have to spell it out, letter for letter. By that time, one of my kids would be dead . . . These are the kinds of fears you go with, every single day . . ."

"Reading directions, I suffer with. I work with chemicals . . . That's scary to begin with . . ."

"You sit down. They throw the menu in front of you. Where do you go from there? Nine times out of ten you say, 'Go ahead. Pick out something for the both of us.' I've eaten some weird things, let me tell you!"

Menus. Chemicals. A child choking while his mother searches for 35 a word she does not know to find assistance that will come too late. Another mother speaks about the inability to help her kids to read: "I can't read to them. Of course that's leaving them out of something they should have. Oh, it matters. You *believe* it matters! I ordered all these books. The kids belong to a book club. Donny wanted me to read a book to him. I told Donny: 'I can't read,' He said: 'Mommy, you sit down. I'll read it to you.' I tried it one day, reading from the pictures. Donny looked at me. He said, 'Mommy, that's not right.' He's only five. He knew I couldn't read . . ."

A landlord tells a woman that her lease allows him to evict her if her baby cries and causes inconvenience to her neighbors. The consequence of challenging his words conveys a danger which appears, unlikely as it seems, even more alarming than the danger of eviction. Once she admits that she can't read, in the desire to maneuver for the time in which to call a friend, she will have defined herself in terms of an explicit impotence that she cannot endure. Capitulation in this case is preferable to self-humiliation. Resisting the definition of oneself in terms of what one cannot do, what others take for granted, represents a need so great that other imperatives (even one so urgent as the need to keep one's home in winter's cold) evaporate and fall away in face of fear. Even the loss of home and shelter, in this case, is not so terrifying as the loss of self.

"I come out of school. I was sixteen. They had their meetings. The directors meet. They said that I was wasting their school paper. I was wasting pencils . . ."

Another illiterate, looking back, believes she was not worthy of her teacher's time. She believes that it was wrong of her to take up space within her school. She believes that it was right to leave in order that somebody more deserving could receive her place.

Children choke. Their mother chokes another way: on more than chicken bones.

40   People eat what others order, know what others tell them, struggle not to see themselves as they believe the world perceives them. A man in California speaks about his own loss of identity, of selflocation, definition:

"I stood at the bottom of the ramp. My car had broke down on the freeway. There was a phone. I asked for the police. They was nice. They said to tell them where I was. I looked up at the signs. There was one that I had seen before. I read it to them: ONE WAY STREET. They thought it was a joke. I told them I couldn't read. There was other signs above the ramp. They told me to try. I looked around for somebody to help. All the cars was going by real fast. I couldn't make them understand that I was lost. The cop was nice. He told me: 'Try once more.' I did my best. I couldn't read. I only knew the sign above my head. The cop was trying to be nice. He knew that I was trapped. 'I can't send out a car to you if you can't tell me where you are.' I felt afraid. I nearly cried. I'm forty-eight years old. I only said: 'I'm on a one-way street . . .'"

The legal problems and the courtroom complications that confront illiterate adults have been discussed above. The anguish that may underlie such matters was brought home to me this year while I was working on this book. I have spoken, in the introduction, of a sudden phone call from one of my former students, now in prison for a criminal offense. Stephen is not a boy today. He is twenty-eight years old.

He called to ask me to assist him in his trial, which comes up next fall. He will be on trial for murder. He has just knifed and killed a man who first enticed him to his home, then cheated him, and then insulted him—as "an illiterate subhuman."

Stephen now faces twenty years to life. Stephen's mother was illiterate. His grandparents were illiterate as well. What parental curse did not destroy was killed off finally by the schools. Silent violence is repaid with interest. It will cost us $25,000 yearly to maintain this broken soul in prison. But what is the price that has been paid by Stephen's victim? What is the price that will be paid by Stephen?

Perhaps we might slow down a moment here and look at the realities described above. This is the nation that we live in. This is a society that most of us did not create but which our President and other leaders have been willing to sustain by virtue of malign neglect. Do we possess the character and courage to address a problem which so many nations, poorer than our own, have found it natural to correct?

The answers to these questions represent a reasonable test of our 45 belief in the democracy to which we have been asked in public school to swear allegiance.

Responding to Reading

1. According to Kozol, how does illiteracy undermine democracy in the United States? Do you agree with him?
2. Do you think Kozol accurately describes the difficulties illiterates face in their daily lives, or does he seem to be exaggerating? If you think he is exaggerating, what motive might he have?
3. Kozol concludes his essay by asking whether we as a nation have "the character and the courage to address" illiteracy (44). He does not, however, offer any concrete suggestions for doing so. Can you offer any suggestions?

Responding in Writing

Keep a log of your activities for a day. Then, write a few paragraphs discussing which of these activities you could and could not perform if you were illiterate.

PROPAGANDA UNDER A DICTATORSHIP

Aldous Huxley

1894–1963

Despite a serious eye disease that forced him to read with a magnifying glass, Aldous Huxley graduated in 1915 with honors from Balliol College, Oxford. Joining the staff of the Atheneum, he wrote brilliant social and political satires and essays on architecture, science, music, history, philosophy, and religion. Brave New World *(1932), his best-known work, describes a sinister Utopia that depends on scientific breeding and conditioned happiness. In the following essay, from* Brave New World Revisited *(1958), Huxley shows how the manipulation of language in the propaganda of Nazi Germany conditioned the thoughts and behavior of the masses.*

At his trial after the Second World War, Hitler's Minister for Armaments, Albert Speer, delivered a long speech in which, with remarkable acuteness, he described the Nazi tyranny and analyzed its methods. "Hitler's dictatorship," he said, "differed in one fundamental point from all its predecessors in history. It was the first dictatorship in the present period of modern technical development, a dictatorship which made complete use of all technical means for the domination of its own country. Through technical devices like the radio and the loud-speaker, eighty million people were deprived of independent thought. It was thereby possible to subject them to the will of one man. . . . Earlier dictators needed highly qualified assistants even at the lowest level—men who could think and act independently. The totalitarian system in the period of modern technical development can dispense with such men; thanks to modern methods of communication, it is possible to mechanize the lower leadership. As a result of this there has arisen the new type of the uncritical recipient of orders."

In the Brave New World of my prophetic fable technology had advanced far beyond the point it had reached in Hitler's day; consequently the recipients of orders were far less critical than their Nazi counterparts, far more obedient to the order-giving elite. Moreover, they had been genetically standardized and postnatally conditioned to perform their subordinate functions, and could therefore be depended upon to behave almost as predictably as machines. . . . This conditioning of "the lower leadership" is already going on under the Communist dictatorships. The Chinese and the Russians are not relying merely on the indirect effects of advancing technology; they are working directly on the psychophysical organisms of their lower leaders, subjecting minds and bodies to a system of ruthless and, from all accounts, highly effective conditioning. "Many a man," said Speer, "has been haunted by the nightmare that one day nations might be dominated by technical means. That nightmare was almost realized in Hitler's totalitarian system." Almost, but not quite. The Nazis did not have time—and perhaps did not have the intelligence and the necessary knowledge—to brainwash and condition their lower leadership. This, it may be, is one of the reasons why they failed.

Since Hitler's day the armory of technical devices at the disposal of the would-be dictator has been considerably enlarged. As well as the radio, the loud-speaker, the moving picture camera and the rotary press, the contemporary propagandist can make use of television to broadcast the image as well as the voice of his client, and can record both image and voice on spools of magnetic tape. Thanks to techno-logical progress, Big Brother can now be almost as omnipresent as God. Nor is it only on the technical front that the hand of the would-be dictator has been strengthened. Since Hitler's day a great deal of work has been carried out in those fields of applied psychology and neurol-ogy which are the special province of the propagandist, the indoctrina-tor and the brainwasher. In the past these specialists in the art of changing people's minds were empiricists. By a method of trial and error they had worked out a number of techniques and procedures, which they used very effectively without, however, knowing precisely why they were effective. Today the art of mind-control is in process of becoming a science. The practitioners of this science know what they are doing and why. They are guided in their work by theories and hy-potheses solidly established on a massive foundation of experimental evidence. Thanks to the new insights and the new techniques made possible by these insights, the nightmare that was "all but realized in Hitler's totalitarian system" may soon be completely realizable.

But before we discuss these new insights and techniques let us take a look at the nightmare that so nearly came true in Nazi Ger-many. What were the methods used by Hitler and Goebbels[1] for "de-priving eighty million people of independent thought and subjecting them to the will of one man"? And what was the theory of human na-ture upon which those terrifyingly successful methods were based? These questions can be answered, for the most part, in Hitler's own words. And what remarkably clear and astute words they are! When he writes about such vast abstractions as Race and History and Provi-dence, Hitler is strictly unreadable. But when he writes about the Ger-man masses and the methods he used for dominating and directing them, his style changes. Nonsense gives place to sense, bombast to a hard-boiled and cynical lucidity. In his philosophical lucubrations Hitler was either cloudily daydreaming or reproducing other people's half-baked notions. In his comments on crowds and propaganda he was writing of things he knew by firsthand experience. In the words of his ablest biographer, Mr. Alan Bullock, "Hitler was the greatest demagogue in history." Those who add "only a demagogue," fail to appreciate the nature of political power in an age of mass politics. As he himself said, "To be a leader means to be able to move the masses." Hitler's aim was first to move the masses and then, having pried them loose from their traditional loyalties and moralities, to impose upon them (with the hypnotized consent of the majority) a new au-thoritarian order of his own devising. "Hitler," wrote Hermann Rauschning in 1939, "has a deep respect for the Catholic church and the Jesuit order; not because of their Christian doctrine, but because

---

[1] Joseph Paul Goebbels (1897–1945), the propaganda minister under Hitler. [Eds.]

of the 'machinery' they have elaborated and controlled, their hierarchical system, their extremely clever tactics, their knowledge of human nature and their wise use of human weaknesses in ruling over believers." Ecclesiasticism without Christianity, the discipline of a monastic rule, not for God's sake or in order to achieve personal salvation, but for the sake of the State and for the greater glory and power of the demagogue turned Leader—this was the goal toward which the systematic moving of the masses was to lead.

5   Let us see what Hitler thought of the masses he moved and how he did the moving. The first principle from which he started was a value judgment: the masses are utterly contemptible. They are incapable of abstract thinking and uninterested in any fact outside the circle of their immediate experience. Their behavior is determined, not by knowledge and reason, but by feelings and unconscious drives. It is in these drives and feelings that "the roots of their positive as well as their negative attitudes are implanted." To be successful a propagandist must learn how to manipulate these instincts and emotions. "The driving force which has brought about the most tremendous revolutions on this earth has never been a body of scientific teaching which has gained power over the masses, but always a devotion which has inspired them, and often a kind of hysteria which has urged them into action. Whoever wishes to win over the masses must know the key that will open the door of their hearts." . . . In post-Freudian jargon, of their unconscious.

Hitler made his strongest appeal to those members of the lower middle classes who had been ruined by the inflation of 1923, and then ruined all over again by the depression of 1929 and the following years. "The masses" of whom he speaks were these bewildered, frustrated and chronically anxious millions. To make them more masslike, more homogeneously subhuman, he assembled them, by the thousands and the tens of thousands, in vast halls and arenas, where individuals could lose their personal identity, even their elementary humanity, and be merged with the crowd. A man or woman makes direct contact with society in two ways: as a member of some familial, professional or religious group, or as a member of a crowd. Groups are capable of being as moral and intelligent as the individuals who form them; a crowd is chaotic, has no purpose of its own and is capable of anything except intelligent action and realistic thinking. Assembled in a crowd, people lose their powers of reasoning and their capacity for moral choice. Their suggestibility is increased to the point where they cease to have any judgment or will of their own. They become very excitable, they lose all sense of individual or collective responsibility, they are subject to sudden accesses of rage, enthusiasm and panic. In a word, a man in a crowd behaves as though he had swallowed a large dose of some powerful intoxicant. He is a victim of what I have called "herd-poisoning." Like alcohol, herd-poison is an active, extraverted drug. The crowd-intoxicated individual escapes from responsibility, intelligence and morality into a kind of frantic, animal mindlessness.

During his long career as an agitator, Hitler had studied the effects of herd-poison and had learned how to exploit them for his own purposes. He had discovered that the orator can appeal to those "hidden forces" which motivate men's actions, much more effectively than can the writer. Reading is a private, not a collective activity. The writer speaks only to individuals, sitting by themselves in a state of normal sobriety. The orator speaks to masses of individuals, already well primed with herd-poison. They are at his mercy and, if he knows his business, he can do what he likes with them. As an orator, Hitler knew his business supremely well. He was able, in his own words, "to follow the lead of the great mass in such a way that from the living emotion to his hearers the apt word which he needed would be suggested to him and in its turn this would go straight to the heart of his hearers." Otto Strasser called him a "loud-speaker, proclaiming the most secret desires, the least admissible instincts, the sufferings and personal revolts of a whole nation." Twenty years before Madison Avenue embarked upon "Motivational Research," Hitler was systematically exploring and exploiting the secret fears and hopes, the cravings, anxieties and frustrations of the German masses. It is by manipulating "hidden forces" that the advertising experts induce us to buy their wares—a toothpaste, a brand of cigarettes, a political candidate. And it is by appealing to the same hidden forces—and to others too dangerous for Madison Avenue to meddle with—that Hitler induced the German masses to buy themselves a Fuehrer, an insane philosophy and the Second World War.

Unlike the masses, intellectuals have a taste for rationality and an interest in facts. Their critical habit of mind makes them resistant to the kind of propaganda that works so well on the majority. Among the masses "instinct is supreme, and from instinct comes faith. . . . While the healthy common folk instinctively close their ranks to form a community of the people" (under a Leader, it goes without saying) "intellectuals run this way and that, like hens in a poultry yard. With them one cannot make history; they cannot be used as elements composing a community." Intellectuals are the kind of people who demand evidence and are shocked by logical inconsistencies and fallacies. They regard oversimplification as the original sin of the mind and have no use for the slogans, the unqualified assertions and sweeping generalizations which are the propagandist's stock in trade. "All effective propaganda," Hitler wrote, "must be confined to a few bare necessities and then must be expressed in a few stereotyped formulas." These stereotyped formulas must be constantly repeated, for "only constant repetition will finally succeed in imprinting an idea upon the memory of a crowd." Philosophy teaches us to feel uncertain about the things that seem to us self-evident. Propaganda, on the other hand, teaches us to accept as self-evident matters about which it would be reasonable to suspend our judgment or to feel doubt. The aim of the demagogue is to create social coherence under his own leadership. But, as Bertrand Russell has pointed out, "systems of dogma without empirical foundations, such as scholasticism, Marxism and fascism, have the advantage of producing a great deal of social coherence among their disciples." The demagogic propagandist must therefore be consistently dogmatic. All his statements are made without qualification. There are no grays in his picture of the world; everything is either diabolically black or celestially white. In Hitler's words, the propagandist should adopt "a systematically one-sided attitude towards every problem that has to be dealt with." He must never admit that he might be wrong or that people with a different point of view might be even partially right. Opponents should not be argued with; they should be attacked, shouted down, or, if they become too much of a nuisance, liquidated. The morally squeamish intellectual may be shocked by this kind of thing. But the masses are always convinced that "right is on the side of the active aggressor."

Such, then, was Hitler's opinion of humanity in the mass. It was a very low opinion. Was it also an incorrect opinion? The tree is known by its fruits, and a theory of human nature which inspired the kind of techniques that proved so horribly effective must contain at least an element of truth. Virtue and intelligence belong to human beings as individuals freely associating with other individuals in small groups. So do sin—and stupidity. But the subhuman mindlessness to which the demagogue makes his appeal, the moral imbecility on which he relies when he goads his victims into action, are characteristic not of men and women as individuals, but of men and women in masses. Mindlessness and moral idiocy are not characteristically human attributes; they are symptoms of herd-poisoning. In all the world's higher religions, salvation and enlightenment are for individuals. The kingdom of heaven is within the mind of a person, not within the collective mindlessness of a crowd. Christ promised to be present where two or three are gathered together. He did not say anything about being present where thousands are intoxicating one another with herd-poison. Under the Nazis enormous numbers of people were compelled to spend an enormous amount of time marching in serried ranks from point A to point B and back again to point A. "This keeping of the whole population on the march seemed to be a senseless waste of time and energy. Only much later," adds Hermann Rauschning, "was there revealed in it a subtle intention based on a well-judged adjustment of ends and means. Marching diverts men's thoughts. Marching kills thought. Marching makes an end of individuality. Marching is the indispensable magic stroke performed in order to accustom the people to a mechanical, quasi-ritualistic activity until it becomes second nature."

10   From his point of view and at the level where he had chosen to do his dreadful work, Hitler was perfectly correct in his estimate of

human nature. To those of us who look at men and women as individuals rather than as members of crowds, or of regimented collectives, he seems hideously wrong. In an age of accelerating over-population, of accelerating over-organization and even more efficient means of mass communication, how can we preserve the integrity and reassert the value of the human individual? This is a question that can still be asked and perhaps effectively answered. A generation from now it may be too late to find an answer and perhaps impossible, in the stifling collective climate of that future time, even to ask the question.

Responding to Reading

1. According to Huxley, why was Hitler's dictatorship different from its predecessors? What techniques did Hitler use to manipulate the German people? Why do you think he was so successful?
2. What was Hitler's opinion of the masses? Does Huxley agree with this evaluation?
3. In paragraph 3, Huxley says, "Since Hitler's day the armory of technical devices at the disposal of the would-be dictator has been considerably enlarged." What are some of these devices, and how have they made a dictator's job easier?

Responding in Writing

Do you think the existence of the Internet makes it easier or more difficult for a dictator to control the masses?

POLITICS AND THE ENGLISH LANGUAGE

George Orwell

1903–1950

George Orwell was born Eric Arthur Blair in Bengal, India, the son of a British colonial civil servant. He joined the Indian Imperial Police in Burma, where he came to question the British methods of colonialism. (See "Shooting an Elephant" in Chapter 11.) An enemy of totalitarianism and a spokesperson for the oppressed, Orwell criticized totalitarian regimes in his bitterly satirical novels Animal Farm *(1945) and* 1984 *(1949). He wrote many literary essays and is much admired for his lucid prose style. The following essay was written at the end of World War II, when jingoistic praise for "our democratic institutions" and blindly passionate defenses of Marxist ideology were the two common extremes of public political discourse. Orwell's plea for clear thinking and writing at a time when "political language . . . [was] designed to make lies sound truthful and murder respectable, and to give an appearance of solidity to pure wind" is as relevant today as it was when it was written.*

Most people who bother with the matter at all would admit that the English language is in a bad way, but it is generally assumed that we cannot by conscious action do anything about it. Our civilization is decadent and our language—so the argument runs—must inevitably share in the general collapse. It follows that any struggle against the abuse of language is a sentimental archaism, like preferring candles to electric light or hansom cabs to airplanes. Underneath this lies the half-conscious belief that language is a natural growth and not an instrument which we shape for our own purposes.

Now, it is clear that the decline of a language must ultimately have political and economic causes: it is not due simply to the bad influence of this or that individual writer. But an effect can become a cause, reinforcing the original cause and producing the same effect in an intensified form, and so on indefinitely. A man may take to drink because he feels himself to be a failure, and then fail all the more completely because he drinks. It is rather the same thing that is happening to the English language. It becomes ugly and inaccurate because our thoughts are foolish, but the slovenliness of our language makes it easier for us to have foolish thoughts. The point is that the process is reversible. Modern English, especially written English, is full of bad habits which spread by imitation and which can be avoided if one is willing to take the necessary trouble. If one gets rid of these habits one can think more clearly, and to think clearly is a necessary first step towards political regeneration: so that the fight against bad English is not frivolous and is not the exclusive concern of professional writers. I will come back to this presently, and I hope that by that time the meaning of what I have said here will have become clearer. Meanwhile, here are five specimens of the English language as it is now habitually written.

These five passages have not been picked out because they are especially bad—I could have quoted far worse if I had chosen—but because they illustrate various of the mental vices from which we now suffer. They are a little below the average, but are fairly representative samples. I number them so that I can refer back to them when necessary:

> "(1) I am not, indeed, sure whether it is not true to say that the Milton who once seemed not unlike a seventeenth-century Shelley had not become, out of an experience ever more bitter in each year, more alien (*sic*) to the founder of that Jesuit sect which nothing could induce him to tolerate."
>
> Professor Harold Laski (Essay in *Freedom of Expression*).

> "(2) Above all, we cannot play ducks and drakes with a native battery of idioms which prescribes such egregious collocations of vocables as the Basic *put up with* for *tolerate or put at a loss for bewilder.*"
>
> Professor Lancelot Hogben (*Interglossa*).

> "(3) On the one side we have the free personality: by definition it is not neurotic, for it has neither conflict nor dream. Its desires, such as

they are, are transparent, for they are just what institutional approval keeps in the forefront of consciousness; another institutional pattern would alter their number and intensity; there is little in them that is natural, irreducible, or culturally dangerous. But *on the other side,* the social bond itself is nothing but the mutual reflection of these selfse-cure integrities. Recall the definition of love. Is not this the very pic-ture of a small academic? Where is there a place in this hall of mirrors for either personality or fraternity?"

Essay on psychology in Politics (New York).

"(4) All the 'best people' from the gentlemen's clubs, and all the fran-tic fascist captains, united in common hatred of Socialism and bestial horror of the rising tide of the mass revolutionary movement, have turned to acts of provocation, to foul incendiarism, to medieval leg-ends of poisoned wells, to legalize their own destruction of proletarian organizations, and rouse the agitated petty-bourgeoisie to chauvinistic fervor on behalf of the fight against the revolutionary way out of the crisis."

Communist pamphlet.

"(5) If a new spirit is to be infused into this old country, there is one thorny and contentious reform which must be tackled, and that is the humanization and galvanization of the B.B.C. Timidity here will be-speak cancer and atrophy of the soul. The heart of Britain may be sound and of strong beat, for instance, but the British lion's roar at present is like that of Bottom in Shakespeare's *Midsummer Night's Dream*—as gentle as any sucking dove. A virile new Britain cannot continue indefinitely to be traduced in the eyes, or rather ears, of the world by the effete languors of Langham Place, brazenly masquerad-ing as 'standard English.' When the Voice of Britain is heard at nine o'clock, better far and infinitely less ludicrous to hear aitches honestly dropped than the present priggish, inflated, inhibited, school-ma'amish arch braying of blameless bashful mewing maidens!"

Letter in Tribune.

Each of these passages has faults of its own, but, quite apart from avoidable ugliness, two qualities are common to all of them. The first is staleness of imagery: the other is lack of precision. The writer either has a meaning and cannot express it, or he inadver-tently says something else, or he is almost indifferent as to whether his words mean anything or not. This mixture of vagueness and sheer incompetence is the most marked characteristic of modern English prose, and especially of any kind of political writing. As soon as certain topics are raised, the concrete melts into the abstract and no one seems able to think of turns of speech that are not hack-neyed: prose consists less and less of *words* chosen for the sake of their meaning, and more and more of *phrases* tacked together like the sections of a prefabricated hen-house. I list below, with notes and examples, various of the tricks by means of which the work of prose-construction is habitually dodged:

Dying Metaphors

5   A newly invented metaphor assists thought by evoking a visual image, while on the other hand a metaphor which is technically "dead" (e.g. *iron resolution*) has in effect reverted to being an ordinary word and can generally be used without loss of vividness. But in between these two classes there is a huge dump of worn-out metaphors which have lost all evocative power and are merely used because they save people the trouble of inventing phrases for themselves. Examples are: *Ring the changes on, take up the cudgels for, toe the line, ride roughshod over, stand shoulder to shoulder with, play into the hands of, no axe to grind, grist to the mill, fishing in troubled waters, on the order of the day, Achilles' heel, swan song, hotbed*. Many of these are used without knowledge of their meaning (what is a "rift,"[1] for instance?), and incompatible metaphors are frequently mixed, a sure sign that the writer is not interested in what he is saying. Some metaphors now current have been twisted out of their original meaning without those who use them even being aware of the fact. For example, *toe the line* is sometimes written *tow the line*. Another example is the *hammer and the anvil*, now always used with the implication that the anvil gets the worst of it. In real life it is always the anvil that breaks the hammer, never the other way about: a writer who stopped to think what he was saying would be aware of this, and would avoid perverting the original phrase.

Operators or Verbal False Limbs

These save the trouble of picking out appropriate verbs and nouns, and at the same time pad each sentence with extra syllables which give it an appearance of symmetry. Characteristic phrases are: *render inoperative, militate against, make contact with, be subjected to, give rise to, give grounds for, have the effect of, play a leading part (role) in, make itself felt, take effect, exhibit a tendency to, serve the purpose of, etc., etc.* The keynote is the elimination of simple verbs. Instead of being a single word, such as *break, stop, spoil, mend, kill,* a verb becomes a *phrase,* made up of a noun or adjective tacked on to some general-purposes verb such as *prove, serve, form, play, render*. In addition, the passive voice is wherever possible used in preference to the active, and noun constructions are used instead of gerunds (*by examination of* instead of *by examining*). The range of verbs is further cut down by means of the *-ize* and *de-* formation, and the banal statements are given an appearance of profundity by means of the *not un-* formation. Simple conjunctions and prepositions are replaced by such phrases as *with respect to, having regard to, the fact that, by dint of, in view of, in the interests of, on the hypothesis that;* and the ends of

---

[1]Originally *rift* referred to a geological fault or fissure. Now it is commonly used to indicate a breach or estrangement. [Eds.]

sentences are saved from anticlimax by such resounding common-places as *greatly to be desired, cannot be left out of account, a development to be expected in the near future, deserving of serious consideration, brought to a satisfactory conclusion,* and so on and so forth.

Pretentious Diction

Words like *phenomenon, element, individual* (as noun), *objective, categorical, effective, virtual, basic, primary, promote, constitute, exhibit, exploit, utilize, eliminate, liquidate,* are used to dress up simple statements and give an air of scientific impartiality to biased judgments. Adjectives like *epoch-making, epic, historic, unforgettable, triumphant, age-old, inevitable, inexorable, veritable,* are used to dignify the sordid processes of international politics, while writing that aims at glorifying war usually takes on an archaic color, its characteristic words being: *realm, throne, chariot, mailed fist, trident, sword, shield, buckler, banner, jackboot, clarion.* Foreign words and expressions such as *cul de sac, ancien régime, deus ex machina, mutatis mutandis, status quo, gleichschaltung, weltanschauung,* are used to give an air of culture and elegance. Except for the useful abbreviations *i.e., e.g.,* and *etc.,* there is no real need for any of the hundreds of foreign phrases now current in English. Bad writers, and especially scientific, political and sociological writers, are nearly always haunted by the notion that Latin or Greek words are grander than Saxon ones, and unnecessary words like *expedite, ameliorate, predict, extraneous, deracinated, clandestine, subaqueous* and hundreds of others constantly gain ground from their Anglo-Saxon opposite numbers.[2] The jargon peculiar to Marxist writing (*hyena, hangman, cannibal, petty bourgeois, these gentry, lacquey, flunkey, mad dog, White Guard,* etc.) consists largely of words and phrases translated from Russian, German or French; but the normal way of coining a new word is to use a Latin or Greek root with the appropriate affix and, where necessary, the *-ize* formation. It is often easier to make up words of this kind (*deregionalize, impermissible, extra-marital, nonfragmentatory* and so forth) than to think up the English words that will cover one's meaning. The result, in general, is an increase in slovenliness and vagueness.

Meaningless Words

In certain kinds of writing, particularly in art criticism and literary criticism, it is normal to come across long passages which are almost

---

[2]An interesting illustration of this is the way in which the English flower names which were in use till very recently are being ousted by Greek ones, *snapdragon* becoming *antirrhinum, forget-me-not* becoming *myosotis,* etc. It is hard to see any practical reason for this change in fashion: it is probably due to an instinctive turning-away from the more homely word and a vague feeling that the Greek word is scientific.

completely lacking in meaning.[3] Words like *romantic, plastic, values, human, dead, sentimental, natural, vitality,* as used in art criticism, are strictly meaningless in the sense that they not only do not point to any discoverable object, but are hardly ever expected to do so by the reader. When one critic writes, "The outstanding feature of Mr. X's work is its living quality," while another writes, "The immediately striking thing about Mr. X's work is its peculiar deadness," the reader accepts this as a simple difference of opinion. If words like *black* and *white* were involved, instead of the jargon words *dead* and *living,* he would see at once that language was being used in an improper way. Many political words are similarly abused. The word *Fascism* has now no meaning except in so far as it signifies "something not desirable." The words *democracy, socialism, freedom, patriotic, realistic, justice,* have each of them several different meanings which cannot be reconciled with one another. In the case of a word like *democracy,* not only is there no agreed definition, but the attempt to make one is resisted from all sides. It is almost universally felt that when we call a country democratic we are praising it: consequently the defenders of every kind of regime claim that it is a democracy, and fear that they might have to stop using the word if it were tied down to any one meaning. Words of this kind are often used in a consciously dishonest way. That is, the person who uses them has his own private definition, but allows his hearer to think he means something quite different. Statements like *Marshal Pétain was a true patriot, The Soviet Press is the freest in the world, The Catholic Church is opposed to persecution,* are almost always made with intent to deceive. Other words used in variable meanings, in most cases more or less dishonestly, are: *class, totalitarian, science, progressive, reactionary, bourgeois, equality.*

Now that I have made this catalogue of swindles and perversions, let me give another example of the kind of writing that they lead to. This time it must of its nature be an imaginary one. I am going to translate a passage of good English into modern English of the worst sort. Here is a well-known verse from *Ecclesiastes:*

> "I returned and saw under the sun, that the race is not to the swift, nor the battle to the strong, neither yet bread to the wise, nor yet riches to men of understanding, nor yet favor to men of skill; but time and chance happeneth to them all."

10   Here it is in modern English:

> "Objective consideration of contemporary phenomena compels the conclusion that success or failure in competitive activities exhibits no

---

[3]Example: "Comfort's catholicity of perception and image, strangely Whitmanesque in range, almost the exact opposite in aesthetic compulsion, continues to evoke that trembling atmospheric accumulative hinting at a cruel, an inexorably serene timelessness. . . . Wrey Gardiner scores by aiming at simple bull's-eyes with precision. Only they are not so simple, and through this contended sadness—runs more than the surface bittersweet of resignation" (*Poetry Quarterly*).

tendency to be commensurate with innate capacity, but that a considerable element of the unpredictable must invariably be taken into account."

This is a parody, but not a very gross one. Exhibit (3), above, for instance, contains several patches of the same kind of English. It will be seen that I have not made a full translation. The beginning and ending of the sentence follow the original meaning fairly closely, but in the middle the concrete illustrations—race, battle, bread—dissolve into the vague phrase "success or failure in competitive activities." This had to be so, because no modern writer of the kind I am discussing— no one capable of using phrases like "objective consideration of contemporary phenomena"—would ever tabulate his thoughts in that precise and detailed way. The whole tendency of modern prose is away from concreteness. Now analyze these two sentences a little more closely. The first contains forty-nine words but only sixty syllables, and all its words are those of everyday life. The second contains thirty-eight words of ninety syllables: eighteen of its words are from Latin roots, and one from Greek. The first sentence contains six vivid images, and only one phrase ("time and chance") that could be called vague. The second contains not a single fresh, arresting phrase, and in spite of its ninety syllables it gives only a shortened version of the meaning contained in the first. Yet without a doubt it is the second kind of sentence that is gaining ground in modern English. I do not want to exaggerate. This kind of writing is not yet universal, and outcrops of simplicity will occur here and there in the worst-written page. Still, if you or I were told to write a few lines on the uncertainty of human fortunes, we should probably come much nearer to my imaginary sentence than to the one from *Ecclesiastes.*

As I have tried to show, modern writing at its worst does not consist in picking out words for the sake of their meaning and inventing images in order to make the meaning clearer. It consists in gumming together long strips of words which have already been set in order by someone else, and making the results presentable by sheer humbug. The attraction of this way of writing is that it is easy. It is easier—even quicker, once you have the habit—to say *In my opinion it is a not unjustifiable assumption that* than to say *I think.* If you use ready-made phrases, you not only don't have to hunt about for words; you also don't have to bother with the rhythms of your sentences, since these phrases are generally so arranged as to be more or less euphonious. When you are composing in a hurry—when you are dictating to a stenographer, for instance, or making a public speech—it is natural to fall into a pretentious, Latinized style. Tags like *a consideration which we should do well to bear in mind* or *a conclusion to which all of us would readily assent* will save many a sentence from coming down with a bump. By using stale metaphors, similes and idioms, you save much mental effort, at the cost of leaving your meaning vague, not only for your reader but for yourself. This is the significance of mixed metaphors. The sole aim of a metaphor is to call up a visual image. When these images clash—as in *The Fascist octopus has sung its swan song, the jackboot is thrown into the melting pot*—it can be taken as certain that the writer is not seeing a mental image of the objects he is naming; in other words he is not really thinking. Look again at the examples I gave at the beginning of this essay. Professor Laski (1) uses five negatives in fifty-three words. One of these is superfluous, making nonsense of the whole passage, and in addition there is the slip *alien* for *akin*, making further nonsense, and several avoidable pieces of clumsiness which increase the general vagueness. Professor Hogben (2) plays ducks and drakes with a battery which is able to write prescriptions, and, while disapproving of the everyday phrase *put up with*, is unwilling to look *egregious* up in the dictionary and see what it means. (3), if one takes an uncharitable attitude towards it, is simply meaningless: probably one could work out its intended meaning by reading the whole of the article in which it occurs. In (4), the writer knows more or less what he wants to say, but an accumulation of stale phrases chokes him like tea leaves blocking a sink. In (5), words and meaning have almost parted company. People who write in this manner usually have a general emotional meaning—they dislike one thing and want to express solidarity with another—but they are not interested in the detail of what they are saying. A scrupulous writer, in every sentence that he writes, will ask himself at least four questions, thus: What am I trying to say? What words will express it? What image or idiom will make it clearer? Is this image fresh enough to have an effect? And he will probably ask himself two more: Could I put it more shortly? Have I said anything that is avoidably ugly? But you are not obliged to go to all this trouble. You can shirk it by simply throwing your mind open and letting the ready-made phrases come crowding in. They will construct your sentences for you—even think your thoughts for you, to a certain extent—and at need they will perform the important service of partially concealing your meaning even from yourself. It is at this point that the special connection between politics and the debasement of language becomes clear.

In our time it is broadly true that political writing is bad writing. Where it is not true, it will generally be found that the writer is some kind of rebel, expressing his private opinions and not a "party line." Orthodoxy, of whatever color, seems to demand a lifeless, imitative style. The political dialects to be found in pamphlets, leading articles, manifestos, White Papers and the speeches of under-secretaries do, of course, vary from party to party, but they are all alike in that one almost never finds in them a fresh, vivid, home-made turn of speech. When one watches some tired hack on the platform mechanically repeating the familiar phrases—*bestial atrocities, iron heel, bloodstained tyranny, free peoples of the world, stand shoulder to shoulder*—one often has a curious feeling that one is not watching a live human being but some kind of dummy: a feeling which suddenly becomes stronger at moments when the light catches the speaker's spectacles and turns them into blank discs which seem to have no eyes behind them. And this is not altogether fanciful. A speaker who uses that kind of phraseology has gone some distance towards turning himself into a machine. The appropriate noises are coming out of his larynx, but his brain is not involved as it would be if he were choosing his words for himself. If the speech he is making is one that he is accustomed to make over and over again, he may be almost unconscious of what he is saying, as one is when one utters the responses in church. And this reduced state of consciousness, if not indispensable, is at any rate favorable to political conformity.

In our time, political speech and writing are largely the defense of the indefensible. Things like the continuance of British rule in India, the Russian purges and deportations, the dropping of the atom bombs on Japan, can indeed be defended, but only by arguments which are too brutal for most people to face, and which do not square with the professed aims of political parties. Thus political language has to consist largely of euphemism, question-begging and sheer cloudy vagueness. Defenseless villages are bombarded from the air, the inhabitants driven out into the countryside, the cattle machine-gunned, the huts set on fire with incendiary bullets: this is called *pacification.* Millions of peasants are robbed of their farms and sent trudging along the roads with no more than they can carry: this is called *transfer of population* or *rectification of frontiers.* People are imprisoned for years without trial, or shot in the back of the neck or sent to die of scurvy in Arctic lumber camps: this is called *elimination of unreliable elements.* Such phraseology is needed if one wants to name things without calling up mental pictures of them. Consider for instance some comfortable English professor defending Russian totalitarianism. He cannot say outright, "I believe in killing off your opponents when you can get good results by doing so." Probably, therefore, he will say something like this:

"While freely conceding that the Soviet régime exhibits certain fea- 15 tures which the humanitarian may be inclined to deplore, we must, I think, agree that a certain curtailment of the right to political opposition is an unavoidable concomitant of transitional periods, and that the rigors which the Russian people have been called upon to undergo have been amply justified in the sphere of concrete achievement."

The inflated style is itself a kind of euphemism. A mass of Latin words falls upon the facts like soft snow, blurring the outlines and covering up all the details. The great enemy of clear language is insincerity. When there is a gap between one's real and one's declared aims, one turns as it were instinctively to long words and exhausted idioms, like a cuttlefish squirting out ink. In our age there is no such thing as "keeping out of politics." All issues are political issues, and politics itself is a mass of lies, evasions, folly, hatred and schizophrenia. When the general atmosphere is bad, language must suffer. I should expect to find—this is a guess which I have not sufficient knowledge to verify—that the German, Russian and Italian languages have all deteriorated in the last ten to fifteen years, as a result of dictatorship.

But if thought corrupts language, language can also corrupt thought. A bad usage can spread by tradition and imitation, even among people who should and do know better. The debased language that I have been discussing is in some ways very convenient. Phrases like *a not unjustifiable assumption, leaves much to be desired, would serve no good purpose, a consideration which we should do well to bear in mind*, are a continuous temptation, a packet of aspirins always at one's elbow. Look back through this essay, and for certain you will find that I have again and again committed the very faults I am protesting against. By this morning's post I have received a pamphlet dealing with conditions in Germany. The author tells me that he "felt impelled" to write it. I open it at random, and here is almost the first sentence that I see: "(The Allies) have an opportunity not only of achieving a radical transformation of Germany's social and political structure in such a way as to avoid a nationalistic reaction in Germany itself, but at the same time of laying the foundations of a cooperative and unified Europe." You see, he "feels impelled" to write—feels, presumably, that he has something new to say—and yet his words, like cavalry horses answering the bugle, group themselves automatically into the familiar dreary pattern. This invasion of one's mind by ready-made phrases (*lay the foundations, achieve a radical transformation*) can only be prevented if one is constantly on guard against them, and every such phrase anesthetizes a portion of one's brain.

I said earlier that the decadence of our language is probably curable. Those who deny this would argue, if they produced an argument at all, that language merely reflects existing social conditions, and that we cannot influence its development by any direct tinkering with words and constructions. So far as the general tone or spirit of a language goes, this may be true, but it is not true in detail. Silly words and expressions have often disappeared, not through any evolutionary process but owing to the conscious action of a minority. Two recent examples were *explore every avenue* and *leave no stone unturned*, which were killed by the jeers of a few journalists. There is a long list of flyblown metaphors which could similarly be got rid of if enough people would interest themselves in the job; and it should also be possible to laugh the *not un-* formation out of existence,[4] to reduce the amount of Latin and Greek in the average sentence, to drive out foreign phrases and strayed scientific words, and, in general, to make pretentiousness unfashionable. But all these are minor

---

[4]One can cure oneself of the *not un-* formation by memorizing this sentence: *A not unblack dog was chasing a not unsmall rabbit across a not ungreen field.*

points. The defense of the English language implies more than this, and perhaps it is best to start by saying what it does *not* imply.

To begin with it has nothing to do with archaism, with the salvaging of obsolete words and turns of speech, or with the setting up of a "standard English" which must never be departed from. On the contrary, it is especially concerned with the scrapping of every word or idiom which has outworn its usefulness. It has nothing to do with correct grammar and syntax, which are of no importance so long as one makes one's meaning clear, or with the avoidance of Americanisms, or with having what is called a "good prose style." On the other hand it is not concerned with fake simplicity and the attempt to make written English colloquial. Nor does it even imply in every case preferring the Saxon word to the Latin one, though it does imply using the fewest and shortest words that will cover one's meaning. What is above all needed is to let the meaning choose the word and not the other way about. In prose, the worst thing one can do with words is to surrender to them. When you think of a concrete object, you think wordlessly, and then, if you want to describe the thing you have been visualizing you probably hunt about till you find the exact words that seem to fit. When you think of something abstract you are more inclined to use words from the start, and unless you make a conscious effort to prevent it, the existing dialect will come rushing in and do the job for you, at the expense of blurring or even changing your meaning. Probably it is better to put off using words as long as possible and get one's meaning as clear as one can through pictures or sensations. Afterwards one can choose—not simply accept—the phrases that will best cover the meaning, and then switch round and decide what impression one's words are likely to make on another person. This last effort of the mind cuts out all stale or mixed images, all prefabricated phrases, needless repetitions, and humbug and vagueness generally. But one can often be in doubt about the effect of a word or a phrase, and one needs rules that one can rely on when instinct fails. I think the following rules will cover most cases:

(i)   Never use a metaphor, simile or other figure of speech which you are used to seeing in print.

(ii) Never use a long word where a short one will do.

(iii) If it is possible to cut a word out, always cut it out.

(iv) Never use the passive where you can use the active.

(v)   Never use a foreign phrase, a scientific word, or a jargon word if you can think of an everyday English equivalent.

(vi) Break any of these rules sooner than say anything outright barbarous.

These rules sound elementary, and so they are, but they demand a 20 deep change of attitude in anyone who has grown used to writing in the style now fashionable. One could keep all of them and still write bad English, but one could not write the kind of stuff that I quoted in those five specimens at the beginning of this article.

I have not here been considering the literary use of language, but merely language as an instrument for expressing and not for concealing or preventing thought. Stuart Chase[5] and others have come near to claiming that all abstract words are meaningless, and have used this as a pretext for advocating a kind of political quietism. Since you don't know what Fascism is, how can you struggle against Fascism? One need not swallow such absurdities as this, but one ought to recognize that the present political chaos is connected with the decay of language, and that one can probably bring about some improvement by starting at the verbal end. If you simplify your English, you are freed from the worst follies of orthodoxy. You cannot speak any of the necessary dialects, and when you make a stupid remark its stupidity will be obvious, even to yourself. Political language—and with variations this is true of all political parties, from Conservatives to Anarchists— is designed to make lies sound truthful and murder respectable, and to give an appearance of solidity to pure wind. One cannot change this all in a moment, but one can at least change one's own habits, and from time to time one can even, if one jeers loudly enough, send some worn-out and useless phrase, some *jackboot, Achilles' heel, hotbed, melting pot, acid test, veritable inferno* or other lump of verbal refuse—into the dustbin where it belongs.

Responding to Reading

1. According to Orwell, what is the relationship between politics and the English language?
2. What does Orwell mean in paragraph 14 when he says, "In our time, political speech and writing are largely the defense of the indefensible"? Do you believe his statement applies to current political speech and writing as well?
3. Locate some examples of dying metaphors used in the popular press. Do you agree with Orwell that they undermine clear thought and expression? Why or why not?

Responding in Writing

As you listen to the local news on TV, write down several sentences that contain words and phrases that are vague, repetitious, or meaningless. Then, substitute your own clearer, more explicit words for the ones you identified.

---

[5]Writer known for his advocacy of clear writing and clear thinking. [Eds.]

Focus

How Free Should Free Speech Be?

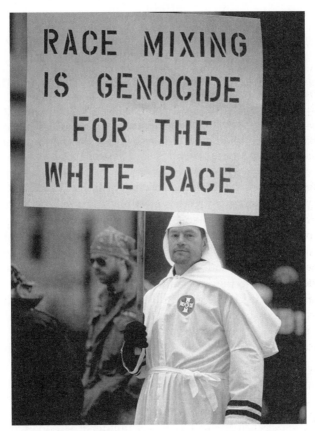

Ku Klux Klan member carrying sign outside Capitol
building, Washington, D.C

Responding to the Image

1. The image above depicts a Ku Klux Klan member in full regalia, looking
   directly at the camera. Which do you find more disturbing, the man or the
   sign he is holding? Explain.
2. The Supreme Court has repeatedly affirmed the right of groups such as the
   Ku Klux Klan to express their views in public—for example, in protest
   marches or in parades. Do you agree with this position? Given the nature
   of their message, what limitations (if any) do you think should be placed
   on such hate groups?

THE FREE-SPEECH FOLLIES

Stanley Fish

1939–

Stanley Fish is a literary scholar best known for his writings about the rela-
tionship between the reader and a literary text and for his work on inter-
pretive communities, a branch of reader-response theory. *His books*
include There's No Such Thing as Free Speech, and It's a Good Thing,
Too *(1994),* Professional Correctness: Literary Studies and Political Change
(1995), The Stanley Fish Reader *(1999), and* How Milton Works *(2001).*
In the following essay, Fish examines free-speech issues on college
campuses and concludes that despite claims to the contrary, many of
these issues have little to do with First Amendment rights.

The modern American version of crying wolf is crying First Amendment. If you want to burn a cross on a black family's lawn or buy an
election by contributing millions to a candidate or vilify Jerry Falwell
and his mother in a scurrilous "parody," and someone or some government agency tries to stop you, just yell "First Amendment rights" and
you will stand a good chance of getting to do what you want to do.

In the academy, the case is even worse: Not only is the First
Amendment pressed into service at the drop of a hat (especially whenever anyone is disciplined for anything), it is invoked ritually when
there are no First Amendment issues in sight.

Take the case of the editors of college newspapers who will always
cry First Amendment when something they've published turns out to
be the cause of outrage and controversy. These days the offending piece
or editorial or advertisement usually involves (what is at least perceived to be) an attack on Jews. In January of this year, the *Daily Illini,* a
student newspaper at the University of Illinois at Urbana-Champaign,
printed a letter from a resident of Seattle with no university affiliation.
The letter ran under the headline "Jews Manipulate America" and argued that because their true allegiance is to the state of Israel, the president should "separate Jews from all government advisory positions";
otherwise, the writer warned, "the Jews might face another Holocaust."

When the predictable firestorm of outrage erupted, the newspaper's editor responded by declaring, first, that "we are committed to
giving all people a voice"; second, that, given this commitment, "we
print the opinions of others with whom we do not agree"; third, that to
do otherwise would involve the newspaper in the dangerous acts of
"silencing" and "self-censorship"; and, fourth, that "what is hate speech
to one member of a society is free speech to another."

5   Wrong four times.

I'll bet the *Daily Illini* is not committed to giving all people a
voice—the KKK? man-boy love? advocates of slavery? would-be

Unabombers? Nor do I believe that the editors sift through submissions looking for the ones they disagree with and then print those. No doubt they apply some principles of selection, asking questions like, Is it relevant, or Is it timely, or Does it get the facts right, or Does it present a coherent argument?

That is, they exercise judgment, which is quite a different thing from silencing or self-censorship. No one is silenced because a single outlet declines to publish him; silencing occurs when that outlet (or any other) is forbidden by the state to publish him on pain of legal action; and that is also what censorship is.

As for self-censoring, if it is anything, it is what we all do whenever we decide it would be better not to say something or cut a sentence that went just a little bit too far or leave a manuscript in the bottom drawer because it is not yet ready. Self-censorship, in short, is not a crime or a moral failing; it is a responsibility.

And, finally, whatever the merits of the argument by which all assertions are relativised—your hate speech is my free speech—this incident has nothing to do with either hate speech or free speech and everything to do with whether the editors are discharging or defaulting on their obligations when they foist them off on an inapplicable doctrine, saying in effect, "The First Amendment made us do it."

More recently, the same scenario played itself out at Santa Rosa Junior College. This time it was a student who wrote the offending article. Titled "Is Anti-Semitism Ever the Result of Jewish Behavior?" it answered the question in the affirmative, creating an uproar that included death threats, an avalanche of hate mail, and demands for just about everyone's resignation. The faculty adviser who had approved the piece said, "The First Amendment isn't there to protect agreeable stories." 10

He was alluding to the old saw that the First Amendment protects unpopular as well as popular speech. But what it protects unpopular speech *from* is abridgment by the government of its free expression; it does not protect unpopular speech from being rejected by a newspaper, and it confers no positive obligation to give your pages over to unpopular speech, or popular speech, or any speech.

Once again, there is no First Amendment issue here, just an issue of editorial judgment and the consequences of exercising it. (You can print anything you like; but if the heat comes, it's yours, not the Constitution's.)

In these controversies, student editors are sometimes portrayed, or portray themselves, as First Amendment heroes who bravely risk criticism and censure in order to uphold a cherished American value. But they are not heroes; they are merely confused and, in terms of their understanding of the doctrine they invoke, rather hapless.

Not as hapless, however, as the Harvard English department, which made a collective fool of itself three times when it invited, disinvited and then reinvited poet Tom Paulin to be the Morris Gray

CHAPTER 3 FOCUS

lecturer. Again the flash point was anti-Semitism. In his poetry and in public comments, Paulin had said that Israel had no right to exist, that settlers on the West Bank "should be shot dead," and that Israeli police and military forces were the equivalent of the Nazi SS. When these and other statements came to light shortly before Paulin was to give his lecture, the department voted to rescind the invitation. When the inevitable cry of "censorship, censorship" was heard in the land, the department flip-flopped again, and a professor-spokesman declared, "This was a clear affirmation that the department stood strongly by the First Amendment."

15   It was of course nothing of the kind; it was a transparent effort of a bunch that had already put its foot in its mouth twice to wriggle out of trouble and regain the moral high ground by striking the pose of First Amendment defender. But, in fact, the department and its members were not First Amendment defenders (a religion they converted to a little late), but serial bunglers.

What should they have done? Well, it depends on what they wanted to do. If they wanted to invite this particular poet because they admired his poetry, they had a perfect right to do so. If they were aware ahead of time of Paulin's public pronouncements, they could have chosen either to say something by way of explanation or to remain silent and let the event speak for itself; either course of action would have been at once defensible and productive of risk. If they knew nothing of Paulin's anti-Israel sentiments (difficult to believe of a gang of world-class researchers) but found out about them after the fact, they might have said, "Oops, never mind" or toughed it out—again alternatives not without risk. But at each stage, whatever they did or didn't do would have had no relationship whatsoever to any First Amendment right— Paulin had no right to be invited—or obligation—there was no obligation either to invite or disinvite him, and certainly no obligation to reinvite him, unless you count the obligations imposed on yourself by a succession of ill-thought-through decisions. Whatever the successes or failures here, they were once again failures of judgment, not doctrine.

In another case, it looked for a moment that judgment of an appropriate kind was in fact being exercised. The University of California at Berkeley houses the Emma Goldman Papers Project, and each year the director sends out a fund-raising mailer that always features quotations from Goldman's work. But this January an associate vice chancellor edited the mailer and removed two quotations that in context read as a criticism of the Bush administration's plans for a war in Iraq. He explained that the quotations were not randomly chosen and were clearly intended to make a "political point, and that is inappropriate in an official university situation."

The project director (who acknowledged that the quotes were selected for their contemporary relevance) objected to what she saw as an act of censorship and a particularly egregious one given Goldman's strong advocacy of free expression.

But no one's expression was being censored. The Goldman quotations are readily available and had they appeared in the project's literature in a setting that did not mark them as political, no concerns would have been raised. It is just, said the associate vice chancellor, that they are inappropriate in this context, and, he added, "It is not a matter of the First Amendment."

Right, it's a matter of whether or not there is even the appearance 20 of the university's taking sides on a partisan issue; that is, it is an empirical matter that requires just the exercise of judgment that associate vice chancellors are paid to perform. Of course he was pilloried by members of the Berkeley faculty and others who saw First Amendment violations everywhere.

But there were none. Goldman still speaks freely through her words. The project director can still make her political opinions known by writing letters to the editor or to everyone in the country, even if she cannot use the vehicle of a university flier to do so. Everyone's integrity is preserved. The project goes on unimpeded, and the university goes about its proper academic business. Or so it would have been had the administration stayed firm. But it folded and countermanded the associate vice chancellor's decision.

At least the chancellor had sense enough to acknowledge that no one's speech had been abridged. It was just, he said, an "error in judgment." Aren't they all?

Are there then no free-speech issues on campuses? Sure there are; there just aren't very many. When Toni Smith, a basketball player at Manhattanville College, turned her back to the flag during the playing of the national anthem in protest against her government's policies, she was truly exercising her First Amendment rights, rights that ensure that she cannot be compelled to an affirmation she does not endorse (see *West Virginia v. Barnette*). And as she stood by her principles in the face of hostility, she truly was (and is) a First Amendment hero, as the college newspaper editors, the members of the Harvard English department, and the head of the Emma Goldman Project are not. The category is a real one, and it would be good if it were occupied only by those who belong in it.

Responding to Reading

1. What does Fish mean when he says, "The modern American version of crying wolf is crying First Amendment" (1)?
2. According to Fish, what constitutes a "First Amendment issue" (12)? In what way is a First Amendment issue different from an issue of "editorial judgment"?
3. How convincing are the examples Fish presents to support his argument? For example, why is the case of Toni Smith a free speech issue? Why does Fish think that she is "a First Amendment hero" and that "the college newspaper editors, the members of the Harvard English department, and the head of the Emma Goldman Project are not" (23)?

Responding in Writing

Do you believe that all viewpoints should be allowed to reach an audience? Or, do you believe that some ideas are so repugnant or dangerous that they should be censored? Explain.

A CHILL WIND IS BLOWING IN THIS NATION
Tim Robbins
1958–

Actor, director, screenwriter, producer—and husband of actress Susan Sarandon—Tim Robbins began acting at age twelve. Robbins has directed and appeared in many films and is best known for his roles that depict individuals wronged by the system (The Shawshank Redemption, 1994); *individuals who abuse power* (Bob Roberts, 1992); *and individuals caught up in a system gone awry* (The Hudsucker Proxy, 1994). *Robbins wrote and directed* Dead Man Walking (1995), *for which he received an Oscar nomination, and he won the best supporting actor award for his role in the 2003 film* Mystic River. *Robbins gave the following speech at the National Press Club in Washington, D.C., on April 15, 2003, just after his invitation to speak at The Baseball Hall of Fame had been withdrawn.*

I can't tell you how moved I have been at the overwhelming support I have received from newspapers throughout the country in these past few days. I hold no illusions that all of these journalists agree with me on my views against the war. While the journalists' outrage at the cancellation of our appearance in Cooperstown is not about my views, it is about my right to express these views. I am extremely grateful that there are those of you out there still with a fierce belief in constitutionally guaranteed rights. We need you, the press, now more than ever. This is a crucial moment for all of us.

For all of the ugliness and tragedy of 9/11, there was a brief period afterward where I held a great hope, in the midst of the tears and shocked faces of New Yorkers, in the midst of the lethal air we breathed as we worked at Ground Zero, in the midst of my children's terror at being so close to this crime against humanity, in the midst of all this, I held on to a glimmer of hope in the naive assumption that something good could come out of it.

I imagined our leaders seizing upon this moment of unity in America, this moment when no one wanted to talk about Democrat versus Republican, white versus black, or any of the other ridiculous divisions that dominate our public discourse. I imagined our leaders going on television telling the citizens that although we all want to be at Ground

Zero, we can't, but there is work that is needed to be done all over America. Our help is needed at community centers to tutor children, to teach them to read. Our work is needed at old-age homes to visit the lonely and infirmed; in gutted neighborhoods to rebuild housing and clean up parks, and convert abandoned lots to baseball fields. I imagined leadership that would take this incredible energy, this generosity of spirit and create a new unity in America born out of the chaos and tragedy of 9/11, a new unity that would send a message to terrorists everywhere: If you attack us, we will become stronger, cleaner, better educated, and more unified. You will strengthen our commitment to justice and democracy by your inhumane attacks on us. Like a Phoenix out of the fire, we will be reborn.

And then came the speech: You are either with us or against us. And the bombing began. And the old paradigm was restored as our leader encouraged us to show our patriotism by shopping and by volunteering to join groups that would turn in their neighbor for any suspicious behavior.

In the 19 months since 9/11, we have seen our democracy compro-   5
mised by fear and hatred. Basic inalienable rights, due process, the sanctity of the home have been quickly compromised in a climate of fear. A unified American public has grown bitterly divided, and a world population that had profound sympathy and support for us has grown contemptuous and distrustful, viewing us as we once viewed the Soviet Union, as a rogue state.

This past weekend, Susan and I and the three kids went to Florida for a family reunion of sorts. Amidst the alcohol and the dancing, sugar-rushing children, there was, of course, talk of the war. And the most frightening thing about the weekend was the amount of times we were thanked for speaking out against the war because that individual speaking thought it unsafe to do so in their own community, in their own life. Keep talking, they said; I haven't been able to open my mouth.

A relative tells me that a history teacher tells his 11-year-old son, my nephew, that Susan Sarandon is endangering the troops by her opposition to the war. Another teacher in a different school asks our niece if we are coming to the school play. They're not welcome here, said the molder of young minds.

Another relative tells me of a school board decision to cancel a civics event that was proposing to have a moment of silence for those who have died in the war because the students were including dead Iraqi civilians in their silent prayer.

A teacher in another nephew's school is fired for wearing a T-shirt with a peace sign on it. And a friend of the family tells of listening to the radio down South as the talk radio host calls for the murder of a prominent anti-war activist. Death threats have appeared on other prominent anti-war activists' doorsteps for their views. Relatives of ours have received threatening e-mails and phone calls. And my 13-year-old boy, who has done nothing to anybody, has recently been embarrassed and humiliated by a sadistic creep who writes—or, rather, scratches his column with his fingernails in dirt.

10   Susan and I have been listed as traitors, as supporters of Saddam, and various other epithets by the Aussie gossip rags masquerading as newspapers, and by their fair and balanced electronic media cousins, 19th Century Fox. (Laughter.) Apologies to Gore Vidal.(Applause.)

Two weeks ago, the United Way canceled Susan's appearance at a conference on women's leadership. And both of us last week were told that both we and the First Amendment were not welcome at the Baseball Hall of Fame.

A famous middle-aged rock-and-roller called me last week to thank me for speaking out against the war, only to go on to tell me that he could not speak himself because he fears repercussions from Clear Channel. "They promote our concert appearances," he said. "They own most of the stations that play our music. I can't come out against this war."

And here in Washington, Helen Thomas finds herself banished to the back of the room and uncalled on after asking Ari Fleischer whether our showing prisoners of war at Guantanamo Bay on television violated the Geneva Convention.

A chill wind is blowing in this nation. A message is being sent through the White House and its allies in talk radio and Clear Channel and Cooperstown. If you oppose this administration, there can and will be ramifications.

15   Every day, the air waves are filled with warnings, veiled and unveiled threats, spewed invective and hatred directed at any voice of dissent. And the public, like so many relatives and friends that I saw this weekend, sit in mute opposition and fear.

I am sick of hearing about Hollywood being against this war. Hollywood's heavy hitters, the real power brokers and cover-of-the-magazine stars, have been largely silent on this issue. But Hollywood, the concept, has always been a popular target.

I remember when the Columbine High School shootings happened. President Clinton criticized Hollywood for contributing to this terrible tragedy—this, as we were dropping bombs over Kosovo. Could the violent actions of our leaders contribute somewhat to the violent fantasies of our teenagers? Or is it all just Hollywood and rock and roll?

I remember reading at the time that one of the shooters had tried to enlist to fight the real war a week before he acted out his war in real life at Columbine. I talked about this in the press at the time. And curiously, no one accused me of being unpatriotic for criticizing Clinton. In fact, the same radio patriots that call us traitors today engaged in daily personal attacks on their president during the war in Kosovo.

Today, prominent politicians who have decried violence in movies—the "Blame Hollywooders," if you will—recently voted to give our current president the power to unleash real violence in our current war. They want us to stop the fictional violence but are okay with the real kind.

And these same people that tolerate the real violence of war don't [20] want to see the result of it on the nightly news. Unlike the rest of the world, our news coverage of this war remains sanitized, without a glimpse of the blood and gore inflicted upon our soldiers or the women and children in Iraq. Violence as a concept, an abstraction—it's very strange.

As we applaud the hard-edged realism of the opening battle scene of "*Saving Private Ryan*," we cringe at the thought of seeing the same on the nightly news. We are told it would be pornographic. We want no part of reality in real life. We demand that war be painstakingly realized on the screen, but that war remain imagined and conceptualized in real life.

And in the midst of all this madness, where is the political opposition? Where have all the Democrats gone? Long time passing, long time ago. (Applause.) With apologies to Robert Byrd, I have to say it is pretty embarrassing to live in a country where a five-foot-one comedian has more guts than most politicians. (Applause.) We need leaders, not pragmatists that cower before the spin zones of former entertainment journalists. We need leaders who can understand the Constitution, congressman who don't in a moment of fear abdicate their most important power, the right to declare war to the executive branch. And, please, can we please stop the congressional sing-a-longs? (Laughter.)

In this time when a citizenry applauds the liberation of a country as it lives in fear of its own freedom, when an administration official releases an attack ad questioning the patriotism of a legless Vietnam veteran running for Congress, when people all over the country fear reprisal if they use their right to free speech, it is time to get angry. It is time to get fierce. And it doesn't take much to shift the tide. My 11-year-old nephew, mentioned earlier, a shy kid who never talks in class, stood up to his history teacher who was questioning Susan's patriotism. "That's my aunt you're talking about. Stop it." And the stunned teacher backtracks and began stammering compliments in embarrassment.

Sportswriters across the country reacted with such overwhelming fury at the Hall of Fame that the president of the Hall admitted he made a mistake and Major League Baseball disavowed any connection to the actions of the Hall's president. A bully can be stopped, and so can a mob. It takes one person with the courage and a resolute voice.

The journalists in this country can battle back at those who would [25] rewrite our Constitution in Patriot Act II, or "Patriot, The Sequel," as we would call it in Hollywood. We are counting on you to star in that movie. Journalists can insist that they not be used as publicists by this administration. (Applause.) The next White House correspondent to be called on by Ari Fleischer should defer their question to the back of the room, to the banished journalist du jour. (Applause.) And any instance of intimidation to free speech should be battled against. Any acquiescence or intimidation at this point will only lead to more intimidation.

You have, whether you like it or not, an awesome responsibility and an awesome power: the fate of discourse, the health of this republic is in your hands, whether you write on the left or the right. This is your time, and the destiny you have chosen.

We lay the continuance of our democracy on your desks, and count on your pens to be mightier. Millions are watching and waiting in mute frustration and hope—hoping for someone to defend the spirit and letter of our Constitution, and to defy the intimidation that is visited upon us daily in the name of national security and warped notions of patriotism.

Our ability to disagree, and our inherent right to question our leaders and criticize their actions define who we are. To allow those rights to be taken away out of fear, to punish people for their beliefs, to limit access in the news media to differing opinions is to acknowledge our democracy's defeat. These are challenging times. There is a wave of hate that seeks to divide us—right and left, pro-war and anti-war. In the name of my 11-year-old nephew, and all the other unreported victims of this hostile and unproductive environment of fear, let us try to find our common ground as a nation. Let us celebrate this grand and glorious experiment that has survived for 227 years. To do so we must honor and fight vigilantly for the things that unite us—like freedom, the First Amendment and, yes, baseball. (Applause.)

Responding to Reading

1. What does Robbins believe America's public leaders should have done after the 9/11 attacks? Do you agree that his suggestions would have created "a new unity" that would have said to terrorists, "If you attack us, we will become stronger, cleaner, better educated, and more unified" (3)?

2. What does Robbins mean when he says, "A chill wind is blowing in this nation" (14)? What evidence does he give to support this assertion? What does Robbins think should be done "to shift the tide" (23)?

3. In paragraph 1, Robbins implies that his constitutional rights were taken away when his scheduled appearance at the Baseball Hall of Fame in Cooperstown was cancelled because of his opposition to the war in Iraq. Would Stanley Fish (p. 202) agree that this action deprived Robbins of his "constitutionally guaranteed" right (1) to express his views?

Responding in Writing

Do you believe that the government should be able to suspend or limit citizens' constitutional rights of privacy and free speech in time of war? How far should such limitations go?

IT'S TIME TO JUNK
THE DOUBLE STANDARD
ON FREE SPEECH

Stuart Taylor, Jr.

1948–

Stuart Taylor, Jr., is a senior writer and weekly opinion columnist for the
National Journal *and a contributing editor at* Newsweek. *His writing
focuses on national legal, political, and policy issues. Taylor practiced law
and then worked as a legal affairs reporter and Supreme Court reporter for
the Washington Bureau of the* New York Times. *In the following essay,
Taylor argues that the media show concern for First Amendment rights
only when someone on the Left is prevented from expressing his or her
views.*

It made news when hecklers booed *Sacramento Bee* publisher Janis
Besler Heaphy so loudly and long—for suggesting that the government
had gone too far in curbing civil liberties since September 11—that she
could not finish her December 15 commencement speech at California
State University (Sacramento). "Many interpret it as a troubling example of rising intolerance for public discourse that questions the nation's
response to the September 11 terror attacks," reported the *Los Angeles
Times. The New York Times* and other major newspapers weighed in
with similar articles. ABC News' *Nightline* did a special report.

Another burst of publicity—and more worries about threats to First
Amendment rights—attended the University of New Mexico's repri-
mand of professor Richard Berthold for opening his September 11 history class with what he later admitted to be a "stupid" remark:
"Anyone who can blow up the Pentagon gets my vote." Berthold also
received death threats.

It's nice to see the media showing some concern for the freedom of
speech. But where have they been during the past two decades of
efforts coming from the politically correct Left—and especially from
devotees of identity politics, racial preferences, and the male-bashing
brand of feminism—to suppress unwelcome speech on our campuses
and elsewhere? Examples:

- Ward Connerly, the black California businessman who has cam-
  paigned across the nation to outlaw racial preferences, has been
  shouted down and drowned out so abusively as to cut short his remarks on at least five campuses since 1996, he recalls, including Atlanta's Emory University in 1998 and the University of Texas
  School of Law in 1999. The consequence, he says, is that "it totally

throws you off your stride. Freedom of speech is not just being able to complete your speech, it's being able to speak without fear of personal harm being done to you. . . . I am not free to speak openly and honestly." College administrators, Connerly adds, "almost go out of their way to make me out as a monster, which incites the audience all the more." Taunts of "Uncle Tom" are routine and, more than once, Connerly notes, hecklers have threatened violence or announced menacingly, "We know where you live."

- Linda Chavez, another leading critic of racial preferences, says: "I have been disinvited, harassed, shouted down, threatened, and [on one occasion] physically assaulted at campuses around the country," including the University of Northern Colorado and the University of Illinois (Urbana-Champaign). Chavez says that while the most-menacing hecklers appeared to be "street thugs" brought in from outside the campuses, students who join in "are being primed by the professors, being told that I'm the devil incarnate, that I want to do terrible things to Hispanics."

- Christina Hoff Sommers, a trenchant critic of liberal feminism, was speaking as an invited panelist at a November 1 conference on preventing substance abuse, organized by the Health and Human Services Department, when some officials, academics, and others took offense at her doubts about a program called "Girl Power." A department official named Linda Bass interrupted and angrily ordered Sommers to stop talking about Girl Power. Later, Sommers said, Fordham University psychology professor (and paid department consultant) Jay Wade told Sommers, "Shut the f—up, bitch," amid mocking laughter from the crowd. Sommers, effectively silenced, left. "As Stanley Kurtz pointed out in *National Review*," Sommers notes, "if Catharine MacKinnon or Carol Gilligan had been treated that way in a government meeting, it would have been reported." Very widely.

But none of these efforts to silence Connerly, Chavez, and Sommers by heckler's veto has ever been reported in any national newspaper, as far as I can find, excepting some coverage in the conservative *Washington Times*, a few opinion columns, *Wall Street Journal* editorials, and a passing mention of Connerly's complaint deep in *The New York Times*. Nor have the national media paid much attention to the pervasive use of speech codes to chill politically incorrect expression on campus. They have likewise ignored the long-running epidemic of thefts of campus newspapers for carrying politically incorrect commentary or advertisements.

5   "University PR and spin has led too many of the media into a terrible double standard" in dealing with such heckler's vetoes and other

forms of censorship, says Thor L. Halvorssen, executive director of the Foundation for Individual Rights in Education Inc. (FIRE). "When it's a conservative [being shouted down], the university will downplay this as a free speech protest, and the media will agree."

The Philadelphia-based FIRE was created two years ago by Boston civil liberties lawyer Harvey Silverglate and University of Pennsylvania professor Alan Charles Kors to protect free speech and other liberties on the nation's campuses. And Halvorssen seethes with the same passionate indignation in denouncing censorial efforts coming from the political Right as those from the Left. But before September 11, he says, the campus censorship came mostly from the Left. And the big media were not interested.

"Close to three-quarters of the colleges and universities, private and public, have speech codes," Halvorssen stresses. "They are applied selectively, with a double standard depending on your blood and culture. I've never heard of a case of anyone being suspended or fired or expelled for insulting a born-again Christian. On a college campus, Andres Serrano's photograph of a crucifix in urine, titled *Piss Christ*, is a work of art. Immerse a photograph of Martin Luther King Jr. in urine, and the sky would fall and the entire school would be put through sensitivity training. There is also a ferocious assault on due process and fairness on campus."

Administrators mete out discipline for offending remarks, for other alleged "harassment," and even for disputed charges of date rape with no semblance of a fair hearing. "We hear a lot of people talking about military tribunals," Halvorssen notes. "We have the equivalent on campus. . . . I see this stuff on a daily basis, and it is a real struggle to get it into the media. Speech codes, thought reform, due process—where have these folks been?"

Since September 11, with leftist critics of the war against terrorism complaining of efforts to intimidate and punish them both on campus and elsewhere, the media have paid a bit more attention—although, Halvorssen says, "it's the equivalent of reporting on how many people are getting into the boats rather than reporting that the *Titanic* is sinking." The coverage has also been more balanced, if only because it would be hard to chronicle the punitive measures against anti-war leftists and Islamists without noticing that, on the campuses, efforts to silence forcefully hawkish statements deemed offensive by Muslims seem about as common.

The reporting on the Berthold "blow up the Pentagon" case, for example, has been paralleled by extensive coverage of a case at Orange Coast College in California in which Professor Kenneth Hearlson was suspended for 11 weeks without a hearing and threatened with dismissal after four Muslim students complained that he had called them terrorists and murderers in class. When other students produced

tape-recordings proving this charge to be false, the college reprimanded Hearlson anyway, for accusing Muslims in general of condon-
ing terrorism against Israel.

Meanwhile, the University of South Florida is seeking to fire Sami
Al-Arian—a tenured Palestinian professor of computer science who is
suspected (but not formally accused) of links to Islamic extremists—
for courting publicity (amid dozens of death threats) about his views
and controversial past. On the other end of the spectrum, a library assistant at UCLA was suspended for a week without pay for calling Israel an "apartheid state" in an e-mail. An Ethiopian student at San
Diego State University was warned that he could be suspended or expelled for "harassment" after he had confronted and criticized a group
of Saudi students for celebrating the destruction of the World Trade
Center. And so on.

Many campus administrators, notes Halvorssen, bend according to
"where the political winds are blowing." And now that some of the
winds are blowing against the Left, even on a lot of campuses, the left-
liberal *Nation* sees the danger. "The last generation's wave of campus
speech codes and anti-harassment policies," wrote David Glenn in December, "may have done more to suppress freedom than to remedy injustice in any meaningful way—and it may be only now, after
September 11, that the full costs will become apparent."

The rediscovery, by some in the media and the Left, of the case for
free speech makes FIRE's Halvorssen optimistic about the future. But
will politically powerful conservatives—some of whom have become
First Amendment stalwarts while seeing their own oxes gored by campus censors—prove equally selective in their devotion to free speech?
"We have to be careful," says Christina Hoff Sommers, "not to play by
the rules written by the intolerant Left."

Responding to Reading

1. According to Taylor, the media is concerned about freedom of speech only
   when someone on the Left cannot express his or her views. What examples
   does he present to support this contention? Do you think he presents
   enough examples to establish his case?
2. What examples of censorship on college campuses does Taylor give? How
   does Taylor think things have changed since September 11? Would Tim
   Robbins (p. 206) agree with Taylor's assessment?
3. Do you think Taylor presents a balanced view of his subject, or do you
   think he favors one group over another?

Responding in Writing

Does your college or university encourage all ideas, or does it favor one political or social viewpoint over another?

WIDENING THE FOCUS

For Critical Thinking and Writing

Write an essay in which you answer the Focus question, "How free should free speech be?" In your essay, refer to the ideas in Stanley Fish's "The Free-Speech Follies," Tim Robbins's "A Chill Wind Is Blowing in This Nation," and Stuart Taylor, Jr.'s "It's Time to Junk the Double Standard on Free Speech".

For Further Reading

The following readings can suggest additional perspectives for thinking and writing about freedom of speech.

- Christina Hoff Sommers, "For More Balance on Campuses" (p. 121)

- James Fallows, "Who Shot Mohammed al-Dura?" (p. 257)

- Lawrence Summers, "Remarks at NBER Conference on Diversifying the Science and Engineering Work force"(p. 613)

For Internet Research

Should the United States have an official language policy? According to *Ethnologue* < http://www.ethnologue.com/>, 162 languages are spoken in the United States. How should the federal government respond to this situation? Do minority languages threaten our national interest and democratic traditions? Should the Congress introduce a constitutional amendment that makes English the official language of the United States? Or, do you see language diversity as a national asset? Should the government encourage speakers of other languages while providing them with ample opportunities to learn English? Write an essay in which you outline a national language policy, basing your argument on information from one of the following Web pages:

- "Bilingual Education: a Critique," an essay published by the Hoover Institution <http://www-hoover.stanford.edu/publications/he/22/22a.html>

- James Crawford's Language Policy Web site <http://ourworld. compuserve.com/homepages/JWcrawford/>

- The "Analysis and Information" pages of the Web site run by English for the Children, a group lobbying to end bilingual education nationwide <http://onenation.org/>

─────────────────────── **WRITING** ───────────────────────

The Politics of Language

1. Currently, there is a great deal of debate about the value of home schooling. What might Richard Rodriguez (p. 139) and Frederick Douglass (p. 150) think of this practice? What advantages do you think they would they see? What problems do you think they would identify? Be specific, and use material from their essays as well as from Daniel Pink's "School's Out" (p. 91) to support your points.

2. Assume that you are the editor of your school newspaper and that you have received an editorial taking the position that to make up for past injustices, minorities and women should have points added to their test scores. Several days after rejecting the article, you receive a letter from the author, who accuses you of depriving him of his First Amendment right to freedom of expression. Write a response to this letter. You can either justify your previous position or reconsider your position and accept the editorial for publication. When formulating your answer, be sure to refer to at least one of the essays in the Focus section of this chapter.

3. In "Mother Tongue" (p. 170), Amy Tan distinguishes between the English she speaks to her mother and the English she speaks to the rest of the world. Write an essay in which you describe the various types of English you speak—at home, at school, at work, to your friends, and so on. In what ways are these Englishes alike, and in what ways are they different? What ideas are you able to express best with each type of English?

4. Over fifty years ago, both Aldous Huxley and George Orwell wrote essays in which they discussed how governments use language to control their citizens. Write an essay in which you discuss how today's governments do this. Do you think such control is easier or more difficult to achieve than it was fifty years ago? In your essay, be sure you refer specifically to "Propaganda under a Dictatorship" (p. 183) and "Politics and the English Language" (p. 189).

5. Both Amy Tan in "Mother Tongue" (p. 170) and Richard Rodriguez in "Aria" (p. 139) talk about how education can change one's use of language. Write an essay discussing the effect education has had on your own spoken and written language. What do you think you have gained and lost as your language has changed?

6. Which of your daily activities would you be unable to carry out if, like the people Jonathan Kozol describes in "The Human Cost of an Illiterate Society" (p. 175), you could neither read nor write? Write

an article for your local newspaper in which you report on a typical day, being sure to identify specific tasks you could not do. In addition, explain some strategies you would use to hide the fact that you couldn't read or write.

7. In paragraph 21 of "Politics and the English Language" (p. 189), Orwell says, "Political language . . . is designed to make lies sound truthful and murder respectable, and to give an appearance of solidity to pure wind." Write an essay in which you agree or disagree with this statement. Support your position with examples of political language you find in newspapers and magazines, on TV, or on the Internet.

8. List some of the words you use to refer to women, minorities, and other groups. Then, write a letter to Alleen Pace Nilsen (p. 158), in which you agree or disagree with her assertion that the words people use tell a lot about their values and beliefs. In addition to Nilsen's essay, consider Diane Ravitch's essay "You Can't Say That" (p. 155) as well as your own ideas.

9. Recently, there has been a great deal of debate about the benefits and drawbacks of a multilingual society. Supporters say that a multilingual society allows people to preserve their own cultures and thus fosters pride. Detractors say that a multilingual society reinforces differences and ultimately tears a country apart. What do you see as the benefits and drawbacks of a multilingual society? As a country, what would we gain if we encouraged multilingualism? What would we lose? Refer to the essays in this chapter by Richard Rodriguez (p. 139), Louise Erdrich (p. 146), and Amy Tan (p. 170) to support your position.

CHAPTER 3 FOCUS

4

MEDIA AND SOCIETY

Many forms of popular media—newspapers and magazines, radio, television, and film—have been around for a long time, and over the years, they have had a powerful and significant impact on our lives. Cable television brought us literally hundreds of stations—along with sitcom reruns that endlessly recycle our childhoods (and our parents' childhoods). Satellites brought immediacy: the Vietnam War was the first televised war, but we had to wait for the evening news to see it; during the Iraq war, journalists have actually been "embedded" with military units, bringing us events in real time on 24-hour cable news programs. Other innovations also appeared: film special effects that have the power to mystify or terrify; newspapers that seem to have more color and graphics than words; and, on television, tabloid journalism, home shopping, reality TV, infomercials, and music videos. Most dramatically,

Fifteenth-century illuminated manuscript depicting the angel Gabriel speaking to Mary

the Internet has made available a tremendous amount of information—and the ability to communicate this information almost instantly to millions of people all over the planet—in news articles, blogs, personal home pages, and e-mail, as well as in audio and video clips.

Over the years, the increasing power and scope of the media have helped to turn the world into what Canadian cultural critic Marshall McLuhan called a "global village," a world of nations that are more and more interconnected and interdependent. This is seen by many as a positive development. Ideally, as citizens of the global village, we should be able to understand one another as we increasingly come to share a common culture, with access to the same music, films, Web sites, and television programs. But the power of the media has also brought problems. The tool that can unite, inform, instruct, entertain, and inspire can also deceive, stereotype, and brainwash—and, perhaps, even incite violence.

As the Focus section of this chapter, "Has the Internet Doomed the Newspaper?", (p. 274) suggests, the rise of the Internet, and our increasing reliance on it, may pose a threat to print media, particularly the daily newspaper. Even before the Internet existed, newspaper readership was on the decline, replaced by television news; cities that used to have several different daily newspapers, with varying editorial positions, now have only a few—and, in some cases, only one. (In fact,

Amazon. com home page

over 98 percent of U.S. cities have just one major daily paper.) Whether or not the Internet is to blame for this situation—and whether or not a problem actually exists—is discussed in the essays in the Focus section.

——————— PREPARING TO READ AND WRITE ———————

As you read and prepare to write about the essays in this chapter, you may consider the following questions:

- Does the essay focus on one particular medium or on the media in general?

- Does the writer see the media as a positive, negative, or neutral force? Why?

- If the writer sees negative effects, where does he or she place blame? Do you agree?

- Does the writer make any recommendations for change? Do these recommendations seem reasonable?

- Is the writer focusing on the media's effects on individuals or on society?

- Does the writer discuss personal observations or experiences? If so, are they similar to or different from your own?

- When was the essay written? Has the situation the writer describes changed since then?

- Which writers' positions on the impact of the media (or on the media's shortcomings) are most alike? Most different? Most like your own?

SPEECH TO RADIO-TELEVISION NEWS DIRECTORS ASSOCIATION

Edward R. Murrow

1908–1965

Credited with founding modern journalism, Edward R. Murrow was an American radio and television broadcaster whose gripping World War II radio reports from London established him as a leading news authority. He produced the radio news digest Hear It Now *and ushered in television news broadcasting with* See It Now *and* Person to Person. *In the following speech, delivered to the 1958 convention of the Radio-Television News Directors Association, Murrow urges members of the radio and television news industry to carefully consider their influence on the United States and the world.*

This just might do nobody any good. At the end of this discourse a few people may accuse this reporter of fouling his own comfortable nest, and your organization may be accused of having given hospitality to heretical and even dangerous thoughts. But the elaborate structure of networks, advertising agencies and sponsors will not be shaken or altered. It is my desire, if not my duty, to try to talk to you journeymen with some candor about what is happening to radio and television.

I have no technical advice or counsel to offer those of you who labor in this vineyard that produces words and pictures. You will forgive me for not telling you that instruments with which you work are miraculous, that your responsibility is unprecedented or that your aspirations are frequently frustrated. It is not necessary to remind you that the fact that your voice is amplified to the degree where it reaches from one end of the country to the other does not confer upon you greater wisdom or understanding than you possessed when your voice reached only from one end of the bar to the other. All of these things you know.

You should also know at the outset that, in the manner of witnesses before Congressional committees, I appear here voluntarily— by invitation—that I am an employee of the Columbia Broadcasting System [CBS], that I am neither an officer nor a director of that corporation and that these remarks are of a "do-it-yourself" nature. If what I have to say is responsible, then I alone am responsible for the saying of it. Seeking neither approbation from my employers, nor new sponsors, nor acclaim from the critics of radio and television, I cannot well be disappointed. Believing that potentially the commercial system of broadcasting as practiced in this country is the best and freest yet devised, I have decided to express my concern about what I believe to be happening to radio and television. These instruments have been good to me beyond my due. There exists in mind no reasonable grounds for personal complaint. I have no feud, either with my employers, any sponsors, or with the professional critics of radio and television. But I am seized with an abiding fear regarding what these two instruments are doing to our society, our culture and our heritage.

Our history will be what we make it. And if there are any historians about fifty or a hundred years from now, and there should be preserved the kinescopes for one week of all three networks, they will there find recorded in black and white, or color, evidence of decadence, escapism and insulation from the realities of the world in which we live. I invite your attention to the television schedules of all networks between the hours of 8 and 11 P.M., Eastern Time. Here you will find only fleeting and spasmodic reference to the fact that this nation is in mortal danger. There are, it is true, occasional informative programs presented in that intellectual ghetto on Sunday afternoons. But during the daily peak viewing periods, television in the main insulates us from the realities of the world in which we live. If this state of affairs continues, we may alter an advertising slogan to read: LOOK NOW, PAY LATER.

For surely we shall pay for using this most powerful instrument of communication to insulate the citizenry from the hard and demanding realities which must be faced if we are to survive. I mean the word survive literally. If there were to be a competition in indifference, or perhaps in insulation from reality, then Nero and his fiddle, Chamberlain and his umbrella, could not find a place on an early afternoon sustaining show. If Hollywood were to run out of Indians, the program schedules would be mangled beyond all recognition. Then some courageous soul with a small budget might be able to do a documentary telling what, in fact, we have done—and are still doing—to the Indians in this country. But that would be unpleasant. And we must at all costs shield the sensitive citizens from anything that is unpleasant.

I am entirely persuaded that the American public is more reasonable, restrained and more mature than most of our industry's program planners believe. Their fear of controversy is not warranted by the evidence. I have reason to know, as do many of you, that when the evidence on a controversial subject is fairly and calmly presented, the public recognizes it for what it is—an effort to illuminate rather than to agitate.

Several years ago, when we undertook to do a program on Egypt and Israel, well-meaning, experienced and intelligent friends shook their heads and said, "This you cannot do—you will be handed your head. It is an emotion-packed controversy, and there is no room for reason in it." We did the program. Zionists, anti-Zionists, the friends of the Middle East, Egyptian and Israeli officials said, with a faint tone of surprise, "It was a fair count. The information was there. We have no complaints."

Our experience was similar with two half-hour programs dealing with cigarette smoking and lung cancer. Both the medical profession and the tobacco industry cooperated in a rather wary fashion. But in the end of the day they were both reasonably content. The subject of radioactive fall-out and the banning of nuclear tests was, and is, highly controversial. But according to what little evidence there is, viewers were prepared to listen to both sides with reason and restraint. This is not said to claim any special or unusual competence in the presentation of controversial subjects, but rather to indicate that timidity in these areas is not warranted by the evidence.

Recently, network spokesmen have been disposed to complain that the professional critics of television have been "rather beastly." There have been hints that somehow competition for the advertising dollar has caused the critics of print to gang up on television and radio. This reporter has no desire to defend the critics. They have space in which to do that on their own behalf. But it remains a fact that the newspapers and magazines are the only instruments of mass communication which remain free from sustained and regular critical comment. If the network spokesmen are so anguished about what appears in print, let them come forth and engage in a little sustained and regular comment regarding newspapers and magazines. It is an ancient and sad fact that most people in network television, and radio, have an exaggerated regard for what appears in print. And there have been cases where executives have refused to make even private comment or on a program for which they were responsible until they heard'd the reviews in print. This is hardly an exhibition confidence.

The oldest excuse of the networks for their timidity is their youth. Their spokesmen say, "We are young; we have not developed the traditions nor acquired the experience of the older media." If they but knew it, they are building those traditions, creating those precedents every day. Each time they yield to a voice from Washington or any political pressure, each time they eliminate something that might offend some section of the community, they are creating their own body of precedent and tradition. They are, in fact, not content to be "half safe."

Nowhere is this better illustrated than by the fact that the chair- 10 man of the Federal Communications Commission [FCC] publicly prods broadcasters to engage in their legal right to editorialize. Of course, to undertake an editorial policy, overt and clearly labeled, and obviously unsponsored, requires a station or a network to be responsible. Most stations today probably do not have the manpower to assume this responsibility, but the manpower could be recruited. Editorials would not be profitable; if they had a cutting edge, they might even offend. It is much easier, much less troublesome, to use the money-making machine of television and radio merely as a conduit through which to channel anything that is not libelous, obscene or defamatory. In that way one has the illusion of power without responsibility.

So far as radio—that most satisfying and rewarding instrument—is concerned, the diagnosis of its difficulties is rather easy. And obviously I speak only of news and information. In order to progress, it need only go backward. To the time when singing commercials were not allowed on news reports, when there was no middle commercial in a 15-minute news report, when radio was rather proud, alert and fast. I recently asked a network official, "Why this great rash of five-minute news reports (including three commercials) on weekends?" He replied, "Because that seems to be the only thing we can sell."

In this kind of complex and confusing world, you can't tell very much about the why of the news in broadcasts where only three minutes is available for news. The only man who could do that was Elmer Davis, and his kind aren't about any more. If radio news is to be regarded as a commodity, only acceptable when saleable, then I don't care what you call it—I say it isn't news.

My memory also goes back to the time when the fear of a slight reduction in business did not result in an immediate cutback in bodies in the news and public affairs department, at a time when network profits had just reached an all-time high. We would all agree, I think, that whether on a station or a network, the stapling machine is a poor substitute for a newsroom typewriter.

One of the minor tragedies of television news and information is that the networks will not even defend their vital interests. When my employer, CBS, through a combination of enterprise and good luck, did an interview with Nikita Khrushchev, the President uttered a few ill-chosen, uninformed words on the subject, and the network practically apologized. This produced a rarity. Many newspapers defended the CBS right to produce the program and commended it for initiative. But the other networks remained silent.

15   Likewise, when John Foster Dulles,[1] by personal decree, banned American journalists from going to Communist China, and subsequently offered contradictory explanations, for his fiat the networks entered only a mild protest. Then they apparently forgot the unpleasantness. Can it be that this national industry is content to serve the public interest only with the trickle of news that comes out of Hong Kong, to

---

[1]Secretary of state under President Dwight D. Eisenhower, 1953–59 [Eds.]

leave its viewers in ignorance of the cataclysmic changes that are occurring in a nation of six hundred million people? I have no illusions about the difficulties reporting from a dictatorship, but our British and French allies have been better served—in their public interest—with some very useful information from their reporters in Communist China.

One of the basic troubles with radio and television news is that both instruments have grown up as an incompatible combination of show business, advertising and news. Each of the three is a rather bizarre and demanding profession. And when you get all three under one roof, the dust never settles. The top management of the networks with a few notable exceptions, has been trained in advertising, research, sales or show business. But by the nature of the coporate structure, they also make the final and crucial decisions having to do with news and public affairs. Frequently they have neither the time nor the competence to do this. It is not easy for the same small group of men to decide whether to buy a new station for millions of dollars, build a new building, alter the rate card, buy a new Western, sell a soap opera, decide what defensive line to take in connection with the latest Congressional inquiry, how much money to spend on promoting a new program, what additions or deletions should be made in the existing covey or clutch of vice-presidents, and at the same time— frequently on the same long day—to give mature, thoughtful consideration to the manifold problems that confront those who are charged with the responsibility for news and public affairs.

Sometimes there is a clash between the public interest and the corporate interest. A telephone call or a letter from the proper quarter in Washington is treated rather more seriously than a communication from an irate but not politically potent viewer. It is tempting enough to give away a little air time for frequently irresponsible and unwarranted utterances in an effort to temper the wind of criticism.

Upon occasion, economics and editorial judgment are in conflict. And there is no law which says that dollars will be defeated by duty. Not so long ago the President of the United States delivered a television address to the nation. He was discoursing on the possibility or probability of war between this nation and the Soviet Union and Communist China—a reasonably compelling subject. Two networks CBS and NBC, delayed that broadcast for an hour and fifteen minutes. If this decision was dictated by anything other than financial reasons, the networks didn't deign to explain those reasons. That hour-and-fifteen-minute delay, by the way, is about twice the time required for an ICBM to travel from the Soviet Union to major targets in the United States. It is difficult to believe that this decision was made by men who love, respect and understand news.

So far, I have been dealing largely with the deficit side of the ledger, and the items could be expanded. But I have said, and I believe, that potentially we have in this country a free enterprise system of radio and television which is superior to any other. But to achieve its promise, it must be both free and enterprising. There is no suggestion here that networks or individual stations should operate as philanthropies. But I can find nothing in the Bill of Rights or the Communications Act which says that they must increase their net profits each year, lest the Republic collapse. I do not suggest that news and information should be subsidized by foundations or private subscriptions. I am aware that the networks have expended, and are expending, very considerable sums of money on public affairs programs from which they cannot hope to receive any financial reward. I have had the privilege at CBS of presiding over a considerable number of such programs. I testify, and am able to stand here and say, that I have never had a program turned down by my superiors because of the money it would cost.

25   But we all know that you cannot reach the potential maximum audience in marginal time with a sustaining program. This is so because so many stations on the network—any network—will decline to carry it. Every licensee who applies for a grant to operate in the public interest, convenience and necessity makes certain promises as to what he will do in terms of program content. Many recipients of licenses have, in blunt language, welshed on those promises. The money-making machine somehow blunts their memories. The only remedy for this is closer inspection and punitive action by the FCC. But in the view of many this would come perilously close to supervision of program content by a federal agency.

So it seems that we cannot rely on philanthropic support or foundation subsidies; we cannot follow the "sustaining route"—the networks cannot pay all the freight—and the F.C.C. cannot or will not discipline those who abuse the facilities that belong to the public. What, then, is the answer? Do we merely stay in our comfortable nests, concluding that the obligation of these instruments has been discharged when we work at the job of informing the public for a minimum of time? Or do we believe that the preservation of the Republic is a seven-day-a-week job, demanding more awareness, better skills and more perseverance than we have yet contemplated.

I am frightened by the imbalance, the constant striving to reach the largest possible audience for everything; by the absence of a sustained study of the state of the nation. Heywood Broun once said, "No body politic is healthy until it begins to itch." I would like television to produce some itching pills rather than this endless outpouring of tranquilizers. It can be done. Maybe it won't be, but it could. Let us not shoot the wrong piano player. Do not be deluded into believing that the titular heads of the networks control what appears on their networks. They all have better taste. All are responsible to stockholders, and in my experience all are honorable men. But they must schedule what they can sell in the public market.

And this brings us to the nub of the question. In one sense it rather revolves around the phrase heard frequently along Madison Avenue: The Corporate Image. I am not precisely sure what this phrase means, but I would imagine that it reflects a desire on the part of the corporations who pay the advertising bills to have the public image, or believe that they are not merely bodies with no souls, panting in pursuit of elusive dollars. They would like us to believe that they can distinguish between the public good and the private or corporate gain. So the question is this: Are the big corporations who pay the freight for radio and television programs wise to use that time exclusively for the sale of goods and services? Is it in their own interest and that of the stockholders so to do? The sponsor of an hour's television program is not buying merely the six minutes devoted to commercial message. He is determining, within broad limits, the sum total of the impact of the entire hour. If he always, invariably, reaches for the largest possible audience, then this process of insulation, of escape from reality, will continue to be massively financed, and its apologist will continue to make winsome speeches about giving the public what it wants, or "letting the public decide."

I refuse to believe that the presidents and chairmen of the boards of these big corporations want their corporate image to consist exclusively of a solemn voice in an echo chamber, or a pretty girl opening the door of a refrigerator, or a horse that talks. They want something better, and on occasion some of them have demonstrated it. But most of the men whose legal and moral responsibility it is to spend the stockholders' money for advertising are removed from the realities of the mass media by five, six, or a dozen contraceptive layers of vice-presidents, public relations counsel and advertising agencies. Their business is to sell goods, and the competition is pretty tough.

But this nation is now in competition with malignant forces of evil who are using every instrument at their command to empty the minds of their subjects and fill those minds with slogans, determination and faith in the future. If we go on as we are, we are protecting the mind of the American public from any real contact with the menacing world that squeezes in upon us. We are engaged in a great experiment to discover whether a free public opinion can devise and direct methods of managing the affairs of the nation. We may fail. But we are handicapping ourselves needlessly.

Let us have a little competition. Not only in selling soap, cigarettes and automobiles, but in informing a troubled, apprehensive but receptive public. Why should not each of the 20 or 30 big corporations which dominate radio and television decide that they will give up one or two of their regularly scheduled programs each year, turn the time over to the networks and say in effect: "This is a tiny tithe, just a little bit of our profits. On this particular night we aren't going to try to sell cigarettes or automobiles; this is merely a gesture to indicate our belief in the importance of ideas." The networks should, and I think would, pay for the cost of producing the program. The advertiser, the sponsor, would get name credit but would have nothing to do with the content of the program. Would this blemish the corporate image? Would the stockholders object? I think not. For if the premise upon which our pluralistic society rests, which as I understand it is that if the people are given sufficient undiluted information, they will then somehow, even after long, sober second thoughts, reach the right decision—if that premise is wrong, then not only the corporate image but the corporations are done for.

There used to be an old phrase in this country, employed when someone talked too much. It was: "Go hire a hall." Under this proposal the sponsor would have hired the hall; he has bought the time; the local station operator, no matter how indifferent, is going to carry the program—he has to. Then it's up to the networks to fill the hall. I am not here talking about editorializing but about straightaway exposition as direct, unadorned and impartial as falliable human beings can make it. Just once in a while let us exalt the importance of ideas and information. Let us dream to the extent of saying that on a given Sunday night the time normally occupied by Ed Sullivan[2] is given over to a clinical survey of the state of American education, and a week or two later the time normally used by Steve Allen[3] is devoted to a thoroughgoing study of American policy in the Middle East. Would the corporate image of their respective sponsors be damaged? Would the stockholders rise up in their wrath and complain? Would anything happen other than that a few million people would have received a little illumination on subjects that may well determine the future of this country, and therefore the future of the corporations?

This method would also provide real competition between the networks as to which could outdo the others in the palatable presentation of information. It would provide an outlet for the young men of skill, and there are some even of dedication, who would like to do something other than devise methods of insulating while selling.

There may be other and simpler methods of utilizing these instruments of radio and television in the interests of a free society. But I know of none that could be so easily accomplished inside the framework of the existing commercial system. I don't know how you would measure the success or failure of a given program. And it would be hard to prove the magnitude of the benefit accruing to the corporation which gave up one night of a variety or quiz show in order that the network might marshal its skills to do a thoroughgoing job on the present status of NATO,[4] or plans for controlling

---

[2]Host of long-running TV variety show [Eds.]

[3]Television personality and formet host of *Tonight* show [Eds.]

[4]North Atlantic Treaty Organization [Eds.]

nuclear tests. But I would reckon that the president, and indeed the majority of shareholders of the corporation who sponsored such a venture, would feel just a little bit better about the corporation and the country.

It may be that the present system, with no modifications and no experiments, can survive. Perhaps the money-making machine has some kind of built-in perpetual motion, but I do not think so. To a very considerable extent the media of mass communications in a given country reflect the political, economic and social climate in which they flourish. That is the reason ours differ from the British and French, or the Russian and Chinese. We are currently wealthy, fat, comfortable and complacent. We have currently a built-in allergy to unpleasant or disturbing information. Our mass media reflect this. But unless we get up off our fat surpluses and recognize that television in the main is being used to distract, delude, amuse and insulate us, then television and those who finance it, those who look at it and those who work at it, may see a totally different picture too late.

I do not advocate that we turn television into a 27-inch wailing 30
wall, where longhairs constantly moan about the state of our culture and our defense. But I would just like to see it reflect occasionally the hard, unyielding realities of the world in which we live. I would like to see it done inside the existing framework, and I would like to see the doing of it redound to the credit of those who finance and program it. Measure the results by Nielsen, Trendex or Silex—it doesn't matter. The main thing is to try. The responsibility can be easily placed, in spite of all the mouthings about giving the public what it wants. It rests on big business, and on big television, and it rests at the top. Responsibility is not something that can be assigned or delegated. And it promises its own reward: good business and good television.

Perhaps no one will do anything about it. I have ventured to outline it against a background of criticism that may have been too harsh only because I could think of nothing better. Someone once said—I think it was Max Eastman—that "that publisher serves his advertiser best who best serves his readers." I cannot believe that radio and television, or the corporation that finance the programs, are serving well or truly their viewers or listeners, or themselves.

I began by saying that our history will be what we make it. If we go on as we are, then history will take its revenge, and retribution will not limp in catching up with us.

We are to a large extent an imitative society. If one or two or three corporations would undertake to devote just a small traction of their advertising appropriation along the lines that I have suggested, the procedure would grow by contagion; the economic burden would be bearable, and there might ensure a most exciting adventure—exposure to ideas and the bringing of reality into the homes of the nation.

To those who say people wouldn't look; they wouldn't be interested; they're too complacent, indifferent and insulated, I can only reply: There is, in one reporter's opinion, considerable evidence against that contention. But even if they are right, what have they got to lose? Because if they are right, and this instrument is good for nothing but to entertain, amuse and insulate, then the tube is flickering now and we will soon see that the whole struggle is lost.

35   This instrument can teach, it can illuminate; yes, and it can even inspire. But it can do so only to the extent that humans are determined to use it to those ends. Otherwise it is merely wires and lights in a box. There is a great and perhaps decisive battle to be fought against ignorance, intolerance and indifference. This weapon of television could be useful.

Stonewall Jackson, who knew something about the use of weapons, is reported to have said, "When war comes, you must draw the sword and throw away the scabbard." The trouble with television is that it is rusting in the scabbard during a battle for survival.

Responding to Reading

1. Murrow begins his speech with the words, "This just might do nobody any good." Considering his audience—radio and TV news directors—do you see this as an effective opening strategy? What "good" do you think he wanted his speech to do?
2. What are Murrow's primary criticisms of the radio and television industry? To what does he attribute the problems he identifies? What changes does he recommend?
3. In paragraph 22, Murrow says, "I am frightened by the imbalance, the constant striving to reach the largest possible audience for everything; . . ." What trends in TV news coverage do you think Murrow would find most frightening today? Would he find any trends encouraging?

Responding in Writing

Watch a half-hour national news program on one of the major TV networks. Do the problems Murrow identified still exist, or do you see evidence that TV news has changed for the better?

TELEVISION: THE PLUG-IN DRUG

Marie Winn

1936–

*Born in Prague, Marie Winn immigrated to the United States with her
family in 1939. She has written on a variety of subjects, but she is probably
best known for her three critiques of television's effects on children and families:* The Plug-In Drug: Television, Children and Family *(1977, revised 2002), from which the following selection was taken;* Children
Without Childhood *(1983); and* Unplugging the Plug-In Drug *(1987).
Winn has also published* Red-Tails in Love: A Wildlife Drama in Central Park *(1998) and* Central Park in the Dark *(2004) as well as several
children's books. In the following widely reprinted essay, Winn considers
how television has affected the family.*

Not much more than fifty years after the introduction of television
into American society, the medium has become so deeply ingrained in
daily life that in many states the TV set has attained the rank of a legal
necessity, safe from repossession in case of debt along with clothes
and cooking utensils. Only in the early years after television's introduction did writers and commentators have sufficient perspective to
separate the activity of watching television from the actual content it
offers the viewer. In those days writers frequently discussed the effects of television on family life. However, a curious myopia afflicted
those first observers: almost without exception they regarded television as a favorable, beneficial, indeed, wondrous influence upon the
family.

"Television is going to be a real asset in every home where there
are children," predicted a writer in 1949.

"Television will take over your way of living and change your
children's habits, but this change can be a wonderful improvement,"
claimed another commentator.

"No survey's needed, of course, to establish that television has
brought the family together in one room," wrote the *New York Times*'s
television critic in 1949.

The early articles about television were almost invariably accom-   5
panied by a photograph or illustration showing a family cozily sitting
together before the television set, Sis on Mom's lap, Buddy perched
on the arm of Dad's chair, Dad with his arm around Mom's shoulder.
Who could have guessed that twenty or so years later Mom would be
watching a drama in the kitchen, the kids would be looking at cartoons in their room, while Dad would be taking in the ball game in
the living room?

Of course television sets were enormously expensive when they first came on the market. The idea that by the year 2000 more than three quarters of all American families would own two or more sets would have seemed preposterous. The splintering of the multiple-set family was something the early writers did not foresee. Nor did anyone imagine the number of hours children would eventually devote to television, the changes television would effect upon child-rearing methods, the increasing domination of family schedules by children's viewing requirements—in short, the power of television to dominate family life.

As children's consumption of the new medium increased together with parental concern about the possible effects of so much television viewing, a steady refrain helped soothe and reassure anxious parents. "Television always enters a pattern of influences that already exist: the home, the peer group, the school, the church and culture generally," wrote the authors of an early and influential study of television's effects on children. In other words, if the child's home life is all right, parents need not worry about the effects of too much television watching.

But television did not merely influence the child; it deeply influenced that "pattern of influences" everyone hoped would ameliorate the new medium's effects. Home and family life have changed in important ways since the advent of television. The peer group has become television-oriented, and much of the time children spend together is occupied by television viewing. Culture generally has been transformed by television. Participation in church and community activities has diminished, with television a primary cause of this change. Therefore it is improper to assign to television the subsidiary role its many apologists insist it plays. Television is not merely one of a number of important influences upon today's child. Through the changes it has made in family life, television emerges as *the* important influence in children's lives today.

The Quality of Life

Television's contribution to family life has been an equivocal one. For while it has, indeed, kept the members of the family from dispersing, it has not served to bring them together. By its domination of the time families spend together, it destroys the special quality that distinguishes one family from another, a quality that depends to a great extent on what a family does, what special rituals, games, recurrent jokes, familiar songs, and shared activities it accumulates.

10   Yet parents have accepted a television-dominated family life so completely that they cannot see how the medium is involved in whatever problems they might be having. A first-grade teacher reports:

I have one child in the group who's an only child. I wanted to find out more about her family life because this little girl was quite isolated from the group, didn't make friends, so I talked to her mother. Well, they don't have time to do anything in the evening, the mother said. The parents come home after picking up the child at the baby-sitter's. Then the mother fixes dinner while the child watches TV. Then they have dinner and the child goes to bed. I said to this mother. "Well, couldn't she help you fix dinner? That would be a nice time for the two of you to talk," and the mother said, "Oh, but I'd hate to have her miss *Zoom.* It's such a good program!"

Several decades ago a writer and mother of two boys aged three and seven described her family's television schedule in a newspaper article. Though some of the programs her kids watched then have changed, the situation she describes remains the same for great numbers of families today:

We were in the midst of a full-scale War. Every day was a new battle and every program was a major skirmish. We agreed it was a bad scene all around and were ready to enter diplomatic negotiations. . . . In principle we have agreed on $2\frac{1}{2}$ hours of TV a day, *Sesame Street, Electric Company* (with dinner gobbled up in between) and two half-hour shows between 7 and 8:30, which enables the grown-ups to eat in peace and prevents the two boys from destroying one another. Their pre-bedtime choice is dreadful, because, as Josh recently admitted, "There's nothing much on I really like." So . . . it's *What's My Line* or *To Tell the Truth.* . . . Clearly there is a need for first-rate children's shows at this time. . . .

Consider the "family life" described here: Presumably the father comes home from work during the *Sesame Street–Electric Company* stint. The children are either watching television, gobbling their dinner, or both. While the parents eat their dinner in peaceful privacy, the children watch another hour of television. Then there is only a half-hour left before bedtime, just enough time for baths, getting pajamas on, brushing teeth, and so on. The children's evening is regimented with an almost military precision. They watch their favorite programs, and when there is "nothing much on I really like," they watch whatever else is on—because *watching* is the important thing. Their mother does not see anything amiss with watching programs just for the sake of watching; she only wishes there were some first-rate children's shows on at those times.

Without conjuring up fantasies of bygone eras with family games and long, leisurely meals, the question arises: isn't there a better family life available than this dismal, mechanized arrangement of children watching television for however long is allowed them, evening after evening?

Of course, families today still do things together at times: go camping in the summer, go to the zoo on a nice Sunday, take various trips and expeditions. But their ordinary daily life together is diminished—those hours of sitting around at the dinner table, the spontaneous taking up of an activity, the little games invented by children on the spur of the moment when there is nothing else to do, the scribbling, the chatting, and even the quarreling, all the things that form the fabric of a family, that define a childhood. Instead, the children have their regular schedule of television programs and bedtime, and the parents have their peaceful dinner together.

15   The author of the quoted newspaper article notes that "keeping a family sane means mediating between the needs of both children and adults." But surely the needs of the adults in that family were being better met than the needs of the children. The kids were effectively shunted away and rendered untroublesome, while their parents enjoyed a life as undemanding as that of any childless couple. In reality, it is those very demands that young children make upon a family that lead to growth, and it is the way parents respond to those demands that builds the relationships upon which the future of the family depends. If the family does not accumulate its backlog of shared experiences, shared everyday experiences that occur and recur and change and develop, then it is not likely to survive as anything other than a caretaking institution.

Family Rituals

Ritual is defined by sociologists as "that part of family life that the family likes about itself, is proud of and wants formally to continue." Another text notes that "the development of a ritual by a family is an index of the common interest of its members in the family as a group."

What has happened to family rituals, those regular, dependable, recurrent happenings that gave members of a family a feeling of belonging to a home rather than living in it merely for the sake of convenience, those experiences that act as the adhesive of family unity far more than any material advantages?

Mealtime rituals, going-to-bed rituals, illness rituals, holiday rituals—how many of these have survived the inroads of the television set?

A young woman who grew up near Chicago reminisces about her childhood and gives an idea of the effects of television upon family rituals:

> As a child I had millions of relatives around—my parents both come from relatively large families. My father had nine brothers and sisters.

And so every holiday there was this great swoop-down of aunts, uncles, and millions of cousins. I just remember how wonderful it used
to be. These thousands of cousins would come and everyone would
play and ultimately, after dinner, all the women would be in the front
of the house, drinking coffee and talking, all the men would be in the
back of the house, drinking and smoking, and all the kids would be all
over the place, playing hide and seek. Christmas time was particularly
nice because everyone always brought all their toys and games. Our
house had a couple of rooms with go-through closets, so there were
always kids running in a great circle route. I remember it was just
wonderful.

And then all of a sudden one year I remember becoming suddenly aware of how different everything had become. The kids were
no longer playing Monopoly or Clue or the other games we used to
play together. It was because we had a television set which had been
turned on for a football game. All of that socializing that had gone
on previously had ended. Now everyone was sitting in front of the
television set, on a holiday, at a family party! I remember being
stunned by how awful that was. Somehow the television had become more attractive.

As families have come to spend more and more of their time to- 20
gether engaged in the single activity of television watching, those rituals and pastimes that once gave family life its special quality have
become more and more uncommon. Not since prehistoric times,
when cave families hunted, gathered, ate, and slept, with little time
remaining to accumulate a culture of any significance, have families
been reduced to such a sameness.

Real People

The relationships of family members to each other are affected by
television's powerful competition in both obvious and subtle ways.
For surely the hours that children spend in a one-way relationship
with television people, an involvement that allows for no communication or interaction, must have some effect on their relationships
with real-life people.

Studies show the importance of eye-to-eye contact, for instance,
in real-life relationships, and indicate that the nature of one's eye-contact
patterns, whether one looks another squarely in the eye or looks to
the side or shifts one's gaze from side to side, may play a significant
role in one's success or failure in human relationships. But no eye
contact is possible in the child-television relationship, although in certain children's programs people purport to speak directly to the child
and the camera fosters this illusion by focusing directly upon the person being filmed. How might such a distortion affect a child's development of trust, of openness, of an ability to relate well to *real* people?

Bruno Bettelheim suggested an answer:

Children who have been taught, or conditioned, to listen passively most of the day to the warm verbal communications coming from the TV screen, to the deep emotional appeal of the so-called TV personality, are often unable to respond to real persons because they arouse so much less feeling than the skilled actor. Worse, they lose the ability to learn from reality because life experiences are much more complicated than the ones they see on the screen. . . .

A teacher makes a similar observation about her personal viewing experiences:

I have trouble mobilizing myself and dealing with real people after watching a few hours of television. It's just hard to make that transition from watching television to a real relationship. I suppose it's because there was no effort necessary while I was watching, and dealing with real people always requires a bit of effort. Imagine, then, how much harder it might be to do the same thing for a small child, particularly one who watches a lot of television every day.

25   But more obviously damaging to family relationships is the elimination of opportunities to talk and converse, or to argue, to air grievances between parents and children and brothers and sisters. Families frequently use television to avoid confronting their problems, problems that will not go away if they are ignored but will only fester and become less easily resolvable as time goes on.

A mother reports:

I find myself, with three children, wanting to turn on the TV set when they're fighting. I really have to struggle not to do it because I feel that's telling them this is the solution to the quarrel—but it's so tempting that I often do it.

A family therapist discusses the use of television as an avoidance mechanism:

In a family I know the father comes home from work and turns on the television set. The children come and watch with him and the wife serves them their meal in front of the set. He then goes and takes a shower, or works on the car or something. She then goes and has her own dinner in front of the television set. It's a symptom of a deeper-rooted problem, sure. But it would help them all to get rid of the set. It would be far easier to work on what the symptom really means without the television. The television simply encourages a double avoidance of each other. They'd find out more quickly what was going on if they weren't able to hide behind the TV. Things wouldn't necessarily be better, of course, but they wouldn't be anesthetized.

A number of research studies done when television was a relatively new medium demonstrated that television interfered with family activities and the formation of family relationships. One survey showed that 78 percent of the respondents indicated no conversation taking place during viewing except at specified times such as commercials. The study noted: "The television atmosphere in most households is one of quiet absorption on the part of family members who are present. The nature of the family social life during a program could be described as 'parallel' rather than interactive, and the set does seem to dominate family life when it is on." Thirty-six percent of the respondents in another study indicated that television viewing was the only family activity participated in during the week.

The situation has only worsened during the intervening decades. When the studies were made, the great majority of American families had only one television set. Though the family may have spent more time watching TV in those early days, at least they were all together while they watched. Today the vast majority of all families have two or more sets, and nearly a third of all children live in homes with four or more TVs. The most telling statistic: almost 60 percent of all families watch television during meals, and not necessarily at the same TV set. When do they talk about what they did that day? When do they make plans, exchange views, share jokes, tell about their triumphs or little disasters? When do they get to be a real family?

Undermining the Family

Of course television has not been the only factor in the decline of family life in America. The steadily rising divorce rate, the increase in the number of working mothers, the trends towards people moving far away from home, the breakdown of neighborhoods and communities—all these have seriously affected the family.

Obviously the sources of family breakdown do not necessarily come from the family itself, but from the circumstances in which the family finds itself and the way of life imposed upon it by those circumstances. As Urie Bronfenbrenner[1] has suggested:

> When those circumstances and the way of life they generate undermine relationships of trust and emotional security between family members, when they make it difficult for parents to care for, educate, and enjoy their children, when there is no support or recognition from the outside world for one's role as a parent, and when time spent with one's family means frustration of career, personal fulfillment, and peace of mind, then the development of the child is adversely affected.

---

[1]Developmental psychologist who co-founded the US Head Start Program [Eds.]

Certainly television is not the single destroyer of American family life. But the medium's dominant role in the family serves to anesthetize parents into accepting their family's diminished state and prevents them from struggling to regain some of the richness the family once possessed.

One research study alone seems to contradict the idea that television has a negative impact on family life. In their important book *Television and the Quality of Life,* sociologists Robert Kubey and Mihaly Csikszentmihalyi observe that the heaviest viewers of TV among their subjects were "no less likely to spend time with their families" than the lightest viewers. Moreover, those heavy viewers reported feeling happier, more relaxed, and satisfied when watching TV with their families than light viewers did. Based on these reports, the researchers reached the conclusion that "television viewing harmonizes with family life."

Using the same data, however, the researchers made another observation about the heavy and light viewers: ". . . families that spend substantial portions of their time together watching television are likely to experience greater percentages of their family time feeling relatively passive and unchallenged compared with families who spend small proportions of their time watching TV."

35 At first glance the two observations seem at odds: the heavier viewers feel happy and satisfied, yet their family time is more passive and unchallenging—less satisfying in reality. But when one considers the nature of the television experience, the contradiction vanishes. Surely it stands to reason that the television experience is instrumental in preventing viewers from recognizing its dulling effects, much as a mind-altering drug might do.

In spite of everything, the American family muddles on, dimly aware that something is amiss but distracted from an understanding of its plight by an endless stream of television images. As family ties grow weaker and vaguer, as children's lives become more separate from their parents', as parents' educational role in their children's lives is taken over by the media, the school, and the peer group, family life becomes increasingly more unsatisfying for both parents and children. All that seems to be left is love, an abstraction that family members know is necessary but find great difficulty giving to each other since the traditional opportunities for expressing it within the family have been reduced or eliminated.

Responding to Reading

1. Winn says, "Home and family life have changed in important ways since the advent of television" (8). How, according to Winn, has family life changed? What kind of support does she offer for this conclusion? Is it enough?

2. Do you agree with Winn that television is an evil, addictive drug that has destroyed cherished family rituals, undermined family relationships, and
"[anesthetized] parents into accepting their family's diminished state and
[prevented] them from struggling to regain some of the richness the family
once possessed" (32)? Or, do you think she is exaggerating the dangers of TV?
3. Although it was updated in 2002, Winn's essay was written almost thirty
years ago. In light of how much time has passed, do you think she needs to
change any of her examples or add any new information?

Responding in Writing

Do you consider any other item—for example, your cell phone, iPod, or
computer—to be a "plug-in drug" for you? Do you see any danger in your
dependence on this object, or do you consider it just a routine part of your life?

REALITY TV: A DEARTH OF TALENT AND THE DEATH OF MORALITY

Salman Rushdie

1947–

Born in Bombay, India, Salman Rushdie is perhaps best known for his novel
The Satanic Verses *(1988), which infuriated Muslims around the world.*
The book was banned in a dozen countries, caused riots in several, and led to
a multimillion-dollar bounty being offered for Rushdie's assassination. In
1998, the fatwa *(death sentence) was lifted by the Iranian government (al-*
though some fundamentalist Muslim groups increased the reward for killing
him). Rushdie lives in seclusion and continues to publish articles, essays,
and books, including Fury *(2001),* Step Across This Line: Collected
Nonfiction 1992–2002 *(2002), and* Shalimar the Clown *(2005). In* the
following selection, which appeared in The Guardian *in 2001, Rushdie of-*
fers his criticisms of reality TV and suggests some dangerous trends to
come.

I've managed to miss out on reality TV until now. In spite of all the
talk in Britain about nasty Nick and flighty Mel, and in America about
the fat, naked bastard Richard manipulating his way to desert-island
victory, I have somehow preserved my purity. I wouldn't recognise
Nick or Mel if I passed them in the street, or Richard if he was standing in front of me unclothed.

Ask me where the Big Brother house is, or how to reach Temptation Island, and I have no answer. I do remember the American
Survivor contestant who managed to fry his own hand so that the skin
peeled away until his fingers looked like burst sausages, but that's

because he got on to the main evening news. Otherwise, search me. Who won? Who lost? Who cares?

The subject of reality TV shows, however, has been impossible to avoid. Their success is the media story of the (new) century, along with the ratings triumph of the big-money game shows such as *Who Wants to Be a Millionaire?* Success on this scale insists on being examined, because it tells us things about ourselves; or ought to.

And what tawdry narcissism is here revealed! The television set, once so idealistically thought of as our window on the world, has become a dime-store mirror instead. Who needs images of the world's rich otherness, when you can watch these half-familiar avatars of yourself—these half-attractive half-persons—enacting ordinary life under weird conditions? Who needs talent, when the unashamed self-display of the talentless is constantly on offer?

5   I've been watching *Big Brother 2,* which has achieved the improbable feat of taking over the tabloid front pages in the final stages of a general election campaign. This, according to the conventional wisdom, is because the show is more interesting than the election. The "reality" may be even stranger. It may be that *Big Brother* is so popular because it's even more boring than the election. Because it is the most boring, and therefore most "normal," way of becoming famous, and, if you're lucky or smart, of getting rich as well.

"Famous" and "rich" are now the two most important concepts in western society, and ethical questions are simply obliterated by the potency of their appeal. In order to be famous and rich, it's OK—it's actually "good"—to be devious. It's "good" to be exhibitionistic. It's "good" to be bad. And what dulls the moral edge is boredom. It's impossible to maintain a sense of outrage about people being so trivially self-serving for so long.

Oh, the dullness! Here are people becoming famous for being asleep, for keeping a fire alight, for letting a fire go out, for videotaping their cliched thoughts, for flashing their breasts, for lounging around, for quarrelling, for bitching, for being unpopular, and (this is too interesting to happen often) for kissing! Here, in short, are people becoming famous for doing nothing much at all, but doing it where everyone can see them.

Add the contestants' exhibitionism to the viewers' voyeurism and you get a picture of a society sickly in thrall to what Saul Bellow called "event glamour." Such is the glamour of these banal but brilliantly spotlit events that anything resembling a real value—modesty, decency, intelligence, humour, selflessness; you can write your own list—is rendered redundant. In this inverted ethical universe, worse is better. The show presents "reality" as a prize fight, and suggests that in life, as on TV, anything goes, and the more deliciously contemptible it is, the more we'll like it. Winning isn't everything, as Charlie Brown once said, but losing isn't anything.

The problem with this kind of engineered realism is that, like all fads, it's likely to have a short shelf-life, unless it finds ways of renewing itself. The probability is that our voyeurism will become more demanding. It won't be enough to watch somebody being catty, or weeping when evicted from the house of hell, or "revealing everything" on subsequent talk shows, as if they had anything left to reveal.

What is gradually being reinvented is the gladiatorial combat. 10 The TV set is the Colosseum and the contestants are both gladiators and lions; their job is to eat one another until only one remains alive. But how long, in our jaded culture, before "real" lions, actual dangers, are introduced to these various forms of fantasy island, to feed our hunger for more action, more pain, more vicarious thrills?

Here's a thought, prompted by the news that the redoubtable Gore Vidal has agreed to witness the execution by lethal injection of the Oklahoma bomber Timothy McVeigh. The witnesses at an execution watch the macabre proceedings through a glass window: a screen. This, too, is a kind of reality TV, and—to make a modest proposal—it may represent the future of such programmes. If we are willing to watch people stab one another in the back, might we not also be willing to actually watch them die?

In the world outside TV, our numbed senses already require increasing doses of titillation. One murder is barely enough; only the mass murderers make the front pages. You have to blow up a building full of people or machine-gun a whole royal family to get our attention. Soon, perhaps, you'll have to kill off a whole species of wildlife or unleash a virus that wipes out people by the thousand, or else you'll be small potatoes. You'll be on an inside page.

And as in reality, so on "reality TV." How long until the first TV death? How long until the second? By the end of Orwell's great novel 1984, Winston Smith has been brainwashed. "He loved Big Brother." As, now, do we. We are the Winstons now.

Responding to Reading

1. Salman Rushdie, a respected novelist with an international reputation, admits here that he knows little about reality TV and has only recently begun to watch *Big Brother 2*. Considering these admissions, do you think he has the credibility to criticize reality TV?

2. Rushdie's fear is that "our voyeurism will become more demanding" (9), leading to shows that will "feed our hunger for more action, more pain, more vicarious thrills" (10). Has this fear been realized in any way since this essay was published in 2001? Do you think Rushdie is correct to be alarmed, or do you think viewers will continue to be satisfied with the present level of thrills and action?

3. How are the trends in reality TV shows that Rushdie describes similar to trends in television in general? Can you think of any dangerous trends that might develop on other kinds of TV shows?

Responding in Writing

Consulting a newspaper's TV listings, read the program descriptions of several different reality shows. List the features these programs seem to have in common. Then, write a paragraph in which you explain what it is about these shows that seems to appeal to viewers.

IS MUSIC PIRACY STEALING?

Charles W. Moore

1951–

Charles W. Moore is contributing editor at Applelinks.com, which offers news and reviews of Apple Macintosh products and trends. In the following essay, Moore argues that the free music downloading and sharing made possible by portable listening devices such as Apple's iPod is a victimless crime.

> The law is wiser than cabal or interest.
>
> Edmund Burke, 1794

This week the Motion Picture Association of America (MPAA) launched an ad campaign using the slogan "copying is stealing," attempting to convey the message that digital copying is as serious and criminal as stealing a CD from a record shop or a DVD from a video shop.

So, is music (and video) piracy stealing? The short answer, as the MPAA and the Recording Industry Association of America (RIAA) will be quick to tell you, is "yes." Under current copyright legislation, downloading music for free is definitely theft under letter of the law. But is the law just and fair? That's the operative question, and the long answer is more complex.

Two-thirds of Internet users who download music are unconcerned that they are violating copyright laws, while only 29 percent say they do care and 6 percent have no opinion on the issue according to a new Pew Internet and American Life Project survey released last Thursday. Not only that, the number of downloaders who say they don't care about copyright has increased over the past year, from 61 percent to 67 percent. A slightly smaller percentage (65%) of respondents who share files online (music or video) say they don't care whether the files they swap are copyrighted or not.

Pew estimates that roughly 35 million American adults use file-sharing software, about 29 percent of Internet users, and that 26 million share files online. The survey notes:

> Young adults are the least likely to express concern about the copy-   5
> rights of the files they share with others, with 82% of file-sharers aged
> 18–29 saying they don't care much about the copyright status of the
> files they share. Those aged 30 to 64 are more likely to express concern
> about copyrights, with about 2 in 5 file-sharers in those age groups
> saying as much. Nevertheless, in each age group, a plurality if not an
> out right majority of each group say that they are unconcerned about
> the copyright of the files they share online.
>
> Students, both full-time and part-time, who share files, say they
> are not concerned about the copyright status of the files they share
> with others online. Eighty percent of full-time students and almost
> three-quarters of part-time students say they do not care whether the
> files they share are copyrighted or not. Fifty-nine percent of non-
> students say the same.
>
> Full-time students overwhelmingly express a lack of concern over
> the copyrights of the files they download—4 out of 5 say they are un-
> concerned. . . .
>
> College grads are the most likely to express concern over copy-
> right amongst file-sharers. Those with lower levels of education are
> much more likely to express very little concern, and even amongst
> college grads, a majority (56%) say they don't care much about
> copyright.

In an AP[1] article on the Pew survey, the RIAA comments that its recent blitz to "educate" file-swappers and music downloaders by randomly suing them will result in more compliant attitudes. I beg to differ. The litigation fascism drive will mainly serve to further alienate and polarize a consuming public which already is growing to despise the recording industry. Some people may be deterred from sharing and downloading music, etcetera, out of fear, but that amounts to legal terrorism—not "education."

As the Pew report notes, "Americans' attitude towards copyrighted material online has remained dismissive, even amid a torrent of media coverage and legal cases aimed at educating the public about the threat file-sharing poses to the intellectual property industries."

I don't think very many folks are unaware that music is copy-   10
righted, or that unauthorized copying is illegal. It's just that, as the Pew survey indicates, they don't care, just as most people in my experience suffer no ethical pangs about photocopying pages from reference books

---

[1]Associated Press [Eds.]

borrowed from the library, or song sheets for their church choir, or copyrighted materials to distribute to their school or college classes, all of which are just as illegal under copyright legislation as downloading pirate MP3s. Literally millions of people who would never dream of shoplifting a book, album, or packaged software item, seem to have no ethical qualms about photocopying books and magazine articles, or downoading music. How do we explain this?

I think one reason is that it is perceived as a victimless crime. I know that music industry people will vigorously disagree, but if someone copies a song, the copyright-holder may or may not be out of revenue he or she might have realized if the item had been purchased, but is not left without something he or she once possessed and now doesn't. That is, the copyright holder is no worse off materially than he or she was prior to the piracy. I'm not trying to construct a moral justification or rationalization for piracy here—just illustrating that it is a stretch to call software or music piracy "stealing" in the sense most people think of theft.

The average person would regard going into a store and pocketing a tangible piece of physical property is as something essentially different from copy piracy. The human mind finds the concept of intellectual property much more abstract, slippery, and nebulous than the concept of physical property. I think it would be accurate to suggest that when most consumers buy a book or CD recording, their gut perception is of having purchased a physical item more than the concept of its intellectual content. Of course, with say, a CD, the cost of the physical medium represents a small fraction of the purchase price, but that gut-perception is still that property is something one can see and touch and keep, even for people who intellectually know better.

And of course, if a burglar breaks in and steals your CD collection, there is no mechanism in place by which you can restore it for the cost of the lost physical media, so perhaps, in practical terms, the ol' gut has a point.

Intellectual property piracy is a tough issue to sort out ethically, and I suspect that most people don't really bother to try. My guess would be that very few people reading this could honestly say that they have never made a photocopy of copyrighted material, taped a favorite song from a friend's record or CD, pirated a piece of software, or "forgotten" to pay a shareware fee. So are we all thieves or not? Some would emphatically answer "yes!," and they have current legality on their side, but as I said going in, I think it's more complex than that.

15   Personally music piracy is not a big part of my life. Like many people with a computer and an Internet hookup, I experimented with downloading MP3s during the Napster era, but didn't do a whole lot of it, and I think in the past two years I've downloaded a grand total of two songs, while testing file-sharing client software for review.

However, like many people, I used to make mixed audio cassette tapes of music I like from LPs belonging to friends and relatives, and I confess to taping movies and sports events on TV to watch later. So, I'm a copyright pirate of sorts I guess, just like virtually every other North American in one context or another. As I said, there are few computer users and Internet surfers who could look you straight in the eye and honestly tell you they have never pirated anything.

However, my central interest in this issue is philosophy, not piracy, per se, to wit: the threat to the free exchange of information over the Internet and otherwise that draconian copyright laws engender. I have come to question conventional wisdom as to the philosophical legitimacy of copyright laws as they're currently written in a broader context as they pertain to the public interest and to inhibition of information exchange.

Some people tell me, that music piracy is just plain wrong, period. I think that in this instance they may be confusing the distinction between "it's against the law," and "it's wrong," since the moral basis for determining that it is wrong is the legitimacy or otherwise of copyright legislation.

Now some people would argue that whatever the law says— breaking it is always wrong. That is a philosophical stance with some integrity, but it founders in the instance of unjust laws. History is littered with bad legislation, and many laws have been downright immoral.

One that isn't law yet, but soon could be is Congress's proposed Author, Consumer and Computer Owner Protection and Security Act, which proposes to make it a felony if you upload even just one measly infringing copyrighted work to the Internet. [20]

Got that? One contraband MP3 in your shared peer-to-peer software directory, and you're a felon. Hello jail! Post a newspaper article or copyrighted photo to your blogsite—whoops!—you're a felon too.

As CNET News.com's Eric Goldman noted this week.

> Congress has been completely convinced that rampant copyright infringement threatens to destroy the American economy. Having internalized this threat, Congress is now determined to fix that problem the only way it knows how—threaten ordinary citizens with jail, despite collateral consequences. . . .
>
> Congress needs to develop an integrated policy about criminal copyright infringement. To do so, Congress needs to realize two things. First, it is not acceptable to put average Americans at the peril of going to jail for doing everyday activities. Second, if the existing laws are not yielding the desired results, perhaps they were bad policy, in which case making them tougher only compounds the initial policy failure. . . .

Indeed, whatever the morality and ethics or lack of that music piracy represents, ruining the lives of individuals for petty noncommercial copyright infringement is vastly worse. It is plain wrong, however legal. Elected representatives need to do some serious soul-searching about who, and whose interests, they really represent, and lose the indignant anger at the American public for continuing to infringe.

It's just not that simple. Particularly in the area of laws governing commerce, the law usually has more to do with protecting vested interests that enjoy political influence, often bought and paid for, then it does with morality.

A good analogy is that of genetically modified (GM) foodstuffs, which enjoy intellectual property protection analogous to that pertaining to music, pictures, or prose. Currently 80% of the patents on GM foods are owned by just 13 corporations globally. Companies engaged in bio-technology pressured government for, and got copyright-like intellectual property law to cover life forms, and in 1985, the U.S. Patent & Trademark Office allowed genetically modified plants, seeds and plant tissue to be patented. Corporations can now acquire the knowledge of generations of indigenous farmers, and then, after subjecting this knowledge to scientific analysis, take out patents on the resulting product. Each "improvement" in farm crops, whether by hybridization or genetic modification, tends to reduce bio-diversity and to marginalize those crops which in the present agricultural and economic context are regarded as unprofitable. These varieties are also the traditional crops on which the poor depend. That would be bad enough.

25 However, transnational companies have acquired the right to patent GM seeds, which means that farmers will be locked into contracts to buy both seeds and chemicals, and not allowed to plant the farm-saved seed. Farmers who switch to GM seed will have to sign a gene licensing agreement, which specifies royalty fees and dictates the seed, fertilizer and chemicals to be used. These agreements prohibit the storing of seed for the following season, locking the farmers into a perpetual, subservient, client relationship with the big chemical companies. It's all perfectly legal, but don't try to convince me that it's ethical or moral.

In genetic engineering, only a tiny fraction of the make-up of the organism can be said to be a product of the scientist. The organism is still essentially a living entity, not an invention. Notwithstanding the considerable investment involved in research and development, the identification of a gene's function is not an ethical ground for claiming exclusive rights. Even though intellectual effort has been used, it is of the nature of discovery, not of invention. I would say the same applies to music, which some consider food for the soul. Music is an arrangement of notes and sometimes words as well, but the vast majority of it is highly derivative. The notion that sounds or combinations of sounds can be private property is a nebulous one at best that no one should accept uncritically at face value.

Listening to rhetoric from the RIAA, et al., you might infer that copyright laws had been handed down on stone tablets by the Almighty. They were not, of course, and not everyone in the world bestows upon the abstract concept of intellectual property rights the quasi-religious reverence they are accorded in corporate boardrooms, litigation lawyers' offices, and the U.S. Congress. Copyright laws are merely an arbitrary and mutable legislative construct, and do not necessarily carry any objective moral weight.

The view that "theft" of intellectual property is tantamount to grand larceny of the highest order, that should be subject to commensurate penalties, is a reflection of a particular philosophical mindset, but unlike theft of real, tangible property, it involves a necessary value judgment.

Copyright laws pertaining to music are especially draconian. I am no expert, but as I understand it, even quoting a few words or a phrase from the lyrics of a copyrighted song is illegal without permission, unlike prose, where fair use can run to hundreds of words. That speaks volumes about the success of the music-biz lobby in getting legislators on side.

This fight is ultimately about money and power and control— 30 over what you will be able to see and read and watch and listen to, and how it will be delivered, and who will make money from it. It is about protection of vested interests, not just protection of artists' intellectual property.

In the U.S. context, Article I, section 8, clause 8 of the United States Constitution gives Congress the obligation to "promote the Progress of Science and useful Arts, by securing for limited times to Authors and Inventors the exclusive Right to their respective Writings and Discoveries."

The original U.S. Copyright Act granted copyright-holders the exclusive right to print, publish, and sell a copyrighted work for fourteen years with a second fourteen-year term possible. There were no rights given to the copyright holder regarding the public performance of the work nor could the holder control adaptations or derivative works.

Thus, rather than representing some sort of categorical moral imperative, copyright legislation is rooted in monopolism and censorship, and has, in our time, been expanded in scope far beyond its original intent. In an era of digital communication, I also submit that it has been expanded well beyond its enforceability and sustainability, let alone desirability.

Why should the private interests of corporations exert a veto on entire technologies that offer benefit to the common public good? That is what happened with Digital Audio Tape, which had the recording interests wetting themselves in fearful anticipation of easy, unauthorized, high-quality copying of music until they successfully and selfishly lobbied in the name of copyright protection for restrictions that effectively killed the technology for widespread use, even though it would have offered many legitimate benefits that had nothing to do with piracy. Meanwhile, MP3 technology was ramping up to blindside them, and I have to say that whatever happens now, it has been delicious seeing the cartels get their comeuppance.

35   There is also a Common Law aspect to the development of our system of law, which in the context of music copyright has been recognized to some degree under the law in both Canada and the US., copyright holders used to insist that ANY unauthorized copying of music recordings was unacceptable, and under the law so it was at the time. The political process and acknowledgment of the reality that music was going to be copied anyway, law or no law, caused the law to be changed. It became legal to make copies for personal use. I expect that there will be further legal developments along these lines driven by popular practice.

The U.S. Constitution and legal system are based on British Common Law, which by definition derives from the common people, as opposed to legislation, which, comes from the "experts." Ergo: Common Law develops at the root levels of society, and is grounded in precedent and tradition as well as reason; it is not law that is imposed by some authority from on high. Congresspeople: are you paying attention?

I contend that copyright legislation as it evolved through the twentieth century has no grounding in Common Law, and was indeed imposed by authorities on high at the behest of vested interests. Consequently, its legitimacy is questionable, at least at the philosophical level.

An aspect of Common Law begins to obtain when a high enough proportion of society decides that a law is unjust or unfair and chooses to ignore it. The Pew survey estimates that 26 million Americans are music file swappers and downloaders. In practical terms, the RIAA will be able to legally harass and persecute a tiny minority of them under current copyright legislation, which *is* unjust and unfair, and as noted above grants rights to copyright holders light years beyond what the U.S. founders ever intended copyrights to do. However, they will not ultimately be able to turn the tide of popular sentiment on this issue.

The development of Common Law is at work when schoolteachers and college professors routinely photocopy copyrighted material to use in class, and advise their students to do the same; when ministers of religion photocopy copyrighted material to distribute in church services; when everybody and their dog photocopies stuff from magazines and library books for personal reference or to hand out to their friends (not to mention all the stuff that gets scanned into computers and distributed over the Internet); I submit that copyright law in its late-twentieth-century iteration is no longer working or workable.

The real conundrum is how to ensure that creators of intellectual 40 property can be fairly compensated for their work given the technological realities of our time. I don't have the answer to that question, but perhaps the orientation should be to abandon the futile fixation on prohibiting unauthorized private copying and think of more innovative means of compensation and protection. As I said, I haven't got the answer, but it surely isn't the tactics and strategy being pursued by the RIAA and its fellow travelers in government.

In summary, the point I have been trying to make over several years now of writing and commenting about copyright issues: The letter of copyright law, as it is currently written, is becoming irrelevant in practical terms. Recording companies and publishers are never, ever, going to be able to regain the tight, top-down control they once had over copying and distribution of intellectual property, no matter how many lawsuits they launch or friends they make (buy?) in Congress.

I guess, ultimately, my argument is that legalities, ethics, and so on aside, in practical terms you can't defy gravity. The litigants will be able to punish some pirates through great legal effort, but they won't end piracy, and even if they could it would be tragically bad news for the freedoms of speech and information exchange.

Copyright as we knew it in the twentieth century is doomed. It will still be able to thrash and writhe for a while yet in its death throes, and cause a lot of collateral damage in the lives of certain individuals, but it is ultimately dead meat.

Responding to Reading

1. How does Moore defend the practice of downloading music? In what respects does he see music copyright laws as unfair? Do you agree with his statement in his conclusion that "Copyright as we knew it in the twentieth century is doomed"?

2. In paragraph 5, Moore calls random lawsuits against those who share and download music "litigation fascism"; he believes that such lawsuits will alienate the public and will not be effective. Do you agree?

3. In paragraph 21, Moore discusses genetically engineered food. How is this discussion related to his comments about music piracy? Do you see the analogy he makes as a sound one?

Responding in Writing

According to Moore, many people see downloading music as essentially a "victimless crime" (7). Do you see it this way? Do you see it as different from stealing a CD from a store? If so, how?

EMINEM IS RIGHT

Mary Eberstadt

Research fellow at the Hoover Institution and associate member of the Fellowship of Catholic Scholars, Mary Eberstadt is a consulting editor at Policy Review *and author of numerous magazine and newspaper articles on various American cultural issues. Originally published in her 2004 book* Home-Alone America: The Hidden Toll of Day Care, Behavioral Drugs, and Other Parent Substitutes, *the essay excerpted here examines the meanings and social implications of contemporary American popular music.*

If there is one subject on which the parents of America passionately agree, it is that contemporary adolescent popular music, especially the subgenres of heavy metal and hip-hop/rap, is uniquely degraded—and degrading—by the standards of previous generations. At first blush this seems slightly ironic. After all, most of today's baby-boom parents were themselves molded by rock and roll, bumping and grinding their way through adolescence and adulthood with legendary abandon. Even so, the parents are correct: Much of today's music *is* darker and coarser than yesterday's rock. Misogyny, violence, suicide, sexual exploitation, child abuse—these and other themes, formerly rare and illicit, are now as common as the surfboards, drive-ins, and sock hops of yesteryear.

In a nutshell, the ongoing adult preoccupation with current music goes something like this: *What is the overall influence of this deafening, foul, and often vicious-sounding stuff on children and teenagers?* This is a genuinely important question, and serious studies and articles, some concerned particularly with current music's possible link to violence, have lately been devoted to it. In 2000, the American Academy of Pediatrics, the American Medical Association, the American Psychological Association, and the American Academy of Child & Adolescent Psychiatry all weighed in against contemporary lyrics and other forms of violent entertainment before Congress with a first-ever "Joint Statement on the Impact of Entertainment Violence on Children."

Nonetheless, this is not my focus here. Instead, I would like to turn that logic about influence upside down and ask this question: *What is it about today's music, violent and disgusting though it may be, that resonates with so many American kids?*

As the reader can see, this is a very different way of inquiring about the relationship between today's teenagers and their music. The first question asks what the music *does* to adolescents; the second asks what it *tells* us about them. To answer that second question is necessarily to enter the roiling emotional waters in which that music is created and consumed in other words, actually to listen to some of it and read the lyrics.

As it turns out, such an exercise yields a fascinating and little un- 5 derstood fact about today's adolescent scene. If yesterday's rock was the music of abandon, today's is that of abandon*ment.* The odd truth about contemporary teenage music—the characteristic that most separates it from what has gone before—is its compulsive insistence on the damage wrought by broken homes, family dysfunction, checked-out parents, and (especially) absent fathers. Papa Roach, Everclear, Blink-182, Good Charlotte, Eddie Vedder and Pearl Jam, Kurt Cobain and Nirvana, Tupac Shakur, Snoop Doggy Dogg, Eminem—these and other singers and bands, all of them award-winning top-40 performers who either are or were among the most popular icons in America, have their own generational answer to what ails the modern teenager. Surprising though it may be to some, that answer is: dysfunctional childhood. Moreover, and just as interesting, many bands and singers explicitly link the most deplored themes in music today—suicide, misogyny, and drugs—with that lack of a quasi-normal, intact-home personal past.

To put this perhaps unexpected point more broadly, during the same years in which progressive-minded and politically correct adults have been excoriating Ozzie and Harriet as an artifact of 1950s-style oppression, many millions of American teenagers have enshrined a new generation of music idols whose shared generational signature in song after song is to rage about what *not* having had a nuclear family has done to them. This is quite a fascinating puzzle of the times. The self-perceived emotional damage scrawled large across contemporary music may not be statistically quantifiable, but it is nonetheless among the most striking of all the unanticipated consequences of our home-alone world....

[An] Example of the rage in contemporary music against irresponsible adults—perhaps the most interesting—is that of genre-crossing bad-boy rap superstar Marshall Mathers or Eminem (sometime stage persona "Slim Shady"). Of all the names guaranteed to send a shudder down the parental spine, his is probably the most effective. In fact, Eminem has single-handedly, if inadvertently, achieved the otherwise ideologically impossible: He is the object of a vehemently disapproving public consensus shared by the National Organization for Women the Gay & Lesbian Alliance Against Defamation, William J. Bennett, Lynne Cheney, Bill O'Reilly, and a large number of other social conservatives as well as feminists and gay activists. In sum, this rapper—"as harmful to America as any al Qaeda fanatic," in O'Reilly's opinion—unites adult polar opposites as perhaps no other single popular entertainer has done.

There is small need to wonder why. Like other rappers, Eminem mines the shock value and gutter language of rage, casual sex, and violence. Unlike the rest, however, he appears to be a particularly attractive target of opprobrium for two distinct reasons. One, he is white and therefore politically easier to attack. (It is interesting to note that black rappers have not been targeted by name anything like Eminem has.) Perhaps even more important, Eminem is one of the largest commercially visible targets for parental wrath. Wildly popular among teenagers these last several years, he is also enormously successful in commercial terms. Winner of numerous Grammys and other music awards and a perpetual nominee for many more, he has also been critically (albeit reluctantly) acclaimed for his acting performance in the autobiographical 2003 movie *8 Mile*. For all these reasons, he is probably the preeminent rock/rap star of the last several years, one whose singles, albums, and videos routinely top every chart. His 2002 album, *The Eminem Show*, for example, was easily the most successful of the year, selling more than 7.6 million copies.

5   This remarkable market success, combined with the intense public criticism that his songs have generated, makes the phenomenon of Eminem particularly intriguing. Perhaps more than any other current musical icon, he returns repeatedly to the same themes that fuel other success stories in contemporary music: parental loss, abandonment, abuse, and subsequent child and adolescent anger, dysfunction, and violence (including self-violence). Both in his raunchy lyrics as well as in *8 Mile*, Mathers's own personal story has been parlayed many times over: the absent father, the troubled mother living in a trailer park, the series of unwanted maternal boyfriends, the protective if impotent feelings toward a younger sibling (in the movie, a baby sister; in real life, a younger brother), and the fine line that a poor, ambitious, and unguided young man might walk between catastrophe and success. Mathers plumbs these and related themes with a verbal savagery that leaves most adults aghast.

10   Yet Eminem also repeatedly centers his songs on the crypto-traditional notion that children need parents and that *not* having them has made all hell break loose. In the song "8 Mile" from the

movie soundtrack, for example, the narrator studies his little sister as she colors one picture after another of an imagined nuclear family, failing to understand that *"mommas got a new man."* *"Wish I could be the daddy that neither one of us had,"* he comments. Such wistful lyrics juxtapose oddly and regularly with Eminem's violent other lines. Even in one of his most infamous songs, "Cleaning Out My Closet (Mama, I'm Sorry)," what drives the vulgar narrative is the insistence on seeing abandonment from a child's point of view. *"My faggot father must have had his panties up in a bunch / 'Cause he split. I wonder if he even kissed me good-bye."*

As with other rappers, the vicious narrative treatment of women in some of Eminem's songs is part of this self-conception as a child victim. Contrary to what critics have intimated, the misogyny in current music does not spring from nowhere; it is, often linked to the larger theme of having been abandoned several times—left behind by father, not nurtured by mother, and betrayed again by faithless womankind. One of the most violent and sexually aggressive songs in the last few years is "Kill You" by the popular metal band known as Korn. Its violence is not directed toward just any woman or even toward the narrator's girlfriend; it is instead a song about an abusive stepmother whom the singer imagines going back to rape and murder.

Similarly, Eminem's most shocking lyrics about women are not randomly dispersed; they are largely reserved for his mother and ex-wife, and the narrative pose is one of despising them for not being better women—in particular, better mothers. The worst rap directed at his own mother is indeed gut-wrenching: *"But how dare you try to take what you didn't help me to get? / You selfish bitch, I hope you'f—burn in hell for this shit!"* It is no defense of the gutter to observe the obvious: This is not the expression of random misogyny but, rather, of primal rage over alleged maternal abdication and abuse.

Another refrain in these songs runs like this: Today's teenagers are a mess, and the parents who made them that way refuse to get it. In one of Eminem's early hits, for example, a song called "Who Knew," the rapper pointedly takes on his many middle- and upper-middle-class critics to observe the contradiction between their reviling him and the parental inattention that feeds his commercial success. *"What about the make-up you allow your 12 year-old daughter to wear?"* he taunts.

This same theme of AWOL parenting is rapped at greater length in another award-nominated 2003 song called "Sing for the Moment," whose lyrics and video would be recognized in an instant by most teenagers in America. That song spells out Eminem's own idea of what connects him to his millions of fans—a connection that parents, in his view, just don't (or is that won't?) understand. It details the case of one more "problem child" created by "*His f—dad walkin' out.*" "Sing for the Moment," like many other songs of Eminem's, is also a popular video. The "visuals" show clearly what the lyrics depict—hordes of disaffected kids, with flashbacks to bad home lives, screaming for the singer who feels their pain. It concludes by rhetorically turning away from the music itself and toward the emotionally desperate teenagers who turn out for this music by the millions. If the demand of all those empty kids wasn't out there, the narrator says pointedly, then rappers wouldn't be supplying it the way they do.

15   If some parents still don't get it—even as their teenagers elbow up for every new Eminem CD and memorize his lyrics with psalmist devotion—at least some critics observing the music scene have thought to comment on the ironies of all this. In discussing The *Marshall Mathers* LP in 2001 for Music Box, a daily online newsletter about music, reviewer John Metzger argued, "Instead of spewing the hate that he is so often criticized of doing, Eminem offers a cautionary tale that speaks to our civilization's growing depravity. Ironically, it's his teenage fans who understand this, and their all-knowing parents that miss the point." Metzger further specified "the utter lack of parenting due to the spendthrift necessity of the two-income family."[1]

That insight raises the overlooked fact that in one important sense Eminem . . . would agree with many of today's adults about one thing: The kids *aren't* all right out there after all. Recall, for just one example, Eddie Vedder's rueful observation about what kind of generation would make him or Kurt Cobain its leader. Where parents and entertainers disagree is over who exactly bears responsibility for this moral chaos. Many adults want to blame the people who create and market today's music and videos. Entertainers, Eminem most prominently, blame the absent, absentee, and generally inattentive adults whose deprived and furious children (as they see it) have catapulted today's singers to fame. (As he puts the point in one more in-your-face response to parents: "*Don't blame me when lil' Eric jumps off of the terrace / You shoulda been watchin him—apparently you ain't parents.*")

The spectacle of a foul-mouthed bad-example rock icon instructing the hardworking parents of America in the art of child-rearing is indeed a peculiar one, not to say ridiculous. The single mother who is working frantically because she must and worrying all the while about what her 14-year-old is listening to in the headphones is entitled to a certain fury over lyrics like those. In fact, to read through most rap lyrics is to wonder which adults or political constituencies *wouldn't* take offense. Even so, the music idols who point the finger away from themselves and toward the emptied-out homes of America

---

[1]John Metzger, review of "Eminem: the Marshall Mathers I.P"., *Music Box* 8:6 (June 2001).

are telling a truth that some adults would rather not hear. In this limited sense at least, Eminem is right.

To say that today's popular music is uniquely concerned with broken homes, abandoned children, and distracted or incapable parents is not to say that this is what all of it is about. Other themes remain a constant, too, although somewhat more brutally than in the alleged golden era recalled by some baby boomers.

Much of today's metal and hip-hop, like certain music of yesterday, romanticizes illicit drug use and alcohol abuse, and much of current hip-hop sounds certain radical political themes, such as racial separationism and violence against the police. And, of course, the most elementally appealing feature of all, the sexually suggestive beat itself, continues to lure teenagers and young adults in its own right—including those from happy homes. Today as yesterday, plenty of teenagers who don't know or care what the stars are raving about find enough satisfaction in swaying to the sexy music. As professor and intellectual Allan Bloom observed about rock in his bestseller, *The Closing of the American Mind* (Simon & Schuster, 1987), the music "gives children, on a silver platter, with all the public authority of the entertaining industry, everything their parents always used to tell them they had to wait for until they grew up and would understand later."

Even so, and putting aside such obvious continuities with previous generations, there is no escaping the fact that today's songs are musically and lyrically unlike any before. What distinguishes them most clearly is a the fixation on having been abandoned personally by the adults supposedly in charge, with consequences ranging from bitterness to rage to bad, sick, and violent behavior. 20

And therein lies a painful truth about an advantage that many teenagers of yesterday enjoyed but their own children often do not. Baby boomers and their music rebelled against parents *because* they were parents—nurturing, attentive, and overly present (as those teenagers often saw it) authority figures. Today's teenagers and their music rebel against parents because they are *not* parents—not nurturing, not attentive, and often not even there. This difference in generational experience may not lend itself to statistical measure, but it is as real as the platinum and gold records that continue to capture it. What those records show compared to yesteryear's rock is emotional downward mobility. Surely if some of the current generation of teenagers and young adults had been better taken care of, then the likes of Kurt Cobain, Eminem, Tupac Shakur, and certain other parental nightmares would have been mere footnotes to recent music history rather than rulers of it.

To step back from the emotional immediacy of those lyrics and to juxtapose the ascendance of such music alongside the long-standing sophisticated assaults on what is sardonically called "family values" is to meditate on a larger irony. As today's music stars and their raving fans likely do not know, many commentators and analysts have been rationalizing every aspect of the adult exodus from home—sometimes celebrating it full throttle, as in the example of working motherhood—longer than most of today's singers and bands have been alive.

Nor do they show much sign of second thoughts. Representative sociologist Stephanie Coontz greeted the year 2004 with one more op-ed piece aimed at burying poor metaphorical Ozzie and Harriet for good. She reminded America again that "changes in marriage and family life" are here to stay and aren't "necessarily a problem"; that what is euphemistically called "family diversity" is or ought to be cause for celebration. Many other scholars and observers—to say nothing of much of polite adult society—agree with Coontz. Throughout the contemporary nonfiction literature written of, by, and for educated adults, a thousand similar rationalizations about family "changes" bloom on.

Meanwhile, a small number of emotionally damaged former children, embraced and adored by millions of teenagers like them, rage on in every commercial medium available about the multiple damages of the disappearance of loving, protective, attentive adults—and they reap a fortune for it. If this spectacle alone doesn't tell us something about the ongoing emotional costs of parent-child separation on today's outsize scale, it's hard to see what could.

Responding to Reading

1. Eberstadt acknowledges in her first paragraph that "contemporary adolescent popular music, especially the subgenre of heavy metal and hip-hop/rap," commonly includes themes of "Misogyny, violence, suicide, sexual exploitation, [and] child abuse. . . ." How does she explain the presence of these themes? In what sense is Eminem "right"?

2. Eberstadt's focus here is not on the effects of music on adolescents but on what it reveals about them. In paragraph 3, she asks, *"What is it about today's music, violent and disgusting though it may be, that resonates with so many American kids?"* How does she answer this question? How would you answer it?

3. In what sense does Eberstadt see today's adolescent music as the music of "abandon*ment*" rather than as the "music of abandon" (5)? How does she believe what she calls "our home-alone world" (6) helps to explain Eminem's violent, misogynistic lyrics? Do you see this essay primarily as a defense of the music of performers like Eminem or as an attack on "irresponsible adults" (7)?

Responding in Writing

Elsewhere, Eberstadt discusses the lyrics of other musical artists who appeal to today's adolescents, and she argues that their lyrics, like Eminem's, also reveal a preoccupation with family dysfunction and abandonment by parents. Give examples of such lyrics and explain how they support her position.

WHO SHOT MOHAMMED AL-DURA?
James Fallows
1949–

Journalist James Fallows, known for his insightful analysis of social and political issues, has written on a wide range of subjects, including computer software, immigration, economics, and national defense. He is currently the Atlantic Monthly's *Washington-based national correspondent. His book* National Defense *won the American Book Award in 1981; he has also written* Breaking the News: How the Media Undermine American Democracy (1996) *and* Free Flight! From Airline Hell to a New Age of Travel (2001). *In the following essay, Fallows examines the incendiary power of television news coverage.*

The name Mohammed al-Dura is barely known in the United States. Yet to a billion people in the Muslim world it is an infamous symbol of grievance against Israel and—because of this country's support for Israel—against the United States as well.

Al-Dura was the twelve-year-old Palestinian boy shot and killed during an exchange of fire between Israeli soldiers and Palestinian demonstrators on September 30, 2000. The final few seconds of his life, when he crouched in terror behind his father, Jamal, and then slumped to the ground after bullets ripped through his torso, were captured by a television camera and broadcast around the world. Through repetition they have become as familiar and significant to Arab and Islamic viewers as photographs of bombed-out Hiroshima are to the people of Japan—or as footage of the crumbling World Trade Center is to Americans. Several Arab countries have issued postage stamps carrying a picture of the terrified boy. One of Baghdad's main streets was renamed The Martyr Mohammed Aldura Street. Morocco has an al-Dura Park. In one of the messages Osama bin Laden released after the September 11 attacks and the subsequent U.S. invasion of Afghanistan, he began a list of indictments against "American arrogance and Israeli violence" by saying, "In the epitome of his arrogance and the peak of his media campaign in which he boasts of 'enduring freedom,' Bush must not forget the image of Mohammed al-Dura and his fellow Muslims in Palestine and Iraq. If he has forgotten, then we will not forget, God willing."

But almost since the day of the episode evidence has been emerging in Israel, under controversial and intriguing circumstances, to indicate that the official version of the Mohammed al-Dura story is not true. It now appears that the boy cannot have died in the way reported by most of the world's media and fervently believed throughout the Islamic world. Whatever happened to him, he was not shot by the Israeli soldiers who were known to be involved in the day's fighting—or so I am convinced, after spending a week in Israel talking with those examining the case. The exculpatory evidence comes not from government or military officials in Israel, who have an obvious interest in claiming that their soldiers weren't responsible, but from other sources. In fact, the Israel Defense Forces, or IDF, seem to prefer to soft-pedal the findings rather than bring any more attention to this gruesome episode. The research has been done by a variety of academics, ex-soldiers, and Web-loggers who have become obsessed with the case, and the evidence can be cross-checked.

No "proof" that originates in Israel is likely to change minds in the Arab world. The longtime Palestinian spokesperson Hanan Ashrawi dismissed one early Israeli report on the topic as a "falsified version of reality [that] blames the victims." Late this spring Said Hamad, a spokesman at the PLO office in Washington, told me of the new Israeli studies, "It does not surprise me that these reports would come out from the same people who shot Mohammed al-Dura. He was shot of course by the Israeli army, and not by anybody else."

Even if evidence that could revise the understanding of this particular death were widely accepted (so far it has been embraced by a few Jewish groups in Europe and North America), it would probably have no effect on the underlying hatred and ongoing violence in the region. Nor would evidence that clears Israeli soldiers necessarily support the overarching Likud policy of sending soldiers to occupy territories and protect settlements. The Israelis still looking into the al-Dura case do not all endorse Likud occupation policies. In fact, some strongly oppose them.

The truth about Mohammed al-Dura is important in its own right, because this episode is so raw and vivid in the Arab world and so hazy, if not invisible, in the West. Whatever the course of the occupation of Iraq, the United States has guaranteed an ample future supply of images of Arab suffering. The two explosions in Baghdad markets in the first weeks of the war, killing scores of civilians, offered an initial taste. Even as U.S. officials cautioned that it would take more time and study to determine whether U.S. or Iraqi ordnance had caused the blasts, the Arab media denounced the brutality that created these new martyrs. More of this lies ahead. The saga of Mohammed al-Dura illustrates the way the battles of wartime imagery may play themselves out.

The harshest version of the al-Dura case from the Arab side is that it proves the ancient "blood libel"—Jews want to kill gentile children—and shows that Americans count Arab life so cheap that they will let the Israelis keep on killing. The harshest version from the Israeli side is that the case proves the Palestinians' willingness to deliberately sacrifice even their own children in the name of the war against Zionism. In Tel Aviv I looked through hour after hour of videotape in an attempt to understand what can be known about what happened, and what it means.

The Day

The death of Mohammed al-Dura took place on the second day of what is now known as the second intifada, a wave of violent protests throughout the West Bank and Gaza. In the summer of 2000 Middle East peace negotiations had reached another impasse. On September 28 of that year, a Thursday, Ariel Sharon, then the leader of Israel's Likud Party but not yet Prime Minister, made a visit to the highly contested religious site in Jerusalem that Jews know as the Temple Mount and Muslims know as Haram al-Sharif, with its two mosques. For Palestinians this was the trigger—or, in the view of many Israelis, the pretext—for the expanded protests that began the next day.

On September 30 the protest sites included a crossroads in the occupied Gaza territory near the village of Netzarim, where sixty families of Israeli settlers live. The crossroads is a simple right-angle intersection of two roads in a lightly developed area. Three days earlier a roadside bomb had mortally wounded an IDF soldier there. At one corner of the intersection were an abandoned warehouse, two six-story office buildings known as the "twin towers," and a two-story building. (These structures and others surrounding the crossroads have since been torn down.) A group of IDF soldiers had made the two-story building their outpost, to guard the road leading to the Israeli settlement.

Diagonally across the intersection was a small, ramshackle building and a sidewalk bordered by a concrete wall. It was along this wall that Mohammed al-Dura and his father crouched before they were shot. (The father was injured but survived.) The other two corners of the crossroads were vacant land. One of them contained a circular dirt berm, known as the Pita because it was shaped like a pita loaf. A group of uniformed Palestinian policemen, armed with automatic rifles, were on the Pita for much of the day.

10   Early in the morning of Saturday, September 30, a crowd of Palestinians gathered at the Netzarim crossroads. TV crews, photographers, and reporters from many news agencies, including Reuters, AP, and the French television network France 2, were also at the ready. Because so many cameras were running for so many hours, there is abundant documentary evidence of most of the day's events—with a few strange and crucial exceptions, most of them concerning Mohammed al-Dura.

"Rushes" (raw footage) of the day's filming collected from these and other news organizations around the world tell a detailed yet confusing story. The tapes overlap in some areas but leave mysterious gaps in others. No one camera, of course, followed the day's events from beginning to end; and with so many people engaged in a variety of activities simultaneously, no one account could capture everything. Gabriel Weimann, the chairman of the communications department at the University of Haifa, whose book *Communicating Unreality* concerns the media's distorting effects, explained to me on my visit that the footage in its entirety has a *"Rashomon* effect."[1] Many separate small dramas seem to be under way. Some of the shots show groups of young men walking around, joking, sitting and smoking and appearing to enjoy themselves. Others show isolated moments of intense action, as protesters yell and throw rocks, and shots ring out from various directions. Only when these vignettes are packaged together as a conventional TV news report do they seem to have a narrative coherence.

---

[1]*Rashomon,* a 1950 film by Japanese director Akira Kurosawa, in which different people give varying accounts of a murder. [Eds.]

Off and on throughout the morning some of the several hundred Palestinian civilians at the crossroads mounted assaults on the IDF outpost. They threw rocks and Molotov cocktails. They ran around waving the Palestinian flag and trying to pull down an Israeli flag near the outpost. A few of the civilians had pistols or rifles, which they occasionally fired; the second intifada quickly escalated from throwing rocks to using other weapons. The Palestinian policemen, mainly in the Pita area, also fired at times. The IDF soldiers, according to Israeli spokesmen, were under orders not to fire in response to rocks or other thrown objects. They were to fire only if fired upon. Scenes filmed throughout the day show smoke puffing from the muzzles of M-16s pointed through the slits of the IDF outpost.

To watch the raw footage is to wonder, repeatedly, What is going on here? In some scenes groups of Palestinians duck for cover from gunfire while others nonchalantly talk or smoke just five feet away. At one dramatic moment a Palestinian man dives forward clutching his leg, as if shot in the thigh. An ambulance somehow arrives to collect him exactly two seconds later, before he has stopped rolling from the momentum of his fall. Another man is loaded into an ambulance—and, in footage from a different TV camera, appears to jump out of it again some minutes later.

At around 3:00 P.M. Mohammed al-Dura and his father make their first appearance on film. The time can be judged by later comments from the father and some journalists on the scene, and by the length of shadows in the footage. Despite the number of cameras that were running that day, Mohammed and Jamal al-Dura appear in the footage of only one cameraman—Talal Abu-Rahma, a Palestinian working for France 2.

Jamal al-Dura later said that he had taken his son to a used-car 15 market and was on the way back when he passed through the crossroads and into the crossfire. When first seen on tape, father and son are both crouched on the sidewalk behind a large concrete cylinder, their backs against the wall. The cylinder, about three feet high, is referred to as "the barrel" in most discussions of the case, although it appears to be a section from a culvert or a sewer system. On top of the cylinder is a big paving stone, which adds another eight inches or so of protection. The al-Duras were on the corner diagonally opposite the Israeli outpost. By hiding behind the barrel they were doing exactly what they should have done to protect themselves from Israeli fire.

Many news accounts later claimed that the two were under fire for forty-five minutes, but the action captured on camera lasts a very brief time. Jamal looks around desperately. Mohammed slides down behind him, as if to make his body disappear behind his father's. Jamal clutches a pack of cigarettes in his left hand, while he alternately waves and cradles his son with his right. The sound of gunfire is heard, and four bullet holes appear in the wall just to the left of the pair. The father starts yelling. There is another burst. Mohammed goes limp and falls forward across his father's lap, his shirt stained with blood. Jamal, too, is hit, and his head starts bobbling. The camera cuts away. Although France 2 or its cameraman may have footage that it or he has chosen not to release, no other visual record of the shooting or its immediate aftermath is known to exist. Other Palestinian casualties of the day are shown being evacuated, but there is no known on-tape evidence of the boy's being picked up, tended to, loaded into an ambulance, or handled in any other way after he was shot.

The footage of the shooting is unforgettable, and it illustrates the way in which television transforms reality. I have seen it replayed at least a hundred times now, and on each repetition I can't help hoping that this time the boy will get himself down low enough, this time the shots will miss. Through the compression involved in editing the footage for a news report, the scene acquired a clear story line by the time European, American, and Middle Eastern audiences saw it on television: Palestinians throw rocks. Israeli soldiers, from the slits in their outpost, shoot back. A little boy is murdered.

What is known about the rest of the day is fragmentary and additionally confusing. A report from a nearby hospital says that a dead boy was admitted on September 30, with two gun wounds to the left side of his torso. But according to the photocopy I saw, the report also says that the boy was admitted at 1:00 P.M.; the tape shows that Mohammed was shot later in the afternoon. The doctor's report also notes, without further explanation, that the dead boy had a cut down his belly about eight inches long. A boy's body, wrapped in a Palestinian flag but with his face exposed, was later carried through the streets to a burial site (the exact timing is in dispute). The face looks very much like Mohammed's in the video footage. Thousands of mourners lined the route. A BBC TV report on the funeral began, "A Palestinian boy has been martyred." Many of the major U.S. news organizations reported that the funeral was held on the evening of September 30, a few hours after the shooting. Oddly, on film the procession appears to take place in full sunlight, with shadows indicative of midday.

The Aftermath

Almost immediately news media around the world began reporting the tragedy. Print outlets were generally careful to say that Mohammed al-Dura was killed in "the crossfire" or "an exchange of fire" between Israeli soldiers and Palestinians. *The New York Times,* for instance, reported that he was "shot in the stomach as he crouched behind his father on the sidelines of an intensifying battle between Israeli and Palestinian security forces." But the same account included Jamal al-Dura's comment that the fatal volley had come from Israeli soldiers. Jacki Lyden said on NPR's *Weekend All Things Considered* that the boy had been "caught in crossfire." She then interviewed the France 2 cameraman, Talal Abu-Rahma, who said that he thought the Israelis had done the shooting.

> ABU-RAHMA: I was very sad. I was crying. And I was remembering my children. I was afraid to lose my life. And I was sitting on my knees and hiding my head, carrying my camera, and I was afraid from the Israeli to see this camera, maybe they will think this is a weapon, you know, or I am trying to shoot on them. But I was in the most difficult situation in my life. A boy, I cannot save his life, and I want to protect myself.

> LYDEN: Was there any attempt by the troops who were firing to cease fire to listen to what the father had to say? Could they even see what they were shooting at?
> ABU-RAHMA: Okay. It's clear it was a father, it's clear it was a boy over there for ever who [presumably meaning "whoever"] was shooting on them from across the street, you know, in front of them. I'm sure from that area, I'm expert in that area, I've been in that area many times. I know every [unintelligible] in that area. Whoever was shooting, he got to see them, because that base is not far away from the boy and the father. It's about a hundred and fifty meters [about 500 feet].

On that night's broadcast of *ABC World News Tonight*, the correspondent Gillian Findlay said unambiguously that the boy had died "under Israeli fire." Although both NBC and CBS used the term "crossfire" in their reports, videos of Israeli troops firing and then the boy dying left little doubt about the causal relationship. Jamal al-Dura never wavered in his view that the Israelis had killed his son. "Are you sure they were Israeli bullets?" Diane Sawyer, of ABC News, asked him in an interview later that year. "I'm a hundred percent sure," he replied, through his translator. "They were Israelis." In another interview he told the Associated Press, "The bullets of the Zionists are the bullets that killed my son."

By Tuesday, October 3, all doubt seemed to have been removed. After a hurried internal investigation the IDF concluded that its troops were probably to blame. General Yom-Tov Samia, then the head of the IDF's Southern Command, which operated in Gaza, said, "It could very much be—this is an estimation—that a soldier in our position, who has a very narrow field of vision, saw somebody hiding behind a cement block in the direction from which he was being fired at, and he shot in that direction." General Giora Eiland, then the head of IDF operations, said on an Israeli radio broadcast that the boy was apparently killed by "Israeli army fire at the Palestinians who were attacking them violently with a great many petrol bombs, rocks, and very massive fire."

The further attempt to actually justify killing the boy was, in terms of public opinion, yet more damning for the IDF. Eiland said, "It is known that [Mohammed al-Dura] participated in stone throwing in the past." Samia asked what a twelve-year-old was doing in such a dangerous place to begin with. Ariel Sharon, who admitted that the footage of the shooting was "very hard to see," and that the death was "a real tragedy," also said, "The one that should be blamed is only the one . . . that really instigated all those activities, and that is Yasir Arafat."

Palestinians, and the Arab-Islamic world in general, predictably did not agree. Sweatshirts, posters, and wall murals were created showing the face of Mohammed al-Dura just before he died. "His face, stenciled three feet high, is a common sight on the walls of Gaza," Matthew McAllester, of *Newsday,* wrote last year. "His name is known to every Arab, his death cited as the ultimate example of Israeli military brutality." In modern warfare, Bob Simon said on CBS's *60 Minutes,* "one picture can be worth a thousand weapons," and the picture of the doomed boy amounted to "one of the most disastrous setbacks Israel has suffered in decades." Gabriel Weimann, of Haifa University, said that when he first heard of the case, "it made me sick to think this was done in my name." Amnon Lord, an Israeli columnist who has investigated the event, told me in an e-mail message that it was important "on the mythological level," because it was "a framework story, a paradigmatic event," illustrating Israeli brutality. Dan Schueftan, an Israeli strategist and military thinker, told me that the case was uniquely damaging. He said, "[It was] the ultimate symbol of what the Arabs want to think: the father is trying to protect his son, and the satanic Jews—there is no other word for it—are trying to kill him. These Jews are people who will come to kill our children, because they are not human."

Two years after Mohammed al-Dura's death his stepmother, Amal, became pregnant with another child, the family's eighth. The parents named him Mohammed. Amal was quoted late in her pregnancy as saying, "It will send a message to Israel: 'Yes, you've killed one, but God has compensated for him. You can't kill us all.' "

Second Thoughts

25 In the fall of last year Gabriel Weimann mentioned the Mohammed al-Dura case in a special course that he teaches at the Israeli Military

Academy, National Security and Mass Media. Like most adults in Israel, Weimann, a tall, athletic-looking man in his early fifties, still performs up to thirty days of military-reserve duty a year. His reserve rank is sergeant, whereas the students in his class are lieutenant colonels and above.

To underscore the importance of the media in international politics, Weimann shows some of his students a montage of famous images from past wars: for World War II the flag raising at Iwo Jima; for Vietnam the South Vietnamese officer shooting a prisoner in the head and the little girl running naked down a path with napalm on her back. For the current intifada, Weimann told his students, the lasting iconic image would be the frightened face of Mohammed al-Dura.

One day last fall, after he discussed the images, a student spoke up. "I was there," he said. "We didn't do it."

"Prove it," Weimann said. He assigned part of the class, as its major research project, a reconsideration of the evidence in the case. A surprisingly large amount was available. The students began by revisiting an investigation undertaken by the Israeli military soon after the event.

Shortly after the shooting General Samia was contacted by Nahum Shahaf, a physicist and engineer who had worked closely with the IDF on the design of pilotless drone aircraft. While watching the original news broadcasts of the shooting Shahaf had been alarmed, like most viewers inside and outside Israel. But he had also noticed an apparent anomaly. The father seemed to be concerned mainly about a threat originating on the far side of the barrel behind which he had taken shelter. Yet when he and his son were shot, the barrel itself seemed to be intact. What, exactly, did this mean?

Samia commissioned Shahaf and an engineer, Yosef Duriel, to 30 work on a second IDF investigation of of the case. "The reason from my side is to check and clean up our values," Samia later told Bob Simon, of CBS. He said he wanted "to see that we are still acting as the IDF." Shahaf stressed to Samia that the IDF should do whatever it could to preserve all physical evidence. But because so much intifada activity continued in the Netzarim area, the IDF demolished the wall and all related structures. Shahaf took one trip to examine the crossroads, clad in body armor and escorted by Israeli soldiers. Then, at a location near Beersheba, Shahaf, Duriel, and others set up models of the barrel, the wall, and the IDF shooting position, in order to re-enact the crucial events.

Bullets had not been recovered from the boy's body at the hospital, and the family was hardly willing to agree to an exhumation to re-examine the wounds. Thus the most important piece of physical evidence was the concrete barrel. In the TV footage it clearly bears a mark from the Israeli Bureau of Standards, which enabled investigators to determine its exact dimensions and composition. When they placed the equivalent in front of a concrete wall and put mannequins representing father and son behind it, a conclusion emerged: soldiers in the Israeli outpost could not have fired the shots whose impact was shown on TV. The evidence was cumulative and reinforcing. It involved the angle, the barrel, the indentations, and the dust.

Mohammed al-Dura and his father looked as if they were sheltering themselves against fire from the IDF outpost. In this they were successful. The films show that the barrel was between them and the Israeli guns. The line of sight from the IDF position to the pair was blocked by concrete. Conceivably, some other Israeli soldier was present and fired from some other angle, although there is no evidence of this and no one has ever raised it as a possibility; and there were Palestinians in all the other places, who would presumably have noticed the presence of additional IDF troops. From the one location where Israeli soldiers are known to have been, the only way to hit the boy would have been to shoot through the concrete barrel.

This brings us to the nature of the barrel. Its walls were just under two inches thick. On the test range investigators fired M-16 bullets at a similar barrel. Each bullet made an indentation only two fifths to four fifths of an inch deep. Penetrating the barrel would have required multiple hits on both sides of the barrel's wall. The videos of the shooting show fewer than ten indentations on the side of the barrel facing the IDF, indicating that at some point in the day's exchanges of fire the Israelis did shoot at the barrel. But photographs taken after the shooting show no damage of any kind on the side of the barrel facing the al-Duras—that is, no bullets went through.

Further evidence involves the indentations in the concrete wall. The bullet marks that appear so ominously in the wall seconds before the fatal volley are round. Their shape is significant because of what it indicates about the angle of the gunfire. The investigators fired volleys into a concrete wall from a variety of angles. They found that in order to produce a round puncture mark, they had to fire more or less straight on. The more oblique the angle, the more elongated and skidlike the hole became.

35   The dust resulting from a bullet's impact followed similar rules. A head-on shot produced the smallest, roundest cloud of dust. The more oblique the angle, the larger and longer the cloud of dust. In the video of the shooting the clouds of dust near the al-Duras' heads are small and round. Shots from the IDF outpost would necessarily have been oblique.

In short, the physical evidence of the shooting was in all ways inconsistent with shots coming from the IDF outpost—and in all ways consistent with shots coming from someplace behind the France 2 cameraman, roughly in the location of the Pita. Making a positive case for who might have shot the boy was not the business of the investigators hired by the IDF. They simply wanted to determine whether the soldiers in the outpost were responsible. Because the investigation was overseen by the IDF and run wholly by Israelis, it stood no chance of being taken seriously in the Arab world. But its fundamental point—that the concrete barrel lay between the outpost and the boy, and no bullets had gone through the barrel—could be confirmed independently from news footage.

It was at this point that the speculation about Mohammed al-Dura's death left the realm of geometry and ballistics and entered the world of politics, paranoia, fantasy, and hatred. Almost as soon as the second IDF investigation was under way, Israeli commentators started questioning its legitimacy and Israeli government officials distanced themselves from its findings. "It is hard to describe in mild terms the stupidity of this bizarre investigation," the liberal newspaper *Ha'aretz* said in an editorial six weeks after the shooting. The newspaper claimed that Shahaf and Duriel were motivated not by a need for dispassionate inquiry but by the belief that Palestinians had staged the whole shooting. (Shahaf told me that he began his investigation out of curiosity but during the course of it became convinced that the multiple anomalies indicated a staged event.) "The fact that an organized body like the IDF, with its vast resources, undertook such an amateurish investigation—almost a pirate endeavor—on such a sensitive issue, is shocking and worrying," *Ha'aretz* said.

As the controversy grew, Samia abbreviated the investigation and subsequently avoided discussing the case. Most government officials, I was told by many sources, regard drawing any further attention to Mohammed al-Dura as self-defeating. No new "proof" would erase images of the boy's death, and resurrecting the discussion would only ensure that the horrible footage was aired yet again. IDF press officials did not return any of my calls, including those requesting to interview soldiers who were at the outpost.

So by the time Gabriel Weimann's students at the Israeli Military Academy, including the one who had been on the scene, began looking into the evidence last fall, most Israelis had tried to put the case behind them. Those against the Likud policy of encouraging settlements in occupied territory think of the shooting as one more illustration of the policy's cost. Those who support the policy view Mohammed al-Dura's death as an unfortunate instance of "collateral damage," to be weighed against damage done to Israelis by Palestinian terrorists. Active interest in the case was confined mainly to a number of Israelis and European Jews who believe the event was manipulated to blacken Israel's image. Nahum Shahaf has become the leading figure in this group.

40   Shahaf is a type familiar to reporters: the person who has given himself entirely to a cause or a mystery and can talk about its ramifications as long as anyone will listen. He is a strongly built man of medium height, with graying hair combed back from his forehead. In photos he always appears stern, almost glowering, whereas in the time I spent with him he seemed to be constantly smiling, joking, having fun. Shahaf is in his middle fifties, but like many other scientists and engineers, he has the quality of seeming not quite grown up. He used to live in California, where, among other pursuits, he worked as a hang-gliding instructor. He moves and gesticulates with a teenager's lack of self-consciousness about his bearing. I liked him.

Before getting involved in the al-Dura case, Shahaf was known mainly as an inventor. He was only the tenth person to receive a medal from the Israeli Ministry of Science, for his work on computerized means of compressing digital video transmission. "But for two and a half years I am spending time only on the al-Dura case," he told me. "I left everything for it, because I believe that this is most important." When I arrived at his apartment, outside Tel Aviv, to meet him one morning, I heard a repeated sound from one room that I assumed was from a teenager's playing a violent video game. An hour later, when we walked into that room—which has been converted into a video-research laboratory, with multiple monitors, replay devices, and computers—I saw that it was one mob scene from September 30, being played on a continuous loop.

Shahaf's investigation for the IDF showed that the Israeli soldiers at the outpost did not shoot the boy. But he now believes that everything that happened at Netzarim on September 30 was a ruse. The boy on the film may or may not have been the son of the man who held him. The boy and the man may or may not actually have been shot. If shot, the boy may or may not actually have died. If he died, his killer may or may not have been a member of the Palestinian force, shooting at him directly. The entire goal of the exercise, Shahaf says, was to manufacture a child martyr, in correct anticipation of the damage this would do to Israel in the eyes of the world—especially the Islamic world. "I believe that one day there will be good things in common between us and the Palestinians," he told me. "But the case of Mohammed al-Dura brings the big flames between Israel and the Palestinians and Arabs. It brings a big wall of hate. They can say this is the proof, the ultimate proof, that Israeli soldiers are boy-murderers. And that hatred breaks any chance of having something good in the future."

The reasons to doubt that the al-Duras, the cameramen, and hundreds of onlookers were part of a coordinated fraud are obvious. Shahaf's evidence for this conclusion, based on his videos, is essentially an accumulation of oddities and unanswered questions about the chaotic events of the day. Why is there no footage of the boy after he was shot? Why does he appear to move in his father's lap, and to clasp a hand over his eyes after he is supposedly dead? Why is one Palestinian policeman wearing a Secret Service-style earpiece in one ear? Why is another Palestinian man shown waving his arms and yelling at others, as if "directing" a dramatic scene? Why does the funeral appear—based on the length of shadows—to have occurred before the apparent time of the shooting? Why is there no blood on the father's shirt just after they are shot? Why did a voice that seems to be that of the France 2 cameraman yell, in Arabic, "The boy is dead" before he had been hit? Why do ambulances appear instantly for seemingly everyone else and not for al-Dura?

A handful of Israeli and foreign commentators have taken up Shahaf's cause. A Web site called masada2000.org says of the IDF's initial apology, "They acknowledged guilt, for never in their collective minds would any one of them have imagined a scenario whereby Mohammed al-Dura might have been murdered by his *own* people . . . a cruel plot staged and executed by Palestinian sharp-shooters and a television cameraman!" Amnon Lord, writing for the magazine *Makor Rishon*, referred to a German documentary directed by Esther Schapira that was "based on Shahaf's own decisive conclusion" and that determined "that Muhammad Al-Dura was not killed by IDF gunfire at Netzarim junction." "Rather," Lord continued, "the Palestinians, in cooperation with foreign journalists and the UN, arranged a well-staged production of his death." In March of this year a French writer, Gérard Huber, published a book called *Contre expertise d'une mise en scène* (roughly, *Re-evaluation of a Re-enactment*). It, too, argues that the entire event was staged. In an e-mail message to me Huber said that before knowing of Shahaf's studies he had been aware that "the images of little Mohammed were part of the large war of images between Palestinians and Israelis." But until meeting Shahaf, he said, "I had not imagined that it involved a fiction"—a view he now shares. "The question of 'Who killed little Mohammed?' " he said, "has become a screen to disguise the real question, which is: 'Was little Mohammed actually killed?' "

The truth about this case will probably never be determined. Or, 45 to put it more precisely, no version of truth that is considered believable by all sides will ever emerge. For most of the Arab world, the rights and wrongs of the case are beyond dispute: an innocent boy was murdered, and his blood is on Israel's hands. Mention of contrary evidence or hypotheses only confirms the bottomless dishonesty of the guilty parties—much as Holocaust-denial theories do in the the Western world. For the handful of people collecting evidence of a staged event, the truth is also clear, even if the proof is not in hand. I saw Nahum Shahaf lose his good humor only when I asked him what he thought explained the odd timing of the boy's funeral, or the contradictions in eyewitness reports, or the other loose ends in the case. "I don't 'think,' I know!" he said several times. "I am a physicist. I work from the evidence." Schapira had collaborated with him for the German documentary and then produced a film advancing the "minimum" version of his case, showing that the shots did not, could not have, come from the IDF outpost. She disappointed him by not embracing the maximum version—the all-encompassing hoax—and counseled him not to talk about a staged event unless he could produce a living boy or a cooperative eyewitness. Shahaf said that he still thought well of her, and that he was not discouraged. "I am only two and a half years into this work," he told me. "It took twelve years for the truth of the Dreyfus case to come out."

For anyone else who knows about Mohammed al-Dura but is not in either of the decided camps—the Arabs who are sure they know what happened, the revisionists who are equally sure—the case will remain in the uncomfortable realm of events that cannot be fully explained or understood. "Maybe it was an accidental shooting," Gabriel Weimann told me, after reading his students' report, which, like the German documentary, supported the "minimum" conclusion—the Israeli soldiers at the outpost could not have killed the boy. (He could not show the report to me, he said, on grounds of academic confidentiality.) "Maybe even it was staged—although I don't think my worst enemy is so inhuman as to shoot a boy for the sake of publicity. Beyond that, I do not know." Weimann's recent work involves the way that television distorts reality in attempting to reconstruct it, by putting together loosely related or even random events in what the viewer imagines is a coherent narrative flow. The contrast between the confusing, contradictory hours of raw footage from the Netzarim crossroads and the clear, gripping narrative of the evening news reports assembled from that footage is a perfect example, he says.

The significance of this case from the American perspective involves the increasingly chaotic ecology of truth around the world. In Arab and Islamic societies the widespread belief that Israeli soldiers shot this boy has political consequences. So does the belief among some Israelis and Zionists in Israel and abroad that Palestinians will go to any lengths to smear them. Obviously, these beliefs do not create the basic tensions in the Middle East. The Israeli policy of promoting settlements in occupied territory, and the Palestinian policy of terror, are deeper obstacles. There would never have been a showdown at the Netzarim crossroads, or any images of Mohammed al-Dura's shooting to be parsed in different ways, if there were no settlement nearby for IDF soldiers to protect. Gabriel Weimann is to the left of Dan Schueftan on Israel's political spectrum, but both believe that Israel should end its occupation. I would guess that Nahum

Shahaf thinks the same thing, even though he told me that to preserve his "independence" as a researcher, he wanted to "isolate myself from any kind of political question."

The images intensify the self-righteous determination of each side. If anything, modern technology has aggravated the problem of mutually exclusive realities. With the Internet and TV, each culture now has a more elaborate apparatus for "proving," dramatizing, and disseminating its particular truth.

In its engagement with the Arab world the United States has assumed that what it believes are noble motives will be perceived as such around the world. We mean the best for the people under our control; stability, democracy, prosperity, are our goals; why else would we have risked so much to help an oppressed people achieve them? The case of Mohammed al-Dura suggests the need for much more modest assumptions about the way other cultures—in particular today's embattled Islam—will perceive our truths.

Responding to Reading

1. Do you think Fallows is presenting an unbiased report, or do you believe he has a particular agenda in reporting the events the way he does?
2. As Fallows notes, "To watch the raw footage is to wonder, repeatedly, What is going on here?" (13); a media expert he consults sees the footage as having a " '*Rashomon* effect' " (11); and Fallows repeatedly acknowledges information gaps, inconsistencies, and confusion. Do you accept Fallows's conclusion that "The truth about this case will probably never be determined" (45)? What do you think actually happened?
3. If, as Fallows admits, the "proof" he assembles here is not at all "likely to change minds in the Arab world" (4), where the image of Mohammed al-Dura has been so inflammatory, what positive outcome can Fallows's article possibly have?

Responding in Writing

In paragraph 17, Fallows describes the footage of the shooting as "unforgettable," adding that "it illustrates the way television transforms reality." Later, he notes that "modern technology has aggravated the problem of mutually exclusive realities. With the Internet and TV, each culture now has a more elaborate apparatus for 'proving,' dramatizing, and disseminating its particular truth" (48). How, specifically, have you seen TV and the Internet "transform reality"?

FICTION

LOVE AND OTHER CATASTROPHES: A MIX TAPE
Amanda Holzer
1981–

An Emerson College graduate, Amanda Holzer published the following short-short story in Story Quarterly's *2002 issue and again in* The Best American Nonrequired Reading *(2003). "Love and Other Catastrophes: A Mix Tape" explores the ways in which popular song titles create a narrative about identity and personal relationships.*

"All By Myself" (Eric Carmen). "Looking for Love" (Lou Reed). "I Wanna Dance With Somebody" (Whitney Houston). "Let's Dance" (David Bowie). "Let's Kiss" (Beat Happening). "Let's Talk About Sex" (Salt N' Pepa). "Like A Virgin" (Madonna). "We've Only Just Begun" (The Carpenters). "I Wanna Be Your Boyfriend" (The Ramones). "I'll Tumble 4 Ya" (Culture Club). "Head Over Heels" (The Go-Go's). "Nothing Compares To You" (Sinéad O'Connor). "My Girl" (The Temptations). "Could This Be Love?" (Bob Marley). "Love and Mar-riage" (Frank Sinatra). "White Wedding" (Billy Idol). "Stuck in the Middle with You" (Steelers Wheel). "Tempted" (The Squeeze). "There Goes My Baby" (The Drifters). "What's Going On?" (Marvin Gaye). "Where Did You Sleep Last Night?" (Leadbelly). "Whose Bed Have Your Boots Been Under?" (Shania Twain). "Jealous Guy" (John Lennon). "Your Cheatin' Heart" (Tammy Wynette). "Shot Through the Heart" (Bon Jovi). "Don't Go Breaking My Heart" (Elton John and Kiki Dee). "My Achy Breaky Heart" (Billy Ray Cyrus). "Heart-break Hotel" (Elvis Presley), "Stop, In the Name of Love" (The Supremes). "Try a Little Tenderness" (Otis Redding). "Try (Just a Little Bit Harder)" (Janis Joplin). "All Apologies" (Nirvana). "Hanging on the Telephone" (Blondie). "I Just Called to Say I Love You" (Stevie Won-der). "Love Will Keep Us Together" (Captain and Tennille). "Let's Stay Together" (Al Green). "It Ain't Over 'Till It's Over" (Lenny Kravitz). "What's Love Got To Do With It? (Tina Turner). "You Don't Bring Me Flowers Anymore" (Barbara Streisand and Neil Diamond). "I Wish You Wouldn't Say That" (Talking Heads). "You're So Vain" (Carly Simon). "Love is a Battlefield" (Pat Benatar). "Heaven Knows I'm Miserable Now" (The Smiths). "(Can't Get No) Satisfaction" (Rolling Stones). "Must Have Been Love (But It's Over Now)" (Rox-ette). "Breaking Up is Hard to Do" (Neil Sedaka). "I Will Survive"

(Gloria Gaynor). "Hit the Road, Jack" (Mary McCaslin and Jim Ringer). "These Boots Were Made for Walking" (Nancy Sinatra). "All Out of Love" (Air Supply). "All By Myself" (Eric Carmen).

Responding to Reading

1. In one sentence, summarize the "plot" of this story. How do you picture the story's setting? How do you picture its characters?
2. How would you characterize the role of popular music in the protagonist's life? Is it simply background, or do the songs have a causal relationship with life events?
3. Does this story have a definite beginning, middle, and end? Could any of the song titles be eliminated? Relocated?

Responding in Writing

Create a "mix tape" that describes a personal crisis of your own—or, compile a "mix tape" that describes a political or social crisis (local, national, or international).

--------------------------------- Focus ---------------------------------

Has the Internet Doomed the Newspaper?

A woman reads the April 1, 1968 *New York Times.* The headline refers to President Lyndon B. Johnson's decision not to seek or accept his party's nomination for another term as president and to his decision to cease U.S. bombing of North Vietnam

Responding to the Image

1. Where is the reader located? Why do you think she is reading the newspaper in this setting? What does her location tell you about the news story? About the newspaper?
2. For what kind of news do most people today turn to newspapers? Give some examples of stories you consider to be "breaking news." Does this kind of news still come from newspapers?

BAD NEWS
Richard A. Posner
1939–

Judge of the U.S. Court of Appeals for the Seventh Circuit and senior lec-
turer at the University of Chicago Law School, Richard A. Posner is a legal
expert whose work has focused on the economics of intellectual property and
health policy. Contributor to the Becker-Posner Blog, he has written numer-
ous academic articles, book reviews, and books, most recently Not a Suicide
Pact: The Constitution in a Time of National Emergency *and* Uncertain
Shield: The U.S. Intelligence System in the Throes of Reform *(both*
2006). In the following book review, Posner explores the changing nature of
the American news media and the ways in which news sources such as blogs
have ushered in a new era of journalism.

The conventional news media are embattled. Attacked by both left and
right in book after book, rocked by scandals, challenged by upstart
bloggers, they have become a focus of controversy and concern. Their
audience is in decline, their credibility with the public in shreds. In a recent poll conducted by the Annenberg Public Policy Center, 65 percent
of the respondents thought that most news organizations, if they discover they've made a mistake, try to ignore it or cover it up, and 79 percent opined that a media company would hesitate to carry negative
stories about a corporation from which it received substantial advertising revenues.

The industry's critics agree that the function of the news is to inform people about social, political, cultural, ethical and economic issues
so that they can vote and otherwise express themselves as responsible
citizens. They agree on the related point that journalism is a profession
rather than just a trade and therefore that journalists and their employers must not allow profit considerations to dominate, but must acknowledge an ethical duty to report the news accurately, soberly,
without bias, reserving the expression of political preferences for the
editorial page and its radio and television counterparts. The critics further agree, as they must, that 30 years ago news reporting was dominated by newspapers and by television network news and that the
audiences for these media have declined with the rise of competing
sources, notably cable television and the Web.

The audience decline is potentially fatal for newspapers. Not only
has their daily readership dropped from 52.6 percent of adults in 1990
to 37.5 percent in 2000, but the drop is much steeper in the 20-to-49-
year-old cohort, a generation that is, and as it ages will remain, much
more comfortable with electronic media in general and the Web in particular than the current elderly are.

At this point the diagnosis splits along political lines. Liberals, including most journalists (because most journalists are liberals), believe that the decline of the formerly dominant "mainstream" media has caused a deterioration in quality. They attribute this decline to the rise of irresponsible journalism on the right, typified by the Fox News Channel (the most-watched cable television news channel), Rush Limbaugh's radio talk show and right-wing blogs by Matt Drudge and others. But they do not spare the mainstream media, which, they contend, provide in the name of balance an echo chamber for the right. To these critics, the deterioration of journalism is exemplified by the attack of the "Swift boat" Vietnam veterans on Senator John Kerry during the 2004 election campaign. The critics describe the attack as consisting of lies propagated by the new right-wing media and reported as news by mainstream media made supine by anxiety over their declining fortunes.

5   Critics on the right applaud the rise of the conservative media as a long-overdue corrective to the liberal bias of the mainstream media, which, according to Jim A. Kuypers, the author of "Press Bias and Politics," are "a partisan collective which both consciously and unconsciously attempts to persuade the public to accept its interpretation of the world as true." Fourteen percent of Americans describe themselves as liberals, and 26 percent as conservatives. The corresponding figures for journalists are 56 percent and 18 percent. This means that of all journalists who consider themselves either liberal or conservative, 76 percent consider themselves liberal, compared with only 35 percent of the public that has a stated political position.

So politically one-sided are the mainstream media, the right complains (while sliding over the fact that the owners and executives, as distinct from the working journalists, tend to be far less liberal), that not only do they slant the news in a liberal direction; they will stop at nothing to defeat conservative politicians and causes. The right points to the "60 Minutes II" broadcast in which Dan Rather paraded what were probably forged documents concerning George W. Bush's National Guard service, and to Newsweek's erroneous report, based on a single anonymous source, that an American interrogator had flushed a copy of the Koran down the toilet (a physical impossibility, one would have thought).

Strip these critiques of their indignation, treat them as descriptions rather than as denunciations, and one sees that they are consistent with one another and basically correct. The mainstream media *are* predominantly liberal—in fact, more liberal than they used to be. But not because the politics of *journalists* have changed. Rather, because the rise of new media, itself mainly an economic rather than a political phenomenon, has caused polarization, pushing the already liberal media farther left.

The news media have also become more sensational, more prone to scandal and possibly less accurate. But note the tension between sensationalism and polarization: the trial of Michael Jackson got tremendous coverage, displacing a lot of political coverage, but it had no political valence.

The interesting questions are, first, the why of these trends, and, second, so what?

The why is the vertiginous decline in the cost of electronic commu-   10 nication and the relaxation of regulatory barriers to entry, leading to the proliferation of consumer choices. Thirty years ago the average number of television channels that Americans could receive was seven; today, with the rise of cable and satellite television, it is 71. Thirty years ago there was no Internet, therefore no Web, hence no online newspapers and magazines, no blogs. The public's consumption of news and opinion used to be like sucking on a straw; now it's like being sprayed by a fire hose.

To see what difference the elimination of a communications bottleneck can make, consider a town that before the advent of television or even radio had just two newspapers because economies of scale made it impossible for a newspaper with a small circulation to break even. Each of the two, to increase its advertising revenues, would try to maximize circulation by pitching its news to the median reader, for that reader would not be attracted to a newspaper that flaunted extreme political views. There would be the same tendency to political convergence that is characteristic of two-party political systems, and for the same reason—attracting the least committed is the key to obtaining a majority.

One of the two newspapers would probably be liberal and have a loyal readership of liberal readers, and the other conservative and have a loyal conservative readership. That would leave a middle range. To snag readers in that range, the liberal newspaper could not afford to be too liberal or the conservative one too conservative. The former would strive to be just liberal enough to hold its liberal readers, and the latter just conservative enough to hold its conservative readers. If either moved too close to its political extreme, it would lose readers in the middle without gaining readers from the extreme, since it had them already.

But suppose cost conditions change, enabling a newspaper to break even with many fewer readers than before. Now the liberal newspaper has to worry that any temporizing of its message in an effort to attract moderates may cause it to lose its most liberal readers to a new, more liberal newspaper; for with small-scale entry into the market now economical, the incumbents no longer have a secure base. So the liberal newspaper will tend to become even more liberal and, by the same process, the conservative newspaper more conservative. (If economies of scale increase, and as a result the number of newspapers grows, the opposite ideological change will be observed, as happened in the 19th century. The introduction of the "penny press" in the 1830's enabled newspapers to obtain large circulations and thus finance themselves by selling advertising; no longer did they have to depend on political patronage.)

The current tendency to political polarization in news reporting is thus a consequence of changes not in underlying political opinions but in costs, specifically the falling costs of new entrants. The rise of the conservative Fox News Channel caused CNN to shift to the left. CNN was going to lose many of its conservative viewers to Fox anyway, so it made sense to increase its appeal to its remaining viewers by catering more assiduously to their political preferences.

15   The tendency to greater sensationalism in reporting is a parallel phenomenon. The more news sources there are, the more intense the struggle for an audience. One tactic is to occupy an overlooked niche— peeling away from the broad-based media a segment of the consuming public whose interests were not catered to previously. That is the tactic that produces polarization. Another is to "shout louder" than the competitors, where shouting takes the form of a sensational, attention-grabbing discovery, accusation, claim or photograph. According to James T. Hamilton in his valuable book "All the News That's Fit to Sell," this even explains why the salaries paid news anchors have soared: the more competition there is for an audience, the more valuable is a celebrity newscaster.

The argument that competition increases polarization assumes that liberals want to read liberal newspapers and conservatives conservative ones. Natural as that assumption is, it conflicts with one of the points on which left and right agree—that people consume news and opinion in order to become well informed about public issues. Were this true, liberals would read conservative newspapers, and conservatives liberal newspapers, just as scientists test their hypotheses by confronting them with data that may refute them. But that is not how ordinary people (or, for that matter, scientists) approach political and social issues. The issues are too numerous, uncertain and complex, and the benefit to an individual of becoming well informed about them too slight, to invite sustained, disinterested attention. Moreover, people don't like being in a state of doubt, so they look for information that will support rather than undermine their existing beliefs. They're also uncomfortable seeing their beliefs challenged on issues that are bound up with their economic welfare, physical safety or religious and moral views.

So why *do* people consume news and opinion? In part it is to learn of facts that bear directly and immediately on their lives—hence the greater attention paid to local than to national and international news.

They also want to be entertained, and they find scandals, violence, crime, the foibles of celebrities and the antics of the powerful all mightily entertaining. And they want to be confirmed in their beliefs by seeing them echoed and elaborated by more articulate, authoritative and prestigious voices. So they accept, and many relish, a partisan press. Forty-three percent of the respondents in the poll by the Annenberg Public Policy Center thought it "a good thing if some news organizations have a decidedly political point of view in their coverage of the news."

Being profit-driven, the media respond to the actual demands of their audience rather than to the idealized "thirst for knowledge" demand posited by public intellectuals and deans of journalism schools. They serve up what the consumer wants, and the more intense the competitive pressure, the better they do it. We see this in the media's coverage of political campaigns. Relatively little attention is paid to issues. Fundamental questions, like the actual difference in policies that might result if one candidate rather than the other won, get little play. The focus instead is on who's ahead, viewed as a function of campaign tactics, which are meticulously reported. Candidates' statements are evaluated not for their truth but for their adroitness; it is assumed, without a hint of embarrassment, that a political candidate who levels with voters disqualifies himself from being taken seriously, like a racehorse that tries to hug the outside of the track. News coverage of a political campaign is oriented to a public that enjoys competitive sports, not to one that is civic-minded.

We saw this in the coverage of the selection of Justice Sandra Day O'Connor's successor. It was played as an election campaign; one article even described the jockeying for the nomination by President Bush as the "primary election" and the fight to get the nominee confirmed by the Senate the "general election" campaign. With only a few exceptions, no attention was paid to the ability of the people being considered for the job or the actual consequences that the appointment was likely to have for the nation.

Does this mean that the news media were better before competition 20 polarized them? Not at all. A market gives people what they want, whether they want the same thing or different things. Challenging areas of social consensus, however dumb or even vicious the consensus, is largely off limits for the media, because it wins no friends among the general public. The mainstream media do not kick sacred cows like religion and patriotism.

Not that the media *lie* about the news they report; in fact, they have strong incentives not to lie. Instead, there is selection, slanting, decisions as to how much or how little prominence to give a particular news item. Giving a liberal spin to equivocal economic data when conservatives are in power is, as the Harvard economists Sendhil Mullainathan and Andrei

Shleifer point out, a matter of describing the glass as half empty when conservatives would describe it as half full.

Journalists are reluctant to confess to pandering to their customers' biases; it challenges their self-image as servants of the general interest, unsullied by commerce. They want to think they inform the public, rather than just satisfying a consumer demand no more elevated or consequential than the demand for cosmetic surgery in Brazil or bull-fights in Spain. They believe in "deliberative democracy"—democracy as the system in which the people determine policy through delibera-tion on the issues. In his preface to "The Future of Media" (a collection of articles edited by Robert W. McChesney, Russell Newman and Ben Scott), Bill Moyers writes that "democracy can't exist without an in-formed public." If this is true, the United States is not a democracy (which may be Moyers's dyspeptic view). Only members of the intelli-gentsia, a tiny slice of the population, deliberate on public issues.

The public's interest in factual accuracy is less an interest in truth than a delight in the unmasking of the opposition's errors. Conserva-tives were unembarrassed by the errors of the Swift Boat veterans, while taking gleeful satisfaction in the exposure of the forgeries on which Dan Rather had apparently relied, and in his resulting fall from grace. They reveled in Newsweek's retracting its story about flushing the Koran down a toilet yet would prefer that American abuse of pris-oners be concealed. Still, because there is a market demand for correct-ing the errors and ferreting out the misdeeds of one's enemies, the media exercise an important oversight function, creating accountability and deterring wrongdoing. That, rather than educating the public about the deep issues, is their great social mission. It shows how a mar-ket produces a social good as an unintended byproduct of self-interested behavior.

The limited consumer interest in the truth is the key to understand-ing why both left and right can plausibly denounce the same media for being biased in favor of the other. Journalists are writing to meet a con-sumer demand that is not a demand for uncomfortable truths. So a newspaper that appeals to liberal readers will avoid exposés of bad be-havior by blacks or homosexuals, as William McGowan charges in "Coloring the News"; similarly, Daniel Okrent, the first ombudsman of The New York Times, said that the news pages of The Times "present the social and cultural aspects of same-sex marriage in a tone that ap-proaches cheerleading." Not only would such exposés offend liberal readers who are not black or homosexual; many blacks and homosexu-als are customers of liberal newspapers, and no business wants to of-fend a customer.

25   But the same liberal newspaper or television news channel will pull some of its punches when it comes to reporting on the activities of government, even in Republican administrations, thus giving credence

to the left critique, as in Michael Massing's "Now They Tell Us," about the reporting of the war in Iraq. A newspaper depends on access to officials for much of its information about what government is doing and planning, and is reluctant to bite too hard the hand that feeds it. Nevertheless, it is hyperbole for Eric Alterman to claim in "What Liberal Media?" that "liberals are fighting a near-hopeless battle in which they are enormously outmatched by most measures" by the conservative media, or for Bill Moyers to say that "the market-place of political ideas" is dominated by a "quasi-official partisan press ideologically linked to an authoritarian administration." In a sample of 23 leading newspapers and news-magazines, the liberal ones had twice the circulation of the conservative. The bias in some of the reporting in the liberal media, acknowledged by Okrent, is well documented by McGowan, as well as by Bernard Goldberg in "Bias" and L. Brent Bozell III in "Weapons of Mass Distortion."

Journalists minimize offense, preserve an aura of objectivity and cater to the popular taste for conflict and contests by—in the name of "balance"—reporting both sides of an issue, even when there aren't two sides. So "intelligent design," formerly called by the oxymoron "creation science," though it is religious dogma thinly disguised, gets almost equal billing with the theory of evolution. If journalists admitted that the economic imperatives of their industry overrode their political beliefs, they would weaken the right's critique of liberal media bias.

The latest, and perhaps gravest, challenge to the journalistic establishment is the blog. Journalists accuse bloggers of having lowered standards. But their real concern is less high-minded—it is the threat that bloggers, who are mostly amateurs, pose to professional journalists and their principal employers, the conventional news media. A serious newspaper, like The Times, is a large, hierarchical commercial enterprise that interposes layers of review, revision and correction between the reporter and the published report and that to finance its large staff depends on advertising revenues and hence on the good will of advertisers and (because advertising revenues depend to a great extent on circulation) readers. These dependences constrain a newspaper in a variety of ways. But in addition, with its reputation heavily invested in accuracy, so that every serious error is a potential scandal, a newspaper not only has to delay publication of many stories to permit adequate checking but also has to institute rules for avoiding error—like requiring more than a single source for a story or limiting its reporters' reliance on anonymous sources—that cost it many scoops.

Blogs don't have these worries. Their only cost is the time of the blogger, and that cost may actually be negative if the blogger can use the publicity that he obtains from blogging to generate lecture fees and book royalties. Having no staff, the blogger is not expected to be accurate. Having no advertisers (though this is changing), he has no reason

CHAPTER 4 FOCUS

to pull his punches. And not needing a large circulation to cover costs, he can target a segment of the reading public much narrower than a newspaper or a television news channel could aim for. He may even be able to pry that segment away from the conventional media. Blogs pick off the mainstream media's customers one by one, as it were.

And bloggers thus can specialize in particular topics to an extent that few journalists employed by media companies can, since the more that journalists specialized, the more of them the company would have to hire in order to be able to cover all bases. A newspaper will not hire a journalist for his knowledge of old typewriters, but plenty of people in the blogosphere have that esoteric knowledge, and it was they who brought down Dan Rather. Similarly, not being commercially constrained, a blogger can stick with and dig into a story longer and deeper than the conventional media dare to, lest their readers become bored. It was the bloggers' dogged persistence in pursuing a story that the conventional media had tired of that forced Trent Lott to resign as Senate majority leader.

30   What really sticks in the craw of conventional journalists is that although individual blogs have no warrant of accuracy, the blogosphere as a whole has a better error-correction machinery than the conventional media do. The rapidity with which vast masses of information are pooled and sifted leaves the conventional media in the dust. Not only are there millions of blogs, and thousands of bloggers who specialize, but, what is more, readers post comments that augment the blogs, and the information in those comments, as in the blogs themselves, zips around blogland at the speed of electronic transmission.

This means that corrections in blogs are also disseminated virtually instantaneously, whereas when a member of the mainstream media catches a mistake, it may take weeks to communicate a retraction to the public. This is true not only of newspaper retractions—usually printed inconspicuously and in any event rarely read, because readers have forgotten the article being corrected—but also of network television news. It took CBS so long to acknowledge Dan Rather's mistake because there are so many people involved in the production and supervision of a program like "60 Minutes II" who have to be consulted.

The charge by mainstream journalists that blogging lacks checks and balances is obtuse. The blogosphere has *more* checks and balances than the conventional media; only they are different. The model is Friedrich Hayek's classic analysis of how the economic market pools enormous quantities of information efficiently despite its decentralized character, its lack of a master coordinator or regulator, and the very limited knowledge possessed by each of its participants.

In effect, the blogosphere is a collective enterprise—not 12 million separate enterprises, but one enterprise with 12 million reporters, feature writers and editorialists, yet with almost no costs. It's as if The Associated

Press or Reuters had millions of reporters, many of them experts, all working with no salary for free newspapers that carried no advertising.

How can the conventional news media hope to compete? Especially when the competition is not entirely fair. The bloggers are parasitical on the conventional media. They copy the news and opinion generated by the conventional media, often at considerable expense, without picking up any of the tab. The degree of parasitism is striking in the case of those blogs that provide their readers with links to newspaper articles. The links enable the audience to read the articles without buying the newspaper. The legitimate gripe of the conventional media is not that bloggers undermine the overall accuracy of news reporting, but that they are free riders who may in the long run undermine the ability of the conventional media to finance the very reporting on which bloggers depend.

Some critics worry that "unfiltered" media like blogs exacerbate so- 35 cial tensions by handing a powerful electronic platform to extremists at no charge. Bad people find one another in cyberspace and so gain confidence in their crazy ideas. The conventional media filter out extreme views to avoid offending readers, viewers and advertisers; most bloggers have no such inhibition.

The argument for filtering is an argument for censorship. (That it is made by liberals is evidence that everyone secretly favors censorship of the opinions he fears.) But probably there is little harm and some good in unfiltered media. They enable unorthodox views to get a hearing. They get 12 million people to *write* rather than just stare passively at a screen. In an age of specialization and professionalism, they give amateurs a platform. They allow people to blow off steam who might otherwise adopt more dangerous forms of self-expression. They even enable the authorities to keep tabs on potential troublemakers; intelligence and law enforcement agencies devote substantial resources to monitoring blogs and Internet chat rooms.

And most people are sensible enough to distrust communications in an unfiltered medium. They know that anyone can create a blog at essentially zero cost, that most bloggers are uncredentialed amateurs, that bloggers don't employ fact checkers and don't have editors and that a blogger can hide behind a pseudonym. They know, in short, that until a blogger's assertions are validated (as when the mainstream media acknowledge an error discovered by a blogger), there is no reason to repose confidence in what he says. The mainstream media, by contrast, assure their public that they make strenuous efforts to prevent errors from creeping into their articles and broadcasts. They ask the public to trust them, and that is why their serious errors are scandals.

A survey by the National Opinion Research Center finds that the public's confidence in the press declined from about 85 percent in 1973 to 59 percent in 2002, with most of the decline occurring since 1991. Over both the longer and the shorter period, there was little change in public confidence in other major institutions. So it seems there are special factors eroding trust in the news industry. One is that the blogs have exposed errors by the mainstream media that might otherwise have gone undiscovered or received less publicity. Another is that competition by the blogs, as well as by the other new media, has pushed the established media to get their stories out faster, which has placed pressure on them to cut corners. So while the blogosphere is a marvelous system for prompt error correction, it is not clear whether its net effect is to reduce the amount of error in the media as a whole.

But probably the biggest reason for declining trust in the media is polarization. As media companies are pushed closer to one end of the political spectrum or the other, the trust placed in them erodes. Their motives are assumed to be political. This may explain recent Pew Research Center poll data that show Republicans increasingly regarding the media as too critical of the government and Democrats increasingly regarding them as not critical enough.

40   Thus the increase in competition in the news market that has been brought about by lower costs of communication (in the broadest sense) has resulted in more variety, more polarization, more sensationalism, more healthy skepticism and, in sum, a better matching of supply to demand. But increased competition has not produced a public more oriented toward public issues, more motivated and competent to engage in genuine self-government, because these are not the goods that most people are seeking from the news media. They are seeking entertainment, confirmation, reinforcement, emotional satisfaction; and what consumers want, a competitive market supplies, no more, no less. Journalists express dismay that bottom-line pressures are reducing the quality of news coverage. What this actually means is that when competition is intense, providers of a service are forced to give the consumer what he or she wants, not what they, as proud professionals, think the consumer should want, or more bluntly, what *they* want.

Yet what of the sliver of the public that does have a serious interest in policy issues? Are these people less well served than in the old days? Another recent survey by the Pew Research Center finds that serious magazines have held their own and that serious broadcast outlets, including that bane of the right, National Public Radio, are attracting ever larger audiences. And for that sliver of a sliver that invites challenges to its biases by reading The New York Times *and* The Wall Street Journal, that watches CNN *and* Fox, that reads Brent Bozell and Eric Alterman and everything in between, the increased polarization of the media provides a richer fare than ever before.

So when all the pluses and minuses of the impact of technological and economic change on the news media are toted up and compared, maybe there isn't much to fret about.

Responding to Reading

1. In the opening sentence of this book review, Posner states, "The conventional news media are embattled." He continues, "Their audience is in decline, their credibility with the public in shreds." In his last paragraph, however, he concludes, "So when all the pluses and minuses of the impact of technological and economic change on the news media are toted up and compared, maybe there isn't much to fret about." Given these contradictory views, do you think Posner believes that the decline of conventional news media is a serious problem?

2. In paragraph 10, Posner comments, "The public's consumption of news and opinion used to be like sucking on a straw; now it's like being sprayed by a fire hose." What does he mean? Which kind of consumption does he think is more valuable? Why?

3. What, according to Posner, is the relationship between the increase in the number of news sources and "political polarization in news reporting" (14)? What role does the increase in news outlets play in "the tendency to greater sensationalism in reporting" (15)? In what sense do blogs pose a "challenge to the journalistic establishment" (24)?

Responding in Writing

Do you agree with Posner that "most people are sensible enough to distrust communications in an unfiltered medium" (37)—that is, that they can distinguish between information in an amateur's blog and information in a respected newspaper?

A LOSER'S GAME

Reuven Frank

1920–2006

A pioneer in American television broadcasting, Reuven Frank was a trusted journalist, executive at NBC News, and producer of numerous television series and specials. He wrote articles on media issues and a memoir, Out of Thin Air: The Brief Wonderful Life of Network News *(1991). In the following essay, Frank challenges the view of Richard A. Posner, who, in "Bad News" (p. 275), sees the blog as a valid and influential source of news.*

A popular cartoon, available on wallpaper, cocktail napkins and an animated screen saver, has a small fish being devoured by a slightly larger fish, which in turn is consumed by a bigger fish that is overtaken by a still larger fish, and so on for half a dozen or more iterations. There is also an old doggerel about fleas that have smaller fleas to bite 'em, and the smaller fleas have smaller fleas, so on ad infinitum.

CHAPTER 4 FOCUS

Either of the above could serve as a metaphor for the evolving conventional wisdom about the current state of the media, as each successive technology overwhelms its predecessor. TV news is said to have diminished the printed press, virtually wiping out afternoon newspapers. (One could more reasonably argue, however, that this resulted from the difficulty of delivering papers during afternoon city traffic.) Cable grabbed the news prize from network TV, and now the Internet—with its trumpeted blogs-is trumping cable. It is all so logical, so pat.

This kind of analysis has been rattling around for a couple of years. But its most prominent-and perhaps most magisterial-recent expression was an essay in the *New York Times Book Review* by Federal Judge Richard A. Posner that filled the cover page and four more inside. Salted with passing references to eight books to justify its placement, the piece postulated that newspapers are surely about to die; that the success of Fox' Right-wing cable news channel has pushed CNN and its other rivals to the Left to pick up viewers alienated by Fox; and that the multiplicity of sources and the competition for breaking stories has increased the number of errors in the news we get.

Writing in the Web magazine *Slate*, Jack Shafer found these positions easy to demolish. Newspapers have been dying since they were born, and today, in fact, are a very profitable business. CNN, MSNBC and the others have veered Right, not Left, hoping to emulate Fox' success. (Subjecting yourself to a couple of hours of jabber on any of those cable networks drives this home.) That many newspapers, including the New York Times, are on the Web too means their online versions may have larger readerships than their print versions, and some of those online readers are quick to bring errors to the attention of editors.

5   Posner's approach is, understandably, lawyerly. Like other self-proclaimed disinterested media observers, lawyers tend to look upon news dissemination as exclusively part of the political process. Or, as Posner puts it, "The industry's critics agree that the function of the news is to inform people about social, political, cultural, ethical, and economic issues so that they can vote and otherwise express themselves as responsible citizens. They agree on the related point that journalism is a profession rather than just a trade and therefore that journalists and their employers must not allow profit considerations to dominate, but must acknowledge an ethical duty to report the news accurately, soberly, without bias, reserving the expression of political preferences for the editorial page and its radio and television counterparts."

How does that track with, to take one example, the notably intense interest among ordinary Americans this past August in the rescue of a Russian submarine and its crew by a British unit with American help? News may (or may not) fit the definitions offered by Posner and other detractors, but only partly.

News is also about hurricanes and automobile pileups and unseasonable blizzards; about marital discord, abandoned children and drug pushers; about malnutrition in Bangladesh and conspicuous consumption in Shanghai; about foster homes, nursing homes, hospitals, and homeless shelters; about locusts, bald eagles and missing persons; about co-ops, condos and rentals; about runaway taxicabs, illegal gamblers and people on death row; about fire walls, retaining walls and the Great Wall of China; about polio and SARS, tuberculosis and AIDS, Ebola virus and avian flu; about earthquakes, tidal waves and drought; about workmen falling off scaffolding, Fourth of July fireworks and St. Patrick's Day parades. And more.

Defining news is a loser's game, yet people keep trying. The only definition I ever found useful was given by an adjunct professor of journalism who was an assistant managing editor at the *New York Herald-Tribune,* of cherished memory. He said, "News is what your city editor tells you it is."

Nevertheless, Posner and the others are right, to a degree. There is no doubt that the audience for news in all media is shrinking at present, or that technological change affects which medium is favored by those who want news. Neither is a new phenomenon, though. Moreover, the critics are mistaken in treating them as the two sides of one coin. They are really separate issues.

When there is interesting news people are interested. Those outside 10 the craft tend to think news is judged by what is important, but journalists are not specialists in such determinations. There is a vague (elite?) consensus on what is considered important, but the true measurement of importance is the province of historians not yet born. A professional journalist's expertise lies in recognizing what is interesting, what (enough) people would want to know if they were told.

The history of American network television news, where the most funeral wreaths are being laid these days, tells the story. Television as a commercial enterprise was postponed by World War II's needs for its technicians and technologies. Its advent coincided with the early days of the Cold War, making for an astounding symbiosis. The Manichean simplicity of the conflict suited TV's favoring narrative pictures that were not only graphic but symbolic. The good people of North Podunk became as familiar with West Berlin, the news capital of the Cold War, as they were with South Podunk.

Starting with the Truman Doctrine and the Marshall Plan, the American majority was willingly enlisted in a battle validated by television's reporting and images. This lasted until Vietnam, when what was then described as the "first living room war" dragged on and became a matter of bitter contention. In addition to the pictures of young GIs wounded and dying, draft card burnings and the disorder outside the 1968 Democratic convention in Chicago prompted Americans who

CHAPTER 4 FOCUS

had accepted, even respected what television had brought them, to turn the other way. Inside the trade we learned the price of showing viewers what they did not want to see.

The case can be made that the "first living room war" took place a decade earlier in Korea. TV coverage was equally detailed and dramatic, and was avidly followed. Some evenings NEC's newscast drew more viewers than the era's ultimate TV entertainer, Milton Berle. But the reaction to the Korean fighting did not parallel the response to Vietnam. Perhaps this was because the Korean War did not last so long, no violent opposition appeared on TV every night, and there was no generational conflict. Nor should it be forgotten that far fewer American homes had TV sets, and those tended to be the homes of the well-to-do.

In any event, since Vietnam the audience for television network news has declined, as it indeed has for news in all media. Most observers cite polls that show the worst decline setting in around 1990. Posner writes, "A survey by the National Opinion Research Center finds that the public's confidence in the press declined from about 85 per cent in 1973 to 59 per cent in 2002, with most of the decline occurring since 1991."

15   Not mentioned by Posner or others is the obvious fact that the dropoff coincided with the implosion of the Soviet Union. After the Berlin Wall came down in 1989, foreign news became multipolar and more difficult to follow. The tired businessman returning home in the evening was assaulted with accounts of fratricide in "former Yugoslavia," starvation, corruption and genocide in African countries he did not know existed, convoluted and bloody antagonisms in remote shards of what we once comfortably lumped together as the Soviet Union. Further, we are told that any news at all turns off the post-baby boom generations, adding to the growing number of people no longer paying attention to the news.

Is this a steady decline or a trough in a rhythmic cycle? People who opine about news seem to have (acquired) memories reaching back only to the years leading up to World War II, when events abroad—in Russia, Italy and Germany—alerted the chattering classes to looming troubles. Major newspapers, like the Chicago Daily News, built reputations on skilled foreign staffs. After the War started and before Pearl Harbor, interest intensified. The U.S. was caught up in bitter debate between Interventionists and Isolationists, but Hollywood was Anglophile. Alfred Hitchcock made a movie called Foreign Correspondent, starring Joel McCrea in a trenchcoat. Radio, rather piddling as a news medium until then, took front position with names like H.V. Kaltenborn, Robert St. John and George Hicks. CBS, an also-ran in entertainment, made its name on its reporting staff in Europe, with Edward R. Murrow broadcasting from London during Nazi bombing raids.

But before that, there were the '20s—the Jazz Age, flappers, prohibition, a sensationalist press, William Randolph Hearst's Right-wing editorials, Floyd Collins trapped for days in a cave, the kidnapping of the Lindbergh baby and the trial and execution of Bruno Richard Hauptmann, Mary Pickford and Douglas Fairbanks Sr., Tammany Hall and New York Mayor James J. Walker, Al Capone and the Half Moon hotel. Sound familiar? Medium aside, it is startling to contemplate how close the profile of what is now considered news comes to the model for news after World War I. Those passing prophetic judgments on the state of journalism would do well to consider the similarity. It might calm their nerves.

As for the technology of the journalism of tomorrow, the consensus of disinterested observers has determined the future belongs to blogs, Internet sites that are virtually uncontrolled. Anyone can start one, and millions do. Academics, even deans of journalism, find them fascinating and hail them as the democratization of news. Newspapers assign staff reporters to cull them for story tips or to write about them.

"The latest, and perhaps gravest, challenge to the journalistic establishment," Posner writes, "is the blog. . . . In effect, the blogosphere is a collective enterprise—not 12 million separate enterprises, but one enterprise with 12 million reporters, feature writers and editorialists, yet with almost no costs. It's as if the Associated Press or Reuters had millions of reporters working with no salary for free newspapers that carried no advertising. . . . They enable unorthodox views to get a hearing. They get 12 million people to write rather than just stare passively at a screen. In an age of specialization and professionalism, they give amateurs a platform."

Always cited is the blogosphere's capacity to detect errors perpe- [20] trated by the mainstream media. The most telling example, and the one most often mentioned, is the blogger who recognized that the documents about George W. Bush's Vietnam-era service in the Air National Guard were composed on a typewriter using a typeface not available until long after the service supposedly took place. It was the first thread in the unraveling of a mighty edifice.

But it is no substitute for a rounded and comprehensive professional news service. From the Christian Science Monitor to the Online Journalism Review, there has lately been a growing recognition that viewing blogs as a freestanding and pervasive form of journalism is simply romantic twaddle.

To begin with, Forrester Research of Cambridge, Massachusetts, reported in early August that only 2 per cent of Americans who go online read a blog once a week or more. Then there is the often repeated concern that blogs are unedited and therefore irresponsible—that for every corrective contribution the blogosphere makes to journalism it imposes at least one egregious mistake on the news-consuming public. There is no way, either, to know how many of the 12 million blogs are alive. Those who are literate in such matters say that many people start a blog, never go back to it, and do not bother to cancel it. The statistics, naturally, do not account for scores of blogs lying dormant in the vast expanse of cyberspace as so much invisible digital debris.

A journalism instructor at Louisiana State University writes in *Editor & Publisher* of a young woman in his class wishing to start up a Web journal for "college women thinking about engineering careers." She told him the responses she received included "spam and 50-year-old men asking for dates, nude pictures, or both. Who needs that?" She deserted her blog after one entry, and it floats in the ether with the other orphans.

Is this the journalism of tomorrow? Hardly.

Responding to Reading

1. In paragraphs 3–5 and elsewhere, Frank summarizes arguments made by Richard A. Posner in "Bad News" (p. 275). On what points does he disagree with Posner? Does he agree with any of Posner's conclusions?
2. Frank believes blogs are "no substitute for a rounded and comprehensive professional news service" (21), and therefore he does not see them as a threat. Do Frank's arguments in paragraphs 19–23 convince you that blogs pose no threat to traditional news media? Why or why not?
3. In reviewing the history of American TV news coverage (paragraphs 11–17), (287,288) Frank asks, "Is this a steady decline or a trough in a rhythmic cycle" (16)? What is Frank's answer to this question?

Responding in Writing

What do you expect "the journalism of tomorrow" (24) to be like? Why?

NOT JUST ANOTHER COLUMN ABOUT BLOGGING

Jack Shafer

Editor at large for Slate *magazine and 2004 Hearst New Media Professional-in-Residence at Columbia Journalism School, Jack Shafer writes* Slate's Press Box *column, where he critiques various issues related to media and politics. In the following Press Box column, Shafer argues that new and traditional media alike must adapt if they are to survive in the age of Internet journalism.*

Six months ago, I stumbled upon a brilliant 16, 241-word paper about press consolidation, and it didn't occur to me until this week, while attending yet another blogger conference, how to spin it into a column.

The whale was written by Elizabeth MacIver Neiva for the spring 1996 issue of Harvard Business School's *Business History Review,* and it's titled "Chain Building: The Consolidation of the American Newspaper Industry, 1953–1980." To the best of my knowledge it's never been cited in the popular press.

The paper isn't online, but the speed-metal, five-page version is. To summarize Neiva's summary, she looks at the consolidation of the newspaper industry over the aforementioned 27-year period, when the number of dallies independently owned by families fell from 1,300 to 700. (There were 1,785 dailies in 1953.) She finds three entrepreneurs who capitalized on three of the external changes in the market that were responsible for the trend. They are Prescott Low of the Quincy, Mass., *Patriot Ledger,* who seized on electronic typesetting; Lloyd Schermer of the Missoula, Mont., *Missoulian,* who broke labor union hegemony; and Paul Miller of Gannett, who exploited IRS-mandated changes in estate-tax appraisal.

According to Neiva, newspaper technology remained stable in the 70 years before the post–WWII era, with the "massive, noisy mechanical contraption called a Linotype machine" that had more than 10,000 moving parts and took as much skill to operate as a nuclear power plant (my hyperbole, not Neiva's) dominating newspaper production. Then postwar inflation and the end of wage freezes sent publishers searching for ways to cut costs.

In 1953, Low of the *Patriot Ledger* placed his bet on a newfangled photocomposition device—the Photon—that set type on film instead of lead, did it six times faster, and did it tons cheaper. By 1956, the *Patriot Ledger* had fully integrated the Photon into its operation. This allowed Low to replace skilled workers with the unskilled, who could set more type in less time at much less cost, eventually displacing "a method of production that newspapers had been using for nearly a hundred years."

Strong trade unions kept photocomposition machines out of many pressrooms, fearing correctly that they would destroy jobs. Schermer's only alternative to photocomposition machines was bankruptcy, so he outwitted the unions with a negotiation strategy that got the machines into his newspaper on his terms, not theirs. To simplify the story, other publishers imitated Schermer, and by the early 1980s many had routed the unions and become hugely profitable.

Family-owned newspapers celebrated their new profitability until the IRS started appraising newspapers by their soaring market values instead of their assets. In the 1960s and 1970s, gift and inheritance taxes stood at about 70 percent, Neiva writes, and under the new IRS rules most newspaper heirs didn't have the cash to pay the new tax bill. Paul Miller of Gannett helped aging owners and their heirs dodge the IRS by trading shares in Gannett for their papers, building the chain out to 79 papers by the time he retired in 1979. Other chains imitated Gannett, accelerating newspaper consolidation.

This is where blogs come in. The union-destroying technology Neiva describes continued to evolve, reducing newspaper costs. Ultimately, the technology trickled down to individual desktops in the form of affordable personal computers. When the Web arrived in the mid-1990s as an alternative publishing system, big media organizations and other well-funded entities were the only ones that could afford to build high-traffic, fancy Web sites.

As John Battelle points out, the prices of hardware, software, and bandwidth have fallen so dramatically in the last six years that the Web has experienced a "second coming," which he and others call "Web 2.0." Writing in the *New York Times* (Nov. 18, 2005), Battelle notes that one can "lease a platform that can handle millions of customers for less than $500 a month. In the 90's, such a platform would have run tens of thousands of dollars or more a month." Here's another astonishing marker: The price of one gigabyte of hard-disk storage has dropped from about $9 in October 2000 (nominal terms) to about 45 cents (retail) or less today. And it's not just a matter of falling prices but of who is catching the technology as it falls: individuals and institutions that couldn't afford the spiffy technologies only moneyed corporations could afford previously.

10   Battelle extols what a new business can accomplish with $200,000 that would have taken millions just six years ago. If you combine Neiva's findings with Battelle's argument, you can make the case that the next entrenched "guild" that technology is likely to bulldoze is the "newspaper guild." I'm not speaking of the union of the same name, but of those who work in the news business—reporters, editors, publishers, radio and TV broadcasters, etc.

Like the long-gone typesetters, today's newspaper guild members believe that their job is somehow their "property," and that no amateur can step in to perform their difficult and arduous tasks. On one level, they're right. John Q. Blogger can't fly to Baghdad or Bosnia and do the work of a John F. Burns.

But what a lot of guild members miss is that not *everybody* wants to read John F. Burns, not *everybody* who wants to read about Baghdad is going to demand coverage of the quality he produces, and not *everybody* wants Baghdad coverage, period. If you loosely define journalism as words and graphics about current events deliverable on tight deadline to a mass audience, the price of entry into the craft has dropped to a few hundred dollars. Hell, I can remember renting an IBM Selectric for $100 a month in the late 1970s just to make my free-lance articles look more "professional" to my editors.

So, when newspaper reporters bellyache about shoot-from-the-hip bloggers who don't fully Investigate the paper trail before writing a story or double-check their facts before posting, they're telling a valuable truth. Bad bloggers are almost as bad as bad journalists. But the prospect of a million amateurs doing something akin to their job unsettles the guild, making it feel like Maytag's factory rats whose jobs were poached by low-paid Chinese labor.

It's not just the *best* of the blogasphere drawing away big audiences that the guild need worry about. If Chris Anderson's Long Tail intuitions are right, the *worst* of the blogosphere—if it's big enough—presents just as much (or more) competition. Michael Kinsley made me laugh a decade ago when he argued against Web populists replacing professional writers, saying that when he goes to a restaurant, he wants the chef to cook his entree, not the guy sitting at the next table. I'm not laughing anymore: When there are millions of aspiring chefs in the room willing to make your dinner for free, a least a hundred of them are likely to deal a good meal. Mainstream publishers no longer have a lock on the means of production, making the future of reading and viewing anybody's game. To submit a tortured analogy, it's like the Roman Catholic Church after Gutenberg. Soon, everyone starts thinking he's a priest.

I'm not about to predict what the collapsing cost of media creation 15 will ultimately do to the news business, if only because my track record at prophecy is terrible. But this much I know: The newspaper guild (again, reporters, editors, publishers) can't compete by adding a few blogs here, blogging up coverage over there, and setting up "comment" sections. If newspapers, magazines, and broadcasters don't produce spectacular news coverage no blogger can match, they have no right to survive.

But instead of improving their product by deploying technology bloggers can't afford (yet), newspapers are devolving. Many are cutting staff. Dally newspapers are growing smaller and uglier, with no paper looking anywhere near as lovely as Joseph Pulitzer's *New York World* from the late 1800s. Comic strips have gotten so tiny you need a magnifying glass to read them. I'm fine with newspapers cutting back on stock tables, but they aren't adding something new to the package. Most newspapers claim they've shrunk their dimensions to combat steep increases in newsprint prices, but that's a lie.

What else do I want? I want a daily newspaper that looks as good as *Vogue* but smells like a cinnamon bun instead of perfume. I want smarter newspaper headlines. I want a Mike Rovko in every daily newspaper. I want editorials signed by people, so I know who to yell at. I want newspapers to restore editorial cartoonists to their place of honor instead of eliminating them. To broaden the answer, I want the newsmagazines to give me a better reason to read them than remixes of the last four days' news cycle, and I want them to look like Harry N. Abrams' coffee-table books.

I want Arthur Sulzberger Jr. to straighten out the production problems at the Washington-area plant that prints the *New York Times* so it arrives on my doorstep more reliably. I also want more for my *Times* subscription than TimesSelect and its stingy 100 "free" searches a month from the archives, its News Tracker, and the paper's columnists.

And that's just for starters. If my fellow guild members want to save their jobs, they'd best meet my needs.

Responding to Reading

1. Why does Shafer open his essay with a discussion of Elizabeth MacIver Neiva's article about the consolidation of newspapers? What point does it help him make? What is the connection between "the union-destroying technology Neiva describes" (8) and the rise of the blog?
2. According to Shafer, what advantages do traditional news reporters have over bloggers? Despite these advantages, why do bloggers continue to threaten the survival of print media? Review Shafer's arguments in paragraphs 12–15. How do you think Richard A. Posner (p. 275) and Reuven Frank (p. 285) would counter the arguments Shafer raises here?
3. What does Shafer believe newspapers should do to save themselves? Are all his suggestions meant to be taken seriously? Do you have any additional suggestions?

Responding in Writing

Do you see the print newspaper as an endangered species? Why or why not?

WIDENING THE FOCUS

✴ For Critical Reading and Writing

Do you think the rise of the Internet in general (and of blogs in particular) threatens the survival of newspapers, news magazines, and television news programs? After reading the three essays in the Focus section, write an essay that answers this question, referring to the readings by Richard A. Posner ("Bad News,") Reuven Frank ("A Loser's Game,"), and Jack Shafer ("Not Just Another Column about Blogging,").

For Further Reading

The following readings can suggest additional perspectives for thinking and writing about the threat the Internet poses to newspapers and other traditional print media.

- Aldous Huxley, "Propaganda under a Dictatorship" (p. 183)
- Tom Standage, "The Internet in a Cup" (p. 351)
- Richard Wright, "The Library Card" (p. 427)

For Internet Research

Has the Internet doomed the newspaper, or has it ushered in important changes in the way the print media industry reaches its audience? As Jack Shafer argues in his essay "Not Just Another Column about Blogging," Web logs, or blogs, are increasingly pervasive and influential news outlets and forums for threaded discussions on current issues. Read the blog posting "Are Newspapers Doomed?" by Jeff Alworth at the BlueOregon blog <http://www.blueoregon.com/2005/09/are_newspapers_.html,>, which includes links to online sources that support his argument as well as several reader responses. Then, write an essay in which you evaluate the arguments presented by Alworth and his readers, and explain which arguments you find most effective and why.

─────────────────────── **WRITING** ───────────────────────

Media and Society

1. What do you think the impact of the various media discussed in this chapter will be in the years to come? What trends do you see emerging that you believe will change the way you think or the way you live? Write an essay in which you speculate about future trends and their impact, using essays in this chapter to support the points you make.

2. Write an essay in which you consider the representation of women, the elderly, or people with disabilities—in movies, on television, or in magazine ads. Do you believe the group you have chosen to write about is adequately represented? Do you think its members are portrayed fairly and accurately, or do you think they are stereotyped? Support your conclusions with specific examples.

3. Keep a daily log of the programs you watch on television, the movies you see, the Web sites you visit, and the newspapers and magazines you read (in print and online). After one week, review your log, and write an essay explaining how these different kinds of media informed, provoked, or entertained you.

4. Do films and television shows present an accurate image of your race, religion, or ethnic group? In what ways, if any, is the image you see unrealistic? In what ways, if any, is it demeaning? If possible, include recommendations for improving the media image of the group you discuss. What should be done to challenge—or change—simplistic or negative images? Whose responsibility should it be to effect change?

5. Should the government continue to support public television and radio? What, if anything, do public radio and television provide that commercial programming does not offer? (Before beginning this essay, compare newspaper listings of public and commercial programming, and try to spend a few hours screening public television and radio programs if you are not familiar with them.)

6. What kind of "family values" are promoted on television? Would you say that TV is largely "profamily" or "antifamily"? Using the essays in this chapter by Winn (p. 231) and Rushdie (p. 239) for background, choose several films and television programs that support your position. Then, write an essay that takes a strong stand on this issue. (Be sure to define exactly what you mean by *family* and *family values*.)

7. To what extent, if any, should explicitly sexual or violent images in magazine ads, on TV, or on the Internet be censored? Write an essay

in which you take a stand on this issue and explain why you believe such censorship is (or is not) necessary.

8. What danger, if any, do you see for young people in the seductive messages of the music they listen to? Do you believe that parents and educators are right to be concerned about the effect the messages in rock and rap music have on teenagers and young adults, or do you think they are overreacting? Support your position with quotations from popular music lyrics. If you like, you can also interview friends and relatives and use their responses to help you develop your argument. Before you begin, read Mary Eborstadt's "Eminem Is Right" (p. 250).

9. Some argue that the Internet brings people together—for example, by providing constant dialogue in e-mail exchanges and chat rooms and by creating a common cultural frame of reference. Others believe that the Internet actually divides and isolates people, enabling them to receive only information that appeals to their own narrow interests and making it possible for them to avoid face-to-face contact. Do you see the Internet as a unifying or a dividing force in our society?

10. Write an analysis of a Web site or a blog, considering the techniques it uses to appeal to its target audience. What message is conveyed, and how successfully is this message communicated?

5

■ ■ ■ ■ □ ■ ■ ■ ■

LIFE AND LIFESTYLE

■ ■ □ ■ ■

The way we live now is very different from the way we lived just a generation or two ago. Early science fiction writers imagined time travel, but few envisioned the scope of the changes that would occur in how we live, what we wear and eat, how we spend our leisure time, and what electronic "toys" we rely on.

In Rick Moody's 1995 novel *The Ice Storm*, set in 1973, the narrator sets the scene in a way that reminds readers how different things were just twenty years earlier:

> No answering machines. And no call waiting. No Caller I.D. No compact disc recorders or laser discs or holography or cable television or MTV. No multiplex cinemas or word processors or laser printers or modems. No virtual reality. No grand unified theory or Frequent

People in airport pay-phone booths, St. Louis, Missouri, 1966

Flyer mileage or fuel injection systems or turbo or premenstrual syndrome or rehabilitation centers or Adult Children of Alcoholics. No codependency. No punk rock, or postpunk, or hardcore, or grunge. No hip-hop. No Acquired Immune Deficiency Syndrome or Human Immunodeficiency Virus or mysterious AIDS-like illnesses. No computer viruses. No cloning or genetic engineering or biospheres or full-color photocopying or desktop copying and especially no facsimile transmission. . . .

And, of course, the world has continued to change in the years since Moody wrote these words in 1995. Now, in the early years of the new millennium, life as we know it would hold surprises not only for a time traveler from 100 years ago or from the 1973 of Moody's novel, but for one from ten years ago as well: houses, televisions, SUVs, and portion sizes have gotten bigger; computers, cell phones, and other electronic gadgets have gotten smaller; and, of course, the popularity of the Internet has increased tremendously.

With these and other changes, both sudden and gradual, have come inevitable problems: As we applaud technology, we fear its misuse; as we discover new forms of entertainment, we find we must work harder to afford them (leaving us with less time to enjoy them); as we live in an increasingly diverse society, we struggle to find common ground while retaining our unique cultures; and even as we learn more about health and nutrition, we have less time to exercise or to monitor our diets.

Businesspeople talking on cell phones, 2001

The essays in this chapter look at some of these (and other) issues, commenting on how our lives have changed and suggesting
changes still to come. The essays in the chapter's Focus section,
"Can We Build Real Communities Online?"(p. 340) examine one important lifestyle change that is already underway: the rise of the Internet as a supplement to (and, sometimes, as a substitute for)
traditional face-to-face communication.

──────── PREPARING TO READ AND WRITE ────────

As you read the selections in this chapter and prepare to write about
them, you may consider the following questions:

- Does the writer present a primarily positive or negative picture
  of society?

- Is the writer looking back at the past or forward to the future?

- On what social issue or issues does the writer focus?

- Would you say the writer's primary objective is to understand an
  issue and its effect, to inform readers, or to change readers'
  minds?

- Does the writer have a personal stake in the issue? If so, does
  your awareness of this involvement weaken or strengthen the selection's impact on you?

- If the selection identifies a problem, does it focus on finding solutions, speculating about long-term effects, or warning about consequences?

- Does the writer stress the need for change—for example, in basic
  attitudes, in habits, or in the law? Is the writer optimistic or pessimistic about the possibility of change?

- Are you emotionally connected to the issue under discussion, or
  are you relatively detached from it?

- What areas of common concern do the writers explore? How are
  their views alike? How are they different? In what ways are they
  like and unlike your own?

- How are the writers' hopes and dreams for the future alike? How
  are they different? In what ways are they like and unlike your
  own?

THE WORLD IS TOO MUCH WITH US
William Wordsworth
1770–1850

One of the best-known English poets, William Wordsworth graduated from Cambridge University in 1791, traveled abroad, and returned to live in the rural Lake District of England, where he stayed for the remainder of his life. Wordsworth's work was deeply influenced by his natural surroundings and by a close association with another English poet, Samuel Taylor Coleridge. Together they led the English Romantic movement in literature, writing poetry in the language of ordinary people and focusing on ideas of freedom, individualism, and Nature. In the following 1807 sonnet, written long before fast food, interstates, shopping malls, and suburban living, Wordsworth laments human separation from the natural world.

The world is too much with us; late and soon,
Getting and spending, we lay waste our powers;
Little we see in Nature that is ours;
We have given our hearts away, a sordid boon!
This Sea that bares her bosom to the moon;   5
The winds that will be howling at all hours,
And are up-gathered now like sleeping flowers;
For this, for everything, we are out of tune;
It moves us not. Great God! I'd rather be
A Pagan suckled in a creed outworn;   10
So might I, standing on this pleasant lea,
Have glimpses that would make me less forlorn;
Have sight of Proteus[1] rising from the sea;
Or hear old Triton[2] blow his wreathèd horn.

Responding to Reading

1. What does the poem's speaker think is wrong with the world in which he lives? Do his complaints apply to the twenty-first-century world as well?
2. What do you think the speaker means by "Getting and spending" (2)?
3. With whom, or what, is the speaker "out of tune" (8)?

Responding in Writing

What in our own world is "too much with us" (1)? Can you suggest a solution for this problem?

---

[1]A Greek sea god capable of assuming different forms. [Eds.]
[2]A son of Poseidon, the Greek god of the sea, described as a demigod of the sea with the lower part of his body like that of a fish. [Eds].

THE TRANSFORMATION OF EVERYDAY LIFE
Richard Florida
1957–

Currently the Heinz professor of economic development at Carnegie Mellon University, Richard Florida has published more than 100 articles in academic journals as well as several books, most recently The Flight of the Creative Class: The New Global Competition for Talent *(2005). In the following selection, from* The Rise of the Creative Class: And How It's Transforming Work, Leisure, Community, and Everyday Life *(2002), Florida explains how the "rise of the creative class" has transformed the workplace, American culture, and people's everyday lives.*

Something's happening here but you don't know what it is, do you, Mr. Jones?

—Bob Dylan

Here's a thought experiment. Take a typical man on the street from the year 1900 and drop him into the 1950s. Then take someone from the 1950s and move him Austin Powers–style into the present day. Who would experience the greater change?

At first glance the answer seems obvious. Thrust forward into the 1950s, a person from the turn of the twentieth century would be awestruck by a world filled with baffling technological wonders. In place of horse-drawn carriages, he would see streets and highways jammed with cars, trucks and buses. In the cities, immense skyscrapers would line the horizon, and mammoth bridges would span rivers and inlets where once only ferries could cross. Flying machines would soar overhead, carrying people across the continent or the oceans in a matter of hours rather than days. At home, our 1900-to-1950s time-traveler would grope his way through a strange new environment filled with appliances powered by electricity: radios and televisions emanating musical sounds and even human images, refrigerators to keep things cold, washing machines to clean his clothes automatically, and much more. A massive new super market would replace daily trips to the market with an array of technologically enhanced foods, such as instant coffee or frozen vegetables to put into the refrigerator. Life itself would be dramatically extended. Many once-fatal ailments could be prevented with an injection or cured with a pill. The newness of this time-traveler's physical surroundings—the speed and power of everyday machines—would be profoundly disorienting.

On the other hand, someone from the 1950s would have little trouble navigating the physical landscape of today. Although we like to think ours is the age of boundless technological wonders, our second time-traveler would find himself in a world not all that different from the one he left. He would still drive a car to work. If he took the train, it would likely be on the same line leaving from the same station. He could probably board an airplane at the same airport. He might still live in a suburban house, though a bigger one. Television would have more channels, but it would basically be the same, and he could still catch some of his favorite 1950s shows on reruns. He would know how, or quickly learn how, to operate most household appliances— even the personal computer, with its familiar QWERTY keyboard. In fact with just a few exceptions, such as the PC, the Internet, CD and DVD players, the cash machine and a wireless phone he could carry with him, he would be familiar with almost all current-day technology. Perhaps disappointed by the pace of progress, he might ask: "Why haven't we conquered outer space?" or "Where are all the robots?"

On the basis of big, obvious technological changes alone, surely the 1900-to-1950s traveler would experience the greater shift, while the other might easily conclude that we'd spent the second half of the twentieth century doing little more than tweaking the great waves of the first half.[1]

But the longer they stayed in their new homes, the more each time-traveler would become aware of subtler dimensions of change. Once the glare of technology had dimmed, each would begin to notice their respective society's changed norms and values, and the ways in which everyday people live and work. And here the tables would be turned. In terms of adjusting to the social structures and the rhythms and patterns of daily life, our second time-traveler would be much more disoriented.

Someone from the early 1900s would find the social world of the 1950s remarkably similar to his own. If he worked in a factory, he might find much the same divisions of labor, the same hierarchical systems of control. If he worked in an office, he would be immersed in the same bureaucracy, the same climb up the corporate ladder. He would come to work at 8 or 9 each morning and leave promptly at 5, his life neatly segmented into compartments of home and work. He would wear a suit and tie. Most of his business associates would be white and male. Their values and office politics would hardly have changed. He would seldom see women in the workplace, except as secretaries, and almost never interact professionally with someone of another race. He would marry young, have children quickly thereafter, stay married to the same person and probably work for the same company for the rest of his life. In his leisure time, he'd find that movies and TV had largely superseded live stage shows, but otherwise his recreational activities would be much the same as they were in 1900: taking in a baseball game or a boxing match, maybe playing a round of golf. He would join the clubs and civic groups befitting his socioeconomic class, observe the same social distinctions, and fully expect his children to do likewise. The tempo of his life would be structured by the values and norms of organizations. He would find himself living the life of the "company man" so aptly chronicled by writers from Sinclair Lewis and John Kenneth Galbraith to William Whyte and C. Wright Mills.[2]

Our second time-traveler, however, would be quite unnerved by the dizzying social and cultural changes that had accumulated between the 1950s and today. At work he would find a new dress code, a new schedule, and new rules. He would see office workers dressed like folks relaxing on the weekend, in jeans and open-necked shirts, and be shocked to learn they occupy positions of authority. People at the office would seemingly come and go as they pleased. The younger ones might sport bizarre piercings and tattoos. Women and even non-whites would be managers. Individuality and self-expression would be valued over conformity to organizational norms—and yet these people would seem strangely puritanical to this time-traveler. His ethnic jokes would fall embarrassingly flat. His smoking would get him banished to the parking lot, and his two-martini lunches would raise genuine concern. Attitudes and expressions he had never thought about would cause repeated offense. He would continually suffer the painful feeling of not knowing how to behave.

Out on the street, this time-traveler would see different ethnic groups in greater numbers than he ever could have imagined—Asian, Indian-, and Latin-Americans and others—all mingling in ways he found strange and perhaps inappropriate. There would be mixed-race couples, and same-sex couples carrying the upbeat-sounding moniker "gay." While some of these people would be acting in familiar ways— a woman shopping while pushing a stroller, an office worker having lunch at a counter—others, such as grown men clad in form-fitting gear whizzing by on high-tech bicycles, or women on strange new roller skates with their torsos covered only by "brassieres"—would appear to be engaged in alien activities.

People would seem to be always working and yet never working when they were supposed to. They would strike him as lazy and yet obsessed with exercise. They would seem career-conscious yet fickle—doesn't anybody stay with the company more than three years?—and caring yet anti-social: What happened to the ladies' clubs, Moose Lodges and bowling leagues? While the physical surroundings would be relatively familiar, the *feel* of the place would be bewilderingly different.

10   Thus, although the first time-traveler had to adjust to some drastic technological changes, it is the second who experiences the deeper,

more pervasive transformation. It is the second who has been thrust into a time when lifestyles and worldviews are most assuredly changing—a time when the old order has broken down, when flux and uncertainty themselves seem to be part of the everyday norm.

The Force Behind the Shift

What caused this transformation? What happened between the 1950s and today that did not happen in the earlier period? Scholars and pundits have floated many theories, along with a range of opinions on whether the changes are good or bad. Some bemoan the passing of traditional social and cultural forms, while others point to a rosy future based largely on new technology. Yet on one point most of them agree. Most tend to see the transformation as something that's being done to us unwittingly. Some complain that certain factions of society have imposed their values on the rest of us; others say that our own inventions are turning around to reshape us. They're wrong.

Society is changing in large measure because we want it to. Moreover it is changing neither in random chaotic ways nor in some mysterious collective-unconscious way, but in ways that are perfectly sensible and rational. The logic behind the transformation has been unclear to this point because the transformation is still in progress. But lately a number of diverse and seemingly unconnected threads are starting to come together. The deeper pattern, the force behind the shift, can now be discerned.

That driving force is the rise of human creativity as the key factor in our economy and society. Both at work and in other spheres of our lives, we value creativity more highly than ever, and cultivate it more intensely. The creative impulse—the attribute that distinguishes us, as humans, from other species—is now being let loose on an unprecedented scale. The purpose of this book is to examine how and why this is so, and to trace its effects as they ripple through our world.

Consider first the realm of economics. Many say that we now live in an "information" economy or a "knowledge" economy. But what's more fundamentally true is that we now have an economy powered by human creativity. Creativity—"the ability to create meaningful new forms," as Webster's dictionary puts it—is now the *decisive* source of competitive advantage. In virtually every industry, from automobiles to fashion, food products, and information technology itself, the winners in the long run are those who can create and keep creating. This has always been true, from the days of the Agricultural Revolution to the Industrial Revolution. But in the past few decades we've come to recognize it clearly and act upon it systematically.

Creativity is multidimensional and comes in many mutually rein- 15
forcing forms. It is a mistake to think, as many do, that creativity can

be reduced to the creation of new blockbuster inventions, new products and new firms. In today's economy creativity is pervasive and ongoing: We constantly revise and enhance every product, process and activity imaginable, and fit them together in new ways. Moreover, technological and economic creativity are nurtured by and interact with artistic and cultural creativity. This kind of interplay is evident in the rise of whole new industries from computer graphics to digital music and animation. Creativity also requires a social and economic environment that can nurture its many forms. Max Weber said long ago that the Protestant ethic provided the underlying spirit of thrift, hard work and efficiency that motivated the rise of early capitalism. In similar fashion, the shared commitment to the creative spirit in its many, varied manifestations underpins the new creative ethos that powers our age.

Thus creativity has come to be the most highly prized commodity in our economy—and yet it is not a "commodity." Creativity comes from people. And while people can be hired and fired, their creative capacity cannot be bought and sold, or turned on and off at will. This is why, for instance, we see the emergence of a new order in the workplace. Hiring for diversity, once a matter of legal compliance, has become a matter of economic survival because creativity comes in all colors, genders and personal preferences. Schedules, rules and dress codes have become more flexible to cater to how the creative process works. Creativity must be motivated and nurtured in a multitude of ways, by employers, by people themselves and by the communities where they locate. Small wonder that we find the creative ethos bleeding out from the sphere of work to infuse every corner of our lives.

At the same time, entirely new forms of economic infrastructure, such as systematic spending on research and development, the high-tech startup company and an extensive system of venture finance, have evolved to support creativity and mobilize creative people around promising ideas and products. Capitalism has also expanded its reach to capture the talents of heretofore excluded groups of eccentrics and nonconformists. In doing so, it has pulled off yet another astonishing mutation: taking people who would once have been viewed as bizarre mavericks operating at the bohemian fringe and setting them at the very heart of the process of innovation and economic growth. These changes in the economy and in the workplace have in turn helped to propagate and legitimize similar changes in society at large. The creative individual is no longer viewed as an iconoclast. He—or she—is the new mainstream.

In tracing economic shifts, I often say that our economy is moving from an older corporate-centered system defined by large companies to a more people-driven one. This view should not be confused with the unfounded and silly notion that big companies are dying off. Nor do I buy the fantasy of an economy organized around small enterprises and independent "free agents."[3] Companies, including very big ones, obviously still exist, are still influential and probably always will be. I simply mean to stress that as the fundamental source of creativity, people are the critical resource of the new age. This has far-reaching effects—for instance, on our economic and social geography and the nature of our communities.

It's often been said that in this age of high technology, "geography is dead" and place doesn't matter any more.[4] Nothing could be further from the truth: Witness how high-tech firms themselves concentrate in specific places like the San Francisco Bay Area or Austin or Seattle. Place has become the central organizing unit of our time, taking on many of the functions that used to be played by firms and other organizations. Corporations have historically played a key economic role in matching people to jobs, particularly given the long-term employment system of the post–World War II era. But today corporations are far less committed to their employees and people change jobs frequently, making the employment contract more contingent. In this environment, it is geographic place rather than the corporation that provides the organizational matrix for matching people and jobs. Access to talented and creative people is to modern business what access to coal and iron ore was to steelmaking. It determines where companies will choose to locate and grow, and this in turn changes the ways cities must compete. As Hewlett-Packard CEO Carley Fiorina once told this nation's governors: "Keep your tax incentives and highway interchanges; we will go where the highly skilled people are."[5]

Creative people, in turn, don't just cluster where the jobs are. 20 They cluster in places that are centers of creativity and also where they like to live. From classical Athens and Rome, to the Florence of the Medici and Elizabethan London, to Greenwich Village and the San Francisco Bay Area, creativity has always gravitated to specific locations. As the great urbanist Jane Jacobs pointed out long ago, successful places are multidimensional and diverse—they don't just cater to a single industry or a single demographic group; they are full of stimulation and creativity interplay.[6] In my consulting work, I often tell business and political leaders that places need a people climate—or a creativity climate—as well as a business climate. Cities like Seattle, Austin, Toronto and Dublin recognize the multidimensional nature of this transformation and are striving to become broadly creative communities, not just centers of technological innovation and high-tech industry. If places like Buffalo, Grand Rapids, Memphis and Louisville do not follow suit, they will be hard-pressed to survive.

Our fundamental social forms are shifting as well, driven by forces traceable to the creative ethos. In virtually every aspect of life, weak ties have replaced the stronger bonds that once gave structure to society. Rather than live in one town for decades, we now move about. Instead of communities defined by close associations and deep commitments to family, friends and organizations, we seek places where we can make friends and acquaintances easily and live quasi-anonymous lives. The decline in the strength of our ties to people and institutions is a product of the increasing number of ties we have. As a retired industrialist who was the head of a technology transfer center in Ottawa, Canada, told me: "My father grew up in a small town and worked for the same company. He knew the same fourteen people in his entire life. I meet more people than that in any given day."[7] Modern life is increasingly defined by contingent commitments. We progress from job to job with amazingly little concern or effort. Where people once found themselves bound together by social institutions and formed their identities in groups, a fundamental characteristic of life today is that we strive to create our own identities. It is this creation and re-creation of the self, often in ways that reflect our creativity, that is a key feature of the creative ethos.

In this new world, it is no longer the organizations we work for, churches, neighborhoods or even family ties that define us. Instead, we do this ourselves, defining our identities along the varied dimensions of our creativity. Other aspects of our lives—what we consume, new forms of leisure and recreation, efforts at community-building—then organize themselves around this process of identity creation.

Notes

1. For a careful empirical comparison of technological change at the turn of the twentieth century versus modern times, see Robert Gordon, "Does the New Economy Measure Up to the Great Inventions of the Past?" Cambridge, Mass.: National Bureau of Economic Research, Working Paper No. 7833, August 2000. His answer is a resounding no. The great majority of the technological inventions in the National Academy of Engineering's "Greatest Engineering Accomplishments of the 20th Century" occurred prior to 1950. Only two of the top ten occurred after World War II (semiconductor electronics, no. 5, and computers, no. 8), while the Internet, the subject of so much New Economy hype, ranks thirteenth. See www.greatachievements.org.

2. Among the most popular, indeed classic works in this vein, see Sinclair Lewis, *Main Street*. New York: Harcourt, Brace and Company, 1920; and *Babbitt*. New York: Harcourt, Brace and World, 1922; William H. Whyte, Jr., *The Organization Man*. New York: Simon and Schuster, 1956; David Riesman, *The Lonely Crowd: A Study of the Changing American Character*. New Haven: Yale University Press, 1950; C. Wright Mills, *White Collar: The American Middle Classes*. New York: Oxford University Press, 1951; John Kenneth

Galbraith, *The New Industrial State.* New York: Houghton-Mifflin, 1967. Also see Anthony Sampson, *Company Man: The Rise and Fall of Corporate Life.* New York: Times Books, 1995.

3. There are many statements of the free agent view, but the most notable is Daniel Pink, *Free Agent Nation: How America's New Independent Workers Are Transforming the Way We Live.* New York: Warner Books, 2001.

4. Again there are many statements of this view, but for a contemporary one see Kevin Kelly, *New Rules for the New Economy: 10 Radical Strategies for a Connected World.* New York: Viking, 1998.

5. Fiorina preceded me in speaking to the Annual Meeting of the National Governors Association in Washington, D.C., in winter 2000, where she made these remarks.

6. Jacobs's work is the classic statement of these themes. See Jane Jacobs, *The Death and Life of Great American Cities.* New York: Random House, 1961; *The Economy of Cities.* New York: Random House, 1969; *Cities and the Wealth of Nations.* New York: Random House, 1984.

7. Personal interview by author, Ottawa, Canada, September 2001.

Responding to Reading

1. In answering the question he poses in paragraph 1, do you think Florida is correct to emphasize the importance of "society's changed norms and values, and the ways in which everyday people live and work" (5) rather than the technological changes that have occurred? Do you think he might be underestimating the importance of the impact of technology and overestimating the impact of "dizzying social and cultural changes" (7)?

2. According to Florida, the "driving force" behind the social and cultural transformation that occurred between 1950 and the present is "the rise of human creativity" (13). What does he mean?

3. How, according to Florida, have "our economic and social geography and the nature of our communities" (18) been transformed in recent years? What role have "creative" individuals played in this transformation?

Responding in Writing

Interview one or both of your parents (in person or by phone or email), and ask them to list five items they rely on now but had never heard of when they were children and five social or cultural changes they have observed over the past twenty years. Which do they see as more important, the technological changes or the social changes? Why?

THE BOREDOM EFFECT
Ellen Ruppel Shell
1952–

Ellen Ruppel Shell is a correspondent for the Atlantic Monthly *and writes regularly for the* New York Times Magazine, *the* New York Times Book Review, Smithsonian, *and the* Washington Post. *Her focus is generally on science and public policy, including public health, infectious diseases, and environmental issues. Currently, Shell is a co-director of the Science Journalism Program at Boston University, where she is an associate professor of journalism. Her most recent book,* The Hungry Gene: The Science of Fat and the Future of Thin *(2002), is a study of the worldwide obesity epidemic. In the following essay, she discusses the disappearance of unstructured, unsupervised time from children's lives.*

As a child I loved a vacant lot we called "the woods." I went there alone, to read or to wander around. I went there with friends, to build tree forts. Sometimes, one of us would bring a magnifying glass to burn ants or to light little teepee fires. Sometimes, one of the boys would pee on the fire to put it out, and we'd laugh our heads off. Our parents knew none of this, of course, but that was the point. Back then, parents pretty much stayed out of children's business, which is to say they stayed out of our play.

Play went mostly unsupervised, and it was deliciously freeform. Our parents wouldn't have thought of making "play dates" for us, or cramming our schedules with lessons. After school and on weekends we hung out on the street until another kid showed up. If no one showed up, we bounced a ball off a stoop, or played solitary jacks, or lolled on the grass. If we had roller skates or a bike, we'd use them, If it rained, we roamed around the house, bored. But most of us avoided letting on that we were bored, for fear that our parents would find us something to do. I'm not talking about a trip to the amusement park or an afternoon of miniature golf. Something to do meant scrubbing the kitchen floor or mowing the lawn or washing the family car. So, unlike many kids today, we took charge of our boredom. According to child development experts, this was probably a good thing.

Last April, Ann O'Bar, president of the American Association on the Child's Right to Play told *The New York Times:* "There's nothing wrong with letting children be bored. Boredom leads to exploration, which leads to creativity." One day last spring I decided to put Ms. O'Bar's theory to the test. My younger daughter Joanna, who's eight, was very, very bored. Her best friend was out of town, none of her other friends was free, and, to heap insult on injury, it was sunny outside. So rather than entertain her, I insisted she find something to do out of doors. I watched from the window, feeling a little guilty as she stomped, sulking, to the play structure in our backyard. She sat on the swing, scowling down at her bare feet (out of defiance, she'd refused to put on shoes). After a few minutes, boredom got the best of her. She had to do something. She twisted and twisted in the swing, then let go, twirling like a dervish. She did this a few more times, throwing her head back to study the cloudless sky. Then she climbed out of the swing and up to the top of the monkey bars, and peered over at the neighbor's parking lot. (We live behind a condominium complex.) She watched a neighbor scrub down his Honda for a while, until she spotted a squirrel. She followed the squirrel up a tree with her eyes, then did a skin-the-cat maneuver down from the monkey bars, back to solid ground. She gathered a bunch of pine cones and sticks, and made a tiny fort for her stuffed armadillo, Jessica. She got the hose and flooded the fort with water. She learned that stuffed armadillos can't swim. She charged into the house for her doctor's bag, then hustled back outside just in time to bring Jessica back to life. I watched all this with one eye, my other trained on the Sunday paper. Gradually my guilt dissolved into pride. Clearly, Ms. O'Bar is onto something.

It seems to me that we've lost trust in our kids. We don't believe that they can navigate the world, so we try to navigate it for them. We muck around in the details of their lives. We load them up with lessons and organized sports overseen by adults. We monitor their every move, demanding to know how and where and with whom they spend their time. And we schedule them so tightly that they lose their natural-born knack for spontaneous play. Put these over-scheduled kids in a room with crayons and markers and scissors and paper and, rather than dig in, they'll ask you what the assignment is. Stick them on a field with a ball, and they'll ask you about the rules. Put them in a room filled with blocks and dolls and trucks and they'll demand a television set or a video game, anything that will organize and structure their time for them.

I'm not sure why this happened, or when, but I am almost certain 5 it has something to do with marketing. Making sure children are endlessly stimulated costs money—money that we are told we must spend if our kids are to be successful, productive adults. We are told that computer games will sharpen their minds, karate lessons will make them assertive, and that gymnastics classes will teach them "invaluable social skills." Many of us are ripe for this kind of argument. We are incredibly busy, juggling careers and community service and parenting like so many hot potatoes. We fear that if we miss a beat, look away for a second, the whole mess will come crashing down. We worry about our children wasting time, missing an opportunity that could, some day, help them get ahead, or even just get by. Most of us know intuitively that children need the opportunity to experiment, to fail. But we are afraid to allow them to do so for fear of their falling behind. In these achievement-oriented times, we parents want our kids to work as hard as we do.

Earlier this year, the Atlanta public schools eliminated recess in elementary schools. Other districts have turned to "socialized recess," where children are supervised in structured activities. Games that teach reading and math, frequently with the help of a computer, are encouraged, as is physical education instruction to "enhance motor skills." Many parents support this trend. We like the idea of our children spending all of the school day in structured learning situations. And we don't mind that new schools are being built without playgrounds. As one school administrator put it, you don't improve academic performance "by having kids hanging on the monkey bars."

I beg to differ. Half a century ago, Swiss child psychologist Jean Piaget identified play as critical to the emotional, moral, and intellectual development of children. According to Piaget, kids learn a whole lot while hanging upside down from their knees. They learn that gravity makes their blood rush to their heads. They learn that all that rushing of blood can make them dizzy. And they learn that if they hang too long another kid will push them off. Play and the restless questing energy that provokes it, is, in a sense, childhood's greatest gift. As Susan Isaacs, a pioneering researcher in child development wrote in 1929: "How large a value children's play has for all sides of their growth. And how fatal to go against this great stream of healthy and active impulse in our children! That 'restlessness' and inability to sit still; that 'mischievousness' and 'looking inside' and eternal 'Why?' That indifference to soiled hands and torn clothes for the sake of running and climbing and digging and exploring—these are not unfortunate and accidental ways of childhood which are to be shed as soon as we can get rid of them. They are the glory of the human child, his human heritage. They are at once the representatives in him of human adventurousness and hard-won wisdom, and the means by which he in his turn will lay hold of knowledge and skill, and add to them."

The best play is spontaneous and unpredictable. Adults cannot control it, they can only sit back and let it happen. While we may spend hours building an architecturally correct structure, as pictured on the box of an expensive construction set, our children would rather brainstorm and build their own shaky pile of blocks. It is the *process* of creation, not the product, that naturally interests children, and it is this process that encourages their development as independent thinkers. But it's terribly easy to dampen a child's creativity, especially by insisting that there is a right and wrong way of doing everything, that life is a sort of multiple-choice quiz with adults holding the answer key. By forcing children to follow rules imposed by others, even during what is supposed to be their leisure time, adults can effectively discourage them from believing that they have anything significant to offer. They can turn them from confident and curious explorers, to cautious over-achievers intent on getting it right. Kids like this grow into adults who are edgy and averse to risk, adults who have difficulty thinking for themselves, difficulty creating. Adults like this make awfully good corporate cogs, because they do what they are told. But they don't make particularly good participants in a democratic system because they fail to grasp that "getting it" in the truest sense often has nothing to do with "getting it right."

And "getting it right" is often what "structured play" is all about—organized sports being a prime example. Last fall, Joanna enrolled in a local soccer league. Not surprisingly, neither she nor many of the other seven-year-olds on her team were terribly interested in the rules of the game. What they wanted to do was kick the ball around, schmooze with their friends, and pick three-leaf clovers on the field. But the coaches and the parents would have none of this. Girls whose attention wandered were called back to focus. Girls who stooped to pick a clover were commanded to keep their eyes on the ball. One father, a professor of mathematics who, from his appearance, has spent little time on playing fields himself, pulled his daughter onto his lap and barked in her ear "be A-G-G-R-E-S-S-I-V-E, AGGRESSIVE!" Another dad threw up his hands in disgust when his daughter kicked the ball into the opposing team's goal. Later I heard her promise that she'd "do better" next time. If kept to a minimum, this sort of adult meddling will probably do the girls little harm. But we're fooling ourselves when we gush over all the good such sessions can do for the pre-preteen set. Team spirit and competition are wonderful things, of course, but no thinking person would consider them essential to the psychic or moral development of a second grader. By projecting our own ambitions and needs onto our kids, by insisting, for instance, that kicking a soccer ball into a goal is more important than searching out clovers, we are making implicit judgments—judgments we may come to regret.

Which returns me to the concept of boredom. Maybe it's time we 10 reconsider the concept. Perhaps boredom is not, as we often regard it, a symptom of neglect. Perhaps it's every child's natural-born right. Rather than supervise and coach and guide our children toward some predetermined goal, perhaps we should encourage them to follow their fancy to a goal we can't even imagine. Maybe it's time we gave childhood back to children. Maybe it's time we let them play.

Responding to Reading

1. How does Shell explain why children today are so much more closely supervised than she was as a child? How, specifically, do the lives of today's children differ from the life Shell led as a child?
2. What kinds of structured activities does Shell mention? What others can you think of? What does Shell see as the disadvantages of these kinds of activity? What does she see as the advantages of boredom?
3. This essay, written in 1998, does not mention additional barriers to boredom created in recent years—for example, TV screens installed in back seats of minivans. Can you list other such innovations? Do you see these as positive or negative?

Responding in Writing

Do you think Shell's childhood world still exists anywhere today? Do you think overstructured, overscheduled children can still be "rescued" and taught to use their boredom creatively? If so, how? If not, why not?

PUTTING UP THE GATES

Edward J. Blakely

1938–

Mary Gail Snyder

1965–

Edward J. Blakely is dean of the Robert J. Milano Graduate School of Management and Urban Policy at New School University in New York City. His books include Planning Local Economic Development *(1994) and* Separate Societies *(1993). Mary Gail Snyder, senior research fellow at the National Housing Institute, has written articles and book reviews as well as reports for municipalities. Blakely and Snyder are the coauthors of* Fortress America: Gated Communities in the United States *(1997). In the following essay, an excerpt from their book, they identify different kinds of gated communities and discuss what they see as the negative implications of such communities.*

Gated communities provoke impassioned reactions from supporters and critics alike. In our book, *Fortress America: Gated Communities in the United States,* . . . we question the ability of this increasingly pervasive design tool to meet its security goals and strengthen the sense of community in America.

Over eight million Americans have sought refuge from crime and other problems of urbanization by installing gates and fences to limit access to their communities—and their numbers are growing. Since the mid-1980s, gates have become ubiquitous in many areas of the country. New towns are routinely built with gated villages, and some entire incorporated cities feature guarded entrances. Along with the trend toward gating in new residential developments, existing neighborhoods are increasingly installing barricades and gates to seal themselves off.

Gated communities physically restrict access so that normally public spaces are privatized. They differ from apartment buildings with guards or doormen, which exclude public access to the private space of lobbies and hallways. Instead, gated communities exclude people from traditionally public areas like sidewalks and streets.

Gates—along with fences, private security forces, "residents only" restrictions on public parks, policies to control the homeless, land use policies, large-lot zoning, and other planning tools—are part of a trend throughout the country to restrict or limit access to residential, commercial, and public areas. These turf wars, representing a retreat from the public realm, are a troubling trend. Gated communities are a dramatic manifestation of the fortress mentality growing in America.

The context for the gated community trend is an America increasingly separated by income, race, and economic opportunity, although people with a range of backgrounds live in gated communities. In *Fortress America: Gated Communities in the United States,* we classify gated communities into three major categories. First are the Lifestyle communities, where the gates provide security and separation for the leisure activities within. These include retirement communities and golf and country club leisure developments. Second are the Prestige communities, which lack the amenities of the Lifestyle communities, but where the gates still are valued as markers of distinction and status. The Lifestyle and Prestige communities are developer-built, and primarily suburban. They range from the enclaves of the rich and famous to the subdivisions of the working class.

The third category is the Security Zone, where trouble with crime or traffic and fear of outsiders are the most common motivations. In these cases residents, not developers, install gates and fences to their previously open neighborhoods. While the image of the neighborhood that retrofits itself with gates or barricades is of the embattled moderate-income city community, such closures occur in the inner city and in the suburbs, in neighborhoods of great wealth and in areas of great poverty. Gating is easily done in open private-street subdivisions. In neighborhoods with public streets, it is usually very controversial, as the streets must be taken over from the city before they can be gated off.

This third type of gated community also includes areas, such as Dayton's Five Oaks . . . , with street barricades that create mazes of blocked streets to reduce vehicular access and deter outsiders. Such street barricading occurs in very wealthy neighborhoods and very poor ones, in places where crime is very high and where it is low. This partial solution is used most often in cases of public streets where residents cannot privatize their streets, either because they cannot afford to or they are not legally allowed to. The street barricaded neighborhoods lack the private amenities and complete closure of the others, but are a form of gated community nonetheless. The reasons given for the gates are usually the same—to reduce traffic, deter crime, and make the neighborhood more livable.

Movements to gate public streets in Los Angeles, Houston, Miami, Chicago, and other large cities often lead to bitter battles within and between neighborhoods. Proponents support street closures as an effective crime deterrent that helps maintain neighborhoods, homeownership, and curb middle-class flight to the suburbs. Opponents point to division, the displacement of crime and traffic, and other negative impacts on neighboring areas. Some opponents charge that racism or classism is the real root of a barricade plan, as in the case of the upscale community of Miami Shores, which borders on a poor African-American section of Miami. And when a small, middle-class, ethnically diverse neighborhood in Maplewood, New Jersey, decided to install five barricades near its border with Newark, ostensibly to reduce the flow of traffic using the neighborhood as a short cut, charges by Newark's mayor and other opponents that the closures were elitist and destructive caused a national media stir.

Exclusion and Control

Social distance has long been a goal of American settlement patterns; the suburbs were built on separation and segregation. Today, with a new set of problems pressing on our metropolitan areas, Americans still turn to separation as a solution.

10   Suburbanization has not meant a lessening of segregation, but only a redistribution of the urban patterns of discrimination. Gated communities are a microcosm of the larger spatial pattern of segmentation and separation. In the suburbs, gates are the logical extension of the original suburban drive. In the city, gates and barricades are sometimes called "cul-de-sac-ization," a term that clearly reflects the design goal to create out of the existing urban grid a street pattern as close to the suburbs as possible.

Exclusion imposes social costs on those left outside. It reduces the number of public spaces that all can share, and thus the contacts that people from different socioeconomic groups might otherwise have with each other. The growing divisions between city and suburb and rich and poor are creating new patterns which reinforce the costs that isolation and exclusion impose on some at the same time that they benefit others. Even where the dividing lines are not clearly ones of wealth, this pattern of fragmentation affects us all.

Forts or Communities?

Some argue that gates and barricades are unfortunate but necessary. They feel that such measures are the only way for beleaguered neighborhoods to reclaim their streets and for better-off neighborhoods to protect themselves in the future. But are these expectations realistic? In the course of our field work, we interviewed local law enforcement and analyzed local studies of streets closures. We found no firm evidence of any general permanent reductions of crime in fully gated communities or in the barricaded streets of the Security Zone. In part, this is because most evidence is anecdotal, and it varies greatly. Some Security Zone communities report drops in crime after streets are closed. Some report only temporary drops, and some no change at all. And still other places have removed barricades as failures, such as in Sepulveda, California, where local gangs used the maze of blocked streets to evade police and control their turf.

In addition to this wide variation in the reported effects of street closures, there is the problem that many available reports simply give "before and after" crime rates. Because such information often does not include comparisons with the crime rate in the overall area, or with longer-term trends, it is hard to conclude what effect the barricades themselves really had.

Gates and fences are not impenetrable to serious criminals, and they do nothing to reduce crime arising from residents. They do not necessarily protect, and they often cause dissension and controversy.

Efforts of neighborhoods to take back their streets are inspirational and sorely needed. That many are turning to barricades is understandable. But the issues that stimulate gates, walls, and private security stem in part from the inattention we have paid to building communities. Without community, we have no hope of solving our social problems, or ever really gaining control of our deteriorated neighborhoods. Physical design does have a place in building community and fighting crime; our choices in architecture, street layout, landscaping and design, and lighting all can help neighborhoods to protect themselves from threats. But these physical design choices are best used to facilitate and encourage social, community responses.

Ever since Jane Jacobs,[1] urban designers and planners have recognized that "eyes on the street" are basic defenses against crime. This is

---

[1]Writer and activist Jane Jacobs (1916–) has been credited with changing the way many Americans view cities and their future. Her books, which examine the ways in which cities operate, include *Death and Life of Great American Cities* (1961), *The Economy of Cities* (1969), and *Cities and the Wealth of Nations* (1984). For decades, Jacobs has advocated a common-sense approach to urban development. [Eds.]

the social control of a tightly-knit community. Overall, such socially-based mechanisms are more effective than additional hardware like gates.

We must also remember that the reasons for gating are not always entirely, or even primarily, the laudable reasons of crime and traffic control. Hopes of rising property values, the lure of prestige, and even the desire to build barriers against a poorer neighborhood or one of different race are also common reasons behind gated communities.

What is the measure of nationhood when the divisions between neighborhoods require security patrols and fencing to keep out other citizens? When public services and even local government are privatized, when the community of responsibility stops at the gates, the function and the very idea of democracy is threatened. Gates and barricades that separate people from one another also reduce people's potential to understand one another and commit to any common or collective purpose. In short, gates reduce the opportunity for social contact, and without social contact, this nation becomes less likely to fulfill its social contract.

Responding to Reading

1. What three kinds of gated communities do Blakely and Snyder identify? What do the three have in common? How are they different? Do you see any one of the three as more desirable, or more justifiable, than the others?
2. How do Blakely and Snyder explain the recent trend in the United States toward a "fortress mentality" (4)? Can you think of additional explanations?
3. Blakely and Snyder see the rise of gated communities as an alarming trend. What specific problems do they think such barricades create? Do you agree that gated communities pose more problems than solutions?

Responding in Writing

To what extent are your home, school, and workplace "gated communities"?

SUPERSIZE ME[1]

Greg Critser
1954–

Journalist Greg Critser writes on nutrition, obesity, health, and medical issues. His work has appeared in the New York Times, *the* Wall Street Journal, *and* Harper's Magazine, *and he also writes regularly for* USA Today. *Critser is the author of* National Geographic California *(2000),* Fat

---

[1] In 2004, McDonald's announced that it would phase out supersized portions by the end of the year, citing "menu simplification" as its reason. [Eds.]

Land: How Americans Became the Fattest People in the World *(2003)*, *and, most recently,* Generation Rx: How Prescription Drugs Are Altering American Lives, Minds, and Bodies *(2006). In this excerpt from* Fat Land, *Critser discusses the alarming trend among Americans to consume more and more calories.*

If the wobbly economy of the 1970s had left consumers fulminating over high food prices and the forces that caused them, the same economy had driven David Wallerstein, a peripatetic director of the McDonald's Corporation, to rage against a force even more primal: cultural mores against gluttony. He hated the fifth deadly sin because it kept people from buying more hamburgers.

Wallerstein had first waged war on the injunction against gluttony as a young executive in the theater business. At the staid Balaban Theaters chain in the early 1960s, Wallerstein had realized that the movie business was really a margin business; it wasn't the sale of low-markup movie tickets that generated profits but rather the sale of high-markup snacks like popcorn and Coke. To sell more of such items, he had, by the mid-1960s, tried about every trick in the conventional retailer's book: two-for-one specials, combo deals, matinee specials, etc. But at the end of any given day, as he tallied up his receipts, Wallerstein inevitably came up with about the same amount of profit.

Thinking about it one night, he had a realization: People did not want to buy two boxes of popcorn *no matter what.* They didn't want to be seen eating two boxes of popcorn. It looked . . . piggish. So Wallerstein flipped the equation around: Perhaps he could get more people to spend just a little more on popcorn if he made the boxes bigger and increased the price only a little. The popcorn cost a pittance anyway, and he'd already paid for the salt and the seasoning and the counter help and the popping machine. So he put up signs advertising jumbo-size popcorn.

The results after the first week were astounding. Not only were individual sales of popcorn increasing; with them rose individual sales of that other high-profit item, Coca-Cola.

Later, at McDonald's in the mid-1970s, Wallerstein faced a similar   5 problem: With consumers watching their pennies, restaurant customers were coming to the Golden Arches less and less frequently. Worse, when they did, they were "cherry-picking," buying only, say, a small Coke and a burger, or, worse, just a burger, which yielded razor-thin profit margins. How could he get people back to buying more fries? His popcorn experience certainly suggested one solution—sell them a jumbo-size bag of the crispy treats.

Yet try as he may, Wallerstein could not convince Ray Kroc, McDonald's founder, to sign on to the idea. As recounted in interviews with his associates and in John F. Love's 1985 book, *McDonald's: Behind the Arches,* the exchange between the two men could be quite contentious on the issue. "If people want more fries," Kroc would say, "they can buy two bags."

"But Ray," Wallerstein would say, "they don't want to eat two bags—they don't want to look like a glutton."

To convince Kroc, Wallerstein decided to do his own survey of customer behavior, and began observing various Chicago-area McDonald's. Sitting in one store after another, sipping his drink and watching hundreds of Chicagoans chomp their way through their little bag of fries, Wallerstein could see: People *wanted* more fries.

"How do you know that?" Kroc asked the next morning when Wallerstein presented his findings.

10 "Because they're eating the entire bagful, Ray," Wallerstein said. "They even scrape and pinch around at the bottom of the bag for more and eat the salt!"

Kroc gave in. Within months receipts were up, customer counts were up, and franchisees—the often truculent heart and soul of the McDonald's success—were happier than ever.

Many franchisees wanted to take the concept even further, offering large-size versions of other menu items. At this sudden burst of entrepreneurism, however, McDonald's mid-level managers hesitated. Many of them viewed large-sizing as a form of "discounting," with all the negative connotations such a word evoked. In a business where "wholesome" and "dependable" were the primary PR watchwords, large-sizing could become a major image problem. Who knew what the franchisees, with their primal desires and shortcutting ways, would do next? No, large-sizing was something to be controlled tightly from Chicago, if it were to be considered at all.

Yet as McDonald's headquarters would soon find out, large-sizing was a new kind of marketing magic—a magic that could not so easily be put back into those crinkly little-size bags.

Max Cooper, a Birmingham franchisee, was not unfamiliar with marketing and magic; for most of his adult life he had been paid to conjure sales from little more than hot air and smoke. Brash, blunt-spoken, and witty, Cooper had acquired his talents while working as an old-fashioned public relations agent—the kind, as he liked to say, who "got you into the newspaper columns instead of trying to keep you out." In the 1950s with his partner, Al Golin, he had formed what later became Golin Harris, one of the world's more influential public relations firms. In the mid-1960s, first as a consultant and later as an executive, he had helped create many of McDonald's most successful early campaigns. He had been the prime mover in the launch of Ronald McDonald.

15 By the 1970s Cooper, tired of "selling for someone else," bought a couple of McDonald's franchises in Birmingham, moved his split-off ad agency there, and set up shop as an independent businessman. As

he began expanding, he noticed what many other McDonald's operators were noticing: declining customer counts. Sitting around a table and kibitzing with a few like-minded associates one day in 1975, "we started talking about how we could build sales—how we could do it and be profitable," Cooper recalled in a recent interview. "And we realized we could do one of three things. We could cut costs, but there's a limit to that. We could cut prices, but that too has its limits. Then we could raise sales profitably—sales, after all, could be limitless when you think about it. We realized we could do that by taking the high-profit drink and fry and then packaging it with the low-profit burger. We realized that if you could get them to buy three items for what they perceived as less, you could substantially drive up the number of walk-ins. Sales would follow."

But trying to sell that to corporate headquarters was next to impossible. "We were maligned! Oh were we maligned," he recalls. "A 99-cent anything was heresy to them. They would come and say 'You're just cutting prices! What are we gonna look like to everybody else?'"

"No no no," Cooper would shoot back. "You have to think of the analogy to a fine French restaurant. You always pay less for a *table d'hôte* meal than you pay for *à la carte*, don't you?"

"Yes, but—"

"Well, this is a *table d'hôte*, dammit! You're getting more people to the table spending as much as they would before—and coming more often!"

Finally headquarters relented, although by now it hardly mattered. 20 Cooper had by then begun his own rogue campaign. He was selling what the industry would later call "value meals"—the origin of what we now call supersizing. Using local radio, he advertised a "Big Mac and Company," a "Fish, Fry, Drink and Pie," a "4th of July Value Combo."

Sales, Cooper says, "went through the roof. Just like I told them they would."

Selling more for less, of course, was hardly a revolutionary notion, yet in one sense it was, at least to the purveyors of restaurant food in post-Butzian[2] America. Where their prewar counterparts sold individual meals, the profitability of which depended on such things as commodity prices and finicky leisure-time spending, the fast-food vendors of the early 1980s sold a product that obtained its profitability from a consumer who increasingly viewed their product as a necessity. Profitability came by maintaining the total average tab.

The problem with maintaining spending levels was inflation. By the early Reagan years, inflation—mainly through rising labor costs—had

---

[2]Earl L. Butz (1909–) served as U.S. Secretary of Agriculture from 1971 to 1976. In 1981, he was sentenced to five years in prison for tax evasion. [Eds.]

driven up the average fast-food tab, causing a decline in the average head count. To bring up the customer count by cutting prices was thus viewed as a grand and—despite the anecdotal successes of people like Wallerstein and Cooper—largely risky strategy. But one thing was different: Thanks to Butz, the baseline costs of meat, bread, sugar, and cheese were rising much more slowly. There was some "give" in the equation if you could somehow combine that slight advantage with increased customer traffic. But how to get them in the door?

In 1983 the Pepsi Corporation was looking for such a solution when it hired John Martin to run its ailing Taco Bell fast-food operation. A Harley-riding, Hawaiian shirt–wearing former Burger King executive, Martin arrived with few attachments to fast-food tradition. "Labor, schmabor!" he liked to say whenever someone sat across from him explaining why, for the millionth time, you couldn't get average restaurant payroll costs down.

25   But Martin quickly found out that, as Max Cooper had divined a decade before, traditional cost-cutting had its limits. If you focused on it too much, you were essentially playing a zero-sum game, cutting up the same pie over and over again. You weren't creating anything new. And all the while there were those customers—just waiting to chomp away if you could give them just a nudge to do so.

But did Americans really want to eat more tacos? "We had always viewed ourselves as a kind of 'one-off' brand," Martin recalled in a recent interview. Tacos—or, for that matter, pizza—would always be the second choice to buying a burger. "That caused us to view ourselves as in a small pond—that the competition was other Mexican outlets."

Then Martin met a young marketing genius named Elliot Bloom. A student of the so-called "smart research" trend in Europe, which emphasized the placing of relative "weights" on consumer responses so as to understand what really mattered to a customer, Bloom had completely different ideas about the market for Mexican food. Almost immediately he began running studies on Taco Bell customers. What he found startled: Fast-food consumers were much more sophisticated and open to innovation than previously thought. In fact, they were bored with burgers. Martin loved the idea of competing with McDonald's, and immediately launched a $200 million national ad campaign, the centerpiece of which was a commercial depicting a man threatening to jump off a ledge if he had to eat another hamburger. The results of the campaign were mixed. Sales of some new products, most notably the taco salad, blossomed, but overall customer counts remained vexingly low.

Meantime, Bloom was still playing with consumer surveys, which now revealed something even more surprising: While almost 90 percent of fast-food buyers had already tried Taco Bell, the repeat visit rate of the average consumer was flat. "Reach" wasn't the problem. Frequency was. And when you started studying the customers who *were* coming back—the "heavy users"—price and value—not taste and presentation—were the key. "That was shocking," Martin recalls. "Value was the number-one issue for these guys—and there were a lot of them—30 percent of our customers accounted for 70 percent of sales. For a lot of us, that was disturbing. Our whole culture was sort of 'out of the kitchen,' you know, the notion that taste, cleanliness, and presentation was the key. But that's not what this new kind of customer was about. His message was loud and clear: more for less. So the business question became—how do you create *more* of these guys?"

One way, of course, was to give them what they wanted. But that was discounting, Martin's financial people warned. "I argued with them. I said, 'Look, this isn't stupid discounting, this is a way to right-price the business after a decade of inflation.'"

Bloom suggested an unscientific test of the idea. Let's not make a 30 lot of national noise about this, he said. Let's go someplace where we might get some clean data. There was, in fact, an ideal place to do so. It was Texas, which in the mid-1980s was suffering from one of the worst recessions the oil patch had seen for decades. "We went in and really cut prices and got a dramatic increase in business," Martin says. "We did not make money but it showed us the potential for upping the number of visits per store."

After Martin widened the test, Bloom reported something even better. "Everyone had thought that if we cut 25 percent off the average price of, say, a taco, that the average check size would drop," Martin says. "I never believed that—that satiety was satiety—and, in fact, I was right. Within seven days of initiating the test, the average check was right back to where it was before—it was just four instead of three items." In other words, the mere presence of more for less induced people to eat more.

To get the profit margins back up, Martin turned to what he knew best: cost-cutting. He fired whole swaths of middle managers, then looked at the stores themselves. In them he found what he called a "just plain weird thing, when you thought about it: 30 percent of the typical Taco Bell store was dining area, 70 percent was kitchen. What was that about?" Martin reversed the ratio, ripping out old-fashioned kitchens and sending the bulk of the cooking to off-site preparation centers.

With his margins back up enough to quell upper management fears, Martin took the value meal concept nationwide in 1988. The response was rapid, dramatic, and, ultimately for Taco Bell, transformative. Between 1988 and 1996 sales grew from $1.6 billion to $3.4 billion.

And the value meal was spreading—to Burger King, to Wendy's, to Pizza Hut and Domino's and just about every player worth its salt except . . . David Wallerstein's McDonald's Corporation.

35   Not that McDonald's was hurting. Its aggressive advertising and marketing had by the late 1980s turned it into a global force unparalleled in the history of the restaurant business. It could, in a sense, afford to call its own tune. (Or at least deal with PR disasters, as was the case in the late 1980s, when the firm was under attack by nutritionists and public health advocates for its use of saturated fats.) But by 1990, Martin's Taco Bell value meals were taking their toll on McDonald's sales. Worse, McDonald's lack of a value meal had become a hot topic on Wall Street, where its stock was slumping. Analysts were restless. On December 17, 1990, one of them, a sharp-eyed fast-food specialist at Shearson Lehman named Carolyn Levy, gave an uncharacteristically frank interview to a reporter at *Nation's Restaurant News.* "McDonald's must bite the bullet," she said. "Some people I know in Texas told me it's cheaper to take their kids for a burger and fries at Chili's than to take them to McDonald's." In McDonald's board meetings, Wallerstein and his supporters used the bad press to good effect. Two weeks later the front page of the same newspaper read: "MCDONALD'S KICKS OFF VALUE MENU BLITZ!"

Though it is difficult to gauge the exact impact of supersizing upon the appetite of the average consumer, there are clues about it in the now growing field of satiety—the science of understanding human satisfaction. A 2001 study by nutritional researchers at Penn State University, for example, sought to find out whether the presence of larger portions *in themselves* induced people to eat more. Men and women volunteers, all reporting the same level of hunger, were served lunch on four separate occasions. In each session, the size of the main entree was increased, from 500 to 625 to 750 and finally to 1000 grams. After four weeks, the pattern became clear: As portions increased, all participants ate increasingly larger amounts, despite their stable hunger levels. As the scholars wrote: "Subjects consumed approximately 30 percent more energy when served the largest as opposed to the smallest portion." They had documented exactly what John Martin had realized fifteen years earlier: that satiety is not satiety. Human hunger could be expanded by merely offering more and bigger options.

Certainly the best nutritional data suggest so as well. Between 1970 and 1994, the USDA reports, the amount of food available in the American food supply increased 15 percent—from 3300 to 3800 calories or by about 500 calories per person per day. During about the same period (1977–1995), average individual caloric intake increased by almost 200 calories, from 1876 calories a day to 2043 calories a day. One could argue which came first, the appetite or the bigger burger, but the calories—they were on the plate and in our mouths.

By the end of the century, supersizing—the ultimate expression of the value meal revolution—reigned. As of 1996 some 25 percent of the $97 billion spent on fast food came from items promoted on the basis of either larger size or extra portions. A serving of McDonald's french fries had ballooned from 200 calories (1960) to 320 calories (late 1970s) to 450 calories (mid-1990s) to 540 calories (late 1990s) to the present 610 calories. In fact, everything on the menu had exploded in size. What was once a 590-calorie McDonald's meal was now . . . 1550 calories. By 1999 heavy users—people who eat fast food more than twenty times a month and Martin's holy grail—accounted for $66 billion of the $110 billion spent on fast food. Twenty times a month is now McDonald's marketing goal for every fast-food eater. The average Joe or Jane thought nothing of buying Little Caesar's pizza "by the foot," of supersizing that lunchtime burger or supersupersizing an afternoon snack. Kids had come to see bigger everything—bigger sodas, bigger snacks, bigger candy, and even bigger doughnuts—as the norm; there was no such thing as a fixed, immutable size for anything, because anything could be made a lot bigger for just a tad more.

There was more to all of this than just eating more. Bigness: The concept seemed to fuel the marketing of just about everything, from cars (SUVs) to homes (mini-manses) to clothes (super-baggy) and then back again to food (as in the Del Taco Macho Meal, which weighed four pounds). The social scientists and the marketing gurus were going crazy trying to keep up with the trend. "Bigness is addictive because it is about power," commented Irma Zall, a teen marketing consultant, in a page-one story in *USA Today*. While few teenage boys can actually finish a 64-ounce Double Gulp, she added, "it's empowering to hold one in your hand."

The pioneers of supersize had achieved David Wallerstein's dream. They had banished the shame of gluttony and opened the maw of the American eater wider than even they had ever imagined.

Responding to Reading

1. The original subtitle of this essay was, "Who Got the Calories into Our Bellies?" According to Critser, who got us to consume these calories? Why?
2. Assuming his readers will be familiar with the key terms he mentions, Critser does not define them. Define the terms *fast food, supersizing,* and *value meal,* and give several examples of each.
3. Critser does not consider the long-term effects of supersizing here. What might those effects be? How does satiety, "the science of understanding human satisfaction" (36), explain the probable long-term effects of supersizing?

Responding in Writing

Just as former smokers have successfully sued tobacco makers, several individuals have recently sued McDonald's for contributing to their obesity. Based on what you have read here about supersizing and satiety, do you think McDonald's owes these individuals compensation? Or, do you believe that they themselves are responsible for their weight problems?

THE FASHION VICTIM'S TEN COMMANDMENTS

Michelle Lee

Michelle Lee, a frequent contributor to leading fashion publications, has held editorial positions at several national magazines, including Glamour, Us Weekly, *and* CosmoGirl. *She is also the author of* Fashion Victim: Our Love-Hate Relationship with Dressing, Shopping, and the Cost of Style *(2003). In the following essay from that book, Lee explains the rules that guide those (herself included) whom she calls "Fashion Victims."*

We Fashion Victims hold certain truths to be self-evident. Without so much as a raised eyebrow, we allow a set of ridiculous, yet compelling, rules to govern our wardrobes, our purchases, our desires, even our own sense of self-worth. It's these unquestioned tenets that have helped bring us to the sorry state we find ourselves in today.

Thou Shalt Pay More to Appear Poor

It takes a great deal of time and money to look as though you put no effort into dressing. Since a garment today rarely remains a popular item in our wardrobes beyond a few months, we require it to be worn out before we buy it. Fabrics are prewashed and grayed out to appear less new. Designers sew on decorative patches, slash gaping holes into the knees of jeans, and fray the hems. Dresses and shirts are prewrinkled. Jeans are stonewashed, sandblasted, acid-washed, and lightened; they're iron-creased and bleached to "whisker" at the upper-thigh as if they were passed down to you by your mother, who inherited them from her father, who had worn them in the wheat fields a century ago. Designers add "character" to clothes by messing them up, like Helmut Lang's famous $270 paint-spattered jeans. Jeans, blasted and stained dust-brown, by CK, Levi's, and Dolce & Gabbana, cost up to $200. In fact, Calvin Klein's "dirty" jeans sold for $20 more than a pair of his basic, unblemished ones. In 2001, Commes des Garçons produced a peasant dress, priced at a very unpeasantlike $495, described by discount shopping website Bluefly.com as "given a chic tattered look."

Fashion may be bent on newness, but we apparently can't stand it when something looks *too* new (who can bear the blinding whiteness of new sneakers?). The industry has taken to calling the shabby, imperfect look "distressed"—a word that carries a connotation of pain and suffering. This fashion agony doesn't come cheap, from Jean-Paul Gaultier's distressed leather pants for $1,560 and two-piece distressed leather jacket and bustier for $2,740 to Versace's distressed ball gowns and midpriced shoe maker Aldo's distressed leather pumps for $70.

On most new clothes, a flaw is reason to return a garment to the store; on others, it's a reason to love the garment with even more fervor. The Fashion Victim understands that ready-to-wear clothes are mostly mass produced, and that a handsewn article somehow possesses more soul and uniqueness. Minute blemishes in a fabric's color prove that a gown was hand-dipped by a dressmaker in Paris; slightly raised threads on a vest attest that it was handcrafted by the real wives of authentic sherpas in Nepal. Some clothes, like a sweater I bought years ago, come with tags explaining how the pills and flecks you may see in the fabric are not flaws at all but rather intentional imperfections, there to add to the garment's charm.

In our hunt for substance in style, we covet clothes that evoke the blue-collar world, like the Authentic Prison Blues shirts (actually made by inmates!) that Bruce Willis and Billy Bob Thornton wore in the 2001 movie *Bandits*. Why do we do it? Fashion is our way of visually signaling to others how we want to be seen, and even though we all want to be considered stylish, we don't want to look like we've put too much planning and money into doing so. Glamour and neatness have their place, but premeditated nonchalance is the Fashion Victim's Holy Grail. We shop at stores like Filthmart, the Manhattan vintage store co-owned by Drea de Matteo of *The Sopranos* and featuring Hell's Angels–meets–Jewel wares. Hip-hop fans spend exorbitant amounts of cash on urbanwear to prove they're still "street": a pair of denim and Ultrasuede pants from Phat Farm for $150, an Enyce "bulletproof" nylon vest for $97, puffy down jackets from the North Face for $199. Even a simple wifebeater tank top can sell for over $100 if it has the right label. We buy peasant blouses at faux-boho Anthropologie because we want to look like we churn butter on a farm in Provence, or grungy $80 pants at Urban Outfitters to show our downtown cool. For his fall 2002 Marc by Marc Jacobs show, Jacobs sent models down the runway in mismatched grandma knits, oversized seventies scarves, rainbow-striped sweaters, jeans, and corduroys— the ultimate home-grown poor-girl look for the woman who has everything. In early 2000, John Galliano took the dressed-down look one step further: he stunned the fashion crowd in Paris with his Homeless Chic couture show for Christian Dior, featuring models draped in torn clothes held together by string and strewn with kitchen utensils and miniature liquor bottles.

In the world of the Fashion Victim, shopping at a thrift store is cool . . . unless you're actually on welfare and have to buy *all* your clothes there. Some hard-core fashionistas insist they only shop second hand. But it's usually not all from the buck-a-pound bin at the local thrift store. In recent years, designers like Imitation of Christ who rework vintage and thrift have become hip. The Fashion Victim drools over these born-again garments, which still possess some of the old, dirty charm but at twenty times the price. Today, even the mere implication that a garment is old can suffice. Gap and Abercrombie & Fitch have pilfered the word "vintage" for use on their fresh-from-the-factory shirts and jeans to suggest classic style. Are we really fooled by a crisp new T-shirt that spells Gap Vintage in faded letters?

Today, it's fun to think you're shopping downmarket. "Cheap chic" stores like H&M, Target, Japan's Uniqlo, and Spain's Mango have made fortunes in recent years selling cut-rate trends. But no true fashionista worth her salt would buy her entire wardrobe at one of these stores, so she engages in cheap chic in her own way, to the point at which "cheap" becomes a completely relative term. Moschino's lower-priced line, called Moschino Cheap & Chic, is far from cheap for most shoppers. A "Leopard" coat and scarf retails for $1,340, and a Petal Trim Sweater for $615. Frugality at its finest, indeed.

Thou Shalt Covet Useless Utility

To the Fashion Victim, there's nothing wrong with clothes that serve no purpose other than looking cool. But if a garment can create the illusion that it's functional as well, it's all the better. A part of us knows that fashion is frivolous, so we attempt to justify our participation in it by making our clothes seem useful. We're grasping at straws to rationalize making some of our unnecessary purchases. Shirts come with hoods whose sole purpose is to hang behind one's neck. The polar fleece vest was pitched as functional in a climbing-the-Alps sort of way, but if you really wanted something to keep you warm, wouldn't you give it sleeves? Cargo pants, with their multitude of pockets, seemed infinitely useful . . . imagine all the odds and ends you could carry. Countless designers, including Calvin Klein, Gucci, and Versace, interpreted the military style for the runway, and mall retailers followed suit with their versions, like Abercrombie's Paratroops and American Eagle's Cargo Trek Pant. Ralph Lauren even produced an army-green cargo bikini with pockets at the hip (for toting beach grenades?). The fashion world's idealized image of the utilitarian future appears to involve lots of zippers, buckles, Velcro, pull closures, straps, and strings—no matter if they actually serve a purpose or not.

Judging by the creations we've seen of late, fashions of the future won't serve just one purpose—they'll serve purposes we never knew needed serving. In 2001, women's magazines touted a new pair of panty hose that dispense a tiny bit of lotion onto the legs with each wearing. The Fuji Spinning Company in Japan has developed a T-shirt and lace underwear that will give wearers their daily dose of vitamin C. Newly developed shirts can monitor vital signs like heart rate and breathing patterns by using optical fibers that send and receive electrical impulses. For years, techies have drooled over the advent of "smart clothes," ultramodern garments with fully operational computers implanted in them. The first samples, furnished with round-the-clock Internet access, have been revealed in fashion shows at tech conferences, with models wearing headset microphones and built-in keyboard sleeves. For all the innovation that's been shoveled into fashion, you'd think inventors would be able to come up with something truly useful—like snag-proof cashmere sweaters. Is that so much to ask?

Thou Shalt Own Minutely Differing Variations of the Same Thing

At least part of the Fashion Victim's closet looks like that of a cartoon 10 character, with rows of essentially identical items hanging next to one another. There are multiple pairs of sneakers: a pair for running, a pair for walking, a pair for shopping, a pair for going out, a pair for jeans, a pair for shorts. Then there are the multiple pairs of black pants: wide-legged, skinny-legged, fitted, baggy, flat-front, zipper, button-fly, pleated, wool, stretch, rayon, linen. Former Filipino first lady Imelda Marcos, who once famously defended herself by stating, "I did not have three thousand pairs of shoes, I had one thousand and sixty," surely had some overlapping styles hanging in her gigantic closet.

Fashion Victims own duplicates of items that are just different enough to not be *exactly* the same. The average American owns seven pairs of blue jeans. Certainly, each pair could be cut and colored differently, but are those seven pairs really that different? Rosa, a twenty-six-year-old office manager in Chicago, owns more than fifteen pairs of navy-blue jeans that she's amassed over the last two years, picking up one or two pairs a month. "Some are regular-waisted, some are boot-cut, others are tapered, one has red stitching on the sides and on the pockets, some are button-fly, some are a bit darker," she explains. "Even though they all look the same, they each have their special style." All that variety means she doesn't wear each pair very often. "I have a few clothes that I have in my closet that I've only worn once or twice," she says. "But it's hard to part with them because I always feel like, 'Maybe I'll wear it *one* more time.'" Fashion Victims all share in this mind-set, and as a result, we could have two walk-in closets stuffed to the gills and still never feel like we have enough. So we continue to buy.

Fashion Victims convince themselves that they need variety in their wardrobes; often they aren't aware of how similar all their clothes really are. "Many of my clients are really surprised at the end of an organizing project to learn they own five pairs of black slacks," says Debbie Williams, a personal organizing coach in Houston, Texas, and publisher of *Organized Times.* "They wouldn't dream of wearing black slacks each and every day of the work week, so having five pairs is overkill to say the least—they really could get by with two or three pairs." When the time comes that our closets begin to burst at the seams and a clean-out is necessary, we moan about the effort it takes to dispose of all our unwanted items.

Nevertheless, it's the nature of the Fashion Victim to be a clothing pack rat, to act as an apparel archivist, to collect superfluous garments for the sake of collecting superfluous garments, to fool herself into thinking she needs a new jacket—even though she already owns its lookalike.

Thou Shalt Believe Submissively in the Fashion Label's Reach

Today when you buy a designer's clothes, you're also buying a lifestyle. Ralph Lauren (a.k.a. Ralph Lifschitz from the Bronx) knew this when he created Polo, a brand meant to evoke the image of the affluent, holiday-in-Hyannisport set. As a result, our favorite clothing brands can sell us practically anything else—hand cream, lipstick, perfume, nail polish, dishes, pillows, candles, duvets, music. You can not only wear Ralph Lauren, Calvin Klein, Banana Republic, Eddie Bauer, Donna Karan, Liz Claiborne, Nautica, and Versace, but you can dress your bedroom in them, too. Love how Club Monaco clothes look? Buy the retailer's line of cosmetics. Hooked on Victoria's Secret bras? Well, they must have good skin-care products if they make good bras, right? Like Armani suits? Buy their line of gourmet chocolates. Just as automakers like Jaguar, Vespa, and Harley-Davidson have their own branded clothing lines, retailers and designers have left their mark on the automotive world with special-edition cars like the Eddie Bauer Ford Explorer and Expedition, the Coach-edition Lexus, the Subaru Outback LL Bean edition, the Joseph Abboud Special Edition Buick Regal, and the Louis Vuitton edition of Chrysler's PT Cruiser.

15   A fashion label may be able to excel at auxiliary products, but don't always assume they're made by who you think they are. For decades, designers have known that their illustrious names alone can sell nearly anything, so they engage in multimillion-dollar licensing deals, offering their names for use by others to make and promote a variety of products. In the 1970s, designers like Valentino and Pierre Cardin began to license their names for everything from sheets to luggage to toilet-seat covers (by 1970, the House of Cardin had licensed its name for use on more than six hundred products). Donna Karan reported that its fastest growth segment was in its licensing division—including

accessories, jeans, home, and bath—which grew to over a billion dollars in sales in 2000. Kenneth Cole has admitted that his company licenses out most of what it does, except for shoes and women's handbags.

Some well-known brands actually make the products of *other* well-known brands. Fossil designs, manufactures, markets, and distributes Burberry watches. Perry Ellis manufactures apparel, bags, and accessories under the Nautica label. Liz Claiborne holds the exclusive license to design and produce DKNY jeans. Estée Lauder holds exclusive licensing agreements to make fragrances for both Tommy Hilfiger and Donna Karan. Procter and Gamble, home of Noxzema, Oil of Olay, and Old Spice, also holds licenses for Hugo Boss, Giorgio, Helmut Lang, and Hervé Leger fragrances. Luxottica makes eyewear for Armani, Brooks Brothers, Anne Klein, Moschino, Ungaro, and Ferragamo. Women's outerwear for Kenneth Cole and Nine West is made by the same company—G-III Apparel, which also holds the license for Tommy Hilfiger's leather outerwear for men.

Licensing may help designers expand their businesses, but it's historically been frowned upon in the fashion world. Cardin's newfound middle-brow appeal made him the world's richest couturier but also got him booted out of the Chambre Syndicale, the exclusive supervisory body for haute couture in Paris. By the late 1990s, licensing had fallen out of favor with many luxury designers, with many like Gucci and Armani beginning to buy back their licensing agreements in an attempt to regain brand control. Then there was the much-publicized lawsuit between Calvin Klein and licensee Warnaco in 2000. In his countersuit, Klein alleged that Warnaco CEO Linda Wachner damaged his brand's image by selling to discount stores and putting his name on designs he hadn't approved. Prior to the lawsuit, an unbelievable 90 percent of Klein's revenues came from licenses. The case shed much unwanted light on the practice of licensing. Consumers fretted, "Could our designer clothes actually be made by lesser manufacturers?" Quite the contrary, say designers—licensing actually improves the quality of products, because they pair with the pros. For instance, an expert in hosiery may do a better job at creating a line of silk stockings under the designer's name than the designer could do himself. Frankly, it works both ways. A good number of licensed products are well made while others are essentially generics with designer labels slapped on them. Luckily for them, either will do just fine for the Fashion Victim.

Thou Shalt Require Validation of Thine Own Stylishness

I've always wondered how people felt after they appeared in one of those "On the Street" photos in the *New York Times* Sunday Styles

section, taken by fashion historian/scholar/journalist Bill Cunningham, a thirty-year veteran of the paper, a man whose job it is to
catch the latest fashion trends on real people on the street.
Clotheshorses are snapped as they're walking to Saks during their
lunch break or browsing an outdoor vendor or exiting a bistro with
co-workers. Some of the subjects are unknown; others, like Ivana
Trump, *Vogue* editor Anna Wintour, and socialite/painter Anh
Duong are career fashion plates. Some are clearly posing for the
camera; others are caught unexpectedly, typically engaging in the
Manhattanite's favorite outdoor pastime—nattering on the cell
phone.

Cunningham, who camps out on the sidewalk day in and day out
for up to a month just to photograph enough subjects for one story,
says he never consciously goes out with a specific trend in mind. During Spring Fashion Week 2001, his discerning lens fell upon a former
co-worker of mine outside one of the shows as she flaunted her cute
metal-studded handbag. It was perhaps the least flattering angle at
which I've ever seen her, but ego stroking nonetheless, in a "you have
good enough taste in bags to be in the *New York Times*" kind of way.
Many "On the Street" subjects are proud to be featured there. Cunningham has photographed Patrick McDonald, a public-relations director for a dressmaker, at least a dozen times. McDonald, who keeps
a book of all his clips, told *New York* magazine in 2000, "I have friends
who say, 'I look in the Style section as soon as I get home from the
Hamptons to see if you're in it.'"

20   The art of dress is quite frequently built on the opinions of others.
We may like to think that how we dress is an extension of how we see
ourselves, but more commonly, it's an expression of how we want
others to see us. "We dress to communicate our social identities to others," says Kim Johnson, Ph.D., a professor at the University of Minnesota who teaches courses on the social psychology of clothing.
"Dress informs others of how willing you are to participate in fashion
and at what levels you're playing." In our appearance-centered society, one of the most common ways we butter up strangers and acquaintances is to compliment them on their clothes. We shower
people with praise for their sense of style and expect to receive praise
in return, like the sometimes sincere "You look great," which never
fails to elicit the awkward yet gushing "You do *too.*"

Fashion Victims dress deliberately, and whether the validation of
their stylishness comes in the form of a photograph or a random compliment, that confirmation is all they need to keep going. A few years
back I attended *Paper* magazine's "Beautiful People Party," held at the
ultra-swanky restaurant of the moment, The Park, in Manhattan's
meatpacking district. As guests entered, a photographer selected certain fashionable people to snap, letting others pass. To be waved

through sans photo was like being dissed by the doorman at some snooty nightclub. I was swept up into the crowd and ended up standing next to a six-foot-five-inch gentleman dressed in full Dandy garb, complete with white jacket and chapeau. Sure enough, the photographer thought I was the dapper Dandy's date and encouraged us to smile for the camera. Was it because I, in my rather plain strapless dress, looked particularly smashing that night? Unfortunately, no. I had simply become fashionable by association. Did I feel like one of the Beautiful People that night? You bet.

Thou Shalt Dress Vicariously Through Thy Children and Pets

It's not enough for Fashion Victims to dress themselves in designer clothes; they often feel it necessary to share their impeccable taste with others. Someone once told me, "You give what you want to receive." People choose items for others that reflect their own taste, rather than the recipient's. We Fashion Victims live by this. We dress our kids (and others' children when we buy gifts) in mini-me lines like Moschino kids, GapKids, babyGap, Old Navy Kids, Diesel Kids, Ralph Lauren kids, Prada kids, and Guess? Kids. Small sizes don't mean small prices. A baby leather jacket costs $200 at Polo. A jean jacket from Diesel Kids costs $109—more than a grown-up size at many stores. Then there's the $125 tulle dress for girls by Christian Dior, the $175 sweater by Missoni Kids, the pink knit pant set by Baby Dior, $93 trousers by Young Versace, and $68 bootleg jeans by Diesel. Before Dolce & Gabbana's kiddy line, D&G Junior, ran into some trouble in 2000 when its licensee Nilva went belly up, it carried several categories of clothing like "Denim Rock Star," "Lord Rapper," and "Logomania." There were gold denim jackets, tiny shearling coats, and a red leather racing-team jacket for $599. With most kids' clothes, there's not even the possibility of an outfit becoming a long-lasting part of a wardrobe because they outgrow things so quickly, so laying out exorbitant amounts of cash is truly like throwing money into a bottomless pit.

Fashion Victims also know that true style must rub off on one's pets. We ooh and ahh over cutesy pet fashions, not just the doggy sweaters, bandannas, and plastic booties sold in most pet stores, but rather real designer duds that mirror our own dress. Illustrious labels like Hermès, Louis Vuitton, Prada, Salvatore Ferragamo, and Gucci have gotten in on the act, offering high-priced beds, bags, collars, and leashes. Gucci ignited the trend in 1997 when it released a collar and leash. Louis Vuitton and Prada followed in 1998, and Coach and Burberry in the following years. Gucci sells a brown doggy raincoat for $117. Louis Vuitton introduced LV-monogram leather dog carriers in the seventies; they are still available today for just under $1,000.

And for those with financial constraints, there's always Old Navy's line of poochy fashions. In L.A., Hollywood's pet owners shop at chi-chi Fifi & Romeo, a luxurious boutique that sells a line of hand-knitted cashmere sweaters and wool coats for little dogs that come in sizes like "teacup" and "mini," priced from $100 to $300.

Models tote their grapefruit-sized Yorkies in their Fendi bags as they sit in the makeup chairs at fashion shows. And fashionable folk dine at sidewalk cafés with their debonair doggies fastened to a table leg with $300 leashes. If it's true what they say about dogs looking like their owners, the Fashion Victim must be quite the pampered human.

Thou Shalt Feign Athleticism

25 Today, our fascination with sports goes beyond wearing the jerseys and caps of athletes and teams we like. Shoppers at American Eagle Outfitters can lounge around the house on a Sunday afternoon wearing one of the store's football shirts, a Vintage Rugby, Spin Cycle Trek T, or Motocross T. Few of us have ever taken a hit on the rugby field, but we can dress like those robust lads with rugby shirts from stores like J. Crew, Polo Ralph Lauren, H&M, and the Gap.

Abercrombie & Fitch carries such faux-sporty wares as the Morrill Athletic Knit with a number eight stitched over the heart, Field Events Vintage Track Pants, Mountaineering Windpant, Rock Climbing Crew, Sculling Hooded Fleece (basically just a hooded sweatshirt with a big green 9 sewn on), and the Goal Keeper Nylon Pant for women. Gap carries an entire Gap Athletic line. There's Prada Sport, Polo Sport, and Tommy Sport. Designers even create sport perfumes and colognes that emit clean scents fitting for the fashion-conscious wannabe athlete, like Escada Sport, Benetton Sport, Boss Sport, and Liz Sport. We wear shoes with technical-sounding names like Reebok's Trailzilla III and Nike's Air Terra Humara Slip-on. Fila's Pininfarina shoe was designed in conjunction with the sports car manufacturer of the same name.

Most of our lives are wholly un-rugged, so we attempt to reinsert that missing ruggedness through our wardrobes. Labels like the North Face and Patagonia, which create functional garb for the mountaineering über-athlete, have become fashionable brands to traipse around town in. Timberland boots are as ideal for digging through CDs at the Virgin Megastore as they are for hiking through backwoods Montana. Columbia Sportswear recently produced a parka that detects when the wearer's skin temperature has dropped and releases stored body heat, which will no doubt become a must-have item for those climbing the Himalayas—or picking up an iced latte at Starbucks (*brrrr*).

Those of us who aren't triathletes or marathoners still enjoy examining the sole of a sneaker and seeing very scientific-looking springs, air pockets, gel, and pumps. Employees at the Nike Sport Research Laboratory hold Ph.D.'s or master's degrees in human biomechanics and bioengineering. In March 2002, Adidas introduced ClimaCool sneakers, designed to keep feet cool with a "360-degree ventilation system." Athletic shoe makers spend millions of dollars on research to develop supersneakers that add more bounce, absorb shock, improve traction, and cushion arches. And when the Fashion Victim buys these supersneakers, he is delighted over his purchase and can't wait to wear them when he meets his buddies for a drink, no doubt at the local sports bar.

Thou Shalt Be a Walking Billboard

The fashion industry is filled with bright ideas thought up by marketing opportunists, from the famous logo print of Louis Vuitton to the ubiquitous Polo emblem, the conspicuous A/X printed on Armani Exchange T-shirts, the unmistakable Nike swoosh, and the name of skatewear company Fuct emblazoned on a sweatshirt. In 2001, Kenneth Cole, Tommy Hilfiger, and Aldo shoes released lines of handbags that touted their designers' names in Steven Sprouse—like graffiti. When Ja Rule wears Burberry's signature plaid in his videos, he provides the company with a free subliminal ad that reaches millions of people, without even uttering the word *Burberry.*

Logophilia hit a high in the 1980s, then dipped in the less showy 30 1990s. But in 2000, it kicked into full gear again with brand names and logo prints splashed across everything from the most downmarket to the most luxurious items. "Quite a bizarre trend if you analyze it too deeply," says Shelly Vella, fashion director of *Cosmopolitan* UK. "People normally associate wearing logoed merchandise with the need to advertise wealth and buying power: 'Look at my Versace sweatshirt, Gucci jeans, etc.' In decades past, sophisticated designer-ism was about quiet elegance and style—connoisseurs could recognize the cut of a good designer garment. Somehow, in the late nineties, Louis Vuitton logo-itis caught on and everything from Macs to bags, shoes, and tops bore a logo. I saw that whole trend as an attempt—very successful—by designers to reestablish the 'cult of the designer' and to market conspicuous consumption as cool."

In a way, wearing a logo is like wearing gang colors. Just as the Bloods and Crips brandish red and blue bandannas, the Fashion Victim wears the designer logo as a proud badge of membership. It's an act that's tribal at its core. "It's like schoolchildren all nagging for the coolest trainers [sneakers, for you non-Anglophiles]," says Vella. "If you're seen to be wearing the right thing, you're in."

A brand name can add immediate "worth" to two identical products. "Branding is unfortunately the cornerstone of many fashion labels today—not the design, the innovation, the cut, or any other skill honed by the designer. And what the brand stands for is everything," says Debi Hall, fashion-branding strategist for JY&A Consulting in London. "As the Japanese say, name is the first thing—without a name, a garment in today's highly capitalistic, value-added culture is worth very little. Take the vintage phenomenon: even if a secondhand YSL dress is without a label, because it once had a name, it is still worth something. If, however, it is simply a secondhand dress with a name nobody has heard of, then it will go for pennies."

Still, not every Fashion Victim is so taken with the visible logo. Some fashion-conscious folk have been known to consider a visible label such a dealbreaker that they'll take the time to remove it. A few years back, hipsters in London started a trend by tearing the *N* off their New Balance sneakers. And according to *New York* magazine, the late Carolyn Bessette Kennedy once had employees cut the labels out of skiwear she had bought. Emily Cinader Woods, cofounder and chairman of J. Crew, says that unlike her friend Michael Jeffries—CEO of Abercrombie & Fitch, a company notorious for slapping its name conspicuously on everything—she's always been adamant about no logos. "There are so many brands that you might love an item or the color but the logo keeps you from buying it," she says. On the other hand, when you're around people who are familiar with various brands—as is typical for the Fashion Victim—it's possible to be a walking billboard without ever displaying the brand name on your body. I once wore a sleeveless J. Crew top to the office, and two co-workers that day remarked in passing, "I like that—J. Crew?" The brand's familiar look and prevalence in their mail-order catalogs had made the clothes recognizable enough that they didn't need an obvious swoosh, polo player, or little green alligator sewn across the chest. I had been a moving J. Crew billboard all day without the presence of any visible logos.

Thou Shalt Care about Paris Hilton's Gaultier Micro-Mini

Although some might argue that the socialite as we once knew her is dead, her successor's social calendar is still jam packed, and her list of contacts in the fashion industry is growing by the New York minute. Fashion glossies like *W* and *Vogue* regularly feature young butterflies like Alexandra Von Furstenberg, Rena Sindi, Aerin Lauder, Brooke de Ocampo, and the Hilton sisters mugging for photographers amid the hip DJs, models, movie stars, and artists who are typically their fellow revelers. The Fashion Victim devours the photos with delight, checking out the Dior gown that Karen Groos wore to an AIDS benefit or the Celine sheath that Pia Getty wore to a summer soiree, knowing little about who these people are except that they're in a magazine, they're rich, and they're incredibly well dressed.

Our fascination with the Junior Jet-setter is somewhat puzzling. 35 She sometimes holds a glamorous job, like contributing editor at a magazine, or even perhaps heads up a relative's business empire, but it's an occupation that would not necessarily garner the same level of press attention for some other person in a similar position. For example, Aerin Lauder may be the executive director of creative marketing for family biz Estée Lauder, but you certainly wouldn't see someone with the same title at Lancôme or Elizabeth Arden in the pages of *Vogue* eight times a year. The Junior Jet-setter often has a famous last name, like Rockefeller or Von Furstenberg, but, again, a well-known surname on its own doesn't necessarily guarantee anyone an overwhelming number of glam photo ops (just look at Sean Lennon).

The socialite's role in the fashion game is to look stunning at events in couture gowns, and casually upper class when attending a summer soiree in the Hamptons. A gossipworthy socialite should be trailed by at least one rumor of out-of-control partying, like making out with someone other than her date or accidentally letting her Galliano gown slip down and flashing her fellow partygoers. Her job is to *be* the answer to the question: "Who actually wears those clothes?" These are the women who can afford the Fendi furs and Gucci pantsuits, but like celebrities, they are also the frequent recipients of loans and freebies from designers—residing below the A-List celebrity, but above B-List TV actresses and pop stars in the fashion hierarchy. In magazines, they seem somehow superhuman. Mostly whippet-thin (perfect for fitting into the sample size), the pretty and privileged attend trunk shows, where they're wined, dined, and shown exquisite new designs. Their job description also includes sitting front row at catwalk shows. Of course, these women are expected to do something in return: they are obliged to wear (and showcase) the designer's clothes. It would be social suicide for a Junior Jet-setter to show up in a Gucci dress at a Versace show. The smart socialite knows this: a few seasons back in Paris, Brooke de Ocampo was seen in Celine at the Celine show and then Dior at the Dior show—both on the same day.

The fashion system is built on want. Looking at socialites' clothes in *Vogue* is like drooling over the estates in *Architectural Digest* or flipping through the *DuPont Registry* to catch a glimpse of the Bentleys and Aston Martins you'll never be able to afford. We live vicariously through the socialite—who has deep enough pockets to buy designer threads of a caliber most of us will never even see in person. Perplexing as our interest may be, the Fashion Victim eats up every morsel, but not without a tinge of jealousy, of course. "I *love* looking at those rich bitches," says Rita, a forty-nine-year-old website editor in Stamford, Connecticut. "But what kills me is that a lot of them don't really have great taste—they just have great resources. If they had to put together a wardrobe like the rest of us mere mortals—from the Gap, Banana Republic, etc.—I doubt they'd be so fabulous. But you do get good fashion ideas from looking and it's nice to daydream."

Thou Shalt Want without Seeing

Curiously, selling clothes today does not always require actually *showing* the clothes. "Sex sells, sells, and keeps selling," says Marc Berger, fashion director of *GQ.* "A sexy woman in an ad will always grab the attention of a man. It's a great marketing ploy." The no-show advertising technique is frequently justified with "We're selling an image." Ads are another example of fashion's hypnotic power over us. All a company needs to do is get our attention—whether or not we love the clothes is insignificant. In recent years, Abercrombie & Fitch's controversial magalog, the *A&F Quarterly,* has raised eyebrows with its photos of tanned all-American dudes and dudettes, often with zero body fat and zero clothing—a buff naked guy holding a film reel in front of his privates, a couple wearing nothing but body paint, a group of disrobed guys flashing their smiles (and nearly everything else) by the pool. The image: cool, horny coeds. In 1999, a Sisley campaign shot by Terry Richardson simply showed the faces of two female models in a half-sexy, half-goofy liplock. Two years later, an ad for the retailer featured a self-portrait of the moustached Richardson wearing a snake around his neck and nothing else. The image: sexy, slightly dirty. Then there was an Ungaro print ad a few years back showing a werewolf licking a woman's bare body, which was widely condemned for being overly graphic. The image? Anyone's guess. Perhaps the most controversial campaign of late comes from French Connection. To announce the opening of its largest store ever, the retailer took out a full-page ad in a London paper that read. "The World's Biggest FCUK," flaunting the company's easily misread acronym (think of the poor dyslexics!).

Some industry experts think the sex pitch has gone too far. Others say it's all in the *way* it's done. Fashion straddles the line between art and commerce, and so do its ads. In 2001, a magazine and billboard ad campaign for Yves Saint Laurent featuring a nude Sophie Dahl laid out on her back as if in orgasmic rapture created a firestorm of controversy. Some people viewed it as art, like a nude painting or sculpture, while others considered it a shameless ploy for attention. *Vogue* Australia editor Kirstie Clements has nixed ads in the past for being too overtly sexual. "Sex sells *Cosmo,* but not so much *Vogue,*" says

Clements. "I've rejected an ad for sex aids, but I have no problem with the Sophie Dahl YSL ads. I think they're very chic. Sexy for us has to be chic and sexy. A sexy-looking Gisele sells, yes. But a girl in bondage, no. Depends on your product."

Sex isn't the only trick in the book. Today, premeditated weird- 40 ness has just as much pull as a gratuitous glimpse of flesh. In 2000, menswear label Daniel Christian's fall ad campaign showed only the face of a wrinkly old woman with the message "buy a Daniel Christian shirt or pair of jeans and the bag comes free." Who *wouldn't* want to buy a pair of jeans after seeing that? "These ads also work because there's so much word of mouth and so many articles about them in the newspapers and other media," says Arthur Asa Berger, author of *Ads, Fads and Consumer Culture*. "If you can create an ad that gets talked about in television news shows and written about in newspapers, you're getting a lot of free publicity . . . for the brand." One of the revolutionaries in this seemingly illogical method of advertising was Benetton, whose ads in the eighties and nineties ranged from the harmless (two smiling children) to the provocative (a duck covered in crude oil) to the controversial (death row inmates). Oliviero Toscani, who photographed the confrontational ads and was dropped shortly after the death row campaign, always maintained that it wasn't *his* duty to sell the clothes—it was the company's. Oh, Oliviero, how we miss you.

Responding to Reading

1. Lee begins her essay by stating that fashion victims like herself "allow a set of ridiculous, yet compelling, rules to govern our wardrobes, our purchases, our desires, even our sense of self-worth" (1). In what sense are the rules she lists "compelling"? In what sense are they "ridiculous"? Who (or what) do you think is responsible for creating "fashion victims"?
2. Which of Lee's rules do you see as essentially harmless? Which, if any, do you find depressing, or even alarming? What is Lee's attitude toward the "ten commandments" she lists? Does she actually accept these commandments as articles of faith, or does she convey impatience or even contempt?
3. Look through some images in a fashion magazine (including advertising photos). Which of Lee's "ten commandments" could each image illustrate?

Responding in Writing

Write a paragraph that uses the second sentence of Lee's essay as your topic sentence. Support this topic sentence with ten additional sentences, each of which paraphrases one of Lee's "ten commandments" and supplies an illustration. Add a final sentence that summarizes the paragraph's main idea. When you edit your paragraph, make sure you have included appropriate transitions between sentences.

—— Focus ——

Can We Build Real Communities Online?

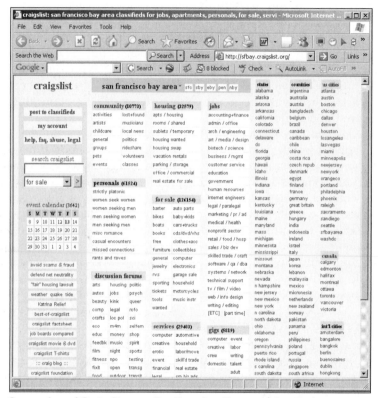

Screen shot of Craigslist.com San Francisco Bay area classifieds

Responding to the Image

1. The image above shows classified ads on the Web site Craigslist.com. Study the categories by which information is arranged visually. What kinds of information can be found through this site? What kinds of connections might visitors to the site make?

2. In what sense does the Craigslist site help to create a community? How is this community different from traditional ones? What advantages and disadvantages does it have over traditional communities?

CONNECTING COMMUNITIES: ON AND OFFLINE

Barry Wellman

1942–

Sociology professor and director of NetLab at the University of Toronto, Barry Wellman has been studying the nature of communities and social networks for decades. He has coauthored numerous articles and coedited three books, most recently, with Caroline Haythornthwaite, The Internet in Everyday Life *(2002). The following essay explores the ways in which traditional and Internet communities intersect to enhance relationships and lifestyles.*

The 2004 documentary film *Almost Real* tells true-life Internet stories. For some characters, the Internet provides an escape from human interaction. A recluse living alone on an abandoned North Sea oil rig runs a data storage haven supposedly free of government interference. An antisocial 8-year-old boy hides from his schoolmates through home schooling and the Web. Meanwhile, the Internet brings other people together. A man and woman in a bondage and domination relationship communicate daily over webcams thousands of miles apart. And teenagers socialize by incessantly playing a cooperative online game.

These stories are fascinating but misleading because they describe people whose social lives are wholly online. Few people dedicate most of their waking lives to the Internet. The Internet usually supplants solitary activities, like watching television, rather than other forms of social life. Most uses of the Internet are not "almost real," but are actual, quite normal interactions. The Internet has become an ordinary part of life.

Consider my own use. I have received several email messages in the past hour. Friends confirm dinner for tonight. Even though it is the weekend, a student sends a question and expects a quick answer. So does a graduate student from Europe, with an urgent request for a letter of recommendation. Cousin Larry shares some political thoughts from Los Angeles. I arrange to meet friends at a local pub later in the week. My teenage niece avoids email as "for adults," so I send her an instant message. And one of my most frequent correspondents writes twice: Ms. Miriam Abacha from Nigeria, wanting yet again to share her millions with me.

In addition to communication, the Internet has become an important source of information. To check facts for this article, I use Google to search the Web. It is too rainy to go out and buy a newspaper, so I skim my personalized Yahoo! News instead. My friend Joe is driving to my house for the first time and gets his directions online from MapQuest.

5   The Internet has burrowed into my life, but is not separate from the rest of it. I integrate offline and online activities. I email, chat, web search and instant message—but I also walk, drive, bike, bus, fly, phone and send an occasional greeting card. I am not unique. Both the exotic aura of the Internet in the 1990s and the fear that it would undermine "community" have faded. The reality is that using the Internet both expands community and changes it in subtle ways.

Digital Divides

Between 1997 and 2001, the number of Americans using computers increased by 27 percent—from 137 million to 174 million—while the online population rose by 152 percent. Nielsen NetRatings reported in March 2004 that three-quarters of Americans over the age of two had accessed the Internet. Many used the Internet both at home and at work, and about half went online daily. Instant messaging (IM) has spread from teenagers to adults in growing popularity, with more than one-third of all American adults now IM-ing.

A decade ago, the Internet was mainly North American, and largely the domain of young, educated, urban, white men. It has since become widely used. About one-third of users live in North America, one-third in Europe and Japan, and one-third elsewhere. India and China host many users, although the percentages of their population who are online remain small. China now has the second largest number of Internet users, growing from half a million in 1997 to 80 million in January 2004. Although the proliferation of computers is no longer headline news, 41 million PCs were shipped to retailers and customers worldwide in the first quarter of 2004.

As more people go online, the digital divide recedes. Yet even as the overall percentage of people online rises, differences in usage rates persist: between affluent and poor, young and old, men and women, more and less educated, urban and rural and English and non-English readers. Moreover, there are substantial international differences, even among developed countries. For instance, the digital divide between high-income households and low-income households ranges from a gap of more than 60 percentage points in the United Kingdom to less than 20 percentage points in Denmark. In the United States, 79 percent of relatively affluent people (family income of $75,000 or more) were Internet users in September 2001, when just 25 percent of poor people (family income of less than $15,000) were online. And while the gender gap is shrinking in many developed countries, it is increasing in Italy and Germany as men get connected at a higher rate than women. Moreover, the digital divide cuts several ways. For instance, even among affluent Americans, there was a 31 percentage point gap in Internet access between those with a university education (82 percent) and those with less than a high school education (51 percent).

Digital divides are particularly wide in developing countries, where users tend to be wealthy, students, employees of large corporations or people with easy access to cybercafes. The risk of a "digital penalty" grows as Internet use among organizations and individuals becomes routine. Those without access to the Internet will increasingly miss out on information and communication about jobs, social and political news and community events.

The many who are using the Internet and the many more who will eventually use it face the question of how the experience might affect their lives. Fast messages, quick shopping and instant reference works aside, widespread concerns focus on the deeper social and psychological implications of a brave new computer-mediated world.

Hopes, Fears and Possibilities

Just a few years ago, hope for the Internet was utopian. Entrepreneurs saw it as a way to get rich, policy makers thought it could remake society, and business people hoped that online sales would make stock prices soar. Pundits preached the gospel of the new Internet millennium. For example, in 1995, John Perry Barlow, co-leader of the Electronic Frontier Foundation, said, "We are in the midst of the most transforming technological event since the capture of fire. I used to think that it was just the biggest thing since Gutenberg, but now I think you have to go back farther."

The media generally saw the Internet as a weird, wonderful and sometimes scary thing. The cover of the December 1999 issue of *Wired* depicted a lithesome cyber-angel leaping off a cliff into the glorious unknown. Major newspapers unveiled special Internet sections, and new computer magazines became fat with ads, advice and influence. The meltdown of the dot-com boom in March 2000 snuffed out many dreams of a radiant Internet future. The pages of *Wired* magazine shrank by 25 percent from September 1996 to September 2001 and another 22 percent by September 2003. Revenue and subscription rates also plummeted. The editors ruefully noted in February 2004 that their magazine "used to be as thick as a phone book."

The advent of the Internet also provoked fears of personal danger and the loss of community. News media warned of men posing as women online, cyber-stalking, identity theft and dangerous cyber-addiction. As recently as March 2004, computer scientist John Messerly warned that "computer and video games . . . ruin the social and scholastic lives of many students."

Much of the hype and fear about the Internet has been both *presentist*—thinking that the world started anew with its advent—and *parochial*—thinking that only things that happened on the Internet were relevant to understanding it. Yet, sociologists have long known that technology by itself does not determine anything. Rather, people take technology and use it (or discard it) in ways its developers never dreamed. For example, the early telephone industry marketed its technology simply as a tool for practical business and spurned the notion that it could be a device for sociability. Indeed, telephones, airplanes and automobiles enabled far-flung communities to flourish well before the coming of the Internet.

Technologies themselves neither make nor break communities. Rather, they create possibilities, opportunities, challenges and constraints for what people and organizations can do. For example, automobiles and expressways make it possible for people to live in sprawling suburbs, but they do not determine that people will do so. Compare the sprawl of American cities with the more compact suburbs of neighboring Canada. The Internet's low cost, widespread use, asynchronicity (people do not have to be connected simultaneously), global connectivity, and attachments (pictures, music, text) make it possible to communicate quickly and cheaply across continents and oceans. For example, emigrants use email to chat with family and friends back home and visit Web sites to learn home news. *Yahoo! India Matrimonial* links brides and grooms in India, Europe and North America. In countries with official censorship, emigrants use email to gather news from back home and post it on Web sites for information hungry readers. Thus, the Internet allows mobile people to maintain community ties to distant places and also supports face-to-face ties closer to home.

Community Online and Offline

15 Online communication—email, instant messaging and chat rooms—does not replace more traditional offline forms of contact—face-to-face and telephone. Instead, it complements them, increasing the overall volume of contact. Where some had feared that involvement in the Internet would detract from "real life" ties with friends and relatives, intensive users of email contact others in person or by phone at least as frequently as those who rarely or never use the Internet. People who frequently use the Internet to contact others also tend to be in frequent contact with people in other ways (even after taking into account differences of age, gender and education). Extroverts especially benefit from its use, simply adding another means of communication to their contact repertoire. For example, a 2001 National Geographic survey reports that North Americans who use email to discuss important matters do so an average of 41 times per month, in addition to having an average of 84 face-to-face discussions and 58 phone discussions. Those who do not use email to discuss important matters have about the same number of monthly face-to-face discussions, 83, but only 36 phone discussions. Thus, those who use email report 183 significant discussions per month, 54 percent more than for those who do not use email. The result: the more email, the more overall communication.

This is not surprising, because the Internet is not a separate world. When we talk to people about what they do on the Internet, we find out that the great majority of the people they email are people they know already. They are keeping in touch between visits, often by exchanging jokes, sharing gossip or arranging to get together. If they email someone they have not already met in person, they are frequently arranging a face-to-face meeting. Telephone calls also get intermixed with emails, because phone chats better convey nuances, provide more intrinsic enjoyment and better accommodate complex discussions. Andrea Baker's book *Double-Click* reports that few cyberdates stay online; they either proceed to in-person meetings or fade away. People also bring to their online interactions such offline baggage as their gender, age, family situation, lifestyle, ethnicity, jobs, wealth and education.

Email is not inherently better or worse than other modes of communication. It is just different. Emails are less intrusive than visits or phone calls and often come with useful attachments, be they baby pictures or maps to someone's home. The spread of high-speed ("broadband") Internet access makes it easier for people to integrate the Internet into the rest of their lives without long waits. By April 2004, 39 percent of U.S. Internet users had broadband at home and 55 percent either at work or home. Broadband means that people can always leave their Internet connection on so that they can spontaneously send emails and search Web sites. Broadband connections also make it easier to surf the Web and download large image, music and video files.

The longer people have been on the Internet, the more they use it. Most Americans—and many in the developed world—have online experience. According to the Pew Internet and American Life study, by February 2004 the average American had been using the Internet for six years. Internet use is becoming even more widespread as home users get access to broadband networks and as access proliferates from deskbound computers to small portable devices such as "third-generation" mobile phones and personal digital assistants (Palm, Pocket PC). Yet, these small-screen, small-keyboard, lower-speed instruments are used differently than computers: to contact a small number of close friends or relatives or to coordinate in-person meetings. Far from homogenizing people's communications, Internet technology is used in different ways by different people.

The Internet Globally and Locally

A decade ago analysts believed that as the rest of the world caught up to the United States in Internet use, they would use it in similar ways. Experience shows that this is not always so. For example, in Scandinavia and Japan, people frequently use advanced mobile phones to exchange email and short text messages. Their Internet use is much less desktop-bound than that of Americans. Teens and young adults are especially heavy users of email on their Internet-connected mobile telephones. Time will tell whether young people continue their heavy mobile use as they get older. Manuel Castells and his associates have shown that people in Catalonia, Spain use the Internet more for information and services than for communication. They extensively search the Web to answer questions and book tickets, but they are much less likely to exchange emails. This may be because many Catalans live near each other and prefer to meet in cafés at night. Mobile phones sit beside them, ready to incorporate other close friends and relatives into conversations via short text messages. Many developing countries exhibit a different mode of use. Even if people can afford to connect to the Internet from their homes, they often do not have reliable electrical, telephone or broadband service. In such situations, they often use public access points such as Internet cafés or schools. They are connecting to the Internet while their neighbors sit next to them in person.

20   Such complexities illuminate the role the Internet can play in specifically local communities. The issue is whether the Internet has fostered a "global village," to use Marshall McLuhan's phrase, and thereby weakened local community. Some intensive and engrossing online communities do exist, such as the "BlueSky" group of young male friends who appear to live online, as described by Lori Kendall in her book *Hanging Out in the Virtual Pub*. Yet, they are a small minority. Despite the Internet's ability to connect continents at a single bound, it does not appear to be destroying local community.

For example, in the late 1990s Keith Hampton and I studied "Netville" near Toronto, a suburban housing tract of middle-priced single-family homes. The teachers, social workers, police officers and technicians who lived there were typical people buying homes to raise young families. The community was exceptional in one important way: As part of an experiment by the telephone company, many residents were given free, high-speed Internet access and became members of a neighborhood email discussion group.

When we compared those who were given this Internet access with those who did not receive it, we found that those on the Internet knew the names of three times as many neighbors as those without Internet access. The "wired" residents had been invited into the homes of an average of 4 neighbors, compared to 2.5 for the unwired, and they regularly talked with twice as many neighbors. The Internet gave wired residents opportunities to identify others in the neighborhood whom they might want to know better. Email and the discussion group made it easier for them to meet fellow residents who were not their immediate neighbors: the wired residents' local friends were more widely dispersed throughout Netville than those of the unwired. The email discussion group was frequently used to discuss common concerns.

These included household matters such as plumbing and yardwork, advice on setting up home computer networks, finding a local doctor, and skills for hire such as those of a tax accountant or carpenter. As one resident commented on the discussion group: "I have walked around the neighborhood a lot lately and I have noticed a few things. I have noticed neighbors talking to each other like they have been friends for a long time. I have noticed a closeness that you don't see in many communities."

Not only did these wired residents talk to and meet one another more, they did most of Netville's civic organizing online, for example, by warning neighbors about suspicious cars in the development and inviting neighbors to social events such as barbeques and block parties. One typical message read: "For anybody interested there is a Sunday night bowling league looking for new people to join. It's lots of fun with prizes, playoffs and more. For both ladies and gents. If interested e-mail me back or give me a call."

These community activities built bonds for political action. When irate Netville residents protested at City Hall against the developer's plans to build more houses, it was the wired Internet members who organized the protest and showed up to make their voices heard. Others grumbled, just like new residents of housing developments have often grumbled, but the Internet supplied the social bonds and tools for organizing, for telling residents what the issues were, who the key players were and when the protest would be.

The Netville experience suggests that when people are offered an easier way of networking with the Internet, the scope and amount of neighborly contact can increase. Evidence from other studies also shows that the Internet supports nearby relationships. For example, the National Geographic Society asked visitors to its website about their communication with friends and relatives living within a distance of 30 miles. Daily Internet users contacted nearby friends and relatives 73 percent more often per year than they contacted those living further away.

At the same time, the Internet helped Netville's wired residents to maintain good ties with, and get help from, friends and relatives who lived in their former neighborhoods. The evidence shows that Internet users are becoming "glocalized," heavily involved in both local and long-distance relationships. They make neighborly contacts—on- and offline—and they connect with far-flung friends and relatives—mostly online.

"Networked Individualism"

As the Internet has been incorporated into everyday life, it has fostered subtle changes in community. In the old days, before the 1990s, places were largely connected—by telephone, cars, planes and railroads. Now with the Internet (and mobile phones), people are connected. Where before each household had a telephone number, now each person has a unique email address. Many have several, in order to keep different parts of their lives separate online. This change from place-based community to person-based community had started before the Internet, but the developing personalization, portability and ubiquitous connectivity of the Internet are facilitating the change. By April 2004, 17 percent of American users could access the Internet wirelessly from their laptop computers and the percentage is growing rapidly. As wireless portability develops from desktops to laptops and handheld devices, an individual's whereabouts become less important for contact with friends and relatives.

The Internet and other new communication technologies are facilitating a basic change in the nature of community—from physically fixed and bounded groups to social networks, which I call "networked individualism." These technologies are helping people to personalize their own communities. Instead of being rooted in homes, cafés and workplaces, people are becoming connected as individuals, available for contact anywhere and at anytime. Instead of being bound up in a neighborhood community where all know all, each person is becoming an individualized switchboard, linking a unique set of ties and networks. In a society where people rarely know friends of friends, there is more uncertainty about who will be supportive under what circumstances, more need to navigate among partial social networks and more opportunity to access a variety of resources. The Internet provides communication and information resources to keep in closer touch with loved ones—from new friends to family members left behind in international migrations.

Responding to Reading

1. How does Wellman refute the idea that the Internet offers "an escape from human interaction" (1)? Do you think his own experience with the Internet, described in paragraphs 3–5, constitutes convincing support for his view that "using the Internet both expands community and changes it in subtle ways" (5)? What other support does he offer for this position?
2. What does the "Netville" experiment described in paragraphs 21–26 show about the role of the Internet in building community?
3. What does Wellman mean by "'networked individualism'" (28)? In what sense does he see it as superior to traditional social networks? How is it different from the social interaction in coffeehouses as described in "The Internet in a Cup" (p. 351)?

Responding in Writing

In paragraph 15, Wellman says, "Online communication—email, instant messaging and chat rooms—does not replace traditional offline forms of contact—face-to-face and telephone. Instead, it complements them, increasing the overall volume of contact." Using examples from your own experience and observations, support or refute Wellman's statement.

WHAT ADOLESCENTS MISS WHEN WE LET THEM GROW UP IN CYBERSPACE

Brent Staples

1951–

After earning a Ph.D. in psychology from the University of Chicago in 1977, Brent Staples turned to journalism, writing for the Chicago Sun-Times *and the* New York Times. *In 1990, he joined the editorial board of the* New York Times, *where his columns now appear regularly. In the following* Times *column, Staples argues that so-called online communities isolate adolescents and hinder their social development.*

My 10th-grade heartthrob was the daughter of a fearsome steel-worker who struck terror into the hearts of 15-year-old boys. He made it his business to answer the telephone—and so always knew who was calling—and grumbled in the background when the conversation went on too long. Unable to make time by phone, the boy either gave up or appeared at the front door. This meant submitting to the intense scrutiny that the girl's father soon became known for.

He greeted me with a crushing handshake, then leaned in close in a transparent attempt to find out whether I was one of those *bad* boys who smoked. He retired to the den during the visit, but cruised by the living room now and then to let me know he was watching. He let up after some weeks, but only after getting across what he expected of a boy who spent time with his daughter and how upset he'd be if I disappointed him.

This was my first sustained encounter with an adult outside my family who needed to be convinced of my worth as a person. This, of course, is a crucial part of growing up. Faced with same challenge to day, however, I would probably pass on meeting the girl's father—and outflank him on the Internet.

Thanks to e-mail, online chat rooms and instant messages—which permit private, real-time conservations—adolescents have at last succeeded in shielding their social lives from adult scrutiny. But this comes at a cost: teenagers nowadays are both more connected to the world at large than ever, and more cut off from the social encounters that have historically prepared young people for the move into adulthood.

The Internet was billed as a revolutionary way to enrich our social 5 lives and expand our civic connections. This seems to have worked well for elderly people and others who were isolated before they got access to the World Wide Web. But a growing body of research is showing that heavy use of the Net can actually isolate younger socially connected people who unwittingly allow time online to replace face-to-face interactions with their families and friends.

CHAPTER 5 FOCUS

Online shopping, checking e-mail and Web surfing—mainly solitary activities—have turned out to be more isolating than watching television, which friends and family often do in groups. Researchers have found that the time spent in direct contact with family members drops by as much as half for every hour we use the Net at home.

This should come as no surprise to the two-career couples who have seen their domestic lives taken over by e-mail and wireless tethers that keep people working around the clock. But a startling body of research from the Human-Computer Interaction Institute at Carnegie Mellon has shown that heavy Internet use can have stunting effect outside the home as well.

Studies show that gregarious, well-connected people actually lost friends, and experienced symptoms of loneliness and depression, after joining discussion groups and other activities. People who communicated with disembodied strangers online found the experience empty and emotionally frustrating but were nonetheless seduced by the novelty of the new medium. As Prof. Robert Kraut, a Carnegie Mellon researcher, told me recently, such people allowed low-quality relationships developed in virtual reality to replace higher-quality relationships in the real world.

No group has embraced this socially impoverishing trade-off more enthusiastically than adolescents, many of whom spend most of their free hours cruising the Net in sunless rooms. This hermetic existence has left many of these teenagers with nonexistent social skills—a point widely noted in stories about the computer geeks who rose to prominence in the early days of Silicon Valley.

10   Adolescents are drawn to cyberspace for different reasons than adults. As the writer Michael Lewis observed in his book "Next: The Future Just Happened," children see the Net as a transformational device that lets them discard quotidian identities for more glamorous ones. Mr. Lewis illustrated the point with Marcus Arnold, who, as a 15-year-old, adopted a pseudonym a few years ago and posed as a 25-year-old legal expert for an Internet information service. Marcus did not feel the least bit guilty, and wasn't deterred, when real-world lawyers discovered his secret and accused him of being a fraud. When asked whether he had actually read the law, Marcus responded that he found books "boring," leaving us to conclude that he had learned all he needed to know from his family's big-screen TV.

Marcus is a child of the Net, where everyone has a pseudonym, telling a story makes it true, and adolescents create older, cooler, more socially powerful selves any time they wish. The ability to slip easily into a new, false self is tailor-made for emotionally fragile adolescents, who can consider a bout of acne or a few excess pounds an unbearable tragedy.

But teenagers who spend much of their lives hunched over computer screens miss the socializing, the real-world experience that would allow them to leave adolescence behind and grow into adulthood. These vital experiences, like much else, are simply not available in a virtual form.

Responding to Reading

1. In paragraph 4, Staples says that "teenagers nowadays are both more connected to the world at large than ever, and more cut off from the social encounters that have historically prepared young people for the move into adulthood." What does he mean? Do you think he is right?
2. Staples believes that the Internet essentially isolates adolescents, who "unwittingly allow time online to replace face-to-face interactions" (5); in paragraph 9, he refers to this replacement as a "socially impoverishing trade-off." How would Barry Wellman (p. 341) respond to the notion of the Internet as a "replacement" for social interaction?
3. Throughout his essay, Staples refers to "a growing body of research" (5) that supports his position. What research does he cite? Do you find it convincing? Why or why not?

Responding in Writing

Write a paragraph with the title, "What Adolescents Gain when We Let Them Grow Up in Cyberspace."

· THE INTERNET IN A CUP

Tom Standage

1969–

Technology editor at the Economist *magazine, Tom Standage has authored four books and recently edited* The Future of Technology *(2005). Before joining the* Economist, *he wrote for the* Guardian, Wired, *and other publications. In the following essay, Standage compares seventeenth- and eighteenth-century coffee-house communities with modern-day computer networks.*

Where do you go when you want to know the latest business news, follow commodity prices, keep up with political gossip, find out what others think of a new book, or stay abreast of the latest scientific and technological developments? Today, the answer is obvious you log on to the internet. Three centuries ago, the answer was just as easy; you went to a coffee-house. There, for the price of a cup of coffee, you could read the latest pamphlets, catch up on news and gossip, attend scientific lectures, strike business deals, or chat with like-minded people about literature or politics.

The coffee-houses that sprang up across Europe, starting around 1650, functioned as information exchanges for writers, politicians, businessmen and scientists. Like today's websites, weblogs and discussion boards, coffee-houses were lively and often unreliable sources of information that typically specialised in a particular topic or political viewpoint. They were outlets for a stream of newsletters, pamphlets, advertising free-sheets and broadsides. Depending on the interests of their customers, some coffee-houses displayed commodity prices, share prices and shipping lists, whereas others provided foreign newsletters filled with coffee-house gossip from abroad.

Rumours, news and gossip were also carried between coffee-houses by their patrons, and sometimes runners would flit from one coffee house to another within a particular city to report major events such as the outbreak of a war or the death of a head of state. Coffee-houses were centres of scientific education, literary and philosophical speculation, commercial innovation and, sometimes, political fermentation. Collectively, Europe's interconnected Web of coffee-houses formed the Internet of the Enlightenment era.

The Great Soberer

Coffee, the drink that fuelled this network, originated in the highlands of Ethiopia, where its beans were originally chewed rather than infused for their invigorating effects. It spread into the Islamic world during the 15th century, where it was embraced as an alternative to alcohol, which was forbidden (officially, at least) to Muslims. Coffee came to be regarded as the very antithesis of alcoholic drinks, sobering rather than intoxicating, stimulating mental activity and heightening perception rather than dulling the senses.

5   This reputation accompanied coffee as it spread into western Europe during the 17th century, at first as a medicine, and then as a social drink in the Arab tradition. An anonymous poem published in London in 1674 denounced wine as the "sweet Poison of the Treacherous Grape" that drowns "our Reason and our Souls." Beer was condemned as "Foggy Ale" that "besieg'd our Brains." Coffee, however, was heralded as

> . . . that Grave and Wholesome Liquer,
> that heals the Stomach, makes the Genius quicker,
> Relieves the Memory, revives the Sad,
> and cheers the Spirits, without making Mad.

The contrast between coffee and alcoholic drinks was reflected in the decor of the coffee-houses that began to appear in European cities. London in particular. They were adorned with bookshelves, mirrors, gilt-framed pictures and good furniture, in contrast to the rowdiness, gloom and squalor of taverns. According to custom, social differences were left at the coffee-house door, the practice of drinking healths was banned, and anyone who started a quarrel had to atone for it by buying an order of coffee for all present. In short, coffee-houses were calm, sober and well ordered establishments that promoted police conversation and discussion.

With a new rationalism abroad in the spheres of both philosophy and commerce, coffee was the ideal drink. Its popularity owed much to the growing middle class of information workers—clerks, merchants and businessmen—who did mental work in offices rather than performing physical labour in the open, and found that coffee sharpened their mental faculties. Such men were not rich enough to entertain lavishly at home, but could afford to spend a few pence a day on coffee. Coffee-houses provided a forum for education, debate and self-improvement. They were nicknamed "penny universities" in a contemporary English verse which observed. "So great a Universitie. I think there ne'er was any, in which you may a Scholar be, for spending of a Penny."

As with modern Web sites, the coffee-houses you went to depended on your interests, for each coffee-house attracted a particular clientele, usually by virtue of its location. Though coffee-houses were also popular in Paris. Venice and Amsterdam, this characteristic was particularly notable in London, where 82 coffee-houses had been set up by 1663, and more than 500 by 1700. Coffee-houses around the Royal Exchange were frequented by businessmen: those around St James's and Westminster by politicians; those near St Paul's Cathedral by clergymen and theologians. Indeed, so closely were some coffee-houses associated with particular topics that the *Tatler*, a London newspaper founded in 1709, used the names of coffee-houses as subject headings for its articles. Its first issue declared:

> All accounts of Gallantry, Pleasure, and Entertainment shall be under the Article of White's Chocolate-house: Poetry, under that of Will's Coffee-house, Learning, under . . . Grecian; Foreign and Domestick News, you will have from St James's Coffee-house.

Richard Steele, the *Tatler*'s editor, gave its postal address as the Grecian coffee-house, which he used as his office. In the days before street numbering or regular postal services, it became a common practice to use a coffee-house as a mailing address. Regulars could pop in once or twice a day, hear the latest news, and check to see if any post awaited them. That said, most people frequented several coffee-houses, the choice of which reflected their range of interests. A merchant, for example, would generally oscillate between a financial coffee-house and one specialising in Baltic. West Indian or East Indian shipping. The wide-ranging interests of Robert Hooke, a scientist and polymath, were reflected in his visits to around 60 coffee-houses during the 1670s.

10   As the *Tatler*'s categorisation suggests, the coffee-house most closely associated with science was the Grecian, the preferred coffee-house of the members of the Royal Society. Britain's pioneering scientific institution. On one occasion a group of scientists including Isaac Newton and Edmund Halley dissected a dolphin on the premises. Scientific lectures and experiments also took place in coffee-houses, such as the Marine, near St Paul's, which were frequented by sailors and navigators. Seamen and merchants realised that science could contribute to improvements in navigation, and hence to commercial success, whereas the scientists were keen to show the practical value of their work. It was in coffee-houses that commerce and new technology first became intertwined.

The more literary-minded, meanwhile, congregated at Will's coffee-house in Covent Garden, where for three decades the poet John Dryden and his circle reviewed and discussed the latest poems and plays. Samuel Pepys recorded in his diary on December 3rd 1663 that he had looked in at Will's and seen Dryden and "all the wits of the town" engaged in "very witty and pleasant discourse." After Dryden's death many of the literatured shifted to Button's, which was frequented by Alexander Pope and Jonathan Swift, among others. Pope's poem "The Rape of the Lock" was based on coffee-house gossip, and discussions in coffee-houses inspired a new, more colloquial and less ponderous prose style, conversational in tone and clearly visible in the journalism of the day.

Other coffee-houses were hotbeds of financial innovation and experimentation, producing new business models in the form of innumerable novel variations on insurance, lottery or joint-stock schemes. The best-known example was the coffee-house opened in the late 1680s by Edward Lloyd. It became a meetingplace for ships' captains, shipowners and merchants, who went to hear the latest maritime news and to attend auctions of ships and their cargoes. Lloyd began to collect and summarise this information, supplemented with reports from a network of foreign correspondents, in the form of a regular newsletter, at first handwritten and later printed and sent to subscribers. Lloyd's thus became the natural meeting place for shipowners and the underwriters who insured their ships. Some underwriters began to rent booths at Lloyd's, and in 1771 a group of 79 of them collectively established the Society of Lloyd's, better known as Lloyd's of London.

Similarly, two coffee-houses near London's Royal Exchange. Jonathan's and Garraway's, were frequented by stockbrokers and jobbers. Attempts to regulate the membership of Jonathan's, by charging an annual subscription and barring non-members, were successfully blocked by traders who opposed such exclusivity. So in 1773 a group of traders from Jonathan's broke away and decamped to a new building, the forerunner of the London Stock Exchange. Garraway's was a less reputable coffee-house, home to auctions of all kinds and much dodgy dealing, particularly during the South Sea Bubble of 1719-21. It was said of Garraway's that no other establishment "fostered so great a quantity of dishonoured paper."

Far more controversial than the coffee-houses' functions as centres of scientific, literary and business exchange, however, was their potential as centres of political dissent. Coffee's reputation as a seditious beverage goes back at least as far as 1511, the date of the first known attempt to ban the consumption of coffee, in Mecca. Thereafter, many attempts were made to prohibit coffee and coffee-houses in the Muslim world. Some claimed it was intoxicating and therefore subject to the same religious prohibition as alcohol. Others claimed it was harmful to the health. But the real problem was the coffee-houses' alarming potential for facilitating political discussion and activity.

This was the objection raised in a proclamation by Charles II of 15 England in 1675. Coffee-houses, it declared, had produced

> very evil and dangerous effects . . . for that in such House . . . divers False. Malitious and Scandalous Reports are devised and spread abroad, to the Delamation of His Majestie's Government, and to the Disturbance of the Peace and Quiet of the Realm.

The result was a public outcry, for coffee-houses had become central to commercial and political life. When it became clear that the proclamation would be widely ignored and the government's authority thus undermined, a further proclamation was issued, announcing that coffee-sellers would be allowed to stay in business for six months if they paid £500 and agreed to sweat an oath of allegiance. But the fee and time limit were soon dropped in favour of vague demands that coffee-houses should refuse entry to spies and mischief makers.

Dark rumours of plots and counter plots swirled in London's coffee-houses, but they were also centres of informed political debate. Swift remarked that he was "not yet convinced that any Access to men in Power gives a man more Truth or Light than the Politicks of a Coffee House." Miles's coffee-house was the meeting-place of a discussion group, founded in 1659 and known as the Amateur Parliament. Pepys observed that its debates were "the most ingeniose, and smart, that I ever heard, or expect to heare, and bandied with great eagernesse; the arguments in the Parliament howse were but flatte to it." After debates, he noted, the group would hold a vote using a "wooden oracle," or ballot-box—a novelty at the time.

Sweet Smell of Sedition

The contrast with France was striking. One French visitor to London, the Abbé Prévost, declared that coffee-houses, "where you have the right to read all the papers for and against the government," were the "seats of English liberty." Coffee-houses were popular in Paris, where 380 had been established by 1720. As in London, they were associated with particular topics or lines of business. But with strict curbs on press freedom and a bureaucratic system of state censorship. France had far fewer sources of news than did England, Holland or Germany. This led to the emergence of handwritten newsletters of Paris gossip, transcribed by dozens of copyists and sent by post to subscribers in Paris and beyond. The lack of a free press also meant that poems and songs passed around on scraps of paper, along with coffee-house gossip, were important sources of news for many Parisians.

Little wonder then that coffee-houses, like other public places in Paris, were stuffed with government spies. Anyone who spoke out against the state risked being hauled off to the Bastille, whose archives contain reports of hundreds of coffee-house conversations, noted down by informers. "At the Café de Foy someone said that the king had taken a mistress, that she was named Gontaut, and that she was a beautiful woman, the niece of the Duc de Noailles," runs one report from the 1720s. Another, from 1749, reads. "Jean-Louis Le Clerc made the following remarks in the Café de Procope: that there never has been a worse king: that the court and the ministers make the king do shameful things, which utterly disgust his people."

20   Despite their reputation as breeding-grounds for discontent, coffee-houses seem to have been tolerated by the French government as a means of keeping track of public opinion. Yet it was at the Café de Foy, eyed by police spies while standing on a table brandishing two pistols, that Camille Desmoulins roused his country-men with his historic appeal—"*Aux armes, citoyens!*"—on July 12th 1789. The Bastille fell two days later, and the French revolution had begun. Jules Michelet, a French historian, subsequently noted that those "who assembled day after day in the Café de Procope saw, with penetrating glance, in the depths of their black drink, the illumination of the year of the revolution."

Can the coffee-houses' modern equivalent, the internet, claim to have had such an impact? Perhaps not. But the parallels are certainly striking. Originally the province of scientists, the internet has since grown to become a nexus of commercial, journalistic and political interchange.

In discussion groups and chatrooms, gossip passes freely—a little too freely, think some regulators and governments, which have tried and generally failed to rein them in. Snippets of political news are rounded up and analysed in weblogs, those modern equivalents of pamphlets and broadsides. Obscure scientific and medical papers, once available only to specialists, are just clicks away; many scientists explain their work, both to their colleagues and to the public at large, on Web pages.

Countless new companies and business models have emerged, not many of them successful, though one or two have become household names. Online exchanges and auction houses, from eBay to industry-specific marketplaces, match buyers and sellers of components, commodities and household bric-à-brac.

Coffee, Meet WiFi

The kinship between coffee-houses and the internet has recently been underlined by the establishment of wireless "hot spots" which provide internet access, using a technology called WiFi, in modern day coffee-shops. T. Mobile, a wireless network operator, has installed hotspots in thousands of Starbucks coffee-shops across America and Europe. Coffee-shop WiFi is particularly popular in Seattle—home to both Starbucks and such leading Internet firms as Amazon and Microsoft.

Such hotspots allow laptop-toting customers to check their e-mail and read the news as they sip their lattes. But history provides a cautionary tale for those hotspot operators that charge for access. Coffee-houses used to charge for coffee, but gave away access to reading materials. Many coffee-shops are now following the same model, which could undermine the prospects for fee based hotspots. Information, both in the 17th century and today, wants to be free—and coffee-drinking customers, it seems, expect it to be.

Responding to Reading

1. In paragraph 2, Standage says that seventeenth- and eighteenth-century coffee-houses "functioned as information exchanges." How else are the coffee-houses described here similar to Web sites?
2. Most of this essay is devoted to describing the history of European coffee-houses. What specific functions did these coffee-houses serve? Is the essay's purpose primarily to enlighten readers about the role of coffee-houses or to compare them to the Internet? Do you think Standage should have devoted more space to the Internet? To the role played by coffee-houses today?
3. Does Standage see the Internet as superior to coffeehouses? What does he see as the advantages and disadvantages of these two forms of social networking? What would Barry Wellman (p. 341) see as the advantages and disadvantages of each?

Responding in Writing

Other than Web sites, what places today serve the function that European coffee-houses used to serve? How are these places similar to the coffee-houses? How are they different?

WIDENING THE FOCUS

For Critical Thinking and Writing

Do you think it is possible to build real communities online? Do you see online communities as supplements to traditional social networks or substitutes for them? Do you see the rise of online communities as essentially a positive or a negative development? After reading the three essays in the Focus section, write an essay that answers these questions.

For Further Reading

The following readings can suggest additional perspectives for thinking and writing about the kinds of communities created online and how they are like and unlike traditional communities.

- Lynda Barry, "The Sanctuary of School" (p. 83)

- Marie Winn, "Television: The Plug-in Drug" (p. 231)

- Edward J. Blakely and Mary Gail Snyder, "Putting Up the Gates" (p. 314)

For Internet Research

For some, the terms *community* and *online* may seem antithetical, but others have made meaningful connections and established intricate social networks from behind the computer screen. In his essay "What Adolescents Miss When We Let Them Grow Up in Cyberspace"(p. 349), Brent Staples cites research conducted by Carnegie Mellon's Human-Computer Interaction Institute that supports his claim that Internet users are more isolated than nonusers. Visit the Web site of Carnegie Mellon's HomeNet Project, the research project to which Staples refers in his essay, at <http://homenet.hcii.cs.cmu.edu/>, and read the project's research highlights. Then, visit the Web site of another research group, the Stanford Institute for the Quantitative Study of Society, which has reported similar findings in its studies of Internet use, at <http://www.stanford.edu/group/siqss/itandsociety/v01i01/v01i01 a18.pdf>. Finally, read the following rebuttals to the two research projects by *Salon.com* Senior Editor of Technology, Scott Rosenberg:

- "Let's Get This Straight: Sad and Lonely in Cyberspace?"<http://archive.salon.com/21st/rose/1998/09/03straight.html>

- "Lonesome Internet Blues, Take 2" <http://archive.salon.com/tech/col/rose/2000/02/18/stanford_study/index.html>

Finally, write an essay in which you evaluate the arguments presented by the HomeNet Project and the Stanford Institute for the Quantitative Study of Society, on the one hand, and Scott Rosenberg, on the other. Which arguments do you find most effective? Why?

WRITING

Life and Lifestyle

1. Who are the heroes for the way we live now? Are they real or fictional? Are they famous? Are they living? Write an essay in which you establish some criteria to define *heroism* and explain why the figures you chose qualify as heroes.

2. Identify several visual "signs of the times," familiar images from advertising, movies, or Web sites, which you believe typify the way we live today, and write an essay explaining what these images tell you about your world.

3. Many contemporary writers have expressed concern about the gap beween the poor and the rest of society, a gap that is widening along with the expansion of computer technology. How do you think the dramatic technological changes the nation is experiencing will affect those who live in poverty? Do you see the "savage inequalities" between rich and poor (identified by Jonathan Kozol in his essay "The Human Cost of an Illiterate Society" on page 175) as inevitably widening? Explain what you believe needs to be done to resolve any problems you identify.

4. Several of the selections in this chapter suggest that some of modern-day society's problems are caused (or at least aggravated) by the media. Do you believe the media make social problems worse—or even create social problems? Support your conclusion with examples from essays in this chapter and Chapter 4 as well as from your own experence.

5. In an essay called "The Making of a Generation" (published in *Change* magazine's September-October 1993 issue), writer Arthur Levine says, "Every . . . generation is defined by the social events of its age." Identify several pivotal social and political events—local or national—that have had an impact on you and others your age, and explain how these events define your generation.

6. What do you predict for our society's future? In light of these predictions, are you optimistic or pessimistic about what lies ahead? You may focus on any of the issues discussed in this chapter.

7. Although none of the essays in this chapter focus on the role of the family in the twenty-first century, the trends they discuss might certainly be seen to have an impact (positive or negative) on family life. Do you believe the ties that connect family members are weakening? If so, what contemporary social forces do you hold responsible? If not, how do you explain the family's continued strength in light of all that has changed in our society?

8. Keep a diary in which you record all the food you eat in a week (including brand names and approximate portion size). What do your food choices reveal about who you are and the way you live? Which of these choices do you suppose might surprise a time traveler from the 1950s? from the 1970s?

9. Richard Florida (p. 302), Edward J. Blakely and Mary Gail Snyder (p. 314), and Ellen Ruppel Shell (p. 310) discuss the concept of community in very different ways. Write an essay in which you use their observations to help you develop and support a thesis of your own about how our concept of community is changing.

10. Which of Michelle Lee's "ten commandments" do you follow? Why? Write an essay in which you explain your motivation and consider the consequences of your decisions. For example, what message does your attire send to others? Is this the message you *want* to send?

6

■ ■ ■ ■ □ ■ ■ ■

GENDER
AND IDENTITY

■ ■ □ ■ ■

Attitudes about gender have changed dramatically over the past forty years, and they continue to change. For some, these changes have resulted in confusion as well as liberation. One reason for this confusion is that people can no longer rely on fixed gender roles to tell them how to behave in public and how to function within their families. Still, many men and women—uncomfortable with the demands of confining gender roles and unhappy with the expectations those roles create— yearn for even less rigidity, for an escape from stereotypes into a society where roles are not strictly defined by gender.

Interestingly, many people still see men and women in terms of outdated or unrealistic stereotypes. Men are strong, tough, and brave,

Two young boys fighting with toy swords

and women are weak, passive, and in need of protection. Men understand mathematics and science and have a natural aptitude for mechanical tasks. They also have the drive, the aggressiveness, the competitive edge, and the power to succeed. They are never sentimental and never cry. Women are better at small, repetitive tasks and shy away from taking bold, decisive actions. They enjoy, and are good at, domestic activities, and they have a natural aptitude for nurturing. Although women may like their jobs, they will leave them to devote themselves to husband and children.

As you read the preceding list of stereotypes, you may react neutrally (or even favorably), or you may react with annoyance; how we react tells us something about our society and something about ourselves. As a number of writers in this chapter point out, however, stereotypes can limit the way people think, the roles they chose to assume, and, ultimately, the positions they occupy in society.

The Focus section of this chapter (p. 399) asks the question, "Is There a Gender Crisis in Education?" As the essays in this section suggest, a performance gap exists between males and females when it comes to education. For example, males are more likely to drop out of school, and they attend college in lower numbers than females do.

When it comes to the causes of this disparity, social critics are not in agreement. Some believe that, contrary to popular opinion, it is boys, not girls, who are being short-changed by the current educational system. These critics say that as parents and teachers have focused on the needs of girls, they have neglected the specific educational needs of

Two girls playing with dolls

boys. Others say that complex social, behavioral, and biological factors hold boys back. For this reason, they say, remedies that do not take these factors into consideration cannot help close the performance gap between boys and girls. Still others assert that before the problems boys face in school can be addressed, society—especially educators—must reexamine the conventional wisdom concerning gender differences and discard those ideas that are either misleading or incorrect. Only by "broadening the dialogue," and by challenging conventional wisdom, will we as a society be able to ensure that both male and female students are able to realize their full potential.

PREPARING TO READ AND WRITE

As you read and prepare to write about the essays in this chapter, you may consider the following questions:

- Is the writer male or female? Are you able to determine the writer's gender without reading his or her name or the headnote? Does the writer's gender matter?

- Is the writer's focus on males, on females, or on both?

- When was the essay written? Does the date of publication affect its content?

- Does the essay seem fair? Balanced?

- Does the writer discuss gender as a sexual, political, economic, or social issue?

- What does the writer suggest are the specific advantages or disadvantages of being male? Of being female? Of being gay or straight?

- Does the writer support the status quo, or does he or she suggest that change is necessary? That change is possible? That change is inevitable?

- Does the writer recommend specific societal changes? What are they?

- Does the writer express the view that men and women are fundamentally different? If so, does he or she suggest that these differences can (or should) be overcome, or at least lessened?

- Does the writer see gender differences as the result of environment, heredity, or both?

- Does the essay challenge any of your ideas about male or female roles?

- In what ways is the essay like other essays in this chapter?

BARBIE DOLL

Marge Piercy

1936–

Marge Piercy's work includes the novels Small Changes *(1972)*; He, She, and It *(1991)*; Three Women *(1999)*; *and* Sex Wars: A Novel of The Turbulent Post–Civil War Period *(2005)*; *and the poetry collections* Mars and Her Children *(1992) and* The Art of Blessing the Day *(1999)*. *According to Piercy, who has been active in the women's movement since 1969, the movement "has been a great source (as well as energy sink!) and healer of the psyche for me." The following poem from* Circles in the Water *(1988), is an ironic look at the influence of the doll that has become a controversial icon.*

This girlchild was born as usual
and presented dolls that did pee-pee
and miniature GE stoves and irons
and wee lipsticks the color of cherry candy.
Then in the magic of puberty, a classmate said:
You have a great big nose and fat legs.   5

She was healthy, tested intelligent,
possessed strong arms and back,
abundant sexual drive and manual dexterity.
She went to and fro apologizing.
Everyone saw a fat nose on thick legs.   10
She was advised to play coy,
exhorted to come on hearty,
exercise, diet, smile and wheedle.
Her good nature wore out
like a fan belt.   15
So she cut off her nose and her legs
and offered them up.

In the casket displayed on satin she lay
with the undertaker's cosmetics painted on,
a turned-up putty nose,   20
dressed in a pink and white nightie.
Doesn't she look pretty? everyone said.
Consummation at last.
To every woman a happy ending.   25

Responding to Reading

1. What is the significance of the poem's title? To whom or what does it refer? What toys was the "girlchild" (1) given after she was born? What effect does Piercy imply that these toys had on the child?
2. What happens to the "girlchild" when she reaches "the magic of puberty" (5)? Do you think this change is inevitable? Explain.
3. Piercy ends on a cynical note. Is this an effective conclusion? What does she gain (or lose) with this kind of ending?

Responding in Writing

What toy (or toys) did you have as a child that defined your "femaleness" or "maleness"? Do you think Piercy accurately portrays the impact of such toys on children, or do you think she exaggerates?

RITE OF PASSAGE

Sharon Olds

1942–

Sharon Olds was thirty-seven years old when she published her first book of poems. Her collections include The Dead and The Living *(1984);* The Gold Cell *(1987);* The Wellspring *(1996);* Blood, Tin, Straw *(1999);* The Unswept Room *(2002); and* Strike Sparks: Selected Poems 1980–2002 *(2004). Much of her poetry focuses on family relationships. Olds is active in community outreach programs, such as the writing workshop at Goldwater Hospital in New York City. In her poetry, Olds often dwells on family and relationships among parents and children, using plain language that reveals surprising emotional depths. In the following poem, Olds implies that her young son and his male friends already possess the violent tendencies of adult men.*

As the guests arrive at my son's party
they gather in the living room—
short men, men in first grade
with smooth jaws and chins.
5 Hands in pockets, they stand around
jostling, jockeying for place, small fights
breaking out and calming. One says to another
How old are you? Six. I'm seven. So?
They eye each other, seeing themselves
10 tiny in the other's pupils. They clear their
throats a lot, a room of small bankers,
they fold their arms and frown. *I could beat you*

up, a seven says to a six,
the dark cake, round and heavy as a
turret, behind them on the table. My son,   15
freckles like specks of nutmeg on his cheeks,
chest narrow as the balsa keel[1] of a
model boat, long hands
cool and thin as the day they guided him
out of me, speaks up as a host   20
for the sake of the group.
We could easily kill a two-year-old,
he says in his clear voice. The other
men agree, they clear their throats
like Generals, they relax and get down to   25
playing war, celebrating my son's life.

Responding to Reading

1. What is a "rite of passage"? Why do you think Olds gives her poem this title?
2. Why does Olds refer to the children at her son's birthday party as "men"?
3. What comment do you think Olds is making about what it means to be male in contemporary American society?

Responding in Writing

Do you think that Olds's portrayal of boys is accurate, or do you think it is exaggerated? Why do you think that she characterizes boys as she does?

GARDENLAND, SACRAMENTO, CALIFORNIA

Michael Nava

1954–

Currently working as an attorney for the California Supreme Court, Michael Nava has written seven mystery novels, and won Lambda Literary Awards for LGBT (lesbian, gay, bisexual, and transgendered) literary achievement. Coauthor of Created Equal: Why Gay Rights Matter to America *(1994), Nava often writes about outsider perspectives, the subject of the following essay.*

I grew up in a neighborhood of Sacramento called Gardenland, a poor community, almost entirely Mexican, where my maternal family, the

---

[1]The long, narrow bottom of a wooden ship. [Eds.]

Acunas, had lived since the 1920s. Sacramento's only distinction used to be that it was the state capital. Today, because it frequently appears on lists of the country's most livable cities, weary big-town urbanites have turned it into a boomtown rapidly becoming unlivable. But when I was a child, in the late fifties and early sixties, the only people who lived in Sacramento were the people who'd been born there.

Downtown the wide residential neighborhoods were lined with oaks shading turreted, run-down Victorian mansions, some partitioned into apartments, others still of a piece, but all of them exuding a shadowy small-town melancholy. The commercial district was block after block of shabby brick buildings housing small businesses. The city's skyline was dominated by the gold-domed capitol, a confectioner's spun-sugar dream of a building. It was set in a shady park whose grass seemed always to glisten magically, as if hidden under each blade of grass were an Easter egg.

Sacramento's only other landmarks of note were its two rivers, the American and the Sacramento. They came together in muddy confluence beneath the slender iron joints of railroad bridges. Broad and shallow, the rivers passed as slowly as thought between the thick and tumble of their banks.

A system of levees fed into the rivers. One of these tributaries was called the Bannon Slough. Gardenland was a series of streets carved out of farmland backed up against the slough. It flowed south, curving east behind a street called Columbus Avenue, creating Gardenland's southern and eastern boundaries. The northern boundary was a street called El Camino. Beyond El Camino was middle-class tract housing. To the west, beyond Bowman Street, were fields and then another neighborhood that may just as well have existed on another planet for all I knew of it.

5   What I knew were the nine streets of Gardenland: Columbus, Jefferson, Harding, Cleveland, El Camino, Peralta, Wilson, Haggin, and Bowman; an explorer, an odd lot of presidents, an unimaginative Spanish phrase, and three inexplicable proper names, one in Spanish, two in English. It was as if the streets had been named out of a haphazard perusal of a child's history text. There were two other significant facts about the streets in Gardenland; they all dead-ended into the levee and their names were not continued across El Camino Boulevard into the Anglo suburb, called Northgate. Gardenland's streets led, literally, nowhere.

Unlike El Camino, where little square houses sat on little square lots, Gardenland had not been subdivided to maximum utility. Broad uncultivated fields stretched between and behind the ramshackle houses. Someone's "front yard" might consist of a quarter acre of tall grass and the remnants of an almond orchard. The fields were littered with abandoned farming implements and the foundations of long-gone houses. For a dreamy boy like me, these artifacts were magical. Finding my own world often harsh, I could imagine from these rusted pieces of metal and fragments of walls a world in which I would have been a prince.

But princes were hard to come by in Gardenland. Almost everyone was poor, and most residents continued to farm after a fashion, keeping vegetable gardens and flocks of chickens. There were neither sidewalks nor streetlights, and the roads, cheaply paved, were always crumbling and narrow as country lanes. At night, the streets and fields were lit by moonlight and the stars burned with millennial intensity above the low roofs of our houses.

The best way to think of Gardenland is not as an American suburb at all, but rather as a Mexican village, transported perhaps from Guanajuato, where my grandmother's family originated, and set down lock, stock, and chicken coop in the middle of California.

My cousin Josephine Robles had divided her tiny house in half and ran a beauty shop from one side. Above her porch was a wooden sign that said in big blue letters GARDENLAND and, in smaller print below, BEAUTY SALON. Over the years the weather took its toll and the bottom half faded completely, leaving only the word GARDENLAND in that celestial blue, like a road sign to a cut-rate Eden.

By the time I was born, in 1954, my family had lived in Gardenland 10 for at least twenty-five years. Virtually all I know of my grandfather's family, the Acunas, was that they were Yaqui Indians living in northern Mexico near the American border at Yuma, Arizona. My grandmother's family, the Trujillos, had come out of central Mexico in 1920, escaping the displacements caused by the Mexican Revolution of 1910. I have dim memories of my great-grandparents, Ygnacio and Phillipa Trujillo, doll-like, white-haired figures living in a big, dark two-story house in east Sacramento.

My grandparents settled on Haggin Avenue in a house they built themselves. My cousins, the Robles, lived two doors down. My family also eventually lived on Haggin Avenue, next door to my grandparents. Our house was the pastel plaster box that became standard suburban architecture in California in the fifties and sixties but it was the exception in Gardenland.

Most houses seemed to have begun as shacks to which rooms were added to accommodate expanding families. They were not built with privacy in mind but simply as shelter. We lived in a series of such houses until our final move to Haggin Avenue. In one of them, the living room was separated from the kitchen by the narrow rectangular bedroom in which my brothers and sisters and I slept. Adults were always walking through it while we were trying to sleep. This made for jittery children, but no one had patience for our complaints. It was enough that we had a place to live.

By the standards of these places, my grandparents' house was luxurious. It was a four-bedroom, **L**-shaped building that they had built themselves. My grandmother put up the original three rooms while my grandfather was in the navy during World War II. My aunt Socorro told me that my grandmother measured the rooms by having her children lie head to toe across a plot of ground. She bought the cement for the foundations, mixed and troweled it, and even installed pipes for plumbing. Later, when my grandfather returned, they added a series of long, narrow rooms paneled in slats of dark-stained pine, solid and thick walled.

Massive, dusty couches upholstered in a heavy maroon fabric, oversize beds soft as sponges, and a leather-topped dining room table furnished the house. Like the rusted combines in the field, these things seemed magical in their antiquity. I would slip into the house while my grandparents were both at work and wander through it, opening drawers and inspecting whatever presented itself to my attention. It was in this fashion that I opened a little-used closet and found it full of men's clothes that obviously were not my grandfather's. Later I learned that they had belonged to my uncle Raymond who had been killed in a car accident. In a subsequent exploration I found pictures of his funeral, including a picture taken of him in his casket, a smooth-faced, dark-skinned, pretty boy of fifteen.

15   Another time, I found a voluminous red petticoat in a cedar chest. Without much hesitation, I put it on and went into my grandmother's bedroom where I took out her face powder and lipstick. I applied these in the careful manner of my grandmother, transforming myself in the dressing mirror beneath the grim gaze of a crucified Christ. Looking back, I don't think I was trying to transform myself into a girl, but only emulating the one adult in my family who loved me without condition. Because she was the soul of kindness, it never occurred to me, as a child, that my grandmother might be unhappy. Only looking back do I see it.

She and my grandfather slept in separate rooms at opposite ends of their house. In the evening, my grandfather would sit on a couch in front of the television quietly drinking himself into a stupor while my grandmother did needlework at the kitchen table. They barely spoke. I would sit with my grandmother, looking at pictures in the *Encyclopedia Americana,* comfortable with the silence, which, to her, must have been a deafening indictment of a failed marriage.

In my parents' house, the marriage of my mother and stepfather was as noisily unhappy as my grandparents' was quietly miserable. In each shabby house where we lived I would be awakened by their fights. I learned to turn myself into a stone, or become part of the bed or the walls so as to abate the terror I felt. No one ever spoke of it. There was only one house in which my family lived together peaceably but it only existed as a blueprint that had come somehow into my stepfather's possession.

In the evening, he would take it down from a shelf and unroll it on the kitchen table. Together we would study it, laying claim to rooms, planning alterations. At the time, we lived in a tiny one-bedroom cinder-block house. My brother and I slept on a bunk bed in an alcove off the kitchen. At night, I could hear mice scampering across the cement floor, terrifying me when I woke up having to pee and pick my way through the darkness to the bathroom.

When we finally moved from the cinder-block house, it was to another, bigger version of that house rather than to the dream house of the blueprint. One night, my mother's screaming woke me. I hurried into the bedroom she and my stepfather occupied and found him beating her. When I tried to stop him, he threw me across the room. The next morning my mother told me he was sorry, but it was too late. Where I lived no longer mattered to me because I learned to live completely within myself in rooms of rage and grief. Now I think these rooms were not so different from the rooms we all occupied, my unhappy family and I.

Although not literally cut off from the outside world, Gardenland was 20 little touched by it. We were tribal in our outlook and our practices. Anglos were generically called "paddies," whether or not they were Irish. All fair-skinned people were mysterious but also alike. Even TV, that great equalizer, only emphasized our isolation since we never saw anyone who looked remotely like us, or lived as we did, on any of the popular shows of the day. At school, the same homogeneity prevailed. Until I was nine I attended a neighborhood grade school where virtually every other child was like me, dark eyed and dark skinned, answering to names like Juarez, Delgadillo, Robles, Martinez. My own name, Michael Angel, was but an Anglicized version of Miguel Angel, a name I shared with at least three other of my classmates.

I had a remarkable amount of freedom as a child. As I said, we eventually lived on the same street as other members of my maternal family and I roamed their houses as unself-consciously as a Bedouin child might move among the tents of his people. I ate in whatever house I found myself at mealtime and the meals were the same in each of my relatives' houses—rice, beans, lettuce and tomato salad, stewed or fried meat, tortillas, salsa. My grandparents did not lock their doors at night—who did? what was there to steal?—so that I could slip into their house quietly and make my bed on their sofa when my parents were fighting.

But most of the time I spent outdoors, alone or with my friends. In spring, the field behind my house was overrun with thistles. We neighborhood kids put in long days cutting trails through them and hacking out clearings that became our forts. Tiring of the fields, we'd lurk in abandoned houses, empty barns, and chicken coops. When all other amusements failed, there was always Bannon Slough, a muddy brown creek that flowed between thickly wooded banks. It was too filthy to swim in. Instead, in the steep shadows of bridges and railroad trestles we taught each other how to smoke and to swear.

Just as often I would be off by myself. Early on, I looked for ways to escape my family. I found it in the stillness of the grass and the slap of the slough's brown water against the shore. There I discovered my own capacity for stillness. Lying on the slope of the levee, I could hear my own breath in the wind and feel my skin in the warm blades of grass that pressed against my neck. In those moments, Gardenland *was* Eden, and I felt the wonder and loneliness of the first being.

For, like Adam, I was lonely. Being everyone's child, I was no one's child. I could disappear in the morning and stay out until dusk and my absence went unnoticed. Children barely counted as humans in our tribe. We were more like livestock and our parents' main concern was that the head count at night matched the head count in the morning.

25   My loneliness became as much a part of me as my brown hair and the mole above my lip, something unremarkable. When I came out, I missed that sense of joining a community of others like me that so many of my friends describe. My habits of secrecy and loneliness were too deeply ingrained. I had become like my grandfather, who, in a rare moment of self-revelation, told me he was a "lone wolf"; the most unsociable of an unsociable tribe. Though I've changed as I've grown older, I still sometimes wonder if one reason I write is because I am filled with all the words I never spoke as a child.

Two things opened up for me the narrow passage through which I finally escaped Gardenland for good. The first was books. I learned to read early and, once started, could not get enough of books. In this affinity, I was neither encouraged nor discouraged by my family. Education beyond its most basic functions, learning how to read and write, to do sums, had absolutely no interest for them. My love of reading became simply another secret part of me.

There wasn't a library in Gardenland. Instead, a big white van pulled up to the corner of Wilson and El Camino, the city Bookmobile. Inside, patrons squeezed into a narrow passageway between tall shelves of books. The children's books occupied the bottom shelves. At the exit, a woman checked out books from a standing desk. The Bookmobile came once a week and I was a regular customer, always taking my limit of books.

Everything about the process pleased me. I was proud of my library card, a yellow piece of cardboard with my name typed on it, which I carried in a cowhide wallet that was otherwise empty. I liked taking books from the shelves, noting their heft and volume, the kind of type, whether they were illustrated, and I studied the record of their circulation, the checkout dates stamped in blue on stiff white cards in paper pockets on the inside covers. I loved the books as much as I loved reading. To me, they were organic things, as alive in their way as I was.

Like so many other bright children growing up in the inarticulate world of the poor, books fueled my imagination, answered my questions, led me to new ones, and helped me conceive of a world in which I would not feel so set apart. Yet I do not believe that my brains alone, even aided by my bookish fantasies, would have been enough to escape Gardenland. For this, I needed the kind of courage that arises out of desperation.

I found this courage in my homosexuality. Early on, I acquired a 30 taste for reading history, particularly ancient history. I suppose that pictures of ruined Greek cities reminded me of the crumbling, abandoned houses in the fields of Gardenland. But I was also fascinated by pictures of the nude male statues. There was something about the smooth, headless torsos, the irisless eyes of ephebes that made me stop my idle flipping through pages and touch the paper where these things were depicted. By the time I was twelve I understood that my fascination was rooted in my sexual nature. One day, walking to school, clutching my books to my chest, girl-style, I heard myself say, "I'm a queer."

It was absolutely clear to me that Gardenland could not accommodate this revelation. Gardenland provided the barest of existences for its people. What made it palatable was the knowledge that everyone was about the same, united in ethnicity and poverty and passivity. The only rituals were the rituals of family, and family was everything there. But I knew that I was not the same as everyone else. And I was certain that my family, already puzzled by my silent devotion to books, would reject me entirely if it became known exactly what thoughts occupied my silence.

Had I been a different child I would have run away from home. Instead, I ran away without leaving home. I escaped to books, to sexual fantasy, to painful, unrequited crushes on male classmates. No one ever knew. I turned myself into an outsider, someone at the margins of a community that was itself outcast. Paradoxically, by doing this, I learned the peasant virtues of my hometown, endurance and survival. As a member of yet another embattled community, those virtues I absorbed as a child continue to serve me.

Responding to Reading

1. In his conclusion, Nava says that he was an outsider living in a community that was itself an outcast; he sees Gardenland as a Mexican village set

down in the middle of California. What are the disadvantages of such cultural isolation? What, if any, are the advantages?

2. Nava grew up both Chicano and gay. Which of these two cultures do you think defined his childhood identity more clearly?

3. What did Nava learn in Gardenland that prepared him for the outside world? Did his experiences ultimately help him or hurt him?

Responding in Writing

Nava says that the fact that he read books marked him as different. How did his reading separate him from his community?

THE M/F BOXES

E. J. Graff

1958–

Senior researcher at the Brandeis Institute for Investigative Journalism and resident scholar at the Brandeis Women's Studies Research Center, E. J. Graff is a widely published author of articles on gender equality and family issues. She is a senior correspondent at the American Prospect, *a contributor to* Out *magazine and TPMCafe.com, and the author of two books— most recently, with Evelyn F. Murphy,* Getting Even: Why Women Don't Get Paid Like Men—and What to Do about It *(2005). The following essay questions conventional male/female distinctions and argues that either/or labels falsely prepackage identity and gender.*

A 15-year-old girl is incarcerated in a Chicago mental hospital in 1981 and kept there for three years because she won't wear a dress. A Winn-Dixie truck driver is fired from a job he held for twenty years when his boss learns that he wears women's clothes at home. A small-time hustler in Falls City, Nebraska, is raped and then murdered when he's discovered to be physically female. A woman bleeds to death after a Washington, DC, hit-and-run accident when, after finding male genitals under her clothes, paramedics stand by laughing.

M or F? For most of us that's a simple question, decided while we were in utero. Checking off that box—at the doctor's, on the census, on a driver's license—takes scarcely a thought. But there's an emerging movement of increasingly vocal people whose bodies or behavior unsettle that clear division. They're calling themselves "transgendered": It's a spongy neologism that, at its broadest, absorbs everyone from medically reassigned transsexuals to cross-dressing men to women so masculine that security guards are called to eject them from women's restrooms. Fellow travelers include intersexuals (once called hermaphrodites), whose bodies are both/and rather than either/or. The slash between M/F cuts painfully through these lives.

And so they've started to organize. Brought together by the Internet, inspired by the successes of the gay rights movement, and with national sympathy gained from the movie *Boys Don't Cry*, intersex and transgender activists are starting to get a hearing in organizations ranging from college campuses to city councils, from lesbian and gay rights groups to pediatric conferences. And, like the feminist and gay rights movements before them, the new sex-and-gender activists may force us to rethink, in life and in law, how we define and interpret the basics of sex.

A first clue to how zealously the M/F border is guarded—to how sex is literally constructed—comes at birth. One in 2,000 infants is born with genitalia ambiguous enough to make doctors hem and haw when parents ask that first question: boy or girl? Since the late 1950s/early 1960s, standard medical procedure has been to lie and obfuscate. Rather than explain that the child is "a mixture of male and female," writes Anne Fausto-Sterling, author of *Sexing the Body*, medical manuals advise physicians to reassign the child surgically to one sex or another, telling parents only that "the gonads were incompletely developed . . . and therefore required removal." A large clitoris may be cut down; a micropenis may be removed and a vagina built; a testis or testes are sliced out—sometimes over the parents' explicit objections.

Now some of those children have come of age and are telling their stories: severe depression, sexual numbness and a long-time despair at having been folded, spindled and mutilated. The leader of this nascent movement is Cheryl Chase, who in 1993 organized the Intersex Society of North America. ISNA opposes reassignment surgery on intersex infants and advocates raising intersex children as social males or females, educating them about their bodies and letting them choose at puberty whether they'd like surgical assistance or a shift in social sex. ISNA's cause was helped when Johns Hopkins sex researcher and PhD John Money, who wrote the intersex silence-and-reassignment protocol, was profoundly discredited. After a child he called "John" was accidentally castrated soon after birth, Money advised his parents to have him undergo surgery to construct a vagina, raise him as "Joan" and give him female hormones at puberty. Money reported this involuntary sex reassignment as fully successful. But in 1997, both a medical journal report and a Rolling Stone article revealed that the reassignment had been a disaster. Despite the insistence of parents, doctors, psychologists and teachers, "Joan" had always insisted that she was "just a boy with long hair in girl's clothes." In adolescence, John took back his manhood.

How did John "know" he was male—and by extension, how do any of us decide we're girls or boys? One theory is that, in utero, John had undergone the androgen bath that turns an undifferentiated fetus—which otherwise becomes female—male, giving him a male identity and masculine behavior. In the other rare cases where XY infants lose penises and are raised as girls, some insist on being boys—but others happily identify as (masculine, lesbian) women, which suggests that things aren't quite so simple. Scientists recognize that our brains and nervous systems are somewhat plastic, developing in response to environmental stimuli. Sexuality—all of it, from identity to presentation to sexual orientation—is no exception; it develops as a biological interaction between inborn capacities and outside influences. As a result, most of us have a narrow range in which we feel "natural" as we gender ourselves daily through clothes, stance, stride, tone. For most, that gendered behavior is consonant with biological sex: Girls present as female, if not feminine, and fall in love with boys; boys present as male or masculine and fall in love with girls. But those in whom gendered behavior is vice versa—feminine boys, highly masculine girls—get treated as unnatural, even though their gendering is just as biological as the rest of ours. What happens to these transgendered folks can be so brutal that the pediatric surgeons who cut off infant clitorises or penises look like merely the advance guard of the M/F border patrol.

Take, for instance, Daphne Scholinski, so masculine that at age 6, strangers chastised her when she tried to use women's restrooms. In her dry, pitiless memoir *The Last Time I Wore a Dress*, Scholinski tells the story of being committed to a mental hospital at 15 for some very real problems, including severe neglect, her father's violence and her own delinquency. The hospital ignored her shocking childhood and instead "treated" her masculinity. Scholinski got demerits if she didn't wear makeup. She was put on a boys' ward, where she was twice raped, to encourage her to be more feminine. Her confinement was so disturbing that she still gets posttraumatic stress flashbacks, including nightmares so terrifying that she wakes up and vomits. And so Scholinski is starting an organization dedicated to reforming the diagnosis of childhood GID, or gender identity disorder, under which she was treated.

Or consider the treatment of Darlene Jespersen and Peter Oiler. After working for Harrah's Reno casino for eighteen years, in the summer of 2000, Jespersen was fired from her bar-tending job when Harrah's launched a new policy requiring all its female employees to wear foundation, powder, eye-liner, lipstick and so on. "I tried it," says Jespersen in a plaintive voice, "but I felt so naked." The obverse happened to Peter Oiler, a weathered, middle-aged man with large aviator glasses, a pleasant drawl and a bit of an overbite. After twenty years of being rotated through progressively more responsible jobs in Winn-Dixie's shipping yards, in 1999 Oiler was driving a fifty-foot truck delivering grocery supplies throughout southeastern Louisiana—until Winn-Dixie learned that he called himself "transgendered." Oiler tried to explain that he simply wore women's clothes on the weekends: He wasn't going to become a woman; he didn't want to wear makeup and heels on company time. In January 2000 Oiler was fired.

Jespersen and Oiler are stunned. Jespersen is suing Harrah's. Says Oiler, "I was raised to believe that if you do an honest day's work, you'll get an honest day's pay." The ACLU Lesbian and Gay Rights Project has taken up his case, in part because of the sheer injustice— and in part to get courts to treat discrimination against people who violate sex stereotypes as illegal sex discrimination. If a woman can wear a dress, or if a man can refuse makeup, why not vice versa? In doing so; the ACLU, like the three national lesbian and gay legal organizations, would be building on the 1989 Supreme Court decision *Price Waterhouse v. Ann Hopkins.* Price Waterhouse had told Hopkins that she wasn't going to make partner because she was too masculine— and, in actual written memos, advised her to wear jewelry and makeup, to go to charm school, to be less aggressive. The Supreme Court declared such stereotyping to be sex discrimination.

Will judges see Peter Oiler's dismissal as illegal sex stereotyping? 10 There have been some recent hints that they might. In Massachusetts, for instance, the US Court of Appeals for the First Circuit said Lucas Rosa could sue a bank that instructed feminine Rosa, who had shown up to apply for a loan wearing a dress, to go home and come back in men's clothes; a female, after all, would have been considered for the loan. Another Massachusetts judge said that a male student could come to school in a dress, since female students could. A Washington transsexual prisoner raped by a prison guard, and two New York municipal employees harassed for being gay, were allowed to sue when judges ruled they'd been attacked for violating stereotyped expectations of their sex.

Our society has learned to see why women would want masculine privileges like playing soccer and serving on the Supreme Court, but there's been no matching force expanding the world for males. Boys and men still patrol each other's masculinity with a Glengarry Glen Ross level of ridicule and violence that can seem, to women, nearly surreal. Those males who violate the M-box's limits on behavior are quite literally risking their lives.

Which means that, if you're a performing drag queen, a cross-dressing straight man like Peter Oiler, or a transsexual who still has some male ID, do not under any circumstances get stopped by a cop. In New York City, says Pauline Park, a co-founder of NYAGRA (New York Association for Gender Rights Advocacy), even if the police don't actually beat you, "you could be arrested and detained for days or weeks. They don't let people out until they plead guilty to prostitution. They put them in the men's cell, where they're often assaulted and some-times raped, as a tactic to get people to plead guilty."

And don't turn to emergency medical personnel. In August 1995 Tyra Hunter's car crashed in Washington, DC. When firefighting paramedics cut away her dress and found male genitals, they laughed and mocked her. She bled to death in the hospital. In August 2000 a jury awarded Hunter's mother $1.75 million in a wrongful-death ac-tion. Hunter's experience, unfortunately, is not unusual. Once a month, someone transgendered is murdered, and those are just the documented cases. Transgender activists are beginning to mark November 28, the anniversary of another such death, as a Day of Re-membrance, with candlelight vigils and a determination to slow the steady drumbeat of murder.

"We're despised. We're pariahs in this society," says Miranda Stevens-Miller, chair of the transgender rights organization It's Time, Illinois, about transsexuals and otherwise transgendered people. Many transsexuals are fired once they begin to transition. Others lose custody and visitation rights, houses, leases. Many are shut out of of-fice and other public restrooms for years—an indignity that cuts to the very core of being human, since every living body needs to pee. And so the most urgent transgender organizing is happening locally, in organizations such as TGNet Arizona, NYAGRA and It's Time, Oregon. They're teaching Trans 101 to local employers, doctors, city councils, lesbian and gay organizations, judges, families, landlords, friends. They're attempting to collect statistics on firings, beatings, murders, bathroom harassment, police abuse. Often these groups are driven by the energy and determination of one or two people who spend their own time and pennies writing and photocopying leaflets, giving workshops for corporate and college groups, and lobbying city councils and lesbian and gay organizations for inclusion in hate-crimes and antidiscrimination laws. Lately, they're having remarkable success at adding "gender identity and expression" to the protected categories in local and state employment nondiscrimination and hate-crimes laws; they've won in locales ranging from Portland, Oregon, to DeKalb, Illinois, to the state of Rhode Island.

15   Nationally, trans groups are still in the skirmishing phase faced by any new movement, with the inevitable splits over strategy and person-ality. The group with the most name recognition, GenderPAC, angers some transgender activists by avoiding the "T" word in its advocacy, saying that it aims at gender freedom for everyone; it acts on behalf of such people as Darlene Jespersen and Peter Oiler, or boys called "fag-got" for not being noticeably masculine. Currently the most significant transgender organizations nationally are IFGE (International Founda-tion for Gender Education), GEA (Gender Education and Advocacy) and the Working Group on Trans Equality, a loose network of grass-roots

trans activists aiming at a coordinated national presence. Perhaps the biggest success so far is that all the major lesbian and gay organizations and many smaller ones have added transgendered folks to their mission statements as folks who are equally, if differently, queer.

Or is it so different? All of us deviate from what's expected from our sex. While the relationship between transgender activists and lesbian and gay groups has at times been contentious, some lesbian and gay activists, notably Chai Feldblum, Georgetown law professor, are starting to urge that we all organize around our common deviance from sex stereotypes. The differences between homosexual, transgender and transsexual experiences are not that great: All are natural variations on the brain's gendered development that have cropped up throughout human history, from Tiresias to Radclyffe Hall, from Billy Tipton to Quentin Crisp. For the most part, the mainstream sees us on one sliding scale of queerness. And occasionally our struggles and goals intersect quite neatly. For instance, homos can't always tell whether we're harassed at work because someone figures out that we date others of the same sex, or simply because we're too butch or too fey.

And none of us can rely on having our marriages recognized by the institutions around us when we need them—because marriage is one of the last laws on the books that discriminate based on sex. Recently, Joe Gardiner asked a Kansas court to invalidate his dead father's marriage to transwoman (born male, medically and legally reassigned as female) J'Noel Gardiner, saying J'Noel was "really" a man—and therefore could not have legally married a man. The lower court agreed with the son that XY = man, which meant the son would inherit his father's fat estate. But the Kansas appeals judge remanded the case back down for a new trial. Sex, the appeals court declared, isn't decided simply by a chromosome test. Rather, sex is a complex constellation of characteristics that includes not only chromosomes but also "gonadal sex, internal morphologic sex, external morphologic sex, hormonal sex, phenotypic sex, assigned sex and gender of rearing, and sexual identity." The court approvingly quoted Johns Hopkins researcher and medical doctor William Reiner, who wrote, "The organ that appears to be critical to psychosexual development and adaptation is not the external genitalia, but the brain."

Responding to Reading

1. How does Graff define the term *transgendered?* What does she mean when she says, "The slash between M/F cuts painfully though these lives" (2)?
2. In paragraph 4, Graff says that the border between male and female is "zealously guarded." What does she mean by this statement? How effectively does her essay support it?

3. Graff says that boys and men "patrol each other's masculinity with a . . . level of ridicule and violence that can seem, to women, nearly surreal" (11). Do agree with this contention? Do you believe that "males who violate the M-box's limits on behavior are quite literally risking their lives" (11)?

Responding in Writing

In paragraph 3, Graff says, "like the feminist and gay rights movements before them, the new sex-and-gender activists may force us to rethink, in life and in law, how we define and interpret the basics of sex." Do you agree with this statement? How is the situation of transgendered individuals similar to and different from that of women and gays?

WHY I WANT A WIFE

Judy Brady

1937–

Judy Brady studied art before getting married, having a family, and starting her writing career. A breast cancer survivor, Brady co-founded the Toxic Links Coalition, an environmental advocacy group based in California. She has edited two books about cancer, including Women and Cancer *(1980), and a collection of essays and poems written by cancer victims,* One in Three: Women with Cancer Confront an Epidemic *(1991). The following essay, "Why I Want a Wife," appeared in the first issue of* Ms. Magazine *in 1972. In this essay, Brady takes a satrical look at what it means to be a wife and mother.*

I belong to that classification of people known as wives. I am A Wife. And, not altogether incidentally, I am a mother.

Not too long ago a male friend of mine appeared on the scene fresh from a recent divorce. He had one child, who is, of course, with his ex-wife. He is looking for another wife. As I thought about him while I was ironing one evening, it suddenly occurred to me that I, too, would like to have a wife. Why do I want a wife?

I would like to go back to school so that I can become economically independent, support myself, and, if need be, support those dependent upon me. I want a wife who will work and send me to school. And while I am going to school I want a wife to take care of my children. I want a wife to keep track of the children's doctor and dentist appointments. And to keep track of mine, too. I want a wife to make sure my children eat properly and are kept clean. I want a wife who will wash the children's clothes and keep them mended. I want a wife who is a good nurturant attendant to my children, who arranges for their schooling, makes sure that they have an adequate social life with their peers, takes them to the park, the zoo, etc. I want a wife who takes care of the children when they are sick, a wife who arranges to be around when the children need special care, because, of course, I cannot miss classes at school. My wife must arrange to lose time at work and not lose the job. It may mean a small cut in my wife's income from time to time, but I guess I can tolerate that. Needless to say, my wife will arrange and pay for the care of the children while my wife is working.

I want a wife who will take care of *my* physical needs. I want a wife who will keep my house clean. A wife who will pick up after me. I want a wife who will keep my clothes clean, ironed, mended, replaced when need be, and who will see to it that my personal things are kept in their proper place so that I can find what I need the minute I need it. I want a wife who cooks the meals, a wife who is a *good* cook. I want a wife who will plan the menus, do the necessary grocery shopping, prepare the meals, serve them pleasantly, and then do the cleaning up while I do my studying. I want a wife who will care for me when I am sick and sympathize with my pain and loss of time from school. I want a wife to go along when our family takes a vacation so that someone can continue to care for me and my children when I need a rest and change of scene.

I want a wife who will not bother me with rambling complaints   5 about a wife's duties. But I want a wife who will listen to me when I feel the need to explain a rather difficult point I have come across in my course of studies. And I want a wife who will type my papers for me when I have written them.

I want a wife who will take care of the details of my social life. When my wife and I are invited out by friends, I want a wife who will take care of the babysitting arrangements. When I meet people at school that I like and want to entertain, I want a wife who will have the house clean, will prepare a special meal, serve it to me and my friends, and not interrupt when I talk about the things that interest me and my friends. I want a wife who will have arranged that the children are fed and ready for bed before my guests arrive so that the children do not bother us. I want a wife who takes care of the needs of my guests so that they feel comfortable, who makes sure that they have an ashtray, that they are passed the hors d'oeuvres, that they are offered a second helping of the food, that their wine glasses are replenished when necessary, that their coffee is served to them as they like it. And I want a wife who knows that sometimes I need a night out by myself.

I want a wife who is sensitive to my sexual needs, a wife who makes love passionately and eagerly when I feel like it, a wife who makes sure that I am satisfied. And, of course, I want a wife who will not demand sexual attention when I am not in the mood for it. I want a wife who assumes the complete responsibility for birth control, because I do not want more children. I want a wife who will remain sexually faithful to me so that I do not have to clutter up my intellectual life with jealousies. And I want a wife who understands that *my* sexual needs may entail more than strict adherence to monogamy. I must, after all, be able to relate to people as fully as possible.

If, by chance, I find another person more suitable as a wife than the wife I already have, I want the liberty to replace my present wife with another one. Naturally, I will expect a fresh, new life; my wife will take the children and be solely responsible for them so that I am left free.

When I am through with school and have a job, I want my wife to quit working and remain at home so that my wife can more fully and completely take care of a wife's duties.

10　My God, who *wouldn't* want a wife?

Responding to Reading

1. Why does Brady begin her essay by saying that she is both a wife and a mother? How does her encounter with a male friend lead her to decide that she would like to have a wife?
2. This essay, written more than thirty years ago, has been anthologized many times. To what do you attribute its continued popularity? In what ways, if any, is the essay dated? In what ways is it still relevant?
3. Brady wrote her essay to address a stereotype and a set of social conventions that she thought were harmful to women. Could you make the case that Brady's characterization of a "wife" is harmful both to women and to feminism?

Responding in Writing

What is your definition of a wife? How is it different from (or similar to) Brady's?

Stay-at-Home Dads
Glenn Sacks
1964–

Glenn Sacks is a columnist who writes about men's and fathers' issues and hosts the radio talk show "His Side" in Los Angeles. His columns have appeared in the Chicago Tribune, *the* Los Angeles Times, Newsday, *the*

Philadelphia Inquirer, Insight Magazine, *and other publications. Before embarking on a career as a columnist and radio personality, Sacks taught high school, elementary school, and adult education courses in Los Angeles and Miami. In the following essay, Sacks discusses the difficulties men (as well as their wives) face if they want to devote themselves to childrearing and housework.*

The subtext to the wave of concern over the recently announced epidemic of childlessness in successful career women is that women can't have it all after all—and it's men's fault. Why? Because men interfere with their wives' career aspirations by their refusal to become their children's primary caregivers, forcing women to sidetrack their careers if they want children.

Despite the criticism, men generally focus on their careers not out of selfishness but because most women still expect men to be their family's primary breadwinners. For women willing to shoulder this burden themselves, replacing the two-earner couple with a female breadwinner and a stay-at-home dad (SAHD) can be an attractive option. I became a SAHD with the birth of my daughter four years ago, and the arrangement has benefited my family immensely.

My wife and I sometimes remark that if we had met in the era before women had real career opportunities, we'd both be pretty unhappy. As a lone breadwinner I would feel deprived of time with my children. My wife, an ambitious woman who loves her career, would feel stifled as a stay-at-home mom. Since each of us would want to be doing what the other is doing, we would probably resent each other. Instead, the freedom to switch gender roles has allowed each of us to gravitate towards what we really want in life.

Men need not fear a loss of power when they become a SAHD. While SAHDs are sometimes stereotyped as being at the mercy of their stronger wives' commands, in reality, I have more power in the family now than I ever did when I was the family breadwinner. The most important issue in any marriage is deciding how to raise the children. While my wife is an equal partner in any major decision regarding the children, I supervise the children on a day to day basis and I make sure that things are done the way I want them done.

Women also benefit from SAHDs because, with reduced familial   5 responsibilities, they can compete on a level playing field with career-oriented men. For men, it is an opportunity to witness the countless magical, irreplaceable moments of a young child's life, and to enjoy some of the subtle pleasures our fathers never knew, like making dinner with a three year-old's "help," or putting the baby down for a midday nap in a hammock.

Still, there are adjustments that both men and women will need to make. Women will need to discard the popular yet misguided notion that men "have it all," and understand that being the breadwinner comes with disadvantages as well as advantages.

One disadvantage can be the loss of their primary status with their young children. Mom is #1 not because of biology or God's law but because mom is the one who does most of the child care. This can change when dad becomes the primary caregiver. When my young daughter has a nightmare and cries at 2 AM, my wife is relieved that she's not the one who has to get up and comfort her. The price that my wife has had to accept is that her child insists on being comforted not by her but by "yaddy."

Another disadvantage is that taking on the main breadwinner role reduces a woman's ability to cut back her work schedule or look for a more rewarding job if her career disappoints her. This is one of the reasons many women prefer life as a frazzled two-earner couple— keeping the man on career track as the main breadwinner helps to preserve women's options.

Men will also have to make adjustments. For one, they will have to endure the unconscious hypocrisy of a society which often wrings its hands over the lot of the housewife yet at the same time views SAHDs as freeloaders who have left their working wives holding the bag.

10   SAHDs also have to contend with the societal perception that being a househusband is unmanly. The idea is so pervasive that even I still tend to think "wimp" when I first hear about a SAHD.

Working women sometimes complain that men in the workplace don't take them as seriously as they take men. As a SAHD I have the same complaint. For example, last year I attended a school meeting with my wife, my son's elementary school teacher, and some school officials, most of whom knew that I drove my son to and from school, met with his teachers, and did his spelling words with him every day. Yet the woman who chaired the meeting introduced herself to my wife, began the meeting, and then, only as an afterthought, looked at me and said "and who might you be?"

In addition, while many stay-at-home parents face boredom and social isolation, it can be particularly acute for SAHDs, since there are few other men at home, and connections with stay-at-home moms can be difficult to cultivate.

None of these hurdles are insurmountable, and they pale in comparison to the benefits children derive from having a parent as a primary caregiver—particularly a parent grateful for the once-in-a-lifetime opportunity that he never knew he wanted, and never thought he would have.

Responding to Reading

1. According to Sacks, what is the "subtext to the wave of concern over the recently announced epidemic of childlessness in successful career women"

(1)? Why does he think most men concentrate on their careers? What does he think is a good alternative to this situation?

2. What are the advantages of being a stay-at-home dad? What does Sacks see as the disadvantages? How practical do you think his solution is?

3. Could you make the argument that Sacks and his wife are simply switching traditional male/female roles? Are there any other models for work and childcare that Sacks and his wife could use? Do any of these seem preferable to the one they currently employ?

Responding in Writing

Would you want your husband to be (or would you want to be) a stay-at-home dad? Why or why not?

WITHOUT APOLOGY: GIRLS, WOMEN, AND THE DESIRE TO FIGHT

Leah Hager Cohen

1967–

Leah Hager Cohen has published six books, including four works of nonfiction and two novels. Her most recent book, Without Apology: Girls, Women, and the Desire to Fight *(2005), from which the following essay is drawn, explores the link between female aggression and desire.*

My first impulse was to dismiss her. Whatever my idea of how a boxing coach should look, it was nothing like this woman standing above me on the ring apron, elbows on the ropes, calling out to her boxer in the ring. She wore a pink tank top, red shorts, white socks, and black boxing shoes, and her hair, wavy and fine and light brown, was held back with a pink scrunchie, and her limbs looked tender and ungainly and very white. She was little, Raphaëlla Johnson, five-four and not much over a hundred pounds. But it wasn't just her physical size, it was her voice, too, a girl's voice, indelibly gentle and light.

"You're dropping your hands!" she yelled. "Jab! Keep firing the jab! Work!"

In the ring, a teenage Latina girl was sparring with a white man in his thirties. The girl wore red headgear and gloves, and a thick white mouthguard that made it look as if she couldn't suppress a smile. Her tank top said DON'T EVEN DON'T EVEN DON'T EVEN DON'T EVEN DON'T EVEN DON'T EVEN THINK ABOUT IT. Her sparring partner, broadly muscular, wore black headgear and gloves. His bare torso was a gallery of sweat-glazed tattoos, the most magnificent of which—an

American flag in the shape of the United States, with portraits of a woman and three children set inside the borders—rippled across his trapezius muscles and caught the light as he danced. Whenever the girl seemed to tire, the man would yell at her, provoke her, hit her in the face.

"C'mon, *move!*" yelled the coach. "Thirty seconds!" Clustered around her on the ring apron, variously standing or kneeling, were three other girls and a woman, all drinking in the spectacle with unchecked merriment, erupting in bursts of excited laughter, hoots of encouragement, and sharp exhortations that echoed those of the coach. Their obvious pleasure in the event seemed to me incongruous and complicated. But no more so than the sheer physical presence of the coach, to whom my gaze kept returning, even as the action in the ring commanded my attention. She was thirty-two, I would later learn, but she looked half that. She was so small, that was the thing. She was the size of me.

5   I'd never before been in a boxing gym. It was late October, late in the day, when I first pulled up, just a few minutes earlier, in the shabby lot behind the building. Through the windshield I could see a feeble growth of weeds, then cement steps leading to a wide metal door, with a sign forbidding its use. ONLY ENTRANCE TO BOXING CLUB GYM, it said, above a long arrow pointing off to the left. Below that a second sign read NO PARKING AT ALL OUT BACK. Beside me, a couple of other cars and a pickup truck had been left on the chewed-up asphalt in apparent disregard of the warning. It had begun to drizzle. I considered the other vehicles for a long moment, and turned off my engine.

The windows had been boarded up and painted over, and save for the two rather stern signs, the whole side of the building was featureless. From the other side of the concrete exterior came a sort of pumping sound, impressively rhythmic, like machinery operating beyond a factory wall. I'd followed the arrow to an unmarked door, yanked it open. Smells of leather and sweat, a short flight up, then into a musty, unpopulated office with an open door at the other end, and I'd found myself quickening my steps toward the noise beyond that door, my timorousness overtaken by a building curiosity until I stood where I was now, astonished by what I was seeing.

I had come prepared to meet this woman boxer and the girls she coached, but I was expecting to find them—I don't know, doing drills, stretching, throwing punches in the air, maybe, not actually sparring in the ring, battling, getting hit in the face, pounding their own gloved fists against another sweating body. When the time clock blared three times, signaling the end of the round, the girl fell to the floor for comic effect and when her headgear and mouthguard were removed, she was grinning. But the next girl who climbed through the ropes and sparred with the man had something wild about her. She was frightening to watch and at the same time I felt frightened for her; her pupils were dilated, and the force of her blows seemed fueled by something uncontrolled. Her gloves crashed against the man's headgear with a wrecking sound. When her headgear came off at the end of sparring, it seemed the coach had to speak with her for a minute, touch her hair and make eye contact, rub her shoulders and hug her, before the girl resurfaced, like a small child returning to waking life by degrees from a night terror.

With the sparring finished, for the first time I took a look around the room beyond the ring. Everyone else in the gym was male. A handful of men and not-really-yet-men worked out in pairs or solo along the periphery of the gym, signaling with their inattention the relative normality of what had just happened in the ring. But it had my heart pounding my breath shallow. I knew I had entered a foreign land.

The Somerville Boxing Club had been around for over twenty years but on that first evening it had been in its current location, the back of a large stone church built in 1917, for only two weeks. Filling the rear sanctuary of what had most recently housed a Brazilian evangelical ministry, it looked more lived-in than that. The space projected a heady confusion of functions, a few sheets of plywood having transformed the altar into locker rooms of unequal size, one for each gender, with a weight-lifting area sandwiched between them. Three flags—Irish, Puerto Rican, and Italian—provided vertical drapes above the dais and evoked a certain theatricality. A couple of old pews, covered in blue velvet and leaking stuffing out the back, bordered, respectively, the weight area and the bloodstained ring, behind which hung a huge American flag and a dozen fight posters. The rest was equipment: heavy bags and speed bags, a double-end bag, a hook for jump ropes; some mats, medicine balls, cracked mirrors for shadow boxing propped against the walls; Vaseline, paper towels, water bottles; a greenish doctor's-office scale; spit buckets rigged with plastic funnels and tubing and duct tape. The time clock beeped at clear, dispassionate intervals, and skin and leather connected soundly, beating out their own, more complex counterpoint. The boom box played salsa or hip-hop or techno or pop, or static when the dial slipped between stations and no one bothered to go tune it for a while. When I got there that evening, it was playing, of all things, "Calling All Angels."

Now the coach was squirting water into the white girl's mouth, 10 which was tipped open in the manner of a baby bird's beak. The girl's hands, still gloved, hung limp at her sides. The coach spoke to her, too softly for me to hear the words, but in a tone that was tender and intimate. The girl, looking down, listened with all her being, nodding occasionally, panting a little. Their heads were almost touching. I got a better look at the coach's face, which—even though what I had witnessed her boxers doing made it impossible to be dismissive—only completed my idea of an unboxerly persona: open, guileless, undefended. Raphaëlla's features don't seem set or sleek; there is a haphazard quality to them, an artlessness, which is her beauty. When she smiles at you, the smile floods her face, every muscle giving itself over to the action, and you feel yourself the recipient of something tangible, an actual object with heft.

Later I would learn that she was the first female New England Golden Gloves champion, that she was a painter as well as a fighter, that she was working toward a master's degree in education, not with the intent of getting a teaching job but for the sole purpose of becoming a better coach, that she'd been to five funerals in the past year, that she had been harmed, that she believed everyone who made his or her way into the gym was in some way broken inside. That night it seemed all I knew was her size, and the knowledge was profound.

I was impatient to meet her and the four girls with whom she was obviously so intensely engaged. But even as the tattooed man stepped out of the ring (a former pro boxer, I later learned, he sometimes sparred with the girls as a personal favor to Raphaëlla), one of the younger girls stepped into the ring to work one-on-one with her coach. The other three girls moved onto the mats for push-ups and sit-ups. So I bided my time, waiting for them to finish.

As the dinner hour ended, more bodies came through the gym doors, from wiry boys to grizzled men, and outside the heavy fire door, which was eventually propped open in defiance of a handwritten sign taped on it, a wedge of sky showed blue-black, throwing into high relief the light, the heat, the fleshly congregation within. Everybody, as he entered, fell wordlessly into the shifting landscape of activity. A boy with an orange bandanna around his head, one foot up on a velvet pew, wrapped his hands. A tall white man worked the speed bag, shifting his weight from one hip to the other with unlikely grace. A barrel-chested man in glasses, arms folded across his formidable girth, scrutinized a lithesome kid on the double-end bag. A couple of brothers jumped rope with the finesse and footwork of circus acrobats. Someone fed the boom box a techno CD and cranked the volume. A trainer greased up a guy's face with fine, utilitarian speed: the nose, the chin, the cheek, the cheek. None of them betrayed the slightest interest in the presence of the girls training among them.

I turned 360 degrees, reading the motivational slogans tacked to the walls: VICTORY GOES TO THOSE WILLING TO PAY THE PRICE; THE WILL TO WIN IS NOT NEARLY IMPORTANT AS THE WILL TO PREPARE TO WIN! I tried to eavesdrop on the bits of conversation between trainers and boxers, but the room was too loud. I cut wide swaths around the multiplying numbers of men working out on the main floor of the gym, so as not to get slapped by anyone's jump rope. It was plain to me that I didn't belong yet the boxers' attitude toward me seemed one of easy indifference.

At last the girls finished their workout and came tumbling 15 down like cubs from the ring and the free-weight area. I met them then: Jacinta and Josefina and Candida Rodriguez, three sisters, ages fifteen, twelve, and ten, respectively; Nikki Silvano, also fifteen and Jacinta's best friend; and Maria, mother to the Rodriguezes. Five people, and they seemed like a dozen that night, talking in bursts, reaching out to slap or pinch or muss one another even as they chatted with me. Maria talked to me as though well accustomed to speaking with reporters, which she was not, but she was roundly and assertively expressive, an agent for her daughters at all times. We were standing over by one of the speed bags, the one by the door to the parking lot, and she and some of the girls took turns swatting at it. Josefina, the middle daughter (known as Sefina), swung herself up on the recently erected wooden supports from which the gym equipment hung, and Maria interrupted herself to snap at the girl to get her butt *down.* She was telling me the story of the Women's Nationals that August, how Raphaëlla had taken the two big girls down to Augusta, Georgia, and how Jacinta had come home with a silver medal and left her opponent a bloody nose and two black eyes.

Candida—Candi—at ten the littlest, and too short to hit the speed bag even at its lowest adjustment without standing on something, burst out, "I want to hit a boy!" She'd been training with Raphaëlla for eight months and hadn't even had a proper sparring session yet: tough to find anyone her size.

Maria regarded her with proud amusement. "You want to fight a boy?"

"Hit. I said hit. Hit is different than fight."

Jacinta calmly grabbed her little sister and turned her upside down. Candi, her knees hooked at Jacinta's middle, her hands folded behind her head, began to do sit-ups from that vertical position.

"A moth!" cried Sefina. It fluttered on the floor. "Kill it! Step on it!" 20

"Don't kill it," said Maria, sucking her teeth derisively.

Sefina got down on her knees and poked at the quivering body.

Nikki told me she'd come home from Augusta with a bronze, that her legs were wobbling in the ring because she hadn't been training that long, that the ref stopped her fight and gave it to the other girl, and that she'd been mad. She explained that she and Jacinta had known each other since attending the same day-care program as little kids, and that Maria had given them matching cornrows for their bouts in Augusta. "I'm five things," said Nikki, ticking them off for me on her fingers: "Irish, Italian, Dutch, Cherokee, French." She had a lightness of presentation and demeanor that made her seem deceptively uncomplicated.

Sefina came over, bawling hoarsely. Jacinta had given her a fat lip, playing. Maria rolled her eyes. "This one cries a lot," she said.

25   "Sorry," said Jacinta, laughter quivering all about her dark eyes and dimples.

"Shut up!" Sefina lunged for the older girl, who yelped in mock fright and darted out of range. "*Mira, mira, Mami!*" Gingerly she lifted back the injured lip.

"*Callete,*" shushed Maria, pretending to slap her with the back of her hand. Then, to me, "This one's better at gymnastics. She can do flips and everything. Go, show her a cartwheel." But Sefina had drifted over to one of the full-length mirrors propped against the wall to examine her wound.

Someone had switched the music from Top Forty to hip-hop, something with a lot of *fuck you, bitch* in it and a solid, galvanizing bass line, and the outside air sifted chilly and pinpricked with rain through the doorway, and inside the sweat ran and ran and the time clock rode on, insistent, above everything else, dictating intervals of work and rest. Jacinta hit Nikki in the back with a medicine ball, and Nikki pretended, halfheartedly, to be mad. I tried to keep up with Maria's amiable, expansive narration of her own childhood, in Puerto Rico and Boston, and her own adolescent wish to fight, to box, to work out with the boys. Around us, the girls fought and played and finally retreated to the locker room to change.

Raphaëlla emerged in jeans and a jacket, a gym bag slung over her shoulder, car keys out. I'd been eager to shake her hand and introduce myself properly. I asked whether I could be in touch for an interview. She asked how long it would take, and recited her number at work. She was not impolite. But her manner contrasted sharply with the easy accessibility offered by Maria and the girls. I felt chastened by her aloofness, all the more so because it felt deserved.

30   The unsettled feeling I'd had out in the parking lot earlier, the anxiety I'd needed to stuff aside in order to make myself go into the building, had not been based on anything so literal as the fear of coming to harm from the boxers within. It wasn't that I was intimidated by the thought of mingling with people who inflict pain for sport. I think it was the product of my own barely acknowledged scorn for the idea of boxing and for those who choose to identify themselves with it. I was about to enter a club whose members I had never met but whom I secretly held in a measure of contempt. How fitting, then, that I had felt nervous about coming inside. And now it was as though Raphaëlla had seen through me.

I had come expecting to find something alien, and found instead, in the person before me, an eerie and shocking resemblance. We might have been sisters, this woman and I. I watched her bid the others farewell with all the warmth and openness she'd kept from her contact with me, and then she was gone, out the side door into the wedge of darkness. The girls left soon after, but I stayed awhile. I was reeling, embarrassed at all that I was feeling.

What *was* this place? I prowled around a bit, unable to go home just yet. The church's main sanctuary was locked up tight, but its lights were on. Peeking through the crack between the doors, I could catch stained-glass silvers of high, arched windows: This was where the Masons, who owned the building, convened. The basement held a social hall with a large adjacent kitchen that smelled of age and damp. That was all, really. Some bathrooms, a boiler room. And the great incongruity of its upstairs tenant, the boxing club.

Going back through the office, I found a man sitting behind the desk. He was short and stocky, with a cleft chin and a toothpick in his mouth and a backward baseball cap. He had dark pebble eyes that didn't hold my gaze. A grandmotherly woman in a green suit sat on the other side of the desk, on which had been laid wads of hundred-dollar bills. Her name was Ann Cooper, and she was recently back from Las Vegas, where the gym's star fighter had just relocated. Her hand was soft and cool, and she smelled like face powder. She seemed something like a den mother, but when I tried to get her actual title, she waved her hand modestly. "Oh, we're all just volunteers. Aren't we, Vinny?" The man with the pebble eyes shrugged and worked his toothpick to the other side of his mouth.

The money, apparently, had come from the boxer in Las Vegas, John "The Quiet Man" Ruiz, who had won the World Boxing Association heavyweight title from Evander Holyfield some seven months earlier—the first Latino ever to hold a world heavyweight title. His portrait hung, several times over, around the shabby little room. (Later I would learn that Raphaëlla had contributed one; she often painted portraits of the boxers she loved.) Ann Cooper's eyes teared up when she talked about John Ruiz. "'Cause we've struggled, you know," she said. "Everybody always said we'd never have a world champion out of our club. Not that that's the most important thing— we're here for the kids, first. But it doesn't hurt." She touched a wad of bills with her long polished fingernails. Rent. Gym fees were twenty-five dollars a month for kids who could afford to pay. As it happened, almost none of them could.

The warmth of this woman, and the sorrow shimmering about her, intrigued me. As did the gross unease of the toothpick man. And the man who emerged pink-skinned from the gym's single bathroom, wearing a little white towel around his waist and concern for no one's gaze as he trod past us on his way to the locker room. And the noble-warrior image of the Quiet Man in the pictures, somber-eyed, naked to the waist, girded by a championship belt of almost burdensome dimensions. And the live-fuse beat of the music inside the gym, and the sharp percussion of fists at their own nonmusical purpose. The idea of all these young boxers bent on being here because they loved—what? Fighting? Hitting? Survival? The odd—*absurd*—impression of wholesomeness about the club, of something nurturing, nourishing, as though this were still a sanctuary, a place of healing instead of hurting. And above all: the fact that girls and women had dug out a place here.

I went back inside the gym proper, sat on a pew, and watched the men. What I am used to, when I report on a story, is disappearing inside it. I could feel that happening now, but only imperfectly. Something unfamiliar was getting in the way, asserting itself amid the rhythms and sweat and brewing questions. This unfamiliar thing was my awareness of *me*. It was as though I'd had ten cups of coffee before coming, as though I'd swallowed some sort of radioactive dye that made my physical presence irrefutable. It was as though, on some cellular level, my body knew what was to come, that this would not be a place where I could lose myself inside the story. That the opposite would prove true.

I sat there, watching the boxers, and floated in the din and the kinesthetic swirl. After a while I became aware of something specific leaping and burning within me, and when I went to put a name to it, it was jealousy.

Responding to Reading

1. What does Cohen mean when she says, "I knew I had entered a foreign land"(8)? What is "foreign" about the Somerville Boxing Club? What does this statement indicate about Cohen?
2. What were Cohen's preconceptions about female boxers? How do the people she meets conform (or not conform) to these stereotypes?
3. Cohen sees the Somerville Boxing Club as a place of contradictions. On the one hand, it is devoted to fighting and hitting. One the other hand, it is "something nourishing," a sanctuary (35). Does she ever resolve her difficulties with these differences? Why, at the end of the essay, does she feel jealousy?

Responding in Writing

In her 1987 book *On Boxing,* Joyce Carol Oates observes, "Boxing is a purely masculine activity and it inhabits a purely male world." The female boxer she says, she "cannot be taken seriously—she is a parody, she is cartoon, she is monstrous." Would Cohen agree with this sentiment? Do you?

MARKED WOMEN

Deborah Tannen

1945–

Deborah Tannen, a professor of linguistics at Georgetown University, has written books for both scholarly and popular audiences, with most of her work focusing on communication between men and women. Tannen is best known for her bestseller You Just Don't Understand: Women and Men in Conversation *(1990); her most recent book is* You're Wearing That?: Mothers and Daughters in Conversation *(2006). The following essay, written in 1993, is a departure from Tannen's usual work. Here she focuses not on different communication styles but on the contrast she finds between the neutral way men in our culture present themselves to the world and the more message-laden way women present themselves.*

Some years ago I was at a small working conference of four women and eight men. Instead of concentrating on the discussion I found myself looking at the three other women at the table, thinking how each had a different style and how each style was coherent.

One woman had dark brown hair in a classic style, a cross between Cleopatra and Plain Jane. The severity of her straight hair was softened by wavy bangs and ends that turned under. Because she was beautiful, the effect was more Cleopatra than plain.

The second woman was older, full of dignity and composure. Her hair was cut in a fashionable style that left her with only one eye, thanks to a side part that let a curtain of hair fall across half her face. As she looked down to read her prepared paper, the hair robbed her of bifocal vision and created a barrier between her and the listeners.

The third woman's hair was wild, a frosted blond avalanche falling over and beyond her shoulders. When she spoke she frequently tossed her head, calling attention to her hair and away from her lecture.

Then there was makeup. The first woman wore facial cover that 5 made her skin smooth and pale, a black line under each eye and mascara that darkened already dark lashes. The second wore only a light gloss on her lips and a hint of shadow on her eyes. The third had blue bands under her eyes, dark blue shadow, mascara, bright red lipstick and rouge; her fingernails flashed red.

I considered the clothes each woman had worn during the three days of the conference: In the first case, man-tailored suits in primary colors with solid-color blouses. In the second, casual but stylish black T-shirts, a floppy collarless jacket and baggy slacks or a skirt in neutral colors. The third wore a sexy jump suit; tight sleeveless jersey and tight yellow slacks; a dress with gaping armholes and an indulged tendency to fall off one shoulder.

Shoes? No. 1 wore string sandals with medium heels; No. 2, sensible, comfortable walking shoes; No. 3, pumps with spike heels. You can fill in the jewelry, scarves, shawls, sweaters—or lack of them.

As I amused myself finding coherence in these styles, I suddenly wondered why I was scrutinizing only the women. I scanned the eight men at the table. And then I knew why I wasn't studying them. The men's styles were unmarked.

The term "marked" is a staple of linguistic theory. It refers to the way language alters the base meaning of a word by adding a linguistic particle that has no meaning on its own. The unmarked form of a word carries the meaning that goes without saying—what you think of when you're not thinking anything special.

10   The unmarked tense of verbs in English is the present—for example, *visit*. To indicate past, you mark the verb by adding *ed* to yield *visited*. For future, you add a word: *will visit*. Nouns are presumed to be singular until marked for plural, typically by adding *s* or *es*, so *visit* becomes *visits* and *dish* becomes *dishes*.

The unmarked forms of most English words also convey "male." Being male is the unmarked case. Endings like *ess* and *ette* mark words as "female." Unfortunately, they also tend to mark them for frivolousness. Would you feel safe entrusting your life to a doctorette? Alfre Woodard, who was an Oscar nominee for best supporting actress, says she identifies herself as an actor because "actresses worry about eyelashes and cellulite, and women who are actors worry about the characters we are playing." Gender markers pick up extra meanings that reflect common associations with the female gender: not quite serious, often sexual.

Each of the women at the conference had to make decisions about hair, clothing, makeup and accessories, and each decision carried meaning. Every style available to us was marked. The men in our group had made decisions, too, but the range from which they chose was incomparably narrower. Men can choose styles that are marked, but they don't have to, and in this group none did. Unlike the women, they had the option of being unmarked.

Take the men's hair styles. There was no marine crew cut or oily longish hair falling into eyes, no asymmetrical, two-tiered construction to swirl over a bald top. One man was unabashedly bald; the others had hair of standard length, parted on one side, in natural shades of brown or gray or graying. Their hair obstructed no views, left little to toss or push back or run fingers through and, consequently, needed and attracted no attention. A few men had beards. In a business setting, beards might be marked. In this academic gathering, they weren't.

There could have been a cowboy shirt with string tie or a three-piece suit or a necklaced hippie in jeans. But there wasn't. All eight men wore brown or blue slacks and nondescript shirts of light colors. No man wore sandals or boots; their shoes were dark, closed, comfortable and flat. In short, unmarked.

Although no man wore makeup, you couldn't say the men didn't 15 wear makeup in the sense that you could say a woman didn't wear makeup. For men, no makeup is unmarked.

I asked myself what style we women could have adopted that would have been unmarked, like the men's. The answer was none. There is no unmarked woman.

There is no woman's hair style that can be called standard, that says nothing about her. The range of women's hair styles is staggering, but a woman whose hair has no particular style is perceived as not caring about how she looks, which can disqualify her for many positions, and will subtly diminish her as a person in the eyes of some.

Women must choose between attractive shoes and comfortable shoes. When our group made an unexpected trek, the woman who wore flat, laced shoes arrived first. Last to arrive was the woman in spike heels, shoes in hand and a handful of men around her.

If a woman's clothing is tight or revealing (in other words, sexy), it sends a message—an intended one of wanting to be attractive, but also a possibly unintended one of availability. If her clothes are not sexy, that too sends a message, lent meaning by the knowledge that they could have been. There are thousands of cosmetic products from which women can choose and myriad ways of applying them. Yet no makeup at all is anything but unmarked. Some men see it as a hostile refusal to please them.

Women can't even fill out a form without telling stories about 20 themselves. Most forms give four titles to choose from. "Mr." carries no meaning other than that the respondent is male. But a woman who checks "Mrs." or "Miss" communicates not only whether she has been married but also whether she has conservative tastes in forms of address—and probably other conservative values as well. Checking "Ms." declines to let on about marriage (checking "Mr." declines nothing since nothing was asked), but it also marks her as either liberated or rebellious, depending on the observer's attitudes and assumptions.

I sometimes try to duck these variously marked choices by giving my title as "Dr."—and in so doing risk marking myself as either uppity (hence sarcastic responses like *"Excuse me!"*) or an overachiever (hence reactions of congratulatory surprise like "Good for you!").

All married women's surnames are marked. If a woman takes her husband's name, she announces to the world that she is married and has traditional values. To some it will indicate that she is less herself, more identified by her husband's identity. If she does not take her husband's name, this too is marked, seen as worthy of comment: she has done something; she has "kept her own name." A man is never said to have "kept his own name" because it never occurs to anyone that he might have given it up. For him using his own name is unmarked.

A married woman who wants to have her cake and eat it too may use her surname plus his, with or without a hyphen. But this too announces her marital status and often results in a tongue-tying string. In a list (Harvey O'Donovan, Jonathan Feldman, Stephanie Woodbury McGillicutty), the woman's multiple name stands out. It is marked.

I have never been inclined toward biological explanations of gender differences in language, but I was intrigued to see Ralph Fasold bring biological phenomena to bear on the question of linguistic marking in his book "The Sociolinguistics of Language." Fasold stresses that language and culture are particularly unfair in treating women as the marked case because biologically it is the male that is marked. While two X chromosomes make a female, two Y chromosomes make nothing. Like the linguistic markers *s, es* or *ess*, the Y chromosome doesn't "mean" anything unless it is attached to a root form—an X chromosome.

25   Developing this idea elsewhere, Fasold points out that girls are born with fully female bodies, while boys are born with modified female bodies. He invites men who doubt this to lift up their shirts and contemplate why they have nipples.

In his book, Fasold notes "a wide range of facts which demonstrates that female is the unmarked sex." For example, he observes that there are a few species that produce only females, like the whiptail lizard. Thanks to parthenogenesis, they have no trouble having as many daughters as they like. There are no species, however, that produce only males. This is no surprise, since any such species would become extinct in its first generation.

Fasold is also intrigued by species that produce individuals not involved in reproduction, like honeybees and leaf-cutter ants. Reproduction is handled by the queen and a relatively few males; the workers are sterile females. "Since they do not reproduce," Fasold says, "there is no reason for them to be one sex or the other, so they default, so to speak, to female."

Fasold ends his discussion of these matters by pointing out that if language reflected biology, grammar books would direct us to use "she" to include males and females and "he" only for specifically male referents. But they don't. They tell us that "he" means "he or she," and that "she" is used only if the referent is specifically female. This use of "he" as the sex-indefinite pronoun is an innovation introduced into English by grammarians in the 18th and 19th centuries, according to Peter Mühlhäusler and Rom Harré in "Pronouns and People." From at least about 1500, the correct sex-indefinite pronoun was "they," as it still is in casual spoken English. In other words, the female was declared by grammarians to be the marked case.

Writing this article may mark me not as a writer, not as a linguist, not as an analyst of human behavior, but as a feminist—which will have positive or negative, but in any case powerful, connotations for readers. Yet I doubt that anyone reading Ralph Fasold's book would put that label on him.

I discovered the markedness inherent in the very topic of gender ₃₀ after writing a book on differences in conversational style based on geographical region, ethnicity, class, age and gender. When I was interviewed, the vast majority of journalists wanted to talk about the differences between women and men. While I thought I was simply describing what I observed—something I had learned to do as a researcher—merely mentioning women and men marked me as a feminist for some.

When I wrote a book devoted to gender differences, in ways of speaking, I sent the manuscript to five male colleagues, asking them to alert me to any interpretation, phrasing or wording that might seem unfairly negative toward men. Even so, when the book came out, I encountered responses like that of the television talk show host who, after interviewing me, turned to the audience and asked if they thought I was male-bashing.

Leaping upon a poor fellow who affably nodded in agreement, she made him stand and asked, "Did what she said accurately describe you?" "Oh, yes," he answered. "That's me exactly." "And what she said about women—does that sound like your wife?" "Oh yes," he responded. "That's her exactly." "Then why do you think she's male-bashing?" He answered, with disarming honesty, "Because she's a woman and she's saying things about men."

To say anything about women and men without marking oneself as either feminist or anti-feminist, male-basher or apologist for men seems as impossible for a woman as trying to get dressed in the morning without inviting interpretations of her character.

Sitting at the conference table musing on these matters, I felt sad to think that we women didn't have the freedom to be unmarked that the men sitting next to us had. Some days you just want to get dressed and go about your business. But if you're a woman, you can't, because there is no unmarked woman.

Responding to Reading

1. Tannen notes that men "can choose styles that are marked, but they don't have to" (12); however, she believes that women do not have the "option of being unmarked" (12). What does she mean? Can you give some examples of women's styles that you believe are unmarked? (Note that in paragraph 16, Tannen says there are no such styles.)

2. In paragraph 33, Tannen says, "To say anything about women and men without marking oneself as either feminist or anti-feminist, male-basher or apologist for men seems as impossible for a woman as trying to get dressed in the morning without inviting interpretations of her character." Do you agree?

3. In paragraphs 24–28, Tannen discusses Ralph Fasold's book *The Sociolinguistics of Language*. Why does she include this material? Could she have made her point just as effectively without it?

Responding in Writing

Consider the men and women you see every day at school or in your neighborhood. Does their appearance support Tannen's thesis?

—————————— Focus ——————————

Is There a Gender Crisis in Education?

Advertisement showing girl in museum looking at
dinosaur skull

Responding to the Image

1. The advertisement above is designed to encourage girls to study math and
   science. What elements in the picture emphasize these subjects? In what
   way do they reinforce the message, "See the world through math and science"?
2. How does this ad attempt to reach its target audience—girls below the age
   of twelve? Do you think it is successful? What changes, if any, would you
   make to the ad?

THE WAR AGAINST BOYS
Christina Hoff Sommers
1950–

Christina Hoff Sommers is a fellow at the American Enterprise Institute in Washington, D.C. A frequent television commentator, Sommers is also the author of essays in a wide variety of periodicals and has published several books, including Who Stole Feminism? How Women Have Betrayed Women *(1994) and* The War against Boys: How Misguided Feminism Is Harming Our Young Men *(2000). Her latest book is* One Nation under Therapy: How The Helping Culture is Eroding Self-Reliance *(2005). In the following, the opening section of a long essay that appeared in the* Atlantic Monthly, *Sommers examines what she calls "the myth of girls in crisis" and demonstrates that contrary to popular opinion, boys, not girls, are short-changed by today's educational establishment.*

It's a bad time to be a boy in America. The triumphant victory of the U.S. women's soccer team at the World Cup last summer has come to symbolize the spirit of American girls. The shooting at Columbine High last spring might be said to symbolize the spirit of American boys.

That boys are in disrepute is not accidental. For many years women's groups have complained that boys benefit from a school system that favors them and is biased against girls. "Schools shortchange girls," declares the *American Association of University Women*. Girls are "undergoing a kind of psychological foot-binding," two prominent educational psychologists say. A stream of books and pamphlets cite research showing not only that boys are classroom favorites but also that they are given to schoolyard violence and sexual harassment.

In the view that has prevailed in American education over the past decade, boys are resented, both as unfairly priviledged sex and as obstacles on the path to gender justice for girls. This perspective is promoted in schools of education, and many a teacher now feels that girls need and deserve special indemnifying condsideration. "It is really clear that boys are Number One in this society and in most of the world," says Patricia O'Reilly, a professor of education and the director of the Gender Equity Center, at the University of Cincinnati.

The idea that schools and society grind girls down has given rise to an array of laws and policies intended to curtail the advantage boys have and to redress the harm done to girls. That girls are treated as the second sex in school and consequently suffer, that boys are accorded privileges and consequently benefit—these are things everyone is presumed to know. But they are not true.

The research commonly cited to support claims of male privilege   5
and male sinfulness is riddled with errors. Almost none of it has been
published in peer-reviewed professional journals. Some of the data
turn out to be mysteriously missing. A review of the facts shows boys,
not girls, on the weak side of an education gender gap. The typical boy
is a year and a half behind the typical girl in reading and writing; he is
less committed to school and less likely to go to college. In 1997 college
fulltime enrollments were 45 percent male and 55 percent female. The
Department of Education predicts that the proportion of boys in college
classes will continue to shrink.

Data from the U.S. Department of Education and from several recent university studies show that far from being shy and demoralized,
today's girls outshine boys. They get better grades. They have higher
educational aspirations. They follow more rigorous academic programs
and participate in advanced-placement classes at higher rates. According to the National Center for Education Statistics, slightly more girls
than boys enroll in high-level math and science courses. Girls, allegedly
timorous and lacking in confidence, now outnumber boys in student
government, in honor societies, on school newspapers, and in debating
clubs. Only in sports are boys ahead, and women's groups are targeting
the sports gap with a vengeance. Girls read more books. They outper-
form boys on tests for artistic and musical ability. More girls than boys
study abroad. More join the Peace Corps. At the same time, more boys
than girls are suspended from school. More are held back and more
drop out. Boys are three times as likely to receive a diagnosis of
attention-deficit hyperactivity disorder. More boys than girls are involved in crime, alcohol, and drugs. Girls attempt suicide more often
than boys, but it is boys who more often succeed. In 1997, a typical year,
4,483 young people aged five to twenty-four committed suicide: 701 females and 3,782 males.

In the technical language of education experts, girls are academically more "engaged." Last year an article in *The CQ Researcher* about
male and female academic achievement described a common parental
observation: "Daughters want to please their teachers by spending
extra time on projects, doing extra credit, making homework as neat as
possible. Sons rush through homework assignments and run outside to
play, unconcerned about how the teacher will regard the sloppy work."

School engagement is a critical measure of student success. The U.S.
Department of Education gauges student commitment by the following
criteria: "How much time do students devote to homework each night?"
and "Do students come to class prepared and ready to learn? (Do they
bring, books and pencils? Have they completed their homework?)". According to surveys of fourth, eighth, and twelfth graders, girls consistently do more homework than boys. By the twelfth grade boys are four
times as likely as girls not to do homework. Similarly, more boys than

girls report that they "usually" or "often" come to school without supplies or without having done their homework.

The performance gap between boys and girls in high school leads directly to the growing gap between male and female admissions to college. The Department of Education reports that in 1996 there were 8.4 million women but only 6.7 million men enrolled in college. It predicts that women will hold on to and increase their lead well into the next decade, and that by 2007 the numbers will be 9.2 million women and 6.9 million men.

Deconstructing the Test-Score Gap

10 Feminists cannot deny that girls get better grades, are more engaged academically, and are now the majority sex in higher education. They argue, however, that these advantages are hardly decisive. Boys, they point out, get higher scores than girls on almost every significant standardized test—especially the Scholastic Assessment Test and law school, medical school, and graduate school admissions tests.

In 1996 I wrote an article for *Education Week* about the many ways in which girl students were moving ahead of boys. Seizing on the test-score data that suggest boys are doing better than girls, David Sadker, a professor of education at American University and a co-author with his wife, Myra, of *Failing at Fairness: How America's Schools Cheat Girls* (1994), wrote, "If females are soaring in school, as Christina Hoff Sommers writes, then these tests are blind to their flight." On the 1998 SAT boys were thirty-five points (out of 800) ahead of girls in math and seven points ahead in English. These results seem to run counter to all other measurements of achievement in school. In almost all other areas boys lag behind girls. Why do they test better? Is Sadker right in suggesting that this is a manifestation of boys' privileged status?

The answer is no. A careful look at the pool of students who take the SAT and similar tests shows that the girls' lower scores have little or nothing to do with bias or unfairness. Indeed, the scores do not even signify lower achievement by girls. First of all, according to *College Bound Seniors,* an annual report on standardized-test takers published by the College Board, many more "at risk" girls than "at risk" boys take the SAT—girls from lower-income homes or with parents who never graduated from high school or never attended college. "These characteristics," the report says, "are associated with lower than average SAT scores." Instead of wrongly using SAT scores as evidence of bias against girls, scholars should be concerned about the boys who never show up for the tests they need if they are to move on to higher education.

Another factor skews test results so that they appear to favor boys. Nancy Cole, the president of the Educational Testing Service, calls it the "spread" phenomenon. Scores on almost any intelligence or achievement test are more spread out for boys than for girls—boys include more prodigies and more students of marginal ability. Or, as the political scientist James Q. Wilson once put it, "There are more male geniuses and more male idiots."

Boys also dominate dropout lists, failure lists, and learning-disability lists. Students in these groups rarely take college-admissions tests. On the other hand, exceptional boys who take school seriously show up in disproportionately high numbers for standardized tests. Gender-equity activists like Sadker ought to apply their logic consistently: if the shortage of girls at the high end of the ability distribution is evidence of unfairness to girls, then the excess of boys at the low end should be deemed evidence of unfairness to boys.

Suppose we were to turn our attention away from the highly motivated, self-selected two fifths of high school students who take the SAT and consider instead a truly representative sample of American schoolchildren. How would girls and boys then compare? Well, we have the answer. The National Assessment of Educational Progress started in 1969 and mandated by Congress, offers the best and most comprehensive measure of achievement among students at all levels of ability. Under the NAEP program 70,000 to 100,000 students, drawn from forty-four states, are tested in reading, writing, math, and science at ages nine, thirteen, and seventeen. In 1996, seventeen-year-old boys outperformed seventeen-year-old girls by five points in math and eight points in science, whereas the girls outperformed the boys by fourteen points in reading and seventeen points in writing. In the past few years girls have been catching up in math and science while boys have continued to lag far behind in reading and writing.

In the July, 1995, issue of *Science,* Larry V. Hedges and Amy Nowell, researchers at the University of Chicago, observed that girls' deficits in math were small but not insignificant. These deficits, they noted, could adversely affect the number of women who "excel in scientific and technical occupations." Of the deficits in boys' writing skills they wrote, "The large sex differences in writing . . . are alarming. . . . The data imply that males are, on average, at a rather profound disadvantage in the performance of this basic skill." They went on to warn,

> The generally larger numbers of males who perfom near the bottom of the distribution on reading comprehension and writing also have policy implications. It seems likely that individuals with such poor literacy skills will have difficulty finding employment in an increasingly information-driven economy. Thus, some intervention may be required to enable them to participate constructively.

Hedges and Nowell were describing a serious problem of national scope, but because the focus elsewhere has been on girls' deficits, few Americans know much about the problem or even suspect that it exists.

CHAPTER 6 FOCUS

Indeed, so accepted has the myth of girls in crisis become that even teachers who work daily with male and female students tend to reflexively dismiss any challenge to the myth, or any evidence pointing to the very real crisis among boys. Three years ago Scarsdale High School, in New York, held a gender-equity workshop for faculty members. It was the standard girls-are-being-shortchanged fare, with one notable difference. A male student gave a presentation in which he pointed to evidence suggesting that girls at Scarsdale High were well ahead of boys. David Greene, a social-studies teacher, thought the student must be mistaken, but when he and some colleagues analyzed department grading patterns, they discovered that the student was right. They found little or no difference in the grades of boys and girls in advanced-placement social-studies classes. But in standard classes the girls were doing a lot better.

And Greene discovered one other thing: few wanted to hear about his startling findings. Like schools everywhere, Scarsdale High has been strongly influenced by the belief that girls are systematically deprived. That belief prevails among the school's gender-equity committee and has led the school to offer a special senior elective on gender equity. Greene has tried to broach the subject of male underperformance with his colleagues. Many of them concede that in the classes they teach, the girls seem to be doing better than the boys, but they do not see this as part of a larger pattern. After so many years of hearing about silenced, diminished girls, teachers do not take seriously the suggestion that boys are not doing as well as girls even if they see it with their own eyes in their own classrooms.

Responding to Reading

1. In paragraph 4, Sommers states her essay's thesis: "That girls are treated as the second sex in school and consequently suffer, that boys are accorded privileges and consequently benefit—these are things everyone is presumed to know. But they are not true." Do you agree that the supposed privileged position of boys is something "everyone is presumed to know"?

2. Paragraph 6 of this essay presents a long list of areas in which "girls outshine boys." Do you find this list convincing? What other information could Sommers have provided to support her case?

3. Sommers believes that "the myth of girls in crisis" is so entrenched that "even teachers who work daily with male and female students tend to reflexively dismiss any challenge to the myth" (17). If what she says is true, would you expect this belief among teachers to benefit boys or girls in the long run? Why?

Responding in Writing

Based on your experience, who is more successful in school—girls or boys?

BOY PROBLEMS
Ann Hulbert

A contributing writer for the New York Times Magazine, *Ann Hulbert is the author of two books, most recently* Raising America: Experts, Parents, and a Century of Advice about Children *(2003). Her work focuses on the American educational system as well as economic and gender inequality, the subjects of the following essay.*

"It's her future. Do the math," instructs a poster that is part of the Girl Scouts of the U.S.A.'s two-year-old "Girls Go Tech" campaign. Accompanying the message—which belongs to a series of public service announcements also sponsored by the Ad Council—is a photograph of an adorable little girl reading a book called "Charlotte's Web Site." The cover of the E. B. White takeoff shows Fern and Wilbur looking intently at Charlotte on a computer screen. The text below warns that "by sixth grade, an alarming number of girls lose interest in math, science and technology. Which means they won't qualify for most future jobs."

But they don't lose interest in reading, this particular ad presumes—nor do girls lose interest in school, certainly not at the rate boys do. The recent controversy over comments made by Lawrence Summers, the president of Harvard, about the gender gap in science and engineering has eclipsed a different educational disparity: boys perform consistently below girls on most tests of reading and verbal skills and lag in college enrollment and degree attainment. After dominating postsecondary education through the late 1970's, young American men now earn 25 percent fewer bachelor's degrees than young women do.

Who knows what Summers would say about this phenomenon, which is the flip side of the underrepresentation of female scientists at the top that he was addressing. Male achievement, as he explained, tends toward the extremes when it comes to testing, while females' scores are more concentrated in the middle of the range. What Summers didn't spell out is that boys owe their edge in math to the unusually high performance of a relatively small number of boys in a pool that also has more than its share of low-scoring students. In assessments of verbal literacy, the clumping of boys toward the bottom is more pronounced.

The gender disparity widens among low-income and minority students. And it is especially dramatic among African-Americans, a recent Urban Institute study shows. Black women now earn twice as many college degrees as black men do. They also receive double the number of master's degrees. But the female lead isn't just a black phenomenon; among whites, women earn 30 percent more bachelor's degrees than men and some 50 percent more master's degrees.

5   It's his future. Do the math—but, as the Boy Scouts warn, be prepared. This trend doesn't lend itself to clear-cut treatment. Ignore the male lag, some advocates of girls are inclined to argue, on the grounds that men on average still end up outearning women. Bring back old-fashioned competition and more hard-boiled reading matter, urge advocates for boys like Christina Hoff Sommers, who in "The War Against Boys: How Misguided Feminism Is Harming Our Young Men" (2000) denounces a touchy-feely, cooperative, progressive ethos that she says undermines boys' performance and school engagement. Males come from Mars and thrive instead on no-nonsense authority, accountability, clarity and peer rivalry.

What both of these views—feminist and antifeminist alike—fail to appreciate is how much patient attentiveness (in the Venus vein) it takes to boost stragglers rather than strivers. In the "do the math" mission under way with girls, the overarching goal has been surprisingly competitive: to maintain the momentum of female math students (who do just as well as boys early on in school) and to keep the top achievers in the academic pipeline for those "future jobs" in our technological world. The payoff for efforts that have been directed toward school performance has been gratifying. Girls are taking more math and science courses in high school and majoring with greater frequency in those fields in college. (Look at the 40 Intel finalists: this year 38 percent of them were girls.)

The educational predicament of boys is fuzzier by comparison and likely to elude tidy empirical diagnosis and well-focused remedies. At the National Bureau of Economic Research (under whose auspices Summers delivered his remarks about women), analysts have been puzzling over the whys behind "Where the Boys Aren't." the title of one working paper. There are some obvious explanations: men in the Army and in prison and more job options for males (in construction and manufacturing) that don't require a college education but pay relatively well.

Yet there are also murkier social and behavioral—and biological—issues at stake that don't augur well for a quick-fix approach. On the front end, boys appear to be later verbal bloomers than girls, which sets them up for early encounters with academic failure—and which makes early-intervention gambits like the Bush administration's push to emphasize more literacy skills in preschool look misdirected. Down the road, there is evidence that poorer "noncognitive skills" (not academic capacity but work habits and conduct) may be what hobble males most, and that growing up in single-parent families takes more of an educational roll on boys than girls.

Those are challenges that beg for more than school-based strategies. To give her credit, Laura Bush hasn't shied away from them as she starts a boy-focused youth initiative, which runs the gamur from dealing with gangs to financing fatherhood programs to improving remedial English programs. Rewards for such efforts aren't likely to be prompt and aren't aimed at the top—two reasons they deserve the spotlight. Females have yet more strides to make in the sciences, but they're building on success. A boost-the-boys educational endeavor faces the challenge of dealing with downward drift. Clearly the nation needs an impetus to tackle the larger problem of growing social inequality. Worries that it is boys who are being left behind could be the goad we need.

Responding to Reading

1. What "educational disparity"(2) does the gender gap in math and science overshadow? According to Hulbert, to what do boys owe their edge in math testing? What happens to gender disparity among low-income and minority students?
2. What effect has the "do the math" mission had on girls' school performance in math and science? Why, according to Hulbert, is the "educational predicament" of boys "fuzzier" (7)? How does the situation of boys make it difficult to institute programs that could help them?
3. What does Hulbert mean in her conclusion when she says, "clearly, the nation needs an impetus to tackle the larger problem of growing social inequality" (9)? What does she think this impetus might be?

Responding in Writing

Hulbert seems to think that social and behavioral factors may be what hold boys back the most. Do you agree?

MEN ARE FROM EARTH, AND SO ARE WOMEN. IT'S FAULTY RESEARCH THAT SETS THEM APART

Rosalind C. Barnett
1937–

Caryl Rivers
1937–

Senior Scientist at Brandeis University's Women's Studies Research Center and Executive Director of the center's Community, Families & Work Program, Rosalind C. Barnett is a widely published author on gender-related issues. Caryl Rivers, Professor of Journalism at Boston University, has written numerous books and articles exploring the nature of gender, family, work, and religion. Like Barnett and Rivers's most recent book, Same Difference: How Gender Myths Are Hurting Our Relationships, Our Children, and Our Jobs *(2004), the following essay reexamines popular (and damaging) beliefs about gender difference.*

Are American college professors unwittingly misleading their students by teaching widely accepted ideas about men and women that are scientifically unsubstantiated?

Why is the dominant narrative about the sexes one of difference, even though it receives little support from carefully designed peer-reviewed studies?

One reason is that findings from a handful of small studies with nonrepresentative samples have often reported wildly overgeneralized but headline-grabbing findings about gender differences. Those findings have then been picked up by the news media—and found their way back into the academy, where they are taught as fact. At the same time, research that tends to debunk popular ideas is often ignored by the news media.

Even worse, many researchers have taken untested hypotheses at face value and used them to plan their studies. Many have also relied exclusively on statistical tests that are designed to find difference, without using tests that would show the degree of overlap between men and women. As a result, findings often suggest—erroneously—that the sexes are categorically different with respect to some specific variable or other.

5   Yet in the latest edition of its publications manual, the American Psychological Association explicitly asks researchers to consider and report the degree of overlap in statistical studies. For good reason: Even if the mean difference between groups being compared is statistically significant, it may be of trivial consequence if the distributions show a

high degree of overlap. Indeed, most studies that do report the size of effects indicate that the differences between the sexes are trivial or slight on a host of personality traits and cognitive and social behaviors.

Because of such serious and pervasive problems, we believe that college students get a distorted picture about the sexes, one that over-states differences while minimizing the more accurate picture—that of enormous overlap and similarity.

It is easy to understand why college professors might spread myths about gender differences. Many of the original studies on which such findings were based have been embraced by both the academy and the wider culture. As Martha T. Mednick, an emerita professor of psychology at Howard University, pointed out in an article some years ago, popular ideas that are intuitively appealing, even if inadequately documented, all too often take on lives of their own. They may have shaky research foundations; they may be largely disproved by later— and better—studies. But bandwagon concepts that have become un-hitched from research moorings are rampant in academe, particularly in the classroom. For example:

Women Are Inherently More Caring and More "Relational" than Men

The chief architect of this essentialist idea is Carol Gilligan, the longtime Harvard University psychologist who is now at New York University. In the early 1980s, she laid out a new narrative for women's lives that theo-rized that women have a unique, caring nature not shared by men. Her ideas have revolutionized the psychology of women and revamped cur-ricula to an unprecedented degree, some observers say. Certainly, al-most every student in women's studies and the psychology of women is familiar with Gilligan. But how many are aware of the critics of her the-ories about women's moral development and the relational self?

Many scholarly reviews of Gilligan's research contend that it does not back up her claims, that she simply created an intriguing hypothe-sis that needs testing. But the relational self has become near-sacred writ, cited in textbooks, classrooms, and the news media.

Anne Alonso, a Harvard psychology professor and director of the Center for Psychoanalytic Studies at Massachusetts General Hospital, told us recently that she is dismayed by the lightning speed at which Gilligan's ideas, based on slender evidence, have been absorbed into psychotherapy. Usually new theories go through a long and rigorous process of publication in peer-reviewed journals before they are ac-cepted by the field. "None of this work has been published in such journals. It's hard to take seriously a whole corpus of work that hasn't been peer-reviewed," Alonso said. The idea of a relational self, she charged, is simply an "idea du jour," one that she called "penis scorn."

10

Men Don't Value Personal Relations

According to essentialist theorists, men are uncomfortable with any kind of communication that has to do with personal conflicts. They avoid talking about their problems. They avoid responding too deeply to other people's problems, instead giving advice, changing the subject, making a joke, or giving no response. Unlike women, they don't react to troubles talk by empathizing with others and expressing sympathy. These ideas are often cited in textbooks and in popular manuals, like those written by John Gray, a therapist, and Deborah Tannen, a linguistics professor at Georgetown University. Men are from Mars, women are from Venus, we are told. They just don't understand each other. But systematic research does not support those ideas.

An important article, "The Myth of Gender Cultures: Similarities Outweigh Differences in Men's and Women's Provision of and Responses to Supportive Communication," was published this year in *Sex Roles: A Journal of Research.* Erina L. MacGeorge, of Purdue University, and her colleagues at the University of Pennsylvania find no support for the idea that women and men constitute different "communication cultures." Their article, based on three studies that used questionnaires and interviews, sampled 738 people—417 women and 321 men.

In fact, the authors find, the sexes are very much alike in the way they communicate: "Both men and women view the provision of support as a central element of close personal relationships; both value the supportive communication skills of their friends, lovers, and family members; both make similar judgments about what counts as sensitive, helpful support; and both respond quite similarly to various support efforts."

Yet, MacGeorge and her colleagues point out, we still read in textbooks that:

- "Men's and women's communication styles are startlingly dissimilar"—*The Interpersonal Communication Reader,* edited by Joseph A. DeVito (Allyn and Bacon, 2002).

- "American men and women come from different sociolinguistic subcultures, having learned to do different things with words in a conversation"—a chapter by Daniel N. Maltz and Ruth A. Borker in *Language and Social Identity* (Cambridge University Press, 1982), edited by John J. Gumperz.

- "Husbands and wives, especially in Western societies, come from two different cultures with different learned behaviors and communication styles"—a chapter by Carol J. S. Bruess and Judy C. Pearson in *Gendered Relationships* (Mayfield, 1996), edited by Julia T. Wood.

Gender differences in mate selection are pervasive and well established.

Evolutionary psychologists like David M. Buss, a professor at the 15
University of Texas at Austin, tell us in such books as *The Evolution of
Desire: Strategies of Human Mating* (Basic Books, 1994) that men and
women differ widely with respect to the traits they look for in a potential mate. Men, such writers claim, lust after pretty, young, presumably
fertile women. Pop culture revels in this notion: Men want young and
beautiful mates. There is, it is presumed, a universal female type
beloved by men—young, unlined, with features that are close to those
of an infant—that signals fertility. If there were a universal male preference for beautiful young women, it would have to be based on a strong
correlation between beauty and reproductive success. Sure, Richard
Gere chose Julia Roberts in Pretty Woman because of her beauty and
youth. But would those qualities have assured enhanced fertility?

The answer, according to empirical research, seems to be no. Having a pretty face as a young adult has no relationship to the number of
children a woman produces or to her health across the life span.
Among married women, physical attractiveness is unrelated to the
number of children they produce. If beauty has little to do with reproductive success, why would nature insist that men select for it? It seems
more likely that having a young beauty on his arm indicates, instead,
that a man is living up to certain cultural and social norms.

According to some who take what we call an ultra-Darwinist stance,
there is no mystery about whom women prefer as a mate: The man with
resources to feed and protect her future children. The combination of
wealth, status, and power (which usually implies an older man) makes
"an attractive package in the eyes of the average woman," as Robert
Wright, a journalist and author of *The Moral Animal: The New Science of
Evolutionary Psychology* (Pantheon, 1994), sums up the argument.

But those who believe that gender roles are shaped at least as much
by culture and environment as by biology point out that women's preference for older good providers fits perfectly with the rise of the Industrial state. That system, which often called for a male breadwinner and
a female working at home, arose in the United States in the 1830s, was
dominant until the 1970s, and then declined.

If that is correct, then we should see a declining preference for
older men who are good providers, particularly among women with
resources. In fact, a study by Alice Eagley, a psychologist at Northwestern University, and Wendy Wood, of Duke University, suggests that as
gender equality in society has increased, women have expressed less of
a preference for older men with greater earning potential. The researchers have found that when women have access to their own resources, they do not look for age in mates, but prefer qualities like
empathy, understanding, and the ability to bond with children. The
desire for an older "provider" is evidently not in women's genes. Terri
D. Fisher, a psychologist at Ohio State University, told a reporter last

year that whenever she teaches her college students the ultra-Darwinian take on the power of youth and beauty, the young men smile and nod and the young women look appalled.

For Girls, Self-Esteem Plummets at Early Adolescence

20 Girls face an inevitable crisis of self-esteem as they approach adolescence. They are in danger of losing their voices, drowning, and facing a devastating dip in self-regard that boys don't experience. This is the picture that Carol Gilligan presented on the basis of her research at the Emma Willard School, a private girls' school in Troy, N.Y. While Gilligan did not refer to genes in her analysis of girls' vulnerability, she did cite both the "wall of Western culture" and deep early childhood socialization as reasons.

Her theme was echoed in 1994 by the clinical psychologist Mary Pipher's surprise best seller, *Reviving Ophelia* (Putnam, 1994), which spent three years on *The New York Times* best-seller list. Drawing on case studies rather than systematic research, Pipher observed how naturally outgoing, confident girls get worn down by sexist cultural expectations. Gilligan's and Pipher's ideas have also been supported by a widely cited study in 1990 by the American Association of University Women. That report, published in 1991, claimed that teenage girls experience a "free-fall in self-esteem from which some will never recover."

The idea that girls have low self-esteem has by now become part of the academic canon as well as fodder for the popular media. But is it true? No.

Critics have found many faults with the influential AAUW study. When children were asked about their self-confidence and academic plans, the report said 60 percent of girls and 67 percent of boys in elementary school responded, "I am happy the way I am." But by high school, the percentage of girls happy with themselves fell to 29 percent. Could it be that 71 percent of the country's teenage girls were low in self-esteem? Not necessarily. The AAUW counted as happy only those girls who checked "always true" to the question about happiness. Girls who said they were "sometimes" happy with themselves or "sort of" happy with themselves were counted as unhappy.

A sophisticated look at the self-esteem data is far more reassuring than the headlines. A new analysis of all of the AAUW data, and a meta-analysis of hundreds of studies, done by Janet Hyde, a psychologist at the University of Wisconsin at Madison, showed no huge gap between boys and girls. Indeed, Hyde found that the self-esteem scores of boys and girls were virtually identical. In particular there was no plunge in scores for girls during the early teen years—the supposed basis for the idea that girls "lost their voices" in that period. Parents, understandably concerned about noxious, hypersexual media images, may gaze in horror at those images while underestimating the resilience of their daughters, who are able to thrive in spite of them.

Boys Have a Mathematics Gene, Or at Least a Biological Tendency to Excel in Math, That Girls Do Not Possess

Do boys have a mathematics gene—or at least a biological tendency to 25
excel in math—that girls lack, as a popular stereotype has it? Suffice it
to say that, despite being discouraged from pursing math at almost
every level of school, girls and women today are managing to perform
in math at high levels.

Do data support arguments for hard-wired gender differences? No.
In 2001 Erin Leahey and Guang Guo, then a graduate student and an assistant professor of sociology, respectively, at the University of North Carolina at Chapel Hill, looked at some 20,000 math scores of children ages 4
to 18 and found no differences of any magnitude, even in areas that are
supposedly male domains, such as reasoning skills and geometry.

The bandwagon concepts that we have discussed here are strongly
held and dangerous. Even though they have been seriously challenged, they continue to be taught by authority figures in the classroom. These ideas are embedded in the curricula of courses in child
and adolescent development, moral development, education, moral
philosophy, feminist pedagogy, evolutionary psychology, gender studies, and the psychology of women.

Few students have the ability to investigate the accuracy of the
claims on their own. And since these ideas resonate with the cultural
zeitgeist, students would have little reason to do so in any case. The essentialist perspective has so colored the dialogue about the sexes that
there is scant room for any narrative other than difference.

Obviously the difference rhetoric can create harm for both men
and women. Men are taught to believe that they are deficient in caring
and empathy, while women are led to believe that they are inherently
unsuited for competition, leadership, and technological professions.
Given how little empirical support exists for essentialist ideas, it's crucial that professors broaden the dialogue, challenging the conventional
wisdom and encouraging their students to do so as well.

Responding to Reading

1. According to Barnett and Rivers, what problems cause college students to "get
   a distorted picture about the sexes . . ." (6)? In what sense is the view distorted?
2. What specific misleading ideas do Barnett and Rivers identify? How do
   they challenge these ideas? How effective are their responses to these ideas?
3. Why do Barnett and Rivers see the "bandwagon concepts" they discuss as
   dangerous (27)? Why do teachers continue to spread these ideas? What do
   Barnett and Rivers think should be done about this situation?

Responding in Writing

Barnett and Rivers do not specifically address the issue of academic performance in their essay. Do you think they should have? How do you think they
would respond to the discussion of academic performance in Christina Hoff
Sommers's essay "The War against Boys" (p. 400)?

CHAPTER 6 FOCUS

WIDENING THE FOCUS

For Critical Thinking and Writing

After reading the three essays in the Focus section of this chapter—Christian Hoff Sommers's "The War against Boys", Ann Hulbert's "Boy Problems", and Rosalind C. Barnett and Caryl Rivers's "Men Are from Earth, and So Are Women"—write an essay in which you answer the question, "Is there a gender crisis in education?" You may use your own ideas as well as those in the three essays.

For Further Reading

The following readings can suggest additional perspectives for thinking and writing about the roles of men and women:

- Alleen Pace Nilsen, "Sexism in English: Embodiment and Language" (p. 158)

- Michelle Lee, "The Fashion Victim's Ten Commandments" (p. 326)

- Judith Ortiz Cofer, "The Myth of the Latin Woman: I Just Met a Girl Named Maria" (p. 442)

- Arlie Hochschild, "The Second Shift" (p. 505)

- Andrew Sullivan, "The Truth about Men and Women" (p. 630)

For Internet Research

Differences in the ways men and women are treated in school remain a contentious discussion topic. In preparation for writing an essay about the gender gap in education, open one of the popular Web search engines that compiles news stories— <http://news.google.com> or <http://news.yahoo.com>—and enter the search term *gender gap and education*. From the search results, select readings about your topic, and use information from these sources to support your essay. You can begin by reading one or all of the following readings, which were found through the Google news site:

- Conlin, Michelle. "The New Gender Gap." *Business Week Online.* May 26, 2003. <http://www.businessweek.com/print/magazine/content/03_21/b3834001_mz001.htm?mz>

- Guerrero, Lucio, and Maureen Jenkins. "Once and for All, It's Men vs. Women." *Chicago Sun-Times.* May 5, 2006. <http://www.suntimes.com/output/lifestyles/cst_ft_sexes05.html>.

- "Girls Get Extra School Help while Boys Get Ritalin." *USA Today.* Aug. 29, 2003. <http://www.usatoday.com/news/opinion/editorials/2003-08-28-our-view_x.htm>.

WRITING

Gender and Identity

1. In her well-known work *A Room of One's Own,* novelist and critic Virginia Woolf observes that "any woman born with a great gift in the sixteenth century would certainly have gone crazed, shot herself, or ended her days in some lonely cottage outside the village, half witch, half wizard, feared and mocked at." Write an essay in which you discuss in what respects this statement may still apply to gifted women of your own generation or of your parents' generation. You may want to read Marge Piercy's poem "Barbie Doll" (p. 365) and Deborah Tannen's "Marked Women" (p. 395) before you plan your paper.

2. List all the stereotypes of women—and of men—identified in the selections you read in this chapter. Then, write an essay in which you discuss those that have had the most negative effects on your life. Do you consider these stereotypes just annoying, or actually dangerous?

3. Several of the selections in this chapter—for example, "Stay-at-Home Dads" (p. 382) and "Why I Want a Wife" (p. 380)—draw distinctions, implicitly or explicitly, between "men's work" and "women's work." Write an essay in which you consider the extent to which such distinctions exist today, and explain how they have affected your professional goals.

4. The title of a best-selling self-help book by John Gray, *Men Are from Mars, Women Are from Venus,* suggests that men and women are so completely different that they may as well be from different planets. Write an essay in which you support or contradict this title's claim. You may focus on men's and women's actions, tastes, values, preferences, or behavior.

5. Write a letter to Judy Brady in which you update (or challenge) her characterization of a wife in "Why I Want a Wife" (p. 380).

6. Could all-male (or all-female) schools solve the problems encountered by boys and girls in school? Write an essay in which you present your views on this issue.

7. In her essay "Marked Women" (p. 395), Deborah Tannen discusses the distinction between the terms *marked* and *unmarked.* Study the men and women around you, or those you see in films or on television, and determine whether or not your observations support Tannen's point that unlike women, men have "the option of being unmarked." Write an essay in which you agree or disagree with Tannen's conclusion, citing her essay as well as your own observations. (Be sure to define the terms *marked* and *unmarked* in your introduction.)

8. A number of the writers in this chapter examine current ideas about what it means to be male and what it means to be female. Write an essay in which you develop your own definitions of these terms. You may want to consider Sharon Olds's "Rite of Passage"(p. 366), Michael Nava's "Gardenland, Sacramento, California"(p. 367), E. J. Graff's "The M/F Boxes"(p. 377), Glenn Sacks's "Stay at Home Dads"(p. 382), and Christina Hoff Sommers's "The War against Boys"(p. 400).

9. In "Without Apology"(p. 385), Leah Hager Cohen describes her visit to a gym where female boxers train. Throughout her essay, she keeps trying to deal with the fact that the women she sees want to hit and to be hit. Choose two or three traditionally male sports that have female participants—basketball, tennis, and soccer, for example. Then, discuss how the female players challenge (or possibly reinforce) traditional stereotypes.

7

THE AMERICAN DREAM

The American Dream—of political and religious freedom, equal access to education, equal opportunity in the workplace, and ultimately, success and wealth—is often elusive. In the process of working toward the dream, individuals and groups struggle to overcome their status as newcomers or outsiders—to fit in, to belong, to be accepted. As they work toward their goals, however, some must make painful decisions, for full participation in American society may mean assimilating, giving up language, custom, and culture and becoming more like others. Thus, although the American Dream may ultimately mean winning something, it can often mean losing something—a vital part of oneself—as well.

For many people, an important part of the American Dream is the possibility of reinventing themselves—the opportunity to become

Italian immigrant family on ferry from docks to Ellis Island, New York City, 1905

someone different, someone better. From Benjamin Franklin to Malcolm X, Americans have a long tradition of reinvention, which can involve anything from undertaking a program of self-improvement to undergoing a complete change of social identity.

In a free and mobile society, people can (theoretically, at least) become whatever they want to be. In the United States, reinvention has often come about through education and hard work, but Americans have also been able to change who they are and how they are perceived by changing their professions, their associations, or their places of residence. Along with this process of reinvention comes a constant self-analysis, as we Americans continue to question who we are and what we can become.

Many of the essays in this chapter are written from the point of view of outsiders looking in. These writers want to be accepted, to belong. Still, while some eagerly anticipate full acceptance, with all the rights and responsibilities that this entails, others are more cautious, afraid of the personal or cultural price they will have to pay for full acceptance into the American mainstream.

In "What Is the American Dream?"(p. 000), the Focus section that concludes this chapter, Thomas Jefferson, poet Emma Lazarus, President John F. Kennedy, and Martin Luther King, Jr., explore the political, historical, and emotional ties that bind Americans to their country and to one another. These readings showcase the idealism with which Americans approach their dream, reminding us that achieving this dream is worth the struggle.

Italian-American couple celebrating fiftieth wedding anniversary with family

─────────── **Preparing to Read and Write** ───────────

As you read and prepare to write about the essays in this chapter, you may consider the following questions:

- What does the American Dream mean to the writer?

- Is the essay a personal narrative? An analysis of a problem facing a group? Both of these?

- Has the writer been able to achieve the American Dream? If so, by what means? If not, why not?

- What are the greatest obstacles that stand between the writer (or the group he or she writes about) and the American Dream? Would you characterize these obstacles as primarily cultural, social, political, racial, economic, religious, or educational?

- Who has the easiest access to the American Dream? For whom is access most difficult? Why?

- Is the writer looking at the United States from the point of view of an insider or an outsider?

- Does the writer want to change his or her status? To change the status of others? What steps, if any, does he or she take to do so? What additional steps could he or she take?

- With what ethnic, racial, geographic, or economic group does the writer most identify? What is the writer's attitude toward this group? What is the writer's attitude toward what he or she identifies as mainstream American culture?

- Does the writer speak as an individual or as a representative of a particular group?

- Which writers' views of the American Dream are most similar? Most different? Most like your own?

WE MAY BE BROTHERS

Chief Seattle

1786?–1866

Son of a Suquamish chief and a Duwamish chief's daughter, Seattle was chief of the Suquamish, Duwamish, and other saltwater tribes occupying the area around Puget Sound in what is now the state of Washington. As white settlers arrived in the region in the early 1850s, Seattle used his diplomacy and speaking skills to help maintain peace between his followers and the settlers. (Unable to pronounce his name in the original Salish tongue, the whites changed its pronunciation to "Seattle" and eventually named their new settlement after him.) In 1854, during treaty negotiations with the U.S. territorial governor, the chief delivered a moving speech in which he described the inevitable displacement of his people by the better-armed, more technologically advanced newcomers. This speech was not transcribed until some thirty years later, and then by a white on-looker who wrote in the flowery English popular at the time. As a result, it is impossible to say how closely what is reprinted here corresponds to Seat-tle's words. The message, however, is a timeless one that very likely reflects Seattle's passionate beliefs.

Yonder sky that has wept tears of compassion upon my people for centuries untold, and which to us appears changeless and eternal, may change. Today is fair. Tomorrow it may be overcast with clouds. My words are like the stars that never change. Whatever Seattle says the great chief at Washington can rely upon with as much certainty as he can upon the return of the sun or the seasons. The White Chief says that Big Chief at Washington sends us greetings of friendship and goodwill. That is kind of him for we know he has little need of our friendship in return. His people are many. They are like the grass that covers vast prairies. My people are few. They resemble the scat-tering trees of a storm-swept plain. . . . I will not dwell on, nor mourn over, our untimely decay, nor reproach our paleface brothers with hastening it, as we too may have been somewhat to blame. . . .

Your God is not our God. Your God loves your people and hates mine. He folds his strong and protecting arms lovingly about the paleface and leads him by the hand as a father leads his infant son— but He has forsaken His red children—if they really are His. Our God, the Great Spirit, seems also to have forsaken us. Your God makes your people strong every day. Soon they will fill the land. Our people are ebbing away like a rapidly receding tide that will never return. The white man's God cannot love our people or He would protect them. They seem to be orphans who can look nowhere for help. How then can we be brothers? . . . We are two distinct races with separate origins and separate destinies. There is little in common between us.

To us the ashes of our ancestors are sacred and their resting place is hallowed ground. You wander far from the graves of your ancestors and seemingly without regret. Your religion was written upon tables of stone by the iron finger of your God so that you could not forget. The Red Man could never comprehend nor remember it. Our religion is the traditions of our ancestors—the dreams of our old men, given them in solemn hours of night by the Great Spirit; and the visions of our sachems; and it is written in the hearts of our people.

Your dead cease to love you and the land of their nativity as soon as they pass the portals of the tomb and wander way beyond the stars. They are soon forgotten and never return. Our dead never forget the beautiful world that gave them being.

5 Day and night cannot dwell together. The Red Man has ever fled the approach of the White Man, as the morning mist flees before the morning sun. However, your proposition seems fair and I think that my people will accept it and will retire to the reservation you offer them. Then we will dwell apart in peace. . . . It matters little where we pass the remnant of our days. They will not be many. A few more moons; a few more winters—and not one of the descendants of the mighty hosts that once moved over this broad land or lived in happy homes, protected by the Great Spirit, will remain to mourn over the graves of a people once more powerful and hopeful than yours. But why should I mourn at the untimely fate of my people? Tribe follows tribe, and nation follows nation, like the waves of the sea. It is the order of nature, and regret is useless. Your time of decay may be distant, but it will surely come, for even the White Man whose God walked and talked with him as friend with friend cannot be exempt from the common destiny. We may be brothers after all. We will see. . . .

Every part of this soil is sacred in the estimation of my people. Every hillside, every valley, every plain and grove, has been hallowed by some sad or happy event in days long vanished. The very dust upon which you now stand responds more lovingly to their footsteps than to yours, because it is rich with the blood of our ancestors and our bare feet are conscious of the sympathetic touch. Even the little children who lived here and rejoiced here for a brief season will love these somber solitudes and at eventide they greet shadowy returning spirits. And when the last Red Man shall have perished, and the memory of my tribe shall have become a myth among the White Men, these shores will swarm with the invisible dead of my tribe, and when your children's children think themselves alone in the field, the store, the shop, upon the highway, or in the silence of the pathless woods, they will not be alone. At night when the streets of your cities and villages are silent and you think them deserted, they will throng with the returning hosts that once filled and still love this beautiful land. The White Man will never be alone.

Let him be just and deal kindly with my people, for the dead are not powerless. Dead, did I say? There is no death, only a change of worlds.

Responding to Reading

1. The point is made in paragraph 2 that Native Americans and whites are "two distinct races with separate origins and separate destinies." What differences are then identified? Are there any similarities between the two groups?
2. Would you characterize the tone of this speech as primarily hopeful, resigned, conciliatory, angry, or bitter? What dreams, if any, does the speech suggest for Chief Seattle's people? Do you think these dreams have been realized?
3. Paragraph 5 offers the observation, "We may be brothers after all. We will see." What do you suppose Chief Seattle means? Do you agree?

Responding in Writing

Chief Seattle's comments were delivered in a speech. How do you picture the setting and audience for this speech?

WHY THE AMERICANS ARE SO RESTLESS IN THE MIDST OF THEIR PROSPERITY
Alexis de Tocqueville
1805–1859

Historian and political scientist Alexis de Tocqueville was born in Verneuil, France. After studying law, he entered politics and went on to serve in the Chamber of Deputies and as minister of foreign affairs. In 1831, the French government sent him on a mission to the United States to draft a report on the penal system. His stay led him to write De la Democratie en Amérique *(1835), the first comprehensive study of the political and social institutions of the United States as well as of the character of the American people. Translated as* Democracy in America, *the book was published here between 1835 and 1840 and remains a classic political science text. In this excerpt from the book, de Tocqueville tries to understand why Americans are dissatisfied despite their many advantages.*

In certain remote corners of the Old World you may still sometimes stumble upon a small district that seems to have been forgotten amid the general tumult, and to have remained stationary while everything around it was in motion. The inhabitants, for the most part, are extremely ignorant and poor; they take no part in the business of the country and are frequently oppressed by the government, yet their countenances are generally placid and their spirits light.

In America I saw the freest and most enlightened men placed in the happiest circumstances that the world affords; it seemed to me as if a cloud habitually hung upon their brow, and I thought them serious and almost sad, even in their pleasures.

The chief reason for this contrast is that the former do not think of the ills they endure, while the latter are forever brooding over advantages they do not possess. It is strange to see with what feverish ardor the Americans pursue their own welfare, and to watch the vague dread that constantly torments them lest they should not have chosen the shortest path which may lead to it.

A native of the United States clings to this world's goods as if he were certain never to die; and he is so hasty in grasping at all within his reach that one would suppose he was constantly afraid of not living long enough to enjoy them. He clutches everything, he holds nothing fast, but soon loosens his grasp to pursue fresh gratifications.

5   In the United States a man builds a house in which to spend his old age, and he sells it before the roof is on; he plants a garden and lets it just as the trees are coming into bearing; he brings a field into tillage and leaves other men to gather the crops; he embraces a profession and gives it up; he settles in a place, which he soon afterwards leaves to carry his changeable longings elsewhere. If his private affairs leave him any leisure, he instantly plunges into the vortex of politics; and if at the end of a year of unremitting labor he finds he has a few days' vacation, his eager curiosity whirls him over the vast extent of the United States, and he will travel fifteen hundred miles in a few days to shake off his happiness. Death at length overtakes him, but it is before he is weary of his bootless chase of that complete felicity which forever escapes him.

At first sight there is something surprising in this strange unrest of so many happy men, restless in the midst of abundance. The spectacle itself, however, is as old as the world; the novelty is to see a whole people furnish an exemplification of it.

Their taste for physical gratifications must be regarded as the original source of that secret disquietude which the actions of the Americans betray and of that inconstancy of which they daily afford fresh examples. He who has set his heart exclusively upon the pursuit of worldly welfare is always in a hurry, for he has but a limited time at his disposal to reach, to grasp, and to enjoy it. The recollection of the shortness of life is a constant spur to him. Besides the good things that he possesses, he every instant fancies a thousand others that death will prevent him from trying if he does not try them soon. This thought fills him with anxiety, fear, and regret and keeps his mind in ceaseless trepidation, which leads him perpetually to change his plans and his abode.

If in addition to the taste for physical well-being a social condition be added in which neither laws nor customs retain any person in his place, there is a great additional stimulant to this restlessness of temper. Men will then be seen continually to change their track for fear of missing the shortest cut to happiness.

It may readily be conceived that if men passionately bent upon physical gratifications desire eagerly, they are also easily discouraged; as their ultimate object is to enjoy, the means to reach that object must be prompt and easy or the trouble of acquiring the gratification would be greater than the gratification itself. Their prevailing frame of mind, then, is at once ardent and relaxed, violent and enervated. Death is often less dreaded by them than perseverance in continuous efforts to one end.

The equality of conditions leads by a still straighter road to several 10 of the effects that I have here described. When all the privileges of birth and fortune are abolished, when all professions are accessible to all, and a man's own energies may place him at the top of any one of them, an easy and unbounded career seems open to his ambition and he will readily persuade himself that he is born to no common destinies. But this is an erroneous notion, which is corrected by daily experience. The same equality that allows every citizen to conceive these lofty hopes renders all the citizens less able to realize them; it circumscribes their powers on every side, while it gives freer scope to their desires. Not only are they themselves powerless, but they are met at every step by immense obstacles, which they did not at first perceive. They have swept away the privileges of some of their fellow creatures which stood in their way, but they have opened the door to universal competition; the barrier has changed its shape rather than its position. When men are nearly alike and all follow the same track, it is very difficult for any one individual to walk quickly and cleave a way through the dense throng that surrounds and presses on him. This constant strife between the inclination springing from the equality of condition and the means it supplies to satisfy them harasses and wearies the mind.

It is possible to conceive of men arrived at a degree of freedom that should completely content them; they would then enjoy their independence without anxiety and without impatience. But men will never establish any equality with which they can be contented. Whatever efforts a people may make, they will never succeed in reducing all the conditions of society to a perfect level; and even if they unhappily attained that absolute and complete equality of position, the inequality of minds would still remain, which, coming directly from the hand of God, will forever escape the laws of man. However democratic, then, the social state and the political constitution of a people may be, it is certain that every member of the community will always find out several points about him which overlook his own position; and we may foresee that his looks will be doggedly fixed in that direction. When inequality of conditions is the common law of society, the most marked inequalities do not strike the eye; when everything is nearly on the same level, the slightest are marked enough to hurt it. Hence the desire of equality always becomes more insatiable in proportion as equality is more complete.

Among democratic nations, men easily attain a certain equality of condition, but they can never attain as much as they desire. It perpetually retires from before them, yet without hiding itself from their sight, and in retiring draws them on. At every moment they think they are about to grasp it; it escapes at every moment from their hold. They are near enough to see its charms, but too far off to enjoy them; and before they have fully tasted its delights, they die.

To these causes must be attributed that strange melancholy which often haunts the inhabitants of democratic countries in the midst of their abundance, and that disgust at life which sometimes seizes upon them in the midst of calm and easy circumstances. Complaints are made in France that the number of suicides increases; in America suicide is rare, but insanity is said to be more common there than anywhere else. These are all different symptoms of the same disease. The Americans do not put an end to their lives, however disquieted they may be, because their religion forbids it; and among them materialism may be said hardly to exist, notwithstanding the general passion for physical gratification. The will resists, but reason frequently gives way.

In democratic times enjoyments are more intense than in the ages of aristocracy, and the number of those who partake in them is vastly larger: but, on the other hand, it must be admitted that man's hopes and desires are oftener blasted, the soul is more stricken and perturbed, and care itself more keen.

Responding to Reading

1. De Tocqueville's essay was published in 1835. Does his characterization of Americans' "unrest" hold true today? If so, do you see this restlessness as a problem?
2. De Tocqueville speaks about Americans in very general, abstract terms. Can you supply concrete, specific examples to support (or contradict) his characterizations?
3. What does de Tocqueville see as the cause of Americans' restlessness? In what sense is "equality" to blame? Does he offer a cure for the national malady? Given the premise of equality upon which our society rests, do you think a cure is possible? Explain.

Responding in Writing

Write a brief letter to de Tocqueville supporting or challenging his characterization of Americans.

THE LIBRARY CARD
Richard Wright
1908–1960

Born on a former plantation near Natchez, Mississippi, Richard Wright spent much of his childhood in an orphanage or with various relatives. He attended schools in Jackson and in 1934 moved to Chicago, where he worked at a number of unskilled jobs before joining the Federal Writers' Project. When his politics became radical, he wrote poetry for leftist publications. In 1938, he published his first book, Uncle Tom's Children: Four Novellas; *two years later, his novel* Native Son *made him famous. After World War II, Wright lived as an expatriate in Paris, where he wrote* Black Boy (1945), *an autobiography that celebrates African-American resilience and courage much as nineteenth-century slave narratives do. In this excerpt from* Black Boy, *Wright tells how he took advantage of an opportunity to feed his hunger for an intellectual life.*

One morning I arrived early at work and went into the bank lobby where the Negro porter was mopping. I stood at a counter and picked up the Memphis *Commercial Appeal* and began my free reading of the press. I came finally to the editorial page and saw an article dealing with one H. L. Mencken.[1] I knew by hearsay that he was the editor of the *American Mercury,* but aside from that I knew nothing about him. The article was a furious denunciation of Mencken, concluding with one hot, short sentence: Mencken is a fool.

I wondered what on earth this Mencken had done to call down upon him the scorn of the South. The only people I had ever heard denounced in the South were Negroes, and this man was not a Negro. Then what ideas did Mencken hold that made a newspaper like the *Commercial Appeal* castigate him publicly? Undoubtedly he must be advocating ideas that the South did not like. Were there, then, people other than Negroes who criticized the South? I knew that during the Civil War the South had hated northern whites, but I had not encountered such hate during my life. Knowing no more of Mencken than I did at that moment, I felt a vague sympathy for him. Had not the South, which had assigned me the role of a non-man, cast at him its hardest words?

Now, how could I find out about this Mencken? There was a huge library near the riverfront, but I knew that Negroes were not allowed to patronize its shelves any more than they were the parks

---

[1]Henry Louis Mencken (1880–1956), journalist, critic, and essayist, who was known for his pointed, outspoken, and satirical comments about the blunders and imperfections of democracy and the cultural awkwardness of Americans. [Eds.]

and playgrounds of the city. I had gone into the library several times to get books for the white men on the job. Which of them would now help me to get books? And how could I read them without causing concern to the white men with whom I worked? I had so far been successful in hiding my thoughts and feelings from them, but I knew that I would create hostility if I went about this business of reading in a clumsy way.

I weighed the personalities of the men on the job. There was Don, a Jew; but I distrusted him. His position was not much better than mine and I knew that he was uneasy and insecure; he had always treated me in an offhand, bantering way that barely concealed his contempt. I was afraid to ask him to help me to get books; his frantic desire to demonstrate a racial solidarity with the whites against Negroes might make him betray me.

5   Then how about the boss? No, he was a Baptist and I had the suspicion that he would not be quite able to comprehend why a black boy would want to read Mencken. There were other white men on the job whose attitudes showed clearly that they were Kluxers or sympathizers, and they were out of the question.

There remained only one man whose attitude did not fit into an anti-Negro category, for I had heard the white men refer to him as a "Pope lover." He was an Irish Catholic and was hated by the white Southerners. I knew that he read books, because I had got him volumes from the library several times. Since he, too, was an object of hatred, I felt that he might refuse me but would hardly betray me. I hesitated, weighing and balancing the imponderable realities.

One morning I paused before the Catholic fellow's desk.

"I want to ask you a favor," I whispered to him.

"What is it?"

10   "I want to read. I can't get books from the library. I wonder if you'd let me use your card?"

He looked at me suspiciously.

"My card is full most of the time," he said.

"I see," I said and waited, posing my question silently.

"You're not trying to get me into trouble, are you, boy?" he asked, staring at me.

15   "Oh, no, sir."

"What book do you want?"

"A book by H. L. Mencken."

"Which one?"

"I don't know. Has he written more than one?"

20   "He has written several."

"I didn't know that."

"What makes you want to read Mencken?"

"Oh, I just saw his name in the newspaper," I said.

"It's good of you to want to read," he said. "But you ought to read the right things."

I said nothing. Would he want to supervise my reading?   25

"Let me think," he said. "I'll figure out something."

I turned from him and he called me back. He stared at me quizzically.

"Richard, don't mention this to the other white men," he said.

"I understand," I said. "I won't say a word."

A few days later he called me to him.   30

"I've got a card in my wife's name," he said. "Here's mine."

"Thank you, sir."

"Do you think you can manage it?"

"I'll manage fine," I said.

"If they suspect you, you'll get in trouble," he said.   35

"I'll write the same kind of notes to the library that you wrote when you sent me for books," I told him. "I'll sign your name."

He laughed.

"Go ahead. Let me see what you get," he said.

That afternoon I addressed myself to forging a note. Now, what were the names of books written by H. L. Mencken? I did not know any of them. I finally wrote what I thought would be a foolproof note: *Dear Madam: Will you please let this nigger boy*—I used the word "nigger" to make the librarian feel that I could not possibly be the author of the note—*have some books by H. L. Mencken?* I forged the white man's name.

I entered the library as I had always done when on errands for 40
whites, but I felt that I would somehow slip up and betray myself. I doffed my hat, stood a respectful distance from the desk, looked as unbookish as possible, and waited for the white patrons to be taken care of. When the desk was clear of people, I still waited. The white librarian looked at me.

"What do you want, boy?"

As though I did not possess the power of speech, I stepped forward and simply handed her the forged note, not parting my lips.

"What books by Mencken does he want?" she asked.

"I don't know, ma'am," I said, avoiding her eyes.

"Who gave you this card?"

"Mr. Falk," I said.   45

"Where is he?"

"He's at work, at the M——Optical Company," I said. "I've been in here for him before."

"I remember," the woman said. "But he never wrote notes like this."

Oh, God, she's suspicious. Perhaps she would not let me have the books? If she had turned her back at that moment, I would have 50 ducked out the door and never gone back. Then I thought of a bold idea.

"You can call him up, ma'am," I said, my heart pounding.

"You're not using these books, are you?" she asked pointedly.

"Oh, no, ma'am. I can't read."

"I don't know what he wants by Mencken," she said under her breath.

55 I knew now that I had won; she was thinking of other things and the race question had gone out of her mind. She went to the shelves. Once or twice she looked over her shoulder at me, as though she was still doubtful. Finally she came forward with two books in her hand.

"I'm sending him two books," she said. "But tell Mr. Falk to come in next time, or send me the names of the books he wants. I don't know what he wants to read."

I said nothing. She stamped the card and handed me the books. Not daring to glance at them, I went out of the library, fearing that the woman would call me back for further questioning. A block away from the library I opened one of the books and read a title: *A Book of Prefaces*. I was nearing my nineteenth birthday and I did not know how to pronounce the word "preface." I thumbed the pages and saw strange words and strange names. I shook my head, disappointed. I looked at the other book; it was called *Prejudices*. I knew what that word meant; I had heard it all my life. And right off I was on guard against Mencken's books. Why would a man want to call a book *Prejudices?* The word was so stained with all my memories of racial hate that I could not conceive of anybody using it for a title. Perhaps I had made a mistake about Mencken? A man who had prejudices must be wrong.

When I showed the books to Mr. Falk, he looked at me and frowned.

"That librarian might telephone you," I warned him.

60 "That's all right," he said. "But when you're through reading those books, I want you to tell me what you get out of them."

That night in my rented room, while letting the hot water run over my can of pork and beans in the sink, I opened *A Book of Prefaces* and began to read. I was jarred and shocked by the style, the clear, clean, sweeping sentences. Why did he write like that? And how did one write like that? I pictured the man as a raging demon, slashing with his pen, consumed with hate, denouncing everything American, extolling everything European or German, laughing at the weaknesses of people, mocking God, authority. What was this? I stood up, trying to realize what reality lay behind the meaning of the words. . . . Yes, this man was fighting, fighting with words. He was using words as a weapon, using them as one would use a club. Could words be weapons? Well, yes, for here they were. Then, maybe, perhaps, I could use them as a weapon? No. It frightened me. I read on and what amazed me was not what he said, but how on earth anybody had the courage to say it.

Occasionally I glanced up to reassure myself that I was alone in the room. Who were these men about whom Mencken was talking so passionately? Who was Anatole France? Joseph Conrad? Sinclair Lewis, Sherwood Anderson, Dostoevski, George Moore, Gustave Flaubert, Maupassant, Tolstoy, Frank Harris, Mark Twain, Thomas Hardy, Arnold Bennett, Stephen Crane, Zola, Norris, Gorky, Bergson, Ibsen, Balzac, Bernard Shaw, Dumas, Poe, Thomas Mann, O. Henry, Dreiser, H. G. Wells, Gogol, T. S. Eliot, Gide, Baudelaire, Edgar Lee Masters, Stendhal, Turgenev, Huneker, Nietzsche, and scores of others? Were these men real? Did they exist or had they existed? And how did one pronounce their names?

I ran across many words whose meanings I did not know, and I either looked them up in a dictionary or, before I had a chance to do that, encountered the word in a context that made its meaning clear. But what strange world was this? I concluded the book with the conviction that I had somehow overlooked something terribly important in life. I had once tried to write, had once reveled in feeling, had let my crude imagination roam, but the impulse to dream had been slowly beaten out of me by experience. Now it surged up again and I hungered for books, new ways of looking and seeing. It was not a matter of believing or disbelieving what I read, but of feeling something new, of being affected by something that made the look of the world different.

As dawn broke I ate my pork and beans, feeling dopey, sleepy. I went to work, but the mood of the book would not die; it lingered, coloring everything I saw, heard, did. I now felt that I knew what the white men were feeling. Merely because I had read a book that had spoken of how they lived and thought, I identified myself with that book. I felt vaguely guilty. Would I, filled with bookish notions, act in a manner that would make the whites dislike me?

I forged more notes and my trips to the library became frequent. Reading grew into a passion. My first serious novel was Sinclair Lewis's *Main Street*.[2] It made me see my boss, Mr. Gerald, and identify him as an American type. I would smile when I saw him lugging his golf bags into the office. I had always felt a vast distance separating me from the boss, and now I felt closer to him, though still distant. I felt now that I knew him, that I could feel the

65

---

[2]*Main Street*, published in 1920, examines the smugness, intolerance, and lack of imagination that characterize small-town American life. [Eds.]

very limits of his narrow life. And this had happened because I had read a novel about a mythical man called George F. Babbitt.[3]

The plots and stories in the novels did not interest me so much as the point of view revealed. I gave myself over to each novel without reserve, without trying to criticize it; it was enough for me to see and feel something different. And for me, everything was something different. Reading was like a drug, a dope. The novels created moods in which I lived for days. But I could not conquer my sense of guilt, my feeling that the white men around me knew that I was changing, that I had begun to regard them differently.

Whenever I brought a book to the job, I wrapped it in newspaper— a habit that was to persist for years in other cities and under other circumstances. But some of the white men pried into my packages when I was absent and they questioned me.

"Boy, what are you reading those books for?"

"Oh, I don't know, sir."

70   "That's deep stuff you're reading, boy."

"I'm just killing time, sir."

"You'll addle your brains if you don't watch out."

I read Dreiser's *Jennie Gerhardt* and *Sister Carrie*[4] and they revived in me a vivid sense of my mother's suffering; I was overwhelmed. I grew silent, wondering about the life around me. It would have been impossible for me to have told anyone what I derived from these novels, for it was nothing less than a sense of life itself. All my life had shaped me for the realism, the naturalism of the modern novel, and I could not read enough of them.

Steeped in new moods and ideas, I bought a ream of paper and tried to write; but nothing would come, or what did come was flat beyond telling. I discovered that more than desire and feeling were necessary to write and I dropped the idea. Yet I still wondered how it was possible to know people sufficiently to write about them. Could I ever learn about life and people? To me, with my vast ignorance, my Jim Crow station in life, it seemed a task impossible of achievement. I now knew what being a Negro meant. I could endure the hunger. I had learned to live with hate. But to feel that there were feelings denied me, that the very breath of life itself was beyond my reach, that more than anything else hurt, wounded me. I had a new hunger.

75   In buoying me up, reading also cast me down, made me see what was possible, what I had missed. My tension returned, new, terrible,

---

[3]The central character in Sinclair Lewis's *Babbit* (1922), who believed in the virtues of home, the Republican Party, and middle-class conventions. To Wright, Babbitt symbolizes the mindless complacency of white middle-class America. [Eds.]

[4]Both *Jennie Gerhardt* (1911) and *Sister Carrie* (1900), by Theodore Dreiser, tell the stories of working women who struggle against poverty and social injustice. [Eds.]

bitter, surging, almost too great to be contained. I no longer *felt* that the world about me was hostile, killing; I *knew* it. A million times I asked myself what I could do to save myself, and there were no answers. I seemed forever condemned, ringed by walls.

I did not discuss my reading with Mr. Falk, who had lent me his library card; it would have meant talking about myself and that would have been too painful. I smiled each day, fighting desperately to maintain my old behavior, to keep my disposition seemingly sunny. But some of the white men discerned that I had begun to brood.

"Wake up there, boy!" Mr. Olin said one day.

"Sir!" I answered for the lack of a better word.

"You act like you've stolen something," he said.

I laughed in the way I knew he expected me to laugh, but I re- 80 solved to be more conscious of myself, to watch my every act, to guard and hide the new knowledge that was dawning within me.

If I went north, would it be possible for me to build a new life then? But how could a man build a life upon vague, unformed yearnings? I wanted to write and I did not even know the English language. I bought English grammars and found them dull. I felt that I was getting a better sense of the language from novels than from grammars. I read hard, discarding a writer as soon as I felt that I had grasped his point of view. At night the printed page stood before my eyes in sleep.

Mrs. Moss, my landlady, asked me one Sunday morning: "Son, what is this you keep on reading?"

"Oh, nothing. Just novels."

"What you get out of 'em?"

"I'm just killing time," I said. 85

"I hope you know your own mind," she said in a tone which implied that she doubted if I had a mind.

I knew of no Negroes who read the books I liked and I wondered if any Negroes ever thought of them. I knew that there were Negro doctors, lawyers, newspapermen, but I never saw any of them. When I read a Negro newspaper I never caught the faintest echo of my preoccupation in its pages. I felt trapped and occasionally, for a few days, I would stop reading. But a vague hunger would come over me for books, books that opened up new avenues of feeling and seeing, and again I would forge another note to the white librarian. Again I would read and wonder as only the naïve and unlettered can read and wonder, feeling that I carried a secret, criminal burden about with me each day.

That winter my mother and brother came and we set up housekeeping, buying furniture on the installment plan, being cheated and yet knowing no way to avoid it. I began to eat warm food and to my surprise found that regular meals enabled me to read faster. I may have lived through many illnesses and survived them, never suspecting that I was ill. My brother obtained a job and we began to save toward the trip north, plotting our time, setting tentative dates for departure. I told none of the white men on the job that I was planning to go north; I knew that the moment they felt I was thinking of the North they would change toward me. It would have made them feel that I did not like the life I was living, and because my life was completely conditioned by what they said or did, it would have been tantamount to challenging them.

I could calculate my chances for life in the South as a Negro fairly clearly now.

90   I could fight the southern whites by organizing with other Negroes, as my grandfather had done. But I knew that I could never win that way; there were many whites and there were but few blacks. They were strong and we were weak. Outright black rebellion could never win. If I fought openly I would die and I did not want to die. News of lynchings were frequent.

I could submit and live the life of a genial slave, but that was impossible. All of my life had shaped me to live by my own feelings and thoughts. I could make up to Bess and marry her and inherit the house. But that, too, would be the life of a slave; if I did that, I would crush to death something within me, and I would hate myself as much as I knew the whites already hated those who had submitted. Neither could I ever willingly present myself to be kicked, as Shorty had done. I would rather have died than do that.

I could drain off my restlessness by fighting with Shorty and Harrison. I had seen many Negroes solve the problem of being black by transferring their hatred of themselves to others with a black skin and fighting them. I would have to be cold to do that, and I was not cold and I could never be.

I could, of course, forget what I had read, thrust the whites out of my mind, forget them; and find release from anxiety and longing in sex and alcohol. But the memory of how my father had conducted himself made that course repugnant. If I did not want others to violate my life, how could I voluntarily violate it myself?

I had no hope whatever of being a professional man. Not only had I been so conditioned that I did not desire it, but the fulfillment of such an ambition was beyond my capabilities. Well-to-do Negroes lived in a world that was almost as alien to me as the world inhabited by whites.

95   What, then, was there? I held my life in my mind, in my consciousness each day, feeling at times that I would stumble and drop it, spill it forever. My reading had created a vast sense of distance between me and the world in which I lived and tried to make a living, and that sense of distance was increasing each day. My days and

nights were one long, quiet, continuously contained dream of terror, tension, and anxiety. I wondered how long I could bear it.

Responding to Reading

1. In what sense did access to books bring Wright closer to achieving the American Dream? What new obstacles did books introduce?
2. In paragraph 74, Wright mentions his "Jim Crow station in life." The term *Jim Crow,* derived from a character in a minstrel show, refers to laws enacted in Southern states that legalized racial segregation. What is Wright's "station in life"? In what ways does he adapt his behavior to accommodate this Jim Crow image? In what ways does he defy this stereotype?
3. After World War II, Wright left the United States to live in Paris. Given what you have read in this essay, does his decision surprise you? Do you think he made the right choice? What other options did he have?

Responding in Writing

If Wright were alive today, what books and magazines would you recommend he read? Why?

BECOMING AMERICAN

Dinesh D'Souza

1961–

Dinesh D'Souza was born in Bombay, India, and immigrated to the United States with his family in 1978. He now works as a fellow at the Hoover Institution of Stanford University and writes articles on culture and politics. D'Souza's books include the bestseller Illiberal Education *(1991),* The Virtue of Prosperity: Finding Values in an Age of Techno-Affluence *(2000), and the bestseller* What's So Great About America *(2002), from which the following essay is taken. Here he tries to explain exactly why America is so appealing to immigrants like himself.*

Critics of America, both at home and abroad, have an easy explanation for why the American idea is so captivating, and why immigrants want to come here. The reason, they say, is money. America represents "the bitch goddess of success." That is why poor people reach out for the American idea: they want to touch some of that lucre. As for immigrants, they allegedly flock to the United States for the sole purpose of getting rich. This view, which represents the appeal of America as the appeal of the almighty dollar, is disseminated on Arab streets and in multicultural textbooks taught in U.S. schools. It is a way of demeaning the United States by associating it with what is selfish, base, and crass: an unquenchable appetite for gain.

It is not hard to see why this view of America has gained a wide currency. When people in foreign countries turn on American TV shows, they are stupefied by the lavish displays of affluence: the sumptuous homes, the bejeweled women, the fountains and pools, and so on. Whether reruns of *Dallas* and *Dynasty* are true to the American experience is irrelevant here; the point is that this is how the United States appears to outsiders who have not had the chance to come here. And even for those who do, it is hard to deny that America represents the chance to live better, even to become fantastically wealthy. For instance, there are several people of Indian descent on the *Forbes* 400 list. And over the years I have heard many Indians now living in the United States say, "We want to live an Indian lifestyle, but at an American standard of living."

If this seems like a crass motive for immigration, it must be evaluated in the context of the harsh fate that poor people endure in much of the Third World. The lives of many of these people are defined by an ongoing struggle to exist. It is not that they don't work hard. On the contrary, they labor incessantly and endure hardships that are almost unimaginable to people in the West. In the villages of Asia and Africa, for example, a common sight is a farmer beating a pickax into the ground, women wobbling under heavy loads, children carrying stones. These people are performing very hard labor, but they are getting nowhere. The best they can hope for is to survive for another day. Their clothes are tattered, their teeth are rotted, and disease and death constantly loom over their horizon. For the poor of the Third World, life is characterized by squalor, indignity, and brevity.

I emphasize the plight of the poor, but I recognize, of course, that there are substantial middle classes even in the underdeveloped world. For these people basic survival may not be an issue, but still, they endure hardships that make everyday life a strain. One problem is that the basic infrastructure of the Third World is abysmal: the roads are not properly paved, the water is not safe to drink, pollution in the cities has reached hazardous levels, public transportation is overcrowded and unreliable, and there is a two-year waiting period to get a telephone. Government officials, who are very poorly paid, are inevitably corrupt, which means that you must pay bribes on a regular basis to get things done. Most important, there are limited prospects for the children's future.

5   In America, the immigrant immediately recognizes, things are different. The newcomer who sees America for the first time typically experiences emotions that alternate between wonder and delight. Here is a country where *everything works:* the roads are clean and paper smooth, the highway signs are clear and accurate, the public toilets function properly, when you pick up the telephone you get a dial tone, you can even buy things from the store and then take them

back. For the Third World visitor, the American supermarket is a thing to behold: endless aisles of every imaginable product, fifty different types of cereal, multiple flavors of ice cream. The place is full of countless unappreciated inventions: quilted toilet paper, fabric softener, cordless telephones, disposable diapers, roll-on luggage, deodorant. Most countries even today do not have these benefits: deodorant, for example, is unavailable in much of the Third World and unused in much of Europe.

What the immigrant cannot help noticing is that America is a country where the poor live comparatively well. This fact was dramatized in the 1980s, when CBS television broadcast an anti-Reagan documentary, "People Like Us," which was intended to show the miseries of the poor during an American recession. The Soviet Union also broadcast the documentary, with a view to embarrassing the Reagan administration. But by the testimony of former Soviet leaders, it had the opposite effect. Ordinary people across the Soviet Union saw that the poorest Americans have television sets and microwave ovens and cars. They arrived at the same perception of America that I witnessed in a friend of mine from Bombay who has been unsuccessfully trying to move to the United States for nearly a decade. Finally I asked him, "Why are you so eager to come to America?" He replied, "Because I really want to live in a country where the poor people are fat."

The point is that the United States is a country where the ordinary guy has a good life. This is what distinguishes America from so many other countries. Everywhere in the world, the rich person lives well. Indeed, a good case can be made that if you are rich, you live better in countries other than America. The reason is that you enjoy the pleasures of aristocracy. This is the pleasure of being treated as a superior person. Its gratification derives from subservience: in India, for example, the wealthy enjoy the satisfaction of seeing innumerable servants and toadies grovel before them and attend to their every need.

In the United States the social ethic is egalitarian, and this is unaffected by the inequalities of wealth in the country. Tocqueville noticed this egalitarianism a century and a half ago, but it is, if anything, more prevalent today. For all his riches, Bill Gates could not approach a homeless person and say, "Here's a $100 bill. I'll give it to you if you kiss my feet." Most likely the homeless guy would tell Gates to go to hell! The American view is that the rich guy may have more money, but he isn't in any fundamental sense better than you are. The American janitor or waiter sees himself as performing a service, but he doesn't see himself as inferior to those he serves. And neither do the customers see him that way: they are generally happy to show him respect and appreciation on a plane of equality. America is the only country in the world where we call the waiter "Sir," as if he were a knight.

The moral triumph of America is that it has extended the benefits of comfort and affluence, traditionally enjoyed by very few, to a large segment of society. Very few people in America have to wonder where their next meal is coming from. Even sick people who don't have proper insurance can receive medical care at hospital emergency rooms. The poorest American girls are not humiliated by having to wear torn clothes. Every child is given an education, and most have the chance to go on to college. The common man can expect to live long enough and have free time to play with his grandchildren.

10   Ordinary Americans enjoy not only security and dignity, but also comforts that other societies reserve for the elite. We now live in a country where construction workers regularly pay $4 for a nonfat latte, where maids drive very nice cars, where plumbers take their families on vacation to Europe. As Irving Kristol once observed, there is virtually no restaurant in America to which a CEO can go to lunch with the absolute assurance that he will not find his secretary also dining there. Given the standard of living of the ordinary American, it is no wonder that socialist or revolutionary schemes have never found a wide constituency in the United States. As sociologist Werner Sombart observed, all socialist utopias in America have come to grief on roast beef and apple pie.*

Thus it is entirely understandable that people would associate the idea of America with a better life. For them, money is not an end in itself; money is the means to a longer, healthier, and fuller life. Money allows them to purchase a level of security, dignity, and comfort that they could not have hoped to enjoy in their native countries. Money also frees up time for family life, community involvement, and spiritual pursuits: thus it produces not just material, but also moral, gains. All of this is true, and yet in my view it offers an incomplete picture of why America is so appealing to so many. Let me illustrate with the example of my own life.

Not long ago, I asked myself: what would my life have been like if I had never come to the United States, if I had stayed in India? Materially, my life has improved, but not in a fundamental sense. I grew up in a middle-class family in Bombay. My father was a chemical engineer; my mother, an office secretary. I was raised without great luxury, but neither did I lack for anything. My standard of living in America is higher, but it is not a radical difference. My life has changed far more dramatically in other ways.

If I had remained in India, I would probably have lived my entire existence within a one-mile radius of where I was born. I would undoubtedly have married a woman of my identical religious, socioeconomic,

*Werner Sombart, *Why Is There No Socialism in the United States?* (White Plains: International Arts and Sciences Press, 1976), 109–10.

and cultural background. I would almost certainly have become a medical doctor, an engineer, or a software programmer. I would have socialized within my ethnic community and had cordial relations, but few friends, outside that group. I would have a whole set of opinions that could be predicted in advance; indeed, they would not be very different from what my father believed, or his father before him. In sum, my destiny would to a large degree have been given to me.

This is not to say that I would have no choice; I would have choice, but within narrowly confined parameters. Let me illustrate with the example of my sister, who got married several years ago. My parents began the process by conducting a comprehensive survey of all the eligible families in our neighborhood. First they examined primary criteria, such as religion, socioeconomic position, and educational background. Then my parents investigated subtler issues: the social reputation of the family, reports of a lunatic uncle, the character of the son, and so on. Finally my parents were down to a dozen or so eligible families, and they were invited to our house for dinner with suspicious regularity. My sister was, in the words of Milton Friedman, "free to choose." My sister knew about, and accepted, the arrangement; she is now happily married with two children. I am not quarreling with the outcome, but clearly my sister's destiny was, to a considerable extent, choreographed by my parents.

By coming to America, I have seen my life break free of these traditional confines. I came to Arizona as an exchange student, but a year later I was enrolled at Dartmouth College. There I fell in with a group of students who were actively involved in politics; soon I had switched my major from economics to English literature. My reading included books like Plutarch's *Moralia*; Hamilton, Madison, and Jay's *Federalist Papers*; and Evelyn Waugh's *Brideshead Revisited*. They transported me to places a long way from home and implanted in my mind ideas that I had never previously considered. By the time I graduated, I decided that I should become a writer, which is something you can do in this country. America permits many strange careers: this is a place where you can become, say, a comedian. I would not like to go to my father and tell him that I was thinking of becoming a comedian. I do not think he would have found it funny.

Soon after graduation I became the managing editor of a policy magazine and began to write freelance articles in the *Washington Post*. Someone in the Reagan White House was apparently impressed by my work, because I was called in for an interview and promptly hired as a senior domestic policy analyst. I found it strange to be working at the White House, because at the time I was not a United States citizen. I am sure that such a thing would not happen in India or anywhere else in the world. But Reagan and his people didn't seem to mind; for them, ideology counted more than nationality. I also met my future wife in the Reagan administration, where she was at the time a White House intern. (She has since deleted it from her résumé.) My wife was born in Louisiana and grew up in San Diego; her ancestry is English, French, Scotch-Irish, German, and American Indian.

I notice that Americans marry in a rather peculiar way: by falling in love. You may think that I am being ironic, or putting you on, so let me hasten to inform you that in many parts of the world, romantic love is considered a mild form of insanity. Consider a typical situation: Anjali is in love with Arjun. She considers Arjun the best-looking man in the world, the most intelligent, virtually without fault, a paragon of humanity! But everybody else can see that Arjun is none of these things. What, then, persuades Anjali that Arjun possesses qualities that are nowhere in evidence? There is only one explanation: Anjali is deeply deluded. It does not follow that her romantic impulses should be ruthlessly crushed. But, in the view of many people and many traditions around the world, they should be steered and directed and prevented from ruining Anjali's life. This is the job of parents and the community, to help Anjali see beyond her delusions and to make decisions that are based on practical considerations and common sense.

If there is a single phrase that encapsulates life in the Third World, it is that "birth is destiny." I remember an incident years ago when my grandfather called in my brother, my sister, and me, and asked us if we knew how lucky we were. We asked him why he felt this way: was it because we were intelligent, or had lots of friends, or were blessed with a loving family? Each time he shook his head and said, "No." Finally we pressed him: why did he consider us so lucky? Then he revealed the answer: "Because you are Brahmins!"

The Brahmin, who is the highest ranking in the Hindu caste system, is traditionally a member of the priestly class. As a matter of fact, my family had nothing to do with the priesthood. Nor are we Hindu: my ancestors converted to Christianity many generations ago. Even so, my grandfather's point was that before we converted, hundreds of years ago, our family used to be Brahmins. How he knew this remains a mystery. But he was serious in his insistence that nothing that the three of us achieved in life could possibly mean more than the fact that we were Brahmins.

20   This may seem like an extreme example, revealing my grandfather to be a very narrow fellow indeed, but the broader point is that traditional cultures attach a great deal of importance to data such as what tribe you come from, whether you are male or female, and whether you are the eldest son. Your destiny and your happiness hinge on these things. If you are a Bengali, you can count on other Bengalis to help you, and on others to discriminate against you; if you are female, then certain forms of society and several professions are

closed to you; and if you are the eldest son, you inherit the family house and your siblings are expected to follow your direction. What this means is that once your tribe, caste, sex, and family position have been established at birth, your life takes a course that is largely determined for you.

In America, by contrast, you get to write the script of your own life. When your parents say to you, "What do you want to be when you grow up?" the question is open-ended; it is you who supply the answer. Your parents can advise you: "Have you considered law school?" "Why not become the first doctor in the family?" It is considered very improper, however, for them to try and force your decision. Indeed, American parents typically send their teenage children away to college, where they live on their own and learn independence. This is part of the process of forming your mind and choosing a field of interest for yourself and developing your identity. It is not uncommon in the United States for two brothers who come from the same gene pool and were raised in similar circumstances to do quite different things: the eldest becomes a gas station attendant, the younger moves up to be vice president at Oracle; the eldest marries his high-school sweetheart and raises four kids, the youngest refuses to settle down, or comes out of the closet as a homosexual; one is the Methodist that he was raised to be, the other becomes a Christian Scientist or a Buddhist. What to be, where to live, whom to love, whom to marry, what to believe, what religion to practice—these are all decisions that Americans make for themselves.

In most parts of the world your identity and your fate are to a large extent handed to you; in America, you determine them for yourself. In America your destiny is not prescribed; it is constructed. Your life is like a blank sheet of paper, and you are the artist. This notion of you being the architect of your own destiny is the incredibly powerful idea that is behind the worldwide appeal of America. Young people especially find irresistible the prospect of being in the driver's seat, of authoring the narrative of their own lives. So too the immigrant discovers that America permits him to break free of the constraints that have held him captive, so that the future becomes a landscape of his own choosing.

Responding to Reading

1. D'Souza seems to agree with those who claim that many immigrants come to the United States "for the sole purpose of getting rich" (1), but he does not criticize these immigrants who are motivated by dreams of wealth. How does he justify their motivation?
2. What is D'Souza's purpose in introducing the story of his own life? Does he achieve this purpose?

3. What specific differences does D'Souza observe between life in America and life in Third World nations? Between his own life in the United States and the life he would have led in India?

Responding in Writing

In paragraph 21, D'Souza says, "In America, . . . you get to write the script of your own life." Do you think this is true, or do you think D'Souza is too optimistic about what his adopted country has to offer?

THE MYTH OF THE LATIN WOMAN: I JUST MET A GIRL NAMED MARIA

Judith Ortiz Cofer

1952–

Born in Hormigueros, Puerto Rico, and raised in Paterson, New Jersey, Judith Ortiz Cofer teaches creative writing at the University of Georgia. She is an award-winning poet and novelist whose books include the novels The Line of the Sun *(1989) and* Silent Dancing *(1990) as well as a collection of biographical essays. Her most recent work is* A Love Story Beginning in Spanish: Poems *(2005). In the following essay from her collection* The Latin Deli: Prose and Poetry *(1993), Cofer describes the stereotypes she has confronted as a Latina.*

On a bus trip to London from Oxford University where I was earning some graduate credits one summer, a young man, obviously fresh from a pub, spotted me and as if struck by inspiration went down on his knees in the aisle. With both hands over his heart he broke into an Irish tenor's rendition of "Maria" from *West Side Story.*[1] My politely amused fellow passengers gave his lovely voice the round of gentle applause it deserved. Though I was not quite as amused, I managed my version of an English smile: no show of teeth, no extreme contortions of the facial muscles—I was at this time of my life practicing reserve and cool. Oh, that British control, how I coveted it. But "Maria" had followed me to London, reminding me of a prime fact of my life: you can leave the island, master the English language, and travel as far as you can, but if you are a Latina, especially one like me who so

---

[1]A popular Broadway musical, loosely based on *Romeo and Juliet,* about two rival street gangs, one Anglo and one Puerto Rican, in New York City. [Eds.]

obviously belongs to Rita Moreno's[2] gene pool, the island travels with you.

This is sometimes a very good thing—it may win you that extra minute of someone's attention. But with some people, the same things can make *you* an island—not a tropical paradise but an Alcatraz, a place nobody wants to visit. As a Puerto Rican girl living in the United States[3] and wanting like most children to "belong," I resented the stereotype that my Hispanic appearance called forth from many people I met.

Growing up in a large urban center in New Jersey during the 1960s, I suffered from what I think of as "cultural schizophrenia." Our life was designed by my parents as a microcosm of their *casas*[4] on the island. We spoke in Spanish, ate Puerto Rican food bought at the *bodega*,[5] and practiced strict Catholicism at a church that allotted us a one-hour slot each week for mass, performed in Spanish by a Chinese priest trained as a missionary for Latin America.

As a girl I was kept under strict surveillance by my parents, since my virtue and modesty were, by their cultural equation, the same as their honor. As a teenager I was lectured constantly on how to behave as a proper *senorita*. But it was a conflicting message I received, since the Puerto Rican mothers also encouraged their daughters to look and act like women and to dress in clothes our Anglo friends and their mothers found too "mature" and flashy. The difference was, and is, cultural; yet I often felt humiliated when I appeared at an American friend's party wearing a dress more suitable to a semi-formal than to a playroom birthday celebration. At Puerto Rican festivities, neither the music nor the colors we wore could be too loud.

I remember Career Day in our high school, when teachers told us 5 to come dressed as if for a job interview. It quickly became obvious that to the Puerto Rican girls "dressing up" meant wearing their mother's ornate jewelry and clothing, more appropriate (by mainstream standards) for the company Christmas party than as daily office attire. That morning I had agonized in front of my closet, trying to figure out what a "career girl" would wear. I knew how to dress for school (at the Catholic school I attended, we all wore uniforms), I knew how to dress for Sunday mass, and I knew what dresses to wear for parties at my relatives' homes. Though I do not recall the precise details of my Career Day outfit, it must have been a composite of

---

[2]Puerto Rico–born actress who won an Oscar for her role in the 1960 movie version of *West Side Story*. [Eds.]

[3]Although it is an island, Puerto Rico is part of the United States (it is a self-governing commonwealth). [Eds.]

[4]Homes. [Eds.]

[5]Small grocery store. [Eds.]

these choices. But I remember a comment my friend (an Italian American) made in later years that coalesced my impressions of that day. She said that at the business school she was attending, the Puerto Rican girls always stood out for wearing "everything at once." She meant, of course, too much jewelry, too many accessories. On that day at school we were simply made the negative models by the nuns, who were themselves not credible fashion experts to any of us. But it was painfully obvious to me that to the others, in their tailored skirts and silk blouses, we must have seemed "hopeless" and "vulgar." Though I now know that most adolescents feel out of step much of the time, I also know that for the Puerto Rican girls of my generation that sense was intensified. The way our teachers and classmates looked at us that day in school was just a taste of the cultural clash that awaited us in the real world, where prospective employers and men on the street would often misinterpret our tight skirts and jingling bracelets as a "come-on."

Mixed cultural signals have perpetuated certain stereotypes—for example, that of the Hispanic woman as the "hot tamale" or sexual firebrand. It is a one-dimensional view that the media have found easy to promote. In their special vocabulary, advertisers have designated "sizzling" and "smoldering" as the adjectives of choice for describing not only the foods but also the women of Latin America. From conversations in my house I recall hearing about the harassment that Puerto Rican women endured in factories where the "bossmen" talked to them as if sexual innuendo was all they understood, and worse, often gave them the choice of submitting to their advances or being fired.

It is custom, however, not chromosomes, that leads us to choose scarlet over pale pink. As young girls, it was our mothers who influenced our decisions about clothes and colors—mothers who had grown up on a tropical island where the natural environment was a riot of primary colors, where showing your skin was one way to keep cool as well as to look sexy. Most important of all, on the island, women perhaps felt freer to dress and move more provocatively since, in most cases, they were protected by the traditions, mores, and laws of a Spanish/Catholic system of morality and machismo whose main rule was: *You may look at my sister, but if you touch her I will kill you.* The extended family and church structure could provide a young woman with a circle of safety in her small pueblo on the island; if a man "wronged" a girl, everyone would close in to save her family honor.

My mother has told me about dressing in her best party clothes on Saturday nights and going to the town's plaza to promenade with her girlfriends in front of the boys they liked. The males were thus given an opportunity to admire the women and to express their admiration in the form of *piropos:* erotically charged street poems they composed on the spot. (I have myself been subjected to a few *piropos* while visiting the island, and they can be outrageous, although custom dictates that they must never cross into obscenity.) This ritual, as I understand it, also entails a show of studied indifference on the woman's part; if she is "decent," she must not acknowledge the man's impassioned words. So I do understand how things can be lost in translation. When a Puerto Rican girl dressed in her idea of what is attractive meets a man from the mainstream culture who has been trained to react to certain types of clothing as a sexual signal, a clash is likely to take place. I remember the boy who took me to my first formal dance leaning over to plant a sloppy, over-eager kiss painfully on my mouth; when I didn't respond with sufficient passion, he remarked resentfully: "I thought you Latin girls were supposed to mature early," as if I were expected to *ripen* like a fruit or vegetable, not just grow into womanhood like other girls.

It is surprising to my professional friends that even today some people, including those who should know better, still put others "in their place." It happened to me most recently during a stay at a classy metropolitan hotel favored by young professional couples for weddings. Late one evening after the theater, as I walked toward my room with a colleague (a woman with whom I was coordinating an arts program), a middle-aged man in a tuxedo, with a young girl in satin and lace on his arm, stepped directly into our path. With his champagne glass extended toward me, he exclaimed "Evita!"[6]

Our way blocked, my companion and I listened as the man half- 10 recited, half-bellowed "Don't Cry for Me, Argentina." When he finished, the young girl said: "How about a round of applause for my daddy?" We complied, hoping this would bring the silly spectacle to a close. I was becoming aware that our little group was attracting the attention of the other guests. "Daddy" must have perceived this too, and he once more barred the way as we tried to walk past him. He began to shout-sing a ditty to the tune of "La Bamba"—except the lyrics were about a girl named Maria whose exploits rhymed with her name and gonorrhea. The girl kept saying "Oh, Daddy" and looking at me with pleading eyes. She wanted me to laugh along with the others. My companion and I stood silently waiting for the man to end his offensive song. When he finished, I looked not at him but at his daughter. I advised her calmly never to ask her father what he had done in the army. Then I walked between them and to my room. My friend complimented me on my cool handling of the situation, but I confessed that I had really wanted to push the jerk into the swimming

---

[6]A Broadway musical, later made into a movie, about Eva Duarte de Perón, the former first lady of Argentina. [Eds.]

pool. This same man—probably a corporate executive, well-educated, even worldly by most standards—would not have been likely to regale an Anglo woman with a dirty song in public. He might have checked his impulse by assuming that she could be somebody's wife or mother, or at least *somebody* who might take offense. But, to him, I was just an Evita or a Maria: merely a character in his cartoon-populated universe.

Another facet of the myth of the Latin woman in the United States is the menial, the domestic—Maria the housemaid or countergirl. It's true that work as domestics, as waitresses, and in factories is all that's available to women with little English and few skills. But the myth of the Hispanic menial—the funny maid, mispronouncing words and cooking up a spicy storm in a shiny California kitchen—has been perpetuated by the media in the same way that "Mammy" from *Gone with the Wind* became America's idea of the black woman for generations. Since I do not wear my diplomas around my neck for all to see, I have on occasion been sent to that "kitchen" where some think I obviously belong.

One incident has stayed with me, though I recognize it as a minor offense. My first public poetry reading took place in Miami, at a restaurant where a luncheon was being held before the event. I was nervous and excited as I walked in with notebook in hand. An older woman motioned me to her table, and thinking (foolish me) that she wanted me to autograph a copy of my newly published slender volume of verse, I went over. She ordered a cup of coffee from me, assuming that I was the waitress. (Easy enough to mistake my poems for menus, I suppose.) I know it wasn't an intentional act of cruelty. Yet of all the good things that happened later, I remember that scene most clearly, because it reminded me of what I had to overcome before anyone would take me seriously. In retrospect I understand that my anger gave my reading fire. In fact, I have almost always taken any doubt in my abilities as a challenge, the result most often being the satisfaction of winning a convert, of seeing the cold, appraising eyes warm to my words, the body language change, the smile that indicates I have opened some avenue for communication. So that day as I read, I looked directly at that woman. Her lowered eyes told me she was embarrassed at her faux pas, and when I willed her to look up at me, she graciously allowed me to punish her with my full attention. We shook hands at the end of the reading and I never saw her again. She has probably forgotten the entire incident, but maybe not.

Yet I am one of the lucky ones. There are thousands of Latinas without the privilege of an education or the entrees into society that I have. For them life is a constant struggle against the misconceptions perpetuated by the myth of the Latina. My goal is to try to replace the old stereotypes with a much more interesting set of realities. Every time I give a reading, I hope the stories I tell, the dreams and fears I examine in my work, can achieve some universal truth that will get my audience past the particulars of my skin color, my accent, or my clothes.

I once wrote a poem in which I called all Latinas "God's brown daughters." This poem is really a prayer of sorts, offered upward, but also, through the human-to-human channel of art, outward. It is a prayer for communication and for respect. In it, Latin women pray "in Spanish to an Anglo God/with a Jewish heritage," and they are "fervently hoping/that if not omnipotent,/at least He be bilingual."

Responding to Reading

1. What exactly is the "myth of the Latin woman"? According to Cofer, what has perpetuated this stereotype? Do you see this "myth" as simply demeaning, or as potentially dangerous?
2. In paragraph 1, Cofer says, "you can leave [Puerto Rico], master the English language, and travel as far as you can, but if you are a Latina, . . . the island travels with you." What does she mean? Do you think this is also true of people from other ethnic groups (and other nations)?
3. Throughout this essay, Cofer speaks of the "'cultural schizophrenia'" (3) she felt, describing the "conflicting message" (4), the "cultural clash" (5), and the "mixed cultural signals" (6) she received from the two worlds she inhabited. Do you see this kind of "schizophrenia" as inevitable? Do you see it as an obstacle to the American Dream? Explain.

Responding in Writing

What stereotypes are associated with your own ethnic group? Do you see these stereotypes as benign or harmful?

COMING INTO THE COUNTRY

Gish Jen

1956–

Gish Jen is the author of a short-story collection and three novels, most recently The Love Wife *(2004). Her work is frequently anthologized and published in the* New York Times Magazine, the New Yorker, *and the* New Republic. *Jen, born to Chinese immigrants, writes primarily about the challenges of cultural assimilation faced by American immigrants and descendants of recent immigrants. The following essay explores the immigrant's process of shaping a distinctly American identity.*

In the Old World, there was one way of life, or 2, maybe 10. Here there are dozens, hundreds, all jammed in together, cheek by jowl, especially in the dizzying cities. Everywhere has a somewhere else just around the corner. We newish Americans leap-frog from world to world, reinventing ourselves en route. We perform our college selves, our waitress selves, our dot-com selves, our parent selves, our downtown selves, our Muslim, Greek, Hindi, South African selves. Even into the second or third generation, we speak different languages— more languages, often, than we know we know. We sport different names. I am Gish, Geesh, Jen, Lillian, Lil, Bilien, Ms. Jen, Miss Ren, Mrs. O'Connor. Or maybe we insist on one name. The filmmaker Mira Nair, for example, will be called *NIGH-ear*, please; she is not a depilatory product.

Of course, there are places where she does not have to insist, and places that don't get the joke, that need—that get—other jokes. It's a kind of high, switching spiels, eating Ethiopian, French, Thai, getting around. And the inventing! The moments of grand inspiration: *I think I will call myself Houdini.* Who could give up even the quotidian luxury of choosing, that small swell of power: to walk or to drive? The soup or the salad? The green or the blue? We bubble with pleasure. *It's me. I'm taking the plane. I'll take the sofa, the chair, the whole shebang—why not?*

Why not, indeed? A most American question, a question that comes to dominate our most private self-talk. In therapy-speak, we Americans like *to give ourselves permission.* To do what? To take care of ourselves, to express ourselves, to listen to ourselves. We tune out the loudspeaker of duty, tune in to the whisper of desire. This is faint at first, but soon proves easily audible; indeed, irresistible. *Why not go to town? Why not move away? Why not marry out? Why not? Why not? Why not?*

To come to America is to be greatly disoriented for many a day. The smell of the air is wrong, the taste of the water, the strength of the sun, the rate the trees grow. The rituals are strange—the spring setting out of mulch, the summer setting out of barbecues. How willingly the men heat themselves with burgers! Nobody eats the wildlife, certainly not the bugs or leaves. And beware, beware the rules about smoking. Your skin feels tight, your body fat or thin, your children stranger than they were already. Your sensations are exhausting.

5   Yet one day a moment comes—often, strangely, abroad—when we find ourselves missing things. Our choice of restaurants, perhaps, or our cheap gas and good roads; or, more tellingly, our rights. To be without freedom of movement, to be without freedom of speech— these things pain everyone. But to be without *our* freedom of movement, without *our* freedom of speech is an American affliction; and in this, as in many facets of American life, possession matters. The moment we feel certain rights to be inalienable, when we feel them to be ours as our lungs are ours, so that their loss is an excision and a death, we have become American.

It's not always a happy feeling. For the more at home we become with our freedom, the more we become aware of its limits. There's much true opportunity in the land of opportunity, but between freedom in theory and freedom in practice gapes a grand canyon. As often as not, what we feel is the burn of injustice. A rise of anger, perhaps followed by a quick check on our impulse to act rashly; perhaps followed by a decision to act courageously. *We gather here today to make known our grievance. For is this not America?*

We wonder who we are—what does it mean to be Irish-American, Cuban-American, Armenian-American?—and are amazed to discover that others wonder, too. Indeed, nothing seems more typically American than to obsess about identity. Can so many people truly be so greatly confused? We feel very much a part of the contemporary gestalt.

Yet two or three generations later, we still may not be insiders. Recently, I heard about a basketball game starring a boy from the Cochiti pueblo in Santa Fe. The kids on his team, a friend reported, had one water bottle, which they passed around, whereas the kids on the other team each had his own. This was a heartening story, signaling the survival of a communal culture against the pressures of individualism. But did the Cochiti boy notice the other team? I couldn't help wondering. Did he feel the glass pane between himself and the mainstream, so familiar, so tangible, so bittersweet? *Nobody has been here longer than we; how come our ways need protecting?* Later a member of the pueblo told me that the Cochiti have started a language-immersion program for the younger generation, and that it has been a success. They are saving their language from extinction.

Hooray! The rest of us cheer. How awed we feel in the presence of tradition, of authenticity. How avidly we will surf to such sites, some of us, and what we will pay to do so! We will pay for bits of the Southwest the way we will pay handsomely, in this generation or the next, for a home. Whatever that looks like; we find ourselves longing for some combination of Martha Stewart and what we can imagine, say, of our family seat in Brazil. At any rate, we can say this much: the home of our dreams is a safe place, a still place. A communal place, to which we contribute; to which we have real ties; a place that feels more stable, perhaps, than ourselves. How American this is—to long, at day's end, for a place where we belong more, invent less; for a heartland with more heart.

Responding to Reading

1. In paragraph 1, Jen says, "We newish Americans leapfrog from world to world, reinventing ourselves en route." Is the concept of reinvention as she describes it limited to "newish Americans," or could it also apply to more assimilated Americans?

2. Jen says, "the more at home we become with our freedom, the more we become aware of its limits" (6). What does she mean? Do you think she is correct?

3. In paragraph 7, Jen observes that "nothing seems more typically American than to obsess about identity." Why, according to Jen, is this obsession "typically American"?

Responding in Writing

Do you consider yourself an American (in Jen's terms, an "insider"), a "hyphenated American" (for example, Irish-American or Cuban-American), or something else?

Just Walk On By

Brent Staples

1951–

After earning a Ph.D. in psychology from the University of Chicago (1977), Brent Staples turned to journalism, writing for the Chicago Sun-Times *and the* New York Times. *In 1990, he joined the editorial board of the* Times, *where his columns now appear regularly. His memoir* Parallel Time *(1994), which was sparked by his brother's murder in a dispute over a cocaine deal, describes Staples's own internal struggles as he straddled the black and white worlds. Originally published in* Ms. *in 1986, the following essay conveys Staples's reactions to white people's images of black men.*

My first victim was a woman—white, well dressed, probably in her early twenties. I came upon her late one evening on a deserted street in Hyde Park, a relatively affluent neighborhood in an otherwise mean, impoverished section of Chicago. As I swung onto the avenue behind her, there seemed to be a discreet, uninflammatory distance between us. Not so. She cast back a worried glance. To her, the youngish black man—a broad six feet two inches with a beard and billowing hair, both hands shoved into the pockets of a bulky military jacket—seemed menacingly close. After a few more quick glimpses, she picked up her pace and was soon running in earnest. Within seconds she disappeared into a cross street.

That was more than a decade ago. I was 22 years old, a graduate student newly arrived at the University of Chicago. It was in the echo of that terrified woman's footfalls that I first began to know the unwieldy inheritance I'd come into—the ability to alter public space in ugly ways. It was clear that she thought herself the quarry of a mugger, a rapist, or worse. Suffering a bout of insomnia, however, I was stalking sleep, not defenseless wayfarers. As a softy who is scarcely able to take a knife to a raw chicken—let alone hold it to a person's throat—I was surprised, embarrassed, and dismayed all at once. Her flight made me feel like an accomplice in tyranny. It also made it clear that I was indistinguishable from the muggers who occasionally seeped into the area from the surrounding ghetto. That first encounter, and those that followed, signified that a vast, unnerving gulf lay between nighttime pedestrians—particularly women—and me. And I soon gathered that being perceived as dangerous is a hazard in itself. I only needed to turn a corner into a dicey situation, or crowd some frightened, armed person in a foyer somewhere, or make an errant move after being pulled over by a policeman. Where fear and weapons meet—and they often do in urban America—there is always the possibility of death.

In that first year, my first away from my hometown, I was to become thoroughly familiar with the language of fear. At dark, shadowy intersections in Chicago, I could cross in front of a car stopped at a traffic light and elicit the *thunk, thunk, thunk, thunk* of the driver—black, white, male, or female—hammering down the door locks. On less traveled streets after dark, I grew accustomed to but never comfortable with people who crossed to the other side of the street rather than pass me. Then there were the standard unpleasantries with police, doormen, bouncers, cab drivers, and others whose business it is to screen out troublesome individuals *before* there is any nastiness.

I moved to New York nearly two years ago and I have remained an avid night walker. In central Manhattan, the near-constant crowd cover minimizes tense one-on-one street encounters. Elsewhere—visiting friends in SoHo, where sidewalks are narrow and tightly spaced buildings shut out the sky—things can get very taut indeed.

Black men have a firm place in New York mugging literature. 5 Norman Podhoretz in his famed (or infamous) 1963 essay, "My Negro Problem—And Ours," recalls growing up in terror of black males; they "were tougher than we were, more ruthless," he writes—and as an adult on the Upper West Side of Manhattan, he continues, he cannot constrain his nervousness when he meets black men on certain streets. Similarly, a decade later, the essayist and novelist Edward Hoagland extols a New York where once "Negro bitterness bore down mainly on other Negroes." Where some see mere panhandlers, Hoagland sees "a mugger who is clearly screwing up his nerve to do more than just *ask* for money." But Hoagland has "the New Yorker's quickhunch posture for broken-field maneuvering," and the bad guy swerves away.

I often witness that "hunch posture," from women after dark on the warrenlike streets of Brooklyn where I live. They seem to set their faces on neutral and, with their purse straps strung across their chests bandolier style, they forge ahead as though bracing themselves against being tackled. I understand, of course, that the danger they perceive is not a hallucination. Women are particularly vulnerable to street violence, and young black males are drastically overrepresented among the perpetrators of that violence. Yet these truths are no solace against the kind of alienation that comes of being ever the suspect, against being set apart, a fearsome entity with whom pedestrians avoid making eye contact.

It is not altogether clear to me how I reached the ripe old age of 22 without being conscious of the lethality nighttime pedestrians attributed to me. Perhaps it was because in Chester, Pennsylvania, the small, angry industrial town where I came of age in the 1960s, I was scarcely noticeable against a backdrop of gang warfare, street knifings, and murders. I grew up one of the good boys, had perhaps a half-dozen fist fights. In retrospect, my shyness of combat has clear sources.

Many things go into the making of a young thug. One of those things is the consummation of the male romance with the power to intimidate. An infant discovers that random flailings send the baby bottle flying out of the crib and crashing to the floor. Delighted, the joyful babe repeats those motions again and again, seeking to duplicate the feat. Just so, I recall the points at which some of my boyhood friends were finally seduced by the perception of themselves as tough guys. When a mark cowered and surrendered his money without resistance, myth and reality merged—and paid off. It is, after all, only manly to embrace the power to frighten and intimidate. We, as men, are not supposed to give an inch of our lane on the highway; we are to seize the fighter's edge in work and in play and even in love; we are to be valiant in the face of hostile forces.

Unfortunately, poor and powerless young men seem to take all this nonsense literally. As a boy, I saw countless tough guys locked away; I have since buried several, too. They were babies, really—a teenage cousin, a brother of 22, a childhood friend in his mid-twenties—all gone down in episodes of bravado played out in the streets. I came to doubt the virtues of intimidation early on. I chose, perhaps even unconsciously, to remain a shadow—timid, but a survivor.

10   The fearsomeness mistakenly attributed to me in public places often has a perilous flavor. The most frightening of these confusions occurred in the late 1970s and early 1980s when I worked as a journalist in Chicago. One day, rushing into the office of a magazine I was writing for with a deadline story in hand, I was mistaken for a burglar. The office manager called security and, with an ad hoc posse, pursued me through the labyrinthine halls, nearly to my editor's door. I had no way of proving who I was. I could only move briskly toward the company of someone who knew me.

Another time I was on assignment for a local paper and killing time before an interview. I entered a jewelry store on the city's affluent

Near North Side. The proprietor excused herself and returned with an enormous red Doberman pinscher straining at the end of a leash. She stood, the dog extended toward me, silent to my questions, her eyes bulging nearly out of her head. I took a cursory look around, nodded, and bade her good night. Relatively speaking, however, I never fared as badly as another black male journalist. He went to nearby Waukegan, Illinois, a couple of summers ago to work on a story about a murderer who was born there. Mistaking the reporter for the killer, police hauled him from his car at gunpoint and but for his press credentials would probably have tried to book him. Such episodes are not uncommon. Black men trade tales like this all the time.

In "My Negro Problem—And Ours," Podhoretz writes that the hatred he feels for blacks makes itself known to him through a variety of avenues—one being his discomfort with that "special brand of paranoid touchiness" to which he says blacks are prone. No doubt he is speaking here of black men. In time, I learned to smother the rage I felt at so often being taken for a criminal. Not to do so would surely have led to madness—via that special "paranoid touchiness" that so annoyed Podhoretz at the time he wrote the essay.

I began to take precautions to make myself less threatening. I move about with care, particularly late in the evening. I give a wide berth to nervous people on subway platforms during the wee hours, particularly when I have exchanged business clothes for jeans. If I happen to be entering a building behind some people who appear skittish, I may walk by, letting them clear the lobby before I return, so as not to seem to be following them. I have been calm and extremely congenial on those rare occasions when I've been pulled over by the police.

And on late-evening constitutionals along streets less traveled by, I employ what has proved to be an excellent tension-reducing measure: I whistle melodies from Beethoven and Vivaldi and the more popular classical composers. Even steely New Yorkers hunching toward nighttime destinations seem to relax, and occasionally they even join in the tune. Virtually everybody seems to sense that a mugger wouldn't be warbling bright, sunny selections from Vivaldi's *Four Seasons*. It is my equivalent of the cowbell that hikers wear when they know they are in bear country.

Responding to Reading

1. Staples speaks quite matter-of-factly of the fear he inspires. Does your experience support his assumption that black men have the "ability to alter public space" (2)? Why or why not? Do you believe white men also have this ability?

2. In paragraph 13, Staples suggests some strategies that he believes make him "less threatening." What else, if anything, do you think he could do? Do you believe he *should* adopt such strategies?

3. Although Staples says he arouses fear in others, he also admits that he him-
    self feels fearful. Why? Do you think he has reason to be fearful? What
    does this sense of fear say about his access to the American Dream?

Responding in Writing

Imagine you are the woman Staples describes in paragraph 1. Write a letter to
Staples in which you explain why you reacted as you did.

ON DUMPSTER DIVING

Lars Eighner

1948–

*When Lars Eighner was eighteen years old, his mother threw him out of her
house after she learned he was gay. Then a student at the University of Texas
at Austin (1966–1969), Eighner began a series of part-time and dead-end
jobs that ended in 1988, when he was fired from his position at an Austin
mental hospital and soon after was evicted from his apartment. At that
point, he headed for Los Angeles and spent three years homeless on the
streets, shuttling between California and Texas with Lizbeth, his Labrador
retriever. During his travels, he kept a journal and later published these entries, along with letters he wrote to a friend, as* Travels with Lizbeth:
Three Years on the Road and on the Streets *(1993), portions of which
had been published previously in several different magazines and journals.
The essay that follows, a chapter from this book, describes the steps he took to
survive on the streets. Eighner's most recent book is the novel* Pawn to
Queen Four *(1995).*

*This chapter was composed while the author was homeless. The present
tense has been preserved.*

Long before I began Dumpster diving I was impressed with Dumpsters, enough so that I wrote the Merriam-Webster research service to
discover what I could about the word *Dumpster*. I learned from them
that it is a proprietary word belonging to the Dempsey Dumpster
company. Since then I have dutifully capitalized the word, although it
was lowercased in almost all the citations Merriam-Webster photocopied for me. Dempsey's word is too apt. I have never heard these
things called anything but Dumpsters. I do not know anyone who
knows the generic name for these objects. From time to time I have
heard a wino or hobo give some corrupted credit to the original and
call them Dipsy Dumpsters.

I began Dumpster diving about a year before I became homeless.

I prefer the word *scavenging* and use the word *scrounging* when I
mean to be obscure. I have heard people, evidently meaning to be

polite, use the word *foraging,* but I prefer to reserve that word for gathering nuts and berries and such which I do also according to the season and the opportunity. *Dumpster diving* seems to me to be a little too cute and, in my case, inaccurate because I lack the athletic ability to lower myself into the Dumpsters as the true divers do, much to their increased profit.

I like the frankness of the word *scavenging,* which I can hardly think of without picturing a big black snail on an aquarium wall. I live from the refuse of others. I am a scavenger. I think it a sound and honorable niche, although if I could I would naturally prefer to live the comfortable consumer life, perhaps—and only perhaps—as a slightly less wasteful consumer, owing to what I have learned as a scavenger.

While Lizbeth and I were still living in the shack on Avenue B as 5 my savings ran out, I put almost all my sporadic income into rent. The necessities of daily life I began to extract from Dumpsters. Yes, we ate from them. Except for jeans, all my clothes came from Dumpsters. Boom boxes, candles, bedding, toilet paper, a virgin male love doll, medicine, books, a typewriter, dishes, furnishings, and change, sometimes amounting to many dollars—I acquired many things from the Dumpsters.

I have learned much as a scavenger. I mean to put some of what I have learned down here, beginning with the practical art of Dumpster diving and proceeding to the abstract.

What is safe to eat?

After all, the finding of objects is becoming something of an urban art. Even respectable employed people will sometimes find something tempting sticking out of a Dumpster or standing beside one. Quite a number of people, not all of them of the bohemian type, are willing to brag that they found this or that piece in the trash. But eating from Dumpsters is what separates the dilettanti from the professionals. Eating safely from the Dumpsters involves three principles: using the senses and common sense to evaluate the conditions of the found materials, knowing the Dumpsters of a given area and checking them regularly, and seeking always to answer the question "Why was this discarded?"

Perhaps everyone who has a kitchen and a regular supply of groceries has, at one time or another, made a sandwich and eaten half of it before discovering mold on the bread or got a mouthful of milk before realizing the milk had turned. Nothing of the sort is likely to happen to a Dumpster diver because he is constantly reminded that most food is discarded for a reason. Yet a lot of perfectly good food can be found in Dumpsters.

Canned goods, for example, turn up fairly often in the Dumpsters 10 I frequent. All except the most phobic people would be willing to eat from a can, even if it came from a Dumpster. Canned goods are among the safest of foods to be found in Dumpsters but are not utterly foolproof.

Although very rare with modern canning methods, botulism is a possibility. Most other forms of food poisoning seldom do lasting harm to a healthy person, but botulism is most certainly fatal and often the first symptom is death. Except for carbonated beverages, all canned goods should contain a slight vacuum and suck air when first punctured. Bulging, rusty, and dented cans and cans that spew when punctured should be avoided, especially when the contents are not very acidic or syrupy.

Heat can break down the botulin, but this requires much more cooking than most people do to canned goods. To the extent that botulism occurs at all, of course, it can occur in cans on pantry shelves as well as in cans from Dumpsters. Need I say that home-canned goods are simply too risky to be recommended.

From time to time one of my companions, aware of the source of my provisions, will ask, "Do you think these crackers are really safe to eat?" For some reason it is most often the crackers they ask about.

This question has always made me angry. Of course I would not offer my companion anything I had doubts about. But more than that, I wonder why he cannot evaluate the condition of the crackers for himself. I have no special knowledge and I have been wrong before. Since he knows where the food comes from, it seems to me he ought to assume some of the responsibility for deciding what he will put in his mouth. For myself I have few qualms about dry foods such as crackers, cookies, cereal, chips, and pasta if they are free of visible contaminants and still dry and crisp. Most often such things are found in the original packaging, which is not so much a positive sign as it is the absence of a negative one.

15   Raw fruits and vegetables with intact skins seem perfectly safe to me, excluding of course the obviously rotten. Many are discarded for minor imperfections that can be pared away. Leafy vegetables, grapes, cauliflower, broccoli, and similar things may be contaminated by liquids and may be impractical to wash.

Candy, especially hard candy, is usually safe if it has not drawn ants. Chocolate is often discarded only because it has become discolored as the cocoa butter de-emulsified. Candying, after all, is one method of food preservation because pathogens do not like very sugary substances.

All of these foods might be found in any Dumpster and can be evaluated with some confidence largely on the basis of appearance. Beyond these are foods that cannot be correctly evaluated without additional information.

I began scavenging by pulling pizzas out of the Dumpster behind a pizza delivery shop. In general, prepared food requires caution, but in this case I knew when the shop closed and went to the Dumpster as soon as the last of the help left.

Such shops often get prank orders; both the orders and the products made to fill them are called *bogus.* Because help seldom stays long at these places, pizzas are often made with the wrong topping, refused on delivery for being cold, or baked incorrectly. The products to be discarded are boxed up because inventory is kept by counting boxes: A boxed pizza can be written off; an unboxed pizza does not exist.

I never placed a bogus order to increase the supply of pizzas and I 20 believe no one else was scavenging in this Dumpster. But the people in the shop became suspicious and began to retain their garbage in the shop overnight. While it lasted I had a steady supply of fresh, sometimes warm pizza. Because I knew the Dumpster I knew the source of the pizza, and because I visited the Dumpster regularly I knew what was fresh and what was yesterday's.

The area I frequent is inhabited by many affluent college students. I am not here by chance; the Dumpsters in this area are very rich. Students throw out many good things, including food. In particular they tend to throw everything out when they move at the end of a semester, before and after breaks, and around midterm, when many of them despair of college. So I find it advantageous to keep an eye on the academic calendar.

Students throw food away around breaks because they do not know whether it has spoiled or will spoil before they return. A typical discard is a half jar of peanut butter. In fact, nonorganic peanut butter does not require refrigeration and is unlikely to spoil in any reasonable time. The student does not know that, and since it is Daddy's money, the student decides not to take a chance. Opened containers require caution and some attention to the question "Why was this discarded?" But in the case of discards from student apartments, the answer may be that the item was thrown out through carelessness, ignorance, or wastefulness. This can sometimes be deduced when the item is found with many others, including some that are obviously perfectly good.

Some students, and others, approach defrosting a freezer by chucking out the whole lot. Not only do the circumstances of such a find tell the story, but also the mass of frozen goods stays cold for a long time and items may be found still frozen or freshly thawed.

Yogurt, cheese, and sour cream are items that are often thrown out while they are still good. Occasionally I find a cheese with a spot of mold, which of course I just pare off, and because it is obvious why such a cheese was discarded, I treat it with less suspicion than an apparently perfect cheese found in similar circumstances. Yogurt is often discarded, still sealed, only because the expiration date on the carton had passed. This is one of my favorite finds because yogurt will keep for several days, even in warm weather.

25   Students throw out canned goods and staples at the end of semesters and when they give up college at midterm. Drugs, pornography, spirits, and the like are often discarded when parents are expected—Dad's day, for example. And spirits also turn up after big party weekends, presumably discarded by the newly reformed. Wine and spirits, of course, keep perfectly well even once opened, but the same cannot be said of beer.

My test for carbonated soft drinks is whether they still fizz vigorously. Many juices or other beverages are too acidic or too syrupy to cause much concern, provided they are not visibly contaminated. I have discovered nasty molds in vegetable juices, even when the product was found under its original seal; I recommend that such products be decanted slowly into a clear glass. Liquids always require some care. One hot day I found a large jug of Pat O'Brien's Hurricane mix. The jug had been opened, but it was still ice cold. I drank three large glasses before it became apparent to me that someone had added the rum to the mix, and not a little rum. I never tasted the rum, and by the time I began to feel the effects I had already ingested a very large quantity of the beverage. Some divers would have considered this a boon, but being suddenly intoxicated in a public place in the early afternoon is not my idea of a good time.

I have heard of people maliciously contaminating discarded food and even handouts, but mostly I have heard of this from people with vivid imaginations who have had no experience with Dumpsters themselves. Just before the pizza shop stopped discarding its garbage at night, jalapeños began showing up on most of the discarded pizzas. If indeed this was meant to discourage me it was a wasted effort because I am native Texan.

For myself, I avoid game, poultry, pork, and egg-based foods, whether I find them raw or cooked. I seldom have the means to cook what I find, but when I do I avail myself of plentiful supplies of beef, which is often in very good condition. I suppose fish becomes disagreeable before it becomes dangerous. Lizbeth is happy to have any such thing that is past its prime and, in fact, does not recognize fish as food until it is quite strong.

Home leftovers, as opposed to surpluses from restaurants, are very often bad. Evidently, especially among students, there is a common type of personality that carefully wraps up even the smallest leftover and shoves it into the back of the refrigerator for six months or so before discarding it. Characteristic of this type are the reused jars and margarine tubs to which the remains are committed. I avoid ethnic foods I am unfamiliar with. If I do not know what it is supposed to look like when it is good, I cannot be certain I will be able to tell if it is bad.

No matter how careful I am I still get dysentery at least once a 30 month, oftener in warm weather. I do not want to paint too romantic a picture. Dumpster diving has serious drawbacks as a way of life.

I learned to scavenge gradually, on my own. Since then I have initiated several companions into the trade. I have learned that there is a predictable series of stages a person goes through in learning to scavenge.

At first the new scavenger is filled with disgust and self-loathing. He is ashamed of being seen and may lurk around, trying to duck behind things, or he may try to dive at night. (In fact, most people instinctively look away from a scavenger. By skulking around, the novice calls attention to himself and arouses suspicion. Diving at night is ineffective and needlessly messy.)

Every grain of rice seems to be a maggot. Everything seems to stink. He can wipe the egg yolk off the found can, but he cannot erase from his mind the stigma of eating garbage.

That stage passes with experience. The scavenger finds a pair of running shoes that fit and look and smell brand-new. He finds a pocket calculator in perfect working order. He finds pristine ice cream, still frozen, more than he can eat or keep. He begins to understand: People throw away perfectly good stuff, a lot of perfectly good stuff.

At this stage, Dumpster shyness begins to dissipate. The diver, 35 after all, has the last laugh. He is finding all manner of good things that are his for the taking. Those who disparage his profession are the fools, not he.

He may begin to hang on to some perfectly good things for which he has neither a use nor a market. Then he begins to take note of the things that are not perfectly good but are nearly so. He mates a Walkman with broken earphones and one that is missing a battery cover. He picks up things that he can repair.

At this stage he may become lost and never recover. Dumpsters are full of things of some potential value to someone and also of things that never have much intrinsic value but are interesting. All the Dumpster divers I have known come to the point of trying to acquire everything they touch. Why not take it, they reason, since it is all free? This is, of course, hopeless. Most divers come to realize that they must restrict themselves to items of relatively immediate utility. But in some cases the diver simply cannot control himself. I have met several of these pack-rat types. Their ideas of the values of various pieces of junk verge on the psychotic. Every bit of glass may be a diamond, they think, and all that glistens, gold.

I tend to gain weight when I am scavenging. Partly this is because I always find far more pizza and doughnuts than water-packed tuna, nonfat yogurt, and fresh vegetables. Also I have not developed much faith in the reliability of Dumpsters as a food source, although it has been proven to me many times. I tend to eat as if I have no idea where my next meal is coming from. But mostly I just hate to see food go to waste and so I eat much more than I should. Something like this drives the obsession to collect junk.

As for collecting objects, I usually restrict myself to collecting one kind of small object at a time, such as pocket calculators, sunglasses, or campaign buttons. To live on the street I must anticipate my needs to a certain extent: I must pick up and save warm bedding I find in August because it will not be found in Dumpsters in November. As I have no access to health care, I often hoard essential drugs, such as antibiotics and antihistamines. (This course can be recommended only to those with some grounding in pharmacology. Antibiotics, for example, even when indicated are worse than useless if taken in in-sufficient amounts.) But even if I had a home with extensive storage space, I could not save everything that might be valuable in some contingency.

40   I have proprietary feelings about my Dumpsters. As I have men-tioned, it is no accident that I scavenge from ones where good finds are common. But my limited experience with Dumpsters in other areas suggests to me that even in poorer areas, Dumpsters, if attended with sufficient diligence, can be made to yield a livelihood. The rich students discard perfectly good kiwi fruit; poorer people discard per-fectly good apples. Slacks and Polo shirts are found in the one place; jeans and T-shirts in the other. The population of competitors rather than the affluence of the dumpers most affects the feasibility of sur-vival by scavenging. The large number of competitors is what puts me off the idea of trying to scavenge in places like Los Angeles.

Curiously, I do not mind my direct competition, other scavengers, so much as I hate the can scroungers.

People scrounge cans because they have to have a little cash. I have tried scrounging cans with an able-bodied companion. Afoot a can scrounger simply cannot make more than a few dollars a day. One can extract the necessities of life from the Dumpsters directly with far less effort than would be required to accumulate the equivalent value in cans. (These observations may not hold in places with container re-demption laws.)

Can scroungers, then, are people who must have small amounts of cash. These are drug addicts and winos, mostly the latter because the amounts of cash are so small. Spirits and drugs do, like all other commodities, turn up in Dumpsters and the scavenger will from time to time have a half bottle of a rather good wine with his dinner. But the wino cannot survive on these occasional finds; he must have his daily dose to stave off the DTs. All the cans he can carry will buy about three bottles of Wild Irish Rose.

I do not begrudge them the cans, but can scroungers tend to tear up the Dumpsters, mixing the contents and littering the area. They become so specialized that they can see only cans. They earn my contempt by passing up change, canned goods, and readily hockable items.

There are precious few courtesies among scavengers. But it is 45 common practice to set aside surplus items: pairs of shoes, clothing, canned goods, and such. A true scavenger hates to see good stuff go to waste, and what he cannot use he leaves in good condition in plain sight.

Can scroungers lay waste to everything in their path and will stir one of a pair of good shoes to the bottom of a Dumpster, to be lost or ruined in the muck. Can scroungers will even go through individual garbage cans, something I have never seen a scavenger do.

Individual garbage cans are set out on the public easement only on garbage days. On other days going through them requires trespassing close to a dwelling. Going through individual garbage cans without scattering litter is almost impossible. Litter is likely to reduce the public's tolerance of scavenging. Individual cans are simply not as productive as Dumpsters; people in houses and duplexes do not move so often and for some reason do not tend to discard as much useful material. Moreover, the time required to go through one garbage can that serves one household is not much less than the time required to go through a Dumpster that contains the refuse of twenty apartments.

But my strongest reservation about going through individual garbage cans is that this seems to me a very personal kind of invasion to which I would object if I were a householder. Although many things in Dumpsters are obviously meant never to come to light, a Dumpster is somehow less personal.

I avoid trying to draw conclusions about the people who dump in the Dumpsters I frequent. I think it would be unethical to do so, although I know many people will find the idea of scavenger ethics too funny for words.

Dumpsters contain bank statements, correspondence, and other 50 documents, just as anyone might expect. But there are also less obvious sources of information. Pill bottles, for example. The labels bear the name of the patient, the name of the doctor, and the name of the drug. AIDS drugs and antipsychotic medicines, to name but two groups, are specific and are seldom prescribed for any other disorders. The plastic compacts for birth-control pills usually have complete label information.

Despite all of this sensitive information, I have had only one apartment resident object to my going through the Dumpster. In that case it turned out the resident was a university athlete who was taking bets and who was afraid I would turn up his wager slips.

Occasionally a find tells a story. I once found a small paper bag containing some unused condoms, several partial tubes of flavored sexual lubricants, a partially used compact of birth-control pills, and the torn pieces of a picture of a young man. Clearly she was through with him and planning to give up sex altogether.

Dumpster things are often sad—abandoned teddy bears, shredded wedding books, despaired-of sales kits. I find many pets lying in state in Dumpsters. Although I hope to get off the streets so that Lizbeth can have a long and comfortable old age, I know this hope is not very realistic. So I suppose when her time comes she too will go into a Dumpster. I will have no better place for her. And after all, it is fitting, since for most of her life her livelihood has come from the Dumpster. When she finds something I think is safe that has been spilled from a Dumpster, I let her have it. She already knows the route around the best ones. I like to think that if she survives me she will have a chance of evading the dog catcher and of finding her sustenance on the route.

Silly vanities also come to rest in the Dumpsters. I am a rather accomplished needleworker. I get a lot of material from the Dumpsters. Evidently sorority girls, hoping to impress someone, perhaps themselves, with their mastery of a womanly art, buy a lot of embroider-by-number kits, work a few stitches horribly, and eventually discard the whole mess. I pull out their stitches, turn the canvas over, and work an original design. Do not think I refrain from chuckling as I make gifts from these kits.

55   I find diaries and journals. I have often thought of compiling a book of literary found objects. And perhaps I will one day. But what I find is hopelessly commonplace and bad without being, even unconsciously, camp. College students also discard their papers. I am horrified to discover the kind of paper that now merits an A in an undergraduate course. I am grateful, however, for the number of good books and magazines the students throw out.

In the area I know best I have never discovered vermin in the Dumpsters, but there are two kinds of kitty surprise. One is alley cats whom I meet as they leap, claws first, out of Dumpsters. This is especially thrilling when I have Lizbeth in tow. The other kind of kitty surprise is a plastic garbage bag filled with some ponderous, amorphous mass. This always proves to be used cat litter.

City bees harvest doughnut glaze and this makes the Dumpster at the doughnut shop more interesting. My faith in the instinctive wisdom of animals is always shaken whenever I see Lizbeth attempt to catch a bee in her mouth, which she does whenever bees are present. Evidently some birds find Dumpsters profitable, for birdie surprise is almost as common as kitty surprise of the first kind. In hunting season all kinds of small game turn up in Dumpsters, some of it, sadly, not entirely dead. Curiously, summer and winter, maggots are uncommon.

The worst of the living and near-living hazards of the Dumpsters are the fire ants. The food they claim is not much of a loss, but they are vicious and aggressive. It is very easy to brush against some surface of the Dumpster and pick up half a dozen or more fire ants, usually in some sensitive area such as the underarm. One advantage of bringing Lizbeth along as I make Dumpster rounds is that, for obvious reasons, she is very alert to ground-based fire ants. When Lizbeth recognizes a fire-ant infestation around our feet, she does the Dance of the Zillion Fire Ants. I have learned not to ignore this warning from Lizbeth, whether I perceive the tiny ants or not, but to remove ourselves at Lizbeth's first pas de bourrée.[1] All the more so because the ants are the worst in the summer months when I wear flip-flops if I have them. (Perhaps someone will misunderstand this. Lizbeth does the Dance of the Zillion Fire Ants when she recognizes more fire ants than she cares to eat, not when she is being bitten. Since I have learned to react promptly, she does not get bitten at all. It is the isolated patrol of fire ants that falls in Lizbeth's range that deserves pity. She finds them quite tasty.)

By far the best way to go through a Dumpster is to lower yourself into it. Most of the good stuff tends to settle at the bottom because it is usually weightier than the rubbish. My more athletic companions have often demonstrated to me that they can extract much good material from a Dumpster I have already been over.

To those psychologically or physically unprepared to enter a 60 Dumpster, I recommend a stout stick, preferably with some barb or hook at one end. The hook can be used to grab plastic garbage bags. When I find canned goods or other objects loose at the bottom of a Dumpster, I lower a bag into it, roll the desired object into the bag, and then hoist the bag out—a procedure more easily described than executed. Much Dumpster diving is a matter of experience for which nothing will do except practice.

Dumpster diving is outdoor work, often surprisingly pleasant. It is not entirely predictable; things of interest turn up every day and some days there are finds of great value. I am always very pleased

---

[1]A short walking or running step in ballet. [Eds.]

when I can turn up exactly the thing I most wanted to find. Yet in spite of the element of chance, scavenging more than most other pursuits tends to yield returns in some proportion to the effort and intelligence brought to bear. It is very sweet to turn up a few dollars in change from a Dumpster that has just been gone over by a wino.

The land is now covered with cities. The cities are full of Dumpsters. If a member of the canine race is ever able to know what it is doing, then Lizbeth knows that when we go around to the Dumpsters, we are hunting. I think of scavenging as a modern form of self-reliance. In any event, after having survived nearly ten years of government service, where everything is geared to the lowest common denominator, I find it refreshing to have work that rewards initiative and effort. Certainly I would be happy to have a sinecure again, but I am no longer heartbroken that I left one.

I find from the experience of scavenging two rather deep lessons. The first is to take what you can use and let the rest go by. I have come to think that there is no value in the abstract. A thing I cannot use or make useful, perhaps by trading, has no value however rare or fine it may be. I mean useful in a broad sense—some art I would find useful and some otherwise.

I was shocked to realize that some things are not worth acquiring, but now I think it is so. Some material things are white elephants that eat up the possessor's substance. The second lesson is the transience of material being. This has not quite converted me to a dualist,[2] but it has made some headway in that direction. I do not suppose that ideas are immortal, but certainly mental things are longer lived than other material things.

65   Once I was the sort of person who invests objects with sentimental value. Now I no longer have those objects, but I have the sentiments yet.

Many times in our travels I have lost everything but the clothes I was wearing and Lizbeth. The things I find in Dumpsters, the love letters and rag dolls of so many lives, remind me of this lesson. Now I hardly pick up a thing without envisioning the time I will cast it aside. This I think is a healthy state of mind. Almost everything I have now has already been cast out at least once, proving that what I own is valueless to someone.

Anyway, I find my desire to grab for the gaudy bauble has been largely sated. I think this is an attitude I share with the very wealthy—we both know there is plenty more where what we have came from. Between us are the rat-race millions who nightly scavenge the cable channels looking for they know not what.

I am sorry for them.

---

[2]One who believes that material things also exist as spiritual ideals or abstractions. [Eds.]

Responding to Reading

1. In paragraph 6, Eighner explains, "I have learned much as a scavenger. I mean to put some of what I have learned down here, beginning with the practical art of Dumpster diving and proceeding to the abstract." Do you think Eighner's purpose goes beyond educating his readers? What other purpose do you think he might have?
2. What surprised you most about Eighner's essay? Did any information disturb you? Repulse you? Make you feel guilty? Arouse your sympathy? Arouse your pity? Do you think Eighner intended you to feel the way you do?
3. How do you suppose Eighner would define the American Dream? What do you think he might have to say about its limits?

Responding in Writing

Assuming that Eighner wished to continue living on the streets, what could he do to make his life easier? Write a flyer, to be distributed to the homeless, advising them of resources available to them in your community (for example, public rest rooms).

TWO KINDS

Amy Tan

1952–

Amy Tan was born in Oakland, California, to parents who had emigrated from China only a few years earlier. After earning a master's degree in linguistics and doing some postgraduate work, she began a career as a business and technical writer but soon turned to fiction, driven by her need to tell stories. Her first novel, The Joy Luck Club *(1987), about Chinese-born mothers and their American-born daughters, became a best-seller and won the National Book Award. She has also written* The Kitchen God's Wife *(1991),* The Hundred Secret Senses *(1995),* The Bonesetter's Daughter *(2001),* The Opposite of Fate: A Book of Musings *(2003) and* Saving Fish from Drowing, *(2006). The following short story, a chapter of* The Joy Luck Club, *offers several perspectives on the American Dream—the mother's, the narrator's as a young girl, and the narrator's as an adult.*

My mother believed you could be anything you wanted to be in America. You could open a restaurant. You could work for the government and get good retirement. You could buy a house with almost no money down. You could become rich. You could become instantly famous.

"Of course you can be prodigy, too," my mother told me when I was nine. "You can be best anything. What does Auntie Lindo know? Her daughter, she is only best tricky."

America was where all my mother's hopes lay. She had come here in 1949 after losing everything in China: her mother and father, her family home, her first husband, and two daughters, twin baby girls. But she never looked back with regret. There were so many ways for things to get better.

We didn't immediately pick the right kind of prodigy. At first my mother thought I could be a Chinese Shirley Temple. We'd watch Shirley's old movies on TV as though they were training films. My mother would poke my arm and say, *"Ni kan"*—You watch. And I would see Shirley tapping her feet, or singing a sailor song, or pursing her lips into a very round O while saying, "Oh my goodness."

5   *"Ni kan,"* said my mother as Shirley's eyes flooded with tears. "You already know how. Don't need talent for crying!"

Soon after my mother got this idea about Shirley Temple, she took me to a beauty training school in the Mission district and put me in the hands of a student who could barely hold the scissors without shaking. Instead of getting big fat curls, I emerged with an uneven mass of crinkly black fuzz. My mother dragged me off to the bathroom and tried to wet down my hair.

"You look like Negro Chinese," she lamented, as if I had done this on purpose.

The instructor of the beauty training school had to lop off these soggy clumps to make my hair even again. "Peter Pan is very popular these days," the instructor assured my mother. I now had hair the length of a boy's, with straight-across bangs that hung at a slant two inches above my eyebrows. I liked the haircut and it made me actually look forward to my future fame.

In fact, in the beginning, I was just as excited as my mother, maybe even more so. I pictured this prodigy part of me as many different images, trying each one on for size. I was a dainty ballerina girl standing by the curtains, waiting to hear the right music that would send me floating on my tiptoes. I was like the Christ child lifted out of the straw manger, crying with holy indignity. I was Cinderella stepping from her pumpkin carriage with sparkly cartoon music filling the air.

10   In all of my imaginings, I was filled with a sense that I would soon become *perfect*. My mother and father would adore me. I would be beyond reproach. I would never feel the need to sulk for anything.

But sometimes the prodigy in me became impatient. "If you don't hurry up and get me out of here, I'm disappearing for good," it warned. "And then you'll always be nothing."

Every night after dinner, my mother and I would sit at the Formica kitchen table. She would present new tests, taking her examples from stories of amazing children she had read in *Ripley's Believe It or Not*, or *Good Housekeeping, Reader's Digest,* and a dozen other magazines she kept in a pile in our bathroom. My mother got these magazines from people whose houses she cleaned. And since she cleaned many houses each week, we had a great assortment. She would look through them all, searching for stories about remarkable children.

The first night she brought out a story about a three-year-old boy who knew the capitals of all the states and even most of the European countries. A teacher was quoted as saying the little boy could also pronounce the names of the foreign cities correctly.

"What's the capital of Finland?" my mother asked me, looking at the magazine story.

All I knew was the capital of California, because Sacramento was 15 the name of the street we lived on in Chinatown. "Nairobi!" I guessed, saying the most foreign word I could think of. She checked to see if that was possibly one way to pronounce "Helsinki" before showing me the answer.

The tests got harder—multiplying numbers in my head, finding the queen of hearts in a deck of cards, trying to stand on my head without using my hands, predicting the daily temperatures in Los Angeles, New York, and London.

One night I had to look at a page from the Bible for three minutes and then report everything I could remember. "Now Jehoshaphat had riches and honor in abundance and . . . that's all I remember, Ma," I said.

And after seeing my mother's disappointed face once again, something inside of me began to die. I hated the tests, the raised hopes and failed expectations. Before going to bed that night, I looked in the mirror above the bathroom sink and when I saw only my face staring back—and that it would always be this ordinary face—I began to cry. Such a sad, ugly girl! I made high-pitched noises like a crazed animal, trying to scratch out the face in the mirror.

And then I saw what seemed to be the prodigy side of me— because I had never seen that face before. I looked at my reflection, blinking so I could see more clearly. The girl staring back at me was angry, powerful. This girl and I were the same. I had new thoughts, willful thoughts, or rather thoughts filled with lots of won'ts. I won't let her change me, I promised myself. I won't be what I'm not.

So now on nights when my mother presented her tests, I per- 20 formed listlessly, my head propped on one arm. I pretended to be bored. And I was. I got so bored I started counting the bellows of the foghorns out on the bay while my mother drilled me in other areas. The sound was comforting and reminded me of the cow jumping over the moon. And the next day, I played a game with myself, seeing if my mother would give up on me before eight bellows. After a while I usually counted only one, maybe two bellows at most. At last she was beginning to give up hope.

Two or three months had gone by without any mention of my being a prodigy again. And then one day my mother was watching *The Ed Sullivan Show* on TV. The TV was old and the sound kept shorting out. Every time my mother got halfway up from the sofa to adjust the set, the sound would go back on and Ed would be talking. As soon as she sat down, Ed would go silent again. She got up, the TV broke into loud piano music. She sat down. Silence. Up and down, back and forth, quiet and loud. It was like a stiff embraceless dance between her and the TV set. Finally she stood by the set with her hand on the sound dial.

She seemed entranced by the music, a little frenzied piano piece with this mesmerizing quality, sort of quick passages and then teasing lilting ones before it returned to the quick playful parts.

"*Ni kan*," my mother said, calling me over with hurried hand gestures, "Look here."

I could see why my mother was fascinated by the music. It was being pounded out by a little Chinese girl, about nine years old, with a Peter Pan haircut. The girl had the sauciness of a Shirley Temple. She was proudly modest like a proper Chinese child. And she also did this fancy sweep of a curtsy, so that the fluffy skirt of her white dress cascaded slowly to the floor like the petals of a large carnation.

25   In spite of these warning signs, I wasn't worried. Our family had no piano and we couldn't afford to buy one, let alone reams of sheet music and piano lessons. So I could be generous in my comments when my mother bad-mouthed the little girl on TV.

"Play note right, but doesn't sound good! No singing sound," complained my mother.

"What are you picking on her for?" I said carelessly. "She's pretty good. Maybe she's not the best, but she's trying hard." I knew almost immediately I would be sorry I said that.

"Just like you," she said. "Not the best. Because you not trying." She gave a little huff as she let go of the sound dial and sat down on the sofa.

The little Chinese girl sat down also to play an encore of "Anitra's Dance" by Grieg. I remember the song, because later on I had to learn how to play it.

Three days after watching *The Ed Sullivan Show,* my mother told ₃₀
me what my schedule would be for piano lessons and piano practice.
She had talked to Mr. Chong, who lived on the first floor of our apartment building. Mr. Chong was a retired piano teacher and my mother
had traded housecleaning services for weekly lessons and a piano for
me to practice on every day, two hours a day, from four until six.

When my mother told me this, I felt as though I had been sent to
hell. I whined and then kicked my foot a little when I couldn't stand it
anymore.

"Why don't you like me the way I am? I'm *not* a genius! I can't
play the piano. And even if I could, I wouldn't go on TV if you paid
me a million dollars!" I cried.

My mother slapped me. "Who ask you be genius?" she shouted.
"Only ask you be your best. For you sake. You think I want you be genius? Hnnh! What for! Who ask you!"

"So ungrateful," I heard her mutter in Chinese. "If she had as
much talent as she has temper, she would be famous now."

Mr. Chong, whom I secretly nicknamed Old Chong, was very ₃₅
strange, always tapping his fingers to the silent music of an invisible orchestra. He looked ancient in my eyes. He had lost most of
the hair on top of his head and he wore thick glasses and had eyes
that always looked tired and sleepy. But he must have been
younger than I thought, since he lived with his mother and was
not yet married.

I met Old Lady Chong once and that was enough. She had this
peculiar smell like a baby that had done something in its pants. And
her fingers felt like a dead person's, like an old peach I once found in
the back of the refrigerator; the skin just slid off the meat when I
picked it up.

I soon found out why Old Chong had retired from teaching
piano. He was deaf. "Like Beethoven!" he shouted to me. "We're both
listening only in our head!" And he would start to conduct his frantic
silent sonatas.

Our lessons went like this. He would open the book and point to
different things, explaining their purpose: "Key! Treble! Bass! No
sharps or flats! So this is C major! Listen now and play after me!"

And then he would play the C scale a few times, a simple chord,
and then, as if inspired by an old, unreachable itch, he gradually
added more notes and running trills and a pounding bass until the
music was really something quite grand.

I would play after him, the simple scale, the simple chord, and ₄₀
then I just played some nonsense that sounded like a cat running up
and down on top of garbage cans. Old Chong smiled and applauded
and then said, "Very good! But now you must learn to keep time!"

So that's how I discovered that Old Chong's eyes were too slow to keep up with the wrong notes I was playing. He went through the motions in half-time. To help me keep rhythm, he stood behind me, pushing down on my right shoulder for every beat. He balanced pennies on top of my wrists so I would keep them still as I slowly played scales and arpeggios. He had me curve my hand around an apple and keep that shape when playing chords. He marched stiffly to show me how to make each finger dance up and down, staccato like an obedient little soldier.

He taught me all these things, and that was how I also learned I could be lazy and get away with mistakes, lots of mistakes. If I hit the wrong notes because I hadn't practiced enough, I never corrected myself. I just kept playing in rhythm. And Old Chong kept conducting his own private reverie.

So maybe I never really gave myself a fair chance. I did pick up the basics pretty quickly, and I might have become a good pianist at that young age. But I was so determined not to try, not to be anybody different that I learned to play only the most ear-splitting preludes, the most discordant hymns.

Over the next year, I practiced like this, dutifully in my own way. And then one day I heard my mother and her friend Lindo Jong both talking in a loud bragging tone of voice so others could hear. It was after church, and I was leaning against the brick wall wearing a dress with stiff white petticoats. Auntie Lindo's daughter, Waverly, who was about my age, was standing farther down the wall about five feet away. We had grown up together and shared all the closeness of two sisters squabbling over crayons and dolls. In other words, for the most part, we hated each other. I thought she was snotty. Waverly Jong had gained a certain amount of fame as "Chinatown's Littlest Chinese Chess Champion."

45   "She bring home too many trophy," lamented Auntie Lindo that Sunday. "All day she play chess. All day I have no time do nothing but dust off her winnings." She threw a scolding look at Waverly, who pretended not to see her.

"You lucky you don't have this problem," said Auntie Lindo with a sigh to my mother.

And my mother squared her shoulders and bragged: "Our problem worser than yours. If we ask Jing-mei wash dish, she hear nothing but music. It's like you can't stop this natural talent."

And right then, I was determined to put a stop to her foolish pride.

A few weeks later, Old Chong and my mother conspired to have me play in a talent show which would be held in the church hall. By then, my parents had saved up enough to buy me a secondhand piano, a black Wurlitzer spinet with a scarred bench. It was the showpiece of our living room.

For the talent show, I was to play a piece called "Pleading Child" 50 from Schumann's *Scenes from Childhood.* It was a simple, moody piece that sounded more difficult than it was. I was supposed to memorize the whole thing, playing the repeat parts twice to make the piece sound longer. But I dawdled over it, playing a few bars and then cheating, looking up to see what notes followed. I never really listened to what I was playing. I daydreamed about being somewhere else, about being someone else.

The part I liked to practice best was the fancy curtsy: right foot out, touch the rose on the carpet with a pointed foot, sweep to the side, left leg bends, look up and smile.

My parents invited all the couples from the Joy Luck Club[1] to witness my debut. Auntie Lindo and Uncle Tin were there. Waverly and her two older brothers had also come. The first two rows were filled with children both younger and older than I was. The littlest ones got to go first. They recited simple nursery rhymes, squawked out tunes on miniature violins, twirled Hula Hoops, pranced in pink ballet tutus, and when they bowed or curtsied, the audience would sigh in unison, "Awww," and then clap enthusiastically.

When my turn came, I was very confident. I remember my childish excitement. It was as if I knew, without a doubt, that the prodigy side of me really did exist. I had no fear whatsoever, no nervousness. I remember thinking to myself, This is it! This is it! I looked out over the audience, at my mother's blank face, my father's yawn, Auntie Lindo's stiff-lipped smile, Waverly's sulky expression. I had on a white dress layered with sheets of lace, and a pink bow in my Peter Pan haircut. As I sat down I envisioned people jumping to their feet and Ed Sullivan rushing up to introduce me to everyone on TV.

And I started to play. It was so beautiful. I was so caught up in how lovely I looked that at first I didn't worry how I would sound. So it was a surprise to me when I hit the first wrong note and I realized something didn't sound quite right. And then I hit another and another followed that. A chill started at the top of my head and began to trickle down. Yet I couldn't stop playing, as though my hands were bewitched. I kept thinking my fingers would adjust themselves back, like a train switching to the right track. I played this strange jumble through two repeats, the sour notes staying with me all the way to the end.

When I stood up, I discovered my legs were shaking. Maybe I 55 had just been nervous and the audience, like Old Chong, had seen me go through the right motions and had not heard anything wrong

---

[1] A name denoting the mother's circle of friends, all of whom were Chinese immigrants to the United States. [Eds.]

at all. I swept my right foot out, went down on my knee, looked up and smiled. The room was quiet, except for Old Chong, who was beaming and shouting, "Bravo! Bravo! Well done!" But then I saw my mother's face, her stricken face. The audience clapped weakly, and as I walked back to my chair, with my whole face quivering as I tried not to cry, I heard a little boy whisper loudly to his mother, "That was awful," and the mother whispered back, "Well, she certainly tried."

And now I realized how many people were in the audience, the whole world it seemed. I was aware of eyes burning into my back. I felt the shame of my mother and father as they sat stiffly throughout the rest of the show.

We could have escaped during intermission. Pride and some strange sense of honor must have anchored my parents to their chairs. And so we watched it all: the eighteen-year-old boy with a fake mustache who did a magic show and juggled flaming hoops while riding a unicycle. The breasted girl with white makeup who sang from *Madama Butterfly* and got honorable mention. And the eleven-year-old boy who won first prize playing a tricky violin song that sounded like a busy bee.

After the show, the Hsus, the Jongs, and the St. Clairs from the Joy Luck Club came up to my mother and father.

"Lots of talented kids," Auntie Lindo said vaguely, smiling broadly.

60   "That was somethin' else," said my father, and I wondered if he was referring to me in a humorous way, or whether he even remembered what I had done.

Waverly looked at me and shrugged her shoulders. "You aren't a genius like me," she said matter-of-factly. And if I hadn't felt so bad, I would have pulled her braids and punched her stomach.

But my mother's expression was what devastated me: a quiet, blank look that said she had lost everything. I felt the same way, and it seemed as if everybody were now coming up, like gawkers at the scene of an accident, to see what parts were actually missing. When we got on the bus to go home, my father was humming the busy-bee tune and my mother was silent. I kept thinking she wanted to wait until we got home before shouting at me. But when my father unlocked the door to our apartment, my mother walked in and then went to the back, into the bedroom. No accusations. No blame. And in a way, I felt disappointed. I had been waiting for her to start shouting, so I could shout back and cry and blame her for all my misery.

I assumed my talent-show fiasco meant I never had to play the piano again. But two days later, after school, my mother came out of the kitchen and saw me watching TV.

"Four clock," she reminded me as if it were any other day. I was stunned, as though she were asking me to go through the talent-show torture again. I wedged myself more tightly in front of the TV.

"Turn off TV," she called from the kitchen five minutes later.   65

I didn't budge. And then I decided. I didn't have to do what my mother said anymore. I wasn't her slave. This wasn't China. I had listened to her before and look what happened. She was the stupid one.

She came out from the kitchen and stood in the arched entryway of the living room. "Four clock," she said once again, louder.

"I'm not going to play anymore," I said nonchalantly. "Why should I? I'm not a genius."

She walked over and stood in front of the TV. I saw her chest was heaving up and down in an angry way.

"No!" I said, and I now felt stronger, as if my true self had finally   70 emerged. So this was what had been inside me all along.

"No! I won't!" I screamed.

She yanked me by the arm, pulled me off the floor, snapped off the TV. She was frighteningly strong, half pulling, half carrying me toward the piano as I kicked the throw rugs under my feet. She lifted me up and onto the hard bench. I was sobbing by now, looking at her bitterly. Her chest was heaving even more and her mouth was open, smiling crazily as if she were pleased I was crying.

"You want me to be someone that I'm not!" I sobbed. "I'll never be the kind of daughter you want me to be!"

"Only two kinds of daughters," she shouted in Chinese. "Those who are obedient and those who follow their own mind! Only one kind of daughter can live in this house. Obedient daughter!"

"Then I wish I wasn't your daughter. I wish you weren't my   75 mother," I shouted. As I said these things I got scared. It felt like worms and toads and slimy things crawling out of my chest, but it also felt good, as if this awful side of me had surfaced, at last.

"Too late change this," said my mother shrilly.

And I could sense her anger rising to its breaking point. I wanted to see it spill over. And that's when I remembered the babies she had lost in China, the ones we never talked about. "Then I wish I'd never been born!" I shouted. "I wish I were dead! Like them."

It was as if I had said the magic words. Alakazam!—and her face went blank, her mouth closed, her arms went slack, and she backed out of the room, stunned, as if she were blowing away like a small brown leaf, thin, brittle, lifeless.

It was not the only disappointment my mother felt in me. In the years that followed, I failed her so many times, each time asserting my own will, my right to fall short of expectations. I didn't get straight As. I didn't become class president. I didn't get into Stanford. I dropped out of college.

80   For unlike my mother, I did not believe I could be anything I wanted to be. I could only be me.

And for all those years, we never talked about the disaster at the recital or my terrible accusations afterward at the piano bench. All that remained unchecked, like a betrayal that was now unspeakable. So I never found a way to ask her why she had hoped for something so large that failure was inevitable.

And even worse, I never asked her what frightened me the most: Why had she given up hope?

For after our struggle at the piano, she never mentioned my playing again. The lessons stopped. The lid to the piano was closed, shutting out the dust, my misery, and her dreams.

So she surprised me. A few years ago, she offered to give me the piano, for my thirtieth birthday. I had not played in all those years. I saw the offer as a sign of forgiveness, a tremendous burden removed.

85   "Are you sure?" I asked shyly. "I mean, won't you and Dad miss it?"

"No, this your piano," she said firmly. "Always your piano. You only one can play."

"Well, I probably can't play anymore," I said. "It's been years."

"You pick up fast," said my mother, as if she knew this was certain. "You have natural talent. You could been genius if you want to."

"No I couldn't."

90   "You just not trying," said my mother. And she was neither angry nor sad. She said it as if to announce a fact that could never be disproved. "Take it," she said.

But I didn't at first. It was enough that she had offered it to me. And after that, every time I saw it in my parents' living room, standing in front of the bay windows, it made me feel proud, as if it were a shiny trophy I had won back.

Last week I sent a tuner over to my parents' apartment and had the piano reconditioned, for purely sentimental reasons. My mother had died a few months before and I had been getting things in order for my father, a little bit at a time. I put the jewelry in special silk pouches. The sweaters she had knitted in yellow, pink, bright orange—all the colors I hated—I put those in moth-proof boxes. I found some old Chinese silk dresses, the kind with little slits up the sides. I rubbed the old silk against my skin, then wrapped them in tissue and decided to take them home with me.

After I had the piano tuned, I opened the lid and touched the keys. It sounded even richer than I remembered. Really, it was a very good piano. Inside the bench were the same exercise notes with handwritten scales, the same secondhand music books with their covers held together with yellow tape.

I opened up the Schumann book to the dark little piece I had played at the recital. It was on the left-hand side of the page, "Pleading Child." It looked more difficult than I remembered. I played a few bars, surprised at how easily the notes came back to me.

And for the first time, or so it seemed, I noticed the piece on the 95 right-hand side. It was called "Perfectly Contented." I tried to play this one as well. It had a lighter melody but the same flowing rhythm and turned out to be quite easy. "Pleading Child" was shorter but slower; "Perfectly Contented" was longer, but faster. And after I played them both a few times, I realized they were two halves of the same song.

Responding to Reading

1. Why does the narrator's mother believe that her daughter can become a prodigy? Does the daughter agree that this is possible?
2. What are the "two kinds" to which the story's title refers? Are these two categories completely irreconcilable, or do you see any common ground between them?
3. In what respects are the story's plot and characters unique to the Chinese-American experience? In what respects does the story reveal truths about other immigrant families as well?

Responding in Writing

The narrator's mother sees the child actress Shirley Temple as typically American. What prominent contemporary figures—entertainers, politicians, sports figures, and so on—do you see as typically American? Why?

Focus

What Is the American Dream?

Immigrant families on board ship approaching Statue of Liberty, c. 1900

Responding to the Image

1. What does this photograph suggest to you about the power of the American Dream? How might the immigrants pictured here define the American Dream?
2. What do you think the Statue of Liberty symbolizes to the people in the picture? Do you think the statue means something different to today's Americans? (Note that most immigrants no longer come to the United States by ship.)

THE DECLARATION OF INDEPENDENCE
Thomas Jefferson
1743–1826

Thomas Jefferson—lawyer, statesman, diplomat, architect, scientist, politician, writer, education theorist, and musician—graduated from William and Mary College in 1762 and went on to lead an impressive political life. Jefferson served as a member of the Continental Congress, governor of Virginia, Secretary of State to George Washington, and Vice-President to John Adams and also served two terms as the U.S. President (1801–1809), during which he oversaw the Louisiana Purchase. After retiring from public office, Jefferson founded the University of Virginia in 1819. He was an avid collector of books and owned nearly ten thousand, which later became the foundation of the Library of Congress. A firm believer in reason and the natural rights of individuals, Jefferson drafted The Declaration of Independence, which was later amended by the Continental Congress. In this document, he presents the colonists' grievances in order to justify their decision to declare their independence from England.

In Congress, July 4, 1776: The Unanimous Declaration of the Thirteen United States of America

When in the Course of human events it becomes necessary for one people to dissolve the political bands which have connected them with another, and to assume among the powers of the earth, the separate and equal station to which the Laws of Nature and of Nature's God entitle them, a decent respect to the opinions of mankind requires that they should declare the causes which impel them to the separation.

We hold these truths to be self-evident, that all men are created equal, that they are endowed by their Creator with certain unalienable Rights, that among these are Life, Liberty and the pursuit of Happiness. That to secure these rights, Governments are instituted among Men, deriving their just powers from the consent of the governed. That whenever any Form of Government becomes destructive of these ends, it is the Right of the People to alter or to abolish it, and to institute new Government, laying its foundation on such principles and organizing its powers in such form, as to them shall seem most likely to effect their Safety and Happiness. Prudence, indeed, will dictate that Governments long established should not be changed for light and transient causes; and accordingly all experience hath shewn, that mankind are more disposed to suffer, while evils are sufferable, than to right themselves by abolishing the forms to which they are accustomed. But when a long train of abuses and usurpations, pursuing invariably the same Object, evinces a design to reduce them under absolute Despotism, it is their right, it is their duty, to throw off such Government, and to provide new Guards for their future security. Such has been the patient sufferance of these Colonies; and such is now the necessity which constrains them to alter their former Systems of Governors. The history of the present King of Great Britain is a history of repeated injuries and usurpations, all having in direct object the establishment of an absolute Tyranny over these States. To prove this, let Facts be submitted to a candid world.

He has refused his Assent to Laws, the most wholesome and necessary for the public good.

He has forbidden his Governors to pass laws of immediate and pressing importance, unless suspended in their operation till his Assent should be obtained; and when so suspended, he has utterly neglected to attend to them.

5   He has refused to pass other Laws for the accommodation of large districts of people, unless those people would relinquish the right of Representation in the Legislature, a right inestimable to them and formidable to tyrants only.

He has called together legislative bodies at places unusual, uncomfortable, and distant from the depository of their Public Records, for the sole purpose of fatiguing them into compliance with his measures.

He has dissolved Representative Houses repeatedly, for opposing with manly firmness his invasions on the rights of the people.

He has refused for a long time, after such dissolutions, to cause others to be elected; whereby the Legislative Powers, incapable of Annihilation, have returned to the People at large for their exercise; the State remaining in the mean time exposed to all the dangers of invasion from without, and convulsions within.

He has endeavored to prevent the population of these States; for that purpose obstructing the Laws for Naturalization of Foreigners; refusing to pass others to encourage their migration hither, and raising the conditions of new Appropriations of Lands.

10   He has obstructed the Administration of Justice, by refusing his Assent to Laws for establishing Judiciary Powers.

He has made Judges dependent on his Will alone, for the tenure of their offices, and the amount and payment of their salaries.

He has erected a multitude of New Offices, and sent hither swarms of Officers to harass our people, and eat out their substance.

He has kept among us, in times of peace, Standing Armies without the Consent of our legislatures.

He has affected to render the Military independent of and superior to the Civil Power.

15   He has combined with others to subject us to a jurisdiction foreign to our constitution, and unacknowledged by our laws; giving his Assent to their Acts of pretended Legislation: For quartering large bodies

of armed troops among us: For protecting them, by a mock Trial, from punishment for any Murders which they should commit on the Inhabitants of these States: For cutting off our Trade with all parts of the world: For imposing Taxes on us without our Consent: For depriving us in many cases, of the benefits of Trial by Jury; For transporting us beyond Seas to be tried for pretended offenses: For abolishing the free System of English Laws in a neighboring Province, establishing therein an Arbitrary government, and enlarging its Boundaries so as to render it at once an example and fit instrument for introducing the same absolute rule into these Colonies: For taking away our Charters, abolishing our most valuable Laws and altering fundamentally the Forms of our Governments: For suspending our own Legislatures, and declaring themselves invested with power to legislate for us in all cases whatsoever.

He has abdicated Government here, by declaring us out of his Protection and waging War against us.

He has plundered our seas, ravaged our Coasts, burnt our towns, and destroyed the lives of our people.

He is at this time transporting large Armies of foreign Mercenaries to complete the works of death, desolation and tyranny, already begun with circumstances of Cruelty & Perfidy scarcely paralleled in the most barbarous ages, and totally unworthy the Head of a civilized nation.

He has constrained our fellow Citizens taken Captive on the high Seas to bear Arms against their Country, to become the executioners of their friends and Brethren, or to fall themselves by their Hands.

He has excited domestic insurrections amongst us, and has endeav- 20
ored to bring on the inhabitants of our frontiers, the merciless Indian Savages, whose known rule of warfare, is an undistinguished destruction of all ages, sexes, and conditions.

In every stage of these Oppressions We have Petitioned for Redress in the most humble terms: Our repeated Petitions have been answered only by repeated injury. A Prince, whose character is thus marked by every act which may define a Tyrant, is unfit to be the ruler of a free people.

Nor have We been wanting in attention to our British brethren. We have warned them from time to time of attempts by their legislature to extend an unwarrantable jurisdiction over us. We have reminded them of the circumstances of our emigration and settlement here. We have appealed to their native justice and magnanimity, and we have conjured them by the ties of our common kindred to disavow these usurpations, which would inevitably interrupt our connections and correspondence. They too have been deaf to the voice of justice and of consanguinity. We must, therefore, acquiesce in the necessity, which denounces our Separation, and hold them, as we hold the rest of mankind, Enemies in War, in Peace Friends.

We, THEREFORE, the Representatives of the UNITED STATES OF AMERICA, in General Congress, Assembled, appealing to the Supreme Judge of the world for the rectitude of our intentions, do, in the Name, and by Authority of the good People of these Colonies, solemnly publish and declare, That these United Colonies are, and of Right ought to be FREE AND INDEPENDENT STATES; that they are Absolved from all Allegiance to the British Crown, and that all political connection between them and the State of Great Britain, is and ought to be totally dissolved; and that as Free and Independent States, they have full Power to levy War, conclude Peace, contract Alliances, establish Commerce, and to do all other Acts and Things which Independent States may of right do. And for the support of this Declaration, with a firm reliance on the protection of Divine Providence, we mutually pledge to each other our Lives, our Fortunes, and our sacred Honor.

Responding to Reading

1. The Declaration of Independence was written in the eighteenth century, a time when logic and reason were thought to be the supreme achievements of human beings. Do you think this document appeals just to reason, or does it also appeal to the emotions?
2. Paragraphs 3 through 20 consist of a litany of grievances, expressed in forceful parallel language. How is this use of parallelism similar to (or different from) the language used by Kennedy (p. 481) and King (p. 485)?
3. Do you think it is fair, as some have done, to accuse the framers of the Declaration of Independence of being racist? Of being sexist?

Responding in Writing

Rewrite five or six sentences from paragraphs 3–20 of The Declaration of Independence in modern English, substituting contemporary examples for the injustices Jefferson enumerates.

THE NEW COLOSSUS

Emma Lazarus

1849–1887

Born to a wealthy family in New York City and educated by private tutors, Emma Lazarus became one of the foremost poets of her day. Today, she is remembered solely for her poem "The New Colossus," a sonnet written in 1883 as part of an effort to raise funds for the Statue of Liberty. The poem was later inscribed on the statue's base, and it remains a vivid reminder of the immigrant's American dream.

Not like the brazen giant of Greek fame,
With conquering limbs astride from land to land;

Here at our sea-washed, sunset gates shall stand
A mighty woman with a torch, whose flame
Is the imprisoned lightning, and her name   5
Mother of Exiles. From her beacon-hand
Glows world-wide welcome; her mild eyes command
The air-bridged harbor that twin cities frame.
"Keep, ancient lands, your storied pomp!" cries she
With silent lips. "Give me your tired, your poor,   10
Your huddled masses yearning to breathe free,
The wretched refuse of your teeming shore.
Send these, the homeless, tempest-tost to me,
I lift my lamp beside the golden door!"

Responding to Reading

1. The Colossus of Rhodes, an enormous statue of the Greek god Apollo, was considered one of the seven wonders of the ancient world. It stood at the mouth of the harbor at Rhodes. Why do you think this poem is called "The New Colossus"?
2. Who is the poem's speaker? Who is being addressed?
3. What is the "golden door" to which the last line refers?

Responding in Writing

Look at the photograph on page 476. What elements of the Statue of Liberty has Lazarus captured in this poem? What characteristics, if any, has she failed to capture?

INAUGURAL ADDRESS
John F. Kennedy
1917–1963

Born in Brookline, Massachusetts, John Fitzgerald Kennedy received a bachelor's degree from Harvard University and served in the Navy as a PT boat commander in the South Pacific. A highly charismatic politician, he was elected to the United States House of Representatives in 1947 and to the Senate in 1953. In 1960, defeating Republican candidate (and later President) Richard Nixon, Kennedy became the youngest man and the first Catholic to be elected President. During his tenure, he supported policies promoting racial equality, aid to the poor and to education, and increased availability of medical care; he also conceived of the idea of the Peace Corps. However, Kennedy was also responsible for involving the country further in the doomed Vietnam conflict. He was assassinated in November of 1963, a year before the end of his first term.

Vice President Johnson, Mr. Speaker, Mr. Chief Justice, President Eisenhower, Vice President Nixon, President Truman, Reverend Clergy, fellow citizens:

We observe today not a victory of party but a celebration of freedom—symbolizing an end as well as a beginning—signifying renewal as well as change. For I have sworn before you and Almighty God the same solemn oath our forebears prescribed nearly a century and three-quarters ago.

The world is very different now. For man holds in his mortal hands the power to abolish all forms of human poverty and all forms of human life. And yet the same revolutionary beliefs for which our forebears fought are still at issue around the globe—the belief that the rights of man come not from the generosity of the state but from the hand of God.

We dare not forget today that we are the heirs of that first revolution. Let the word go forth from this time and place, to friend and foe alike, that the torch has been passed to a new generation of Americans—born in this century, tempered by war, disciplined by a hard and bitter peace, proud of our ancient heritage—and unwilling to witness or permit the slow undoing of those human rights to which this nation has always been committed, and to which we are committed today at home and around the world.

5   Let every nation know, whether it wishes us well or ill, that we shall pay any price, bear any burden, meet any hardship, support any friend, oppose any foe to assure the survival and the success of liberty.

This much we pledge—and more.

To those old allies whose cultural and spiritual origins we share, we pledge the loyalty of faithful friends. United there is little we cannot do in a host of cooperative ventures. Divided there is little we can do—for we dare not meet a powerful challenge at odds and split asunder.

To those new states whom we welcome to the ranks of the free, we pledge our word that one form of colonial control shall not have passed away merely to be replaced by a far more iron tyranny. We shall not always expect to find them supporting our view. But we shall always hope to find them strongly supporting their own freedom—and to remember that, in the past, those who foolishly sought power by riding the back of the tiger ended up inside. To those people in the huts and villages of half the globe struggling to break the bonds of mass misery, we pledge our best efforts to help them help themselves, for whatever period is required—not because the communists may be doing it, not because we seek their votes, but because it is right. If a free society cannot help the many who are poor, it cannot save the few who are rich.

To our sister republics south of our border, we offer a special pledge—to convert our good words into good deeds—in a new alliance for progress—to assist free men and free governments in casting off the chains of poverty. But this peaceful revolution of hope cannot become the prey of hostile powers. Let all our neighbors know that we shall join with them to oppose aggression or subversion anywhere in the

Americas. And let every other power know that this Hemisphere intends to remain the master of its own house.

To that world assembly of sovereign states, the United Nations, our 10 last best hope in an age where the instruments of war have far outpaced the instruments of peace, we renew our pledge of support—to prevent it from becoming merely a forum for invective—to strengthen its shield of the new and the weak—and to enlarge the area in which its writ may run.

Finally, to those nations who would make themselves our adversary, we offer not a pledge but a request: that both sides begin anew the quest for peace, before the dark powers of destruction unleashed by science engulf all humanity in planned or accidental self-destruction.

We dare not tempt them with weakness. For only when our arms are sufficient beyond doubt can we be certain beyond doubt that they will never be employed.

But neither can two great and powerful groups of nations take comfort from our present course—both sides overburdened by the cost of modern weapons, both rightly alarmed by the steady spread of the deadly atom, yet both racing to alter that uncertain balance of terror that stays the hand of mankind's final war.

So let us begin anew—remembering on both sides that civility is not a sign of weakness, and sincerity is always subject to proof. Let us never negotiate out of fear. But let us never fear to negotiate.

Let both sides explore what problems unite us instead of belabor- 15 ing those problems which divide us.

Let both sides, for the first time, formulate serious and precise proposals for the inspection and control of arms and bring the absolute power to destroy other nations under the absolute control of all nations.

Let both sides seek to invoke the wonders of science instead of its terrors. Together let us explore the stars, conquer the deserts, eradicate disease, tap the ocean depths and encourage the arts and commerce.

Let both sides unite to heed in all corners of the earth the command of Isaiah—to "undo the heavy burdens . . . (and) let the oppressed go free."

And if a beachhead of cooperation may push back the jungle of suspicion, let both sides join in creating a new endeavor, not a new balance of power, but a new world of law, where the strong are just and the weak secure and the peace preserved.

All this will not be finished in the first one hundred days. Nor will 20 it be finished in the first one thousand days, nor in the life of this Administration, nor even perhaps in our lifetime on this planet. But let us begin.

In your hands, my fellow citizens, more than mine, will rest the final success or failure of our course. Since this country was founded, each generation of Americans has been summoned to give testimony to its national loyalty. The graves of young Americans who answered the call to service surround the globe.

Now the trumpet summons us—again not as a call to bear arms, though arms we need—not as a call to battle, though embattled we are—but a call to bear the burden of a long twilight struggle, year in and year out, "rejoicing in hope, patient in tribulation"—a struggle against the common enemies of man: tyranny, poverty, disease and war itself. Can we forge against these enemies a grand and global alliance, North and South, East and West, that can assure a more fruitful life for all mankind? Will you join in that historic effort?

In the long history of the world, only a few generations have been granted the role of defending freedom in its hour of maximum danger. I do not shrink from this responsibility—I welcome it. I do not believe that any of us would exchange places with any other people or any other generation. The energy, the faith, the devotion which we bring to this endeavor will light our country and all who serve it—and the glow from that fire can truly light the world. And so, my fellow Americans: ask not what your country can do for you—ask what you can do for your country. My fellow citizens of the world: ask not what America will do for you, but what together we can do for the freedom of man.

Finally, whether you are citizens of America or citizens of the world, ask of us here the same high standards of strength and sacrifice which we ask of you. With a good conscience our only sure reward, with history the final judge of our deeds, let us go forth to lead the land we love, asking His blessing and His help, but knowing that here on earth God's work must truly be our own.

Responding to Reading

1. At the beginning of his speech, Kennedy alludes to the "revolutionary beliefs" of Jefferson (p. 477) and asserts, "We are the heirs of that first revolution" (4). What does he mean? Do you think his speech offers adequate support for this statement?
2. What, according to Kennedy, must we still achieve in order to fulfill Jefferson's dreams? What other problems do you believe must still be solved before we can consider the American Dream a reality?
3. Near the end of his speech, Kennedy says, "And so, my fellow Americans: ask not what your country can do for you—ask what you can do for your country" (23). What does this famous, often-quoted passage actually mean in practical terms? Do you think this exhortation is realistic? Do you think it is fair? Explain.

Responding in Writing

Exactly what do you expect America to do for you, and what do you expect to do for your country?

I HAVE A DREAM

Martin Luther King, Jr.

1929–1968

One of the greatest civil rights leaders and orators of this century, Baptist minister Martin Luther King, Jr. earned a B.A. degree from Morehouse College (1948), a B.D. degree from Crozer Theological Seminary in Pennsylvania (1951), and a Ph.D. from Boston University (1955). Influenced by Thoreau and Gandhi, King altered the spirit of African-American protest in the United States by advocating nonviolent civil disobedience to achieve racial equality. King was arrested more than twenty times and assaulted at least four times for his activities, but he also was awarded five honorary degrees, was named Man of the Year by Time *magazine in 1963, and the following year was awarded the Nobel Peace Prize. King was assassinated on April 4, 1968, in Memphis, Tennessee. He delivered the following speech from the steps of the Lincoln Memorial on August 28, 1963, during the March on Washington in support of civil rights.*

I am happy to join with you today in what will go down in history as the greatest demonstration for freedom in the history of our nation.

Fivescore years ago, a great American, in whose symbolic shadow we stand today, signed the Emancipation Proclamation. This momentous decree came as a great beacon light of hope to millions of Negro slaves who had been seared in the flames of withering injustice. It came as a joyous daybreak to end the long night of their captivity.

But one hundred years later, the Negro still is not free; one hundred years later, the life of the Negro is still sadly crippled by the manacles of segregation and the chains of discrimination; one hundred years later, the Negro lives on a lonely island of poverty in the midst of a vast ocean of material prosperity; one hundred years later, the Negro is still languishing in the corners of American society and finds himself in exile in his own land.

So we've come here today to dramatize a shameful condition. In a sense we've come to our nation's capital to cash a check. When the architects of our republic wrote the magnificent words of the Constitution and the Declaration of Independence, they were signing a promissory note to which every American was to fall heir. This note was the promise that all men, yes, black men as well as white men, would be guaranteed the unalienable rights of life, liberty, and the pursuit of happiness.

It is obvious today that America has defaulted on this promissory note in so far as her citizens of color are concerned. Instead of honoring this sacred obligation, America has given the Negro people a bad check; a check which has come back marked "insufficient funds." We refuse to believe that there are insufficient funds in the great vaults of opportunity of this nation. And so we've come to cash this check, a check that will give us upon demand the riches of freedom and the security of justice.

We have also come to this hallowed spot to remind America of the fierce urgency of now. This is no time to engage in the luxury of cooling off or to take the tranquilizing drug of gradualism. Now is the time to make real the promises of democracy; now is the time to rise from the dark and desolate valley of segregation to the sunlit path of racial justice; now is the time to lift our nation from the quicksands of racial injustice to the solid rock of brotherhood; now is the time to make justice a reality for all God's children. It would be fatal for the nation to overlook the urgency of the moment. This sweltering summer of the Negro's legitimate discontent will not pass until there is an invigorating autumn of freedom and equality.

Nineteen sixty-three is not an end, but a beginning. And those who hope that the Negro needed to blow off steam and will now be content, will have a rude awakening if the nation returns to business as usual.

There will be neither rest nor tranquility in America until the Negro is granted his citizenship rights. The whirlwinds of revolt will continue to shake the foundations of our nation until the bright day of justice emerges.

But there is something that I must say to my people who stand on the warm threshold which leads into the palace of justice. In the process of gaining our rightful place we must not be guilty of wrongful deeds.

10   Let us not seek to satisfy our thirst for freedom by drinking from the cup of bitterness and hatred. We must forever conduct our struggle on the high plane of dignity and discipline. We must not allow our creative protest to degenerate into physical violence. Again and again we must rise to the majestic heights of meeting physical force with soul force.

The marvelous new militancy which has engulfed the Negro community must not lead us to a distrust of all white people, for many of our white brothers, as evidenced by their presence here today, have come to realize that their destiny is tied up with our destiny and they have come to realize that their freedom is inextricably bound to our freedom. This offense we share mounted to storm the battlements of injustice must be carried forth by a biracial army. We cannot walk alone.

And as we walk, we must make the pledge that we shall always march ahead. We cannot turn back. There are those who are asking the devotees of civil rights, "When will you be satisfied?" We can never be satisfied as long as the Negro is the victim of the unspeakable horrors of police brutality.

We can never be satisfied as long as our bodies, heavy with fatigue of travel, cannot gain lodging in the motels of the highways and the hotels of the cities. We cannot be satisfied as long as the Negro's basic mobility is from a smaller ghetto to a larger one.

We can never be satisfied as long as our children are stripped of their selfhood and robbed of their dignity by signs stating "for whites only." We cannot be satisfied as long as a Negro in Mississippi cannot vote and a Negro in New York believes he has nothing for which to vote. No, we are not satisfied, and we will not be satisfied until justice rolls down like waters and righteousness like a mighty stream.

I am not unmindful that some of you have come here out of excessive 15 trials and tribulation. Some of you have come fresh from narrow jail cells. Some of you have come from areas where your quest for freedom left you battered by the storms of persecution and staggered by the winds of police brutality. You have been the veterans of creative suffering. Continue to work with the faith that unearned suffering is redemptive.

Go back to Mississippi; go back to Alabama; go back to South Carolina; go back to Georgia; go back to Louisiana; go back to the slums and ghettos of the northern cities, knowing that somehow this situation can, and will be changed. Let us not wallow in the valley of despair.

So I say to you, my friends, that even though we must face the difficulties of today and tomorrow, I still have a dream. It is a dream deeply rooted in the American dream that one day this nation will rise up and live out the true meaning of its creed—we hold these truths to be self-evident, that all men are created equal.

I have a dream that one day on the red hills of Georgia, sons of former slaves and sons of former slave-owners will be able to sit down together at the table of brotherhood.

I have a dream that one day, even the state of Mississippi, a state sweltering with the heat of injustice, sweltering with the heat of oppression, will be transformed into an oasis of freedom and justice.

I have a dream my four little children will one day live in a nation 20 where they will not be judged by the color of their skin but by the content of their character. I have a dream today!

I have a dream that one day, down in Alabama, with its vicious racists, with its governor having his lips dripping with the words of interposition and nullification, that one day, right there in Alabama, little black boys and black girls will be able to join hands with little white boys and white girls as sisters and brothers. I have a dream today!

I have a dream that one day every valley shall be exalted, every hill and mountain shall be made low, the rough places shall be made plain, and the crooked places shall be made straight and the glory of the Lord will be revealed and all flesh shall see it together.

This is our hope. This is the faith that I go back to the South with.

With this faith we will be able to hew out of the mountain of despair a stone of hope. With this faith we will be able to transform the jangling discords of our nation into a beautiful symphony of brotherhood.

25   With this faith we will be able to work together, to pray together, to struggle together, to go to jail together, to stand up for freedom together, knowing that we will be free one day. This will be the day when all of God's children will be able to sing with new meaning—"my country 'tis of thee; sweet land of liberty; of thee I sing; land where my fathers died, land of the pilgrim's pride; from every mountain side, let freedom ring"—and if America is to be a great nation, this must become true.

So let freedom ring from the prodigious hilltops of New Hampshire.

Let freedom ring from the mighty mountains of New York.

Let freedom ring from the heightening Alleghenies of Pennsylvania.

Let freedom ring from the snow-capped Rockies of Colorado.

30   Let freedom ring from the curvaceous slopes of California.

But not only that.

Let freedom ring from Stone Mountain of Georgia.

Let freedom ring from Lookout Mountain of Tennessee.

Let freedom ring from every hill and molehill of Mississippi, from every mountainside, let freedom ring.

35   And when we allow freedom to ring, when we let it ring from every village and hamlet, from every state and city, we will be able to speed up that day when all of God's children—black men and white men, Jews and Gentiles, Catholics and Protestants—will be able to join hands and to sing in the words of the old Negro spiritual, "Free at last, free at last; thank God Almighty, we are free at last."

Responding to Reading

1. What exactly is King's dream? Do you believe it has come true in any sense?

2. Speaking as a representative of his fellow African-American citizens, King tells his audience that African Americans find themselves "in exile in [their] own land" (3). Do you believe this is still true of African Americans? Of members of other minority groups? Which groups? Why?

3. Jefferson (p. 477) wrote in the eighteenth century; King, in the twentieth. Jefferson wrote as an insider, a man of privilege; King, as an outsider. What do their dreams have in common? How did each man intend to achieve his dream?

Responding in Writing

What dreams do you have for yourself and for your family? What dreams do you have for your country? Do you expect these dreams to be realized?

WIDENING THE FOCUS

For Critical Thinking and Writing

Read the selections by Jefferson (The Declaration of Independence), Lazarus ("The New Colossus"), Kennedy (Inaugural Address), and King ("I Have a Dream") in this chapter's Focus section. Then, try to answer the question, "What is the American Dream?"

For Further Reading

The following readings can suggest additional perspectives for thinking and writing about the American Dream:

- Sherman Alexie, "The Unauthorized Autobiography of Me" (p. 47)
- Jonathan Kozol, "The Human Cost of an Illiterate Society" (p. 175)
- Martin Luther King, Jr., "Letter from Birmingham Jail" (p. 741)

For Internet Research

The American Dream was first defined more than two centuries ago, and over the years it has changed along with our society. How would you define today's American Dream? For example, does it include access for all to education, employment, healthcare, and home ownership? Visit some Web sites that offer their visions of the American Dream, such as the following:

- *The Center for a New American Dream,* <http://www.newdream.org/>
- *A World Connected,* <http://www.aworldconnected.org/>
- *The American Dream Group,* <http://achieve-the dream.net/index.htm>
- *America's Promise,* <http://www.americaspromise.org/>
- *The "I Have a Dream"®️ Foundation,* <http://www.ihad.org/>

Or, use a search engine to find discussion of the American Dream in online political magazines listed on the Yahoo! Directory, <http://dir.yahoo.com/Government/U_S_Government/Politics/News_and_Media/Magazines/>.

Then, write an essay in which you define what you think the American Dream should be for the twenty-first century.

--- **WRITING** ---

The American Dream

1. Write an essay in which you support the idea that the strength of the United States comes from its ability to assimilate many different groups. In your essay, discuss specific contributions your own ethnic group and others have made to American society.

2. Some of the writers in this chapter respond to their feelings of being excluded from American society with anger and protest; others respond with resignation and acceptance. Considering several different writers and situations, write an essay in which you contrast these two kinds of responses. Under what circumstances, if any, does each kind of response make sense?

3. Several of the readings in this chapter—for example, "The Library Card" (p. 427) and "Two Kinds" (p. 465)—deal with the uniquely American concept of reinventing oneself, taking on a new identity. Some Americans reinvent themselves through education; others do so simply by changing their appearance. Write an essay in which you outline the options available to newcomers to the United States who wish to achieve this kind of transformation. Whenever possible, give examples from the readings in this chapter.

4. What do you see as the greatest obstacle to full access to the American Dream? (You might, for example, consider the limitations posed by gender, race, religion, language, social class, ethnicity, physical disability, sexual orientation, lack of education, or poverty.) Support your thesis with references to several selections in this chapter—and, if you like, to your own experiences.

5. Interview a first-generation American, a second-generation American, and a third-generation American. How are their views of the American Dream different? How are they like and unlike the dreams of various writers represented in this chapter? How do you account for those similarities and differences?

6. The mother in Amy Tan's "Two Kinds" (p. 465) believes that "you could be anything you wanted to be in America" (1); in "Becoming American" (p. 435), Dinesh D'Souza says, "In America your destiny is not prescribed; it is constructed. Your life is like a blank sheet of paper, and you are the artist" (22). Do you agree? That is, do you think the United States is really a land of opportunity? Support your position on this issue with references to readings in this chapter and elsewhere in this book.

7. Using the readings in this chapter as source material, write a manifesto that sets forth the rights and responsibilities of all Americans. (Begin by reading Kennedy's inaugural address, p. 481.)

8. Some Americans believe that before the American Dream can become a reality, the nation has an obligation to compensate members of minority groups for past injustices—in particular, to compensate African Americans for the evils of slavery. Do you believe that blacks are owed such compensation, or do you see the payment of reparations as inherently unfair, impractical, or unnecessary? For additional background, read Jonathan Kozol's "The Human Cost of an Illiterate Society" (p. 175) and Maya Angelou's "Graduation" (p. 103) as well as the essays in this chapter by Richard Wright ("The Library Card," p. 427) and Brent Staples ("Just Walk On By," p. 450).

9. Most of the writers whose works appear in this chapter are Americans, people who view the American Dream as something of their own. De Tocqueville, however, was clearly an outsider, looking at American institutions and aspirations from an objective point of view ("Why the Americans Are So Restless in the Midst of Their Prosperity," p. 423). What special insights did his outsider status give him? How might the various writers in this chapter respond to de Tocqueville's insights?

10. Both Gish Jen and Dinesh D'Souza identify the ability to make choices—what Jen calls "the luxury of choosing" (2)—as a distinctly American advantage. Do you agree that Americans truly have this luxury? Consider what choices Americans have and what they are *not* free to choose. What factors limit our choices? Family or cultural expectations? Religious beliefs? Prejudice? Financial pressures? Government regulations or laws? Given these limitations, do you agree with D'Souza that in America, "you get to write the script of your own life" (21)?

CHAPTER 7 FOCUS

8

WHY WE WORK

Although work has always been a part of the human experience, the nature of work has evolved considerably—especially over the last two hundred years. During the Middle Ages and the Renaissance, work was often done by family units. Whether it involved planting and harvesting crops, tending livestock, or engaging in the manufacture of goods, parents, grandparents, and children (and possibly an apprentice or two) worked together, at home. With the Industrial Revolution, however, the nature of work changed. Manufacturing became centralized in factories, and tasks that were formerly divided among various members of a family were now carried out more efficiently by machines. People worked long hours—in many cases twelve to fifteen hours a day, six and sometimes seven days a week—and could be fired for any reason. By the middle of the nineteenth

Auto workers making car radiators on assembly line, circa 1915

century, most of the great manufacturing cities of Europe were over-crowded and polluted, teeming with unskilled factory workers. It is no wonder that labor unions became increasingly popular as they or-ganized workers to fight for job security, shorter workdays, and min-imum safety standards

Thanks to the labor struggles of the past, many workers today have pension plans, health insurance, sick leave, paid vacations, life insurance, and other benefits. In some respects, American workers are more secure and more highly compensated than they have ever been, but there is a dark side to their situation: Workers in the United States work longer and harder than those in any other Western country—often working long hours without overtime and routinely forgoing va-cation and personal leave days. Add to this the tendency of American companies to move manufacturing jobs overseas and to see workers as entities whose jobs can be phased out as the need arises, and it is no surprise that employees are often stressed, insecure, and unhappy. The result is that many of today's workers question the role that work plays in their lives and wonder if it is in their best interests to invest so much time and effort in their jobs.

The essays Focus section of this chapter (p.538) address the ques-tion, "Is outsourcing bad for America?" These essays examine outsourc-ing and the effect it has on the American economy. For example, businesses that engage in this practice say that by shifting jobs to coun-tries that have lower wages, they are able to remain competitive in a global business environment. In addition, they say that outsourcing not

Automotive manufacturing line with robotic arms, 1999

only benefits American consumers, but it also benefits countries in the developing world by giving them desperately needed capital. The essays in this section ask important questions. Is the United States becoming a nation of outsourcers, shifting the responsibility for everything from education to health care to others? Does outsourcing really represent a danger to the American economy, or is its effect being exaggerated? How should we as a society respond to the plight of workers whose jobs are lost to outsourcing? Finally, what moral responsibility do both American companies and the American government have to the poor in nations of the world who could benefit from outsourcing?

PREPARING TO READ AND WRITE

As you read and prepare to write about the essays in this chapter, you may consider the following questions:

- What do you know about the writer? In what way does the writer's economic and social position affect his or her definition of work?

- Is the writer male or female? Does the writer's gender affect his or her attitude toward work?

- When was the essay written? Does the date of publication affect its content?

- Does the essay seem fair? Balanced? Does the writer have any preconceived ideas about work and its importance?

- Is the writer generally sympathetic or unsympathetic toward workers?

- Does the writer have a realistic or unrealistic view of work?

- On what specific problems does the writer focus?

- What specific solutions does the writer suggest? Are these solutions practical?

- Is your interpretation of the problem the same as or different from the interpretation presented in the essay?

- Are there any aspects of the problem that the writer ignores?

- Does the essay challenge any of your ideas about work?

- In what ways is the essay like other essays in this chapter?

WHY WE WORK
Andrew Curry
1976–

Andrew Curry writes and reports for U.S. News and World Report.
*"Why We Work" was the cover story of the February 24, 2003 issue. In this
essay, Curry examines the nature of work and explains why many workers
today feel unfulfilled.*

In 1930, W. K. Kellogg made what he thought was a sensible decision,
grounded in the best economic, social, and management theories of
the time. Workers at his cereal plant in Battle Creek, Mich., were told
to go home two hours early. Every day. For good.

The Depression-era move was hailed in Factory and Industrial
Management magazine as the "biggest piece of industrial news since
[Henry] Ford announced his five-dollar-a-day policy." President Her-
bert Hoover summoned the eccentric cereal magnate to the White
House and said the plan was "very worthwhile." The belief: Industry
and machines would lead to a workers' paradise where all would
have less work, more free time, and yet still produce enough to meet
their needs.

So what happened? Today, work dominates Americans' lives as
never before, as workers pile on hours at a rate not seen since the Industrial Revolution. Technology has offered increasing productivity
and a higher standard of living while bank tellers and typists are replaced by machines. The mismatch between available work and those
available to do it continues, as jobs go begging while people beg for
jobs. Though Kellogg's six-hour day lasted until 1985, Battle Creek's
grand industrial experiment has been nearly forgotten. Instead of
working less, our hours have stayed steady or risen—and today many
more women work so that families can afford the trappings of suburbia. In effect, workers chose the path of consumption over leisure.

But as today's job market shows so starkly, that road is full of pot-
holes. With unemployment at a nine-year high and many workers worried about losing their jobs—or forced to accept cutbacks in pay and
benefits—work is hardly the paradise economists once envisioned.

Instead, the job market is as precarious today as it was in the early   5
1980s, when business began a wave of restructurings and layoffs to
maintain its competitiveness. Many workers are left feeling unsecure,
unfulfilled, and underappreciated. It's no wonder surveys of today's
workers show a steady decline in job satisfaction. "People are very
emotional about work, and they're very negative about it," says David
Rhodes, a principal at human resource consultants Towers Perrin.
"The biggest issue is clearly workload. People are feeling crushed."

The backlash comes after years of people boasting about how hard they work and tying their identities to how indispensable they are. Ringing cellphones, whirring faxes, and ever present E-mail have blurred the lines between work and home. The job penetrates every aspect of life. Americans don't exercise, they work out. We manage our time and work on our relationships. "In reaching the affluent society, we're working longer and harder than anyone could have imagined," says Rutgers University historian John Gillis. "The work ethic and identifying ourselves with work and through work is not only alive and well but more present now than at any time in history."

Stressed Out

It's all beginning to take a toll. Fully one third of American workers—who work longer hours than their counterparts in any industrialized country—felt overwhelmed by the amount of work they had to do, according to a 2001 Families and Work Institute survey. "Both men and women wish they were working about 11 hours [a week] less," says Ellen Galinsky, the institute's president. "A lot of people believe if they do work less they'll be seen as less committed, and in a shaky economy no one wants that."

The modern environment would seem alien to pre-industrial laborers. For centuries, the household—from farms to "cottage" craftsmen—was the unit of production. The whole family was part of the enterprise, be it farming, blacksmithing, or baking. "In pre-industrial society, work and family were practically the same thing," says Gillis.

The Industrial Revolution changed all that. Mills and massive iron smelters required ample labor and constant attendance. "The factory took men, women and children out of the workshops and homes and put them under one roof and timed their movements to machines," writes Sebastian de Grazia in *Of Time, Work and Leisure.* For the first time, work and family were split. Instead of selling what they produced, workers sold their time. With more people leaving farms to move to cities and factories, labor became a commodity, placed on the market like any other.

10   Innovation gave rise to an industrial process based on machinery and mass production. This new age called for a new worker. "The only safeguard of order and discipline in the modern world is a standardized worker with interchangeable parts," mused one turn-of-the-century writer.

Business couldn't have that, so instead it came up with the science of management. The theories of Frederick Taylor, a Philadelphia factory foreman with deep Puritan roots, led to work being broken down into component parts, with each step timed to coldly quantify jobs that skilled craftsmen had worked a lifetime to learn. Workers resented Taylor and his stopwatch, complaining that his focus on process stripped their jobs of creativity and pride, making them irritable. Long before anyone knew what "stress" was, Taylor brought it to the workplace—and without sympathy. "I have you for your strength and mechanical ability, and we have other men paid for thinking," he told workers.

Long Hours

The division of work into components that could be measured and easily taught reached its apex in Ford's River Rouge plant in Dearborn, Mich., where the assembly line came of age. "It was this combination of a simplification of tasks . . . with moving assembly that created a manufacturing revolution while at the same time laying waste human potential on a massive scale," author Richard Donkin writes in *Blood, Sweat and Tears*.

To maximize the production lines, businesses needed long hours from their workers. But it was no easy sell. "Convincing people to work 9 to 5 took a tremendous amount of propaganda and discipline," says the University of Richmond's Joanne Ciulla, author of *The Working Life: The Promise and Betrayal of Modern Work*. Entrepreneurs, religious leaders, and writers like Horatio Alger created whole bodies of literature to glorify the work ethic.

Labor leaders fought back with their own propaganda. For more than a century, a key struggle for the labor movement was reducing the amount of time workers had to spend on the job. "They were pursuing shorter hours and increased leisure. In effect, they were buying their time," says University of Iowa Prof. Benjamin Hunnicutt, author of *Work Without End: Abandoning Shorter Hours for the Right to Work*.

The first labor unions were organized in response to the threat of 15 technology, as skilled workers sought to protect their jobs from mechanization. Later, semi- and unskilled workers began to organize as well, agitating successfully for reduced hours, higher wages, and better work conditions. Unions enjoyed great influence in the early 20th century, and at their height in the 1950s, 35 percent of U.S. workers belonged to one.

Union persistence and the mechanization of factories gradually made shorter hours more realistic. Between 1830 and 1930, work hours were cut nearly in half, with economist John Maynard Keynes famously predicting in 1930 that by 2030 a 15-hour workweek would be standard. The Great Depression pressed the issue, with job sharing proposed as a serious solution to widespread unemployment. Despite business and religious opposition over worries of an idle populace, the Senate passed a bill that would have mandated a 30-hour week in 1933; it was narrowly defeated in the House.

Franklin Delano Roosevelt struck back with a new gospel that lives to this very day: consumption. "The aim . . . is to restore our rich domestic market by raising its vast consuming capacity," he said. "Our first purpose is to create employment as fast as we can." And so began the modern work world. "Instead of accepting work's continuing decline and imminent fall from its dominant social position, businessmen, economists, advertisers, and politicians preached that there would never be 'enough,'" Hunnicutt writes in *Kellogg's Six-Hour Day*. "The entrepreneur and industry could invent new things for advertising to sell and for people to want and work for indefinitely."

The New Deal dumped government money into job creation, in turn encouraging consumption. World War II fueled the fire, and American workers soon found themselves in a "golden age"—40-hour workweeks, plenty of jobs, and plenty to buy. Leisure was the road not taken, a path quickly forgotten in the postwar boom of the 1950s and 1960s.

Discontent

Decades of abundance, however, did not bring satisfaction. "A significant number of Americans are dissatisfied with the quality of their working lives," said the 1973 report "Work in America" from the Department of Health, Education and Welfare. "Dull, repetitive, seemingly meaningless tasks, offering little challenge or autonomy, are causing discontent among workers at all occupational levels." Underlying the dissatisfaction was a very gradual change in what the "Protestant work ethic" meant. Always a source of pride, the idea that hard work was a calling from God dated to the Reformation and the teachings of Martin Luther. While work had once been a means to serve God, two centuries of choices and industrialization had turned work into an end in itself, stripped of the spiritual meaning that sustained the Puritans who came ready to tame the wilderness.

20   By the end of the '70s, companies were reaching out to spiritually drained workers by offering more engagement while withdrawing the promise of a job for life, as the American economy faced a stiff challenge from cheaper workers abroad. "Corporations introduced feel-good programs to stimulate jaded employees with one hand while taking away the elements of a 'just' workplace with the other," says Andrew Ross, author of *No Collar: The Humane Workplace and Its Hidden Costs*. Employees were given more control over their work and schedules, and "human relations" consultants and motivational speakers did a booming business. By the 1990s, technology made working from home possible for a growing number of people. Seen as a boon at first, telecommuting and the rapidly proliferating "electronic leash" of cellphones made work inescapable, as employees found themselves on

call 24/7. Today, almost half of American workers use computers, cell-phones, E-mail, and faxes for work during what is supposed to be nonwork time, according to the Families and Work Institute. Home is no longer a refuge but a cozier extension of the office.

The shift coincided with a shortage of highly skilled and educated workers, some of whom were induced with such benefits as stock options in exchange for their putting the company first all the time. But some see a different explanation for the rise in the amount of time devoted to work. "Hours have crept up partly as a consequence of the declining power of the trade-union movement," says Cornell University labor historian Clete Daniel. "Many employers find it more economical to require mandatory overtime than hire new workers and pay their benefits." Indeed, the trend has coincided with the steady decline in the percentage of workers represented by unions, as the labor movement failed to keep pace with the increasing rise of white-collar jobs in the economy. Today fewer than 15 percent of American workers belong to unions.

Nirvana?

The Internet economy of the '90s gave rise to an entirely new corporate climate. The "knowledge worker" was wooed with games, gourmet chefs, and unprecedented freedom over his schedule and environment. Employees at Intuit didn't have to leave their desks for massages; Sun Microsystems offered in-house laundry, and Netscape workers were offered an on-site dentist. At first glance, this new corporate world seemed like nirvana. But "for every attractive feature, workers found there was a cost," says Ross. "It was both a worker's paradise and a con game."

When the stock market bubble burst and the economy fell into its recent recession, workers were forced to re-evaluate their priorities. "There used to be fat bonuses and back rubs, free bagels and foosball tables—it didn't really feel like work," says Allison Hemming, who organizes "pink-slip parties" for laid-off workers around the country and has written *Work It! How to Get Ahead, Save Your Ass, and Land a Job in Any Economy.* "I think people are a lot wiser about their choices now. They want a better quality of life; they're asking for more flex-time to spend with their families."

In a study of Silicon Valley culture over the past decade, San Jose State University anthropologist Jan English-Lueck found that skills learned on the job were often brought home. Researchers talked to families with mission statements, mothers used conflict-resolution buzzwords with their squabbling kids, and engineers used flowcharts to organize Thanksgiving dinner. Said one participant: "I don't live life; I manage it."

25   In some ways, we have come full circle. "Now we're seeing the return of work to the home in terms of telecommuting," says Gillis. "We may be seeing the return of households where work is the central element again."

But there's still the question of fulfillment. In a recent study, human resources consultants Towers Perrin tried to measure workers' emotions about their jobs. More than half of the emotion was negative, with the biggest single factor being workload but also a sense that work doesn't satisfy their deeper needs. "We expect more and more out of our jobs," says Hunnicutt. "We expect to find wonderful people and experiences all around us. What we find is Dilbert."

Responding to Reading

1. Why is it that "work dominates Americans' lives as never before" (3)? According to Curry, what toll does this situation take on American workers?
2. How did the Industrial Revolution change the nature of work? What effect did Fredrick Taylor have on work? According to Curry, why were the first labor unions formed? Why was the New Deal "the golden age" for workers (18)?
3. Why does Curry think that workers today are unfulfilled? What evidence does he offer to support this contention? What view of work do you think he has? Do you agree or disagree with his assessment?

Responding in Writing

Why do the people you know work? Do their motives support or challenge Curry's conclusion?

PROFESSIONS FOR WOMEN

Virginia Woolf

1882–1941

Virginia Woolf was born into a literary family in London, England. Largely self-educated, she began writing criticism for the Times Literary Supplement *when she was in her early twenties and published her first novel,* The Voyage Out, *in 1915. In later novels, including* Mrs. Dalloway *(1925),* To the Lighthouse *(1927), and* The Waves *(1931), she experimented with stream of consciousness and other stylistic and narrative innovations. She published two collections of her essays under the title* The Common Reader *(1925, 1932) and two feminist tracts,* A Room of One's Own *(1929) and* Three Guineas *(1938). The following essay was originally composed as a speech delivered in 1931 to a British women's organization, the Women's League of Service. In her remarks, Woolf discusses employment opportunities for women, focusing on the experience of women writers.*

When your secretary invited me to come here, she told me that your Society is concerned with the employment of women and she suggested that I might tell you something about my own professional experiences. It is true I am a woman; it is true I am employed, but what professional experiences have I had? It is difficult to say. My profession is literature; and in that profession there are fewer experiences for women than in any other, with the exception of the stage—fewer, I mean, that are peculiar to women. For the road was cut many years ago—by Fanny Burney, by Aphra Behn, by Harriet Martineau, by Jane Austen, by George Eliot—many famous women, and many more unknown and forgotten, have been before me, making the path smooth, and regulating my steps. Thus, when I came to write, there were very few material obstacles in my way. Writing was a reputable and harmless occupation. The family peace was not broken by the scratching of a pen. No demand was made upon the family purse. For ten and sixpence one can buy paper enough to write all the plays of Shakespeare—if one has a mind that way. Pianos and models, Paris, Vienna and Berlin, masters and mistresses, are not needed by a writer. The cheapness of writing paper is, of course, the reason why women have succeeded as writers before they have succeeded in the other professions.

But to tell you my story—it is a simple one. You have only got to figure to yourselves a girl in a bedroom with a pen in her hand. She had only to move that pen from left to right—from ten o'clock to one. Then it occurred to her to do what is simple and cheap enough after all—to slip a few of those pages into an envelope, fix a penny stamp in the corner, and drop the envelope in the red box at the corner. It was thus that I became a journalist; and my effort was rewarded on the first day of the following month—a very glorious day it was for me—by a letter from an editor containing a check for one pound ten shillings and sixpence. But to show you how little I deserve to be called a professional woman, how little I know of the struggles and difficulties of such lives, I have to admit that instead of spending that sum upon bread and butter, rent, shoes and stockings, or butcher's bills, I went out and bought a cat—a beautiful cat, a Persian cat, which very soon involved me in bitter disputes with my neighbors.

What could be easier than to write articles and to buy Persian cats with the profits? But wait a moment. Articles have to be about something. Mine, I seem to remember, was about a novel by a famous man. And while I was writing this review, I discovered that if I were going to review books I should need to do battle with a certain phantom. And the phantom was a woman, and when I came to know her better I called her after the heroine of a famous poem, The Angel in the House. It was she who used to come between me and my paper when I was writing reviews. It was she who bothered me and wasted my time and so tormented me that at last I killed her. You who come of a younger and happier generation may not have heard of her—you may not know what I mean by the Angel in the House. I will describe her as shortly as I can. She was intensely sympathetic. She was immensely charming. She was utterly unselfish. She excelled in the difficult arts of family life. She sacrificed herself daily. If there was chicken, she took the leg; if there was a draught she sat in it—in short she was so constituted that she never had a mind or a wish of her own but preferred to sympathize always with the minds and wishes of others. Above all—I need not say it—she was pure. Her purity was supposed to be her chief beauty—her blushes, her great grace. In those days—the last of Queen Victoria—every house had its Angel. And when I came to write I encountered her with the very first words. The shadow of her wings fell on my page; I heard the rustling of her skirts in the room. Directly, that is to say, I took my pen in hand to review that novel by a famous man, she slipped behind me and whispered: "My dear, you are a young woman. You are writing about a book that has been written by a man. Be sympathetic; be tender; flatter; deceive; use all the arts and wiles of our sex. Never let anybody guess that you have a mind of your own. Above all, be pure." And she made as if to guide my pen. I now record the one act for which I take some credit to myself, though the credit rightly belongs to some excellent ancestors of mine who left me a certain sum of money—shall we say five hundred pounds a year?—so that it was not necessary for me to depend solely on charm for my living. I turned upon her and caught her by the throat. I did my best to kill her. My excuse, if I were to be had up in a court of law, would be that I acted in self-defense. Had I not killed her she would have killed me. She would have plucked the heart out of my writing. For, as I found, directly I put pen to paper, you cannot review even a novel without having a mind of your own, without expressing what you think to be the truth about human relations, morality, sex. And all these questions, according to the Angel in the House, cannot be dealt with freely and openly by women; they must charm, they must conciliate, they must—to put it bluntly—tell lies if they are to succeed. Thus, whenever I felt the shadow of her wing or the radiance of her halo upon my page, I took up the inkpot and flung it at her. She died hard. Her fictitious nature was of great assistance to her. It is far harder to kill a phantom than a reality. She was always creeping back when I thought I had dispatched her. Though I flatter myself that I killed her in the end, the struggle was severe; it took much time that had better have been spent upon learning Greek grammar; or in roaming the world in search of adventures. But it was a real experience; it was an experience that was bound to befall all women writers at that time. Killing the Angel in the House was part of the occupation of a woman writer.

But to continue my story. The Angel was dead; what then remained? You may say that what remained was a simple and common object—a young woman in a bedroom with an inkpot. In other words, now that she had rid herself of falsehood, that young woman had only to be herself. Ah, but what is "herself"? I mean, what is a woman? I assure you, I do not know. I do not believe that you know. I do not believe that anybody can know until she has expressed herself in all the arts and professions open to human skill. That indeed is one of the reasons why I have come here—out of respect for you, who are in process of showing us by your experiments what a woman is, who are in process of providing us, by your failures and successes, with that extremely important piece of information.

But to continue the story of my professional experiences. I made 5 one pound ten and six by my first review; and I bought a Persian cat with the proceeds. Then I grew ambitious. A Persian cat is all very well, I said; but a Persian cat is not enough. I must have a motor car. And it was thus that I became a novelist—for it is a very strange thing that people will give you a motor car if you will tell them a story. It is a still stranger thing that there is nothing so delightful in the world as telling stories. It is far pleasanter than writing reviews of famous novels. And yet, if I am to obey your secretary and tell you my professional experiences as a novelist, I must tell you about a very strange experience that befell me as a novelist. And to understand it you must try first to imagine a novelist's state of mind. I hope I am not giving away professional secrets if I say that a novelist's chief desire is to be as unconscious as possible. He has to induce in himself a state of perpetual lethargy. He wants life to proceed with the utmost quiet and regularity. He wants to see the same faces, to read the same books, to do the same things day after day, month after month, while he is writing, so that nothing may break the illusion in which he is living—so that nothing may disturb or disquiet the mysterious nosings about, feelings round, darts, dashes and sudden discoveries of that very shy and illusive spirit, the imagination. I suspect that this state is the same both for men and women. Be that as it may, I want you to imagine me writing a novel in a state of trance. I want you to figure to yourselves a girl sitting with a pen in her hand, which for minutes, and indeed for hours, she never dips into the inkpot. The image that comes to my mind when I think of this girl is the image of a fisherman lying sunk in dreams on the verge of a deep lake with a rod held out over the water. She was letting her imagination sweep unchecked round every rock and cranny of the world that lies submerged in the depths of our unconscious being. Now came the experience, the experience that I believe to be far commoner with women writers than with men. The line raced through the girl's fingers. Her imagination had rushed away. It had sought the pools, the depths, the dark places where the largest fish slumber. And then there was a smash. There was an explosion. There was foam and confusion. The imagination had dashed itself against something hard. The girl was roused from her dream. She was indeed in a state of the most acute and difficult distress. To speak without figure she had thought of something, something about the body, about the passions which it was unfitting for her as a woman to say. Men, her reason told her, would be shocked. The consciousness of what men will say of a woman who speaks the truth about her passions had roused her from her artist's state of unconsciousness. She could write no more. The trance was over. Her imagination could work no longer. This I believe to be a very common experience with women writers—they are impeded by the extreme conventionality of the other sex. For though men sensibly allow themselves great freedom in these respects, I doubt that they realize or can control the extreme severity with which they condemn such freedom in women.

These then were two very genuine experiences of my own. These were two of the adventures of my professional life. The first—killing the Angel in the House—I think I solved. She died. But the second, telling the truth about my own experiences as a body, I do not think I solved. I doubt that any woman has solved it yet. The obstacles against her are still immensely powerful—and yet they are very difficult to define. Outwardly, what is simpler than to write books? Outwardly, what obstacles are there for a woman rather than for a man? Inwardly, I think the case is very different; she has still many ghosts to fight, many prejudices to overcome. Indeed it will be a long time still, I think, before a woman can sit down to write a book without finding a phantom to be slain, a rock to be dashed against. And if this is so in literature, the freest of all professions for women, how is it in the new professions which you are now for the first time entering?

Those are the questions that I should like, had I time, to ask you. And indeed, if I have laid stress upon these professional experiences of mine, it is because I believe that they are, though in different forms, yours also. Even when the path is nominally open—when there is nothing to prevent a woman from being a doctor, a lawyer, a civil servant—there are many phantoms and obstacles, as I believe, looming in her way. To discuss and define them is I think of great value and importance; for thus only can the labor be shared, the difficulties be solved. But besides this, it is necessary also to discuss the ends and the aims for which we are fighting, for which we are doing battle with these formidable obstacles. Those aims cannot be taken for granted; they must be perpetually questioned and examined. The whole position, as I see it—here in this hall surrounded by women practising for the first time in history I know not how many different professions—is one of extraordinary interest and importance. You have won rooms of your own in the house hitherto exclusively owned by men. You are able, though not without great labor and effort, to pay the rent. You are earning your five hundred pounds a year. But this freedom is only a beginning; the room is your own, but it is still bare. It has to be furnished; it has to be decorated; it has to be shared. How are you going to furnish it, how are you going to decorate it? With whom are you going to share it, and upon what terms? These, I think, are questions of the utmost importance and interest. For the first time in history you are able to ask them; for the first time you are able to decide for yourselves what the answers should be. Willingly would I stay and discuss those questions and answers—but not tonight. My time is up; and I must cease.

Responding to Reading

1. According to Woolf, why have women found success in writing? How does Woolf's explanation shed light on the fact that there were few female doctors, lawyers, or corporate executives in 1931—the year she delivered her address?
2. What does Woolf mean in paragraph 3 when she says that if she were going to review books, she would have to "do battle with a . . . phantom"? Why does she call this phantom "The Angel in the House"? What does Woolf mean when she says, "Killing the Angel in the House was part of the occupation of a woman writer" (3)?
3. In paragraph 7, Woolf says that women writers now have a room in a house that was once "exclusively owned by men." What must women do to make the room their own? What does Woolf mean when she says, "It has to be furnished; it has to be decorated; it has to be shared" (7)?

Responding in Writing

In what ways would Woolf's speech be different if she were delivering it today to a graduating class at your college or university?

THE SECOND SHIFT

Arlie Hochschild

1940–

Arlie Hochschild is co-director of the Center for Working Families and has done extensive research into the role of work in personal and family life. Hochschild has published The Second Shift: Working Parents and the Revolution at Home *(1989) and* The Time Bind: When Work Becomes Home and Home Becomes Work *(1997). Her latest book,* The Commercialization of Intimate Life *(2003), is a collection of essays written over the last thirty years. The following essay, taken from* The Second Shift, *makes the point that most working women have two jobs: one that lasts from nine to five and another that begins the moment they return home.*

Every American household bears the footprints of economic and cultural trends that originate far outside its walls. A rise in inflation eroding the earning power of the male wage, an expanding service sector opening for women, and the inroads made by women into many professions—all these changes do not simply go on around the American family. They occur *within* a marriage or living-together arrangement and transform it. Problems between couples, problems that seem "unique" or "marital," are often the individual ripples of powerful economic and cultural shock waves. Quarrels between husbands and wives in households across the nation result mainly from a friction between faster-changing women and slower-changing men.

The exodus of women from the home to the workplace has not been accompanied by a new view of marriage and work that would make this transition smooth. Most workplaces have remained inflexible in the face of the changing needs of workers with families, and most men have yet to really adapt to the changes in women. I call the strain caused by the disparity between the change in women and the absence of change elsewhere the "stalled revolution."

If women begin to do less at home because they have less time, if men do little more, and if the work of raising children and tending a home requires roughly the same effort, then the questions of who does what at home and of what "needs doing" become a source of deep tension in a marriage.

Over the past 30 years in the United States, more and more women have begun to work outside the home, and more have divorced. While some commentators conclude that women's work *causes* divorce, my research into changes in the American family suggests something else. Since all the wives in the families I studied (over an eight-year period) worked outside the home, the fact that they worked did not account for why some marriages were happy and others were not. What *did* contribute to happiness was the husband's willingness to do the work at home. Whether they were traditional or more egalitarian in their relationship, couples were happier when the men did a sizable share of housework and child care.

5   In one study of 600 couples filing for divorce, researcher George Levinger found that the second most common reason women cited for wanting to divorce—after "mental cruelty"—was their husbands' "neglect of home or children." Women mentioned this reason more often than financial problems, physical abuse, drinking, or infidelity.

A happy marriage is supported by a couple's being economically secure, by their enjoying a supportive community, and by their having compatible needs and values. But these days it may also depend on a shared appreciation of the work it takes to nurture others. As the role of the homemaker is being abandoned by many women, the homemaker's work has been continually devalued and passed on to low-paid house-keepers, baby-sitters, or day-care workers. Long devalued by men, the contribution of cooking, cleaning, and care-giving is now being devalued as mere drudgery by many women, too.

In the era of the stalled revolution, one way to make housework and child care more valued is for men to share in that work. Many working mothers are already doing all they can at home. Now it's time for men to make the move.

If more mothers of young children are working at full-time jobs outside the home, and if most couples can't afford household help, who's doing the work at home? Adding together the time it takes to do a paid job and to do housework and child care and using estimates from major studies on time use done in the 1960s and 1970s, I found that women worked roughly 15 more hours each week than men. Over a year, they worked an extra month of 24-hour days. Over a dozen years, it was an extra year of 24-hour days. Most women without children spend much more time that men on housework. Women with children devote more time to both housework and child care. Just as there is a wage gap between men and women in the workplace, there is a "leisure gap" between them at home. Most women work one shift at the office or factory and a "second shift" at home.

In my research, I interviewed and observed 52 couples over an eight-year period as they cooked dinner, shopped, bathed their children, and in general struggled to find enough time to make their complex lives work. The women I interviewed seemed to be far more deeply torn between the demands of work and family than were their husbands. They talked more about the abiding conflict between work and family. They felt the second shift was *their* issue, and most of their husbands agreed. When I telephoned one husband to arrange an interview with him, explaining that I wanted to ask him how he managed work and family life, he replied genially, "Oh, this will *really* interest my *wife*."

Men who shared the load at home seemed just as pressed for time 10 as their wives, and as torn between the demands of career and small children. But of the men I surveyed, the majority did not share the load at home. Some refused outright. Others refused more passively, often offering a loving shoulder to lean on, or an understanding ear, as their working wife faced the conflict they both saw as hers. At first it seemed to me that the problem of the second shift *was* hers. But I came to realize that those husbands who helped very little at home were often just as deeply affected as their wives—through the resentment their wives felt toward them and through their own need to steel themselves against that resentment.

A clear example of this phenomenon is Evan Holt, a warehouse furniture salesman who did very little housework and played with his four-year-old son, Joey, only at his convenience. His wife, Nancy, did the second shift, but she resented it keenly and half-consciously expressed her frustration and rage by losing interest in sex and becoming overly absorbed in Joey.

Even when husbands happily shared the work, their wives *felt* more responsible for home and children. More women than men kept track of doctor's appointments and arranged for kids playmates to come over. More mothers than fathers worried about a child's Halloween costume or a birthday present for a school friend. They were more likely to think about their children while at work and to check in by phone with the baby-sitter.

Partly because of this, more women felt torn between two kinds of urgency, between the need to soothe a child's fear of being left at day-care and the need to show the boss she's "serious" at work. Twenty percent of the men in my study shared housework equally. Seventy percent did a substantial amount (less than half of it, but more than a third), and 10 percent did less than a third. But even when couples more equitably share the work at home, women do two thirds of the daily jobs at home, such as cooking and cleaning up—jobs that fix them into a rigid routine. Most women cook dinner, for instance, while men change the oil in the family car. But, as one mother pointed out, dinner needs to be prepared every evening around six o'clock, whereas the car oil needs to be changed every six months, with no particular deadline. Women do more child care than men, and men repair more household appliances. A child needs to be tended to daily, whereas the repair of household appliances can often wait, said the men, "until I have time." Men thus have more control over when they make their contributions than women do. They may be very busy with family chores, but, like the executive who tells his secretary to "hold my calls," the man has more control over his time.

Another reason why women may feel under more strain than men is that women more often do two things at once—for example, write checks and return phone calls, vacuum and keep an eye on a three-year-old, fold laundry and think out the shopping list. Men more often will either cook dinner *or* watch the kids. Women more often do both at the same time.

15   Beyond doing more at home, women also devote proportionately, more of their time at home to housework than men and proportionately less of it to child care. Of all the time men spend working at home, a growing amount of it goes to child care. Since most parents prefer to tend to their children than to clean house, men do more of what they'd rather do. More men than women take their children on "fun" outings to the park, the zoo, the movies. Women spend more time on maintenance, such as feeding and bathing children—enjoyable activities, to be sure, but often less leisurely or "special" than going to the zoo. Men also do fewer of the most undesirable household chores, such as scrubbing the toilet.

As a result, women tend to talk more intensely about being over-tired, sick, and emotionally drained. Many women interviewed were fixated on the topic of sleep. They talked about how much they could "get by on" six and a half, seven, seven and a half, less, more. They talked about who they knew who needed more or less. Some apologized for how much sleep they needed—"I'm afraid I need eight hours of sleep"—as if eight was "too much." They talked about how to avoid fully waking up when a child called them at night, and how to get back to sleep. These women talked about sleep the way a hungry person talks about food.

If, all in all, the two-job family is suffering from a speedup of work and family life, working mothers are its primary victims. It is ironic, then, that often it falls to women to be the time-and-motion experts of family life. As I observed families inside their homes, I noticed it was often the mother who rushed children, saying, "Hurry up! It's time to go." "Finish your cereal now," "You can do that later," or "Let's go!" When a bath needed to be crammed into a slot between 7:45 and 8:00, it was often the mother who called out "Let's see who can take their bath the quickest." Often a younger child would rush out, scurrying to be first in bed, while the older and wiser one stalled, resistant, sometimes resentful: "Mother is always rushing us." Sadly, women are more often the lightning rods for family tensions aroused by this speedup of work and family life. They are the villains in a process in which they are also the primary victims. More than the longer hours and the lack of sleep, this is the saddest cost to women of their extra month of work each year.

Raising children in a nuclear family is still the overwhelming preference of most people. Yet in the face of new problems for this family mode we have not created an adequate support system so that the nuclear family can do its job well in the era of the two-career couple. Corporations have done little to accommodate the needs of working parents, and the government has done little to prod them.

We really need, as sociologist Frank Furstenberg has suggested, a Marshall Plan for the family. After World War II we saw that it was in our best interests to aid the war-torn nations of Europe. Now—it seems obvious in an era of growing concern over drugs, crime, and family instability—is in our best interests to aid the overworked two-job families right here at home. We should look to other nations for a model of what could be done. In Sweden, for example, upon the birth of a child every working couple is entitled to 12 months of paid parental leave—nine months at 90 percent of the worker's salary, plus an additional three months at about three hundred dollars a month. The mother and father are free to divide this year off between them as they wish. Working parents of a child under eight have the opportunity to work no more than six hours a day, at six hours' pay. Parental insurance offers parents money for work time lost while visiting a child's school or caring for a sick child. That's a true pro-family policy.

20   A pro-family policy in the United States could give tax breaks to companies that encourage job sharing, part-time work, flex time, and family leave for new parents. By implementing comparable worth policies we could increase pay scales for "women's" jobs. Another key element of a pro-family policy would be instituting, fewer-hour, more flexible options—called "family phases"—for all regular jobs filled by parents of young children.

Day-care centers could be made more warm and creative through generous public and private funding. If the best form of day-care comes from the attention of elderly neighbors, students, or grandparents, these people could be paid to care for children through social programs.

In these ways, the American government would create a safer environment for the two-job family. If the government encouraged corporations to consider the long-ranged interests of workers and their families, they would save on long-range costs caused by absenteeism, turnover, juvenile delinquency, mental illness, and welfare support for single mothers.

These are real pro-family reforms. If they seem utopian today, we should remember that in the past the eight-hour day, the abolition of child labor, and the vote for women seemed utopian, too. Among top rated employees listed in *The 100 Best Companies to Work for in America* are many offering country-club memberships, first-class air travel, and million-dollar fitness centers. But only a handful offer job sharing, flex time, or part-time work. Not one provides on-site day-care, and only three offer child-care deductions: Control Data, Polaroid, and Honeywell. In his book *Megatrends*, John Naisbitt reports that 83 percent of corporate executives believed that more men feel the need to share the responsibilities of parenting; yet only 9 percent of corporations offer paternity leave.

Public strategies are linked to private ones. Economic and cultural trends bear on family relations in ways it would be useful for all of us to understand. The happiest two-job marriages I saw during my research were ones in which men and women shared the housework and parenting. What couples called good communication often meant that they were good at saying thanks to one another for small aspects of taking care of the family. Making it to the school play, helping a child read, cooking dinner in good spirit, remembering the grocery list, taking responsibility for cleaning up the bedrooms—these were the silver and gold of the marital exchange. Until now, couples committed to an equal sharing of house-work and child care have been rare. But, if we as a culture come to see the urgent need of meeting the new problems posed by the second shift, and if society and government begin to shape new policies that allow working parents more flexibility then we will be making some progress toward happier times at home and work. And as the young learn by example, many more women and men will be able to enjoy the pleasure that arises when family life is family life, and not a second shift.

Responding to Reading

1. Hochschild coined the terms "second shift" and "stalled revolution." Define each of these terms. Are they appropriate for what they denote? Would other terms—for example, *late shift* or *swing shift* and *postponed revolution* or *failed revolution*—be more appropriate? Explain.

2. According to Hochschild, women *think* that they are "under more strain than men" (14), even when their husbands do their share of housework and child care. How does Hochschild account for this impression?

3. Beginning with paragraph 18, Hochschild recommends changes that she believes will ease the strain on working families—because, as she says in paragraph 24, "public strategies are linked to private ones." Given what Hochschild has said about the basic differences in men's and women's approaches to family roles, do you believe that government and corporations can solve the problem she identifies?

Responding in Writing

Would you say that your parents are committed to equal sharing of housework and childcare? What changes, if any, would you suggest?

BEHIND THE COUNTER
Eric Schlosser
1960–

Eric Schlosser became a full-time journalist after writing a two-part article for Rolling Stone *magazine, which was later expanded into the book* Fast Food Nation *(2001). Schlosser is a correspondent for the* Atlantic Monthly *and has written about the families of homicide victims and the "prison-industrial complex." His magazine investigations into migrant labor, pornography, and marijuana gave him the background for his most recent book,* Reefer Madness: Sex, Drugs, and Cheap Labor in the American Black Market *(2003). In the following essay, Schlosser examines the working conditions of those who prepare and serve the food at fast-food restaurants.*

Every Saturday Elisa Zamot gets up at 5:15 in the morning. It's a struggle, and her head feels groggy as she steps into the shower. Her little sisters, Cookie and Sabrina, are fast asleep in their beds. By 5:30,

Elisa's showered, done her hair, and put on her McDonald's uniform. She's sixteen, bright-eyed and olive-skinned, pretty and petite, ready for another day of work. Elisa's mother usually drives her the half-mile or so to the restaurant, but sometimes Elisa walks, leaving home before the sun rises. Her family's modest townhouse sits beside a busy highway on the south side of Colorado Springs, in a largely poor and working-class neighborhood. Throughout the day, sounds of traffic fill the house, the steady whoosh of passing cars. But when Elisa heads for work, the streets are quiet, the sky's still dark, and the lights are out in the small houses and rental apartments along the road.

When Elisa arrives at McDonald's, the manager unlocks the door and lets her in. Sometimes the husband-and-wife cleaning crew are just finishing up. More often, it's just Elisa and the manager in the restaurant, surrounded by an empty parking lot. For the next hour or so, the two of them get everything ready. They turn on the ovens and grills. They go downstairs into the basement and get food and supplies for the morning shift. They get the paper cups, wrappers, cardboard containers, and packets of condiments. They step into the big freezer and get the frozen bacon, the frozen pancakes, and the frozen cinnamon rolls. They get the frozen hash browns, the frozen biscuits, the frozen McMuffins. They get the cartons of scrambled egg mix and orange juice mix. They bring the food upstairs and start preparing it before any customers appear, thawing some things in the microwave and cooking other things on the grill. They put the cooked food in special cabinets to keep it warm.

The restaurant opens for business at seven o'clock, and for the next hour or so, Elisa and the manager hold down the fort, handling all the orders. As the place starts to get busy, other employees arrive. Elisa works behind the counter. She takes orders and hands food to customers from breakfast through lunch. When she finally walks home, after seven hours of standing at a cash register, her feet hurt. She's wiped out. She comes through the front door, flops onto the living room couch, and turns on the TV. And the next morning she gets up at 5:15 again and starts the same routine.

Up and down Academy Boulevard, along South Nevada, Circle Drive, and Woodman Road, teenagers like Elisa run the fast food restaurants of Colorado Springs. Fast food kitchens often seem like a scene from *Bugsy Malone*, a film in which all the actors are children pretending to be adults. No other industry in the United States has a workforce so dominated by adolescents. About two-thirds of the nation's fast food workers are under the age of twenty. Teenagers open the fast food outlets in the morning, close them at night, and keep them going at all hours in between. Even the managers and assistant managers are sometimes in their late teens. Unlike Olympic gymnastics— an activity in which teenagers consistently perform at a higher level than adults—there's nothing about the work in a fast food kitchen that requires young employees. Instead of relying upon a small, stable, well-paid, and well-trained workforce, the fast food industry seeks out part-time, unskilled workers who are willing to accept low pay. Teenagers have been the perfect candidates for these jobs, not only because they are less expensive to hire than adults, but also because their youthful inexperience makes them easier to control.

The labor practices of the fast food industry have their origins in the assembly line systems adopted by American manufacturers in the early twentieth century. Business historian Alfred D. Chandler has argued that a high rate of "throughput" was the most important aspect of these mass production systems. A factory's throughput is the speed and volume of its flow—a much more crucial measurement, according to Chandler, than the number of workers it employs or the value of its machinery. With innovative technology and the proper organization, a small number of workers can produce an enormous amount of goods cheaply. Throughput is all about increasing the speed of assembly, about doing things faster in order to make more.

Although the McDonald brothers had never encountered the term "throughput" or studied "scientific management," they instinctively grasped the underlying principles and applied them in the Speedee Service System. The restaurant operating scheme they developed has been widely adopted and refined over the past half century. The ethos of the assembly line remains at its core. The fast food industry's obsession with throughput has altered the way millions of Americans work, turned commercial kitchens into small factories, and changed familiar foods into commodities that are manufactured.

At Burger King restaurants, frozen hamburger patties are placed on a conveyer belt and emerge from a broiler ninety seconds later fully cooked. The ovens at Pizza Hut and at Domino's also use conveyer belts to ensure standardized cooking times. The ovens at McDonald's look like commercial laundry presses, with big steel hoods that swing down and grill hamburgers on both sides at once. The burgers, chicken, french fries, and buns are all frozen when they arrive at a McDonald's. The shakes and sodas begin as syrup. At Taco Bell restaurants the food is "assembled," not prepared. The guacamole isn't made by workers in the kitchen; it's made at a factory in Michoàcán, Mexico, then frozen and shipped north. The chain's taco meat arrives frozen and precooked in vacuum-sealed plastic bags. The beans are dehydrated and look like brownish corn flakes. The cooking process is fairly simple. "Everything's add water," a Taco Bell employee told me. "Just add hot water."

Although Richard and Mac McDonald introduced the division of labor to the restaurant business, it was a McDonald's executive named Fred Turner who created a production system of unusual thoroughness and attention to detail. In 1958, Turner put together an operations and training manual for the company that was seventy-five pages long, specifying how almost everything should be done. Hamburgers were always to be placed on the grill in six neat rows; french fries had to be exactly 0.28 inches thick. The McDonald's operations manual today has ten times the number of pages and weighs about four pounds. Known within the company as "the Bible," it contains precise instructions on how various appliances should be used, how each item on the menu should look, and how employees should greet customers. Operators who disobey these rules can lose their franchises. Cooking instructions are not only printed in the manual, they are often designed into the machines. A McDonald's kitchen is full of buzzers and flashing lights that tell employees what to do.

At the front counter, computerized cash registers issue their own commands. Once an order has been placed, buttons light up and suggest other menu items that can be added. Workers at the counter are told to increase the size of an order by recommending special promotions, pushing dessert, pointing out the financial logic behind the purchase of a larger drink. While doing so, they are instructed to be upbeat and friendly. "Smile with a greeting and make a positive first impression," a Burger King training manual suggests. "Show them you are GLAD TO SEE THEM. Include eye contact with the cheerful greeting."

10   The strict regimentation at fast food restaurants creates standardized products. It increases the throughput. And it gives fast food companies an enormous amount of power over their employees. "When management determines exactly how every task is to be done . . . and can impose its own rules about pace, output, quality, and technique," the sociologist Robin Leidner has noted, "[it] makes workers increasingly interchangeable." The management no longer depends upon the talents or skills of its workers—those things are built into the operating system and machines. Jobs that have been "de-skilled" can be filled cheaply. The need to retain any individual worker is greatly reduced by the ease with which he or she can be replaced.

Teenagers have long provided the fast food industry with the bulk of its workforce. The industry's rapid growth coincided with the baby-boom expansion of that age group. Teenagers were in many ways the ideal candidates for these low-paying jobs. Since most teenagers still lived at home, they could afford to work for wages too low to support an adult, and until recently, their limited skills attracted few other employers. A job at a fast food restaurant became an American rite of passage, a first job soon left behind for better things. The flexible terms of employment in the fast food industry also attracted housewives who needed extra income. As the number of baby-boom teenagers declined, the fast food chains began to hire other marginalized workers: recent immigrants, the elderly, and the handicapped.

English is now the second language of at least one-sixth of the nation's restaurant workers, and about one-third of that group speaks no English at all. The proportion of fast food workers who cannot speak English is even higher. Many know only the names of the items on the menu; they speak "McDonald's English."

The fast food industry now employs some of the most disadvantaged members of American society. It often teaches basic job skills— such as getting to work on time—to people who can barely read, whose lives have been chaotic or shut off from the mainstream. Many individual franchisees are genuinely concerned about the well-being of their workers. But the stance of the fast food industry on issues involving employee training, the minimum wage, labor unions, and overtime pay strongly suggests that its motives in hiring the young, the poor, and the handicapped are hardly altruistic.

At a 1999 conference on foodservice equipment, top American executives from Burger King, McDonald's, and Tricon Global Restaurants, Inc. (the owner of Taco Bell, Pizza Hut, and KFC) appeared together on a panel to discuss labor shortages, employee training, computerization, and the latest kitchen technology. The three corporations now employ about 3.7 million people worldwide, operate about 60,000 restaurants, and open a new fast food restaurant every two hours. Putting aside their intense rivalry for customers, the executives had realized at a gathering the previous evening that when it came to labor issues, they were in complete agreement. "We've come to the conclusion that we're in support of each other," Dave Brewer, the vice president of engineering at KFC, explained. "We are aligned as a team to support this industry." One of the most important goals they held in common was the redesign of kitchen equipment so that less money needed to be spent training workers. "Make the equipment intuitive, make it so that the job is easier to do right than to do wrong," advised Jerry Sus, the leading equipment systems engineer at McDonald's. "The easier it is for him [the worker] to use, the easier it is for us not to have to train him." John Reckert—director of strategic operations and of research and development at Burger King—felt optimistic about the benefits that new technology would bring the industry. "We can develop equipment that only works one way," Reckert said. "There are many different ways today that employees can abuse our product, mess up the flow . . . If the equipment only allows one process, there's very little to train." Instead of giving written instructions to crew members, another panelist suggested, rely as much as possible on photographs of menu items, and "if there are instructions, make them very simple, write them at a fifth-grade level, and write them in Spanish and English." All of the executives agreed that "zero training" was the fast food industry's ideal, though it might not ever be attained.

15   While quietly spending enormous sums on research and technology to eliminate employee training, the fast food chains have accepted hundreds of millions of dollars in government subsidies for "training" their workers. Through federal programs such as the Targeted Jobs Tax Credit and its successor, the Work Opportunity Tax Credit, the chains have for years claimed tax credits of up to $2,400 for each new low-income worker they hired. In 1996 an investigation by the U.S. Department of Labor concluded that 92 percent of these workers would have been hired by the companies anyway—and that their new jobs were part-time, provided little training, and came with no benefits. These federal subsidy programs were created to reward American companies that gave job training to the poor.

Attempts to end these federal subsidies have been strenuously opposed by the National Council of Chain Restaurants and its allies in Congress. The Work Opportunity Tax Credit program was renewed in 1996. It offered as much as $385 million in subsidies the following year. Fast food restaurants had to employ a worker for only four hundred hours to receive the federal money—and then could get more money as soon as that worker quit and was replaced. American taxpayers have in effect subsidized the industry's high turnover rate, providing company tax breaks for workers who are employed for just a few months and receive no training. The industry front group formed to defend these government subsidies is called the "Committee for Employment Opportunities." Its chief lobbyist, Bill Signer, told the *Houston Chronicle* there was nothing wrong with the use of federal subsidies to create low-paying, low-skilled, short-term jobs for the poor. Trying to justify the minimal amount of training given to these workers, Signer said, "They've got to crawl before they can walk."

The employees whom the fast food industry expects to crawl are by far the biggest group of low-wage workers in the United States today. The nation has about 1 million migrant farm workers and about 3.5 million fast food workers. Although picking strawberries is orders of magnitude more difficult than cooking hamburgers, both jobs are now filled by people who are generally young, unskilled, and willing to work long hours for low pay. Moreover, the turnover rates for both jobs are among the highest in the American economy. The annual turnover rate in the fast food industry is now about 300 to 400 percent. The typical fast food worker quits or is fired every three to four months.

The fast food industry pays the minimum wage to a higher proportion of its workers than any other American industry. Consequently, a low minimum wage has long been a crucial part of the fast food industry's business plan. Between 1968 and 1990, the years when the fast food chains expanded at their fastest rate, the real value of the U.S. minimum wage fell by almost 40 percent. In the late 1990s, the real value of the U.S. minimum wage still remained about 27 percent lower than it was in the late 1960s. Nevertheless, the National Restaurant Association (NRA) has vehemently opposed any rise in the minimum wage at the federal, state, or local level. About sixty large food-service companies—including Jack in the Box, Wendy's, Chevy's, and Red Lobster—have backed congressional legislation that would essentially eliminate the federal minimum wage by allowing states to disregard it. Pete Meersman, the president of the Colorado Restaurant Association, advocates creating a federal guest worker program to import low-wage foodservice workers from overseas.

While the real value of the wages paid to restaurant workers has declined for the past three decades, the earnings of restaurant company executives have risen considerably. According to a 1997 survey in *Nation's Restaurant News*, the average corporate executive bonus was $131,000, an increase of 20 percent over the previous year. Increasing the federal minimum wage by a dollar would add about two cents to the cost of a fast food hamburger.

In 1938, at the height of the Great Depression, Congress passed 20 legislation to prevent employers from exploiting the nation's most vulnerable workers. The Fair Labor Standards Act established the first federal minimum wage. It also imposed limitations on child labor. And it mandated that employees who work more than forty hours a week be paid overtime wages for each additional hour. The overtime wage was set at a minimum of one and a half times the regular wage.

Today few employees in the fast food industry qualify for overtime—and even fewer are paid it. Roughly 90 percent of the nation's fast food workers are paid an hourly wage, provided no benefits, and scheduled to work only as needed. Crew members are employed "at will." If the restaurant's busy, they're kept longer than usual. If business is slow, they're sent home early. Managers try to make sure that each worker is employed less than forty hours a week, thereby avoiding any overtime payments. A typical McDonald's or Burger King restaurant has about fifty crew members. They work an average of thirty hours a week. By hiring a large number of crew members for each restaurant, sending them home as soon as possible, and employing them for fewer than forty hours a week whenever possible, the chains keep their labor costs to a bare minimum.

A handful of fast food workers are paid regular salaries. A fast food restaurant that employs fifty crew members has four or five managers and assistant managers. They earn about $23,000 a year and usually receive medical benefits, as well as some form of bonus or profit sharing. They have an opportunity to rise up the corporate ladder. But they also work long hours without overtime—fifty, sixty, seventy hours a week. The turnover rate among assistant managers is extremely high. The job offers little opportunity for independent decision-making. Computer programs, training manuals, and the machines in the kitchen determine how just about everything must be done.

Fast food managers do have the power to hire, fire, and schedule workers. Much of their time is spent motivating their crew members. In the absence of good wages and secure employment, the chains try to inculcate "team spirit" in their young crews. Workers who fail to work hard, who arrive late, or who are reluctant to stay extra hours are made to feel that they're making life harder for everyone else, letting their friends and coworkers down. For years the McDonald's Corporation has provided its managers with training in "transactional analysis," a set of psychological techniques popularized in the book *I'm OK—You're OK* (1969). One of these techniques is called "stroking"—a form of positive reinforcement, deliberate praise, and recognition that many teenagers don't get at home. Stroking can make a worker feel that his or her contribution is sincerely valued. And it's much less expensive than raising wages or paying overtime.

The fast food chains often reward managers who keep their labor costs low, a practice that often leads to abuses. In 1997 a jury in Washington State found that Taco Bell had systematically coerced its crew members into working off the clock in order to avoid paying them overtime. The bonuses of Taco Bell restaurant managers were tied to their success at cutting labor costs. The managers had devised a number of creative ways to do so. Workers were forced to wait until things got busy at a restaurant before officially starting their shifts. They were forced to work without pay after their shifts ended. They were forced to clean restaurants on their own time. And they were sometimes compensated with food, not wages. Many of the workers involved were minors and recent immigrants. Before the penalty phase of the Washington lawsuit, the two sides reached a settlement; Taco Bell agreed to pay millions of dollars in back wages, but admitted no wrongdoing. As many as 16,000 current and former employees were owed money by the company. One employee, a high school dropout named Regina Jones, regularly worked seventy to eighty hours a week but was paid for only forty. In 2001, Taco Bell settled a class-action lawsuit in California, agreeing to pay $9 million in back wages for overtime and an Oregon jury found that Taco Bell managers had falsified the time cards of thousands of workers in order to get productivity bonuses.

Responding to Reading

1. Why does Schlosser begin his essay with a description of Eliza Zamot's daily routine? What does Schlosser mean when he says, "Fast food kitchens often seem like a scene from *Bugsy Malone,* a film in which all the actors are children pretending to be adults" (4)?
2. In what way do the labor practices of the Speedee Service system resemble those of an assembly line? What are the advantages of this system? What are the disadvantages?
3. Why are teenagers the ideal candidates for the fast-food workforce? What other types of worker does this industry employ? Overall, would you say that Schlosser presents a positive picture of the fast-food industry?

Responding in Writing

Have you (or has anyone you have known) worked in a fast-food restaurant? Do your experiences (or the experiences of someone you know) support Schlosser's conclusions?

SELLING IN MINNESOTA
Barbara Ehrenreich
1941–

Barbara Ehrenreich labels herself an unabashed "feminist, populist, social-ist, and secular humanist." Ehrenreich has written about social, political, and economic issues for Mother Jones *magazine,* Time *magazine, and the* Guardian. *Her books of social criticism include* Fear of Falling: The Inner Life of the Middle Class *(1989);* The Worst Years of Our Lives: Irreverent Notes on a Decade of Greed *(1990);* Nickel and Dimed: On (Not) Getting by in America *(2001);* Global Woman: Nannies, Maids, and Sex Workers in the New Economy *(2003), and* Bait and Switch: The (Futile) Pursuit of the American Dream *(2005). The fol-lowing essay, taken from* Nickel and Dimed, *describes a Wal-Mart cor-porate orientation that Ehrenreich took part in when she was hired as a sales associate.*

For sheer grandeur, scale, and intimidation value, I doubt if any cor-porate orientation exceeds that of Wal-Mart. I have been told that the process will take eight hours, which will include two fifteen-minute breaks and one half-hour break for a meal, and will be paid for like a regular shift. When I arrive, dressed neatly in khakis and clean T-shirt, as befits a potential Wal-Mart "associate," I find there are ten new hires besides myself, mostly young and Caucasian, and a team of three, headed by Roberta, to do the "orientating." We sit around a long table in the same windowless room where I was interviewed, each with a thick folder of paperwork in front of us, and hear Roberta tell once again about raising six children, being a "people person," discovering that the three principles of Wal-Mart philosophy were the same as her own, and so on. We begin with a video, about fifteen minutes long, on the history and philosophy of Wal-Mart, or, as an anthropological observer might call it, the Cult of Sam. First young Sam Walton, in uniform, comes back from the war. He starts a store, a sort of five-and-dime; he marries and fathers four attractive children; he receives a Medal of Freedom from President Bush, after which he promptly dies, making way for the eulogies. But the company goes on, yes indeed. Here the arc of the story soars upward unstoppably, pausing only to mark some fresh milestone of corporate expansion. 1992: Wal-Mart becomes the largest retailer in the world. 1997: Sales top $100 billion. 1998: The number of Wal-Mart associates hits 825,000, making Wal-Mart the largest private employer in the nation. Each landmark date is accompanied by a clip showing throngs of shoppers, swarms of associates, or scenes of handsome new stores and their adjoining parking lots. Over and over we hear in voiceover or see in graphic display the "three principles," which are maddeningly, even defiantly, nonparallel: "respect for the individual, exceeding customers' expectations, strive for excellence."

"Respect for the individual" is where we, the associates, come in, because vast as Wal-Mart is, and tiny as we may be as individuals, everything depends on us. Sam always said, and is shown saying, that "the best ideas come from the associates"—for example, the idea of having a "people greeter," an elderly employee (excuse me, associate) who welcomes each customer as he or she enters the store. Three times during the orientation, which began at three and stretches to nearly eleven, we are reminded that this brainstorm originated in a mere associate, and who knows what revolutions in retailing each one of us may propose? Because our ideas are welcome, more than welcome, and we are to think of our managers not as bosses but as "servant leaders," serving us as well as the customers. Of course, all is not total harmony, in every instance, between associates and their servant-leaders. A video on "associate honesty" shows a cashier being caught on videotape as he pockets some bills from the cash register. Drums beat ominously as he is led away in handcuffs and sentenced to four years.

The theme of covert tensions, overcome by right thinking and positive attitude, continues in the twelve-minute video entitled *You've Picked a Great Place to Work*. Here various associates testify to the "essential feeling of family for which Wal-Mart is so well-known," leading up to the conclusion that we don't need a union. Once, long ago, unions had a place in American society, but they "no longer have much to offer workers," which is why people are leaving them "by the droves." Wal-Mart is booming; unions are declining: judge for yourself. But we are warned that "unions have been targeting Wal-Mart for years." Why? For the dues money of course. Think of what you would lose with a union: first, your dues money, which could be $20 a month "and sometimes much more." Second, you would lose "your voice" because the union would insist on doing your talking for you. Finally, you might lose even your wages and benefits because they would all be "at risk on the bargaining table." You have to wonder—and I imagine some of my teenage fellow orientees may be doing so—why such fiends as these union organizers, such outright extortionists, are allowed to roam free in the land.

There is more, much more than I could ever absorb, even if it were spread out over a semester-long course. On the reasonable assumption that none of us is planning to go home and curl up with the "Wal-Mart Associate Handbook," our trainers start reading it out loud to us, pausing every few paragraphs to ask, "Any questions?" There never are. Barry, the seventeen-year-old to my left, mutters that his "butt hurts." Sonya, the tiny African American woman across from me, seems frozen in terror. I have given up on looking perky and am fighting to keep my eyes open. No nose or other facial jewelry, we learn; earrings must be small and discreet, not dangling; no blue jeans except on Friday, and then you have to pay $1 for the privilege of wearing them. No "grazing," that is, eating from food packages that somehow become open; no "time theft." This last sends me drifting off in a sci-fi direction: *And as the time thieves headed back to the year 3420, loaded with weekends and days off looted from the twenty-first century* . . . Finally, a question. The old guy who is being hired as a people greeter wants to know, "What is time theft?" Answer: Doing anything other than working during company time, anything at all. Theft of *our* time is not, however, an issue. There are stretches amounting to many minutes when all three of our trainers wander off, leaving us to sit there in silence or take the opportunity to squirm. Or our junior trainers go through a section of the handbook, and then Roberta, returning from some other business, goes over the same section again. My eyelids droop and I consider walking out. I have seen time move more swiftly during seven-hour airline delays. In fact, I am getting nostalgic about seven-hour airline delays. At least you can read a book or get up and walk around, take a leak.

On breaks, I drink coffee purchased at the Radio Grill, as the in- 5 house fast-food place is called, the real stuff with caffeine, more because I'm concerned about being alert for the late-night drive home than out of any need to absorb all the Wal-Mart trivia coming my way. Now, here's a drug the drug warriors ought to take a little more interest in. Since I don't normally drink it at all—iced tea can usually be counted on for enough of a kick—the coffee has an effect like reagent-grade Dexedrine: my pulse races, my brain overheats, and the result in this instance is a kind of delirium. I find myself overly challenged by the little kindergarten-level tasks we are now given to do, such as affixing my personal bar code to my ID card, then sticking on the punch-out letters to spell my name. The letters keep curling up and sticking to my fingers, so I stop at "Barb," or more precisely, "BARB," drifting off to think of all the people I know who have gentrified their names in recent years—Patsy to Patricia, Dick to Richard, and so forth—while I am going in the other direction. Now we start taking turns going to the computers to begin our CBL, or Computer-Based Learning, and I become transfixed by the HIV-inspired module entitled "Bloodborne Pathogens," on what to do in the event that pools of human blood should show up on the sales floor. All right, you put warning cones around the puddles, don protective gloves, etc., but I can't stop trying to envision the circumstances in which these pools might arise: an associate uprising? a guest riot? I have gone through six modules, three more than we are supposed to do tonight—the rest are to be done in our spare moments over the next few weeks—when one of the trainers gently pries me away from the computer. We are allowed now to leave.

Responding to Reading

1. Ehrenreich begins her essay with the statement, "For sheer grandeur, scale, and intimidation value, I doubt if any corporate orientation exceeds that of Wal-Mart" (1). Do you think Ehrenreich wants her readers to take this statement seriously? In what way do these opening remarks set the tone for the rest of the essay?
2. Why does Ehrenreich describe the orientation process in such detail? What does she hope to accomplish with this strategy?
3. How would you describe Ehrenreich's attitude toward the orientation process? Toward Wal-Mart? Toward her co-workers? What words and phrases in the essay convey these attitudes?

Responding in Writing

Assume you are one of the trainers at Wal-Mart's orientation section. Write a one- or two-paragraph memo that explains the orientation process and its goals.

DELUSIONS OF GRANDEUR
Henry Louis Gates, Jr.
1950–

Henry Louis Gates, Jr. earned a Ph.D. (1979) in English Literature from Clare College at the University of Cambridge, where he was the first African American to do so. At age thirty, he received a MacArthur Foundation Genius Grant (1980). He has taught at Yale, Cornell, Duke, and Harvard. One of Gates's best-known works is Loose Canons: Notes on the Culture Wars (1992), *in which he discusses gender, literature, and multiculturalism in American arts and letters. His latest book is* America Behind the Color Line: Dialogues with African Americans *(2004). He is general editor of* The Norton Anthology of African-American Literature, *second edition (2003); a staff writer for the* New Yorker; *and the author of essays, reviews, and profiles in many other publications. In the following essay, Gates points out how few African Americans actually succeed as professional athletes and argues that the schools should do more to encourage young black men to pursue more realistic goals.*

Standing at the bar of an all-black VFW post in my hometown of Piedmont, W.Va., I offered five dollars to anyone who could tell me how many African-American professional athletes were at work today. There are 35 million African-Americans, I said.

"Ten million!" yelled one intrepid soul, too far into his cups.

"No way . . . more like 500,000," said another.

"You mean *all* professional sports," someone interjected, "including golf and tennis, but not counting the brothers from Puerto Rico?" Everyone laughed.

"Fifty thousand, minimum," was another guess.   5

Here are the facts:

There are 1,200 black professional athletes in the U.S.
There are 12 times more black lawyers than black athletes.
There are $2\frac{1}{2}$ times more black dentists than black athletes.
There are 15 times more black doctors than black athletes.

Nobody in my local VFW believed these statistics; in fact, few people would believe them if they weren't reading them in the pages of *Sports Illustrated*. In spite of these statistics, too many African-American youngsters still believe that they have a much better chance of becoming another Magic Johnson or Michael Jordan than they do of matching the achievements of Baltimore Mayor Kurt Schmoke or neurosurgeon Dr. Benjamin Carson, both of whom, like Johnson and Jordan, are black.

In reality, an African-American youngster has about as much chance of becoming a professional athlete as he or she does of winning the lottery. The tragedy for our people, however, is that few of us accept that truth.

Let me confess that I love sports. Like most black people of my generation—I'm 40—I was raised to revere the great black athletic heroes, and I never tired of listening to the stories of triumph and defeat that, for blacks, amount to a collective epic much like those of the ancient Greeks: Joe Louis's demolition of Max Schmeling; Satchel Paige's dazzling repertoire of pitches; Jesse Owens's in-your-face performance in Hitler's 1936 Olympics; Willie Mays's over-the-shoulder basket catch; Jackie Robinson's quiet strength when assaulted by racist taunts; and a thousand other grand tales.

10   Nevertheless, the blind pursuit of attainment in sports is having a devastating effect on our people. Imbued with a belief that our principal avenue to fame and profit is through sport, and seduced by a win-at-any-cost system that corrupts even elementary school students, far too many black kids treat basketball courts and football fields as if they were classrooms in an alternative school system. "O.K., I flunked English," a young athlete will say. "But I got an A plus in slamdunking."

The failure of our public schools to educate athletes is part and parcel of the schools' failure to educate almost everyone. A recent survey of the Philadelphia school system, for example, stated that "more than half of all students in the third, fifth and eighth grades cannot perform minimum math and language tasks." One in four middle school students in that city fails to pass to the next grade each year. It is a sad truth that such statistics are repeated in cities throughout the nation. Young athletes—particularly young black athletes—are especially ill-served. Many of them are functionally illiterate, yet they are passed along from year to year for the greater glory of good old Hometown High. We should not be surprised to learn, then, that only 26.6% of black athletes at the collegiate level earn their degrees. For every successful educated black professional athlete, there are thousands of dead and wounded. Yet young blacks continue to aspire to careers as athletes, and it's no wonder why; when the University of North Carolina recently commissioned a sculptor to create archetypes of its student body, guess which ethnic group was selected to represent athletes?

Those relatively few black athletes who do make it in the professional ranks must be prevailed upon to play a significant role in the education of all of our young people, athlete and nonathlete alike. While some have done so, many others have shirked their social obligations: to earmark small percentages of their incomes for the United Negro College Fund; to appear on television for educational purposes rather than merely to sell sneakers; to let children know the message that becoming a lawyer, a teacher or a doctor does more good for our people than winning the Super Bowl; and to form productive liaisons with educators to help forge solutions to the many ills that beset the black community. These are merely a few modest proposals.

A similar burden falls upon successful blacks in all walks of life. Each of us must strive to make our young people understand the realities. Tell them to cheer Bo Jackson but to emulate novelist Toni Morrison or businessman Reginald Lewis or historian John Hope Franklin or Spelman College president Johnetta Cole—the list is long.

Of course, society as a whole bears responsibility as well. Until colleges stop using young blacks as cannon fodder in the big-business wars of so-called nonprofessional sports, until training a young black's mind becomes as important as training his or her body, we will continue to perpetuate a system akin to that of the Roman gladiators, sacrificing a class of people for the entertainment of the mob.

Responding to Reading

1. Why does Gates begin his essay with an anecdote? What does this story reveal about African-American assumptions about sports? According to Gates, what harm do these assumptions do?
2. What does Gates mean when he says, "The failure of our public schools to educate athletes is part and parcel of the schools' failure to educate almost everyone" (11)? Do you agree? In addition to the public schools, who or what else could be responsible for the situation Gates describes?
3. What does Gates mean when he says that colleges are using young blacks as "cannon fodder" (14)? According to Gates, how are young black athletes like Roman gladiators? Do you think that this comparison is accurate? Fair?

Responding in Writing

What were your reactions to the statistics presented in paragraph 6? Write the text of a children's picture book designed to convey this information accurately to preschoolers.

WHAT NURSES STAND FOR

Suzanne Gordon

1945–

*Suzanne Gordon, a freelance writer and editor, writes frequently about so-
cial issues and health care. She is coeditor of* Caregiving: Readings in
Knowledge, Practice, Ethics, and Politics *(1996); author of* Life Support: Three Nurses on the Front Lines *(1997); and coauthor of* From Silence to Voice: What Nurses Know and Must Communicate to the
Public *(2000). Her latest book is* Nursing Against the Odds: How
Health Care Cost Cutting, Media Stereotypes, and Medical Hubris
Undermine Nurses and Patient Care (2005). *In the following excerpt
from* Life Support, *Gordon explains that nurses play a far greater role in
medical caregiving than most people realize.*

At four o'clock on a Friday afternoon the hematology-oncology clinic
at Boston's Beth Israel Hospital is quiet. Paddy Connelly and Frances
Kiel, two of the eleven nurses who work in the unit, sit at the nurses'
station—an island consisting of two long desks equipped with
phones, which ring constantly, and computers. They are encircled by
thirteen blue-leather reclining chairs, in which patients may spend
only a brief time, for a short chemotherapy infusion, or an entire afternoon, to receive more complicated chemotherapy or blood products. At one of the chairs Nancy Rumplik is starting to administer
chemotherapy to a man in his mid-fifties who has colon cancer.

Rumplik is forty-two and has been a nurse on the unit for seven
years. She stands next to the wan-looking man and begins to hang the
intravenous [IV] drugs that will treat his cancer. As the solution drips
through the tubing and into his vein, she sits by his side, watching to
make sure that he has no adverse reaction.

Today she is acting as triage nurse—the person responsible for
patients who walk in without an appointment, for patients who call
with a problem but can't reach their primary nurse, for the smooth
functioning of the unit, and, of course, for responding to any emergencies. Rumplik's eyes thus constantly sweep the room to check on
the other patients. She focuses for a moment on a heavy-set African-
American woman in her mid-forties, dressed in a pair of navy slacks
and a brightly colored shirt, who is sitting in the opposite corner. Her
sister, who is younger and heavier, is by her side. The patient seems
fine, so Rumplik returns her attention to the man next to her. Several
minutes later she looks up again, checks the woman, and stiffens.
There is now a look of anxiety on the woman's face. Rumplik, leaning
forward in her chair, stares at her.

"What's she getting?" she mouths to Kiel.

Looking at the patient's chart, Frances Kiel names a drug that has ₅
been known to cause severe allergic reactions. In that brief moment,
as the two nurses confer, the woman suddenly clasps her chest. Her
look of anxiety turns to terror. Her mouth opens and shuts in silent
panic. Rumplik leaps up from her chair, as do Kiel and Connelly, and
sprints across the room.

"I can't breathe," the woman sputters when Rumplik is at her
side. Her eyes bulging, she grasps Rumplik's hand tightly; her eyes
roll back as her head slips to the side. Realizing that the patient is
having an anaphylactic reaction (her airway is swelling and closing),
Rumplik immediately turns a small spigot on the IV tubing to shut off
the drip. At the same instant Kiel calls a physician and the emergency-
response team. By this time the woman is struggling for breath.

Kiel slips an oxygen mask over the woman's head and wraps a
blood-pressure cuff around her arm. Connelly administers an antihis-
tamine to stop the allergic reaction, and cortisone to decrease the in-
flammation blocking her airway. The physician, an oncology fellow,
arrives within minutes. He assesses the situation and then notices the
woman's sister standing paralyzed, watching the scene. "Get out of
here!" he commands sharply. The woman moves away as if she had
been slapped.

Just as the emergency team arrives, the woman's breathing returns to normal and the look of terror fades from her face. Taking
Rumplik's hand again, she looks up and says, "I couldn't breathe. I
just couldn't breathe." Rumplik gently explains that she has had an
allergic reaction to a drug and reassures her that it has stopped.

After a few minutes, when the physician is certain that the patient
is stable, he and the emergency-response team walk out of the treatment area, but the nurses continue to comfort the shaken woman.
Rumplik then crosses the room to talk with her male patient, who is
ashen-faced at this reminder of the potentially lethal effects of the
medication that he and others are receiving. Responding to his unspo-
ken fears, Rumplik says quietly, "It's frightening to see something like
that. But it's under control."

He nods silently, closes his eyes, and leans his head back against ₁₀
the chair. Rumplik goes over to the desk where Connelly and Kiel are
breathing a joint sigh of relief. One of the nurses comments on the
physician's treatment of the patient's sister. "Did you hear him? He
just told her to get out."

Wincing with distress, Rumplik looks around for the sister. She
goes into the waiting room, where the woman is sitting in a corner,
looking bereft and frightened. Rumplik sits down next to her, explains
what happened, and suggests that the patient could probably benefit
from some overnight company. Then she adds, "I'm sorry the doctor
talked to you like that. You know, it's a very anxious time for all of us."

At this gesture of respect and recognition the woman, who has every strike—race, class, and sex—against her when dealing with elite white professionals in this downtown hospital, smiles solemnly. "I understand. Thank you."

Nancy Rumplik returns to her patient.

"I Am Ready to Die"

It is 6:00 P.M. Today Jeannie Chaisson, a clinical nurse specialist, arrived at her general medical unit at seven in the morning and cared for patients until three-thirty in the afternoon. At home now, she makes herself a pot of coffee and sits down in the living room, cradling her cup. Just as she is shedding the strain of the day, the phone rings.

15   It's the husband of one of Chaisson's patients—a sixty-three-year-old woman suffering from terminal multiple myeloma, a cancer of the bone marrow. When Chaisson left the hospital, she knew the family was in crisis. Having endured the cancer for several years, the woman is exhausted from the pain, from the effects of the disease and failed treatments, and from the pain medication on which she has become increasingly dependent. Chaisson knows she is ready to let death take her. But her husband and daughter are not.

Now the crisis that was brewing has exploded. Chaisson's caller is breathless, frantic with anxiety, as he relays his wife's pleas. She wants to die. She is prepared to die. She says the pain is too much. "You've got to do something," he implores Chaisson. "Keep her going—stop her from doing this."

Chaisson knows that it is indeed time for her to do something—but, sadly, not what the anguished husband wishes. "Be calm," she tells him. "Please hold on. We'll all talk together. I'm coming right in." Leaving a note for her family, she gets into her car and drives back to the hospital.

When Chaisson walks into the patient's room, she is not surprised by what she finds. Seated next to the bed is the visibly distraught husband. Behind him the patient's twenty-five-year-old daughter paces in front of a picture window with a view across Boston. The patient is lying in a state somewhere between consciousness and coma, shrunken by pain and devoured by the cancer's progress. Chaisson has seen scenes like this many times before in her fifteen-year career as a nurse.

As she looks at the woman, she can understand why her husband and her daughter are so resistant. They remember her as she first appeared to Chaisson, three years ago—a bright, feisty sixty-year-old woman, her nails tapered and polished, her hair sleekly sculpted into a perfect silver pouf. Chaisson remembers the day, during the first of many admissions to the unit, when she asked the woman if she wanted her hair washed.

The woman replied in astonishment, "I do not wash my hair. I have it done. Once a week." 20

Now her hair is unkempt, glued to her face with sweat. Her nails are no longer polished. Their main work these days is to dig into her flesh when the pain becomes too acute. The disease has slowly bored into her bones. Simply to stand is painful and could even be an invitation to a fracture. Her pelvis is disintegrating. The nurses have inserted an indwelling catheter, because having a bedpan slipped underneath her causes agony, but she has developed a urinary-tract infection. Because removing the catheter will make the infection easier to treat, doctors suggest this course of action. Yet if the catheter is removed, the pain will be intolerable each time she has to urinate.

When the residents and interns argued that failure to treat the infection could mean the patient would die, Chaisson responded, "She's dying anyway. It's her disease that is killing her, not a urinary tract infection." They relented.

Now the family must confront this reality.

Chaisson goes to the woman's bed and gently wakes her. Smiling at her nurse, the woman tries to muster the energy to explain to her husband and her daughter that the pain is too great and she can no longer attain that delicate balance, so crucial to dying patients, between fighting off pain and remaining alert for at least some of the day. Only when she is practically comatose from drugs can she find relief.

"I am ready to die," she whispers weakly. 25

Her husband and daughter contradict her—there is still hope.

Jeannie Chaisson stands silent during this exchange and then intervenes, asking them to try to take in what their loved one is telling them. Then she repeats the basic facts about the disease and its course. "At this point there is no treatment for the disease," she explains, "but there is treatment for the pain, to make the patient comfortable and ease her suffering." Chaisson spends another hour sitting with them, answering their questions and allowing them to feel supported. Finally the family is able to heed the patient's wishes—leave the catheter in and do not resuscitate her if she suffers a cardiac arrest. Give her enough morphine to stop the pain. Let her go.

The woman visibly relaxes, lies back, and closes her eyes. Chaisson approaches the husband and the daughter, with whom she has worked for so long, and hugs them both. Then she goes out to talk to the medical team.

Before leaving for home, Chaisson again visits her patient. The husband and the daughter have gone for a cup of coffee. The woman is quiet. Chaisson sits down at the side of her bed and takes her hand.

The woman opens her eyes. Too exhausted to say a word, she merely squeezes the nurse's hand in gratitude. For the past three years Chaisson has helped her to fight her disease and live as long as possible. Now she is here to help her die.

The Endangered RN

30   When we hear the word "hospital," technology and scientific invention spring to mind: mechanical ventilators, dialysis machines, intravenous pumps, biomedical research, surgery, medication. These, many believe, are the life supports in our health-care system. This technology keeps people alive, and helps to cure and heal them.

In fact there are other, equally important life supports in our health care system: the 2.2 million nurses who make up the largest profession in health care, the profession with the highest percentage of women, and the second largest profession after teaching. These women and men weave a tapestry of care, knowledge, and trust that is critical to patients' survival.

Nancy Rumplik and Jeannie Chaisson have between them more than a quarter century's experience caring for the sick. They work in an acute-care hospital, one of Harvard Medical School's teaching hospitals. Beth Israel not only is known for the quality of its patient care but also is world-renowned for the quality of its nursing staff and its institutional commitment to nursing.

The for-profit, market-driven health care that is sweeping the nation is threatening this valuable group of professionals. To gain an advantage in the competitive new health-care marketplace, hospitals all over the country are trying to cut their costs. One popular strategy is to lay off nurses and replace them with lower-paid, less-skilled workers.

American hospitals already use 20 percent fewer nurses than their counterparts in other industrialized countries. Nursing does provide attractive middle-income salaries. In 1992 staff nurses earned, on average, $33,000 a year. Clinical nurse specialists, who have advanced education and specialize in a particular field, earned an average of $41,000, and nurse practitioners, who generally have a master's degree and provide primary-care services, earned just under $44,000. Yet RN salaries and benefits altogether represent only about 16 percent of total hospital costs.

35   Nevertheless, nurses are a major target of hospital "restructuring" plans, which in some cases have called for a reduction of 20 to 50 percent in registered nursing staff.

The process of job elimination, deskilling, and downgrading seriously erodes opportunities for stable middle-class employment in nursing as in other industries. However, as the late David Gordon documented in his book *Fat and Mean: The Corporate Squeeze of Working*

Americans and the Myth of Managerial "Downsizing," reduced "head counts" among production or service workers don't necessarily mean that higher-level jobs (and the pay and perquisites associated with them) are being chopped as well. In fact, Gordon argued, many head-line grabbing exercises in corporate cost-cutting leave executive compensation untouched, along with other forms of managerial "bloat."

Even in this era of managed-care limits on physicians' compensation, nurses' pay is relatively quite modest. And the managers of care themselves—particularly hospital administrators and health-maintenance-organization executives—are doing so well that even doctors look underpaid by comparison.

According to the business magazine *Modern Healthcare's* 1996 physician-compensation report, the average salary in family practice is $128,096, in internal medicine $135,755, in oncology $164,621, in anesthesiology $193,242, and in general surgery $199,342. Some specialists earn more than a million dollars a year.

A survey conducted in 1995 by *Hospitals & Health Networks*, the magazine of the American Hospital Association, found that the average total cash compensation for hospital CEOs was $188,500. In large hospitals the figure went up to $280,900, and in for-profit chains far higher. In 1995, at age forty-three, Richard Scott, the CEO of Columbia/Healthcare Corporation, received a salary of $2,093,844. He controlled shares in Columbia/HCA worth $359.5 million.

In 1994 compensation for the CEOs of the seven largest for-profit HMOs averaged $7 million. Even those in the not-for-profit sector of insurance earn startling sums: in 1995 John Burry Jr., the chairman and CEO of Ohio Blue Cross and Blue Shield, was paid $1.6 million. 40

According to a report in *Modern Healthcare*, a proposed merger with the for-profit Columbia/HCA would have paid him $3 million "for a decade-long no-compete contract . . . [and] up to $7 million for two consulting agreements."

At the other end of the new health-care salary spread are "unlicensed assistive personnel" (UAPs), who are now being used instead of nurses. They usually have little background in health care and only rudimentary training. Yet UAPs may insert catheters, read EKGs, suction tracheotomy tubes, change sterile dressings, and perform other traditional nursing functions. To keep patients from becoming unduly alarmed about—or even aware of—this development, some hospitals now prohibit nurses from wearing any badges that identify them as RNs. Thus everyone at the bedside is some kind of generic "patient-care technician"—regardless of how much or how little training and experience she or he has.

In some health-care facilities other nonprofessional staff—janitors, housekeepers, security guards, and aides—are also being "cross-trained" and transformed into "multi-skilled" workers who can be assigned to nursing duties. One such employee was so concerned about the impact of this on patient care that he recently wrote a letter to Timothy McCall, M.D., a critic of multi-skilling, after reading a magazine article the latter had written on the subject.

> I am an employee of a 95-bed, long-term care facility. My position is that of a security guard. Ninety-five percent of my job consists of maintenance, housekeeping, admitting persons into clinical lab to pick-up & leave specimens. Now a class, 45 minutes, is being given so employees can feed, give bedpans & move patients. My expertise is in law enforcement & security, 25 years. I am not trained or licensed in patient care, maintenance, lab work, etc. . . . This scares me. Having untrained, unlicensed people performing jobs, in my opinion, is dangerous.

Training of RN replacements is indeed almost never regulated by state licensing boards. There are no minimum requirements governing the amount of training that aides or cross-trained workers must have before they can be redeployed to do various types of nursing work. Training periods can range from a few hours to six weeks. One 1994 study cited in a 1996 report by the Institute of Medicine on nursing staffing found that

> 99 percent of the hospitals in California reported less than 120 hours of on-the-job training for newly hired ancillary nursing personnel. Only 20 percent of the hospitals required a high school diploma. The majority of hospitals (59 percent) provided less than 20 hours of classroom instruction and 88 percent provided 40 hours or less of instruction time.

45   Because the rapidly accelerating UAP trend is so new, its impact on patient care has not yet been fully documented. However, in a series of major studies over the past twenty years researchers have directly linked higher numbers and greater qualifications of registered nurses on hospital units to lower mortality rates and decreased lengths of hospital stay. Reducing the number of expert nurses in the hospital, the community, and homes endangers patients' lives and wastes scarce resources. Choosing to save money by reducing nursing care aggravates the impersonality of a medical system that tends to turn human beings into their diseases and the doctors who care for them into sophisticated clinical machines. When they're sick, patients do not ask only what pills they should take or what operations they should have. They are preoccupied with questions such as Why me? Why now? Nurses are there through this day-by-day, minute-by-minute attack on the soul. They know that for the patient not only a sick or infirm body but also a life, a family, a community, a society, needs to heal.

Media Stereotypes

Although nurses help us to live and die, in the public depiction of health-care patients seem to emerge from hospitals without ever having benefited from their assistance. Whether patients are treated in an emergency room in a few short hours or on a critical-care unit for months on end, we seem to assume that physicians are responsible for all the successes—and failures—in our medical system. In fact, we seem to believe that they are responsible not only for all of the curing but also for much of the caring.

Nurses remain shadowy figures moving mysteriously in the background. In television series they often appear as comic figures. On TV's short-lived *Nightingales*, on the sitcom *Nurses*, and on the medical drama *Chicago Hope* nurses are far too busy pining after doctors or racing off to aerobics classes to care for patients.

ER gives nurses more prominence than many other hospital shows, but doctors on *ER* are constantly barking out commands to perform the simplest duties—get a blood pressure, call the OR—to experienced emergency-room nurses. In reality the nurses would have thought of all this before the doctor arrived. In an emergency room as busy and sophisticated as the one on *ER*, the first clinician a patient sees is a triage nurse, who assesses the patient and dictates what he needs, who will see him, and when. Experienced nurses will direct less-experienced residents (and have sometimes done so on *ER*), suggesting a medication, a test, consultation with a specialist, or transfer to the operating room. The great irony of *ER* is that Carol Hathaway, the nurse in charge, is generally relegated to comforting a child or following a physician's orders rather than, as would occur in real life, helping to direct the staff in saving lives.

Not only do doctors dominate on television but they are the focus of most hard-news health-care coverage. Reporters rarely cover innovations in nursing, use nurses as sources, or report on nursing research. The health-care experts whom reporters or politicians consult are invariably physicians, representatives of physician organizations, or policy specialists who tend to look at health care through the prism of economics. "Who Counts in New Coverage of Health Care?," a 1990 study by the Women, Press & Politics Project, in Cambridge, Massachusetts, of health-care coverage in *The New York Times*, the *Los Angeles Times*, and *The Washington Post*, found that out of 908 quotations that appeared in three months' worth of health-care stories, nurses were the sources for ten.

The revolution in health care has become big news. Occasionally 50 reporters will turn their attention to layoffs in nursing, but the story is rarely framed as an important public-health issue. Rather, it is generally depicted as a labor-management conflict. Nursing unions are battling with management. Nurses say this; hospital administrators claim that. Whom can you believe?

Worse still, this important issue may be couched in the stereotypes of nursing or of women's work in general. A typical example appeared on NBC Nightly News in September of 1994. The show ran a story that involved a discussion of the serious problems, including deaths, resulting from replacing nurses with unlicensed aides. The anchor introduced it as "a new and controversial way of administering TLC."[1] Imagine how the issue would be characterized if 20 to 50 percent of staff physicians were eliminated in thousands of American hospitals. Would it not be front-page news, a major public-health catastrophe? Patients all over the country would be terrified to enter hospitals. Yet we learn about the equivalent in nursing with only a minimum of concern. If laying off thousands of nurses results only in the loss of a little TLC, what difference does it make if an aide replaces a nurse?

Nursing is not simply a matter of TLC. It's a matter of life and death. In hospitals, which employ 66 percent of America's nurses, nurses monitor a patient's condition before, during, and after high-tech medical procedures. They adjust medication, manage pain and the side effects of treatment, and instantly intervene if a life-threatening change occurs in a patient's condition.

In our high-tech medical system nurses care for the body and the soul. No matter how sensitive, caring, and attentive physicians are, nurses are often closer to the patient's needs and wishes. That's not because they are inherently more caring but because they spend far more time with patients and are likely to know them better. This time and knowledge allows them to save lives. Nurses also help people to adjust to the lives they must live after they have recovered. And when death can no longer be delayed, nurses help patients confront their own mortality with at least some measure of grace and dignity.

The Stigma of Sickness

There is another reason that nurses' work so often goes unrecognized. Even some of the patients who have benefited the most from nurses' critical care are unable to credit its importance publicly. Because nurses observe and cushion what the physician and writer Oliver Sacks has called human beings' falling "radically into sickness," they are a reminder of the pain, fear, vulnerability, and loss of control that adults find difficult to tolerate and thus to discuss. A man who has had a successful heart bypass will boast of his surgeon's accomplishments to friends at a dinner party. A woman who has survived a

---

[1]That is, "tender, loving care." [Eds.]

bone-marrow transplant will extol her oncologist's triumph in the war against cancer to her friends and relatives. But what nurses did for those two patients will rarely be mentioned. It was a nurse who bathed the cardiac patient and comforted him while he struggled with the terror of possible death. It was a nurse who held the plastic dish under the cancer patient's lips as she was wracked with nausea, and who wiped a bottom raw from diarrhea. As Claire Fagin and Donna Diers have explained in an eloquent essay titled "Nursing as Metaphor," nurses stand for intimacy. They are our secret sharers. Even though they are lifelines during illness, when control is restored the residue of our anxiety and mortality clings to them like dust, and we flee the memory.

At one moment a nurse like Nancy Rumplik or Jeannie Chaisson 55 may be involved in a sophisticated clinical procedure that demands expert judgment and advanced training in the latest technology. The next moment she may do what many people consider trivial or menial work, such as emptying a bedpan, giving a sponge bath, administering medication, or feeding or walking a patient.

The fact that nurses' work incorporates many so-called menial tasks that don't demand total attention is not a reason to replace nurses with less-skilled workers. This hands-on care allows nurses to explore patients' physical condition *and* to register their anxiety and fear. It allows them to save lives *and* to ascertain when it's appropriate to help patients die. It is only in watching nurses weave the tapestry of care that we grasp its integrity and its meaning for a society that too easily forgets the value of things that are beyond price.

Responding to Reading

1. Gordon begins her essay with two long narratives. What does each of these stories illustrate? How do they help Gordon make her point about nurses? How is this section of the essay different from the rest of the essay?
2. What new positions have for-profit health-care corporations created to save money? According to Gordon, how are the actions of these corporations compromising health care in the United States?
3. Why does Gordon think the work of nurses so often goes unnoticed? How do the media contribute to this situation? How do people's attitudes toward "nurses' work" add to the problem?

Responding in Writing

What attitude do you have toward nurses? Do you think your attitude "adds to the problem" that Gordon identifies?

FICTION

GIRL

Jamaica Kincaid
1949–

Born Elaine Potter Richardson in Saint Johns, Antigua-Barbuda, Jamaica, Kincaid moved to the United States and worked as a nanny and a reception-ist before attending the New School for Social Research in New York and Franconia College in New Hampshire. She has written for the New Yorker *since 1976 and has taught at Bennington College and Harvard University. Kincaid writes novels, essays, and short stories and has published* At the Bottom of the River *(1983),* Annie John *(1985),* Lucy *(1991),* The Auto-biography of My Mother *(1996), and* Talk Stories *(2000). Her latest book is* Amors Flowers: A Walk in the Himalaya *(2003). In the following short story, published in 1978, a young girl is being taught a lesson in life.*

Wash the white clothes on Monday and put them on the stone heap; wash the color clothes on Tuesday and put them on the clothesline to dry; don't walk barehead in the hot sun; cook pumpkin fritters in very hot sweet oil; soak your little cloths right after you take them off; when buying cotton to make yourself a nice blouse, be sure that it doesn't have gum on it, because that way it won't hold up well after a wash; soak salt fish overnight before you cook it; is it true that you sing benna in Sunday school?; always eat your food in such a way that it won't turn someone else's stomach; on Sundays try to walk like a lady and not like the slut you are so bent on becoming; don't sing benna in Sunday school; you mustn't speak to wharf-rat boys, not even to give directions; don't eat fruits on the street—flies will follow you; *but I don't sing benna on Sundays at all and never in Sunday school;* this is how to sew on a button; this is how to make a buttonhole for the button you have just sewed on; this is how to hem a dress when you see the hem coming down and so to prevent yourself from look-ing like the slut I know you are so bent on becoming; this is how you iron your father's khaki shirt so that it doesn't have a crease; this is how you iron your father's khaki pants so that they don't have a crease; this is how you grow okra—far from the house, because okra tree harbors red ants; when you are growing dasheen, make sure it gets plenty of water or else it makes your throat itch when you are eating it; this is how you sweep a corner; this is how you sweep a whole house; this is how you sweep a yard; this is how you smile to someone you don't like too much; this is how you smile to someone you don't like at all; this is how you smile to someone you like completely; this is how you set a table for tea; this is how you set a table for dinner; this is how you set a table for dinner with an important guest; this is how you set a table for lunch; this is how you set a table for breakfast; this is how to behave in the presence of men who don't know you very well, and this way they won't recognize immediately the slut I have warned you against becoming; be sure to wash every day, even if it is with your own spit; don't squat down to play marbles—you are not a boy, you know; don't pick people's flowers—you might catch something; don't throw stones at blackbirds, because it might not be a blackbird at all; this is how to make a bread pudding; this is how to make doukona; this is how to make pepper pot; this is how to make a good medicine for a cold; this is how to make a good medicine to throw away a child before it even becomes a child; this is how to catch a fish; this is how to throw back a fish you don't like, and that way something bad won't fall on you; this is how to bully a man; this is how a man bullies you; this is how to love a man, and if this doesn't work there are other ways, and if they don't work don't feel too bad about giving up; this is how to spit up in the air if you feel like it, and this is how to move quick so that it doesn't fall on you; this is how to make ends meet; always squeeze bread to make sure it's fresh; *but what if the baker won't let me feel the bread?*; you mean to say that after all you are really going to be the kind of women who the baker won't let near the bread?

Responding to Reading

1. How would you describe the kind of work the narrator of the story is being taught to do? Who is instructing her? Why must she learn the tasks she is being taught?
2. How old do you think the narrator is? Does she like the work she is being taught to do? What choices in life does she seem to have? What kind of future do you envision for her?
3. To whom is the narrator speaking? What clues in the story indicate what the listener is thinking?

Responding in Writing

Rewrite a portion of the story, filling in the responses of the silent listener to the narrator.

Focus

Is Outsourcing Bad for America?

Kashmiris at computers in a business process outsourcing centre in Rangreth, on the outskirts of Srinagar

Responding to the Image

1. What is your initial response to this photograph? After reading the essays in this Focus section, has your response changed in any way?
2. Do you think outsourcing is good for the United States? For the people of Kashmir? What impression of outsourcing does the photo convey?

LET SOMEONE ELSE DO IT: THE IMPULSE
BEHIND EVERYTHING.

Cullen Murphy

1952–

Managing editor at the Atlantic Monthly *magazine, Cullen Murphy has written numerous articles on political, linguistic, and religious issues. He has published three books, most recently* The Word According to Eve: Women and the Bible in Ancient Times and Our Own *(1998). In the following essay, Murphy examines the social, political, and religious implications of outsourcing.*

The terminology of economics—marginal utility," "vertical equity," "asymmetric information"—is not, by and large, the stuff of deep public passion. But in recent years one economic term has become hot to the touch. The term is "outsourcing," which refers to the spinning off of job functions from one place to another, and especially to the export of jobs from high-wage America to low-wage countries such as India and China. Both presidential candidates have expressed concern about outsourcing, which has devastated some of the most vigorously contested swing states, even as economists debate the overall pluses and minuses of outsourcing in the long run. What nobody disputes is that outsourcing has been occurring, that the pace is picking up, and that it affects all economic sectors and levels of management. Indeed, much of the job of President of the United States seems to have been outsourced to a lower-wage Vice President.

But it would be a mistake to think of outsourcing as simply an economic transaction; it is a universal tendency, like gravity, that exerts a pull on everything. It may be helpful to think in terms of a fourth law of thermodynamics. The first law, you'll recall, holds that the amount of matter and energy in the universe is constant. The second holds that the default direction of everything is toward entropy. The third law . . . well, never mind. The fourth law, newly postulated, holds that outsourcing—getting others to do things for you—is the intrinsic vector of all human activity.

National governments, for instance, once cherished their vaunted "monopoly on violence"; this was among the chief attributes of sovereignty. The war in Iraq has made Americans aware of the extent to which military functions have been outsourced to corporations like Halliburton, Bechtel, and DynCorp. Of course, armies never provided everything for themselves (the toilet paper inside meals-ready-to-eat, for example, comes from a $1.4 million contract to the Rose Resnick Lighthouse for the Blind and Visually Impaired, in Oakland), but core military functions such as building bases, guarding depots, and conducting surveillance are increasingly private-sector affairs. So, too, sometimes, is torture, as the Abu Ghraib scandal reveals, although the more common practice is for squeamish governments (i.e., ours) to outsource problematic interrogations to less squeamish governments (Cairo, Manila)—a practice that goes by the artfully bland term "rendition." Even the political task of educating Iraqis about the virtues of democracy has been outsourced—in this instance not to an American company but to a British public-relations firm, Bell Pottinger, which received a $5.6 million contract to produce promotional commercials for use on Iraqi television. (Bell Pottinger's chairman, Lord Tim Bell, previously oversaw publicity for Margaret Thatcher.)

Outsourcing extends into areas one might never have expected. The United States, seemingly self-sufficient in its own territory, has been outsourcing itself for years, at least when it comes to movie and television locales. New York is often played by (cheap) Toronto. The Appalachian settings in the movie Cold Mountain were played by (even cheaper) Romania. It used to be that standing in line for a driver's license or a government hearing, or to buy tickets, was the sort of thing one pretty much had to do for oneself. This function, too, is outsourceable. Today the "service expediter" industry provides human substitutes (for up to $30 an hour) who will save a place until your turn arrives. It's hard to see how this industry could ever be moved offshore to people in Thailand or Indonesia, but God help anyone needing a license if it is.

5   According to The Chronicle of Higher Education, the diploma-mill industry is being outsourced. There have long been unaccredited educational institutions in America willing for a fee to offer fast-track doctorates, and fly-by-night companies willing to send out handsome facsimile transcripts ("for amusement purposes only"), but the nation's homegrown diploma mills are now being undermined by competition from abroad. The Jerusalem-based University Degree Program has sold more than 30,000 advanced degrees of various kinds, from nonexistent institutions such as Ashbourne University and the University of Palmers Green. (There is even a phone number employers can call to confirm a job applicant's claims.) A China-based company called BackAlleyPress.com sells official-looking fake transcripts from real universities, custom-made to suit every educational need.

Demographic realities create urgent outsourcing needs. The shortage of Catholic priests in America has resulted in a grave backlog of prayers and masses. When the devout request special prayers of thanksgiving or remembrance, often to be said for years at a time, the requests (and monetary offerings) are increasingly outsourced to India, whose Catholic priests are giving the notion of service expediter a whole new dimension. Asked about this by The New York Times, a spokesman for the Catholic Church commented, "The prayer is heart-felt, and every prayer is treated as the same whether it is paid for in dollars, euros, or rupees."

If spiritual succor can be outsourced, so, presumably, can other inef-fable qualities and pursuits. A bit of a fuss was caused some years ago when it was revealed that clergymen in the United States had been out-sourcing their sermons—buying them from an online "sermon mill." But the entire range of human expression, from toasts by a best man to eulogies by a grieving friend, can now be acquired at a factory outlet. InstantWeddingToasts.com sells fill-in-the-blank templates to help clients create a memorable wedding speech. "In about five painless min-utes, you'll have a wedding speech ready to go . . . without writing!"

In America we've been outsourcing the idea of personal responsi-bility for years. The old-fashioned moral stance is the one articulated in Julius Caesar: "The fault, dear Brutus, is not in the stars but in our-selves." That was before the "Twinkle defense," which attributed a murderer's actions to elevated blood-sugar levels brought on by vigor-ous snacking on junk food. The dispositions of diet, the lash of up-bringing, the twist of genetics—targets of other-directed blame have become only more plentiful. A killer in Eustis, Florida, cited the fantasy role-playing game Vampire: The Masquerade as the catalyst of the al-leged mental illness that formed the basis of his defense. In another case, according to a newspaper account, a man in Panama City, Florida, "claimed drinking jasmine tea caused him to go temporarily insane be-fore he smashed his way into a neighbor's house and chased the woman with a large dagger." The charges against him were dropped.

Outsourcing has been with us from the very beginning. Think of slavery, a fundamental form of outsourcing. On a macro scale, the great imperial systems of history have been exercises in outsourcing. No doubt one of the earliest forms of outsourcing was the delegation of one's intellectual chores to a support staff of consultants.

Middle-class Americans today have typically outsourced a vast 10 proportion of child care, food preparation, and money handling. With the help of personal concierges, many higher-end Americans also have outsourced the great bulk of their interpersonal relationships. Repro-duction itself is often outsourced (by means of sperm and egg donors and in vitro fertilization), and people needing various kinds of human tissue for purposes of repair increasingly seek outsourced components in the developing world, where life is cheap and so are kidneys.

And I must confess that much of this column was in fact out-sourced to subcontracting facilities in Bangalore and Nogales, where I've been told that quality control is adequate and language issues should present no cause for concern. To be sure, there are glitches still to be worked out (for instance, the previous sentence originally came off the assembly line as "where I've been told that quality control is jolly good and language issues should present no problema"). But I can assure you that the sentiments expressed herein remain heartfelt, whether paid for in dollars, euros, or rupees.

Responding to Reading

1. What is meaning of the term *outsourcing*? What does Murphy mean when he says that outsourcing "is a universal tendency, like gravity, that exerts a pull on everything" (2)?
2. Murphy applies the concept of outsourcing to areas such as politics, the war in Iraq, education, religion, and childcare. Are these applications of the term justified? Convincing?
3. Murphy makes several references to contemporary politics. Do these references strengthen or weaken his case? What do these remarks tell you about his view of his audience?

Responding in Writing

Do you think the government should act to limit outsourcing? Or, do you believe that the decision to outsource should be left up to private industry?

MISSED TARGET: IS OUTSOURCING REALLY SO BAD?

Clay Risen

Clay Risen is managing editor at Democracy: A Journal of Ideas, *opinion editor at* Flak *magazine, and a contributing writer for* Morning News *magazine. His work includes articles about various political and economic issues as well as film, television, book, and music reviews. In the following essay, Risen considers the problem of outsourcing and attempts to allay Americans' fears about its scope and its impact.*

Ask folks in Silicon Valley these days about their biggest fear, and you likely won't hear about Osama bin Laden, global warming, or failing schools. These days, everyone's afraid of offshore outsourcing—the movement of white-collar jobs, especially in the high-tech sector, from the United States to foreign countries, where the labor is cheap, plentiful, and, increasingly, well-educated. "There's an increased level of anxiety about what the economy's going to be like," says Marcus Courtney, president of the Washington Alliance of Technology Workers. "People who entered this field thought it was going to be a career for twenty years, and now their jobs are gone." And they may not be coming back. "America is short of jobs as never before, and the major candidates for our offshore outsourcing are ramping up employment as never before," Stephen Roach, chief economist at Morgan Stanley, recently told the *New York Times*. "[T]hese jobs are, by [and] large, lost forever."

Predictably, politicians and the media have been quick to pick up on these fears. "tech workers struggle to answer overseas threat," noted a *New York Times* headline in November. And United Press International claimed recently that the financial benefits of offshoring would "come with a hefty price tag, with significant economic as well as social consequences." In turn, a growing number in Congress have called for a raft of anti-offshoring measures, from tax incentives to keep jobs offshore to bans on using foreign labor for government projects; Senators George Voinovich and Craig Thomas, for example, added an amendment to the 2004 Transportation and Treasury appropriations bil that would prevent contractors from using overseas labor to complete some federal contracts. And, on the op-ed page of the *New York Times*, Senator Charles Schumer recently asked "whether the case for free trade . . . is undermined by the changes now evident in the modern global economy," particularly offshore outsourcing. His answer? A resounding "yes." Offshore outsourcing, especially to developing powerhouses like China and India, has become this decade's "giant sucking sound."

But, like the fears that surrounded NAFTA, those around offshoring are mostly baseless. While offshoring is definitely an economic trend, there is no statistical evidence pointing to the massive employment drain activists call the "coring out" of America's best jobs. In fact, recent studies show that the opposite is true: While offshoring may displace some workers in the short term, in the medium and long terms it represents a net benefit for both domestic businesses and their workers. In fact, the greatest threat from outsourcing is that its opponents will use it to force a new wave of protectionism.

The frenzy over offshoring got going in late 2002, when Forrester Research released a startling study showing that 3.3 million white-collar jobs would move overseas by 2015. Then, in July of last year, the research firm Gartner trotted out its own study saying that as many as 5 percent of all information technology (I.T.) jobs could move abroad between mid-2003 and the end of 2004. And a 2003 report from Deloitte Research said that the top 100 financial-services firms plan to move $356 billion in operations and two million job overseas in the next five years.

But those numbers aren't as scary as they sound. For one thing, 5 while offshore outsourcing is definitely occurring, it's difficult to say just how large a trend it is at present. The Forrester research is based primarily on surveys of business leaders who are merely speculating about future offshoring decisions they might make: "There is no objective data to prove all these jobs are going overseas," says Michaela Platzer of the AeA (formerly the American Electronics Association).

"There's just a lot of anecdotal evidence." Some point to the jobless recovery as evidence of offshoring's impact, but the lack of jobs is just as likely the result of booming productivity and the economy's (until recently) anemic pace. "I think people are confusing the business cycle with long-term trends," says Daniel Griswold, an economist at the Cato Institute. "People are looking fo someone to blame. They say, 'Aha, it's because our jobs are moving to India.' If you look at the late 1990s, though, all these globalizing phenomena were going on." In other words, it wasn't that offshoring practices changed; it was that the economy slowed.

What's more, economists don't even agree on how such data could be collected—for example, many offshoring moves represent not a direct shift of a given job overseas but rather its restructuring, which in turn might create a new job overseas as well as a new job, with a new job description, in the United States. Such restructuring is particularly prevalent in high-tech fields like software and data management—for example, an America employee might be tasked with the design, implementation, and testing of a software program; under restructuring, his employer might hire an Indian, at one-tenth the cost, to do the implementation and testing and then hire an American to do the design work. IBM for example, plans to offshore 3,000 programming jobs this year. But, at the same time, it will also create 5,000 jobs in the United States. Does that count as jobs lost, jobs gained, or both? "[Offshoring is] going to lead to individual job loss," says Gary Burtless, an economist at Brookings, "but that does not mean it will lead to aggregate loss of employment in the United States."

Even if there were a short-term loss of jobs, the losses would likely have a more muted effect on the economy than the factory flight of the 1980s and '90s, when most factory workers had to undergo intensive retraining in order to find new jobs. White-collar workers tend to be, both in terms of skills and career perspective, more capable of moving on to other jobs. Another mitigating factor is the wide dispersal of high-tech jobs throughout the country; unlike manufacturing, which tends to clump hundreds or thousands of jobs in the same factory or town, high-tech work can be done anywhere. For example, one of the job sectors frequently cited as "offshoring prone" is medical transcription. Although it's a $15 billion industry, medical-transcription work is almost always farmed out to small firms around the country; even if all of them closed, the impact on any one community would be small.

And, while Forrester's 3.3 million jobs estimate may sound like a lot, keep in mind that it's a loss spread out over 15 years (2000–2015)—just 220,000 jobs annually. Furthermore, Forrester isn't talking about net job loss, but rather gross loss. In fact, even during periods of fast job growth, the U.S. economy sheds hundreds of thousands of jobs each year; it's simply robust enough to make up for the loss. In 1999, a year the economy produced a net 1.13 million jobs, it shed 2.5 million. But few argued that those job cuts were bad for the economy; in fact, most economists would argue they were beneficial, because they allowed companies to structure their operations more efficiently.

Offshoring is no different. In a sense, offshoring is simply the radical extension of the "creative destruction" processes that many credit as a driving force behind the '90s boom. Under the mantra "focus on what you do best," companies have been outsourcing non-core operations (such as human resources and call centers) for years; it is only with the emergence of high-quality telecommunications links that those operations have begun to move offshore. Unburdened by such ancillary concerns, companies are free to focus on—and innovate within—their core businesses, in turn creating new jobs, even new industries. "The standard arguments for free trade exist in this case," says Josh Bivens, an economist at the Economy Policy Institute. "I think the United States could see a productivity gain through this kind of trade." Meanwhile, the bulk of jobs that the Forrester survey claims will be outsourced are hardly the sorts of jobs on which the U.S. economy depends. "The lower-level jobs, the programming jobs, a lot of them will not be done in this country," says Stephanie Moore, an outsourcing expert at Giga, an economic research firm. In their place, she says, "New jobs are going to be created. Citibank will never let an Indian vendor manage its retail-banking operations."

Indeed, recent studies delving beyond the Forrester and Gartner numbers indicate that, despite the impact of short-term job loss, offshore outsourcing represents a net economic benefit for the United States. According to the McKinsey Global Institute, for every dollar a U.S. company spends on offshoring to India, the U.S. economy gains $1.14, thanks to a number of factors: savings from the increased operational efficiency, equipment sales to Indian outsourcers, the value of American labor reemployed to higher-wage jobs, and repatriated earnings by U.S. companies that own Indian outsourcing firms. "The recent changes driving offshoring are not that different or radical from the changes that dynamic, competitive, technologically evolving economies have experienced for the last few decades," the report concludes.

None of this, of course, has stopped antioffshoring critics from calling for restrictions. In 2002, after Shirley Turner, a New Jersey state representative, learned that calls to the state's welfare and food-stamps programs were being routed to a call center in Mumbai, she introduced a bill that would block foreign firms from working on state-funded projects. The bill created a firestorm in the I.T. community, with most workers supporting Turner. "I've been in the legislature now for ten years, and I have never received as much correspondence from people as I have with this bill," she told *USA Today*. Similar legislation has popped up in six other states. And, though none of those bills have been approved, observers say they'll likely pick up steam as the November elections approach. "I would expect that those bills will reemerge," says Information Technology Association of America President Harris Miller. "And, given it's an election year in most states, the likelihood of passage will be much higher." Anti-outsourcing fever is also growing in Congress, where a raft of bills has been introduced to limit the number of visas available for skilled laborers. The USA Jobs Protection Act, introduced by Senator Chris Dodd and Representative Nancy Johnson, would prevent U.S. companies from hiring foreign workers when American workers are available for the same job.

But there's little reason to believe these sorts of plans could stanch job contractions, even if they did manage to prevent jobs from going offshore. Particularly during rough economic times, the need to cut costs is an absolute priority, and, if offshoring weren't a possibility, domestic jobs would still likely be cut. "The choice isn't outsourcing or keeping jobs here," says Griswold. "It's outsourcing or going out of business. Which isn't good for jobs. This is an absolute necessity for many companies." If companies were somehow prevented from shipping jobs offshore, they would likely turn to other methods of reducing labor costs, such as technological upgrades—a process that has resulted in job loss since the birth of capitalism. "It's striking that people have less sympathy if those people are replaced by machines than if they are replaced by foreign workers," says Burtless. "It's all part of the same phenomenon of trying to squeeze value out of the same resources."

But, while offshoring-related protectionism may stifle economic development and unnecessarily force business closures, its biggest impact may be longer term. That's because, as the baby-boomers move into retirement, the size of the working population will decline precipitously, by 5 percent by 2015, according to the McKinsey report. Without a readily available source of high-quality, young labor—i.e., the sort provided by offshore outsourcing—the country could find itself in a sort of economic sclerosis. Growth could be permanently hamstrung by the high labor costs and booming social spending that have turned Germany, where it's extraordinarily difficult for companies to lay off employees, from an economic engine into a plodding giant. As Carl Steidtmann, chief economist for Deloitte Research, wrote recently, "Restrictive employment laws in Europe go a long way toward explaining why Europe consistently runs a higher rate of unemployment when contrasted with the U.S. or Britain."

Nevertheless, the fact that there are benefits to offshore outsourcing doesn't mean we should sit back and let it ride. At the individual level, job loss is a painful process, and there is no guarantee that even a relatively mobile white-collar worker whose job is outsourced will be able to find a new one, let alone at the same wage. The response, however, isn't to fight against offshoring but to find ways to alleviate its negative effects. One approach—advocated by Lori Kletzer, a senior fellow at the Institute for International Economics, and Robert Litan of the Brookings Institution—is to require companies to purchase "outsourcing insurance," which would cover a portion of displaced employees' salaries for a fixed period of time in the event their jobs are outsourced. Not only would this help alleviate the pain of layoffs, but it would force companies to internalize the economic cost of their outsourcing decisions. The McKinsey report, which also favors this approach, argues that, "as offshoring volumes rise, the insurance premiums will increase, cutting into the gains from offshoring and, thereby, making offshoring less attractive to companies in periods of high unemployment."

The most obvious and, in the global economy, most necessary solution, however, is worker training. The Trade Adjustment Assistance program already provides assistance to workers displaced by nafta-related factory closings; a similar program could easily be crafted to respond to offshore outsourcing. Indeed, requiring companies that outsource to contribute a portion of their savings to training programs would both internalize the cost and provide the necessary funds. And job training would not only alleviate periods of protracted unemployment; by making workers more agile, it would also make the U.S. economy more efficient and productive. Indeed, thanks to its combination of high job mobility and a highly educated work force, one of the U.S. economy's greatest strengths is its ability to redeploy workers quickly without dramatic cuts in their wages. And, thanks to that flexibility, notes the McKinsey report, "Over the past 10 years, the U.S. economy has created a total of 35 million new private sector jobs." It would be ironic if, in an effort to protect jobs, we closed off one of the most powerful means by which they are created.

Responding to Reading

1. According to Risen, why are workers concerned about outsourcing? How have politicians responded to these fears?
2. Why does Risen think that the fears surrounding outsourcing are "mostly baseless" (3)? What evidence does he present to support this opinion?
3. According to Risen, what is the best way to respond to outsourcing? Why is he against protectionism? What does he mean when he says, "It would

be ironic if, in an effort to protect jobs, we closed off one of the most powerful means by which they are created" (14)?

Responding in Writing

Do you see people who lose their jobs because of outsourcing as different from other unemployed Americans? Do you think they should get special help from the government?

FAIR EXCHANGE: WHO BENEFITS FROM OUTSOURCING?

Albino Barrera

Professor of economics and theology at Providence College, Albino Barrera often writes about the religious implications of economic policy. He has written three books, most recently Economic Compulsion and Christian Ethics *(2005) and* God and the Evil of Scarcity: Moral Foundations of Economic Agency *(2005). The following essay makes a moral argument about the nature of outsourcing.*

The Outsourcing of U.S. jobs overseas, the subject of much discussion in this year's presidential campaign, is part of an economic movement that promises a better life—indeed, a new beginning—for many people in developing countries. It gives technologically savvy young people in countries like India livelihoods that move them into the ranks of the middle class. On the other hand, workers in industrialized nations are being displaced in large numbers. Comparably well-paying jobs are not being created fast enough to make up for the positions headed offshore.

How does one morally evaluate this complex situation? Since international trade by its nature entails shifting resources for comparative advantage, the phenomenon of international outsourcing is not really new. The U.S. imports goods that would have cost more to produce domestically, and it manufactures and sells to other countries commodities that would have been more expensive for them to supply themselves. It is a win-win situation for nations, providing gains in consumption, production and exchange.

Cheaper imports mean that incomes can be stretched to buy more goods and services. Trade increases real income because it improves people's purchasing power. It also brings gains in production, since it allows countries to manufacture only those commodities that provide them the best possible earnings.

It makes sense for the U.S. to use its scarce natural and human resources to manufacture airplanes, high-end computer chips and advanced software—products that command better prices than do less complex things like shoes or textiles. Why produce something ourselves that we can get more cheaply elsewhere? Why use our resources to manufacture something of lesser value when we could use them to make something of greater value?

The world reaps enormous benefits from letting countries specialize in what they do best and most cheaply. Not only does this system increase efficiency and achieve economies of scale (both of which lead to a drop in costs), but it lays the groundwork for even more pathbreaking technological changes in processes and products.

Economic history makes clear that openness to the global marketplace is a significant determiner of a nation's economic well-being. Thus, the promotion of trade liberalization has been a perennial part of the World Bank's and the International Monetary Fund's assistance packages.

Yet assertions about the advantages of international trade (and, by extension, international outsourcing) must be heavily qualified. They refer only to overall gains and do not acknowledge how benefits are disbursed. One error in economic reasoning is the fallacy of division: the assumption that what is good for the whole is necessarily good for its individual parts. Not everybody gains from trade. The benefits of international trade come at the price of creating an economic life in constant flux and even disequilibrium.

Concern over the deleterious impact of trade (or technological change) is also not new. Tensions arising from market innovations and expansion began with the onset of the Industrial Revolution. British master weavers' hard-won and highly paid skills were rendered obsolete overnight by the introduction of machinery that quickly and abundantly produced textiles of comparable and uniform quality. Some of these disaffected weavers (eventually known as the Luddites) rioted, destroyed textile machinery and heavily lobbied parliament to ban or regulate the use of labor-displacing equipment (all to no avail).

Earlier, through contentious, drawn-out debates, "free-traders" succeeded in convincing the British parliament to repeal the Corn Laws and allow the unrestricted entry of cheaper grains from abroad. Industrialists asserted that this approach kept food prices (and wages) low, thereby making British industrial products more competitive abroad. Urban workers and industrialists benefited from the liberalization of the food market, but at the expense of farmers and landowners.

Technological change and market expansion can precipitate radical overnight changes in income distribution. They can produce a profound reallocation of burdens and benefits across local communities

CHAPTER 8 FOCUS

and even nations. No wonder international trade has always been a contentious issue.

Outsourcing has gained notoriety in recent months because of the accelerating volume of job transfers overseas and the sudden vulnerability of high-tech and service occupations that were once thought immune to trade displacement. Services that used to be nontradable (back-office operations, call centers, data management and accounting sectors) have now been made fully tradable because of advances in communications and computational technologies. Location is increasingly insignificant in the provision of these services. Moreover, the ready availability of large pools of technically capable and computer-savvy workers overseas has eroded what traditionally had been considered the distinct preserve of the U.S. and other developed countries: sophisticated, high-end technologies.

Many people have come to expect that blue-collar workers will sometimes be displaced as a consequence of trade. The fact that the same fate can descend on highly skilled and educated professionals is a new concern. Developed countries are torn between the steady call to stay the course with international trade and the ever-growing clamor to slow down or even ban outsourcing.

According to the standards of procedural justice, which calls for treating similar cases in a similar fashion, nations should not be selective in implementing trade rules but should simply let mutually agreed-upon processes and procedures run their course. Since World War II, developed countries, especially the U.S., have championed trade liberalization, having learned from the ill effects of trade protectionism during the interwar years. The spectacular economic growth in the second half of the 20th century reflects the enormous benefits reaped from the free trade of goods and services. The Asian Tigers (South Korea, Taiwan, Hong Kong and Singapore) and Japan became economic powerhouses. China owes its current economic boom to the open Western markets for its products and services.

Developed countries, too, have been major beneficiaries, since their comparative advantage lies in the trade of manufactures, services, intellectual property and capital. Industrialized countries have been vocal in promoting trade openness in these areas and have fiercely defended the need to respect and enforce intellectual property rights (e.g., pharmaceutical patents and software). There are, of course, adjustment costs that accompany trade, since segments of local populations are hurt by open markets. Despite these costs, poor countries have subscribed to international trade rules and have slowly but steadily opened their markets in those economic sectors (especially manufactures and services) where industrialized countries have much to gain.

Having reaped enormous profits from free trade in those areas 15 where they enjoy a distinct comparative advantage, developed countries violate procedural justice whenever they curtail or suppress the liberalization of markets in which they have a comparative disadvantage. This is exactly what the European Union, Japan and the U.S. have done in food markets, making poor countries unable fully to reap the gains of their comparative advantage (agricultural crops). The industrialized nations have steadfastly refused to open up trade in farm goods in an effort to protect farmers from being displaced by global trade. This is the proverbial case of wanting to have one's cake and eat it too.

A second conception of justice, justice as mutual advantage, calls for an equitable disposition of costs and benefits for all involved. Relationships should not be one-sided; gains and liabilities should be shared according to some mutually approved criteria. There are many variants of this school of thought, one of the best known being John Rawls's conception of justice as fairness: every person has the maximum freedoms consistent with others' enjoyment of the same liberties; and inequalities are permitted only to the extent that such disparities benefit the most disadvantaged.

The quickest and easiest way to understand the second condition is to use its theological analog, the preferential option for the poor: the more disadvantage are, the greater should be the assistance and solicitude extended to them by those in a position to help.

The promise that outsourcing holds for many impoverished people is vividly seen in India. Computer-related industries around Bangalore have spavined a wide and beneficial ripple effect across the nation. Human capital has replaced physical capital and natural resources as the primary creator of wealth in this postindustrial era. This augurs well for many nations poor in financial capital and natural resources but richly endowed with an educated workforce. They can leapfrog the traditional process of industrial development and parlay their human capital into much-needed foreign exchange. In other words, the technological advances that have made outsourcing possible have created a new global market for what used to be "nontradable" services.

In assessing mutual advantage in economic exchange, second-order effects should also be considered. U.S. consumers benefit from outsourcing through their gains in consumption. Moreover, a leaner cost structure makes U.S. producers more competitive in global markets, which should create more jobs. Blocking outsourcing thus imposes hidden costs ("taxes") on other Americans.

Future generations are the biggest beneficiaries of the dynamic 20 gains from trade brought on by technological advances. Innovation is price-sensitive and responds to incentives and increased earnings.

Trade distortions would erode future gains from efficiency, and succeeding generations would be adversely affected if outsourcing were impeded. The efficient use of finite resources benefits not only contemporary market participants but future economic agents as well. Justice requires mutual advantages across different generations.

Despite these arguments against obstructing outsourcing, a laissez-faire approach is also not right. Justice calls for remedial action for the negative unintended consequences of market operations. Those who map the benefits of international trade have duties toward those who bear the costs of making such market exchanges possible.

The claim that trade is ultimately beneficial because it creates new jobs even as it destroys old ones runs into two problems. First, disparities in skills or in geographic location may make for a bad fit between displaced workers and new jobs. Finding a new job, getting retrained, shifting to a new field or securing age-appropriate employment can be difficult and costly. A second problem is the time lag between job destruction and job creation.

Who should bear these unavoidable and significant costs? A laissez-faire approach to outsourcing simply leaves people to fend for themselves. Justice as mutual advantage requires a transfer of resources and assistance between beneficiaries and losers in market exchange. Relief cannot be limited to unemployment payments, food stamps or other stopgap measures, but must be substantive and geared toward reintegrating displaced workers back into the economy. This can take many forms, such as the provision of trade adjustment assistance grants, retraining, tuition assistance, extended health care benefits and career counseling,

Funding these programs will be a contentious issue because of the difficulty of identifying and then compelling beneficiaries (e.g., firms and consumers) to give up some of their gains from outsourcing. Government should not be viewed as the sole provider of these measures. Unions and local communities have an obligation to do whatever they can for themselves. Higher bodies should not arrogate functions that lower bodies can provide for themselves. Involving nongovernmental organizations can elicit new and creative ways of providing assistance to those who have been hurt by outsourcing.

25   Theological ethics arrives at the same conclusion as philosophical ethics: though outsourcing must take its course as part of the normal workings of international trade, the beneficiaries of this market exchange must help displaced workers make the transition to new place in the economy. We have a dual obligation to be efficient in our use of the goods of the earth and to cooperate with one another in our economic work. God entrusted the earth to our care as we use it to fill our needs. International trade fulfils these twin duties by satisfying human

needs in the most effective way while eliciting collaborative work through the division of labor.

The formation of ancient Israel provides insights into how the global economy ought to approach the dilemmas posed by outsourcing. Yahweh not only liberates the oppressed He brews from their slavery in Egypt but also brings them into a land "flowing with milk and honey." God offers his people a life both free and abundant, but only if they live up to their covenantal responsibility. The covenant code (Exod. 20:22–23:33), the Deuteronomic law (Deut. 12–26) and the code of holiness (Lev. 17–26) present a formidable array of statutes governing economic life: mandatory lending, interest-free loans, sabbatical rest and festivals, jubilee releases and land tenure, gleaning restrictions, tithing, debt remission, slave manumission, and the preferential treatment of widows, orphans and strangers.

We can draw various insights from these divine initiatives. Divine providence fills our needs; God intended us to have a bounteous life. But this abundant life is possible only if we truly care for each other. Our mutual solicitude is God's channel for providing us with plenty. Consequently, we must take responsibility for those who are in economic distress, reintegrating them into the community's economic life. Globalization affords us unique opportunities to take responsibility for each other's welfare. We are on the cusp of a global economy that requires humans to function as a single interdependent family. If we embrace the claim that we are all brothers and sisters in Christ, then national borders cannot limit our solicitude for others.

We cannot end outsourcing simply because local jobs are lost; outsourcing has an immense upside in its effect on the lives of poor people. It presents a unique opportunity to assist people mired in poverty. Economists and policymakers know that the best and most enduring form of assistance developed countries can give to poor nations is not in direct grants but in open markets. The global economy can be the "land flowing with milk and honey" entrusted to us all. Nevertheless, neither outsourcing nor trade should be completely unfettered. The moral obligations that tell us to assist the poor of the world by opening our markets also call us to help displaced workers find another place in the economy. Our duties toward poor nations and displaced domestic workers are not mutually exclusive. They can be satisfied simultaneously, but only if people are willing to sacrifice for each other's well-being.

Responding to Reading

1. What is "procedural justice" (13)? What does Barrera mean when he says, "developed countries violate procedural justice whenever they curtail or

suppress the liberalization of markets in which they have a comparative disadvantage" (15)?

2. What is "justice as mutual advantage" (16)? What promise does outsourcing hold for impoverished people? Why does Barrera believe that despite the arguments in favor of outsourcing, "a laissez-faire approach is also not right" (21)?

3. According to Barrera, how does globalization offer us "unique opportunities to take responsibility for each other's welfare" (27)? What does he mean when he says, "Our duties toward poor nations and displaced domestic workers are not mutually exclusive" (28)?

Responding in Writing

What moral argument does Barrera make? Do you think his allusions to the Bible and his appeals to divine providence strengthen or weaken his case?

WIDENING THE FOCUS

For Critical Thinking and Writing

Write an essay in which you answer the Focus question, "Is outsourcing bad for America"? In your essay, refer to the ideas in Cullen Murphy's "Let Someone Else Do It: The Impulse Behind Everything," Clay Risen's "Missed Target: Is Outsourcing Really So Bad?", and Albino Barrera', "Fair Exchange: Who Benefits from Outsourcing?"

For Further Reading

The following readings can suggest additional perspectives for thinking and writing about how to address the issue of outsourcing and its effects:

- Daniel Pink, "School's Out" (p. 91)

- Jonathan Kozol, "The Human Cost of an Illiterate Society" (p. 175)

- Richard Florida, "The Transformation of Everyday Life" (p. 302)

- Andrew Curry, "Why We Work" (p. 495)

For Internet Research

As the essays in the Focus section indicate, outsourcing is a source of debate. Proponents see outsourcing as a way of increasing productivity while at the same time reducing costs. In addition, they see outsourcing as a way of helping developing countries gain desperately needed capital. Opponents see outsourcing as an insidious activity that damages the American economy by permanently transferring jobs to other countries, where workers are exploited and underpaid. To gain greater insight into the issue of outsourcing, read the information on the following Web sites:

- <*www.blogsource.org/*> Offshore Outsourcing World, a site that promotes outsourcing

- <*http://www.topix.net/business/outsourcing*>, a site that provides updated outsourcing news from various sources on the Web.

Then, write an essay in which you discuss the advantages and disadvantages of outsourcing. As you do so, consider these questions: Is outsourcing really a less expensive alternative to domestic labor? Are there hidden costs that make outsourcing less desirable than it appears to be? Do companies that try outsourcing actually achieve the benefits that they expected?

CHAPTER 8 FOCUS

─────────────── **WRITING** ───────────────

Why We Work

1. In "Professions for Women," (p. 500) Virginia Woolf speaks of the difficulties women writers face—the "many ghosts to fight, many prejudices to overcome" (6). Apply Woolf's ideas about the struggle of women artists to a contemporary woman writer or artist with whose career you are familiar.

2. In "What Nurses Stand For" (p. 526), Suzanne Gordon says that the public's lack of concern about the layoffs of nurses "may be couched in the stereotypes of nursing or of women's work in general" (51). Interview several of your friends and family members about their attitudes toward nurses. Find out whether they see them as highly trained professionals or as people who perform menial tasks. Then, write an essay in which you discuss your findings.

3. Write an essay in which you describe the worst job you ever had.

4. Considering the essays in this chapter—especially "Why We Work (p. 495)," "Behind the Counter," (p. 511), and "The Second Shift" (p. 505)—write an essay in which you discuss what you believe the purpose of work should be. For example, should it be to earn money, or should it be to gain personal satisfaction and fulfillment? Are these two goals mutually exclusive? Does the way we work in this country help people achieve these goals? Would alternative arrangements—such as working fewer days with longer hours or having two people share one job—be better? Given the challenges of the global economy, are these changes in the way we work possible?

5. In "The Second Shift" (p. 505), Arlie Hochschild says that both society and the government should institute new policies that would allow workers to have more time at home. Write an essay in which you briefly summarize Hochschild's ideas and then go on to explain in detail why people need more time with their families.

6. In "Professions for Women" (p. 500), Virginia Woolf sees work as a way to achieve her full potential as a human being. In "Why We Work," (p. 495), however, Andrew Curry makes the point that most workers dislike their jobs. Which of these two views of work do you hold? Write an essay in which you give the reasons for your belief. Illustrate your points with your own experiences as well as with references to the essays by Woolf and Curry.

7. Imagine that you have been asked by your former high school to address this year's graduating class about how to get part-time and summer jobs to offset the high cost of college. Write a speech that is inspirational, but also offers specific advice.

8. Do you agree with Henry Louis Gates's contention in "Delusions of Grandeur" that colleges place too much emphasis on sports—especially when it concerns the African-American athlete? If you agree with Gates, present specific suggestions for rectifying the situation. If you do not agree, show where in the essay he is in error.

9. Suppose that you were attending the Wal-Mart orientation with Barbara Ehrenreich (p. 519). Write a letter to the manager of the store in which you point out the shortcomings of the program as well as your suggestions for improving it. Support your points with specific references to Ehrenreich's essay.

9

■ ■ ■ ■ ☐ ■ ■ ■

SCIENCE AND HUMAN VALUES

■ ■ ☐ ■ ■

We are living in a unique era. Diseases such as polio and smallpox, which plagued human beings for centuries, have been all but eradicated in the West. The power of the atom has been used to generate electricity as well as to diagnose and to cure diseases. More recent developments—such as human cloning, stem-cell research, and wireless technology—have had a profound impact on the way we see our society and ourselves. It is remarkable to consider that during the past hundred years, scientists have made more advances than they had made since the beginning of human history. Even more remarkable, there is no reason to think that this exponential growth of knowledge will not continue.

Scientific progress comes at a cost, however. Every new discovery presents new challenges—both technological and ethical. For example, in

A nuclear power plant in Cruas, France

the nineteenth century, mechanization enabled workers to increase their output and thus to raise the standard of living of millions of people. Maintaining this technology, however, requires a tremendous amount of energy from fossil fuels, and this energy use may be responsible for increasing the temperature of the earth. Is this advance worth the price we pay for it, or is the cost too high? The same question may be asked of other, more recent scientific discoveries. What are the moral implications of stem-cell research, of human cloning, of organ transplants, and of space exploration? What problems do these discoveries create? What benefits do they offer? Do the benefits outweigh the possible harm? In the final analysis, we are left with one overriding question: Does scientific progress put us in touch with what is best in ourselves, or does it simply overwhelm us with increasingly difficult moral dilemmas?

This chapter focuses on issues that scientific progress has forced us to confront. Unlike other chapters in this book, this chapter consists of three Focus sections, each asking a question about a specific scientific issue. The first Focus question (p. 563) asks, "Is global warming fact or fiction?" In this section, the essays consider whether global warming is a man-made disaster, a natural phenomenon, or simply a creation of environmental activists. The second Focus question (p. 000) asks, "Can the energy crisis be solved?" The essays in this section discuss alternative energy sources and consider whether they can meet the country's future energy needs. The third Focus question (p. 000) asks, "Are men better in math and science than women?" The essays in this section discuss why math and science careers seem to be dominated by men and whether men are more proficient in math and science than women.

A mushroom cloud above Hiroshima after the dropping of the first atomic bomb

PREPARING TO READ AND WRITE

As you read and prepare to write about the selections in this chapter, you may consider the following questions:

- Is the writer a scientist? A layperson? A journalist? Does the writer's background make you more or less receptive to his or her ideas?

- On what issue does the writer focus?

- What position does the writer take on the issue? Do you agree or disagree with this position?

- Is the writer's emphasis theoretical or practical?

- What preconceptions do you have about the issue? Does the essay reinforce or challenge these preconceptions?

- What background in science does the writer assume readers have?

- Does the writer think science alone will be able to solve the problems he or she mentions? Does the writer believe other kinds of solutions are necessary? Is the writer optimistic or pessimistic about the future?

- What is the writer's purpose? Is it to make readers think about a controversial idea? To persuade readers? To educate them? To warn them?

- In what ways is the essay similar or different from the others in its Focus section?

APOLLO

Elizabeth Alexander
1962–

Associate Professor of African-American Studies at Yale University, Elizabeth Alexander is a poet, fiction writer, and essayist whose works have appeared in Signs, American Poetry Review, *the* Village Voice, *the* Women's Review of Books, *and the* Washington Post, *among other publications. She has written and edited six books, most recently* American Sublime *(2005), a collection of poems. The following poem offers a unique look into NASA's 1960s–1970s moon-landing program.*

We pull off
to a road shack
in Massachusetts
to watch men walk

on the moon. We did   5
the same thing
for three two one
blast off, and now

we watch the same men
bounce in and out   10
of craters. I want
a Coke and a hamburger.

Because the men
are walking on the moon
which is now irrefutably   15
not green, not cheese,

not a shiny dime floating
in a cold blue,
the way I'd thought,
the road shack people don't   20

notice we are a black
family not from there,
the way it mostly goes.
This talking through

static, bouncing in space-   25
boots, tethered
to cords is much
stranger, stranger

even than we are.

Responding to Reading

1. What is the speaker's response to the moon landing? Does she seem excited? Awed? Thrilled? Bored? Something else?
2. What does the speaker mean when she says the moon is "not green, not cheese" (16) and not "a shiny dime" (17)?
3. Why don't the people in the "road shack" notice that the speaker and her family are black? What does the speaker mean when she says that the men walking on the moon are "stranger, stranger / even than we are" (28–29)?

Responding in Writing

What would your reaction be to watching a group of astronauts walking on the moon today? Would your response be similar to or different from the reaction of the people in the road shack?

—— Focus ——

Is Global Warming Fact or Fiction?

A tidal wave batters New York City in the film *The Day After Tomorrow*

Responding to the Image

1. The visual above is a still from *The Day After Tomorrow,* a movie that shows the possible effects of global warming. What does this visual suggest about global warming? To what emotions is the filmmaker appealing in order to get his point across?
2. Would the visual's impact be different if the city dominated more of the picture?

GLOBAL WARMING: IS IT ALREADY TOO LATE?

Mark Lynas

1973–

Climatologist and social activist Mark Lynas has written the book High Tide: News from a Warming World *(2004) and is currently working on his second,* Six Degrees. *He has also written numerous articles for publications such as the* Observer *and the* Guardian. *Lynas strives in his work to raise social awareness on the issue of global warming, the focus of the following essay.*

The first warning signs would have come from the sunsets. Weird splashes of red, yellow and purple-painted evening horizons all around the globe. Only those living near the eruption site would have seen the cause—vast volcanic outgassings of carbon dioxide, ash and sulphur. The end-Permian apocalypse had begun. By its conclusion, up to 95 per cent of species had been wiped out, the oceans transformed into black, oxygen-starved graveyards as millions of animal carcasses and uprooted plants rotted in the inky depths. It was the worst mass extinction ever to hit the planet, and it happened 251 million years ago because of global warming. (For a full description, see Michael Benton's *When Life Nearly Died*, published by Thames & Hudson last year.)

Today, the world stands on the brink of a similar cataclysm, with one crucial difference. The agent of death at the end of the Permian period was volcanism. Now the agent of death is man.

But how close are we to this catastrophe? Is it still avoidable? In the pre-industrial era, levels of carbon dioxide per cubic metre of air stood at roughly 278 parts per million (ppm). Today, they have soared to 376 ppm, the highest in at least 420,000 years, and probably much longer. This means that every breath of air we take is chemically different from the air breathed throughout the evolutionary history of the human species. And if the current rate of carbon accumulation continues, the rise in temperature could be as much as 6° Celsius by the end of the century, according to the UN Intergovernmental Panel on Climate Change. That is roughly the same as the temperature increase that delivered the coup de grace to the prehistoric world of the Permian.

All the efforts of the climate-change panel, all the international conferences and protocols, all the green campaigning, are based on the assumption that, if we act now, the worst can be avoided. Although some global warming is already inescapable—temperatures will continue to rise for many years, and there is no power on earth that can stop them—we assume, none the less, that it is not too late; if we do the right things within the next couple of decades, temperatures will eventually stabilise.

But what if this is wrong? What if global warming is already un- 5
stoppable and is now accelerating uncontrollably? What if we have
reached the point of no return and there is nothing we can do except
wait for the end? Scientists are naturally cautious people, but a growing
number fear that this may be the case. One ominous indicator comes
from a US atmospheric sampling station 3,000 metres up on the northern flank of the Mauna Loa volcano in Hawaii. Since the 1950s, this station—and dozens of others dotted around the globe from Alaska to the
South Pole—have recorded a steady increase in carbon-dioxide concentrations. The average year-on-year rise is 1.5 ppm. Over the past two
years, the rate of accumulation has doubled—to nearly 3 ppm. This
could mean that the rate of fossil-fuel burning has doubled—but it hasn't.
The alternative explanation is that the biosphere "sinks," which used to
absorb carbon, have suddenly shut down.

To understand the implications of this second possibility, we need
to look at how global warming works. Every year, humans burn
enough coal, oil and gas to add roughly six billion tonnes of carbon to
the global atmosphere. This carbon was formerly trapped underground, laid down between rock deposits from much earlier (and wan-
ner) phases in the earth's history. About half of this extra annual dose
of carbon—three billion tonnes—is soaked up by oceans and plants. It
is the other half that steadily accumulates in the atmosphere and causes
all the trouble.

The fear is that, as temperatures rise, global warming, in a process
that scientists call "positive feedback," will itself increase the amount of
carbon released into the atmosphere, regardless of what humans do: in
other words, the oceans and plants will stop soaking up those three billion tonnes. The UK Meteorological Office's Hadley Centre, which spe-
cialises in climate-change research, published an alarming paper in
Nature in 2000 which gave the results of a computer simulation of the
future global carbon cycle. It showed that if green-house-gas emissions
continued, the Amazon rainforest ecosystem would begin to collapse,
releasing vast quantities of stored carbon into the atmosphere in addition to the man-made carbon emissions. After about 2050, even more
carbon would pour into the air from warming soils around the world.
The combined effect would be enough to increase CO_2 in the atmosphere by another 250 ppm—equivalent to a temperature rise of an extra
1.5° Celsius above previous predictions.

There is an even more chilling possibility. Deep under oceanic continental shelves right around the world, from Peru to Norway, huge
quantities of methane are stored in "hydrate" form, kept solid by a
combination of low temperatures and pressure from the water and sed-
iment piled above them. It has been estimated that this methane hydrate store contains 10,000 gigatonnes—that is, ten thousand billion
tonnes—of carbon, more than double the world's entire combined

fossil-fuel reserves. Like carbon dioxide, methane is a greenhouse gas—in fact, it is 21 times more potent than CO_2. If even a small quantity were to escape into the atmosphere, runaway global warming might become inevitable.

This nightmare, scientists say, is increasingly likely. Warming ocean temperatures will destabilise the hydrates, allowing them to bubble up to the surface. This new methane will increase temperatures further, leading to still more release from the sea floor in a potentially unstoppable spiral. In fact, geologists increasingly think this feedback to have been the mechanism that drove the end-Permian cataclysm: carbon dioxide from volcanoes first raised world temperatures enough to destabilise methane hydrates, after which prehistoric global warming gained its own deadly momentum.

10   A more recent geological event, 55 million years ago at the end of the Palaeocene epoch, provides even stronger evidence that a "methane burp" from the oceans has indeed happened before. Although less dramatic than the end-Permian, it was also accompanied by mass extinctions. Indeed, it was in the recovery period from this second crisis that mammals—including our primate forebears—first exploded on to the scene. The government's chief scientist, Professor Sir David King, was referring to this period when he told reporters at Tony Blair's Climate Group launch on 27 April that "Antarctica was the best place for mammals to live, and the rest of the globe would not sustain human life." He warned that these conditions, with CO_2 levels as high as 1,000 ppm and no ice left on earth, could again be reached by 2100.

How seriously should we take these warnings? It must be emphasised that, while scientists are now virtually unanimous about the reality of man-made global warming—new evidence published in *Nature* that the troposphere, the lowest level of the atmosphere, is warming at roughly the same rate as the earth's surface has removed the last doubts—they are far more cautious about suggestions that it is already moving out of control. The increase in carbon-dioxide concentrations detected by the Hawaii station, says Pieter Tans of the US National Oceanic and Atmospheric Administration, may not continue. In warmer years, he explains, the rate of bacterial decomposition in the ground speeds up, and more carbon is released from soils. Over more than a few years, he says, ecosystems adjust. However, his colleague Ralph Keeling, while agreeing that the recent change "might not be such a big deal," points out that "there is no past period where the average carbon accumulation has stayed this high." Another expert on the carbon cycle—who was prepared to speak only on condition of anonymity—said: "We simply don't have a way to tell from just one year if a positive feedback is kicking in. But if it was happening, this is what it would look like."

That is the trouble with global warming. Human beings respond to events on a daily and weekly basis, not an annual, still less a decadal one. But according to a paper from the Benfield Hazard Research Centre, to be published shortly, the impact of methane hydrate failure could be very dramatic indeed. If enough gas is released, entire continental slopes could collapse in enormous submarine landslides, triggering tsunami waves of up to 15 metres in height—enough to level entire coastal cities. Again, there is a precedent: just 7,000 years ago, an area of continental slope the size of Wales slid downhill between Norway and Iceland, triggering a tsunami that wiped out neolithic communities on the north-east coast of Scotland.

If such an event happens again, the only certainty is that there will be no warning. And yet, the danger signs are already all around: 2003 was the second-warmest year on record. Last summer's heatwave across Europe was so far off the normal statistical scale that climatologists logged it as a once-in-10,000-years event. Sea-level rise is accelerating, according to the latest satellite measurements. And last month, a truly unprecedented weather event occurred. Hurricanes were thought to be an entirely north Atlantic phenomenon. But on this occasion an Atlantic hurricane formed south of the Equator and struck Brazil with 90 mph winds. Tropical meteorologists were so baffled that they had no idea what to call it, and hurricane monitoring systems may now have to be extended a thousand miles further south.

So is there any hope of persuading politicians to treat global warming with the urgency it requires? Perhaps so, now that the story has reached Hollywood, with the disaster movie *The Day After Tomorrow* due out this summer. Unfortunately, the events in the film are premised on an effect of global warming that remains contentious among scientists, and tends to confuse the public. This is the possibility that global warming, by increasing rainfall and ice-melt at high latitudes, shuts down the Atlantic's circulation, plunging Europe into a new ice age. A current known as the Gulf Stream transports a staggering amount of heat northwards, equivalent to the energy produced by about a million nuclear power stations. Without it, our climate would be between 5° Celsius and 10° Celsius colder—similar to that of Newfoundland. Again, the warning signs are clear: the "subpolar gyre" part of the current has already begun to slow, and through-flow of water between Iceland and the Faroes has declined by 20 per cent over the past 50 years.

However, *The Day After Tomorrow*'s storyline—where New York is 15 flooded and then frozen solid within a week—is not even remotely likely. Most scientists, whilst quietly approving of Hollywood's sudden conversion to an issue that many have been battling to get into the media for years, give the film itself short shrift. Writing last month in *Science* magazine, the oceanographer Andrew Weaver pooh-poohed the "new ice age" scenario, pointing out that such a drastic cooling of the climate would be impossible with greenhouse gases at today's elevated levels.

But whatever its flaws, there is at least a chance that the film will put global warming on the US political agenda. Indeed, the former vice-president Al Gore, who frequently delivers speeches warning of the dangers of climate change, is planning a mass rally in New York City to capitalise on the sudden media interest.

The more common mood among environmentalists, however, is one of pessimism. At the annual UN climate-change talks, scheduled for Buenos Aires in December, negotiators, instead of discussing "mitigation" (reducing greenhouse-gas emissions), are likely to focus mainly on "adaptation." In other words, having lost the battle to stop global warming, the best we can all now hope for is desperate rearguard actions to protect coastal land from flooding and to ward off large-scale starvation. Even the Pentagon is having to take note. A recent report for America's military top brass warned that mass refugee flows and competition for water and food could plunge the world into nuclear conflict. "Humans fight when they outstrip the carrying capacity of their natural environment," it warns. "The most combative societies are the ones that survive."

The report charts some of the "potential military implications of climate change," including the collapse of the EU [European Union], civil war in China and the takeover of US borders by the army to prevent refugee incursions from the Caribbean and Mexico. The report's title, Abrupt Climate Change, reflects an increasing awareness among scientists and policy-makers alike that global warming is more likely to lead to sudden climatic shifts than to slow, linear change. Once more, the earth's climate history gives a precedent: the planet swung between cold and warm periods at the end of the most recent ice age in as little as a decade.

Sudden, unanticipated events—which climatologists drily term "surprises"—could include, for example, the collapse of the west Antarctic ice sheet and the catastrophic inundation of low-lying areas all around the world. This is the scenario that causes giant waves to flood Manhattan in The Day After Tomorrow. In reality, even the most dramatic rise in sea level would still take years rather than minutes to flood coastal cities.

20   A better storyline might have run as follows. Rapid melting of the Greenland ice sheet causes the offshore continental shelf to rebound upwards, releasing huge quantities of methane hydrates with explosive force. The entire shelf slumps downward, triggering 15 m-high tsunamis right across the north Atlantic, wiping out Reykjavik, Lisbon and—ultimately—New York City itself. The new methane adds rapidly to global warming, causing mega-droughts and mass starvation across

Asia, Africa and South America. Don't forget: it's happened before, so it could happen again.

Three months ago, scientists would have laughed if a film had portrayed a freak hurricane forming in the south Atlantic. Now nobody's smiling.

Responding to Reading

1. What evidence does Lynas present to support the idea that global warming is taking place? How convincing is this evidence? Does he ever actually establish that global warming has a human cause?
2. Does Lynas believe that the "warnings" he presents are to be taken seriously? According to him, "is there any hope of persuading politicians to treat global warming with the urgency it requires" (14)?
3. What does Lynas think of the movie *The Day After Tomorrow*? What good does he hope will come out of the film? What kind of story line would he rather have seen?

Responding in Writing

Rent a DVD of the movie *The Day After Tomorrow*. Do you believe it offers a believable view of the effects of global warming?

CLIMATE CHANGE: MENACE OR MYTH?

Fred Pearce

Fred Pearce has written and coauthored numerous books on environmental issues such as global warming and water conservation. His latest book, When the Rivers Run Dry: Water, the Defining Crisis of the Twenty-First Century, *was published in 2006. In the following essay, Pearce considers the complexities of global warming.*

On 16 February, the Kyoto protocol comes into force. Whether you see this as a triumph of international cooperation or a case of too little, too late, there is no doubt that it was only made possible by decades of dedicated work by climate scientists. Yet as these same researchers celebrate their most notable achievement, their work is being denigrated as never before.

The hostile criticism is coming from sceptics who question the reality of climate change. Critics have always been around, but in recent months their voices have become increasingly prominent and influential. One British newspaper called climate change a "global fraud" based on "left-wing, anti-American, anti-west ideology." A London-based think tank described the UK's chief scientific adviser, David King, as "an embarrassment" for believing that climate change is a bigger threat than terrorism. And the bestselling author Michael Crichton, in his much publicised new novel *State of Fear*, portrays global warming as an evil plot perpetrated by environmental extremists.

If the sceptics are to be believed, the evidence for global warming is full of holes and the field is riven with argument and uncertainty. The apparent scientific consensus over global warming only exists, they say, because it is enforced by a scientific establishment riding the gravy train, aided and abetted by governments keen to play the politics of fear. It's easy to dismiss such claims as politically motivated and with no basis in fact—especially as the majority of sceptics are economists, business people or politicians, not scientists. (see "Meet the sceptics," page 40.) But there are nagging doubts. Could the sceptics be onto something? Are we, after all, being taken for a ride?

This is perhaps the most crucial scientific question of the 21st century. The winning side in the climate debate will shape economic, political and technological developments for years, even centuries, to come. With so much at stake, it is crucial that the right side wins. But which side is right? What is the evidence that human activity is warming the world, and how reliable is it?

5　First, the basic physics. It is beyond doubt that certain gases in the atmosphere, most importantly water vapour and carbon dioxide, trap infrared radiation emitted by the Earth's surface and so have a greenhouse effect. This in itself is no bad thing. Indeed, without them the planet would freeze. There is also no doubt that human activity is pumping CO_2 into the atmosphere, and that this has caused a sustained year-on-year rise in CO_2 concentrations. For almost 60 years, measurements at the Mauna Loa observatory in Hawaii have charted this rise, and it is largely uncontested that today's concentrations are about 35 per cent above preindustrial levels.

The effect this has on the planet is also measurable. In 2000, researchers based at Imperial College London examined satellite data covering almost three decades to plot changes in the amount of infrared radiation escaping from the atmosphere into space an indirect measure of how much heat is being trapped. In the part of the infrared spectrum trapped by CO_2—wavelengths between 13 and 19 micrometres—they found that between 1970 and 1997 less and less radiation was escaping. They concluded that the increasing quantity of atmospheric CO_2 was trapping energy that used to escape, and storing it in the atmosphere as heat. The results for the other greenhouse gases were similar.

These uncontested facts are enough to establish that "anthropogenic" greenhouse gas emissions are tending to make the atmosphere warmer. What's more, there is little doubt that the climate is changing right now. Temperature records from around the world going back 150 years suggest that 19 of the 20 warmest years—measured in terms of average global temperature, which takes account of all available thermometer data—have occurred since 1980, and that four of these occurred in the past seven years.

The only serious question mark over this record is the possibility that measurements have been biased by the growth of cities near the sites where temperatures are measured, as cities retain more heat than rural areas. But some new research suggests there is no such bias. David Parker of the UK's Met Office divided the historical temperature data into two sets: one taken in calm weather and the other in windy weather. He reasoned that any effect due to nearby cities would be more pronounced in calm conditions, when the wind could not disperse the heat. There was no difference.

It is at this point, however, that uncertainty starts to creep in. Take the grand claim made by some climate researchers that the 1990s were the warmest decade in the warmest century of the past millennium. This claim is embodied in the famous "hockey stick" curve, produced by Michael Mann of the University of Virginia in 1998, based on "proxy" records of past temperature, such as air bubbles in ice cores and growth rings in tree and coral. Sceptics have attacked the findings over poor methodology used, and their criticism has been confirmed by climate modellers, who have recently recognised that such proxy studies systematically underestimate past variability. As one Met Office scientist put it: "We cannot make claims as to the 1990s being the warmest decade."

There is also room for uncertainty in inferences drawn from the rise 10 in temperature over the past 150 years. The warming itself is real enough, but that doesn't necessarily mean that human activity is to blame. Sceptics say that the warming could be natural, and again they have a point. It is now recognised that up to 40 per cent of the climatic variation since 1890 is probably due to two natural phenomena. The first is solar cycles, which influence the amount of radiation reaching the Earth, and some scientists have argued that increased solar activity can account for most of the warming of the past 150 years. The second is the changing frequency of volcanic eruptions, which produce airborne particles that can shade and hence cool the planet for a year or more. This does not mean, however, that the sceptics can claim victory, as no known natural effects can explain the 0.5°C warming seen in the past 30 years. In fact, natural changes alone would have caused a marginal global cooling.

How hot will it get?

In the face of such evidence, the vast majority of scientists, even sceptical ones, now agree that our activities are making the planet warmer, and that we can expect more warming as we release more CO_2 into the atmosphere. This leaves two critical questions. How much

CHAPTER 9 FOCUS 1

warming can we expect? And how much should we care about it? Here the uncertainties begin in earnest.

The concentration of CO_2 in the atmosphere now stands at around 375 parts per million. A doubling of CO_2 from pre-industrial levels of 280 parts per million, which could happen as early as 2050, will add only about 1°C to average global temperatures, other things being equal. But if there's one thing we can count on, it is that other things will not be equal; some important things will change.

All experts agree that the planet is likely to respond in a variety of ways, some of which will dampen down the warming (negative feedback) while others will amplify it (positive feedback). Assessing the impacts of these feedbacks has been a central task of the UN's Intergovernmental Panel on Climate Change [IPCC], a co-operative agency set up 17 years ago that has harnessed the work of thousands of scientists. Having spent countless hours of supercomputer time creating and refining models to simulate the planet's climate system, the IPCC concludes that the feedbacks will be overwhelmingly positive. The only question, it says, is just how big this positive feedback will be.

15   The latest IPCC assessment is that doubling CO_2 levels will warm the world by anything from 1.4 to 5.8°C. In other words, this predicts a rise in global temperature from pre-industrial levels of around 14.8°C to between 16.2 and 20.6°C. Even at the low end, this is probably the biggest fluctuation in temperature that has occurred in the history of human civilisation. But uncertainties within the IPCC models remain, and the sceptics charge that they are so great that this conclusion is not worth the paper it is written on. So what are the positive feedbacks and how much uncertainty surrounds them?

Melting of polar ice is almost certainly one. Where the ice melts, the new, darker surface absorbs more heat from the sun, and so warms the planet. This is already happening. The second major source of positive feedback is water vapour. As this is responsible for a bigger slice of today's greenhouse effect than any other gas, including CO_2, any change in the amount of moisture in the atmosphere is critical. A warmer world will evaporate more water from the oceans, giving an extra push to warming. But there is a complication. Some of the water vapour will turn to cloud, and the net effect of cloudier skies on heat coming in and going out is far from clear. Clouds reflect energy from the sun back into space, but they also trap heat radiated from the surface, especially at night. Whether warming or cooling predominates depends on the type and height of clouds. The IPCC calculates that the combined effect of extra water vapour and clouds will increase warming, but accepts that clouds are the biggest source of uncertainty in the models.

Sceptics who pounce on such uncertainties should remember, however, that they cut both ways. Indeed, new research based on thousands of different climate simulation models run using the spare computing capacity of idling PCs, suggest that doubling CO_2 levels could increase temperatures by as much as 11°C (*Nature,* vol 434, p 403).

Recent analysis suggests that clouds could have a more powerful warming effect than once thought—possibly much more powerful (*New Scientist,* 24 July 2004, p 44). And there could be other surprise positive feedbacks that do not yet feature in the climate models. For instance, a release of some of the huge quantities of methane, a potent greenhouse gas, that are frozen into the Siberian permafrost and the ocean floor could have a catastrophic warming effect. And an end to ice formation in the Arctic could upset ocean currents and even shut down the Gulf Stream the starting point for the blockbuster movie *The Day After Tomorrow.*

There are counterbalancing negative feedbacks, some of which are already in the models. These include the ability of the oceans to absorb heat from the atmosphere, and of some pollutants—such as the sulphate particles that make acid rain—to shade the planet. But both are double-edged. The models predict that the ocean's ability to absorb heat will decline as the surface warms, as mixing between less dense, warm surface waters and the denser cold depths becomes more difficult. Meanwhile, sulphate and other aerosols could already be masking far stronger underlying warming effects than are apparent from measured temperatures. Aerosols last only a few weeks in the atmosphere, while greenhouse gases last for decades. So efforts to cut pollution by using technologies such as scrubbers to remove sulphur dioxide from power station stacks could trigger a surge in temperatures.

Sceptics also like to point out that most models do not yet include [20] negative feedback from vegetation, which is already growing faster in a warmer world, and soaking up more CO_2. But here they may be onto a loser, as the few climate models so far to include plants show that continued climate change is likely to damage their ability to absorb CO_2, potentially turning a negative feedback into a positive one.

Achilles' heel?

More credible is the suggestion that some other important negative feedbacks have been left out. One prominent sceptic, meteorologist Richard Lindzen of the Massachusetts Institute of Technology, has made an interesting case that warming may dry out the upper levels of the innermost atmospheric layer, the troposphere, and less water means a weaker greenhouse effect. Lindzen, who is one of the few sceptics with a research track record that most climate scientists respect, says this drying effect could negate all the positive feedbacks and bring the warming effect of a doubling of CO_2 levels back to 1°C. While there is little data to back up his idea, some studies suggest that these outer reaches are not as warm as IPCC models predict. This could be a mere wrinkle in the models or something more important. But if catastrophists have an Achilles' heel, this could be it.

Where does this leave us? Actually, with a surprising degree of consensus about the basic science of global warming—at least among scientists. As science historian Naomi Oreskes of the University of California, San Diego, wrote in *Science* late last year (vol 306, p 1686): "Politicians, economists, journalists and others may have the impression of confusion, disagreement or discord among climate scientists, but that impression is incorrect."

Her review of all 928 peer-reviewed papers on climate change published between 1993 and 2003 showed the consensus to be real and near universal. Even sceptical scientists now accept that we can expect some warming. They differ from the rest only in that they believe most climate models overestimate the positive feedback and underestimate the negative, and they predict that warming will be at the bottom end of the IPCC's scale.

25　For the true hard-liners, of course, the scientific consensus must, by definition, be wrong. As far as they are concerned the thousands of scientists behind the IPCC models have either been seduced by their own doom-laden narrative or are engaged in a gigantic conspiracy. They say we are faced with what the philosopher of science Thomas Kuhn called a "paradigm problem."

"Most scientists spend their lives working to shore up the reigning world view—the dominant paradigm—and those who disagree are always much fewer in number," says climatologist Patrick Michaels of the University of Virginia in Charlottesville, a leading proponent of this view. The drive to conformity is accentuated by peer review, which ensures that only papers in support of the paradigm appear in the literature, Michaels says, and by public funding that gives money to research into the prevailing "paradigm of doom." Rebels who challenge prevailing orthodoxies are often proved right, he adds.

But even if you accept this sceptical view of how science is done, it doesn't mean the orthodoxy is always wrong. We know for sure that human activity is influencing the global environment, even if we don't know by how much. We might still get away with it: the sceptics could be right, and the majority of the world's climate scientists wrong. It would be a lucky break. But how lucky do you feel?

Responding to Reading

1. What are the "uncontested facts" that establish that "greenhouse gas emissions are tending to make the atmosphere warmer" (7)? According to Pearce, what uncertainties are there in the inferences drawn from the increase in the earth's temperature over the last 150 years?

2. What do the vast majority of scientists believe about global warming? According to Pearce, what arguments do skeptics put forth against global warming? How effectively does Pearce counter these arguments?

3. What does Pearce conclude about global warming? Does his conclusion seem reasonable? Balanced? Tentative? Forced?

Responding in Writing

In paragraph 3, Pearce asks, "Could the skeptics be onto something? Are we, after all, being taken for a ride?" Does he answer these questions?

THE FALSE ALERT OF GLOBAL WARMING

Tom Bethell

Senior editor at the American Spectator *and visiting media fellow at the Hoover Institution, Tom Bethell has published numerous articles in magazines such as the* New York Times Magazine, *the* Atlantic, *and* Fortune. *He has also written five books, most recently* The Politically Incorrect Guide to Science *(2005). In the following essay, Bethell examines what he considers to be flawed arguments in support of global warming.*

Global warming became the environmentalists' *cause célèbre* in the late 1980s. They had turned on a dime, for only a few years earlier global cooling had been their mantra. They didn't know what had caused that earlier "cooling trend," but its effects were sure to be bad. "The drop in food output could begin quite soon, perhaps only in ten years," *Newsweek* reported in 1975. "The resulting famines could be catastrophic."

Now warming is the specter, with its melting glaciers, inundated cities, and the Gulf Stream reversing course. But I doubt if the enviros can keep on fomenting the scare much longer. It has been based on little more than extrapolated temperatures and spurious charts. What are the facts? Surface temperature measurements show a global warming period from about 1910 to 1940, followed by a cooling period until 1975. Since then we have experienced a slight warming trend. These three periods add up to a surface-temperature increase of perhaps one-degree Fahrenheit for the entire 20th century.

Satellite measurements of *atmospheric* temperatures do not agree, however. They began only in 1979, and have shown no significant increase over the last quarter century. Balloon readings did show an abrupt, one-time increase in 1976–1977. Since then, those temperatures have stabilized.

Environmentalists believe that the 20th-century warming was caused by human activity, primarily the burning of fossil fuels. That produces carbon dioxide—one of several "greenhouse gases." The argument is that their release into the atmosphere wraps the Earth in an invisible shroud. This makes the escape of heat into outer space slightly more difficult than its initial absorption from sunlight. This is the Greenhouse Effect. So the Earth warms up.

5   But whether *man-made* carbon-dioxide emissions have caused measurable temperature increases over the last 30 years is debated. Carbon dioxide is itself a benign and essential substance, incidentally. Without it, plants would not grow, and without plant-life animals could not live. Any increase of carbon dioxide in the atmosphere causes plants, trees, and forests to grow more abundantly. It should be a tree-hugger's delight.

The surface data suggest that man-made carbon dioxide has not in fact increased global temperatures. From 1940 to 1975, coal-fired plants emitted fumes with great abandon and without restraint by Greens. Yet the Earth cooled slightly in that time. And if man-made global warming is real, atmospheric as well as surface temperatures should have increased steadily. But they haven't. There was merely that one-time increase, possibly caused by a solar anomaly. In addition, an "urban heat island effect" has been identified. Build a tarmac runway near a weather station, and the nearby temperature readings will go up.

Global warming became the focus of activism at the time of the Earth Summit in Rio, in 1992. Bush the elder signed a climate-change treaty, with signatories agreeing to reduce carbon dioxide emissions below 1990 levels. The details were worked out in Kyoto, Japan. But America was the principal target, everyone knew it, and Clinton didn't submit the treaty to the Senate for ratification. The 1990 date had been carefully chosen. Emissions in Germany and the Soviet Union were still high; Germany had just absorbed East Germany, then still using inefficient coal-fired plants. After they were modernized, Germany's emissions dropped, so the demand that they be reduced below 1990 levels had already been met and became an exercise in painless moralizing.

The same was true for the Soviet Union. After its collapse, in 1991, economic activity fell by about one-third. As for France, most of its electricity comes from nuclear power, which has no global-warming effects but has been demonized for other reasons. If the enviros were serious about reducing carbon dioxide they would be urging us to build nuclear power plants, but that is not on their agenda. They want windmills (whether or not they kill golden eagles).

Under the Kyoto Protocol, U.S. emissions would have to be cut so much that economic depression would have been the only certain outcome. We were expected to reduce energy use by about 35 percent within ten years, which might have meant eliminating one-third of all cars. You can see why the enviros fell in love with the idea.

10   Third World countries are exempt, as are China and India. Australia, like the U.S., has refused to ratify. Thirty-five countries, mostly in Europe,

have agreed to reduce emissions. But there are no enforcement mechanisms, the potential for cheating is unlimited, and the principal irritation today is that the main enemy, the United States, slipped the noose.

Any unusual event is now likely to be linked to climate change. Within 24 hours of the tsunami in December, the CBS evening news displayed a graphic that had only the words "global warming" and "tsunamis." Citing unnamed "climate experts," Dan Rather intoned:

> Climate experts warned today that tsunamis could become more common around the world and more dangerous. They cite a number of factors, including a creeping rise in sea levels believed to come from global warming and growing populations along coastal areas.

The claim that the globe is warming depends on knowing earlier temperatures. Such information can only be obtained indirectly. Climate scientists depend on tree rings, bore holes, ice cores, the skeletons of marine organisms. The graph that was most effective in persuading policy-makers became known as the hockey stick. The temperature line is mostly horizontal, perhaps declining slightly for 900 years, then abruptly heading up into a warmer range over the last 100 years. The 900 years are the handle, the last hundred are the blade.

The "Hockey Stick" was first published in 1998 by the climatologist Michael Mann of the University of Virginia, and co-authors. It was immediately used by the United Nations to promote the idea that we have an unprecedented crisis on our hands. But the chart also aroused suspicions, because for years there had been a broad agreement among climatologists that global temperatures had not been as unvarying as the chart implied. There had been something called the Medieval Warm Period, which persisted until the "Little Ice Age" took hold in the 14th and 15th centuries. Both periods lasted for several hundred years.

The warmer period, accompanied by a flowering of prosperity, knowledge, and art in Europe, seems to have been wholly beneficial. Agricultural yields increased, marshes and swamps—today called wetlands—dried up, removing the breeding grounds of malaria-spreading mosquitoes. Infant mortality fell, the population grew. Greenland was settled by the Vikings, who reached a peak of prosperity in the 12th and 13th centuries. They began declining in the late 14th century, with the colder weather. Then the settlements perished.

The warm period has been recognized in the climate textbooks for 15 decades, and it was an obvious embarrassment to those claiming that the 20th-century warming was a true anomaly. Also, the earlier changes occurred when fossil-fuel consumption could hardly have been the culprit. They would prove that warming could occur without human intervention.

Consider, in this context, the experience of David Deming with the University of Oklahoma's College of Geosciences. In 1995, he published

CHAPTER 9 FOCUS 1

a paper in the journal *Science,* reviewing the evidence showing that bore hole data showed a warming of about one degree Celsius in North America over the last 100 to 150 years. Deming continues:

> With the publication of the article in *Science,* I gained significant credibility in the community of scientists working on climate change. They thought I was one of them, someone who would pervert science in the service of social and political causes. So one of them let his guard down. A major person working in the area of climate change and global warming sent me an astonishing email that said, "We have to get rid of the Medieval Warm Period."

Whether intentionally or not, that is exactly what Mann's "hockey stick" did.

Once doomsayers convince us that we are experiencing something new, they feel free to claim that we face a catastrophe. They can extrapolate from the minor and beneficial warming that we may (or may not) have experienced in the last generation and argue that temperatures will keep on rising until the ice caps melt and cities flood.

Then the hockey stick was challenged by a Toronto minerals consultant named Stephen McIntyre, who, remarkably, had no credentials as a climatologist. He spent two years and $5,000 of his own money trying to uncover Mann's methods. Mann at first did give him some information, but then cut him off saying he didn't have time to respond to "every frivolous note" from nonscientists. McIntyre was joined by another Canadian, and in 2003 they published a critical article. Mann had "used flawed methods that yield meaningless results."

20   In a rebuttal, Mann revealed new information that had not appeared in his original paper. It had been published in the British journal *Nature,* which later published a correction. McIntyre thinks there may be more errors but still doesn't know how the graph was generated. Mann has refused to release his secret formula. A *Wall Street Journal* reporter doggedly pursued the matter and contacted Mann. He told the reporter: "Giving them the algorithm would be giving in to the intimidation tactics that these people are engaged in."

Michael Mann now concedes it is plausible that past temperature variations may have been larger than thought. Fred Singer, a leading critic of warming scares and founder of the Science and Environmental Policy Project, says that "the hockey stick is dead." He was recently nominated by warmists to receive the First Annual Flat Earth Award for being "the year's most prominent global warming denier." Nominated along with him were Rush Limbaugh and Michael Crichton, the thriller writer.

In his recent book *State of Fear,* Crichton unexpectedly emerged as a powerful critic of modish conclusions about global warming. He studied the subject for a couple of years before writing his recent book, to which he added an appendix comparing global-warming science to eugenics. Earlier, in a speech at Caltech, he had compared it to the search for extraterrestrials (which he says is based on bogus science). There may have been some warming as a part of a natural trend, Crichton allows. But "no one knows how much of the present trend might be natural or how much man-made."

"Open and frank discussion" of global warming is being suppressed, he believes. One indication is that "so many of the outspoken critics of global warming are retired professors." They can speak freely because they are no longer seeking grants or facing colleagues "whose grant applications and career advancement may be jeopardized by their criticisms."

Environmentalists have become adept at de-legitimizing their opponents by saying they are "supported by industry," but studies funded by environmentalist organizations are "every bit as biased," Crichton added. They have become a special interest like any other, with legislative goals and millions spent on lobbying.

Myron Ebell, who works for the Competitive Enterprise Institute 25 (CEI) in Washington, D.C., one of the few groups that examines global-warming claims skeptically, says that environmentalism is now a $1.5 billion industry. In Washington, skeptics (like himself) are outnumbered by global warming advocates perhaps by a margin of 300 to one. Yet CEI, greatly underfunded by comparison with groups like the Sierra Club, tends to be characterized in the media as "industry supported." The enviros' problem is that they have "everything going for them except the facts," Ebell says.

Some environmentalists have begun to echo the complaint that they are a special interest. A few months ago, Michael Shellenberger and Ted Norhaus wrote a widely circulated 14,000-word essay called "The Death of Environmentalism." It "provoked a civil war among tree huggers," Nicholas D. Kristof wrote in the *New York Times*. In effect, it was a cry of anguish: Why have we been unable to win on our top issues, especially global warming? They called it "the world's most serious ecological crisis," which "may kill hundreds of millions of human beings over the next century." They looked back to their golden age in the 1970s—the time when they began "using science to define the problem as 'environmental.' "

"Using science" is what they were doing, all right, and the rest of us were blinded by it, for about 25 years. But the problem wasn't that the use of science had led them to propose unattractive "technical fixes," when they should have been appealing to something larger in the human spirit. The problem was that their science was never very good to begin with. And as its inadequacies became more apparent, their scare tactics became more apparent, too.

To keep the money rolling in, environmentalists always need a crisis. It looks as though they will have to cook up a new one.

Responding to Reading

1. Global warming became the focus of environmentalists in the late 1980s. According to Bethell, what motivates of the environmentalists? Why does he think the United States has refused to ratify the Kyoto Protocol? Does Bethell agree or disagree with this decision?
2. How does the "Little Ice Age" undercut arguments in support of global warming? What is the "Hockey Stick"? According to Bethell, what is wrong with this model of global warming?
3. Bethell uses the opinions of the novelist Michael Crichton to support his argument. Is this a good idea? What are the advantages and disadvantages of this strategy?

Responding in Writing

Bethell uses terms like *enviros* and *tree huggers* to describe environmentalists. How does his use of such terms affect the tone of his essay? Do they strengthen or weaken his argument?

——— Focus ———

Can the Energy Crisis Be Solved?

A row of wind turbines stands on a slope on an empty plain.

Responding to the Image

1. Wind turbines, such as the ones pictured above, are a clean source of electricity. Do these turbines seem to fit into the environment, or do they seem alien to it? What elements in the photograph lead you to your conclusion?
2. Does the photograph seem comforting or disquieting? Do you think the photographer has a neutral view of his subject, or does he seem to be trying to make a point?

OVER A BARREL

Paul Roberts

1955–

A novelist and essayist who focuses on various political, religious, and environmental issues, Paul Roberts has written numerous articles for Harper's, *the* Washington Post, *and other publications. He has also written seven books, most recently* The End of Oil: On the Edge of a Perilous New World *(2004). In the following essay, Roberts proposes ways to avert a potentially devastating energy crisis.*

It's eight o'clock on a fresh summer morning in Denver, and I'm at a podium before a hundred executives from regional energy companies. Having spent the last few years closely observing trends in the oil industry, I'm often asked to speak about the decline of global energy supplies, the way oil has corrupted U.S. foreign policy, and why the worldwide energy economy needs a radical transformation if we want to avoid catastrophic climate change. Yet while these themes play well to liberal audiences in Boulder and Berkeley, I worry my reception here will be much cooler. Most of these weather-beaten men (and a few women) spend their days squeezing hydrocarbons from the sand and stone beneath the Rockies; if my past observations of the energy industry are any guide, they voted for Bush, support the Iraq war, think climate change is a leftist hoax, and believe the main cause of America's energy crisis is that overzealous regulation keeps drillers like themselves from tapping the most promising reserves of oil and natural gas.

But as I finish my spiel and take questions, my initial assumptions vanish. When I suggest that the Iraq war might not have been motivated *entirely* by America's thirst for oil, many in the room openly smirk, as if I've just suggested that the world is flat. Likewise, few here seem to share the White House's Panglossian view that the United States is sitting atop some massive, but politically off-limits, reserve of natural gas. In fact, as much as these executives would love to sink their drills anywhere they want—and as much as they detest environmentalists for stopping them—no one here believes the volume of natural gas yet to be discovered in the Rockies, or anywhere else in America, would reverse the nation's decline of gas production or let the United States move to a cleaner, more secure "gas" economy. As one executive tells me, "even if all the off-limits land were opened for drilling, all the new gas we could bring on-line wouldn't be enough to replace all the production we're losing from older fields. We'd barely keep production flat."

For those who wonder where the world will be getting its energy a decade from now, confessions like these only confirm what many have feared for some time: namely, that the cheap, "easy" oil and natural gas that powered industrial growth for a century no longer exist in such easy abundance; and that we may have a lot less time than we thought to replace that system with something cleaner, more sustainable, and far less vulnerable to political upheaval.

The evidence is certainly piling up. Pollution levels from cars and power plants are on the rise. Climate change, another energy-related disaster, has begun impacting crop yields and water supplies and may soon provoke political strife. In fact, according to a Pentagon report last October, global warming could make key resources so scarce, and nations so desperate, that "disruption and conflict will be endemic" and "warfare would define human life."

Yet the most alarming symptoms of an energy system on the verge of collapse are found in the oil markets. Today, even as global demand for oil, led by the economic boom in Asia, is rising far faster than anticipated, our ability to pump more oil is falling. Despite assurances from oil's two biggest players—the House of Bush and the House of Saud—that supplies are plentiful (and, as George W. Bush famously put it, that getting the oil is just a matter of "jaw-boning" "our friends in OPEC to open the spigots"), it's now clear that even the Saudis lack the physical capacity to bring enough oil to desperate consumers. As a result, oil markets are now so tight that even a minor disturbance—accelerated fighting in Iraq, another bomb in Riyadh, more unrest in Venezuela or Nigeria—could send prices soaring and crash the global economy into a recession. "The world really has run out of production capacity," a veteran oil analyst warned me in late August. "Iraq is producing less than a third of the oil that had been forecast, the Saudis are maxed out, and there is no place else to go. And America is still relying on an energy policy that hasn't changed significantly in 20 years."

Nor is it any longer a matter of simply drilling new wells or laying new pipe. Oil is finite, and eventually, global production must peak, much as happened to domestic supplies in the early 1970s. When it does, oil prices will leap, perhaps as high as $100 per barrel—a disaster if we don't have a cost-effective alternative fuel or technology in place. When the peak is coming is impossible to predict with precision. Estimates range from the ultra-optimistic, which foresee a peak no sooner than 2035, to the pessimistic, which hold that the peak may have already occurred. In any case, the signs are clear that the easy oil is harder to find and what remains is increasingly difficult and expensive to extract. Already, Western oil companies are struggling to discover new supplies fast enough to replace the oil they are selling. (Royal/Dutch Shell was so concerned about how declining discovery rates would devastate its stock price that it inflated its reserves figures by 20 percent.)

Worse, according to a new study in the respected *Petroleum Review,* in the United Kingdom, Indonesia, Gabon, and 15 other oil-rich nations that now supply 30 percent of the world's daily crude, oil production—that is, the number of barrels that are pumped each day—is declining by 5 percent a year. That's double the rate of decline of even a year ago, and it has forced other oil producers to pump extra simply to keep global supplies steady. "Those producers still with expansion potential are having to work harder and harder just to make up for the accelerating losses of the large number that have clearly peaked and are now in continuous decline," writes Chris Skrebowski, editor of *Petroleum Review* and a former analyst with BP and the Saudi national oil company. "Though largely unrecognized, [depletion] may be contributing to the rise in oil prices."

If there is one positive sign, it's that the high prices seem to have finally broken through America's wall of energy denial. In fact, while energy experts like Skrebowski have been fretting about oil dependency and depleting reserves since the 1970s, today's energy anxiety is no longer coming simply from academia or the political margins. In recent months, energy problems have come under intense focus by the mainstream media, filling radio and TV talk shows and newsmagazines. Whereas official U.S. policy still blames OPEC for our oil woes, even right-of-center, pro-business outlets like *Business Week, The Economist,* and *Fortune* have acceded that the biggest risk for U.S. energy security isn't "foreign" producers or even environmentalists, but rather a

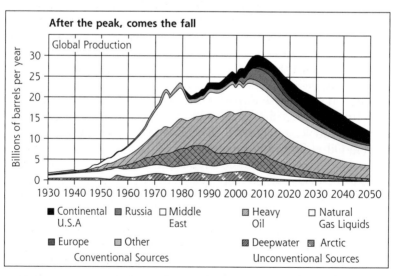

When conventional oil production peaks—this chart presents a 2005 scenario—nations will increasingly turn to much more difficult-to-extract sources, such as reserves found under the Arctic ice caps or far out to sea, heavy oil distilled from sand tar, or natural gas liquids such as butane. But eventually, these sources, too, will peter out

decades-old domestic energy policy that remains focused almost entirely on finding new supplies while doing nothing to curb demand. "Much as we might like to, we can't blame it on OPEC," noted *Fortune* in August. "After all, Americans have been on a two-decade oil pig-out, gorging like oversized vacationers at a Vegas buffet."

What's more, while a powerful, ideologically driven minority— led, sadly, by the Bush administration—continues to insist that energy security is simply a question of drilling in the Arctic National Wildlife Refuge (ANWR) or browbeating OPEC, outside the White House, and certainly outside the Beltway, there's a growing push to build a fundamentally new energy system. Thus, while the Bush administration dithered on climate change and the future of energy, individual states, like California and New York, enacted their own alternative energy policies and even sued utilities over carbon dioxide emissions. The corporate world, once a stalwart opponent of any policy reform, has become startlingly progressive. Toyota and Honda are busily rolling out hybrid cars. Agriculture and insurance firms warn of the future costs of oil-price swings and climate change. And energy companies like BP and Shell, eager to profit in the new energy order, are developing new fuels and technologies to help reduce oil use and emissions.

And if most U.S. consumers still share the administration's energy 10 obliviousness (U.S. gasoline consumption continues to rise, despite high oil prices), some in Congress have become downright activist. Last year in the Senate, Republican John McCain and Democrat Joseph Lieberman came close to passing a climate policy far beyond anything the White House has countenanced. In fact, even some traditional oil-and-gas politicians appear to see the writing on the wall. For example, U.S. Senator Lisa Murkowski, a Republican from Alaska and still an ardent supporter of drilling for oil in ANWR, nonetheless concedes "this nation needs to do a far better job of energy conservation and needs to develop alternative energy technologies to wean us from fossil fuels."

Unfortunately, as encouraging as all this new energy awareness is, actually weaning the United States from fossil fuels is far easier said than done. To begin with, our current energy infrastructure—the pipelines and refineries, the power plants and grids, the gasoline stations, and, of course, the cars, trucks, planes, and ships—is a massive, sprawling asset that took more than a century to build and is worth some $1 trillion. Replacing that hydrocarbon monster with "clean" technologies and fuels before our current energy problems escalate into catastrophes will likely be the most complex and expensive challenge this country has ever faced.

And just as we've tended to underplay the flaws in our hydrocarbon energy system, we've also held far too rosy a notion of the various energy alternatives that are supposed to replace oil. In fact, to the extent that most politicians even discuss alternative energy, it tends to be in the rhetoric of American Can-Doism, a triumphant vision in which the same blend of technological prowess, entrepreneurial spirit, and market forces that helped us build an atom bomb, put a man on the moon, and produce the TV dinner and the microchip can now be counted on to yield a similar miracle in energy. Thus we find ourselves imagining a future powered by solar cells, bio-diesel, wind farms, tidal power, cold fusion, and, of course, hydrogen fuel cells, all currently being created in busy research labs and brought to us by a Free Market that is responding naturally, efficiently, and inexorably to the rising price of oil.

Yet the hard truth is that this hyper-optimistic dream is plagued by a variety of potentially killer flaws. First, many of these new technologies are nowhere near ready for prime time, and exist mainly in the conceptual stage, if that. Second, of the alternative fuels and gadgets that are technically viable today, many simply cannot compete with fossil fuels or existing technologies. Third, while the market is indeed a marvelous mechanism for bringing innovation to life, the modern economy doesn't even recognize that the current energy system needs replacing. You and I may know that hydrocarbons cost us dearly, in terms of smog, climate change, corruption, and instability, not to mention the billions spent defending the Middle East. But because these "external" costs aren't included in the price of a gallon of gasoline, the market sees no reason to find something other than oil, gas, or coal.

In late July 2004, financial analysts from across North America joined a conference call with Dennis Campbell, the embattled president of a shrinking Canadian company called Ballard Power Systems. Just a few years before, Ballard had been the toast of energy investors and the acknowledged leader in the campaign to move beyond oil. Its main product, a compact hydrogen fuel cell that could power a car, was widely hailed as the breakthrough that would smash the century-long reign of the gasoline-powered internal combustion engine. In early 2000, Ballard shares were trading for $120, allowing the company to raise a near-record $340.7 million in financing and touching off a wave of expectations that a fuel-cell revolution was imminent.

15   Since then, however, as fuel cells have been hobbled by technical problems, Ballard has seen its share value plummet to $8, as energy investors have all but abandoned hydrogen in favor of the latest energy darling, the gas-electric hybrid. During the conference call, Campbell insisted that hybrids were only a temporary fix, and that fuel cells remained the only long-term solution to problems like climate change and declining energy supplies. He was, however, forced to acknowledge that consumers and businesses alike were "discouraged by the long wait and the uncertain timelines" for fuel cells and had been "seduced by the lure of an easier solution to the energy and environmental challenges that we face."

In many respects, Ballard is the perfect cautionary tale for the entire roster of alternative fuels and energy technologies, which, for all their huge promise, are, upon closer inspection, plagued by problems. For example, many energy experts see natural gas as the most logical interim step in eventually weaning ourselves from oil. Natural gas emits less carbon dioxide and pollutants than does oil (and certainly coal); it can be used in everything from cars to power plants; it's also easily refined into hydrogen—all of which make it the perfect "bridge" fuel between the current oil-based economy and something new. But even as demand for gas grows in the United States, domestic production is in decline, meaning we'll have to import an increasing volume via pipelines from Canada or through liquefied natural gas terminals in port cities. Even assuming we overcome the political hurdles, simply building this costly new infrastructure will take years, and, once completed, will leave us dependent on many of the same countries that now control the oil business. (The biggest gas reserves are in the Middle East and Russia.)

Above all, gas doesn't solve the climate problem; it merely slows the rate at which we emit carbon dioxide. According to the United Nations Intergovernmental Panel on Climate Change, in order to cut CO_2 emissions fast enough to actually prevent catastrophic warming, we eventually need to produce most of our energy with carbon-free technology. And we're a long way from "most." Today, hydrocarbons own the energy market—40 percent of our energy comes from oil, 23 percent each from gas and coal. Nuclear provides around 8 percent, while renewable, carbon-free energy accounts for barely 5 percent of our total energy supply. Of that "good" energy, nearly 90 percent comes from hydroelectric dams, which are so expensive and environmentally nasty that their future role is extremely limited. The rest comes mainly from "biomass," usually plants and crop waste that are either refined into fuels, like ethanol, or burned to make steam.

And what about solar and wind? As it turns out, the two most famous alternative energy technologies together generate less than half a percent of the planet's energy. Here's a depressing fact: The entire output of every solar photovoltaic (PV) cell currently installed worldwide—about 2,000 megawatts total—is less than the output of just two conventional, coal-fired power plants.

Why do alternatives own such a puny share of the market? According to conventional wisdom, Big Oil and Big Coal use their massive economic power to corrupt Big Government, which then hands out massive subsidies and tax breaks for oil and coal, giving hydrocarbons an unbeatable advantage over alternatives. In truth, much of the fault lies with the new energy technologies themselves, which simply cannot yet compete effectively with fossil fuels.

Consider the saga of the solar cell. Despite decades of research and 20 development, solar power still costs more than electricity generated from a gas- or coal-fired power plant. And although PV cell costs will continue to fall, there remains the problem of "intermittency"—solar only works when the sun is shining, whereas a conventional power plant can crank out power 24 hours a day, 365 days a year. (Wind presents a similar problem.) To use solar and wind, utilities must have backup power, probably coal- or gas-fired plants.

Eventually, utilities will solve the intermittency problem—probably with superfast "smart" power grids that can connect wind or solar farms built across the nation, or even the hemisphere, effectively getting power from wherever the sun is shining or the wind is blowing and delivering it to customers. But the very scale of this solution illustrates an even more serious weakness for wind and other renewables: They lack the "power density" of the fossil fuels they seek to replace. Coal, for example, packs a great deal of stored energy in a relatively small volume. As a result, a coal-fired plant requires only a few hundred acres of space, yet can supply electricity for 200,000 homes. By contrast, to generate equal power from wind, which is far less power-dense, you'd need a wind farm of more than 200 square miles in size. Given that by 2030, almost 60 percent of the global population is expected to live in cities of 1 million or more, meeting our power needs with wind, solar, or other renewables will be challenging indeed. "Supplying those buildings from locally generated renewable energies is either impractical or impossible," says Vaclav Smil, an expert in energy economics at the University of Manitoba. The "power-density mismatch is simply too large."

The most dramatic example of the mismatch between fossil fuels and their would-be competitors, however, can be found in the fuel cell. For decades, hydrogen proponents have argued that fuel cells, which turn hydrogen and oxygen into electricity while emitting only water vapor, are the key to the next energy economy. Like a battery that never needs charging, fuel cells can power office buildings, laptops, and especially cars, where they are roughly three times as efficient as a traditional internal combustion engine. And because you can make hydrogen by running electric current through water, advocates envisioned a global system in which power from solar, wind, and other renewables would be turned into hydrogen.

This compelling vision helps explain why the "hydrogen economy" was so touted during the 1990s, and why companies like Ballard Power Systems could partner with giants like Daimler-Chrysler and Ford, igniting a fuel-cell mania that dazzled investors and policymakers alike. Indeed, in his 2003 State of the Union address, President Bush vowed that, within 20 years, fuel cells would "make our air significantly cleaner, and our country much less dependent on foreign sources of oil."

In truth, even as the president was promising better living through hydrogen, the reality of a hydrogen economy was moving farther and farther away. While the basic technology remains promising, making hydrogen turns out to be far more difficult than advertised. The easiest and by far cheapest method—splitting natural gas into carbon and hydrogen—is hampered by domestic shortages of natural gas. And while it is possible to extract hydrogen from water using renewably generated electricity, that concept suffers from the power-density problem. Studies by Jim MacKenzie, a veteran energy analyst with the World Resources Institute, show that a solar-powered hydrogen economy in the United States would require at least 160,000 square miles of photovoltaic panels—an area slightly larger than the state of California—and would increase national water consumption by 10 percent. "We could do it," MacKenzie told me last year. "But it would be expensive."

But hydrogen's biggest problem is the fuel cell itself, which, despite decades of research, is still too expensive and unreliable to compete with the internal combustion engine. As of last year, the best fuel cells were still 10 times as costly as an equivalently powered gasoline engine. Hydrogen advocates argue that once fuel cells can be mass-produced, costs will drop dramatically. Yet while that's true, it's also true that gasoline engines will also improve over time—in fact, they already have. With the gasoline-electric hybrid, for example, the internal combustion engine has, in a stroke, doubled its fuel economy and halved its emissions—but without forcing consumers to use a complicated new technology or fuel. Barring some technological breakthrough that dramatically lowers costs or improves performance, the fuel cell may remain one step behind the gasoline engine for a long time, further delaying the moment it can begin displacing its hydrocarbon rival.

This, then, is the central dilemma facing the architects of the next energy economy. Left to themselves, markets will indeed move us to new energy technologies, but these technologies may not be the ones we ultimately want or need. For example, while the hybrid does cut emissions and fuel use, as Ballard's Campbell testily points out, hybrids "still require fossil fuel" and thus can only be an interim solution. To be sure, interim solutions are essential, but if we concentrate only on half-measures, long-term technologies may not become economically viable fast enough to stave off an implosion of our energy system—be it from runaway climate change in 2015 or the collapse of the Saudi government in 2005.

Thus a true energy revolution—one that begins moving away from fossil fuels entirely—can't succeed or even get started until we can somehow induce the market to "see" the true costs of energy, and, specifically, just how environmentally and politically expensive "cheap" fossil fuels really are.

One approach would be to copy the European Union's "cap-and-trade" system, which sets a cap on how much CO_2 companies can emit, but allows firms that cut emissions faster to sell their carbon "credits"

25

CHAPTER 9 FOCUS 2

to companies that can't. As carbon becomes a cost to avoid, companies have a huge incentive to cut CO_2 emissions—first by burning hydrocarbons more efficiently, but eventually by developing technologies and fuels that are entirely carbon-free.

What the European experience suggests, however, is that even if the United States were to adopt a cap-and-trade regime (which the Bush administration has been in no hurry to do), the markets would still need help developing these new technologies—especially in the early, expensive stages of development. With massive public investment, new energy technologies could be advanced to the point that private companies were willing to take the risks and bring them to market. The fuel cell is an ideal candidate. Another is something called cellulosic ethanol, a bio-fuel that is almost as energy-dense as gasoline, but that burns more cleanly and can be refined into hydrogen. Unlike traditional, corn-brewed ethanol, which is so uneconomical that it requires permanent federal subsidies, cellulosic ethanol is made from a specially bred crop, known as switchgrass, that thrives on marginal lands, needs little water and no fertilizer, and is easily processed into fuel. "Once we have mature cellulosic ethanol technology," says Lee Lynd, a researcher at Dartmouth College and one of the top bio-fuels experts in the world, "we could reasonably expect the new fuel to cost no more than gasoline to produce." Under some scenarios, by 2025 up to one-fifth of all cars and light trucks could be running on cellulosic ethanol. The point, says Lynd, is that "if the world is looking for an alternative to gasoline, hydrogen is not the only candidate."

30   Of course, market-altering steps like these would require a phenomenal amount of political will, which thus far has been lacking. Despite expressing interest in a carbon-trading regime before 9/11, the Bush administration refused to push for such a system for fear it would alienate utilities and coal states. (When John Kerry said that he backed a carbon-trading regime, Bush's energy secretary, Spencer Abraham, thundered that such a plan "would likely devastate the coal sector.") Most energy experts say the U.S. government would need to spend on the order of $5-$10 billion a year for several decades to have any hope of boosting promising new energy technologies into viability. (For comparison, last year the government spent roughly $900 million on research into renewables, hydrogen, and efficiency—chump change compared with the billions the U.S. has spent in research on fossil fuels and especially nuclear energy.)

Still, as the price of oil and natural gas has skyrocketed, and as the risks of continued reliance on producers like Iraq and Russia have become more obvious, some energy advocates have begun to quietly wonder whether the political currents might begin to run the other way. According to David Portalatin, an auto industry analyst with the NPD Group, a sizable number of consumers have reported that they would definitely buy a more fuel-efficient car or begin taking mass transit if gas prices stayed high for at least 12 months. Portalatin sees this as a significant change in attitude. Whether and how soon we can expect consumers to take the next step—actually buying the hybrid—won't be clear until quarterly sales data are in. But Portalatin says that consumer anxiety is much higher than a year ago. "If prices remain high and if consumers follow through on what they told us, then, yes, we'll get there."

The danger, of course, is that the same economic currents that are pushing America into a new energy consciousness may themselves become too strong to control. High oil prices could indeed unlock the political logjam that has long blocked developments in alternative energy. Yet keep in mind that those high prices aren't benign; rather, they reflect an energy market that might be so close to a melt-down that no amount of research dollars, carbon policies, or energy consciousness will make much of a difference. Supply and demand are today so tightly balanced that even the smallest incident in an oil-producing country could send prices into the stratosphere, destroying economies and forcing big, oil-dependent nations like the United States and China to opt for emergency short-term fixes—fixes that aren't likely to involve methodical programs to improve automotive efficiency or develop cost-effective ethanol. Rather, once the United States finds itself in a real energy emergency, it will do what desperate states have always done when resources turn scarce: fight for them. In other words, the most pressing question may not be whether we have the right technologies, but whether we have enough time.

Responding to Reading

1. According to Roberts, we are running out of the inexpensive, easy-to-obtain oil and gas that have powered our industrial growth. What evidence does he present to support this conclusion? Is his evidence convincing?

2. What alternatives to our current energy sources does Roberts discuss? What does he mean when he says, "Replacing that hydrocarbon monster with 'clean' technologies and fuels before our current energy problems escalate into catastrophes will likely be the most complex and expensive challenge this country has ever faced" (11)?

3. Why does Roberts think that the free market will not be able to solve America's energy problems? What course of action does he suggest? Do you find his suggestions reasonable? Practical?

Responding in Writing

Do you think that the United States will be able to solve its energy problem before it becomes a crisis?

ENERGY'S FUTURE

Dennis Behreandt

Dennis Behreandt writes on political, environmental, and healthcare issues. In the following essay, written for The New American *magazine, Behreandt envisions an optimistic energy future for America.*

It's hard to escape the conclusion that America faces a new, and perhaps serious, energy crisis. Home heating costs have risen dramatically, the price of gasoline at the pump is rising rapidly, and the price of crude oil is on the increase. The rising cost of fuel will affect consumers of all goods, as the cost of bringing those goods to market will rise in concert with the rise in the cost of fuel.

At least for now, there does not appear to be any relief in sight, as demand for oil is expected to continue to grow. On March 11, the Paris-based International Energy Agency (IEA) announced its latest forecast for energy demand. The agency expects that global consumption of oil will climb this year to 84.3 million barrels per day, a 2.2 percent increase over the previous year.

Importantly, the world is not running out of oil. The current crisis stems not from the depletion of the Earth's oil resources, but from the inability of current infrastructure to support the increased demand. "The reality is that oil consumption has caught up with installed crude and refining capacity," the IEA said. "If supply continues to struggle to keep up, more policy attention may come to be directed at oil demand intensity in our economies and alternatives."

The IEA is partially correct: more effort is needed to develop energy technologies, whether that effort is within the fossil fuels industry or in advancements in alternative technologies. The answer, though, does not lie with "more policy attention" directed by governments at influencing market trends. In fact, government regulations are directly responsible for limiting our refinery capacity.

5   If left alone, the market demand for energy will spur competition to invest in new infrastructure and new technologies. The current energy environment, marked by strong demand, will result in increased spending on exploration for new energy sources and on new energy technologies. Similar "crises" in the past were alleviated through just this type of investment and innovation. If left unhampered by government, there is no telling what energy technologies will be achieved in the near future by innovators eager to supply the world's increasing appetite for energy.

--------------------- **TALES OF SHORTAGES PAST** ---------------------

In many ways, the current energy environment bears similarities with an era that seems far removed from our current technological age. In the late Renaissance and early modern period, Europe underwent a technological revolution in energy and productivity.

The early modern Europe that emerged from the Renaissance is often thought of in one of two distinct ways. For some, it is the era of the Reformation, when much thought and vitality went into constructing the theologies and denominations of Protestantism. For others, it was the age of exploration, when adventurers followed the path blazed by Columbus into the deep recesses of the Atlantic and then Pacific Oceans. It was also an era of great commercial expansion, and this commercial expansion was driven by energy.

Prior to this period, the primary motive energy source in Europe was muscle power, either human or animal. For heating and cooking, wood played a primary role. Later, following the Renaissance, Europe's commercial success continued to expand, and with it population expanded. Growth was sustained by energy. At sea, naval technology was increasingly able to harness the power of the wind, allowing European nations to engage in ever more vigorous trade with distant lands.

Within Europe itself, forests provided plenty of wood for domestic energy needs. But demand eventually began to outstrip the ability of the existing infrastructure to bring energy to market, and costs rose. "The agrarian regime . . . encountered inherent limits that it could not transcend without a fundamental transformation of its social metabolic basis," wrote German historian Rolf Peter Sieferle about energy availability in the 1700s. "These observations speak for the fact that in the 18th century the preindustrial . . . system stood at a threshold impeding the growth of important physical parameters (population size, material flow). The energy potential of the given area was in a sense exhausted."

The preindustrial energy system was heavily dependent on wood. 10 The rising demand for wood reduced the supply, causing prices to rise. "Pundits rang the alarm bells about the soaring cost of wood for heating and for the iron industry; the price of charcoal [made from wood] doubled in real terms between 1630 and 1700," writes business journalist Vijay V. Vaitheeswaran in his recent book *Power to the People*. The rise in prices spurred by the increased demand for energy led to the development of new and previously little-used energy sources. "Enticed by rising prices, entrepreneurs rose to the occasion," wrote Vaitheeswaran. "They found a way to bring to market a substance that had largely been overlooked until then: coal. That was a turning point in history, for without coal there would have been no industrial revolution."

THE RISE OF INDUSTRY

The industrial revolution may have seen the rise of all manner of innovation, but it was without doubt built on the back of King Coal, which replaced wood as the most dominant energy source. "Day by day it becomes more evident that the Coal we happily possess in excellent quality and abundance is the mainspring of modern material civilization." British economist William Stanley Jevons wrote in his book *The Coal Question*, published in 1865. "As the source of fire, it is the source at once of mechanical motion and of chemical change. Accordingly it is the chief agent in almost every improvement or discovery in the arts which the present age brings forth."

However, Jevons did not think that the rapid increase in coal production to support the "present age" was sustainable. He opined that England's rapacious appetite for energy would soon consume the nation's coal reserves. "I draw the conclusion that I think any one would draw, that *we cannot long maintain our present rate of increase of consumption; that we can never advance to the higher amounts of consumption supposed.*" In the end, Jevons thought, England would run out of coal by 1900.

Jevons needn't have worried. As before, demand for energy made innovation worthwhile, and another form of fuel was brought to market. It was time to turn to crude oil.

This fuel had been known for centuries. The Romans burned it as a fumigant. In Borneo, it had been used for heat and light. But as the 20th century drew near, this fuel would become the lifeblood of the world's economy. Early wells were shallow, limited by insufficient drill technology. All that changed on January 10, 1901. Two brothers. Al and Curt Hammil, using a new rotary drill technology, bored through more than 1,000 feet of Texas soil on a small hill called Spindletop. Just when it seemed as if they should give up, the drill punctured a pressurized dome of fossil fuel. Methane gas came howling from the drill with a roar, followed by a geyser of oil.

15   There was more oil than anyone had ever imagined. Most wells of the day were shallow and produced from 50 to 100 barrels per day. Spindletop produced 100,000 barrels per day. A confluence of events was now occurring that would make oil the most important fuel in the world. The internal combustion engine would shortly be combined with a horseless carriage, and diesel and gasoline refined from crude oil would power the new transportation device. Coal had been used to power steam engines, but oil quickly became the fuel of choice for those too. "As oil prices fell, coal users began switching in droves to the more efficient oil," author Paul Roberts wrote in his recent book. *The End of Oil*. "Railroads converted their coal-fired locomotives to burn cheap Texas crude. Shipping companies, quickly recognizing that oil

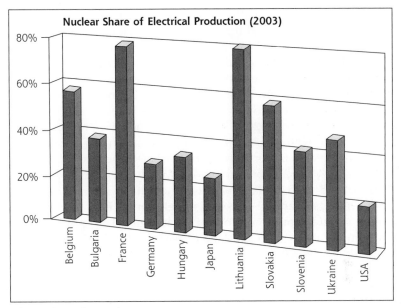

The nuclear alternative

About 20 percent of total U.S. electrical production now comes from nuclear power. But the percentage could be much higher, if the political roadblocks were removed. In 2003, 19 nations (including the ones shown here) produced a higher percentage of their electricity from nuclear power than did the United States

made their ships go faster—and also that it took up less storage room onboard than coal did—refitted cargo vessels to run on oil."

Since Spindletop, oil has been king. And, for a good part of the 20th century, the United States was both the top producer and consumer of oil. By 1946, however, the nation was actually consuming more oil than it produced, a condition that has persisted to the present. Since then, there has been an ever-present chorus of those claiming that the world is about to run out of oil.

"Ever since oil was first harvested in the 1800s, people have said we'd run out of the stuff," noted John Felmy, the chief economist at the American Petroleum Institute. These predictions have come to naught, says science journalist Kevin Kelleher. "In the 1880s a Standard Oil executive sold off shares in the company out of fear that its reserves were close to drying up." Kelleher wrote in the August 2004 issue of *Popular Science*. Similarly, in 1977, President Jimmy Carter warned that mankind "could use up all the proven reserves of oil in the entire world by the end of the next decade." That wasn't true then, and it isn't true now.

CHAPTER 9 FOCUS 2

It is, of course, true that there is more demand for oil today from other quarters of the world than there was previously. Whereas North America and Europe had been far and away the major consumers of energy throughout most of the last century, now emerging industrialized economies in Asia, notably China, are competing for the resource. And yet, the world is not running out of oil. There is, in fact, quite a large amount of oil remaining.

In the U.S. alone in 2003, according to the U.S. Energy Information Agency, proved reserves (meaning oil that can be recovered from existing reservoirs under current operational and economic conditions) totaled some 21.8 billion barrels. Worldwide, in 2003 proved reserves totaled 1.15 trillion barrels, enough to last for 41 years, according to the giant oil firm British Petroleum (BP). "Despite those who say we are about to run out of oil and gas, the figures in the review confirm there is no shortage of reserves," said BP chief economist Peter Davies.

20   At the current rate of consumption, it appears that the world's proved reserves will be consumed in approximately 30 or 40 years. This, however, may not be likely. Proved reserves are only those reserves that are feasibly recoverable, both economically and technologically, at a given time. As technology improves and demand increases, it will become practical to recover more oil, increasing proved reserves. In fact, this has happened in the past, and proved reserves figures have gone up. The total amount of the resource available, though not necessarily accessible under current conditions, is vastly larger than proved reserves. According to the U.S. Energy Information Agency, "technically recoverable resources" of crude oil in the U.S. alone total 105.05 billion barrels—five times the "proved reserves" subset.

It is worth considering, in addition, that many domestic resources have been placed off-limits by government regulation. In fact, according to the EIA, 78.6 percent of technically recoverable resources are located on federal land. The Arctic National Wildlife Refuge (ANWR) is a case in point. The ANWR sits upon vast amounts of recoverable oil on a par with the current largest U.S. oil field at Prudhoe Bay. The oil could be recovered with negligible impact to the environment of the area, yet opening the ANWR to drilling continues to be resisted.

Similarly, much of the outer continental shelf off the nation's coasts has been made off-limits, despite the very real possibility that important energy resources may be located there. In addition, other deposits of oil and other substances in the contiguous states have been made off-limits by virtue of the fact that they are located on federal land. The energy future, in fact, would be very bright—if government would simply get out of the way and allow entrepreneurs to develop our known energy resources and discover new ones.

————————————— **OLD FUELS AND NEW TRICKS** —————————————

Despite government interference, new technologies are constantly putting more oil within man's reach. Because it hasn't always been possible to recover all the oil from an oil field, some of the oil, sometimes large amounts, remained out of reach. "As recently as the 1970s," writes author Paul Roberts, "drillers were lucky to extract 30 percent of the oil from a field, while effectively leaving 70 percent in the ground as 'unrecoverable'." That may be changing. Studies have shown, for instance, that injecting carbon dioxide (CO_2) into "depleted" oil fields

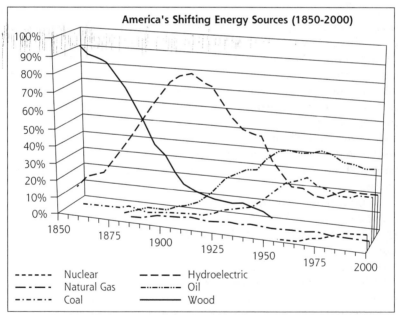

America's Shifting Energy Sources (1850-2000)

- - - - - - Nuclear   - - - - Hydroelectric
— · — · Natural Gas   - - ··· - - Oil
- · - · - · Coal   ———— Wood

The energy we consume comes from different sources, the most significant of which are shown here. Our reliance on these sources has changed radically since 1850, when about 90 percent of the energy we consumed was generated by wood power. These changes resulted from various factors, including supply and demand and technological advances. Because of these changes, we have not run out of wood or any other resource. Nor will we run out, if entrepreneurs are allowed to develop existing and new technologies allows for the recovery of additional oil, sometimes in substantial quantities.

Other new techniques may also improve access to oil. New seismic survey techniques allow scientists to pinpoint oil reserves with greater accuracy: new deep sea drilling technologies are bringing offshore sources within reach, intelligent well systems are giving operators and engineers more finely tuned control of wells: even the drills themselves are improving. According to *Popular Science*, "Flexible, coiled-tube drills that carve out horizontal side paths are a marked improvement over conventional, rigid drills that move only straight down. Using such technology, companies hope to soon harvest 50 to 60 percent of oil from existing wells, up from today's 35 percent."

25   Even though technology will make it possible to continue to supply the world's oil needs, the increased demand for energy may make other fuels attractive. The United States sits atop an almost unimaginably vast store of relatively high quality coal. As an energy source, coal is supposed to be passé. Widely regarded as a dirty substance that kills miners and pollutes the air with choking soot and poisonous sulphur dioxide, it was supposed to have been relegated to the dustbin of history by cleaner burning oil and natural gas.

That coal is still vital is illustrated by the career of Corbin Robertson, Jr. Robertson's family turned oil into a billion dollar business with Quintana Petroleum. But the young Corbin gave it all up for coal. "I bet the ranch and all the cows on it," Robertson told *Forbes* magazine in 2003. "I even hocked the Tom O'Conner [oil] Field."

In part, the attraction of coal is its sheer quantity. According to the National Mining Association, in 2003 U.S. coal reserves stood at a staggering 496 billion tons. At present rates of consumption, these reserves will supply U.S. coal needs for more than 200 years. Coal is presently, and will continue to be, important to the U.S. energy supply. According to the Energy Information Agency. "Coal is projected to fuel roughly 50% of electricity generation through 2025." Even so, coal prices are expected to hold steady or even decline over the same period, making it an ever more attractive fuel option.

Innovation may make coal even more essential. Coal can be turned into a gas. Many years ago, this gas was used to provide fuel for gaslights. But now some generating stations are being built that use the gas to generate electricity. Integrated Gasification Combined Cycle (IGCC) power plants first turn coal into gas, then use the gas to power gas-fired turbines, making electricity. In the process, they produce CO_2 that could be used in efforts to recover oil from "depleted" wells. Moreover, the process of gasification produces hydrogen, itself an energy source with vast potential for the future. Finally, the procedure works with fuels other than coal. Under parts of Canada, for instance, are vast quantities of tar sands. The province of Alberta, for example, sits upon tar sands holding the equivalent of a trillion barrels of oil, fuel that can augment coal in IGCC plants. Another otherwise difficult to harness fuel, heavy oil (and there are large concentrations in South America), can also be used by the process. "A $1.2 billion IGCC plant in Italy, for example, turns sixteen million tons of heavy oil into 550 megawatts of electricity and several tons of hydrogen, which could be used to run fuel cell cars," writes journalist Paul Roberts.

Of Fuel Cells and Fission

Fuel cell-powered cars may prove to be the most important technological innovation since the internal combustion engine. Currently, much of the oil recovered from the world's oil fields is refined into the fuels used by the internal combustion engines powering the world's fleet of cars and trucks. Naturally, the demand for oil for this purpose would be significantly diminished if fuel cell-powered vehicles live up to their promise. There are, however, difficulties to be overcome.

Fuel cells are deceptively simple. They work by combining hydrogen with oxygen to create water, producing electricity in the process. The only byproduct is water. Because the process is silent and results in electricity, automobile designers are presented with design possibilities never before attainable due to constraints imposed by the internal combustion engine and the gearing mechanisms needed to harness its power. Suddenly, completely silent automobiles featuring "fly-by-wire" controls become feasible.

The chief problem with fuel cells is the fuel. Hydrogen is difficult to store and not easily accessible at present. Though hydrogen is the most abundant element in the universe, it is almost invariably found in combination with other elements and must be freed for use. This itself takes energy. Fortunately, this can be overcome by coal-fired IGCC power plants. Still, the infrastructure needed to store and distribute the hydrogen will be needed. Another option will be to power fuel cells with more complex hydrocarbons, like methane, and reform them "onboard" for use in the fuel cell. This less efficient method may be an intermediate solution.

So are fuel cells just some futurist's pipe dream? Based on the fact that they are being employed commercially, the answer must be "no." General Motors, for instance, has entered into a deal with Dow Chemical to provide fuel cell technology to power a Dow plant. According to a GM overview of the plan, "The initial GM fuel cell will generate 75 kilowatts of power. This is enough electricity for fifty average homes. Dow and GM plan to ultimately install up to 400 fuel cells to generate 35 megawatts of electricity. That would be enough power for 25,000 average sized American homes."

Fuel cells aren't the only futuristic energy technology that will probably play a significant role in the near future. Another is a technology

CHAPTER 9 Focus 2

that has already been producing power for nearly 50 years but still seems futuristic nonetheless; nuclear energy. Prior to the nuclear age, splitting the atom was considered an impossibility. Albert Einstein, the famous physicist, argued, "There is not the slightest indication that [nuclear] energy will ever be obtainable. It would mean that the atom would have to be shattered at will." Work completed by Enrico Fermi and others, though, caused Einstein to change his mind.

Nuclear power, an American innovation, has been brought to a virtual standstill in this country, because of political, not technological, obstacles. Yet it is still a viable and important energy source. According to the federal Energy Information Agency. U.S. nuclear facilities had a record year in 2004. The EIA reported: "The U.S. nuclear industry generated 788.556 million kilowatt hours of electricity in 2004, a new U.S. (and international) record. Although no new U.S. nuclear power plants have come online since 1996, this is the industry's fifth annual record since 1998." There are currently 104 licensed nuclear power generating stations operating within the United States. The energy they produce accounts for about 20 percent of the nation's electricity and about 8 percent of the total energy we consume.

35   These figures could be higher, as evidenced by the fact that many other nations, taking full advantage of the technology the United States developed, are using nuclear technology to produce a much higher percentage of their electricity from nuclear power than we are.

Japan plans to increase its nuclear capacity so that 41 percent of its total energy needs can be met with atomic energy. What's more, despite setbacks. Japanese industry is committed to advancements in nuclear technology. Japan invested heavily in fast breeder technology, completing the "Monju" fast breeder reactor that would get dramatically more energy out of a given amount of uranium than a conventional nuclear power plant. The Monju reactor suffered a coolant leak and was shut down, but plans exist for bringing the facility back online soon.

Nuclear energy may even play a role in smaller-scale remote installations. The town of Galena, Alaska, suffers from an erratic energy supply and wants to install a small, Japanese-made nuclear reactor. The liquid-sodium cooled. Toshiba-built reactor would produce 10 megawatts of electricity and would run almost unattended and underground. It would not need to be refueled for 30 years. Whether in small-town Alaska or in the lower 48 states, nuclear power can provide a relatively inexpensive, clean, and nearly unlimited source of energy.

THE FUTURE IS BRIGHT

The future is not limited to the fossil fuels and nuclear fission of the past century. Just as the last 100 years have witnessed almost unimaginable advances in technology, the next 100 years will almost certainly be just as revolutionary. "[O]ver the next few decades, we are very likely to see all kinds of technological advances that have nothing to do with hydrocarbons, or solar, or wind, for that matter—advances that most of us, brought up in the age of oil, probably can't even imagine," writes journalist Paul Roberts in his book, *The End of Oil*.

In the fall of 1984, two chemists. Stanley Pons and Martin Fleischman, suspended a solid palladium electrode measuring one cubic centimeter in a beaker filled with a mixture of deuterium and lithium. Inserting another electrode, they passed a current through the mixture, forcing the deuterium into the palladium. One evening that winter (the exact date is unclear), the experiment appeared to have come to a violent end. To Pons it seemed as if there had been an explosion. The palladium block may have been vaporized. Or, parts of it, becoming superheated, melted through the beaker, the table on which the beaker sat, and, spilling onto the floor below, produced a hole four inches deep in the lab's concrete floor. Accounts of the accident differ, but it seemed as if something violently energetic might have occurred.

The chemists became convinced that they had achieved the impos- 40 sible: a fusion reaction at room temperature. Fusion is the reaction that powers the sun and all other stars. If a fusion reaction occurred in the lab that night, as Pons and Fleischman suspected, it would mean a future of limitless, cheap energy. After a series of further experiments, the cold fusion duo went public March 23, 1989 to a chorus of worldwide acclaim and wonder.

In the end, attempts to duplicate the results proved fruitless. Cold fusion had not been achieved. Nevertheless, it is just this pioneering spirit that will likely usher in further advancements in energy technology. And fusion itself is not dead. Experiments with "hot" fusion, both in tokomak (magnetic) reactors and with inertial (laser powered) technologies, could still bring the power of the sun to Earth. But even the power of fusion would pale before the possibilities of another exotic, futuristic power: antimatter. The material that powers the fictional starship *Enterprise* on TV was actually first predicted based on work done in 1928 by physicist Paul Dirac. Though it has been the stuff of science fiction for years, antimatter really does exist.

Antimatter is, essentially, the same as regular matter. The only difference is that its charge is reversed. A normal, positively charged proton, for instance, finds its antimatter counterpart in a negatively charged antiproton. Similarly, the normal, negatively charged electron's antimatter counterpart is the positron. The existence of the positron was discovered in 1932.

Antimatter has immense potential for energy generation. Should a particle of antimatter encounter a particle of ordinary matter, the result is the complete annihilation of both particles and their complete conversion into energy. According to senior science writer Robert Roy Britt of *Space.com*, "A solar flare in July 2002 created about a pound of anti-matter, or half a kilo, according to new NASA-led research. That's enough to power the United States for two days." So far, only small amounts of antimatter can be made in the lab using incredibly high-energy particle accelerators.

Still, there's no telling what these advances and others yet unimagined may bring. One thing is certain, though. The current energy crisis marked by the rapidly rising cost of petroleum will be like other such crises in the past. It will not be an indication that a resource is being depleted, because, like wood and coal of earlier days, oil continues to exist in abundance. The rising cost does mean, though, that vast opportunities exist for innovators and investors who seek to bring new technologies to market. The risks are high, but the rewards are great. If the past is a guide, the current, robust demand for energy will lead to a new age of energy innovation and abundance.

Responding to Reading

1. Beginning with paragraph 7, Behreandt compares the current energy situation with that of Europe in the late Renaissance. Does this comparison shed light on the current energy situation? Do you find the comparison useful?
2. In addition to coal, what other sources of energy does Behreandt think will be important in the future? What are the advantages and disadvantages of each of these energy sources?
3. Do you find Behreandt's assessment of the future realistic or overly optimistic? Do you agree that new technology and free market innovation will make for a bright future? Is Behreandt correct when he says, "If the past is a guide, the current, robust demand for enery will lead to a new age of energy innovation and abundance" (44)?

Responding in Writing

Do you think Behreandt presents an accurate scenario of America's energy future?

THE END OF OIL

James Howard Kunstler

1948–

Novelist, nonfiction writer, and lecturer James Howard Kunstler is a contributing writer for the New York Times. *His work centers on social, urban, economic, and environmental concerns. His recent book* The Long Emergency: Surviving the Converging Catastrophes of the Twenty-First Century *(2005), from which the following essay is adapted, examines what he calls the "Long Emergency."*

A few weeks ago, the price of oil ratcheted above fifty-five dollars a barrel, which is about twenty dollars a barrel more than a year ago. The next day, the oil story was buried on page six of the *New York Times* business section. Apparently, the price of oil is not considered significant news, even when it goes up five bucks a barrel in the span of ten days. That same day, the stock market shot up more than a hundred points because, CNN said, government data showed no signs of inflation. Note to clueless nation: Call planet Earth.

Carl Jung, one of the fathers of psychology, famously remarked that "people cannot stand too much reality." What you're about to read may challenge your assumptions about the kind of world we live in, and especially the kind of world into which events are propelling us. We are in for a rough ride through uncharted territory.

It has been very hard for Americans—lost in dark raptures of non-stop infotainment, recreational shopping and compulsive motoring—to make sense of the gathering forces that will fundamentally alter the terms of everyday life in our technological society. Even after the terrorist attacks of 9/11, America is still sleepwalking into the future. I call this coming time the Long Emergency.

Most immediately we face the end of the cheap-fossil-fuel era. It is no exaggeration to state that reliable supplies of cheap oil and natural gas underlie everything we identify as the necessities of modern life—not to mention all of its comforts and luxuries: central heating, air conditioning, cars, airplanes, electric lights, inexpensive clothing, recorded music, movies, hip-replacement surgery, national defense—you name it.

The few Americans who are even aware that there is a gathering 5 global-energy predicament usually misunderstand the core of the argument. That argument states that we don't have to run out of oil to start having severe problems with industrial civilization and its dependent systems. We only have to slip over the all-time production peak and begin a slide down the arc of steady depletion.

The term "global oil-production peak" means that a turning point will come when the world produces the most oil it will ever produce in a given year and, after that, yearly production will inexorably decline. It is usually represented graphically in a bell curve. The peak is the top of the curve, the halfway point of the world's all-time total endowment, meaning half the world's oil will be left. That seems like a lot of oil, and it is, but there's a big catch: It's the half that is much more difficult to extract, far more costly to get, of much poorer quality and located mostly in places where the people hate us. A substantial amount of it will never be extracted.

The United States passed its own oil peak—about 11 million barrels a day—in 1970, and since then production has dropped steadily. In 2004 it ran just above 5 million barrels a day (we get a tad more from natural-gas condensates). Yet we consume roughly 20 million barrels a day now. That means we have to import about two-thirds of our oil, and the ratio will continue to worsen.

The U.S. peak in 1970 brought on a portentous change in geoeconomic power. Within a few years, foreign producers, chiefly OPEC, were setting the price of oil, and this in turn led to the oil crises of the 1970s. In response, frantic development of non-OPEC oil, especially the North Sea fields of England and Norway, essentially saved the West's ass for about two decades. Since 1999, these fields have entered depletion. Meanwhile, worldwide discovery of new oil has steadily declined to insignificant levels in 2003 and 2004.

Some "cornucopians" claim that the Earth has something like a creamy nougat center of "abiotic" oil that will naturally replenish the great oil fields of the world. The facts speak differently. There has been no replacement whatsoever of oil already extracted from the fields of America or any other place.

10   Now we are faced with the global oil-production peak. The best estimates of when this will actually happen have been somewhere between now and 2010. In 2004, however, after demand from burgeoning China and India shot up, and revelations that Shell Oil wildly misstated its reserves, and Saudi Arabia proved incapable of goosing up its production despite promises to do so, the most knowledgeable experts revised their predictions and now concur that 2005 is apt to be the year of alltime global peak production.

It will change everything about how we live.

To aggravate matters, American natural-gas production is also declining, at five percent a year, despite frenetic new drilling, and with the potential of much steeper declines ahead. Because of the oil crises of the 1970s, the nuclear-plant disasters at Three Mile Island and Chernobyl and the acid-rain problem, the U.S. chose to make gas its first choice for electric-power generation. The result was that just about every power plant built after 1980 has to run on gas. Half the homes in America are heated with gas. To further complicate matters, gas isn't easy to import. Here in North America, it is distributed through a vast pipeline network. Gas imported from overseas would have to be compressed at minus 260 degrees Fahrenheit in pressurized tanker ships and unloaded (re-gasified) at special terminals, of which few exist in America. Moreover, the first attempts to site new terminals have met furious opposition because they are such ripe targets for terrorism.

Some other things about the global energy predicament are poorly understood by the public and even our leaders. This is going to be a permanent energy crisis, and these energy problems will synergize with the disruptions of climate change, epidemic disease and population overshoot to produce higher orders of trouble.

We will have to accommodate ourselves to fundamentally changed conditions.

No combination of alternative fuels will allow us to run American 15
life the way we have been used to running it, or even a substantial fraction of it. The wonders of steady technological progress achieved
through the reign of cheap oil have lulled us into a kind of Jiminy
Cricket syndrome, leading many Americans to believe that anything
we wish for hard enough will come true. These days, even people who
ought to know better are wishing ardently for a seamless transition
from fossil fuels to their putative replacements.

The widely touted "hydrogen economy" is a particularly cruel
hoax. We are not going to replace the U.S. automobile and truck fleet
with vehicles run on fuel cells. For one thing, the current generation of
fuel cells is largely designed to run on hydrogen obtained from natural
gas. The other way to get hydrogen in the quantities wished for would
be electrolysis of water using power from hundreds of nuclear plants.
Apart from the dim prospect of our building that many nuclear plants
soon enough, there are also numerous severe problems with hydrogen's nature as an element that present forbidding obstacles to its use
as a replacement for oil and gas, especially in storage and transport.

Wishful notions about rescuing our way of life with "renewables"
are also unrealistic. Solar-electric systems and wind turbines face not
only the enormous problem of scale but the fact that the components
require substantial amounts of energy to manufacture and the probability that they can't be manufactured at all without the underlying support platform of a fossil-fuel economy. We will surely use solar and
wind technology to generate some electricity for a period ahead but
probably at a very local and small scale.

Virtually all "biomass" schemes for using plants to create liquid
fuels cannot be scaled up to even a fraction of the level at which things
are currently run. What's more, these schemes are predicated on using
oil and gas "inputs" (fertilizers, weed-killers) to grow the biomass
crops that would be converted into ethanol or bio-diesel fuels. This is a
net energy loser—you might as well just burn the inputs and not bother
with the biomass products. Proposals to distill trash and waste into oil
by means of thermal depolymerization depend on the huge waste
stream produced by a cheap oil and gas economy in the first place.

Coal is far less versatile than oil and gas, extant in less abundant
supplies than many people assume and fraught with huge ecological
drawbacks—as a contributor to greenhouse "global warming" gases
and many health and toxicity issues ranging from widespread mercury
poisoning to acid rain. You can make synthetic oil from coal, but the
only time this was tried on a large scale was by the Nazis under
wartime conditions, using impressive amounts of slave labor.

If we wish to keep the lights on in America after 2020, we may in- 20
deed have to resort to nuclear power, with all its practical problems and
eco-conundrums. Under optimal conditions, it could take ten years to

CHAPTER 9 FOCUS 2

get a new generation of nuclear power plants into operation, and the price may be beyond our means. Uranium is also a resource in finite supply. We are no closer to the more difficult project of atomic fusion, by the way, than we were in the 1970s.

The upshot of all this is that we are entering a historical period of potentially great instability, turbulence and hardship. Obviously, geopolitical maneuvering around the world's richest energy regions has already led to war and promises more international military conflict. Since the Middle East contains two-thirds of the world's remaining oil supplies, the U.S. has attempted desperately to stabilize the region by, in effect, opening a big police station in Iraq. The intent was not just to secure Iraq's oil but to modify and influence the behavior of neighboring states around the Persian Gulf, especially Iran and Saudi Arabia. The results have been far from entirely positive, and our future prospects in that part of the world are not something we can feel altogether confident about.

And then there is the issue of China, which, in 2004, became the world's second-greatest consumer of oil, surpassing Japan. China's surging industrial growth has made it increasingly dependent on the imports we are counting on. If China wanted to, it could easily walk into some of these places—the Middle East, former Soviet republics in central Asia—and extend its hegemony by force. Is America prepared to contest for this oil in an Asian land war with the Chinese army? I doubt it. Nor can the U.S. military occupy regions of the Eastern Hemisphere indefinitely, or hope to secure either the terrain or the oil infrastructure of one distant, unfriendly country after another. A likely scenario is that the U.S. could exhaust and bankrupt itself trying to do this, and be forced to withdraw back into our own hemisphere, having lost access to most of the world's remaining oil in the process.

We know that our national leaders are hardly uninformed about this predicament. President George W. Bush has been briefed on the dangers of the oil-peak situation as long ago as before the 2000 election and repeatedly since then. In March, the Department of Energy released a report that officially acknowledges for the first time that peak oil is for real and states plainly that "the world has never faced a problem like this. Without massive mitigation more than a decade before the fact, the problem will be pervasive and will not be temporary."

Most of all, the Long Emergency will require us to make other arrangements for the way we live in the United States. America is in a special predicament due to a set of unfortunate choices we made as a society in the twentieth century. Perhaps the worst was to let our towns and cities rot away and to replace them with suburbia, which had the additional side effect of trashing a lot of the best farmland in America. Suburbia will come to be regarded as the greatest misallocation of resources in the history of the world. It has a tragic destiny. The psychology of previous investment suggests that we will defend our drive-in utopia long after it has become a terrible liability.

Before long, the suburbs will fail us in practical terms. We made the ongoing development of housing subdivisions, highway strips, fried-food shacks and shopping malls the basis of our economy, and when we have to stop making more of those things, the bottom will fall out.

The circumstances of the Long Emergency will require us to down-scale and rescale virtually everything we do and how we do it, from the kind of communities we physically inhabit to the way we grow our food to the way we work and trade the products of our work. Our lives will become profoundly and intensely local. Daily life will be far less about mobility and much more about staying where you are. Anything organized on the large scale, whether it is government or a corporate business enterprise such as Wal-Mart, will wither as the cheap energy props that support bigness fall away. The turbulence of the Long Emergency will produce a lot of economic losers, and many of these will be members of an angry and aggrieved former middle class.

Food production is going to be an enormous problem in the Long Emergency. As industrial agriculture fails due to a scarcity of oil- and gas-based inputs, we will certainly have to grow more of our food closer to where we live, and do it on a smaller scale. The American economy of the mid-twenty-first century may actually center on agriculture, not information, not high tech, not "services" like real estate sales or hawking cheeseburgers to tourists. Farming. This is no doubt a startling, radical idea, and it raises extremely difficult questions about the reallocation of land and the nature of work. The relentless subdividing of land in the late twentieth century has destroyed the contiguity and integrity of the rural landscape in most places. The process of readjustment is apt to be disorderly and improvisational. Food production will necessarily be much more labor-intensive than it has been for decades. We can anticipate the re-formation of a native-born American farm-laboring class. It will be composed largely of the aforementioned economic losers who had to relinquish their grip on the American dream. These masses of disentitled people may enter into quasifeudal social relations with those who own land in exchange for food and physical security. But their sense of grievance will remain fresh, and if mistreated they may simply seize that land.

The way that commerce is currently organized in America will not survive far into the Long Emergency. Wal-Mart's "warehouse on wheels" won't be such a bargain in a non-cheap-oil economy. The national chain stores' 12,000-mile manufacturing supply lines could easily be interrupted by military contests over oil and by internal conflict in the nations that have been supplying us with ultracheap manufactured goods, because they, too, will be struggling with similar issues of energy famine and all the disorders that go with it.

As these things occur, America will have to make other arrangements for the manufacture, distribution and sale of ordinary goods. They will probably be made on a "cottage industry" basis rather than the factory system we once had, since the scale of available energy will be much lower—and we are not going to replay the twentieth century. Tens of thousands of the common products we enjoy today, from paints to pharmaceuticals, are made out of oil. They will become increasingly scarce or unavailable. The selling of things will have to be reorganized at the local scale. It will have to be based on moving merchandise shorter distances. It is almost certain to result in higher costs for the things we buy and far fewer choices.

30   The automobile will be a diminished presence in our lives, to say the least. With gasoline in short supply, not to mention tax revenue, our roads will surely suffer. The interstate highway system is more delicate than the public realizes. If the "level of service" (as traffic engineers call it) is not maintained to the highest degree, problems multiply and escalate quickly. The system does not tolerate partial failure. The interstates are either in excellent condition, or they quickly fall apart.

America today has a railroad system that the Bulgarians would be ashamed of. Neither of the two major presidential candidates in 2004 mentioned railroads, but if we don't refurbish our rail system, then there may be no long-range travel or transport of goods at all a few decades from now. The commercial aviation industry, already on its knees financially, is likely to vanish. The sheer cost of maintaining gigantic airports may not justify the operation of a much-reduced air-travel fleet. Railroads are far more energy efficient than cars, trucks or airplanes, and they can be run on anything from wood to electricity. The rail-bed infrastructure is also far more economical to maintain than our highway network.

The successful regions in the twenty-first century will be the ones surrounded by viable farming hinterlands that can reconstitute locally sustainable economies on an armature of civic cohesion. Small towns and smaller cities have better prospects than the big cities, which will probably have to contract substantially. The process will be painful and tumultuous. In many American cities, such as Cleveland, Detroit and St. Louis, that process is already well advanced. Others have further to fall. New York and Chicago face extraordinary difficulties, being oversupplied with gigantic buildings out of scale with the reality of declining energy supplies. Their former agricultural hinterlands have long been paved over. They will be encysted in a surrounding fabric of necrotic suburbia that will only amplify and reinforce the cities' problems. Still, our cities occupy important sites. Some kind of urban entities will exist where they are in the future, but probably not the colossi of twentieth-century industrialism.

Some regions of the country will do better than others in the Long Emergency. The Southwest will suffer in proportion to the degree that it prospered during the cheap-oil blowout of the late twentieth century. I predict that Sunbelt states like Arizona and Nevada will become significantly depopulated, since the region will be short of water as well as gasoline and natural gas. Imagine Phoenix without cheap air conditioning.

I'm not optimistic about the Southeast, either, for different reasons. I think it will be subject to substantial levels of violence as the grievances of the formerly middle class boil over and collide with the delusions of Pentecostal Christian extremism. The latent encoded behavior of Southern culture includes an outsized notion of individualism and the belief that firearms ought to be used in the defense of it. This is a poor recipe for civic cohesion.

The Mountain States and Great Plains will face an array of prob- 35 lems, from poor farming potential to water shortages to population loss. The Pacific Northwest, New England and the Upper Midwest have somewhat better prospects. I regard them as less likely to fall into lawlessness, anarchy or despotism and more likely to salvage the bits and pieces of our best social traditions and keep them in operation at some level.

These are daunting and even dreadful prospects. The Long Emergency is going to be a tremendous trauma for the human race. We will not believe that this is happening to us, that 200 years of modernity can be brought to its knees by a world-wide power shortage. The survivors will have to cultivate a religion of hope—that is, a deep and comprehensive belief that humanity is worth carrying on. If there is any positive side to stark changes coming our way, it may be in the benefits of close communal relations, of having to really work intimately (and physically) with our neighbors, to be part of an enterprise that really matters and to be fully engaged in meaningful social enactments instead of being merely entertained to avoid boredom. Years from now, when we hear singing at all, we will hear ourselves, and we will sing with our whole hearts.

Responding to Reading

1. In paragraph 3, Kunstler refers to the future as the "Long Emergency." What does he mean by this term? How effective is this term in defining the problems we face? Can you think of another term that would be more effective?
2. In paragraph 16, Kunstler dismisses the use of hydrogen to offset the energy crisis as a "cruel hoax." He goes on to say that there are many problems with hydrogen, "especially in storage and transport" (16). Should he have discussed these problems in more detail?

3. In what ways will the Long Emergency cause us to change our lives? What regions of the country does Kunstler think will be successful in the coming years? Which does he think will be unsuccessful?

Responding in Writing

Of the three writers in this Focus section, who do you think is most pessimistic? Who do you think is most optimistic? Which of the three do you believe presents the most accurate picture of the future?

---------------------------------- Focus ----------------------------------

Are Men Better in Math and Science than Women?

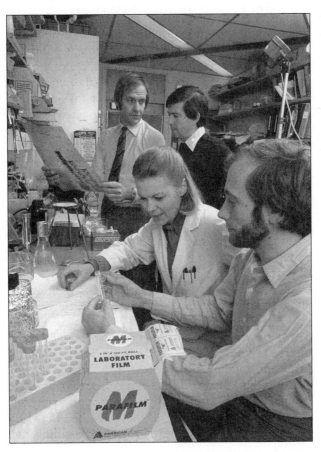

Biologists in UCSF Laboratory (1980)

Responding to the Image

1. How does the photograph portray scientists? What assumptions does the photographer make about the above audience? Do the people pictured conform to your idea of what scientists look like?
2. This photograph was taken in 1980. How do you think people might have reacted to the photo in 1980? How would they be likely to react today?

REMARKS AT NBER CONFERENCE ON DIVERSIFYING THE SCIENCE AND ENGINEERING WORKFORCE

Lawrence Summers

1954–

Former president of Harvard University, economist, and former secretary of the United States treasury, Lawrence Summers has written numerous articles and has written, coauthored, and edited several books focusing on economic and social issues. In January 2005, Summers delivered the following controversial remarks about male and female propensities toward math and science at the National Bureau of Economic Research (NBER) Conference on Diversifying the Science and Engineering Workforce. (Summers stepped down as president of Harvard in 2006).

I asked Richard [Harvard economist Richard Freeman, conference organizer] when he invited me to come here and speak, whether he wanted an institutional talk about Harvard's policies toward diversity or whether he wanted some questions asked and some attempts at provocation, because I was willing to do the second and didn't feel like doing the first. And so we have agreed that I am speaking unofficially and not using this as an occasion to lay out the many things we're doing at Harvard to promote the crucial objective of diversity. There are many aspects of the problems you're discussing and it seems to me they're all very important from a national point of view. I'm going to confine myself to addressing one portion of the problem, or of the challenge we're discussing, which is the issue of women's representation in tenured positions in science and engineering at top universities and research institutions, not because that's necessarily the most important problem or the most interesting problem, but because it's the only one of these problems that I've made an effort to think in a very serious way about. The other prefatory comment that I would make is that I am going to, until most of the way through, attempt to adopt an entirely positive, rather than normative approach, and just try to think about and offer some hypothese as to why we observe what we observe without seeing this through the kind of judgmental tendency that inevitably is connected with all our common goals of equality. It is after all not the case that the role of women in science is the only example of a group that is significantly underrepresented in an important activity and whose underrepresentation contributes to a shortage of role models for others who are considering being in that group. To take a set of diverse examples, the data will, I am confident, reveal that Catholics are substantially underrepresented in investment banking, which is an enormously high-paying profession in our society; that white men are very substantially underrepresented in the National Basketball Association; and that Jews are very substantially underrepresented in farming and in agriculture. These are all phenomena in which one observes underrepresentation, and I think it's important to try to think systematically and clinically about the reasons for underrepresentation.

There are three broad hypotheses about the sources of the very substantial disparities that this conference's papers document and have been documented before with respect to the presence of women in high-end scientific professions. One is what I would call the—I'll explain each of these in a few moments and comment on how important I think they are—the first is what I call the high-powered job hypothesis. The second is what I would call different availability of aptitude at the high end, and the third is what I would call different socialization and patterns of discrimination in a search. And in my own view, their importance probably ranks in exactly the order that I just described.

Maybe it would be helpful to just, for a moment, broaden the problem, or the issue, beyond science and engineering. I've had the opportunity to discuss questions like this with chief executive officers at major corporations, the managing partners of large law firms, the directors of prominent teaching hospitals, and with the leaders of other prominent professional service organizations, as well as with colleagues in higher education. In all of those groups, the story is fundamentally the same. Twenty or twenty-five years ago, we started to see very substantial increases in the number of women who were in graduate school in this field. Now the people who went to graduate school when that started are forty, forty-five, fifty years old. If you look at the top cohort in our activity, it is not only nothing like fifty-fifty, it is nothing like what we thought it was when we started having a third of the women, a third of the law school class being female, twenty or twenty-five years ago. And the relatively few women who are in the highest ranking places are disproportionately either unmarried or without children, with the emphasis differing depending on just who you talk to. And that is a reality that is present and that one has exactly the same conversation in almost any high-powered profession. What does one make of that? I think it is hard—and again, I am speaking completely descriptively and non-normatively—to say that there are many professions and many activities, and the most prestigious activities in our society expect of people who are going to rise to leadership positions in their forties near total commitments to their work. They expect a large number of hours in the office, they expect a flexibility of schedules to respond to contingency, they expect a continuity of effort through the life cycle, and they expect—and this is harder to measure—but they expect that the mind is always working on the problems that are in the job, even when the job is not taking place. And it is a fact about our society that that is a level of commitment that a much higher fraction of married men have been historically prepared to make than of married women. That's not a judgment about how it should be, not a judgment about what they should expect. But it seems to me that it is very hard to look at the data and escape the conclusion that that expectation is meeting with the choices that people make and is contributing substantially to the outcomes that we observe. One can put it differently. Of a class, and the work that Claudia Goldin and Larry Katz are doing will, I'm sure, over time, contribute greatly to our understanding of these issues and for all I know may prove my conjectures completely wrong. Another way to put the point is to say, what fraction of young women in their mid-twenties make a decision that they don't want to have a job that they think about eighty hours a week. What fraction of young men make a decision that they're unwilling to have a job that they think about eighty hours a week, and to observe what the difference is. And that has got to be a large part of what is observed. Now that begs entirely the normative questions—which I'll get to a little later—of, is our society right to expect that level of effort from people who hold the most prominent jobs? Is our society right to have familial arrangements in which women are asked to make that choice and asked more to make that choice than men? Is our society right to ask of anybody to have a prominent job at this level of intensity, and I think those are all questions that I want to come back to. But it seems to me that it is impossible to look at this pattern and look at its pervasiveness and not conclude that something of the sort that I am describing has to be of significant importance. To buttress conviction and theory with anecdote, a young woman who worked very closely with me at the Treasury and who has subsequently gone on to work at Google highly successfully, is a 1994 graduate of Harvard Business School. She reports that of her first year section, there were twenty-two women, of whom three are working full time at this point. That may, the dean of the Business School reports to me, that that is not an implausible observation given their experience with their alumnae. So I think in terms of positive understanding, the first very important reality is just what I would call the, who wants to do high-powered intense work?

The second thing that I think one has to recognize is present is what I would call the combination of, and here, I'm focusing on something that would seek to answer the question of why is the pattern different in science and engineering, and why is the representation even lower and more problematic in science and engineering than it is in other fields. And here, you can get a fair distance, it seems to me, looking at a relatively simple hypothesis. It does appear that on many, many different human attributes-height, weight, propensity for criminality, overall IQ, mathematical ability, scientific ability-there is relatively clear evidence that whatever the difference in means-which can be debated-there is a difference in the standard deviation, and variability of a male and a female population. And that is true with respect to attributes that are and are not plausibly, culturally determined. If one supposes, as I think is reasonable, that if one is talking about physicists at a top twenty-five research university, one is not talking about people who are two standard deviations above the mean. And perhaps it's not even talking about somebody who is three standard deviations above the mean. But it's talking about people who are three and a half, four standard deviations above the mean in the one in 5,000, one in 10,000 class. Even small differences in the standard deviation will translate into very large differences in the available pool substantially out. I did a very crude calculation, which I'm sure was wrong and certainly was un-subtle, twenty different ways. I looked at the Xie and Shauman paper—looked at the book, rather—looked at the evidence on the sex ratios in the top 5% of twelfth graders. If you look at those—they're all over the map, depends on which test, whether it's math, or science, and so forth—but 50% women, one woman for every two men, would be a high-end estimate from their estimates. From that, you can back out a difference in the implied standard deviations that works out to be about 20%. And from that, you can work out the dif-ference out several standard deviations. If you do that calculation—and I have no reason to think that it couldn't be refined in a hundred ways—you get five to one, at the high end. Now, it's pointed out by one of the papers at this conference that these tests are not a very good measure and are not highly predictive with re-spect to people's ability to do that. And that's absolutely right. But I don't think that resolves the issue at all. Because if my reading of the data is right—it's something people can argue about—that there are some systematic differences in variability in different popula-tions, then whatever the set of attributes are that are precisely de-fined to correlate with being an aeronautical engineer at MIT or being a chemist at Berkeley, those are probably different in their standard deviations as well. So my sense is that the unfortunate truth—I would far prefer to believe something else, because it would be easier to address what is surely a serious social problem if something else were true—is that the combination of the high-pow-ered job hypothesis and the differing variances probably explains a fair amount of this problem.

CHAPTER 9 FOCUS 3

5   There may also be elements, by the way, of differing, there is some, particularly in some attributes, that bear on engineering, there is reasonably strong evidence of taste differences between little girls and little boys that are not easy to attribute to socialization. I just returned from Israel, where we had the opportunity to visit a kibbutz, and to spend some time talking about the history of the kibbutz movement, and it is really very striking to hear how the movement started with an absolute commitment, of a kind one doesn't encounter in other places, that everybody was going to do the same jobs. Sometimes the women were going to fix the tractors, and the men were going to work in the nurseries, sometimes the men were going to fix the tractors and the women were going to work in the nurseries, and just under the pressure of what everyone wanted, in a hundred different kibbutzes, each one of which evolved, it all moved in the same direction. So, I think, while I would prefer to believe otherwise, I guess my experience with my two and a half year old twin daughters who were not given dolls and who were given trucks, and found themselves saying to each other, look, daddy truck is carrying the baby truck, tells me something. And I think it's just something that you probably have to recognize. There are two other hypotheses that are all over. One is socialization. Somehow little girls are all socialized towards nursing and little boys are socialized towards building bridges. No doubt there is some truth in that. I would be hesitant about assigning too much weight to that hypothesis for two reasons. First, most of what we've learned from empirical psychology in the last fifteen years has been that people naturally attribute things to socialization that are in fact not attributable to socialization. We've been astounded by the results of separated twins studies. The confident assertions that autism was a reflection of parental characteristics that were absolutely supported and that people knew from years of observational evidence have now been proven to be wrong. And so, the human mind has a tendency to grab to the socialization hypothesis when you can see it, and it often turns out not to be true. The second empirical problem is that girls are persisting longer and longer. When there were no girls majoring in chemistry, when there were no girls majoring in biology, it was much easier to blame parental socialization. Then, as we are increasingly finding today, the problem is what's happening when people are twenty, or when people are twenty-five, in terms of their patterns, with which they drop out. Again, to the extent it can be addressed, it's a terrific thing to address.

       The most controversial in a way, question, and the most difficult question to judge, is what is the role of discrimination? To what extent is there overt discrimination? Surely there is some. Much more tellingly, to what extent are there pervasive patterns of passive discrimination and stereotyping in which people like to choose people like themselves, and the people in the previous group are disproportionately white male, and so they choose people who are like themselves, who are disproportionately white male. No one who's been in a university department or who has been involved in personnel processes can deny that this kind of taste does go on, and it is something that happens, and it is something that absolutely, vigorously needs to be combated. On the other hand, I think before regarding it as pervasive, and as the dominant explanation of the patterns we observe, there are two points that should make one hesitate. The first is the fallacy of composition. No doubt it is true that if any one institution makes a major effort to focus on reducing stereotyping, on achieving diversity, on hiring more people, no doubt it can succeed in hiring more. But each person it hires will come from a different institution, and so everyone observes that when an institution works very hard at this, to some extent they are able to produce better results. If I stand up at a football game and everybody else is sitting down, I can see much better, but if everybody stands up, the views may get a little better, but they don't get a lot better. And there's a real question as to how plausible it is to believe that there is anything like half as many people who are qualified to be scientists at top ten schools and who are now not at top ten schools, and that's the argument that one has to make in thinking about this as a national problem rather than an individual institutional problem. The second problem is the one that Gary Becker very powerfully pointed out in addressing racial discrimination many years ago. If it was really the case that everybody was discriminating, there would be very substantial opportunities for a limited number of people who were not prepared to discriminate to assemble remarkable departments of high quality people at relatively limited cost simply by the act of their not discriminating, because of what it would mean for the pool that was available. And there are certainly examples of institutions that have focused on increasing their diversity to their substantial benefit, but if there was really a pervasive pattern of discrimination that was leaving an extraordinary number of high-quality potential candidates behind, one suspects that in the highly competitive academic marketplace, there would be more examples of institutions that succeeded substantially by working to fill the gap. And I think one sees relatively little evidence of that. So my best guess, to provoke you, of what's behind all of this is that the largest phenomenon, by far, is the general clash between people's legitimate family desires and employers' current desire for high power and high intensity, that in the special case of science and engineering, there are issues of intrinsic aptitude, and particularly of the variability of aptitude, and that those considerations are reinforced by what are in fact lesser factors involving socialization and continuing discrimination. I would like nothing better than to be proved wrong, because I would like nothing better than for these problems to be addressable simply by everybody understanding what they are, and working very hard to address them.

What's to be done? And what further questions should one know the answers to? Let me take a second, first to just remark on a few questions that it seems to me are ripe for research, and for all I know, some of them have been researched. First, it would be very useful to know, with hard data, what the quality of marginal hires are when major diversity efforts are mounted. When major diversity efforts are mounted, and consciousness is raised, and special efforts are made, and you look five years later at the quality of the people who have been hired during that period, how many are there who have turned out to be much better than the institutional norm who wouldn't have been found without a greater search. And how many of them are plausible compromises that aren't unreasonable, and how many of them are what the right-wing critics of all of this suppose represent clear abandonments of quality standards. I don't know the answer, but I think if people want to move the world on this question, they have to be willing to ask the question in ways that could face any possible answer that came out. Second, and by the way, I think a more systematic effort to look at citation records of male and female scholars in disciplines where citations are relatively well-correlated with academic rank and with people's judgments of quality would be very valuable. Of course, most of the critiques of citations go to reasons why they should not be useful in judging an individual scholar. Most of them are not reasons why they would not be useful in comparing two large groups of scholars and so there is significant potential, it seems to me, for citation analysis in this regard. Second, what about objective versus subjective factors in hiring? I've been exposed, by those who want to see the university hiring practices changed to favor women more and to assure more diversity, to two very different views. One group has urged that we make the processes consistently more clear-cut and objective, based on papers, numbers of papers published, numbers of articles cited, objectivity, measurement of performance, no judgments of potential, no reference to other things, because if it's made more objective, the subjectivity that is associated with discrimination and which invariably works to the disadvantage of minority groups will not be present. I've also been exposed to exactly the opposite view, that those criteria and those objective criteria systematically bias the comparisons away from many attributes that those who contribute to the diversity have: a greater sense of collegiality, a greater sense of institutional responsibility. Somebody ought to be able to figure out the answer to the question of, if you did it more objectively versus less objectively, what would happen. Then you can debate whether you should or whether you shouldn't, if objective or subjective is better. But that question ought to be a question that has an answer, that people can find. Third, the third kind of question is, what do we know about search procedures in universities? Is it the case that more systematic comprehensive search processes lead to minority group members who otherwise would have not been noticed being noticed? Or does fetishizing the search procedure make it very difficult to pursue the targets of opportunity that are often available arising out of particular family situations or particular moments, and does fetishizing and formalizing search procedures further actually work to the disadvantage of minority group members. Again, everybody's got an opinion; I don't think anybody actually has a clue as to what the answer is. Fourth, what do we actually know about the incidence of financial incentives and other support for child care in terms of what happens to people's career patterns. I've been struck at Harvard that there's something unfortunate and ironic about the fact that if you're a faculty member and you have a kid who's 18 who goes to college, we in effect, through an interest-free loan, give you about $9,000. If you have a six-year-old, we give you nothing. And I don't think we're very different from most other universities in this regard, but there is something odd about that strategic choice, if the goal is to recruit people to come to the university. But I don't think we know much about the child care issue. The fifth question—which it seems to me would be useful to study and to actually learn the answer to—is what do we know, or what can we learn, about the costs of career interruptions. There is something we would like to believe. We would like to believe that you can take a year off, or two years off, or three years off, or be half-time for five years, and it affects your productivity during the time, but that it really doesn't have any fundamental effect on the career path. And a whole set of conclusions would follow from that in terms of flexible work arrangements and so forth. And the question is, in what areas of academic life and in what ways is it actually true. Somebody reported to me on a study that they found, I don't remember who had told me about this—maybe it was you, Richard—that there was a very clear correlation between the average length of time, from the time a paper was cited. That is, in fields where the average papers cited had been written nine months ago, women had a much harder time than in fields where the average thing cited had been written ten years ago. And that is suggestive in this regard. On the discouraging side of it, someone remarked once that no economist who had gone to work at the President's Council of Economic Advisors for two years had done highly important academic work after they returned. Now, I'm sure there are counterexamples to that, and I'm sure people are kind of processing that Tobin's Q is the best-known counterexample to that proposition, and there are obviously different kinds of effects that happen from working in Washington for two years. But it would be useful to explore a variety of kinds of natural interruption experiments, to see what actual difference it makes, and to see whether it's actually true, and to see in what ways interruptions can be managed, and in what fields it makes a difference. I think it's an area in which there's conviction but where it doesn't seem to me there's an enormous amount of evidence. What should we all do? I think the case is overwhelming for employers trying to be the [unintelligible] employer who responds to everybody else's discrimination by competing effectively to locate people who others are discriminating against, or to provide different compensation packages that will attract the people who would otherwise have enormous difficulty with child care. I think a lot of discussion of issues around child care, issues around extending tenure clocks, issues around providing family benefits, are enormously important. I think there's a strong case for monitoring and making sure that searches are done very carefully and that there are enough people looking and watching that that pattern of choosing people like yourself is not allowed to take insidious effect. But I think it's something that has to be done with very great care because it slides easily into pressure to achieve given fractions in given years, which runs the enormous risk of people who were hired because they were terrific being made to feel, or even if not made to feel, being seen by others as having been hired for some other reason. And I think that's something we all need to be enormously careful of as we approach these issues, and it's something we need to do, but I think it's something that we need to do with great care.

Let me just conclude by saying that I've given you my best guesses after a fair amount of reading the literature and a lot of talking to people. They may be all wrong. I will have served my purpose if I have provoked thought on this question and provoked the marshalling of evidence to contradict what I have said. But I think we all need to be thinking very hard about how to do better on these issues and that they are too important to sentimentalize rather than to think about in as rigorous and careful ways as we can. That's why I think conferences like this are very, very valuable. Thank you.

Responding to Reading

1. According to Summers, what do the most prestigious activities in our society expect of people who want to rise to leadership positions? How do these expectations work against women?
2. At one point in his speech, Summers says that evidence seems to indicate that males and females have different aptitudes for math and science. He

also says that taste differences between males and females might account for their career choices. How strong is his evidence in support of these ideas?

3. Summers says that he does not want to solve the problems he mentions. Instead, he wants to raise issues that people should think long, hard, and rigorously about. Do you think he achieved his purpose? Or, do you think his remarks were ill-timed and ill-conceived?

Responding in Writing

Assume you are a female faculty member listening to Summers deliver his remarks. Write a response to Summers in which you agree or disagree with his ideas.

RESPONSE TO LAWRENCE SUMMERS

Women in Science and Engineering Leadership Institute

The Women in Science and Engineering Leadership Institute (WISELI) of the University of Wisconsin, College of Engineering, has as its mission "to address a number of impediments to women's academic advancement." The Institute seeks to increase female presence and influence in the traditionally male fields of science and engineering. Shortly after Lawrence Summers, President of Harvard University, delivered his January 2005 speech on the disparity between male and female scientists and engineers (see page 613) the Institute, one of many organizations that objected to Summers's remarks, issued the following response.

At a recent private, invitation-only conference on women and minorities in science, Harvard University president, Lawrence Summers, gave a controversial luncheon talk offering three possible explanations for the small numbers of women in high-level positions in science and engineering. Because Summers' "explanations" are being widely reported in the press and because the conference organizer and Harvard economist, Richard B. Freeman, has characterized Summers' critics as "very sensitive" and as over-reacting, WISELI feels compelled to address and counter the arguments Summers' made.

The reasons for women's inadequate representation at the highest levels of academic science are indeed complex and we whole-heartedly agree with Summers' contention that "raising questions, discussing multiple factors that may explain a difficult problem, and seeking to understand how they interrelate is vitally important" (Summers, 1/18).

Indeed WISELI—the Women in Science and Engineering Leadership Institute, funded by the National Science Foundation's (NSF) AD-VANCE Institutional Transformation grant program—is committed to conducting research that seeks to identify such complex and interacting factors and to implement remedies based on research findings. WISELI is joined in this effort by eighteen other universities funded by NSF's ADVANCE Program. In addition, the efforts of all these institutions are based on and supplemented by the work of several reputable scholars who have devoted years of research to the question of women's achievements in science and engineering and who have published numerous books and scholarly articles on the subject. Several of these scholars were in attendance at the conference in question. The problem is not that the question of women's representation and achievement in science be analyzed and discussed; indeed that was the point of the conference. The problem is that Lawrence Summers appears to be ignorant of the vast body of scholarship that already exists on the subject.

Summers began by positing that one reason for women's inadequate representation in high-level positions in science is the reluctance or inability of women who have children to work 80-hour weeks. As Virginia Valian, author of *Why So Slow: The Advancement of Women,* notes in an as yet unpublished opinon piece submitted to *The New York Times,* Summers' explanation assumes that "80-hour work weeks are a necessary condition for intellectual creativity and excellence" and that "women who *do* put in 80-hour weeks receive the same rewards as men." Both assumptions, Valian argues, are faulty. According to Valian, there is no data showing that an 80-hour workweek is essential for academic excellence; "it is a folk belief still awaiting verification" (Valian). There is also a vast array of data indicating that women who do put in 80-hour weeks do not reap the same rewards as men. Numerous controlled studies show that women's successes are frequently attributed to luck rather than skill and that women are more poorly evaluated than men with precisely the same experience and credentials (Deaux and Emswiller, Martell, Eagly and Karau, Heilman, Ridgeway, Valian). In one such study, 238 academic psychologists, 118 male and 120 female, evaluated a résumé submitted in application for an assistant professorship that was randomly assigned a male or female name. Both male and female participants gave the male applicant better evaluations for teaching and research and were more likely to hire the male applicant (Steinpreis et al.).

Summers continued by arguing that fewer girls than boys have top scores on science and math tests in late high school years. He acknowledged no one really understands the reasons for this, but went on to contend that genetics may provide the explanation. Women, he argued, do not have the same "intrinsic aptitude" as men in some fields. This lack of "intrinsic aptitude" presumably explains women's inadequate representation in senior positions on science faculty across the nation (Summers, 1/14). Summers glosses over a vast body of research on gender differences in science and math tests, including recent studies indicating that gender differences in performance on mathematical tests are small and decreasing and that a variety of complex and as yet not fully understood factors, including expectations and stereotype threat, influence performance (Leahey and Guo, Hyde et al., Spencer, Steele, and Quinn). To rely upon genetics as the explanatory factor is irresponsible and unscientific. Though genetic research has indeed made incredible advances and has shown, as Summers argued, that there is a genetic component to autism, it is highly unscientific to extrapolate from such research to conclude that genetics is also responsible for women's disproportionate representation in the higher echelons of math and science. Our past experience with eugenics, the effort to apply simple genetic concepts to solve and explain complex socially constructed conditions, should warn us against such simplistic extrapolation. Summers' comments on women's innate inabilities are insulting not only to women in general and women scientists in particular, but also to geneticists who struggle to meticulously research the highly complex interactions between genes and the environment.

Finally, Summers makes an argument based in his own field of expertise, economics. If discrimination was the main factor limiting the advancement of women in science and engineering, Summers argues, economic theory suggests that a school that does not discriminate would gain an advantage by hiring away the top women who were discriminated against elsewhere (Bombardieri, *Boston Globe*). Unfortunately, this theory posts a model of rational decision-making that frequently does not hold in practice, and does not take into consideration real world constraints that prevent talented and exceptional women scientists from seeking positions at other universities. For example, several studies indicate that women scientists, especially married women scientists with children, are more geographically constrained than their male counterparts (Kulis and Sicotti, Schauman and Xie). Summers' reliance on this neoclassical economic theory also fails to recognize the fact that discriminatory treatment may be widespread across academe; that there may not be a school that does not discriminate. Summers might also consider, as Virginia Valian points out, that particularly well-endowed private universities such as Harvard have considerable resources with which to indulge their "taste for discrimination" (to use the language of economists).

If Summers were more well-versed in the vast body of psychological and sociological research on the nature of discrimination, including the research of the members of his audience, perhaps he would have realized that our shared and deeply ingrained cultural expectations about gender, already internalized by his daughters who at a very young age named their toy trucks "daddy truck" and "baby truck," contribute to unintentional discriminatory treatment of women, particularly when they seek to enter fields traditionally dominated by men.

Are Summers' critics, including ourselves, "over reacting" and "very sensitive"? We think not. In response to his critics, Summers claimed that he was trying to be provocative. There is a difference, we argue, between provoking stimulating intellectual debate and discussion and ignoring research findings and questioning women's competence to excel in science.

Summers' failure to engage with the scholarly work in this field should be an embarrassment to Harvard University, for it tramples upon the proud tradition of intellectual excellence that Harvard University claims to uphold. Summers needs a thorough education in the issues confronting women in academe. For the sake of Harvard University, its women students who aspire to positions in science, and its female faculty members, we hope he gets it.

> Molly Carnes, M.D., M.S., Co-Director, WISELI; Professor, Departments of Medicine, Psychiatry, and Industrial & Systems Engineering; Director, Center for Women's Health Research
>
> Jo Handelsman, Ph.D., Co-Director, WISELI, Howard Hughes Medical Institute Professor, Department of Plant Pathology
>
> Eve Fine, M.A., Researcher, WISELI
>
> Jennifer Sheridan, Ph.D., Research Director, WISELI
>
> Deveny Benting, B.A., Researcher and Evaluator, WISELI
>
> Vicki Bier, Ph.D., Professor, Department of Industrial and Systems Engineering; Member, WISELI Leadership Team
>
> Patricia F. Brennan, Ph.D., M.S.N., Professor, Departments of Industrial Engineering, Biomedical Engineering, and School of Nursing; Member, WISELI Leadership Team
>
> Pat Farrell, Ph.D., Associate Dean for Academic Affairs, College of Engineering; Professor, Departments of Mechanical Engineering; Member, WISELI Leadership Team
>
> Cecilia Ford, Ph.D., Professor, English Language and Linguistics, Department of English; Member, WISELI Leadership Team
>
> Catherine Middlecamp, Ph.D., Distinguished Faculty Associate, Department of Chemistry; Member, WISELI Leadership Team
>
> Gary Sandefur, Ph.D., Dean, College of Letters and Sciences; Professor, Department of Sociology; Member, WISELI Leadership Team

Amy Stambach, Ph.D., Associate Professor of Educational Policy Studies and Anthropology; Member, WISELI Leadership Team

Lillian Tong, Ph.D., Faculty Associate, Undergraduate Education Coordinator; Director of Faculty/Staff Programs, Center for Biology Education; Member, WISELI Leadership Team

References

Biernat, Monica and Kathleen Fuegen. "Shifting Standards and the Evaluation of Competence: Complexity in Gender-Based Judgment and Decision Making." *J Social Issues* 57 (2001): 707–724.

Bombardieri, Marcella. "Summers' remarks on women draw fire." *Boston Globe.* January 17, 2005. http://www.boston.com/news/education/higher/articles/2005/01/17/summers_remarks_on_women_draw_fire/

Eagly, Alice H. and Steven J. Karau. "Role Congruity Theory of Prejudice toward Female Leaders." *Psychological Review* 109 (2002): 573–598.

Heilman, Madeline E. "Description and Prescription: How Gender Stereotypes Prevent Women's Ascent up the Organizational Ladder." *J Social Issues* 57 (2001): 657–674.

Heilman, Madeline E., et al. "Penalties for Success: Reactions to Women Who Succeed at Male Gender-Typed Tasks." *J Applied Psychology* 89 (2004): 416–427.

Hyde, Janet, et al. "Gender Differences in Mathematics Performance: A Meta-Analysis." *Psychological Bulletin* 107(1990): 139–155.

Kulis, Stephen and Diane Sicotti. "Women Scientists in Academia: Geographically Constrained to Big Cities, College Clusters, or the Coasts?" *Research in Higher Education* 43 (2002): 1–30.

Leahey, Erin and Guang Guo. "Gender Differences in Mathematical Trajectories." *Social Forces* 80 (2001): 713–732.

Martell, Richard F. "Sex Bias at Work: The Effects of Attentional and Memory Demands on Performance Ratings of Men and Women." *J Applied Social Psychology* 21 (1991): 1939–1960.

Harvard Chief Defends His Talk on Women

Ridgeway, Cecilia L. "Gender, Status, and Leadership." *J Social Issues* 57 (2001): 637–655.

Shaumann, Kimberlee A. and Yu Xie. "Geographic Mobility of Scientists: Sex Differences and Family Constraints." *Demography* 33 (1996): 455–468.

Spencer, Stephen J., Claude M. Steele, and Diane M. Quinn. "Stereotype Threat and Woman's Math Performance." *Journal of Experimental Social Psychology* 35(1999): 4–28.

CHAPTER 9 FOCUS 3

Steinpreis, Rita E., Katie A. Ander, and Dawn Ritzke. "The Impact of Gender on the Review of the Curricula Vitae of Job Applicants and Tenure Candidates: A National Empirical Study." *Sex Roles* 41 (1999): 509–528.

Summers, Lawrence, Remarks at NBER Conference on Diversifying the Science & Engineering Workforce, January 14, 2005. (http://www .president.harvard.edu/speeches/2005/nber.html)

Summers, Lawrence as quoted in Sam Dillon. "Harvard Chief Defends His Talk on Women." *New York Times* January 18, 2005. (http://www .nytimes.com/2005/01/18/national/18harvard.html?8bl)

Valian, Virginia. "Who Belongs at Harvard." Unpublished. January 18, 2005. (http://wiseli.engr.wisc.edu/news/ValianonSummers.rtf)

Valian, Virginia. *Why So Slow? The Advancement of Women.* Cambridge, MA: MIT Press, 1998.

Responding to Reading

1. Why do the members of WISELI feel compelled to address Summers's comments about women in science?
2. In its statement, WISELI says that it does not object to a discussion that focuses on the representation and achievement of women in science. What specifically does it object to?
3. How does WISELI respond to the following points made by Lawrence Summers?

   - Women who have children will not work 80-hour weeks.
   - Fewer girls than boys have high scores on high school science and math tests.
   - Schools that do not discriminate against women would have an economic advantage over schools that do discriminate.

Responding in Writing

In their response to Summers, WISELI says that his critics have been accused of overreacting. Do you think they *are* overreacting?

SUMMERS OF OUR DISCONTENT

Katha Pollitt

1949–

Feminist critic, essayist, and poet Katha Pollitt has written four books, most recently Virginity or Death! and Other Social and Political Issues of Our Time *(2006). She writes a bimonthly column in the* Nation, *"Subject to Debate," where the following counterargument to Lawrence Summers's now infamous January 2005 speech (see page 613) originally appeared.*

As the saying goes, behind every successful woman is a man who is surprised. Harvard president Larry Summers apparently is that man. A distinguished economist who was Treasury Secretary under Clinton, Summers caused a firestorm on January 14 when, speaking from notes at a conference on academic diversity, he argued that tenured women are rare in math and science for three reasons, which he listed in descending order of importance. One, women choose family commitments over the eighty-hour weeks achievement in those fields requires; two, fewer women than men have the necessary genetic gifts; and three, women are discriminated against. Following standard economic theory, Summers largely discounted discrimination: A first-rate woman rejected by one university would surely be snapped up by a rival. We're back to women's lack of commitment and brainpower.

On campus, Summers has lost big—he has had to apologize, appoint a committee and endure many a hairy eyeball from the faculty, and complaints from furious alumnae like me. In the press, he's done much better: Provocative thinker brought down by PC feminist mob! Women *are* dumber! Steven Pinker says so! The *New York Times* even ran a supportive op-ed by Charles Murray without identifying him as the co-author of *The Bell Curve,* the discredited farrago of racist claptrap. While much was made of MIT biologist Nancy Hopkins walking out of his talk—what about free speech, what about Truth?—we heard little about how Summers, who says he only wanted to spark a discussion, has refused to release his remarks. The bold challenger of campus orthodoxy apparently doesn't want the world to know what he actually said.

Do men have an innate edge in math and science? Perhaps someday we will live in a world free of the gender bias and stereo-typing we know exists today both in and out of the classroom, and we will be able to answer that question, if anyone is still asking it. But we know we don't live in a bias-free world now: Girls are steered away from math and science from the moment they are born. The interesting fact is that, thanks partly to antidiscrimination laws that have forced open closed doors, they have steadily increased their performance nonetheless. Most of my Radcliffe classmates remember being firmly discouraged from anything to do with numbers or labs; one was flatly told that women couldn't be physicians—at her Harvard med school interview. Today women obtain 48 percent of BAs in math, 57 percent in biology and agricultural science, half of all places in med school, and they are steadily increasing their numbers as finalists in the Intel high school science contest (fifteen out of forty this year, and three out of four in New York City).

Every gain women have made in the past 200 years has been in the face of experts insisting they couldn't do it and didn't really want to. Biology, now trotted out to "prove" women's incapacity for math and

CHAPTER 9   FOCUS 3

science, used to "prove" that they shouldn't go to college at all. As women progress, the proponents of innate inferiority simply adapt their arguments to explain why further advancement is unlikely. But how can we know that in 2005, any more than we knew it in 1905? I'd like to hear those experts explain this instead: The number of tenure offers to women at Harvard has gone down in each of Summers's three years as president, from nine in thirty-six tenures to three in thirty-two. (The year before his arrival, it was thirteen women out of thirty-six.) Surely women's genes have not deteriorated since 2001?

5   Whatever they may be in theory, in the workplace, biological incapacity and natural preference are the counters used to defend against accusations of discrimination. Summers argues that competition makes discrimination irrational; that wouldn't hold, though, if an entire field is pervaded with discrimination, if there's a consensus that women don't belong there and if female candidates are judged more harshly by all potential employers. It also doesn't work if the threat of competition isn't so credible: It will be a long time before the Ivies feel the heat from Northwestern, which has improved its profile by hiring the first-rate women they foolishly let go. The history of women and minorities in the workplace shows that vigorous enforcement of antidiscrimination law is what drives progress. Moreover, the competition argument can be turned against Summers: After all, given its prestige and wealth, Harvard could "compete" for women with any university on the planet. So why doesn't it?

This brings us to that eighty-hour week and women's domestic "choices." It's a truism that career ladders are based on the traditional male life plan—he knocks himself out in his 20s and 30s while his wife raises the kids, mends his socks and types his papers. If women had been included from the start, the ladder would look rather different—careers might peak later, taking a semester off to have a baby would not blot your copybook, women would not be expected to do huge amounts of academic service work and then be blamed at tenure time for not publishing more. By treating this work culture as fixed, and women as the problem, Summers lets academia off the hook. Yet Harvard, with its $23 billion endowment, doesn't even offer free daycare to grad students.

There's a ton of research on all the subjects raised by Summers—the socialization of girls; conscious and unconscious gender bias in teaching, hiring and promotion; what makes talented females, like Intel finalists, drop out of science at every stage; what makes motherhood so hard to combine with a career. We are past the day when brilliant women could be expected to sit quietly while a powerful man parades his ignorance of that scholarship and of their experience. It is not "provocative" when the president of Harvard justifies his university's lamentable record by recalling that his toddler daughter treated toy trucks like dolls. It's an insult to his audience. What was his point, anyway? That she'll grow up and flunk calculus? That she'll get a job in a daycare center?

If Summers wants to know why women are underrepresented in math and science, he should do his homework, beginning with Nancy Hopkins's pathbreaking 1999 study of bias against female faculty at MIT. And then he should ask them.

Responding to Reading

1. In paragraph 1, Pollitt asserts that Lawrence Summers caused controversy when he "argued that tenured women are rare in math and science" because they choose family commitments over work; because they do not have the genetic makeup for math and science; and because they are discriminated against. Does Pollitt accurately characterize Summers's remarks? (See "Remarks at NBER Conference on Diversifying the Science and Engineering Workforce," p. 613.)
2. In paragraph 3, Pollitt asks, "Do men have an innate edge in math and science?" How effectively does she answer this question? What evidence does she supply to support her arguments?
3. What preconceived ideas does Pollitt have about her subject? How do you know? Does she consider her readers friendly or hostile to her arguments? Explain.

Responding in Writing

According to Pollitt, "Every gain women have made in the past 200 years has been in the face of experts insisting they couldn't do it and didn't really want to" (4). Do you think she is correct?

THE TRUTH ABOUT MEN AND WOMEN

Andrew Sullivan

1963–

A former editor-in-chief of the New Republic, *Andrew Sullivan is a contributor to the* New York Times Magazine, *an essayist for* Time, *and a columnist for the* Sunday Times *of London as well as a prolific blogger. He has written and edited several books, most recently* The Conservative Soul: How We Lost It, How to Get It Back *(2006). In this* Sunday Times *column, Sullivan defends Lawrence Summers's controversial January 2005 speech.*

We should perhaps be grateful that Kingsley Amis is not around to write a novel about the current president of Harvard, Larry Summers. But "Larry and the Women" would be a great read—along with "Larry and the African-Americans" or even "Larry and the Gays."

Most provocateurs tend toward the dense. Summers is one of the sharpest minds of his generation. When he speaks, it's hard to ignore him. In Washington, where he worked as an economics adviser to the Clinton administration, he left politicians and bureaucrats agape with his energy and arrogance.

Then, in some stroke of unusual brilliance, he was appointed president of Harvard. One of his first moves was pointedly to ask Cornel West, the African-American scholar, when he was going to produce a new, solid body of work. West quit in outrage. Then Summers backed allowing military recruiters on campus, despite a boycott because of their ban on gays. Some of the faculty have been regretting Summers's appointment ever since.

They should get over it. Summers is the best thing to happen to American higher education in a very long time. The latest flap reveals why. Summers was speaking in a private capacity at a seminar that was supposed to be off the record. He had no text and spoke from notes. His topic was why women are not equally represented at the very top of the sciences in the American academy.

5   Women make up 35% of the faculty in US higher education (and a majority of students). But they make up only 20% of top positions in science. Summers prefaced his remarks by saying they were designed to provoke. He spoke of the fact that some women might prefer to spend critical research years bringing up children.

Then he made the mistake of pointing to some interesting research by the University of Michigan sociologist Yu Xie and his University of California–Davis colleague Kimberlee A Shauman. Their hypothesis was that in science tests the median score for men and women was roughly the same. But for some reason men were disproportionately represented at the very bottom and the very top of the table.

Or, as the *Harvard Crimson* reported: "There are more men who are at the top and more men who are utter failures."

One possible explanation for this is genetics. Summers raised the possibility that this might have something to do with male preponderance at the very top of research science. And he immediately added: "I'd like to be proven wrong on this one."

This was too much for one of the attendees, Professor Nancy Hopkins. "When he started talking about innate differences in aptitude between men and women, I just couldn't breathe because this kind of bias makes me physically ill," Hopkins told a sympathetic *New York Times*. "Let's not forget that people used to say that women couldn't drive an automobile."

10   Okay, let's not forget that. But, honestly, what does it say that a leading academic finds the mere positing of an empirical theory of a complex problem something that makes her "physically ill"? And to leap immediately from Summers's subtle question to the crudest

accusations of sexism is a form of emotional blackmail. It's a sublime example of the left-liberal academy's preference for feeling over argument.

The Massachusetts Institute of Technology's brilliant scientist Steven Pinker put it better than I can: "Look, the truth cannot be offensive. Perhaps the hypothesis is wrong, but how would we ever find out whether it is wrong if it is 'offensive' even to consider it? People who storm out of a meeting at the mention of a hypothesis, or declare it taboo or offensive without providing arguments or evidence, don't get the concept of a university or free inquiry."

Is Summers's supposition outrageous? Hardly. Scientists are finding out more and more about the differences between the male and female brains. One thing that endures across cultures and populations is a male edge at the very top of the bell curve for spatial and mathematical reasoning. Ever wonder why boys are more likely to suffer from autism? Some researchers are investigating whether autism isn't an extreme case of this specialisation.

Scientists have also discovered correlations between certain behavioural traits and levels of testosterone. Testosterone exists in both men and women but it is far more plentiful in men. Among testosterone-related characteristics are aggression, lack of focus and edginess.

No big surprise then that 95% of all hyperactive kids are boys; or that four times as many boys are dyslexic and learning-disabled as girls. There is a greater distinction between the right and left brains among boys than girls, and worse linguistic skills. These are generalisations, of course. There are many boys who are great linguists and model students, and vice versa. Some boys even prefer, when left to their own devices, to play with dolls as well as trucks. But we are talking of generalities.

All this is the subject of cutting-edge scientific debate. It cannot be 15 illegitimate to conduct it. In a university it shouldn't be illegitimate to have any debate that is rooted in evidence, reason and argument. That's what universities are for.

Of course, discussion of human natural inequality will always be sensitive. It's a hard fact to absorb that some people will never be as intelligent as some others, or as musically gifted, or as mathematically skilled. Americans in particular hate the notion that there is some natural limit on what people can and cannot achieve.

But there is a distinction between moral and political equality for all—the bedrock of a liberal society—and unavoidable natural inequalities between human beings and, in a few narrow areas, between social groups. This cannot and should not mean that any individual should be prejudged or denied opportunity. But it does mean that some imbalances in certain professions may not be entirely a function of prejudice or bigotry.

Summers would be in a stronger position if Harvard didn't have a much worse record in hiring women professors than some other universities. There were 32 tenured members of faculty hired last year at Harvard, of which only four were women. He'd also be better off if he had silky social skills. But by raising interesting questions Summers is leading by example. True scholars are afraid of no hypothesis; they go where others fear to think.

For all the offence he has created, Summers has revealed one important fact: the truth sometimes is controversial. And if you aren't sometimes challenged and appalled by some ideas, you haven't really begun to grapple with them.

Responding to Reading

1. In paragraph 4, Sullivan says, "Summers is the best thing to happen to American higher education in a very long time." Does Sullivan support this assertion? Do you agree with him?
2. In paragraph 12, Sullivan asks, "Is Summers's supposition outrageous?" What "supposition" is he referring to? He then answers, "Hardly." Do you agree?
3. In paragraph 17, Sullivan says, "Some imbalances in certain professions may not be entirely a function of prejudice or bigotry." Do you think he is right?

Responding in Writing

Do you believe there are innate differences between men and women that affect their choice of careers?

WIDENING THE FOCUS

For Critical Thinking and Writing

Write an essay in which you answer one of the three Focus questions in this chapter:

- Is global warming fact or fiction?
- Can the energy crisis be solved?
- Are men better in math and science than women?

In your essay, refer to the essays in the appropriate Focus section of this chapter.

For Further Reading

The following readings can suggest additional perspectives for thinking and writing about science and human values:

- Virginia Woolf, "Professions for Women" (p. 500)
- Tenzin Gyatso, "Our Faith in Science" (p. 641)
- Christoph Schonborn, "Finding Design in Nature" (p. 680)
- Claire McCarthy, "Dog Lab" (p. 756)
- Stanley Milgrim, "The Perils of Obedience" (p. 764)

For Internet Research

This chapter presents views across the spectrum on three important topics in science and human values: global warming, the energy crisis, and gender equality in math and science. Visit the Web site for Science Friday, a weekly National Public Radio program that engages discussion on various scientific issues, at <http://www.sciencefriday.com/>. Read blog postings, such as "Global Warming: The Object Speaks for Itself," and listen to streaming audio for archived Science Friday programs. Select one scientific issue, and write an essay in which you evaluate the arguments and evidence presented in the blog posting or audio archive on your topic. Be sure to explain which arguments you find most effective and why.

CHAPTER 9 FOCUS 3

--- **Writing** ---

Science and Human Values

1. Identify a scientific or technological advance that has changed your life or the life of someone you know. Write an essay in which you discuss how this development has affected you or the person you know.
2. On the Web, find some political speeches that address one of the three issues considered in this chapter. Write an essay in which you evaluate the politicians' arguments.
3. Assume you are moderating a debate about global warming. Read the essays about global warming in this chapter. Then, write an essay in which you assess the arguments presented by the writers. Which writer do you think makes the strongest case? Who makes the weakest case? (Remember, you do not necessarily have to agree with a writer whose arguments you find effective).
4. Search the Internet for information about the alternative energy sources mentioned in "Over a Barrel" by Paul Roberts (p. 582) and "Energy's Future" by Dennis Behreandt (p. 592). Do you believe these alternative sources can ease the energy problems of this country? Why or why not?
5. Do you believe that Lawrence Summers disparaged women in "Remarks at NBER Conference on Diversifying the Science and Engineering Workforce" (p. 613)? Is the WISELI "Response to Lawrence Summers' Remarks on Women in Science" justified (p. 622)? Or, do you agree with Andrew Sullivan's assessment in "The Truth about Men and Women" (p. 630)?
6. Are you generally optimistic or pessimistic about America's technological future? Do you think that the United States will be able to deal with the technological and moral problems that technology creates? Or, do you think that these problems will continue to plague us? Use several of the essays in this chapter to support your position.
7. Write a proposal addressed to the president of your college or university in which you suggest ways to encourage more women to take advanced math and science courses. Use the essays by lawrence Summers (p. 613), WISELI (p. 622), and katha pollitt (p. 627) to support your ideas.
8. Visit several Web sites that take a position on alternate energy sources. Read the arguments each site presents to support its case, and look at the visuals these sites use to reinforce their positions. Then, write an essay in which you evaluate one of these sites. Discuss your impressions of the site as well as your evaluation of its fairness and effectiveness.

9. In "The False Alert of Global Warming" (p. 575), Tom Bethell says that environmentalists have created global warming "to keep the money rolling in" (28). Write an essay in which you agree or disagree with his contention. Be sure you discuss which of his specific arguments are convincing and which are not.

10

■ ■ ■ ■ □ ■ ■ ■ ■

RELIGION IN AMERICA

■ ■ □ ■ ■

Since its inception, the United States has been a country in which religion was important. Historical figures such as George Washington, Benjamin Franklin, and Abraham Lincoln routinely called on God for guidance, and many of our founding documents invoke the deity. As Alexis de Toqueville, the nineteenth-century social philosopher, observed in 1830, "There is no country in the world where the Christian religion retains a greater influence over the souls of men than in America." Although the United States has become a much more secular country since de Toqueville wrote *Democracy in America,* we are still a nation in which religion is extremely influential. Even though the Constitution expressly forbids the establishment of a state religion, religion plays a significant role in our public life. For example, our currency carries the

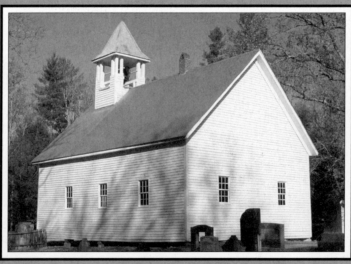

A simple white church at Great Smoky Mountains National Park in Tennessee

phrase "In God we trust," the Pledge of Allegiance includes the words "One nation under God," and the President takes the oath of office with a hand on the Bible.

Moreover, organized religion plays a strong role in everyday American life. According to a survey conducted at the University of Michigan, the United States has a higher level of church attendance than any other country at a comparable level of development. Over 44 percent of Americans say they attend church, synagogue, or another house of worship once a week. This figure compares to 16 percent in Britain, 14 percent in France, and 13 percent in Germany. (In some areas of Sweden and The Netherlands, church attendance is less than 10 percent.) In addition, 53 percent of Americans say religion is very important in their lives, 80 percent say they pray regularly, and almost 80 percent believe God either created or guided the development of human beings. Over 60 percent of Americans say faith is critical to their lives, and almost 40 percent read the Bible at least once a week. Despite the fact that some scholars consider these figures somewhat inflated, they suggest the strength of religious belief in the United States. Even so, a secular view of the world also manifests itself in American thought, sometimes complementing religious interpretations and sometimes challenging them.

The Focus section of this chapter (p. 659) examines the conflicting claims of science and religion as they apply to Darwin's Theory of Evolution. Specifically, it asks the question, "Is there intelligent design in nature?" In "Finding Design in Nature," Christoph Schönborn

The 7,000-seat Willow Creek Community church during a service in South Barrington, Illinois

argues that science alone cannot explain the complex design of nature. In "Why Intelligent Design Isn't," H. Allen Orr refutes two major critics of Darwinian evolution. Finally, in "Finding Darwin's God," Kenneth R. Miller attempts to bridge the gap between evolution and intelligent design.

PREPARING TO READ AND WRITE

- Is the writer examining religion or spirituality in general, or does he or she have a narrower focus?

- Is the writer's focus on morality? Ethics? Values?

- Does the writer focus on a particular social or political issue?

- Does the writer present opposing opinions fairly? Respectfully?

- Does the writer acknowledge the limitations of his or her own positions?

- Is the writer discussing his or her own beliefs or considering the broader impact of religion on society?

- What role does the writer think religion should play in society?

- Are the writer's sympathies with science or with religion?

- Does the writer think that the gap between science and religion can be bridged?

- Does the writer interpret religious doctrine literally or figuratively?

- In what way do the writer's beliefs affect his or her discussion?

- Which of the writers' ideas are most similar? Which are most like your own?

SALVATION

Langston Hughes

1902–1967

Poet, novelist, dramatist, and nonfiction writer Langston Hughes was central to the 1920s Harlem Renaissance, which helped to shape the genre of African-American literature. His work focuses largely on the social plight of African Americans and their rich and vibrant culture, especially their contributions of jazz and blues to American music. In the following autobiographical essay, Hughes explores his own religious experience as a young boy.

I was saved from sin when I was going on thirteen. But not really saved. It happened like this. There was a big revival at my Auntie Reed's church. Every night for weeks there had been much preaching, singing, praying, and shouting, and some very hardened sinners had been brought to Christ, and the membership of the church had grown by leaps and bounds. Then just before the revival ended, they held a special meeting for children, "to bring the young lambs to the fold." My aunt spoke of it for days ahead. That night I was escorted to the front row and placed on the mourners' bench with all the other young sinners, who had not yet been brought to Jesus.

My aunt told me that when you were saved you saw a light, and something happened to you inside! And Jesus came into your life! And God was with you from then on! She said you could see and hear and feel Jesus in your soul. I believed her. I had heard a great many old people say the same thing and it seemed to me they ought to know. So I sat there calmly in the hot, crowded church, waiting for Jesus to come to me.

The preacher preached a wonderful rhythmical sermon, all moans and shouts and lonely cries and dire pictures of hell, and then he sang a song about the ninety and nine safe in the fold, but one little lamb was left out in the cold. Then he said: "Won't you come? Won't you come to Jesus? Young lambs, won't you come?" And he held out his arms to all us young sinners there on the mourners' bench. And the little girls cried. And some of them jumped up and went to Jesus right away. But most of us just sat there.

A great many old people came and knelt around us and prayed, old women with jet-black faces and braided hair, old men with work-gnarled hands. And the church sang a song about the lower lights are burning, some poor sinners to be saved. And the whole building rocked with prayer and song.

Still I kept waiting to *see* Jesus.

5

Finally all the young people had gone to the altar and were saved, but one boy and me. He was a rounder's[1] son named Westley. Westley and I were surrounded by sisters and deacons praying. It was very hot in the church, and getting late now. Finally Westley said to me in a whisper: "God damn! I'm tired o' sitting here. Let's get up and be saved." So he got up and was saved.

Then I was left all alone on the mourners' bench. My aunt came and knelt at my knees and cried, while prayers and song swirled all around me in the little church. The whole congregation prayed for me alone, in a mighty wail of moans and voices. And I kept waiting serenely for Jesus, waiting, waiting—but he didn't come. I wanted to see him, but nothing happened to me. Nothing! I wanted something to happen to me, but nothing happened.

I heard the songs and the minister saying: "Why don't you come? My dear child, why don't you come to Jesus? Jesus is waiting for you. He wants you. Why don't you come? Sister Reed, what is this child's name?"

"Langston," my aunt sobbed.

10   "Langston, why don't you come? Why don't you come and be saved? Oh, Lamb of God! Why don't you come?"

Now it was really getting late. I began to be ashamed of myself, holding everything up so long. I began to wonder what God thought about Westley, who certainly hadn't seen Jesus either, but who was now sitting proudly on the platform, swinging his knickerbockered[2] legs and grinning down at me, surrounded by deacons and old women on their knees praying. God had not struck Westley dead for taking his name in vain or for lying in the temple. So I decided that maybe to save further trouble, I'd better lie, too, and say that Jesus had come, and get up and be saved.

So I got up.

Suddenly the whole room broke into a sea of shouting, as they saw me rise. Waves of rejoicing swept the place. Women leaped in the air. My aunt threw her arms around me. The minister took me by the hand and led me to the platform.

When things quieted down, in a hushed silence, punctuated by a few ecstatic "Amens," all the new young lambs were blessed in the name of God. Then joyous singing filled the room.

15   That night, for the first time in my life but one for I was a big boy twelve years old—I cried. I cried, in bed alone, and couldn't stop. I buried my head under the quilts, but my aunt heard me. She woke up and told my uncle I was crying because the Holy Ghost had come into my life, and because I had seen Jesus. But I was really crying because I couldn't bear to tell her that I had lied, that I had deceived everybody

---

[1] a dissolute person [Eds.]
[2] wearing short full trousers gathered at the knees

in the church, that I hadn't seen Jesus, and that now I didn't believe there was a Jesus anymore, since he didn't come to help me.

Responding to Reading

1. Hughes opens his essay by saying, "I was saved from sin when I was going on thirteen. But not really saved." What does he mean? Was he "saved" or not?
2. Paraphrase the explanation of salvation in paragraph 2. How is his aunt's description of this process different from what young Langston expects to experience?
3. Do you think Langston's motivation for accepting salvation is any different from Westley's? Explain.

Responding in Writing

The young Langston Hughes cries because he believes he has lied and "deceived everybody in the church" (15). Do you think he is being too hard on himself, or do you think he really has committed a sin?

OUR FAITH IN SCIENCE

Tenzin Gyatso, Dalai Lama XIV
1935–

The fourteenth Dalai Lama, Tenzin Gyatso is the spiritual and political leader of Tibetan Buddhism. In 1959, he was forced into exile when the Chinese military occupied Tibet. Literally the "Ocean of Wisdom," the Dalai Lama is a scholar, diplomat, politician, and civil servant who travels the world to foster peace and understanding among different cultures and religions. Gyatso has written numerous books, including The Universe in a Single Atom: The Controversy of Science and Spirituality *(2006), in which he explores the intersection of faith and science, also the topic of the following essay.*

Science has always fascinated me. As a child in Tibet, I was keenly curious about how things worked. When I got a toy I would play with it a bit, then take it apart to see how it was put together. As I became older, I applied the same scrutiny to a movie projector and an antique automobile.

At one point I became particularly intrigued by an old telescope, with which I would study the heavens. One night while looking at the moon I realized that there were shadows on its surface. I corralled my two main tutors to show them, because this was contrary to the ancient version of cosmology I had been taught, which held that the moon was a heavenly body that emitted its own light.

But through my telescope the moon was clearly just a barren rock, pocked with craters. If the author of that fourth-century treatise were writing today, I'm sure he would write the chapter on cosmology differently.

If science proves some belief of Buddhism wrong, then Buddhism will have to change. In my view, science and Buddhism share a search for the truth and for understanding reality. By learning from science about aspects of reality where its understanding may be more advanced, I believe that Buddhism enriches its own worldview.

5   For many years now, on my own and through the Mind and Life Institute, which I helped found, I have had the opportunity to meet with scientists to discuss their work. World-class scientists have generously coached me in subatomic physics, cosmology, psychology, biology.

It is our discussions of neuroscience, however, that have proved particularly important. From these exchanges a vigorous research initiative has emerged, a collaboration between monks and neuroscientists, to explore how meditation might alter brain function.

The goal here is not to prove Buddhism right or wrong—or even to bring people to Buddhism—but rather to take these methods out of the traditional context, study their potential benefits, and share the findings with anyone who might find them helpful.

After all, if practices from my own tradition can be brought together with scientific methods, then we may be able to take another small step toward alleviating human suffering.

Already this collaboration has borne fruit. Dr. Richard Davidson, a neuroscientist at the University of Wisconsin, has published results from brain imaging studies of lamas meditating. He found that during meditation the regions of the brain thought to be related to happiness increase in activity. He also found that the longer a person has been a meditator, the greater the activity increase will be.

10   Other studies are under way. At Princeton University, Dr. Jonathan Cohen, a neuroscientist, is studying the effects of meditation on attention. At the University of California Medical School at San Francisco, Dr. Margaret Kemeny has been studying how meditation helps develop empathy in school teachers.

Whatever the results of this work, I am encouraged that it is taking place. You see, many people still consider science and religion to be in opposition. While I agree that certain religious concepts conflict with scientific facts and principles, I also feel that people from both worlds can have an intelligent discussion, one that has the power ultimately to generate a deeper understanding of challenges we face together in our interconnected world.

One of my first teachers of science was the German physicist Carl von Weizsäcker, who had been an apprentice to the quantum theorist

Werner Heisenberg. Dr. Weizsäcker was kind enough to give me some formal tutorials on scientific topics. (I confess that while listening to him I would feel I could grasp the intricacies of the full argument, but when the sessions were over there was often not a great deal of his explanation left behind.)

What impressed me most deeply was how Dr. Weizsäcker worried about both the philosophical implications of quantum physics and the ethical consequences of science generally. He felt that science could benefit from exploring issues usually left to the humanities.

I believe that we must find a way to bring ethical considerations to bear upon the direction of scientific development, especially in the life sciences. By invoking fundamental ethical principles, I am not advocating a fusion of religious ethics and scientific inquiry.

Rather, I am speaking of what I call "secular ethics," which embrace the principles we share as human beings: compassion, tolerance, consideration of others, the responsible use of knowledge and power. These principles transcend the barriers between religious believers and nonbelievers; they belong not to one faith, but to all faiths.

Today, our knowledge of the human brain and body at the cellular and genetic level has reached a new level of sophistication. Advances in genetic manipulation, for example, mean scientists can create new genetic entities—like hybrid animal and plant species—whose long-term consequences are unknown.

Sometimes when scientists concentrate on their own narrow fields, their keen focus obscures the larger effect their work might have. In my conversations with scientists I try to remind them of the larger goal behind what they do in their daily work.

This is more important than ever. It is all too evident that our moral thinking simply has not been able to keep pace with the speed of scientific advancement. Yet the ramifications of this progress are such that it is no longer adequate to say that the choice of what to do with this knowledge should be left in the hands of individuals.

This is a point I intend to make when I speak at the annual meeting of the Society for Neuroscience today in Washington. I will suggest that how science relates to wider humanity is no longer of academic interest alone. This question must assume a sense of urgency for all those who are concerned about the fate of human existence.

A deeper dialogue between neuroscience and society—indeed between all scientific fields and society—could help deepen our understanding of what it means to be human and our responsibilities for the natural world we share with other sentient beings.

Just as the world of business has been paying renewed attention to ethics, the world of science would benefit from more deeply considering the implications of its own work. Scientists should be more than merely technically adept; they should be mindful of their own motivation and the larger goal of what they do: the betterment of humanity.

Responding to Reading

1. The author of this essay, a Buddhist and the spiritual leader of the people of Tibet, makes the following statement: "If science proves some belief of Buddhism wrong, then Buddhism will have to change" (4). Do you accept this statement at face value, or do you find it insincere or unrealistic?
2. Do you think the primary purpose of this essay is to explain how religion might be influenced by science, to explain how science might be influenced by religion, or to explain how science and religion can work together to improve people's lives? Explain.
3. What does Gyatso mean by " 'secular ethics' " (15)? Do you agree that the principles he mentions "transcend the barriers between religious believers and nonbelievers" (15)?

Responding in Writing

What specific values do you think "religious believers and nonbelievers" (15) might share? Why?

AMONG THE BELIEVERS

Tayari Jones

1970–

An assistant professor of English at the University of Illinois, Urbana— Champaign, Tayari Jones has written two novels, both of which explore coming of age, family, and identity. In the following essay, Jones describes the religious and irreligious transformation she experienced while she was growing up in the American South.

In elementary school, I spent a great deal of energy trying to explain the difference between atheism and devil worship. Until second grade I answered the commonplace query: "Where do you go to church?" with this: "My father says that we don't believe in God." Adults took this information with shocked silence, but children lack restraint. "You're a devil worshiper?," they asked. I didn't think I was but I asked Daddy who assured me that we were not. "Atheists," he explained, "don't believe in the devil either."

Though most of the other children found this argument to be convincing, they still demonstrated the difference between chilly tolerance and the warmth that came from actually fitting in. But I remained true to my faithlessness for the same reasons most children are true to a faith: because it is what their parents tell them.

My father, a preacher's son, had not been so obedient. When I visited his hometown, Oakdale, La., I was constantly aware that I was the daughter of the son who strayed.

During my summers in Oakdale, I understood what an outsider I really was. Unable to sing hymns from memory, not knowing when to stand or sit during the sermon—all of these things marked me as an infidel among believers. The most humiliating moment came at meals, when we all bowed our heads and one-by-one recited a Bible verse before starting to eat. My cousin Shunda—three years older, supremely disdainful and thus intimidatingly sophisticated—possessed a vast repertoire of premeal utterances. When my turn came, I could say only, "Jesus wept," which is like the tricycle of verses.

The summer before I entered fifth grade, my visit to Oakdale happened to coincide with vacation Bible school. At last, I could receive the remedial religious instruction I'd been longing for!   5

I looked forward to discussions in which I could ask some of the questions that I had previously posed to my father who gave the most unsatisfying responses:

Q. If God made the world, who made God?

A. God didn't make the world.

Q. Then why does it say so in the Bible?

A. Makes people feel better.

Q. How do the angels get their clothes on? Don't the wings get in the way?

A. The same way Santa gets down the chimney.

To my chagrin, there was little theological analysis in vacation Bible school. Mostly we used stumpy crayons to color bizarre pictures: line drawing of animals in pairs, dead giants, bread and fish. There weren't even captions saying who was who and what was what. We didn't learn any good hymns. By the third day of the five-day program, the only useful thing I had learned was that Job rhymed with "robe", not with "bob." On the fourth day, we used Popsicle sticks and yarn to make ornamental crucifixes called "God's Eyes." On the last day, the Bible school teacher pulled me aside and asked what was troubling me.

I blurted my most pressing question: "If God made the world, who made God?"

She squinted: "Are you trying to be funny?"

"No," I told her. I just wanted to understand religion and be like everyone else for a change. The teacher gave me a little smile and handed me a mimeographed sheet to read at home. It was the text of the 23rd Psalm. I read the opening line, "The Lord is my Shepherd; I shall not want." I knew this verse; it was Shunda's. Oh, the wonder of punctuation. When she quoted the verse, I thought it a bit rude, rejecting the Lord as one's shepherd, whatever that meant. But now I understood.

10   Feeling something akin to faith, I vowed to learn at least a verse or two. I imagined the adoring faces of my relatives as I surprised them at Sunday dinner. I smiled back at the teacher and she probably imagined that she had converted me, the daughter of Oakdale's best-known nonbelieving son.

The 23rd Psalm is not terribly long; before I knew it, I'd memorized the whole thing. Had I not won a prize the previous school year for reciting both "Hiawatha" and "Annabel Lee"? In Bible school we'd been told that God gives each person a special gift, a ministry. Perhaps dramatic recitation was mine.

At Grandmother's house the next Sunday, we all gathered around the table with our heads bowed. Beside me, my cousin said demurely, "Peace, be still." It was now my turn. Although most people pray with their eyes closed, I opened mine, wanting to see their expressions as I let loose with my Psalm.

"The Lord is my shepherd; I shall not want." Working my way through the first stanza, carefully pronouncing the "th" on "maketh," I felt something real. I pictured myself lying down in green pastures. In my mind's eye, I saw myself eating at the table prepared by the Lord. I'll never forget that moment of connection between myself and the glorious words; the comfort they described, was the warmth of well-being that I felt. By the time I got to the good part, I'd whipped myself into a fine crescendo: "Yea, though I walk through the valley of the shadow of death . . . "

At this instant, Shunda released a disapproving gasp-sigh. "Shut up," she said without saying. "The food is getting cold, you boring, annoying, little freak."

15   Chastened, I closed my eyes, but I continued my recitation, oblivious to the reaction of the others at the table, and the food cooling on the platters, riding the buoyancy of the words, filling my mind and heart with the lyrics of this strange and powerful song.

Now people think it charming when they find out that I grew up black, Southern and atheist. At a recent cocktail party, on hearing about my background, a woman said to me, "How idiosyncratic!" I suppose she is right. Left to find my own way in matters of religion, I have a quirky collection of experiences that have helped me sort out my relationship with the divine.

The 23rd Psalm mimeographed on cheap paper gave me my first glimpse into spirituality, but the moment was not marked by the speaking of tongues. That moment will be forever etched in my memory as the day that language revealed to me if not its full power, its awesome potential. Maybe this is the day it was decided that I would be a writer, when I saw in the beauty of a poem the true glory of God.

Responding to Reading

1. In paragraph 2, Jones says that she "remained true to [her] faithlessness for the same reasons most children are true to a faith: because it is what their parents tell them." In what other respects does Jones see atheism as similar to religious faith?
2. When she was a child, why did Jones want to learn more about religion? How satisfied was she with what she learned from her family? From Bible school?
3. What was it about the 23rd Psalm that enabled Jones to feel "something akin to faith" (11)? How did it give her her "first glimpse into spirituality" (18)?

Responding in Writing

Do you think Jones is an atheist today? Why or why not?

KICKING THE SECULARIST HABIT
David Brooks
1961–

David Brooks is an Atlantic *correspondent, a* New York Times *columnist, a* Weekly Standard *senior editor, a* Newsweek *contributing editor, and a radio and television political commentator. A widely published writer on various American political issues, he has written two books, most recently* On Paradise Drive: How We Live Now (and Always Have) in the Future Tense *(2004). In the following essay, Brooks considers America's burgeoning religiosity.*

Like a lot of people these days, I'm a recovering secularist. Until September 11 I accepted the notion that as the world becomes richer and better educated, it becomes less religious. Extrapolating from a tiny and unrepresentative sample of humanity (in Western Europe and parts of North America), this theory holds that as history moves forward, science displaces dogma and reason replaces unthinking obedience. A region that has not yet had a reformation and an enlightenment, such as the Arab world, sooner or later will.

It's now clear that the secularization theory is untrue. The human race does not necessarily get less religious as it grows richer and better educated. We are living through one of the great periods of scientific progress and the creation of wealth. At the same time, we are in the midst of a religious boom.

Islam is surging. Orthodox Judaism is growing among young people, and Israel has gotten more religious as it has become more affluent. The growth of Christianity surpasses that of all other faiths. In 1942 this magazine published an essay called "Will the Christian Church Survive?" Sixty years later there are two billion Christians in the world; by 2050, according to some estimates, there will be three billion. As Philip Jenkins, a Distinguished Professor of History and Religious Studies at Pennsylvania State University, has observed, perhaps the most successful social movement of our age is Pentecostalism (see "The Next Christianity," October *Atlantic*). Having gotten its start in Los Angeles about a century ago, it now embraces 400 million people—a number that, according to Jenkins, could reach a billion or more by the half-century mark.

Moreover, it is the denominations that refuse to adapt to secularism that are growing the fastest, while those that try to be "modern" and "relevant" are withering. Ecstatic forms of Christianity and "anti-modern" Islam are thriving. The Christian population in Africa, which was about 10 million in 1900 and is currently about 360 million, is expected to grow to 633 million by 2025, with conservative, evangelical, and syncretistic groups dominating. In Africa churches are becoming more influential than many nations, with both good and bad effects.

5   Secularism is not the future; it is yesterday's incorrect vision of the future. This realization sends us recovering secularists to the bookstore or the library in a desperate attempt to figure out what is going on in the world. I suspect I am not the only one who since September 11 has found himself reading a paperback edition of the Koran that was bought a few years ago in a fit of high-mindedness but was never actually opened. I'm probably not the only one boning up on the teachings of Ahmad ibn Taymiyya, Sayyid Qutb, and Muhammad ibn Abd al-Wahhab.

There are six steps in the recovery process. First you have to accept the fact that you are not the norm. Western foundations and universities send out squads of researchers to study and explain religious movements. But as the sociologist Peter Berger has pointed out, the phenomenon that really needs explaining is the habits of the American professoriat: religious groups should be sending out researchers to try to understand why there are pockets of people in the world who do not feel the constant presence of God in their lives, who do not fill their days with rituals and prayers and garments that bring them into contact with the divine, and who do not believe that God's will should shape their public lives.

Once you accept this—which is like understanding that the earth revolves around the sun, not vice-versa—you can begin to see things in a new way.

The second step toward recovery involves confronting fear. For a few years it seemed that we were all heading toward a benign end of history, one in which our biggest worry would be boredom. Liberal democracy had won the day. Yes, we had to contend with globalization and inequality, but these were material and measurable concepts. Now we are looking at fundamental clashes of belief and a truly scary situation—at least in the Southern Hemisphere—that brings to mind the Middle Ages, with weak governments, missionary armies, and rampant religious conflict.

The third step is getting angry. I now get extremely annoyed by the secular fundamentalists who are content to remain smugly ignorant of enormous shifts occurring all around them. They haven't learned anything about religion, at home or abroad. They don't know who Tim La-Haye and Jerry B. Jenkins are, even though those co-authors have sold 42 million copies of their books. They still don't know what makes a Pentecostal a Pentecostal (you could walk through an American newsroom and ask that question, and the only people who might be able to answer would be the secretaries and the janitorial staff). They still don't know about Michel Aflaq, the mystical Arab nationalist who served as a guru to Saddam Hussein. A great Niagara of religious fervor is cascading down around them while they stand obtuse and dry in the little cave of their own parochialism—and many of them are journalists and policy analysts, who are paid to keep up with these things.

The fourth step toward recovery is to resist the impulse to find a 10 materialistic explanation for everything. During the centuries when secularism seemed the wave of the future, Western intellectuals developed social-science models of extraordinary persuasiveness. Marx explained history through class struggle, other economists explained it through profit maximization. Professors of international affairs used conflict-of-interest doctrines and game theory to predict the dynamics between nation-states.

All these models are seductive and partly true. This country has built powerful institutions, such as the State Department and the CIA, that use them to try to develop sound policies. But none of the models can adequately account for religious ideas, impulses, and actions, because religious fervor can't be quantified and standardized. Religious motivations can't be explained by cost-benefit analysis.

Over the past twenty years domestic-policy analysts have thought hard about the roles that religion and character play in public life. Our foreign-policy elites are at least two decades behind. They go for months ignoring the force of religion; then, when confronted with something inescapably religious, such as the Iranian revolution or the Taliban, they begin talking of religious zealotry and fanaticism, which suddenly explains everything. After a few days of shaking their heads over the fanatics, they revert to their usual secular analyses. We do not yet have, and sorely need, a mode of analysis that attempts to merge the spiritual and the material.

The recovering secularist has to resist the temptation to treat religion as a mere conduit for thwarted economic impulses. For example, we often say that young Arab men who have no decent prospects turn to radical Islam. There's obviously some truth to this observation. But it's not the whole story: neither Mohammed Atta nor Osama bin Laden, for example, was poor or oppressed. And although it's possible to construct theories that explain their radicalism as the result of alienation or some other secular factor, it makes more sense to acknowledge that faith is its own force, independent of and perhaps greater than economic resentment.

Human beings yearn for righteous rule, for a just world or a world that reflects God's will—in many cases at least as strongly as they yearn for money or success. Thinking about that yearning means moving away from scientific analysis and into the realm of moral judgment. The crucial question is not What incentives does this yearning respond to? but Do individuals pursue a moral vision of righteous rule? And do they do so in virtuous ways, or are they, like Saddam Hussein and Osama bin Laden, evil in their vision and methods?

15   Fifth, the recovering secularist must acknowledge that he has been too easy on religion. Because he assumed that it was playing a diminishing role in public affairs, he patronized it. He condescendingly decided not to judge other creeds. They are all valid ways of approaching God, he told himself, and ultimately they fuse into one. After all, why stir up trouble by judging another's beliefs? It's not polite. The better option, when confronted by some nasty practice performed in the name of religion, is simply to avert one's eyes. Is Wahhabism a vicious sect that perverts Islam? Don't talk about it.

But in a world in which religion plays an ever larger role, this approach is no longer acceptable. One has to try to separate right from wrong. The problem is that once we start doing that, it's hard to say where we will end up. Consider Pim Fortuyn, a left-leaning Dutch politician and gay-rights advocate who criticized Muslim immigrants for their attitudes toward women and gays. When he was assassinated, last year, the press described him, on the basis of those criticisms, as a rightist in the manner of Jean-Marie Le Pen,[1] which was

---

[1]1928– . French politician, founder of the far–right National Front Party. [Eds.]

far from the truth. In the post-secular world today's categories of left and right will become inapt and obsolete.

The sixth and final step for recovering secularists is to understand that this country was never very secular anyway. We Americans long for righteous rule as fervently as anybody else. We are inculcated with the notion that, in Abraham Lincoln's words, we represent the "last, best hope of earth." Many Americans have always sensed that we have a transcendent mission, although, fortunately, it is not a theological one. We instinctively feel, in ways that people from other places do not, that history is unfulfilled as long as there are nations in which people are not free. It is this instinctive belief that has led George W. Bush to respond so ambitiously to the events of September 11, and that has led most Americans to support him.

Americans are as active as anyone else in the clash of eschatologies. Saddam Hussein sees history as ending with a united Arab nation globally dominant and with himself revered as the creator of a just world order. Osama bin Laden sees history as ending with the global imposition of sharia. Many Europeans see history as ending with the establishment of secular global institutions under which nationalism and religious passions will be quieted and nation-states will give way to international law and multilateral cooperation. Many Americans see history as ending in the triumph of freedom and constitutionalism, with religion not abandoned or suppressed but enriching democratic life.

We are inescapably caught in a world of conflicting visions of historical destiny. This is not the same as saying that we are caught in a world of conflicting religions. But understanding this world means beating the secularist prejudices out of our minds every day.

Responding to Reading

1. What does Brooks mean when he calls himself a "recovering secularist" (1)? What exactly is the habit he is trying to kick? Why?
2. What evidence does Brooks offer to support his claim that "we are in the midst of a religious boom" (2)? Can you offer examples of your own? Does Brooks see this rise of religion as a positive trend? Do you?
3. Summarize the six steps in Brooks's recovery program.

Responding in Writing

Adapt Brooks's "recovery program" for your peers, adding brief examples appropriate for your audience.

TURNING FAITH INTO ELEVATOR MUSIC
William J. Stuntz
1958–

Professor and Vice-Dean for Intellectual Life at Harvard Law School and contributing writer for TCS *[Technology Commerce Society]* Daily, *William J. Stuntz specializes in Christian legal theory and criminal justice. He coauthored the 1995 book* Constitutional Criminal Procedure: An Examination of the Fourth, Fifth, and Sixth Amendments, and Related Areas. *In the following essay, Stuntz examines the legality of government-sanctioned religious displays.*

The Supreme Court has spoken, and then some: ten separate opinions in a pair of Ten Commandments cases, which seems nicely symmetrical. What all those opinions add up to, predictably, is a muddle. The Ten Commandments can stay on the Texas State Capitol grounds—but not in Kentucky's courthouses. Moses hangs in the balance. So does baby Jesus: Come December, you can bet on a raft of manger scenes on courthouse lawns across the South and Midwest, in all the places Michael Moore likes to call "Jesusland"—and a raft of lawsuits seeking to take them down.

I'm rooting for the lawsuits.

That's a little odd, since I'm part of the target audience, the constituency that is supposed to like these things. I live in Massachusetts (which Michael Moore likes to call "Canada"), but my natural sympathies belong to Jesusland. I'm a Christian. I believe the Bible is a true account of who God is and who we are. I believe the Ten Commandments lie at the core of wisdom. I believe the Incarnation, the event all those manger scenes celebrate, is incomparably the best and most important event in human history. If it matters, I even voted for George W. Bush, twice. So if anyone should want the Ten Commandments in state capitols and "in God we trust" on the coins and manger scenes on courthouse lawns, I should.

But I don't want any of those things. I'd much rather give them back.

5   Here's a thought experiment. Test the decision to put that monument on the Texas capitol grounds against another Biblical principle: the Golden Rule, the idea C. S. Lewis liked to call "do as you would be done by." Take the people who want symbols of their faith on government property, and put them in a society where passionate atheism is the majority view. Suppose all those passionate atheists want to put up monuments in every courthouse and state capitol saying that there is no God, that all good law consists of human wisdom and nothing more. Would my fellow believers like that state of affairs? I

don't think so. I know I wouldn't like it. It would make me feel, just a little, like a stranger in my own home, someone who doesn't belong. It would be a tiny reminder that other people with beliefs hostile to mine own this country, and that I'm here at their sufferance. I wouldn't like that at all.

If that's right, then turning around and doing the same thing to people who don't believe what I do when my crowd is in the majority is wrong. Not wrong by the measure of the First Amendment or some legal theory or secular philosophy, but wrong by the measure of "do as you would be done by." That might be tolerable if the monuments and manger scenes satisfied some religious duty. If anything, though, duty cuts the other way. There is a passage in the book of Revelations that bears on this point. The risen Jesus is speaking of, and to, the church in Laodicea. He tells them: "I know your deeds, that you are neither cold nor hot. I wish you were either one or the other! So, because you are lukewarm—neither hot nor cold—I am about to spit you out of my mouth." Symbolic acknowledgments like the Texas monument and the Kentucky plaques, like religious mottoes on money or public manger scenes (usually accompanied by Santa and his reindeer), are quintessentially lukewarm. They do not so much honor God as try to buy him off, cheap. This was precisely the problem with most mandatory school prayers in the days when such things were allowed. The prayers were so vapid as to insult believers, yet still managed to offend non-believers. Just like baby Jesus with a stable full of reindeer.

Seeing the Ten Commandments in public spaces is a little like hearing the *Miranda* warnings on *Law and Order* which doesn't make anyone think about the real meaning of *Miranda* (whatever that is) because it doesn't make anyone think at all. It's the social equivalent of elevator music. Religious people shouldn't want their faith to be elevator music.

That leads to an even worse problem. Symbols like the ones the Supreme Court haggled about give the impression that Christianity and the government are somehow in cahoots with each other. That's a dangerous impression, and a false one. It's a small step from the idea that the government endorses Christianity to an idea that is much worse: that *Christianity* endorses the *government*. Christians are the big losers in that transaction. Western Europe is filled with Christian symbols—Christian Democrats are a leading political party in several countries—but almost entirely devoid of Christians. Christianity does not thrive when political parties take its name and capitol lawns showcase its precepts. On the contrary, it thrives when it stays as far from those things as possible.

The government thrives, too. Religious conservatives and secular liberals should be able to agree on this much: teaching good morals is

not a job for the Texas legislature or the Kentucky courts—or any legislature or court. Making just laws is hard enough, and our government isn't so good at that. Teaching virtue is incomparably harder.
Personally, I'd rather they stuck to the laws.

10   But the question shouldn't be what I'd rather. It shouldn't be
what is or isn't to my side's advantage. If the Golden Rule means anything in this context, the question should be, what is to the *other side's*
advantage? Twenty-first century America is a land full of legal rights,
and lawyers to make the most of them. The most Christian thing to do
in a place like that is to make the *least* of them. Somewhere, sometime
I'd like to hear that my fellow believers, when given the opportunity
to erect some watered-down monument or display, said: "Thank you,
but no. I don't want to exercise my rights." That would communicate
more Christian faith than all the monuments and plaques and graduation prayers put together.

Then the Supreme Court could quit wasting its time on these
cases (and, given the way the Supreme Court works, start wasting its
time on something else). There are plenty of issues worth fighting
about in America's courtrooms and legislative hallways. This isn't
one of them.

Responding to Reading

1. Why is Stuntz, a self-described Christian, "rooting for the lawsuits" (2) that
    challenge the legality of public displays of religion on government prop-
    erty? Why does he go to the trouble of explaining his religious and political
    views in paragraph 3? Is this explanation necessary? Does it strengthen his
    arguments?
2. In paragraph 7, Stuntz says, "Religious people shouldn't want their faith to
    be elevator music." Explain this analogy. Do you think it is valid?
3. How does Stuntz use the Golden Rule to support his arguments? Do you
    find this strategy helpful? Convincing? Simplistic? Condescending? Ex-
    plain.

Responding in Writing

Stuntz believes that "symbols of faith on government property" (5) might make
nonbelievers feel uncomfortable. Is there any government-sanctioned symbol,
slogan, or practice that makes you feel like "someone who doesn't belong" (5)?
If so, do you see this as something the government should change, or something you should adjust to?

Muslim in America
Jeffery Sheler
Michael Betzold

Author of Is the Bible True? How Modern Debates and Discoveries Af-firm the Essence of the Scriptures *(1999), Jeffery Sheler is a religion writer at* U.S. News & World Report *and a correspondent for PBS's* Religion & Ethics NewsWeekly *television news program. Freelance writer Michael Betzold has written several articles, three nonfiction books, and a novel. In the following essay, Sheler and Betzold explore what it means to be a Muslim in America.*

Inside a storefront on West Warren Avenue, a gritty Dearborn, Mich., neighborhood of modest shops with hand-painted Arabic signs, a handful of men respond to the high-pitched chant of the muezzin[1] and form a line facing Mecca. They bow, sit, and prostrate on colorful rugs in a mostly silent rendition of the salat, the daily prayers Muslims have recited for nearly 1,400 years. In a smaller room, a cluster of women with head coverings also recite the prayers in response to the voice of the imam, which they can hear from across the hall. Most of the worshipers are recent refugees from Iraq who want a link to the country they still consider home. "They thank God they are here" in America, says Imam Hushan Al-Husainy, the mosque leader. "But their heart is back home with their loved ones who are suffering."

Meanwhile, 68 miles away, beneath a gleaming white dome and twin minarets that tower over the Ohio cornfields southwest of Toledo, hundreds of families assemble for worship—a largely upper-middle-class flock that represents some 22 nationalities, most U.S. citizens and some second- or third-generation Americans. Few of the women wear head coverings outside of the prayer hall, where only a 3-foot-high partition separates men and women, side by side. After prayers, they all gather for a potluck. The Toledo center, says its president, Cherrefe Kadri, represents a "progressive and middle-of-the-road" brand of Islam that, she says, is "very much at home in Middle America."

This, then, is American Islam: The modern Islamic Center of Greater Toledo and the traditionalist Karbala Islamic Education Center are but two examples of its wide-ranging diversity. And even though it is

---

[1]At a mosque, the person who leads the call to prayer.

the nation's fastest-growing faith, with an estimated 7 million adherents here—nearly double from a decade ago—Islam remains widely misunderstood in this country. The religion of more than a fifth of the world's population is viewed by many Americans as foreign, mysterious, even threatening to the nation's "Judeo-Christian heritage"—certainly no less so since the events of September 11—despite the fact that it shares common roots with Christianity and Judaism and has been present in North America for centuries.

The rules. Indeed, Islam embraces the monotheism of Christianity and Judaism, accepts the Hebrew Bible, and venerates Jesus as a prophet. It is centered on the Koran—the Islamic scriptures, which Muslims believe were revealed to the prophet Mohammed—which commands five basic devotional duties, called the "Five Pillars": a declaration of belief that "there is no God but Allah [Arabic for "the God"] and Mohammed is his prophet"; prayers offered five times a day; daytime fasting during the month of Ramadan; charitable giving; and at least one pilgrimage to Mecca. Muslims are forbidden to consume alcohol, illicit drugs, pork, or any meat that is not halal—the Islamic equivalent of kosher. Premarital sex and extramarital sex are sternly prohibited, as are most forms of unchaperoned dating. Emphasis on public modesty prompts many Muslims to cover themselves from the wrists to the ankles. Muslims also may not gamble or pay or accept interest on loans or savings accounts. It is a regimen that often runs in conflict with the dominant culture. Most American Muslims have no choice but to break the prohibition on usury to buy homes and automobiles, for example.

5   But if the intense scrutiny focused on world Islam since September 11 has revealed anything, it is that the faith is no monolith. While there is much that binds the world's 1.2 billion Muslims together, there is no authoritative hierarchy—no pope, no central group of elders—that speaks to them or for them. And American Islam, it emerges, is its own special brand. A recent study sponsored by the Council on American-Islamic Relations [CAIR] in cooperation with the Hartford Institute for Religion Research found that American Muslims generally are more accepting of differences, less inclined to fundamentalism, and more at home in a secular society than most Muslims elsewhere. They are also ethnically diverse: Most are immigrants or their descendants from Islamic countries in Asia, Africa, and the Middle East. About a third are African-Americans, and a small number are whites of European descent.

Connections? But while diversity may naturally include the extremes, the question on many people's minds has been what exactly the relationship is between American Islam and the kind of terror and anti-Americanism that came so horribly into focus last month under the guise of religious zealotry. One moderate American Islamic leader,

Sheik Muhammad Hisham Kabbani, told a State Department forum in 1999 that 80 percent of the nation's mosques are headed by clerics who espouse "extremist ideology"—which Kabbani associates with Wahhabism, an Islamic fundamentalist movement that began in Saudi Arabia in the 18th century. But Kabbani, head of the Islamic Supreme Council of America, a Washington, D.C.–based advocacy group, added that "a majority of American Muslims do not agree" with the extremist ideology.

Other American Muslim leaders say Kabbani's estimate of Wahhabi influence in U.S. mosques is exaggerated. "I don't know where he came up with that," says Ingrid Mattson, a Hartford Seminary professor and vice president of the Islamic Society of North America [ISNA]. African-Americans alone account for a third of the mosques, she notes, "and they clearly are not Wahhabis." The CAIR-Hartford study found that about 20 percent of mosques say they interpret the Koran literally, but 7 in 10 follow a more nuanced, nonfundamentalist approach.

Scholars say the democratic structure and autonomy of many American mosques protect them from extremist takeovers. Modern Islamic centers, like the one in Toledo, are "less likely to be dominated by a single teacher or viewpoint," says Frederick Denny, a scholar of Islam at the University of Colorado. That describes at least 60 percent of American mosques, according to the CAIR-Hartford study. Those that are more fundamentalist, he says, often are smaller, with transient members, such as those that "cater to foreign students who want something that feels like home." Even where fundamentalism exists, says Mattson, "there is a huge distinction between fundamentalist ideology and support of terrorism."

What divides American Muslims most often, says Denny, "is not liberal-versus-conservative ideology but how best to domesticate Islam in a Western society without doing violence to either." What, for example, are American Muslims to do with sharia, the Islamic legal and ethical codes that tradition says should undergird Islamic society? Radical clerics say it is a Muslim's duty to impose sharia throughout the world, by force if necessary. But moderates argue that Islamic law must be internalized. "It shouldn't be taken literally," says Imam Farooq Aboelzahab of the Toledo mosque. "The way sharia was applied 1,400 years ago may not always fit. It must be applied to the place and time where you live."

One indication that many Muslims are feeling more at home in 10 America is their growing involvement in the nation's public life. During the past five years, Islamic leaders and groups have become increasingly outspoken on social- and foreign-policy issues. Groups like CAIR, ISNA, the American Muslim Council, and the Islamic Institute maintain a high-visibility Washington presence, working to rally

Muslim political activism and acting as media watchdogs. While American Islamic groups were virtually unanimous in condemning the terrorist attacks on New York and Washington, they remain vociferous critics of U.S. policy in the Middle East.

Stronger rhetoric, of course, has its price in this country. In late September, a prominent imam at a Cleveland mosque nearly lost his job over anti-Jewish remarks he had made in a speech 10 years ago. The board at the Islamic Center of Cleveland voted to keep Fawaz Damra after he apologized for the remarks, which appeared on a tape that surfaced recently, but local Jewish leaders are still upset. Incendiary rhetoric. Meanwhile, a leading Muslim teacher in Northern California has apologized for his own rhetorical excesses. Hamza Yusuf, who was invited to the White House to pray with President Bush after the attacks, later came under criticism for saying in a speech two days before the attacks that the United States "stands condemned" and faced "a terrible fate" because of rampant immorality and injustice in its treatment of minorities. While their causes may be just, says Yusuf, "the rhetoric of some Muslim leaders has been too incendiary— I myself have been guilty of it." September 11, he says, "was a wake-up call to me. I don't want to contribute to the hate in any shape or form."

A decade ago, Sulayman Nyang, professor of African studies at Howard University in Washington, D.C., warned in a speech that Islam will be accepted in America only when Muslims fully take their place alongside other citizens, participating in the nation's civic life, and when what the Islamic faith can offer Western culture is recognized widely as something of value. Neither, he says, will be easy to accomplish. But in times like these, such hard work is more important than ever.

Responding to Reading

1. This essay appeared in a newsmagazine on October 29, 2001, just weeks after the 9/11 terrorist attacks. What do you suppose the writers' purpose was? How can you tell?
2. According to Sheler and Betzold, is Islam like other widely followed U.S. religions? How is it different?
3. In paragraph 5, the writers assert that the Muslim faith is "no monolith." What do they mean? What evidence do they offer to support this claim?

Responding in Writing

What do you think it would take for Muslims to truly feel "at home in America" (10)?

EARTHLY EMPIRES

William C. Symonds
Brian Grow
John Cady

Writers for BusinessWeek *magazine, William C. Symonds is Boston bureau chief, Brian Grow is Atlanta bureau correspondent, and John Cady is New York bureau correspondent. The following essay discusses the business aspects of the "megachurch" phenomenon.*

There's no shortage of churches in Houston, deep in the heart of the Bible Belt. So it's surprising that the largest one in the city—and in the entire country—is tucked away in a depressed corner most Houstonians would never dream of visiting. Yet 30,000 people endure punishing traffic on the narrow roads leading to Lakewood Church every weekend to hear Pastor Joel Osteen deliver upbeat messages of hope. A youthful-looking 42-year-old with a ready smile, he reassures the thousands who show up at each of his five weekend services that "God has a great future in store for you." His services are rousing affairs that often include his wife, Victoria, leading prayers and his mother, Dodie, discussing passages from the Bible.

Osteen is so popular that he has nearly quadrupled attendance since taking over the pulpit from his late father in 1999, winning over believers from other churches as well as throngs of the "unsaved." Many are drawn first by his ubiquitous presence on television. Each week 7 million people catch the slickly produced broadcast of his Sunday sermons on national cable and network channels, for which Lakewood shells out $15 million a year. Adherents often come clutching a copy of Osteen's best-seller, Your Best Life Now, which has sold 2.5 million copies since its publication last fall.

To keep them coming back, Lakewood offers free financial counseling, low-cost bulk food, even a "fidelity group" for men with "sexual addictions." Demand is brisk for the self-help sessions. Angie Mosqueda, 34, who was brought up a Catholic, says she and her husband, Mark, first went to Lakewood in 2000 when they were on the brink of a divorce. Mark even threw her out of the house after she confessed to infidelity. But over time, Lakewood counselors "really helped us to forgive one another and start all over again," she says.

Disney Look

Osteen's flourishing Lakewood enterprise brought in $55 million in contributions last year, four times the 1999 amount, church officials say. Flush with success, Osteen is laying out $90 million to transform the massive Compaq Center in downtown Houston—former home of the NBA's Houston Rockets—into a church that will seat 16,000, complete with a high-tech stage for his TV shows and Sunday School for 5,000 children. After it opens in July, he predicts weekend attendance will rocket to 100,000. Says Osteen: "Other churches have not kept up, and they lose people by not changing with the times."

5   Pastor Joel is one of a new generation of evangelical entrepreneurs transforming their branch of Protestantism into one of the fastest-growing and most influential religious groups in America. Their runaway success is modeled unabashedly on business. They borrow tools ranging from niche marketing to MBA hiring to lift their share of U.S. churchgoers. Like Osteen, many evangelical pastors focus intently on a huge potential market—the millions of Americans who have drifted away from mainline Protestant denominations or simply never joined a church in the first place.

To reach these untapped masses, savvy leaders are creating Sunday Schools that look like Disney World and church cafes with the appeal of Starbucks. Although most hold strict religious views, they scrap staid hymns in favor of multimedia worship and tailor a panoply of services to meet all kinds of consumer needs, from divorce counseling to help for parents of autistic kids. Like Osteen, many offer an upbeat message intertwined with a religious one. To make newcomers feel at home, some do away with standard religious symbolism—even basics like crosses and pews—and design churches to look more like modern entertainment halls than traditional places of worship.

Branding Whiz

So successful are some evangelicals that they're opening up branches like so many new Home Depots or Subways. This year, the 16.4 million-member Southern Baptist Convention plans to "plant" 1,800 new churches using by-the-book niche-marketing tactics. "We have cowboy churches for people working on ranches, country music churches, even several motorcycle churches aimed at bikers," says Martin King, a spokesman for the Southern Baptists' North American Mission Board.

Branding whizzes that they are, the new church leaders are spreading their ideas through every available outlet. A line of "Biblezines" packages the New Testament in glossy magazines aimed at different market segments—there's a hip-hop version and one aimed at teen girls. Christian music appeals to millions of youths, some of whom otherwise might never give church a second thought, serving up everything from alternative rock to punk and even "screamo" (they scream religious lyrics). California megachurch pastor Rick Warren's 2002 book, *The Purpose-Driven Life,* has become the fastest-selling non-fiction book of all time, with more than 23 million copies sold, in part through a novel "pyro marketing" strategy. Then there's the Left Behind phenomenon, a series of action-packed, apocalyptic page-turners about those left on earth after Christ's second coming, selling more than 60 million copies since 1995.

Evangelicals' eager embrace of corporate-style growth strategies is giving them a tremendous advantage in the battle for religious market share, says Roger Finke, a Pennsylvania State University sociology professor and co-author of a new book, *The Churching of America, 1776–2005: Winners and Losers in Our Religious Economy.* A new Pope has given Catholicism a burst of global publicity, but its nominal membership growth in the U.S. stems largely from the influx of Mexican immigrants. Overall, the Catholic Church's long-term decline in U.S. attendance accelerated after the recent sex-abuse scandals, there's a severe priest shortage, and parish churches and schools are closing in the wake of a financial crisis.

Similarly, the so-called mainline Protestants who dominated 10 20th century America have become the religious equivalent of General Motors Corp. The large denominations—including the United Methodist Church and the Episcopal Church—have been shrinking for decades and have lost more than 1 million members in the past 10 years alone. Today, mainline Protestants account for just 16% of the U.S. population, says University of Akron political scientist John C. Green.

In contrast, evangelicalism's theological flexibility gives it the freedom to adapt to contemporary culture. With no overarching authority like the Vatican, leaders don't need to wrestle with a bureaucratic hierarchy that dictates acceptable behavior. "If you have a vision for ministry, you just do it, which makes it far easier to respond to market demand," says University of North Carolina at Chapel Hill sociology professor Christian Smith.

With such low barriers to entry, the number of evangelical megachurches—defined as those that attract at least 2,000 weekly worshippers—has shot up to 880 from 50 in 1980, figures John N. Vaughan, founder of research outfit Church Growth Today in Bolivar, Mo. He calculates that a new megachurch emerges in the U.S. an average of every two days. Overall, white evangelicals make up more than a quarter of Americans today, experts estimate. The figures are fuzzy because there's no common definition of evangelical, which typically refers to Christians who believe the Bible is the literal work of God. They may include many Southern Baptists, nondenominational churches, and some Lutherans and Methodists. There are also nearly 25 million black Protestants who consider themselves evangelicals but largely don't share the conservative politics of most white ones. Says pollster George Gallup, who has studied religious trends for decades: "The evangelicals are the most vibrant branch of Christianity."

The triumph of evangelical Christianity is profoundly reshaping many aspects of American politics and society. Historically, much of the U.S. political and business elite has been mainline Protestant. Today, President George W. Bush and more than a dozen members of Congress, including House Speaker Dennis Hastert, are evangelicals. More important, the Republican Right has been fueled by the swelling ranks of evangelicals, whose leaders tend to be conservative politically despite their progressive marketing methods. In the 1960s and '70s, prominent evangelicals like Billy Graham kept a careful separation of pulpit and politics—even though he served as a spiritual adviser to President Richard M. Nixon. That began to change in the early 1980s, when Jerry Falwell formed the Moral Majority to express evangelicals' political views. Many of today's evangelicals hope to expand their clout even further. They're also gaining by taking their views into Corporate America. Exhibit A: the recent clash at software giant Microsoft.

As they thrive, though, there are growing tensions, with some mainline Protestants offended by their conservative politics and brazen marketing. "Jesus was not a capitalist; check out what [He] says about how hard it is to get into heaven if you're a rich man," says the Reverend Robert W. Edgar, general secretary of the liberal National Council of Churches.

15   Especially controversial are leaders like Osteen and the flamboyant Creflo A. Dollar, pastor of World Changers Church International in College Park, Ga., who preach "the prosperity gospel." They endorse material wealth and tell followers that God wants them to be prosperous. In his book, Osteen talks about how his wife, Victoria, a striking blonde who dresses fashionably, wanted to buy a fancy house some years ago, before the money rolled in. He thought it wasn't possible. "But Victoria had more faith," he wrote. "She convinced me we could live in an elegant home . . . and several years later, it did come to pass." Dollar, too, defends materialistic success. Dubbed "Pass-the-Dollar" by critics, he owns two Rolls Royces and travels in a Gulfstream 3 jet. "I practice what I preach, and the Bible says . . . that God takes pleasure in the prosperity of his servants," says Dollar, 43, nattily attired in French cuffs and a pinstriped suit.

Hucksters?

Some evangelical leaders acknowledge that flagrant materialism can raise the specter of religious hucksterism à la Sinclair Lewis' fictional

Elmer Gantry[1] or Jim and Tammy Faye Bakker.[2] Our goal is not to turn the church into a business," insists Warren, the founder of Saddleback megachurch in Lake Forest, Calif. After *The Purpose-Driven Life* made him millions, he repaid Saddleback all the salary he had taken over the years and still lives modestly. Cautions Kurt Frederickson, a director of the Fuller Theological Seminary in Pasadena, Calif.: "We have to be careful when a pastor moves into the CEO mode and becomes too market-oriented, or there might be a reaction against megachurches just as there is against Wal-Mart."

Many evangelicals say they're just trying to satisfy demands not met by traditional churches. Craig Groeschel, who launched Life Church in Edmond, Okla., in 1996, started out doing market research with non-churchgoers in the area—and got an earful. "They said churches were full of hypocrites and were boring," he recalls. So he designed Life Church to counter those preconceptions, with lively, multimedia-filled services in a setting that's something between a rock concert and a coffee shop.

Once established, some ambitious churches are making a big business out of spreading their expertise. Willow Creek Community Church in South Barrington, Ill., formed a consulting arm called Willow Creek Assn. It earned $17 million last year, partly by selling marketing and management advice to 10,500 member churches from 90 denominations. Jim Mellado, the hard-charging Harvard MBA who runs it, last year brought an astonishing 110,000 church and lay leaders to conferences on topics such as effective leadership. "Our entrepreneurial impulse comes from the Biblical mandate to get the message out," says Willow Creek founder Bill Hybels, who hired Stanford MBA Greg Hawkins, a former McKinsey & Co. consultant, to handle the church's day-to-day management. Willow Creek's methods have even been lauded in a Harvard Business School case study.

Hybel's consumer-driven approach is evident at Willow Creek, where he shunned stained glass, Bibles, or even a cross for the 7,200-seat, $72 million sanctuary he recently built. The reason? Market research suggested that such traditional symbols would scare away non-churchgoers. He also gives practical advice. On a recent Wednesday evening, one of his four "teaching" pastors gave a service that started with 20 minutes of music, followed by a lengthy sermon about the Christian approach to personal finances. He told the 5,000 listeners about resisting advertising aimed at getting people to buy things

---

[1]Evangelical preacher and con man [Eds.]

[2]Jim Bakker, Assemblies of God minister and former host (with his wife Tammy Faye Bakker) of the evangelical christian TV program *The PTL Club*. Indicted on federal charges of fraud and tax evasion.

they don't need and suggested they follow up at home by e-mailing questions. Like Osteen, Hybel packages self-help programs with a positive message intended to make people feel good about themselves. "When I walk out of a service, I feel completely relieved of any stress I walked in with," says Phil Earnest, 38, a sales manager who in 2003 switched to Willow Creek from the Methodist Church he found too stodgy.

20 So adept at the sell are some evangelicals that it can be difficult to distinguish between their religious aims and the secular style they mimic. Last December, Prestonwood Baptist Church in Plano, Tex., staged a spectacular Christmas festival, including a 500-person choir, that attracted 70,000 people even though the cheapest ticket was $20. Throughout the year, some 16,000 people take part in its sports program, which uses eight playing fields and six gyms on its $100 million, 140-acre campus. The teams, coached by church members, bring in converts, many of them children, says Executive Pastor Mike Buster.

Gushers of Cash

Kids are often a prime target audience for megachurches. The main campus of Groeschel's Life Church in Edmond, Okla., includes a "Toon Town" of 3D buildings, a 16-foot high slide, and an animatronic police chief who recites rules. All the razzmatazz has helped Life Church quadruple its Sunday school attendance to more than 2,500 a week. "The kids are bringing their parents to church," says children's pastor Scott Werner.

Such marketing and services help to create brand loyalty any CEO would envy. Willow Creek ranks in the top 5% of 250 major brands, right up with Nike and John Deere, says Eric Arnson. He helped develop a consumer-brand practice that McKinsey then bought and recently did a pro bono study for Willow Creek using that methodology.

Other megachurches are franchising their good name. Life Church now has five campuses in Oklahoma and will expand into Phoenix this fall. Pastor Groeschel jumped the 1,000 miles to Arizona after market research pinpointed Phoenix as an area with a large population but few effective churches. Atlanta's Dollar, who is African American, has pushed into five countries, including Nigeria and South Africa.

All this growth, plus the tithing many evangelicals encourage, is generating gushers of cash. A traditional U.S. church typically has fewer than 200 members and an annual budget of around $100,000. The average megachurch pulls in $4.8 million, according to a 1999 study by the Hartford Seminary, one of the few surveys on the topic.

The money is also fueling a megachurch building boom. First Baptist Church of Woodstock, near Atlanta, for example, has just finished a $62 million, 7,000-seat sanctuary.

Megachurch business ventures sometimes grow beyond the 25 bounds of the church itself. In the mid-1990s, Kirbyjon Caldwell, a Wharton MBA who sold bonds for First Boston before he enrolled in seminary, formed an economic development corporation that revived a depressed neighborhood near Houston's 14,000-member Windsor Village United Methodist Church, which he heads. A former Kmart now houses a mix of church and private businesses employing 270 people, including a Christian school and a bank. New plans call for a massive center with senior housing, retailing, and a public school.

For all their seemingly unstoppable success, evangelicals must contend with powerful forces in U.S. society. The ranks of Americans who express no religious preference have quadrupled since 1991, to 14%, according to a recent poll. Despite the megachurch surge, overall church attendance has remained fairly flat. And if anything, popular culture has become more vulgar in recent years. Still, experts like pollster Gallup see clear signs of a rising fascination with spirituality in the U.S. The September 11 attacks are one reason. So is the aging of the culturally influential Baby Boom, since spirituality tends to increase with age, he says. If so, no one is better poised than evangelicals to capitalize on the trend.

Responding to Reading

1. Is this essay's purpose essentially informative or persuasive? Can you tell whether the writers have a positive, negative, or neutral view of the evangelical churches they describe? Of those who worship there? Of Pastor Osteen? (Before you answer this question, look carefully at the essay's subject headings and at the analogies the writers make between religious institutions and businesses.)
2. What does Lakewood Church offer its parishioners? What do you think attracts worshippers to this church and to its pastor?
3. This essay appeared in *BusinessWeek*, and the writers use business terms and concepts to describe the rise of evangelical churches like Lakewood. Give some examples of such language. Do you think it is effective? Do you think it is appropriate?

Responding in Writing

What do you see as the advantages of a "megachurch" like Lakewood? What do you see as the disadvantages?

CATHEDRAL

Raymond Carver
1938–1988

*A talented short story writer, Raymond Carver led a troubled life. Through-
out his adult life, Carver struggled with alcoholism and marital problems,
but he remained sober and productive during the last ten years of his life.
His story collections include* Will You Please Be Quiet, Please? *(1976);*
What We Talk About When We Talk About Love *(1981);* Short Cuts
(1984); and Cathedral *(1984), in which the following short story originally
appeared.*

This blind man, an old friend of my wife's, he was on his way to
spend the night. His wife had died. So he was visiting the dead wife's
relatives in Connecticut. He called my wife from his in-laws'.
Arrangements were made. He would come by train, a five-hour trip,
and my wife would meet him at the station. She hadn't seen him since
she worked for him one summer in Seattle ten years ago. But she and
the blind man had kept in touch. They made tapes and mailed them
back and forth. I wasn't enthusiastic about his visit. He was no one I
knew. And his being blind bothered me. My idea of blindness came
from the movies. In the movies, the blind moved slowly and never
laughed. Sometimes they were led by seeing-eye dogs. A blind man in
my house was not something I looked forward to.

That summer in Seattle she had needed a job. She didn't have any
money. The man she was going to marry at the end of the summer
was in officers' training school. He didn't have any money, either. But
she was in love with the guy, and he was in love with her, etc. She'd
seen something in the paper: HELP WANTED—*Reading to Blind Man,*
and a telephone number. She phoned and went over, was hired on
the spot. She'd worked with this blind man all summer. She read
stuff to him, case studies, reports, that sort of thing. She helped him
organize his little office in the county social-service department.
They'd become good friends, my wife and the blind man. How do I
know these things? She told me. And she told me something else. On
her last day in the office, the blind man asked if he could touch her
face. She agreed to this. She told me he touched his fingers to every
part of her face, her nose—even her neck! She never forgot it. She
even tried to write a poem about it. She was always trying to write a

poem. She wrote a poem or two every year, usually after something really important had happened to her.

When we first started going out together, she showed me the poem. In the poem, she recalled his fingers and the way they had moved around over her face. In the poem, she talked about what she had felt at the time, about what went through her mind when the blind man touched her nose and lips. I can remember I didn't think much of the poem. Of course, I didn't tell her that. Maybe I just don't understand poetry. I admit it's not the first thing I reach for when I pick up something to read.

Anyway, this man who'd first enjoyed her favors, the officer-to-be, he'd been her childhood sweetheart. So okay. I'm saying that at the end of the summer she let the blind man run his hands over her face, said goodbye to him, married her childhood etc., who was now a commissioned officer, and she moved away from Seattle. But they'd kept in touch, she and the blind man. She made the first contact after a year or so. She called him up one night from an Air Force base in Alabama. She wanted to talk. They talked. He asked her to send a tape and tell him about her life. She did this. She sent the tape. On the tape, she told the blind man about her husband and about their life together in the military. She told the blind man she loved her husband but she didn't like it where they lived and she didn't like it that he was part of the military-industrial thing. She told the blind man she'd written a poem and he was in it. She told him that she was writing a poem about what it was like to be an Air Force officer's wife. The poem wasn't finished yet. She was still writing it. The blind man made a tape. He sent her the tape. She made a tape. This went on for years. My wife's officer was posted to one base and then another. She sent tapes from Moody AFB, McGuire, McConnell, and finally Travis, near Sacramento, where one night she got to feeling lonely and cut off from people she kept losing in that moving-around life. She got to feeling she couldn't go it another step. She went in and swallowed all the pills and capsules in the medicine chest and washed them down with a bottle of gin. Then she got into a hot bath and passed out.

But instead of dying, she got sick. She threw up. Her officer—   5 why should he have a name? he was the childhood sweetheart, and what more does he want?—came home from somewhere, found her, and called the ambulance. In time, she put it all on a tape and sent the tape to the blind man. Over the years, she put all kinds of stuff on tapes and sent the tapes off lickety-split. Next to writing a poem every year, I think it was her chief means of recreation. On one tape, she told the blind man she'd decided to live away from her officer for a time. On another tape, she told him about her divorce. She and I began going out, and of course she told her blind man about it. She told him everything, or so it seemed to me. Once she asked me if I'd like to hear the latest tape from the blind man. This was a year ago. I was on the tape, she said. So I said okay, I'd listen to it. I got us drinks and we settled down in the living room. We made ready to listen. First she inserted the tape into the player and adjusted a couple of dials. Then she pushed a lever. The tape squeaked and someone began to talk in this loud voice. She lowered the volume. After a few minutes of harmless chitchat, I heard my own name in the mouth of this stranger, this blind man I didn't even know! And then this: "From all you've said about him, I can only conclude—" But we were interrupted, a knock at the door, something, and we didn't ever get back to the tape. Maybe it was just as well. I'd heard all I wanted to.

Now this same blind man was coming to sleep in my house.

"Maybe I could take him bowling," I said to my wife. She was at the draining board doing scalloped potatoes. She put down the knife she was using and turned around.

"If you love me," she said, "you can do this for me. If you don't love me, okay. But if you had a friend, any friend, and the friend came to visit, I'd make him feel comfortable." She wiped her hands with the dish towel.

"I don't have any blind friends," I said.

10   "You don't have *any* friends," she said. "Period. Besides," she said, "goddamn it, his wife's just died! Don't you understand that? The man's lost his wife!"

I didn't answer. She'd told me a little about the blind man's wife. Her name was Beulah. Beulah! That's a name for a colored woman.

"Was his wife a Negro?" I asked.

"Are you crazy?" my wife said. "Have you just flipped or something?" She picked up a potato. I saw it hit the floor, then roll under the stove. "What's wrong with you?" she said. "Are you drunk?"

"I'm just asking," I said.

15   Right then my wife filled me in with more detail than I cared to know. I made a drink and sat at the kitchen table to listen. Pieces of the story began to fall into place.

Beulah had gone to work for the blind man the summer after my wife had stopped working for him. Pretty soon Beulah and the blind man had themselves a church wedding. It was a little wedding—who'd want to go to such a wedding in the first place?—just the two of them, plus the minister and the minister's wife. But it was a church wedding just the same. It was what Beulah had wanted, he'd said. But even then Beulah must have been carrying the cancer in her glands. After they had been inseparable for eight years—my wife's word, *inseparable*—Beulah's health went into a rapid decline. She died in a Seattle hospital room, the blind man sitting beside the bed and holding on to her hand. They'd married, lived and worked together, slept together—had sex, sure—and then the blind man had to bury her. All this without his having ever seen what the goddamned woman looked like. It was beyond my understanding. Hearing this, I felt sorry for the blind man for a little bit. And then I found myself thinking what a pitiful life this woman must have led. Imagine a woman who could never see herself as she was seen in the eyes of her loved one. A woman who could go on day after day and never receive the smallest compliment from her beloved. A woman whose husband could never read the expression on her face, be it misery or something better. Someone who could wear makeup or not—what difference to him? She could, if she wanted, wear green eye-shadow around one eye, a straight pin in her nostril, yellow slacks, and purple shoes, no matter. And then to slip off into death, the blind man's hand on her hand, his blind eyes streaming tears—I'm imagining now—her last thought maybe this: that he never even knew what she looked like, and she on an express to the grave. Robert was left with a small insurance policy and a half of a twenty-peso Mexican coin. The other half of the coin went into the box with her. Pathetic.

So when the time rolled around, my wife went to the depot to pick him up. With nothing to do but wait—sure, I blamed him for that—I was having a drink and watching the TV when I heard the car pull into the drive. I got up from the sofa with my drink and went to the window to have a look.

I saw my wife laughing as she parked the car. I saw her get out of the car and shut the door. She was still wearing a smile. Just amazing. She went around to the other side of the car to where the blind man was already starting to get out. This blind man, feature this, he was wearing a full beard! A beard on a blind man! Too much, I say. The blind man reached into the backseat and dragged out a suitcase. My wife took his arm, shut the car door, and, talking all the way, moved him down the drive and then up the steps to the front porch. I turned off the TV. I finished my drink, rinsed the glass, dried my hands. Then I went to the door.

My wife said, "I want you to meet Robert. Robert, this is my husband. I've told you all about him." She was beaming. She had this blind man by his coat sleeve.

The blind man let go of his suitcase and up came his hand.   20

I took it. He squeezed hard, held my hand, and then he let it go.

"I feel like we've already met," he boomed.

"Likewise," I said. I didn't know what else to say. Then I said, "Welcome. I've heard a lot about you." We began to move then, a little group, from the porch into the living room, my wife guiding him by the arm. The blind man was carrying his suitcase in his other hand. My wife said things like, "To your left here, Robert. That's right. Now watch it, there's a chair. That's it. Sit down right here. This is the sofa. We just bought this sofa two weeks ago."

I started to say something about the old sofa. I'd liked that old sofa. But I didn't say anything. Then I wanted to say something else, small-talk, about the scenic ride along the Hudson. How going *to* New York, you should sit on the right-hand side of the train, and coming *from* New York, the left-hand side.

25 "Did you have a good train ride?" I said. "Which side of the train did you sit on, by the way?"

"What a question, which side!" my wife said. "What's it matter which side?" she said.

"I just asked," I said.

"Right side," the blind man said. "I hadn't been on a train in nearly forty years. Not since I was a kid. With my folks. That's been a long time. I'd nearly forgotten the sensation. I have winter in my beard now," he said. "So I've been told, anyway. Do I look distinguished, my dear?" the blind man said to my wife.

"You look distinguished, Robert," she said. "Robert," she said. "Robert, it's just so good to see you."

30 My wife finally took her eyes off the blind man and looked at me. I had the feeling she didn't like what she saw. I shrugged.

I've never met, or personally known, anyone who was blind. This blind man was late forties, a heavy-set, balding man with stooped shoulders, as if he carried a great weight there. He wore brown slacks, brown shoes, a light-brown shirt, a tie, a sports coat. Spiffy. He also had this full beard. But he didn't use a cane and he didn't wear dark glasses. I'd always thought dark glasses were a must for the blind. Fact was, I wished he had a pair. At first glance, his eyes looked like anyone else's eyes. But if you looked close, there was something different about them. Too much white in the iris, for one thing, and the pupils seemed to move around in the sockets without his knowing it or being able to stop it. Creepy. As I stared at his face, I saw the left pupil turn in toward his nose while the other made an effort to keep in one place. But it was only an effort, for that eye was on the roam without his knowing it or wanting it to be.

I said, "Let me get you a drink. What's your pleasure? We have a little of everything. It's one of our pastimes."

"Bub, I'm a Scotch man myself," he said fast enough in this big voice.

"Right," I said. Bub! "Sure you are. I knew it."

35 He let his fingers touch his suitcase, which was sitting alongside the sofa. He was taking his bearings. I didn't blame him for that.

"I'll move that up to your room," my wife said.

"No, that's fine," the blind man said loudly. "It can go up when I go up."

"A little water with the Scotch?" I said.

"Very little," he said.

"I knew it," I said.

He said, "Just a tad. The Irish actor, Barry Fitzgerald? I'm like that 40 fellow. When I drink water, Fitzgerald said, I drink water. When I drink whiskey, I drink whiskey." My wife laughed. The blind man brought his hand up under his beard. He lifted his beard slowly and let it drop.

I did the drinks, three big glasses of Scotch with a splash of water in each. Then we made ourselves comfortable and talked about Robert's travels. First the long flight from the West Coast to Connecticut, we covered that. Then from Connecticut up here by train. We had another drink concerning that leg of the trip.

I remembered having read somewhere that the blind didn't smoke because, as speculation had it, they couldn't see the smoke they exhaled. I thought I knew that much and that much only about blind people. But this blind man smoked his cigarette down to the nubbin and then lit another one. This blind man filled his ashtray and my wife emptied it.

When we sat down at the table for dinner, we had another drink. My wife heaped Robert's plate with cube steak, scalloped potatoes, green beans. I buttered him up two slices of bread. I said, "Here's bread and butter for you." I swallowed some of my drink. "Now let us pray," I said, and the blind man lowered his head. My wife looked at me, her mouth agape. "Pray the phone won't ring and the food doesn't get cold," I said.

We dug in. We ate everything there was to eat on the table. We ate 45 like there was no tomorrow. We didn't talk. We ate. We scarfed. We grazed that table. We were into serious eating. The blind man had right away located his foods, he knew just where everything was on his plate. I watched with admiration as he used his knife and fork on the meat. He'd cut two pieces of meat, fork the meat into his mouth, and then go all out for the scalloped potatoes, the beans next, and then he'd tear off a hunk of buttered bread and eat that. He'd follow this up with a big drink of milk. It didn't seem to bother him to use his fingers once in a while, either.

We finished everything, including half a strawberry pie. For a few moments, we sat as if stunned. Sweat beaded on our faces. Finally, we got up from the table and left the dirty plates. We didn't look back. We took ourselves into the living room and sank into our places again. Robert and my wife sat on the sofa. I took the big chair. We had us two or three more drinks while they talked about the major things that had come to pass for them in the past ten years. For the most part, I just listened. Now and then I joined in. I didn't want him to think I'd left the room, and I didn't want her to think I was feeling left out. They talked of things that had happened to them—to them!— these past ten years. I waited in vain to hear my name on my wife's sweet lips: "And then my dear husband came into my life"—something like that. But I heard nothing of the sort. More talk of Robert. Robert had done a little of everything, it seemed, a regular blind jack-of-all-trades. But most recently he and his wife had had an Amway distributorship, from which, I gathered, they'd earned their living, such as it was. The blind man was also a ham radio operator.[1] He talked in his loud voice about conversations he'd had with fellow operators in Guam, in the Philippines, in Alaska, and even in Tahiti. He said he'd have a lot of friends there if he ever wanted to go visit those places. From time to time, he'd turn his blind face toward me, put his hand under his beard, ask me something. How long had I been in my present position? (Three years.) Did I like my work? (I didn't.) Was I going to stay with it? (What were the options?) Finally, when I thought he was beginning to run down, I got up and turned on the TV.

My wife looked at me with irritation. She was heading toward a boil. Then she looked at the blind man and said, "Robert, do you have a TV?"

The blind man said, "My dear, I have two TVs. I have a color set and a black-and-white thing, and old relic. It's funny, but if I turn the TV on, and I'm always turning it on, I turn on the color set. It's funny, don't you think?"

I didn't know what to say to that. I had absolutely nothing to say to that. No opinion. So I watched the news program and tried to listen to what the announcer was saying.

50   "This is a color TV," the blind man said. "Don't ask me how, but I can tell."

"We traded up a while ago," I said.

The blind man had another taste of his drink. He lifted his beard, sniffed it, and let it fall. He leaned forward on the sofa. He positioned his ashtray on the coffee table, then put the lighter to his cigarette. He leaned back on the sofa and crossed his legs at the ankles.

My wife covered her mouth, and then she yawned. She stretched. She said, "I think I'll go upstairs and put on my robe. I think I'll change into something else. Robert, you make yourself comfortable," she said.

"I'm comfortable," the blind man said.

55   "I want you to feel comfortable in this house," she said.

"I am comfortable," the blind man said.

After she'd left the room, he and I listened to the weather report and then to the sports roundup. By that time, she'd been gone so long I didn't know if she was going to come back. I thought she might have gone to bed. I wished she'd come back downstairs. I didn't want

---

[1]Amateur short-wave radio operator.

to be left alone with a blind man. I asked him if he wanted another drink, and he said sure. Then I asked if he wanted to smoke some dope with me. I said I'd just rolled a number. I hadn't, but I planned to do so in about two shakes.

"I'll try some with you," he said.

"Damn right," I said. "That's the stuff."

I got our drinks and sat down on the sofa with him. Then I rolled 60 us two fat numbers. I lit one and passed it. I brought it to his fingers. He took it and inhaled.

"Hold it as long as you can," I said. I could tell he didn't know the first thing.

My wife came back downstairs wearing her pink robe and her pink slippers.

"What do I smell?" she said.

"We thought we'd have us some cannabis," I said.

My wife gave me a savage look. Then she looked at the blind man 65 and said, "Robert, I didn't know you smoked."

He said, "I do now, my dear. There's a first time for everything. But I don't feel anything yet."

"This stuff is pretty mellow," I said. "This stuff is mild. It's dope you can reason with," I said. "It doesn't mess you up."

"Not much it doesn't, bub," he said, and laughed.

My wife sat on the sofa between the blind man and me. I passed her the number. She took it and toked and then passed it back to me. "Which way is this going?" she said. Then she said, "I shouldn't be smoking this. I can hardly keep my eyes open as it is. That dinner did me in. I shouldn't have eaten so much."

"It was the strawberry pie," the blind man said. "That's what did 70 it," he said, and he laughed his big laugh. Then he shook his head.

"There's more strawberry pie," I said.

"Do you want some more, Robert?" my wife said.

"Maybe in a little while," he said.

We gave our attention to the TV. My wife yawned again. She said, "Your bed is made up when you feel like going to bed, Robert. I know you must have had a long day. When you're ready to go to bed, say so." She pulled his arm. "Robert?"

He came to and said, "I've had a real nice time. This beats tapes, 75 doesn't it?"

I said, "Coming at you," and I put the number between his fingers. He inhaled, held the smoke, and then let it go. It was like he'd been doing it since he was nine years old.

"Thanks, bub," he said. "But I think this is all for me. I think I'm beginning to feel it," he said. He held the burning roach out for my wife.

"Same here," she said. "Ditto. Me, too." She took the roach and passed it to me. "I may just sit here for a while between you two guys with my eyes closed. But don't let me bother you, okay? Either one of you. If it bothers you, say so. Otherwise, I may just sit here with my eyes closed until you're ready to go to bed," she said. "Your bed's made up, Robert, when you're ready. It's right next to our room at the top of the stairs. We'll show you up when you're ready. You wake me up now, you guys, if I fall asleep." She said that and then she closed her eyes and went to sleep.

The news program ended. I got up and changed the channel. I sat back down on the sofa. I wished my wife hadn't pooped out. Her head lay across the back of the sofa, her mouth open. She'd turned so that her robe slipped away from her legs, exposing a juicy thigh. I reached to draw her robe back over her, and it was then that I glanced at the blind man. What the hell! I flipped the robe open again.

80   "You say when you want some strawberry pie," I said.

"I will," he said.

I said, "Are you tired? Do you want me to take you up to your bed? Are you ready to hit the hay?"

"Not yet," he said. "No, I'll stay up with you, bub. If that's all right. I'll stay up until you're ready to turn in. We haven't had a chance to talk. Know what I mean? I feel like me and her monopolized the evening." He lifted his beard and he let it fall. He picked up his cigarettes and his lighter.

"That's all right," I said. Then I said, "I'm glad for the company."

85   And I guess I was. Every night I smoked dope and stayed up as long as I could before I fell asleep. My wife and I hardly ever went to bed at the same time. When I did go to sleep, I had these dreams. Sometimes I'd wake up from one of them, my heart going crazy.

Something about the church and the Middle Ages was on the TV. Not your run-of-the-mill TV fare. I wanted to watch something else. I turned to the other channels. But there was nothing on them, either. So I turned back to the first channel and apologized.

"Bub, it's all right," the blind man said. "It's fine with me. Whatever you want to watch is okay. I'm always learning something. Learning never ends. It won't hurt me to learn something tonight. I got ears," he said.

We didn't say anything for a time. He was leaning forward with his head turned at me, his right ear aimed in the direction of the set. Very disconcerting. Now and then his eyelids drooped and then they snapped open again. Now and then he put his fingers into his beard and tugged, like he was thinking about something he was hearing on the television.

On the screen, a group of men wearing cowls was being set upon and tormented by men dressed in skeleton costumes and men dressed as devils. The men dressed as devils wore devil masks, horns, and long tails. This pageant was part of a procession. The Englishman who was narrating the thing said it took place in Spain once a year. I tried to explain to the blind man what was happening.

"Skeletons," he said. "I know about skeletons," he said, and nodded.

The TV showed this one cathedral. Then there was a long, slow look at another one. Finally, the picture switched to the famous one in Paris, with its flying buttresses and its spires reaching up to the clouds. The camera pulled away to show the whole of the cathedral rising above the skyline.

There were times when the Englishman who was telling the thing would shut up, would simply let the camera move around the cathedrals. Or else the camera would tour the countryside, men in fields walking behind oxen. I waited as long as I could. Then I felt I had to say something. I said, "They're showing the outside of this cathedral now. Gargoyles. Little statues carved to look like monsters. Now I guess they're in Italy. Yeah, they're in Italy. There's paintings on the walls of this one church."

"Are those fresco paintings,[2] bub?" he asked, and he sipped from his drink.

I reached for my glass. But it was empty. I tried to remember what I could remember. "You're asking me are those frescoes?" I said. "That's a good question. I don't know."

The camera moved to a cathedral outside Lisbon. The differences in the Portuguese cathedral compared with the French and Italian were not that great. But they were there. Mostly the interior stuff. Then something occurred to me, and I said, "Something has occurred to me. Do you have any idea what a cathedral is? What they look like, that is? Do you follow me? If somebody says cathedral to you, do you have any notion what they're talking about? Do you know the difference between that and a Baptist church, say?"

He let the smoke dribble from his mouth. "I know they took hundreds of workers fifty or a hundred years to build," he said. "I just heard the man say that, of course. I know generations of the same families worked on a cathedral. I heard him say that, too. The men who began their life's work on them, they never lived to see the completion of their work. In that wise, bub, they're no different from the rest of us, right?" He laughed. Then his eyelids drooped again. His head nodded. He seemed to be snoozing. Maybe he was imagining himself in Portugal. The TV was showing another cathedral now. This one was in Germany. The Englishman's voice droned on. "Cathedrals," the blind man said. He sat up and rolled his head back and forth. "If you want the truth, bub, that's about all I know. What I just said. What I heard him say. But maybe you could describe one to me?

---

[2]Paintings on plaster.

I wish you'd do it. I'd like that. If you want to know, I really don't have a good idea."

I stared hard at the shot of the cathedral on the TV. How could I even begin to describe it? But say my life depended on it. Say my life was being threatened by an insane guy who said I had to do it or else.

I stared some more at the cathedral before the picture flipped off into the countryside. There was no use. I turned to the blind man and said, "To begin with, they're very tall." I was looking around the room for clues. "They reach way up. Up and up. Toward the sky. They're so big, some of them, they have to have these supports. To help hold them up, so to speak. These supports are called buttresses. They remind me of viaducts,[3] for some reason. But maybe you don't know viaducts, either? Sometimes the cathedrals have devils and such carved into the front. Sometimes lords and ladies. Don't ask me why this is," I said.

He was nodding. The whole upper part of his body seemed to be moving back and forth.

100   "I'm not doing so good, am I?" I said.

He stopped nodding and leaned forward on the edge of the sofa. As he listened to me, he was running his fingers through his beard. I wasn't getting through to him, I could see that. But he waited for me to go on just the same. He nodded, like he was trying to encourage me. I tried to think what else to say. "They're really big," I said. "They're massive. They're built of stone. Marble, too, sometimes. In those olden days, when they built cathedrals, men wanted to be close to God. In those olden days, God was an important part of everyone's life. You could tell this from their cathedral-building. I'm sorry," I said, "but it looks like that's the best I can do for you. I'm just no good at it."

"That's all right, bub," the blind man said. "Hey, listen. I hope you don't mind my asking you. Can I ask you something? Let me ask you a simple question, yes or no. I'm just curious and there's no offense. You're my host. But let me ask if you are in any way religious? You don't mind my asking?"

I shook my head. He couldn't see that, though. A wink is the same as a nod to a blind man. "I guess I don't believe in it. In anything. Sometimes it's hard. You know what I'm saying?"

"Sure, I do," he said.

105   "Right," I said.

The Englishman was still holding forth. My wife sighed in her sleep. She drew a long breath and went on with her sleeping.

"You'll have to forgive me," I said. "But I can't tell you what a cathedral looks like. It just isn't in me to do it. I can't do any more than I've done."

The blind man sat very still, his head down, as he listened to me.

---

[3]Long elevated roadways.

I said, "The truth is, cathedrals don't mean anything special to me. Nothing. Cathedrals. They're something to look at on late-night TV. That's all they are."

It was then that the blind man cleared his throat. He brought something up. He took a handkerchief from his back pocket. Then he said, "I get it, bub. It's okay. It happens. Don't worry about it," he said. "Hey, listen to me. Will you do me a favor? I got an idea. Why don't you find us some heavy paper? And a pen. We'll do something. We'll draw one together. Get us a pen and some heavy paper. Go on, bub, get the stuff," he said.

So I went upstairs. My legs felt like they didn't have any strength in them. They felt like they did after I'd done some running. In my wife's room, I looked around. I found some ballpoints in a little basket on her table. And then I tried to think where to look for the kind of paper he was talking about.

Downstairs, in the kitchen, I found a shopping bag with onion skins in the bottom of the bag. I emptied the bag and shook it. I brought it into the living room and sat down with it near his legs. I moved some things, smoothed the wrinkles from the bag, spread it out on the coffee table.

The blind man got down from the sofa and sat next to me on the carpet.

He ran his fingers over the paper. He went up and down the sides of the paper. The edges, even the edges. He fingered the corners.

"All right," he said. "All right, let's do her."

He found my hand, the hand with the pen. He closed his hand over my hand. "Go ahead, bub, draw," he said. "Draw. You'll see. I'll follow along with you. It'll be okay. Just begin now like I'm telling you. You'll see. Draw," the blind man said.

So I began. First I drew a box that looked like a house. It could have been the house I lived in. Then I put a roof on it. At either end of the roof, I drew spires. Crazy.

"Swell," he said. "Terrific. You're doing fine," he said. "Never thought anything like this could happen in your lifetime, did you, bub? Well, it's a strange life, we all know that. Go on now. Keep it up."

I put in windows with arches. I drew flying buttresses. I hung great doors. I couldn't stop. The TV station went off the air. I put down the pen and closed and opened my fingers. The blind man felt around over the paper. He moved the tips of his fingers over the paper, all over what I had drawn, and he nodded.

"Doing fine," the blind man said.

I took up the pen again, and he found my hand. I kept at it. I'm no artist. But I kept drawing just the same.

My wife opened up her eyes and gazed at us. She sat up on the sofa, her robe hanging open. She said, "What are you doing? Tell me, I want to know."

I didn't answer her.

The blind man said, "We're drawing a cathedral. Me and him are working on it. Press hard," he said to me. "That's right. That's good," he said. "Sure. You got it, bub, I can tell. You didn't think you could. But you can, can't you? You're cooking with gas now. You know what I'm saying? We're going to really have us something here in a minute. How's the old arm?" he said. "Put some people in there now. What's a cathedral without people?"

125   My wife said, "What's going on? Robert, what are you doing? What's going on?"

"It's all right," he said to her. "Close your eyes now," the blind man said to me.

I did it. I closed them just like he said.

"Are they closed?" he said. "Don't fudge."

"They're closed," I said.

130   "Keep them that way," he said. He said, "Don't stop now. Draw."

So we kept on with it. His fingers rode my fingers as my hand went over the paper. It was like nothing else in my life up to now.

Then he said, "I think that's it. I think you got it," he said. "Take a look. What do you think?"

But I had my eyes closed. I thought I'd keep them that way for a little longer. I thought it was something I ought to do.

"Well?" he said. "Are you looking?"

135   My eyes were still closed. I was in my house. I knew that. But I didn't feel like I was inside anything.

"It's really something," I said.

Responding to Reading

1. What is the narrator's first impression of the blind man? How does his attitude change? How do you account for this change?
2. Why do you think the blind man asks the narrator to draw a cathedral? Why does the blind man ask the narrator to close his eyes? What does the blind man hope to teach the narrator?
3. What is the significance of the story's title? In what sense is "Cathedral" a religious story? In what sense is it *not* a religious story?

Responding in Writing

How would you characterize the narrator's marriage? What effect do you think the blind man has on the marriage?

Focus

Is There Intelligent Design in Nature?

The "ascent" of man from Simian through Prehominid to Neanderthal and finally to *Homo sapiens*

Responding to the Image

1. Do you think this image accurately represents the theory of evolution? In what sense could the artist be accused of oversimplifying?
2. In what ways is the last figure similar to the other species pictured above? In what sense is he different?

FINDING DESIGN IN NATURE

Christoph Schönborn

1945–

Roman Catholic Cardinal–Archbishop of Vienna Christoph Schönborn edited the 1992 Catechism of the Catholic Church, *contributing significantly to the works that have come to define Catholicism. In the following essay, Schönborn attempts to reconcile Catholic doctrine with theories of evolution.*

Ever since 1996, when Pope John Paul II said that evolution (a term he did not define) was "more than just a hypothesis," defenders of neo-Darwinian dogma have often invoked the supposed acceptance—or at least acquiescence—of the Roman Catholic Church when they defend their theory as somehow compatible with Christian faith.

But this is not true. The Catholic Church, while leaving to science many details about the history of life on earth, proclaims that by the light of reason the human intellect can readily and clearly discern purpose and design in the natural world, including the world of living things.

Evolution in the sense of common ancestry might be true, but evolution in the neo-Darwinian sense—an unguided, unplanned process of random variation and natural selection—is not. Any system of thought that denies or seeks to explain away the overwhelming evidence for design in biology is ideology, not science.

Consider the real teaching of our beloved John Paul. While his rather vague and unimportant 1996 letter about evolution is always and everywhere cited, we see no one discussing these comments from a 1985 general audience that represents his robust teaching on nature:

5   "All the observations concerning the development of life lead to a similar conclusion. The evolution of living beings, of which science seeks to determine the stages and to discern the mechanism, presents an internal finality which arouses admiration. This finality which directs beings in a direction for which they are not responsible or in charge, obliges one to suppose a Mind which is its inventor, its creator."

He went on: "To all these indications of the existence of God the Creator, some oppose the power of chance or of the proper mechanisms of matter. To speak of chance for a universe which presents such a complex organization in its elements and such marvelous finality in its life would be equivalent to giving up the search for an explanation of the world as it appears to us. In fact, this would be equivalent to admitting effects without a cause. It would be to abdicate human intelligence, which would thus refuse to think and to seek a solution for its problems."

Note that in this quotation the word "finality" is a philosophical term synonymous with final cause, purpose or design. In comments at another general audience a year later, John Paul concludes, "It is clear that the truth of faith about creation is radically opposed to the theories of materialistic philosophy. These view the cosmos as the result of an evolution of matter reducible to pure chance and necessity."

Naturally, the authoritative Catechism of the Catholic Church agrees: "Human intelligence is surely already capable of finding a response to the question of origins. The existence of God the Creator can be known with certainty through his works, by the light of human reason." It adds: "We believe that God created the world according to his wisdom. It is not the product of any necessity whatever, nor of blind fate or chance."

In an unfortunate new twist on this old controversy, neo-Darwinists recently have sought to portray our new pope, Benedict XVI, as a satisfied evolutionist. They have quoted a sentence about common ancestry from a 2004 document of the International Theological Commission, pointed out that Benedict was at the time head of the commission, and concluded that the Catholic Church has no problem with the notion of "evolution" as used by mainstream biologists—that is, synonymous with neo-Darwinism.

The commission's document, however, reaffirms the perennial 10 teaching of the Catholic Church about the reality of design in nature. Commenting on the widespread abuse of John Paul's 1996 letter on evolution, the commission cautions that "the letter cannot be read as a blanket approbation of all theories of evolution, including those of a neo-Darwinian provenance which explicitly deny to divine providence any truly causal role in the development of life in the universe."

Furthermore, according to the commission, "An unguided evolutionary process—one that falls outside the bounds of divine providence—simply cannot exist."

Indeed, in the homily at his installation just a few weeks ago, Benedict proclaimed: "We are not some casual and meaningless product of evolution. Each of us is the result of a thought of God. Each of us is willed, each of us is loved, each of us is necessary."

Throughout history the church has defended the truths of faith given by Jesus Christ. But in the modern era, the Catholic Church is in the odd position of standing in firm defense of reason as well. In the 19th century, the First Vatican Council taught a world newly enthralled by the "death of God" that by the use of reason alone mankind could come to know the reality of the Uncaused Cause, the First Mover, the God of the philosophers.

Now at the beginning of the 21st century, faced with scientific claims like neo-Darwinism and the multiverse hypothesis in cosmology invented to avoid the overwhelming evidence for purpose and

CHAPTER 10 FOCUS

design found in modern science, the Catholic Church will again defend human reason by proclaiming that the immanent design evident in nature is real. Scientific theories that try to explain away the appearance of design as the result of "chance and necessity" are not scientific at all, but, as John Paul put it, an abdication of human intelligence.

Responding to Reading

1. According to Schönborn, what is Pope John Paul's position on evolution? How is it different from that of neo-Darwinists?
2. Why do neo-Darwinists attempt to characterize Pope Benedict XVI "as a satisfied evolutionist" (9)? Why does Schönborn think this characterization is false?
3. How does the Catholic Church "defend human reason" (14)? In what sense is this defense antithetical to modern scientific theory?

Responding in Writing

Do you think it is possible, as Schönborn asserts, to defend human reason and at the same time to reject the neo-Darwinist view of the universe?

WHY INTELLIGENT DESIGN ISN'T

H. Allen Orr

1960–

A biology professor at the University of Rochester, H. Allen Orr studies genetic evolution and adaptation. A respected biologist, he has published numerous articles in various scientific journals. In the following New Yorker *essay, Orr characterizes intelligent design as "junk science."*

If you are in ninth grade and live in Dover, Pennsylvania, you are learning things in your biology class that differ considerably from what your peers just a few miles away are learning. In particular, you are learning that Darwin's theory of evolution provides just one possible explanation of life, and that another is provided by something called intelligent design. You are being taught this not because of a recent breakthrough in some scientist's laboratory but because the Dover Area School District's board mandates it. In October, 2004, the board decreed that "students will be made aware of gaps/problems in Darwin's theory and of other theories of evolution including, but not limited to, intelligent design."*

---

*In December 2005, a U.S. District Count barred the Dover schools from teaching intelligent design, saying the concept is creationism in disguise.

While the events in Dover have received a good deal of attention as a sign of the political times, there has been surprisingly little discussion of the science that's said to underlie the theory of intelligent design, often called I.D. Many scientists avoid discussing I.D. for strategic reasons. If a scientific claim can be loosely defined as one that scientists take seriously enough to debate, then engaging the intelligent-design movement on scientific grounds, they worry, cedes what it most desires: recognition that its claims are legitimate scientific ones.

Meanwhile, proposals hostile to evolution are being considered in more than twenty states; earlier this month, a bill was introduced into the New York State Assembly calling for instruction in intelligent design for all public-school students. The Kansas State Board of Education is weighing new standards, drafted by supporters of intelligent design, that would encourage schoolteachers to challenge Darwinism. Senator Rick Santorum, a Pennsylvania Republican, has argued that "intelligent design is a legitimate scientific theory that should be taught in science classes." An I.D.-friendly amendment that he sponsored to the No Child Left Behind Act—requiring public schools to help students understand why evolution "generates so much continuing controversy"—was overwhelmingly approved in the Senate. (The amendment was not included in the version of the bill that was signed into law, but similar language did appear in a conference report that accompanied it.) In the past few years, college students across the country have formed Intelligent Design and Evolution Awareness chapters. Clearly, a policy of limited scientific engagement has failed. So just what is this movement?

First of all, intelligent design is not what people often assume it is. For one thing, I.D. is not Biblical literalism. Unlike earlier generations of creationists—the so-called Young Earthers and scientific creationists—proponents of intelligent design do not believe that the universe was created in six days, that Earth is ten thousand years old, or that the fossil record was deposited during Noah's flood. (Indeed, they shun the label "creationism" altogether.) Nor does I.D. flatly reject evolution: adherents freely admit that some evolutionary change occurred during the history of life on Earth. Although the movement is loosely allied with, and heavily funded by, various conservative Christian groups—and although I.D. plainly maintains that life was created—it is generally silent about the identity of the creator.

The movement's main positive claim is that there are things in the world, most notably life, that cannot be accounted for by known natural causes and show features that, in any other context, we would attribute to intelligence. Living organisms are too complex to be explained by any natural—or, more precisely, by any mindless—process. Instead, the design inherent in organisms can be accounted for only by invoking a designer, and one who is very, very smart.

CHAPTER 10 FOCUS

All of which puts I.D. squarely at odds with Darwin. Darwin's theory of evolution was meant to show how the fantastically complex features of organisms—eyes, beaks, brains—could arise without the intervention of a designing mind. According to Darwinism, evolution largely reflects the combined action of random mutation and natural selection. A random mutation in an organism, like a random change in any finely tuned machine, is almost always bad. That's why you don't, screwdriver in hand, make arbitrary changes to the insides of your television. But, once in a great while, a random mutation in the DNA that makes up an organism's genes slightly improves the function of some organ and thus the survival of the organism. In a species whose eye amounts to nothing more than a primitive patch of light-sensitive cells, a mutation that causes this patch to fold into a cup shape might have a survival advantage. While the old type of organism can tell only if the lights are on, the new type can detect the *direction* of any source of light or shadow. Since shadows sometimes mean predators, that can be valuable information. The new, improved type of organism will, therefore, be more common in the next generation. That's natural selection. Repeated over billions of years, this process of incremental improvement should allow for the gradual emergence of organisms that are exquisitely adapted to their environments and that look for all the world as though they were designed. By 1870, about a decade after *The Origin of Species* was published, nearly all biologists agreed that life had evolved, and by 1940 or so most agreed that natural selection was a key force driving this evolution.

Advocates of intelligent design point to two developments that in their view undermine Darwinism. The first is the molecular revolution in biology. Beginning in the nineteen-fifties, molecular biologists revealed a staggering and unsuspected degree of complexity within the cells that make up all life. This complexity, I.D.'s defenders argue, lies beyond the abilities of Darwinism to explain. Second, they claim that new mathematical findings cast doubt on the power of natural selection. Selection may play a role in evolution, but it cannot accomplish what biologists suppose it can.

These claims have been championed by a tireless group of writers, most of them associated with the Center for Science and Culture at the Discovery Institute, a Seattle-based think tank that sponsors projects in science, religion, and national defense, among other areas. The center's fellows and advisers—including the emeritus law professor Phillip E. Johnson, the philosopher Stephen C. Meyer, and the biologist Jonathan Wells—have published an astonishing number of articles and books that decry the ostensibly sad state of Darwinism and extol the virtues of the design alternative. But Johnson, Meyer, and Wells, while highly visible, are mainly strategists and popularizers. The scientific leaders of the design movement are two scholars, one a biochemist and the other a mathematician. To assess intelligent design is to assess their arguments.

Michael J. Behe, a professor of biological sciences at Lehigh University (and a senior fellow at the Discovery Institute), is a biochemist who writes technical papers on the structure of DNA. He is the most prominent of the small circle of scientists working on intelligent design, and his arguments are by far the best known. His book *Darwin's Black Box* (1996) was a surprise best-seller and was named by *National Review* as one of the hundred best nonfiction books of the twentieth century. (A little calibration may be useful here; *The Starr Report* also made the list.)

Not surprisingly, Behe's doubts about Darwinism begin with biochemistry. Fifty years ago, he says, any biologist could tell stories like the one about the eye's evolution. But such stories, Behe notes, invariably began with cells, whose own evolutionary origins were essentially left unexplained. This was harmless enough as long as cells weren't qualitatively more complex than the larger, more visible aspects of the eye. Yet when biochemists began to dissect the inner workings of the cell, what they found floored them. A cell is packed full of exceedingly complex structures—hundreds of microscopic machines, each performing a specific job. The "Give me a cell and I'll give you an eye" story told by Darwinists, he says, began to seem suspect: starting with a cell was starting ninety per cent of the way to the finish line.

Behe's main claim is that cells are complex not just in degree but in kind. Cells contain structures that are "irreducibly complex." This means that if you remove any single part from such a structure, the structure no longer functions. Behe offers a simple, nonbiological example of an irreducibly complex object: the mousetrap. A mousetrap has several parts—platform, spring, catch, hammer, and hold-down bar—and all of them have to be in place for the trap to work. If you remove the spring from a mousetrap, it isn't slightly worse at killing mice; it doesn't kill them at all. So, too, with the bacterial flagellum, Behe argues. This flagellum is a tiny propeller attached to the back of some bacteria. Spinning at more than twenty thousand r.p.m.s, it motors the bacterium through its aquatic world. The flagellum comprises roughly thirty different proteins, all precisely arranged, and if any one of them is removed the flagellum stops spinning.

In *Darwin's Black Box*, Behe maintained that irreducible complexity presents Darwinism with "unbridgeable chasms." How, after all, could a gradual process of incremental improvement build something like a flagellum, which needs *all* its parts in order to work? Scientists, he argued, must face up to the fact that "many biochemical systems cannot be built by natural selection working on mutations." In the end, Behe concluded that irreducibly complex cells arise the same way as irreducibly complex mousetraps—someone designs them. As he put it in a recent *Times* Op-Ed piece: "If it looks, walks, and quacks like a duck, then, absent compelling evidence to the contrary, we have warrant to conclude it's a duck. Design should not be overlooked simply because it's so obvious." In *Darwin's Black Box,* Behe speculated that the designer might have assembled the first cell, essentially solving the problem of irreducible complexity, after which evolution might well have proceeded by more or less conventional means. Under Behe's brand of creationism, you might still be an ape that evolved on the African savanna; it's just that your cells harbor micro-machines engineered by an unnamed intelligence some four billion years ago.

But Behe's principal argument soon ran into trouble. As biologists pointed out, there are several different ways that Darwinian evolution can build irreducibly complex systems. In one, elaborate structures may evolve for one reason and then get co-opted for some entirely different, irreducibly complex function. Who says those thirty flagellar proteins weren't present in bacteria long before bacteria sported flagella? They may have been performing other jobs in the cell and only later got drafted into flagellum-building. Indeed, there's now strong evidence that several flagellar proteins once played roles in a type of molecular pump found in the membranes of bacterial cells.

Behe doesn't consider this sort of "indirect" path to irreducible complexity—in which parts perform one function and then switch to another—terribly plausible. And he essentially rules out the alternative possibility of a direct Darwinian path: a path, that is, in which Darwinism builds an irreducibly complex structure while selecting all along for the same biological function. But biologists have shown that direct paths to irreducible complexity are possible, too. Suppose a part gets added to a system merely because the part improves the system's performance; the part is not, at this stage, essential for function. But, because subsequent evolution builds on this addition, a part that was at first just advantageous might *become* essential. As this process is repeated through evolutionary time, more and more parts that were once merely beneficial become necessary. This idea was first set forth by H. J. Muller, the Nobel Prize–winning geneticist, in 1939, but it's a familiar process in the development of human technologies. We add new parts like global-positioning systems to cars not because they're necessary but because they're nice. But no one would be surprised if, in fifty years, computers that rely on G.P.S. actually drove our cars. At that point, G.P.S. would no longer be an attractive option; it would be an essential piece of automotive technology. It's important to see that this process is thoroughly Darwinian: each change might well be small and each represents an improvement.

15   Design theorists have made some concessions to these criticisms. Behe has confessed to "sloppy prose" and said he hadn't meant to imply that irreducibly complex systems "by definition" cannot evolve gradually. "I quite agree that my argument against Darwinism does not

add up to a logical proof," he says—though he continues to believe that Darwinian paths to irreducible complexity are exceedingly unlikely. Behe and his followers now emphasize that, while irreducibly complex systems can in principle evolve, biologists can't reconstruct in convincing detail just how any such system did evolve.

What counts as a sufficiently detailed historical narrative, though, is altogether subjective. Biologists actually know a great deal about the evolution of biochemical systems, irreducibly complex or not. It's significant, for instance, that the proteins that typically make up the parts of these systems are often similar to one another. (Blood clotting—another of Behe's examples of irreducible complexity—involves at least twenty proteins, several of which are similar, and all of which are needed to make clots, to localize or remove clots, or to prevent the runaway clotting of all blood.) And biologists understand why these proteins are so similar. Each gene in an organism's genome encodes a particular protein. Occasionally, the stretch of DNA that makes up a particular gene will get accidentally copied, yielding a genome that includes two versions of the gene. Over many generations, one version of the gene will often keep its original function while the other one slowly changes by mutation and natural selection, picking up a new, though usually related, function. This process of "gene duplication" has given rise to entire families of proteins that have similar functions; they often act in the same biochemical pathway or sit in the same cellular structure. There's no doubt that gene duplication plays an extremely important role in the evolution of biological complexity.

It's true that when you confront biologists with a particular complex structure like the flagellum they sometimes have a hard time saying which part appeared before which other parts. But then it can be hard, with any complex historical process, to reconstruct the exact order in which events occurred, especially when, as in evolution, the addition of new parts encourages the modification of old ones. When you're looking at a bustling urban street, for example, you probably can't tell which shop went into business first. This is partly because many businesses now depend on each other and partly because new shops trigger changes in old ones (the new sushi place draws twenty-somethings who demand wireless Internet at the café next door). But it would be a little rash to conclude that all the shops must have begun business on the same day or that some Unseen Urban Planner had carefully determined just which business went where.

The other leading theorist of the new creationism, William A. Dembski, holds a Ph.D. in mathematics, another in philosophy, and a master of divinity in theology. He has been a research professor in the conceptual foundations of science at Baylor University, and was recently appointed to the new Center for Science and Theology at Southern Baptist Theological Seminary. (He is a longtime senior fellow at the

Discovery Institute as well.) Dembski publishes at a staggering pace. His books—including *The Design Inference, Intelligent Design, No Free Lunch,* and *The Design Revolution*—are generally well written and packed with provocative ideas.

According to Dembski, a complex object must be the result of intelligence if it was the product neither of chance nor of necessity. The novel *Moby Dick,* for example, didn't arise by chance (Melville didn't scribble random letters), and it wasn't the necessary consequence of a physical law (unlike, say, the fall of an apple). It was, instead, the result of Melville's intelligence. Dembski argues that there is a reliable way to recognize such products of intelligence in the natural world. We can conclude that an object was intelligently designed, he says, if it shows "specified complexity"—complexity that matches an "independently given pattern." The sequence of letters "JKXVCJUDOPLVM" is certainly complex: if you randomly type thirteen letters, you are very unlikely to arrive at this particular sequence. But it isn't *specified:* it doesn't match any independently given sequence of letters. If, on the other hand, I ask you for the first sentence of "Moby Dick" and you type the letters "CALLMEISHMAEL," you have produced something that is both complex and specified. The sequence you typed is unlikely to arise by chance alone, and it matches an independent target sequence (the one written by Melville). Dembski argues that specified complexity, when expressed mathematically, provides an unmistakable signature of intelligence. Things like "CALLMEISHMAEL," he points out, just don't arise in the real world without acts of intelligence. If organisms show specified complexity, therefore, we can conclude that they are the handiwork of an intelligent agent.

20   For Dembski, it's telling that the sophisticated machines we find in organisms match up in astonishingly precise ways with recognizable human technologies. The eye, for example, has a familiar, cameralike design, with recognizable parts—a pinhole opening for light, a lens, and a surface on which to project an image—all arranged just as a human engineer would arrange them. And the flagellum has a motor design, one that features recognizable O-rings, a rotor, and a drive shaft. Specified complexity, he says, is there for all to see.

Dembski's second major claim is that certain mathematical results cast doubt on Darwinism at the most basic conceptual level. In 2002, he focussed on so-called No Free Lunch, or N.F.L., theorems, which were derived in the late nineties by the physicists David H. Wolpert and William G. Macready. These theorems relate to the efficiency of different "search algorithms." Consider a search for high ground on some unfamiliar, hilly terrain. You're on foot and it's a moonless night; you've got two hours to reach the highest place you can. How to proceed? One sensible search algorithm might say, "Walk uphill in the steepest possible direction; if no direction uphill is available, take a couple of steps to the left and try again." This algorithm insures that you're generally moving upward. Another search algorithm—a so-called blind search algorithm—might say, "Walk in a random direction." This would sometimes take you uphill but sometimes down. Roughly, the N.F.L. theorems prove the surprising fact that, averaged over all possible terrains, no search algorithm is better than any other. In some landscapes, moving uphill gets you to higher ground in the allotted time, while in other landscapes moving randomly does, but on average neither outperforms the other.

Now, Darwinism can be thought of as a search algorithm. Given a problem—adapting to a new disease, for instance—a population uses the Darwinian algorithm of random mutation plus natural selection to search for a solution (in this case, disease resistance). But, according to Dembski, the N.F.L. theorems prove that this Darwinian algorithm is no better than any other when confronting all possible problems. It follows that, over all, Darwinism is no better than blind search, a process of utterly random change unaided by any guiding force like natural selection. Since we don't expect blind change to build elaborate machines showing an exquisite coördination of parts, we have no right to expect Darwinism to do so, either. Attempts to sidestep this problem by, say, carefully constraining the class of challenges faced by organisms inevitably involve sneaking in the very kind of order that we're trying to explain—something Dembski calls the displacement problem. In the end, he argues, the N.F.L. theorems and the displacement problem mean that there's only one plausible source for the design we find in organisms: intelligence. Although Dembski is somewhat noncommittal, he seems to favor a design theory in which an intelligent agent programmed design into early life, or even into the early universe. This design then unfolded through the long course of evolutionary time, as microbes slowly morphed into man.

Dembski's arguments have been met with tremendous enthusiasm in the I.D. movement. In part, that's because an innumerate public is easily impressed by a bit of mathematics. Also, when Dembski is wielding his equations, he gets to play the part of the hard scientist busily correcting the errors of those soft-headed biologists. (Evolutionary biology actually features an extraordinarily sophisticated body of mathematical theory, a fact not widely known because neither of evolution's great popularizers—Richard Dawkins and the late Stephen Jay Gould—did much math.) Despite all the attention, Dembski's mathematical claims about design and Darwin are almost entirely beside the point.

The most serious problem in Dembski's account involves specified complexity. Organisms aren't trying to match any "independently given pattern": evolution has no goal, and the history of life isn't trying to get anywhere. If building a sophisticated structure like an eye increases

CHAPTER 10 FOCUS

the number of children produced, evolution may well build an eye. But if destroying a sophisticated structure like the eye increases the number of children produced, evolution will just as happily destroy the eye. Species of fish and crustaceans that have moved into the total darkness of caves, where eyes are both unnecessary and costly, often have degenerate eyes, or eyes that begin to form only to be covered by skin—crazy contraptions that no intelligent agent would design. Despite all the loose talk about design and machines, organisms aren't striving to realize some engineer's blueprint; they're striving (if they can be said to strive at all) only to have more offspring than the next fellow.

25   Another problem with Dembski's arguments concerns the N.F.L. theorems. Recent work shows that these theorems don't hold in the case of co-evolution, when two or more species evolve in response to one another. And most evolution is surely co-evolution. Organisms do not spend most of their time adapting to rocks; they are perpetually challenged by, and adapting to, a rapidly changing suite of viruses, parasites, predators, and prey. A theorem that doesn't apply to these situations is a theorem whose relevance to biology is unclear. As it happens, David Wolpert, one of the authors of the N.F.L. theorems, recently denounced Dembski's use of those theorems as "fatally informal and imprecise." Dembski's apparent response has been a tactical retreat. In 2002, Dembski triumphantly proclaimed, "The No Free Lunch theorems dash any hope of generating specified complexity via evolutionary algorithms." Now he says, "I certainly never argued that the N.F.L. theorems provide a direct refutation of Darwinism."

Those of us who have argued with I.D. in the past are used to such shifts of emphasis. But it's striking that Dembski's views on the history of life contradict Behe's. Dembski believes that Darwinism is incapable of building anything interesting; Behe seems to believe that, given a cell, Darwinism might well have built you and me. Although proponents of I.D. routinely inflate the significance of minor squabbles among evolutionary biologists (did the peppered moth evolve dark color as a defense against birds or for other reasons?), they seldom acknowledge their own, often major differences of opinion. In the end, it's hard to view intelligent design as a coherent movement in any but a political sense.

It's also hard to view it as a real research program. Though people often picture science as a collection of clever theories, scientists are generally staunch pragmatists: to scientists, a good theory is one that inspires new experiments and provides unexpected insights into familiar phenomena. By this standard, Darwinism is one of the best theories in the history of science: it has produced countless important experiments (let's re-create a natural species in the lab—yes, that's been done) and sudden insight into once puzzling patterns (*that's* why there are no native land mammals on oceanic islands). In the nearly ten years since the publication of Behe's book, by contrast, I.D. has inspired no nontrivial experiments and has provided no surprising insights into biology. As the years pass, intelligent design looks less and less like the science it claimed to be and more and more like an extended exercise in polemics.

In 1999, a document from the Discovery Institute was posted, anonymously, on the Internet. This Wedge Document, as it came to be called, described not only the institute's long-term goals but its strategies for accomplishing them. The document begins by labelling the idea that human beings are created in the image of God "one of the bedrock principles on which Western civilization was built." It goes on to decry the catastrophic legacy of Darwin, Marx, and Freud— the alleged fathers of a "materialistic conception of reality" that eventually "infected virtually every area of our culture." The mission of the Discovery Institute's scientific wing is then spelled out: "nothing less than the overthrow of materialism and its cultural legacies." It seems fair to conclude that the Discovery Institute has set its sights a bit higher than, say, reconstructing the origins of the bacterial flagellum.

The intelligent-design community is usually far more circumspect in its pronouncements. This is not to say that it eschews discussion of religion; indeed, the intelligent-design literature regularly insists that Darwinism represents a thinly veiled attempt to foist a secular religion— godless materialism—on Western culture. As it happens, the idea that Darwinism is yoked to atheism, though popular, is also wrong. Of the five founding fathers of twentieth-century evolutionary biology— Ronald Fisher, Sewall Wright, J. B. S. Haldane, Ernst Mayr, and Theodosius Dobzhansky—one was a devout Anglican who preached sermons and published articles in church magazines, one a practicing Unitarian, one a dabbler in Eastern mysticism, one an apparent atheist, and one a member of the Russian Orthodox Church and the author of a book on religion and science. Pope John Paul II himself acknowledged, in a 1996 address to the Pontifical Academy of Sciences, that new research "leads to the recognition of the theory of evolution as more than a hypothesis." Whatever larger conclusions one thinks *should* follow from Darwinism, the historical fact is that evolution and religion have often coexisted. As the philosopher Michael Ruse observes, "It is simply not the case that people take up evolution in the morning, and become atheists as an encore in the afternoon."

Biologists aren't alarmed by intelligent design's arrival in Dover 30 and elsewhere because they have all sworn allegiance to atheistic materialism; they're alarmed because intelligent design is junk science. Meanwhile, more than eighty per cent of Americans say that God either created human beings in their present form or guided their development. As a succession of intelligent-design proponents appeared before the Kansas State Board of Education earlier this month, it was possible to wonder whether the movement's scientific coherence was beside the point. Intelligent design has come this far by faith.

Responding to Reading

1. What is intelligent design? How is it different from creationism? How is it different from Darwinism?
2. What is Michael J. Behe's major argument against Darwinsim? How does Orr counter this argument? How convincing is he?
3. What two points does William A. Dembski make to support intelligent design? What is Orr's response to these points? According to Orr, why are biologists alarmed by intelligent design?

Responding in Writing

Do you believe intelligent design is legitimate scientific theory, or do you think it is simply a way to bring religion into public schools?

FINDING DARWIN'S GOD

Kenneth R. Miller

1948–

A biology professor at Brown University, Kenneth R. Miller is a widely published writer and expert on the intersection of religion and evolution. He has coauthored three biology textbooks and most recently published the book Finding Darwin's God: A Scientist's Search for Common Ground between God and Evolution *(1999), from which the following essay is exerpted.*

The great hall of the Hynes Convention Center in Boston looks nothing like a church. And yet I sat there, smiling amid an audience of scientists, shaking my head and laughing to myself as I remembered another talk, given long ago, inside a church to an audience of children.

Without warning, I had experienced one of those moments in the present that connects with the scattered recollections of our past. Psychologists tell us that things happen all the time. Five thousand days of childhood are filed, not in chronological order, but as bits and pieces linked by words, or sounds, or even smells that cause us to retrieve them for no apparent reason when something "refreshes" our memory. And just like that, a few words in a symposium on developmental biology had brought me back to the day before my first communion. I was eight years old, sitting with the boys on the right side of our little church (the girls sat on the left), and our pastor was speaking.

Putting the finishing touches on a year of preparation for the sacrament, Father Murphy sought to impress us with the reality of God's power in the world. He pointed to the altar railing, its polished marble gleaming in sunlight, and firmly assured us that God himself had fashioned it. "Yeah, right," whispered the kid next to me. Worried that there might be the son or daughter of a stonecutter in the crowd, the good Father retreated a bit. "Now, he didn't carve the railing or bring it here or cement it in place . . . but God himself *made* the marble, long ago, and left it for someone to find and make into part of our church."

I don't know if our pastor sensed that his description of God as craftsman was meeting a certain tide of skepticism, but no matter. He had another trick up his sleeve, a can't-miss, sure-thing argument that, no doubt, had never failed him. He walked over to the altar and picked a flower from the vase.

"Look at the beauty of a flower," he began. "The Bible tells us that even Solomon in all his glory was never arrayed as one of these. And do you know what? Not a single person in the world can tell us what makes a flower bloom. All those scientists in their laboratories, the ones who can split the atom and build jet planes and televisions, well, not one of them can tell you how a plant makes flowers." And why should they be able to? "Flowers, just like you, are the work of God." 5

I was impressed. No one argued, no one wisecracked. We filed out of the church like good little boys and girls, ready for our first communion the next day. And I never thought of it again, until this symposium on developmental biology. Sandwiched between two speakers working on more fashionable topics in animal development was Elliot M. Meyerowitz, a plant scientist at Caltech. A few of my colleagues, uninterested in research dealing with plants, got up to stretch their legs before the final talk, but I sat there with an ear-to-ear grin on my face. I jotted notes furiously; I sketched the diagrams he projected on the screen and wrote additional speculations of my own in the margins. Meyerowitz, you see, had explained how plants make flowers.

The four principal parts of a flower—sepals, petals, stamens, and pistils—are actually modified leaves. This is one of the reasons why plants can produce reproductive cells just about anywhere, while animals are limited to a very specific set of reproductive organs. Your little finger isn't going to start shedding reproductive cells anytime soon. But in springtime, the tip of any branch on an apple tree may very well blossom and begin scattering pollen. Plants can produce new flowers anywhere they can grow new leaves. Somehow, however, the plant must find a way to "tell" an ordinary cluster of leaves that they should develop into floral parts. That's where Meyerowitz's lab took over.

Several years of patient genetic study had isolated a set of mutants that could only form two or three of the four parts. By crossing the various mutants, his team was able to identify four genes that had to be

CHAPTER 10 FOCUS

turned on or off in a specific pattern to produce a normal flower. Each of these genes, in turn, sets off a series of signals that "tell" the cells of a brand new bud to develop as sepals or petals rather than ordinary leaves. The details are remarkable, and the interactions between the genes are fascinating. To me, sitting in the crowd thirty-seven years after my first communion, the scientific details were just the icing on the cake. The real message was "Father Murphy, you were wrong." God doesn't make a flower. The floral induction genes do.

Our pastor's error, common and widely repeated, was to seek God in what science has not yet explained. His assumption was that God is best found in territory unknown, in the corners of darkness that have not yet seen the light of understanding. These, as it turns out, are exactly the wrong places to look.

Searching the Shadows

10 By pointing to the process of making a flower as proof of the reality of God, Father Murphy was embracing the idea that God finds it necessary to cripple nature. In his view, the blooming of a daffodil requires not a self-sufficient material universe, but direct intervention by God. We can find God, therefore, in the things around us that lack material, scientific explanations. In nature, elusive and unexplored, we will find the Creator at work.

The creationist opponents of evolution make similar arguments. They claim that the existence of life, the appearance of new species, and, most especially, the origins of mankind have not and cannot be explained by evolution or any other natural process. By denying the self-sufficiency of nature, they look for God (or at least a "designer") in the deficiencies of science. The trouble is that science, given enough time, generally explains even the most baffling things. As a matter of strategy, creationists would be well-advised to avoid telling scientists what they will never be able to figure out. History is against them. In a general way, we really do understand how nature works.

And evolution forms a critical part of that understanding. Evolution really does explain the very things that its critics say it does not. Claims disputing the antiquity of the earth, the validity of the fossil record, and the sufficiency of evolutionary mechanisms vanish upon close inspection. Even to the most fervent anti-evolutionists, the pattern should be clear—their favorite "gaps" are filling up: the molecular mechanisms of evolution are now well-understood, and the historical record of evolution becomes more compelling with each passing season. This means that science can answer their challenges to evolution in an obvious way. Show the historical record, provide the data, reveal the mechanism, and highlight the convergence of theory and fact.

There is, however, a deeper problem caused by the opponents of evolution, a problem for religion. Like our priest, they have based their search for God on the premise that nature is *not* self-sufficient. By such logic, only God can make a species, just as Father Murphy believed only God could make a flower. Both assertions support the existence of God *only* so long as these assertions are true, but serious problems for religion emerge when they are shown to be false.

If we accept a *lack* of scientific explanation as proof for God's existence, simple logic would dictate that we would have to regard a successful scientific explanation as an argument *against* God. That's why creationist reasoning, ultimately, is much more dangerous to religion than to science. Elliot Meyerowitz's fine work on floral induction suddenly becomes a threat to the divine, even though common sense tells us it should be nothing of the sort. By arguing, as creationists do, that nature cannot be self-sufficient in the formation of new species, the creationists forge a logical link between the limits of natural processes to accomplish biological change and the existence of a designer (God). In other words, they show the proponents of atheism exactly how to disprove the existence of God—show that evolution works, and it's time to tear down the temple. This is an offer that the enemies of religion are all too happy to accept.

Putting it bluntly, the creationists have sought God in darkness. 15 What we have not found and do not yet understand becomes their best—indeed their only—evidence for the divine. As a Christian, I find the flow of this logic particularly depressing. Not only does it teach us to fear the acquisition of knowledge (which might at any time disprove belief), but it suggests that God dwells only in the shadows of our understanding. I suggest that, if God is real, we should be able to find him somewhere else—in the bright light of human knowledge, spiritual and scientific.

Faith and Reason

Each of the great Western monotheistic traditions sees God as truth, love, and knowledge. This should mean that each and every increase in our understanding of the natural world is a step toward God and not, as many people assume, a step away. If faith and reason are both gifts from God, then they should play complementary, not conflicting, roles in our struggle to understand the world around us. As a scientist and as a Christian, that is exactly what I believe. True knowledge comes only from a combination of faith and reason.

A nonbeliever, of course, puts his or her trust in science and finds no value in faith. And I certainly agree that science allows believer and nonbeliever alike to investigate the natural world through a common lens of observation, experiment, and theory. The ability of science to transcend cultural, political, and even religious differences is part of its genius, part of its value as a way of knowing. What science cannot do is assign either meaning or purpose to the world it explores. This leads

CHAPTER 10 FOCUS

some to conclude that the world as seen by science is devoid of meaning and absent of purpose. It is not. What it does mean, I would suggest, is that our human tendency to assign meaning and value must transcend science and, ultimately, must come from outside it. The science that results can thus be enriched and informed from its contact with the values and principles of faith. The God of Abraham does not tell us which proteins control the cell cycle. But he does give us a reason to care, a reason to cherish that understanding, and above all, a reason to prefer the light of knowledge to the darkness of ignorance.

As more than one scientist has said, the truly remarkable thing about the world is that it actually does make sense. The parts fit, the molecules interact, the darn thing works. To people of faith, what evolution says is that nature is complete. Their God fashioned a material world in which truly free and independent beings could evolve. He got it right the very first time.

To some, the murderous reality of human nature is proof that God is absent or dead. The same reasoning would find God missing from the unpredictable branchings of an evolutionary tree. But the truth is deeper. In each case, a deity determined to establish a world that was truly independent of his whims, a world in which intelligent creatures would face authentic choices between good and evil, would have to fashion a distinct, material reality and then let his creation run. Neither the self-sufficiency of nature nor the reality of evil in the world mean God is absent. To a religious person, both signify something quite different—the strength of God's love and the reality of our freedom as his creatures.

The Weapons of Disbelief

20 As a species, we like to see ourselves as the best and brightest. We are the intended, special, primary creatures of creation. We sit at the apex of the evolutionary tree as the ultimate products of nature, self-proclaimed and self-aware. We like to think that evolution's goal was to produce us.

In a purely biological sense, this comforting view of our own position in nature is false, a product of self-inflating distortion induced by the imperfect mirrors we hold up to life. Yes, we are objectively among the most complex of animals, but not in every sense. Among the systems of the body, we are the hands-down winners for physiological complexity in just one place—the nervous system—and even there, a nonprimate (the dolphin) can lay down a claim that rivals our own.

More to the point, any accurate assessment of the evolutionary process shows that the notion of one form of life being more highly evolved than another is incorrect. Every organism, every cell that lives today, is the descendant of a long line of winners, of ancestors who used successful evolutionary strategies time and time again, and therefore lived to tell about it—or, at least, to reproduce. The bacterium perched on the lip of my coffee cup has been through as much evolution as I have. I've got the advantage of size and consciousness, which matter when I write about evolution, but the bacterium has the advantage of numbers, of flexibility, and most especially, of reproductive speed. That single bacterium, given the right conditions, could literally fill the world with its descendants in a matter of days. No human, no vertebrate, no animal could boast of anything remotely as impressive.

What evolution tells us is that life spreads out along endless branching pathways from any starting point. One of those tiny branches eventually led to us. We think it remarkable and wonder how it could have happened, but any fair assessment of the tree of life shows that our tiny branch is crowded into insignificance by those that bolted off in a thousand different directions. Our species, *Homo sapiens,* has not "triumphed" in the evolutionary struggle any more than has a squirrel, a dandelion, or a mosquito. We are all here, now, and that's what matters. We have all followed different pathways to find ourselves in the present. We are all winners in the game of natural selection. *Current* winners, we should be careful to say.

That, in the minds of many, is exactly the problem. In a thousand branching pathways, how can we be sure that one of them, historically and unavoidably, would lead for sure to us? Consider this: we mammals now occupy, in most ecosystems, the roles of large, dominant land animals. But for much of their history, mammals were restricted to habitats in which only very small creatures could survive. Why? Because another group of vertebrates dominated the earth—until, as Stephen Jay Gould has pointed out, the cataclysmic impact of a comet or asteroid drove those giants to extinction. "In an entirely literal sense," Gould has written, "we owe our existence, as large and reasoning animals, to our lucky stars."

So, what if the comet had missed? What if our ancestors, and not 25 dinosaurs, had been the ones driven to extinction? What if, during the Devonian period, the small tribe of fish known as rhipidistians had been obliterated? Vanishing with them would have been the possibility of life for the first tetrapods. Vertebrates might never have struggled onto the land, leaving it, in Gould's words, forever "the unchallenged domain of insects and flowers."

Surely this means that mankind's appearance on this planet was *not* pre-ordained, that we are here not as the products of an inevitable procession of evolutionary success, but as an afterthought, a minor detail, a happenstance in a history that might just as well have left us out. What follows from this, to skeptic and true believer alike, is a conclusion whose logic is rarely challenged—that no God would ever have used such a process to fashion his prize creatures. How could he have been sure that leaving the job to evolution would lead things to working out the "right" way? If it was God's will to produce us, then by showing that we are the products of evolution, we would rule God as Creator. Therein lies the value or the danger of evolution.

Not so fast. The biological account of lucky historical contingencies that led to our own appearance on this planet is surely accurate. What does not follow is that a perceived lack of inevitability translates into something that we should regard as incompatibility with a divine will. To do so seriously underestimates God, even as this God is understood by the most conventional of Western religions.

Yes, the explosive diversification of life on this planet was an unpredictable process. But so were the rise of Western civilization, the collapse of the Roman Empire, and the winning number in last night's lottery. We do not regard the indeterminate nature of any of these events in human history as antithetical to the existence of a Creator; why should we regard similar events in natural history any differently? There is, I would submit, no reason at all. If we can view the contingent events in the families that produced our individual lives as consistent with a Creator, then certainly we can do the same for the chain of circumstances that produced our species.

The alternative is a world where all events have predictable outcomes, where the future is open neither to chance nor to independent human action. A world in which we would always evolve is a world in which we would never be free. To a believer, the particular history leading to us shows how truly remarkable we are, how rare is the gift of consciousness, and how precious is the chance to understand.

Certainty and Faith

30 One would like to think that all scientific ideas, including evolution, would rise or fall purely on the basis of the evidence. If that were true, evolution would long since have passed, in the public mind, from controversy into common sense, which is exactly what has happened within the scientific community. This is, unfortunately, not the case—evolution remains, in the minds of much of the American public, a dangerous idea, and for biology educators, a source of never-ending strife.

I believe much of the problem is the fault of those in the scientific community who routinely enlist the findings of evolutionary biology in support of their own philosophical pronouncements. Sometimes these take the form of stern, dispassionate pronouncements about the meaninglessness of life. Other times we are lectured that the contingency of our presence on this planet invalidates any sense of human purpose. And very often we are told that the raw reality of nature strips the authority from any human system of morality.

As creatures fashioned by evolution, we are filled, as the biologist E. O. Wilson has said, with instinctive behaviors important to the survival of our genes. Some of these behaviors, though favored by natural

CHAPTER 10 FOCUS

selection, can get us into trouble. Our desires for food, water, reproduction, and status, our willingness to fight, and our tendencies to band together into social groups, can all be seen as behaviors that help ensure evolutionary success. Sociobiology, which studies the biological basis of social behaviors, tells us that in some circumstances natural selection will favor cooperative and nurturing instincts—"nice" genes that help us get along together. Some circumstances, on the other had, will favor aggressive self-centered behaviors, ranging all the way from friendly competition to outright homicide. Could such Darwinian ruthlessness be part of the plan of a loving God?

Yes, it could. To survive on this planet, the genes of our ancestors, like those of any other organism, had to produce behaviors that protected, nurtured, defended, and ensured the reproductive successes of the individuals that bore them. It should be no surprise that we carry such passions within us, and Darwinian biology cannot be faulted for giving their presence a biological explanation. Indeed, the Bible itself gives ample documentation of such human tendencies, including pride, selfishness, lust, anger, aggression, and murder.

Darwin can hardly be criticized for pinpointing the biological origins of these drives. All too often, in finding the sources of our "original sins," in fixing the reasons why our species displays the tendencies it does, evolution is misconstrued as providing a kind of justification for the worst aspects of human nature. At best, this is a misreading of the scientific lessons of sociobiology. At worst, it is an attempt to misuse biology to abolish any meaningful system of morality. Evolution may explain the existence of our most basic biological drives and desires, but that does not tell us that it is always proper to act on them. Evolution has provided me with a sense of hunger when my nutritional resources are running low, but evolution does not justify my clubbing you over the head to swipe your lunch. Evolution explains our biology, but it does not tell us what is good, or right, or moral. For those answers, however informed we may be by biology, we must look somewhere else.

What Kind of World?

Like it or not, the values that any of us apply to our daily lives have 35 been affected by the work of Charles Darwin. Religious people, however, have a special question to put to the reclusive naturalist of Down House. Did his work ultimately contribute to the greater glory of God, or did he deliver human nature and destiny into the hands of a professional scientific class, one profoundly hostile to religion? Does Darwin's work strengthen or weaken the idea of God?

The conventional wisdom is that whatever one may think of his science, having Mr. Darwin around certainly hasn't helped religion very much. The general thinking is that religion has been weakened by Darwinism and has been constrained to modify its view of the Creator in order to twist doctrine into conformity with the demands of evolution. As Stephen Jay Gould puts it, with obvious delight, "Now the conclusions of science must be accepted *a priori,* and religious interpretations must be finessed and adjusted to match unimpeachable results from the magisterium of natural knowledge!" Science calls the tune, and religion dances to its music.

This sad specter of a weakened and marginalized God drives the continuing opposition to evolution. This is why the God of the creationists requires, above all, that evolution be shown not to have functioned in the past and not to be working now. To free religion from the tyranny of Darwinism, creationists need a science that shows nature to be incomplete; they need a history of life whose events can only be explained as the result of supernatural processes. Put bluntly, the creationists are committed to finding permanent, intractable mystery in nature. To such minds, even the most perfect being we can imagine would not have been perfect enough to fashion a creation in which life would originate and evolve on its own. Nature must be flawed, static, and forever inadequate.

Science in general, and evolutionary science in particular, gives us something quite different. It reveals a universe that is dynamic, flexible, and logically complete. It presents a vision of life that spreads across the planet with endless variety and intricate beauty. It suggests a world in which our material existence is not an impossible illusion propped up by magic, but the genuine article, a world in which things are exactly what they seem. A world in which we were formed, as the Creator once told us, from the dust of the earth itself.

It is often said that a Darwinian universe is one whose randomness cannot be reconciled with meaning. I disagree. A world truly without meaning would be one in which a deity pulled the string of every human puppet, indeed of every material particle. In such a world, physical and biological events would be carefully controlled, evil and suffering could be minimized, and the outcome of historical processes strictly regulated. All things would move toward the Creator's clear, distinct, established goals. Such control and predictability, however, comes at the price of independence. Always in control, such a Creator would deny his creatures any real opportunity to know and worship him—authentic love requires freedom, not manipulation. Such freedom is best supplied by the open contingency of evolution.

40   One hundred and fifty years ago it might have been impossible not to couple Darwin to a grim and pointless determinism, but things look different today. Darwin's vision has expanded to encompass a new world of biology in which the links from molecule to cell and from cell to organism are becoming clear. Evolution prevails, but it does so with a richness and subtlety its original theorist may have found surprising and could not have anticipated.

We know from astronomy, for example, that the universe had a beginning, from physics that the future is both open and unpredictable, from geology and paleontology that the whole of life has been a process of change and transformation. From biology we know that our tissues are not impenetrable reservoirs of vital magic, but a stunning matrix of complex wonders, ultimately explicable in terms of biochemistry and molecular biology. With such knowledge we can see, perhaps for the first time, why a Creator would have allowed our species to be fashioned by the process of evolution.

If he so chose, the God whose presence is taught by most Western religions could have fashioned anything, ourselves included, *ex nihilo,* from his wish alone. In our childhood as a species, that might have been the only way in which we could imagine the fulfillment of a divine will. But we've grown up, and something remarkable has happened: we have begun to understand the physical basis of life itself. If a string of constant miracles were needed for each turn of the cell cycle or each flicker of a cilium, the hand of God would be written directly into every living thing—his presence at the edge of the human sandbox would be unmistakable. Such findings might confirm our faith, but they would also undermine our independence. How could we fairly choose between God and man when the presence and the power of the divine so obviously and so literally controlled our every breath? Our freedom as his creatures requires a little space and integrity. In the material world, it requires self-sufficiency and consistency with the laws of nature.

Evolution is neither more nor less than the result of respecting the reality and consistency of the physical world over time. To fashion material beings with an independent physical existence, any Creator would have had to produce an independent material universe in which our evolution over time was a contingent possibility. A believer in the divine accepts that God's love and gift of freedom are genuine—so genuine that they include the power to choose evil and, if we wish, to freely send ourselves to Hell. Not all believers will accept the stark conditions of that bargain, but our freedom to act has to have a physical and biological basis. Evolution and its sister sciences of genetics and molecular biology provide that basis. In biological terms, evolution is the only way a Creator could have made us the creatures we are—free beings in a world of authentic and meaningful moral and spiritual choices.

Those who ask from science a final argument, an ultimate proof, an unassailable position from which the issue of God may be decided will always be disappointed. As a scientist I claim no new proofs, no revolutionary data, no stunning insight into nature that can tip the balance in one direction or another. But I do claim that to a believer, even in the most traditional sense, evolutionary biology is not at all the obstacle we often believe it to be. In many respects, evolution is the key to understanding our relationship with God.

45   When I have the privilege of giving a series of lectures on evolutionary biology to my freshman students, I usually conclude those lectures with a few remarks about the impact of evolutionary theory on other fields, from economics to politics to religion. I find a way to make clear that I do not regard evolution, properly understood, as either antireligious or antispiritual. Most students seem to appreciate those sentiments. They probably figure that Professor Miller, trying to be a nice guy and doubtlessly an agnostic, is trying to find a way to be unequivocal about evolution without offending the University chaplain.

There are always a few who find me after class and want to pin me down. They ask me point-blank: "Do you believe in God?"

And I tell each of them, "Yes."

Puzzled, they ask: "What kind of God?"

Over the years I have struggled to come up with a simple but precise answer to that question. And, eventually I found it. I believe in Darwin's God.

Responding to Reading

1. Why does Miller begin his essay with a story from his childhood? How does this story lead him to his larger point? What does Miller mean when he says, "By pointing to the process of making a flower as proof of the reality of God, Father Murphy was embracing the idea that God finds it necessary to cripple nature" (10)?
2. Why does Miller believe that scientists are to blame for the public's distrust of evolution? Why does Miller disagree with the idea that a "Darwinian universe is one whose randomness cannot be reconciled with meaning" (39)?
3. What does Miller mean when he says, "In many respects, evolution is the key to understanding our relationship with God" (44)?

Responding in Writing

Do you think it is possible both to believe in God and to accept evolution? Explain.

WIDENING THE FOCUS

For Critical Thinking and Writing

Write an essay in which you answer the focus question, "Is there intelligent design in nature?" In your essay, refer to the ideas in Christoph Schönborn's "Finding Design in Nature," H. Allen Orr's "Why Intelligent Design Isn't," and Kenneth R. Miller's "Finding Darwin's God."

For Further Reading

The following readings can suggest additional perspectives for thinking and writing about how to address the issues surrounding the conflict between religion and science:

- Richard Florida, "The Transformation of Everyday Life"(p. 302)

- Albino Barrera, "Fair Exchange: Who Benefits from Outsourcing?" (p. 548)

- Tenzin Gyatso, "Our Faith in Science" (p. 641)

For Internet Research

The intelligent design debate has sparked heated discussion between scientists and philosophers on the questions, "Who are we?" and "Where do we come from?" Proponents of evolution, on the one hand, argue that life as we know it came to be through a series of random mutations and the process of natural selection; advocates of intelligent design, on the other hand, argue that organisms such as ourselves are not the result of chance occurrences, but rather the work of an intelligent creator. Read the 2002 *Natural History* magazine report *Intelligent Design?* at <http://www.actionbioscience.org/evolution/nhmag.html>, in which supporters of the intelligent design and evolution theories debate this important topic. Then, write a paper in which you evaluate this report. Is it effective in presenting the complexities of the issue? What arguments and evidence are presented? Which arguments do you find most convincing? Why?

WRITING

Religion in America

1. In Langston Hughes's "Salvation" (p. 639) and Tayari Jones's "Among the Believers" (p. 644), the writers recount childhood experiences in which they struggled to understand what religion and spirituality meant to them. Write an essay in which you trace your own struggle to come to terms with your family's faith (or lack of faith).

2. Do you see religion and science as compatible, or do you see them as inevitably in conflict? After reading "Our Faith in Science" (p. 641) try to answer this question as it applies to a particular moral or ethical issue. (If you like, you can write about one of the issues in Chapter 9, "Science and Human Values.")

3. Is there a place in American society for a strictly secular view of moral and social issues, or is this view somehow incomplete? Read "Kicking the Secularist Habit" (p. 647), and then write an essay in which you consider whether it is possible to live a moral life by following guidelines that are secular rather than religious.

4. Do you believe religious instruction and prayer—for example, Bible study groups or prayer among football players before a game—should be permitted in our nation's public schools? What advantages do you see in officially sanctioning such activities? What problems might it cause?

5. Do you think religious institutions should continue to be exempt from paying federal income tax? Why or not? In your essay, consider the contributions religious organizations make to society and the services they provide—but also consider the fact that many religious groups take positions on political issues.

6. Is it appropriate for churches to take positions on political issues, such as abortion, the death penalty, or aiding illegal immigrants? Why or why not?

7. Fewer and fewer young people are becoming priests and nuns; as a result, the Catholic Church is facing a crisis. What do you think might be done to attract more young people to consider devoting their lives to the Church?

8. Because more than 75 percent of the U.S. population is Christian, many people consider the United States to be a Christian nation— even though the population also includes significant numbers of

Jews, Muslims, Buddhists, and Hindus (well over a million each), as well as people follow to numerous other religions. In what respects do you see the United States as a Christian nation? In what respects is it not a Christian nation? How do you think it *should* be perceived?

9. After reading "Earthly Empires" (p. 659), write a proposal for a new "megachurch" (or mosque or synagogue) that might attract worshippers in your community. What should this new institution offer in the way of religious services and instruction, facilities, social programs, and community outreach services? How would the programs you suggest help individual members of the community? How would they strengthen the institution? Be sure to explain *why* the programs and services you describe would be beneficial.

10. The title of Raymond Carver's short story "Cathedral" (p. 666) suggests that its focus is on religion. Is this actually the case? Is it about a religious experience or about something else? Write an essay in which you explore the themes of this story.

11

MAKING CHOICES

As Robert Frost suggests in his poem "The Road Not Taken" (p. 709), making choices is fundamental to our lives. The ability—and, in fact, the need—to make complex decisions is part of what makes us human. On a practical level, we choose friends, mates, careers, and places to live. On a more abstract level, we struggle to make the moral and ethical choices that people have struggled with for many years.

Many times, complex questions have no easy answers; occasionally, they have no answers at all. For example, should we abide by a law even if we believe it to be morally wrong? Should we stand up to authority even if our stand puts us at risk? Should we help less fortunate individuals if such help threatens our own social or economic status? Should we strive to do well or to do good? Should we tell the

Peace Corps teacher with pupils in Botswana

truth even if the truth may hurt us—or hurt someone else? Which road should we take, the easy one or the hard one?

Most of the time, the choice we (and the writers whose works appear in this chapter) face is the same: to act or not to act. To make a decision, we must understand both the long- and short-term consequences of acting in a particular way or of choosing not to act. We must struggle with the possibility of compromise—and with the possibility of making a morally or ethically objectionable decision. And, perhaps most important, we must learn to take responsibility for our decisions.

The writers whose essays are included in the Focus section of this chapter, "Can We Be Both Free and Safe?"(p. 783), consider the difficult question of how to achieve a balance between liberty and security. In the wake of the terrible events of September 11, 2001, many strongly believe that it is necessary to sacrifice some of our rights and institute measures (such as racial and ethnic profiling, increased electronic surveillance, and limitations on immigration) that may protect us. Others feel just as strongly that to sacrifice any of our precious rights (for example, the right to privacy), even in the name of personal safety or national security, is to sacrifice what it means to be an American. Now more than ever, the Focus question is one that we must struggle to answer.

Young businessman at work

————————— PREPARING TO READ AND WRITE —————————

As you read and prepare to write about the selections in this chapter, you may consider the following questions:

- On what specific choice or choices does the essay focus? Is the decision to be made moral? Ethical? Political? Theoretical?

- Does the writer introduce a **dilemma,** a choice between two equally problematic alternatives?

- Does the choice the writer presents apply only to one specific situation or case, or does it also have a wider application?

- Is the writer emotionally involved with the issue he or she is discussing? Does this involvement (or lack of involvement) affect the writer's credibility?

- What social, political, or religious ideas influence the writer? How can you tell? Are these ideas similar to or different from your own views?

- Does the choice being considered cause the writer to examine his or her own values? The values of others? The values of the society at large? Does the writer lead you to examine your own values?

- Does the writer offer a solution? If so, do you find it reasonable?

- Does the choice the writer advocates require sacrifice? If so, does the sacrifice seem worth it?

- Which writers' views seem most alike? Which seem most different?

THE ROAD NOT TAKEN

Robert Frost

1874–1963

Robert Frost, four-time Pulitzer Prize–winning poet of rural New England, lived most of his life in New Hampshire and taught at Amherst College, Harvard University, and Dartmouth College. His subjects at first seem familiar and comfortable, as does his language, but the symbols and allusions and underlying meanings in many of his poems are quite complex. Some of Frost's most famous poems are "Birches," "Mending Wall," and "Stopping by Woods on a Snowy Evening." In the poem that follows the speaker hesitates before making a choice.

Two roads diverged in a yellow wood,
And sorry I could not travel both
And be one traveller, long I stood
And looked down one as far as I could
To where it bent in the undergrowth;   5

Then took the other, as just as fair,
And having perhaps the better claim,
Because it was grassy and wanted wear;
Though as for that the passing there
Had worn them really about the same,   10

And both that morning equally lay
In leaves no step had trodden black.
Oh, I kept the first for another day!
Yet knowing how way leads on to way,
I doubted if I should ever come back.   15

I shall be telling this with a sigh
Somewhere ages and ages hence:
Two roads diverged in a wood, and I—
I took the one less travelled by,
And that has made all the difference.   20

Responding to Reading

1. What is the difference between the two paths Frost's speaker considers? Why does he make the choice he does?
2. Is "The Road Not Taken" simply about two paths in the wood, or does it suggest more? What makes you think so? To what larger choices might the speaker be alluding?
3. What does the speaker mean by "that has made all the difference" (line 20)?

Responding in Writing

In your own words, write a short summary of this poem. Use first person and past tense (as Frost does).

Ethics

Linda Pastan

1932–

The winner of numerous prizes for her poetry, Linda Pastan often focuses on the complexity of domestic life, using intense imagery to bring a sense of mystery to everyday matters. She has been a lecturer at the Breadloaf Writers Conference in Vermont and an instructor at American University, and she has published numerous collections of poetry, including Waiting for My Life *(1981),* PM/AM: New and Selected Poems *(1983),* Carnival Evening: New and Selected Poems 1968–1998 *(1998), and* The Last Uncle: Poems *(2002). In "Ethics," from* Waiting for My Life, *the speaker introduces an ethical dilemma.*

In ethics class so many years ago
our teacher asked this question every fall:
if there were a fire in a museum
which would you save, a Rembrandt painting

5   or an old woman who hadn't many
years left anyhow? Restless on hard chairs
caring little for pictures or old age
we'd opt one year for life, the next for art
and always half-heartedly. Sometimes

10 the woman borrowed my grandmother's face
leaving her usual kitchen to wander
some drafty, half imagined museum.
One year, feeling clever, I replied
why not let the woman decide herself?

15 Linda, the teacher would report, eschews
the burdens of responsibility.
This fall in a real museum I stand
before a real Rembrandt, old woman,
or nearly so, myself. The colors

20 within this frame are darker than autumn,
darker even than winter—the browns of earth,
though earth's most radiant elements burn
through the canvas. I know now that woman
and painting and season are almost one

25 and all beyond saving by children.

Responding to Reading

1. What choice actually confronts Pastan's speaker? What answer do you think the teacher expects the students to give?

2. Do you agree with the teacher that refusing to choose means avoiding responsibility? Does Frost's speaker (p. 709) have the option not to choose?
3. When the speaker says that "woman / and painting and season are almost one" (lines 23–24), what does she mean? Does she imply that the teacher's question really has no answer? That the children who would "opt one year for life, the next for art" (8) are right?

Responding in Writing

Confronted with the choice facing the speaker, would you save the Rembrandt painting or the elderly woman? Why? Would you find this a difficult choice to make?

THE DEER AT PROVIDENCIA
Annie Dillard
1945–

Naturalist and essayist Annie Dillard wrote of the Roanoke Valley of Virginia in her first book, Pilgrim at Tinker Creek, *for which she won the Pulitzer Prize in 1975. Dillard calls herself a "stalker" of nature and its mysteries, and she delights in both the wonders and the terrors it inspires. Her books include* Teaching a Stone to Talk *(1982),* An American Childhood *(1987),* The Writing Life *(1989),* The Living *(1992),* Mornings Like This: Found Poems *(1995), and* For the Time Being *(1999). Her articles have been published in* Harper's *and the* Atlantic Monthly, *among other magazines. In "The Deer at Providencia," first published in 1982, Dillard explores the paradoxical nature of suffering for animals and humans.*

There were four of us North Americans in the jungle, in the Ecuadoran jungle on the banks of the Napo River in the Amazon watershed. The other three North Americans were metropolitan men. We stayed in tents in one riverside village, and visited others. At the village called Providencia we saw a sight which moved us, and which shocked the men.

The first thing we saw when we climbed the riverbank to the village of Providencia was the deer. It was roped to a tree on the grass clearing near the thatch shelter where we would eat lunch.

The deer was small, about the size of a whitetail fawn, but apparently full-grown. It had a rope around its neck and three feet caught in the rope. Someone said that the dogs had caught it that morning and the villagers were going to cook and eat it that night.

This clearing lay at the edge of the little thatched-hut village. We could see the villagers going about their business, scattering feed corn for hens about their houses, and wandering down paths to the river to bathe. The village headman was our host; he stood beside us as we watched the deer struggle. Several village boys were interested in the deer; they formed part of the circle we made around it in the clearing. So also did four businessmen from Quito[1] who were attempting to guide us around the jungle. Few of the very different people standing in this circle had a common language. We watched the deer, and no one said much.

5   The deer lay on its side at the rope's very end, so the rope lacked slack to let it rest its head in the dust. It was "pretty," delicate of bone like all deer, and thin-skinned for the tropics. Its skin looked virtually hairless, in fact, and almost translucent, like a membrane. Its neck was no thicker than my wrist; it was rubbed open on the rope, and gashed. Trying to paw itself free of the rope, the deer had scratched its own neck with its hooves. The raw underside of its neck showed red stripes and some bruises bleeding inside the muscles. Now three of its feet were hooked in the rope under its jaw. It could not stand, of course, on one leg, so it could not move to slacken the rope and ease the pull on its throat and enable it to rest its head.

Repeatedly the deer paused, motionless, its eyes veiled, with only its rib cage in motion, and its breaths the only sound. Then, after I would think, "It has given up; now it will die," it would heave. The rope twanged; the tree leaves clattered; the deer's free foot beat the ground. We stepped back and held our breaths. It thrashed, kicking, but only one leg moved; the other three legs tightened inside the rope's loop. Its hip jerked; its spine shook. Its eyes rolled; its tongue, thick with spittle, pushed in and out. Then it would rest again. We watched this for fifteen minutes.

Once three young native boys charged in, released its trapped legs, and jumped back to the circle of people. But instantly the deer scratched up its neck with its hooves and snared its forelegs in the rope again. It was easy to imagine a third and then a fourth leg soon stuck, like Brer Rabbit and the Tar Baby.[2]

We watched the deer from the circle, and then we drifted on to lunch. Our palm-roofed shelter stood on a grassy promontory from which we could see the deer tied to the tree, pigs and hens walking under village houses, and black-and-white cattle standing in the river. There was even a breeze.

Lunch, which was the second and better lunch we had that day, was hot and fried. There was a big fish called *doncella,* a kind of cat-fish, dipped whole in corn flour and beaten egg, then deep fried. With our fingers we pulled soft fragments of it from its sides to our plates,

---

[1]Capital of Ecuador. [Eds.]

[2]Characters created by southern writer Joel Chandler Harris. In one of Harris's stories, Brer Rabbit becomes stuck to a figure made of tar. [Eds.]

and ate; it was delicate fish-flesh, fresh and mild. Someone found the roe, and I ate of that too—it was fat and stronger, like egg yolk, naturally enough, and warm.

There was also a stew of meat in shreds with rice and pale brown 10 gravy. I had asked what kind of deer it was tied to the tree; Pepe had answered in Spanish, *"Gama."* Now they told us this was *gama* too, stewed. I suspect the word means merely game or venison. At any rate, I heard that the village dogs had cornered another deer just yesterday, and it was this deer which we were now eating in full sight of the whole article. It was good. I was surprised at its tenderness. But it is a fact that high levels of lactic acid, which builds up in muscle tissues during exertion, tenderizes.

After the fish and meat we ate bananas fried in chunks and served on a tray; they were sweet and full of flavor. I felt terrific. My shirt was wet and cool from swimming; I had had a night's sleep, two decent walks, three meals, and a swim—everything tasted good. From time to time each one of us, separately, would look beyond our shaded roof to the sunny spot where the deer was still convulsing in the dust. Our meal completed, we walked around the deer and back to the boats.

That night I learned that while we were watching the deer, the others were watching me.

We four North Americans grew close in the jungle in a way that was not the usual artificial intimacy of travelers. We liked each other. We stayed up all that night talking, murmuring, as though we rocked on hammocks slung above time. The others were from big cities: New York, Washington, Boston. They all said that I had no expression on my face when I was watching the deer—or at any rate, not the expression they expected.

They had looked to see how I, the only woman, and the youngest, was taking the sight of the deer's struggles. I looked detached, apparently, or hard, or calm, or focused, still. I don't know. I was thinking. I remember feeling very old and energetic. I could say like Thoreau that I have traveled widely in Roanoke, Virginia.[3] I have thought a great deal about carnivorousness; I eat meat. These things are not issues; they are mysteries.

Gentlemen of the city, what surprises you? That there is suffering 15 here, or that I know it?

We lay in the tent and talked, "If it had been my wife," one man said with special vigor, amazed, "she wouldn't have cared what was going on; she would have dropped *everything* right at that moment

---

[3]In *Walden,* Henry David Thoreau (see p. 722) says, "I have traveled a good deal in Concord." [Eds.]

and gone in the village from here to there to there, she would not have *stopped* until that animal was out of its suffering one way or another. She couldn't *bear* to see a creature in agony like that."

I nodded.

Now I am home. When I wake I comb my hair before the mirror above my dresser. Every morning for the past two years I have seen in that mirror, beside my sleep-softened face, the blackened face of a burnt man. It is a wire-service photograph clipped from a newspaper and taped to my mirror. The caption reads: "Alan McDonald in Miami hospital bed." All you can see in the photograph is a smudged triangle of face from his eyelids to his lower lip; the rest is bandages. You cannot see the expression in his eyes; the bandages shade them.

The story, headed MAN BURNED FOR SECOND TIME, begins:

> "Why does God hate me?" Alan McDonald asked from his hospital bed.
>
> "When the gunpowder went off, I couldn't believe it," he said. "I just couldn't believe it. I said, 'No, God couldn't do this to me again.'"

20   He was in a burn ward in Miami, in serious condition. I do not even know if he lived. I wrote him a letter at the time, cringing.

He had been burned before, thirteen years previously, by flaming gasoline. For years he had been having his body restored and his face remade in dozens of operations. He had been a boy, and then a burnt boy. He had already been stunned by what could happen, by how life could veer.

Once I read that people who survive bad burns tend to go crazy; they have a very high suicide rate. Medicine cannot ease their pain; drugs just leak away, soaking the sheets, because there is no skin to hold them in. The people just lie there and weep. Later they kill themselves. They had not known, before they were burned, that the world included such suffering, that life could permit them personally such pain.

This time a bowl of gunpowder had exploded on McDonald.

> "I didn't realize what had happened at first," he recounted. "And then I heard that sound from 13 years ago. I was burning. I rolled to put the fire out and I thought, 'Oh God, not again.'"
>
> "If my friend hadn't been there, I would have jumped into a canal with a rock around my neck."

His wife concludes the piece, "Man, it just isn't fair."

25   I read the whole clipping again every morning. This is the Big Time here, every minute of it. Will someone please explain to Alan McDonald in his dignity, to the deer at Providencia in his dignity, what is going on? And mail me the carbon.

When we walked by the deer at Providencia for the last time, I said to Pepe, with a pitying glance at the deer, "*Pobrecito*"—"poor little thing." But I was trying out Spanish. I knew at the time it was a ridiculous thing to say.

Responding to Reading

1. Could Dillard have done anything to free the deer? Why do you think she chose to do nothing? Does she regret her decision not to act? Do you think she *should* regret it?
2. In paragraph 14, Dillard says, "I have thought a great deal about carnivorousness; I eat meat. These things are not issues; they are mysteries." What does she mean? Do you find this statement a satisfactory explanation of her ability to enjoy deer meat while she watches the trapped deer "convulsing in the dust" (11)? Why or why not?
3. What connection does Dillard see between Alan McDonald and the deer at Providencia? Do you see this as a reasonable association, or do you believe Dillard has exploited (or even invented) a connection?

Responding in Writing

Reread paragraphs 5 and 6, in which Dillard describes the deer's suffering. Rewrite this passage from the deer's point of view, paraphrasing Dillard's language and deleting information that the deer could not know or observe.

SHOOTING AN ELEPHANT

George Orwell

1903–1950

This detailed account of an incident with an elephant in Burma is George Orwell's most powerful criticism of imperialism and the impossible position of British police officers—himself among them—in the colonies. Orwell says about the incident, "It was perfectly clear to me what I ought to do," but then he thinks of "the watchful yellow faces from behind" and realizes that his choice is not so simple. (Also see Orwell's essay in Chapter 3, p. 189.)

In Moulmein, in lower Burma, I was hated by large numbers of people—the only time in my life that I have been important enough for this to happen to me. I was sub-divisional police officer of the town, and in an aimless, petty kind of way anti-European feeling was very bitter. No one had the guts to raise a riot, but if a European woman went through the bazaars alone somebody would probably spit betel juice over her dress. As a police officer I was an obvious target and was baited whenever it seemed safe to do so. When a nimble Burman tripped me up on the football field and the referee (another Burman) looked the other way, the crowd yelled with hideous laughter. This happened more than once. In the end the sneering yellow faces of young men that met me everywhere, the insults hooted after me when I was at a safe distance, got badly on my nerves. The young Buddhist priests were the worst of all. There were several thousands of them in the town and none of them seemed to have anything to do except stand on street corners and jeer at Europeans.

All this was perplexing and upsetting. For at that time I had already made up my mind that imperialism was an evil thing and the sooner I chucked up my job and got out of it the better. Theoretically— and secretly, of course—I was all for the Burmese and all against their oppressors, the British. As for the job I was doing, I hated it more bitterly than I can perhaps make clear. In a job like that you see the dirty work of Empire at close quarters. The wretched prisoners huddling in the stinking cages of the lock-ups, the grey, cowed faces of the long-term convicts, the scarred buttocks of the men who had been flogged with bamboos—all these oppressed me with an intolerable sense of guilt. But I could get nothing into perspective. I was young and ill-educated and I had had to think out my problems in the utter silence that is imposed on every Englishman in the East. I did not even know that the British Empire is dying, still less did I know that it is a great deal better than the younger empires that are going to supplant it.[1] All I knew was that I was stuck between my hatred of the empire I served and my rage against the evil-spirited little beasts who tried to make my job impossible. With one part of my mind I thought of the British Raj[2] as an unbreakable tyranny, as something clamped down, in *saecula saeculorum*,[3] upon the will of prostrate peoples; with another part I thought that the greatest joy in the world would be to drive a bayonet into a Buddhist priest's guts. Feelings like these are the normal by-products of imperialism; ask any Anglo-Indian official, if you can catch him off duty.

One day something happened which in a roundabout way was enlightening. It was a tiny incident in itself, but it gave me a better glimpse than I had had before of the real nature of imperialism—the real motives for which despotic governments act. Early one morning the sub-inspector at a police station the other end of the town rang me up on the phone and said that an elephant was ravaging the bazaar.

---

[1] This essay was written in 1936, three years before the start of World War II; Stalin and Hitler were in power. [Eds.]

[2] Sovereignty

[3] From time immemorial. [Eds.]

Would I please come and do something about it? I did not know what I could do, but I wanted to see what was happening and I got on to a pony and started out. I took my rifle, an old .44 Winchester and much too small to kill an elephant, but I thought the noise might be useful in *terrorem.* Various Burmans stopped me on the way and told me about the elephant's doings. It was not, of course, a wild elephant, but a tame one which had gone "must." It had been chained up, as tame elephants always are when their attack of "must"[4] is due, but on the previous night it had broken its chain and escaped. Its mahout,[5] the only person who could manage it when it was in that state, had set out in pursuit, but had taken the wrong direction and was now twelve hours' journey away, and in the morning the elephant had suddenly reappeared in the town. The Burmese population had no weapons and were quite helpless against it. It had already destroyed somebody's bamboo hut, killed a cow, and raided some fruit-stalls and devoured the stock; also it had met the municipal rubbish van and, when the driver jumped out and took to his heels, had turned the van over and inflicted violences upon it.

The Burmese sub-inspector and some Indian constables were waiting for me in the quarter where the elephant had been seen. It was a very poor quarter, a labyrinth of squalid bamboo huts, thatched with palm-leaf, winding all over a steep hillside. I remember that it was a cloudy, stuffy morning at the beginning of the rains. We began questioning the people as to where the elephant had gone and, as usual, failed to get any definite information. That is invariably the case in the East; a story always sounds clear enough at a distance, but the nearer you get to the scene of events the vaguer it becomes. Some of the people said that the elephant had gone in one direction, some said that he had gone in another, some professed not even to have heard of any elephant. I had almost made up my mind that the whole story was a pack of lies, when we heard yells a little distance away. There was a loud, scandalized cry of "Go away, child! Go away this instant!" and an old woman with a switch in her hand came round the corner of a hut, violently shooing away a crowd of naked children. Some more women followed, clicking their tongues and exclaiming; evidently there was something that the children ought not to have seen. I rounded the hut and saw a man's dead body sprawling in the mud. He was an Indian, a black Dravidian coolie,[6] almost naked, and he could not have been dead many minutes. The people said that the elephant had come suddenly upon him round the corner of the hut, caught him with its trunk, put its foot on his back, and

---

[4]Frenzy. [Eds.]
[5]Keeper. [Eds.]
[6]An unskilled laborer. [Eds.]

ground him into the earth. This was the rainy season and the ground was soft, and his face had scored a trench a foot deep and a couple of yards long. He was lying on his belly with arms crucified and head sharply twisted to one side. His face was coated with mud, the eyes wide open, the teeth bared and grinning with an expression of unendurable agony. (Never tell me, by the way, that the dead look peaceful. Most of the corpses I have seen looked devilish.) The friction of the great beast's foot had stripped the skin from his back as neatly as one skins a rabbit. As soon as I saw the dead man I sent an orderly to a friend's house nearby to borrow an elephant rifle. I had already sent back the pony, not wanting it to go mad with fright and throw me if it smelt the elephant.

5 The orderly came back in a few minutes with a rifle and five cartridges, and meanwhile some Burmans had arrived and told us that the elephant was in the paddy fields below, only a few hundred yards away. As I started forward practically the whole population of the quarter flocked out of the houses and followed me. They had seen the rifle and were all shouting excitedly that I was going to shoot the elephant. They had not shown much interest in the elephant when he was merely ravaging their homes, but it was different now that he was going to be shot. It was a bit of fun to them, as it would be to an English crowd; besides they wanted the meat. It made me vaguely uneasy. I had no intention of shooting the elephant—I had merely sent for the rifle to defend myself if necessary—and it is always unnerving to have a crowd following you. I marched down the hill, looking and feeling a fool, with the rifle over my shoulder and an ever-growing army of people jostling at my heels. At the bottom, when you got away from the huts, there was a metalled road and beyond that a miry waste of paddy fields a thousand yards across, not yet ploughed but soggy from the first rains and dotted with coarse grass. The elephant was standing eight yards from the road, his left side towards us. He took not the slightest notice of the crowd's approach. He was tearing up bunches of grass, beating them against his knees to clean them and stuffing them into his mouth.

I had halted on the road. As soon as I saw the elephant I knew with perfect certainty that I ought not to shoot him. It is a serious matter to shoot a working elephant—it is comparable to destroying a huge and costly piece of machinery—and obviously one ought not to do it if it can possibly be avoided. And at that distance, peacefully eating, the elephant looked no more dangerous than a cow. I thought then and I think now that his attack of "must" was already passing off; in which case he would merely wander harmlessly about until the mahout came back and caught him. Moreover, I did not in the least want to shoot him. I decided that I would watch him for a little while to make sure that he did not turn savage again, and then go home.

But at that moment I glanced round at the crowd that had followed me. It was an immense crowd, two thousand at the least and growing every minute. It blocked the road for a long distance on either side. I looked at the sea of yellow faces above the garish clothes—faces all happy and excited over this bit of fun, all certain that the elephant was going to be shot. They were watching me as they would watch a conjurer about to perform a trick. They did not like me, but with the magical rifle in my hands I was momentarily worth watching. And suddenly I realized that I should have to shoot the elephant after all. The people expected it of me and I had got to do it; I could feel their two thousand wills pressing me forward, irresistibly. And it was at this moment, as I stood there with the rifle in my hands, that I first grasped the hollowness, the futility of the white man's dominion in the East. Here was I, the white man with his gun, standing in front of the unarmed native crowd—seemingly the leading actor of the piece; but in reality I was only an absurd puppet pushed to and fro by the will of those yellow faces behind. I perceived in this moment that when the white man turns tyrant it is his own freedom that he destroys. He becomes a sort of hollow, posing dummy, the conventionalized figure of a sahib.[7] For it is the condition of his rule that he shall spend his life in trying to impress the "natives," and so in every crisis he has got to do what the "natives" expect of him. He wears a mask, and his face grows to fit it. I had got to shoot the elephant. I had committed myself to doing it when I sent for the rifle. A sahib has got to act like a sahib; he has got to appear resolute, to know his own mind and do definite things. To come all that way, rifle in hand, with two thousand people marching at my heels, and then to trail feebly away, having done nothing—no, that was impossible. The crowd would laugh at me. And my whole life, every white man's life in the East, was one long struggle not to be laughed at.

But I did not want to shoot the elephant. I watched him beating his bunch of grass against his knees, with that preoccupied grandmotherly air that elephants have. It seemed to me that it would be murder to shoot him. At that age I was not squeamish about killing animals, but I had never shot an elephant and never wanted to. (Somehow it always seems worse to kill a *large* animal.) Besides, there was the beast's owner to be considered. Alive, the elephant was worth at least a hundred pounds; dead, he would only be worth the value of his tusks, five pounds, possibly. But I had got to act quickly. I turned to some experienced looking Burmans who had been there when we arrived, and asked them how the elephant had been behaving. They all said the same thing: he took no notice of you if you left him alone, but he might charge if you went too close to him.

---

[7] Term used by natives of colonial India when referring to a European of rank. [Eds.]

It was perfectly clear to me what I ought to do. I ought to walk up to within, say, twenty-five yards of the elephant and test his behavior. If he charged, I could shoot; if he took no notice of me, it would be safe to leave him until the mahout came back. But also I knew that I was going to do no such thing. I was a poor shot with a rifle and the ground was soft mud into which one would sink at every step. If the elephant charged and I missed him, I should have about as much chance as a toad under a steam-roller. But even then I was not thinking particularly of my own skin, only of the watchful yellow faces behind. For at that moment, with the crowd watching me, I was not afraid in the ordinary sense, as I would have been if I had been alone. A white man mustn't be frightened in front of "natives"; and so, in general, he isn't frightened. The sole thought in my mind was that if anything went wrong those two thousand Burmans would see me pursued, caught, trampled on, and reduced to a grinning corpse like that Indian up the hill. And if that happened it was quite probable that some of them would laugh. That would never do. There was only one alternative. I shoved the cartridges into the magazine and lay down on the road to get a better aim.

10   The crowd grew very still, and a deep, low, happy sigh, as of people who see the theatre curtain go up at last, breathed from innumerable throats. They were going to have their bit of fun after all. The rifle was a beautiful German thing with cross-hair sights. I did not then know that in shooting an elephant one would shoot to cut an imaginary bar running from ear-hole to ear-hole. I ought, therefore, as the elephant was sideways on, to have aimed straight at his ear-hole; actually I aimed several inches in front of this, thinking the brain would be further forward.

When I pulled the trigger I did not hear the bang or feel the kick—one never does when a shot goes home—but I heard the devilish roar of glee that went up from the crowd. In that instant, in too short a time, one would have thought, even for the bullet to get there, a mysterious, terrible change had come over the elephant. He neither stirred nor fell, but every line of his body had altered. He looked suddenly stricken, shrunken, immensely old, as though the frightful impact of the bullet had paralysed him without knocking him down. At last, after what seemed a long time—it might have been five seconds, I dare say—he sagged flabbily to his knees. His mouth slobbered. An enormous senility seemed to have settled upon him. One could have imagined him thousands of years old. I fired again into the same spot. At the second shot he did not collapse but climbed with desperate slowness to his feet and stood weakly upright, with legs sagging and head dropping. I fired a third time. That was the shot that did for him. You could see the agony of it jolt his whole body and knock the last remnant of strength from his legs. But in falling he seemed for a moment to rise, for as his hind legs collapsed beneath him he seemed to tower upward like a huge rock toppling, his trunk reaching skywards like a tree. He trumpeted, for the first and only time. And then down he came, his belly towards me, with a crash that seemed to shake the ground even where I lay.

I got up. The Burmans were already racing past me across the mud. It was obvious that the elephant would never rise again, but he was not dead. He was breathing very rhythmically with long rattling gasps, his great mound of a side painfully rising and falling. His mouth was wide open—I could see far down into caverns of pale pink throat. I waited a long time for him to die, but his breathing did not weaken. Finally I fired my two remaining shots into the spot where I thought his heart must be. The thick blood welled out of him like red velvet, but still he did not die. His body did not even jerk when the shots hit him, the tortured breathing continued without a pause. He was dying, very slowly and in great agony, but in some world remote from me where not even a bullet could damage him further. I felt that I had got to put an end to that dreadful noise. It seemed dreadful to see the great beast lying there, powerless to move and yet powerless to die, and not even to be able to finish him. I sent back for my small rifle and poured shot after shot into his heart and down his throat. They seemed to make no impression. The tortured gasps continued as steadily as the ticking of a clock.

In the end I could not stand it any longer and went away. I heard later that it took him half an hour to die. Burmans were bringing dahs[8] and baskets even before I left, and I was told they had stripped his body almost to the bones by the afternoon.

Afterwards, of course, there were endless discussions about the shooting of the elephant. The owner was furious, but he was only an Indian and could do nothing. Besides, legally I had done the right thing, for a mad elephant has to be killed, like a mad dog, if its owner fails to control it. Among the Europeans opinion was divided. The older men said I was right, the younger men said it was a damn shame to shoot an elephant for killing a coolie, because an elephant was worth more than any damn Coringhee coolie. And afterwards I was very glad that the coolie had been killed; it put me legally in the right and it gave me a sufficient pretext for shooting the elephant. I often wondered whether any of the others grasped that I had done it solely to avoid looking a fool.

Responding to Reading

1. The central focus of this essay is Orwell's struggle to decide how to control the elephant. Do you think he really has a choice?

---

[8]Large knives. [Eds.]

2. Orwell says that his encounter with the elephant, although "a tiny incident in itself," gave him an understanding of "the real nature of imperialism—the real motives for which despotic governments act" (3). In light of this statement, do you think his purpose in this essay is to explore something about himself or something about the nature of British colonialism—or both?

3. In paragraphs 5–6, Orwell introduces the elephant as peaceful and innocent; in paragraphs 11–12, he describes the animal's misery. What do these paragraphs contribute to the essay?

Responding in Writing

Compare paragraphs 11–12 with paragraphs 5–6 of Annie Dillard's essay (p. 711). How are the descriptions alike? How are they different?

CIVIL DISOBEDIENCE

Henry David Thoreau
1817–1862

American essayist, journalist, and intellectual Henry David Thoreau was a social rebel who loved nature and solitude. A follower of transcendentalism, a philosophic and literary movement that flourished in New England, he contributed to the Dial, *a publication that gave voice to the movement's romantic, idealistic, and individualistic beliefs. For three years, Thoreau lived in a cabin near Walden Pond in Concord, Massachusetts, and he recorded his experiences there in his most famous book,* Walden *(1854). He left* Walden, *however, because, according to him, he had "several more lives to live and could not spare any more for that one." A canoe excursion in 1839 resulted in the chronicle* A Week on the Concord and Merrimack Rivers, *and other experiences produced books about Maine and Cape Cod. The following impassioned and eloquent defense of civil disobedience, published in 1849, has influenced such leaders as Gandhi and Martin Luther King, Jr.*

I heartily accept the motto,—"That government is best which governs least;" and I should like to see it acted up to more rapidly and systematically. Carried out, it finally amounts to this, which also I believe,—"That government is best which governs not at all"; and when men are prepared for it, that will be the kind of government which they will have. Government is at best but an expedient; but most governments are usually, and all governments are sometimes, inexpedient. The objections which have been brought against a standing army, and they are many and weighty, and deserve to prevail, may also at last be brought against a standing government. The standing army is only an arm of the standing government. The government itself, which is only the mode which the people have chosen to execute their will, is equally liable to be abused and perverted before the people can act through it. Witness the present Mexican war,[1] the work of comparatively a few individuals using the standing government as their tool; for, in the outset, the people would not have consented to this measure.

This American Government,—what is it but a tradition, though a recent one, endeavoring to transmit itself unimpaired to posterity, but each instant losing some of its integrity? It has not the vitality and force of a single living man; for a single man can bend it to his will. It is a sort of wooden gun to the people themselves. But it is not the less necessary for this; for the people must have some complicated machinery or other, and hear its din, to satisfy that idea of government which they have. Governments show thus how successfully men can be imposed on, even impose on themselves, for their own advantage. It is excellent, we must all allow. Yet this government never of itself furthered any enterprise, but by the alacrity with which it got out of its way. *It* does not keep the country free. *It* does not settle the West. *It* does not educate. The character inherent in the American people has done all that has been accomplished; and it would have done somewhat more, if the government had not sometimes got in its way. For government is an expedient by which men would fain succeed in letting one another alone; and, as has been said, when it is most expedient, the governed are most let alone by it. Trade and commerce, if they were not made of India-rubber, would never manage to bounce over the obstacles which legislators are continually putting in their way; and, if one were to judge these men wholly by the effects of their actions and not partly by their intentions, they would deserve to be classed and punished with those mischievous persons who put obstructions on the railroads.

But, to speak practically and as a citizen, unlike those who call themselves no-government men, I ask for, not at once no government, but *at once* a better government. Let every man make known what kind of government would command his respect, and that will be one step toward obtaining it.

After all, the practical reason why, when the power is once in the hands of the people, a majority are permitted, and for a long period continue, to rule is not because they are most likely to be in the right, nor because this seems fairest to the minority, but because they are physically the strongest. But a government in which the majority rule in all cases cannot be based on justice, even as far as men understand

---

[1]In December 1845, the US annexation of Texas, led to a war between the United States and Mexico (1846–1848). Thoreau opposed this war, thinking it served the interests of slaveholders, who believed that the land won from Mexico would be slave territory. In protest, he refused to pay the Massachusetts poll tax and was arrested for his act of civil disobedience. [Eds.]

it. Can there not be a government in which majorities do not virtually decide right and wrong, but conscience?—in which majorities decide only those questions to which the rule of expediency is applicable? Must the citizen ever for a moment, or in the least degree, resign his conscience to the legislator? Why has every man a conscience, then? I think that we should be men first, and subjects afterward. It is not desirable to cultivate a respect for the law, so much as for the right. The only obligation which I have a right to assume is to do at any time what I think right. It is truly enough said, that a corporation has no conscience; but a corporation of conscientious men is a corporation *with* a conscience. Law never made men a whit more just; and, by means of their respect for it, even the well-disposed are daily made the agents of injustice. A common and natural result of any undue respect for law is, that you may see a file of soldiers, colonel, captain, corporal, privates, powder-monkeys, and all, marching in admirable order over hill and dale to the wars, against their wills, ay, against their common sense and consciences, which makes it very steep marching indeed, and produces a palpitation of the heart. They have no doubt that it is a damnable business in which they are concerned; they are all peaceably inclined. Now, what are they? Men at all? or small movable forts and magazines, at the service of some unscrupulous man in power? Visit the Navy-Yard, and behold a marine, such a man as an American government can make, or such as it can make a man with its black arts,—a mere shadow and reminiscence of humanity, a man laid out alive and standing, and already, as one may say, buried under arms with funeral accompaniments, though it may be,—

> "Not a drum was heard, not a funeral note,
> As his corse to the rampart we hurried;
> Not a soldier discharged his farewell shot
> O'er the grave where our hero we buried."[2]

5   The mass of men serve the state thus, not as men mainly, but as machines, with their bodies. They are the standing army, and the militia, jailers, constables, posse comitatus, etc. In most cases there is no free exercise whatever of the judgment or of the moral sense; but they put themselves on a level with wood and earth and stones; and wooden men can perhaps be manufactured that will serve the purpose as well. Such command no more respect than men of straw or a lump of dirt. They have the same sort of worth only as horses and dogs. Yet such as these even are commonly esteemed good citizens. Others—as most legislators, politicians, lawyers, ministers, and office-holders—serve

---

[2]From "The Burial of Sir John Moore at Corunna," by Irish poet Charles Wolfe (1791–1823). [Eds.]

the state chiefly with their heads; and, as they rarely make any moral distinctions, they are as likely to serve the Devil, without intending it, as God. A very few, as heroes, patriots, martyrs, reformers in the great sense, and men, serve the state with their consciences also, and so necessarily resist it for the most part; and they are commonly treated as enemies by it. A wise man will only be useful as a man, and will not submit to be "clay," and "stop a hole to keep the wind away,"[3] but leave that office to his dust at least:—

"I am too high-born to be propertied,
To be a secondary at control,
Or useful serving-man and instrument
To any sovereign state throughout the world."[4]

He who gives himself entirely to his fellow-men appears to them useless and selfish; but he who gives himself partially to them is pronounced a benefactor and philanthropist.

How does it become a man to behave toward this American government to-day? I answer, that he cannot without disgrace be associated with it. I cannot for an instant recognize that political organization as *my* government which is the *slave's* government also.

All men recognize the right of revolution; that is, the right to refuse allegiance to, and to resist, the government, when its tyranny or its inefficiency are great and unendurable. But almost all say that such is not the case now. But such was the case, they think, in the Revolution of '75. If one were to tell me that this was a bad government because it taxed certain foreign commodities brought to its ports, it is most probable that I should not make an ado about it, for I can do without them. All machines have their friction; and possibly this does enough good to counterbalance the evil. At any rate, it is a great evil to make a stir about it. But when the friction comes to have its machine, and oppression and robbery are organized, I say, let us not have such a machine any longer. In other words, when a sixth of the population of a nation which has undertaken to be the refuge of liberty are slaves, and a whole country is unjustly overrun and conquered by a foreign army, and subjected to military law, I think that it is not too soon for honest men to rebel and revolutionize. What makes this duty the more urgent is the fact that the country so overrun is not our own, but ours is the invading army.

Paley,[5] a common authority with many moral questions, in his chapter on the "Duty of Submission to Civil Government," resolves all civil obligation into expediency; and he proceeds to say, "that so

---

[3]From *Hamlet* (act V, scene i) by William Shakespeare. [Eds.]
[4]From *King John* (act V, scene ii) by William Shakespeare. [Eds.]
[5]William Paley (1743–1805), English clergyman and philosopher. [Eds.]

long as the interest of the whole society requires it, that is, so long as the established government cannot be resisted or changed without public inconveniency, it is the will of God that the established government be obeyed, and no longer. . . . This principle being admitted, the justice of every particular case of resistance is reduced to a computation of the quantity of the danger and grievance on the one side, and of the probability and expense of redressing it on the other." Of this, he says, every man shall judge for himself. But Paley appears never to have contemplated those cases to which the rule of expediency does not apply, in which a people, as well as an individual, must do justice, cost what it may. If I have unjustly wrested a plank from a drowning man, I must restore it to him though I drown myself. This, according to Paley, would be inconvenient. But he that would save his life, in such a case, shall lose it. This people must cease to hold slaves, and to make war on Mexico, though it cost them their existence as a people.

10   In their practice, nations agree with Paley; but does any one think that Massachusetts does exactly what is right at the present crisis?

"A drab of state, a cloth-o'-silver slut,
To have her train borne up, and her soul trail in the dirt."[6]

Practically speaking, the opponents to a reform in Massachusetts are not a hundred thousand politicians at the South, but a hundred thousand merchants and farmers here, who are more interested in commerce and agriculture than they are in humanity, and are not prepared to do justice to the slave and to Mexico, *cost what it may.* I quarrel not with far-off foes, but with those who, near at home, coöperate with, and do the bidding of, those far away, and without whom the latter would be harmless. We are accustomed to say, that the mass of men are unprepared; but improvement is slow, because the few are not materially wiser or better than the many. It is not so important that many should be as good as you, as that there be some absolute goodness somewhere; for that will leaven the whole lump. There are thousands who are *in opinion* opposed to slavery and to the war, who yet in effect do nothing to put an end to them; who, esteeming themselves children of Washington and Franklin, sit down with their hands in their pockets, and say that they know not what to do, and do nothing; who even postpone the question of freedom to the question of free-trade, and quietly read the prices-current along with the latest advices from Mexico, after dinner, and, it may be, fall asleep over them both. What is the price-current of an honest man and patriot to-day? They hesitate, and they regret, and sometimes they petition; but they do nothing in earnest and with effect. They will wait, well disposed,

---

[6]From act IV, scene iv, of Cyril Tourneur's *The Revenger's Tragedy* (1607). [Eds.]

for others to remedy the evil, that they may no longer have it to regret. At most, they give only a cheap vote, and a feeble countenance and Godspeed, to the right, as it goes by them. There are nine hundred and ninety-nine patrons of virtue to one virtuous man. But it is easier to deal with the real possessor of a thing than with the temporary guardian of it.

All voting is a sort of gaming, like checkers or backgammon, with a slight moral tinge to it, a playing with right and wrong, with moral questions; and betting naturally accompanies it. The character of the voters is not staked. I cast my vote, perchance, as I think right; but I am not vitally concerned that that right should prevail. I am willing to leave it to the majority. Its obligation, therefore, never exceeds that of expediency. Even voting *for the right* is *doing* nothing for it. It is only expressing to men feebly your desire that it should prevail. A wise man will not leave the right to the mercy of chance, nor wish it to prevail through the power of the majority. There is but little virtue in the action of masses of men. When the majority shall at length vote for the abolition of slavery, it will be because they are indifferent to slavery, or because there is but little slavery left to be abolished by their vote. *They* will then be the only slaves. Only *his* vote can hasten the abolition of slavery who asserts his own freedom by his vote.

I hear of a convention to be held at Baltimore, or elsewhere, for the selection of a candidate for the Presidency, made up chiefly of editors, and men who are politicians by profession; but I think, what is it to any independent, intelligent, and respectable man what decision they may come to? Shall we not have the advantage of his wisdom and honesty, nevertheless? Can we not count upon some independent votes? Are there not many individuals in the country who do not attend conventions? But no: I find that the respectable man, so called, has immediately drifted from his position, and despairs of his country, when his country has more reason to despair of him. He forthwith adopts one of the candidates thus selected as the only *available* one, thus proving that he is himself *available* for any purposes of the demagogue. His vote is of no more worth than that of any unprincipled foreigner or hireling native, who may have been bought. O for a man who is a *man*, and, as my neighbor says, has a bone in his back which you cannot pass your hand through! Our statistics are at fault: the population has been returned too large. How many *men* are there to a square thousand miles in this country? Hardly one. Does not America offer any inducement for men to settle here? The American has dwindled into an Odd Fellow,—one who may be known by the development of his organ of gregariousness, and a manifest lack of intellect and cheerful self-reliance; whose first and chief concern, on coming into the world, is to see that

Almshouses[7] are in good repair; and, before yet he has lawfully donned the virile garb, to collect a fund for the support of the widows and orphans that may be; who, in short, ventures to live only by the aid of the Mutual Insurance company, which has promised to bury him decently

It is not a man's duty, as a matter of course, to devote himself to the eradication of any, even the most enormous wrong; he may still properly have other concerns to engage him; but it is his duty, at least, to wash his hands of it, and, if he gives it no thought longer, not to give it practically his support. If I devote myself to other pursuits and contemplations, I must first see, at least, that I do not pursue them sitting upon another man's shoulders. I must get off him first, that he may pursue his contemplations too. See what gross inconsistency is tolerated. I have heard some of my townsmen say, "I should like to have them order me out to help put down an insurrection of the slaves, or to march to Mexico—see if I would go;" and yet these very men have each, directly by their allegiance, and so indirectly, at least, by their money, furnished a substitute. The soldier is applauded who refuses to serve in an unjust war by those who do not refuse to sustain the unjust government which makes the war; is applauded by those whose own act and authority he disregards and sets at naught; as if the state were penitent to that degree that it hired one to scourge it while it sinned, but not to that degree that it left off sinning for a moment. Thus, under the name of Order and Civil Government, we are all made at last to pay homage to and support our own meanness. After the first blush of sin comes its indifference; and from immoral it becomes, as it were, *un*moral, and not quite unnecessary to that life which we have made.

15   The broadest and most prevalent error requires the most disinterested virtue to sustain it. The slight reproach to which the virtue of patriotism is commonly liable, the noble are most likely to incur. Those who, while they disapprove of the character and measures of a government, yield to it their allegiance and support are undoubtedly its most conscientious supporters, and so frequently the most serious obstacles to reform. Some are petitioning the state to dissolve the Union, to disregard the requisitions of the President. Why do they not dissolve it themselves,—the union between themselves and the state,—and refuse to pay their quota into its treasury? Do not they stand in the same relation to the state that the state does to the Union? And have not the same reasons prevented the state from resisting the Union which have prevented them from resisting the state?

---

[7]Poorhouses; county homes that provided for the needy. [Eds.]

How can a man be satisfied to entertain an opinion merely, and enjoy *it*? Is there any enjoyment in it, if his opinion is that he is aggrieved? If you are cheated out of a single dollar by your neighbor, you do not rest satisfied with knowing that you are cheated, or with saying that you are cheated, or even with petitioning him to pay you your due; but you take effectual steps at once to obtain the full amount, and see that you are never cheated again. Action from principle, the perception and the performance of right, changes things and relations; it is essentially revolutionary, and does not consist wholly with anything which was. It not only divides states and churches, it divides families; ay, it divides the *individual,* separating the diabolical in him from the divine.

Unjust laws exist: shall we be content to obey them, or shall we endeavor to amend them, and obey them until we have succeeded, or shall we transgress them at once? Men generally, under such a government as this, think that they ought to wait until they have persuaded the majority to alter them. They think that, if they should resist, the remedy would be worse than the evil. But it is the fault of the government itself that the remedy is worse than the evil. *It* makes it worse. Why is it not more apt to anticipate and provide for reform? Why does it not cherish its wise minority? Why does it cry and resist before it is hurt? Why does it not encourage its citizens to be on the alert to point out its faults, and *do* better than it would have them? Why does it always crucify Christ, and excommunicate Copernicus and Luther, and pronounce Washington and Franklin rebels?

One would think, that a deliberate and practical denial of its authority was the only offense never contemplated by government; else, why has it not assigned its definite, its suitable and proportionate penalty? If a man who has no property refuses but once to earn nine shillings for the state, he is put in prison for a period unlimited by any law that I know, and determined only by the discretion of those who placed him there; but if he should steal ninety times nine shillings from the state, he is soon permitted to go at large again.

If the injustice is part of the necessary friction of the machine of government, let it go, let it go: perchance it will wear smooth,—certainly the machine will wear out. If the injustice has a spring, or a pulley, or a rope, or a crank, exclusively for itself, then perhaps you may consider whether the remedy will not be worse than the evil; but if it is of such a nature that it requires you to be the agent of injustice to another, then, I say, break the law. Let your life be a counter friction to stop the machine. What I have to do is to see, at any rate, that I do not lend myself to the wrong which I condemn.

As for adopting the ways which the state has provided for reme- 20 dying the evil, I know not of such ways. They take too much time, and a man's life will be gone. I have other affairs to attend to. I came into this world, not chiefly to make this a good place to live in, but to live in it, be it good or bad. A man has not everything to do, but some-thing; and because he cannot do *everything,* it is not necessary that he should do *something* wrong. It is not my business to be petitioning the Governor or the Legislature any more than it is theirs to petition me; and if they should not hear my petition, what should I do then? But in this case the state has provided no way: its very Constitution is the evil. This may seem to be harsh and stubborn and unconciliatory; but it is to treat with the utmost kindness and consideration the only spirit that can appreciate or deserve it. So is all change for the better, like birth and death, which convulse the body.

I do not hesitate to say, that those who call themselves Abolition-ists should at once effectually withdraw their support, both in person and property, from the government of Massachusetts, and not wait till they constitute a majority of one, before they suffer the right to pre-vail through them. I think that it is enough if they have God on their side, without waiting for that other one. Moreover, any man more right than his neighbors constitutes a majority of one already.

I meet this American government, or its representative, the state government, directly, and face to face, once a year—no more—in the person of its tax-gatherer; this is the only mode in which a man situ-ated as I am necessarily meets it; and it then says distinctly, Recognize me; and the simplest, the most effectual, and, in the present posture of affairs, the indispensablest mode of treating with it on this head, of expressing your little satisfaction with and love for it, is to deny it then. My civil neighbor, the tax-gatherer, is the very man I have to deal with,—for it is, after all, with men and not with parchment that I quarrel,—and he has voluntarily chosen to be an agent of the govern-ment. How shall he ever know well what he is and does as an officer of the government, or as a man, until he is obliged to consider whether he shall treat me, his neighbor, for whom he has respect, as a neighbor and well-disposed man, or as a maniac and disturber of the peace, and see if he can get over this obstruction to his neighborliness without a ruder and more impetuous thought or speech correspond-ing with his action. I know this well, that if one thousand; if one hun-dred, if ten men whom I could name,—if ten *honest* men only,—say if *one* HONEST man, in this State of Massachusetts, *ceasing to hold slaves,* were actually to withdraw from this copartnership, and be locked up in the county jail therefor, it would be the abolition of slavery in America. For it matters not how small the beginning may seem to be: what is once well done is done forever. But we love better to talk about it: that we say is our mission. Reform keeps many scores of newspapers in its service, but not one man. If my esteemed neighbor, the State's ambassador, who will devote his days to the settlement of the question of human rights in the Council Chamber, instead of being threatened with the prisons of Carolina, were to sit down the prisoner of Massachusetts, that State which is so anxious to foist the sin of slavery upon her sister,—though at present she can discover only an act of inhospitality to be the ground of a quarrel with her,—the Legislature would not wholly waive the subject the following winter.

Under a government which imprisons any unjustly, the true place for a just man is also a prison. The proper place to-day, the only place which Massachusetts has provided for her freer and less desponding spirits, is in her prisons, to be put out and locked out of the State by her own act, as they have already put themselves out by their principles. It is there that the fugitive slave, and the Mexican prisoner on parole, and the Indian come to plead the wrongs of his race should find them; on that separate, but more free and honorable ground, where the State places those who are not *with* her, but *against* her,—the only house in a slave State in which a free man can abide with honor. If any think that their influence would be lost there, and their voices no longer afflict the ear of the State, that they would not be as an enemy within its walls, they do not know by how much truth is stronger than error, nor how much more eloquently and effectively he can combat injustice who has experienced a little in his own person. Cast your whole vote, not a strip of paper merely, but your whole influence. A minority is powerless while it conforms to the majority; it is not even a minority then; but it is irresistible when it clogs by its whole weight. If the alternative is to keep all just men in prison, or give up war and slavery, the State will not hesitate which to choose. If a thousand men were not to pay their tax-bills this year, that would not be a violent and bloody measure, as it would be to pay them, and enable the State to commit violence and shed innocent blood. This is, in fact, the definition of a peaceable revolution, if any such is possible. If the tax-gatherer, or any other public officer, asks me, as one has done, "But what shall I do?" my answer is, "If you really wish to do anything, resign your office." When the subject has refused allegiance, and the officer has resigned his office, then the revolution is accomplished. But even suppose blood should flow. Is there not a sort of blood shed when the conscience is wounded? Through this wound a man's real manhood and immortality flow out, and he bleeds to an everlasting death. I see this blood flowing now.

I have contemplated the imprisonment of the offender, rather than the seizure of his goods,—though both will serve the same purpose,—because they who assert the purest right, and consequently are most dangerous to a corrupt State, commonly have not spent much time in accumulating property. To such the State renders comparatively small service, and a slight tax is wont to appear exorbitant, particularly if they are obliged to earn it by special labor with their hands. If there were one who lived wholly without the use of money, the State itself would hesitate to demand it of him. But the rich man—not to make any invidious comparison—is always sold to the institution which makes him rich. Absolutely speaking, the more money, the less virtue; for money comes between a man and his objects, and obtains them for him; and it was certainly no great virtue to obtain it. It puts to rest many questions which he would otherwise be taxed to answer; while the only new question which it puts is the hard but superfluous one, how to spend it. Thus his moral ground is taken from under his feet. The opportunities of living are diminished in proportion as what are called the "means" are increased. The best thing a man can do for his culture when he is rich is to endeavor to carry out those schemes which he entertained when he was poor. Christ answered the Herodians according to their condition. "Show me the tribute-money," said he;—and one took a penny out of his pocket;—if you use money which has the image of Caesar on it, which he has made current and valuable, that is, *if you are men of the State,* and gladly enjoy the advantages of Caesar's government, then pay him back some of his own when he demands it. "Render therefore to Caesar that which is Caesar's, and to God those things which are God's,"—leaving them no wiser than before as to which was which; for they did not wish to know.

25   When I converse with the freest of my neighbors, I perceive that, whatever they may say about the magnitude and seriousness of the question, and their regard for the public tranquility, the long and the short of the matter is, that they cannot spare the protection of the existing government, and they dread the consequences to their property and families of disobedience to it. For my own part, I should not like to think that I ever rely on the protection of the State. But, if I deny the authority of the State when it presents its tax-bill, it will soon take and waste all my property, and so harass me and my children without end. This is hard. This makes it impossible for a man to live honestly, and at the same time comfortably, in outward respects. It will not be worth the while to accumulate property; that would be sure to go again. You must hire or squat somewhere, and raise but a small crop, and eat that soon. You must live within yourself, and depend upon yourself always tucked up and ready for a start, and not have many affairs. A man may grow rich in Turkey even, if he will be in all respects a good subject of the Turkish government. Confucius said: "If a state is governed by the principles of reason, poverty and misery are subjects of shame; if a state is not governed by the principles of reason, riches and honors are the subjects of shame." No: until I want the protection of Massachusetts to be extended to me in some distant Southern port, where my liberty is endangered, or until I am bent solely on building up an estate at home by peaceful enterprise, I can

afford to refuse allegiance to Massachusetts, and her right to my property and life. It costs me less in every sense to incur the penalty of disobedience to the State than it would to obey. I should feel as if I were worth less in that case.

Some years ago, the State met me in behalf of the Church, and commended me to pay a certain sum toward the support of a clergyman whose preaching my father attended, but never I myself. "Pay," it said, "or be locked up in the jail." I declined to pay. But, unfortunately, another man saw fit to pay it. I did not see why the schoolmaster should be taxed to support the priest, and not the priest the schoolmaster; for I was not the State's schoolmaster, but I supported myself by voluntary subscription. I did not see why the lyceum should not present its tax-bill, and have the State to back its demand, as well as the Church. However, at the request of the selectmen, I condescended to make some such statement as this in writing:—"Know all men by these presents, that I, Henry Thoreau, do not wish to be regarded as a member of any incorporated society which I have not joined." This I gave to the town clerk; and he has it. The State, having thus learned that I did not wish to be regarded as a member of that church, has never made a like demand on me since; though it said that it must adhere to its original presumption that time. If I had known how to name them, I should have then signed off in detail from all the societies which I never signed on to; but I did not know where to find a complete list.

I have paid no poll-tax for six years. I was put into a jail once on this account, for one night; and, as I stood considering the walls of solid stone, two or three feet thick, the door of wood and iron, a foot thick, and the iron grating which strained the light, I could not help being struck with the foolishness of that institution which treated me as if I were mere flesh and blood and bones, to be locked up. I wondered that it should have concluded at length that this was the best use it could put me to, and had never thought to avail itself of my services in some way. I say that, if there was a wall of stone between me and my townsmen, there was a still more difficult one to climb or break through before they could get to be as free as I was. I did not for a moment feel confined, and the walls seemed a great waste of stone and mortar. I felt as if I alone of all my townsmen had paid my tax. They plainly did not know how to treat me, but behaved like persons who are underbred. In every threat and in every compliment there was a blunder; for they thought that my chief desire was to stand the other side of that stone wall. I could not but smile to see how industriously they locked the door on my meditations, which followed them out again without let or hindrance, and *they* were really all that was dangerous. As they could not reach me, they had resolved to punish my body; just as boys, if they cannot come at some person against whom they have a spite, will abuse his dog. I saw that the State was half-witted, that it was timid as a lone woman with her silver spoons, and that it did not know its friends from its foes, and I lost all my remaining respect for it, and pitied it.

Thus the State never intentionally confronts a man's sense, intellectual or moral, but only his body, his senses. It is not armed with superior wit or honesty; but with superior physical strength. I was not born to be forced. I will breathe after my own fashion. Let us see who is the strongest. What force has a multitude? They only can force me who obey a higher law than I. They force me to become like themselves. I do not hear of *men* being *forced* to live this way or that by masses of men. What sort of life were that to live? When I meet a government which says to me, "Your money or your life," why should I be in haste to give it my money? It may be in a great strait, and not know what to do: I cannot help that. It must help itself; do as I do. It is not worth the while to snivel about it. I am not responsible for the successful working of the machinery of society. I am not the son of the engineer. I perceive that, when an acorn and a chestnut fall side by side, the one does not remain inert to make way for the other, but both obey their own laws, and spring and grow and flourish as best they can, till one, perchance, over-shadows and destroys the other. If a plant cannot live according to its nature, it dies; and so a man.

The night in prison was novel and interesting enough. The prisoners in their shirt-sleeves were enjoying a chat and the evening air in the doorway, when I entered. But the jailer said, "Come, boys, it is time to lock up;" and so they dispersed, and I heard the sound of their steps returning into the hollow apartments. My room-mate was introduced to me by the jailer as "a first-rate fellow and a clever man." When the door was locked, he showed me where to hang my hat, and how he managed matters there. The rooms were whitewashed once a month; and this one, at least, was the whitest, most simply furnished, and probably the neatest apartment in the town. He naturally wanted to know where I came from, and what brought me there; and, when I had told him, I asked him in my turn how he came there, presuming him to be an honest man, of course; and, as the world goes, I believe he was. "Why," said he, "they accuse me of burning a barn; but I never did it." As near as I could discover, he had probably gone to bed in a barn when drunk, and smoked his pipe there; and so a barn was burnt. He had the reputation of being a clever man, had been there some three months waiting for his trial to come on, and would have to wait as much longer; but he was quite domesticated and contented, since he got his board for nothing, and thought that he was well treated.

30   He occupied one window, and I the other; and I saw that if one stayed there long, his principal business would be to look out the window. I had soon read all tracts that were left there, and examined

where former prisoners had broken out, and where a grate had been sawed off, and heard the history of the various occupants of that room; for I found that even here there was a history and a gossip which never circulated beyond the walls of the jail. Probably this is the only house in the town where verses are composed, which are afterward printed in a circular form, but not published. I was shown quite a long list of verses which were composed by some young men who had been detected in an attempt to escape, who avenged themselves by signing them.

I pumped my fellow-prisoner as dry as I could, for fear I should never see him again; but at length he showed me which was my bed, and left me to blow out the lamp.

It was like traveling into a far country, such as I had never expected to behold, to lie there for one night. It seemed to me that I never had heard the town-clock strike before, nor the evening sounds of the village; for we slept with the windows open, which were inside the grating. It was to see my native village in the light of the Middle Ages, and our Concord was turned into a Rhine stream, and visions of knights and castles passed before me. They were the voices of old burghers that I heard in the streets. I was an involuntary spectator and auditor of whatever was done and said in the kitchen of the adjacent village-inn,—a wholly new and rare experience to me. It was a closer view of my native town. I was fairly inside of it. I never had seen its institutions before. This is one of its peculiar institutions; for it is a shire town.[8] I began to comprehend what its inhabitants were about.

In the morning, our breakfasts were put through the hole in the door, in small oblong-square tin pans, made to fit, and holding a pint of chocolate, with brown bread, and an iron spoon. When they called for the vessels again, I was green enough to return what bread I had left; but my comrade seized it, and said that I should lay that up for lunch or dinner. Soon after he was let out to work at haying in a neighboring field, whither he went every day, and would not be back till noon; so he bade me good-day, saying that he doubted if he should see me again.

When I came out of prison,—for some one interfered, and paid that tax,—I did not perceive that great changes had taken place on the common, such as he observed who went in a youth and emerged a tottering and gray-headed man; and yet a change had to my eyes come over the scene,—the town, and State, and country,—greater than any that mere time could effect. I saw yet more distinctly the State in which I lived. I saw to what extent the people among whom I

---

[8]County seat. [Eds.]

lived could be trusted as good neighbors and friends; that their friendship was for summer weather only; that they did not greatly propose to do right; that they were a distinct race from me by their prejudices and superstitions, as the Chinamen and Malays are; that in their sacrifices to humanity they ran no risks, not even to their property; that after all they were not so noble but they treated the thief as he had treated them, and hoped, by a certain outward observance and a few prayers, and by walking in a particular straight though useless path from time to time, to save their souls. This may be to judge my neighbors harshly; for I believe that many of them are not aware that they have such an institution as the jail in their village.

35   It was formerly the custom in our village; when a poor debtor came out of jail, for his acquaintances to salute him, looking through their fingers, which were crossed to represent the grating of a jail window, "How do ye do?" My neighbors did not thus salute me, but first looked at me, and then at one another, as if I had returned from a long journey. I was put into jail as I was going to the shoemaker's to get a shoe which was mended. When I was let out the next morning, I proceeded to finish my errand, and, having put on my mended shoe, joined a huckleberry party, who were impatient to put themselves under my conduct; and in half an hour,—for the horse was soon tackled,—was in the midst of a huckleberry field, on one of our highest hills, two miles off, and then the State was nowhere to be seen.

This is the whole history of "My Prisons."

I have never declined paying the highway tax, because I am as desirous of being a good neighbor as I am of being a bad subject; and as for supporting schools, I am doing my part to educate my fellow-countrymen now. It is for no particular item in the tax-bill that I refuse to pay it. I simply wish to refuse allegiance to the State, to withdraw and stand aloof from it effectually. I do not care to trace the course of my dollar, if I could, till it buys a man or a musket to shoot one with,—the dollar is innocent,—but I am concerned to trace the effects of my allegiance. In fact, I quietly declare war with the State, after my fashion, though I will still make what use and get what advantage of her I can, as is usual in such cases.

If others pay the tax which is demanded of me, from a sympathy with the State, they do but what they have already done in their own case, or rather they abet injustice to a greater extent than the State requires. If they pay the tax from a mistaken interest in the individual taxed, to save his property, or prevent his going to jail, it is because they have not considered wisely how far they let their private feelings interfere with the public good.

This, then, is my position at present. But one cannot be too much on his guard in such a case, lest his action be biased by obstinacy or an undue regard for the opinions of men. Let him see that he does only what belongs to himself and to the hour.

I think sometimes, Why, this people mean well, they are only ig- 40
norant; they would do better if they knew how: why give your neighbors this pain to treat you as they are not inclined to? But I think
again, This is no reason why I should do as they do, or permit others
to suffer much greater pain of a different kind. Again, I sometimes say
to myself, When many millions of men, without heat, without ill will,
without personal feeling of any kind, demand of you a few shillings
only, without the possibility, such is their constitution, of retracting or
altering their present demand, and without the possibility, on your
side, of appeal to any other millions, why expose yourself to this
overwhelming brute force? You do not resist cold and hunger, the
winds and the waves, thus obstinately; you quietly submit to a thousand similar necessities. You do not put your head into the fire. But
just in proportion as I regard this as not wholly a brute force, but
partly a human force, and consider that I have relations to those millions as to so many millions of men, and not of mere brute or inanimate things, I see that appeal is possible, first and instantaneously,
from them to the Maker of them, and, secondly, from them to themselves. But if I put my head deliberately into the fire, there is no appeal to fire or to the Maker of fire, and I have only myself to blame. If
I could convince myself that I have any right to be satisfied with men
as they are, and to treat them accordingly, and not accordingly, in
some respects, to my requisitions and expectations of what they and I
ought to be, then, like a good Mussulman[9] and fatalist, I should endeavor to be satisfied with things as they are, and say it is the will of
God. And, above all, there is this difference between resisting this and
a purely brute or natural force that I can resist this with some effect;
but I cannot expect, like Orpheus,[10] to change the nature of the rocks
and trees and beasts.

I do not wish to quarrel with any man or nation. I do not wish to
split hairs, to make the fine distinctions, or set myself up as better
than my neighbors. I seek rather, I may say, even an excuse for con-
forming to the laws of the land. I am but too ready to conform to
them. Indeed, I have reason to suspect myself on this head; and each
year, as the tax-gatherer comes round, I find myself disposed to review the acts and position of the general and State governments, and
the spirit of the people, to discover a pretext for conformity.

"We must affect our country as our parents,
And if at any time we alienate
Our love or industry from doing it honor,
We must respect effects and teach the soul

---

[9]Muslim. [Eds.]

[10]Legendary Greek poet and musician who played the lyre so beautifully that wild beasts were
transfixed by his music and rocks and trees moved. [Eds.]

Matter of conscience and religion,
And not desire of rule or benefit."[11]

I believe that the State will soon be able to take all my work of this sort out of my hands, and then I shall be no better a patriot than my fellow-countrymen. Seen from a lower point of view, the Constitution, with all its faults, is very good; the law and the courts are very respectable; even this State and this American government are, in many respects, very admirable, and rare things, to be thankful for, such as a great many have described them; but seen from a point of view a little higher, they are what I have described them; seen from a higher still, and the highest, who shall say what they are, or that they are worth looking at or thinking of at all?

However, the government does not concern me much, and I shall bestow the fewest possible thoughts on it. It is not many moments that I live under a government, even in this world. If a man is thought-free, fancy-free, imagination-free, that which *is not* never for a long time appearing *to be* to him, unwise rulers or reformers cannot fatally interrupt him.

I know that most men think differently from myself; but those whose lives are by profession devoted to the study of these or kindred subjects content me as little as any. Statesmen and legislators, standing so completely within the institution, never distinctly and nakedly behold it. They speak of moving society, but have no resting-place without it. They may be men of a certain experience and discrimination, and have no doubt invented ingenious and even useful systems, for which we sincerely thank them; but all their wit and usefulness lie within certain not very wide limits. They are wont to forget that the world is not governed by policy and expediency. Webster[12] never goes behind government, and so cannot speak with authority about it. His words are wisdom to those legislators who contemplate no essential reform in the existing government; but for thinkers, and those who legislate for all time, he never once glances at the subject. I know of those whose serene and wise speculations on this theme would soon reveal the limits of his mind's range and hospitality. Yet, compared with the cheap professions of most reformers, and the still cheaper wisdom and eloquence of politicians in general, his are almost the only sensible and valuable words, and we thank Heaven for him. Comparatively, he is always strong, original, and, above all, practical. Still, his quality is not wisdom, but prudence. The lawyer's truth is not Truth, but consistency or a consistent expediency. Truth is always in harmony with herself, and is not concerned chiefly to reveal the

---

[11]From *The Battle of Alcazar* (1594), a play by George Peele (1558?–1597?). [Eds.]
[12]Daniel Webster (1782–1852), legendary American orator, lawyer, and statesman. [Eds.]

justice that may consist with wrong-doing. He well deserves to be called, as he has been called, the Defender of the Constitution. There are really no blows to be given to him but defensive ones. He is not a leader, but a follower. His leaders are the men of '87.[13] "I have never made an effort," he says, "and never propose to make an effort; I have never countenanced an effort, and never mean to countenance an effort, to disturb the arrangement as originally made, by which the various States came into the Union." Still thinking of the sanction which the Constitution gives to slavery, he says, "Because it was a part of the original compact,—let it stand." Notwithstanding his special acuteness and ability, he is unable to take a fact out of its merely political relations, and behold it as it lies absolutely to be disposed of by the intellect,—what, for instance, it behooves a man to do here in America to-day with regard to slavery,—but ventures, or is driven, to make some such desperate answer as the following, while professing to speak absolutely, and as a private man,—from which what new and singular code of social duties might be inferred? "The manner," says he, "in which the governments of those States where slavery exists are to regulate it is for their own consideration, under their responsibility to their constituents, to the general laws of propriety, humanity, and justice, and to God. Associations formed elsewhere, springing from a feeling of humanity, or any other cause, have nothing whatever to do with it. They have never received any encouragement from me, and they never will."

They who know of no purer sources of truth, who have traced up 45 its stream no higher, stand, and wisely stand, by the Bible and the Constitution, and drink at it there with reverence and humility; but they who behold where it comes trickling into this lake or that pool, gird up their loins once more, and continue their pilgrimage toward its fountain-head.

No man with a genius for legislation has appeared in America. They are rare in the history of the world. There are orators, politicians, and eloquent men, by the thousand; but the speaker has not yet opened his mouth to speak who is capable of settling the much-vexed questions of the day. We love eloquence for its own sake, and not for any truth which it may utter, or any heroism it may inspire. Our legislators have not yet learned the comparative value of free-trade and of freedom, of union, and of rectitude, to a nation. They have no genuis or talent for comparatively humble questions of taxation and finance, commerce and manufacturers and agriculture. If we were left solely to the wordy wit of legislators in Congress for our guidance, uncorrected by the seasonable experience and the effectual complaints of

---

[13]The 1787 framers of the Constitution. [Eds.]

the people, America would not long retain her rank among the nations. For eighteen hundred years, though perchance I have no right to say it, the New Testament has been written; yet where is the legislator who has wisdom and practical talent enough to avail himself of the light which it sheds on the science of legislation?

The authority of government, even such as I am willing to submit to,—for I will cheerfully obey those who know and can do better than I, and in many things even those who neither know nor can do so well,—is still an impure one: to be strictly just, it must have the sanction and consent of the governed. It can have no pure right over my person and property but what I concede to it. The progress from an absolute to a limited monarchy, from a limited monarchy to a democracy, is a progress toward a true respect for the individual. Even the Chinese philosopher was wise enough to regard the individual as the basis of the empire. Is a democracy, such as we know it, the last improvement possible in government? Is it not possible to take a further step towards recognizing and organizing the rights of man? There will never be a really free and enlightened State until the State comes to recognize the individual as a higher and independent power, from which all its own power and authority are derived, and treats him accordingly. I please myself with imagining a State at last which can afford to be just to all men, and to treat the individual with respect as a neighbor; which even would not think it inconsistent with its own repose if a few were to live aloof from it, not meddling with it, nor embraced by it, who fulfilled all the duties of neighbors and fellow-men. A State which bore this kind of fruit, and suffered it to drop off as fast as it ripened, would prepare the way for a still more perfect and glorious State, which also I have imagined, but not yet anywhere seen.

Responding to Reading

1. What moral or political choice does each of the following statements by Thoreau imply?

   - " 'That government is best which governs least' " (1).
   - "All men recognize the right of revolution" (8).
   - "All voting is a sort of gaming, like checkers or backgammon" (12).
   - "Under a government which imprisons any unjustly, the true place for a just man is also a prison" (23).
   - "I did not see why the schoolmaster should be taxed to support the priest, and not the priest the schoolmaster" (26).

2. Do you believe civil disobedience is ever necessary? If so, under what circumstances?

3. Do you see any advantages in obeying a law, however unjust, rather than disobeying it? Explain.

Responding in Writing

Thoreau, like Martin Luther King, Jr. (below), was jailed for his beliefs (Thoreau for refusing to pay his taxes, King for refusing to cease his civil rights demonstrations). What different kinds of peaceful protest can you think of? Select several causes you believe in, and suggest an appropriate form of civil disobedience for each. Explain how each action might achieve the result you desire.

LETTER FROM BIRMINGHAM JAIL
Martin Luther King, Jr.
1929–1968

One of the greatest civil rights leaders and orators of this century, Martin Luther King, Jr., was a Baptist minister and winner of the 1964 Nobel Peace Prize. Influenced by Thoreau and Gandhi, King altered the spirit of African-American protest in the United States by advocating nonviolent civil disobedience to achieve racial equality. His books include Letter from Birmingham Jail *(1963) and* Where Do We Go From Here: Chaos or Community? *(1967). King was assassinated on April 4, 1968. The following letter, written in 1963, is his eloquent and impassioned response to a public statement by eight fellow clergymen in Birmingham, Alabama, who appealed to the citizenry of the city to "observe the principles of law and order and common sense" rather than join in the principled protests that King was leading. (Also see King's essay in Chapter 7, p. 485.)*

MY DEAR FELLOW CLERGYMEN:[1]

While confined here in the Birmingham city jail, I came across your recent statement calling my present activities "unwise and untimely." Seldom do I pause to answer criticism of my work and ideas. If I sought to answer all the criticisms that cross my desk, my secretaries would have little time for anything other than such correspondence in the course of the day, and I would have no time for constructive work. But since I feel that you are men of genuine good will and that your criticisms are sincerely set forth, I want to try to answer your statement in what I hope will be patient and reasonable terms.

---

[1]This response to a published statement by eight fellow clergymen from Alabama (Bishop C. C. J. Carpenter, Bishop Joseph A. Durick, Rabbi Milton L. Grafman, Bishop Paul Hardin, Bishop Holan B. Harmon, the Reverend George M. Murray, the Reverend Edward V. Ramage and the Reverend Earl Stallings) was composed under somewhat constricting circumstances. Begun on the margins of the newspaper in which the statement appeared while I was in jail, the letter was continued on scraps of writing paper supplied by a friendly Negro trusty, and concluded on a pad my attorneys were eventually permitted to leave me. Although the text remains in substance unaltered, I have indulged in the author's prerogative of polishing it for publication.

I think I should indicate that I am here in Birmingham, since you have been influenced by the view which argues against "outsiders coming in." I have the honor of serving as president of the Southern Christian Leadership Conference, an organization operating in every southern state, with headquarters in Atlanta, Georgia. We have some eighty-five affiliated organizations across the South, and one of them is the Alabama Christian Movement for Human Rights. Frequently we share staff, educational, and financial resources with our affiliates. Several months ago the affiliate here in Birmingham asked us to be on call to engage in a non-violent direct-action program if such were deemed necessary. We readily consented, and when the hour came we lived up to our promise. So I, along with several members of my staff, am here because I was invited here. I am here because I have organizational ties here.

But more basically, I am in Birmingham because injustice is here. Just as the prophets of the eighth century B.C. left their villages and carried their "thus saith the Lord" far beyond the boundaries of their home towns, and just as the Apostle Paul left his village of Tarsus and carried the gospel of Jesus Christ to the far corners of the Greco-Roman world, so am I compelled to carry the gospel of freedom beyond my own home town. Like Paul, I must constantly respond to the Macedonian call for aid.

Moreover, I am cognizant of the interrelatedness of all communities and states. I cannot sit idly by in Atlanta and not be concerned about what happens in Birmingham. Injustice anywhere is a threat to justice everywhere. We are caught in an inescapable network of mutuality, tied in a single garment of destiny. Whatever affects one directly, affects all indirectly. Never again can we afford to live with the narrow, provincial "outside agitator" idea. Anyone who lives inside the United States can never be considered an outsider anywhere within its bounds.

5   You deplore the demonstrations taking place in Birmingham. But your statement, I am sorry to say, fails to express a similar concern for the conditions that brought about the demonstrations. I am sure that none of you would want to rest content with the superficial kind of social analysis that deals merely with effects and does not grapple with underlying causes. It is unfortunate that demonstrations are taking place in Birmingham, but it is even more unfortunate that the city's white power structure left the Negro community with no alternative.

In any nonviolent campaign there are four basic steps: collection of the facts to determine whether injustices exist; negotiation; self-purification; and direct action. We have gone through all these steps in Birmingham. There can be no gainsaying the fact that racial injustice engulfs this community. Birmingham is probably the most thoroughly segregated city in the United States. Its ugly record of brutality is widely known. Negroes have experienced grossly unjust treatment in the courts. There have been more unsolved bombings of Negro homes and churches in Birmingham than in any other city in the nation. These are the hard, brutal facts of the case. On the basis of these conditions, Negro leaders sought to negotiate with the city fathers. But the latter consistently refused to engage in good-faith negotiation.

Then, last September, came the opportunity to talk with leaders of Birmingham's economic community. In the course of the negotiations, certain promises were made by the merchants—for example, to remove the stores' humiliating racial signs. On the basis of these promises, the Reverend Fred Shuttlesworth and the leaders of the Alabama Christian Movement for Human Rights agreed to a moratorium on all demonstrations. As the weeks and months went by, we realized that we were the victims of a broken promise. A few signs, briefly removed, returned; the others remained.

As in so many past experiences, our hopes had been blasted, and the shadow of deep disappointment settled upon us. We had no alternative except to prepare for direct action, whereby we would present our very bodies as a means of laying our case before the conscience of the local and the national community. Mindful of the difficulties involved, we decided to undertake a process of self-purification. We began a series of workshops on nonviolence, and we repeatedly asked ourselves: "Are you able to accept blows without retaliating?" "Are you able to endure the ordeal of jail?" We decided to schedule our direct-action program for the Easter season, realizing that except for Christmas, this is the main shopping period of the year. Knowing that a strong economic-withdrawal program would be the by-product of direct action, we felt that this would be the best time to bring pressure to bear on the merchants for the needed change.

Then it occurred to us that Birmingham's mayoral election was coming up in March, and we speedily decided to postpone action until after election day. When we discovered that the Commissioner of Public Safety, Eugene "Bull" Connor,[2] had piled up enough votes to be in the run-off, we decided again to postpone action until the day after the run-off so that the demonstrations could not be used to cloud the issues. Like many others, we wanted to see Mr. Connor defeated, and to this end we endured postponement after postponement. Having aided in this community need, we felt that our direct-action program could be delayed no longer.

You may well ask, "Why direct action? Why sit-ins, marches, and 10 so forth? Isn't negotiation a better path?" You are quite right in calling

---

[2]An ardent segregationist, Connor ordered police officers to use police dogs and fire hoses to break up civil rights demonstrations. (Conner lost his bid for mayor.) [Eds.]

for negotiation. Indeed, this is the very purpose of direct action. Nonviolent direct action seeks to create such a crisis and foster such a tension that a community which has constantly refused to negotiate is forced to confront the issue. It seeks so to dramatize the issue that it can no longer be ignored. My citing the creation of tension as part of the work of the nonviolent-resister may sound rather shocking. But I must confess that I am not afraid of the word "tension." I have earnestly opposed violent tension, but there is a type of constructive, nonviolent tension which is necessary for growth. Just as Socrates felt that it was necessary to create a tension in the mind so that individuals could rise from the bondage of myths and half-truths to the unfettered realm of creative analysis and objective appraisal, so must we see the need for nonviolent gadflies to create the kind of tension in society that will help men rise from the dark depths of prejudice and racism to the majestic heights of understanding and brotherhood.

The purpose of our direct-action program is to create a situation so crisis-packed that it will inevitably open the door to negotiation. I therefore concur with you in your call for negotiation. Too long has our beloved Southland been bogged down in a tragic effort to live in monologue rather than dialogue.

One of the basic points in your statement is that the action that I and my associates have taken in Birmingham is untimely. Some have asked: "Why didn't you give the new city administration time to act?" The only answer that I can give to this query is that the new Birmingham administration must be prodded about as much as the outgoing one, before it will act. We are sadly mistaken if we feel that the election of Albert Boutwell as mayor will bring the millennium to Birmingham. While Mr. Boutwell is a much more gentle person than Mr. Connor, they are both segregationists, dedicated to maintenance of the status quo. I have hoped that Mr. Boutwell will be reasonable enough to see the futility of massive resistance to desegregation. But he will not see this without pressure from devotees of civil rights. My friends, I must say to you that we have not made a single gain in civil rights without determined legal and nonviolent pressure. Lamentably, it is an historical fact that privileged groups seldom give up their privileges voluntarily. Individuals may see the moral light and voluntarily give up their unjust posture; but, as Reinhold Niebuhr[3] has reminded us, groups tend to be more immoral than individuals.

We know through painful experience that freedom is never voluntarily given by the oppressor; it must be demanded by the oppressed. Frankly, I have yet to engage in a direct-action campaign that was "well timed" in the view of those who have not suffered unduly

---

[3] American religious and social thinker (1892–1971). [Eds.]

from the disease of segregation. For years now I have heard the word "Wait!" It rings in the ear of every Negro with piercing familiarity. This "Wait!" has almost always meant "Never." We must come to see, with one of our distinguished jurists, that "justice too long delayed is justice denied."[4]

We have waited for more than 340 years for our constitutional and God-given rights. The nations of Asia and Africa are moving with jetlike speed toward gaining political independence, but we still creep at horse-and-buggy pace toward gaining a cup of coffee at a lunch counter. Perhaps it is easy for those who have never felt the stinging darts of segregation to say, "Wait." But when you have seen vicious mobs lynch your mothers and fathers at will and drown your sisters and brothers at whim; when you have seen hate-filled policemen curse, kick, and even kill your black brothers and sisters; when you see the vast majority of your twenty million Negro brothers smothering in an airtight cage of poverty in the midst of an affluent society; when you suddenly find your tongue twisted and your speech stammering as you seek to explain to your six-year-old daughter why she can't go to the public amusement park that has just been advertised on television, and see tears welling up in her eyes when she is told that Funtown is closed to colored children, and see ominous clouds of inferiority beginning to form in her little mental sky, and see her beginning to distort her personality by developing an unconscious bitterness toward white people; when you have to concoct an answer for a five-year-old son who is asking, "Daddy, why do white people treat colored people so mean?"; when you take a cross-country drive and find it necessary to sleep night after night in the uncomfortable corners of your automobile because no motel will accept you; when you are humiliated day in and day out by nagging signs reading "white" and "colored"; when your first name becomes "nigger," your middle name becomes "boy" (however old you are) and your last name becomes "John," and your wife and mother are never given the respected title "Mrs."; when you are harried by day and haunted by night by the fact that you are a Negro, living constantly at tiptoe stance, never quite knowing what to expect next, and are plagued with inner fears and outer resentments; when you are forever fighting a degenerating sense of "nobodiness"—then you will understand why we find it difficult to wait. There comes a time when the cup of endurance runs over, and men are no longer willing to be plunged into the abyss of despair. I hope, sirs, you can understand our legitimate and unavoidable impatience.

---

[4]Attributed to British statesman William Ewart Gladstone (1809–1898), a stalwart of the Liberal Party who also said, "You cannot fight the future. Time is on our side." [Eds.]

15   You express a great deal of anxiety over our willingness to break laws. This is certainly a legitimate concern. Since we so diligently urge people to obey the Supreme Court's decision of 1954 outlawing segregation in the public schools, at first glance it may seem rather paradoxical for us consciously to break laws. One may well ask: "How can you advocate breaking some laws and obeying others?" The answer lies in the fact that there are two types of laws: just and unjust. I would be the first to advocate obeying just laws. One has not only a legal but a moral responsibility to obey just laws. Conversely, one has a moral responsibility to disobey unjust laws. I would agree with St. Augustine[5] that "an unjust law is no law at all."

Now, what is the difference between the two? How does one determine whether a law is just or unjust? A just law is a man-made code that squares with the moral law or the law of God. An unjust law is a code this is out of harmony with the moral law. To put it in the terms of St. Thomas Aquinas:[6] An unjust law is a human law that is not rooted in eternal law and natural law. Any law that uplifts human personality is just. Any law that degrades human personality is unjust. All segregation statutes are unjust because segregation distorts the soul and damages the personality. It gives the segregator a false sense of superiority and the segregated a false sense of inferiority. Segregation, to use the terminology of the Jewish philosopher Martin Buber,[7] substitutes an "I-it" relationship for an "I-thou" relationship and ends up relegating persons to the status of things. Hence segregation is not only politically, economically, and sociologically unsound, it is morally wrong and sinful. Paul Tillich[8] has said that sin is separation. Is not segregation an existential expression of man's tragic separation, his awful estrangement, his terrible sinfulness? Thus it is that I can urge men to obey the 1954 decision of the Supreme Court, for it is morally right; and I can urge them to disobey segregation ordinances, for they are morally wrong.

Let us consider a more concrete example of just and unjust laws. An unjust law is a code that a numerical or power majority group compels a minority group to obey but does not make binding on itself. This is *difference* made legal. By the same token, a just law is a code that a majority compels a minority to follow and that it is willing to follow itself. This is *sameness* made legal.

Let me give another explanation. A law is unjust if it is inflicted on a minority that, as a result of being denied the right to vote, had no part in enacting or devising the law. Who can say that the legislature

---

[5]Italian-born missionary and theologian (?–c.604) [Eds.]
[6]Italian philosopher and theologian (1225–1274). [Eds.]
[7]Austrian existentialist philosopher and Judaic scholar (1878–1965). [Eds.]
[8]American philosopher and theologian (1886–1965). [Eds.]

of Alabama which set up that state's segregation laws was democratically elected? Throughout Alabama all sorts of devious methods are used to prevent Negroes from becoming registered voters, and there are some counties in which, even though Negroes constitute a majority of the population, not a single Negro is registered. Can any law enacted under such circumstances be considered democratically structured?

Sometimes a law is just on its face and unjust in its application. For instance, I have been arrested on a charge of parading without a permit. Now, there is nothing wrong in having an ordinance which requires a permit for a parade. But such an ordinance becomes unjust when it is used to maintain segregation and to deny citizens the First-Amendment privilege of peaceful assembly and protest.

I hope you are able to see the distinction I am trying to point out. 20 In no sense do I advocate evading or defying the law, as would the rabid segregationist. That would lead to anarchy. One who breaks an unjust law must do so openly, lovingly, and with a willingness to accept the penalty. I submit that an individual who breaks a law that conscience tells him is unjust, and who willingly accepts the penalty of imprisonment in order to arouse the conscience of the community over its injustice, is in reality expressing the highest respect for law.

Of course, there is nothing new about this kind of civil disobedience. It was evidenced sublimely in the refusal of Shadrach, Meshach, and Abednego to obey the laws of Nebuchadnezzar, on the ground that a higher moral law was at stake.[9] It was practiced superbly by the early Christians, who were willing to face hungry lions and the excruciating pain of chopping blocks rather than submit to certain unjust laws of the Roman Empire. To a degree, academic freedom is a reality today because Socrates practiced civil disobedience.[10] In our own nation, the Boston Tea Party represented a massive act of civil disobedience.

We should never forget that everything Adolf Hitler did in Germany was "legal" and everything the Hungarian freedom fighters[11] did in Hungary was "illegal." It was "illegal" to aid and comfort a Jew in Hitler's Germany. Even so, I am sure that, had I lived in Germany at the time, I would have aided and comforted my Jewish brothers. If today I lived in a Communist country where certain principles

---

[9] In the book of Daniel, Nebuchadnezzar commanded the people to worship a golden statue or be thrown into a furnace of blazing fire. When Shadrach, Meshach, and Abednego refused to worship any god but their own, they were bound and thrown into a blazing furnace, but the fire had no effect on them. Their escape led Nebuchadnezzar to make a decree forbidding blasphemy against their god. [Eds.]

[10] The ancient Greek philosopher Socrates was tried by the Athenians for corrupting their youth through his use of questions to teach. When he refused to change his methods of teaching, he was condemned to death. [Eds.]

[11] The Hungarian anti-Communist uprising of 1956 was quickly crushed by the army of the USSR. [Eds.]

dear to the Christian faith are suppressed, I would openly advocate disobeying that country's anti-religious laws.

I must make two honest confessions to you, my Christian and Jewish brothers. First, I must confess that over the past few years I have been gravely disappointed with the white moderate. I have almost reached the regrettable conclusion that the Negro's great stumbling block in his stride toward freedom is not the White Citizen's Counciler or the Ku Klux Klanner, but the white moderate, who is more devoted to "order" than to justice; who prefers a negative peace which is the absence of tension to a positive peace which is the presence of justice; who constantly says, "I agree with you in the goal you seek, but I cannot agree with your methods of direct action"; who paternalistically believes he can set the timetable for another man's freedom; who lives by a mythical concept of time and who constantly advises the Negro to wait for a "more convenient season." Shallow understanding from people of good will is more frustrating than absolute misunderstanding from people of ill will. Lukewarm acceptance is much more bewildering than outright rejection.

I had hoped that the white moderate would understand that law and order exist for the purpose of establishing justice and that when they fail in this purpose they become the dangerously structured dams that block the flow of social progress. I had hoped that the white moderate would understand that the present tension in the South is a necessary phase of the transition from an obnoxious negative peace, in which the Negro passively accepted his unjust plight, to a substantive and positive peace, in which all men will respect the dignity and worth of human personality. Actually, we who engage in nonviolent direct action are not the creators of tension. We merely bring to the surface the hidden tension that is already alive. We bring it out in the open, where it can be seen and dealt with. Like a boil that can never be cured so long as it is covered up but must be opened with all its ugliness to the natural medicines of air and light, injustice must be exposed, with all the tension its exposure creates, to the light of human conscience and the air of national opinion, before it can be cured.

25   In your statement you assert that our actions, even though peaceful, must be condemned because they precipitate violence. But is this a logical assertion? Isn't this like condemning a robbed man because his possession of money precipitated the evil act of robbery? Isn't this like condemning Socrates because his unswerving commitment to truth and his philosophical inquiries precipitated the act by the misguided populace in which they made him drink hemlock? Isn't this like condemning Jesus because his unique God-consciousness and never-ceasing devotion to God's will precipitated the evil act of crucifixion? We must come to see that, as the federal courts have consistently

affirmed, it is wrong to urge an individual to cease his efforts to gain his basic constitutional rights because the quest may precipitate violence. Society must protect the robbed and punish the robber.

I had also hoped that the white moderate would reject the myth concerning time in relation to the struggle for freedom. I have just received a letter from a white brother in Texas. He writes: "All Christians know that the colored people will receive equal rights eventually, but it is possible that you are in too great a religious hurry. It has taken Christianity almost two thousand years to accomplish what it has. The teachings of Christ take time to come to earth." Such an attitude stems from a tragic misconception of time, from the strangely irrational notion that there is something in the very flow of time that will inevitably cure all ills. Actually, time itself is neutral; it can be used either destructively or constructively. More and more I feel that the people of ill will have used time much more effectively than have the people of good will. We will have to repent in this generation not merely for the hateful words and actions of the bad people, but for the appalling silence of the good people. Human progress never rolls in on wheels of inevitability; it comes through the tireless efforts of men willing to be co-workers with God, and without this hard work, time itself becomes an ally of the forces of social stagnation. We must use time creatively, in the knowledge that the time is always ripe to do right. Now is the time to make real the promise of democracy and transform our pending national elegy into a creative psalm of brotherhood. Now is the time to lift our national policy from the quicksand of racial injustice to the solid rock of human dignity.

You speak of our activity in Birmingham as extreme. At first I was rather disappointed that fellow clergymen would see my nonviolent efforts as those of an extremist. I began thinking about the fact that I stand in the middle of two opposing forces in the Negro community. One is a force of complacency, made up in part of Negroes who, as a result of long years of oppression, are so drained of self-respect and a sense of "somebodiness" that they have adjusted to segregation; and in part of a few middle-class Negroes who, because of a degree of academic and economic security and because in some ways they profit by segregation, have become insensitive to the problems of the masses. The other force is one of bitterness and hatred, and it comes perilously close to advocating violence. It is expressed in the various black nationalist groups that are springing up across the nation, the largest and best-known being Elijah Muhammad's Muslim movement. Nourished by the Negro's frustration over the continued existence of racial discrimination, this movement is made up of people who have lost faith in America, who have absolutely repudiated Christianity, and who have concluded that the white man is an incorrigible "devil."

I have tried to stand between these two forces, saying that we need emulate neither the "do-nothingism" of the complacent nor the hatred and despair of the black nationalist. For there is the more excellent way of love and nonviolent protest. I am grateful to God that, through the influence of the Negro church, the way of nonviolence became an integral part of our struggle.

If this philosophy had not emerged, by now many streets of the South would, I am convinced, be flowing with blood. And I am further convinced that if our white brothers dismiss as "rabblerousers" and "outside agitators" those of us who employ nonviolent direct action, and if they refuse to support our nonviolent efforts, millions of Negroes will, out of frustration and despair, seek solace and security in black-nationalist ideologies—a development that would inevitably lead to a frightening racial nightmare.

30   Oppressed people cannot remain oppressed forever. The yearning for freedom eventually manifests itself, and that is what has happened to the American Negro. Something within has reminded him of his birthright of freedom, and something without has reminded him that it can be gained. Consciously or unconsciously, he has been caught up by the *Zeitgeist*,[12] and with his black brothers of Africa and his brown and yellow brothers of Asia, South America, and the Caribbean, the United States Negro is moving with a sense of great urgency toward the promised land of racial justice. If one recognizes this vital urge that has engulfed the Negro community, one should readily understand why public demonstrations are taking place. The Negro has many pent-up resentments and latent frustrations, and he must release them. So let him march; let him make prayer pilgrimages to the city hall; let him go on freedom rides—and try to understand why he must do so. If his repressed emotions are not released in nonviolent ways, they will seek expression through violence; this is not a threat but a fact of history. So I have not said to my people, "Get rid of your discontent." Rather, I have tried to say that this normal and healthy discontent can be channeled into the creative outlet of nonviolent direct action. And now this approach is being termed extremist.

But though I was initially disappointed at being categorized as an extremist, as I continued to think about the matter I gradually gained a measure of satisfaction from the label. Was not Jesus an extremist for love: "Love your enemies, bless them that curse you, do good to them that hate you, and pray for them which despitefully use you, and persecute you." Was not Amos an extremist for justice: "Let justice roll down like waters and righteousness like an ever-flowing stream." Was not Paul an extremist for the Christian gospel: "I bear in

---

[12]The spirit of the times. [Eds.]

my body the marks of the Lord Jesus." Was not Martin Luther an extremist: "Here I stand; I cannot do otherwise, so help me God." And John Bunyan: "I will stay in jail to the end of my days before I make a butchery of my conscience." And Abraham Lincoln: "This nation cannot survive half slave and half free." And Thomas Jefferson: "We hold these truths to be self-evident, that all men are created equal. . . ." So the question is not whether we will be extremists, but what kind of extremists we will be. Will we be extremists for hate or for love? Will we be extremists for the preservation of injustice or for the extension of justice? In that dramatic scene on Calvary's hill three men were crucified. We must never forget that all three were crucified for the same thing—the crime of extremism. Two were extremists for immorality, and thus fell below their environment. The other, Jesus Christ, was an extremist for love, truth, and goodness, and thereby rose above his environment. Perhaps the South, the nation, and the world are in dire need of creative extremists.

I had hoped that the white moderate would see this need. Perhaps I was too optimistic; perhaps I expected too much. I suppose I should have realized that few members of the oppressor race can understand the deep groans and passionate yearnings of the oppressed race, and still fewer have the vision to see that injustice must be rooted out by strong, persistent, and determined action. I am thankful, however, that some of our white brothers in the South have grasped the meaning of this social revolution and committed themselves to it. They are still all too few in quantity, but they are big in quality. Some—such as Ralph McGill, Lillian Smith, Harry Golden, James McBridge Dabbs, Ann Braden, and Sarah Patton Boyle—have written about our struggle in eloquent and prophetic terms. Others have marched with us down nameless streets of the South. They have languished in filthy, roach-infested jails, suffering the abuse and brutality of policemen who view them as "dirty nigger-lovers." Unlike so many of their moderate brothers and sisters, they have recognized the urgency of the moment and sensed the need for powerful "action" antidotes to combat the disease of segregation.

Let me take note of my other major disappointment. I have been so greatly disappointed with the white church and its leadership. Of course, there are some notable exceptions. I am not unmindful of the fact that each of you has taken some significant stands on this issue. I commend you, Reverend Stallings, for your Christian stand on this past Sunday, in welcoming Negroes to your worship service on a non-segregated basis. I commend the Catholic leaders of this state for integrating Spring Hill College several years ago.

But despite these notable exceptions, I must honestly reiterate that I have been disappointed with the church. I do not say this as one of those negative critics who can always find something wrong with the church. I say this as a minister of the gospel, who loves the church; who was nurtured in its bosom; who has been sustained by its spiritual blessings and who will remain true to it as long as the cord of life shall lengthen.

35 When I was suddenly catapulted into the leadership of the bus protest in Montgomery, Alabama, a few years ago, I felt we would be supported by the white church. I felt that the white ministers, priests, and rabbis of the South would be among our strongest allies. Instead, some have been outright opponents, refusing to understand the freedom movement and misrepresenting its leaders; all too many others have been more cautious than courageous and have remained silent behind the anesthetizing security of stained glass windows.

In spite of my shattered dreams, I came to Birmingham with the hope that the white religious leadership of this community would see the justice of our cause and, with deep moral concern, would serve as the channel through which our just grievances could reach the power structure. I had hoped that each of you would understand. But again I have been disappointed.

I have heard numerous southern religious leaders admonish their worshipers to comply with a desegregation decision because it is the law, but I have longed to hear white ministers declare: "Follow this decree because integration is morally right and because the Negro is your brother." In the midst of blatant injustices inflicted upon the Negro, I have watched white churchmen stand on the sideline and mouth pious irrelevancies and sanctimonious trivialities. In the midst of a mighty struggle to rid our nation of racial and economic injustice, I have heard many ministers say: "Those are social issues, with which the gospel has no real concern." And I have watched many churches commit themselves to a completely otherworldly religion which makes a strange, un-Biblical distinction between body and soul, between the sacred and the secular.

I have traveled the length and breadth of Alabama, Mississippi, and all the other southern states. On sweltering summer days and crisp autumn mornings I have looked at the South's beautiful churches with their lofty spires pointing heavenward. I have beheld the impressive outlines of her massive religious-education buildings. Over and over I have found myself asking: "What kind of people worship here? Who is their God? Where were their voices when the lips of Governor Barnett[13] dripped with words of interposition and nullification? Where were they when Governor Wallace[14] gave a clarion call for defiance

---

[13]Ross Barnett, segregationist governor of Mississippi, who strongly resisted the integration of the University of Mississippi in 1962. [Eds.]

[14]George Wallace, segregationist governor of Alabama, best known for standing in the doorway of a University of Alabama building to block the entrance of two black students who were trying to register. [Eds.]

and hatred? Where were their voices of support when bruised and weary Negro men and women decided to rise from the dark dungeons of complacency to the bright hills of creative protest?"

Yes, these questions are still in my mind. In deep disappointment I have wept over the laxity of the church. But be assured that my tears have been tears of love. There can be no deep disappointment where there is not deep love. Yes, I love the church. How could I do otherwise? I am in the rather unique position of being the son, the grandson, and the great-grandson of preachers. Yes, I see the church as the body of Christ. But, oh! How we have blemished and scarred that body through social neglect and through fear of being nonconformists.

There was a time when the church was very powerful—in the time when the early Christians rejoiced at being deemed worthy to suffer for what they believed. In those days the church was not merely a thermometer that recorded the ideas and principles of popular opinion; it was a thermostat that transformed the mores of society. Whenever the early Christians entered a town, the people in power became disturbed and immediately sought to convict the Christians for being "disturbers of the peace" and "outside agitators." But the Christians pressed on, in the conviction that they were "a colony of heaven," called to obey God rather than man. Small in number, they were big in commitment. They were too God-intoxicated to be "astronomically intimidated." By their effort and example they brought an end to such ancient evils as infanticide and gladiatorial contests.

Things are different now. So often the contemporary church is a weak, ineffectual voice with an uncertain sound. So often it is an archdefender to the status quo. Far from being disturbed by the presence of the church, the power structure of the average community is consoled by the church's silent—and often even vocal—sanction of things as they are.

But the judgment of God is upon the church as never before. If today's church does not recapture the sacrificial spirit of the early church, it will lose its authenticity, forfeit the loyalty of millions, and be dismissed as an irrelevant social club with no meaning for the twentieth century. Every day I meet young people whose disappointment with the church has turned into outright disgust.

Perhaps I have once again been too optimistic. Is organized religion too inextricably bound to the status quo to save our nation and the world? Perhaps I must turn my faith to the inner spiritual church, the church within the church, as the true *ekklesia*[15] and the hope of the world. But again I am thankful to God that some noble souls from the ranks of organized religion have broken loose from the paralyzing

---

[15]The Greek word for the early Christian church. [Eds.]

chains of conformity and joined us as active partners in the struggle for freedom. They have left their secure congregations and walked the streets of Albany, Georgia, with us. They have gone down the highways of the South on tortuous rides for freedom. Yes, they have gone to jail with us. Some have been dismissed from their churches, have lost the support of their bishops and fellow ministers. But they have acted in the faith that right defeated is stronger than evil triumphant. Their witness has been the spiritual salt that has preserved the true meaning of the gospel in these troubled times. They have carved a tunnel of hope through the dark mountain of disappointment.

I hope the church as a whole will meet the challenge of this decisive hour. But even if the church does not come to the aid of justice, I have no despair about the future. I have no fear about the outcome of our struggle in Birmingham, even if our motives are at present misunderstood. We will reach the goal of freedom in Birmingham and all over the nation, because the goal of America is freedom. Abused and scorned though we may be, our destiny is tied up with America's destiny. Before the pilgrims landed at Plymouth, we were here. Before the pen of Jefferson etched the majestic words of the Declaration of Independence across the pages of history, we were here. For more than two centuries our forebears labored in this country without wages; they made cotton king; they built the homes of their masters while suffering gross injustice and shameful humiliation—and yet out of a bottomless vitality they continued to thrive and develop. If the inexpressible cruelties of slavery could not stop us, the opposition we now face will surely fail. We will win our freedom because the sacred heritage of our nation and the eternal will of God are embodied in our echoing demands.

45   Before closing I feel impelled to mention one other point in your statement that has troubled me profoundly. You warmly commended the Birmingham police force for keeping "order" and "preventing violence." I doubt that you would have so warmly commended the police force if you had seen its dogs sinking their teeth into unarmed, nonviolent Negroes. I doubt that you would so quickly commend the policemen if you were to observe their ugly and inhumane treatment of Negroes here in the city jail; if you were to watch them push and curse old Negro women and young Negro girls; if you were to see them slap and kick old Negro men and young boys; if you were to observe them, as they did on two occasions, refuse to give us food because we wanted to sing our grace together. I cannot join you in your praise of the Birmingham police department.

It is true that the police have exercised a degree of discipline in handling the demonstrators. In this sense they have conducted themselves rather "nonviolently" in public. But for what purpose? To preserve the evil system of segregation. Over the past few years I have consistently preached that nonviolence demands that the means we use must be as pure as the ends we seek. I have tried to make clear that it is wrong to use immoral means to attain moral ends. But now I must affirm that it is just as wrong, or perhaps even more so, to use moral means to preserve immoral ends. Perhaps Mr. Connor and his policemen have been rather nonviolent in public, as was Chief Pritchett in Albany, Georgia, but they have used the moral means of nonviolence to maintain the immoral end of racial injustice. As T. S. Eliot[16] has said, "The last temptation is the greatest treason: To do the right deed for the wrong reason."

I wish you had commended the Negro sit-inners and demonstrators of Birmingham for their sublime courage, their willingness to suffer, and their amazing discipline in the midst of great provocation. One day the South will recognize its real heroes. They will be the James Merediths,[17] with the noble sense of purpose that enables them to face jeering and hostile mobs, and with the agonizing loneliness that characterizes the life of the pioneer. They will be old, oppressed, battered Negro women, symbolized in a seventy-two-year-old woman in Montgomery, Alabama, who rose up with a sense of dignity and with her people decided not to ride segregated buses, and who responded with ungrammatical profundity to one who inquired about her weariness: "My feets is tired, but my soul is at rest." They will be the young high school and college students, the young ministers of the gospel and a host of their elders, courageously and nonviolently sitting in at lunch counters and willingly going to jail for conscience' sake. One day the South will know that when these disinherited children of God sat down at lunch counters, they were in reality standing up for what is best in the American dream and for the most sacred values in our Judaeo-Christian heritage, thereby bringing our nation back to those great wells of democracy which were dug deep by the founding fathers in their formulation of the Constitution and the Declaration of Independence.

Never before have I written so long a letter. I'm afraid it is much too long to take your precious time. I can assure you that it would have been much shorter if I had been writing from a comfortable desk, but what else can one do when he is alone in a narrow jail cell, other than write long letters, think long thoughts, and pray long prayers?

If I have said anything in this letter that overstates the truth and indicates an unreasonable impatience, I beg you to forgive me. If I have said anything that understates the truth and indicates my having

---

[16]American-born British poet (1888–1965), winner of the 1948 Nobel Prize in Literature. [Eds.]

[17]First African American to enroll at the University of Mississippi, after federal troops were brought in to control demonstrators protesting his enrollment. [Eds.]

a patience that allows me to settle for anything less than brotherhood, I beg God to forgive me.

50   I hope this letter finds you strong in the faith. I also hope that circumstances will soon make it possible for me to meet each of you, not as an integrationist or a civil-rights leader but as a fellow clergyman and a Christian brother. Let us all hope that the dark clouds of racial prejudice will soon pass away and the deep fog of misunderstanding will be lifted from our fear-drenched communities, and in some not too distant tomorrow the radiant stars of love and brotherhood will shine over our great nation with all their scintillating beauty.

Yours for the cause of Peace and Brotherhood,
MARTIN LUTHER KING, JR.

Responding to Reading

1. What decision do the clergy members King addresses believe he should rethink? Do you believe King would have been justified in arguing that he had no alternative other than protest? Would you accept this argument?
2. In paragraph 30, King says, "Oppressed people cannot remain oppressed forever." Do you think world events of the last few years confirm or contradict this statement?
3. Throughout this letter, King uses elaborate diction and a variety of rhetorical devices: he addresses his audience directly; makes frequent use of balance and parallelism, understatement, and metaphor; and makes many historical and religious allusions. What effect do you think King intended these rhetorical devices to have on the letter's original audience of clergymen? Does King's elaborate style enhance his argument, or does it just get in the way?

Responding in Writing

Write a short manifesto advocating civil disobedience for a cause you strongly believe in. To inspire others to follow the course of action you propose, explain the goal you are seeking, and identify the opposing forces that you believe make civil disobedience necessary. Then, outline the form you expect your peaceful protest to take.

DOG LAB
Claire McCarthy
1963–

A graduate of Harvard Medical School, Claire McCarthy is now a faculty member there as well as co-director of the pediatrics department at the Martha Eliot Health Center in Boston and "on-call columnist" for Parenting *magazine. During her medical training, she kept detailed journals, which provided the basis for her books* Learning How the Heart Beats: The

Making of a Pediatrician *(1995) and* Everyone's Children: A Pediatrician's Story of an Inner-City Practice *(1998). In the following essay, a chapter from* Learning How the Heart Beats, *McCarthy recalls her reluctance to attend an optional lab lesson in which students studied the cardiovascular system of a sedated living dog, which was then euthanized.*

When I finished college and started medical school, the learning changed fundamentally. Whereas in college I had been learning mostly for learning's sake, learning in order to know something, in medical school I was learning in order to *do* something, do the thing I wanted to do with my life. It was exhilarating and at the same time a little scary. My study now carried responsibility.

The most important course in the first year besides Anatomy was Physiology, the study of the functions and processes of the human body. It was the most fascinating subject I had ever studied. I found the intricacies of the way the body works endlessly intriguing and ingenious: the way the nervous system is designed to differentiate a sharp touch from a soft one; the way muscles move and work together to throw a ball; the wisdom of the kidneys, which filter the blood and let pass out only waste products and extra fluid, keeping everything else carefully within. It was magical to me that each organ and system worked so beautifully and in perfect concert with the rest of the body.

The importance of Physiology didn't lie just in the fact that it was fascinating, however. The other courses I was taking that semester, like Histology and Biochemistry, were fascinating, too. But because Physiology was the study of how the body actually works, it seemed the most pertinent to becoming a physician. The other courses were more abstract. Physiology was practical, and I felt that my ability to master Physiology would be a measure of my ability to be a doctor.

When the second-year students talked about Physiology, they always mentioned "dog lab." They mentioned it briefly but significantly, sharing knowing looks. I gathered that it involved cutting dogs open and that it was controversial, but that was all I knew. I didn't pursue it, I didn't ask questions. That fall I was living day to day, lecture to lecture, test to test. My life was organized around putting as much information into my brain as possible, and I didn't pay much attention to anything else.

I would get up around six, make coffee, and eat my bowl of cereal   5
while I sat at my desk. There was nowhere else to sit in my dormitory room, and if I was going to sit at my desk, I figured I might as well study, so I always studied as I ate. I had a small refrigerator and a hot plate so that I could fix myself meals. After breakfast it was off to a morning of lectures, back to the room at lunchtime for a yogurt or soup and more studying, then afternoon lectures and labs. Before dinner I usually went for a run or a swim; although it was necessary for

my sanity and my health, I always felt guilty that I wasn't studying instead. I ate dinner at my desk or with other medical students at the cafeteria in Beth Israel Hospital. We sat among the doctors, staff, and patients, eating our food quickly. Although we would try to talk about movies, current affairs, or other "nonmedical" topics, sooner or later we usually ended up talking about medicine; it was fast becoming our whole life. After dinner it was off to the eerie quiet of the library, where I sat surrounded by my textbooks and notes until I got tired or frustrated, which was usually around ten-thirty. Then I'd go back to the dorm, maybe chat with the other students on my floor, maybe watch television, probably study some more, and then fall asleep so that I could start the routine all over again the next morning.

My life had never been so consuming. Sometimes I felt like a true student in the best sense of the word, wonderfully absorbed in learning; other times I felt like an automation. I was probably a combination of the two. It bothered me sometimes that this process of teaching me to take care of people was making me live a very study-centered, self-centered life. However, it didn't seem as though I had a choice.

One day at the beginning of a physiology lecture the instructor announced that we would be having a laboratory exercise to study the cardiovascular system, and that dogs would be used. The room was quickly quiet; this was the infamous "dog lab." The point of the exercise, he explained, was to study the heart and blood vessels in vivo[1] to learn the effects of different conditions and chemicals by seeing them rather than just by reading about them. The dogs would be sedated and the changes in their heart rates, respiratory rates, and blood pressure would be monitored with each experiment. As the last part of the exercise the sleeping dogs' chests would be cut open so we could actually watch the hearts and lungs in action, and then the dogs would be killed, humanely. We would be divided up into teams of four, and each team would work with a teaching assistant. Because so many teaching assistants were required, the class would be divided in half, and the lab would be held on two days.

The amphitheater buzzed.

The lab was optional, the instructor told us. We would not be marked off in any way if we chose not to attend. He leaned against the side of the podium and said that the way he saw it there was a spectrum of morality when it came to animal experimentation. The spectrum, he said, went from mice or rats to species like horses or apes, and we had to decide at which species we would draw our lines. He hoped, though, that we would choose to attend. It was an excellent learning opportunity, and he thought we ought to take advantage of it. Then he walked behind the podium and started the day's lecture.

---

[1]Latin phrase for "in the living being." [Eds.]

It was all anyone could talk about: should we do dog lab or 10 shouldn't we? We discussed it endlessly.

There were two main camps. One was the "excellent learning opportunity" camp, which insisted that dog lab was the kind of science we came to medical school to do and that learning about the cardiovascular system on a living animal would make it more understandable and would therefore make us better doctors.

Countering them was the "importance of a life" camp. The extreme members of this camp insisted that it was always wrong to murder an animal for experimentation. The more moderate members argued that perhaps animal experimentation was useful in certain kinds of medical research, but that dog lab was purely an exercise for our education and didn't warrant the killing of a dog. We could learn the material in other ways, they said.

On and on the arguments went, with people saying the same things over and over again in every conceivable way. There was something very important about this decision. Maybe it was because we were just beginning to figure out how to define ourselves as physicians—were we scientists, eager for knowledge, or were we defenders of life? The dog lab seemed to pit one against the other. Maybe it was because we thought that our lives as physicians were going to be filled with ethical decisions, and this was our first since entering medical school. It was very important that we do the right thing, but the right thing seemed variable and unclear.

I was quiet during these discussions. I didn't want to kill a dog, but I certainly wanted to take advantage of every learning opportunity offered me. And despite the fact that the course instructor had said our grades wouldn't be affected if we didn't attend the lab, I wasn't sure I believed him, and I didn't want to take any chances. Even if he didn't incorporate the lab report into our grades, I was worried that there would be some reference to it in the final exam, some sneaky way that he would bring it up. Doing well had become so important that I was afraid to trust anyone; doing well had become more important than anything.

I found myself waiting to see what other people would decide. I 15 was ashamed not to be taking a stand, but I was stuck in a way I'd never been before. I didn't like the idea of doing the lab; it felt wrong. Yet for some reason I was embarrassed that I felt that way, and the lab seemed so important. The more I thought about it, the more confused I became.

Although initially the students had appeared divided more or less evenly between the camps, as the lab day drew nearer the majority chose to participate. The discussions didn't stop, but they were fewer and quieter. The issue seemed to become more private.

I was assigned to the second lab day. My indecision was becoming a decision since I hadn't crossed my name off the list. I can still change my mind, I told myself. I'm not on a team yet, nobody's counting on me to show up. One of my classmates asked me to join his group. I hedged.

The day before group lists had to be handed in, the course instructor made an announcement. It was brief and almost offhand: he said that if any of us wished to help anesthetize the dogs for the lab, we were welcome to do so. He told us where to go and when to be there for each lab day. I wrote the information down.

Somehow, this was what I needed. I made my decision. I would do the lab, but I would go help anesthetize the dogs first.

20   Helping with the anesthesia, I thought, would be taking full responsibility for what I was doing, something that was very important to me. I was going to *face* what I was doing, see the dogs awake with their tails wagging instead of meeting them asleep and sort of pretending they weren't real. I also thought it might make me feel better to know that the dogs were treated well as they were anesthetized and to be there, helping to do it gently. Maybe in part I thought of it as my penance.

The day of the first lab came. Around five o'clock I went down to the Friday afternoon "happy hour" in the dormitory living room to talk to the students as they came back. They came back singly or in pairs, quiet, looking dazed. They threw down their coats and backpacks and made their way to the beer and soda without talking to anyone. Some, once they had a cup in their hands, seemed to relax and join in conversations; others took their cups and sat alone on the couches. They all looked tired, worn out.

"Well?" I asked several of them. "What was it like?"

Most shrugged and said little. A few said that it was interesting and that they'd learned a lot, but they said it without any enthusiasm. Every one of them said it was hard. I thought I heard someone say that their dog had turned out to be pregnant. Nobody seemed happy.

The morning of my lab was gray and dreary. I overslept, which I hardly ever do. I got dressed quickly and went across the street to the back entrance of the lab building. It was quiet and still and a little dark. The streets were empty except for an occasional cab. I found the open door and went in.

25   There was only one other student waiting there, a blond-haired woman named Elise. I didn't know her well. We had friends in common, but we'd never really talked. She was sweet and soft-spoken; she wore old jeans and plaid flannel shirts and hung out with the activist crowd. She had always intimidated me. I felt as though I weren't political enough when I was around her. I was actually a little surprised that she was doing the lab at all, as many of her friends had chosen not to.

We greeted each other awkwardly, nodding hello and taking our places leaning against the wall. Within a few minutes one of the teaching assistants came in, said good morning, pulled out some keys, and let us into a room down the hall. Two more teaching assistants followed shortly.

The teaching assistants let the dogs out of cages, and they ran around the room. They were small dogs; I think they were beagles. They seemed happy to be out of their cages, and one of them, white with brown spots, came over to me with his tail wagging. I leaned over to pet him, and he licked my hand, looking up at me eagerly. I stood up again quickly.

The teaching assistant who had let us in, a short man with tousled brown hair and thick glasses, explained that the dogs were to be given intramuscular injections of a sedative that would put them to sleep. During the lab they would be given additional doses intravenously as well as other medications to stop them from feeling pain. We could help, he said, by holding the dogs while they got their injections. Elise and I nodded.

So we held the dogs, and they got their injections. After a few minutes they started to stumble, and we helped them to the floor. I remember that Elise petted one of the dogs as he fell asleep and that she cried. I didn't cry, but I wanted to.

When we were finished, I went back to my room. I sat at my desk, 30 drank my coffee, and read over the lab instructions again. I kept thinking about the dogs running around, about the little white one with the brown spots, and I felt sick. I stared at the instructions without really reading them, looking at my watch every couple of minutes. At five minutes before eight I picked up the papers, put them in my backpack with my books, and left.

The lab was held in a big open room with white walls and lots of windows. The dogs were laid out on separate tables lined up across the room; they were on their backs, tied down. They were all asleep, but some of them moved slightly, and it chilled me.

We walked in slowly and solemnly, putting our coats and backpacks on the rack along the wall and going over to our assigned tables. I started to look for the dog who had licked my hand, but I stopped myself. I didn't want to know where he was.

Our dog was brown and black, with soft floppy ears. His eyes were shut. He looked familiar. We took our places, two on each side of the table, laid out our lab manuals, and began.

The lab took all day. We cut through the dog's skin to find an artery and vein, into which we placed catheters. We injected different drugs and chemicals and watched what happened to the dog's heart rate and blood pressure, carefully recording the results. At the end of the day, when we were done with the experiments, we cut open the dog's chest. We cut through his sternum and pulled open his rib cage. His heart and lungs lay in front of us. The heart was a fist-size muscle that squeezed itself as it beat, pushing blood out. The lungs were white and solid and glistening under the pleura that covered them. The instructor pointed out different blood vessels, like the aorta and the superior vena cava. He showed us the stellate ganglion, which really did look like a star. I think we used the electrical paddles of a defibrillator and shocked the dog's heart into ventricular fibrillation, watching it shiver like Jell-O in front of us. I think that's how we killed them—or maybe it was with a lethal dose of one of the drugs. I'm not sure. It's something I guess I don't want to remember.

35　　Dan was the anesthesiologist, the person assigned to making sure that the dog stayed asleep throughout the entire procedure. Every once in a while Dan would get caught up in the experiment and the dog would start to stir. I would nudge Dan, and he would quickly give more medication. The dog never actually woke up, but every time he moved even the slightest bit, every time I had to think about him being a real dog who was never going to wag his tail or lick anyone's hand again because of us, I got so upset that I couldn't concentrate. In fact, I had trouble concentrating on the lab in general. I kept staring at the dog.

As soon as we were finished, or maybe a couple of minutes before, I left. I grabbed my coat and backpack and ran down the stairs out into the dusk of the late afternoon. It was drizzling, and the medical school looked brown and gray. I walked quickly toward the street.

I was disappointed in the lab and disappointed in myself for doing it. I knew now that doing the lab was wrong. Maybe not wrong for everyone—it was clearly a complicated and individual choice—but wrong for me. The knowledge I had gained wasn't worth the life of a dog to me. I felt very sad.

The drizzle was becoming rain. I slowed down; even though it was cold, the rain felt good. A couple of people walking past me put up their umbrellas. I let the rain fall on me. I wanted to get wet.

From the moment you enter the field of medicine as a medical student, you have an awareness that you have entered something bigger and more important than you are. Doctors are different from other people, we are told implicitly, if not explicitly. Medicine is a way of life, with its own values and guidelines for daily living. They aren't bad values; they include things like the importance of hard work, the pursuit of knowledge, and the preservation of life—at least human life. There's room for individuality and variation, but that's something I realized later, much later. When I started medical school I felt that not only did I have to learn information and skills, I had to become a certain kind of person, too. It was very important to me to learn to do the thing that a doctor would do in a given situation. Since the course instructor, who represented Harvard Medical School to me, had recommended that we do the lab, I figured that a doctor would do it. That wasn't the only reason I went ahead with the lab, but it was a big reason.

The rain started to come down harder and felt less pleasant. I 40 walked more quickly, across Longwood Avenue into Vanderbilt Hall. I could hear familiar voices coming from the living room, but I didn't feel like talking to anyone. I ducked into the stairwell.

I got to my room, locked the door behind me, took off my coat, and lay down on my bed. The rain beat against my window. It was the time I usually went running, but the thought of going back out in the rain didn't appeal to me at all. I was suddenly very tired.

As I lay there I thought about the course instructor's discussion of the spectrum of morality and drawing lines. Maybe it's not a matter of deciding which animals I feel comfortable killing, I thought. Maybe it's about drawing different kinds of lines: drawing the lines to define how much of myself I will allow to change. I was proud of being a true student, even if it did mean becoming a little like an automaton. But I still needed to be the person I was before; I needed to be able to make some decisions without worrying about what a doctor would do.

I got up off the bed, opened a can of soup, and put it in a pan on the hot plate to warm. I got some bread and cheese out of the refrigerator, sat down at my desk, and opened my Biochemistry text.

Suddenly I stopped. I closed the text, reached over, and turned on the television, which sat on a little plastic table near the desk. There would be time to study later. I was going to watch television, read a newspaper, and call some friends I hadn't called since starting medical school. It was time to make some changes, some changes back.

Responding to Reading

1. Summarize the two main schools of thought about whether or not to participate in "dog lab." Do the students really have a choice? Explain.
2. Why did McCarthy decide to help anesthetize the dogs? Does her decision make sense to you?
3. Does McCarthy believe that the knowledge she gained was worth the sacrifice of the dog? Do you agree with her? Do you think her experience in "dog lab" changed her? Do you think it made her a better doctor?

Responding in Writing

Do you see a difference in the relative value of the lives of a laboratory animal, an animal in the wild, and a pet? Or, do you think the lives of all three kinds of animals have equal value? Explain your beliefs.

THE PERILS OF OBEDIENCE

Stanley Milgram

1932–1984

Social psychologist Stanley Milgram is best known for his experiments that study aggression and human conformity, especially obedience (he used Nazi Germany as a tragic example of submission to authority). He has said that "it is only the person dwelling in isolation who is not forced to respond, with defiance or submission, to the commands of others." In the following selection, from his book Obedience to Authority *(1974), Milgram's descriptions of some of his experiments on obedience raise perplexing moral questions.*

Obedience is as basic an element in the structure of social life as one can point to. Some system of authority is a requirement of all communal living, and it is only the person dwelling in isolation who is not forced to respond, with defiance or submission, to the commands of others. For many people, obedience is a deeply ingrained behavior tendency, indeed a potent impulse overriding training in ethics, sympathy, and moral conduct.

The dilemma inherent in submission to authority is ancient, as old as the story of Abraham,[1] and the question of whether one should obey when commands conflict with conscience has been argued by Plato, dramatized in *Antigone*,[2] and treated to philosophic analysis in almost every historical epoch. Conservative philosophers argue that the very fabric of society is threatened by disobedience, while humanists stress the primacy of the individual conscience.

The legal and philosophic aspects of obedience are of enormous import, but they say very little about how most people behave in concrete situations. I set up a simple experiment at Yale University to test how much pain an ordinary citizen would inflict on another person simply because he was ordered to by an experimental scientist. Stark authority was pitted against the subjects' strongest moral imperatives against hurting others, and, with the subjects' ears ringing with the screams of the victims, authority won more often than not. The extreme willingness of adults to go to almost any lengths on the command of an authority constitutes the chief finding of the study and the fact most urgently demanding explanation.

In the basic experimental design, two people come to a psychology laboratory to take part in a study of memory and learning. One of

---

[1]Abraham, commanded by God to sacrifice his son Isaac, is ready to do so until an angel stops him. [Eds.]

[2]In Plato's *Apology*, the philosopher Socrates provokes and accepts the sentence of death rather than act against his conscience; the heroine of Sophocles' *Antigone* risks a death sentence in order to give her brother a proper burial. [Eds.]

them is designated as a "teacher" and the other a "learner." The experimenter explains that the study is concerned with the effects of punishment on learning. The learner is conducted into a room, seated in a kind of miniature electric chair; his arms are strapped to prevent excessive movement, and an electrode is attached to his wrist. He is told that he will be read lists of simple word pairs, and that he will then be tested on his ability to remember the second word of a pair when he hears the first one again. Whenever he makes an error, he will receive electric shocks of increasing intensity.

The real focus of the experiment is the teacher. After watching the learner being strapped into place, he is seated before an impressive shock generator. The instrument panel consists of thirty lever switches set in a horizontal line. Each switch is clearly labeled with a voltage designation ranging from 15 to 450 volts. The following designations are clearly indicated for groups of four switches, going from left to right: Slight Shock, Moderate Shock, Strong Shock, Very Strong Shock, Intense Shock, Extreme Intensity Shock, Danger: Severe Shock. (Two switches after this last designation are simply marked XXX.)

When a switch is depressed, a pilot light corresponding to each switch is illuminated in bright red; an electric buzzing is heard; a blue light, labeled "voltage energizer," flashes; the dial on the voltage meter swings to the right; and various relay clicks sound off.

The upper left-hand corner of the generator is labeled SHOCK GENERATOR, TYPE ZLB, DYSON INSTRUMENT COMPANY, WALTHAM, MASS. OUTPUT 15 VOLTS–450 VOLTS.

Each subject is given a sample 45-volt shock from the generator before his run as teacher, and the jolt strengthens his belief in the authenticity of the machine.

The teacher is a genuinely naïve subject who has come to the laboratory for the experiment. The learner, or victim, is actually an actor who receives no shock at all. The point of the experiment is to see how far a person will proceed in a concrete and measurable situation in which he is ordered to inflict increasing pain on a protesting victim.

Conflict arises when the man receiving the shock begins to show that he is experiencing discomfort. At 75 volts, he grunts; at 120 volts, he complains loudly; at 150, he demands to be released from the experiment. As the voltage increases, his protests become more vehement and emotional. At 285 volts, his response can be described only as an agonized scream. Soon thereafter, he makes no sound at all.

For the teacher, the situation quickly becomes one of gripping tension. It is not a game for him; conflict is intense and obvious. The manifest suffering of the learner presses him to quit; but each time he hesitates to administer a shock, the experimenter orders him to continue. To extricate himself from this plight, the subject must make a clear break with authority.[3]

The subject, Gretchen Brandt,[4] is an attractive thirty-one-year-old medical technician who works at the Yale Medical School. She had emigrated from Germany five years before.

On several occasions when the learner complains, she turns to the experimenter coolly and inquires, "Shall I continue"? She promptly returns to her task when the experimenter asks her to do so. At the administration of 210 volts, she turns to the experimenter, remarking firmly, "Well, I'm sorry, I don't think we should continue."

> EXPERIMENTER: The experiment requires that you go on until he has learned all the word pairs correctly.
> BRANDT: He has a heart condition, I'm sorry. He told you that before.
> EXPERIMENTER: The shocks may be painful but they are not dangerous.
> BRANDT: Well, I'm sorry, I think when shocks continue like this, they are dangerous. You ask him if he wants to get out. It's his free will.
> EXPERIMENTER: It is absolutely essential that we continue . . .
> BRANDT: I'd like you to ask him. We came here of our free will. If he wants to continue I'll go ahead. He told you he had a heart condition. I'm sorry. I don't want to be responsible for anything happening to him. I wouldn't like it for me either.
> EXPERIMENTER: You have no other choice.
> BRANDT: I think we are here on our own free will. I don't want to be responsible if anything happens to him. Please understand that.

She refuses to go further and the experiment is terminated.

15   The woman is firm and resolute throughout. She indicates in the interview that she was in no way tense or nervous, and this corresponds to her controlled appearance during the experiment. She feels that the last shock she administered to the learner was extremely painful and reiterates that she "did not want to be responsible for any harm to him."

The woman's straightforward, courteous behavior in the experiment, lack of tension, and total control of her own action seem to make disobedience a simple and rational deed. Her behavior is the very embodiment of what I envisioned would be true for almost all subjects.

Before the experiments, I sought predictions about the outcome from various kinds of people—psychiatrists, college sophomores, middle-class adults, graduate students and faculty in the behavioral

---

[3]The ethical problems of carrying out an experiment of this sort are too complex to be dealt with here, but they receive extended treatment in the book from which this article is adapted. [The book is *Obedience to Authority* (New York: Harper & Row, 1974)—Eds.]
[4]Names of subjects described in this piece have been changed.

sciences. With remarkable similarity, they predicted that virtually all subjects would refuse to obey the experimenter. The psychiatrists specifically predicted that most subjects would not go beyond 150 volts, when the victim makes his first explicit demand to be freed. They expected that only 4 percent would reach 300 volts, and that only a pathological fringe of about one in a thousand would administer the highest shock on the board.

These predictions were unequivocally wrong. Of the forty subjects in the first experiment, twenty-five obeyed the orders of the experimenter to the end, punishing the victim until they reached the most potent shock available on the generator. After 450 volts were administered three times, the experimenter called a halt to the sessions. Many obedient subjects then heaved sighs of relief, mopped their brows, rubbed their fingers over their eyes, or nervously fumbled cigarettes. Others displayed only minimal signs of tension from beginning to end.

When the very first experiments were carried out, Yale undergraduates were used as subjects, and about 60 percent of them were fully obedient. A colleague of mine immediately dismissed these findings as having no relevance to "ordinary" people, asserting that Yale undergraduates are a highly aggressive, competitive bunch who step on each other's necks on the slightest provocation. He assured me that when "ordinary" people were tested, the results would be quite different. As we moved from the pilot studies to the regular experimental series, people drawn from every stratum of New Haven life came to be employed in the experiment: professionals, white-collar workers, unemployed persons, and industrial workers. *The experimental outcome was the same as we had observed among the students.*

Moreover, when the experiments were repeated in Princeton, Munich, Rome, South Africa, and Australia, the level of obedience was invariably somewhat *higher* than found in the investigation reported in this article. Thus one scientist in Munich found 85 percent of his subjects obedient. 20

Fred Prozi's reactions, if more dramatic than most, illuminate the conflicts experienced by others in less visible form. About fifty years old and unemployed at the time of the experiment, he has a good-natured, if slightly dissolute, appearance, and he strikes people as a rather ordinary fellow. He begins the session calmly but becomes tense as it proceeds. After delivering the 180-volt shock, he pivots around in his chair and, shaking his head, addresses the experimenter in agitated tones:

> PROZI: I can't stand it. I'm not going to kill that man in there. You hear him hollering?
> EXPERIMENTER: As I told you before, the shocks may be painful, but . . .
> PROZI: But he's hollering. He can't stand it. What's going to happen to him?

EXPERIMENTER: (his voice is patient, matter-of-fact): The experiment requires that you continue, Teacher.

PROZI: Aaah, but, unh, I'm not going to get that man sick in there—know what I mean?

EXPERIMENTER: Whether the learner likes it or not, we must go on, through all the word pairs.

PROZI: I refuse to take the responsibility. He's in there hollering!

EXPERIMENTER: It's absolutely essential that you continue, Prozi.

PROZI: (indicating the unused questions): There's too many left here, I mean, Jeez, if he gets them wrong, there's too many of them left. I mean, who's going to take the responsibility if anything happens to that gentleman?

EXPERIMENTER: I'm responsible for anything that happens to him. Continue, please.

PROZI: All right. (Consults list of words.) The next one's "Slow—walk, truck, dance, music." Answer, please. (A buzzing sound indicates the learner has signaled his answer.) Wrong. A hundred and ninety-five volts. "Dance." (Zzumph!)

learner (yelling): Let me out of here! My heart's bothering me! (Teacher looks at experimenter.)

EXPERIMENTER: Continue, please.

LEARNER (screaming): Let me out of here! You have no right to keep me here! Let me out of here, my heart's bothering me, let me out!

PROZI: (shakes head, pats the table nervously): You see, he's hollering. Hear that? Gee, I don't know.

EXPERIMENTER: The experiment requires . . .

PROZI: (interrupting): I know it does, sir, but I mean—hunh! He don't know what he's getting in for. He's up to 195 volts! (Experiment continues, through 210 volts, 225 volts, 240 volts, 255 volts, 270 volts, at which point Prozi, with evident relief, runs out of word-pair questions.)

EXPERIMENTER: You'll have to go back to the beginning of that page and go through them again until he's learned them all correctly.

PROZI: Aw, no. I'm not going to kill that man. You mean I've got to keep going up with the scale? No sir. He's hollering in there. I'm not going to give him 450 volts.

EXPERIMENTER: The experiment requires that you go on.

LEARNER: Ohhh. I absolutely refuse to answer anymore. (Shouting urgently now.) Let me out of here! You can't hold me here! Get me out. Get-me-out-of-here!

EXPERIMENTER: Continue. The next word is "Green," please.

PROZI: "Green—grass, hat, ink, apple." (Nothing happens. No answering buzz. Just gloomy silence.)

PROZI: I don't think he is going to answer.

EXPERIMENTER: If the learner doesn't answer in a reasonable time, about four or five seconds, consider the answer wrong. And follow the same procedures you have been doing for wrong answers. Say, "Wrong," tell him the number of volts, give him the punishment, read him the correct answer. Continue, please.

PROZI: "Green—grass, hat, ink, apple." Answer, please. (More silence. Subject just sits there.)

EXPERIMENTER: Go on with the procedure, please.

PROZI: Three hundred and fifteen volts. The answer is "ink." (Zzumph!)

LEARNER: Ohh. Oooohh.

PROZI: (relieved to hear response): Next one . . .

LEARNER: I absolutely refuse to answer.

PROZI: You got to. You get a shock if you don't answer. (Experiment continues with learner refusing to answer, and, finally, failing even to grunt or groan. At 375 volts, the subject stands up.)

PROZI: I think something's happening to that fellow in there. I don't get no answer. He was hollering at less voltage. Can't you check in and see if he's all right, please?

EXPERIMENTER: (with same detached calm): Not once we've started. Please continue, Teacher.

PROZI: (sits down, sighs deeply): "Cool—day, shade, water, paint." Answer, please. Are you all right in there? Are you all right?

EXPERIMENTER: Please continue, Teacher. Continue, please. (Subject pushes lever. Zzumph!)

PROZI: (swiveling around in his chair): Something's happened to that man in there. (Swiveling back.) Next one. "Low—dollar, necklace, moon, paint." (Turning around again.) Something's happened to that man in there. You better check in on him, sir. He won't answer or nothing.

EXPERIMENTER: Continue. Go on, please.

PROZI: You accept all responsibility?

EXPERIMENTER: The responsibility is mine. Correct. Please go on. (Subject returns to his list, starts running through words as rapidly as he can read them, works through to 450 volts.)

PROZI: That's that.

EXPERIMENTER: Continue using the 450 switch for each wrong answer. Continue, please.

PROZI: But I don't get anything!

EXPERIMENTER: Please continue. The next word is "white."

PROZI: Don't you think you should look in on him, please?

EXPERIMENTER: Not once we've started the experiment.

PROZI: What if he's dead in there? (Gestures toward the room with the electric chair.) I mean, he told me he can't stand the shock, sir. I don't mean to be rude, but I think you should look

in on him. All you have to do is look in on him. All you have to
do is look in the door. I don't get no answer, no noise. Something might have happened to the gentleman in there, sir.
EXPERIMENTER: We must continue. Go on, please.
PROZI: You mean keep giving him what? Four-hundred-fifty
volts, what he's got now?
EXPERIMENTER: That's correct. Continue. The next word is "white."
PROZI: (now at a furious pace): "White—cloud, horse, rock,
house." Answer, please. The answer is "horse." Four hundred
and fifty volts. (Zzumph!) Next word, "Bag—paint, music,
clown, girl." The answer is "paint." Four hundred and fifty
volts. (Zzumph!) Next word is "Short—sentence, movie . . ."
EXPERIMENTER: Excuse me, Teacher. We'll have to discontinue
the experiment.

Morris Braverman, another subject, is a thirty-nine-year-old social
worker. He looks older than his years because of his bald head and serious demeanor. His brow is furrowed, as if all the world's burdens
were carried on his face. He appears intelligent and concerned.

When the learner refuses to answer and the experimenter instructs Braverman to treat the absence of an answer as equivalent to a
wrong answer, he takes his instruction to heart. Before administering
300 volts he asserts officiously to the victim, "Mr. Wallace, your silence has to be considered as a wrong answer." Then he administers
the shock. He offers halfheartedly to change places with the learner,
then asks the experimenter. "Do I have to follow these instructions literally?" He is satisfied with the experimenter's answer that he does.
His very refined and authoritative manner of speaking is increasingly
broken up by wheezing laughter.

The experimenter's notes on Mr. Braverman at the last few shocks
are:

25   *Almost breaking up now each time gives shock. Rubbing face to hide
laughter.*

  Squinting, trying to hide face with hand, still laughing.
  Cannot control his laughter at this point no matter what he does.
  Clenching fist, pushing it onto table.

In an interview after the session, Mr. Braverman summarizes the
experiment with impressive fluency and intelligence. He feels the experiment may have been designed also to "test the effects on the
teacher of being in an essentially sadistic role, as well as the reactions
of a student to a learning situation that was authoritative and punitive." When asked how painful the last few shocks administered to
the learner were, he indicates that the most extreme category on the
scale is not adequate (it read EXTREMELY PAINFUL) and places his mark
at the edge of the scale with an arrow carrying it beyond the scale.

It is almost impossible to convey the greatly relaxed, sedate qual- 30
ity of his conversation in the interview. In the most relaxed terms, he
speaks about his severe inner tension.

> EXPERIMENTER: At what point were you most tense or nervous?
> MR. BRAVERMAN: Well, when he first began to cry out in pain,
> and I realized this was hurting him. This got worse when he
> just blocked and refused to answer. There was I. I'm a nice
> person, I think, hurting somebody, and caught up in what
> seemed a mad situation . . . and in the interest of science, one
> goes through with it.

When the interviewer pursues the general question of tension,
Mr. Braverman spontaneously mentions his laughter.

"My reactions were awfully peculiar. I don't know if you were
watching me, but my reactions were giggly, and trying to stifle laughter. This isn't the way I usually am. This was a sheer reaction to a totally impossible situation. And my reaction was to the situation of
having to hurt somebody. And being totally helpless and caught up in
a set of circumstances where I just couldn't deviate and I couldn't try
to help. This is what got me."

Mr. Braverman, like all subjects, was told the actual nature and purpose of the experiment, and a year later he affirmed in a questionnaire
that he had learned something of personal importance: "What appalled
me was that I could possess this capacity for obedience and compliance to
a central idea, i.e., the value of a memory experiment, even after it became
clear that continued adherence to this value was at the expense of violation of another value, i.e., don't hurt someone who is helpless and not
hurting you. As my wife said, 'You can call yourself Eichmann.[5] I hope I
deal more effectively with any future conflicts of values encounter."

One theoretical interpretation of this behavior holds that all people
harbor deeply aggressive instincts continually pressing for expression,
and that the experiment provides institutional justification for the release of these impulses. According to this view, if a person is placed in
a situation in which he has complete power over another individual,
whom he may punish as much as he likes, all that is sadistic and bestial in man comes to the fore. The impulse to shock the victim is seen
to flow from the potent aggressive tendencies, which are part of the
motivational life of the individual, and the experiment, because it provides social legitimacy, simply opens the door to their expression.

It becomes vital, therefore, to compare the subject's performance 35
when he is under orders and when he is allowed to choose the shock
level.

---

[5]Nazi officer, executed in 1962, who engineered the mass extermination of Jews. Many concentration camp officials defended themselves afterward by saying they were "just following orders."
[Eds.]

The procedure was identical to our standard experiment, except that the teacher was told that he was free to select any shock level on any of the trials. (The experimenter took pains to point out that the teacher could use the highest levels on the generator, the lowest, any in between, or any combination of levels.) Each subject proceeded for thirty critical trials. The learner's protests were coordinated to standard shock levels, his first grunt coming at 75 volts, his first vehement protest at 150 volts.

The average shock used during the thirty critical trials was less than 60 volts—lower than the point at which the victim showed the first signs of discomfort. Three of the forty subjects did not go beyond the very low-est level on the board, twenty-eight went no higher than 75 volts, and thirty-eight did not go beyond the first loud protest at 150 volts. Two subjects provided the exception, administering up to 325 and 450 volts, but the overall result was that the great majority of people delivered very low, usually painless, shocks when the choice was explicitly up to them.

This condition of the experiment undermines another commonly of-fered explanation of the subjects' behavior—that those who shocked the victim at the most severe levels came only from the sadistic fringe of so-ciety. If one considers that almost two-thirds of the participants fall into the category of "obedient" subjects, and that they represented ordinary people drawn from working, managerial, and professional classes, the argument becomes very shaky. Indeed, it is highly reminiscent of the issue that arose in connection with Hannah Arendt's 1963 book, *Eichmann in Jerusalem.* Arendt contended that the prosecution's effort to depict Eichmann as a sadistic monster was fundamentally wrong, that he came closer to being an uninspired bureaucrat who simply sat at his desk and did his job. For asserting her views, Arendt became the object of considerable scorn, even calumny. Somehow, it was felt that the mon-strous deeds carried out by Eichmann required a brutal, twisted person-ality, evil incarnate. After witnessing hundreds of ordinary persons submit to the authority in our own experiments, I must conclude that Arendt's conception of the banality of evil comes closer to the truth than one might dare imagine. The ordinary person who shocked the victim did so out of a sense of obligation—an impression of his duties as a sub-ject—and not from any peculiarly aggressive tendencies.

This is, perhaps, the most fundamental lesson of our study: ordi-nary people, simply doing their jobs, and without any particular hos-tility on their part, can become agents in a terrible destructive process. Moreover, even when the destructive effects of their work become patently clear, and they are asked to carry out actions incompatible with fundamental standards of morality, relatively few people have the resources needed to resist authority.

40   Many of the people were in some sense against what they did to the learner, and many protested even while they obeyed. Some were totally convinced of the wrongness of their actions but could not

bring themselves to make an open break with authority. They often derived satisfaction from their thoughts and felt that—within themselves, at least—they had been on the side of the angels. They tried to reduce strain by obeying the experimenter but "only slightly" encouraging the learner, touching the generator switches gingerly. When interviewed, such a subject would stress that he had "asserted my humanity" by administering the briefest shock possible. Handling the conflict in this manner was easier than defiance.

The situation is constructed so that there is no way the subject can stop shocking the learner without violating the experimenter's definitions of his own competence. The subject fears that he will appear arrogant, untoward, and rude if he breaks off. Although these inhibiting emotions appear small in scope alongside the violence being done to the learner, they suffuse the mind and feelings of the subject, who is miserable at the prospect of having to repudiate the authority to his face. (When the experiment was altered so that the experimenter gave his instructions by telephone instead of in person, only a third as many people were fully obedient through 450 volts.) It is a curious thing that a measure of compassion on the part of the subject—an unwillingness to "hurt" the experimenter's feelings—is part of those binding forces inhibiting his disobedience. The withdrawal of such deference may be as painful to the subject as to the authority he defies.

The subjects do not derive satisfaction from inflicting pain, but they often like the feeling they get from pleasing the experimenter. They are proud of doing a good job, obeying the experimenter under difficult circumstances. While the subjects administered only mild shocks on their own initiative, one experimental variation showed that, under orders, 30 percent of them were willing to deliver 450 volts even when they had to forcibly push the learner's hand down on the electrode.

Bruno Batta is a thirty-seven-year-old welder who took part in the variation requiring the use of force. He was born in New Haven, his parents in Italy. He has a rough-hewn face that conveys a conspicuous lack of alertness. He has some difficulty in mastering the experimental procedure and needs to be corrected by the experimenter several times. He shows appreciation for the help and willingness to do what is required. After the 150-volt level, Batta has to force the learner's hand down on the shock plate, since the learner himself refuses to touch it.

When the learner first complains, Mr. Batta pays no attention to him. His face remains impassive, as if to dissociate himself from the learner's disruptive behavior. When the experimenter instructs him to force the learner's hand down, he adopts a rigid, mechanical procedure. He tests the generator switch. When it fails to function he immediately forces the learner's hand onto the shock plate. All the while he maintains the same rigid mask. The learner, seated alongside him, begs him to stop, but with robotic impassivity he continues the procedure.

45   What is extraordinary is his apparent total indifference to the learner; he hardly takes cognizance of him as a human being. Meanwhile, he relates to the experimenter in a submissive and courteous fashion.

At the 330-volt level, the learner refuses not only to touch the shock plate but also to provide any answers. Annoyed, Batta turns to him, and chastises him: "You better answer and get it over with. We can't stay here all night." These are the only words he directs to the learner in the course of an hour. Never again does he speak to him. The scene is brutal and depressing, his hard, impassive face showing total indifference as he subdues the screaming learner and gives him shocks. He seems to derive no pleasure from the act itself, only quiet satisfaction at doing his job properly.

When he administers 450 volts, he turns to the experimenter and asks, "Where do we go from here, Professor?" His tone is deferential and expresses his willingness to be a cooperative subject, in contrast to the learner's obstinacy.

At the end of the session he tells the experimenter how honored he has been to help him, and in a moment of contrition, remarks, "Sir, sorry it couldn't have been a full experiment."

He has done his honest best. It is only the deficient behavior of the learner that has denied the experimenter full satisfaction.

50   The essence of obedience is that a person comes to view himself as the instrument for carrying out another person's wishes, and he therefore no longer regards himself as responsible for his actions. Once this critical shift of viewpoint has occurred, all of the essential features of obedience follow. The most far-reaching consequence is that the person feels responsible to the authority directing him but feels no responsibility *for* the content of the actions that the authority prescribes. Morality does not disappear—it acquires a radically different focus: the subordinate person feels shame or pride depending on how adequately he has performed the actions called for by authority.

Language provides numerous terms to pinpoint this type of morality: *loyalty, duty, discipline* all are terms heavily saturated with moral meaning and refer to the degree to which a person fulfills his obligations to authority. They refer not to the "goodness" of the person per se but to the adequacy with which a subordinate fulfills his socially defined role. The most frequent defense of the individual who has performed a heinous act under command of authority is that he has simply done his duty. In asserting this defense, the individual is not introducing an alibi concocted for the moment but is reporting honestly on the psychological attitude induced by submission to authority.

For a person to feel responsible for his actions, he must sense that the behavior has flowed from "the self." In the situation we have studied, subjects have precisely the opposite view of their actions—namely, they see them as originating in the motives of some other person. Subjects in the experiment frequently said, "If it were up to me, I would not have administered shocks to the learner."

Once authority has been isolated as the cause of the subject's behavior, it is legitimate to inquire into the necessary elements of authority and how it must be perceived in order to gain his compliance. We conducted some investigations into the kinds of changes that would cause the experimenter to lose his power and to be disobeyed by the subject. Some of the variations revealed that:

> *The experimenter's physical presence has a marked impact on his authority.* As cited earlier, obedience dropped off sharply when orders were given by telephone. The experimenter could often induce a disobedient subject to go on by returning to the laboratory.

> *Conflicting authority severely paralyzes action.* When two experimenters of equal status, both seated at the command desk, gave incompatible orders, no shocks were delivered past the point of their disagreement.

> *The rebellious action of others severely undermines authority.* In one variation, three teachers (two actors and a real subject) administered a test and shocks. When the two actors disobeyed the experimenter and refused to go beyond a certain shock level, thirty-six of forty subjects joined their disobedient peers and refused as well.

Although the experimenter's authority was fragile in some respects, it is also true that he had almost none of the tools used in ordinary command structures. For example, the experimenter did not threaten the subjects with punishment—such as loss of income, community ostracism, or jail—for failure to obey. Neither could he offer incentives. Indeed, we should expect the experimenter's authority to be much less than that of someone like a general, since the experimenter has no power to enforce his imperatives, and since participation in a psychological experiment scarcely evokes the sense of urgency and dedication found in warfare. Despite these limitations, he still managed to command a dismaying degree of obedience.

I will cite one final variation of the experiment that depicts a 55 dilemma that is more common in everyday life. The subject was not ordered to pull the lever that shocked the victim, but merely to perform a subsidiary task (administering the word-pair test) while another person administered the shock. In this situation, thirty-seven of forty adults continued to the highest level of the shock generator. Predictably, they excused their behavior by saying that the responsibility belonged to the man who actually pulled the switch. This may illustrate a dangerously typical arrangement in a complex society: it is easy to ignore responsibility when one is only an intermediate link in a chain of action.

The problem of obedience is not wholly psychological. The form and shape of society and the way it is developing have much to do with it. There was a time, perhaps, when people were able to give a fully human response to any situation because they were fully absorbed in it as human beings. But as soon as there was a division of labor things changed. Beyond a certain point, the breaking up of society into people carrying out narrow and very special jobs takes away from the human quality of work and life. A person does not get to see the whole situation but only a small part of it, and is thus unable to act without some kind of overall direction. He yields to authority but in doing so is alienated from his own actions.

Even Eichmann was sickened when he toured the concentration camps, but he had only to sit at a desk and shuffle papers. At the same time the man in the camp who actually dropped Cyclon-b into the gas chambers was able to justify *his* behavior on the ground that he was only following orders from above. Thus there is a fragmentation of the total human act; no one is confronted with the consequences of his decision to carry out the evil act. The person who assumes responsibility has evaporated. Perhaps this is the most common characteristic of socially organized evil in modern society.

Responding to Reading

1. What is the "dilemma inherent in submission to authority" (2)? How do Milgram's experiments illustrate this dilemma? Why do you suppose virtually no one predicted that the subjects would continue to obey the orders of the experimenter?
2. Do you see the subjects as ordinary people—cooperative, obedient, and eager to please—or as weak individuals, too timid to defy authority? Explain.
3. In paragraph 51, Milgram says, "The most frequent defense of the individual who has performed a heinous act under command of authority is that he has simply done his duty." In your opinion, can such a defense ever excuse a "heinous act"? If so, under what circumstances?

Responding in Writing

List all the individuals whom you see as having authority over you. What gives them this authority? Under what circumstances would you feel it was necessary to defy each of these people?

The Ones Who Walk Away from Omelas

Ursula K. Le Guin

1929–

Ursula K. Le Guin has written science fiction and fantasy, fiction, screen-plays, poetry, and essays, some of which reflect her interests in Eastern phi-losophy and Jungian psychology. Her novels include The Left Hand of Darkness *(1969),* The Lathe of Heaven *(1971),* Dispossessed *(1974), A* Fisherman of the Inland Sea *(1994), and* The Telling *(2000); she has also written a book of poetry,* Hard Words *(1981), and children's books. Her lat-est work is* The Earthsea Quartet *(2003). In her book of essays* The Lan-guage of the Night *(1979), Le Guin says that, "the use of imaginative fiction is to deepen your understanding of your world, and your fellow men, and your own feelings, and your destiny." In the 1975 story that follows, she creates a scenario that offers a test of conscience.*

With a clamor of bells that set the swallows soaring, the Festival of Summer came to the city Omelas, bright-towered by the sea. The rig-ging of the boats in harbor sparkled with flags. In the streets between houses with red roofs and painted walls, between old moss-grown gardens and under avenues of trees, past great parks and public buildings, processions moved. Some were decorous: old people in long stiff robes of mauve and grey, grave master workmen, quiet, merry women carrying their babies and chatting as they walked. In other streets the music beat faster, a shimmering of gong and tam-bourine, and the people went dancing, the procession was a dance. Children dodged in and out, their high calls rising like the swallows' crossing flights over the music and the singing. All the processions wound towards the north side of the city, where on the great water-meadow called the Green Fields boys and girls, naked in the bright air, with mud-stained feet and ankles and long lithe arms, exercised their restive horses before the race. The horses wore no gear at all but a halter without bit. Their manes were braided with streamers of sil-ver, gold, and green. They flared their nostrils and pranced and boasted to one another; they were vastly excited, the horse being the only animal who had adopted our ceremonies as its own. Far off to the north and west the mountains stood up half encircling Omelas on her bay. The air of morning was so clear that the snow still crowning the Eighteen Peaks burned with white-gold fire across the miles of sunlit air, under the dark, blue of the sky. There was just enough wind to make the banners that marked the racecourse snap and flutter now and then. In the silence of the broad green meadows one could hear the music winding through the city streets, farther and nearer and ever approaching, a cheerful faint sweetness of the air that from time to time trembled and gathered together and broke out into the great joyous clanging of the bells.

Joyous! How is one to tell about joy! How describe the citizens of Omelas?

They were not simple folk, you see, though they were happy. But we do not say the words of cheer much any more. All smiles have become archaic. Given a description such as this one tends to make certain assumptions. Given a description such as this one tends to look next for the King, mounted on a splendid stallion and surrounded by his noble knights, or perhaps in a golden litter borne by great-muscled slaves. But there was no king. They did not use swords or keep slaves. They were not barbarians. I do not know the rules and laws of their society, but I suspect that they were singularly few. As they did without monarchy and slavery, so they also got on without the stock exchange, the advertisement, the secret police, and the bomb. Yet I repeat that these were not simple folk, not dulcet shepherds, noble savages, bland utopians. They were not less complex than us. The trouble is that we have a bad habit, encouraged by pedants and sophisticates, of considering happiness as something rather stupid. Only pain is intellectual, only evil interesting. This is the treason of the artist: a refusal to admit the banality of evil and the terrible boredom of pain. If you can't lick 'em, join 'em. If it hurts, repeat it. But to praise despair is to condemn delight, to embrace violence is to lose hold of everything else. We have almost lost hold; we can no longer describe a happy man, nor make any celebration of joy. How can I tell you about the people of Omelas? They were not naïve and happy children—though their children were, in fact, happy. They were mature, intelligent, passionate adults whose lives were not wretched. O miracle! but I wish I could describe it better. I wish I could convince you. Omelas sounds in my words like a city, in a fairy tale, long ago and far away, once upon a time. Perhaps it would be best if you imagined it as your own fancy bids, assuming it will rise to the occasion, for certainly I cannot suit you all. For instance, how about technology? I think that there would be no cars or helicopters in and above the streets; this follows from the fact that the people of Omelas are happy people. Happiness is based on a just discrimination of what is necessary, what is neither necessary nor destructive, and what is destructive. In the middle category, however—that of the unnecessary but undestructive, that of comfort, luxury, exuberance, etc.—they could perfectly well have central heating, subway trains, washing machines, and all kinds of marvelous devices not yet invented here, floating light-sources, fuelless power, a cure for the common cold. Or they could have none of that: It doesn't matter. As you like it. I incline to think that people from towns up and down the coast have been coming in to Omelas during the last days before the Festival on very fast little trains and double-decked trams, and that the train station of Omelas is actually the handsomest building in town, though plainer than the magnificent Farmers' Market. But even granted trains, I fear that Omelas so far strikes some of you as goody-goody. Smiles, bells, parades, horses, bleh. If so, please add an orgy. If an orgy would help, don't hesitate. Let us not, however, have temples from which issue beautiful nude priests and priestesses already half in ecstasy and ready to copulate with any man or woman, lover or stranger, who desires union with the deep godhead of the blood, although that was my first idea. But really it would be better not to have any temples in Omelas—at least not manned temples. Religion yes, clergy no. Surely the beautiful nudes can just wander about, offering themselves like divine soufflés to the hunger of the needy and the rapture of the flesh. Let them join the processions. Let tambourines be struck above the copulations, and the glory of desire be proclaimed upon the gongs, and (a not unimportant) let the offspring of these delightful rituals be beloved and looked after by all. One thing I know there is none of in Omelas is guilt. But what else should there be? I thought at first there were no drugs, but that is puritanical. For those who like it, the faint insistent sweetness of *drooz* may perfume the ways of the city, *drooz* which first brings a great lightness and brilliance to the mind and limbs, and then after some hours a dreamy languor, and wonderful visions at last of the very arcana and inmost secrets of the Universe, as well as exciting the pleasure of sex beyond all belief; and it is not habit-forming. For more modest tastes I think there ought to be beer. What else, what else belongs in the joyous city? The sense of victory, surely, the celebration of courage. But as we did without clergy, let us do without soldiers. The joy built upon successful slaughter is not the right kind of joy; it will not do; it is fearful and it is trivial. A boundless and generous contentment, a magnanimous triumph felt not against some outer enemy but in communion with the finest and fairest in the souls of all men everywhere and the splendor of the world's summer: This is what swells the hearts of the people of Omelas, and the victory they celebrate is that of life. I really don't think many of them need to take *drooz*.

Most of the processions have reached the Green Fields by now. A marvelous smell of cooking goes forth from the red and blue tents of the provisioners. The faces of small children are amiably sticky; in the benign grey beard of a man a couple of crumbs of rich pastry are entangled. The youths and girls have mounted their horses and are beginning to group around the starting line of the course. An old woman, small, fat, and laughing, is passing out flowers from a basket, and tall young men wear her flowers in their shining hair. A child of nine or ten sits at the edge of the crowd, alone, playing on a wooden flute. People pause to listen, and they smile, but they do not speak to him, for he never ceases playing and never sees them, his dark eyes wholly rapt in the sweet, thin magic of the tune.

5   He finishes, and slowly lowers his hands holding the wooden flute.

As if that little private silence were the signal, all at once a trumpet sounds from the pavilion near the starting line: imperious, melancholy, piercing. The horses rear on their slender legs, and some of them neigh in answer. Sober-faced, the young riders stroke the horses' necks and soothe them, whispering, "Quiet, quiet, there my beauty, my hope. . . ." They begin to form in rank along the starting line. The crowds along the racecourse are like a field of grass and flowers in the wind. The Festival of Summer has begun.

Do you believe? Do you accept the festival, the city, the joy? No? Then let me describe one more thing.

In a basement under one of the beautiful public buildings of Omelas, or perhaps in the cellar of one of its spacious private homes, there is a room. It has one locked door, and no window. A little light seeps in dustily between cracks in the boards, secondhand from a cobwebbed window somewhere across the cellar. In one corner of the little room a couple of mops, with stiff, clotted, foul-smelling heads, stand near a rusty bucket. The floor is dirt, a little damp to the touch, as cellar dirt usually is. The room is about three paces long and two wide: a mere broom closet or disused tool room. In the room a child is sitting. It could be a boy or a girl. It looks about six, but actually is nearly ten. It is feeble-minded. Perhaps it was born defective, or perhaps it has become imbecile through fear, malnutrition, and neglect. It picks its nose and occasionally fumbles vaguely with its toes or genitals, as it sits hunched in the corner farthest from the bucket and the two mops. It is afraid of the mops. It finds them horrible. It shuts its eyes, but it knows the mops are still standing there; and the door is locked; and nobody ever comes, except that sometimes—the child has no understanding of time or interval—sometimes the door rattles terribly and opens, and a person, or several people, are there. One of them may come in and kick the child to make it stand up. The others never come close, but peer in at it with frightened, disgusted eyes. The food bowl and the water jug are hastily filled, the door is locked, the eyes disappear. The people at the door never say anything, but the child, who has not always lived in the tool room, and can remember sunlight and its mother's voice, sometimes speaks. "I will be good," it says. "Please let me out. I will be good!" They never answer. The child used to scream for help at night, and cry a good deal, but now it only makes a kind of whining, "eh-haa-, ch-haa," and it speaks less and less often. It is so thin there are no calves to its legs; its belly protrudes; it lives on a half-bowl of corn meal and grease a day. It is naked. Its buttocks and thighs are a mass of festered sores, as it sits in its own excrement continually.

They all know it is there, all the people of Omelas. Some of them have come to see it; others are content merely to know it is there. They all know that it has to be there. Some of them understand why, and some do not, but they all understand that their happiness, the beauty of their city, the tenderness of their friendships, the health of their children, the wisdom of their scholars, the skill of their makers, even the abundance of their harvest and the kindly weathers of their skies, depend wholly on this child's abominable misery.

This is usually explained to children when they are between eight 10 and twelve, whenever they seem capable of understanding; and most of those who come to see the child are young people, though often enough an adult comes, or comes back, to see the child. No matter how well the matter has been explained to them, these young spectators are always shocked and sickened at the sight. They feel disgust, which they had thought themselves superior to. They feel anger, outrage, impotence, despite all the explanations. They would like to do something for the child. But there is nothing they can do. If the child were brought up into and sunlight out of that vile place, if it were cleaned and fed and comforted, that would be a good thing, indeed; but if it were done, in that day and hour all the prosperity and beauty and delight of Omelas would wither and be destroyed. Those are the terms. To exchange all the goodness and grace of every life in Omelas for that single, small improvement: to throw away the happiness of thousands for the chance of the happiness of one: that would be to let guilt within the walls indeed.

The terms are strict and absolute; there may not even be a kind word spoken to the child.

Often the young people go home in tears, or in a tearless rage, when they have seen the child and faced this terrible paradox. They may brood over it for weeks or years. But as time goes on they begin to realize that even if the child could be released, it would not get much good of its freedom: a little vague pleasure of warmth and food, no doubt, but little more. It is too degraded and imbecile to know any real joy. It has been afraid too long ever to be free of fear. Its habits are too uncouth for it to respond to humane treatment. Indeed, after so long it would probably be wretched without walls about it to protect it, and darkness for its eyes, and its own excrement to sit in. Their tears at the bitter injustice dry when they begin to perceive the terrible justice of reality, and to accept it. Yet it is their tears and anger, the trying of their generosity and the acceptance of their helplessness, which are perhaps the true source of the splendor of their lives. Theirs is no vapid, irresponsible happiness. They know that they, like the child, are not free. They know compassion. It is the existence of the child, and their knowledge of its existence, that makes possible the nobility of their architecture, the poignancy of their music, the profundity of their science. It is because of the child that they are so gentle with children. They know that if the wretched one were not there snivelling in the dark, the other one, the flute-player, could make no joyful music as the young riders line up in their beauty for the race in the sunlight of the first morning of summer.

Now do you believe in them? Are they not more credible? But there is one more thing to tell, and this is quite incredible.

At times one of the adolescent girls or boys who go to see the child does not go home to weep or rage, does not, in fact, go home at all. Sometimes also a man or woman much older falls silent for a day or two, and then leaves home. These people go out into the street, and walk down the street alone. They keep walking, and walk straight out of the city of Omelas, through the beautiful gates. They keep walking across the farmlands of Omelas. Each one goes alone, youth or girl, man or woman. Night falls; the traveler must pass down village streets, between the houses with yellow-lit windows, and on out into the darkness of the fields. Each alone, they go west or north, towards the mountains. They go on. They leave Omelas, they walk ahead into the darkness, and they do not come back. The place that they go towards is a place even less imaginable to most of us than the city of happiness. I cannot describe it at all. It is possible that it does not exist. But they seem to know where they are going, the ones who walk away from Omelas.

Responding to Reading

1. Why do you think Le Guin's narrator keeps asking readers whether or not they "believe," whether they accept what she is saying as the truth? Do *you* "believe"? Which elements of this story do you find most unbelievable? Which do you find most believable?
2. Are "the ones who walk away from Omelas" any less morally responsible for the child's welfare than those who keep the child imprisoned? In other words, do you believe there is a difference between actively doing something "wrong" and passively allowing it to happen?
3. Why does the logic of the story require that the child be present? Why must the child suffer?

Responding in Writing

Might it be argued that our society has its own equivalent of the child locked in the closet and that we are guilty of failing to act to save this child? If so, what is it?

Focus

Can We Be Both Free and Safe?

July 2002: Passengers going through a metal detector gate at a security checkpoint at Denver International Airport.
Photo by Andre Lambertson/Corbis SABA

Responding to the Image

1. What do you see in this photograph? What do the people in line see? What do you think the photographer wanted you to see?
2. Do you believe it is really necessary to subject every airline passenger to the kind of scrutiny pictured above? Should any group—for example, babies, the elderly, pregnant women, uniformed police officers and military personnel—be exempt? Should any individuals or groups receive *more* scrutiny than others? Explain your reasoning.

THE MOST PATRIOTIC ACT
Eric Foner
1943–

A noted historian who specializes in the Civil War and Reconstruction, slavery, and nineteenth-century America, Eric Foner is currently DeWitt Clinton Professor of History at Columbia University. He has written numerous books, including Who Owns History? Rethinking the Past in a Changing World *(2002) and, most recently,* Forever Free: The Story of Emancipation and Reconstruction *(2005). In the following selection, published in the* Nation *in 2001, Foner asserts the importance of preserving civil liberties.*

The drumbeat now begins, as it always does in time of war: We must accept limitations on our liberties. The FBI and CIA should be "unleashed" in the name of national security. Patriotism means uncritical support of whatever actions the President deems appropriate. Arab-Americans, followers of Islam, people with Middle Eastern names or ancestors, should be subject to special scrutiny by the government and their fellow citizens. With liberal members of Congress silent and the Administration promising a war on terrorism lasting "years, not days," such sentiments are likely to be with us for some time to come.

Of the many lessons of American history, this is among the most basic. Our civil rights and civil liberties—freedom of expression, the right to criticize the government, equality before the law, restraints on the exercise of police powers—are not gifts from the state that can be rescinded when it desires. They are the inheritance of a long history of struggles: by abolitionists for the ability to hold meetings and publish their views in the face of mob violence; by labor leaders for the power to organize unions, picket and distribute literature without fear of arrest; by feminists for the right to disseminate birth-control information without being charged with violating the obscenity laws; and by all those who braved jail and worse to challenge entrenched systems of racial inequality.

The history of freedom in this country is not, as is often thought, the logical working out of ideas immanent in our founding documents or a straight-line trajectory of continual progress. It is a story of countless disagreements and battles in which victories sometimes prove temporary and retrogression often follows progress.

When critics of the original Constitution complained about the absence of a Bill of Rights, the Constitution's "father," James Madison, replied that no list of liberties could ever anticipate the ways government might act in the future. "Parchment barriers" to the abuse of authority, he wrote, would be least effective when most needed. Thankfully, the Bill of Rights was eventually adopted. But Madison's observation was amply borne out at moments of popular hysteria when freedom of expression was trampled in the name of patriotism and national unity.

Americans have notoriously short historical memories. But it is worth recalling some of those moments to understand how liberty has been endangered in the past. During the "quasi war" with France in 1798, the Alien and Sedition Acts allowed deportation of immigrants deemed dangerous by federal authorities and made it illegal to criticize the federal government. During the Civil War, both sides jailed critics and suppressed opposition newspapers.

In World War I German-Americans, socialists, labor leaders and critics of US involvement were subjected to severe government repression and assault by private vigilante groups. Publications critical of the war were banned from the mails, individuals were jailed for antiwar statements and in the Red Scare that followed the war thousands of radicals were arrested and numerous aliens deported. During World War II, tens of thousands of Japanese-Americans, most of them US citizens, were removed to internment camps. Sanctioned by the Supreme Court, this was the greatest violation of Americans' civil liberties, apart from slavery, in our history.

No one objects to more stringent security at airports. But current restrictions on the FBI and CIA limiting surveillance, wiretapping, infiltration of political groups at home and assassinations abroad do not arise from an irrational desire for liberty at the expense of security. They are the response to real abuses of authority, which should not be forgotten in the zeal to sweep them aside as "handcuffs" on law enforcement.

Before unleashing these agencies, let us recall the FBI's persistent harassment of individuals like Martin Luther King Jr. and its efforts to disrupt the civil rights and antiwar movements, and the CIA's history of cooperation with some of the world's most egregious violators of human rights. The principle that no group of Americans should be stigmatized as disloyal or criminal because of race or national origin is too recent and too fragile an achievement to be abandoned now.

Every war in American history, from the Revolution to the Gulf War, with the exception of World War II, inspired vigorous internal dissent. Self-imposed silence is as debilitating to a democracy as censorship. If questioning an ill-defined, open-ended "war on terrorism" is to be deemed unpatriotic, the same label will have to be applied to Abraham Lincoln at the time of the Mexican War, Jane Addams and Eugene V. Debs during World War I, and Wayne Morse and Ernest Gruening, who had the courage and foresight to vote against the Gulf of Tonkin resolution in 1964.

All of us today share a feeling of grief and outrage over the events of September 11 and a desire that those responsible for mass murder be brought to justice. But at times of crisis the most patriotic act of all is the unyielding defense of civil liberties, the right to dissent and equality before the law for all Americans.

Responding to Reading

1. What is "the most patriotic act" to which Foner refers in his title?
2. Writing less than a month after September 11, 2001, Foner predicts that sentiments that call for limitations on civil liberties "are likely to be with us for some time to come" (1). Do you believe that Foner's prediction has come true?
3. In paragraphs 3–6 and paragraph 9, Foner presents examples from history to support his position. How are his examples different from those presented by Declan McCullagh below and Jay Tolson (p. 790)? Do the three writers interpret any historical events differently?

Responding in Writing

In the years since September 11, 2001, what kinds of increased security have you noticed on your campus and workplace and in your community? Do you think this increased security is necessary? Do you think it is effective? Do you believe any of these new security regulations violate your civil liberties?

WHY LIBERTY SUFFERS IN WARTIME

Declan McCullagh

1971–

Journalist and photographer Declan McCullagh writes and speaks frequently about technology, law, and politics. Currently chief political correspondent for CNET's News.com, *he was formerly the Washington bureau chief for* Wired News; *a reporter for* Time Digital Daily, *Time's The Netly News, and* Time Magazine; *and a correspondent for* HotWired. *McCullagh's articles have appeared in the* New Republic *and the* Wall Street Journal. *In the following essay, written in late September 2001, McCullagh gives a historical overview of what he calls "the supremacy of security over liberty" in times of war.*

Anyone worried about the fate of civil liberties during the U.S. government's growing war on terrorism might want to consider this Latin maxim: *Inter arma silent leges.*

It means, "In time of war the laws are silent," and it encapsulates the supremacy of security over liberty that typically accompanies national emergencies.

Consider this: During all of America's major wars—the Civil War, World War I and World War II—the government restricted Americans' civil liberties in the name of quelling dissent, silencing criticism of political decisions and preserving national security.

It's far too soon to predict what additional powers the government will assume after the catastrophic attacks on the World Trade Center and the Pentagon. To their credit, many politicians have already stressed that sacrificing liberty for security, even temporarily, is an unacceptable trade.

"We will not violate people's basic rights as we make this nation   5
more secure," said House Majority Leader Dick Armey (R-Texas). Sen. Max Baucus (D-Montana) said: "This does not mean that we can allow terrorists to alter the fundamental openness of U.S. society or the government's respect for civil liberties. If we do so, they will have won."

These statements come as Congress is deliberating a sweeping set of proposals from the Bush administration that would increase wiretapping of phones and the Internet, boost police authority to detain suspected terrorists, and rewrite immigration laws. In response, a coalition of over 100 groups from across the political spectrum asked Congress to tread carefully in this area last week.

Yet history has shown that during moments of national crisis, real or perceived, politicians have been quick to seize new authority, and courts have been impotent or reluctant to interfere.

1798   In July 1798, Congress enacted the Alien and Sedition Acts, ostensibly to respond to the possible threat posed by the French Revolution, but also in an attempt to punish Thomas Jefferson's Republican party. The laws made it a crime to "write, print, utter or publish" any "false, scandalous and malicious writing or writings against the government of the United States, or either house of the Congress of the United States or the president of the United States."

That enraged Kentucky and Virginia. Kentucky's legislature approved a statement saying, "This commonwealth does upon the most deliberate reconsideration declare, that the said alien and sedition laws, are in their opinion, palpable violations of the Constitution." (An earlier draft, relying on libertarian principles, went so far as to say such laws were "void and of no force.")

Civil War   President Lincoln interfered with freedom of speech and   10
of the press and ordered that suspected political criminals be tried before military tribunals. Much as President Bush now is concerned with protecting airplane safety, Lincoln wanted to preserve the railroads: Rebels were destroying railroad bridges near Baltimore in 1861.

Probably Lincoln's most controversial act was suspending the writ of *habeas corpus*, a safeguard of liberty that dates back to English common law and England's Habeas Corpus Act of 1671. A vital check on the government's power, *habeas corpus* says that authorities must bring a person they arrest before a judge who orders it.

The U.S. Constitution says: "The privilege of the writ of *habeas corpus* shall not be suspended, unless when in cases of rebellion or invasion the public safety may require it." But Lincoln suspended *habeas corpus* without waiting for Congress to authorize it.

Lincoln's decision led to a showdown between the military and United States Chief Justice Roger Taney. After the U.S. Army arrested John Merryman on charges of destroying railroad bridges and imprisoned him in Fort McHenry, Merryman's lawyer drew up a *habeas corpus* petition that Taney quickly signed.

When the Army refused to bring Merryman before the high court, Taney said the U.S. marshals had the authority to haul Army General George Cadwalader into the courtroom on contempt charges—but Taney would not order it since the marshals would likely be outgunned. Instead, Taney protested and called on Lincoln "to perform his constitutional duty to enforce the laws" and the "process of this court."

15   This was a controversial decision: the *New York Times* described Taney's decision the next day as one that "can only be regarded as at once officious and improper."

World War I   Soon after declaring war on Germany and its allies in 1917, Congress banned using the U.S. mail from sending any material urging "treason, insurrection or forcible resistance to any law."

It punished offenders with a fine of up to $5,000 and a five-year prison term, and the government used this new authority to ban magazines such as *The Nation* from the mail.

President Wilson asked Congress to go even further: His draft of the Espionage Act included a $10,000 fine and 10 years imprisonment for anyone publishing information that could be useful to the enemy. The House of Representatives narrowly defeated it by a vote of 184–144.

Even without Wilson's proposals, the Espionage Act gave birth to a famous civil liberties case: *U.S. v. Charles Schenck*. The Supreme Court unanimously upheld his conviction for printing leaflets that urged Americans to resist the draft.

20   The justices ruled: "When a nation is at war, many things that might be said in time of peace are such a hindrance to its effort that their utterance will not be endured so long as men fight and that no court could regard them as protected by any constitutional right."

While there were no trials before military tribunals, the Justice Department unsuccessfully asked Congress to enact a law—punishable by death—that would have authorized such trials for anyone "interfering with the war effort."

World War II   Civil liberties groups recently have repeatedly offered reminders of the internment of Japanese immigrants and their children in walled camps in the aftermath of Pearl Harbor.

In Executive Order 9066, President Roosevelt authorized the military to remove Japanese-Americans from America's west coast, home to many military bases and manufacturing plants—and viewed at the time as vulnerable to Japanese attack. In a remarkable silence, the American Civil Liberties Union did not object to the internment camps until years later.

A collection of challenges to the internment camps found their way to the U.S. Supreme Court. In a brief supporting the camps, the states of Washington, Oregon and California noted that Japanese submarines had attacked oil platforms at Santa Barbara, California, the town of Brookings. Oregon, and a gun installation at Astoria, Oregon. On June 7, 1942, the brief said, the Japanese had invaded North America by occupying some Aleutian islands.

In its response, drafted by Chief Justice Harlan Stone in 1943, the 25 court ducked the constitutionality of internment camps, ruling only on a related curfew requirement.

The justices upheld the action: "Whatever views we may entertain regarding the loyalty to this country of the citizens of Japanese ancestry, we cannot reject as unfounded the judgment of the military authorities and of Congress that there were disloyal members of that population."

Some of America's most respected legal thinkers, while saying that the government went too far in World War II, say that some erosion of freedom in wartime is necessary.

"There is no reason to think that future wartime presidents will act differently from Lincoln, Wilson or Roosevelt, or that future justices of the Supreme Court will decide questions differently from their predecessors," William Rehnquist, chief justice of the United States, wrote in a book published in 1998.

"It is neither desirable nor is it remotely likely that civil liberty will occupy as favored a position in wartime as it does in peacetime," Rehnquist wrote in *All the Laws But One.*

The 100-plus groups whose representatives gathered at the National 30 Press Club on Thursday aren't quite so certain. In a statement posted on a new website, In Defense of Freedom, they say: "We need to ensure that actions by our government uphold the principles of a democratic society, accountable government and international law, and that all decisions are taken in a manner consistent with the Constitution."

CHAPTER 11 FOCUS

Responding to Reading

1. What is McCullagh's position on the balance between liberty and security? In what respects, if any, would he be likely to agree with Eric Foner (p. 784)?

2. In paragraph 7, McCullagh says, "history has shown that during moments of national crisis, real or perceived, politicians have been quick to seize new authority, and courts have been impotent or reluctant to interfere." Does he see this tendency as a bad thing? Do you?

3. The title of McCullagh's essay is "Why Liberty Suffers in Wartime," and in his introduction he quotes the saying, "In time of war the laws are silent" (2). How does he define *war* in this essay? How would you define it? For example, do you consider the "war on terrorism" to be a war? Do you think all the historical examples McCullagh cites qualify as "wars"? Explain.

Responding in Writing

This essay was written less than two weeks after the tragic events of September 11, 2001. Write a short narrative that traces your own experiences on that day: what you saw and heard, and what you did. On that day, were you willing to sacrifice some freedoms for increased security? Do you still feel the way you did then?

IMBALANCE OF POWER

Jay Tolson

1935–

A writer for U.S. News & World Report, *Jay Tolson explores various issues related to society, culture, and politics. In the following essay, he examines what he calls the "imperial" political structure of the American presidency and considers its effect on Americans' civil liberties.*

During the Civil War, Abraham Lincoln got away with suspending habeas corpus and subjecting citizens to military law. Even more famously, he defied the law of the land by freeing enslaved Americans. During World War II, Franklin D. Roosevelt ordered the internment of Japanese-American citizens and received the Supreme Court's subsequent approval. Yet when Harry S. Truman ordered the Commerce Department to take over 87 steel plants crippled by striking workers during the Korean War, the high court ruled that he had pushed executive prerogative beyond acceptable bounds.

So just how imperial can the American president be? And more specifically, how, when, and how far can the powers that the Constitution invested in the commander in chief be extended?

Disclosures about George W. Bush's support for a National Security Agency-run domestic-spying program have pushed those questions to the fore once again. The headlines have fueled charges that his administration has, in post–9/11 measures ranging from indefinite detention of terrorism suspects (including two U.S. citizens) to torture and abuse of detainees around the world,[1] taken presidential discretion to new, possibly illegal extremes. Joining a host of liberal voices, former Vice President Al Gore has decried a "truly breathtaking expansion of executive power" by the Bush administration.

Bush, so far, has gotten a broad pass on his amplification of the commander in chief's prerogatives, which many Americans view as justified in the name of the war on terrorism. But there are growing signs of resistance. Congressional hearings in February will examine the president's rationale for ignoring procedures instituted in the 1978 Foreign Intelligence Surveillance Act, namely the requirement that intelligence agencies secure a warrant from a special court before eavesdropping on U.S. citizens. Another congressional committee says it will oversee implementation of a new ban on the use of torture, which the president, even while signing the bill into law, suggested he would ignore when necessary. For its part, the Supreme Court is mulling over the possibility of hearings on detainee cases, although the Justice Department's solicitor general has argued that the court has no jurisdiction over them.[2]

Whatever the solicitor general argues, cases involving possible executive overreach are almost certain to reach the high court. The American Civil Liberties Union and the Center for Constitutional Rights have filed separate suits to challenge the legality of warrantless domestic spying and to determine whether the NSA monitored lawyers, journalists, and academics involved with the Middle East. One plaintiff in the ACLU suit, journalist Christopher Hitchens, a prominent backer of Bush's war on terrorism and the war in Iraq, says that if the administration wants to engage in domestic spying, it "must ask Congress to change FISA, not ignore it."

Powering Up This in some ways goes to the nub of the historical and theoretical debate about executive authority: How does the commander in chief exercise extraordinary powers within the legal framework of the republic, including the constitutionally ordained separation of powers?

---

[1] In June 2006, the Supreme Court ruled that President Bush overstepped his authority by ordering the use of military tribunals for Guantanamo Bay detainees.
[2] The government's warrantless surveillance program was ruled unconstitutional by a federal court in 2006. The ruling is currently under appeal.

CHAPTER 11 FOCUS

Arguments for and against strong executive authority—"energy in the executive," as Alexander Hamilton phrased it—have been put forth by both sides of the conservative-liberal divide, depending largely on who is in the White House. From the 1950s through the '70s, liberal scholars and pundits were among the aggressive supporters of a stronger executive. Historians Henry Steele Commager and Arthur Schlesinger Jr. both took on critics who attacked Truman for not securing congressional authority when he sent troops to Korea. Richard Neustadt's 1960 study, Presidential Power, exalted FDR's strong leadership and lamented Dwight Eisenhower's allegedly listless presidency. But after both John F. Kennedy and Lyndon Johnson tried, with mixed results, to bring greater élan to the White House, Neustadt grew uneasy that his ideas were seen as providing a warrant for the Vietnam War debacle and Nixon administration abuses, including illegal wiretapping of political foes and antiwar activists. Schlesinger also changed his tune in his book The Imperial Presidency. But as liberals began deploring a lack of balance among government branches, conservative (and particularly neoconservative) thinkers supportive of Ronald Reagan's "morning in America" began to trot out the oldest justifications of a strong executive. "When you own the presidency," acknowledges Harvard political scientist Harvey Mansfield, a leading conservative defender of executive prerogative, "it looks like a far more valuable possession."

Advocates of both sides often rely on the variously authored papers of The Federalist. Collectively, these writings provided the intellectual underpinnings of the Constitution, and, more to the point, they offer differing takes on executive authority. Federalist No. 4, penned by John Jay, cautions that monarchs often make war "for purposes and objects merely personal, such as a thirst for military glory, revenge for personal affronts, ambition, or private compacts to aggrandize or support their particular families or partisans." Monarchs, of course, can be taken to mean any leader who acts autocratically. Small-"d" democrats of the early Jeffersonian Republican party attacked President John Adams and his fellow Federalists as quasi monarchists for suppressing dissent with the Alien and Sedition Acts, instituted during the undeclared naval war with France.

But Federalists like Adams and Hamilton often drew on the reasoning behind Hamilton's own papers (particularly Federalist Nos. 70–75) advocating a strong and "unitary" chief executive. This unity would be diminished, Hamilton argued, by having more than one executive or by vesting power "ostensibly in one man, subject, in whole or in part, to the control and cooperation of others, in the capacity of counsellors to him." Those "others" apparently included other government branches, notably the legislature. As Hamilton observed, "It is one thing [for the executive] to be subordinate to the laws, another to be dependent on the legislative body. The first comports with, the last violates, the fundamental principles of good government."

But, again, the critical nub is how the commander in chief remains 10 subordinate to the laws if he must stretch or even break them to deal with the extraordinary circumstances of war or other emergencies. That was the question Lincoln repeatedly faced during the Civil War, beginning with his orders to call up the militia and expand the Army and the Navy and continuing through his emancipation measures and his suspension of habeas corpus to silence war opponents who were discouraging military enlistment. In each case, argues political scientist Sean Mattie in an article in the Review of Politics, Lincoln overcame the apparently unresolvable conflict between the need for executive prerogative and the rule of law by seeking after-the-fact legislative approval of his emergency-driven measures. And in each case, Congress provided that approval either through explicit statutes or funding bills. "Congress's legislative support strengthened Lincoln's position as executive but also its own as legislature," Mattie writes, "since statutory approval testified to the power of (if not also the need for) Congress to give formal recognition to extraordinary executive power." Bush's reluctance to seek congressional approval of his own extraordinary measures may be one reason for the growing concerns about their legality and possible abuse of his office.

Scrutiny   Then there is the matter of which circumstances call for extraordinary measures. Because World War II was as clear a threat to the republic as the Civil War had been, Roosevelt overcame challenges to his most legally questionable actions. Not only did the Supreme Court accept Japanese-American internment; in Ex Parte Quirin (1942), it upheld Roosevelt's decision to try eight German saboteurs—including an arguably naturalized U.S. citizen—in front of a military tribunal he had appointed. (This ruling is often cited, puzzlingly, as a precedent for the treatment of terrorism suspects Yaser Hamdi and Jose Padilla, even though, as constitutional scholar Louis Fisher points out in Presidential War Power, nothing in that decision "justifies holding a U.S. citizen indefinitely without access to counsel or a trial.") During the Korean War, however, the Supreme Court may have slapped down Truman's attempted steel-plant takeover in part because Congress had never officially declared war. Similarly, as the somewhat ill-defined war on terrorism stretches into the future, historian and Columbia University Provost Alan Brinkley suggests, extraordinary measures will more likely be subjected to closer constitutional scrutiny: "This may go on 20, 30, or 50 years, as the Cold War did, but we didn't let the Cold War serve as a basis for the alteration of our basic rights."

To Robert George, a professor of jurisprudence at Princeton University, questions circling the limits of executive prerogative are less large-"c" constitutional issues than small-"c" ones. By that, he means that these questions tend to be addressed less through close parsing of what the Constitution says about presidential prerogative (which is quite broad and vague) than through the judgments of the court of public opinion. "In the current context," George says, "the public seems to think the president is doing what is necessary."

Polls back that up, but George cautions that such verdicts must stand up against the test of history: "If it turns out this power was used in an abusive way—say, for political reasons—we will think back on it as we do on the way we abused executive power in World War II when we used the War Relocation Authority [to intern Japanese-Americans]. It will be seen as a great stain on our constitutional record. It all depends on whether the power is used responsibly. And," adds George, "the temptation to use it wrongly is very high."

Responding to Reading

1. In paragraph 2, Tolson asks, "So just how imperial can the American president be? And more specifically, how, when, and how far can the powers that the Constitution invested in the commander in chief be extended?" How does Tolson answer these questions?
2. What does the word *imperial* suggest to you? What effect do you think Tolson's use of this word might have on his readers?
3. What examples from history does Tolson present to illustrate the advantages and disadvantages of a strong, even "imperial" presidency? Does Tolson seem to support or oppose "strong executive authority" (7)? How can you tell?

Responding in Writing

Does the knowledge that the United States has a "domestic spying" program make you feel more or less secure?

WIDENING THE FOCUS

For Critical Thinking and Writing

Read the essays in the Focus section of this chapter. Then, write an argumentative essay in which you answer the question, "Can we be both free and safe?" taking a stand on which you believe is more important, freedom or security. Be sure to discuss the possible dangers and sacrifices your position will entail, and support your position with specific examples from your own reading, observations, and experience as well as from the essays by Eric Foner, Declan McCullagh, and Jay Tolson.

For Further Reading

The following readings can suggest additional perspectives for thinking and writing about the conflict between liberty and security:

- Tim Robbins, "A Chill Wind Is Blowing in This Nation" (p. 206)
- Edward J. Blakely and Mary Gail Snyder, "Putting Up the Gates" (p. 314)
- Thomas Jefferson, The Declaration of Independence (p. 477)

For Internet Research

Conflicts between individual freedoms and the security of communities, states, and the nation have been debated throughout US history. During both world wars, the phrase *national security* was used to justify actions that limited (or even revoked) the civil rights of many individuals. Since the passage of the USA Patriot Act following the September 11, 2001, terrorist attacks, the debate over individual liberties and national security has intensified. The US Justice Department has created a Web site to promote the benefits of the USA Patriot Act, <http://www.lifeandliberty.gov/.> The American Civil Liberties Union (ACLU), an organization, criticizes the provisions of the law on its Web site, <http://www.aclu.org/safefree/index.html.> Visit both Web sites, and analyze how each organization presents its position. Then, write an essay in which you evaluate some of the arguments presented on each Web site. Which site do you think is more persuasive, and why?

WRITING

Making Choices

1. What moral and ethical rules govern your behavior? Considering the ethical guidelines set forth by several writers in this chapter, define and explain your own personal moral code.

2. The question of whether or not to act to end another's suffering—possibly at one's own expense—is explored, implicitly or explicitly, in "The Deer at Providencia" by Annie Dillard (p. 711), "Shooting an Elephant" by George Orwell (p. 715), and "The Ones Who Walk Away from Omelas" by Ursula K. Le Guin (p. 777). What are your own feelings about this issue?

3. Henry David Thoreau (p. 722) says, "Unjust laws exist: shall we be content to obey them, or shall we endeavor to amend them, and obey them until we have succeeded, or shall we transgress them at once?" (17). Choose a law or practice that you consider unjust, and write an essay in which you tell why you believe it should be disobeyed. Use ideas from Thoreau's essay to support your points.

4. Stanley Milgram (p. 764) believes that his study illustrates philosopher Hannah Arendt's controversial theory, showing that "ordinary people, simply doing their jobs, and without any particular hostility on their part, can become agents in a terrible destructive process" (39). Cite examples from recent news events or from your own experience to support Arendt's theory.

5. Martin Luther King, Jr. (p. 741), stanley Milgram (p. 764), and Henry David Thoreau (p. 722) all consider the difficulties of resisting majority rule, standing up to authority, and protesting against established rules and laws. Did you ever submit to authority even though you thought you should not have? Write an essay in which you describe your experience. What were the consequences of your act? (Or, describe a time when you stood up to authority. What motivated you? Was your resistance successful? Would you do the same thing again?) Be sure you draw a conclusion from your experience, and state this conclusion as your thesis.

6. What do you believe we gain and lose by using animals in scientific research? Do you believe this practice should be continued? If so, with which animals? Under what circumstances? If not, why not? What alternative do you propose? Reread Claire McCarthy's "Dog Lab" (p. 756) and Annie Dillard's "The Deer at Providencia" (p. 711) before you begin your essay.

7. Which of the two roads identified in Robert Frost's "The Road Not Taken" (p. 709) have you chosen? In what sense has that choice "made all the difference"?

8. Do you believe it is possible both to do good (that is, to help others) and to do well (that is, to be financially successful), or do you believe these two goals are mutually exclusive? Answer this question, citing examples from public figures who have (or have not) managed both to do good and to do well.

CREDITS

■ ■ ■ ■ □ ■ ■ ■ ■

Kincaid, Jamaica, "Girl" from *At the Bottom of the River* by Jamaica Kincaid. Copyright © 1983 by Jamaica Kincaid. Reprinted by permission of Farrar, Straus and Giroux, LLC.

King, Martin Luther, Jr., "I Have A Dream." Copyright © 1963 Dr. Martin Luther King, Jr., copyright renewed 1991 Coretta Scott King. Reprinted by arrangement of the Estate of Martin Luther King, Jr., c/o Writers House as agent for the proprietor, New York, NY.

King, Martin Luther, Jr., "Letter from a Birmingham Jail." Copyright © 1963 Dr. Martin Luther King, Jr., copyright renewed 1991 Coretta Scott King. Reprinted by arrangement of the Estate of Martin Luther King, Jr., c/o Writers House as agent for the proprietor, New York, NY.

Kingston Hong, Maxine, "No Name Woman," from *The Woman Warrior* by Maxine Kingston Hong. Copyright © 1975, 1976 by Maxine Hong Kingston. Used by permission of Alfred A. Knopf, a division of Random House, Inc.

Kozol, Jonathon, "The Human Cost of an Illiterate Society," from *Illiterate America* by Jonathon Kozol, copyright © 1985 by Jonathan Kozol. Used by permission of Doubleday, a division of Random House, Inc.

Kunstler, James Howard, "The End of Oil," *Rolling Stone*, April 7, 2005; 971; pp. 45–48.

Lee, Michelle, "The Fashion Victim's Ten Commandments," from *Fashion Victim: Our Love-Hate Relationship with Dressing, Shopping and the Cost of Style* by Michelle Lee, copyright © 2003 by Michelle Lee. Used by permission of Broadway Books, a division of Random House, Inc.

LeGuin, Ursula, "The Ones Who Walk Away from Omelas." Copyright © 1973, 2001 by Ursula K. LeGuin: first appeared in *The Wind's Twelve Quarters*, permission is granted by the author and the author's agents, the Virginia Kidd Agency, Inc.

Lynas, Mark, "Global Warming: Is It Already Too Late?," *New Statesman*, London, May 17, 2004, Col. 17, Iss. 807; pg. 28, 4 pgs. Reprinted by permission.

McCarthy, Claire, "Dog Lab," from *Learning How the Heart Beats* by Claire McCarthy, copyright © 1995 by Claire McCarthy. Used by permission of Viking Penguin, a division of Penguin Group (USA) Inc.

McCullagh, Declan, "Why Liberty Suffers in Wartime," from *Wired News*, September 24, 2001.

Milgram, Stanley, "The Perils of Obedience," abridged and adapted from *Obedience to Authority* by Stanley Milgram. Published in *Harper's Magazine*. Copyright © 1974 by Stanley Milgram. Reprinted by permission of HarperCollins Publishers, Inc.

Miller, Kenneth R., "Finding Darwin's God," *Brown Alumni Magazine*, November 1999. http://www.brown.edu. Reprinted by permission.

Moore, Charles W., "Is Music Piracy Stealing?," http://www.applelinks.com/mooresviews/pirate.shtml.

Murphy, Cullen, "Let Someone Else Do It: The Impulse Behind Everything," *The Atlantic Monthly*, Nov. 2004 v 294 i4 p173 (2). Reprinted by permission.

Murrow, Edward R., Speech to RTNDA Convention (1958), www.rtnda.org/resources/speeches/murrow.shtml.

Nava, Michael, "Gardenland, Sacramento, California," excerpt from *The Little Death* by Michael Nava. © 1986, 1996 by Michael Nava. All rights reserved. Reprinted by permission.

Nguyen, Bich Minh, "The Good Immigrant Student" by Bich Mihn Nguyen. Reprinted by permission of Russell & Volkening as agents for the author. © 2000 Bich Ninh Nguyen.

Nilsen, Aileen Pace, "Sexism in English: Embodiment and Language" from *Female Studies IV: Closer to the Ground: Women's Classes, Criticism, Programs*, copyright © 1972 by Aileen Pace Nilsen, Arizona State University, Tempe, AZ. Reprinted by permission of the author.

Olds, Sharon, "Rites of Passage," from *The Dead and the Living* by Sharon Olds, copyright © 1987 by Sharon Olds. Used by permission of Alfred A. Knopf, a division of Random House, Inc.

Orr, Allen, "Why Intelligent Design Isn't" from *Devolution*. Reprinted by permission of the author.

Orwell, George, "Politics and the English Language" from *Shooting an Elephant and Other Essays*, by George Orwell, copyright © 1950 by Harcourt, Inc., renewed 1979 by Sonia Brownell Orwell. Reprinted by permission of Harcourt, Inc. and copyright © 1946 by permission of Bill Hamilton as the Literary Executor of the Estate of the Late Sonia Brownell Orwell and Secker & Warburg Ltd.

Orwell, George, "Shooting an Elephant" from *Shooting an Elephant and Other Essays*, by George Orwell, copyright © 1950 by Harcourt, Inc, and renewed 1979 by Sonia Brownell Orwell, reprinted by permission of Harcourt, Inc. and Copyright © George Orwell 1946 by permission of Bill Hamilton as the Literary Executor of the Estate of the Late Sonia Brownell and Secker & Warburg Ltd.

Pastan, Linda, "Ethics" from *Waiting for My Life* by Linda Pastan. Copyright © 1981 by Linda Pastan. Used by permission of W.W. Norton & Company, Inc.

Pearce, Fred, "Climate Change: Menace or Myth?," *New Scientist*, London: Feb 12-Feb 18, 2005, Vol. 185, Iss. 2486; pg. 38, 6 pgs

Pink, Daniel, "School's Out," from *Free Agent Nation* by Daniel Pink. Copyright © 2001 by Daniel H. Pink. By permission of Warner Books, Inc.

Piercy, Marge, "Barbie Doll" from *Circles on the Water* by Marge Piercy, copyright © 1982 by Marge Piercy. Used by permission of Alfred A. Knopf, a division of Random House, Inc.

Pollitt, Katha, "Summers of Our Discontent" by Katha Pollitt. Originally appeared in *The Nation*, February 21, 2005, p. 10. Reprinted by permission of the author.

Posner, Richard A., "Bad News" by Richard A. Posner from *The New York Times Book Review*, July 31, 2005, Copyright © 2005 by The New York Times Co. Reprinted by permission.

Ravitch, Diane, "You Can't Say That," by Diane Ravitch. Originally appeared in the *Wall Street Journal*, February 13, 2004. Reprinted by permission of the author.

Risen, Clay, "Missed Target: Is Outsourcing Really So Bad?," *Missed Target* by Clay Risen. Reprinted by permission of *The New Republic*. © 2004 The New Republic, LLC.

Robbins, Tim, "A Chill Wind is Blowing in This Nation," speech given to the National Press Club, 4/15/03. Reprinted by permission.

Roberts, Paul, "Over a Barrel," from *Mother Jones*, November/December 2004, pp. 65–69. © 2004 Foundation for National Progress.

Rodriguez, Richard, "Aria" from *Hunger of Memory* by Richard Rodriguez. Reprinted by permission of David R. Godine, Publisher, Inc. Copyright © 1982 by Richard Rodriguez.

Rushdie, Salman, "Reality TV: A Dearth of Talent and the Death of Morality," from *The Guardian*, June 9, 2001. Copyright © 2001 by Salman Rushdie. Reprinted with the permission of The Wylie Agency, Inc.

Sacks, Glenn, "Stay-at-Home Dads" as publisher in *Newsday*, May 22, 2002, www.glennsacks.com. Reprinted by permission of Glenn Sacks.

Sagel, Jim, "Baca Grande," *Hispanics in the United States: An Anthology of Creative Literature*, edited by Francisco Jime_nez and Gary D. Keller, Ypsilanti, Mich.: Bilingual Review/Press. Copyright © 1982 Bilingual Press. Reprinted by permission.

Schlosser, Eric, "Behind the Counter," from *Fast Food Nation* by Eric Schlosser. Copyright © 2001 by Eric Schlosser. Reprinted by permission of Houghton Mifflin Company. All rights reserved.

renewed by Marjorie T. Parsons, Executrix, reprinted by permission of the publisher.

Wright, Richard, Chapter XIII (titled "Library Card") from *Black Boy* by Richard Wright. Copyright 1937, 1942, 1944, 1945 by Richard Wright: renewed © 1973 by Ellen Wright. Reprinted by permission of HarperCollins Publishers Inc.

PHOTO CREDITS

Introduction, page 10: Adbusters Media Foundation.

Chapter 1, page 12: Hulton/Archive by Getty Images, Inc.
Chapter 1, page 13: © Bill Bachmann/PhotoEdit. All Rights Reserved.
Chapter 1, page 61: Stone/Getty Images./Photographers: Stone/Getty/Images

Chapter 2, page 80: Erlanson-Messens, Britt J./Getty Images Inc.–Image Bank
Chapter 2, page 81: Rogelio Solis/AP Wide World Photos
Chapter 2, page 130-A: Jim Heemstra
Chapter 2, page 130-A: Michael Kreiser
Chapter 2, page 130-B: Jim Heemstra
Chapter 2, page 130-B: Michael Kreiser
Chapter 2, page 130-C: Jim Heemstra
Chapter 2, page 130-C: Michael Kreiser
Chapter 2, page 130-D: Jim Heemstra
Chapter 2, page 130-D: Michael Kreiser

Chapter 3, page 134: © Peter Blakely/CORBIS SABA.
Chapter 3, page 135: AP Wide World Photos.
Chapter 3, page 201: PhotoEdit Inc./Robert Ginn

Chapter 4, page 218: Geoff Dann © Dorling Kindersley, Courtesy of the Museum of the Order of St John, London.
Chapter 4, page 258: AP Wide World Photos.
Chapter 4, page 274: © Bettmann/CORBIS All Rights Reserved

Chapter 5, page 298: © Bettmann/CORBIS
Chapter 5, page 299: PhotoEdit Inc./Spencer Grant

Chapter 6, page 362: The Image Works/Bob Daemmrich
Chapter 6, page 363: Stone/Getty Images./Photographers: Stone/GettyImages
Chapter 6, page 399: The Advertising Counsel, Inc.

Chapter 7, page 418: Hulton/Archive by Getty Images, Inc.
Chapter 7, page 419: © David Young-Wolff/PhotoEdit Inc.
Chapter 7, page 476: Archive Holdings Inc. Getty Images Inc. - Image Bank

Chapter 8, page 492: Hulton/Archive by Getty Images, Inc.
Chapter 8, page 493: AP Wide World Photos
Chapter 8, page 538: FAYAZ KABLI/Reuters Corbis/Reuters America LLC.

Chapter 9, page 558: Esbin/Anderson/Omni-Photo Communications, Inc.
Chapter 9, page 559: Getty Images Inc. - Hulton Archive Photos.
Chapter 9, page 563: © Courtesy of Twentieth Century Fox/Bureau L.A. Collection/Corbis.
Chapter 9, page 581: Malcolm File/Getty Images, Inc.- Photodisc.
Chapter 9, page 584: © CORBIS All Rights Reserved.

Chapter 9, page 611: Roger Ressmeyer/CORBIS–NY© Photographer/Corbis
Chapter 10, page 636: Omni-Photo Communications, Inc./Jeff Greenberg
Chapter 10, page 637: Corbis/Reuters America LLC./JOHN GRESS/Reuters
Chapter 10, page 679: Photo Researchers, Inc./David Gifford

Chapter 11, page 706: PhotoEdit Inc./Paul Conklin Photography
Chapter 11, page 707: © Jose Luis Pelaez, Inc./CORBIS.
Chapter 11, page 783: © (Photographer) / CORBIS All Rights Reserved.

INDEX OF AUTHORS AND TITLES

■ ■ ■ ■ □ ■ ■ ■ ■

Alexander, Elizabeth, "Apollo," 561

Alexie, Sherman J., Jr., "The Unauthorized Autobiography of Me," 47

Angelou, Maya, "Graduation," 103

Barnett, Rosalind C. and Rivers, Caryl, "Men Are From Earth, and So Are Women," 408

Barrera, Albino, "Fair Exchange: Who Benefits from Outsourcing?" 548

Barry, Lynda, "The Sanctuary of School," 83

Behreandt, Dennis, "Energy's Future," 592

Bethell, Tom, "The False Alert of Global Warming," 575

Blakely, Edward J. and Snyder, Mary Gail, "Putting Up the Gates," 314

Brady, Judy, "Why I Want a Wife," 380

Brooks, David, "Kicking the Secularist Habit," 647

Carver, Raymond, "Cathedral," 666

Chief, Seattle, "We May Be Brothers," 421

Coben, Harlan, "The Key to My Father," 56

Cofer, Judith Ortiz, "The Myth of the Latin Woman: I Just Met a Girl Named Maria," 442

Cohen, Leah Hager, "Without Apology: Girls, Women, and the Desire to Fight," 385

Critser, Greg, "Supersize Me," 318

Curry, Andrew, "Why We Work," 495

de Tocqueville, Alexis, "Why the Americans Are So Restless in the Midst of Their Prosperity," 423

Dillard, Annie, "The Deer at Providencia," 711

Douglass, Frederick, "Learning to Read and Write," 150

D'Souza, Dinesh, "Becoming American," 435

Eberstadt, Mary, "Eminem is Right," 250

Ehrenreich, Barbara, "Selling in Minnesota," 519

Eighner, Lars, "On Dumpster Diving," 454

Erdrich, Louise, "Two Languages in Mind, But Just One in the Heart," 146

Fallows, James, "Who Shot Mohammed al-Dura?" 257

Fish, Stanley, "The Free-Speech Follies," 202

Florida, Richard, "The Transformation of Everyday Life," 302

Foner, Eric, "The Most Patriotic Act," 784

Frank, Reuven, "A Loser's Game," 285

Frost, Robert, "The Road Not Taken," 709

Gallagher, Maggie, "What Marriage Is For," 65

Gates, Henry Louis, Jr.,"Delusions of Grandeur," 523

Gordon, Suzanne, "What Nurses Stand For," 526

Graff, E. J., "The M/F Boxes," 374

Gyatso, Tenzin, "Our Faith in Science," 641

Hayden, Robert, "Those Winter Sundays," 15

Hochschild, Arlie, "The Second Shift," 505

Holt, John, "School Is Bad for Children," 86

Holzer, Amanda, "Love and Other Catastrophes: A Mix Tape," 272

Howley, Kerry, "Marriage Just Lets the State Back In," 72

811

Hughes, Langston, "Salvation," 639

Hulbert, Ann, "Boy Problems," 405

Huxley, Aldous, "Propaganda Under a Dictatorship," 183

Jefferson, Thomas, The Declaration of Independence, 477

Jen, Gish, "Coming Into The Country," 447

Jones, Edward P., "The First Day," 124

Jones, Tayari, "Among the Believers," 644

Kennedy, John F., Inaugural Address, 481

Kincaid, Jamaica, "Girl," 536

King, Martin Luther, Jr., "I Have a Dream," 485

King, Martin Luther, Jr., "Letter from Birmingham Jail," 741

Kingston, Maxine Hong, "No Name Woman," 29

Kozol, Jonathan, "The Human Cost of an Illiterate Society," 175

Kunstler, James Howard, "The End of Oil," 602

Lazarus, Emma, "The New Colossus," 480

Le Guin, Ursula K., "The Ones Who Walk Away from Omelas," 777

Lee, Michelle, "The Fashion Victim's Ten Commandments," 326

Lynas, Mark, "Global Warming: Is It Already Too Late?" 564

McCarthy, Claire, "Dog Lab," 756

McCullagh, Declan, "Why Liberty Suffers in Wartime," 786

Milgram, Stanley, "The Perils of Obedience," 764

Miller, Kenneth R., "Finding Darwin's God," 692

Moore, Charles W., "Is Music Piracy Stealing?" 242

Murphy, Cullen, "Let Someone Else Do It: The Impulse Behind Everything," 539

Murrow, Edward R., Speech to Radio-Television News Directors Association, 221

Nava, Michael, "Gardenland, Sacramento, California," 367

Nguyen, Bich Minh, "The Good Immigrant Student," 113

Nilsen, Alleen Pace, "Sexism in English: Embodiment and Language," 158

Olds, Sharon, "Rite of Passage," 366

Orr, H. Allen, "Why Intelligent Design Isn't," 682

Orwell, George, "Shooting an Elephant," 715

Orwell, George, "Politics and the English Language," 189

Pastan, Linda, "Ethics," 710

Pearce, Fred, "Climate Change: Menace or Myth?," 569

Piercy, Marge, "Barbie Doll," 365

Pink, Daniel H., "School's Out," 91

Pollitt, Katha, "Summers of Our Discontent," 627

Posner, Richard A., "Bad News," 275

Ravitch, Diane, "You Can't Say That," 155

Risen, Clay, "Missed Target: Is Outsourcing Really So Bad?" 542

Robbins, Tim, "A Chill Wind Is Blowing in This Nation," 206

Roberts, Paul, "Over a Barrel," 582

Rodriguez, Richard, "Arial," 139

Rushdie, Salman, "Reality TV: A Dearth of Talent and the Death of Morality," 239

Sacks, Glenn, "Stay-at-Home Dads," 382

Sagel, Jim, "Baca Grande," 137

Schlosser, Eric, "Behind the Counter," 511

Schönborn, Christoph, "Finding Design in Nature," 680

Shafer, Jack, "Not Just Another Column about Blogging," 290

Sheler, Jeffery and Betzold, Michael, "Muslim in America," 655

Shell, Ellen Ruppel, "The Boredom Effect," 310

Sommers, Christina Hoff, "For More Balance on Campuses," 121

Sommers, Christina Hoff, "The War Against Boys," 400

Soto, Gary, "One Last Time," 16

Standage, Tom, "The Internet in a Cup," 351

Staples, Brent, "Just Walk On By," 450

Staples, Brent, "What Adolescents Miss when We Let Them Grow Up in Cyberspace," 349

Stuntz, William J., "Turning Faith into Elevator Music," 652

Sullivan, Andrew, "The Truth about Men and Women," 630

Summers, Lawrence, Remarks at NBER Conference on Diversifying the Science & Engineering Workforce, 613

Symonds, William C., "Earthly Empires," 659

Tan, Amy, "Mother Tongue," 170

Tan, Amy, "Two Kinds," 465

Tannen, Deborah, "Marked Women," 393

Taylor, Stuart, Jr., "It's Time to Junk the Double Standard on Free Speech," 211

Thoreau, Henry David, "Civil Disobedience," 722

Tolson, Jay, "Imbalance of Power," 790

Walker, Alice, "Beauty: When the Other Dancer Is the Self," 40

Wedgwood, Ralph, "What Are We Fighting For?" 62

Wellman, Barry, "Connecting Communities: On and Offline," 341

White, E. B., "Once More to the Lake," 23

Winn, Marie, "Television: The Plug-In Drug," 231

Women in Science and Engineering Leadership Institute, Response to Lawrence Summers, 622

Woolf, Virginia, "Professions for Women," 500

Wordsworth, William, "The World Is Too Much with Us," 301

Wright, Richard, "The Library Card," 427